CALLAGHAN
A Life

CALLAGHAN
A Life

By KENNETH O. MORGAN

OXFORD UNIVERSITY PRESS

1997

Oxford University Press, Great Clarendon Street, Oxford OX2 6DP
Oxford New York
Athens Auckland Bangkok Bogota Bombay
Buenos Aires Calcutta Cape Town Dar es Salaam
Delhi Florence Hong Kong Istanbul Karachi
Kuala Lumpur Madras Madrid Melbourne
Mexico City Nairobi Paris Singapore
Taipei Tokyo Toronto Warsaw
and associated companies in
Berlin Ibadan

Oxford is a trade mark of Oxford University Press

Published in the United States
by Oxford University Press Inc., New York

British Library Cataloguing in Publication Data
Data available

Library of Congress Cataloging in Publication Data
Morgan , Kenneth O.
Callaghan: a life / Kenneth O. Morgan.
p. cm.
Includes bibliographical references (p.).
1. Callaghan, James, 1912– . 2. Prime ministers—Great Britain—Biography. 3. Great Britain—Politics and government—1945–
I. Title.
DA591.C34M67 1997 941.085'092—dc21 97–19750
ISBN 0–19–820216–4

1 3 5 7 9 10 8 6 4 2

Typeset by Hope Services (Abingdon) Ltd.
Printed in Great Britain
on acid free paper by
Bookcraft Ltd., Midsomer Norton
Nr. Bath, Somerset

To
David and Katherine
with love

Preface

THE career of Lord Callaghan is inseparable from British history in the second half of the twentieth century. In many ways he is one of its representative figures. He has played a part in British public life for well over sixty years. He became a union official in 1933 and he is an active peer in 1997. His longevity in politics exceeds that of Lloyd George and rivals that of Gladstone or Churchill. Not even they managed to hold all the major offices of prime minister, foreign secretary, chancellor of the Exchequer, and home secretary which Lord Callaghan uniquely has done. No one else better embodies the rise and decline of the social democratic consensus that largely shaped British history for the three decades after the end of the war in 1945. His fall from power in 1979 was commonly taken as marking the end of an era. Many commentators then saw him as Labour's last prime minister, a prophecy which events in May 1997 were to demolish. Lord Callaghan is a symbol of our present as well as our recent past, New Labour as well as Old. He links the age of Clem Attlee and that of Tony Blair.

The art and craft of biography are subtle and contentious. The relationships of author and subject have been extensively, often passionately, discussed. In my own case, this book is an official biography in the sense that I have had unhindered access to Lord Callaghan's personal archive of 55 boxes and to Lord Callaghan himself. But it remains a totally independent work of history. He has not revised my judgements. Nor indeed, since he has already written a work of autobiography, did he wish to. I do not feel in any way compromised by my own relationship with my subject. I met him intermittently in earlier years, notably when I chaired an election meeting at which he spoke in Swansea West back in 1959. But I had little contact with him over subsequent decades until we met again in early 1989 after my appointment as a vice-chancellor in the University of Wales. I was an academic observer of his career but never in any way a participant in the events described in this book. I do not feel inhibited by the fact that Lord Callaghan is still alive. I hope and believe that I have written in the same spirit of frankness and independence as if he were a figure in the past. In any event, a biography such as David Douglas's fine study of William the Conqueror, or almost any book by Arthur Schlesinger, Jr., reminds us that bias towards one's subject is not confined to the living.

There is, obviously, one colossal gain in writing the biography of a living person, namely the ability to talk freely with my subject on anything I choose. In writing earlier books of mine, how I would have loved to talk to Keir Hardie or David Lloyd George. In the case of Keir Hardie, who died twenty years before I was born (despite his firm belief in spiritualism and a recorded account of a conversation with him at a socialist seance on 26 July 1945), I did at least talk to the late Fenner Brockway. He was able to give me many insights into Hardie (whom he first met in 1906) that I simply could not have obtained elsewhere. The personality of Lloyd George was much illuminated for me by conversations with two of his children, his nephew, and some of his grandchildren. In the case of this contemporary leader, Lord Callaghan, alive, well, and mentally in full vigour during the eight years in which I was writing this book, I needed no such intermediaries.

Biography is a kaleidoscopic art form. In this book, I was concerned to go beyond merely describing the career of one important figure, and to revert in part to an earlier literary tradition. The great majority of my previous books have not been biographies. I have tried here to write something akin to the more traditional 'life and times', to set Lord Callaghan's career against the context of Britain's domestic and international history from the 1930s to the 1990s, and locate it within the distinctive evolution, tradition, and mythology of the British Labour movement. I have greatly benefited from the recent flowering of contemporary history in this country. It is the public man, the national and world figure, who has been my main concern. I do not think that a psycho-biography of Lord Callaghan would be of any great interest, even assuming I was professionally competent to produce one. On the other hand, Lytton Strachey has long taught us that the public and the private are virtually impossible to disentangle. Lord Callaghan's ancestry, personal characteristics, and style of life, his views on religion and culture, on public and personal morality, on family, friendship, and foreign lands are an essential part of trying to explain his career and draw out the fullest implications of his role in the making of the modern world.

My main thanks must be to Lord Callaghan himself for asking me to write a book which has given me such extraordinary enjoyment and stimulation over the past eight years, as well as to Lady Callaghan for much personal kindness and hospitality. In addition to subjecting himself to, I imagine, dozens of meetings (informal open-ended conversations, not tape-recorded interviews) with invariable frankness, courtesy, and good humour, Lord Callaghan also gave me free range over his archive of fifty-five boxes. They form a very substantial collection which spans his life in all its aspects from his career as a trade union official in the early 1930s onwards. It contains a wealth of correspondence, manuscript notes and jottings, transcripts, reports, *aides-mémoires*, and sections of diaries. The Callaghan Papers have gone to the Bodleian Library in Oxford, where they will lie alongside those of Attlee, Macmillan, and Wilson amongst other post-war political figures, and I hope that they will shortly be made available to other scholars. During the writing of this book, I was much indebted to successive keepers of the House of Lords Record Office, Mr H. C. Cobb and Mr D. J. Johnson and their staff of the House of Lords Record Office who looked after the main archive from 1990, and latterly to Mrs Mary Clapinson of the Bodleian and Dr Angela Raspin of the LSE for their help in arranging the transfer of material to the Bodleian.

Beyond this, I have incurred an immense range of obligations over the past eight years. I am much indebted for formal interviews with Lord Allen of Abbeydale, the late Lord Bancroft, Dr Nigel Bowles, Lord Brooks of Tremorfa, Sir Julian Bullard, Sir Alec Cairncross, Michael Callaghan, Baroness Castle, Sir Brian Cubbon, Dr Jack Cunningham MP, Sir Geoffrey de Deney, Lord Donoughue of Ashton, Gwyneth Evans, David Faulkner, Michael Foot, Lord Gladwin of Clee, Geoffrey Goodman, Roy Hattersley, Lord Healey, the late Lord Houghton of Sowerby, Lord Hunt of Tanworth, Lady Jay of Paddington, the late Lord Jay of Battersea, Peter Jay, Lord Jenkins of Hillhead, Jack Jones, Dr Henry Kissinger, His Excellency Lee Kuan Yew, Professor Ian Little, Sir Thomas McCaffrey, Tom McNally, Lord Merlyn-Rees of Cilfynydd, Alun Michael MP, Lord Murray of Epping Forest, Lord Rodgers of Quarrybank, His Excellency Helmut Schmidt, Roger Stott MP, Sir Kenneth Stowe, and Alan Watkins. I have also benefited from information, often extensive, kindly provided by Donald Anderson MP, Kenneth Baker, Lord Blake, Albert Booth, Ken Bovington, Lord Bullock, Natasha Burkhardt, Tony Christopher, Professor Brian Clarkson, Lord Cledwyn of Penrhos, Edmund Dell, Dr N. H. Dimsdale, Mrs Marjorie Durbin, Emrys Evans, Dr Ewen Green, Harry Green, Kenneth Harris, Professor Peter Hennessy, Sir Reginald Hibbert, Lord Hooson, Lord Hunt of Llanfairwaterdine, Lady Jay of Battersea, Rt. Hon. Neil Kinnock, Sir Montague Levine, Robert

Maclennan MP, Professor David Marquand, Leslie Monckton, Mrs Margaret Park (UW Swansea), W. G. A. Raggett, Gerald Rees (Bank of Wales), John Sadden, Dr Jean Seaton, Peter Shore MP, Olive Tanton, Professor Charles Webster, Baroness Williams of Crosby, and Jessie Worrall.

I am very grateful to the following libraries and archive centres for permission to quote from papers in their possession: the Public Record Office; the Bodleian Library, Oxford (Attlee, George-Brown, Greenwood, Boyd of Merton); Rhodes House Library, Oxford (Creech Jones, Welensky); the National Library of Wales (Cledwyn, Donnelly, Griffiths, Tonypandy); British Library of Political and Economic Science (Crosland, Dalton); Modern Records Centre, University of Warwick (Cousins, CBI, IRSF); Clive Brooke (Inland Revenue Staff Federation papers); Lyndon Baines Johnson Library, Austin (Johnson, Fowler); Gerald R. Ford Library (Ford); Jimmy Carter Library (Carter). I am also indebted to Mr John Cousins for access to the Cousins Papers, to Lady George-Brown for access to the George-Brown Papers, and to Lord Cledwyn and Lord Tonypandy for access to their papers. Professor Ian Little kindly let me use his papers on the economics seminars of the early 1960s. My old friend Sir Alec Cairncross, himself an eighth wonder of the world, allowed me to use his MS diary as well as his important study of economic policy in the 1960s, prior to publication. Lord Tonypandy, Rhodri Morgan MP, Baroness Williams, Peter Shore MP, Dr Jack Cunningham MP, David Lipsey, and Sir Goronwy Daniel allowed me to print extracts from letters to which they own the copyright. I can only apologize if, through mischance or inadvertence, I have failed to trace or acknowledge any other authors.

I am also most grateful for help regarding source material to Lord Donoughue, Christine Woodland (Modern Records Centre, Warwick), John Graham Jones (National Library of Wales), Geoffrey Goodman and Tony Christopher (Lord Houghton papers), Stephen Bird (Labour Party archives), Harry Middleton and Michael Parrish (Lyndon Baines Johnson Library), Martin Elzy (Jimmy Carter Library), Leesa Tobin and Nancy Mirshat (Gerald R. Ford Library), Robert Morgan (BBC Today programme), Kirsty White (BBC archive), Hywel Francis (UW Swansea), Nick Crowson and Virginia Preston (Institute of Contemporary British History), and the library of the Athenaeum. Like so many historians I am deep in the debt of the Public Record Office and its good-natured staff over the years.

I have also appreciated the opportunity to try out my ideas on the matters discussed in this book in seminars or public lectures at a variety of institutions. I am therefore most grateful to invitations successively from the University of Malaya (Kuala Lumpur); the National University of Singapore; the Aberystwyth Rotary Club; the Stubbs Society, Oxford; the University of Wales, Swansea; the University of East Anglia; the University of Tübingen (Baden-Württemberg); the University of Wales, Aberystwyth, History Society; the graduate research seminar at St John's College, Oxford; the Universities of the Witwatersrand, Cape Town, and Western Cape, South Africa, and the University of Sheffield.

Many learned colleagues and friends have generously given their time in commenting upon all or part of this book. Professor Vernon Bogdanor of Brasenose College, Oxford, read the entire text and offered a host of stimulating suggestions or corrections; I am deeply in his debt, as also to the anonymous reader for Oxford University Press. I also benefited from the learning of Dr John Darwin of Nuffield College and Dr Nick Owen of Queen's on colonial policy, Dr Nicholas Dimsdale of Queen's on economic policy, Professor Richard Rose of Strathclyde on the premiership, Dr John Rowett of Brasenose on modern political history, Professor Roger Hood of All Souls and my late wife Jane on penal policy, and Dr Nigel Bowles of St Anne's on recent politics, quite apart from his own close association with Lord Callaghan since 1979. I have, as always, benefited from conversation with my friends Dr Alastair Parker of Queen's and Dr Denis Balsom, warden of Gregynog, as well as with Tim Bale of Sheffield University. Obviously, blemishes and errors that remain are my responsibility and mine alone. I would like to mention also the endlessly cheerful help of Gina Page, Lord Callaghan's secretary, and his driver, Alan Currie, and of my two wonderful staff at the university in Aberystwyth, my personal assistant Nan Thomas, and my secretary Beryl Jones. Indeed, Aberystwyth as a whole was remarkably generous in allowing its vice-chancellor the opportunity to retain a foothold in the historical world. My literary agent Bruce Hunter, a mentor and good friend over a quarter of a century, has always been a fount of encouragement. Tony Morris of OUP has once again been the most unstuffy of editors, and my old friend Ivon Asquith a firm rock of reassurance. I am also indebted to the advice of Kim Scott-Walwyn, and the calm efficiency of Mick Belson, Amy Turner, and Juliet New.

To my children, David and Katherine, my debt is beyond words. They have materially helped this book (not least by explaining to a grossly non-technical father how word-processors work!), they have been eternally cheerful, and they have shown immense reserves of courage when the most important person in our lives, my beloved Jane, was so cruelly taken from us. They have shown me and each other love and endless loyalty. At a time when such a thing appeared somewhat elusive, they have given me a reason to live. Diolch o galon!

K.O.M.

Long Hanborough
8 May 1997

Contents

List of Illustrations

(between pages 240–241)

PART ONE

1912–1964

1

NAVAL CHILDHOOD

LIKE Winston Churchill and perhaps with more justification, Jim Callaghan could have adopted the description 'former naval person'. More than any other British prime minister, his view of history and of geography was shaped by the Royal Navy and the mystique of the sea. This, of course, is almost as old as England itself. Historians from J. A. Froude to G. M. Trevelyan regarded British sea power as a key to British (more specifically English) liberty. It warded off would-be Continental invaders and planted the seed of freedom in foreign lands. Froude saw sea power as an essential component of Tudor greatness. He helped mould the imperialist geopolitical views of the American historian Admiral Mahan, author in the 1890s of a book celebrated in its day, *The Influence of Sea Power upon History*. Trevelyan was later to hail the fact that 'Nelson's was the best-loved name' in English history.[1]

Young Jim Callaghan grew up in precisely this tradition, in the shadow of Nelson's own flagship, the *Victory*. His world was one in which Britannia really ruled the waves, by means of the famous 'two-power standard', and where Jolly Jack Tar with his pigtail, in contrast to the soldiers of a potentially oppressive standing army, was the people's instrument of national freedom. His world-view started from here, as did a geographical sense that stemmed from living in a great naval port on the English Channel. It saw Britain's role as a global one rather than being narrowly restricted to Continental societies across the water. In Portsmouth more than most places, the maps glowed with imperial red. Europe was distant for its inhabitants just as it seemed close by for Kentish citizens like the young Edward Heath. All his life, Callaghan was pre-eminently at home in maritime and naval circles. This was to be reinforced by wartime service in the navy, and by early ministerial experience at the Admiralty. It was a bond between him and another erstwhile sailor, President Jimmy Carter. Chancellor Helmut Schmidt, from the historically Anglophile seaport of

Hamburg, claimed to feel particularly at ease with someone from such a background. An event Callaghan treasured during his premiership was attending the naval review at Spithead from on board the royal yacht during the Queen's silver jubilee in 1977. In later life, his Sussex farm would be adorned with a rich variety of naval prints, paintings, and photographs of clippers and schooners and men-of-war. They included HMS *Victoria and Albert* in which his father served. The route up to his farm loft was by way of a ship's rope ladder. His speeches would be sometimes coloured with naval terminology. A famous example was his 1967 budget speech in which the course of future financial policy was set out. 'All seamen know the word of command—"steady as she goes".'

This sea-faring background was the central feature of his upbringing. His home was the great naval base of Portsmouth.[2] It was perhaps at the zenith of its importance in 1912, the year of the birth of Leonard James Callaghan. The roots of its eminence as a maritime town went back many centuries. It had been a naval station in the later Roman period. Since the later Middle Ages, it had been a significant port, with its deep-water facilities and easy access to the Channel via the Solent. Under the early Tudors, it became a major naval base, along with Plymouth and Tilbury. Henry VII built the first naval dry dock there in the 1490s. Henry VIII expanded the fleet there as part of a more adventurous foreign policy in the 1530s and 1540s. It was from Portsmouth that the *Mary Rose* set off on its brief and calamitous maiden voyage to repel an invading French fleet in 1545. In the seventeenth and eighteenth centuries, the naval base and the town surrounding it continued to grow, especially during the French revolutionary wars. At that time, in April 1797, Portsmouth was also to see the first major naval mutiny, on ships stationed at Spithead, which paralysed the British Channel Fleet for a month at a critical moment just after the battle of Cape St Vincent. It was a reasoned appeal for higher pay: not one of the Portsmouth mutineers was punished, unlike their colleagues of the North Sea Fleet who mutinied at The Nore. More positively, Portsmouth Naval College was established for superior shipyard apprentices by Order in Council in 1809. Nelson's *Victory*, of course, was based there. When he visited the Leeward Islands as a senior statesman, Callaghan was to make a point of visiting Nelson's dockyard in English Harbour on the south shore of the small island of Antigua. The rundown state of the small naval museum there, with its relics of Codrington and Nelson, was something he drew to the attention of the Antiguan government.

Throughout the nineteenth century, Portsmouth expanded still further as the naval dockyard grew in importance. The railways brought new development on the north and east of the town, while neighbouring Southsea developed as a popular seaside resort. By the eve of war in 1914, Portsmouth, along with Devonport and Chatham, was pre-eminent amongst bases for the Grand Fleet. Dreadnought battleships, Admiral Fisher's monster iron-clad response to Tirpitz's naval challenge, were built there, culminating in the *Royal Sovereign*, the largest of them all, which was launched in April 1915. The town had a population of 233,929 recorded in the census of 1921. It boasted an imposing Guildhall in the town centre; at a popular level, a successful Southern League football team, familiarly known as 'Pompey' to supporters, was based in Fratton Park. In the summer of 1914, witnessed by thousands of excited and patriotic spectators including the Callaghan family, the King held a review of the Grand Fleet there. It was the mightiest naval force the world had ever seen, with 24 of the new Dreadnought battleships, 35 other battleships, 49 cruisers, 76 submarines, and 78 destroyers on display, manned by around 100,000 sailors. The Commander-in-Chief of the Home Fleet on that day, by a curious twist, was Vice-Admiral Sir George Callaghan. It was in this thrusting, self-confident naval metropolis, at 38 Funtingdon Road, Copnor, Portsmouth, that another Callaghan, Leonard James, was born on 27 March 1912.

James Callaghan's father, also named James, was himself a naval man and a free spirit in many ways. He was the grandson of an Irish weaver born around 1805–7 who had migrated to Coventry after the catastrophe of the Irish potato famine in 1845–6. He had a son, another James, born in 1851, who worked as a silversmith in Coventry. It was his son James, one of ten children and born in January 1877, who was the father of the future prime minister. When Jim Callaghan became premier in April 1976, the *Sun* newspaper displayed the habitual curiosity of the British press about his ancestry.[3] Its researches showed that the family name was not Callaghan at all, but Garoghan. In fact, Jim Callaghan's father joined the Royal Navy under an assumed name as a young lad in the 1890s, hoping that his parents would not be able to trace him—not an unusual event for naval recruits 'running away to sea', then or later. In addition to his father's background being Irish Catholic and the family name not in fact being Callaghan at all, the Prime Minister discovered another interesting detail about his ancestry in 1976. His father's mother was Elizabeth Bernstein, from Sheffield; he was, therefore, a quarter Jewish as well. None of these facts was to his disadvantage. Indeed, in the late 1960s, the very Irishness of the name Callaghan, a name capable of being identified with either community in Northern Ireland (unlike the republican-sounding Garoghan, for instance), was a distinct political asset.

However unorthodox his entry into the navy, Callaghan's father rapidly progressed, rising from boy second class to an eventual rank of chief petty officer. When an Admiralty minister in 1950, Callaghan was able to look up the departmental records which, to his pleasure, consistently described his father's character as 'very good' or even 'superior'.[4] He served in HMS *Benbow* and *St George* in the 1890s and took part in an adventurous, and highly dangerous, expedition to avenge the murder of the deputy British Consul in Benin City in Nigeria in 1895. Several of the expedition were killed by native ambushes or died of disease. Another hazard was that Benin City itself was razed to the ground by a mysterious fire. Colourful stories of these events, including other adventures on the island of Zanzibar, were an essential feature of young Jim's clifftop walks with his father at Brixham later on. These excitements clearly only whetted further the desire of Callaghan senior for ventures new. He applied to join Captain Scott's expedition to the Antarctic in the *Discovery* but, fortunately, his wife (already once widowed) managed to dissuade her adventurous husband.

Instead, he embarked on a more prestigious career, indeed one which greatly raised the family's profile locally, namely service in the royal yacht *Victoria and Albert*, until the outbreak of war in August 1914. Callaghan's father went on several voyages on the royal yacht after Edward VII became King. He was present at the Kaiser's review of the Grand Fleet in the Kiel Canal. It is likely that he took part in the yacht's progress up the Baltic to Riga in June 1908 to visit the Tsar, Nicholas II. This provoked a kind of boycott of royal events, such as garden parties, by the entire Labour Party in the Commons after Keir Hardie and other MPs were suspended from the House for protesting at this British recognition of the hated tyranny of Tsardom.[5] Events like this gesture by impetuous socialists, however, would merely have served to reinforce an instinctive patriotism, indeed imperialism, for the crew and their families. The young Callaghan was to devote some of his spare time, later on, to plotting on maps the progress of Edward, the young Prince of Wales, across the world. On a personal level, he was able to tell the Queen during the naval review in Portsmouth during the jubilee in 1977 that the ornamental binnacle on the royal yacht *Britannia* taken from its predecessor was one that he had been shown over sixty years before, when taken as a toddler in his father's arms.

From his father, Callaghan acquired a profound attachment to the romance of the sea, and the mystique of imperial greatness, along with much technical knowledge of seamanship. His mother's background was somewhat different. Charlotte Gertrude Callaghan (née Cundy) was of West Country nonconformist stock. Her paternal grandfather Robert Cundy was a quarryman from Tavistock; her maternal grandfather was a shoemaker from Devonport, both therefore Devonians. But the sea, inevitably, was in her background too. Her father, born in Tavistock in 1831, was William Henry Cundy, a naval shipwright on HMS *Impregnable*. He married Rosina McDowell of Devonport; their daughter Charlotte, born in 1879 also in Devonport, was one of five children. She married young, almost inevitably to another sailor, Daniel Speare, a seaman on HMS *Defiant*. But she was to be widowed before she was 21 since Speare perished in a naval accident when a destroyer ran down the liberty boat in which he was returning to his ship in Plymouth Sound. She then met and married James Callaghan, who was about to serve on the royal yacht. She was a staunch Baptist, and when Callaghan was refused permission to marry her by the royal naval Catholic chaplain, he left the Catholic Church forthwith. The family thus settled down as Baptists all, their one daughter, Dorothy, born in 1904, and their sole son, Leonard James, eight years younger. Just as Callaghan derived one formative influence from his naval father, his patriotism, so he grew up with an equally powerful inheritance from his Baptist mother, his puritanism.

His early years were spent in the Copnor region of Portsmouth, a densely populated suburb of working-class terraces in the north-east of the town which grew up between the early 1890s and the First World War after the spread of the railways. As it happened, Ian Mikardo, a somewhat older boy born in 1908 to a Yiddish-speaking family resident in the Portsea area near the docks, where his father worked as a naval tailor, was growing up in another part of the town at the same time. He was to study at Aria College, intended to train young Hampshire Jews as rabbis, and then at Portsmouth Grammar School. However, the Mikardos and the Callaghans had no knowledge of each other; nor were Ian and Jim ever in any sense close comrades when they served in the House together as Labour MPs for many decades after 1945. Callaghan's birthplace in Funtingdon Road was an Edwardian terrace house with a single bow window. Almost immediately, the family moved to nearby 28 Westbourne Road, a similar style of house where they lived until 1919, when Callaghan's father was demobilized and moved his employment to Brixham in Devon. When Callaghan received the freedom of the city of Portsmouth in 1991, a day of much civic rejoicing, the event produced something of a rash of blue plaques to commemorate episodes of his childhood.[6] It emerged then that the occupant of 28 Westbourne Road at the time was a staunch

Conservative, but she warmly welcomed the blue plaque nevertheless because the value of her home might thereby increase.

The infant Callaghan's early years were dominated by the outbreak of war. Rumours of war were part of Portsmouth life for some years prior to 1914. There was fear of Admiral Tirpitz's German fleet, and alarmist talk of invasion. The first British Dreadnought had been launched from Portsmouth dockyard by King Edward VII in 1906; Kaiser Wilhelm II of Germany had come to inspect it there in 1907. Nine of the 22 Dreadnoughts of the British Grand Fleet were built in Portsmouth. In August 1914, when war broke out, Callaghan's father was sent to man HMS *Agincourt*, a battleship originally destined for the Turkish fleet and then requisitioned and renamed by the Royal Navy. *Agincourt* sailed to join the Grand Fleet at Scapa Flow and Callaghan senior was then virtually lost to the family's view for the next four years. A photograph survives of Dorothy Callaghan and her 4-year-old brother, sent to their father on the high seas in 1916. In fact, at the age of 2½, Callaghan had appeared in the press for the first time, in an evangelical magazine entitled *Ashore and Afloat*.[7] The writer, Agnes ('Aggie') Weston, well known as the founder of the Royal Sailors' Rest, wrote of meeting baby Leonard in December 1914 and of his saying prayers for his father's safe return. 'Please Jesus bring my daddy safe home again for Leonard, Mamma and Dorothy. Amen.' So enthusiastic was little Leonard to say his prayers that he fell over in the garden in his rush, hitting his head above the eye and scraping his knee, but the prayers were said regardless. Many people in Copnor were connected with either the navy or the dockyards, and events at sea soon filtered back to the local community. The Callaghans' neighbour was widowed when her husband died in *The Good Hope*, sunk by the *Scharnhorst* off the coast of Chile in November 1914. Many more tragedies resulted from the battle of Jutland in June 1916, where indeed Callaghan's father was himself wounded. But the manhood of Portsmouth was represented in the army as well. Three Portsmouth battalions were raised in response to Kitchener's appeal for volunteers. In all, 6,000 men were to lose their lives. During the war years, young Leonard experienced one major change in 1916 when he started off at the local infants' school. It was marked by strict discipline and teaching by rote, with particular reference to the capes and promontories of the British coastline beloved of Edwardian schools inspectors.

His father, however, came back home safely after four years at war, and there then followed an apparently much happier and more secure phase of young Callaghan's life. The family moved to the fishing port of Brixham in Devon, best known historically as the landing place of William of

Orange in 1688. Here his father had a more relaxing post as a local coastguard, a relatively gentle occupation which gave him time to take his son on clifftop walks and instruct the little boy in Morse code or ships' semaphore in the coastguard station high up at Berry Head near the entrance to Torbay. There were always many stories of adventures in Africa, too. For the next two years the young Leonard experienced all the natural pleasures that a seaside childhood can bring, the bustle of the fishing fleet in Brixham harbour, the gulls wheeling over Berry Head, the shells and the sea-moss, the panorama of the ships in Torbay, with excitements like the Torbay and Brixham regatta in high summer. Devon, like south Wales, is rugby territory. Callaghan ardently supported Brixham rugby team: a seat in the stand could be obtained for 3*d.* A radio broadcast in March 1976, made just before Callaghan became Prime Minister, recalled the excitement in 1922 when Brixham won the Devon Senior Cup.[8]

On the other hand, the disaster in March 1922 when a storm struck the Brixham trawler fleet brought home the tragic side of life at sea. Two fishing smacks, the *Love and Unity* and the *Majestic*, were lost with all their crews including a 14-year-old boy with whom Callaghan was friendly. It made a lifelong impression upon him. Events like this, along with the graves in Brixham cemetery recalling maritime disasters in the past, were direct and poignant testimony to the force of J. B. Dykes's noble hymn, a requiem for fisherfolk everywhere, 'Eternal father, strong to save'. Years later, on 18 April 1951, Callaghan, now an Admiralty minister, had to speak to the House immediately after comforting the bereaved in Portsmouth following the accidental sinking of the submarine *Affray* in the English Channel with the loss of all seventy-five men on board. For almost the only time in his life, he nearly broke down in the Commons after this latest tragic testimony to 'those in peril on the sea'.

The local junior school, Furzeham School, Brixham, which Callaghan attended from 1919 to 1923, had several positive features.[9] One teacher that Callaghan was to recall with some affection was Harry 'Spot' Smardon, who organized the local regatta and lived long enough (he died in 1948) to see his former pupil a government minister. Callaghan was to attend a school centenary reunion in 1989 and to unveil a memorial plaque. His attendance at the school became a part of Brixham folklore. Brixham seemed an altogether more open and relaxed place than the terraced streets of Portsmouth. The coastguard's house at Brixham was the only one in Callaghan's childhood years with a proper garden. Then tragedy struck without warning. In October 1921, Callaghan's father died suddenly of a heart attack, along with stomach trouble, at the age of 44. For his 9-year-old son, the impact was devastating, the more so since his mother seemed a more remote, perhaps forbidding,figure and his sister, eight years older, was too far removed in age to be close. Callaghan wrote movingly in his autobiography, sixty-six years on, of the intensity of his grief and sense of loss, as the coffin, draped in the white ensign, made its slow way along the Brixham quayside and the fishermen took off their caps and stood in silent tribute to the passing of one of their own. His father was buried in St Mary's Church: as a nonconformist, he was laid to rest in unconsecrated ground. Callaghan knew very little of his father's family thereafter. He knew that a brother, a little-known uncle of his, emigrated to Australia some time later. He was much surprised in 1994 to have a letter from this uncle's daughter, a long-lost cousin.

The psychological impact of the loss of a parent so early in life may be left to others to explore. In the case of Callaghan, the deprivation seems to have led in time to a peculiar form of toughness and self-reliance that marked his early steps as both a trade unionist and a politician. Yet side by side with this went an abiding need for security. As a young man—to some degree throughout his life—he combined a breezy confidence in his own abilities with a defensive touchiness, especially if slights were being cast on his inadequate educational background, for instance by Hampstead Gaitskellites or Foreign Office mandarins. Almost at the same moment, he could seem both self-assured and insecure. The search for a calm anchorage was a lifelong one. At various times, the Inland Revenue, the union movement, and above all the warmth and solidarity of the Labour movement provided safe havens. He often spoke of the loneliness of his childhood years. Later in life, with the effects of a long and happy marriage, he became a much more relaxed and secure personality. But the very depth of this early grief also made him a strong, emotional person, capable of responding instinctively to the bereavement of others, the more able to commune spontaneously with the victims of life's pain and injustices. As it happened, his later colleague Hugh Gaitskell, born in 1906, also lost his father at the age of 9, but he was at boarding school at the time. Judgements vary as to the importance of the effect of this loss upon the development of his personality. In Callaghan's case, there can be far less doubt.

After two more difficult years, a time of struggle with the family breadwinner suddenly removed and there being effectively no widow's pension for Callaghan's mother, they moved back again to Portsmouth. For young Leonard (the name by which he was habitually known) the move was not a happy one. At a time of mounting recession and mass unemployment in

Portsmouth as elsewhere, the family was on the verge of genuine poverty, even after his mother managed to gain a pension of 16*s.* a week (with a further 10*s.* for her son) after the advent of the first Labour government in 1924 (an event which Callaghan was to claim in later life helped make him a socialist). They stayed in a series of rented rooms in various streets in the Copnor area. The family did not live well, though perhaps a little better than in Brixham, where young Leonard had to survive the school day with a slice of bread and dripping. There were no school meals to be had. His health suffered indirectly; when he entered the navy himself in 1943, traces of tuberculosis were found in his lungs.

Nor was life altogether improved by his experience at school. He was not at all a stupid child and was able to pass the examination to enter the local school, one of three secondary schools in Portsmouth, Northern Secondary School in Fratton Road, not far from the family Baptist church in London Road. In the 1990s, this red-brick building which was Callaghan's school seemed almost attractive with its oriel windows, and it served as the quite imposing offices of the local Housing Association. It was a building owned by the parish church of St Mary's, Kingston, across the road, and began life as St Mary's Institute in 1898. Towering above was St Mary's Church, the mother church of Portsea Island, originally founded in the reign of Henry II. With its 165-feet high tower, it was a new building, designed by Sir Arthur Bromfield, dating from 1887, and the result in large measure of the generosity of a notable citizen of Portsmouth, W. H. Smith MP. A plaque in the aisle notes that Charles Dickens was christened in the earlier St Mary's in 1812.

Kingston is a pleasant, leafy area with no other Dickensian overtones. But for Callaghan, so he wrote later, Portsmouth Northern was not a model of how a secondary school should be run, and he criticized it severely.[10] When as a government minister he attended an old boys' dinner in February 1948—the Old Nortonians Association it was now called—his comments were somewhat barbed. The purpose of such schools, he observed, should be to teach boys to think for themselves. He appeared to imply here that Portsmouth Northern neglected to do so, although he also noted that it gave him a sound academic foundation in the end. It was cramped, with room in the main Institute building only for three subject lessons, others being conducted in huts and in the glebe hall at the back. There was no real play area, save for a small strip of tarmac alongside the road. Apart from Percy Roberts, a nice geography teacher, who allowed young Len the run of his own bookshelves, Callaghan found the teaching dull and the atmosphere frigid. Lavish use was made of the cane, with the head walking around the school with this weapon in his hand for immediate use.[11] The headmaster, 'Buggy' Beeden, a kindly man in many ways, enlivened the week with homilies such as 'Make sure you do not marry beneath yourselves.' For his first three years, according to his own account, Callaghan did very little work even though the payment of his school fees of 2 guineas a term by the Ministry of Pensions depended on his gaining reasonable school reports. Indeed, he later felt himself to have been 'a bad boy' and to have frequently misbehaved. His mother, sorely tried by her circumstances in life, disciplined him severely as a result.

In retrospect, the crimes he recalled seemed more schoolboy boisterousness than anything more heinous. They included running a kind of sweep amongst the pupils based on the weekend football results. On the other hand, he insisted that, for the grave misdemeanour of tying a fish to a master's table, he was wrongly accused and unjustly punished. A high proportion of the pupils were there to be trained for the navy or the dockyards, as engineers and artificers, and this type of vocational instruction Callaghan found to be utterly boring. However, as he discovered the local Carnegie Library a little way along the Fratton Road, and found the works of Dickens, Scott, Thackeray, and other nineteenth-century authors, his interest was kindled in history and English, although his mathematics and science remained poor. In his last two years at school, as he prepared for the Oxford Senior Certificate which could open up some kind of professional career, his work (though not perhaps his attitude to the school) steadily improved.

He was in some ways a lonely boy, or felt himself to be, blushing easily if spoken to. He was acutely and desperately aware of the absence of a father. Other boys found him a large, somewhat tough character, with some interest in physical exercise and games. He took to running in Fratton Park before school began and played in the school football team in 1928, although apparently with limited skill. He also took part in athletics on behalf of Wallington House: he was not a great athlete. Nevertheless, he made a positive impact on several of his school friends. He cannot have been such a 'bad boy' after all, and in general his schooldays became increasingly happy. His range of friends included Cyril Long, a photographer's son, Leonard Palmer, who was to work for a gas company, and perhaps most usefully Clifford Parker, whose father made excellent pork pies. Leslie Monckton, another schoolmate, who kept in close touch afterwards, regarded Len Callaghan as a likeable boy. He recalled in 1992 an expedition on a Harley-Davidson motor bicycle which broke down, though Leonard seems to have accepted this with good humour and did nothing worse than ruffle Leslie's hair. Another contemporary recalls cheerful pranks such as putting the geography teacher's bottle of red ink on a stove during a cold winter's day in 1926–7, with explosive and colourful results.[12] As was the norm in British schools, Leonard's friends seem to have been wholly male, although a tall, fresh-faced young man with dark wavy hair and a cheerful smile attracted the opposite sex in the usual way. Marjorie Fulford and another girl would wave to Leonard and one of his friends, and get a similar response in return. But the relationship never got any further, to Marjorie's long-term regret.[13]

Even at this very early stage, there were some signs of the future politician. Mrs Long, a Scottish landlady of theirs at one time and a fierce socialist, seems to have been a formative influence. She got her young tenant to run errands for the Labour committee rooms in the general elections of 1923 and 1924. Some of his fellow Baptists were Christian socialists. The historic advent of a Labour government under Ramsay MacDonald, in February 1924 shortly after Leonard Callaghan entered Portsmouth Northern, was another factor of importance for him. His mother was much gratified at receiving a widow's pension for the first time from this government, and seems to have voted Labour thereafter. A. E. Strawn, another schoolfellow, recalled an unusually vehement commitment to socialism in the young Callaghan, who showed much facility in school debates and form discussion periods. Percy Harding, one of the English masters, recalled Leonard Callaghan running around the school with a string of boys behind him, shouting aggressively at anyone who would listen, 'We'll soak the rich! We'll soak the rich! You Tories just wait!'[14]

If school offered mixed experiences, the local Carnegie Library, as noted earlier, was a haven of cultural enrichment and private happiness. The young Leonard discovered here the joy of reading. One treasured early possession was a prize from the Sunday school, Joseph Addison's *Coverley Papers*. More recent literature, however, including more politically committed authors like Shaw and Wells, was unknown to him until he left Portsmouth. But it was the influence of the Baptist chapel that was both the most powerful and the most difficult for him. As noted, his mother was an intensely strict Baptist. His sister Dorothy was also religious though less severely so. In time she would marry a Baptist minister, Sidney Carter, and settle in Cornwall.[15] There were services and Sunday schools almost continuously on Sundays, and a variety of activities such as the Band of Hope and Christian Endeavour most evenings of the week. Callaghan's Sunday school was a remarkably large one, with over 600 'scholars'. The Callaghans had attended the Baptist chapel in Brixham: one of the visiting ministers there was the Revd F. Durbin. He was the father of Callaghan's later political friend Evan Durbin, whose Christian name was derived from Evan Roberts, the Welsh religious revivalist of 1905, the year before Evan Durbin was born. The Callaghans attended the London Road Baptist chapel which was conveniently close to all their various rented homes. It was a solid Edwardian brick building, opened in January 1902, with the Revd G. Roberts Hern as its first pastor. Its early membership received a boost from the religious revival in Wales. As a sign of changing mores, in 1996 it stood next door to a pub named 'The Tap'.

Callaghan was made to attend Sunday school scrupulously. When his natural rebelliousness expressed itself, and he questioned the views of his teacher Mr Martin, the poacher was made gamekeeper and he became assistant secretary of the school for his pains. At the age of 15, he was baptized. He also served as a Sunday school teacher himself from the age of 14 onwards. Jessie Worrall, one of his contemporaries, recalled their singing together, 'Hear the pennies dropping, Listen how they fall, Every one for Jesus, He shall have them all.'[16] Intrinsic to the Sunday school was learning by heart lengthy passages from the Bible. Callaghan attended this school faithfully until he left Portsmouth in October 1929. On leaving for his first job at that time, he was formally presented by the superintendent, Mr Woodruff, with a Bible and a framed copy of Psalm 37: 23, 'as a token of love and esteem'. It was a valued memento over the years. Sixty-six years on in 1995, Callaghan had his Portsmouth Bible rebound.

His religious upbringing left a deep imprint upon him. At the time, he often felt it to be a harsh and brooding faith. The chapel was itself sombre, with its dark mullioned windows and veneered pews. The message of evangelicalism and Sabbatarianism he found joyless, and family life in many ways severe. His mother seemed to have an almost fatalistic attitude to life, in which even the passing away of a young child could be half-welcomed since it would bring the infant back to Jesus. On the other hand, she was undoubtedly an affectionate mother and coped bravely with the extreme strain of being a sole parent. His sister Dorothy, being older, had gone off to training college in Truro; she was a high-spirited girl and far more relaxed in personality. But like other products of late Victorian and Edwardian religion, young Leonard Callaghan grew up with a Calvinist sense of guilt, inadequacy, inner torment, and an almost neurotic sense of tragedy which he found deeply unsettling. As a 7-year-old he had experienced a moment of terror when returning home to an empty house. He believed that the Second Coming had dawned, and his mother had been taken away to heaven. The shaming sense of being a sinner remained with him for the rest of his life. 'Even in adult life', he wrote perceptively in his autobiography, 'I have never been able wholly to shake off a sense of guilt.'[17]

But the chapel had a more positive side. It was also an example of neighbourly social Christianity at work, of the fraternal base in which the Labour Party found its roots. The members of the Baptist church were caring people who, in daily life, provided a genuine sense of community and of loving thy neighbour. The Baptist folk in Brixham had looked after the family in a spirit of Christian commitment after the tragedy of the father's death. The London Road Baptists went around the poorest areas of Portsmouth in the depressed years of the 1920s, delivering sugar and margarine to needy families. The chapel was of direct help to a deprived family like the Callaghans, and materially helped in the move to Maidstone where he found his first job. In his unsettled Portsmouth childhood after the death of his father, the Baptists 'acted like an anchor'.[18] Callaghan soon rebelled against the religious imperatives of nonconformity. He lost his religious views altogether when he moved to Maidstone and was not a churchgoer later on. It caused some mirth when Lord Longford attributed the virtues of the 1964 Labour government to the fact that its three main members, Wilson, Callaghan, and Brown, were all practising Christians.[19]

On the other hand, the ethic and style of nonconformity remained embedded in his make-up, his patterns of speech and vocabulary. Sixty years on, his autobiography was to begin with a reference to St John's Gospel, and to be prefaced by a quotation from Ecclesiastes. Long after his Portsmouth years, he could recall in detail the hymns and sermons of his youth. This helped him make his way in the public life of nonconformist Wales after 1945, and also to strike up relationships with such foreign politicians as the largely Presbyterian leaders of black Africa in the 1950s and his fellow Baptist President Jimmy Carter later on. The Christian doctrine may have withered in the vineyard, but the ethic of Christian witness and neighbourly service remained an essential component of his view of the world. So, too, was an inherent suspicion of social, moral, and sexual experiment. Though a tolerant man, aberrations such as divorce, the sexual philandering of an apparently austere colleague like Hugh Gaitskell, or overt homosexual behaviour (such as he encountered in his parliamentary colleague Tom Driberg) disturbed him. In his view of family and personal life, Callaghan embodied a sense of decency and rectitude, what a later generation of Conservative politicians christened (ironically as events turned out) 'back to basics'. His Baptism was at the root of his world-view as was her corner-shop Methodism for Margaret Thatcher. When in 1969 as Home Secretary he rebelled against the permissive doctrine of 'sex, drugs and rock 'n' roll', and declared that 'the tide of permissiveness has gone too far', he not only met with applause from both sides of the House and from conventional middle-class opinion. He was also surely giving passionate voice to the fundamentalist creed of the Portsmouth Baptists, all those long years ago, shouting out in defiance, almost in despair, against what he saw as an amoral, rootless world.

His life in Portsmouth had many compensations. Relatively poor as his family was, there were occasional treats—performances by the Royal Marine band for a *2d.* entrance fee at the Guildhall on Saturday nights, concerts by famous singers like the Australian Peter Dawson at the Wesley Central Hall, perhaps joining some other lads on 'Boilermakers' Hump' at Fratton Park to cheer on Portsmouth Football Club. Callaghan was to treasure his links with the city later on. He was glad to identify himself as a Pompey boy. It was a day of immense pride for him in May 1991 when he received the freedom of the city, making an open-top bus tour of Westbourne Road and other neighbouring streets. There was in return immense civic pride that one of their own should have risen so far. He took the opportunity then in a speech in the Guildhall to attack the Tory government for cuts in the defence budget which would weaken the Royal Navy.[20] Another pleasant event came in 1997 when the old Military Road was renamed 'Callaghan Drive'. Unlike the Cockney tones acquired by that other son of Pompey, Ian Mikardo, the Hampshire burr in his speech reflected his Portsmouth origins for the rest of his life.

But, compared with Brixham, the Portsmouth years were less happy ones for him, inevitably so given his domestic loss. He had to move on and move out, and he determined to do so. In his final two years at school, he pulled himself together. Even his mathematics now began to show a marked improvement. He had a quick intelligence, wrote clearly, and had a command of logical argument. In due time, he passed the Oxford Senior Certificate comfortably with second-class honours. He gained distinctions in English and history, with credits in French, physics, and several branches of mathematics.[21] Theoretically, this could have enabled him to go on to university, but the finances of the Callaghan family made this unthinkable. For the rest of his life, his inability to go to university left him with a deep sense of deprivation. It partly shaped his political priorities thereafter.

So he took instead a further examination to achieve a position in the public service as a civil service clerk. He passed comfortably, coming 190th out of 3,700 candidates. Years later, when he became Chancellor in 1964, he exchanged friendly messages with 'Johnnie' Walker, a stalwart of the masters' football team who had tutored him successfully in mathematics and science for this examination.[22] (In return, Callaghan had apparently been used as messenger boy in taking love letters to a girlfriend of Mr Walker's who lived near his home.) With this examination success, Callaghan thus entered the ranks of the black-coated clerical workers, that new class which increased and multiplied in the early decades of the century. It was not glamorous work and was poorly paid. However, in Portsmouth as elsewhere in the late 1920s, unemployment was immense. There were long queues outside the Labour Exchange in Lake Road, with hundreds of young men waiting to collect their 'dole' or else hanging around listlessly on street corners, filling in time at billiards.[23] The Portsea area around the harbour and the dockyards was caught up in an endemic cycle of poverty, decay, and despair, no less than mining communities were. It was a desperate world: Callaghan had once discussed with a school friend the possibility of emigrating to New Zealand. In these circumstances, the Wellsian career of a civil service clerk offered a rare avenue of security and social advance, as did so many white-collar jobs after the war. For Leonard Callaghan, it meant a job for the first time, in a tax office working for the Inland Revenue—not in Portsmouth though, but (to the initial dismay of his mother) in Maidstone in Kent, a faraway county of which he knew nothing. The prospect of a year's pay of £52, plus a cost-of-living allowance, was manna indeed. The Portsmouth Baptists rallied round loyally to help and arranged lodgings for him in Maidstone through the Baptist community there.

So, at the age of 17, young Len Callaghan moved on to his first job. He did so as a patriotic son of the sea who was showing early evidence of political radicalism, a manufactured puritan with some scant signs of earthy worldliness. Domestic tragedy had given him an unusual toughness, a capacity for enterprise, and a sharp awareness of class inequality. He did not lack self-belief and had shown youthful signs of being able to express his thoughts fluently in public. His formal education was over, and he resented the fact henceforth. Some of the Oxford-bred Gaitskellites claimed to detect the constant intrusive presence of the chip on the shoulder. But, while often identified later on as that increasing rarity, a Labour leader of working-class origin, Callaghan's starting point was different from that of the party's founding fathers. He was *déclassé* rather than proletarian, and the naval origins reinforced the point. Seebohm Rowntree and Charles Booth would have categorized him as 'lower middle class', along with schoolteachers or poorer clergymen, perhaps less well paid than artisans but with higher expectations of social advance. Booth, writing about east London at the turn of the century, noted 'the social feeling which places the clerk's work above manual employment'.[24] Callaghan had been able to complete his secondary education and embark on a professional career, however modest. Indeed, his educational background was somewhat stronger than that of another prime minister who lost his father very young, the popularly styled 'cottage-bred boy' David Lloyd George, and perhaps more comparable to that of another relatively disadvantaged future leader, John Major.

The Portsmouth years brought their meed of hardship but also hopes of a better life. They had served to give young Leonard a chance. Compared with the autodidact labour leaders of an earlier generation, men like Jack Lawson, George Isaacs, or George Tomlinson or, of course, Ernest Bevin, all of whom had a brief elementary education before going into manual work, and with whom he was to serve in Attlee's government, he had prospects of being upwardly mobile. He had given himself an opportunity both to understand and to change his world, and he was determined to take it.

1. G. M. Trevelyan, *History of England* (London, 1926), 578.

2. A very helpful work is John Sadden, *Keep the Home Fires Burning: The Story of Portsmouth and Gosport in World War I* (Portsmouth, 1990). I am much indebted to Mr Sadden for helpful advice and information. Also useful is *British Medical Association: 91st Annual Meeting, Portsmouth 1923. The Book of Portsmouth* (Portsmouth, 1923). I am also grateful to Mr Harry Green, letter to the author, 16 Mar. 1992, for information on Portsmouth at the time of Callaghan's childhood.

3. *Sun*, Apr. 1976 (cutting in Callaghan Papers).

4. James Callaghan, *Time and Chance* (London, 1987), 22.

5. Kenneth O. Morgan, *Keir Hardie: Radical and Socialist* (London, 1975), 258.

6. See *Portsmouth Evening News*, 10 May 1991.

7. *Ashore and Afloat*, Dec. 1914.

8. Peter Gregory to Callaghan, 27 Mar. 1976 (Callaghan Papers, box 18). I am much indebted to Dr Ewen Green, of Magdalen College, Oxford, for information on his native Brixham. It was the home of H. F. Lyte author of 'Abide with me'.

9. *Furzeham School, Brixham, 1889–1989: A Centenary Booklet* (Brixham, 1989), 33 ff.

10. Interesting recollections by former pupils of the school in Callaghan's time there appeared in the *Portsmouth Evening News*, 10 May 1991. Callaghan's own recollections of his schooldays in that newspaper, 2 Apr. 1987, are of much interest. For his later thoughts, see *Guardian*, 1 Jan. 1994. 'We weren't encouraged to use or expand our minds and I wouldn't call it a good school environment.'

11. W. G. A. Raggett to the author, 18 Mar. 1992. 'Jim had painful memories of Buggy Beeden's strong right hand—we had both been caned by him and that usually meant 6 of the best—3 strokes on each hand.'

12. Leslie Monckton to the author, 13 Mar. 1992; letter from E. M. Spreadbury in *Portsmouth Evening News*, 10 May 1991.

13. Marjorie Fulford, ibid.

14. A. E. Strawn, ibid.; Olive Tanton (Percy Harding's sister) to the author, 9 Mar. 1992.

15. Interview with Lord Callaghan; Harry Green to the author, 16 Mar. 1992.

16. Jessie Worrall to the author, 9 Mar. 1992.

17. Callaghan, *Time and Chance*, 25.

18. Ibid., 36.

19. Lord Longford, *Eleven at Number Ten* (London, 1984), 150. When asked by the atheist Tony Crosland around 1966 how he could claim that Wilson's was 'a Christian Cabinet', Pakenham replied, 'I make it eleven Christians, beginning with the top three—Harold Wilson, George Brown and Jim Callaghan—six non- or anti-Christians and four don't knows.' He adds, curiously, 'Jim Callaghan's Christianity, like that of some of the greatest saints (St. Augustine, for example), owes an immeasurable debt to his mother.' I know of no other comparison of Lord Callaghan to St Augustine, author of the famous observation, 'Lord, make me pure, but not yet.'

20. *Portsmouth Evening News*, 10 May 1991.

21. Material in Callaghan Papers, box 31.

22. Ibid.

23. MS material from Dorothy Carter (sister), *c.*1981 (Callaghan Papers, British School of Political Economic Science, box 7, 'Memoirs'). Also see Ian Mikardo, *Backbencher* (London, 1988), 26.

24. Charles Booth, *Life and Labour of the People in London* (2nd edn., London, 1902–3), 2nd series, iii. 275. He adds, 'A clerk differs from an artisan in the claims each makes upon society no less than the claim society makes on them.'

2

UNION MAN

IN the autumn of 1929, Leonard Callaghan entered a new world in more senses than one. From the working-class suburbs of Portsmouth, with its gaunt naval barracks and sprawling dockyards, he moved to the compact county town of Maidstone in Kent. It was a placid rural haven on the river Medway, in which the pace of life seemed slow and stately, especially when errant sheep blocked the main streets of the town. It was a totally unfamiliar scene to the young Inland Revenue clerk who arrived to share lodgings there with another young clerk, clutching a bag of pears given him by the kindly Mr Woodruff, superintendent of the Portsmouth Baptist Sunday school. But in many ways it was also a more stimulating world, healthy, environmentally friendly, and relaxed. Many of the clients at the tax office were local farmers, complaining, as farmers commonly do, about the burdens of tax, but undoubtedly much afflicted by the effects of the agricultural depression that gripped Britain in the inter-war years. Callaghan's pay was just 33*s*. *6d*. (£1.67) a week, out of which he paid 25*s*. for his lodgings. However, he was still able to save enough to rent a wireless set and buy his mother a gold sovereign. Even on a small stipend, Maidstone with its opportunities for open-air games like tennis and friendly tea shops seemed like a pleasant change. Inland Revenue clerks like Callaghan were poorly paid, had no clear avenue of promotion, and worked in dingy surroundings in local offices. Nevertheless, in November 1929—just after 'Black Thursday' and the Wall Street crash in New York with a huge resultant increase in unemployment in Britain with which the new Labour government of Ramsay MacDonald manifestly failed to deal—a job was a job.

As a clerk working in a local tax office, Callaghan was one of hundreds of thousands of young people, men and increasingly women, who formed part of the massive expansion of white-collar workers after the First World War. The clerks and other lower middle-class employees had been a striking feature of the changing and more complex labour structure of later

Victorian Britain as the administrative and professional services expanded. The clerks have been identified as being prominent in the patriotic celebrations of the time, in the popular frenzy which greeted the relief of Mafeking and the defeat of the Boers in the South African War.[1] On a happier note, they provided clients of the new tourist trips to the seaside, and customers of the music hall and football and cricket matches. They were immortalized by H. G. Wells in his sagas of the lower middle class. Politically, while mainly thought to be a conservative force, they also inspired a new thrust towards administrative socialism amongst the Fabians. Sidney Webb, who began his professional life as a clerk for the Inland Revenue, particularly identified with them. One notable socialist crusader was Herbert Morrison, an official for the National Union of Clerks, who was to campaign from his lower middle-class Lewisham constituency later on for Labour to appeal to the black-coated no less than to the blue-collar worker. They, too, counted amongst Morrison's 'useful people'.

The First World War, with its vast increase in the leviathan of central government through the 'war socialism' of the time, witnessed a massive growth of the administrative and other service personnel. This expansion went on in the post-war years. It was calculated that the clerical professions expanded by 1.4 million between 1911 and 1931, 650,000 of these being women. It was to organize their affairs that the Whitley Councils were created.[2] This growth went on during the 1920s, not least amongst the Inland Revenue. Despite the fact that the majority of workers still paid no income tax (which stood at 4*s*. (20 pence) in the pound in 1929), the growing complexity of the tax and revenue system meant that the Inland Revenue needed a steady flow of young recruits to undertake routine and mundane, but essential, tasks. The work was often humdrum, yet employment by the Inland Revenue, a key arm of the machinery of central government, was to carry with it a certain social cachet, with prestige and historic identity thought to compensate young clerks for the dull nature of their activities. They were, in Marxist terms, *petit bourgeois*, not rank and file artisans.

Young Callaghan, while capable and quick in his work, found it anything but riveting. Certainly, the routine experience of office work as a young tax official stayed with him for the rest of his public life. His approach to financial policy, as shadow and then as actual Chancellor of the Exchequer, focused particularly on tax reform in which he always demonstrated a particular expertise. The minutiae of assessment and collection procedures were always a special interest. Not surprisingly, he was to provide his own tax statements for the Inland Revenue later on in life, when others might have turned to the services of an accountant. Still, the office work was boring, with few demands on his intelligence. Much of his time was spent in simply copying out Schedule A assessments. Such excitements as there were came from meetings with often recalcitrant local farmers on market days.

But the mind of the young tax clerk in his eighteenth year was engrossed by a more rewarding opportunity for his talents. This was the world of clerical trade unionism. He joined the Association of the Officers of Taxes on the voluntary basis on which 95 per cent of the clerical employees joined. He did so in part to improve his promotion prospects since the AOT offered correspondence courses on assisting the examination success of young clerks, a useful way of recruiting new members. But he soon became passionately absorbed by the need for union reorganization and internal reform for their own sake. Here he showed a force of personality and clarity of analysis unusual in a totally inexperienced young man of 18. The AOT emerged out of the reorganization of the non-industrial civil service by the national Whitley Council in 1920, which recommended that there should be four general classes of employees—administrative, executive, clerical, and 'female writing assistants' (the last, inevitably perhaps, the most humble and poorly paid of them all). Along with this reorganization came higher pay scales and a sliding scale to cover movements in the cost of living.[3] The Association of Tax Clerks (as it was first called) came into being in May 1921 at a meeting at Liverpool when the 23-year-old A. L. N. D. (Douglas) Houghton, who had joined the Inland Revenue as a boy clerk and served in the Civil Service Rifle Corps during the war, became organizing secretary. The class distinction between the various civil service grades was glaring. The clerical grade, in which Leonard Callaghan served, drew its membership from the ordinary secondary schools; the executive grade members came from the grammar schools; the administrative class derived from the public schools and the universities, invariably Oxford and Cambridge.[4] It was a highly stratified, almost segregated system which precisely mirrored British society as a whole. The young Callaghan, like many other clerks, was bitterly aware of its rigid inequalities.

Even so, the AOT, which numbered just 3,219 members by the spring of 1922, became more effective over time, in large measure because of Houghton's endeavours. Its monthly journal *Taxes*, launched in 1912, became a far more effective vehicle for the union after the war. The new Association was supposed, so its standing orders declared, 'to regulate relations between the tax clerk and the Board of Inland Revenue'—a distinctly unequal match—as well as to deal with matters amongst the clerks themselves, and to relieve members in distressed circumstances such as bereavements. Like all civil service unions, the AOT was officially non-political. The Trades Disputes Act of 1927, passed by the Baldwin government after the General Strike, laid down that it could not affiliate to any political party and that any political fund must be administered by independent trustees. Nevertheless, it had earlier welcomed the return to parliament in a by-election in 1922 of Charles Ammon, the organizing secretary of the Union of Post Office Workers and the first MP from a civil service union. He was much needed to ward off some of the effects of the Geddes axe, the cuts in social and public services imposed by the Lloyd George coalition government in 1922. The official historian of the Post Office Workers has testified to the importance of this priority for his union, and other clerical workers benefited also, or felt that they did.[5]

Callaghan became at once fascinated by, and impatient with, the operations of the AOT. He became a minor office secretary for the union in the course of 1930. He felt the local branch was ill-organized and he expressed this view in the caustic, impatient, perhaps arrogant way characteristic of young would-be reformers frustrated by the perceived inertia of the old guard. In 1932, the same year in which he passed the civil service examination to become a senior tax officer, he became branch secretary for the AOT for Kent. He forced a vote against the sitting officer, E. J. Clark of Folkestone, and, bolstered by the votes of younger members, defeated him. He thus reflected the growing influence of young recruits as the generation of ex-servicemen was being replaced. He was now eligible to attend the annual conference of the AOT and, although only 20, was a potentially important figure in the union. He attended the 1933 conference of the Association at Buxton and spoke there. At this conference, he found himself sitting next to a somewhat older Swansea man, Edgar Heale, and another Welshman and past president, Dai Kneath. Eleven years later, Heale and particularly Kneath were to help in smoothing his progress to becoming a south Wales Labour MP.

As a young union official, based on Ashford, some of his duties were amiable enough: for instance, he part organized a cricket competition for branches in the Kent district.[6] But it soon became clear that the young Turk from Kent was a troublemaker. At least, that is how he was regarded by Douglas Houghton and the established union leadership. He later described himself, with wry exaggeration, as 'a rabid young revolutionary'.[7] He was highly critical of the situation of young entrants such as himself with pay of only £2 10*s*. a week, with no opportunities for promotion for up to twenty years, and only monotonous and undemanding work to do. As early as November 1933, a forceful article of his appeared in *Taxes* which spelt out some of the grievances of the members involved.[8] He attended the annual conference of the Association at Buxton Spa in 1933, as noted, and as a result of a vigorous speech found himself elected to the union's executive. In 1934, he was to be fourth out of seven elected with 99 votes.[9] He now found effective allies among other young union members. In particular, he formed a lively partnership with Stanley Raymond, another clerk more than a year younger than Callaghan, and also the product of a deprived home background since he had been brought up in an orphanage. He and Callaghan now became forceful spokesmen for the younger recruits to the profession. They articulated vigorously at union meetings the grievances of teenage recruits, not least their being inhumanely pitchforked to a quite new part of the country to find their own lodgings at the tender age of perhaps 17. No doubt Callaghan had his own experience in mind.

In February, the dissidents formed a new body, the New Entrants' movement, at a meeting in London. S. E. Raymond of Kingston was elected chairman and L. J. Callaghan of Maidstone its secretary. In a speech to the meeting, Callaghan emphasized that this was not a secessionist movement but one that reflected the genuine grievance of young boys and girls entering civil service employment. Opportunities should be given to those within the service in the administrative class and not simply to *arriviste* Oxford and Cambridge graduates. He was caustically critical of a senior colleague in the columns of *Taxes* in January 1934 for his failure to understand the grievances of the young entrants, and he urged him to enrol in tutorial classes in psychology.[10] By May the New Entrants claimed over 200 members and was presenting a series of formal demands to the AOT executive. It rejected the very modest revision in the tax officers' pay grade endorsed by the executive. In a seven-page memorandum, it argued the case for a rise in the payment to £3 10*s*. a week (from £2 16*s*.) at the age of 22, with an allowance of £30 and a separate allowance of £30 for women tax clerks.[11] A particular grievance was that success in the qualifying examination brought no obvious rewards. In *Taxes* in May 1934 Callaghan spelt out the need to keep the various clerical grades open to boys and girls from the central schools as well as the grammar schools, and to preserve the idea of a career open to talents.[12]

This series of challenges brought Callaghan into sharp conflict with Douglas Houghton. Although still only 38, Houghton was already a senior, almost revered, figure within the ranks of clerical unionism. He was a legendary organizer and strategist, with much success in public bargaining with the Inland Revenue on working conditions and pay. But he was also a man of a notoriously short fuse, and he and Callaghan clashed on several occasions. He did not approve of angry young men. When the New Entrants produced its own paper, *New Outlook*, a pugnacious publication, Houghton and the AOT president, J. R. Simpson, actually brought a libel action against it, and took legal advice to inquire whether the *Outlook* could be lawfully suppressed. After some acrimony, the case was settled out of court on the basis that all copies of one offending issue of the *Outlook* be destroyed. (Fortunately for the historian, copies survive in the British Library.) On the other hand, Houghton drew a distinction between Raymond and Callaghan in personal terms. The former, in Houghton's later view, was 'the bulldozer', blunt-spoken and direct. Callaghan was 'the strategist', with his aggression generally under control and greater political skills.[13] He had a high regard for the young man's abilities even then, and this helped towards a reconciliation in June 1934 when the New Entrants' Committee was wound up, and the reorganization proposed by the executive accepted as a basis for presentation to the Inland Revenue.[14] The following month, the Board of Inland Revenue accepted the executive's proposals. On the other hand, the New Entrants had largely won their point also with assurances about working conditions and promotion procedures offered to new recruits. Callaghan and others offered a message of harmony and the need for a united front.

The New Entrants' movement, however, was of wider importance. It gave early prominence to Raymond and to Callaghan. Raymond went on to have a distinguished career in the war where he rose to the rank of lieutenant-colonel, and then served on the control commission in Germany. He and Callaghan were to meet again in the 1960s as head of British Rail (1965–7), via the British Transport Commission, and Chancellor of the Exchequer respectively. When he went to the Home Office, Callaghan appointed his old friend Raymond to be head of the Gaming Board in 1968, partly to have a tough figure in a sphere where possible Mafia involvement was feared. More remarkably, Douglas Houghton believed that Callaghan also considered Raymond as a unique outside appointment to the Commissionership of the Metropolitan Police. The New Entrants had a wider significance for Callaghan's own career, too. It offered him an opportunity to strike a judicious balance between protest and diplomacy. This was typical of Callaghan throughout his career, with carrots usually predominating over big sticks. He continued to have critical things to say about his union. In February 1935 he wrote in *Taxes* on the congenial theme of widening the Tax Officers' Qualifying Examination, with more general subjects like economics, languages, and English brought in alongside the technical and vocational subjects of the kind he had endured at school at Portsmouth Northern.[15] But he had also achieved a wider recognition and acceptance as an effective speaker and a clear-headed organizer. By now, he had moved his post from Maidstone to London where he served in the City East branch, and became a member of the London Executive Committee of the union. His career, and his lifelong relationship with Douglas Houghton, were to enter a new phase.

His personal life had also been transformed. The youthful stormy petrel of the union was, for the first significant time, in love. He took part in the Sunday school in the Baptist community in Maidstone, who had welcomed him in. Here he met a slim 16-year-old girl, Audrey Moulton, at a formal tea meeting on the first occasion of all.[16] He was sufficiently struck by Audrey to take up the game of tennis with which he had little previous acquaintance, and to join a tennis club. Audrey was a Maidstone girl who had attended the local high school. She played hockey and tennis and had taken holidays in France to develop her linguistic skills. Her parents were both active Baptists. Her father Frank Moulton, a Cambridge man by origin and a local small businessman, was managing director of the Lead Wool company, which contained many Baptists in key positions and was deacon and superintendent of the Sunday school. His wife Clara came from Watford in Hertfordshire. Apart from the presence of Audrey, Leonard Callaghan felt much at ease in the Moulton home. In some ways, perhaps, Frank Moulton became the father he had lost at so early an age. He enjoyed the large garden, the family tea parties, the strolls in the cherry orchard, the Sunday lunches, and the trips to the seaside, all of them delights for a somewhat lonely young man. Audrey herself was from the first deeply attractive to him and it soon became clear that their relationship was going to be a permanent one. They embarked, as was the custom at that time, on a lengthy engagement, punctuated by occasional holidays including somewhat adventurous driving expeditions in a 1921 Wolseley coupé car, and a first visit abroad, a vacation in Switzerland in 1937. When Callaghan moved his job to London in 1934, Audrey followed. She trained at the Battersea College of Domestic Science, and then became a teacher of that subject in Eltham.

In Audrey, Callaghan found the perfect partner. Throughout his career, he would freely acknowledge his dependence on her for love and moral support. An illness for Audrey was a crisis for Jim. He never had to confront the domestic complications that scarred the private lives of Lloyd

George or Harold Macmillan. She would sustain him in difficult political crises, and was a devoted and loving mother of their three children. She was always benevolent, gentle in manner. But she had her own strong views also. In particular, she had a special interest in health and the well-being of children. Her later strong links with Great Ormond Street hospital for children could have been foreseen years earlier. In addition, she was manifestly a political wife, far more so than was the case with earlier Labour prime ministers. Ramsay MacDonald was a long-term widower. Violet Attlee appears to have been, if anything, a Conservative. Mary Wilson was a private person who loved poetry, and disliked politics; she thought that with Harold she had married a don who would settle down happily in the Betjeman land of north Oxford for the rest of his days. Although the Moulton family were anti-socialist (probably nonconformist Liberals who moved to the right), Audrey herself had leftish views, no doubt encouraged by the fiery young union official who was her partner at tennis. She joined the Fabian Society, and went with Leonard to London to hear lectures by Laski, Wells, or Shaw in the Fabians' autumn lecture series at Friends' House, or perhaps exotic celebrities like Krishna Menon. She read the works of the Coles and the Webbs, and was much influenced by an extramural economics course she attended in Eltham High School, conducted by, amongst others, a young lecturer called Hugh Gaitskell. Although she had no idea that her young fiancé would enter politics himself, she viewed the prospect without dismay. In her self-effacing way she contributed to it immensely herself, without ever incurring, in those gentler times, the kind of aggressive and intrusive tabloid attention visited upon Glenys Kinnock or Cherie Blair as alleged powers behind the throne.

They were married at Knightrider Baptist church, Maidstone, on 28 July 1938, with Callaghan's friend Archie Clark, assistant tuition course organizer of the IRSF, as best man. It was followed by a reception at Tudor House, Bearstead. Audrey gave Leonard an Omega watch which he wore for the rest of his life. He gave her a fur wrap. The music that accompanied the signing of the register was, somewhat unusually, a work by Dvořák. Audrey chose this herself and indeed had kindled a growing interest in music in Callaghan himself. Prom concerts and the Old Vic had been part of their lives together for some time, while he chose to inform the readers of *Taxes* of the merits of a woman producer's version of Ibsen's *Master Builder*—'one of the most masterly things I have seen'.[17] They had a honeymoon in Paris and Chamonix and settled to live in a rented house in Upper Norwood. For they could now afford this improved style of life.

The 26-year-old Callaghan, who had entered the civil service only eight years previously, was now a significant trade union official.

His progress had been rapid after the New Entrants dispute. Houghton saw in him not only a lively young prospect, but also a plausible democratic radical to promote, in contrast to the Communists who were beginning to infiltrate some levels of white-collar unionism in the 1930s. In February 1936 the AOT merged with the National Association of Tax Assessing and Collecting Services (NATACS) to form the Inland Revenue Staff Federation. In January 1937 they were to be joined by the Valuation Officers' Clerical Association. They were a distinctly bourgeois group: the class barriers were coming down at last. From that time onwards, the IRSF was the voice of the Inland Revenue staff, and a respected and effective body: in 1996 it was finally wound up or rather transformed into the Inland Revenue group of the newly formed Public Services, Tax and Commerce Union. Callaghan, as AOT delegate from City East, attended the founding meeting of the IRSF council at Central Hall, Westminster, on 24 January 1936, and was appointed to the General Purposes Committee. He had not lost his pugnacity on behalf of the younger entrants. In May he criticized a letter from seventy-five tax officers who had complained at having to compete for promotion with new entrants. Callaghan attacked them for 'wanting to erect a tariff wall 10 years high'. Their letter was 'an ill-considered effusion'.[18] In response, F. R. Oddy told Callaghan, 'The fight is with the Board. Hit hard, keep hitting, but don't hit your own men.'[19] In spite of this, Houghton viewed Callaghan with a cordial eye. Young though he was, he had confidence and style.

In August 1936, Callaghan stood for national office as assistant secretary of the IRSF. This would put him second only to Houghton himself. To prepare the way, he had 'a quiet word' (a characteristic phrase) with Jock Simpson, an executive member who was anxious to defeat a left-wing movement headed by A. Greenway.[20] Callaghan himself, as always, detested extremism in any form. In the event, he defeated with some ease a distinguished group of rivals. The short list consisted, apart from himself, of Stanley Raymond and Cyril Plant, who was collection honorary secretary at the time and was himself to serve as general secretary of the IRSF from 1960 to 1976 and to become a nationally known trade unionist. Plant was to be president of the TUC in 1976 when his old IRSF colleague went to 10 Downing Street. In the columns of *Taxes*, Callaghan's election was greeted by Raymond with generosity and warmth. When he first met Callaghan in 1934, he had thought him 'very much subdued at first', but he soon blossomed to show originality of thought. Raymond urged

Callaghan not to let his health be undermined by the pressures of work in the way that Houghton's had been.[21] But Callaghan was a young man on fire. He cheerfully gave up a secure job with the Inland Revenue for the less certain future of a union secretaryship, though at an enhanced stipend of £350 and with an office at 7 St George's Square, a part-time secretary, and even that comparative rarity, a telephone. As a union man he had arrived.

Many new avenues now opened up for him. There was the happiness and security of his relationship with Audrey and her family. There was the excitement of entertainment and sport in London in which he himself participated. Indeed, on the suggestion of Stan Raymond, he had taken up the unfamiliar game of rugby and, with his burly physique, played for a time as a second-row forward with Streatham. The only mishap he recalled was a collision with another player which resulted in the loss of two front teeth. In October 1939, after he had stopped playing, he recalled on a visit to the Rosslyn Park dressing room how the characteristic smell of the liniment made him nostalgic for his rugby-playing days. He gave a strong impression of rude health and athletic vigour. In 1976, after he had become premier, he told the IRSF delegates of his frustration, as a young tax officer, at having to slave away in a stuffy office during the post-budget work peak in the summer months when other young men were on the cricket field or the tennis court.[22] Not surprisingly, one of his most effective areas of activity as assistant secretary of the union was in organizing the IRSF Youth Group, where a sporting 25-year-old created a far more dynamic image than did his out-of-condition, middle-aged colleagues.

Professionally, his most important relationship was that with Douglas Houghton. He was Houghton's protégé—indeed, his intended successor (although he could not know that Houghton was not to retire until 1960!). He performed important and delicate tasks for his master. One of them was the rewriting of the union rule-book. This was a matter whose importance Callaghan instinctively understood. He would not have made Harold Wilson's mistake in the 1960s of impatiently telling union leaders that their rule-books should be thrown away. At a youthful age, Callaghan knew much better than that. But the relationship with the older man was not an easy one. Houghton was virtually married to the union. The domestic distraction that Leonard's marriage to Audrey brought led to almost a kind of jealousy. Houghton's fiery temper led to many rows with almost everyone, and he was not best pleased during the war when Callaghan chose to enter the navy. The position at the end of the war when Callaghan had become an MP but still wanted an official connection with the IRSF also led to some tension. For all that, the long-term relationship was close and respectful on both sides. Callaghan admired Houghton greatly as a very able, far-sighted, and pioneering figure: one major instance of this was to be Houghton's role in persuading the Inland Revenue during the war to start the system of PAYE. At first, of course, Houghton was the senior figure, and indeed acquired more celebrity during the war with his radio broadcasts *Can I help you?* in which he explained tricky points about social security and welfare to the listeners. But quite soon the roles became reversed. Houghton was anxious for a parliamentary seat himself, and Callaghan tried in vain to get him nominated for Lewisham. What defeated him, apparently, was Houghton's recent divorce, a real political handicap at that time, although he remarried in 1939. Eventually, he was elected for the Yorkshire constituency of Sowerby in a by-election in 1949 and served in parliament until 1974. He was a minister in the first Wilson government. As chairman of the parliamentary Labour Party from 1967 he was a close confidant and backer of Callaghan's, consulted by him over select employment and other taxes while at the Treasury. He backed him strongly, in defiance of Harold Wilson, over the arguments about *In Place of Strife* in 1969, and formed a strong, even unbeatable, troika with Callaghan and Vic Feather of the TUC. Even in the 1990s, the nonagenarian Houghton was a frequent associate of Callaghan's in the Lords, even though appearing to lament that young Jim, his octogenarian colleague, did not share fully his own absorbing passion for animal rights.[23]

The work as assistant secretary of the IRSF was busy but rewarding. The columns of *Taxes* give an impression of a lively, growing union. The cheerfulness extended to its publishing seaside photographs of the more attractive female union members in bathing suits. During this period, Callaghan was brought into wider prominence as delegate to the Trades Union Congress (non-voting), where he was to meet Dalton, Bevin, and other Labour leaders. He spoke out at a conference of black-coated workers organized by the Fabian Society in London where he denounced Clause 5 of the 1927 Trade Disputes Act which forbade political activity. His own performances at the IRSF's conferences were crisp and confident. In June 1937 it was said that he 'made a very good impression' with his presentation.[24] His wedding in 1938 was a major public event, attended by John Jagger and other union notables such as Jock Simpson, W. T. Seddon, and P. H. M. Hoey. Callaghan gained further publicity by writing a secretary's column in *Taxes*. This dealt with matters such as sick pay and compensation for injuries, pay scales, and always the prospects for young entrants, very much his own cause. He discussed practical details of the most minute kind. One column advocated keeping windows shut for fifty-five minutes in an hour, with five minutes of open windows then for the staff to have a break.

He was also a regular participant in hearings with the Civil Service Clerical Association on the Arbitration Tribunal to discuss matters of pay and grading. The staff side nominee on the Tribunal was Harold Laski, a selfless servant of the unions in forums such as these. Callaghan had been much impressed by reading his *Grammar of Politics*, an argument for liberal pluralism, some years earlier. He had gone avidly through its pages at lunchtimes at Tower Hill while he chewed the odd sandwich. Half a century later, Callaghan listed this book in the *Northern Echo* as one of five that had particularly influenced him as a young man. He described Laski's book there as 'an ABC of socialism and a theoretical underpinning to justify practical political action'. (The other four books included Shaw's *Prefaces* to his plays and Arthur Koestler's *Spanish Testament*.[25]) Laski, in turn, was clearly struck by the sheer ability of the young Callaghan's performance in tribunal sessions. He urged him to take an external degree at the London School of Economics which he himself would supervise. He arranged for him to have a reader's ticket for the library there, but Callaghan simply did not have the time to spare. The burden of the assistant secretary's routine was far too heavy. But in addition Laski struck a different note. He suggested that the union official should think about politics. He kept Callaghan's name in mind as a likely future Labour parliamentary candidate, and indeed recommended him to Transport House.[26]

Meanwhile, the Federation, in alliance with the CSCA and help from the Ministry of Labour, managed to promote its specific causes. One constant theme for Callaghan right down to the war was, once again, the situation for young recruits. He also criticized the system of compulsory transfers of employees to other parts of the country at short notice. He laid emphasis on the difficulties caused for young wives, moving to anonymous housing estates on the outskirts of a strange town where they knew nobody. Movement from depressed industrial areas in Wales, Scotland, and the north of England to new posts in the London suburbs could often be demoralizing and stressful for family life, and harmful to the children's education. On balance, the impression is left of a highly competent but also compassionate and thoughtful young union official, energetic and articulate, wholly effective in directing the union's affairs. In short, here was Houghton's natural deputy and future successor.

But, since the early 1930s, his mind had ranged beyond the life of the unions. Despite his youthful forays in the school playground, he was not a notably political animal when he went to Maidstone. There he met socialists in the local branch, including Steve MacWhirter, who directed his interest towards political and economic matters. He quietly joined the Labour Party in Maidstone in 1931, and became more active when he moved to Lewisham with the greater protective anonymity afforded by suburban London. He also joined the Fabians. He strengthened his interest by taking WEA evening classes in economics and social history, and reading voraciously the works of Shaw and Wells, the Webbs, Laski, and Cole. To an instinctive hatred of injustice and the class inequality which he had witnessed in the streets of Portsmouth and even in the clerical union, he now added a much clearer intellectual and dialectical thrust.

The young Callaghan, in short, had got religion and wanted the world to know. He became a passionate, though always democratic, socialist, and shed his old Baptist faith as he did so. The break with Christianity was far from straightforward and evidently produced a crisis of conscience of a somewhat fundamental kind. Somewhat unusually, he wrote a formal letter to the secretary of the Maidstone Baptists declaring that his faith in socialism was incompatible with Christianity. However, a talk with a wise senior deacon appeared to show him that church membership and socialist beliefs were not irreconcilable, and that in any case the strict fundamentalism of his upbringing was far from typical amongst Baptists. As a result, Callaghan withdrew his resignation from chapel membership, but the pull of the union and the Labour Party caused a slow drift from the faith nevertheless.[27] Effectively he ceased to be a practising Christian, though he was to pray at critical moments when in government, notably in his time at the Treasury. He now began to speak at Labour Party meetings, especially when he moved to London. In the 1935 general election he and Audrey manned the Labour Party committee rooms in Lewisham on behalf of Freda Corbett and Michael Stewart in the East and West divisions. Both candidates, however, were heavily defeated in these strongly Conservative middle-class constituencies.[28]

One important stimulus to his political enthusiasm was access to men like Hugh Dalton, ever supportive of the young, at TUC conferences. Laski, as has been seen, was another important influence, not only for his commitment to socialism of an inspirational and libertarian kind, but also for his personal links as a teacher with young students from Africa, India, Australia, and the Caribbean. Callaghan would work closely with many of them in later life. His political sympathies had to be kept on a leash, in line with the traditions of the civil service unions, while in any case the white-collar employees were not overenthusiastic for links with a Labour Party that was largely identified with blue-collar workers in heavy industry. Still, the spark of political engagement was there, and national activities as a union official helped nurture it. Many young idealists like Leonard Callaghan joined the Labour movement or socialist organizations in the 1930s. But, while attention has usually focused on the more left-wing forms of this—the Socialist League, the Popular Front, the Left Book Club—the prevailing trend was undoubtedly for more moderate, gradualist socialists of the Callaghan type. He read the Left Book Club volumes, he devoured the fiercely anti-capitalist critiques of journalists like H. N. Brailsford and Kingsley Martin, he chaired meetings on behalf of Indian self-government addressed by a radical like Krishna Menon. But it was always within the context of constitutionalism and persuasion. As with Ernest Bevin, his socialism was rooted in empirical realities, not in abstract dogma. 'Extremism', he would say in later life, 'only bred extremism.' He was never sentimental about Soviet Russia, and had no time for Cripps's call for a Popular Front. It was this fusion of gradualism and social passion that marked him out for Douglas Houghton as a possible union leader. More broadly, it set him on the road that led to 1945 and indeed to 1976.

Callaghan's political passion was stirred by the international crises of which he read and heard, and which provided the background to his advance as a union leader. The failure of the National Government to defend Abyssinia was a major theme of his speeches in the general election of October 1935. A loyal son of a naval petty officer, he was never any kind of pacifist. On the other hand, he shared the confusions of the British left towards international affairs at that time. He subscribed to the standard opposition to the 'system of Versailles' which he felt had been unjustly punitive to Germany and had been a major cause of the rise of fascism. 'Allied Statesmanship since 1918 had been even more responsible for the Nazis.'[29] He condemned the National Government for failing to lend proper support to the League of Nations and endorsed the findings of the Peace Ballot with its backing for sanctions. On the other hand, he was deeply suspicious of Baldwin's government in all its aspects, at home and abroad, and down to 1939 he opposed military conscription on civil liberties grounds. He also took a somewhat *bienpensant* view of the Peace Ballot (including in his memoirs forty years later) which bypassed the fact that collective security and military sanctions were widely felt to be incompatible. Collective security, many believed, would imply disarmament rather than rearmament while recourse to arms would merely reproduce capitalist great-power rivalries of the old kind which had led to war in 1914.

But what stirred young Callaghan, as it did so many of the centre-left in Britain at that time, was Spain. For him, as for thousands of others, the civil war there was a straightforward struggle between good and evil, between a popularly elected, democratic, socialist-led government and a fascist military dictatorship. W. H. Auden declared in 1937, 'I am your choice, your decision. Yes, I am Spain.' Callaghan spoke out from Labour Party platforms for Britain to join with the newly elected Popular Front government in France under Léon Blum, to end the arms embargo, so one-sided in its effects, and to send arms to defend Spanish democracy against fascism and Franco. He sympathized with the aims of the International Brigade which some young British socialists joined, including the young Jack Jones in Merseyside, and attended a massive Arms for Spain meeting in Shoreditch Town Hall addressed by D. N. Pritt.

More remarkably, he managed as its assistant secretary to help persuade the IRSF to send financial assistance to the Spanish Medical Aid Committee. This was a more complex matter than it might seem, because the civil service unions were not permitted political affiliations.[30] When the Spanish Civil War broke out in July 1936, this factor alone led to a guarded response from the white-collar unions. The most militant of them, the Union of Postal Workers, which sought affiliation to the Labour Party, did demonstrate its support for the 'Spanish Workers' Fund', while the Civil Service Clerical Association, with its radical secretary W. J. Brown, actually donated a small sum to the fund. This, however, provoked some resistance, partly because of the qualms of Roman Catholic members who were sympathetic to the Franco uprising against the anticlerical Republican government. More important, perhaps, was the link of aid for Spain with the Communist Party and fellow-travelling organizations generally. It was, therefore, quite an achievement for Callaghan to have passed on 26 May 1938, at the annual IRSF conference held at Bexhill, an amendment in favour of the Spanish Medical Aid fund, the case being argued on humanitarian rather than political grounds.[31] Here Callaghan pointed out that the Post Office Workers and the Civil Service Clerical Association had already endorsed the principle. Efforts were now made to co-ordinate activity with the other civil service unions. But the white-collar unions in general remained cautious. Even the Union of Postal Workers declined to co-operate, preferring to emphasize its own individual contributions since 1936 on behalf of the Spanish workers. Nor did Callaghan and his colleagues get much sympathy from the Labour Party leadership when he led a six-man deputation from East Lewisham to the Commons. Hugh Dalton, Labour's foreign affairs spokesman, refused to endorse a call for the supply of arms, He was gratuitously offensive to Callaghan personally, a slight which the younger man remembered during their later friendship. Early in 1939 the Republican cause finally collapsed and Franco's régime prevailed in Spain until 1975, by which time Callaghan was Foreign Secretary. Even so, the relatively active stance of the otherwise apolitical IRSF in the Spanish Civil War, in the face of some resistance from the membership voiced in *Taxes*,[32] must have owed a good deal to Callaghan's own energetic advocacy. It indicated his growing passionate commitment to political issues. Union officials like Cyril Plant wondered how long they would be able to retain the services of their energetic and capable young assistant secretary.

As the crises over the *Anschluss* with Austria and then over the Sudetenland brought war steadily nearer in 1938, the Callaghans took a more personal initiative. In response to an appeal to extend hospitality to fugitives from Nazism, they welcomed to their home Bernhard Menne, a leading German Social Democrat who had written a study of the Krupps arms dynasty during a period in Prague, and had fled to Britain after the Munich crisis. Menne was a gentle, intellectual figure; when Callaghan took him to see an England–Ireland rugby international at Twickenham, he was horrified by its ferocity. A former Communist, he had moved over to the Social Democrats after the Soviet state trials in 1927; by 1938 he detested Communists and fascists in equal measure. He and his wife, who joined him in Britain at the outbreak of war, impressed on the Callaghans the strength and durability of Hitler's regime which would, so they prophesied, take years of fighting to overthrow. Without doubt, Callaghan's friendship with Menne added to an increasingly informed concern with the international crisis. It may be added that the Callaghans' hospitable attitude contrasted favourably with that of others in the British Labour movement who treated German Social Democrat émigrés with caution and perhaps suspicion.[33] Ironically, the British authorities were less generous and briefly detained the Mennes as 'enemy aliens' during the war years. They returned to West Germany afterwards with some relief, and Menne was to become editor of the influential left-wing newspaper *Die Welt am Sonntag*.

With the threat of war looming in the summer of 1939, the Callaghans' pleasant suburban life in West Norwood was overtaken by a mood of anxiety. Perhaps because of the ominous nature of the time, Callaghan began to keep an intermittent diary. Its pages reveal a moving, almost pathetic, attempt to keep normal life going while anxiously preparing for what were thought to be inevitable destructive aerial bombardments from the Luftwaffe. At the start of September, he went to see the new world mile record-holder, Sidney Wooderson, and marvelled that one of his puny physique could run so fast. He paid a nostalgic visit to see Rosslyn Park play Harlequins at rugby. At the office, he kept busy, advising union members about problems of compulsory transfer consequent on war, and the technicalities of enlistment into the armed services. There was a suggestion in September 1939 that Callaghan might actually change jobs to become assistant secretary to the Civil Service Alliance and thus contribute to achieving an amalgamation of the various civil service unions. Untypically, he refused to pursue this. He confided in his diary, 'I feel that for 27 years of age I ought to be better than I am & that by this time my powers should be much more developed than they are.'[34] Perhaps his sense of deprivation through not having gone on to higher education was connected with this dissatisfaction.

But the international crisis overshadowed everything else. He was not surprised by the Nazi–Soviet pact and the Russian invasion of Poland, since his expectations of Stalin's Russia were low in any case. His view of foreign affairs, indeed, was more realistic and accurate than that of many better-trained minds—Cripps, Dalton, even Attlee—who continued to hold naive illusions about the Soviet Union down to 1939. Callaghan, by contrast, felt that the Soviet Union had 'betrayed socialist principles', although he felt that a long-lasting Russo-German alliance was unlikely. He also noted the changing situation created at home by the advent of war. Simon's budget showed that Britain might be forced into a war economy. 'Socialists must be ready to take advantage of the war and immediate post-war situation.'[35]

His most complete thoughts were set down on 10 October, more than a month after the war had broken out. It may be taken as a summary of his political philosophy as it had evolved during the 1930s. As was common in leftish analyses of the time, he felt that great-power rivalries and imperial exploitation overseas and social revolution at home were intertwined. He believed that Germany did not want a war of indeterminate length and that Britain had no intention of fighting Russia. He cited the view of Liddell Hart that 'force has never permanently settled anything', an optimistic belief if ever there was one. No peace settlement should humiliate Germany where 'pride of race' was so overwhelmingly powerful. Very reluctantly, he concluded that war was inevitable in the face of 'unprovoked aggression by a bully',[36] even though he greatly doubted whether either Chamberlain or Hitler could be relied upon to tell the truth during the period of half-peace. As with Hugh Gaitskell, his pre-war experience was to inoculate him against any sympathy with unilateralism in the 1950s and beyond. But just as important for the young Callaghan was the purpose for which the war was being fought. On no account should they be fighting to save the British Empire. He called for colonial freedom, a proper self-government for India ('not just a makeshift'), and an end to the system of colonial preference. The empire as 'a closed economic unit' was 'a menace to world peace'.

Equally urgent was a revolution at home. Like George Orwell in *The Lion and the Unicorn*, Callaghan felt that the war offered immense potential for fundamental social change. They must now reorganize the country so that there would no longer be 2 million unemployed workers. The Bank of England must be controlled in the nation's interests. Cotton, coal, the woollen industry, and agriculture should be planned for the public good, and other industry run 'in the National interest and not in the interest of private profit'. Without these changes, Britain would not have clean hands. The war could not be justified without a commitment to major changes in Britain itself and its colonies. 'So here we sit between the Scylla of Toryism and the Charybdis of Hitlerism.' The entire analysis is tormented, with no solution produced. But clearly he felt, reluctantly, that a firm, long-term response to the threat from Hitler was unavoidable. His head in turmoil, as he concluded recording his thoughts at 10.45 p.m. he then turned to hear Beethoven's Eighth Symphony on the radio, the orchestra conducted by 'somebody called Ian Whyte'. Even this did not soothe his fevered and anxious mind. He disapproved of the phrasing, the interpretation, and the conductor—'A most unsatisfying affair.'[37]

More than most young men, Callaghan came of age in the 1930s. Clearly, about the war itself, his mind was in flux. Not surprisingly, it found him unclear about long-term political and economic objectives. A stabilizing factor in 1939 was his commitment to the trade union movement. Thereafter he was constantly to be linked with the unions in his political career, their principled defender over *In Place of Strife*, their ally in drawing up the social contract in 1973–4 and retaining the Labour alliance in 1996. His rebuff by union members during the winter of discontent in 1978–9 was wounding for him as it would have been for no other Labour leader. However, his union experience was of a particular kind. His union, the IRSF, was a small, white-collar union of around 16,000 members in 1939, bourgeoisified, apolitical, unaffiliated to the Labour Party, at a time when all the major unions represented manual workers in manufacturing and service employment in their hundreds of thousands. The IRSF was a fringe body. Only in the 1970s did white-collar unionism explode in size, with massive changes in the labour market, and eventually arrived in the van of union militancy. The later stages of the 'winter of discontent' in 1979 were to be conducted by the government with the Civil Service Alliance, even those who serviced Downing Street itself, on strike.

His experience with the IRSF left Callaghan with an instinctive commitment to negotiation, arbitration, and conciliation, and a resistance to strike action. He developed early on an intuitive bargaining style, adapted later in life to running government departments or handling international conferences. From Houghton and others, he learnt how to parry, how to negotiate, when to threaten or cajole, how much to hold back in reserve. He took to heart the maxim of his old Welsh union friend Dai Kneath, that 'more flies are caught with honey than with vinegar'.[38] It followed that he took a comparatively buoyant view of the capacity of labour representatives to reach agreement and to do so within established bargaining procedures rather than via the pressures of the law. Government should operate in this spirit. Significantly, he developed a kind of admiration for Stanley Baldwin, the apostle of 'peace in our time, O Lord', and always rejected the view that he was a grey or negative politician. Journalists would sometimes see him as a new Baldwin, a consensual centrist figure, when he reached No. 10 himself, and he did not object to the comparison. Manifestly, his early views of industrial relations anticipated the voluntarist philosophy of the Donovan report of 1968. It was unthinkable that the penal sanctions of Barbara Castle's Industrial Relations Bill of 1969 could prove either workable or desirable. After all, the object was to get the law off workers' backs. A major point for all the unions in 1939 was to secure the repeal of the restrictive 1927 Trades Disputes Act. He took the standard Labour view that the state should plan production, distribution, and consumption, but remain essentially aloof from collective bargaining.

On the other hand, his experience of the 1930s convinced him also that trade unionism, like patriotism, was not enough. In the mobilizing of economic power, the political weapon was essential. His commitment to the Labour Party grew throughout the 1930s, and his determination to enter politics steadily crystallized. He had gone far in his union for so young a man. He knew when to impose pressure, when to conciliate; he had shown some skill in mobilizing opinion. An effective, confident speaker, he was a born politician. But he was also largely a home-based one, whose grasp of the international scene was shrewd but incomplete and largely second-hand. He had, after all, been abroad only twice, one occasion being his honeymoon. There was an urgent need to extend his understanding. The war provided it. It was the climacteric of his early development as for other young politicians. Nervously but determinedly, the young tax official was about to draw up his own personal audit of war.

1. See R. Price, *An Imperial War and the British Working Class* (London, 1972), 199: 'Clerks formed the backbone of the Imperial City Volunteers.'

2. For a good general account, see G. S. Bain, *The Growth of White Collar Unionism* (Oxford, 1970).

3. *Tax Clerks' Journal* (1921).

4. Callaghan, *Time and Chance*, 41.

5. Alan Clinton, *Post Office Workers: A Trade Union and Social History* (London, 1984).

6. *Taxes* (Sept. 1933).

7. Video to commemorate the centenary of the IRSF, 1992 (courtesy of Mr Clive Brooke).

8. L. J. Callaghan, 'Reorganization and the New Entrants', *Taxes* (Nov. 1933), 593–4.

9. Ibid. (May 1934), 267 ff.

10. Ibid. (Jan. 1934), 68.

11. AOT 3849. Memorandum on Reorganization submitted by the New Entrant Committee for the consideration of the Executive Committee (Callaghan Papers, box 2).

12. *Taxes* (May 1934), 267 ff.

13. Interview with Lord Houghton of Sowerby, 17 July 1990.

14. *Taxes* (July 1934), 410; cf. Lord Callaghan's memorial address on Lord Houghton, 11 July 1996. On the IRSF in the 1930s and beyond, I am much indebted to Mr K. J. Bovington whom 'Cally' (as he called him) appointed to a junior post as finance clerk to the Federation in 1938 and who worked for the IRSF for forty years, including editing *Taxes* from 1963 to 1980.

15. Ibid. (Feb. 1935), 151–2.

16. Personal knowledge; Diana Farr, *Five at Ten. Prime Minister's Consorts since 1957* (London, 1985), 125 ff.

17. Letter in *Taxes* (Apr. 1936).

18. *Taxes* (May 1936), 342.

19. Ibid. (June 1936), 423.

20. Interview with Lord Callaghan.

21. *Taxes* (Aug. 1936), 537. Article by S. E. Raymond, 'New A.O.T. Assistant Secretary: Welcome to L. J. Callaghan'. Also see Cyril Plant, 'Prime Minister Callaghan', ibid. (Apr. 1976), 155–7.

22. Callaghan diary, 1 Oct. 1939 (Callaghan Papers); communication by K. J. Bovington to the author, 25 Sept. 1996.

23. Interview with Lord Houghton of Sowerby, 17 July 1990.

24. *Taxes* (Nov. 1936), 756; (June 1937), 329.

25. *Northern Echo*, 13 May 1983 (cutting Callaghan Papers (BLPES, box 7).

26. Callaghan, *Time and Chance*, 45. See also his foreword to Granville Eastwood, *Harold Laski* (London, 1977).

27. *Time and Chance*, 39.

28. For Lewisham politics, see Tom Jeffery, 'The Suburban Nation: Politics and Class in Lewisham', in David Feldman and Gareth Stedman Jones (eds.), *Metropolis: London* (London, 1989), 189–218.

29. Callaghan diary, 24 Sept. 1939 (Callaghan Papers).

30. For an interesting discussion, see Tom Buchanan, 'Divided Loyalties: The Impact of the Spanish Civil War on Britain's Civil Service Trade Unions', *Historical Research*, 65/156 (Feb. 1992), 90–107.

31. *Taxes* (June 1938), 136.

32. Ibid. (May 1939), 271.

33. See Anthony Glees, *Exile Politics during the Second World War* (Oxford, 1982).

34. Callaghan diary, 26 Sept. 1939 (Callaghan Papers).

35. Ibid. 1 Oct. 1939.

36. Ibid. 13 Sept. 1939.

37. Ibid. 10 Oct. 1939. Ian Whyte was conductor and part-founder of the BBC Scottish Orchestra.

38. *Time and Chance*, 44.

3

PEOPLE'S WAR

On the outbreak of hostilities, the civil service like the army was put on a war footing. For taxation officers, this meant a massive dislocation of personnel. Clerks and other officials were given new roles in the administrative machinery, and often propelled with little warning to other parts of Britain. Callaghan as assistant secretary was at full stretch in advising members how to cope with the strains that this often created, from new chains of command to the problems of relocating a wife and children in unfamiliar surroundings. He was fiercely critical of the dilatory role, as he saw it, of the Clerks to the Commissioners—'they are just a nuisance and a clog on the machine'. The union was kept busy in enlisting the support of senior Labour MPs such as Arthur Greenwood (a former civil servant himself) and Frederick Pethick-Lawrence in redressing the grievances that resulted.[1]

The assistant secretary himself was not immune to the stresses of war. Shortly after hostilities began, there was a proposal that he be compulsorily transferred to serve the wool secretariat in the relatively unknown terrain of Bradford. But Douglas Houghton managed to prevent this and retain his protégé for the service of the Inland Revenue Staff Federation. Other possible moves, however, arose from Callaghan's own ambition. He applied unsuccessfully (after many rows with Houghton) for a post with the Ministry of Labour Staff Association. He had also been approached by George Higham, as has been seen, to take on the secretaryship of the Civil Service Alliance. In September 1941 he applied to become the secretary of the Federation of Post Office Supervising Officers. In his application he laid emphasis on the rise in IRSF membership during his five years in post, from 13,000 to 20,000, but again he was unsuccessful.[2] In the meantime, he was much preoccupied with official duties. One was the congenial theme of career prospects for young recruits. He clashed vigorously with the Chief Valuer's Office when he condemned the professional valuers for resisting the professional advance of young valuation clerks, male or female. 'The summit of his or her ambition is really the S.V.C. [senior valuation clerk] grade on £400 per annum.' The professional valuers, he complained, treated their junior clerks as personal servants. A more profound issue came when he collaborated with Cyril Plant and other officers and especially with Douglas Houghton, the main driving force, in persuading the Inland Revenue to embark on the PAYE system. There was a struggle to persuade the Revenue that assessment and collection on the previous year's earnings was no longer practical and that a deduction scheme from current earnings would have to replace it. Eventually, both the Inland Revenue and the Chancellor, Kingsley Wood, were convinced and PAYE finally came into effect in the budget of 1943.[3] During the early period of 'phoney war' in the autumn and winter of 1939–40, Callaghan remained busily engaged at his desk in the IRSF offices in St George's Square, Westminster, in time combining this role with that of a fire-watcher in the civil defence services.

In June 1940, just after Dunkirk and with dominant fears of a likely German invasion, the union's offices were moved and the Callaghans' family life was disrupted. They had continued to live in Upper Norwood in the winter of 1939–40, during which time their first child was born, a daughter, Margaret. The birth was uneventful for mother and daughter, though a hospital visit cost Callaghan some minor facial damage when he collided with a pillar box during the London blackout. However, the transfer of the Inland Revenue from Somerset House in the Strand to the coastal resort of Llandudno in north Wales meant that the IRSF must inevitably follow it. Callaghan was dispatched to north Wales, along with Cyril Plant and other colleagues, to find a suitable building to serve as the union offices. Curiously, although the relocation in Llandudno was supposed to be a secret, union officers heard the news from a German broadcast by William Joyce, 'Lord Haw-Haw'. Audrey Callaghan and the infant Margaret were first moved to Welshpool, a small market town in Montgomeryshire in mid-Wales. The family was able to spend a summer holiday together in the Merioneth seaside resort of Aberdyfi. But in December 1940 the family settled down at 'Winchmore', 7 Mostyn Crescent, Llandudno, in a flat above the IRSF offices there. This was to be their temporary home until the latter half of 1944. A second daughter, Julia, was born to them in October 1942. However, as for so many families during these years, the war brought dislocation and disruption. The home in Upper Norwood was shut up for the duration. Callaghan spent one week per month in the flat in Llandudno, and the rest of the time in lodgings in Queen's Gate, Kensington, alternating his time there with fire-watching duties at the Federation offices and sleeping in the basement. Meanwhile, in Llandudno he launched a successful campaign to improve conditions for civil servants in the town, including the opening of a British Restaurant.[4]

As for many young men at this time, the impact of war, and the social upheaval it entailed, impelled Callaghan more and more forcibly towards political ideas and activity. His secretary's column in *Taxes* became more overtly partisan. An important experience for him was attending the famous meeting of trade unionists addressed by Ernest Bevin in Central Hall, Westminster, on 25 May 1940, just before Dunkirk. No such meeting of a government minister and union leaders had taken place since the General Strike in 1926. The purpose was to spell out, more sympathetically than the Asquith government had done in the early months of the First World War, the relationship of the trade unions to the war effort, as the government saw it. This would entail the sacrifice of many historic union rights and practices, with the advent of the dilution of skilled labour, transfers in the labour market, and retraining; there would also, as in 1914, be a massive use of women workers in factories and on farms. Callaghan, like almost all the unionists present, had no difficulty with what appeared to him a voluntary agreement freely entered into. He was impressed both by Bevin's dominating role—'there is no place for weaklings or faint hearts in that school'—and by the immense reserves of untapped strength that the union representatives at the conference symbolized. Only four representatives dissented, and Callaghan was certainly never going to be one of them.[5]

Callaghan's concern for the war effort became more direct and outspoken. In July 1940 he spelt out in *Taxes* the priorities for a 'people's war'.[6] The 'Chamberlain–Wilson–Munich attitude of mind' should be cut out, root and branch, and the economy mobilized to win the war. 'Everything which hinders, preconceived prejudices, out-of-date notions of property, superannuated leaders must be swept away.' Less conventionally, he attacked the hysteria of War Office policy towards 'enemy aliens' and urged the full protection of civil liberties in parliament and the press. In July 1941 his column struck a powerfully socialist note. He attacked wage stabilization while big hotels were full and *The Times* continued to carry advertisements for butlers and footmen. There should be more stringent price controls and some legitimate upward adjustment of wages. 'Is there any reason why the working class should not have a stake in the post-war expenditure which will follow wartime savings?'[7]

Clearly the mind of the assistant secretary of the Federation was moving far beyond the confines of desk or office. He was now active in a local Fabian group and persuaded Labour celebrities like Laski, Ellen Wilkinson, and Margaret Cole to come up to north Wales to address meetings at Llandudno or Colwyn Bay. In the winter of 1940–1 he ran an adult education class in Llandudno for the Workers' Education Trade Union Committee, and held it in his home. It was designed to bring the gospel of workers' education, hitherto largely associated with manual workers through the National Association of Labour Colleges, to clerical employees. His chosen theme was 'The Theory and Practice of Trade Unionism' with the emphasis on the growth of trade unions as free and autonomous voluntary associations. Fifty years later, he still felt that these lectures embodied the essence of his social philosophy, industrial partnership rather than statutory direction by central government and the law.

The war years saw no let-up in the Labour Party's activity in the constituencies, despite the existence of the Coalition. Indeed the idea of an unquestioned wartime consensus is one of the myths prevalent about these years.[8] The social provisions of the Beveridge report, published on 1 December 1942, had been anticipated by Labour's own proposals for social insurance back in February, while the *sub rosa* activities of the Socialist Medical Association had pushed on ideas for a comprehensive national health service, free at the point of delivery, along with a salaried medical profession. Callaghan, with his intimate personal knowledge of the impact of legislation and regulations on the standard of living of union members, responded to the full to these exciting new vistas, as indeed did his wife Audrey. He reflected in his diary on the experiences of 1941 as a whole. 'Had a very pleasant year altogether, apart from some considerable trouble with Houghton who has taken us all on individually and collectively and who is just a dam' nuisance to himself & everybody else.'[9]

His ideas on a possible future career in politics continued to develop. One abiding influence was Harold Laski who kept in touch with the young union official who had so impressed him at civil service tribunals a few years earlier. Another was John Parker, the future MP for Dagenham, whom he had met in the Fabian Society. Socialists on the IRSF were also urging him to keep his options open for the future. One interesting political event in June 1942 was a meeting of Callaghan and some seven or eight other trade unionists with Sir Stafford Cripps, just back from a time as ambassador to Moscow.[10] They met at Cripps's flat in Whitehall Mansions, and were sustained by Cripps's wife, Lady Isobel, with cups of

Horlicks. The Cripps boom was now at its height, coinciding as it did with a severe downturn in the war, the fall of Singapore in February 1942, the capture of Tobruk in north Africa on 25 June, and a subsequent denting of Churchill's own prestige as premier and war leader. Cripps told the assembled trade unionists that the war opened up possibilities of a wider social and economic transformation, possibilities which were of no interest to Churchill himself. Cripps's preferred objective—astonishing for one so recently advocating a Popular Front from a far-left position—was for a post-war 'National' government in which far-reaching radical reforms would be supported by younger Tory MPs 'who have come a long way along the road of planning'. Callaghan was not disposed to accept Cripps's bland certainties. He annoyed the minister by informing him that he had no particular influence on government policy and that his volte face on the coal mines had lessened his national prestige. Callaghan was evidently dismayed at what he saw as a clear shift to the right. 'He is no use to us in his present frame of mind.' Cripps's refusal to rejoin the Labour Party, and his apparent enthusiasm for alliance with Tories such as Eden, Anderson, and Lyttelton after the war, were equally unacceptable. 'Altogether I thought Cripps was in rather a sorry state. . . . He is forced to seek support from different quarters according to every wind that blows and his position rests on an uneasy compromise because his temporary support remains fluid and never congeals.'

The episode had little positive effect for Cripps whose political position remained essentially rootless. By the end of the year, especially after the apparent failure of a visit to India to try to negotiate a settlement with Gandhi and the Congress leaders, his bubble had burst.[11] Churchill felt powerful enough to dismiss him as Lord Privy Seal just after the battle of El Alamein. In the end he had to rejoin the Labour Party after all, which he did just before the general election in 1945. For the young Len Callaghan, the episode merely fortified his socialist zeal, and perhaps his self-confidence, so effective had been his sharp interrogation of a senior worthy like Cripps. 'I feel that mentally I have developed a great deal in the last twelve months,' he wrote. 'I am still "fighting" everything I think wrong—I shan't get too old for that for a long time!'[12]

A mounting passion for politics went with a developing zeal to participate in the war. Callaghan had a reserved occupation as a civil servant, while his comfortable lifestyle and young family offered every inducement to stay where he was. However, his intense preoccupation with the war and its objectives, allied to the natural instinctive patriotism of a product of the Portsmouth naval scene, led him actively to seek involvement in the armed services. In June 1940, a few days after Dunkirk, he applied to the navy, his inevitable target, to enlist as a seaman, and indeed the Admiralty informed him soon after that he could enlist as an ordinary seaman. This, however, led to one of many rows with Douglas Houghton. The latter's towering preoccupation was his union, war or no war. No distraction should deflect its key personnel from its service. As noted, Houghton had even been unhappy at Callaghan's marriage to Audrey at first, and for a time manifested almost a kind of jealousy towards the younger man's new wife, as an unnecessary distraction from office and union. The navy came into the same category. At first, Callaghan submitted and satisfied his inclinations instead in the Local Defence Volunteers, and service as a fire-watcher. In the latter occupation, he met up with Gordon Dennis, a neighbour years later to be instrumental in his move to his Sussex farm. During the London blitz, Callaghan encountered danger and death at first hand, but it was still remote from where he felt the real action lay.

Finally, in the latter end of 1942 Houghton agreed that Callaghan could be released, and he was recruited for the navy. A decisive factor in Houghton's mind was the presence of Cyril Plant, later himself to be secretary of the Federation in 1960 and also to become a peer, as a deputy for Callaghan while he was away on wartime service. In April 1943 Callaghan bid farewell to union members with the kind of reckless gaiety that young men going off to war had shown over the centuries. He expected shortly to be serving on a vessel in the North Sea. He would miss the union after seven years of major office. But 'this new life is a tremendous experience and one that I am proud not to miss. . . . Au revoir everybody!'[13] His father's example, Jutland and all, would light the way ahead.

His time in the navy, however, was to prove distinctly less eventful than his father's service in Jellicoe's Grand Fleet during the First World War, let alone the Benin expedition. Callaghan had hoped to serve on a motor torpedo boat, but found himself confined to the less glamorous role of serving on a mine-sweeper. His training took place first in Lowestoft, then off the west coast of Scotland. He became friendly with some fishermen from the Hebrides who had also enlisted. He attended Church of Scotland services with them, while 'Lofty', as the six-footer Len Callaghan became known, also offered technical advice in filling up their income tax returns.[14] A prolonged period of training then followed. From March 1943 to April 1944, as an ordinary seaman, he was attached successively to a series of base ships, HMS *Europa*, *Fortitude*, *Europa* again, *King Alfred*, and (most evocative of all) HMS *Victory*. He got to sea, however, only on HMS *Malahne* in June–August 1943. At the end of his training in April 1944, he was promoted to the rank of sub-lieutenant and more active service seemed to lie immediately ahead.

But, to his dismay, his move to a fighting ship was frustrated by a medical examination which discovered a minor condition of tuberculosis, a hazard of working-class communities in the 1930s but something he thought he had largely escaped in the terraced streets of Copnor. He found himself in Portsmouth in a naval hospital confined in irritating inactivity while he recovered. More fruitfully, he joined a discussion group to consider current issues of the day. The group included J. P. L. Mallalieu, a future parliamentary colleague of Callaghan's, the future historian Richard Ollard, and the later television actor Jon Pertwee, of *Dr Who* fame. After drifting around briefly, he found himself summoned to the Admiralty where he was told that his promotion to sub-lieutenant was confirmed, but that he would be obliged to stay on shore for the next six months.

To his astonishment the Admiralty told him that his next undertaking would be to write an instructional manual on Japan, with whom Britain had been at war since the end of 1941. Callaghan had no expertise at all in Asian matters: indeed, his knowledge even of the European continent was sketchy in the extreme. But the decision to get him to study Japanese society was an inspired one, and had a fateful effect on his developing international outlook. He worked in the library of Chatham House in St James's Square, and produced his pamphlet *The Enemy: Japan* early in 1944.[15] The subheading is 'Twelve talks edited with notes for discussion group leaders' and it bears the stamp of its origins. Even so, for someone with no formal background in research or higher education, it is a very competent and comprehensive manual of 135 pages, covering the social character of Japan, recent Japanese history ('Japan's career of aggression'), the record of the war in the Far East, and the nature of Japanese totalitarianism. Two final sections give the texts, suitably annotated, of the Atlantic Charter and the Cairo Declaration of 1943. It is fairly conventional in treatment, though a somewhat curious chapter on 'Women in Japan' contained some comments on brothels and the alleged links between prostitution and patriotism. Under the code number BR 1212, it was delivered to the fleet for discussion purposes among the men. Half a century on, when Callaghan was one of three presidents of Chatham House, he was delighted to see that a copy of his pamphlet was retained in its library, and he also had one in his private possession at his Sussex farm.

This pamphlet was deemed to have made him an expert on the Far East, and he was told that he would eventually be dispatched to Australia to serve in the British Pacific Fleet. Tired of what had so far been a remarkably sedentary war, however, he demanded an early involvement in active service, and this took him on board HMS *Activity* to serve in the British East Indies Fleet in Ceylon in 1945. He spent the remaining months of the war under that command. It seemed to be only the start of a prolonged period of naval service. Whatever the fate of Germany (about which the navy in the Far East was poorly informed), there seemed no likelihood of Japan's being defeated within two to three years, and it was anticipated that there would be a long and bloody advance all the way to Japan itself. In the autumn of 1944, as the Allied advance across western Europe reached a decisive stage and the defeat of the Reich appeared ever closer, Callaghan and his shipmates in the Indian Ocean settled down for a long haul.

His war proved to be unremarkable. He saw little active service in the Indian Ocean, and was hardly ever, in his own estimation, in physical danger. The most exciting engagement he saw came immediately after VE Day in May 1945 when his ship, HMS *Queen Elizabeth*, Beatty's flagship at the time of the battle of Jutland in 1916, joined a French battleship, the *Richelieu*, in pursuit of two Japanese cruisers. The Japanese vessels outpaced the aged British ships but they were eventually sunk.

Yet, uneventful though it was for him personally, the war was a major point of reference for Callaghan as for most of his generation. It produced a mixture of responses, conservative and radical. On the one hand, it was to be a fount of nostalgia, which Callaghan himself freely shared at the time of the anniversary of VE and VJ Day in 1995, and which perhaps slowed down Britain's adaptation to the post-war world, especially towards Europe. For up to half a century many Britons seemed stuck in the insular time-warp of Dunkirk and the battle of Britain, a mood faithfully nurtured by popular television programmes such as *Dad's Army* and war films like *The Dambusters*. On the other hand, the war years were a major source of renewal, at home and across the world. Callaghan's awareness of the radicalism on the mess deck and the war-weary cynicism of the ordinary sailor gave new stimulus for his pursuit of a brave new post-war world, one which would eliminate the unemployment and poverty that afflicted the Callaghan family amongst hundreds of thousands of others after 1918. When it was observed how massively the service vote of ordinary soldiers, sailors, and airmen had swung to Labour in the 1945 election, Callaghan was not in the least surprised. For him, therefore, life in the navy was a laboratory of social change. The lower deck had its own informal versions of the army's ABCA classes, where current affairs were discussed. There was also a wider dimension, fostered by first-hand observation of the Ceylon parliament in action in Colombo. It helped to convince Callaghan of the futility of trying to prop up the old empire, and in particular of the need for immediate self-government in the Indian subcontinent and Ceylon, and also in French Indo-China and the Dutch East Indies which he also saw at first hand.

Hostility to the old imperialism, however, went side by side with a warm commitment to a newer sense of commonwealth, founded on interracial partnership, collaboration, and economic development. Ceylon in particular made a deep impression upon him. From this time on, the developing world, with its economic and political complexities, provided a yardstick for his analysis of society. It provided the thrust of his maiden speech in 1945. Callaghan emerged from wartime service as less of a union-centred man, more of a Commonwealth man. Instinctively he linked social transformation in Britain itself with the manifest economic needs of developing societies. Europe, by contrast, was a lesser priority, then and later. It is not too fanciful, perhaps, to draw something of a distinction between post-war Labour politicians such as Callaghan or Denis Healey who fought overseas and developed, however tentatively, an international vision of democratic socialism, and those like Gaitskell or Wilson whose war was spent in the machinery of government in Whitehall and who saw post-war Britain less as an opportunity for social revolution than a laboratory for applied technocracy. This did not mean any automatic sorting out into pro-Europeans or anti-Europeans in the 1960s or 1970s. But it did mean something of a gulf of awareness between the more insular home-bound planners and others who had a more dominant interest in foreign affairs after seeing the wider world as it was.

Long before the end of hostilities, though, Callaghan's life had been fundamentally and permanently transformed. He was now a prospective Labour candidate. At a stormy meeting of the IRSF executive just before he entered the navy, the union had agreed reluctantly to give him permission to seek a parliamentary constituency. Under the 1927 Trades Disputes Act, the Association of the Officers of Taxes was prevented from retaining control of its political fund: around £1,500 was thus placed in the hands of a group of independent trustees, one of whom happened to be Callaghan's friend Dai Kneath. In early 1943 he was thus encouraged by friends to try for nominations in a variety of constituencies. The very vitality of local party organization during the war years encouraged young (invariably male) candidates to enter the fray. Callaghan was approached about seats in county Durham and the Yardley constituency of Birmingham. He actually put his name forward for Reading, but the nomination in the South constituency went to the left-wing figure of Ian Mikardo. This was to prove fortunate since Reading was never the safest of Labour seats: Mikardo was eventually to be defeated there in 1959.

Then, out of the blue, Callaghan received a serious invitation to try for Cardiff South. He had no connection with Cardiff hitherto; his main knowledge of Wales derived from his time working for the union in Llandudno on the north coast. In fact, his connection there was now diminishing: Cyril Plant's taking his place as assistant secretary, at least for the wartime period, meant that the family had no particular reason to stay in Llandudno. In the course of 1944, Audrey Callaghan and her two children moved back to Maidstone so that she could be near her parents. They lived there, in Ashford Road, for the immediate post-war period, the family increasing in 1945 when their son Michael was born. Len Callaghan, then, was not a name to conjure with in the valleys. His introduction to Cardiff, in fact, owed much to sympathetic Labour figures within the Inland Revenue Staff Federation, Edgar Heale of Swansea, the Quaker Leslie Punter of Bath (a former IRSF president), and, more important perhaps, Dai Kneath, then of Swansea, later of Pontnewydd. He was an old colleague on tribunals who had once given him useful (and characteristically Welsh) advice on the subtle arts of persuasion.[16] Kneath it was who introduced Callaghan to Bill Headon, secretary of the Cardiff South Labour Party, and he made a strong impression, not least with his informed criticisms of the 1927 Trades Disputes Act as it affected the trade unions. He was also able to reassure Mrs Headon, a strong chapel-goer, that despite his name he was not Roman Catholic.

Cardiff South was certainly a winnable seat. The sitting member was Colonel Sir Arthur Evans. He was a leading figure in the Territorial Army who had served with the BEF in France in 1940 and had been mentioned in dispatches. He was also a businessman who had been elected as the member in 1923 (when he was just 25) and again since the landslide election of 1931. However, it had been a Labour seat in 1929–31 and Evans's majority over Labour in the last general election, held as long ago as 1935, had been a mere 541. It contained parts of proletarian Cardiff, Adamsdown (the old Irish quarter) in the central areas of the town, and the picaresque dockside areas of Bute Town and Tiger Bay, alongside middle-class areas in central Cardiff and parts of the genteel villadom of Penarth on the coast, with its many retired people.

On balance, it looked like a very possible Labour seat, and inevitably there was a large field of candidates. It was later said that they considered the young Roy Jenkins of Abersychan, a brilliant Oxford graduate whose father had been a long-serving miners' agent and Labour MP, but his name was not pursued. However, it was declared by the local party secretary, Cliff Prothero, that there would be a short list of three. Among them was a local Methodist schoolteacher whose pacifism had bred some controversy, George Thomas. His career and Callaghan's were to be intertwined for half a century, not always with the happiest of results. No one could have foreseen that in the years to come they would encounter one another as Speaker of the House and Prime Minister. The contrast between the pacifist sombre-suited Thomas and the handsome young Lieutenant Callaghan in his gold-braided naval uniform could not have been more stark. The young Callaghan, according to Thomas's controversial memoirs, introduced himself with the words, 'My family call me Leonard but for politics I'm going to use my second name, James.'[17] It was also, of course, his father's name. In a difficult contest, Callaghan gained the nomination by just one vote, twelve to eleven. He also won the approval of the local Fabians who included young Eirene White, daughter of Lloyd George's aide Thomas Jones, and a future parliamentary colleague in Wales. The contest was a close-run thing but it was to ensure a lifetime's commitment to Cardiff, reinforced by the title he took for his peerage. Len had indeed become Jim. He had also become a probable member of parliament. Meanwhile all was far from lost for George Thomas, since he was shortly nominated for Cardiff West, an equally attractive prospect for a Labour candidate.

Obviously, Callaghan on war service in the Far East could campaign only episodically and at very long range. Even so, enough of his outlook comes across from the fragmented evidence of the time. In November 1944 he came home to address the electors of Cardiff for the first time.[18] He stressed three main themes—a national minimum of subsistence; the public ownership of industries and the harnessing of national resources for the benefit of the community; and, perhaps more originally, 'an International Order' involving the pooling of armaments and joint international obligations.

He also had to address himself to the variegated aspects of the Cardiff South constituency. It was the epitome of what Sir Alfred Zimmern had once called 'American Wales' with its immense admixture of peoples typical of a major dockside constituency. He had to tread somewhat warily on the religious issue, where the Catholic Irish of Adamsdown were a major element amongst his prospective constituents. It was widely believed that Callaghan, with his Irish name, was a Catholic himself: the *Catholic Herald* was to include him amongst the Roman Catholic MPs after the 1945 election. Callaghan's denial was unprovocative. Apart from the religious complexities of Cardiff South, its racial admixture was potentially even more explosive. Here Callaghan had no difficulty in associating himself with the various ethnic subgroups of Bute Town and beyond; the majority of them at that time were Arabs, mainly Adenese, Yemenis, and Somalis, and Maltese, rather than Afro-Caribbean, since the major West Indian immigration occurred after 1950. Callaghan spoke out vigorously on behalf of racial equality. His Cardiff address on 27 November 1944 included support for 'the Coloured Peoples' right to a decent life', as well as for a seaman's charter. It was indeed ironic that his stance at Home Secretary over Commonwealth immigration in 1968 was to lead to attacks on Callaghan as a crypto-racialist, since more than most members of parliament he had first-hand knowledge of racial questions, was strongly committed to racial equality, and was genuinely shocked by cases of discrimination.

Perhaps more striking than these activities in his constituency, though, was his first hint of celebrity in British politics as a whole. In December 1944 there took place a Labour Party conference, which Callaghan attended for the first time.[19] His first speech to that assembly, in Central Hall, Westminster, was a notable event. It occurred during a famous debate on nationalization when delegates attacked the Executive in the person of Emanuel Shinwell for apparently retreating from the party's unambiguous commitment to the public ownership of major industries and utilities, central to Labour's programme since 1937. The 'Reading Resolution', moved on behalf of his constituency by the newly nominated Ian Mikardo, was a remarkable episode which confirmed the grass-roots radicalism within the party, even at a time of coalition. It echoed the angry dissatisfaction of Harold Laski and other socialists at the compromise approach apparently identified with Attlee, Morrison, Bevin, and other Labour ministers.

Mikardo's motion won backing from many parts of the conference hall. His supporters included Evelyn (later Lady) Denington and Bessie Braddock of Liverpool. It also had the crisp, forceful endorsement of James Callaghan (Cardiff South), whom Laski as conference chairman took care to call. Callaghan urged a ringing, uncompromising commitment to public ownership (which he claimed servicemen supported), and a 'restatement of our fundamental principles'. Apart from a standard demand for socialist control of the economy, Callaghan also, perhaps more originally, included a demand for more effective forms of management in the industries of the country. His plea for public ownership was couched in terms of efficiency and planning, no doubt a product in part of his experiences of wartime command. Despite a plea from the platform from Philip Noel-Baker to withdraw his motion, Mikardo pressed on with it and it was carried by a show of hands so overwhelming that no card vote was called for. Mikardo was euphoric, Herbert Morrison less so. He put a hand on Mikardo's shoulder. 'Young man, you did very well this morning. That was a good speech you made—but you do realise, don't you, that you've lost us the general election.'[20] The young Jim (formerly Len) Callaghan was amongst the youthful delinquents he had in mind.

When VE Day arrived, Callaghan was attached to HMS *Queen Elizabeth*, sailing from Trincomalee harbour and covering a landing against Japanese troops in Rangoon. But a few days later, on 20 May, a special Labour conference voted unanimously to leave the Coalition. A caretaker Conservative government was then formed by Churchill and a general election called for 5 July. The war against Japan, of course, was still very much in being, and Callaghan was still on naval service in the Indian Ocean at this time. His projected destination was Japan where he would take part in local administration on the surrender of the enemy. But he returned immediately to fight the election, his naval career terminated. His return was agonizingly slow since obtaining transport was a matter of private enterprise or sheer chance. He flew in small hops from Trincomalee to Colombo to Karachi (where he hung around for two precious weeks living in a tent in the desert). Finally he flew back to Britain in the baggage compartment of an RAF bomber. Reunited with his family in Maidstone, he discovered that both his daughters, Margaret and Julia, had measles.

So far as the election was concerned, Callaghan approached the campaign with breezy confidence. He sensed, as did others who had served in the war, that the armed services alone were swinging heavily to Labour. The tide of wartime by-elections, with their return of left-wing candidates such as those of Sir Richard Acland's Common Wealth party, and radical independents such as W. J. Brown, one of Callaghan's great civil service leaders, spoke of a wartime tide of radicalism. Despite this and the evidence of the little-understood Gallup poll which showed Labour anything up to 12 points ahead, the vast majority of Labour's leaders from Attlee downwards were obsessed by the parliamentary dominance of Churchill during the war. They were thus convinced that Labour were in for yet another defeat, even if a recovery from 1935 was generally anticipated. Aneurin Bevan, who had sensed the pent-up anger after the years of depression and defeat, was one of the very few who felt that a great socialist victory lay in store.

Labour in Cardiff was ready for the fight. Cyril Plant and other IRSF officers had been down in Cardiff preparing a plan of campaign with Bill

Headon, the agent, while the candidate was still in the Far East. As soon as he returned, Callaghan launched himself into the fray with immense vigour. This was still an election of open-air meetings, and face-to-face contact between candidate and constituents. Callaghan turned up with a loudspeaker at factory gates, on the dockside, even in business premises committed to Sir Arthur Evans's campaign. The presence of Evans's mistress, a Penarth woman, on his election platform led to Labour choruses of 'Hello! Hello! Who's your lady friend?' Labour held eleven public meetings in the last week of the contest, culminating in an enthusiastic mass rally at the Cory Hall on election eve, 4 July.

His election address listed as its priorities the demobilization of men from the armed service, a new housebuilding programme, full employment and nationalization, price and rent control, social security, and 'an International Armed Force responsible to a World Authority'. More unusually, he also emphasized assistance for the men of the Merchant Navy. The address depicted Labour as a practically minded party, well prepared for the demands of government. It was, all in all, a moderate document: there were no overtones of class war. In his speeches, he spoke confidently of the need for nationalization of the mines, gas, electricity, and also of steel (since East Moors steel works was a major employer in the adjoining constituency). These nationalized industries would be 'publicly owned and managed by expert engineers, chemists and administrators in the national interest'. Labour would also end 'the paradox of Public Transport being privately owned'.[21] He also spoke of the need for a welfare state based on a national health service, and especially for a renewal of housing, a desperate problem in an old industrial area such as the Cardiff dockside community. Working-class voters, he reported, were mainly interested in practicalities such as these, along with full employment. Middle-class voters showed an interest in peace and reconstruction, on which he felt equally confident, along with self-government for India to which he had long been committed.[22]

The words 'socialism' or 'socialist' appear nowhere in his election address, but the thrust in that direction is unambiguous. Certainly once he got into the Commons, he had no hesitation in proclaiming himself a socialist, if a practical and moderate one. Even if some later academics would argue that Labour had never been in any significant sense a socialist party, the speeches of Callaghan and many other young candidates in 1945 suggest that both the idealism and the doctrinal commitment at that unique moment in Labour's history should not be underestimated. The British electors were polarized on grounds of class and of ideas as never before or since.

The voting, as in other constituencies in that unusual election affected by the absence of voters on military service or elsewhere, was relatively high. When the results were declared on 25 July, it was shown that a total of 29,000 electors had voted out of 39,000, including 3,882 on the service register and a small business vote of 194. Callaghan's victory was a comfortable one, 17,489 votes against Evans's 11,545, a majority of almost 6,000 or 20.4 per cent of those voting. Immense delight came from the IRSF which now had its first-ever MP. Callaghan's success was part of a huge Labour sweep across Cardiff. George Thomas captured Cardiff West by 4,524, while Hilary Marquand, an economics professor and a future Labour minister, won Cardiff East, defeating an outgoing minister, Sir P. J. Grigg, by almost 5,000. It was set against a background of 200 Labour gains in all parts of Britain. Labour ended up with 394 seats as against only 210 for the Conservatives and their allies. Churchill and his colleagues were almost humiliated. Attlee went to Buckingham Palace almost immediately, frustrating an attempt by Morrison to question his authority. Callaghan, Thomas, and Marquand were carried shoulder high from Cardiff City Hall amidst scenes of high emotion and mass rejoicing. 'We were unconquerable', Callaghan reflected in his memoirs.[23] Truly, they were the masters now.

Callaghan, of course, won Cardiff South as a speaker and campaigner of proven ability, with a kind of charisma. His union background was invaluable, too, not only in his being able to capture the Cardiff South nomination but also because of union contributions from the AOT to his parliamentary fund. This enabled him to spend £680 on the campaign, in contrast to Evans's £571, a significant sum though well within the legal limit of £819.[24] Cardiff was a highly unionized city and this was reflected in Callaghan's canvassers and campaign staff.

But, beyond that, Callaghan's career to that point had brought together essential strands characteristic of Labour's achievement in its supreme moment of glory. He had a broadly working-class background, and could genuinely claim to have experienced poverty and social deprivation at first hand. He had also become a trade union officer—in a white-collar union, it is true, marginalized in the union movement as a whole, but still a vital preparation for progress within the labour alliance at all levels. His role as assistant secretary, too, had provided him with vital contacts with union and party personalities across the country, including eminences like Harold Laski. The wartime years, with their commitment to social transformation, were crucial. But they also reinforced another element in his make-up—a basic patriotism drawn from the naval background in

Portsmouth, but a patriotism of citizenship and grass-roots populism rather than of edicts handed down by the establishment. In peace and in war, Jim Callaghan, still only 33 in 1945 but with over a decade of public life behind him, had instinctively identified with essential strands of his nation's historic experience. He was an outsider no longer. The wartime service in the Far East had provided yet another dimension, and given him a new breadth of outlook. His self-confidence as a public speaker received an unexpected boost shortly before VJ Day when he made his first radio broadcast in London.[25] He spoke on 'The Royal Navy in the East Indies' and called for the navy to be given priority for equipment now that Germany had been defeated. Then it was on to take his seat in Westminster. As he entered the Commons in 1945, more than most young men he could feel that his brief life had been a preparation for this hour.

1. *Taxes* (Oct. 1939), 585–6.
2. Material in Callaghan Papers, box 2.
3. Cyril Plant, 'Prime Minister Callaghan', *Taxes* (Apr. 1976), 155–6.
4. Diary, 13 July 1942 (Callaghan Papers); J. B. Edwards to Lord Callaghan, 19 Aug. 1993; Lord Callaghan to J. B. Edwards, 1 Sept. 1993 (in private possession).
5. L. J. Callaghan, 'Bevin and the T.U.C.', *Taxes* (June 1940), 227–8.
6. L. J. Callaghan, 'Fighting for our Lives', *Taxes* (July 1940), 281–2.
7. Ibid.
8. See in particular Stephen Brooke, *Labour's War* (Oxford, 1992).
9. Diary, 13 July 1942 (Callaghan Papers).
10. Memo by Callaghan of meeting with Cripps, June 1942 (Callaghan Papers).
11. See Paul Addison, *The Road to 1945* (London, 1975), 190–210. Cripps's moment passed when Churchill won a vote of censure on 2 July by 476 to 25. After Alamein, he was shunted down by Churchill to become Minister of Aircraft Production outside the War Cabinet.
12. Diary, 13 July 1942 (Callaghan Papers).
13. 'L. J. Callaghan Says Au Revoir', *Taxes* (Apr. 1943), 154.
14. Ibid.
15. Pamphlet in Lord Callaghan's possession and also in Chatham House.
16. Callaghan, *Time and Chance*, 44–5.
17. George Thomas, *Mr Speaker* (London, 1985), 49.
18. Note in Callaghan Papers, box 1A.
19. *Report of the 43rd Labour Party Conference, December 1944*, 160 ff.
20. Mikardo, *Backbencher* (London, 1988), 77.
21. Election address in Callaghan Papers.
22. Note in Callaghan Papers, box 1A.
23. Callaghan, *Time and Chance*, 64.
24. *Return of the Expenses of Each Candidate at the General Election of July 1945 in Great Britain and Northern Ireland*, H. of C. 1945–6 (128), xix. 539.
25. Note in Callaghan Papers, box 1A.

4

BACKBENCH CRITIC

TO be a young Labour MP in July 1945 was for Jim Callaghan the fulfilment of a lifetime. Inspired by the landslide majority for their party, 393 Labour MPs (over 200 of them new members) flocked excitedly to Westminster to hail Attlee as party leader and Prime Minister. Oblivious to backstage manœuvres centred on Herbert Morrison to challenge Attlee's leadership, they roared enthusiasm for Labour's formidable new team. A few days later, they crammed into the House of Lords, which the Commons had taken over as a result of war damage during the blitz, and hurled defiance at the diminished Tory rump and Churchill, the fallen leader. Led by George Griffiths, a Yorkshire miner, they greeted Attlee with a noisy rendition of 'The Red Flag', the traditional hymn for the new Jerusalem. From his vantage point on the third bench above the gangway, sitting next to his fellow Cardiff member George Thomas, Jim Callaghan noisily shared in the singing and the mass enthusiasm.

It was possible that a young MP might be swamped in the massive Labour majority. Compared with the trade union officials, articulate journalists, lawyers, and university intellectuals on the Labour benches, Callaghan might easily have been lost to view. In fact, from the start, as an ambitious and articulate backbencher, he began to make his mark. He told IRSF members that he would concentrate on issues such as the civil service and taxes, the royal and merchant navies, and the Far East, on which he was knowledgeable following his work in wartime naval intelligence.[1] He was assiduous in attending the informal gatherings of Labour MPs in the smoking room, and a sociable figure in the tearoom and on the terrace. He made the acquaintance, early on, of prominent figures from journalism or academia such as Dick Crossman, John Strachey, Tom Driberg, and Maurice Webb. One friend was to be Maurice Edelman, a Coventry member like Crossman, and an urbane man of letters and fine linguist. Another was the donnish figure of Dick Mitchison, member for Kettering, who became a QC in 1946; he and his wife Naomi, the daughter of J. B. S. Haldane and herself a distinguished writer, became close to the Callaghans, who enjoyed several family holidays at their home in Argyllshire.

An especially influential new comrade was Evan Durbin, a brilliant Oxford-trained economist whose cogent analysis of *The Case for Democratic Socialism* had appeared during the early years of the war. Durbin, the son of a Baptist minister whom Callaghan had met during his childhood attendances at Baptist chapels in Brixham, became a close colleague. Conscious (probably over-conscious) of his possible disadvantage in handling economic issues as someone who lacked a university background, Callaghan used Durbin as a source of instruction; according to one account, Durbin used to set him essays on economics, but Callaghan himself did not recall this later on.[2] It was Durbin who got him on to the XYZ group of economists assembled by Nicholas Davenport. Here he met Oxford-trained figures like Hugh Gaitkskell and also Douglas Jay, who was to be elected for Battersea North at a by-election in 1946. Academic economists like the Hungarians Nicky Kaldor and Tommy Balogh were also part of the XYZ personnel. The relationship with them endured, with some storms with Balogh at least, until Callaghan became Chancellor nearly twenty years later.

He also had a more senior patron. Attlee and Morrison were remote figures, while Bevin, with his bullying ways with backbench snipers, was not especially congenial. But there was also Hugh Dalton, the new Chancellor, and an ardent promoter of young (invariably male) political talent. Most of his protégés were university figures like Gaitskell, Healey, and later Crosland, but Callaghan was a relatively rare working-class member who enlisted his enthusiasm. Without Dalton's patronage, Callaghan's progress would have been problematic indeed. At a lesser level, John Parker, secretary of the Fabians and junior minister at Dominions, was another encouraging figure, and Callaghan shortly took up a position as (unpaid) parliamentary private secretary to Parker in this department. Beyond the charmed circle of Westminster politics, Callaghan's friendship with old journalistic contacts like Ian Mackay of the *News Chronicle* and Trevor Evans of the *Daily Express* always came in useful.

It was not easy to achieve prominence as a maiden speaker amongst so vast an array of debutants, but Callaghan managed it. His debut in the House on 20 August was a confident performance. It focused on the Far East, reflecting his wartime service experience.[3] Callaghan emphasized the difficulties in establishing a stable regime in Japan after its military defeat, the dangers of backing either side in the civil war in China, and the massive upsurge of the forces of nationalism in Asia generally. It was a crisp, knowledgeable speech which was commended, in more than usually warm terms, by the following speaker, one of the two Conservative members for Brighton, William Teeling, as 'the most interesting of all the maiden speeches we have heard today'. Thereafter Callaghan became an increasingly active and prominent backbencher. He focused variously on foreign and defence affairs, the needs of the south Wales economy, and financial issues which reflected his background in the Inland Revenue. Dalton drafted him onto the Finance Committee of the parliamentary party, while as a prominent ex-service officer, he also joined the Defence and Services Group where he became a vigorous champion of the need for rapid demobilization.

Thereafter, like other young MPs, Callaghan was an excited witness of great events. For perhaps the last time in British history, debates in the House of Commons captured the imagination of the world. Great measures of public ownership were pushed forward. By the end of 1946, the Bank of England, cable and wireless, civil aviation, and, most evocative of all, the coal mines had all been nationalized with remarkably little opposition from the Tories. The major welfare reforms of Beveridge were enacted, with the passage of Jim Griffiths's National Insurance Act and of family allowances in 1946. Even more momentous, Aneurin Bevan took the National Health Service triumphantly through the House, for its launch in May 1948. Overseas, there were the excitements of the birth of the United Nations, the hopes and disillusion inspired by great-power manœuvres between Britain, the United States, and the Soviet Union. In the colonial and Commonwealth area, there was the trauma of Palestine, but also the momentous events that were to lead to the transfer of power in India and Pakistan in August 1947. All of these measures, along with programmes of council house and school building, and measures to promote regional development and protect full employment, met with the almost unanimous endorsement of Labour MPs. Party discipline was not a problem for the whips.

It might have seemed that, as an affable and ambitious young MP, he would have trodden a careful path to attract the notice of the party leadership and keep faithful to the official line. In fact, a striking feature of Callaghan's parliamentary career down to perhaps 1950 was his independence of judgement and his outspokenness. A dramatic early instance of this came in December 1945 when the House discussed the $3.75 bn. loan negotiated with the United States by Maynard Keynes. In fact, the terms of the US loan provoked intense debate. The terms eventually agreed, with commercial interest of 2 per cent to be paid in fifty annual instalments, aroused much disappointment, but more controversial were two longer-term conditions attached. There should be an immediate multilateral liberalization of trade, despite the ravaged condition of the British economy after the war, and the convertibility of sterling into dollars would come into effect in July 1947. The terms of the loan had generated the first intense disagreement in Attlee's Cabinet on 29 November and 3 December. While all the leading ministers, including Dalton, Bevin, and Morrison, backed the terms of the loan, two left-wing ministers, Emanuel Shinwell and Aneurin Bevan, fiercely attacked it as incompatible with a socialist planned economy and for putting Britain in a long-term suppliant position towards capitalist America. At a further meeting on 5 December, their resistance was overborne, although Shinwell remained violently hostile, but the news of Cabinet dissension became widely known on the backbenches.[4]

In the Commons debate on the terms of the loan on 13 December, many Labour backbenchers, not all of them on the left, attacked the terms that were being offered. They included such prominent left-wing figures as Michael Foot, Barbara Castle, Jennie Lee, Hugh Delargy, and Benn Levy. But they were joined by Callaghan. He failed to catch the Speaker's eye in the debate, but in a following debate on the Far East later that evening, he combined a brisk attack on American support for Chiang Kai-shek and endorsement of undemocratic forces in Japan with a retrospective blow at the US loan which he described as 'economic aggression by the United States'.[5] In *Taxes*, he spelt out his reservations more fully. The terms would generate bad faith and international suspicion. 'Must we repeat the story of the War Debt over again?' Britain could not possibly expand its exports to 175 per cent of what they had been in 1938; nor could its economic future be left to the free play of world economic forces. 'As a Socialist' he believed in 'the international control of industrial investment'.[6] Stripped of the left-wing rhetoric, these arguments found support elsewhere, including from many on the Conservative benches. Robert Boothby made a devastating critique of the loan terms, which Callaghan still recalled in detail forty years on. In the debate on 13 December, 23 Labour MPs including Callaghan voted against the government, along with over 70 Conservatives, many of them imperialists anxious about the future of sterling and Britain's international role generally. After the debate, Callaghan resigned his minor post as John Parker's PPS at Dominions.

Even allowing for the overestimate of Britain's economic strength common on the left at this time, the arguments against at least some of the loan's aspects still command respect. If the burden of commercial interest was not to prove onerous, the genuflection to American nostrums of nineteenth-century liberalism in trade was immediately harmful. Worse still, the imposition of convertibility in July 1947 proved to be a disaster which almost destroyed the position of sterling and the Attlee government along with it. For Callaghan, who was in no way anti-American, the decisive aspect seems to have been that Britain was being bullied by a supposed ally with damaging results for its international role as a major power. Politically, Callaghan's rebellion, such as it was, did not do him any particular harm; indeed, before the vote, Dalton had privately indicated that some display of Labour dissent would do no harm in making an impact on the Americans. However, he naturally had to resign as PPS and emerged as a fully-fledged independent backbencher of growing influence.

From this time on, Callaghan's emphasis was increasingly on international matters. He did intervene vigorously in Welsh affairs debates, briefly championing the notion of a secretary of state for Wales popular in Labour circles in 1945–6, though he soon abandoned what he came to regard as a flirtation with nationalism, inappropriate for a Cardiff member.[7] He also took part in financial debates, as one with an expert knowledge on taxation and its implications. In a debate on Pay as You Earn on 1 November 1946 he allowed himself to move into wider ideological realms. He called for a new human relationship between the employer and the employed. 'That is one reason why I am a Socialist because I believe that one gets that ultimate sense of responsibility in a socialist society where a man feels that he is working for the good of the community as a whole and for the communal good which flows from his work in his own particular factory.'[8] Here and elsewhere his commitment to socialism, albeit of a consensual Fabian kind, was unambiguous and unapologetic.

But it was in international affairs, not only the Far East, where his particular expertise lay. In this respect, the first two of many important overseas journeys, to eastern Europe and later to west Africa, played a major part. In December 1945 he went on a delegation of parliamentary and non-parliamentary figures to Russia, a journey for which he kept a full diary.[9] He was invited to go by the First Lord of the Admiralty, A. V. Alexander. His closest colleague on the trip appears to have been John Platts-Mills, later to be expelled from the parliamentary party in 1949 as a far-left fellow-traveller. Another with whom he became friendly was Lawrence Daly, a young Fifeshire miners' official, later to be a close ally during

Callaghan's later career. The young Cardiff MP stood out amongst his colleagues. It had been insisted by the First Lord that Callaghan wear his naval officer's uniform, since he had not yet been discharged. As a result, students in Stalino in the Don basin (a town founded by a Welsh iron-master and previously known therefore as Hughesovska) cheerfully called him 'Admiral'. Callaghan noted in his diary, 'Everywhere I go I seem to be regarded as the typical Englishman of the party—it's amazing what a naval uniform and white shirt and stiff collar can do!'

Despite the austerity of the food and accommodation and the cold of the Russian winter, the visit was far from being wholly disagreeable. Then as always Callaghan was an insatiably curious traveller, fascinated especially by Moscow, but also greatly moved by Stalingrad and other scenes of wartime devastation, notably in Kiev. There were also concerts and visits to the opera. In Moscow Callaghan presented a Russian composer with a suite for orchestra by Inglis Gundry, whom Callaghan had met while on naval service. He particularly enjoyed the company of David Brandt, a 30-year-old Jewish geography lecturer in Moscow. Callaghan saw him as 'a typical Jew, restless, self-confident, ready to correct me on a point on the British economy (he was wrong about that!), quick brained, very intelligent' and 'unable to avoid being a rebel'. This dissident in the making urged Callaghan to press the British government for greater freedom for Soviet citizens. More relaxing was the company of Tamara, a sympathetic young girl guide. She told him 'I was her idea of a typical Englishman—because I have a pug nose, am cunning and use speech to disguise my thoughts. She says I am typical of the high up Englishman who is much too clever for the Russian. But I believe she thinks there is hope for me.' Callaghan reflected, after visits to the opera in Kiev and Donetsk, 'I like the Russian girls very much, and Tamara in particular.'[10]

In many ways, Callaghan seems to have responded to the Russian scene with the enthusiasm for the former wartime ally widespread amongst leftish opinion in Britain in the winter of 1945–6, before the rigours of the cold war descended. He was impressed by the genuine fear of renewed threats from Germany evident in a sombre war crimes trial he attended in Kiev in January 1946.[11] The approval voiced by the accused, a former German official in charge of operations south of Kharkov, of the murder of Jewish children made a devastating impact on the court, and on Callaghan himself. The depth and genuineness of Russian fears for their western border security impressed themselves on him. He was also struck by the genuine signs of Russian economic recovery after the devastation of war. One striking feature for him was the role of women workers in rebuilding the economy. As he left, he reflected that 'Russia has more than turned the corner—she has taken several strides along the road to recovery'. On the other hand, the news from Britain, with its food shortages and likely bread rationing, 'seems to be as gloomy as ever'.[12]

In his diary, Callaghan speculated on whether 'the Soviet state has reached its final form'. He was under no illusions, even then, of the repressive, authoritarian nature of the Soviet regime and noted the difficulties of free expression faced by Soviet writers and Jewish intellectuals such as David Brandt. However, his sanguine conclusion was that 'I do not think that any great numbers of the population feels itself to be in a mental or spiritual strait jacket'.[13] At Fulton, Missouri, that March, Winston Churchill spoke of an Iron Curtain descending across Europe, but the young Callaghan was as yet unable to agree. He was one of 93 Labour MPs who signed a Commons motion denouncing Churchill's speech as a danger to peace. But he was no kind of fellow-traveller. By the end of the year, the continuing deadlock between the western powers and the Russians, headed by the impenetrable Molotov at conference after conference, was leading to a re-evaluation of east–west relations on Callaghan's part.

His insight into eastern Europe was developed further in September 1946 when he visited Czechoslovakia, still then a democratic country ruled by a coalition government which included Communists. It was a Fabian Society group, his colleagues being Shiela Grant Duff, John Parker MP, Carol Johnson, Hector Hughes MP, and Michael Young of Transport House.[14] During its ten-day visit, Callaghan met amongst others President Beneš and Klement Gottwald, the Communist Prime Minister, along with leaders of the Catholic Church. In addition, the baroque splendours of Prague, which had survived both world wars unscathed, made a strong impression on him, and he also saw the medieval city of Brno in Moravia. He told his Cardiff constituents in *Clarion* (perhaps with some adaptation of history) that he felt heartened by visiting 'one of the earliest and best democracies of Europe'.[15] Its leaders after all included distinguished liberal intellectuals like the Foreign Minister, Dr Jan Masaryk. The deputation saw little sign of the Republic's later collapse in February 1948 through a Communist coup headed by Gottwald with Soviet backing. On the contrary, it found much to be optimistic about at that period of Czech history, as was recorded in a book that the Fabian group produced in 1947. Callaghan's own special interest was Czechoslovakian trade unionism which he described in detail from the central negotiating machinery to the district factory groups. 'By contrast with the pre-war position, the future of Czechoslovakian trade unionism looks extremely bright', he concluded.[16] He retained a keen interest in eastern Europe and his expertise here added to his stature as a prominent and independent-minded backbencher.

A further important dimension came in December 1946 when, just after Christmas, he went with three other Labour MPs and three Conservatives including F. J. Erroll and Lord Llewellin, to west Africa as part of an empire parliamentary association delegation. They spent ten days in Nigeria, and eight in the Gold Coast, as well as going to Gambia and Sierra Leone.[17] In Gambia they enjoyed a river expedition, Callaghan dressed in the lightweight tropical kit of a naval officer. He stayed in Sierra Leone with the parents of the later Mrs Judy Steel, wife of his partner in the Lib–Lab pact of 1977. Callaghan had been increasingly fascinated by issues of imperial and colonial government since his wartime visit to Ceylon and the Far East. That experience had convinced him of the inevitability of colonial independence, at least in the Indian subcontinent, but also of the massive need for economic reconstruction and partnership to accompany any transfer of power. West Africa was already in the throes of constitutional change, especially in the Gold Coast. In Nigeria he came across the power of the nationalist movement, and had a private and lengthy talk with its most articulate voice, the secretary of the National Council, Dr Azikiwe. The sophistication of the latter's analysis of the west African scene made it the more galling for Callaghan to encounter well-meaning but blinkered colonial administrators who spoke of Nigerians not being ready for self-government for several decades to come. This was the start of a lifelong connection with Nigeria, culminating in his efforts to secure the liberation of the former head of state, General Obasanjo, in 1997.

A much more positive impression was made in Accra by the Governor of the Gold Coast Sir Alan Burns, who had pioneered significant constitutional advances there the previous year. Callaghan dined with him on New Year's Eve in Governor's House in Christianborg Castle. It was a spectacular fortress built by the Swedes in 1652: 'I shall believe in Hollywood from now on', he wrote in his diary. This near-veteran Governor, in contrast to other colonial officials, told Callaghan and his colleagues of the dangers of being too cautious in giving Africans political responsibility. Callaghan struck up a good relationship with him which indeed he attempted to turn to positive effect in 1947. Burns's relatively liberal approach, together with the scandal resulting from his handling of a so-called 'juju' murder, had led to criticisms from Churchill who, Callaghan felt, 'played a poor part in his incitement against the Secretary of State', Creech Jones. Callaghan, whom Burns later felt was 'one of the few who kept their heads', was able to secure an adjournment debate and Burns was persuaded to withdraw his resignation. However the Governor was later moved anyway, and went on to serve in Nigeria before returning to Britain, where he died in 1980 in his ninety-fourth year.[18]

Callaghan's first visit to Africa, to be followed by scores of others to that continent, began a lifetime's engagement with colonial problems. His friendship with nationalist leaders in Nigeria and other countries was lifelong. But so, too, was his awareness of the complexities of decolonization. Here and elsewhere he drew on the gradualist, developmental message of Rita Hinden and the Fabian Colonial Research Bureau, one sometimes denounced by more fervent nationalists.[19] Callaghan's approach was always a measured, realistic one, free from the simple anti-imperial stereotypes typical of many on the left. As he told the *Daily Guardian* of Freetown, the urgency of political independence could not be divorced from the economic difficulties that would follow. He was also anxious to develop a positive view of relations with the mother country. In Callaghan's view, the conclusion must be that Britain and its colonies in Africa should create a new relationship based on development and partnership. 'Economic self-determination must not be allowed to degenerate into a narrow economic nationalism.'[20] This constructive theme was followed up in a powerful speech he made at the 1947 Labour Party conference, in which he set out his conclusions after his visit to west Africa and explicitly linked political freedom with economic development.[21] He amplified it further in a cogent article, 'What is Britain's Role in West Africa?', in the *West African Review* in June 1947 when he emphasized the need for economic development through partnership. His argument focused particularly on the modernization of agriculture in Nigeria and elsewhere. A new generation of colonial civil servants should be dispatched to west Africa, and the United Africa Company nationalized and run as a public board. But 'the first principle that must underlie all our actions is that the country belongs to the Africans not to us'. In looking at the problems of Africa, perhaps more than in his early views on eastern Europe, Callaghan's analysis was probing and mature. It was to lead in time to the watershed of his career, his time as Labour's colonial spokesman. The visit to west Africa in 1946, then, was a genuinely educative and enlightening one for him. It had also echoes of his childhood. In Nigeria he visited Benin City and the scene of the exciting saga of which his father had told him during their all too brief relationship.

By the end of 1946, many felt that Callaghan was a coming man. He was a handsome, sociable, articulate figure, much sought after by the whips to stabilize opinion in difficult debates on such issues as demobilization. A political opponent, Derek Walker-Smith, Conservative member for Hertford, wrote warmly in August 1946 of the strong impression that Callaghan had made in the House. 'He looks extremely young. This, together with an air of complete assurance, gave some members an impression of smug complacency. In my view this was undeserved and people are begining to realise that. They appreciate his confidence and skill.'[22] Earlier in the year, a columnist in the *Observer* had described him as 'one of the outstanding younger men in this Parliament'. A critic like Barbara Castle was later to see in him 'God's gift to a parliamentary occasion'.[23] Callaghan had his circle of closer colleagues, including people like Durbin, and he continued to enjoy a good relationship with Dalton. The widespread view that he was due for government office of some kind was shared by Callaghan himself, though somewhat guardedly. He was told by the chief whip, William Whiteley, on 8 October 1946 that he might have been appointed to assist Fred Bellenger at the War Office, following the resignation through ill health of the veteran miner Jack Lawson. Unfortunately, he had been abroad in Czechoslovakia at that critical time. Callaghan noted privately, however, 'I'm going to strive constantly to be on my guard against letting my actions be influenced by the prospect of office.' Indeed, he was involved in a potentially damaging protest about the handling of some mutineers in the Malay 13th Parachute Regiment at this very time.[24]

In fact, Callaghan at this pivotal time in his career, with prospects opening of junior office, was anything but a docile sycophant. His growing involvement with foreign and colonial affairs had added to a reputation for awkward dissent. He was a long-established centre-left critic of Bevin's foreign policy. He described the Foreign Secretary, in a private letter to Kingsley Martin, editor of the *New Statesman*, as 'immovable and apparently impenetrable to any influence that he does not wish to acknowledge'. He feared that British socialism 'will find itself bolstering up capitalism abroad'.[25] Amongst a cluster of backbenchers active in mobilizing protest against the government's defence and foreign policies, Callaghan was a prominent figure. Indeed, his stature had grown in this area since he had succeeded General Mason-Macfarlane (the former governor of Gibraltar) as chairman of the PLP Defence and Services Group earlier in 1946. What came to be known as 'Keep Left', the first left-wing dissident group formed in 1947 and in some ways an anticipation of Bevanism later on, was in the making. In October 1946, at a time when relations between the west and the Soviet Union seemed to have reached a frigid impasse, a powerful shot across the government's bows came with a letter signed by twenty-one Labour backbenchers and sent to Attlee. Simultaneously it was released to the press. These twenty-one did not include far-left fellow-travellers like Platts-Mills, Solley, or Zilliacus; their general posture was 'inside left' in the footballing metaphor of the time, including as they did Crossman, Jennie Lee (Bevan's wife), Donald Bruce (his PPS), 'Kim' Mackay, J. P. W. Mallalieu, Michael Foot, Sydney Silverman, and Woodrow Wyatt. Callaghan was amongst them, in what was perhaps the most dangerous challenge to the government on any aspect of policy since the 1945 election.[26]

In effect, this public letter condemned the overall course of Britain's foreign policy. Britain gave the impression, so the critics claimed, of being 'infected by the anti-red virus which is cultivated in the United States'. Instead, they offered an impassioned plea for what was popularly termed 'a socialist foreign policy'. Their argument had five main points. They claimed that the only valid basis for world government was democratic socialism, a 'genuine middle way' between American capitalism and Russian totalitarianism. In passing, western policy in relation to Franco's Spain and royalist Greece was denounced, along with the failure to adopt the views of the German Social Democrats in the economic management of the allied zones of Germany. Secondly, there was strong support for collective security being enforced by the United Nations; plans for a two-year conscription period for Britain were denounced. Thirdly, a socialist foreign policy should hold the balance even in criticizing both Soviet and American policies. Fourth, the vigorous pursuit of socialist policies at home was championed. The western powers 'have become so hypnotised by the fear of Communism establishing itself even where it was indeed the sole alternative to Fascism that we have tended to support the worst species of collaborators and political adventurers'. And finally, the need to support social democratic parties in other European countries was strongly endorsed.

This document was, no doubt, based on a considerable overestimate of British power and influence. But it was also the most assertive statement yet of the idea of a third force, perhaps in alignment with socialist comrades in western Europe, current at that bleak time of the incipient cold war. The ideological range of the twenty-one signatories meant that they could not be dismissed as an incorrigible group of far-left fellow-travellers; many of them, including Callaghan, were amongst the most promising of the 1945 intake. Attlee made no public response to what was a fierce onslaught on all aspects of Bevin's foreign policy, though he did voice his alarm at a Cabinet meeting on 8 November. Emanuel Shinwell responded broadly in defence of the critics.[27] In the House, in the debate on the King's Speech on 18 November there was vocal opposition from Crossman, Jennie Lee, and others to government foreign policy, Crossman denouncing Britain's 'drift into the American camp'. There were seventy Labour abstentions in the vote. Significantly, Callaghan was not amongst them, but nevertheless he had been prominent in a powerful grass-roots attack which shook the government at a critical time. Bevin was away at the Council of Foreign Ministers in New York at the time, but he returned in full majesty at the 1947 party conference at Margate to condemn this 'stab in the back'.

The dissidents, however, were far from being cowed. The foreign affairs amendment now led directly to the formation of the Keep Left group in April 1947.[28] This consisted of fifteen left-wing (though not far-left) MPs, including Crossman, Foot, and Jennie Lee, with Ian Mikardo as secretary. Its main line of attack was the need for an unaligned socialist foreign policy independent of the two major powers, along with more vigorous policies of socialist planning and control of the economy at home. For many of the fifteen, one key priority was a policy of collaboration with socialist parties in western Europe to form a new third force; indeed, the Labour left was in the forefront of moves towards greater European unity in the immediate post-war years. Callaghan was one of several who were thought to be likely recruits for Keep Left, and indeed he continued to work with them on key issues. But he kept to a careful path of support for the government on key issues while continuing to express selective dissent. In any case, the Keep Lefters, almost half of whom were middle-class journalists, represented a somewhat different ideological strand from that of a former trade union official like himself.

On another issue, however, Callaghan was in the forefront of revolt. Indeed, although commonly thought of as a party regular throughout his career, he was now to play a key role in inflicting by far the most serious backbench defeat on the Labour government during its six years in office. This arose over military conscription.[29] As the pressures of the cold war mounted, defence chiefs became more vocal in pressing not only for the rate of demobilization to be slowed down but for numbers in the armed services to be increased. By the end of 1946, almost a year and half after the war had ended, 1,385,000 British men and women were serving in the forces across the world from Hong Kong to Belize; the British zone of Germany and, inevitably, India claimed the vast majority. This alone provoked massive discontent from the Labour Defence and Services Group. It contained several former service officers like Geoffrey Bing, Ashley Bramall, Marcus Lipton, Harry Pursey, Stephen Swingler, George Wigg, and Woodrow Wyatt, as well as Callaghan, its active chairman. It condemned the delay in demobilization both for its human cost and for harmful effects on the economy. Some argued that the very influence of the army in particular was felt to be harmful, even corrupting, on the nation's youth, since the armed services, run by a socially exclusive officer class, maintained archaic patterns of mindless discipline. It manifestly did not reflect the democratic revolution seen at home in the 1945 election returns.

When the government actually proposed reintroducing peacetime conscription for a period of eighteen months in the course of the King's Speech debate in November 1946, there was an explosion of rage. There were divided counsels in the parliamentary party which accepted the eighteen months period by 126 votes to 54, while in the House 45 rebels voted against the government with a further 90 abstaining. At this stage, the protests came mainly from traditional pacifist figures, many of nonconformist background, such as Rhys Davies and Victor Yates. Ernest Bevin declared, 'I realized it was chiefly the Welsh',[30] although in fact the majority of the largely nonconformist Welsh members were loyalists at this time. Callaghan himself did not object to the principle of conscription even in peacetime, and was obviously no kind of pacifist. But he had long been an outspoken critic of the level of manpower retained in the armed forces. Douglas Jay first became aware of Callaghan when he entered the House in 1946, when a defence statement on the rate of demobilization by the mighty Attlee was interrupted by the Cardiff member who called out, 'Not low enough'.[31]

But the duration of the period of conscription proposed was profoundly shocking to him. His objections were various. Industrially, he felt that manpower needs would be seriously affected and the economy held back by a shortage of labour. Politically, he felt that it divided the party and the nation. He also claimed, with reason, that twelve months was more than enough to train a fully equipped fighting man. But, of course, the need for eighteen months was governed by the need not only to train troops but also to station them in Germany, Palestine, and other strategically sensitive areas. What underlay Callaghan's objection to eighteen months' conscription was the foreign policy that gave rise to it. He felt that so lengthy a period of military service was the product of a negative, needlessly provocative, anti-Soviet policy of confrontation maintained by Bevin. Conscription proved to be the highest common denominator for uniting the foreign policy dissidents. In addition, Callaghan, with his keen sense of class distinction, shared to the full the reservations about the snobbish, socially exclusive, and politically reactionary outlook of military and naval chiefs; he had seen them on display himself two years earlier. In a letter to the *New Statesman* on 23 November 1946 he had condemned the rigid class structure of the army and called for a complete overhaul of the King's Regulations. The latter, he declared, were 'devised by nineteenth-century Blimps for eighteenth-century convicts'. He would have agreed with criticisms by Basil Liddell Hart that national service increased the influence of such people over government policy, a view for which there was indeed much evidence notably in the Middle East. It was one of history's ironies that the British Empire had reached its greatest territorial extent under a Labour government. Indeed, Bevin had even suggested in 1946 that it become greater still with the acquisition of the former Italian colonies of Cyrenaica and Tripolitania (modern Libya) and Italian Somaliland, the latter to merge with British Somaliland in a vast new territory in the Horn of Africa. Elgar and Kipling had come again with the ragged-trousered philanthropists of the British labour movement.

In the early months of 1947, Callaghan and his colleagues in the Defence and Services Group waged a powerful campaign to have the period of conscription cut back to twelve months. In the later view of Crossman, no mean plotter himself as the nickname 'double Crossman' suggested, this undercover campaign amounted to a kind of conspiracy, one in which Crossman himself joined.[33] But in the early months of 1947 conscription did not stand alone as an issue. It was a cruelly hard winter with many weeks of snow and freezing weather. This, added to the inadequacy of Shinwell's planning of fuel reserves, led to immense difficulties for the economy and much short-term unemployment. In addition, food rationing had reached new levels of severity. The government's prestige plummeted; Conservatives declared that the citizens were being invited to 'shiver with Shinwell and starve with Strachey'. The campaign to reduce national service, therefore, took place against a background of an economy desperately in need of more labour, especially in the mines, and a government no longer in charge of events.

In these circumstances, all the disciplinary manœuvres of Morrison and the diplomacy of Attlee were insufficient. The replacement of the veteran Jack Lawson at the War Office by Fred Bellenger, a so-called 'soldiers' friend', did not assuage the critics.[34] Further, a key minister like Hugh Dalton, the Chancellor, who had previously accepted the need for national service as a kind of military contract of citizenship equivalent to the welfare state at home, now became deeply anxious at the state of the economy and the pressure on sterling. The advent of convertibility in July was a worrying portent which some feared might even lead to the devaluation of the pound. Despite all Attlee's personal efforts, 72 Labour MPs voted against the government's National Service Bill on 1 April while another 70, including Callaghan, abstained. The Minister of Defence, A. V. Alexander, was hesitant and ineffective in the face of knowledgeable ex-service Labour critics. On 3 April the Cabinet discussed the issue, in the absence of Ernest Bevin, and decided to give way; twelve, not eighteen months, would now be the term. The rebels had triumphed. On 7 May Callaghan welcomed the retreat in a speech in the House, and ridiculed Churchill's claim that it meant a policy of 'scuttle'.[35] However, while the principle of peacetime conscription had indeed been endorsed, it was without doubt a serious setback for the government. With the effective loss of over 100,000 men, their defence plans were in tatters and Montgomery and other defence chiefs furious at what they saw as a loss of nerve. For a moment, at a key point in the cold war, Britain's government had lost credibility through the active sabotage of its own backbenchers.

Callaghan continued to take a distinctly independent line that spring and summer. The government was far from prospering. Its nationalization policies were all going ahead; Bevan gradually overcame his medical critics in the BMA; there was the great achievement of the transfer of power in India and Pakistan on 15 August. But it was almost to no avail. What preoccupied the nation was the deteriorating state of the economy which, among other things, did serious damage to the reputation of Hugh Dalton, previously a commanding figure as Chancellor and Callaghan's patron. The advent of the convertibility of sterling on 15 July was calamitous. Dollar reserves poured out of the country, the stock markets plummeted, and Britain appeared to face bankruptcy. The residue of $400m., all that remained of the original US loan, was frozen by the American Treasury. In desperation, convertibility was stopped on 20 August after only five weeks, and stern deflationary measures followed to shore up the economy. The government was severely shaken. Not only Dalton but also Morrison, supposedly in charge of economic planning, lost face. Attlee himself had seemed irresolute in the crisis and in September there was an unsuccessful attempt to replace him as prime minister with Stafford Cripps, President of the Board of Trade, who alone had come out of the crisis with his reputation intact.[36]

Callaghan's response to the crisis reflected these tensions. The Defence and Services Group widened its activities, linking the role of the services with the travails of the economy and the need for 'scientific methods of operational research' and more effective forms of vocational training to be provided by the armed services. A side issue, though one of much interest to Callaghan himself, was pressure to have the age of entry to Dartmouth naval college raised from 14 to 16 to widen its social base and make the navy's command less exclusive. Callaghan himself was to implement this change as an Admiralty minister in 1950 though it was not to prove a great success.[37] But his main attack was launched against the handling of the economy. In an aggressive speech at the TUC, whose conference he was now able to attend as a delegate (as a former IRSF official), he delivered a fierce onslaught on policies for the concentration of industry and the allocation of key raw materials such as steel. He condemned 'a fatal hesitation in the minds of the political leaders of our movement' and dismissed with contempt a protest from Vincent Tewson, the highly conformist secretary of the TUC, reminding him of his own earlier opposition to the American loan. Herbert Morrison's Economic Planning Board he derided as 'a mockery'. He urged the government to take 'a few decisions' and then 'the political movement will be worthy of the loyalty which the Trade Union movement gives to it'.[38]

It was this anxiety about the handling of the economy that gave renewed impetus to his links with Keep Left. Although still keeping his distance, Callaghan was one of nineteen signatories to a letter to Attlee on 23 July, at the height of the convertibility crisis. Those also signing were Benn Levy, Michael Foot, E. R. Millington, J. P. W. Mallalieu, Geoffrey Bing, Richard Crossman, Donald Bruce, Stephen Swingler, Fred Lee, George Wigg, Woodrow Wyatt, A. J. Champion, Leslie Hale, S. S. Allen, Harold Davies, Barbara Castle, Ian Mikardo, and R. W. G. Mackay. In broad terms, they were a distinctly left-wing group, the majority of whom were to be later Bevanites or members of the Tribune group. It was company that Callaghan at this stage of his backbench career was not afraid to keep. The letter asked for import controls; severe cuts in overseas commitments in Palestine and Germany and a reduction of the armed services to 600,000 by 1948; and a socialist economic policy including taxes on capital appreciation and profits, controls of raw materials, the preservation in full of expenditure on housing and the social services, and the general application of 'socialist principles', left undefined. It was a further sign of discontent in the ranks and some weakening of the credibility of Attlee and his Cabinet colleagues.[39] In the Commons during the Finance Bill committee stage on 18 July Callaghan congratulated Dalton on maintaining a high rate of tax on the rich. With biblical fervour, he denounced the distributed profits that were going to shareholders at a time when the workers were being hard hit. The next speaker, the Conservative Lieutenant-Commander Gurney Braithwaite, commented that Callaghan, with his Inland Revenue background, spoke like a tax gatherer rather than a tax-payer.[40] Some time in mid-August, following a letter from Keep Left to the *Daily Herald* demanding further cuts in the armed services, an end to convertibility, and a capital levy, Callaghan, along with Crossman, Mikardo, and Swingler, went to Attlee and then to Dalton to voice back-bench concern, but with little effect.

Callaghan was an independent spirit, whose outspokenness continued as the troubled summer gave way to an anxious autumn and a belated Cabinet reshuffle. He witnessed with some concern the apparent sidelining of his patron Dalton and the appointment of Cripps as Minister of Economic Affairs in early September; Cripps was not a minister with whom Callaghan had ever been close, and his various political gyrations in the pre-war and wartime years had not impressed the latter. Some commentators continued, however mistakenly, to link Callaghan with Keep Left. But then, instead of banishment to the political equivalent of a Siberian power-station, Callaghan was sent for by Attlee in early October 1947. He was to be given a government post for the first time, parliamentary secretary to the Minister of Transport, Alfred Barnes of the Co-operative Society. Attlee's advice to Callaghan was characteristically succinct. In three sentences he reminded him that he was now in 'the first eleven'. And, perhaps with recent backbench contributions in mind, the Prime Minister added, 'if you are going to negotiate with someone tomorrow, don't insult him today', always useful advice.[41] It was part of a wider Cabinet reshuffle of much importance. Cripps became Minister of Economic Affairs, Herbert Morrison was removed from directing economic strategy, Arthur Greenwood left the Cabinet altogether. The 31-year-old Harold Wilson entered the Cabinet as President of the Board of Trade, the 41-year-old Hugh Gaitskell replaced Shinwell at Fuel and Power, and Philip Noel-Baker also joined the Cabinet. Shinwell was moved to the War Office outside the Cabinet, while George Strauss became Minister of Supply in place of John Wilmot. Callaghan's promotion came later, amongst ministers of the second rank.

In general, the reshuffle was welcomed as strengthening the government. It removed some dead wood and brought in able younger intellectuals like Gaitskell and Wilson. The removal of Morrison from the handling of economic policy, where he was ill at ease, was generally popular. The *New Statesman* was critical of what it saw as a broad move to the right, and a diminution of the number of working-class ministers.

However it also welcomed the advent of leftish newcomers of proven talent, of whom it particularly mentioned John Freeman and James Callaghan.[42] For Callaghan himself it was the fulfilment of a major ambition. In response to a warm welcoming note from Dalton, he wrote, 'This is going to be an exciting job and that is what makes it so fascinating.' He welcomed the return to office life and routine. 'I've already initialled a couple of files and begin to feel like a Civil Servant again.'[43]

If one surveys Callaghan's brief backbench career from his entry into parliament in July 1945 to his entry into government in October 1947, the general impression is one of restlessness and not infrequent revolt. From the vote against the American loan in December 1945, through the criticisms of Bevin's foreign policy in 1946, to the remarkable triumph in defeating the government over conscription in April 1947 and subsequent attacks on the handling of the economy, he had been anything but a docile conformist. On the contrary, he had variously annoyed Morrison, Bevin, and Attlee in turn. No doubt Attlee as a supreme party manager was anxious to minimize discontent by bringing effective critics into the fold, rather than have them (to bowdlerize Lyndon Johnson) outside the tent spitting in. But the record of 1945–51 is full of talented left-wing rebels whose reward was permanent exclusion—Crossman, Foot, Mikardo, and Barbara Castle spring obviously to mind. It is therefore worth speculating why Callaghan's reputation was such that his sins of dissent were felt to be less heinous.

Without doubt, he was a capable backbencher who had made a strong impression both as a Commons speaker of confidence and panache, and as chairman of the Defence and Services Group. The whips from William Whiteley downwards had often found his talents helpful in defusing discontent, for instance on policy towards Germany or on the pace of demobilization. He also had a remarkably wide range, having spoken with authority on defence matters, the Far East and colonial policy, economic policy and especially finance and taxation, housing, and the regional difficulties of south Wales. He was an all-rounder in politics, without showing superficiality in any of his chosen themes, well informed and incisive. Nor was his radicalism unconstrained. In key votes, even on conscription, he sided with the government and always kept his lines open to the whips. He was with Keep Left on some themes but not of them.

Further, his political profile and his concept of socialism were not in themselves seen to be provocative by the administration. His socialism called for the practical management of the nation's resources, not any kind of social revolution. Much of his support of a 'socialist foreign policy' consisted of anxiety to help social democratic parties (as in Czechoslovakia) trying to pursue a similar policy. In general, he could accept the broad lines even of Bevin's foreign policy. Indeed by the autumn of 1947 for Callaghan, as for Crossman and others of the centre-left, the early post-war enthusiasm for the Soviet Union was distinctly on the wane as what seemed to be a threatening and ideologically rigid policy was pursued by Stalin whatever the cost. Already clouds of Russian menace were threatening the Czechoslovak Republic which Callaghan had found so attractive. His concern with colonial issues, too, was comparatively moderate. Instead of launching into simplistic defences of immediate colonial independence, Callaghan's stance was to emphasize the complexity and especially the economic fragility of the prospect for decolonization. He approved of the British withdrawal from Palestine where he steered a judicious middle course more consistently than others of Labour's future leaders. While friendly with Rabin, Peres, and others of the young Israeli Labour leaders, he was never a dogmatic zealot for Zionism, unlike Harold Wilson. Yet, unlike George Brown, he was never one of 'Labour's Arabs' doctrinally committed to the Palestinians either.

In domestic matters, he was broadly a defender of the main lines of government policy on the mixed economy and social welfare. He was a forceful moderate, not any kind of socialist extremist. This emerged in an interesting and reflective chapter he wrote on 'The Approach to Social Equality'. It appeared in a volume, *Socialism: The British Way*, edited by Donald Munro with a foreword by Herbert Morrison (who confessed that he had not actually read the book!), and published in late 1948. Evan Durbin had been the main intellectual driving force behind its appearance. In his chapter, Callaghan took a balanced but challenging stance. He urged the vigorous use of tax policy to eliminate large disparities in financial rewards, while Labour should make 'the inheritance of substantial wealth an impossibility'. But he also took the view that the system of social security did not lead to the transfer of resources between classes since 'most working-class benefits are paid for by the working class'. In the overall redistribution of incomes, the transfer from rich to poor was smaller than that within the lower income groups themselves. He also argued, unfashionably for that time, that high rates of tax in themselves would not generate equality. Indeed, by removing incentives for enterprising ordinary citizens, unduly severe rates of direct taxation would be counterproductive. 'Our fiscal machine has, in the past, been largely geared to the process of transferring money incomes, but it now has the additional task of encouraging the maximum production of wealth.' He added that 'the negative attack on class privilege is not by itself sufficient'. Raising educational standards and improvements in the social services were more fundamental as steps towards an egalitarian society.[44]

When he went to the Ministry of Transport in October 1947 Callaghan certainly did not feel that the momentum of the socialist advance was spent. Consolidation did not mean retreat. His was a different stance even from the Gaitskellite revisionists of the late 1950s let alone Tony Blair's 'New Labour' in the 1990s. On the contrary, there were more important reforms to come, including the nationalization of gas, and iron and steel. All of them Callaghan (whose constituency was in future to include the East Moors steel works) warmly supported. He applauded the wider extension of the welfare state, including the new energy being shown in housing policy. In foreign affairs he believed, as most Labour MPs did, that Britain's democratic socialist middle way offered a beacon of hope for humanity, especially in the third world, even though he was being increasingly disillusioned by the prospects for a peaceful dialogue with the Russians.

But the socialist advance at home and overseas was being seriously threatened, both by Britain's weakening international position and even more by the realities of serious financial difficulties at home. The fervour of 1945 was abating. It was hard to detect England Arising amidst the austerity and shortages of post-war Britain. Callaghan, like most of his colleagues, was a realist; like them, he was a 'consolidationist' in the making. He was also a shrewd tactician able to steer a subtle path between destructive rebellion and quiescent conformity, in the parliamentary party as in the Inland Revenue Staff Federation. Already he had become a professional politician who 'did everything on purpose', though also one with courage and independence of judgement. By October 1947 his protests had shaken the party's leaders but had not shocked them. His executive capacity and clarity of mind had impressed them from the start. The junior post in the Ministry of Transport was not the most charismatic of government appointments, though with road and rail nationalization still going through the Commons it was well within the sound of gunfire. It would provide a vital test not only of the enduring resilience of Britain's experiment with socialism, but of the capacity for growth of the rising backbencher who sat for Cardiff South.

1. *Taxes* (Aug. 1945), 377.
2. Information from Mrs Marjorie Durbin.
3. *Parl. Deb.*, 5th ser., vol. 413, 351–4 (20 Aug. 1945).

4. Cabinet Conclusions, 29 Nov., 3, 5 Dec. 1945 (PRO, CAB 128/2).
5. *Parl. Deb.*, 5th ser., vol. 417, 750–3 (13 Dec. 1945).
6. *Taxes* (Jan. 1946), 20.
7. *Parl. Deb.*, 5th ser., vol. 414, 918 (16 Oct 1945). Attlee gave no reply.
8. Ibid., vol. 428, 102–3 (1 Nov. 1946).
9. Callaghan Papers, box 30.
10. Diary, 19 Jan. 1946 (ibid.).
11. *Time and Chance*, 86–7.
12. Diary, 7 Feb. 1946 (Callaghan Papers, box 30).
13. Ibid.
14. *Czechoslovakia: Six Studies in Reconstruction* (London: Fabian Society and Allen & Unwin, 1947).
15. *Clarion*, 1/1 (Oct. 1946).
16. *Czechoslovakia*, 54.
17. Material in Callaghan Papers, box 4.
18. Callaghan to Sir Alan Burns, 14 Oct. 1949 (ibid.); Sir Alan Burns, *Colonial Civil Servant* (London, 1949), 230.
19. See Partha Sarathi Gupta, *Imperialism and the British Labour Movement, 1914–1964* (London, 1975) for the Bureau.
20. *Daily Guardian*, 7 Aug. 1947.
21. *Report of Annual Labour Party Conference, 1947*, 115.
22. *Daily Express*, 4 Aug. 1946.
23. *Observer*, 10 Mar. 1946; Barbara Castle, *The Castle Diaries, 1974–76* (London, 1980), 432 (23 June 1975), referring to the crisis in Uganda with President Amin.
24. Diary, 8 Oct. 1946 (Callaghan Papers, box 28).
25. Quoted in Jonathan Schneer, *Labour's Conscience* (London, 1988), 55.
26. Letter in Callaghan Papers, box 28.
27. Cabinet Conclusions, 8 Nov. 1946 (CAB 128/8).
28. Schneer, *Labour's Conscience*, 61–3.
29. An excellent analysis is L. V. Scott, *Conscription and the Attlee Governments* (Oxford, 1993).
30. Ibid. 152.
31. Interview with Lord Jay of Battersea, 20 Aug. 1991.
32. *Parl. Deb.*, 5th ser., vol. 437, 461–7 (7 May 1947).
33. *The Backbench Diaries of Richard Crossman*, ed. Janet Morgan (London, 1981), 88.
34. Scott, *Conscription*, 144.
35. *Parl. Deb.*, 5th ser., vol. 437, 461.
36. See Kenneth O. Morgan, *Labour in Power, 1945–1951* (Oxford, 1984), ch. 8.
37. Anthony Seldon, *Churchill's Indian Summer* (London, 1981), 351.
38. *Report of Trades Union Congress, Southport, 1947*.
39. *Daily Herald*, 8 Aug. 1947.
40. *Parl. Deb.*, 5th ser., vol. 440, 777–83.
41. *Time and Chance*, 95.
42. *New Statesman*, 11 Oct. 1947.
43. Callaghan to Dalton, 9 Oct. 1947 (Dalton Papers, 9/3).
44. Donald Munro (ed.), *Socialism: The British Way* (London, 1948), 139–40, 153.

5

JUNIOR MINISTER

FROM the autumn of 1947 the Attlee government entered upon a period of hard slog. It was the high noon of austerity symbolized by the moralistic figure of Sir Stafford Cripps. Following the sterling convertibility crisis, there were massive controls imposed upon consumption. They were accompanied from mid-1948 by a voluntary wage freeze. This led to trade union protests and unofficial strikes in the docks and to a state of emergency being called. For the average citizen, this period meant the full rigours of rationing and controls in the consumption of food, clothing, and fuel. There was in 1948 a weekly allocation of thirteen ounces of meat, six ounces of butter and margarine, eight ounces of sugar, two pints of milk, and a solitary egg; for this bounty housewives had to spend weary hours in lengthy queues. These restrictions on consumption and the direction of industrial production and manufacturing to the export market, especially that of North America to earn precious dollars, seemed to be paying dividends in 1948 and early 1949. There was a huge surge in exports of cars and other manufactured goods, and the balance of payments, previously in massive deficit, moved sharply into equilibrium. Ordinary citizens might have been suffering the rigours of austerity and rationing, but there was full employment, and opportunities to spend growing take-home pay on the delights of the cinema, dance halls, and professional sport, all of which enjoyed a massive boom.

But the economic situation suddenly deteriorated in the summer of 1949 with heavy speculation against sterling. In September Cripps, to his horror, had to devalue the pound against the dollar by a third of its value. As in 1931 (when in fact the devaluation had been carried through by the National Government) a Labour administration was publicly identified with devaluation of the currency, widely regarded as a badge of national surrender and dishonour. It was a lesson that Callaghan and Wilson were to have fully in mind as they considered the options for future policy when they entered office in 1964. The humiliation that Cripps endured in 1949 was a lasting memory for the young parliamentary secretary to the Minister of Transport.

There were many difficulties elsewhere. The Cabinet had been riven by dissent over whether to proceed with the nationalization of iron and steel in the summer of 1947. Eventually the nationalizers, headed by Dalton and Bevan, prevailed over the more cautious Cabinet members including Morrison and (surprisingly) Shinwell. George Strauss as Minister of Supply took over to speed up the transfer of the steel industry into public ownership, but over the next two years the government seemed to make slow and very reluctant progress on what Bevan and others (including Callaghan) regarded as a priority for a socialist government. Overseas, there was an an atmosphere of crisis, culminating in the Russian siege of West Berlin in 1948, which led the Labour government to join President Truman in organizing an airlift. The Communist coup in Czechoslovakia in February 1948 (for all Callaghan's optimism eighteen months earlier), along with the Russian breach with Tito in Yugoslavia in 1949, reinforced the sense of gloom and foreboding as the cold war reached a new level of glacial intensity. In the Commonwealth, such rejoicing as there was with the transfer of power in India in August 1947 was tempered by another, far less honourable, withdrawal (or 'scuttle' to Churchill) from Palestine and the severe damage to Ernest Bevin's reputation as a result.

Even so, Callaghan, like most of the ministers young and old, retained his optimism. In general, Labour's solidarity held. Almost all of the trade unions accepted the rigours of a wage freeze and later of devaluation. Strikes were not widespread. The public seemed prepared to accept austerity in return for full employment and 'fair shares'. The severity of the cold war meant that left-wing dissidents of the Keep Left type virtually disintegrated in the face of clear evidence of Russian aggression. The era of Cripps, for all its painful aspects, seemed to be giving Labour a new lease of life. It was 'consolidating' the achievements of 1945–7, but also keeping up public spending and the socialist forward momentum. By-elections (other than one freak contest in Glasgow determined by the ILP) showed Labour holding on to all its seats, however marginal. Callaghan, bright and breezy at the Ministry of Transport, shared this optimism. In a note written at Christmas time 1949, he concluded that 'the mood of the people is for another period of Labour Government and has been so since the press started bringing the possibility of a General Election to public notice'. However, he added that 'unless we have thought out and got over to people our attitude on the problems of 1950 to 1960 we shall lose the

Election following this one—and will deserve to'. He took comfort in the fact that Crossman and others were working on longer-term planning with this in mind.[1]

At the Ministry of Transport he was in his element, vigorous, commanding, with a direct quarterdeck manner. His position might have been affected very early on. His patron Hugh Dalton, whose prestige had suffered in any case during the convertibility crisis, had to resign following a minor budget leak in November 1947. Callaghan spent some time in comforting the fallen Chancellor, walking with him along Downing Street very late at night to tell him that his friends expected to see him back soon.[2] In May 1948 he greeted Dalton's return to the Cabinet as Chancellor of the Duchy with special responsibility for European affairs with genuine cordiality and enthusiasm. A more severe personal wrench that year was the death through drowning during a holiday accident of his friend Evan Durbin. But his career was now moving on independently of Dalton or other patrons. His departmental chief at Transport, Alfred Barnes, was a reserved trade unionist active in the Co-operative Movement. He made a virtue of the dullness with which he handled departmental affairs in the Commons. It seems that he gave the young Callaghan a free hand in branching out in the variety of areas that concerned his department—road and rail transport, road safety, regional policy, and especially the docks, of direct electoral concern to a Cardiff member.

In his office in Berkeley Square, Callaghan got on well enough with Barnes, and had good relations with his civil servants who appreciated his human directness and diligence ('Jim always did his homework'). He insisted on interviewing each official at length when he began his duties. His secretary Gwyneth Jones, a young Welsh-speaking girl (who was privately a Conservative), found Callaghan stimulating and friendly to work with. Compared with her previous minister, George Strauss, who was laid back and complacent, Callaghan was 'dynamic' and energetic, a young man in a hurry but not unpleasantly so. His obsessive commitment to his department led to his fixing a departmental meeting on the day of the royal wedding in 1947 when the huge crowds meant that getting around London was almost impossible. He took out Gwyneth and two typists for a dinner at Christmas time, and gave her a tea party when she married and left the civil service to return to Aberystwyth. In return, she performed a variety of homely tasks for him, including finding a kitten for the Callaghan children which gave much pleasure, and securing a borrowed bow tie from a civil servant when Callaghan found himself unexpectedly speaking at a formal dinner. Gwyneth later surmised that when she was replaced by a man, the relationship with the minister was not quite so cordial.[3]

The main public area of controversy with which the Ministry had to deal was following up the public ownership of road and rail transport and that of the docks in the latest phase of the government's programme of nationalization. After some difficulty in the Lords, notably over the C licences for short-term road hauliers where the government unexpectedly climbed down, this measure came into effect in the autumn of 1947, as the new junior minister moved into his post. Callaghan was an enthusiastic supporter of this policy. At the same time, he tried to tone down his naturally forceful approach as a government minister of the House and sought, not often successfully, to emulate Barnes's speaking style of paralysing dullness. He was a particularly effective front-bench performer who enjoyed good relations with many of his Conservative opposite numbers. In 1948, he was praised as 'one of the most likeable men in the House'.[4] But there was no lack of commitment on his part. In the Commons in November 1947 he strongly defended the positive effects of the railways being nationalized not only in terms of operational efficiency but also for 'making the fullest use of the people employed in it'.[5] He was able to point both to a huge increase in freight transported on the railways and also to the new 'spirit of co-operation' he detected amongst the workforce.

The docks and shipping were a more complex area. This was particularly because of the enduring problems of dock labour and of casual work which had caused difficulty ever since Ernest Bevin was a youthful officer of the Transport Workers' Union in Bristol before the First World War. As will be seen, the activities of the Dock Labour Board caused many managerial difficulties in which Callaghan himself was to be involved. He was active in trying to use the opportunities of public ownership to secure a nationwide distribution of work for the various docks, through the direction of government-owned cargoes in particular. In 1949, at the Bristol Chamber of Commerce, he hailed the enormous expansion of the opportunities for British shipping during the export boom of the previous twelve months and through the new opportunities for European co-operation following the advent of Marshall Aid and the OEEC.[6] However, the Bristol audience was a difficult one. Callaghan was also very much aware of the needs of his own south Wales region and indeed of his own constituency in Cardiff, which, along with the other Welsh ports, was in rivalry with that of Bristol, not to mention those of Liverpool, Manchester, Southampton, Hull, and especially London further afield. Replying to Lady Megan Lloyd George, then a Liberal, in the Welsh

Affairs debate on 24 November 1947, he hailed the immense rise in imports and exports being handled in the docks of south Wales.[7] He was praised in the Swansea newspaper the *Evening Post*, which described him as a 'young and energetic' minister, for his work in encouraging trade for south Wales ports, as in the timber traffic from Germany and Scandinavia currently being sent through the Swansea docks.[8] In this and other ways, he claimed that 'a flowering of the Welsh spirit' was taking place—this despite the blank reluctance of Herbert Morrison to grant any form of devolution or create an effective Council for Wales.[9] Regional considerations as well as an efficient national plan for the docks and shipping told in favour of an effective distribution of activity across the country by the Ministry of Transport. The intransigence of the shipping industry, however, which had strong influence with the department, and the difficulties created by the labour force in many of the docks led to Callaghan's efforts being somewhat frustrated. By 1950 the bulk of the work was being rerouted to London and Liverpool just the same, although the Cardiff docks continued to work at nearly full capacity for years thereafter.

One particular result of being connected with the nation's ports was that he was brought into Cabinet policy in dealing with industrial disputes in the docks. By the summer of 1948 there were unofficial strikes in Liverpool and the Port of London in particular, and Callaghan attended the Cabinet's Emergencies Committee under the chairmanship of the Home Secretary, Chuter Ede, to deal with them. In June 1948 the strikes in the London docks had led to 16,000 men being on strike and troops were on standby. Arthur Deakin and other Transport Workers' leaders spoke darkly of political motivation by Communist longshoremen though the case was never proved. In the end, Attlee had to use troops and to ask the King to call a state of emergency, and the strike thereafter crumbled.[10] There is no evidence that Callaghan or indeed any government minister, including Aneurin Bevan, had any qualms about this stern policy, which Labour had earlier condemned when used by Lloyd George's coalition government in 1919–21. Ministers and TUC leaders regarded the strikes as an act of industrial betrayal by selfish dissidents against a Labour administration formed to defend the workers.

A more serious episode came in May–July 1949 when again Attlee had to use the 1920 Emergency Powers Act and ask the King to declare a state of emergency. Troops were used to unload deteriorating cargoes on the dockside. The dispute was more difficult because of its connection with industrial action by the Canadian seamen, many of whose leaders were Communists. The affair was also complicated by a dispute between the government and the chairman of the Dock Labour Board, the elderly Labour peer Lord Ammon. After the use of 15,000 troops to break the strike, and a failure to extend it to Tilbury, the men returned to work in late July.[11] Callaghan again took a firm line. But, as will be seen, he also linked the trouble in the docks to genuine grievances in the industry from workers who still regarded themselves as 'casual labour' despite the operation of the Dock Labour Scheme. The men were bound to work on successive ships under the direction of particular master stevedores. It would be far better, he felt, for them to have only one employer for one dock, as happened in the Port of Manchester where there was no sense of dockers being casual labour and where strikes had disappeared in consequence. Even more fundamentally, the role of the unions under the Scheme was ambiguous. They appeared as both advocates and judges, protectors of the workers yet also instruments of the employment system whose control over 'cards' determined the employment pattern. This weakened the hold of elected union officials and handed the initiative over to local unofficial leaders. The problems of the docks continued to plague the government for the remainder of its term, and were unresolved when Callaghan left the Ministry of Transport in February 1950.

Contrasted with the Serbonian bog of dock labour, Callaghan imposed himself on the public consciousness in a highly visible way in relation to the roads. There were political dividends here, too, for instance in Callaghan's opportunities to link the government's road building programme with the building of new factories in the Welsh valleys: he was able to make this point effectively when opening a new 'heads of the valleys' bypass for Merthyr and Dowlais.[12] There was also early speculation about a future Severn crossing. One of his concerns was road safety. He chaired the Ministry's Road Safety Committee which dealt with such matters as speed restrictions and road markings.[13] In this connection he first met the young Princess Elizabeth. Following an early visit by Callaghan to the Road Research Laboratory, two permanent and highly visible reforms took place. Striped crossings, popularly known as 'zebra crossings', were instituted on major thoroughfares. More notable were the illuminated metal studs or 'Cats eyes' which Callaghan had instituted on major roads—this despite fears that they would lead to drivers driving on the middle of the road. At a time when severe fog or 'smog' was still a hazard particularly during the autumn and winter, the new 'Cats eyes' were a major symbol of the Ministry turning its effective attention to problems of road safety. Callaghan himself, handsome and spruce in a dark blue suit, took part in a film made by the Ministry to publicize the value of Cats eyes.

It helped to underline his executive role. The episode, however, could also be taken to show the ways in which civil servants and official 'experts' could try to delay beneficial change, not least through the use of misleading or plainly inaccurate statistics.

Callaghan was, of course, a minor member of the government at this time, though one whose performance drew words of praise from the Prime Minister, Clement Attlee, himself. But he also managed to impose himself on the wider political world in a number of controversial areas. These showed that, even as an ambitious and thrusting junior minister, he had not lost his pugnacity or his ability for independent judgement and self-expression. Perhaps the most striking came in May 1948, when as a minister concerned with the implementation of the government's nationalization programme, he took fierce public issue with a senior minister, albeit one somewhat bruised by his earlier experiences at Fuel and Power, the War Minister, Emanuel Shinwell. At a meeting of the Co-operative Congress on 2 May Shinwell made a remarkably negative speech about the effects of nationalization of industry to date. He complained that there had been too little preparation of the precise methods of running a nationalized industry and also that trying to introduce democratic methods into the workings of nationalized industry had not been a success.[14] This said little more than what many critics on the left had long been pointing out—indeed, Shinwell himself, who chaired the Labour Party's committee on nationalization planning during the latter stages of the war, was one of the main culprits. Callaghan himself was to make many of the same comments later on.

But the political timing caused much anger—not least from Hugh Gaitskell who had succeeded Shinwell at Fuel and Power and suspected him of trying to undermine the Gas Nationalization Bill currently going through the House. Callaghan spoke out belligerently before the parliamentary party on 5 May. It was a meeting at which emotion was already running high because of the disciplining of the MPs who had sent a telegram in support of the left-wing Italian socialist leader Pietro Nenni. Callaghan added to the emotion: he pointed out that Shinwell's current position as chairman of the party gave his comments added authority. Privately, Callaghan told his divisional party in Cardiff South that Shinwell's remarks made it appear that the nationalization of iron and steel was now in the balance. He also checked with Morgan Phillips, Labour's general secretary, to see whether Shinwell's speech had been prepared by Transport House.[15] On balance, Callaghan came out of this row with his reputation enhanced. He had stood up to a notoriously aggressive and combustible minister (boxing was one of Shinwell's particular enthusiasms) with some panache, and had rekindled mass support for public ownership. The *Young Socialist* praised him at this time as 'a man with a bright vision of a better Britain—a socialist Britain'. At the meeting of Labour's National Executive on 11 May Shinwell was, in effect, let off with a caution.[16] The NEC considered his explanation to be 'adequate and complete' but Shinwell did not come well out of the affair. For all the private criticism of senior colleagues like Dai Grenfell, Callaghan refurbished his credentials as a defender of the faith.

Nationalization was an issue where a public stand would undoubtedly do Callaghan some good. But he also took an independent position on a quite different kind of question where the public mood was very different. In April 1948 there was difficulty over the Home Secretary Chuter Ede's Criminal Justice Bill. It was an otherwise unremarkable measure which attracted dissent from a large number of Labour MPs who wanted to abolish the death penalty. Callaghan, with a strong commitment to civil liberties and penal reform, was amongst them. On 14 April 1948 Attlee told a meeting of junior ministers that they should on no account vote against the death penalty since the Cabinet had decided otherwise. A majority of Cabinet ministers, including Attlee and Ede, in fact favoured hanging at this time. There were many protests on what was felt to be a matter of individual conscience, by Lords Chorley and Ammon, and by Evan Durbin, Geoffrey de Freitas, Buchanan, Wheatley, Blenkinsop, and Callaghan himself. 'I believe that looking back in 10 years time I should be ashamed of myself if I had cast a vote in favour of its continuance and in company with a number of others I decided to abstain, as I could not vote as I would like to.'[17] Sydney Silverman's abolitionist amendment was carried in the Commons but perished at the hands of the Lords. When the bill returned to the Commons, Labour's whips compelled the deletion of any reference to ending the death penalty. Again, however, Callaghan, sometimes criticized as an overambitious careerist, had taken a firm stand on grounds of conscience.

In July 1949, during the London dock strike, he was more daring still. In an unusual move for a junior minister, he wrote in protest to Attlee himself about the operations of the Dock Labour Scheme. In effect he was complaining about one of the achievements of the mighty Ernest Bevin himself, the most powerful trade unionist alive and Foreign Secretary. In a letter cleared beforehand with Barnes, Callaghan rehearsed the points of criticism about the Dock Labour Scheme noted above. In particular he urged amending the disciplinary system in the docks 'so that the Union returns to its traditional role of acting as advocate, and ceases to be judge, leaving discipline to be imposed by a body independent of employers and men'. Attlee handed the letter over to Bevin whose somewhat overbearing reply tried to jump on the young junior minister from a great height. 'I feel that you are not well informed regarding the situation in south Wales. I take this opportunity therefore to forward you a brief history.' He added that the suggestion that the union was now an organization which a man had to join to hold a card 'is rather far-fetched' and he disputed that there was a plague of industrial troubles either in the south Wales ports or anywhere else.

Callaghan, however, was far from being overawed. He pointed out that his comments were not applicable to south Wales alone. 'I stick to my point that the Union has less real influence with the Dockers than it used to have. There is plenty of evidence for that.' He reiterated that changes in the disciplinary machinery, giving the unions a more independent role, would be valuable. As a parting shot, he noted, 'By the way, we do not strike in South Wales because we don't get enough ships to fight about. London and Liverpool gorge themselves with shipping to an increasing extent.' Bevin did not respond formally, but Attlee seems to have responded to Callaghan's criticisms equably enough. He proposed to refer his points to the official committee set up by the Ministry of Labour to examine the working of the Dock Labour Scheme.[18] The events of the next few years, which saw unofficial strikes in the docks continue, tended to confirm Callaghan's fears of the ambiguous role of the union leadership and its dangers in maintaining industrial discipline. It also confirmed perhaps an underlying tension between the Ministry of Labour and that of Transport in approaching an issue of this kind, in their different perceptions of the role of the unions. Callaghan's later view was that the Dock Labour Scheme as a whole was beneficial but that large numbers of the underlying problems, caused by slipshod management and antique work practices, remained in full.[19] Politically, it showed again that he was a forceful, unsycophantic minister not to be trifled with.

He was throughout this period making his way through the party and the administration as a coming man. Across the country he was a much sought-after speaker at party gatherings, and was popular with university students. One of his more successful appearances was at the Cambridge Union in February 1948 when he spoke in defence of the idea of socialism in opposition to Sir David Maxwell-Fyfe. The young Peter Shore was among the audience. The student newspaper, *Varsity*, reported that Callaghan was 'wildly acclaimed as he sat down'.[20] He was amongst a number of promising junior ministers who came into the ambit of Cripps, who was probably considered in 1948–9 to be the most likely successor to Attlee should there be a change of leadership. Hugh Gaitskell, now Minister of Fuel and Power and a long-standing admirer of his parliamentary skills,[21] was another with whom he had a reasonably close association. With Keep Left, his links were now over; indeed that body had virtually dissolved when men like Crossman and Foot declared their support for the formation of NATO in view of the belligerent course of Soviet foreign policy. He viewed the expulsion from the party of far-left rebels like Platts-Mills, Pritt, and Zilliacus without distress. One powerful figure on the left, with whom he kept in contact notably on train journeys to their south Wales constituencies on Friday nights, was Aneurin Bevan. They were never particularly close, but in October 1949 Bevan unburdened himself on the inadequacies of government policy at home and abroad as he saw them. Callaghan noted, 'He has his eye on the Prime Minister's job. Surely Ernie Bevin can't hang on? How wrong Herbert Morrison usually is! The P.M.'s job is not enviable but at some stage in your career you become the custodian of the hopes and aspirations of others. Then you are no longer free!' Bevan added that if Attlee and Bevin continued after the election without indicating when they would step down, he would consider not joining the government. 'The way ahead seems dark', Callaghan reflected.[22]

But the most important new dimension that his career acquired at this time came in overseas affairs. This came formally somewhat later in April 1950, when Callaghan was unexpectedly asked by Hugh Dalton to serve as his deputy on the British delegation to the new Council of Europe in Strasbourg.[23] Callaghan had already briefly served as a British delegate there, deputizing for Morrison, in August 1949. He accepted at once, even though it meant rearranging the family's summer holiday. Hitherto, Callaghan's interests in overseas affairs had largely lain elsewhere. He was a strong Commonwealth man and closely identified with African national aspirations since his visit to west Africa early in 1946. In overseas affairs more generally, he was a qualified Atlanticist, critical of the Americans over conditions attached to the loan in 1945 and what sometimes appeared to him a Pavlovian cold-war antagonism to the Soviet Union. But he was also well aware of the immense value of Marshall Aid and of securing a permanent American commitment to the defence of western Europe. Callaghan was not one of those backbenchers particularly associated with overtures to western European socialist parties in 1947–8, while in any case he had little knowledge of European languages. On the other hand, the functional approach to western European union, through economic collaboration and then through defence, under the terms of OEEC and the Brussels Treaty, was wholly congenial to him.

In Strasbourg, he served on the British delegation at an interesting time. Much of the limelight amongst the British delegates was monopolized by the presence on the Conservative delegation of Winston Churchill whose grandiose, if vague, declarations on behalf of some kind of European union at The Hague two years earlier had attracted much publicity. However, the British delegates, who included William Glenvil Hall, Aidan Crawley, Maurice Edelman (a fine linguist), Fred Lee, Lynn Ungoed Thomas, and the 'fanatical Federalist' Kim Mackay, with Denis Healey and Anthony Crosland in attendance as well as Dalton himself, were a lively crew.[24] They enjoyed a cheerful hiking excursion to Le Donon in the Vosges, amongst other diversions congenial to Dalton with his love of the open air and of young male company. Ernest Bevin, a very sick man, briefly joined them there. At Strasbourg, Callaghan acquitted himself well in this unfamiliar setting, full of western European prima donnas such as Monnet, Mollet, Schuman, and Spaak. He spoke out in defence of Britain's economic interests (prefacing his remarks with the phrase 'I am not an economist') and emphasized the dangers of an American recession for the western European economies.[25] He was also happy to defend European functional collaboration, notably in defence, speaking with the added authority now of a service minister.

However, here and in a subsequent visit to Strasbourg in December 1950, Callaghan had to uphold a British position, already well entrenched, of keeping a distance between British national interests and any plans for a more unified or federalist Europe. There was dispute between the British and French delegates, headed by Mollet and Bidault, over the precise terms of a defence resolution in August.[26] Callaghan had to announce the British view that the European Assembly should not attempt to take powers away from national government, and that any deviation in a federalist direction was unacceptable. In particular, the British Labour delegates were adamant against a European army, even if the defeated Germans were excluded.[27] Dalton, no lover of Europeans, was particularly firm on this: he urged that the various working parties and committees could neither instruct nor dictate, but merely put forward resolutions, and Callaghan had to follow this line, too. He faced much opposition from continental Europeans, headed by Robert Schuman, the French Foreign Minister, on this, and indeed had to make the best of a somewhat unsatisfactory brief. He had the solace, however, of much praise from Dalton. 'I consider that Callaghan had handled a difficult situation extremely well,' he wrote. He told Attlee, 'Callaghan was always definitely recognised by me and others as my No. 2. [He] disported himself well and I am sure learned a lot from the experience. On my advice he had worked hard at his French which he now understands quite well and can speak passably.'[28] Bevin himself sent a rare note of congratulations, as did the Conservative Harold Macmillan, writing 'as one country bumpkin to another'.[29] Callaghan's stance throughout was to emphasize Britain's central role in defending western Europe, but through NATO rather than through any elaborate form of united Europe. He was critical of the way that federalists, include apparently some of the British Conservatives, attempted to hijack the discussions, but felt satisfied by the end of the session that they had been held at bay.

The visit to Strasbourg was a major episode for Callaghan. It brought him much closer to the nub of international events than ever before and undoubtedly heightened his awareness of the interconnectedness of the economic, defence, and political relationships of the nations of western Europe, and of all of them with the United States. He got to know younger men like Denis Healey and Anthony Crosland with whom his career was to be so closely intertwined in the future. He also met prominent Conservatives—Macmillan and Sandys, and the mighty Churchill himself, whom he was to alarm by revealing that a proposed European naval force would have a French admiral.

His own views came to reflect some of the prevailing enthusiasm for collaboration with Britain's European partners. In May 1950 the French Foreign Minister Robert Schuman shook the British government by proposing a European Steel and Coal Community, 'the Schuman Plan' as it became popularly known. Callaghan, like Kenneth Younger and some other junior ministers, was immediately sympathetic. But he was then summoned to the presence of Bevin himself. The Foreign Secretary was annoyed at the idea of Britain's being bounced by the French for their own diplomatic purposes. He argued that the real purpose of Schuman's plan was to bind France and Germany together economically and ultimately militarily, while keeping Britain at a distance. 'They don't want us, Callaghan', Bevin declared, pronouncing Callaghan's surname with a hard 'G' as was his wont.[30]

Callaghan was not convinced at the time, but soon he came to share the general suspicion felt by the Attlee government about an apparently industrial plan that was intended to lead the way to federal integration in other forms. Monnet-type federalism, theoretical abstractions by federal idealists were not a kind of political approach with which Callaghan felt comfortable. Strasbourg was to confirm in his mind a pragmatic, Fabian approach towards relations with Europe, notably in defence matters, but its more theoretical passion for political grand designs alienated him. In general, the suspicion of moves towards European union later in the 1950s, which were studiously ignored by Churchill and Eden down to the formation of the Treaty of Rome, kindled the same lack of fervour in Callaghan and his distinctly Eurosceptic Labour comrades also. The Internationale was little more than a rousing refrain, not a call to socialist solidarity.

Before his dispatch to Strasbourg, Callaghan's career had undergone an important turning of the ways. There had been a general election in February 1950, with Cripps as Chancellor magnificently refusing to introduce an electioneering budget before an election was called. This time, Labour was much affected by the redistribution of constituencies. This was generally considered to have cost Labour about sixty seats, a memory which Callaghan recalled as Home Secretary in 1969 when a further redistribution of constituencies was under discussion prior to a general election. His own constituency was renamed Cardiff South-East and its composition was somewhat changed, with the addition of residential Roath. The working-class core of Splott, Adamsdown, and the docks area of Bute Town was balanced to some degree by middle-class Roath and the urban district of Penarth. It did, however, appear a better prospect for Labour than the old Cardiff South constituency had been. Callaghan was swift to claim it at the expense of his diffident professorial colleague Hilary Marquand who, however, found a very safe seat in Middlesbrough East instead. Prior to the election, there had been some difficulty between Callaghan and his old superior officer Douglas Houghton, now returned as Labour member for Sowerby in a by-election. Callaghan was anxious that his position as an officer of the Inland Revenue Staff Federation should be in some sense kept open for him should he be defeated. The union, not unreasonably, pointed out that he had effectively ceased to be assistant secretary since he enlisted in the navy in 1943 and that Cyril Plant had long been installed as a full-time and highly effective secretary in his place.[31] With a young family of three children, the candidate for Cardiff South-East clearly had the usual personal hazards of the political life to confront.

In the election, Callaghan's Conservative opponent was Dr Hayward, a medical practitioner, while there was a further complication this time with the intervention of a 22-year-old recent Oxford undergraduate who stood as a Liberal (and lost his deposit). In dismal winter weather Callaghan fought his usual typically vigorous campaign. In an 'open letter' to Churchill, he attacked the Tories for intending to reduce food subsidies and for their appeals to 'greed' in relation to house purchase. By contrast, he praised Labour policies in building houses, illustrated by the new housing estates in Rumney and along Western Avenue which had led to nearly 3,000 additional families being housed since 1945. The work of his own department in giving work to Cardiff dockers was also emphasized. He ended, as many Labour candidates did in the 1950 election, by referring to Churchill's historic role in suppressing striking miners in Tonypandy back in 1910 and ridiculed Churchill's (historically quite inaccurate) claim that troops were not sent there at all.[32] A problem of an unexpected kind was that Catholic voters (thought to number 10,000) were urged not to vote for him because of his failure to support public funding for Catholic schools, and he probably lost some Irish votes in Adamsdown as a result; the dispute was cleared up in good time for the 1951 election. In the event, Callaghan won with a solid, though not overwhelming, majority of 5,895 over Hayward with 51 per cent of the votes and a majority of 11.8 per cent. He would still have to work to consolidate his base. So, even more, would the Attlee government as a whole since its enormous majority of over 150 in 1945 fell to a mere 6, which meant that it would be a target for opposition harrying tactics from the outset.

The election resulted in an important change of post. Callaghan now became parliamentary and financial secretary to the Admiralty. In effect, he was the junior minister to George, Viscount Hall, an elderly former Welsh miner who sat in the Lords and had succeeded A. V. Alexander as Navy Minister. This was, of course, the most natural of all posts for Callaghan with his naval background and brought immense joy both to him and to his elderly mother. It would add another dimension, that of defence, to his already remarkably varied range of interests, domestic, international, and colonial. It also came at a crucial time for the British armed services and for the Royal Navy in particular. The navy was still a large one in 1950 with five battleships, eight fleet carriers, thirteen light fleet carriers, and twenty-nine cruisers, on active service, in reserve, or being constructed. But it had been run down, inevitably, since the end of the war, indeed more so than either the army or the air force. Older warships were being scrapped, and others brought out of reserve for active service, all the time against a background of financial stringency. The main priorities were held to be the protection of the British commercial fleet across the world and defence against the Soviet Union's submarine fleet, although there was also a service priority for the defence of British

Commonwealth outposts and possessions 'east of Suez' and across the Pacific.

Callaghan's main priorities at first lay at home, in dealing with the equipping and refitting of Britain's fleet, especially the reserve fleet, and the needs of royal naval servicemen. He sat on the historic Board of Admiralty under Hall's chairmanship. His most conspicuous intervention there came in December 1950 when he tried to extend the same rights in disciplinary cases to lower ratings as those enjoyed by petty officers.[33] He did not board a ship for several months. This interlude did enable him to look up files in the Admiralty records relating to his father's naval career which confirmed the accuracy of the colourful boyhood stories of the expedition to Benin City.

However, his earliest activities in his new post served to confirm his rising reputation as an effective junior minister. He handled his first naval estimates with immense aplomb in the Commons on 22 March 1950.[34] Speaking apparently without a note, he had to announce the further reduction of naval manpower from 153,000 to 143,000. On the other hand, the growth of the Far East Fleet required further expenditure, especially following tension with China after the colourful voyage of the *Amethyst* down the Yangtze in 1949. He was able to announce that six carriers were under construction and that the *Eagle* and *Ark Royal*, when completed, would be the largest aircraft carriers Britain had ever possessed. His speech was well received by his Conservative opponent, J. P. L. Thomas, who praised Callaghan's 'extraordinary ability' and referred warmly to the 'distinguished and varied career' of his father in the navy. From his own backbenches, Callaghan also met with praise from Michael Foot, who combined a near-pacifist view of foreign policy with a prudent regard for the needs of his Devonport constituents. He cheerfully (and accurately) praised Callaghan for having 'good Devonshire blood in his veins'.

At last in May 1950, following a pleasant 'Navy Week' inspection of the home fleet in Plymouth Sound, with his wife, children, and mother present, Callaghan got to sea. He had a relaxing and enjoyable time with officers his own age. The experience, however, was not a total success. He sailed in the *Euryalus* to Gibraltar where he discussed with the naval authorities there the need to build smaller carriers able to take helicopters. He found the naval officers alarmingly right-wing, 'even pro-Franco'. Even worse was a visit most reluctantly undertaken, to a bullfight in Málaga. 'It was loathsome . . . The bull never had a chance. The Picadors were cruel and clumsy and the atmosphere was nauseating.'[35] With much relief, he sailed on to Malta where he stayed in the gloomy residence of the

Governor, and met for the first time the vigorous young leader of the Maltese Labour Party, Dom Mintoff, anxious at that time for direct representation for his country at Westminster. He was to appear frequently in Callaghan's career thereafter.

The outlook of the Admiralty was radically transformed in late June 1950 by the outbreak of the Korean War. North Korea invaded the South and the United States fortuitously (in the temporary absence of the Soviet Union) managed to obtain support in the Security Council of the United Nations for the dispatch of American and other troops to assist the government of South Korea. Urged to do so by its highly influential ambassador in Washington, Sir Oliver Franks, the Attlee government unhesitatingly resolved to support the Americans militarily. This would confirm its position in 'the special relationship', 'not just a member of the European queue' as Franks somewhat curiously put it.[36] It meant the early dispatch of British forces, including naval, to the Far East to assist in the defence of South Korea, and, even at a time of constant economic dificulties, a massive increase in the British rearmament programme.

The effects on the policy of the Admiralty, where Callaghan was increasingly taking the initiative from Hall as he had done from Barnes at Transport, were considerable. Busy though he was at Strasbourg at the Council of Europe, he had to attend to the implications of naval expansion. To this end, he sailed with the navy to Greece between 1 and 9 January 1951 to examine naval dispositions in the eastern Mediterranean; among other naval commanders there he met the Duke of Edinburgh who, he considered, 'talked good sense' and remained something of a friend thereafter. He later wrote to Attlee about the Duke and urged that he be given some civilian experience, which Attlee agreed to consider.[37] The main priority, though, was that the Korean War meant a redirection of naval activity to the Far East, including fresh resources for the naval base at Singapore which had been somewhat in the shadows since being liberated from the Japanese in 1945.[38] British warships were soon in action in Korean waters and played a central, and highly distinguished, role in the allied landing at Inchon, working closely with the US Seventh Fleet.

Inevitably, an increase in the defence estimates followed, although the extent of it startled many observers. On 1 August, despite vigorous protests from Aneurin Bevan (which were later conveniently forgotten by Attlee and Gaitskell), a huge new rearmament programme of £3,400m. spread over the three years 1950/1 to 1953/4 was agreed; it meant a larger defence burden per capita than for the United States, and compared with a figure of £2,400m. originally proposed by Alexander, the Defence Minister in

1949.[39] After Attlee's meeting with President Truman in Washington in December, the defence burden became even more immense. The Admiralty had the smallest share of this budget, but there was still a massive increase in its resources. Compared with a figure of £193m. in the original 1950 defence budget, the 1950/1 defence estimates, presented to the Commons in January 1951, showed a global figure of £278.5m. for the Admiralty, including works, production, research and development, and all other headings of expenditure. This compared with £435.33m. for the War Office and £345.75m. for the Air Ministry.[40] When Attlee presented the figures to the Commons in January 1951, his proposed defence budget of £4,700m. over the next three years startled even many Conservatives. After all, the Prime Minister had spoken as recently as 12 September in terms of only £3,600m. Even though it was made clear by ministers (including Callaghan himself) that the successful achievement of this rearmament programme largely depended on massive US assistance, it was nevertheless an immense defence burden for Britain to undertake.

While the main decisions, of course, rested with the First Lord of the Admiralty, Callaghan was directly involved in helping to implement this massive rearmament drive. In introducing the naval estimates in the Commons on 12 March 1951, he gave an indication of how the £278m. allocated to the Admiralty would be spent, including the bringing of sixty more vessels from the reserve into the active fleet, and the construction of four 'Hermes' light carriers.[41] Once again, Callaghan's polished speech, delivered without any notes and showing an impressive command of naval technicalities, met with the warm praise of J. P. L. Thomas, the Opposition spokesman, and encouraged further cheerful references from Michael Foot to his Devonian blood. Privately, Lord Mountbatten congratulated him on 'a tour de force' while Hugh Dalton, who had heard three-quarters of an hour of Callaghan's speech, declared it to be 'clear, confident, attractive . . . You're well set for the upward climb.'[42] There was also much favourable comment in the press; Pendennis in the *Observer* noted Callaghan as a minister who was steadily confirming 'a glowing reputation'.[43] Beyond these courtesies, however, there was a sombre aspect. Callaghan was directly implicated in a hazardous rearmament programme designed as much for political as for defence purposes, to reassure the Americans of Britain's eternal loyalty as a dependable ally. It was also a programme with wider implications. It could put at risk the economic recovery over which Cripps and Gaitskell, his successor as Chancellor from October 1950, had presided during 1950 and which saw the balance of payments in the black for the first time since the end of 1948. Equally serious, it was to push the hitherto largely united Labour government into a divisive crisis that shook it to its foundation. In one way or another, it was to colour personal relations in Labour's high command, between Callaghan himself and Barbara Castle for example, for the next thirty years.

The initial decision to support the rearmament programme imposed on Britain by the Truman administration appeared to have been agreed, although not without much internal argument and soul-searching. In particular, Aneurin Bevan on two occasions (1 August 1950 and 25 January 1951) had explicitly spelt out his misgivings. Other ministers, Chuter Ede, James Griffiths, and George Tomlinson, were also known to have reservations. Bevan had often made known to his wife Jennie Lee and to close friends like Michael Foot that winter his profound unease with the government's foreign and defence policies. In a tense Cabinet on 25 January, Bevan had set out a series of objections to the rearmament programme scheduled for the next three years, based on the harm they would do to the economy, the damage to exports, the distortions to the labour market, the difficulties of raw materials and of essential supplies such as machine tools.[44] Every one of his criticisms was later, to some degree at least, to be vindicated and the Churchill administration took them to heart after October 1951. But he failed to carry the day with Attlee and his colleagues. Bevan's remarkably brilliant speech in defence of the government's rearmament programme on 15 February when he carried the House with him, Churchill included, focused largely on combating the challenge of communism in the realm of democratic ideas and economic reconstruction. However, he certainly did endorse the rearmament drive, even if only in passing, and emphasize that Britain would carry out its commitments to its allies. By March, despite the horrendous economic sacrifices that it would involve, it appeared that the rearmament programme had been agreed to without splitting either the government or the Labour Party. Junior ministers like Callaghan had apparently no grounds for believing that a crisis was at hand.

However, the situation was transformed when Gaitskell proposed, as part of the economies necessary to finance the rearmament drive, to impose charges on the National Health Service, on dentures and spectacles in particular. There was a furious battle between Gaitskell and Bevan on the Cabinet Committee on the Health Service throughout March over the level of expenditure for the next year. Gaitskell insisted on a ceiling of £392m. being imposed, and the charges being imposed along with prescription charges; the dying Ernest Bevin tried desperately to find a compromise.[45] Finally, at two momentous Cabinet meetings on 22

March and 9 April, the Cabinet agreed that the NHS charges would indeed go ahead, despite Bevan's furious protests that a basic socialist achievement was being undermined for the sake of defence spending. He pointed out that the total sum involved was a mere £23m. and that so fundamental a reversal of policy was unnecessary since the cuts could be made elsewhere.[46] He had previously clashed with Cripps over possible NHS charges and prescription charges in 1950 and it was known that he regarded an attack on the Health Service, his own creation, as a fundamental issue. In addition, his anger was fuelled by personal animosity towards Gaitskell, a public-school *arriviste* who had vaulted above him to succeed Cripps as Chancellor of the Exchequer. Bevan found an ally, somewhat unexpectedly, in the person of Harold Wilson, certainly a champion of the Health Service but one whose criticisms focused rather on the damage to an overstretched economy and the fatal shortage of raw materials, of which, as President of the Board of Trade, he was well aware. By 10–11 April, a period at which Attlee was temporarily in hospital for a minor operation and the Cabinet was being chaired by Morrison, Bevan's old enemy, it was known that Bevan was in ferociously angry mood and on the verge of resignation from the government.

Callaghan was only on the margins of this crisis. As regards the substance of the issue, he was of course a strong defender of the Health Service although he had not been prominent in Commons debates on it. He was also very well aware of the problems that the increased rearmament programme would cause for the economy. Indeed his own opposition to an eighteen-month period of national service back in 1947 had focused in part on the damage that it would do to industrial production. He was conscious, too, of how the defence programme depended fundamentally on American assistance, which was always problematic. And he knew of the supplies difficulties since he now chaired a Cabinet committee on the allocation of raw materials. As a service minister, he was familiar with the difficulties of reversing a policy of retrenchment in defence expenditure. On the other hand, he had become a strong Atlanticist, deeply concerned at what he saw as a worldwide Communist threat, from China now as well as the Soviet Union, and he accepted the new rearmament programme as a grim necessity.

On the personal side, he had quite close relations with both Gaitskell and Bevan and admired both in their different ways. He and Gaitskell had become friendly in the course of the 1945–50 parliament; after all, long ago Gaitskell had been Audrey Callaghan's tutor in a WEA class. They were both Dalton protégés. When Gaitskell became Chancellor in October

1950, Callaghan wrote him a fulsome note of congratulations. 'I have not heard a single word of criticism, because it is regarded as a natural and inevitable step. There was no one else. That is a remarkable tribute.'[47] On the other hand, he knew Bevan well also as a fellow south Wales member who had confided in Callaghan his dissatisfactions and ambitions. He certainly had a high regard for Bevan's hold over the movement and his charismatic qualities. But since Callaghan moved neither in Gaitskell's Hampstead set nor in Bevan's world of London journalists and left-wing *littérateurs*, he observed largely from the sidelines.

Unexpectedly, however, he became involved directly on 10 April, budget day. By chance he met up with Arthur Blenkinsop, formerly Bevan's PPS at the Ministry of Health, who told him Bevan was likely to resign. Callaghan was aghast at the news and promptly drafted a letter to his Welsh colleague urging him not to leave the government. Callaghan got this letter signed by Blenkinsop, Alfred Robens, and Michael Stewart of the centre-right, along with Fred Lee, a left-winger. In it, they warned Bevan of the damage to the party that a resignation might inflict. They urged him at least to wait until the parliamentary party meeting on 11 April.[48] Bevan then had a private meeting with Callaghan behind the Speaker's chair; here he paced up and down pouring out his animosity towards Gaitskell ('Hugh is a Tory'). However, he still appeared to keep his options open. Later that day Callaghan had a second meeting with Bevan in which the latter urged that the Health Service charges be dropped. He emphasized the triviality of destroying the government for the sake of £13m. in one financial year and the impossibility of ever carrying the rearmament programme out. These were points with which Callaghan had much sympathy. He also felt that, friendly as he was with Gaitskell, the latter's stubbornness, amounting to intellectual arrogance, was a major factor in the crisis too. Callaghan then went on to see Chuter Ede, who railed against both Gaitskell and Bevan, but suggested a possible compromise to the effect that the NHS charges bill remain, as it were, undated, with no specific time when they would come into effect. Callaghan then relayed this back to Bevan, though perhaps surprisingly he did not see Gaitskell as well. But Bevan remained adamant. Callaghan's effort at shuttle diplomacy, such as it was, had ended.

At a Cabinet meeting on 12 April, Bevan and Wilson announced that they were unable to vote in favour of the NHS charges. Attempts by Dalton and others to mediate failed; the intervening death of Ernest Bevin did not alter the political atmosphere which became increasingly poisonous. Gaitskell's supporters compared Bevan to Mosley; Bevan dismissed

Gaitskell as 'Nothing! Nothing!' On 20 April *Tribune* carried a ferocious leading article, written by Michael Foot, which compared Gaitskell to MacDonald and Snowden, the historic traitors in 1931. Later that day, Bevan and Wilson resigned from the government. On 23 April Bevan made an angry resignation speech in the Commons which misjudged the mood of the House and alienated it. After a violent meeting of the parliamentary party the next day, when Bevan denounced Gaitskell's attacks on 'my Health Service', a meeting of fifteen left-wing Labour MPs was held at the House of Commons; several of them were members of the old Keep Left group. Bevan and Wilson were also present, along with John Freeman, a junior minister who had also resigned. The 'Bevanites' had in effect come into being. Labour was plunged into years of civil war.

Callaghan reacted to these events as a party loyalist first and foremost. Whatever his regard for Bevan and his doubts about the defence programme, he felt that in the end Bevan had been the more intransigent of the two warring Cabinet ministers. His behaviour had been disloyal and unforgivable. Callaghan was from that time a clear opponent of the Bevanite tendency, even if he was never regarded as a root and branch Gaitskellite either. In speeches at Enfield (29 April) and Merthyr Tydfil (6 May 1951) he called for understanding of the problems of Labour defence ministers and spelt out the consequences of rearmament in building up the navy. He felt confident that the United States would recognize that its policy of stockpiling raw materials would prevent Britain from realizing its defence programme, and deplored the fact of ministers resigning from the government. At the party conference in September, he took a middle of the road line. 'The combination of individual freedom and economic controls is the way in which you can best counter the revolutionary march of Communism.' But he derided sentimental notions of 'getting together with Joe'.[49]

It was a tense summer. The build-up of the Bevanite group continued, with the publication in July of *One Way Only*. It is a pamphlet which now reads remarkably moderately in its analysis of the world crisis in raw materials but it also attacked the rearmament programme. At the time it was regarded as a left-wing manifesto by Bevan, Wilson, Freeman, and their friends, and Callaghan did not like it. There were other possible troubles for the Admiralty that summer when the seizure of the Abadan oil refinery in Persia by the government of Dr Mussadiq led to a crisis and a possible dispatch of British troops to defend the United Kingdom's oil interests. Shinwell, now the Minister of Defence, was in belligerent mood, as was Morrison who had succeeded Bevin at the Foreign Office, but other ministers, including not only Dalton but also Gaitskell, urged wiser counsels. The Admiralty did not, therefore, have to dispatch vessels of war to the Persian Gulf. It was in any case busy enough in the Far East.

Callaghan had much else to do at this time. In addition to the naval operations in Korea, he was also engaged in persuading Shinwell to send destroyers to India as a peace-keeping gesture. Lord Mountbatten, the former Viceroy who was now the Fourth Sea Lord, applauded this proposal. 'There could be no question whatever of India ever attacking Pakistan; of that I am convinced', he wrote.[50] There were also negotiations with the Nationalist government in South Africa about the costs of the proposed transfer of the British naval base in Simonstown.[51] The economy again deteriorated as the world crisis in raw materials hugely increased Britain's import bill and sent the balance of payments massively into the red. In September Gaitskell went to Washington to try to get American assistance over the spiralling cost of raw materials, but the Americans, especially John Snyder at the US Treasury, were unsympathetic. Of American assistance with 'burden-sharing' over rearmament or help with vital resources such as machine tools, there was no great sign. Bevan's prophecies were being confirmed by default.

Callaghan shared the prevailing dismay and desperation as the government, harassed with its tiny majority by aggressively confident Tory backbenchers, lurched from one crisis to another. Two more cropped up in September–October. There was pressure in southern Africa for a Central African Federation of the two Rhodesias and Nyasaland. It was a scheme initially endorsed by Labour's ministers Patrick Gordon Walker and James Griffiths. The economic merits of a federation became the prevailing orthodoxy for a time in Labour circles, including for Callaghan. It was, however, a plan likely to inflame black African opinion in the southern part of the continent. Here was an issue to engage much of Callaghan's attention in future years. Then in October a crisis threatened in Egypt with the government of Nahas Pasha threatening to evict the British forces, stationed in the canal zone as they had been since the time of Sir Garnet Wolseley in 1882. Morrison, as in the Abadan crisis, was belligerent. Again an international confrontation loomed. The Royal Navy in the Mediterranean was put on full alert.

Callaghan meanwhile had his personal grievances. When George Hall, the veteran First Lord, had resigned on grounds of age in May, Callaghan had reasonable expectations of replacing him as the Cabinet minister responsible for the navy. After all, his own performance as junior Admiralty Minister had won golden opinions from all sides. Instead, Lord

Pakenham, somewhat improbably, was chosen. Dalton thought it was very unfair. He had mentioned Callaghan's name to Attlee back in February as a putative colonial secretary should Jim Griffiths replace Bevin at the Foreign Office, but Attlee had commented, without further explanation, that Callaghan 'wasn't quite balanced enough yet'. Callaghan wrote to Attlee expressing his extreme disappointment at his lack of promotion. The Prime Minister 'hadn't liked this at all', according to Gaitskell.[52] However an emollient reply came from Attlee which confirmed the excellent impression he had made in two very different departments, but told him to be patient. It was another example of Attlee's reluctance to promote talented younger men (or, indeed, virtually any women) and Callaghan remained somewhat aggrieved. He suspected that Pakenham, with whom he had a good personal relationship, had been selected partly for class reasons, as a polished public-school man who could address naval commanders as tradition dictated. Attlee, a loyal Haileybury product, always had a soft spot for upper-class public schoolboys. On the other hand, a more amusing episode came at a Buckingham Palace garden party that summer when the ever tactless Lady Astor, herself a former member for Plymouth, rushed up to Callaghan and Pakenham, who were together. Ignoring the latter entirely, she commiserated loudly with Callaghan on his being superseded by Pakenham about whom her comments were distinctly less than flattering. Dalton loyally shared in Callaghan's disappointment. He and Hugh Massingham of the *Observer* agreed 'that it was bad to put him under Pakenham who is his own age [*sic*]. To be under George [Hall] hadn't mattered.' Massingham added that Attlee was 'hated' in the party for promoting such élitist figures as Lords Pakenham and Ogmore.[53]

While Gaitskell was in the United States in September, Attlee, who presided over an ageing, tired Cabinet many of whom had been in office for almost eleven years in peace and in war, called a general election. It was a snap decision taken by the Prime Minister and almost certainly a tactical mistake. The reason appears to have been to anticipate a coming visit to Africa by King George VI. In fact, the King was to die shortly after and never went to Africa at all. Had Attlee waited until the summer of 1952 the economic situation would have been much improved, and the Korean War much nearer a settlement, so Labour might well have hung on to office. In the election, Callaghan played his usual vigorous part, even though he complained when Transport House sent him off to Anglesey to speak on behalf of Cledwyn Hughes and against the radical Liberal Lady Megan Lloyd George whom Callaghan regarded as a Labour sympathizer (and who later became a Labour MP herself).[54] There was a Labour campaign to stir up fears of the aged Churchill as a 'war-monger'; in this vein, the *Daily Mirror* was to have a powerful headline, 'Whose finger on the trigger', on the eve of the poll. When the Archbishop of York took it upon himself to condemn a speech by Callaghan in Sunderland along these lines, the latter dismissed him as 'taking too innocent a view'.[55] It was indeed an outwardly calm, but still confrontational, election, even if Bevan and his followers returned as loyalists for the campaign and Bevan himself helped draft the manifesto.

The election was the last still fought in the traditional way in local halls and with door-to-door canvassing, rather than being contested on the media. Callaghan had his work cut out to hold on to Cardiff South-East. This time he had a straight fight against Harry West, an ex-miner and former Liberal who was now Conservative Party organizer in Wales. But Labour's electoral machine stood the strain. In the event, Callaghan retained the seat with a fairly comfortable majority of 4,499, a margin of 8.6 per cent over West. In the country as a whole, the extent of Labour's grass-roots support in working-class areas and amongst its 'own people' remained extraordinarily strong. The party ended up with more votes than the Conservatives, and a total of almost 14 million, the highest poll that any British party was to obtain until the Conservatives' victory in 1992. But there were 21 Conservative gains in some rural and suburban areas and commuter constituencies, tired of rationing, shortages, and austerity, and that, along with the vagaries of the British election system, resulted in the election of 321 Conservatives against 295 Labour. By the narrowest of margins, Churchill returned to office. Britain's socialist experiment was over. Labour returned to the familiar pastures of opposition to contemplate an uncertain future.

Callaghan emerged from the maelstrom as one of the most promising of Labour's second-tier younger ministers. Many of the coming politicians were university-trained middle-class people like Gaitskell, Jay, Jenkins, and newer figures like Crosland and Healey (the latter not yet in the House). Callaghan, along with George Brown and Alf Robens, was a relatively rare instance of a working-class ex-trade unionist, also close to the front rank and likely to graduate to the shadow Cabinet in the immediate future. Dalton looked forward to 'a Young Turk landing on the beaches of Power and Fame—with my three companions at that unforgettable weekend at Le Donon—Jim Callaghan, Tony and Denis—in the van.'[56] In the 1945–51 parliaments, amidst the array of talented Labour backbenchers, he had risen up significantly from obscurity. He had proved himself an excellent communicator in the Commons and on the platform; he had good connections with press and radio (television was still in its comparative infancy); he was well liked throughout the party, and was not so bigoted a partisan that he did not enjoy good relations with Conservatives like Walter Elliot and J. P. L. Thomas also. In the House he had trodden a skilful path between conformity and individuality.

On a variety of issues from the US loan to the troubles in the docks, he had taken a remarkably frank line. But his broad acceptability to the whips led him into government office and here he had shone and created a good, if not outstanding, reputation. He had also shown versatility. He was never a one-issue man but had spoken with authority on taxation, transport, housing, defence, international affairs, and colonial questions. His appearances at Strasbourg had added a valuable European dimension.

Beyond his own career, perhaps what Callaghan showed above all was that, despite the travails of the Bevan–Wilson resignations and the disappointment of defeat in 1951, Labour had the capacity for renewal. The party was still in good heart. Its individual membership continued to rise. The unions were loyal. It still had massive support in the numerous thriving centres of heavy industry and manufacturing, with particular strength in Scotland and Wales. And it could bring forward young men like Callaghan who still felt democratic socialism to be a valid creed, who were still anxious for social and economic change (including some public ownership in Callaghan's case), and who had the energy and the controlled passion to help it on. There was no sense after the polls in 1951 that Labour was in a phase of prolonged opposition, let alone terminal decline. Bevin was dead and Cripps was mortally ill. But there was a new generation of younger leaders to follow on from Attlee, Morrison, Dalton, Alexander, and the revered veterans. The sharp and determined member for Cardiff South was certain that he would be foremost amongst them.

1. Callaghan's MS note, Christmas 1949 (Callaghan Papers, box 28).
2. Callaghan to Dalton, 1 June 1948 (Dalton Papers, LSE, 10/21).
3. Interview with Mrs Gwyneth Evans (née Jones), 17 Apr. 1991.
4. Colin McPhee, 'Young Man with a Plan', *Young Socialist* (May 1948).
5. *Parl. Deb.*, 5th ser., vol. 443, 2209 ff. (7 Nov. 1947).
6. Speech to Bristol Chamber of Commerce, 4 Mar. 1949 (Callaghan Papers, box 28).
7. *Parl. Deb.*, 5th ser., vol. 470, 632 ff.
8. *South Wales Evening Post*, 9 Sept. 1948.
9. *Parl. Deb.*, 5th ser., vol. 470, loc. cit.
10. Minutes of Cabinet Emergencies Committee, 21–8 July 1948 (CAB 134/175, 176).
11. Ibid. 21 June–22 July 1949 (CAB 134/176).

12. *Aberdare Leader*, 25 June 1949.

13. Committee on Road Safety proceedings, 1948–51 (PRO, MT 108/6).

14. *News Chronicle*, 3 May 1948.

15. Callaghan to Cardiff South divisional party, 7 May 1948; Callaghan to Morgan Phillips, 7 May 1948 (Callaghan Papers, box 28).

16. Labour Party NEC minutes, 12 May 1948.

17. Callaghan MS note, 14 Apr. 1948 (Callaghan Papers, box 28).

18. Callaghan to Attlee, ? 18 July 1949; Bevin to Callaghan, 19 July 1948; Callaghan to Bevin, 20 July 1948; Attlee to Callaghan, 21 July 1948 (FO 800/519).

19. Callaghan to J. Phillips, 3 Sept. 1992 (in author's private possession).

20. *Varsity*, 14 Feb. 1948. The account of this debate was written by Humphrey Berkely, the president of the Cambridge Union and a future Conservative MP (and subsequently member of the Labour, SDP, and Labour Party again, in sequence). I am grateful for information from Peter Shore.

21. Philip Williams, *Hugh Gaitskell* (London, 1979), 131.

22. Callaghan MS note, 30 Oct. 1949 (Callaghan Papers, box 28).

23. Callaghan to Dalton, 14 Apr. 1950 (Dalton Papers, 9/9).

24. Hugh Dalton, *High Tide and After* (London, 1962), 327 ff. For this description of Mackay, see Dalton to Attlee, 10 Sept. 1949 (Dalton Papers, 9/7/45).

25. Draft speech to European Assembly, 1950 (Callaghan Papers, box 1A).

26. Dalton to Attlee, 1 Sept. 1950 (Dalton Papers, 9/11).

27. Statement by Callaghan to General Affairs Committee, Strasbourg, Aug. 1950 (Dalton Papers, 9/12).

28. Dalton to Attlee, 1 Sept. 1950.

29. Macmillan to Callaghan, 23 Nov. 1950 (Callaghan Papers, box 28).

30. *Time and Chance*, 79; transcript of interview with Kenneth Younger (Nuffield College library), 27.

31. Callaghan to Houghton, 15 Dec. 1948, and other materials in Callaghan Papers, box 2.

32. *Western Mail*, 17 Feb. 1950.

33. Minutes of the Board of Admiralty, 28 Dec. 1950 (ADM 167/135), 539–40. Callaghan attended the Board regularly from 30 Mar. 1950.

34. *Parl. Deb.*, 5th ser., vol. 472, 1967–84; see comments in *The Times*, 23 Mar. 1950.

35. Callaghan MS note, 11 June 1950 (Callaghan Papers, box 28).

36. Oliver Franks to Attlee, 15 July 1950 (PREM 8/1405, pt. I); Cabinet Conclusions (CAB 128/19). Cf. Franks to Attlee, 20 Sept. 1949 (PREM 8/973).

37. Callaghan diary, 1–9 January 1951 (Callaghan Papers, box 28); private information from Lord Callaghan.

38. See the excellent account in Malcolm H. Murfett, *In Jeopardy: the Royal Navy and Britain's Far Eastern Defence Policy, 1945– 1951* (Oxford, 1995), 109 ff.

39. Cabinet Conclusions, 1 Aug. 1950 (CAB 128/18).

40. Defence Estimates, Jan. 1951 (T/225/123); Note on the Estimates of the Cost of the Korean War, 1950–1 (ADM1/ 21791); 'Navy Estimates, 1951–2' (ADM 167/135), 426.

41. *Parl. Deb.*, 5th ser., vol. 485, 1072 ff. (12 Mar. 1951).

42. Dalton to Callaghan, 12 Mar. 1951 (Callaghan Papers, box 28).

43. *Observer*, 18 Mar. 1951, 'Table Talk'; also cf. *Spectator*, 16 Mar. 1951.

44. Cabinet Conclusions, 25 Jan. 1951 (CAB 128/19).

45. Cabinet Committee on the National Health Service, 14 Mar. 1951 (CAB 134/19); Gaitskell memo on the Health Service, Mar. 1951 (T171/403).

46. Cabinet Conclusions, 22 Mar., 9 Apr. (CAB 128/19).

47. Williams, *Gaitskell*, 236.

48. The letter is printed in full in *Time and Chance*, 110.

49. Notes of speeches in Callaghan Papers, box 28; *Report of Annual Labour Party Conference, 1951*, 110.

50. Mountbatten to Callaghan, 31 Aug. 1951 (Callaghan Papers, box 28).

51. Admiralty brief, July 1951 (ADM1/22534, M01599/51).

52. Interview with Lord Callaghan; *The Political Diary of Hugh Dalton 1918–40; 1945–60*, ed. Ben Pimlott (London, 1986), 507, 549.

53. Dalton, *Political Diary*, 627 (12 May 1954). In fact, Pakenham was over six years older.

54. Callaghan to Dalton, 3 Aug. 1951 (Callaghan Papers, box 28).

55. *Sunderland Echo*, 1 Sept. 1951.

56. Dalton, *Political Diary*, 555 (18 Sept. 1951).

6

OPPOSITION YEARS

PARLIAMENT resumed in November after the general election, with Churchill and the Conservative Party back in office, Callaghan was a vigorous part of Labour's attempt to fight back. Starting in the debate on the King's Speech, he led the charge against what he considered a reactionary government hostile to the interests of the workers. His growing stature was confirmed when he was elected to the shadow Cabinet for the first time, finishing seventh of the twelve elected, with the impressive total of 111 votes. He was to remain a member of either the shadow Cabinet or the Cabinet itself continuously from November 1951 to October 1980, matching the long service of Harold Wilson. Even though Attlee unimaginatively sent him back to the transport portfolio, he could not fail to be prominent in Labour's attack. At first, Labour's tails were up as R. A. Butler, the Conservative Chancellor of the Exchequer, had to grapple with the same balance of payments crisis that had confronted Gaitskell, and Churchill's Cabinet had to confront colonial crises from Egypt to British Guiana. No one imagined that the new Tory government, with its tiny majority, heralded a period of thirteen years of unbroken Conservative ascendancy and that by the end of the decade Labour's strategists would be wondering whether their party could ever regain power again. The years of opposition from the 1951 general election to the Suez crisis in 1956 are a less colourful period of Callaghan's career and receive scant attention in his memoirs. Nevertheless, as a period of consolidation when his reputation as potential leader was further built up, not only in parliament but through the media and in the public consciousness in general, it demands careful attention.

Callaghan certainly had opportunities to shine as transport spokesman, especially in leading the fight against the denationalization of road transport in 1952–3. In general, the Churchill government was content to accept almost all of Labour's measures of public ownership between 1945 and 1951, but it made two exceptions. One was the controversial case of iron and steel; the other was transport, where Labour's attempts to impose controls on small hauliers and local bus companies had brought them some unpopularity. Callaghan, as a believer in an integrated system of public transport, road, rail, sea, and air, had no difficulty in rebutting road denationalization with much vigour. The fact that the main Labour spokesman was Herbert Morrison—an ageing figure with no particular expertise in transport matters any more, following his work in creating the London Passenger Transport Board back in 1931—gave the relatively youthful Callaghan, just into his forties, the more prominence. He felt later that Morrison failed to exert himself in the committee stage, and left matters largely in his own hands.[1] Richard Crossman observed Callaghan and Morrison at work in the committee debate on the guillotine on the Transport Bill in April 1953. 'Once again I marvelled at the parliamentary character of men like Morrison and Callaghan. They live for this sort of thing, in which I can only take the mildest of interest and admire the passion that they manage to feel. But then, they are parliamentarians in the sense that they like Parliament for its own sake, whereas I am only interested in it from the point of view of getting things done.'[2] The patronizing tone of this remark illustrates why Callaghan did not always love Oxford academics.

In the debate on the address in November 1951, Callaghan took the offensive. He denied that the British Transport Commission contained 'an element of monopoly' and belligerently argued that road denationalization was only being introduced because of the contributions from road hauliers to Tory Party funds. In debates on the Transport Bill in 1952–3 he attacked the 'parcelling of investment resources' in transport and promised that the next Labour government would take over such units as were needed to provide an integrated long-distance transport system.[3] However, with the assistance of the Liberals, the government got road denationalization onto the statute book safely enough.

In these debates, Callaghan often sounded like an unregenerate apostle of nationalization whose views had not shifted since 1945. At Colchester in May 1950 he had strongly defended bringing 20 per cent of the economy into public ownership, and had also laid down terms for the acceptable performance of the remaining 80 per cent.[4] Yet at the same time, this speech had also made it clear that there were sharp limits to his view of nationalization. Provided that private enterprise was co-operative, it would be perfectly possible to achieve an effective national industrial policy by other methods—control of the credit operations of the joint-stock banks, the further use of the Distribution of Industry Act to achieve regional balance, the licensing of new building, the development of more democratic procedures within companies for the views of the workforce to be effectively heard, public controls over both earnings and the distribution of dividends to shareholders, the furthering of efficiency through Development Councils, and public controls over credit and investment to safeguard against the effects of falling consumption. Callaghan clearly regarded his recipe as being one to reconcile central direction and business freedom, although whether his proposed battery of controls appealed to private firms as a vision of libertarianism is another matter.

Another theme which Callaghan developed in speeches in the early 1950s is the importance of the consumer and ensuring that producer interests alone did not dictate industrial or commercial policy. Drawing on his experience as a minister under Attlee, he urged that socialism as he understood it was a principle, not 'a blueprint for organization'. Other ways of achieving the same social and economic objectives should be pursued. In a speech in Aberavon in the early 1950s, he declared, 'I am not a nationaliser and I don't believe that nationalisation is the only way through which the soul of a Socialist can be saved.' Nationalization was a means not an end. 'If we can get to socialism by other means then let us do it. Otherwise these nationalised industries can become a sort of Frankenstein because coal, gas and electricity are monopolistic industries.' Again he urged that 'the accent for socialists must be on the consumer', for example effective consumers' consultative committees to ensure that the public was not held to ransom by a nationalized giant and its workers.[5]

These speeches picked up many of the themes on which Callaghan had so fiercely rebuked Shinwell in 1948. They showed that he, like other frontbench colleagues, was moving towards a more flexible approach to achieving their economic objectives, in which public ownership would increasingly be replaced by the central planning of production, distributive services, and credit. More generally, too, Callaghan can be seen hinting at themes later powerfully voiced by his friend Anthony Crosland, in *The Future of Socialism* in 1956, that the route to social change lay less through the control of ownership and more through a combination of financial redistribution allied to measures in education, industrial democracy, and the social services to promote equality. Although Callaghan apparently played no part in the preparation of Crosland's book, he was moving in the same direction. It was a line he took up in the columns of *Socialist Commentary*, a right-wing Labour monthly edited by Rita Hinden from small offices above a café near the British Museum in Great Russell Street. Callaghan, in short, embodied in the early 1950s the drive towards revisionism, completed under Tony Blair forty years later.

His growing reputation extended well beyond parliament now. He was a popular speaker at party meetings up and down the country. Dalton felt in February 1954 that 'he has a first-class public face and platform personality, and is fun as a companion' though he believed also that the younger man's political judgement was not always 'very sure'.[6] He also continued to establish a particular rapport with student audiences. Throughout his career, he had special empathy with the young. Groups such as the Oxford University Labour Club found in Callaghan a friendly, unstuffy senior politician. He seemed genuinely to enjoy the cut and thrust of keen debate with educated young people, with coffee in local cafés all round, after the formal meeting had been concluded.

But his increasing prominence lay in other areas, too. British politics in the early 1950s became media-dominated, and Callaghan was a beneficiary of it. He was a child of the television age, when the medium became the message. Frequently, he appeared in Labour Party political broadcasts and very effectively so. He looked good on television in his dark suits, vigorous, his face unlined, his sleek hair dark and well brushed, his smile warm, his language homely and direct. Women viewers, who considered him 'a good looker',[7] were particularly impressed, while the confident, undeclamatory style that had served him well in the House was equally effective in the television studio and on the air.

One particular venture that brought him more prominence was a weekly political discussion, or argument, the BBC television programme *In the News*. This popular verbal brawl, chaired by Edgar Lustgarten and always preceded by a meal at a good restaurant, usually featured a quartet of political mavericks—W. J. Brown, once a left-wing civil service union leader, now distinctly to the right (including in an anonymous column in the weekly *Time and Tide*, in which as 'Diogenes' he regularly denounced Darwin's theories of evolution); the independently minded and bisexually adventurous Scottish Tory Robert Boothby; the equally independent left-wing Labour MP Michael Foot; and the Oxford historian A. J. P. Taylor, a little-England socialist of a kind who defied all orthodox categories. When their individualistic debates, which included free-wheeling attacks on party orthodoxies of all kinds, fell foul of both the Conservative and Labour whips, the programme was moved to the new Independent television channel in 1955 under the title *Free Speech* and continued to be popular with the viewers. Callaghan was one of a number of MPs often brought in to these programmes, both *In the News* and *Free Speech*. He proved an effective performer, robust and quick-witted in debate but able to keep his temper and sense of humour. Always he played the part of a straight Labour loyalist. It was Callaghan whose partisan contributions on housing so annoyed Alan Taylor on one programme that he folded his arms and sulked, turning away from the cameras and refusing to take any further part in that week's discussions.[8] Even so, Callaghan's regular appearances before millions of viewers added to his celebrity in the public mind.

So, too, to a lesser extent did journalism. He wrote a variety of columns in the popular press at this time. In particular, Hugh Cudlipp got him signed up as a weekly columnist on the pro-Labour *Women's Sunday Mirror*, at a fee of £25 a time. Crossman reported that Callaghan 'was enormously pleased, since this has removed his financial worries. What a difference journalism makes to the outlook of a politician!'[9] Callaghan's column was entitled, in Shavian terms, 'The Intelligent Woman's Guide to World Affairs'. He was not the most lively of writers, but he could range over an immense variety of topics, foreign and domestic, in an authoritative way, and spell out in human terms what they might mean to the average shopper, parent, or citizen. His topics included such varied items as supporting the abolition of the House of Lords, urging that licences be removed from drunken drivers, and demanding that more women delegates be sent to the TUC. Again his career was achieving a wider prominence, although in this case not for long. Sydney Jacobson of Mirror Publications took against his column and abruptly wound it up in September 1955.[10]

But the outstanding feature of the Labour Party between 1952 and 1955 in the popular estimation was not its ability to resist the government on denationalization or proclaim its objectives in the media. To the wider public, Labour was a deeply divided party, as it had been ever since Bevan and Wilson resigned in protest at Gaitskell's budget in April 1951. By mid-1952 there appeared to be a clear group of left-wing socialists acting in some sense as a party within a party, holding their secret gatherings and keeping minutes. They included such formidable communicators as Michael Foot, Richard Crossman, Barbara Castle, Ian Mikardo, and Tom Driberg, most of them old associates of Callaghan in the days of Keep Left. In a disastrous annual party conference at the Lancashire coastal resort of Morecambe, held during a wet week in October 1952, 'Bevanites' as they came to be called, including Bevan himself, swept the constituency section of the elections to the National Executive. They captured six seats out of seven, with only Jim Griffiths to represent the centre-right majority. For the rest of the decade, they continued to dominate the constituency section. In response, the party's centre and right mounted increasingly furious onslaughts on the Bevanites as a politically motivated and malignant group of wreckers. Union bosses like Arthur Deakin of the Transport Workers and Will Lawther of the Miners were even more outspoken. Gaitskell in particular, who had borne the fire of the left for over a year and a half, responded most aggressively. In a speech at Stalybridge just after the Morecambe conference he launched a bitter attack on the Bevanite conspiracy as he saw it; 'an attempt at mob rule by a group of frustrated journalists' was a term that particularly lingered in the public's mind. The unity of purpose and loyalty to the movement which Bevan had long lauded as Labour's secret weapons seemed to have evaporated at a stroke.

Callaghan, as one who had enjoyed good relations with both Gaitskell and Bevan, was amongst those at first anxious to smooth over these violent differences of view. With John Strachey, a former Marxist who had now moved to a centre-right position and had recently been Air Minister, George Strauss, Michael Stewart, and others, Callaghan was part of the so-called 'Keep Calm' group who tried to damp down extremes of animosity. Dalton saw in him 'a careful calculator'.[11] However, Callaghan felt it essential to preserve party unity. He liked to quote a maxim from the world of sailing—'to sail fastest into the wind keep your boat upright'. In politics as in sailing, balance was crucial. But with Crossman in particular being so provocative, Callaghan found his centrist role difficult and he was criticized from both extremes. At the Morecambe conference, he had urged the newly elected six Bevanites on the NEC to educate their followers on the vital need for a military alliance with the United States to defend democratic socialism. On the other hand, the virulence of Gaitskell's Stalybridge speech offended him too, and he said so.

By instinct an incipient revisionist on social and economic policy, a firm advocate of the western alliance in foreign and defence matters, Callaghan was basically in the Gaitskell camp, which was indeed the view of the great majority in the movement, political and industrial. He 'stood up to Nye boldly' at a meeting of the shadow Cabinet in June 1953.[12] On the other hand, he also sided with Bevan on several foreign policy issues. He would not automatically swallow the orthodoxies of a faction. This in turn annoyed Gaitskell—a 'trimmer' and 'fence-sitter' was how he saw Callaghan as a result.[13] A particularly difficult theme was the proposed rearmament of West Germany as part of a European defence force in the EDC. The Attlee government had reluctantly agreed to this in principle in early 1951, but practical acceptance was a very different matter. Throughout 1954, Callaghan was lined up with Dalton, Wilson, the near-pacifist Chuter Ede, and all the Bevanites in a fierce party debate on German rearmament. The issue was highly contentious in that year's party conference and Attlee got the matter resolved only after enormous pressure on some small unions including the unfortunate Woodworkers. Callaghan's view may seem somewhat surprising given his general stance on western defence, but he was evidently influenced by Dalton's view on this, and no doubt by his own wartime attitudes. He did not, however, share at all Dalton's rabid anti-Germanism (the latter apparently argued on one occasion that all Germans were murderers).[14] Rather he tried to link German disarmament to ideas for a wider international settlement including a demilitarized zone between East and West Germany, and moves towards a possible future reunification. However, there was clearly much heat generated in the parliamentary party on this issue, even though in the end German rearmament was backed by the party by 124 votes to 72. As events turned out, the EDC was thrown out by the French national assembly in any case, so Labour's *angst* over a rearmed Germany then subsided.

Callaghan, then, was with the Bevanite left on German rearmament. But by 1955 he was deeply angry at the divisions they were causing. It was a bleak period for Labour, with Attlee unable to reconcile the rival factions, and creating the impression that he was hanging on as leader simply to frustrate the hopes of another veteran, Herbert Morrison. The Bevanite group was beginning to show signs of fragmenting: Harold Wilson actually moved onto the shadow Cabinet when Bevan resigned from it in April 1954. But Bevan himself, in Callaghan's view, was becoming increasingly impossible. He attacked SEATO and NATO; in the defence debate in February 1955 he appeared to defy his own front bench in opposing Labour's commitment to Britain's developing a hydrogen bomb. As in 1939, 1944, and several occasions since November 1951, Bevan's expulsion from the party was clearly on the agenda.

Callaghan, for all his previous Keep Calm credentials, was passionately angry with Bevan and said so. On 24 February, he spoke out in support of Chuter Ede's motion at the Parliamentary Committee (the shadow Cabinet) that the whip should be withdrawn from Bevan immediately. Gaitskell was surprised at his strength of feeling since 'he had also been with Bevan on German rearmament and decidedly equivocal on many occasions'.[15] The vote against Bevan was nine to four, the majority including Callaghan. The issue later went before the parliamentary party where Attlee's motion that the whip be withdrawn was carried, after an angry debate, by 141 to 112. Bevan angrily denounced 'the hatchet-faced men sitting on the platform', having Callaghan and Jay in mind. It was believed to be Callaghan who shouted in reply, 'It's a lie'.[16] But there was evidently much reluctance to force an issue with an election close at hand; Attlee himself was hesitant and unconvincing in proposing the motion. Finally the affair went to the National Executive, of which Callaghan was not yet a member. Here, despite the vehement opposition of union leaders like Arthur Deakin and Tom Williamson, Bevan finally escaped the ignominy of expulsion, after he had made a personal appearance before the Committee. Attlee moved a motion not to expel Bevan but to accept his assurances of better behaviour in the future and this was carried, by the narrowest of margins, 14 to 13, Edith Summerskill, the chairman (who was hostile to Bevan), declining to vote. Bevan thus remained a member of the parliamentary party and Labour went into the general election of May 1955 as a relatively united team. However, it was clear also that the Bevanite movement was now distinctly on the wane, Bevan's erratic conduct alienating even many of his friends. Callaghan, who had moved from being conciliator to prosecuting counsel, was well pleased.

In these years, Callaghan's public interests continued to widen. Thus, although he was very bound up with domestic issues on the shadow Cabinet, he kept up his interests in overseas affairs, especially the Far East. In April and May 1954 he was sent as a journalist by Hugh Cudlipp of the *Daily Mirror* to observe the Geneva international conference set up to resolve the crisis of Indo-China following the defeat of the French. He witnessed Dulles, Molotov, Zhou Enlai, Eden, and Mendès-France operating at first hand, and approved of the outcome. The result was a permanent armistice, and the creation of new states of North and South Vietnam, Laos, and Cambodia. It was a major diplomatic triumph for Eden, the British Foreign Minister, in the face of constant obstruction from John Foster Dulles, the US Secretary of State. But to Callaghan, who knew South-East Asia at first hand, the prospects of a secure peace in the region were still precarious. The later cathartic crisis in Vietnam in the 1960s did not surprise him.

He was also active in Labour discussions during 1955 to try to moderate American hostility towards Communist China on behalf of its protégé Chiang Kaishek, based on Formosa (Taiwan). Labour was united on this issue, as in deploring bellicose American postures later on over the tiny Chinese islands of Quemoy and Matsu. In January 1956, he went to the Middle East for the first time. Over the years, while generally sympathetic to the Israeli cause, he had tended to steer a balanced course, free from the emotional Zionist sympathies of many Labour MPs including Harold

Wilson and Richard Crossman, and the pan-Arabism of figures such as George Brown. On this occasion, Callaghan visited both Jordan and Israel. He met the Prime Minister, David Ben Gurion, and other Israeli Labour leaders with whom he got on well. He also had his first experience of life on a kibbutz.

In April of that year, there was a far more spectacular involvement with international affairs. Callaghan was amongst the Labour shadow ministers who had a stormy encounter with the Russian premier Nikita Khrushchev, when he visited London with President Bulganin. It was, however, George Brown and, perhaps more surprisingly, Aneurin Bevan who were the main combatants on 23 April in the angry discussion at dinner with Khrushchev over the fate of Soviet dissidents. Callaghan was not prominent other than in leading the call for Khrushchev to make a speech, which he then did at much length and in a tone which proved to be highly provocative. The whole affair led to much embarrassing publicity. An angry Khrushchev observed that if these were the British socialists, he was for the Conservatives. Callaghan's most important role at this time, perhaps, was in acting as rapporteur of a meeting at Claridge's Hotel on 24 April between Khrushchev and Ambassador Malik for the Soviet Union, Harold Stassen (US representative on the disarmament commission) and Sir William Hayter, the British ambassador to Moscow. Callaghan was the only other person present as Khrushchev pressed Stassen hard on east–west disarmament in a generally amicable discussion. 'My own reaction is that Khruschev means business on disarmament', Callaghan reported to the shadow Cabinet and NEC.[17] Here and elsewhere, he was continuing to develop an informed, specialist interest in key aspects of international affairs, an interest which he reinforced by his academic contacts with Chatham House and the work of the Wiener Library.

A totally different area which also involved him for a time was Northern Ireland. Hitherto, Callaghan had had no connection at all with Ireland other than through his ancestry. He shared this detachment from the 'other island' with political leaders on both sides of the House. From 4 to 9 November 1954, on the invitation of the Northern Irish TUC and Sam Napier of the Northern Ireland Labour Party, Callaghan and Alfred Robens led a Labour Party delegation to investigate the province. On his return, he made speeches on the need to remedy the endemic unemployment of Northern Ireland, including calling for a development corporation there to start new enterprises. He noted particularly the economic problems of the Catholic areas of Londonderry such as the Bogside. However this was a fleeting visit and he did not dwell on Irish matters thereafter.[18] Nor did he have anything to say publicly about the political and civil rights aspects of the Northern Irish situation, even though the Protestants' domination of the Catholic minority bore directly on many of Ulster's economic problems; this applied especially in the apprenticeships offered in the shipyards of Harland & Wolff in Belfast and the Short Brothers' aircraft factories. Northern Ireland, preserved in aspic since Lloyd George's partition settlement in 1921–2, was a very marginal issue indeed for Westminster politicians. It seemed most improbable that it would ever loom prominently in Callaghan's career.

A much more considerable new interest emerged in a quite different area in the autumn of 1955 after the general election. Callaghan was approached by the Police Federation, the body which represented rank and file policemen or 'the bobby on the beat' in popular parlance, to act as consultant and adviser at a salary of £500 a year with £300 expenses (Tory MPs were later to allege that it was £20,000).[19] Callaghan had had no contact with the police previously but the Federation saw in him a skilled trade union negotiator with a thorough knowledge of the procedures of the Whitley Council. He saw it as an inexperienced body needing help to become organized and remove genuine grievances. The main issue before him was the need for a substantial increase in police officers' pay. In 1935 a constable had been amongst the better paid of workers, with his pay anything between 16 and 55 per cent above the average of industrial earnings. However, rising pay elsewhere along with full employment after the war had meant a rapid deterioration, until in 1960 the Royal Commission on the Police recorded that minimum police pay was no less than 28 per cent below the average. Callaghan's task was to help negotiate a major increase and to help improve the police constable's conditions of work and social status in general. The Police Council of Great Britain, set up in 1949, had so far been unresponsive and police morale suffered accordingly.

Callaghan's role was to assist the Federation, not act as its paid poodle. Forty years on, in January 1995 he gave evidence before the Nolan Committee on Standards in Public Life which was considering the issue of paid consultancy and wider evidence that MPs were using their position to enhance their income in a secret or undeclared way. Here, Callaghan reflected as a senior statesman on his role with the Federation between 1955 and 1964.[20] He argued that he had in no way compromised his independence as a member of parliament. He was acting as an experienced trade unionist. He had given technical advice and specialist assistance to a important group of people, but had never been dictated to. One major instance was the issue of capital punishment, where he invariably voted for abolition despite the Federation's passionate commitment to the hanging of murderers. Except once on the single issue of pensions, he never spoke on their behalf in the House; 'I was certainly not a lobbyist.' In addition, his payment from the Federation had been entirely open, and appeared in the latter's accounts. In July 1964 he told the House that he was not a Federation spokesman but 'preferred to work through friends on both sides'.[21] A basic distinction should be made between this kind of arrangement, widespread and necessary in the 1950s, and the paid advocacy through intermediaries such as Ian Greer in the 1990s. Certainly the openness of Callaghan's arrangement, manifestly in the public domain, and the secret and often disreputable activities of later Conservative MPs in 'cash for questions', arms trafficking, and other scandals were in stark contrast.

At any rate, he worked for the Federation with much success. After the 1959 election the arrangement with the Police Federation became a permanent contract. He had now a similar consultancy with the Scottish Police Federation at a salary of £200, raised to £300 in 1961. He urged the then Home Secretary, R. A. Butler, of the need for a royal commission on the police, to inquire into police pay and perhaps also into the relations of the police with the wider public. In 1960 Callaghan represented them before the Royal Commission along with nine police representatives. The Federation certainly needed Callaghan's trade union expertise. Their core staff consisted of one Metropolitan constable who was seconded from his work on the beat, together with a shorthand typist. The employers were represented by no less a figure than a future Labour Lord Chancellor, Gerald Gardiner QC. Nevertheless, the Federation argued with much effect the case for a considerable increase in basic pay. Callaghan had prepared for the Commission by putting immense pressure on local chief constables to support the Federation's pay claims and the police thus presented an impressive united front. The outcome was very satisfactory. It was, indeed, largely due to Callaghan's influence that Sir Henry Willink, its chairman, included police pay in the Commission's terms of reference in any case. The Commission was to recommend the largest increase in police pay in history. The maximum pay of a constable should go up from £695 to £910 per year, with two increments of £30 each for long service (payable after 17 and 22 years) raising it further to £970. This was close enough to the concept of a £1,000 a year constable for which Callaghan had argued. After years of ineffective advocacy before the Police Council, a loose gathering of local authority and Home Office representatives for whom Callaghan had 'a blunt contempt',[22] action had been achieved and it owed an immense amount to his work as consultant.

His connection with the police, which was wound up when he entered the Wilson government in October 1964, had an important effect on Callaghan's public standing. To many moderate citizens, his calm, 'steady as she goes' approach as a reliable public figure was reinforced by his association with the police. Columnists and cartoonists (often to his irritation) represented him as PC Jim, or as the political reincarnation of the reassuring image of the constabulary embodied by Jack Warner in the popular television series *Dixon of Dock Green* and earlier (in 1949) in the Ealing Studios film *The Blue Lamp*. Conversely, as the public image of the police was dented in the public order confrontations of the 1960s, Callaghan's police connections were sometimes viewed less favourably. He seemed to take a naturally conservative stance, committed to law and order and the legitimacy of an often insensitive police at the expense of demonstrating students, anti-Vietnam protesters, and free associations of citizens in general. It led to some left-wing criticisms of his handling of demonstrations during his time at the Home Office and encouraged a growth in grassroots Labour Party circles of animosity towards the police that endured in some senses until the Smith–Blair era after 1992. Ironically, too, the Federation became far more hostile to Callaghan when he went to the Home Office in 1967 and he found himself booed at their annual conference at Llandudno in 1970 (an experience he shared with virtually every other Home Secretary thereafter). But on balance, it seems quite unjust to see Callaghan's commitment to libertarian protest as being compromised by his links with the police. He saw the constabulary as a vital component of a free democracy, fully entitled to decent pay and working conditions like other workers, and to carry out their duties of protecting the public free from political abuse. In the short-term perspective of the years 1955–64 he showed once again how effective he could be as a vigorous, informed, determined advocate, committed intellectually and morally to the ordinary people he represented.

In the general election of May 1955 Callaghan played an active role in meetings and press conferences, on radio and television. He was one of Labour's main campaigners. In fact, it was a quiet election in which the odds were always heavily in favour of the Conservative government. Their new premier, Anthony Eden, even if a highly familiar, perhaps well-worn figure, gave a sense of fresh leadership after the eventual departure of the aged Churchill. The world seemed a much more tranquil place now. The Korean War had been wound up in 1953, and attempts at 'summit diplomacy' after the death of Stalin in the same year at least gave some promise of peaceful coexistence between east and west. Most important for the voters, the economy was now in a highly robust condition. The terms of trade had moved dramatically in Britain's favour since the end of the Korean War. Unemployment had disappeared and the balance of payments was comfortably in the black. To make doubly sure, Butler, the Chancellor of the Exchequer, introduced an electioneering budget in April which gave away £134m. through cuts in the standard rate of income tax. By the autumn this had led to massive inflationary pressures and a major balance of payments crisis that cost Butler his job in favour of Macmillan. But in winning the general election it did the trick.

Labour, conversely, were still in a somewhat dormant mood after the Bevanite controversies, and Attlee himself was hardly a dynamic leader now for all his great prestige. The Conservatives increased their majority substantially with 345 seats to Labour's 277. It was to prove a rare election defeat down to 1987 which did not drive Labour further to the left. Callaghan himself had as usual a vigorous fight in Cardiff. His opponent this time was an effective one, Michael Roberts, a Llandaff headmaster destined to enter the House himself in future years. In the end, Callaghan won with a majority of 3,240 in a straight fight, gaining 53.4 per cent of the vote to Roberts's 46.6 per cent. The worrying tendency for a gradual fall in his majority thus continued. But it was still comfortable enough.

In the new parliament, as a sterling and balance of payments crisis in September dented the complacency of the new Eden government, Labour had plenty of scope for attack. Mr Butskell had vanished for good. But the most important change as far as Callaghan and other MPs were concerned was an internal one. In November, after twenty years as leader in peace and in war, Attlee resigned. In the following leadership contest, Gaitskell, the forceful standard-bearer of the right, easily defeated Bevan, representing the left, by 157 votes to 70; the veteran Herbert Morrison, who had mistakenly decided to stand for the leadership as he had last done in 1935, polled a somewhat humiliating 40. Callaghan was enthusiastic. For him, Gaitskell was the only conceivable leader and he campaigned for him vigorously as did almost all the former Keep Calm group. He might reasonably expect his reward, even though the rise of Wilson who voted for Gaitskell and became shadow Chancellor complicated the position amongst Labour's main candidates for high office. Callaghan now moved from the transport portfolio, to become shadow spokesman on fuel and power, again a second-ranking position. The alternative portfolio of housing and local government had also been considered for him.[23]

Then in the summer of 1956 Gaitskell gave him a much more interesting post, that of spokesman for education and for science. This was certainly a theme that engaged Callaghan with his own incomplete educational background of which he was acutely conscious. He was interested in the development of scientific and technological education, in the relationship between traditional education and vocational training, and in the need to build up and diversify higher education. His overseas visits had impressed him with how Britain was lagging behind in its educational provision, especially with the rigid social selection imposed on schoolchildren in the maintained sector through the 'eleven plus' examination. On the other hand, with a personal penchant for the grammar schools and also the direct grant schools to which two of his own children eventually went, he would have been unlikely to be a radical, probably less so than the public-school and Oxford-trained Tony Crosland was to prove a decade later. In any case, at this stage comprehensive schools had not been created, other than in a few rural areas such as Anglesey. Education was to emerge as a key theme time and again in Callaghan's career later on. He almost moved to be Secretary of State for Education on resigning from the Treasury in November 1967; his Ruskin College speech in October 1976 on standards of literary and numeracy in the schools was a defining moment during his premiership to which he returned frequently in later years, including in a major twentieth anniversary address in October 1996 to which he devoted much time and care. In addition, his presidency of the University College of Swansea (later the University of Wales, Swansea) from 1986 onwards was important to him. But in 1956 his time as education spokesman was to prove exceptionally brief, a few months only, since political life was again engulfed in turmoil.

The Suez crisis plunged British people into a passionate debate. It reached a climax in early November 1956, in a way unknown since the time of Munich. It did not greatly involve Callaghan, for all his undoubtedly strong views on the issue. He did have, as has been seen, some first-hand knowledge of the Middle East following his visit to Israel in January 1956. On that occasion, the Israeli Prime Minister David Ben Gurion had impressed upon him that Egypt was the main enemy.[24] The nationalization of the Suez Canal by President Nasser of Egypt on 26 July led to the last massive crisis of empire in British history. It had particular repercussions for the Labour shadow Cabinet which combined a strong commitment to the United Nations with a deep-rooted attachment to the Labour government of the new state of Israel. In retrospect, Nasser's actions might well have been anticipated following the decision of the United States not to finance the building of the proposed Aswan high dam on which the Egyptians had set their hearts. But it was a sensation nevertheless, and a particular challenge to Eden, the Prime Minister, who had developed a massive personal animosity towards Nasser whom he variously compared with Napoleon, Mussolini, and Hitler.

In the working out of Labour's response, Callaghan attended all six meetings of the shadow Cabinet that were called by Gaitskell between 30 July and 12 September.[25] There was agreement that Labour could not object to nationalization of the canal as such and that 'we would not back the use of force except in self defence'. Callaghan was satisfied that Gaitskell had made this clear in the House on 2 August although he perhaps underestimated the emotional impact made by the Labour leader's rhetoric about Nasser, whom he compared to Hitler. After pressure from the Foreign Affairs Group, with Wedgwood Benn, John Hynd, and William Warbey as its spokesmen, the shadow Cabinet on 13 August issued a statement which, while condemning Nasser's action as arbitrary, reaffirmed that armed force could be used only in terms of Britain's obligations to the United Nations and called for an international conference to ensure a free and proper operation of the canal for the benefit of all users and of the Egyptian people themselves.

Callaghan played no major part in the later stages of the Suez crisis. After the collapse of the Canal Users' conference in London, there followed the concocting of secret plans to invade Egypt by the British and French governments, in association with the Israelis in late October. The Israelis invaded the Suez area and, on the pretext of 'separating the combatants', the British and French attacked Egypt, bombing and occupying Port Said. By early November, Britain and its two allies stood condemned by the United States, the Commonwealth, and the United Nations, which voted to denounce the Anglo-French action by 64 to 5. Only when massive pressure on the British economy and the pound (deliberately exaggerated by Macmillan, the Chancellor) forced a British withdrawal on 5 November did the pressure ease. Eden retired to Goldeneye, Jamaica, the home of Ian Fleming, to convalesce; his reputation as an authoritative director of foreign policy was in tatters and he resigned as premier in January 1957. Public opinion had been divided over Suez as on no issue since the war. For the Labour Party, Gaitskell led the attack, condemning the Eden government without reservation for a naked, conspiratorial act of aggression that had left Britain with scarcely a friend in the world. Aneurin Bevan, now a front-bench spokesman after returning to the fold, was more measured, concentrating rather on blunders of policy which had in any case led to the Suez Canal being blocked after all and hence to an oil crisis which shortly led to British motorists experiencing petrol rationing for the first time since the 1940s. He congratulated savagely the miserable Foreign Secretary, Selwyn Lloyd, for 'sounding the bugle of advance to cover his retreat'.

Callaghan was away during a few of these events. In August, he and John Strachey took a holiday as a guest of the wealthy and eccentric Labour QC R. T. Paget, who maintained a small yacht on Hayling Island. They had some premonition of the coming crisis when they observed British war vessels moving down the Solent. It was a year when Callaghan himself had been on the move in the Middle East and the Mediterranean area. He had been in Israel and Jordan in January. Later he had gone to Malta as an observer during the referendum. In mid-October he flew briefly to the Middle East himself with Robert Boothby and others, to attend a meeting of a British parliamentary delegation at Abadan, scene of the Persian oil crisis in 1951, before moving on to Kuwait. He commented that 'Abadan is extraordinary—just like Surbiton with privet hedges everywhere'.[26] But his abiding impression was of the growth of American interests in the Gulf region.

In the mounting controversy over the Suez invasion, Callaghan strongly backed up Gaitskell's position, even though privately he felt it to be too intemperate and unduly intellectual in its view of international law. He was strengthened in this view by his first-hand knowledge of both the Arab and Israeli scene. As noted, his view was not swayed by the Zionist sympathies of so many Labour MPs. Bevan, by contrast, he later felt 'understood better the temperament of the British people' in his comments during the crisis.[27] It was indeed the most ardent Gaitskellites, men on the right like Douglas Jay and Denis Healey, who were foremost in denouncing the government. However, in the special sessions of the Commons held in early November, Callaghan sat on the Labour front bench alongside George Brown and Alfred Robens, vigorously heckling Eden's shifty and unconvincing explanations for his government's actions. Callaghan dealt patiently but firmly with various correspondents worried about the Labour Party's stand on Suez. He told one of them that Eden had taken 'decisions that will prove to be more disastrous to Britain than the loss of the American colonies'.[28]

The situation in the country and the party now became fluid once again. While the opinion polls showed short-term support for the government's handling of the Suez crisis, there were political dividends for Labour after so humiliating a defeat. There were dramatic by-election gains for Labour candidates in North Lewisham (where the Callaghans lived) and Carmarthen in February, and a 12.2 per cent swing in Eden's own seat of

Warwick and Leamington. For Gaitskell, a major bonus was his new rapprochement with Aneurin Bevan, clearly back in the mainstream after powerful debating performances, and his solid support of Gaitskell, during the Suez crisis. Alfred Robens had not been impressive in the House as foreign affairs spokesman, where he appeared out of his element, and Gaitskell was now able to replace him with Bevan. Although the two still had differences of view, especially over American policy in the Far East, it gave Gaitskell's position as leader a new legitimacy. Crossman wrote of the 'Gaitskell–Bevan axis'.[29] This move had knock-on effects. Bevan had previously been the spokesman on colonial policy. This key vacancy was now to be filled by James Callaghan.

In future years, this move to a major portfolio at a time of colonial crisis was to be seen as the decisive breakthrough in Callaghan's rise to the front rank. At the time this was much less clear. There were those who wondered precisely what specialist knowledge the new man had in colonial matters; they forgot his strong interest both in the Far East and, since 1946, in African matters. What was clear, however, was that his promotion was recognition of Callaghan's continuing effectiveness in a variety of contexts. He had handled domestic portfolios successfully. He had positioned himself skilfully in the internal party rows over Bevanism and had shown a degree of toughness in the heat of debate that surprised many commentators who had preferred to dwell on his equable and congenial approach. Amiable though he was, Jim Callaghan was without doubt a very hard man, well able to look after himself in the hurly-burly of a rough old trade. He had also developed his wider interests, proved himself an effective consultant, and projected himself skilfully in the media. What remained to be seen was whether he could make the imaginative leap necessary, at a time of recurrent Commonwealth crises from Malaya to Malta, to map out a wider analysis of the geopolitical, economic, and moral aspects of Britain's relationship with the third world. It would show whether he could make the transition from party regular to potential world statesman. As he launched himself into his new department with his invariable breezy self-confidence, an exciting prospect lay ahead.

1. Interview with Lord Callaghan.
2. Crossman, *Backbench Diaries*, 227 (28 Apr. 1953).
3. *Parl. Deb.*, 5th ser., vol. 493, 733–8 (12 Nov. 1951); Vol. 507, 1695–1706 (18 Nov. 1952).
4. Speech of 19 May 1950 (text in Callaghan Papers, box 1A).
5. Text in Callaghan Papers, ibid.
6. Dalton, *Political Diary*, 620 (20 Feb. 1954).
7. Ray Gunter to Callaghan, quoting his wife ?1962 (Callaghan Papers, box 18).

8. A. J. P. Taylor, *A Personal History* (London, 1983), 203–4.

9. Material in Callaghan Papers, box 31; Crossman, *Backbench Diaries*, 384 (15 Feb. 1955).

10. 'Sydney' to Callaghan, 11 Sept. 1955 (Callaghan Papers, box 31). The article calling for the abolition of the Lords appeared in the *Women's Sunday Mirror* on 6 Mar. 1955. Callaghan's final article appeared on 4 Sept. 1955: it was a plea for more women delegates to the TUC.

11. Dalton, *Political Diary*, 565–6 (29 Oct. 1951).

12. Ibid., 612 (23 June 1953).

13. Ibid., 627 (12 May 1954).

14. Ibid., 591–2 (30 June 1952).

15. *The Diary of Hugh Gaitskell, 1945–1956*, ed. Philip Williams (London, 1983), 368 (19 Mar. 1955).

16. Dalton, *Political Diary*, 651–2 (16 Mar. 1955).

17. Callaghan's note, 24 Apr. 1956 (Callaghan Papers, box 1A). The dinner on 23 Apr. was given by Labour's NEC, with the Parliamentary Committee also invited.

18. Material in Callaghan Papers, box 2; speech on Northern Ireland Employment Bill, *Parl. Deb.*, vol. 540, 2035–45 (5 May 1955).

19. For an account of Callaghan's work for the Police Federation, see Anthony Judge, *The First Fifty Years: The Story of the Police Federation* (London, 1968), 88–120. Judge, a constable, gave evidence before the Willink Commission. Cf. *Police Review*, 23 Dec. 1955, which praises Callaghan's 'masterly assistance'.

20. Callaghan's evidence to Nolan Committee, 19 Jan. 1995, *Standards in Public Life. Transcripts of Oral Evidence* (Cm. 2850–II), H. of C. 1994–95, 56–66, and letter on p. 505. Also see Callaghan, letter in *Encounter*, 2 Aug. 1962.

21. Judge, *The First Fifty Years*, 119.

22. *Royal Commission on the Police, 1960: Interim Report* (Cmnd. 1222), H. of C. 1960–1, xx. 347–9, 386–7, 397–8; Judge, *The First Fifty Years*, 101.

23. Dalton, *Political Diary*, 644 (28 Feb. 1955).

24. Notes of visit in Callaghan Papers, box 2.

25. Callaghan to T. Greenstein, 22 Feb. 1995, and enclosures from Callaghan Papers (in author's possession).

26. Note of visit to Abadan, 13–16 Oct. 1956, in Callaghan Papers, box 2.

27. Interview with Lord Callaghan.

28. Callaghan to Kenneth Bryant, 21 Nov. 1956 (Callaghan Papers, BLPES, box 5, file 'Suez').

29. Crossman, *Backbench Diaries*, 356 (18 Dec. 1956).

7

HOUSE AND HOME

WORKING at Westminster makes it hard to enjoy a secure and happy family life.[1] The hours are long and antisocial, the pressures of Commons and constituency difficult to reconcile with domestic priorities. This was undoubtedly the case with James Callaghan. He was highly ambitious, committed to his work at the House or, between 1947 and 1951, in government departments, spending long hours there and returning sometimes in the early hours of the morning. The Commons did not assemble until after lunch, of course, but mornings and lunchtimes were often taken up with political meetings of a formal or informal kind, or briefings with journalists. He was prominent in the Commons smoking room or the lobbies. Most Friday evenings when the House was in session, he took the train to Cardiff. He never missed attending the Management Committee of the Cardiff South constituency. The next day would invariably be spent in Cardiff, starting with a surgery in the morning to meet constituents with problems to discuss, and going on to other meetings perhaps with his agent or local councillors. During the times when parliament was in recess, he would often be on his travels. This reached a climax when he became colonial affairs spokesman, where he was constantly on the move, flying to Africa, South-East Asia, Australasia, or elsewhere. In one year, 1958, he actually flew to Africa or elsewhere in the Commonwealth fourteen times.

The effect on his home and family was not conducive to stability. Yet his family life remained remarkably secure. Not at any stage during an extremely long marriage, marked by a golden wedding anniversary in 1988, was his domestic base anything other than a happy one. It was an important part of his self-assurance and credibility as a politician. For this, an immense amount was owed to Audrey Callaghan. As was the invariable custom with marriages in the unliberated 1940s and 1950s, she took a subordinate role, supporting her husband faithfully in his political activities.

Indeed, they posed little difficulty for her since she had strong political interests herself. In time they were to lead to her election to the London County Council for North Lewisham in 1959. In 1964 she was to become an alderman on the newly formed Greater London Council, which she remained until 1970. Her strongest interest, however, was the welfare of children. She became chairman of the South East London Children's Committee, which had 8,000 children in care, and was later to embark on a strong and abiding connection with Great Ormond Street children's hospital. At home, she took total responsibility for the health and education of the children, and for the running of the household, including the preparation of meals. She was, indeed, an excellent and enthusiastic cook whereas Callaghan himself, like most men of the time, admitted to being helpless in the kitchen. Margaret Jay had to attend to her father's needs in 10 Downing Street when Audrey was briefly in hospital since the most elementary of culinary tasks seemed to be beyond him. As a partner and loyal support Audrey Callaghan could hardly have been surpassed. Unflappable and good-humoured but with a strong will and also a sharp analytical judgement on which her husband often relied, she kept the family on a steady course. This applied even in the particularly difficult circumstances of wartime separation or immediately after Callaghan's return to parliament in 1945, when she was still living in Maidstone with the children and Callaghan himself had to commute.

In the complicated circumstances of a parliamentary life, Callaghan did his best to be the traditional good father, even if at long range. He took a keen interest in the children's education, school reports in particular, and there were happy family summer holidays, always in Britain. The coast of Pembrokeshire was a popular destination in the 1950s, but Norfolk and Cornwall were also favoured, along with private stays with the Mitchisons in Scotland. Callaghan also handled all the family's financial business, drawing on his knowledge as a tax clerk to fill out income tax returns and to attend to family wills.

Callaghan was very seldom ill; a physician's report in March 1960 reported that his overall health was excellent. He had experienced various allergic disorders as a boy, hay fever as a teenager, and more serious asthma in his early thirties during the war. But his asthmatic attacks were a thing of the past. There was no evidence of chest deformity or lung disease remaining, nor any other medical problem. His many overseas trips were negotiated without medical mishap, apart from an ear infection once contracted during a visit to Uganda. He never suffered jet lag. His doctor from the early 1960s, Sir Montague ('Monty') Levine, became a close friend who was to accompany the Callaghans on a trip to China including an expedition to the Great Wall, as well as on prime ministerial visits to India, Pakistan, Bangladesh, Nigeria, Egypt, Guadeloupe, and Barbados. His doctor noted that his patient always liked to have full and precise information about any medicine or tablets he was being given, and how they worked.[2] One useful legacy of Callaghan's wartime service in the navy which remained with him for the remainder of his long life was the ability to take a catnap of perhaps half an hour at various times of the day to renew his energy. After his youthful efforts at rugby and tennis, he played no games and took little exercise apart from some hiking expeditions on holiday. Perhaps in consequence of his own robust health, he seemed at times somewhat impatient with the illnesses of others. It was surmised that his own difficult upbringing as a boy in Portsmouth made him somewhat severe in this aspect of the paternal role. It was Audrey who supplied the tea and sympathy for the family, while her husband pursued his career. In later life, Callaghan, whose capacity for self-criticism was considerable, often excessively so, would say, 'Audrey is a much nicer person than I am.' Of the devotion of the two to each other, there was never any doubt; they were a particularly close partnership for a political family. There was never a hint of difficulty, let alone scandal. When, in later life, Audrey had illnesses or accidents—a minor car accident when Callaghan was Prime Minister, a thrombosis in her leg when in the United States, a particularly frightening mugging in London when she was in her seventies—it was a major crisis for Callaghan in every respect.

The extended family was changing as the years went by. Callaghan's ageing mother lived on in Worthing in Sussex, and died in 1961, just short of her 82nd birthday. She had the joy of seeing her son not merely a government minister, but actually serving in the Admiralty beloved of her late naval husband, and inspecting the Home Fleet in Plymouth Sound. Callaghan's older sister Dorothy, with whom he had a warm but long-range relationship, lived in Cornwall, married to the Revd Sidney Carter, a Baptist minister. Audrey's parents also lived to a good age. Her father, Frank Moulton, lived to see the flowering of his son-in-law's political career which he viewed with much enthusiasm, for all his own non-Labour views. He was to help the Callaghans in meeting the costs of house purchase. He died in his beloved Maidstone, serene and devout to the end, a Bible at his bedside, in 1956. His wife Clara died five years later.

The Callaghans had three children. In addition to their daughters Margaret and Julia, both born during the war, they also had a son, Michael, born in September 1945. All grew up to be healthy and successful young people, each with a strong social conscience. Michael, who took part in the 1979 election campaign team, appeared to be the most political of the three, though he never contemplated a political career himself. Margaret worked rather in the media and for social causes, most prominently especially the Aids Trust from the 1980s. But she also had leftish views, announced early on at Blackheath school when she denounced the Tory government in 1956 during a school debate on Suez. She took the Labour whip when she went to the Lords as Lady Jay of Paddington in 1992, to the joy of her parents. In time she became a whip and then in 1997 a health minister. Julia, also a strong Labour supporter, was notable, among other things, for her fierce professional commitment to the National Health Service and to environmental issues. There was certainly no sign of rebellion against parental influence here.

In determining the children's education, Callaghan, like many other Labour politicians at the time, seems to have had no ideological difficulty in turning to private schooling. Having had what he felt to be an unsatisfactory, old-fashioned, and incomplete education himself, he was determined that his children should do much better, and indeed they did. Margaret started off at the local Maidstone school but at the age of 8 began at Blackheath High School, a direct grant school that came under the Girls' Public Schools Trust. She proved to be a very able student and won an open scholarship to Girton College, Cambridge. Her heart, however, was set on Oxford and she was duly admitted shortly after to Somerville College there. Her time at university was notable in many ways, but particularly perhaps for her meeting and ultimately marrying Peter, the son of Douglas Jay, one of Callaghan's major front-bench colleagues. After the marriage in September 1961, Peter Jay developed a very close and affectionate relationship with his father-in-law, who paid his views the greatest deference when Peter moved first to the Treasury and then to work as economics editor of *The Times*. Callaghan, he declared, was one of his heroes. In many ways he was probably a second father to him as well.

Julia also started off at Blackheath High School but her teachers reported that her abilities seemed to lie particularly in more vocational rather than academic subjects. She finished up her schooling, at her own request, in Kidbrooke, one of the new flagship comprehensives in south London. After school, she went for a time to America and lived for a period with the family of Sir Hugh Foot, then Britain's representative at the UN. She was to marry Ian Hubbard who became in due course a consultant in ophthalmology and they settled happily at Ulverston in the Lake District. Michael started off at a local school, Sherington junior boys' school, but Callaghan then had him transferred to Dulwich, a notable public boarding school on whose merits Callaghan had received advice from Henry Brooke, at the time the Conservative Minister for Housing and Local Government, and knowledgeable on the schools of London. Michael went to Dulwich on a GLC scholarship. Eventually he became a student in the University College of South Wales, Cardiff, close by his father's own constituency, and in time rose to be a director with Ford's Motors. While a student he met and married a Welsh girl, Jenny Morris, who shared lodgings with another young Welsh student, Glenys Parry. The latter married the recent president of the Student Union, Neil Kinnock, around the same time.

The family lived in a series of homes, reflecting a familiar 1950s middle-class pattern of upwards mobility, from rented accommodation to owner-occupation, from anonymous Eltham to salubrious Blackheath, close to Greenwich Park and the architectural splendours of Inigo Jones and Christopher Wren (not to mention the latter's famous naval museum, dear to Callaghan's heart). Immediately after the end of the war, Audrey continued to live with her children at 13 Ashford Road, Maidstone, to be near her ageing parents. She combined this with temporary chairmanship of the Maidstone Labour Party. Then, after Callaghan became junior Transport Minister, the family in 1948 bought 83 Guibal Road, Lee, in south-east London, a 1920s house with five bedrooms, a garage, and an extensive garden with several old apple and pear trees. It was a pleasant detached house, the first they had owned rather than rented. One rare blemish was that Callaghan left instructions about decorating the bedrooms to his secretary, Gwyneth Jones, to communicate over the phone, which led to the wrong colour paint being chosen.

The family experienced some financial difficulty in managing the mortgage payments after the fall of the Labour government, so in early 1952 they went back to renting a house, 40 Maze Hill, an early Victorian house on land facing Greenwich Observatory on Blackheath, rented from the Greenwich Hospital Estate. They moved in there on the day of King George VI's funeral. But they were anxious for something more spacious and devised a plan with architect friends, Gordon and Ursula Bowyer, whom they had met in Blackheath. Callaghan purchased what he later described as 'a bomb site' facing the lower end of Blackheath in 1957. He paid £800 for it at the time of Peter Thorneycroft's 1957 credit squeeze. The Bowyers purchased half for £400 and designed and built two houses there. They did not in fact occupy them, but the Callaghans did move into their new house, 17 Montpellier Row, in October 1958, around the time that

Margaret went up to Oxford. It was bought leasehold on a ninety-year lease with a £3,500 mortgage from the Abbey National. An apparent dispute with the contractors about building repairs took some time to resolve. But it was an agreeable house. William Rodgers, a future director-general of the Royal Institute of British Architects and not yet a Labour MP, was struck by its modernity and attractiveness when he went round to dinner in the late 1950s.[3] The Callaghans were to live there until Labour's election victory in October 1964 sent them to 11 Downing Street.

These developments caused some financial pressure for the Callaghans as for other ordinary families. There were the inevitable costs of bringing up children, involving some payment of school fees. In the late 1940s, there was also a Danish *au pair* to pay for. Much expense was incurred at Maze Hill in meeting the belated costs of bomb damage, apart from financing the £2,600 mortgage with the Burnley Building Society. To help out, Audrey took a part-time job as dietitian at a local clinic for expectant mothers. Clearly, the family's finances were somewhat uncertain after Labour's defeat in 1951, despite a loan from the Moultons, and Callaghan's anxiety about possibly returning to being an official with the IRSF should he lose his seat is very understandable. British MPs were notoriously underpaid and Labour members in particular found it difficult to make ends meet. Not until 1955 did the Callaghans feel more secure, when Callaghan temporarily acquired the extra income from writing his columns in the *Women's Sunday Mirror*. His salary as consultant for the Police Federation from September 1955 brought further comfort. The Moultons also left a significant legacy: it is worth noting that Mr Moulton's doctor had a private practice in Wimpole Street. In addition, Audrey Callaghan benefited from a legacy from an aunt which enabled them to buy a cottage in the Isle of Wight for £850 in 1958. This proved to be an ideal base for family holidays.

Later in his career, as his affluence grew, Callaghan sometimes faced personal attacks from within the Labour movement and in magazines such as *Private Eye* and *Rebecca*, with sarcastic inquiries about the source of the new-found affluence of his lifestyle. His association with capitalist millionaires such as Julian Hodge and Charles Forte was frequently mentioned. These will be dealt with below, but it is worth noting that there was nothing unusual, and certainly nothing remotely sinister, about Callaghan's earlier progression to reasonable financial security. He was always properly careful about money matters, but he had no private business or commercial interests as did so many Tory MPs, no large supplementary income such as fell to colleagues who were in the legal or other professions, nor the steady flow from journalistic activity or other forms of writing that many of his Bevanite critics enjoyed. He had absolutely no inherited wealth of his own; indeed his childhood had been one of comparative poverty. He made his own way financially as he did politically, with no hidden advantages, certainly not the kind of business or commercial links that made the most mediocre American congressmen wealthy men. He was in political life to achieve results and promote social change. His later links with Julian Hodge and the Bank of Credit and Commerce International notwithstanding, he was, and remained, a basically honest man whose approach seemed, in the sleaze and financial and sexual scandals of the 1990s, a reminder of the standards of a bygone age.

Callaghan's social life was geared almost entirely to politics. Almost all his closer friends were fellow members whom he encountered in the Commons, or perhaps journalists he met in the lobby. His architect friends, the Bowyers, were exceptions. There was little private entertaining; Callaghan was in any case modest in his eating and drinking habits. When he went to the Foreign Office, he became a teetotaller. There were those who surmised that Callaghan like other MPs did not really have close friends, but rather political associates, no one with whom he could unwind or commune in private. Richard Crossman recorded a conversation of 27 June 1953 after driving with Gaitskell and Callaghan to address a weekend meeting in Abingdon during a by-election (there was a poor turnout partly because the Lord's test match against the Australians was being televised). Callaghan observed that it was pleasant to spend a day with colleagues on holiday (which is apparently how he estimated a by-election meeting). 'I replied that my idea of a holiday was not to see my colleagues and James said, "But they're such good friends".' Crossman responded, 'Well I've been wondering whether a single one of them would be my friend if I wasn't in politics.'[4]

Probably, Callaghan like other men acquired the arts of intimacy as middle age brought a sense of serenity or self-confidence. With political associates such as Helmut Schmidt or Gerald Ford in later life, the public relationship was substantially reinforced by personal affection. Like most Labour politicians, he invariably got on well with Americans. But always Callaghan was at his best relating to, and communicating with, humbler figures—constituents, ordinary party workers, shy university students, modest secretaries, and personal assistants. He was direct, unpompous, with a good sense of humour, and, up to a point, the ability to take a joke against himself. If he were crossed by political equals, however, it was a different story. Dark clouds would build up and 'Sunny Jim' of the tabloid press would turn stormy.

He admitted that his world was totally circumscribed by political issues and individuals. He liked to say of himself that he had no interests, played no games, indulged in no hobbies. The days when he allegedly sang with a popular dance band were far distant. He took some interest in sport, mainly in connection with the fortunes of Cardiff teams. This meant usually sharing disappointment with Cardiff City football club (which he vainly tried to persuade Henry Kissinger to watch at Ninian Park), joy with Cardiff rugby club now at the zenith of its glory in the Cliff Morgan–Bleddyn Williams era, and modified rapture when a constituent like Joe Erskine became British heavyweight boxing champion. Generally, unlike colleagues like Denis Healey or Roy Jenkins, Callaghan believed that he had no 'hinterland', to adopt Healey's famous term.

But he was being in some ways unfair to himself. Certainly the visits to concerts, plays, and operas of the earlier years of his relationship with Audrey petered out with the pressures of public life, although visits to the opera in Moscow in 1946 were evidently genuinely enjoyed. He always appreciated classical music: ballet, by contrast, he freely admitted that he hated. He read novels (including Tolstoy and Dostoevsky) and some history when he could find time. One substantial interest was visual art. He was a supporter of the Royal Academy. One friend was the sculptor Henry Moore, the son of a Castleford miner who was himself a committed socialist. Callaghan built up a decent collection of paintings and prints which were on display in his various homes. Many of them illustrated maritime or naval themes, often historical. Beyond that, Callaghan's only hobby in the House, useful for filling in time before trooping through the division lobby, was chess, which he played with colleagues such as Douglas Jay, Reginald Paget, and Maurice Edelman. Michael Foot was a more dashing performer, and the backbencher Julius Silverman perhaps the strongest Commons player of all. Callaghan's chess style was unremarkable: he favoured classic openings and endgames such as the Ruy Lopez and the Sicilian Defence (though, as for many others, the full subtleties of the latter often eluded him). He admired the proficiency of the leading Russians, the current world champion Mikhail Botvinnik and his successors Smyslov and Tal. It marginally underlined his early enthusiasm for the Soviet Union. He kept up his interest in chess throughout his life, being a regular attender at the Hastings chess congress. He even took part in a simultaneous contest with the then Russian world champion Gary Kasparov in 1993, with inevitably very brief results. A good-humoured loser, Callaghan concluded that more intelligence was required for chess than for politics.[5]

In two other areas, however, Callaghan found genuine satisfaction with wider interests. One was the Wiener Library in London. Callaghan met Dr Alfred Wiener shortly after visiting Russia in January 1946 and was deeply moved by his immense and unique collection of books and papers relating to the rise of fascism and the consequences of totalitarian horror inflicted upon the Jewish people. Callaghan felt that it was vital, perhaps politically even more than academically, to retain so vital a legacy of the menace of fascism, and was concerned about the financial prospects for the Wiener Library now that it was no longer being used as an information agency by British and Allied governments as it had been up to 1945. The war trials he had witnessed in Kiev reinforced in Callaghan a sense of the continuing threat of totalitarianism and racial ideologies even in a world notionally at peace, and later in 1946 he became a founder member of the Board of the Wiener Library. Among other things he admired the dispassionate way in which the Library presented its holdings. It was not a propagandist anti-German display but merely an indispensable record of the horrors of modern times, irrespective of their source. Callaghan's links with the Wiener, in association with scholars like Alan Bullock, continued for the rest of his life. In 1980, when the Library was in danger of closing down through lack of funds, Callaghan chaired the endowment appeal which soon raised most of the million pounds which was sought. The Wiener connection was important to Callaghan as it was to his generation. It shows him at his most genuine and idealistic.

Another, more prophetic, issue with which he was also involved as a wider interest was that of environmental pollution. This theme which flourished during the 'green' movements of the 1980s and 1990s was in its infancy in the post-war period. But it captured Callaghan's imagination at this early time. It originated from his concern with the problems of the sea during his time as an Admiralty Minister, and no doubt from his feel for the maritime heritage dating from Portsmouth and Brixham days. In late 1951, he wrote a letter to *The Times* drawing attention to the dangers of oil pollution and received an immediate response from two scientists respectively at the Natural History Musuem and the Royal Geographical Society.

In March 1952 he founded a co-ordinating Advisory Committee on Oil Pollution of the Sea (ACOPS) in a meeting in a Commons committee room. It was to bring in a variety of enviromental bodies, and representatives of seaside resorts and of the shipping industry. Callaghan acted as its chairman from 1952 to 1963. Its main objective was to protect shores and wildlife through the total prohibition of the discharge of waste oil into the sea. Callaghan persuaded the then Minister of Transport, Alan Lennox-Boyd, to open a conference in 1953 and thereafter ACOPS remained an active and influential pressure group, enlisting significant academics like Sir Solly Zuckerman and Wilfred Beckerman. Later on in 1960, Callaghan was fiercely to rebuke the Minister of Science, Lord Hailsham, for failing to respond adequately to a complaint from ACOPS about the pollution of beaches by oil deposits.[6] Conventions were held to fight oil pollution of the sea, a Year Book was published, and Tony Crosland, when Environment Secretary in 1970, was persuaded to appoint a royal commission on the subject, drawing on names which Callaghan recommended to him. There was one notable legislative achievement to record, the passage of the Navigable Waters Act in July 1963. ACOPS was an important precursor of the environmental movements of a later period. By the 1990s (when an annual Callaghan lecture was inaugurated) it had some real achievements in stemming the pollution of the sea from oil tankers and in other ways, and in protecting marine wildlife. It was increasingly turning its attention to land-based sources of sea pollution. On the other hand, a series of catastrophes from the *Torrey Canyon* in 1967 to that in Milford Haven in 1996 illustrated the constant threat that remained.

An invaluable personal outcome of these activities was that through ACOPS Callaghan met Ruth Sharpe, originally the secretary of Miss Barclay-Smith of the Natural History Museum. Ruth Sharpe was a poised, gracious, and very able woman who had served with SOE during the war and spoke perfect French. From the mid-1950s she served as joint secretary to Callaghan and John Strachey. When the latter died in 1963 she devoted herself selflessly to Callaghan alone. She became Callaghan's own indispensable secretary and a great family friend, who, unlike some other ministerial secretaries, won great affection from the civil servants with whom she worked.[7] She never aroused the mixture of emotions associated with Marcia Williams. She also became a major figure in the world of Cardiff politics and largely directed operational matters during election campaigns from 1959 onwards. Throughout Callaghan's periods of Cabinet office including his premiership, she was irreplaceable and unique.

Callaghan's concern with environmental matters could lead into other areas. He took pride in the fact that his first budget as Chancellor included provision for £0.5m. to start the purchase of the British coastline to prevent spoliation. Snowdonia was purchased for the public domain. His Dalton-like concern for the countryside led to his name later being immortalized in a National Park in Newfoundland, the James Callaghan Trail in Le Gros Morne. He always loved the country, the flowers and hedgerows, the butterflies and bird life. He also took a vigorous interest in the movement for recycling natural products, at a period when these issues were marginal to public debate. He became involved with the International Bureau of Recycling. This passion carried on into his private life. In 1955–6, when the family was living in Maze Hill, he pressed the town clerk and other authorities in Greenwich about the pollution of the atmosphere from the generating station nearby on Greenwich Reach, which he had been monitoring with a deposit gauge in his garden. He wanted to know what action was being taken: the answer evidently was virtually nothing. 'As you know,' Callaghan wrote, 'I am very keen on this question of the prevention of smoke pollution.'[8] It is another illustration of his capacity for practical idealism, anticipating debate over the Millenium site at Greenwich years later.

The private picture of Callaghan that emerges at this time is in some ways a conventional one—a family man trying to reconcile legitimate professional ambition with the needs of house and home. Like all politicians, he met with a variety of responses. Gaitskell and Crossman, Wykehamists both, were inclined to be snobbishly dismissive of his intellectual abilities. Callaghan seemed disposed to agree; one hears echoes of Stanley Baldwin's defensive comment in response to the Celtic wizardry of Lloyd George, 'I am not a clever man.' Tony Crosland, another powerful mind, did not share this view at all, nor did Douglas Jay, another Wykehamist and Fellow of All Souls, while Dalton, a former university professor, thought Callaghan, along with Crosland and Healey, the most intelligent of the younger generation.[9] When Callaghan became premier, his inductive logic and intellectual clarity much impressed the very able team that formed his policy-making entourage. Certainly, not all the Fellows of Nuffield were to be impressed by his intellectual powers when he became a Visiting Fellow there in 1957. But Callaghan, like George Brown, another product of a working-class background, would have surely been a successful university student.

Some criticized his relentlessly driving ambition; others felt that it was kept in check by a genuine humanity. He had an astonishing memory for the individual circumstances of his Cardiff constituents, however humble their background. His friend and patron Hugh Dalton, who liked him very much, at one time described him as 'first class though with no manners and ruthless ambition'.[10] On the other hand, Dalton, Gaitskell, and others found him a cheerful, buoyant companion: 'gay' (in the 1950s sense) was one of Gaitskell's adjectives for him. His approachable quality was a major factor in his political progress. Temperamentally he could be volatile. The terms 'bully' or even 'thug' were sometimes applied. But then the distinctly uncomradely Labour Party, in the series of seismic upheavals that struck it during the years of the Bevanite controversy, was no place for faint hearts. There seemed no adversary, Shinwell, Morrison, George Brown, the mighty Nye Bevan himself, to whom Callaghan would not stand up if circumstances dictated. He would fight for his views, savagely if need be. But he was usually under control and the public invariably saw the genial front of 'Sunny Jim'.

More broadly, while he could calculate or trim, he could also be a reliable ally. As a former trade union negotiator, he believed trust was an essential attribute and it was one that he himself could inspire. He might not have been a great innovative thinker but his word could usually be relied on. This dependable quality, which served him in difficult phases of diplomacy with foreign statesmen and colonial leaders, and with trade union and business leaders at home, gave him an air of bluff honesty. The firm qualities that were reflected in his relationship with the police had wider implications. Cartoonists like Gerald Scarfe or Cummings were to be less severe towards him than to other premiers such as Macmillan, Hume, Heath, Wilson, Thatcher, or Major.[11] *Private Eye* usually spared him the savagery it reserved for Harold 'Wislon' or 'Grocer' Heath. Nor did it target Audrey Callaghan as it did other prime ministers' spouses in 'Mary Wilson's diary' or the purported saga of Denis Thatcher, 'Dear Bill'. All this could and did transfer to the perceptions of the wider public. As with Stanley Baldwin and Clem Attlee, both politicians he admired in earlier periods, Callaghan somehow seemed to embody, as time went on, some of the solid traditional instincts of an old historic nation. To adopt one of his favourite seafaring phrases, he embodied the philosophy of 'steady as you go'. More plausibly than the Conservatives of the 1990s, Callaghan, husband, family man, good neighbour, and patriot, embodied the comforting ethic of 'Victorian values'. He symbolized the solid fifties, not the swinging sixties. This image would help to make this one-time fiery socialist a reassuring centrist, and turn a routine politician into a figure of national stature. The wider dimension and visibility acquired through his concern with decolonization and the retreat from empire from 1956 onwards served only to make this perception stronger still.

1. This chapter is based largely on materials in the Callaghan Papers, boxes 2, 29, 30, and 31, and on personal knowledge derived from interviews and from other sources.

2. I am very grateful to Sir Montague Levine for information on aspects of these medical matters.

3. Interview with Lord Rodgers.

4. Crossman, *Backbench Diaries*, 251.

5. For Callaghan's interest in chess, see his interview with Cathy Forbes in *Chess* (June 1990), 26–7. For his match with Kasparov, see *Guardian*, 18 Feb. 1993.

6. Callaghan to Hailsham, 11 July 1960 (Callaghan Papers, box 18). 'When I write to you I hope to hear from you personally, not get a stuffy letter from your secretary.'

7. Information from Dr Nigel Bowles; Lord Bancroft to the author, 25 Feb. 1996. Ruth Sharpe died in 1981 and the present writer never met her, but he also should record his immense appreciation for her work in imposing order on Lord Callaghan's private papers.

8. Callaghan to the clerk of the Greenwich Council, 26 July 1955 (Callaghan Papers, box 2).

9. Dalton, *Political Diary*, 511 (entry of 12 Mar. 1951).

10. Ibid. 511 (12 Mar. 1951).

11. Kenneth Baker to the author, 10 Oct. 1994, discussing his book on political cartoons.

8

THE ENDING OF EMPIRE

EMPIRE is at the heart of modern British history. It provided literary inspiration from Conrad and Rider Haggard to Paul Scott and J. G. Ballard. It dominated much of the 1950s as it had done the 1880s and 1890s. But whereas earlier it was the expansion of empire that dominated public debate, uniquely in the 1950s it was the trauma of decolonization and the winding up of the greatest territorial empire the world had known that compelled attention. It was in the late 1950s, not the 1940s (which had seen the independence of the Indian subcontinent but little else), that the retreat from empire really took effect. Successive Conservative colonial ministers, Hopkinson, Lennox-Boyd, and especially Macleod, found themselves compelled to liquidate large colonial obligations to which their party was historically uniquely attached. This was a quite distinct process from the aftermath of Suez, to which too much importance can be attached. Debates about colonial policy, therefore, above all in west, east, and especially southern Africa, achieved a centrality not known before or since. Whether this was a scuttle that amounted to a national humiliation for a once-great power, or a statesmanlike advance to a new concept of a multiracial commonwealth, provoked violent controversy. The residual passions of Suez temporarily fanned the flames.

It was a debate for which Labour and its new colonial spokesman were now much more fully equipped. Until the Second World War, Labour's ideas on colonial and imperial matters had been patchy and derivative. In its earlier years, with the partial exception of Ramsay MacDonald, Labour's spokesmen had little to offer other than a repetitive quasi-Marxist aversion to empire. Labour was against empire just as it was against a capitalist war. The first two Labour governments of 1924 and 1929–31 had little new to say. In the latter administration, Sidney Webb (now Lord Passfield) was not an innovative figure at the Colonial Office, although it should be added that he was then in his seventies. Left-wing publicists like Harold Laski and H. N. Brailsford wrote on Indian independence; many in the ILP had personal links with the Congress movement. There was also an abiding Labour commitment to Zionism, with Poale Zion affiliated to the party. But there was less attention paid to colonial issues than to any other policy area. A radical writing exclusively on aspects of colonial freedom like the young Leonard Barnes in the later 1930s was a rarity.

Only in the war years did Labour begin to evolve a more constructive approach, through the Fabian Colonial Research Bureau. Here, notably through Rita Hinden, a Jewish South African émigré, and Arthur Creech Jones, once of the ILP, new policies were drawn up for long-term patterns of colonial development, economic, educational, and technological, and a programme of partnership in an evolving commonwealth.[1] This approach, more fruitful than the simple-minded anti-imperialism of earlier years, was enshrined in the Colonial Charter adopted at the party conference in 1942. It was substantially put into practice by Creech Jones as Labour's Colonial Secretary in 1946–50 and by his successor James Griffiths in 1950–1. Creech Jones, a dull, prosaic speaker, was also in many ways a visionary committed to an exciting programme of social and economic transformation, along the lines the youthful Callaghan had favoured during his visit to west Africa in 1947. He encouraged a new breed of enlightened civil servants, like Andrew Cohen, head of the Africa division of the Colonial Office. But Creech Jones also suffered from being tainted with the policy failures of Gambia eggs and, more seriously, groundnuts in Tanganyika (although Strachey as Food Minister was equally culpable here). He lost his seat at Shipley in 1950 and, although he later returned in a by-election as member for Wakefield, he was never a political force again. James Griffiths was Labour's spokesman on colonial matters after 1951, and an effective one. Even so, as urgent new colonial problems erupted in the mid-1950s and nationalist movements spread in South-East Asia, the Middle East, and throughout the length and breadth of the African continent, Labour needed a new approach and a powerful voice.

A variety of influences converged on Callaghan as he embarked on his important new portfolio. The main intellectual and policy initiatives still came from the Fabian Colonial Research Bureau with its message of developmental growth and partnership. Its guiding spirit, Rita Hinden, was now mainly involved in editing the monthly periodical *Socialist Commentary*: she retained a keen interest in colonial questions of all kinds. The Bureau's programme of long-term development in Africa and Asia had once been criticized for lack of detail, but it had been fleshed out successfully by Professor Arthur Lewis, an eminent West Indian economist. More controversially, the Bureau was falling foul of critics on the left for its extreme caution, as they saw it, in promoting the idea of colonial independence. Rita Hinden's criticisms of Cheddi Jagan, the left-wing nationalist leader in British Guiana, led to her being attacked for conflating cold-war attitudes with colonial issues.[2] Callaghan was friendly with Rita Hinden and a warm supporter of, and contributor to, *Socialist Commentary*. Her vision of evolution, economic development, and partnership was naturally congenial to him. But he became aware in the late 1950s that the very pace and pressure of African nationalism in particular called for a more urgent approach towards colonial freedom. The dynamics of political change took precedence over developmental advance. Trusteeship like patriotism was not enough.

Transport House was an alternative source of ideas and advice, especially its Commonwealth Officer, John Hatch. Appointed in 1954, Hatch was a man on the party left (he had formerly been an organizer for the ILP) and with a South African background. He was strongly committed to the urgency of self-determination for colonial peoples. Despite their different political backgrounds, he and Callaghan worked together effectively, including sponsoring a series of pamphlets on colonial issues. When Hatch retired in 1961 he was to reflect that his role as public educator had been substantially completed, not simply because of Labour's close relationship with colonial nationalist movements but also through the major reversal of policy undertaken by Iain Macleod in his period as Colonial Secretary.[3] Quite distinct from these essentially political influences was the role of Nuffield College, Oxford. Callaghan became a Visiting Fellow of the college in 1957 and the connection clearly helped him in formulating ideas on the details of colonial policy. In particular, Dr (later Dame) Margery Perham, the leading authority in British universities on colonial administration, was a valued mentor, as were the many visiting academics and others from Commonwealth territories.

More instructive still, perhaps, was the succession of nationalist leaders from a wide variety of Commonwealth countries who came to Britain in the 1950s. For them the Labour Party, along with its links with the Fabians, the London School of Economics, and the *New Statesman*, was the natural home. Labour indeed actively encouraged them with scholarships to visit Britain and attend Labour summer schools. Since before the war, African and Asian nationalists had been involved in grass-roots party activity, as Dr Hastings Banda was in South Shields and Krishna Menon in St Pancras. Indian Congress leaders were well known in party circles. In the 1950s, these visits turned into a flood. A newer generation of younger leaders came to political maturity through contacts of this kind, and Callaghan became friendly with almost all of them. He got to know many of them at an important meeting of Commonwealth socialists in Beatrice Webb House in Dorking in the summer of 1957. In particular, Tom Mboya, the Kenyan trade union activist, and Harry Lee, later Lee Kuan Yew, 'a brilliant young Chinese socialist lawyer' from Singapore, impressed him as leaders of the future. Lee's PAP programme was 'an excellent analysis of Socialist thinking conceived in curiously Western terms'.[4] Along with more senior figures like the Africans Julius Nyerere, Kenneth Kaunda, and Joshua Nkomo, and Caribbean leaders like Michael Manley and Grantley Adams, they provided an indispensable range of contacts with the high command of colonial nationalism pivotal to Callaghan's later career.

Labour reached a natural consensus on colonial issues in the later 1950s. The party was at one in pressing for a rapid end to colonial rule, multiracial participatory democracy, and the economic redevelopment of colonial territories. Callaghan spoke for a party as broadly united on these issues as it was bitterly divided over defence (notably nuclear weapons) and to some degree the nationalization of industry. He had a good relationship with the Colonial Group of the parliamentary party. Nor did his shadow Cabinet colleagues present any difficulty. Gaitskell, who had some expertise in colonial matters acquired from his brother Arthur, a distinguished authority on economic development in the Sudan, was generally supportive, especially on central Africa. Aneurin Bevan, Callaghan's predecessor as colonial spokesman, was benignly helpful, for instance in discussions over Malta and Cyprus, and in chairing the party's Commonwealth subcommittee. In parliamentary debates and in the press, Labour presented a strong and almost united front. By contrast, the Conservatives witnessed the bewildering reversals of policy by Macleod and eventually Butler in Africa with mixed feelings. A minority group of imperialists, stemming in part from the Suez rebels of the mid-1950s, regarded it as a cruel betrayal. The aged Churchill lent them some sympathy, as did ministers like Salisbury and Julian Amery. Macleod, declared Lord Salisbury, was 'too clever by half'. His fury would have been all the greater had he known of Macleod's privately declared intention to be the last Colonial Secretary.[5]

Even so, it was unlikely that Labour would be totally unified on colonial issues, especially given the fractious nature of the party through the 1950s from Bevanism to CND. There were always pressure groups linked to particular countries which could be difficult. Cyprus generated some problems for Callaghan given the links Labour had with the Greek

Cypriot community in London, which made Lena Jeger, who counted many of them amongst her Holborn and St Pancras constituents, a sharp critic. A more troublesome force was Barbara Castle, who became a passionate (and, in Callaghan's view, unduly one-sided) advocate of the Greek Cypriot cause and of 'enosis' with Greece. She responded furiously when Callaghan and Gaitskell failed to react to a message she conveyed from Archbishop Makarios, with whom she had had a secret meeting in Athens in September 1958.[6] In the 1945 parliament she and Callaghan had been friendly. The latter enjoyed the Castles' Christmas parties, which featured high-kicking contests between himself and Geoffrey de Freitas, fortified by Algerian wine. But the row over Cyprus foretold squalls ahead. Another pleader for specialist interests who caused some trouble was Dr Thomas Balogh, the eminent Balliol-based Hungarian economist who, for some reason, became a fervent advocate of the causes of Dom Mintoff and the Maltese Labour Party. Callaghan firmly resisted Balogh's appeal that Labour should 'back Mintoff'. 'I am much opposed to backing people abroad however friendly we may be with them when we have no control over their activities or policies.'[7] Among other objections, Balogh's overtures complicated private discussions Callaghan was having with Lord Perth and the British government over the advance towards the integration of Malta with Britain.

More potentially troublesome for Callaghan was the Movement for Colonial Freedom. This was a powerful pressure group launched in 1954.[8] Its core members were prominent Bevanites like Geoffrey Bing, Ian Mikardo, and Barbara Castle. But it also drew support more widely in the party such as from Sir Leslie Plummer, former chairman of the Overseas Food Corporation, R. T. Paget, a maverick right-winger with whom Callaghan was personally friendly, and the very young, and not yet especially radical, Anthony Wedgwood Benn. Its chairman was the veteran Fenner Brockway, a survivor from the days of Keir Hardie, and a lifelong apostle of pacificism and colonial freedom. More remarkably, it was perhaps the one radical group of the time whose rallies could draw support not only from the predictable London-based intelligentsia but also from trade unionists. Callaghan's public relations with the MCF were courteous enough. He sent a friendly message to it soon after becoming colonial spokesman, to the pleasure of Wedgwood Benn.[9] Brockway, a warm-hearted idealist, could send cheerful words praising 'the democratic and co-operative way' in which Callaghan conducted discussions with the Commonwealth and Colonial Group of the parliamentary party. (In the same letter he called for the immediate withdrawal of all British troops in

Malaya, still then caught up in its state of emergency.[10]) But privately Callaghan regarded the MCF as a well-intentioned but essentially unreliable, if not unstable, group mainly of left-wingers whose views of colonial matters were simplistic. He did not attend their meetings and regarded their approach as 'impulsive'. He refused to attend an MCF meeting in Cardiff to condemn racial discrimination, to coincide with the holding of the 1958 Commonwealth Games in Wales. Among other issues, it sought to point out that the South African team was all white. But Brockway and others, he told the Cardiff Labour Party, aroused much distrust in some of the colonial territories (he did not specify whether it was white or black colonials he had in mind). It was far better for meetings of this type to be held under the official auspices of the Labour Party.[11]

The Movement for Colonial Freedom, which was to take up the cause of Greek Cypriot nationalism in a major way, was a frequent gadfly. It was repugnant to Callaghan's own more measured and gradualist approach towards colonial matters. Left-wing splinter groups like the Congress of Peoples against Imperialism could be dismissed as an unimportant Trotskyist group of fellow-travellers. The MCF clearly was a far more substantial body. By the early 1960s, in fact, it had lost impetus, partly because of internal disputes over Communist infilitration, but much more because Callaghan's Fabian approach on both political and economic questions commanded wide-ranging support right across the party. The MCF could claim in 1964 that the new Labour Cabinet contained some of its prominent members such as Barbara Castle and Anthony Greenwood. The new Prime Minister, Harold Wilson, had been an earlier supporter. But in general, like so many left-wing pressure groups in the past, the MCF had been marginalized whereas the official party spokesman had claimed the bipartisan mantle of responsible statesmanship.

As always, Callaghan's main source of wisdom lay less in the various influences of the Fabian Bureau, Transport House, Nuffield College, or the Movement for Colonial Freedom, and more in his own personal contacts and observation. He kept in close touch with writers on colonial issues in the press such as Colin Legum of the *Observer*. More important still, he travelled incessantly to virtually every one of Britain's Commonwealth territories between 1957 and 1962. Only a few outposts like St Helena (to which he dispatched Cledwyn Hughes) and a handful of Pacific dependencies were left out. In particular, he travelled to various parts of Africa on perhaps two dozen occasions, especially in 1957–8 when the Central African Federation was reaching a critical stage. As always, he enjoyed sightseeing and encountering problems at first hand. In these visits he applied his own particular blend of practical observation and insight. Over time, his conclusions became more measured. An early visit to Rhodesia in September 1957 led to some incautious remarks about the adventurous, bracing tone of life in southern Africa reminiscent of Baden-Powell or Rider Haggard.[12] But even then, the main thrust of his visit was directed towards the implacable opposition of African nationalists to any form of colonial rule, and the urgent need for rapid moves towards independence. His naturally friendly, approachable manner, without pomp, went down well with colonial leaders of all kinds, at a time when Conservative policy found spokesmen in such antique paternalist figures as the Lords Home and Perth. Callaghan never sounded or looked like any kind of imperialist. He also developed a shrewd talent for handling sensitive, proud figures like Nyerere or Kaunda. He spoke their kind of language. At the same time, in Africa or at Westminster, as a shrewd journalist noted, he 'had the trick of sounding more radical than he really is' on colonial issues.[13]

His focus was usually on Africa, but in early 1959 he had the opportunity to take a wider view when he travelled on behalf of his party to New Zealand, Australia, Singapore, Indonesia, Burma, and India.[14] Here he heard the fears of the New Zealand and Australian Labour Parties of Britain's future entry into the European Common Market, which they regarded as almost inevitable. His first impression of New Zealand was not encouraging. It was 'dull' and its communities were too small to sustain cultural activities. He got on well with H. V. Evatt., the Australian Labour leader, and his colleagues, less so with Robert Menzies, the conservative premier of Australia, whom he felt to be a languid character seemingly mainly interested in test matches. In Singapore he had talks with Lee Kuan Yew about the critical relations of the island with Malaya, and the political difficulties of keeping the local Chinese detached from the Communists. Singapore's chief minister Lim Yew Hock wanted union with the Malayan Federation and incongruously urged the island's large Chinese majority to 'Malayanise themselves'. As a naval man Callaghan was anxious to retain links with the naval base there but 'economically, the future of Singapore is not bright'. 'It is of doubtful use to us.' Its future astonishing progress and prosperity were impossible to anticipate at that time. Not that his judgements on the island were wholly negative: his notes commented appreciatively on 'lovely Chinese girls with the entrancing sheath dress and slit skirt'. Later that year, the election victory of the People's Action Party in Singapore under Lee Kuan Yew was to lead to a new crisis in relations with the Malayan government in Kuala Lumpur, and to several years of political and economic instability.

His visit to India helped build up an enduring relationship with its leaders, not only with the Congress but also with Morarji Desai, eventually to be the founder of the opposition Janata Party, which continued vigorously for the next thirty years. He encouraged the idea that India might sponsor a socialist Commonwealth conference. The fact that Callaghan had been a member of the honoured Attlee government which gave India its freedom added to his stature then and later. He reflected on his return, 'For the British and for the Labour Party in particular there is overwhelming friendship. . . . In no other country have I ever felt so proud to tell people that I was a Labour Member of Parliament. It has been an exhilarating experience.'[15]

Then, and in other visits to Australia and elsewhere, Callaghan always tried to project particular Commonwealth themes against the wider background of international relations and the global economy. Colonial development should be viewed as part of a wider programme of raising up the economies, technological base, and educational skills of the third world, and eliminating the problem of endemic colonial poverty and indebtedness. There should be stable world commodity prices, linked to the bulk purchase of foodstuffs, agricultural education to raise productivity, and consumer co-operatives. He called for a Colombo Plan for Africa. 'Political' aid, however, was useless, transparent, and counter-productive. But the economics of the colonies were subordinated to their politics. Callaghan argued that, while smaller colonial territories should also be granted self-government (he had much to do with the independence of Zanzibar and Mauritius, for instance), in each case the issue of the transfer of power should be treated with care. That meant, in practice, that Britain might have to stay in control longer than many African nationalists considered desirable until the social and economic conditions were appropriate for a proper working democracy. The British connection was still felt to be valuable in colonial territories. Britain was 'a steadying influence'. It was a prudent patriotic message, not very different from what moderate Conservatives like Macleod were saying at the time, but articulated with more passion.

In one part of the Commonwealth after another from early 1957 onwards, Callaghan's judgement was put to the test. On issue after issue, he found himself locked in combat of a kind with the Colonial Office. The Colonial Secretary until 1959 was Alan Lennox-Boyd, a somewhat patriarchal representative of the Guinness family whose extreme right-wing views mellowed at the Colonial Office. His personal relations with Callaghan were cordial enough, but the latter, with his fierce sense of independence, kept his distance from what he felt to be a patronizing, social embrace from Lennox-Boyd, designed to draw his fire. On the contrary, on the affairs of central Africa and the atrocities at Hola Camp, Callaghan waded into the Colonial Secretary with extreme ferocity which brought him plaudits right across the political spectrum. Lennox-Boyd's successor in 1959, Iain Macleod, a genuinely liberal figure bent on rapid decolonization, was quite different. He was a man of similar outlook with whom Callaghan enjoyed a perfectly agreeable relationship, both then and when Macleod was shadow Chancellor in the mid-1960s. They worked closely together on some issues, notably when Callaghan tried to dampen down some of Kenneth Kaunda's fiercer assaults on British government in Northern Rhodesia in 1960, which he compared with the chaos of the Congo. On the other hand, Callaghan was careful to keep his distance from Macleod also. He felt him to be abler than Lennox-Boyd but politically less trustworthy. Reginald Maudling, whom he liked, had just begun work as Macleod's successor when Callaghan himself was moved elsewhere.

A variety of crises in different parts of the Commonwealth demanded that Labour take up a position in this period. On South-East Asia, there was no great initiative for Callaghan and Labour to take, despite his personal association with Lee Kuan Yew and other nationalist leaders. The state of emergency came to an end in 1959 and British troops, many of them young national servicemen, could be brought home. The national war memorial in the Lake Garden in Kuala Lumpur today, commemorating three wars, those of 1914, 1939, and 1952, remarkably includes British troops amongst those commemorated. Callaghan resisted pressure from the Movement for Colonial Freedom that Labour should prematurely (as he saw it in 1958) call for the withdrawal of British troops. Through his contacts with Lee Kuan Yew, Prime Minister of Singapore from 1960, he was kept primed on the tense discussions of that island with the Malayan government of Tunku Abdul Rahman about their future constitutional relationship, a matter still unresolved when Callaghan ceased to be colonial affairs spokesman at the end of 1961.[16] Callaghan's view was that Malaya should be encouraged to absorb Singapore, of whose economic prospects he was pessimistic with cutbacks in Britain's naval presence in the Far East. He also noted in neutral terms that in 'Malaysia' (as it was renamed) the idea of a federation was mooted, to include Sarawak and North Borneo (though not Brunei), even though protests from President Sukarno of Indonesia were likely. The federal idea was a Colonial Office panacea at this period, pursued variously in plans for federations in the West Indies, east Africa, central Africa of course, Malaysia, and later southern Arabia. In each case, these federations were frustrated by local patriotisms: thus the successive withdrawal of Jamaica and Trinidad in 1961–2 doomed the West Indies federal structure after only four years. By the end of the 1960s every such scheme had collapsed in bitter disagreement.

Apart from Singapore, two other British bases concerned Callaghan and the British government much more acutely. Malta, which he had visited during the war, unexpectedly became a source of some tension from 1956 onwards. Whereas the right-wing clerical party there demanded self-government, the Maltese Labour Party under its volatile leader Dom Mintoff called for integration with Britain, including Maltese MPs at Westminster. There was also much argument about increased economic aid to Malta. Its economy was overwhelmingly dependent on work from the Royal Navy, which was now being cut back in defence economies. In 1959 the Maltese constitution was suspended and direct British rule imposed. Callaghan faced some pressure to intervene from sympathizers with Mintoff within the British Labour Party. Prominent among them, as has been seen, was Thomas Balogh who 'flooded' Callaghan with letters on the topic.[17] In fact, the latter was anxious to keep his distance from Mintoff, whose political judgement he saw as erratic. On Malta, the gulf between Labour and the Conservative government was not a wide one. Callaghan gave his private approval to Lennox-Boyd's package of economic aid for the island in July 1957 though he demanded more.[18] In July 1958 he had private talks with the government minister, Lord Perth, about policy towards Malta. Perth, who was anxious for a bipartisan approach, reported to Lennox-Boyd that the talks were friendly. 'They are I think at present on our side vis-à-vis Mintoff.' Callaghan was anxious for generous economic assistance to Malta. Apart from wider considerations, Baileys, the ship construction firm, was located in his constituency in Cardiff South-East.

On Maltese constitutional matters, Callaghan urged that a new constitution be introduced as early as possible, preferably before the spring. He added that 'it would be difficult for any Maltese government not to be allowed to control its own island's affairs including police'.[19] In the end, though, Labour (and this applied to Bevan and Gaitskell no less than Callaghan) did not dissent when the British government broke off talks with Dom Mintoff. With Hilary Marquand and George Thomson, he told Macleod that it was important to get a new constitution in being there and to defer Mintoff's request for integration.[20] He told Sam Watson, the Durham miners' leader, that 'I thought the tactics of the Malta Labour

Party had set back their own cause'.[21] In the event, a harmonious constitutional settlement, without integration, was to be reached with the Maltese (though not Mintoff) in 1964. For all his naval connections and British sentimental regard for 'the George Cross island', Callaghan's and Labour's approach towards their Maltese comrades had been watchful.

Far more critical was the problem of Cyprus. The long-standing tension in that island between the Greek majority and the Turkish minority had been further complicated by the demands of the Greek Cypriots and their titular spokesman Archbishop Makarios for 'enosis' or union with Greece. The British government had handled the issue badly: the current Colonial Minister of State, Henry Hopkinson, disastrously stated in 1954 that Cyprus, important as it was for British naval and air forces in the eastern Mediterranean with the bases at Akrotiri and Dhekelia, could 'never' expect self-government. An underground Greek guerrilla organization, EOKA, began operations in the island under the direction of Colonel Grivas. In 1955 a bloody war began between EOKA and the British forces in Cyprus. The Troodos mountains became a killing ground. Archbishop Makarios was condemned for his role by Lennox-Boyd and eventually dispatched to exile in the Seychelles in the Indian Ocean. Like Gandhi, Nehru, and other colonial leaders before him, Makarios completed his political education in a British jail. Callaghan had to tread warily on the issue. There was a natural Labour sympathy for the Greek Cypriots and for colonial self-determination (though not necessarily 'enosis'). The repressive régime of the British governor General Harding led to vehement criticism; allegations of brutality towards Greek Cypriot spokesmen were not being investigated. Callaghan's first major intervention in debate as shadow colonial spokesman was on the emergency regulations in Cyprus on 2 December 1956. On 19 February he moved a critical motion protesting at British policy. He condemned the draconian measures of the Harding régime, the exiling of Archbishop Makarios, and the failure to pursue bilateral talks with the Greek and Turkish community on the basis of the Radcliffe proposals. Partition of Cyprus, he believed, was impossible as a solution. Discussions should begin on the early implementation of self-government.[22]

Then and later, he also attacked the British premiss that Cyprus had a unique value as a military and naval base. Callaghan noted privately that ministers argued that Cyprus was ' "our last foothold" in the Middle East and if we abandon it altogether the Middle East will fall more completely still under American influence'.[23] There was also the sensitive 'scuttle' aspect so soon after Suez. On the contrary, he argued that the existence of the Baghdad pact as an extension of NATO, the new alliances with Libya and Jordan, and the delicate state of Britain's oil supplies after the Suez fiasco made Cyprus far less significant to Britain's strategic interests. The British government rejected these last arguments, which the passage of time was to make seem tenuous, and indeed Callaghan himself was subsequently to abandon them also. Cyprus remained a British base down to the end of the century.

In fact, if one reads Labour's speeches on Cyprus at the time, their criticisms of the government focus less on objectives, since both sides rejected both 'enosis' with Greece and partition, than on methods, the ways in which security was being enforced, and the precise route to be adopted in preparing for talks with the Cypriots. Makarios was released from the Seychelles in 1957 to facilitate this process. On the one hand, Callaghan pressed the government hard on unanswered charges of brutality by the Special Police, charges emanating amongst others from the terrorist leader Nicos Sampson.[24] On the other, he urged that 'enosis' be abandoned as an objective; when Archbishop Makarios did so, it opened up the way for a fresh appraisal of the problem of self-government in Cyprus. There was something else—a blunt patriotic refusal to condemn British security operations too vigorously as the Movement for Colonial Freedom and individuals like Barbara Castle were doing. Callaghan told John Hatch in October 1958, 'I simply will not be a party to condemning the British troops when a much heavier responsibility rests upon Makarios and EOKA as well as with the British government.'[25] In the end, a constitutional agreement was reached for Cyprus in the Zurich accord endorsed in London in February 1959. Cyprus ceased to be a critical problem for Britain and for NATO. The main conflict henceforth was not between the Cypriots and the British but between the Greeks and Turks in Cyprus itself. Years later, when he was Foreign Secretary in 1974, Callaghan was to see war break out between the two communities on the island, with resultant tension between him and Henry Kissinger, the US Secretary of State. Cyprus (and indeed Nicos Sampson) came back to haunt him, and on this occasion the outcome was to be far less clear-cut.

Singapore, Malta, and Cyprus, however, were all essentially localized problems. The continent of Africa had global significance. In 1957 it was said to be 'Africa's year'. So, to a degree, were 1958, 1959, 1960, and 1961. All across the continent, African nationalism and European colonial pretensions came into conflict. It was Africa, therefore, a part of the world of which he had some first-hand experience, which mainly absorbed Callaghan's passionate attention during his period as colonial spokesman.

It was Africa that brought him to the fore as a politician and gave him for the first time an aura of major statesmanship.

West Africa, which he had visited back in January 1947, was not especially critical at this time. Moves for self-government had progressed rapidly in both Nigeria and in the Gold Coast in the early 1950s; in the latter, renamed Ghana, Kwame Nhrumah, head of the Convention People's Party, had built himself up into a major and apparently unassailable figure, with whom the British government had amicable relations. Ghana attained full independence in 1957. Nigeria, on the other hand, was transformed into a federation in which it was hopefully believed that the tribal tensions between the eastern, western, and northern parts of that vast but potentially rich country had been suppressed. It received its independence in 1960. Callaghan, however, was under few illusions as to the extent to which political stability and integrity, and harmony between the Ibo, Yoruba, and other tribes, had been achieved. He retained a close personal contact with Nigerian leaders over the next thirty years. From the civil war involving the breakaway of Biafra in the later 1960s, to the corrupt military dictatorship of the 1990s which saw the atrocious putting to death of the writer Ken Saro-Wiwa in 1995, Callaghan was to find that Nigeria, like other new African nations, was a source of bitter disappointment, through its internal misgovernment, tribal conflict, and corruption. He embarked on a long and sometimes dangerous campaign to try to end the detention without trial of General Obasanjo, the sole head of state who had handed Nigeria back to democratic rule, at the hands of President Abacha. Sierra Leone and Gambia, two other countries he knew at first hand, also shortly became independent, without any dispute.

East Africa was more difficult by far in the later 1950s, especially in Kenya with its large white population of 60,000 including settler-farmers in the 'white highlands' and the bitter war against the 'Mau Mau' which claimed to represent the Kikuyu peoples. Between 1952 and 1956, over 14,000 Kikuyus lost their lives, more due to conflict amongst the native tribe itself than to warfare with the British troops. All three east African territories, Kenya, Uganda, and Tanganyika, were on the move in the later 1950s, as also was the small island of Zanzibar which some sought to merge with Tanganyika. Even so, as late as 1959, Lennox-Boyd was talking in terms of the independence of Kenya, Uganda, and Tanganyika not being achieved until the 1970s. Of these territories, Tanganyika made the most rapid progress, especially after Macleod succeeded Lennox-Boyd at the Colonial Office in October 1959. Callaghan enjoyed a close relationship with Julius Nyerere whose TANU party dominated politics in

Tanganyika. Previous leisurely British timetables were scrapped as the new independent state of Tanzania came into being under Macleod's aegis in December 1961.

Uganda was more complex since it involved an abandonment of the British notion of a unitary state, and the absorption of the kingdom of Buganda within a broader Uganda, eventually under the leadership of Milton Obote. In 1961–2 Uganda also became an independent nation. Callaghan had no serious disagreement with the policy of the Colonial Office, which he regarded as reasonably progressive. He was involved in moves in 1960 to try to frustrate a breakaway by the Kabaka of Buganda.[26] He speculated on the possibility of an Eastern African Federation, but this proved to be another chimera in the abortive history of federal experiments. Later on, when Uganda fell under the dictatorship of President Amin, it was again to become one of Callaghan's preoccupations as Foreign Secretary.

Kenya was a critical area, with much political tension after the ending of the Mau Mau emergency and determined pressure by a significant white settler minority to preserve their rights. There was halting progress towards a constitutional settlement in Kenya in the late 1950s. A further complicating factor was that the Colonial Office claimed that Kenya, like Cyprus, was vital to Britain's defence needs, with the importance of the naval base of Mombasa in particular for the navy's strategic operations in the Indian Ocean. Callaghan knew Kenya at first hand and went there again in late 1961. He was a close friend of Tom Mboya of KANU, on whom he exercised some influence. He was critical of the leisurely approach that Lennox-Boyd and Sir Evelyn Baring, the Governor of Kenya, adopted towards self-government, with ten years set aside for devising a bicameral new constitution, and a Council of State proposed which might well supersede the legislative council.[27] In addition, African political activity was largely curtailed. The Kikuyu leader Jomo Kenyatta, like many nationalist leaders a resident in British jails (where Callaghan visited him), was viewed with intense suspicion as a tribal demagogue.

In the Commons and in private communications with Lennox-Boyd, Callaghan pressed the government for a greater urgency. By 1958 the entire situation in Kenya appeared to be disintegrating with a prospect of serious racial conflict. There should, he urged, be far greater political participation by blacks in Kenya, the powers of the proposed Council of State should be curtailed, and its members appointed for a fixed term of years. Above all, the progress in agricultural development and education originating with the 'Swinnerton plan' in the Kikuyu territory should be actively pursued. On the other hand, he was also anxious that Kenyan nationalism should remain moderate in tone now that the violence of the Mau Mau had been successfully resisted. He told the Committee of African Organizations in March 1958 that Lennox-Boyd's proposed new constitution should be endorsed 'as a stage on the road to full democratic government'.[28] He constantly urged on Mboya the need for negotiation and dialogue with the Governor and the white minority. 'The situation today does present an opportunity for a substantial move forward', he wrote to Tom Mboya in May 1959.[29] Two months later he advised, 'I should proceed on the assumption that you are working towards a full democracy in Kenya. I hold the view that a lot is to be gained by having a constitutional conference at an early date, and I hope this can be arranged.' He urged the importance of 'moving in the main stream of opinion throughout Africa'.[30]

In fact, the advent of Macleod (whose brother Rhoderick was a prominent white moderate in Kenya) brought a rapid advance which Callaghan generally applauded. The relatively moderate stance of Mboya and other KANU leaders was a helpful factor, but perhaps more so was the determination of Michael Blundell, head of the New Kenya Group, to have a genuinely multiracial democracy in Kenya in which whites could freely participate. The white settler population there was more diverse, more commercial than farmers in the white highlands, and the climate was right for change. Following a major conference at Lancaster House in London in January 1960, the road lay open for fuller participation in political opinion by moderate African parties, and for black majority rule in Kenya in the near future. Jomo Kenyatta, with whom Mboya had somewhat mixed relations, was released from jail to head KANU and the British government, anxious to avoid a state of anarchy on the model of the Congo, rapidly moved to granting Kenya independence at the end of 1963. Callaghan gave warm approval to all these moves: he was primed on land developments there by George Brown.[31] He had ceased to be a colonial spokesman when the Kenyan political situation was apparently resolved, although a sad personal loss later on in 1969 was the assassination of Tom Mboya. He was a victim of Kenya's innate tribal factionalism since he was a Luo, not a Kikuyu, while his policies as Minister of Economic Planning had aroused local opposition. With his death Kenya lost a powerful and deeply intelligent force for socio-economic change adapted to the local circumstances. Callaghan also lost perhaps his most valued contact with the African cause. By 1969, too, Callaghan was experiencing as Home Secretary one of the unforeseen consequences of Kenyan independence, when the right to a British passport given to white settlers in the early 1960s was now claimed by a significant number of Kenyan Asians. It proved to be one of his greatest political embarrassments.

But Callaghan's involvement with Kenya went beyond constitutional and economic niceties. There was also a powerful humanitarian aspect which brought him to prominence. In Hola Camp near Mombasa in Coast Province, it was reported in 1959 that eleven Kikuyu, detained after the Mau Mau troubles, had mysteriously died. There were serious allegations of brutality against the camp commander and a public inquiry was eventually held. It emerged that the prisoners had been beaten to death by armed guards. Callaghan reacted with great decisiveness. To him it was another colonial atrocity in a long and dismal story that began with the Amritsar massacre in India in 1919. In a debate on the Hola Camp deaths on 16 June 1959 he launched a furious assault on the government and on Lennox-Boyd in particular.[32] He said that the inquiry had been totally inadequate. The Colonial Secretary was condemned as 'totalitarian': Callaghan went so far as to refer to his pre-war sympathy for Franco in the Spanish Civil War. He linked the treatment of Hola Camp to a long record of Tory failures in colonial policy—Suez, Cyprus, and Nyasaland—and demanded that the Colonial Secretary should resign. Gaitskell amongst others was delighted by his performance and horrified by the evasiveness not only of Lennox-Boyd but also of Macmillan, the Prime Minister. For a time, the bipartisan consensus on African policy was shattered. Alan Lennox-Boyd shortly afterwards left politics, his reputation seriously tarnished. Praise was showered down on Callaghan; equally valuable, politically, were fierce attacks on him in the right-wing press.[33] The Hola Camp affair languished unsatisfactorily without adequate retribution. But, for all its grisly aspects, it had given Callaghan the opportunity to show that, as colonial affairs spokesman, he could be not merely a party tactician or a pragmatic advocate of moderation, but also a powerful moral force who could be an eloquent voice of conscience and the decent opinions of mankind.

It was, however, central Africa above all other areas which dominated Callaghan's time as colonial affairs spokesman. By 1957 the Central African Federation of Northern and Southern Rhodesia, and Nyasaland had been in being for four years.[34] There had been mounting fury from African nationalists, especially in Nyasaland, where the white population was minute (9,000), and in Northern Rhodesia where the white population stood at about 74,000 in 1961. Africans in both territories claimed that a new oppressive white-dominated regime had been set up comparable to the apartheid system in South Africa. There was also tension between the government of Southern Rhodesia, led by the relatively liberal Garfield Todd, and the government of the Federation, headed by Roy Welensky, a tough former trade union leader and advocate of white domination, himself from Northern Rhodesia. The Labour Party had originally favoured the idea of a Central African Federation; Patrick Gordon Walker and James Griffiths, Dominions and Colonial Secretary respectively, had argued the case before African leaders at the Victoria Falls conference in September 1951. The main justification was the economic benefits thought to derive from federation, but there was also a curious belief that the Federation might act as a bulwark of some kind against South African aggression north of the river Zambezi. There was also the unspoken knowledge of the rich uranium deposits in the Rhodesias. Callaghan himself frequently went on record, even as late as 1961, to claim that the economic benefits of federation were indisputable, a case more often stated than proved.[35] But, like the Labour Party in general from 1953 onwards, he was adamant that any federation must founder unless it was acceptable to African opinion. By 1957 it was all too obvious that it was not, and that the entire future of the Federation was in jeopardy, soon after its brief life had begun.

Callaghan had no first-hand knowledge of the Central African territories. But he shortly was to acquire it in a dramatic fashion. In September 1957 he visited the Federation territories for the first time.[36] It was as part of a group of MPs, four Conservative and three Labour, invited by the Commonwealth Parliamentary Association, and headed by the Conservative Richard Wood, the son of Lord Halifax. It had a powerful impact upon his analysis of the situation. He went as still something of an enthusiast for the idea of federation as an instrument for economic advance. Indeed, the delegation's eventual report which he signed was to come down strongly in favour of it.[37] But he returned far more aware of the political and racial difficulties involved. He was to commit Labour, with a clarity never previously voiced by a party spokesman, to the concept of no independence for the Federation before black African majority rule. It was a tense period. African nationalism had been incensed by Lennox-Boyd's proposed Constitutional Amendment Act which, they believed, made transparent the naked political ambition of the white minority, especially in Southern Rhodesia, their main base. Conversely, Roy Welensky, a belligerent man as befitted a former heavyweight boxing champion, was anxious for rapid constitutional change to reinforce the authority of the federal government and was furiously opposed to any threats, by African leaders like Hastings Banda in Nyasaland and Kenneth Kaunda in

Northern Rhodesia, to break away. Callaghan's visit was expected to be delicate and difficult, and so it proved.

In some ways it was a pleasant enough visit. Callaghan told an audience at a joint meeting of the Royal African Society and the Royal Empire Society in London on 7 November, after his return, that he found Southern Rhodesia an exciting place. 'He felt exhilarated the whole time he was there, far better than ever in London.'[38] As ever, he enjoyed the sights and sounds of travel, the colourful jacaranda in Salisbury, the glorious mountains and lakes of Nyasaland. He was impressed by the signs of prosperity in Salisbury, many of whose inhabitants were recent British settlers who had emigrated through distaste for a Labour government after 1945. On a personal level, he got on well with the Conservative MPs in the group, notably Richard Wood, the son of Lord Halifax, whose *noblesse oblige* in coping with the loss of both legs (the result of a wartime tank accident) greatly impressed him.[39] He kept up a friendly relationship with another, the far-right imperial apologist Patrick Wall.

But the political issues that arose were on a quite different plane. He encountered the full impact of white supremacy, especially in Salisbury, and also of discrimination against African workers by the white-run trade unions, 'one of the most evil things I have come across'.[40] He was far from impressed by the Federation's political leaders, and he and Roy Welensky were at odds from the start. Welensky, he felt, was not only politically aggressive, but naive and even dishonest. He was astonished to learn that he had never met leading African politicians at all and was totally ignorant of their ideas. In a press conference towards the end of his tour, Callaghan caused a stir by stating that, if the people of the Federation were unable to produce a constitutional solution acceptable to African opinion, the British government would have to do so, though he coupled this with some criticism of the approach of certain ANC representatives who 'were following a very dangerous course'. He assured Welensky that 'our job is not to be pro- or anti-anybody but to be fair and carry out our obligations'.[41] Somewhat warily, he signed the delegation's report on the visit. This spelt out the economic potential of the Federation 'which could not seriously be challenged', but it also underlined the intense suspicions of the Africans, especially in Nyasaland, and the need for a careful reappraisal of the franchise rolls as they affected the black majority. Callaghan later wrote that he approved of the report since it committed Wood and his fellow Conservatives to an analysis of the endemic political weakness of the Federation. He told J. G. Lockhart, who had accompanied them in central Africa, that it showed that all members of the delegation 'feel that the territories are not ready for dominion status to be conceded in 1960'.[42] Welensky was told by one of his colleagues that 'the report is not nearly as vicious as we had been led to expect. . . . It is only when the report presumes to tender advice to us on how to run the country that one recognised the hand of Callaghan.'[43] But by this time Callaghan had long acquired demonic status amongst Rhodesian whites in general.

In addition to taking part in the activities of the delegation as a whole, Callaghan also chose to branch out on his own. To *Reynolds News*, a pro-Labour Sunday newspaper, he contributed four articles, two of them written while he was in Africa. These strongly criticized political, industrial, and social aspects of the situation in the federal territories. His second article on 22 September, 'Trouble Brewing: The Land of King Copper', condemned working conditions for African miners on the Copperbelt, their poor pay, and lack of skilled training; he anticipated serious industrial trouble. On 29 September he attacked the circumstances of black African women, especially the lack of educational and professional opportunities for young black girls. The final article on 6 October sharply criticized elements of racism in Salisbury, including in its hotels and other institutions. Race relations would have to be put right if the Federation was to have any future. He made it clear that, if a political solution agreeable to all were not found, a future Labour government would not hesitate to wind the Federation up. He had further discussions on this matter with Kenneth Kaunda whom he met soon after his return to London.

Welensky reacted with fury. He accused Callaghan publicly of a 'breach of hospitality' in writing his articles in *Reynolds News*, followed by another in a similar vein in the *Central African Examiner*.[44] Labour, he declared, was proving itself to be pro-African and anti-European, while Callaghan himself had been prejudiced against the Federation from the outset. He told Clyde Sanger, the liberal editor of the *Central African Examiner*, for whom Callaghan had written, that the Labour politician's comments were 'irresponsible' and one-sided. They totally ignored, for instance, the investment in the technical training for African workers, including in previously backward Nyasaland.[45]

Callaghan left a reply to a Labour colleague, James McColl, who defended his actions in *The Times*.[46] The entire affair received much international publicity which, Lord Home told Welensky, had embarrassed the British government. It left a deep vein of resentment in the mind and psychology of Roy Welensky. He had welcomed the delegation with the hope that it would advance his aspiration of full dominion status for the Federation territories. In fact, he concluded that the entire visit was little short of a disaster, however emollient the final report. He unburdened himself to F. S. Joelson, editor of *East Africa and Rhodesia*:

> Of course Richard Wood was no match for Callaghan, Wood is no doubt a very decent person with plenty of intelligence, but Callaghan is a very slick gentleman, much more of a politician, and of course stole the thunder here.... Callaghan told us in as many words that until there were African majorities in the two Northern Territorial legislatures we really had no right to ask for any improvements in the constitutional status. You can imagine how this has gone down in this part of the world.[47]

J. G. Lockhart, the secretary of the Commonwealth Parliamentary Association, wrote apologetically to Welensky to say that he was sorry to hear of the 'brush' with Callaghan. But he also admitted that the latter had asked for formal permission to write his newspaper articles and also to make a broadcast.[48]

In a speech in the House on 25 November, Callaghan opposed the government's Constitutional Amendment Bill for the Federation, although in studiously moderate terms. He continued to agree that the Federation had potential economic benefits, but the Federal Assembly, with a proposed membership of 59, was hopelessly biased against African voters, of whom only a minute fraction appeared on the electoral roll.[49] He opposed an abdication of authority by the British government in favour of a federal government under Welensky in whom Africans had no trust of any kind. For his part, Welensky was almost apoplectic. He was 'shocked', he told Joelson, by the way the Conservative government presented their case during what he called 'the Callaghan debate' and 'I let Home know it'.

> What in God's name has come over the Tories? They are always on the defensive, they agree to things and then are almost ashamed of them. I was livid about their attitude towards Callaghan's remarks in the Convention and I said so. Have they not learnt there is no means of buying off this element in the British Labour Party. Attlee couldn't handle them, much as he tried, and he was a decent, reasonable little man.[50]

In 1958–9 the situation in central Africa went from bad to worse. The patience of Africans in Nyasaland, in particular, reached breaking point. Callaghan, as in Kenya, urged Kenneth Kaunda and his ANC colleagues to keep to a moderate path. As they discussed the future conduct of elections and the future place of minority groups in the Assembly, Callaghan commented, 'I am very glad to see that you are still thinking in terms of all races in Northern Rhodesia. I am sure that this will be the way in which the most rapid political advance will be made.'[51] But the Federation was now being torn apart. Welensky remained an implacable federal premier, while the replacement of the moderate Garfield Todd by Sir Edgar Whitehead in Southern Rhodesia did not improve matters. The majority of black opinion in Northern Rhodesia, following Kaunda's lead, rejected the proposed new constitution for their country, while in Nyasaland, where there were hardly any whites at all, Hastings Banda voiced a universal rejection of the idea of federation. Callaghan had initially urged Hastings Banda back in October 1957 that his country could benefit economically from a federation. 'I would be very averse to its seceding from the Federation and degenerating into an economic and agricultural slum in the heart of Africa', he wrote somewhat bluntly.[52] The object, he wrote later, was to 'try and reconcile Nyasaland's aspirations for self-government with the economic benefits that are flowing from the concept of Federation'. He urged Banda's followers to avoid 'narrow ingrowing racialism'.[53]

But moderation was being left behind as black Africans rejected the idea of federation out of hand. There were strikes by African workers in both Rhodesias, and major trouble in Nyasaland, throughout 1958–9, with many disturbances, Twenty people were killed in one episode at Nkata Bay on 3 March 1959. A state of emergency was declared by the Governor, Sir Robert Armitage, and a conflagration similar to that of the Congo appeared at hand in the green hills of Nyasaland. A report written by the eminent British judge Lord Devlin and published in mid-1959, shortly before the British general election, roundly condemned colonial rule in Nyasaland. Devlin declared it was, 'no doubt temporarily, a police state'. He ridiculed the claims of there being 'a murder plot' and was severe on the Governor, Armitage. Many believed that he had fabricated the idea of a 'plot' at the behest of Welensky in order to suppress African anti-federal nationalism. Black Africa had scored a huge propaganda victory.

The situation in central Africa presented Callaghan with a rare challenge and he seized it with great effect. His speeches on central Africa and on Nyasaland were perhaps the most effective of his career to date, and won him plaudits across the political spectrum in Britain, as well as in black Africa. On 3 March 1959 he fiercely attacked the Colonial Secretary in the Commons in an adjournment debate on the situation in Nyasaland; Lennox-Boyd replied vigorously in kind, but was clearly wounded. Callaghan's speech drew warm congratulations from liberal-minded opinion. The journalist Honor Balfour wrote a warm letter of congratulations: 'your speech was both moving and angry—very fine.'[54] Callaghan detailed the emphatic opposition of Africans in Nyasaland to the idea of federation;

the federal government had made matters worse by foolishly deporting Hastings Banda to Southern Rhodesia. He would remain politically effective and enjoy the aura of martyrdom at the same time. Callaghan pointed out the absurdity of imposing an unacceptable political settlement in a country where there were 2.75 million blacks and a minuscule total of 7,500 whites. Welensky was again furiously angry. 'I am beginning to hate the British Labour Party', he told F. S. Joelson. 'It is, I think, a most serious state of affairs when statements are made, such as Griffiths' and Callaghan's, and ending in the one by Brockway accusing me of having to arrange a show-down with the African people before the Labour Party got back into office.'[55] He told Patrick MacDonagh that it would be 'almost impossible to have reasonable relationships between the two governments if a man like Callaghan were Secretary of State . . . Allegations such as those made by Bevan that we were Fascists and the remarks of Callaghan that the Europeans were frightened etc. have not gone down well and that's putting it mildly.'[56] He took small comfort from a criticism of Callaghan in *The Economist* which said that the latter's attack on Welensky, who was sitting in the gallery at the time, 'went a long way towards disqualifying him as a useful Colonial Secretary'.[57]

Unabashed, on 28 July in the Commons Callaghan moved the acceptance of the Devlin report.[58] A most thorough inquiry chaired by a most eminent judge, which had interrogated 455 individuals and a further 1,300 in groups, now resulted in the Attorney-General refusing to accept its verdict. He argued for Banda's moderation; he had been prepared to endorse Labour's proposals for parity between Africans and Europeans on the new executive council under the constitution. But Welensky, he claimed, had persuaded the British government to reject all the ANC's overtures. He called on the government to release or bring to trial all detainees, to begin constitutional talks, and to give a pledge to the people of Nyasaland that they would have the right to secede. Above all, Lennox-Boyd should go.

By the autumn, the atmosphere had changed if only because Macleod had succeeded Lennox-Boyd at the Colonial Office. The situation now was very serious. Nyasaland was barely governable. Northern Rhodesia was not much better with Kenneth Kaunda now in jail as an agitator. As a sign of a change of policy, a commission was now appointed under the chairmanship of the former Tory Cabinet minister Sir Walter Monckton, to investigate conditions there. The Commission would have twenty-six members, only five of whom would be Africans. It was expected that there would be Labour figures on it, and one, Monckton hoped, would be Callaghan. In fact, Callaghan was something of a personal friend of

Monckton, whom he had got to know when the latter was in 1951–5 a Minister of Labour remarkably benevolent towards the trade unions. Monckton had given him some hospitality, including a dinner invitation to meet the Duke and Duchess of Windsor which Callaghan had evidently enjoyed. However, Macmillan (reflecting Welensky's views) attached a stipulation that members of the Commission should be privy counsellors, which was evidently intended to exclude both Callaghan and Barbara Castle, who had also been thought of as a member. It seemed that the impasse had been resolved when Callaghan was offered a privy counsellorship himself. Welensky was totally opposed to this, but in any case Callaghan himself sternly turned down what he regarded as a cheap political stratagem, intended to separate him from front-bench colleagues. To Gaitskell (who may not have fully grasped a point such as this), he compared it to a Welsh rugby forward being offered a cap by England. Gaitskell went along with this even though he later confided that he privately regretted the decision and would have preferred Callaghan to be on the council. Labour then urged that it would participate if the Commission's terms of reference include the right of a territory to secede, but Macmillan refused. No Labour representatives served under Monckton.

Despite this, after the Commission conducted its inquiries, between February and October 1960, it was unanimous in concluding that African hostility towards Federation was overwhelming. To the fury of Welensky and almost all whites it openly raised the possibility of secession. Clearly, this unhappy experiment in political innovation seemed increasingly destined to fail, with Welensky a beleaguered figure. The Monckton Commission's report called for a federal assembly of sixty seats divided equally between Europeans and Africans, with a common roll of electors. There should be African majorities in the legislatures of both Northern Rhodesia and Nyasaland, and political prisoners must be released. Some powers should be transferred from the federal to the territorial governments. The Commission made a final attempt to inject new life into the Federation which it still approved as a concept. But it also noted 'the almost pathological dislike' of it amongst Africans which surely doomed it to fail. In the debate on the Address on 3 November 1960 Callaghan warmly praised the Monckton Commission for, in effect, endorsing Labour's views on central Africa.[59] He still believed that, theoretically, the Federation could be made to work—but only if the racial policies of Southern Rhodesia were radically amended, if an African majority in the Federal Assembly were accepted, if federal powers were redistributed to the territories, and if there were an agreed right to secede. Together or singly, however, these were virtually unattainable objectives. In the mean time, African leaders like Joshua Nkomo in Southern Rhodesia should be released from prison.

In debates in 1961 Callaghan condemned the continuing racial discrimination in southern Africa. In a rare flight of sentiment, he quoted remarks at the time of the Union of South Africa Bill back in 1909 by the 'revered' Keir Hardie.[60] His final significant Commons speech on central Africa came on 19 October 1961 when he was confronted now with the genial presence of Reginald Maudling who had succeeded Macleod at the Colonial Office. Macleod, despite the famous accusation by Lord Salisbury, was in reality 'not clever enough', declared Callaghan, because he had broken pledges given at the time of the Monckton Commission.[61] In fact, Maudling's arrival heralded the final phase of the increasingly ghostly life of the Central African Federation. Welensky scathingly (but not incorrectly) described him in his memoirs as 'completely ignorant about Africa, not aggressively opinionated, but neither strong enough nor independent enough to make any stand against the wishes of the majority of his senior colleagues'.[62] Certainly never at any stage of his career did Maudling look like a fighter against the odds.

In July 1962 the senior figure of R. A. Butler, a leading Foreign Office exponent of appeasement at the time of Munich, was appointed with special responsibility for central African affairs. In effect he was negotiating another surrender although this time a far more defensible one. It was a vital task but one which he combined with many other key responsibilities including that of deputy prime minister. Nyasaland's secession from the Federation was already inevitable. By the end of March 1963, Northern Rhodesia, it was agreed, should also secede. That left Southern Rhodesia, a self-governing territory since the 1920s, in an anomalous position all its own, to plague British governments for almost another twenty years. The spectral Federation ceased to exist from 1 January 1964. Butler had done his work with rare dispatch indeed. Without doubt, its disappearance, however, immensely improved relations between Britain and black African opinion. Figures like Kaunda and Nyerere were to be pillars of the Commonwealth for years to come.

Callaghan himself could have claimed to have played a major role in this process. He had successfully combined constructive policies for central African development with a mordant critique of government policies. He had made Labour the effective voice of colonial freedom in Africa. There was, however, one curious by-product of his involvement with the troubles of the Central African Federation. In spite of the fierce arguments of 1957–9, his personal relations with Roy Welensky remained quite cordial; he was, after all, a working-class leader in his way. Callaghan wrote to him with some warmth in November 1961, saying that they would always be glad to see Welensky at the Labour Party Colonial Group. 'I shall be giving up Colonies in a few days time (not officially announced yet) & so our paths will not cross so much but I shall always be glad to see you when you are in London.'[63]

Despite everything, Welensky retained an emotional attachment to Britain and became an isolated figure when Ian Smith led the Southern Rhodesians into a unilateral independence from Britain in 1965. His stance had always been one of interracial 'partnership', albeit under white leadership for any foreseeable future, as opposed to the white supremacists of the regime in South Africa. His United Federal Party had included some African members. In the early 1970s, an ageing man who had remarried after the death of his first wife and had young children, he found himself in financial difficulties. He moved to Britain and settled in the West Country. He was able to draw on his friendship with Callaghan who helped arrange a pension for him via the Foreign Office. As a retired man, Welensky finally settled down in Dorset. Callaghan consulted him frequently on aspects of the Rhodesian problem in 1976–7, especially over the Owen–Vance initiative when Callaghan became Prime Minister. The two old adversaries exchanged occasional greetings and Christmas cards. It was a rare episode of harmony in the tense affairs of southern Africa. Lord Home had shrewdly described Callaghan to Welensky on 4 February 1958 as 'a bouncy young customer' who might well become Welensky's friend and so it proved.[64]

Throughout all these controversies, Callaghan built up a strong, authoritative position as Labour's spokesman on colonial and Commonwealth matters. His performance won him strong support right across the party spectrum, including from many in the Movement for Colonial Freedom. In party conference, his speeches on colonial policy were always hailed as oratorical and dialectical triumphs. However, for him and his party, this was a rare area of harmony. In the later 1950s, Labour became embroiled in one of the most vicious periods of internecine warfare in its history. Bevanism was now a thing of the past, and Bevan himself worked well enough with Gaitskell as shadow foreign affairs spokesman from 1957 onwards. But the scars of the Bevanite revolt remained and manifested themselves in a new and damaging form in the emergence of the Campaign for Nuclear Disarmament in 1958. Originally an extra-parliamentary movement of conscience and dissent led by intellectuals such as Bertrand Russell, Canon John Collins, and the historian A. J. P. Taylor, its call for Britain unilaterally to abandon the production or use of nuclear weapons soon found echoes in the Labour Party, including amongst many of them not usually associated with the left. The main attack focused on Gaitskell's own strong attachment to NATO and the nuclear alliance, even though Gaitskell's stand was now endorsed by none other than Nye Bevan who condemned CND as irrational and 'an emotional spasm'. Callaghan was not centrally involved in these arguments. On the other hand, he was now a major figure at all levels, having been elected to the constituency section of the National Executive in 1957. He came in seventh with 565,000 votes, the only non-Bevanite or ex-Bevanite elected, coming in behind Greenwood, Wilson, Barbara Castle, Driberg, Mikardo, and Crossman. Throughout the early months of 1959, as a strong defender of the western alliance and an opponent of what he saw as essentially neutralism or pacifism or both, Callaghan emerged as one of the embattled Gaitskell's most vehement defenders.

At this time, with Labour still in some disarray on its attitude to defence matters, there came the general election of October 1959. The party fought a vigorous and effective campaign under Gaitskell's leadership and hopes were high, even though the current sense of affluence and well-being stacked the odds in favour of Macmillan's government staying in power. Callaghan was a major figure at every level, speeches, broadcasts, press conferences, in October 1959 and did well in all of them. He was sanguine about the result, indeed unduly so. But he faced many problems and this time Cardiff South-East was one of them. His opponent again was Michael Roberts, the Welsh schoolmaster who had reduced his majority to below 3,300 in 1955. It required a swing of 3.5 per cent for the Tories to win, and the result could not be taken for granted. The local Conservatives, under the chairmanship of G. V. Wynne-Jones, a noted radio rugby commentator, had sharpened up their organization, and the mood in the country was confident.

Callaghan spoke out strongly on mainly local issues such as leasehold housing (a major problem in south Wales and especially in Cardiff for historic reasons relating to the Bute estate), old-age pensions, and the repeal of the 1957 Rent Act.[65] He spoke at several public meetings, where Michael Roberts preferred the doorstep approach. One worrying phenomenon of which Callaghan was aware was the 4,000 new voters on the Llanrumney housing estate, potential Labour supporters in the main, but many of them not registered. In the event, it was a close-run thing, the closest of

Callaghan's career. His majority slumped to three figures only, a margin of 868 votes or just 1.6 per cent. Cardiff South-East had become a marginal; clearly a major effort had been put in to unseat Callaghan. It is noticeable that in neighbouring Cardiff West, a somewhat similar constituency, George Thomas's majority (3,132) largely held up.

Undeterred by this narrow escape (which he later attributed to the non-registration of Labour voters in Llanrumney), Callaghan launched himself vigorously into the controversies that now engulfed Labour after its heavy election defeat. This, after all, was the third in a row, and political analysts like Mark Abrams and Robert McKenzie were to speculate whether Labour could ever win again. Gaitskell's first response to the defeat was a disastrous one, of which Callaghan much disapproved, namely to suggest that Labour should delete from its constitution the famous Clause 4 committing the party to nationalization of the means of production, distribution, and exchange. In fact, the bulk of party opinion was opposed to Gaitskell's démarche which appeared to stem from a post-election article by Douglas Jay, and he had to withdraw. A skilful oratorical performance by the dying Aneurin Bevan, which made metaphorical use of Euclidian geometry, saved Gaitskell from humiliation at the post-election party conference.

The civil war over unilateralism, however, reached new levels of fury. In the past, Callaghan had been accused of being a trimmer, and a man with no real convictions. In 1960, the psephologist David Butler (a Nuffield colleague) had asked Hugh Dalton, 'Has he got a resignation inside him?', perhaps an academic question in more senses than one.[66] But in defending Gaitskell and the party leadership against the onslaughts of CND and its supporters, Callaghan was staunch and unequivocal. Indeed, George Brown, himself the most belligerent champion of the western defence alliance, thought at times that Callaghan was going too far. At the party conference at Scarborough in October 1960, one of the most bitter even in Labour's fratricidal history, Gaitskell was defeated on the conference vote. He vowed, in a famous flight of oratory, to 'fight, fight and fight again to save the party we love'.

Callaghan was in deep depression at this time. Rather oddly, he cheered himself up with another visit to Czechoslovakia. Tony Wedgwood Benn reported Audrey Callaghan as saying that he returned feeling 'convinced that socialism can work'.[67] Soon after this, Callaghan wrote gloomily to Guy Clutton-Brock, a noted Rhodesian liberal, 'I am afraid our preoccupation with defence matters is preventing us from spending all the time we might on other issues.'[68] As in the Bevanite period, he tried to mend fences. Before the 1959 election, he had appealed to Frank Cousins of the Transport Workers, a powerful opponent of racialism, not to allow the debates on the hydrogen bomb to prevent the election of a Labour government for which the people of black Africa craved. 'If the Tories are returned, they will do a carve up on South African lines with Welensky. I know the main lines that such an agreement (or more realistically such a betrayal) would take. . . . Frank, we can't let them down! We should lose the whole continent of Africa to racialism of a vicious character on both sides. The H Bomb is not the only thing that matters!'[69] But by the end of 1960 such appeals had clearly failed.

On the NEC and in the parliamentary party, Callaghan led the call for the PLP to dissociate itself entirely from what he regarded as the calamitous view of the conference. He clashed with colleagues like Tony Greenwood who believed that Britain's membership of the North Atlantic alliance should be 'conditional'.[70] He was scathing about the endorsement of unilateralism voiced by Crossman, Michael Foot, and Barbara Castle, and derided Wilson for his opportunism in venturing to oppose Gaitskell in the election of party leader. In one notable meeting in Cardiff in March 1961 Callaghan turned on Crossman, who was present, with a rare ferocity, accusing his parliamentary colleague, among other things, of lies and dishonesty. Even the Gaitskellites were taken aback. Crossman, a ferocious combatant himself, noted in his diary, 'Inside myself I was shaken because Callaghan knows how to lambast and assault and create a foul impression of his opponent.'[71] Frank Cousins was another of Callaghan's adversaries. In an article in *Reynolds News*, 'Labour and the Bomb' in September 1960, Callaghan took on the unilateralists head on, although that did not prevent him and Cousins, fellow trade unionists, from having a reasonably amicable personal relationship. Callaghan, for instance, sympathized with Cousins when he was the target of a vicious newspaper attack by Woodrow Wyatt. 'What have we done to deserve people like this?', Callaghan asked.[72]

By early 1961, however, CND had passed its high tide. It was suffering from internal divisions over strategy between a parliamentary wing and the direct action supporters of the Committee of One Hundred. In reaction to the Scarborough conference decisions, a grass-roots movement was formed by centre-right followers of Gaitskell headed by William Rodgers and Bernard Donoughue, to support the leader and his stand against unilateralism. It adopted the name Campaign for Democratic Socialism, and attracted the support of right-wing figures such as Jenkins, Crosland, Jay, and Gordon Walker. Callaghan was not directly associated with this body, preferring his habitual 'Keep Calm' tactics of refusing to be part of a faction. Even so, in the 1962 NEC elections he was described as 'outstanding among existing members' on the CDS slate.[73] The result was that constituency parties and major unions were recaptured in many instances by CDS and supporters of the leadership. In the 1961 party conference Gaitskell comfortably succeeded in reversing the decision of the previous year and getting Labour again committed to NATO and the nuclear deterrent. Callaghan was a victim of the political fallout. He temporarily lost his place on the NEC in 1962, a result of a determined attempt amongst some unions and constituency parties to punish him for his stand on nuclear weapons. Gaitskell warmly sympathized with him. 'It makes one despair—and it makes one very angry at the same time.'[74] Callaghan's replacement was Anthony Wedgwood Benn towards whom he appears to have felt no resentment.

But more important, without doubt, was his far closer ties with Gaitskell as a result. Around this time, Gaitskell (who addressed him habitually as 'My dear James' but never 'Jim') wrote, 'You were splendid tonight as you have been through all these trying weeks—brave and dignified and gay—when it wasn't at all easy. Such things count among friends—and more widely. Bless you. Hugh.'[75] Shortly after the party conference, in November 1961, Gaitskell moved the unreliable Wilson from being shadow Treasury spokesman which he had been since 1955 to foreign affairs, where he was to prove less at ease. In his place, Callaghan became shadow Treasury spokesman. Roy Welensky had been told of this happening in a report from the Labour Party conference at Blackpool in October 1961. 'Mr. Callaghan seems to be sliding out of dealing with Colonial Affairs. He spoke only on economic matters and I was told refused to have anything to do with the lobbying efforts of James Johnson on behalf of the Africans.'[76] After years of contention, Callaghan was one of Labour's big three at last.

In his years as shadow colonial spokesman, Callaghan had turned himself into a front-ranking political figure. His new stature across the party was indisputable and there were those who even felt him to be a possible coming leader. He did indeed stand for the party deputy leadership in October 1960, being nominated by George Thomson, Arthur Skeffington, and Harold Finch, not the strongest trio of supporters perhaps. Callaghan's candidature was based on 'the traditional Labour Party policy of collective security and multilateral disarmament' and support for Gaitskell's leadership.[77] As things turned out, he polled only 55 as against 118 for George Brown of the right and 73 for Fred Lee of the left; Brown easily defeated Lee 146 to 83 on the second ballot. Callaghan afterwards received letters of sympathy from supporters such as Lord Pakenham, Arthur Skeffington, and Tony Crosland who hailed him as 'the clear and unchallenged No. 3 in the Party'.[78] However, he lacked strong support from the trade union MPs as well as from the party left. Contrary to his situation when he was elected party leader in 1976, his fellow Welsh MPs, headed by Jim Griffiths, tended to prefer George Brown. Hugh Dalton, who had somewhat disloyally expressed private doubts about Callaghan to David Butler, urged his protégé to cheer up. He was a leading figure in the shadow Cabinet and the NEC, apart from his 'political Private Empire in Africa'. He was a high-ranking member of the new younger leadership of the party. 'Out with the TWERPS and TIDDLIES!' Dalton cogently concluded.[79]

Of Callaghan's progress within the party over the period 1957–61 there could be no doubt. To become shadow Chancellor of the Exchequer was a marked sign of new power and prestige. But it went much further than that. In a series of impressive performances in parliament or elsewhere, on domestic and Commonwealth platforms, Callaghan had emerged as a major figure, addressing the central themes of the ending of empire with clarity and confidence. As effectively as Macmillan he had detected the winds of change, and probably with more direct impact on third-world opinion. He had broken out of the mould of being a purely local figure concerned with domestic issues such as transport or fuel and power, and could claim a genuinely international horizon. He had elaborated important new themes on colonial development and their relationship to the global economy, although in the late 1950s it was the constitutional and political aspects of decolonization that largely preoccupied him. He had constructive and important things to say on Cyprus and Malta, Kenya and Tanzania, and especially on central Africa. His critique of the Federation as well as the passion of his attack on affairs in Nyasaland contributed in important ways to public debate, and helped ensure that British decolonization would remain a relatively peaceful process by comparison with what had taken place in Algeria under the French, Indonesia under the Dutch, and, crucially at this period, the Congo after the Belgians had departed. More than with most shadow spokesmen, his views were taken very seriously by the government. He always strove to be constructive and to find ways of reconciling legitimate African demands with the equally legitimate fears of white settler minorities, and to urge nationalist movements of liberation to follow a moderate, inclusive path and to avoid tribal parochialism.

His views inevitably had their limitations. He did not free himself from the prevailing orthodoxy. Like moderate Tories such as Macleod (and indeed the future colonial leaders themselves), he retained a belief that the newly independent colonies would look essentially to Britain for their markets, sources of aid, political and constitutional models, and strategic protection. It was for this reason that he attacked policies too sympathetic to white settler interests which might delay or frustrate this potentially exciting new relationship between Britain and the newly emergent 'developing world'. This view, broadly held by Gaitskell and Labour's front bench as a whole, was in time to be proved far too optimistic. Callaghan was also too uncritical in endorsing the economic arguments on behalf of a federation in central Africa. In later life he would also criticize himself and contemporaries for being unduly wedded to British models of parliamentary constitutionalism, but in the circumstances of the time he could hardly be criticized for holding to what was the conventional wisdom, among African as well as European observers. His speeches on a transfer of power did make a serious attempt to reconcile adult manhood suffrage in colonial territories with the old tribal structure. His attack on the atrocities in Hola Camp was in the grand tradition of critics of empire from Lloyd George and Keir Hardie onwards. It notably added to Labour's reputation in an area where it was traditionally weak or ill-informed. Finally, in the important new links he built up with colonial leaders such as Mboya, Kaunda, Nyerere, Nkomo, and Lee Kuan Yew, representative of the new generation of African and Asian leaders, he added significantly to his political stature. It was to give him a new intellectual range as Foreign Secretary and Prime Minister, to be deployed for the advantage of American leaders such as Kissinger or Jimmy Carter later on. It also provided him with a network of crucial allies across the world which few other British figures could claim. He had a genuine international recognition. At the age of 49 Callaghan was no longer a coming man, but a symbol of the future at work.

1. See Gupta, *Imperialism and the British Labour Movement, 1914–1964*, for this important body.

2. Ibid., 259–64.

3. Stephen Howe, *Anticolonialism in British Politics* (Oxford, 1993), 229.

4. Callaghan's diary of Commonwealth visit, Jan.–Feb. 1959 (Callaghan Papers, box 1A).

5. Robert Shepherd, *Iain Macleod* (London, 1994), 161.

6. Barbara Castle, *Fighting All the Way* (London, 1994), 303–4.

7. Callaghan to Balogh, 23 July 1958 (Callaghan Papers, box 4).

8. Howe, *Anticolonialism*, 231–67.

9. *Tony Benn, Years of Hope: Diaries, Papers and Letters, 1940–1962*, ed. Ruth Winstone (London, 1994), 216 (2 Dec. 1956). 'This was very much appreciated', Benn noted.

10. Fenner Brockway to Callaghan, 7 Apr. 1958 (Callaghan Papers, box 4).

11. Callaghan to Joe Bishop, Cardiff City Labour Party, 3 Apr. 1958 (ibid.).

12. *African Affairs* (Jan. 1958), 28.

13. 'Westminster Commentary', *Evening News*, 20 Mar. 1959.

14. Report of visit in Callaghan Papers, box 4; personal diary, box 1A.

15. Personal diary (ibid.).

16. Interview with His Excellency Lee Kuan Yew, Istana Negara, Singapore, 21 Sept. 1993. See the excellent volume, Ernest C. T. Chew and Edwin Lee (eds.), *A History of Singapore* (Oxford, 1991), 132–49.

17. Notes of conversation of Lord Perth with Callaghan, 17 July 1958 (PRO, CO 926/660).

18. Note in Callaghan Papers, box 4.

19. Lord Perth to Lennox-Boyd, 2 July 1958; Perth to Lord Home, 28 July 1958 (CO 926/660).

20. Callaghan to Dom Mintoff, 18 Sept., 6 Dec. 1961 (Callaghan Papers, box 4).

21. Callaghan to Watson, 18 Aug. 1961. Also cf. Callaghan to Gaitskell, 23 June 1961 (of Mintoff), 'Negotiating with him is such a fruitless and frustrating exercise' (ibid.).

22. *Parl. Deb.*, 5th ser., vol. 565, 217–34.

23. Callaghan to Desmond Young, 9 June 1960 (Callaghan Papers, box 4).

24. Callaghan to Lennox-Boyd, 8 Dec. 1956; Lennox-Boyd to Callaghan, 3 July 1957 (ibid.).

25. Callaghan to John Hatch, 7 Oct. 1958 (ibid.).

26. Materials in Callaghan Papers, ibid.

27. Callaghan note of meeting with Lennox-Boyd and Sir Evelyn Baring, 11 Dec. 1957; Callaghan to Tom Mboya, 18 Dec. 1957 (ibid.).

28. Callaghan to Abu Mayanja, 27 Mar. 1958 (ibid.).

29. Callaghan to Mboya, 28 May 1959 (ibid.).

30. Callaghan to Mboya, 22 July 1959 (ibid.).

31. Callaghan to George Brown, 5 July 1961 (ibid.).

32. *Parl. Deb.*, 5th ser., vol. 607, 352–61. For helpful background, see Richard Lamb, *The Macmillan Years, 1957–1963: The Emerging Truth* (London, 1995), esp. 221 ff.

33. e.g. Collie Knox in *Morning Telegraph* (New York), 1 Aug. 1959 (Bodleian, Boyd of Merton Papers, Ms.Eng.c. 3467).

34. For an excellent account of these matters, see Robert Blake, *A History of Rhodesia* (London, 1977), 295 ff. Also helpful are Donald C. Mulford, *Zambia: The Politics of Independence* (Oxford, 1967) and Ritchie Ovendale, 'Macmillan and the Wind of Change in Africa, 1957–1960', *Historical Journal*, 38/2 (1995), 455–77.

35. e.g. Callaghan to T. D. T. Banda, Blantyre, 10 Dec. 1957 (Callaghan Papers, box 4).

36. Record in Callaghan Papers, box 4.

37. Report of a Commonwealth Parliamentary Association visit to the Federation of Rhodesia and Nyasaland, Sept. 1957 (draft in Welensky Papers, Rhodes House Library, Oxford, 194/5).

38. *African Affairs* (Jan. 1958).

39 *Time and Chance*, 137–8.

40 Report of Callaghan's speech to the Bristol Fabian Society, *Western Daily Press*, 13 Jan. 1958.

41. Callaghan to Welensky, 26 Sept. 1957 (Welensky Papers, 596/5, fo. 5).

42. Callaghan to J. G. Lockhart, 18 Oct. 1957; Callaghan to Clyde Sanger, 24 Oct. 1957 (Callaghan Papers, box 4).

43. Report by John Ross for Welensky, 17 Dec. 1957 (Welensky Papers, 194/5).

44. *Reynolds News*, 8, 22, 29 Sept., 6 Oct. 1957; *Central African Examiner*, 28 Sept. 1957. Also *The Welensky Papers*, ed. J. R. T. Wood (Durban, 1983), 556–68.

45. Welensky to Clyde Sanger, 15 Nov. 1957 (Welensky Papers, 596/5, fos. 14–15).

46. *The Times*, 15, 16, 22 Nov. 1957.

47. Welensky to F. S. Joelson, 23 Oct. 1957 (ibid. 628/5, fo. 56).

48. J. G. Lockhart to Welensky, 19 Nov. 1957 (ibid 596/5, fo. 27).

49. *Parl. Deb.*, 5th ser., vol. 578, 808–20 (25 Nov. 1957).

50. Welensky to F. S. Joelson, 31 Dec. 1957 (Welensky Papers, 628/5, fo. 60).

51. Callaghan to Kenneth Kaunda, 13 Feb. 1958 (Callaghan Papers, box 4).

52. Callaghan to Hastings Banda, 24 Oct. 1957 (ibid.).

53. Callaghan to Hastings Banda, 10 Dec. 1957 (ibid.).

54. *Parl. Deb.*, 5th ser., vol. 601, 279–87 (3 Mar. 1959); Honor Balfour to Callaghan, n.d. (Callaghan Papers, box 4).

55. Welensky to Joelson, 25 Mar. 1959 (Welensky Papers, 628/5, fo. 95).

56. Welensky to MacDonagh, 23 Mar. 1959 (ibid. 640/2, fo. 86).

57. Materials on CPA delegation (ibid. 596/5, fo. 30).

58. *Parl. Deb.*, 5th ser., vol. 610, 335–53 (28 July 1959).

59. Ibid., vol. 629, 378–98 (3 Nov. 1960).

60. Ibid., vol. 642, 1808 (22 June 1961).

61. Ibid., vol. 646, 354–73 (19 Oct. 1961).

62. Roy Welensky, *Welensky's 4,000 Days* (London, 1964), 315.

63. Callaghan to Welensky, 29 Nov. 1961 (Welensky Papers, 596/5, fo. 46), 'Personal'.

64. *The Welensky Papers*, 572.

65. *Western Mail*, 7 Oct. 1959.

66. Dalton, *Political Diary*, 700 (13 July 1960).

67. *Benn, Years of Hope*, 351 (21 Oct. 1960).

68. Callaghan to Guy Clutton-Brock, 24 Oct. 1960 (Callaghan Papers, box 4).

69. Callaghan to Frank Cousins, 2 July 1959 (University of Warwick Modern Records Centre, Cousins Papers).

70. Greenwood to Callaghan, 2 Jan. 1961 (Callaghan Papers, box 31).

71. Crossman, *Backbench Diaries*, 936.

72. Frank Cousins to Callaghan, 29 Sept. 1960 (Callaghan Papers, box 1A); Callaghan to Cousins, 11 June 1960; Cousins to Callaghan, 16 June 1960 (Cousins Papers).

73. Brian Brivati, *Hugh Gaitskell* (London, 1996), 393.

74. Gaitskell to Callaghan, 2 Oct. 1962 (Callaghan Papers, box 31).

75. Gaitskell to Callaghan, n.d. [1960] (ibid., box 1A).

76. W. F. Nicholas to Welensky, 6 Oct. 1961 (Welensky Papers, 522/7, fo. 22).

77. Materials in Callaghan Papers, box 1A.

78. Tony Crosland to Callaghan, 'Friday' [1960] (ibid.).

79. Dalton to Callaghan, n.d. [1960] (ibid.).

9

HUGH TO HAROLD

JAMES CALLAGHAN became shadow Chancellor in November 1961 not because he was an economist but because he was a major politician. He had, of course, a strong professional background in the minutiae of taxation from his days in the Inland Revenue. He had often spoken in budget debates and had written on the need for taxation reform of a redistributive kind to promote equality. Hugh Dalton had brought him on to the XYZ group. But, unlike his predecessors as Labour spokesman on finance, Gaitskell and Wilson, both Oxford-trained economics dons, Callaghan had no known expertise in economic theory or policy-making. Earlier in his career, he had on more than one occasion confessed, somewhat ruefully, that he was not truly an economist. He had not been particularly involved in party debates on economic policy in the 1950s, in which Gaitskell, Jay, Crosland, and Jenkins had been major participants. Given his background in colonial affairs and his long-term interest in the Far East and other areas, the foreign affairs portfolio might have seemed a more natural one for him. Anthony Wedgwood Benn had noted in his diary in 1960 that Callaghan perhaps had his eye on the position of shadow foreign minister. 'The colonies are shrinking and he doesn't want to shrink with them!', Wedgwood Benn shrewdly remarked.[1]

The reason for Callaghan's significant promotion really lay in relations between Gaitskell and Harold Wilson. The latter had taken a somewhat different stance on Labour's view of unilateral nuclear disarmament and had actually challenged Gaitskell for the party leadership in November 1960 (being defeated 166 to 81). After this, Gaitskell determined to move Wilson from his economics portfolio and eventually transferred him sideways to the shadow foreign affairs position. Callaghan, a staunch defender of Gaitskell during the party wrangles over unilateralism (indeed, stauncher than almost anybody, including George Brown) and a proven success on the front bench, was a logical replacement. On this political basis, then, Callaghan took an important step forward. His move was greeted with some scepticism by financial journalists and political commentators, and indeed he himself appeared for a time to lack the panache and self-confidence that he had shown in every previous role. But he gradually asserted himself here too. Nor was his promotion that improbable or risky. After all, the twentieth century has several examples of essentially political chancellors who have been effective from Lloyd George to Kenneth Clarke, as well as some who have not (Winston Churchill or John Simon for instance). There seemed a real possibility that a skilled, articulate figure like Callaghan might also come across positively.

In any case, the opportunities for any shadow chancellor at the start of 1962 were extremely promising. It was becoming clear that the heady growth of affluence and economic advance throughout the 1950s, especially since the end of the Korean War in 1953, was coming to an end. The balance of payments, for many years in surplus, was running into deficit. Britain's fortunate position in improved terms of trade, through a sharp fall in the price of imported raw materials and the opportunities for exports for cars and other products in the Commonwealth and North American markets, was less and less apparent. Potentially dangerous overseas rivals in world markets, Germany and France in Europe, Japan and other Pacific Rim nations in the Far East, previously recovering from the shattering impact of wartime defeat or occupation, were now rapidly overtaking Britain as major-league economic performers.

Keynesianism was still the prevailing orthodoxy on both sides of the political divide—a rare quasi-monetarist dissenter like Peter Thorneycroft in January 1958 had to resign as Chancellor, along with his junior ministers Enoch Powell and Nigel Birch, when the Cabinet resisted cuts of around £150m. in public expenditure. But, equally, many commentators such as Sam Brittan and the youthful Peter Jay, fresh at the Treasury from Oxford, suspected that Keynesianism had already passed its high noon and that a very different international economic and monetary order was beginning to undermine its ascendancy. For Britain, the warning signs were plentiful. In 1950, a quarter of the world's trade in manufactures came from British factories; by 1964, the figure had dropped to 14 per cent. Britain's share of manufacturing exports from the major eleven manufacturing countries was to decline from 20 per cent of the total in 1954 to less than 14 per cent ten years later. Its share of world exports fell from 26.2 per cent in 1953 to 20.6 per cent in 1961. Throughout the 1950s, Britain's growth rate was a mere 58 per cent of the OECD average. Investment was sluggish, product innovation poor, much research and development wasted.

The Germans, French, and Japanese moved confidently into the newer consumer markets. Already, for example, there were signs of a British car industry in some difficulties, while domestic car-owners turned increasingly to the products of Volkswagen, Renault, and Fiat. Labour politicians in 1962–4 would present before the voters tables of exports, production, productivity, capital investment, and much else besides. They all showed Britain shooting down the league like some consistently unsuccessful football team, falling even behind traditionally comic, and allegedly impractical, peoples such as the Italians.

All around were the abiding symbols of 1950s consumer affluence—the expanding house-ownership on cheap mortgages; the glossy building society offices in city centres often replacing cherished older institutions like family grocery stores and newsagents; the massive sale of cars, television sets, and washing machines; the new 'swinging' opportunities for the young with their Vespa scooters, 'bubble cars', 'trendy' new fashions, and cheap holidays on the Costa Brava or Majorca. In 1959 Mary Quant first took root in the King's Road, while the boom years of Carnaby Street were about to begin. Yet, despite all this, the British no longer were convinced that they had never had it so good. From 1961 onwards, the polls revealed that most British people now expressed pessimism about their own and their country's prospects. There was a sharp downturn of economic activity and rising unemployment in 1959–60 led to new government pump-priming measures in the 'regions'. The worst balance of payments crisis since 1950 led to the departure of Derick Heathcoat Amory from the Treasury with a somewhat dented reputation.

Selwyn Lloyd, his successor as Chancellor, moved to that office still bearing the scars of having been Foreign Secretary during the débâcle of Suez in 1956. His subsequent policy was far more disinflationary than the British had been accustomed to since the time of Sir Stafford Cripps in the years of post-war austerity. Lloyd's first budget in April 1961 epitomized the so-called 'stop-go' economics of which the Tory government was accused in Macmillan's last phase. It gave the Treasury 'regulator' powers to raise duties and taxes. Even so, the terms of trade continued to deteriorate and the gold and foreign exchange reserves steadily declined. In July 1961 Lloyd went further, in an attempt to stem domestic inflation. His so-called 'pay pause' stopped pay increases for public sector workers across a wide range. He also raised bank rate to 7 per cent along with a severe credit squeeze. Among other things, the manifest crudity and alleged unfairness of the 'pay pause' aroused intense opposition to the government from highly articulate middle-class professional groups usually sympathetic to the Conservative cause—civil servants, teachers and lecturers, hospital consultants. A wide range of dangerous critics were aroused, while the white-collar unions began spates of industrial action.

When Callaghan began serious operations as shadow Treasury spokesman at the start of 1962, the reputation of the government and of Selwyn Lloyd in particular continued to slump. While domestic inflation was held back to some degree, the comparative decline in exports continued. Lloyd was identified with economic stagnation, and the voters were unhappy. The government suffered a humiliating shock in March 1962 when they lost the safe suburban seat of Orpington to the Liberals, a protest by middle-class, mortgage-holding commuters. The running down of commuter rail services, and the closure of many lines altogether under the Beeching 'axe', was an especial source of grievance. The terrifying spectre of 'Orpington Man' entered the political vocabulary or perhaps demonology. Lloyd, in fact, was attempting something much more positive than merely a policy of disinflation: an attempt at hands-on economic direction. He created the National Economic Development Council, with Sir Robert Shone as director-general and Sir Donald MacDougall as economic director, to set targets for production and investment in a distinctly interventionist way. 'Neddy' was soon followed by 'Nicky' (National Incomes Commission), which purported to relate wage claims to economic growth. Much of this kind of *dirigisme* was congenial to Labour and to Keynesians generally. Indeed, the planning and incomes policies of Selwyn Lloyd's period—the work of an early Keynesian who had been active in Liberal Party summer schools in the later 1920s—were ones with which Callaghan as Chancellor was to be largely associated. But they were imposed on an economy already showing signs of endemic decay, and a state machine unable to cope with the dynamics of development. Apart from the comparative aspects of decline in relation to trading competitors, there was the broader context of the slow disintegration of the post-war system of fixed exchange rates and currency movements agreed in 1944 at Bretton Woods. This meant a massive potential threat to the sterling area, to sterling's role as a world reserve currency, and to the value of the pound, devalued in 1949 yet still in uncertain health. The world in which, politically, Callaghan had grown up was starting to disappear.

Selwyn Lloyd's budget of 1962 was fiercely criticized by Labour and by Callaghan for being almost totally negative and failing to address itself to the problem of growth. Production and exports continued to stagnate. Coal pits were being closed, ironically enough under the aegis of a former

Labour Cabinet member, Alfred Robens. It was no great surprise when Lloyd was removed from the Treasury in favour of Reginald Maudling in July 1962. What caused shock was that Lloyd's departure was part of a massive purge on 13 July, 'the night of the long knives', when Macmillan removed a third of his Cabinet in what looked like a mood of panic. Maudling was a far more economically literate Chancellor than Lloyd but he inherited a difficult legacy. The very severe winter of 1962–3, which saw many closures and severe unemployment of a kind not known since the 1930s for a time, tested him to the full and Maudling was said to be too slow to act, for instance in using the Treasury's regulator. In 1963–4, as will be seen, he embarked on a considerable reversal of policy, a 'dash for growth' which led to a massive surge in exports and production, and a sharp fall in unemployment. But this was achieved at the cost of rising imports and a marked deterioration in the balance of payments. Under 'stop-go' Tory economic policies, it seemed impossible for Britain to keep a steady course, to avoid lurching from disinflation and a credit squeeze on the one hand, to an uncontrollable booming expansion leading to a balance of payments crisis on the other. It was to examining the precise course to be steered between these unpalatable alternatives that Callaghan and his advisers on the Labour side devoted their main energies.

Quite properly, Callaghan as an untried economics spokesman had to build up a team of advisers. He already had a variety of counsellors, Richard Kahn from Cambridge, occasionally Thomas Balogh from Oxford, although the latter was really Harold Wilson's associate (or, as some thought, mole).[2] But the shadow Chancellor felt he needed a more structured form of advice. To the interest (or sarcasm) of contemporaries, he turned to the university world, to Nuffield College, Oxford, the fortress of the social sciences of which he was an Honorary Fellow. The original initiative came from Tony Crosland who felt that Callaghan knew very little about economics and needed to learn fast. As convener, Crosland turned to his friend Ian Little, formerly his successor as economics tutor at Trinity. In May 1962 Callaghan was able to tell Gaitskell of about seven or eight advisers who had been assembled by Little.[3] He was a Fellow of Nuffield and formerly of Trinity College who had written on fiscal policy but was himself politically quite detached. One of his major research interests, however, was aid to underdeveloped countries notably in Africa (he published a book on *Aid to Africa* in 1964) and this gave him a practical point of contact with Callaghan. But Little saw his group as providing authoritative guidance on pure and applied economics for a potential Chancellor as an exercise in public service. He did not regard it as a secretariat to help the Labour Party even though the great majority of the group were Labour sympathizers.

The outstanding feature of the group was its experience of government. Little himself had worked in the Treasury in the 1950s, but the group in general indicated a heavy influence from the Economic Section of the Cabinet, the supreme bastion of Keynesian ideas in central governmental planning machinery. Sir Robert Hall, an Australian who had been active in Labour politics in the 1930s, had headed the Economic Section under Labour and Conservative chancellors from Cripps to Lloyd until he left to become head of Hertford College, Oxford, in 1961, to be succeeded as head of the Economic Section by Alec Cairncross. With him was C. R. Ross of Hertford College, who had worked with Hall in the Economic Section. So had P. D. Henderson of Lincoln College (who had written on the Central African Federation among other topics) and C. W. ('Kit') McMahon of Magdalen College, whose work for the Section included a period in Washington. J. R. Sargent of Worcester College, an authority on Europe and the sterling area who had also written on transport policy for the Fabian Society, would be joining the Economic Section shortly. A major figure was Robert Neild, director of the National Institute of Economic and Social Research, who was seen, in Callaghan's words, as 'general adviser and initiator of ideas and subjects that I shall be taking as spokesman for the Party'. A number of other economists and businessmen also occasionally appeared, including the industrialist Fred Catherwood of British Aluminium, who combined free-market economics with a strong social concern deriving from an evangelical nonconformist faith. Another was John Grieve-Smith, of the research section of the Steel Board, who Callaghan felt could approach Cairncross, Maudling's current key adviser, on the relationship between NEDC and the Treasury.

The group met twice a term at Nuffield at 5 p.m. on Friday afternoons, followed by dinner, to consider aspects of fiscal, industrial, and monetary policy. The first such meeting took place on 4 May 1962 to examine what Callaghan called the 'traffic light' (more familiar as 'stop-go') approach of the Tory government towards industrial expansion. He had written to Little on 2 April, 'I still do not have clear in my head how we can run British industry on a high level and still pay our way overseas.' Incomes policy loomed large, with papers on this topic by Dick Ross, Michael Stewart, and also John Corina, economics Fellow at St Peter's College. One of the latter's papers considered possible penal sanctions such as a tax on recalcitrant employers who disregarded the restraints on wage increases. Ian Little himself read an early paper on steady growth and the regulation of total demand, conceived on strictly Keynesian lines.

Kit McMahon gave a presentation on policies for sterling. It was generally agreed that devaluation of the pound would be dangerous, likely to lead to the inflation of the price of imports and to alter the ratio of assets and liabilities. McMahon conceded that 'if there were no sterling balances, devaluation would undoubtedly be an invaluable weapon of policy' but the existence of the balances made a prospective devaluation of sterling 'genuinely hazardous'. It was important to show that it was in the world's interest that Britain should not devalue. In donnish Oxonian terms, McMahon urged that they keep before the world's bankers 'the awe-inspiring prospect of Callaghan Agonistes!'[4] McMahon was to publish a book in 1964, *Sterling in the Sixties*, which confirmed this view by arguing forcefully against devaluation. It should be noted, however, that other members of the group, including Ian Little himself, took a more flexible view of exchange rates; in the case of Robert Hall, he had after all served under Cripps during the devaluation of 1949. One paper in February 1963, ironically in view of Callaghan's later trials as Prime Minister, was on the high and rising levels of unemployment—the official figure of 814,000 was said to be a considerable underestimate. The main cause of recession was held to be Selwyn Lloyd's credit squeeze and the higher taxes of July 1961. As a result, production was lower at the end of 1962 than in mid-1961. This paper was entitled, as luck would have it, 'the Tory Winter of Discontent'.

The general tone of these seminars was broadly Keynesian. They urged counter-cyclical policies by the government, the management of demand, and an adaptable use of budgetary controls. Planning was a central theme—'there is no substitute for economic planning', one paper declared. An article published by Callaghan himself at this time asserted, in Rooseveltian terms, that 'planning means introducing a sense of purpose into our national life'.[5] Industries should be encouraged to build up a closer relation with government, to create targets for growth, and to improve their efficiency. A mood of expansion must be fostered. Vigorous policies must be applied in the regions and through planning councils for industry. NEDC should be properly exploited and brought directly within the machinery of central government instead of occupying a marginal role. Callaghan himself criticized its attempts to override collective bargaining procedures through a 'guiding light' principle, though he did otherwise endorse the idea of a 'National Plan' to fix production targets for key industries.[6] A stuttering approach, with lurches from extreme stagnation to excessive expansion which would overheat the economy, should be avoided.

On balance, Callaghan was surely wise in taking advice from what appeared to be the best and most scholarly sources available at the time. There was some derision, often of a snobbish nature, heaped on the idea of the untutored Callaghan receiving tutorials to brush up the fundamentals and equip him to discuss the economic issues of the day. But he required intellectual ballast and, unlike many chancellors or shadow chancellors, had the humility and realism to seek it out. At least his advisers were a group with fairly eclectic political and ideological standpoints. They were not blinkered partisans. Little himself, an apolitical figure, resisted swelling the group with outsiders from London and even (or perhaps especially) Cambridge economists. He felt that the group should 'stick to general principles' rather than have specialist talks on specific issues such as when Callaghan proposed that James Meade address them on the workings of GATT. Little murmured to Callaghan on 11 April 1963 that 'we cannot really act as a sort of secretariat to you'.[7] There was tension here between the intellectual priorities of university economics dons and Callaghan's anxiety to bring out the political implications, often prematurely in Little's view. However, other contacts with industrialists and civil servants did materialize through Labour's 'Planning and Industry Group' which, for example, had on 31 October 1962 a talk on 'The Treasury's Role in Planning' by the head of the Economic Section, Alec Cairncross.

On balance, these Nuffield seminars had an indirect influence at best. With their somewhat abstract agenda, they left no obvious trace after he became Chancellor in October 1964. He did not keep up any particular contact thereafter with Ian Little (who indeed became a fierce critic of Callaghan later on at the Home Office for his handling of the issue of the passports of east African Asians). He turned rather to more committed and governmentally orientated figures such as Robert Neild. Nevertheless, the Nuffield experience was undoubtedly a valuable intellectual preparation for the shadow Chancellor. Tory chancellors from Howe to Major, in the 1980s, the heyday of monetarism, could well have profited from a wider range of advice. Callaghan was not one to ask of an economist 'Is he one of us?' In other respects, however, his preparation for his shadow Treasury role was less complete. While he talked to financial journalists, the specialists of the XYZ group, and influential civil servants, he had virtually no contact with the City. Nor, indeed, did any Labour chancellor, from Philip Snowden in 1924 to Denis Healey in 1974–9. A change in stance began only with John Smith and then Gordon Brown, as Labour's shadow chancellors in the late 1980s and early 1990s on a so-called 'prawn cocktail circuit' (causing Michael Heseltine to comment, 'Never have so many crustaceans died in vain'). Callaghan himself felt later on that a knowledge of the workings and psychology of the City would materially have assisted his work as Chancellor.

He also placed a strong reliance, perhaps stronger than was warranted in the light of his experiences in 1964–7, on the background support of the United States. A strong Atlanticist, he operated in 1961–4 on the basis that America, Britain's closest ally, would rescue Britain if the economic going got exceptionally rough. An important episode here was a visit he paid to the United States in May 1963,[8] followed by another twelve months later. At his request, the Nuffield seminar provided briefing papers for him by Sir Robert Hall. They covered possible British attitudes towards aid, defence, and freer trade, apart from measures to protect sterling against an anticipated run on the pound soon after a Labour government took office. Hall also sketched out the personalities whom Callaghan would expect to meet—Douglas Dillon, Walter Heller, George Ball, and Bob Roosa, 'who is a very able man indeed'. Hall's general message was, 'there is no reason to suppose that the US authorities feel at all disturbed at the prospect of a Labour Government'. They would be anxious to defend sterling, although they also hoped that Britain would in time join the EEC. On his first visit to the United States, in May 1963, Callaghan among other things led off faculty seminars at Columbia and Princeton Universities on Labour's economic policies. His talks perhaps impressed some of those present more for their political adroitness than for their economic insight. More important, he got to know leading figures in the banking world such as David Rockefeller of the Chase Manhattan Bank, with whom he discussed the Kennedy round of trade talks. He also met Douglas Dillon, Kennedy's Secretary to the Treasury, and Bob Roosa, Under-Secretary of State for Monetary Affairs. Both were sympathetic. They argued against a British devaluation and spoke instead of the possibility of swapping sterling for Continental currencies along the lines that Robert Hall had previously suggested, and creating a conversion to long-term holdings. With both Dillon and Roosa, Callaghan was to have a close and friendly relationship when he faced the trials of being Chancellor.

During his second visit in May 1964, Callaghan had a long conversation in New York with Al Hayes, president of the Federal Reserve Bank. He too, although politically a Republican, was extremely friendly. He assured Callaghan that the USA would in no way be dismayed by the prospect of a Labour government and that the Federal Reserve would act to stem any serious run on the pound. He was anxious for Britain and the USA to collaborate on lowering tariffs and expanding international liquidity. Callaghan concluded, 'I like him as a man and have struck up a personal relationship with him that would make me feel that I could always be discussing our problems.'[9] On balance, these visits, while valuable in promoting Labour's image across the Atlantic, may have contained something of a trap. They may have led Callaghan and Wilson to place excessive faith in America's helpfulness, especially during the long-running sagas of the British economy and the stability of the pound in 1964–7 and also in the autumn of 1976. Reliance on a safety net of support from our ally under 'the special relationship' could be a short-term diversion from more fundamental restructuring of the ailing British economy.

Callaghan cannot be fairly criticized for setting up his able group of economic advisers, based on Nuffield, nor for making overseas visits to test the temperature amongst the American and European banking and business community. He was more open to the attack that his range of advisers were not so much unduly academic as insufficiently radical. One who pressed this charge, more effectively so than in his earlier forays on behalf of Maltese independence, was Thomas Balogh of Balliol, Oxford. In November 1962 he wrote to Callaghan to urge that he enlarge his Nuffield seminar with Oxford and Cambridge economists of a Labour background; more fundamentally, he was calling for a more overtly socialist approach rather than one governed by Treasury or Economic Section orthodoxy. He constantly pressed for physical controls and a letter he wrote to Callaghan on 7 November 1962 went along with the conclusion that devaluation should be resisted. But he added that the papers from the Nuffield group that he had seen 'obscured the fact essential for a Labour Chancellor, that devaluation of a downward floating pound would not represent a cut in real wages, and thus a terrible defeat (this was not so in 1931 because we had large scale unemployment)'. He did not discuss the merits or demerits of the devaluation of 1949, which Callaghan's generation of politicians had constantly in their minds as a great political setback. Balogh ironically added that he was not surprised that most Labour economists in Oxford were left out of the group. 'After all we had eleven years of Tory rule and support for the Labour Party was not one of the best recommendations for being selected for the Economic Section.'

Callaghan replied tactfully that he would like to have a group that had Balogh's 'political flair'. But the group was self-generating. 'I did not form it and I do not wish to tell them who should belong to it.' He would discuss with them whether they wished to extend the membership, but in any event he would hope to turn to 'your own distinctive point of view which is based on a long knowledge of the Labour Party's philosophy and outlook'.[10] Nicholas Kaldor of Cambridge who was to loom so large in Labour's economic policy-making in 1964–7 was consulted separately, and proved a fount of new ideas, notably on taxation policy. Nevertheless, on balance the composition of Callaghan's group of advisers does not suggest a radical tinge. On such central themes as budgetary policy or the role of sterling, the general tone is Keynesian centrism. That did not mean that radical initiatives might not be expected from a Labour Chancellor, for instance on taxation policy of a redistributive kind, but a challenge to long-held Treasury assumptions about the relation of government policy to the markets was less likely. As colonial spokesman, his advisers had been rather more eclectic.

What mattered most, though, was not whether Callaghan had the approval of Dr Balogh but rather whether he had that of Hugh Gaitskell. The party leader was, in general, good at letting subordinates have their head, and Callaghan was someone in whom, politically, he had the utmost trust. Whether he had similar faith in Callaghan's capacity as an economic spokesman is less certain. Gaitskell was a specialist economist himself and naturally anxious to see progress in Labour's evolving a credible economic policy for its next term in office. On June 1962, soon after the Nuffield group had come into being, Gaitskell asked Callaghan about progress on what he saw as the three key problems, increasing the rate of productivity, increasing exports, and at the same time preventing cost inflation. 'On the third what I have in mind, of course, is the whole question of incomes policy'; he urged the group to study Swedish and Dutch systems as presently applied. Callaghan seems to have interpreted this as an inquiry about the group's work in general, and he replied detailing papers on incomes policy ('a preliminary paper' from Dick Ross), the public accountability of private industry, reform of the civil service, the location of industry, sterling, and taxation. On incomes policy he reported that much was already known about the Swedish and Dutch incomes policies. He had also had discussions with prominent trade unionists such as Frank Cousins, Harry Nicholas, and Dai Davies. 'So you will see that work is moving ahead in all directions.' Gaitskell, clearly, was not wholly satisfied and wanted some more focused work immediately on incomes policy. He was anxious to see Dick Ross's paper and urged Callaghan also to take a wider range of advice. He might find financial journalists more helpful on exports and productivity; he mentioned Andrew Shonfield and people on the *Financial Times* who would be helpful. 'You will appreciate, I know, the absolutely vital character of these projects.'[11]

There has been some suggestion that Gaitskell tended to be less than satisfied with Callaghan as Treasury spokesman.[12] Crossman's frequent captious comments on Callaghan's performance have to be measured against the fact that he himself was no economist. On the other hand, Anthony Crosland, perhaps the most distinguished economist on the Labour benches, was one of Callaghan's keenest supporters. Whether Callaghan would have been the chancellor in a Gaitskell-led government is somewhat debatable. The change of leadership, with the power brokering that it implied, undoubtedly strengthened his position.

On more general matters, Callaghan and Gaitskell saw matters very much as one. The most important priority facing Labour in the latter months was its attitude towards Europe, now that the Conservative government was making a formal bid to enter the European Economic Community. In the end, Gaitskell, mindful of recent savage party infighting on defence matters, came out strongly at the party conference in October 1962 against British membership. He spoke of 'a thousand years of history' and took a strongly pro-Commonwealth line in citing the sacrifices of Commonwealth troops at Gallipoli and Vimy Ridge in the past.

Both the appeals to history and to ties with Commonwealth countries were entirely congenial to Callaghan who was no great Euro-enthusiast now. His sympathy for the Schuman Plan in 1950 was long past. In a speech to his constituents in Cardiff he attacked the potential effects of joining the EEC on the Commonwealth countries. The Six were likely to prove 'inward-looking' and protectionist and to cut themselves off from the rest of the world. He told the Edmonton Labour Party that any move towards federalism would threaten the British identity. 'If we join Europe we cut ourselves adrift from much of the Commonwealth by the very act of accepting the Treaty of Rome.'[13] When President de Gaulle vetoed Britain's application for membership in January 1963, Callaghan took the news less than tragically. He felt that Macmillan's negotiated terms were in any case quite unacceptable. Only 16 per cent of Britain's trade was involved, he argued, while some of the EEC's policies 'savoured of claustrophobia'. He derided the government's attitude as one of 'Moi, je suis content, Jacques'—'I'm all right, Jack' in the popular argot of the time. The key to future British prosperity lay in Britain's boosting the performance of its own domestic economy. Sterling could be protected by international efforts to harmonize interest rates and to provide 'swap' arrangements at times of crisis.[14] Within a protective shield such as this, the economy could safely grow. He rejected criticisms by the strongly pro-European Roy Jenkins of the accuracy of his statistics on British exports to

Europe compared to the Commonwealth. However, he still kept his options open. Shortly after beginning his term as economics spokesman, he had written in the *Statist* that he 'suspended judgment' on the Common Market, since it was essentially a political issue on which the shadow Chancellor chose not to be dogmatic.[15]

In January 1963, the political scene was quite unexpectedly transformed. Gaitskell had gone to hospital in late November with a mysterious virus. He seemed to improve and returned home for Christmas. But then he suddenly deteriorated and on 18 January he died, at the age of 56. Callaghan, like all the Labour leaders, was pole-axed by the news. In personal terms, it was the loss of a close political friend and ally. But, clearly, the election of a new leader opened up all kinds of possibilities: one immediate outcome of Gaitskell's death was that Callaghan automatically returned to the National Executive as runner-up in the last elections. The two clear front-runners for the leadership were Harold Wilson, broadly representative of the left but also a major front-bench spokesman since 1955, and the deputy leader, George Brown. The latter, as the candidate of the right, appeared to be the clear favourite. But things went wrong for Brown from the start. His campaign made a leisurely start, and he was also wrong-footed by Wilson who, with typical machiavellianism, released a leak to the press to the effect that he and Brown had agreed that the winner would automatically appoint the other deputy leader. But worst of all was the news that there was now a third candidate, James Callaghan.

There were many in the centre of the party who found both early candidates unacceptable. Wilson had a long record of deviousness; he was immensely able, especially on economic matters, but felt to be unpredictable and disloyal. Brown was erratic in a different way, temperamentally explosive, especially when under the influence of (not necessarily very much) drink. There were able centre-right figures like Douglas Jay, John Strachey, George Strauss, Michael Stewart, Jack Diamond, and George Thomson who saw Callaghan as an acceptable alternative. They were an imposing group, consisting of past or future ministers. Douglas Jay had the additional personal tie of knowing Callaghan well in family terms; his son Peter had recently married Callaghan's elder daughter Margaret. Nor was the case for Callaghan a wholly negative one. Apart from having the qualification of not being either Wilson or Brown, he was felt to be a major figure who had performed consistently well in parliament and was well liked. Douglas Jay felt certain that Callaghan would make much the best prime minister of the three. He was also a trade unionist by origin, which helped. An important secret meeting was held by prominent former

Gaitskellites active in the CDS in the London flat of Jack Diamond. In effect they were considering how best to stop Wilson, although the personal weaknesses of Brown were also canvassed. The sharp division of view that emerged amongst them in effect heralded the rapid disintegration of the Campaign for Democratic Socialism. Crosland, Jay, and Thomson all argued with some force on behalf of Callaghan: Dick Taverne and the majority still favoured Brown. Christopher Mayhew was unenthusiastic about all three, but declared that 'I'm not going to vote for either a crook or a drunk so I'll vote for Jim.'[16] At first Callaghan was extremely dubious about standing, but the idea became more appealing, even if only as a marker for the future of his emerging status. George Lawson, a Scotsman and a future government whip, served as his campaign manager. In addition, there was deft persuasion exercised by some of Wilson's supporters, notably Sir Leslie Plummer, who saw clearly that a Callaghan candidature would divide the party's right wing and greatly assist Wilson's cause.[17] Meanwhile successful pressure had been put on the leftish Anthony Greenwood not to stand since his candidature would have been as damaging to Wilson as Callaghan's was likely to be to Brown.

Brown regarded the prospect of a Callaghan candidature with much dismay. Henry Brandon, the *Sunday Times* man in Washington, reported Arthur Schlesinger, Jr., as believing that Callaghan (whom he spelt 'Calahan') might emerge as an acceptable third candidate since there was so much conflict between Wilson and Brown. Brown, replying on 15 January, two days before Gaitskell's death, dismissed this as journalistic gossip; in any case he expected Gaitskell to recover.[18] On the day of his leader's death, he was stunned to hear that Callaghan was seriously considering the possibility of standing. Brown told him that this meant the virtual end of his prospects of ever becoming party leader. Callaghan, while warmly congratulating Brown on his public tribute to Gaitskell, added, 'I am sorry that I cannot give you a reply about standing yet. People whose opinion I respect believe that I should do so. I have not given them a reply for the moment.'[19] One of the latter was Anthony Crosland, an emphatic supporter of Callaghan's and a fierce critic of Brown on personal grounds.

Soon after, the inevitable news came that Callaghan was standing. His campaign had no prospect of succeeding, but it was a crucial intervention that shook Brown and his supporters out of their stride. It made sufficient impact to win the endorsement of Alastair Hetherington in the *Guardian*. Brown's campaign never went well, and the unduly forceful tactics of some of his backers (including an attack on Wilson as a religious non-believer) did not go down well with backbenchers. An impromptu observation on

Callaghan from Brown, temporarily located on the backbenches after a good dinner, was said to have alienated several Welsh MPs. On 7 February, it was announced that Wilson led on the first ballot, with 115 votes, as against 88 for Brown and 41 for Callaghan. The latter then dropped out. He had not polled strongly, his backers mainly being senior or front-bench figures. His old trade union patron Douglas Houghton, however, was not amongst them. He got limited Welsh support. George Thomas voted for Harold Wilson, and not for his old Cardiff comrade-in-arms, though he went out of his way to keep this from the press. Jim Griffiths backed Brown as a trade unionist. Few backbenchers voted for Callaghan; his fellow MPs went for Wilson or Brown. In response to a cheering message from Robert Neild, he commented gloomily that he seemed to be everybody's second choice but nobody's first choice.[20]

But, even though there was a natural majority for Brown, Callaghan's intervention was decisive in making Harold Wilson leader. Wilson's campaign manager, George Wigg, was able to report to his master that 20 of Callaghan's supporters had pledged their backing for Wilson in the second ballot; in fact, he needed only 8 of them to win. In the final ballot, therefore, Wilson won comfortably with 144 votes to Brown's 103. Since his vote had gone up by 29 to Brown's 15 it is clear that around two-thirds of Callaghan's supporters, all former Gaitskellites, had swung to Wilson. Crosland certainly did so, disbelieving no doubt (to reverse a famous *Times* leader) that George Brown drunk was a better man than Harold Wilson sober.[21] Callaghan himself also voted for Wilson, though without enthusiasm. Brown was shattered, and spent some time sulking in his tent in miserable isolation. Members of the CDS found that, for all their triumphs in the constituencies since Scarborough, they had ended up with a left-wing, ex-Bevanite leader. Harold Wilson had become leader against all the odds. In an emotional episode that leaked out, he took some of the Bevanite survivors aside, Crossman, Barbara Castle, Greenwood, and others, to salute the memory of the dead champion, Nye Bevan, who had won at the last.[22] Yet it was not the hallowed legacy of Bevan, but the political intervention of another Welsh member, Jim Callaghan, that led to Wilson's triumph.

Therefter, Wilson, Callaghan, and Brown formed a distinctly wary troika of leaders. There was little warmth or, for a time it seemed, trust. Callaghan and Wilson had a somewhat distant relationship even though personally Callaghan probably found the new leader's folksy northern style more generally acceptable than Gaitskell's donnish manner. Unlike some on Labour's front bench, he had no particular problem with Harold

Wilson's powerful and devoted personal assistant Marcia Williams. Indeed, it had been Callaghan who first drew the attention of Transport House to her abilities when he met her at a university students' meeting. (Foremost among her qualities, apparently, was that she 'had beautiful blue eyes'.) She worked briefly for Callaghan before starting her service for Wilson and their relationship over subsequent years remained comparatively warm. With others in Wilson's entourage, it was a rather different story. But not until the 1964 election campaign were the leader and his shadow Chancellor on the way to intimacy and trust. However, Labour's fortunes were soon on the mend. Wilson helped the process by giving a large number of key portfolios to former Gaitskellites; the intensely right-wing figure of Patrick Gordon Walker, for example, became shadow Foreign Secretary. Callaghan's place as shadow Chancellor was, it seemed, assured after the nature of the electoral contest. More important, Wilson soon proved himself to be a quite superb Opposition leader in 1963–4, perhaps the best of the century in any party, with outstanding performances in parliament, on the public platform, and especially on television, whose technical skills he had mastered. He also proved remarkably skilful in capturing the public imagination with his call for purposive planning and scientific modernization.

Equally important, the Macmillan government was now falling into much disarray. The Prime Minister himself, so recently the dominant 'SuperMac' of Vicky cartoons, now became a figure of fun lampooned by the satirists of *Private Eye* and *That Was the Week that Was*. He seemed an ageing figure who confessed, somewhat pathetically, that he did not often move amongst young people. Party morale was already shaken by the 'night of the long knives' in July 1962. The abrupt rejection of British membership of the EEC in January 1963 at the hands of General de Gaulle was seen as a national humiliation. The economic indices continued to go badly. In addition, as often happens with governments in disarray, there were a bewildering series of government scandals, or alleged scandals, including the Vassall case, the Duchess of Argyll trial, and, most shattering of all, the Profumo affair when the War Minister had to resign after admitting lying to the Commons about his sexual involvement with a call-girl. At this point, the Prime Minister himself seemed almost pathetically out of touch. At a calamitous Conservative Party conference, Macmillan, who was in hospital, announced that he was resigning through ill-health (in fact he was to live on for a further twenty-five years and to take an active part in public life until almost the end). There were chaotic scenes in which the party once again turned against R. A. Butler while Quintin

Hogg (despite announcing that he would renounce his peerage) failed to establish his credentials. In the end, to much astonishment, the Conservatives found themselves led by the antique figure of the Earl of Home, shortly to emerge in the Commons as Sir Alec Douglas-Home. Harold Wilson seized this unexpected opportunity: he exploited to the full his own folksy style as opposed to the 'grouse-moor image' of one he joyously referred to as 'the fourteenth earl'. Labour's electoral prospects looked stronger than for over a decade and commentators confidently expected them to achieve the large 6 per cent swing they needed and to form the next government some time in 1964.

This was all very exciting for Callaghan. His authority as shadow Chancellor steadily grew in 1963–4, especially as the results of the overheating of the economy under Maudling's 'dash for growth' became evident. Labour's call for indicative planning was supported by important books by economists like Michael Shanks (*The Stagnant Society*) and Andrew Shonfield (*British Economic Policy since the War*) at this time. On the other hand, Callaghan's own role and remit were now somewhat less certain. The origins of this lay not so much in economic factors as in the internal party politics of the Labour leadership. Labour had long urged, in general terms, the need for somehow separating the direction of production, exports, and economic planning from what was felt to be the negative, if not dead, hand of the Treasury. Callaghan himself, as shadow Chancellor, frequently condemned the reliance on fiscal policy, purchase and other taxes, and the financial regulator to direct industry, with the outcome in so-called 'stop-go' policies and a failure to achieve steady and sustainable growth. 'Neddy' had called for a growth rate of 4 per cent, an ambitious target, and there seemed little chance of achieving it if the Treasury retained sole control.

There was also the practical problem of what to do with George Brown, a strong character in need of a home. As deputy leader he clearly had to be given a significant portfolio commensurate with his status, and the natural area appeared to be a Ministry of Economic Planning to prepare a national plan for the next few years. Wilson, with his attraction to scientific development and planning, encouraged by major scientists like Professor Blackett, was enthusiastic about this idea. In addition, it would resolve, if only by divide and rule tactics, the political problem of the rival roles of Brown and Callaghan. There would be 'creative tension' between them, so Wilson claimed.[23] A Minister of Planning and a Minister of Budget, somewhat on American lines, was one possible scenario discussed in the press. So there came into being the famous division between the Treasury and a Department of Economic Affairs. It duly eventually came into effect in October 1964 when Labour took office.

This presented Callaghan with a dilemma. In his memoirs, rather oddly, he says that he favoured the idea of DEA with the model of Monnet-style French planning in mind. Years later, he confirmed that the concept of having a DEA could be defended.[24] But the implementation was another matter entirely. In fact, it is clear that he viewed the way the idea was worked out with great suspicion. It involved dividing up key functions of policy. In effect, it downgraded the stature of a future Labour Chancellor. It was Brown, not Callaghan, who would chair NEDC. Wilson enjoyed himself in private sessions with both Brown and Callaghan assuring each that his ministry would be the superior. Meanwhile, relations between the latter two became more combustible; interestingly, observers noted that Callaghan, regarded as by far the stabler colleague of the two, was also often the aggressor in public disagreements with the volatile Brown. In any case, even if Brown and Callaghan had been plaster saints, there was no doubting the dangerous vagueness of the arrangement that had been created. The attractive legend of the DEA being cobbled up in the back of a taxi after a meeting in St Ermin's Hotel should be rejected outright. Even so, its origins were wreathed in the utmost confusion. The precise boundaries between a ministry concerned with stimulating growth in the economy and a Treasury involved with taxation, budgetary, and currency policies central to that growth were hardly clear. The further gloss that the DEA would be concerned with the long term and the Treasury with the short term made matters worse, and was also a kind of insult to Callaghan. Crossman was one observer who viewed the entire situation with glee, insisting that Wilson had no great confidence in Callaghan anyway and regarded him as a lightweight in economic matters. If he did not like the new arrangements, he could always switch to becoming Minister for Defence. Gordon Walker reported Wilson immediately after his election as leader as being 'worried about Callaghan. He knew no economics and listened to the last adviser'.[25]

In the winter and spring of 1963–4 George Brown worked to put flesh on the bones of the putative new department. He had a key meeting with William Armstrong on 15 April; as a result, a fully-fledged DEA was agreed on, rather than a Ministry of Production and Planning, with the object of devising a national plan for the economy over the next five years. But immense uncertainty about the relationship of the Treasury and the DEA to each other lingered on until the general election and beyond. Not until the famous 'concordat' worked out in the Treasury in November–

December 1964 and finally set out by Sir Burke Trend, the Cabinet Secretary, was any kind of sense to be made.[26] In the meantime, an observer like Douglas Jay, who recalled the immense confusion in the Attlee government between 1945 and 1947 when Dalton ran the Treasury and Morrison directed economic planning as Lord President, regarded the entire scheme as a disaster created solely to appease two rival personalities.[27] His forebodings were to be amply fulfilled.

In the winter and spring of 1963–4, as Wilson struck out strongly at the economic and other failings of the Douglas-Home government, Callaghan's concern about his future role and the precise direction of the DEA was a constant *leitmotiv*. The party conference at Scarborough—scene of Gaitskell's famous defeat by supporters of CND and his vow to 'fight and fight again' back in 1960—was a triumph for Harold Wilson. His call for Britain to be transformed by a new planned scientific advance in 'the white heat of a new industrial revolution' seemed genuinely inspiring. It bypassed the sterility of old theological debates over public ownership and captured all the headlines. An incidental event was the return of Callaghan to the National Executive at the expense of Wedgwood Benn in the constituency section. But there was also at Scarborough an undercurrent of tension between Callaghan and Brown as to the precise allocation of responsibilities between the Treasury and the new DEA. Callaghan made public his unease, to Wilson's irritation. Public statements were made to the effect that the DEA would deal with devising a national economic plan for growth, while the Treasury would focus on the control of public expenditure and major tax reform—not that that cleared matters up.[28] But it would all be left to Harold to sort out.

In his conference speech on economic policy, Callaghan in effect called for a voluntary incomes policy, couched publicly as 'a planned growth of incomes'. It had been a theme much canvassed at the Nuffield seminars. But key figures like Frank Cousins and Jack Jones of the Transport Workers remained non-committal and fundamentally suspicious. After all, the TUC had boycotted 'Nicky' from the outset. Henceforth, the direction that Labour's economic policy would take after the next election remained unclear in key respects right down to the election campaign. The NEC Economic Policy Subcommittee (chaired by Mikardo but which Callaghan attended) focused on specific issues such as regional policy and the role of the proposed Land Commission, not on grand strategy.[29] One difficult matter that surfaced here was a proposed tax on wealth. Here Callaghan was in the end forced to have the idea put on ice. At first he had given it support on the basis of a 1 per cent levy on individual holdings of capital in excess of £20,000. 'I think the tax on wealth can be a winner if it is properly presented.' His economic advisers were somewhat divided, Ian Little being very doubtful, Nicky Kaldor strongly in favour.[30] But by 1964 the commitment had been reversed, and it did not see light again until 1977 when Callaghan was Prime Minister. The effect of the wealth tax affair was that the left criticized him for caution while Wilson was said by Gordon Walker to be annoyed that the shadow Chancellor made public reference to the issue at all.[31]

In the early months of 1964 the Maudling boom continued. At first it was projected to reach a heady 6 per cent; in the end it seemed to settle down at 4 per cent. Unemployment fell and industrial production rose sharply. What a later generation would term the 'feel-good factor' was widely appreciated by the electors, and Labour's lead in the opinion polls fell slightly though it was still around 10 per cent, while the capture of the Greater London Council, thought to be a prize reserved for the Conservatives after the abolition of the old Labour-dominated LCC, was a further encouragement for Labour. Audrey Callaghan became a member. On the other hand, the Conservatives still felt they had a chance through residual contentment with full employment and consumer affluence. What really began to attract public attention in May and June was the mounting feeling that the Maudling boom was in many respects illusory, or rather being created artificially at a grave underlying cost. Britain could not operate on the basis of 'Keynesianism in one country'. On 29 April Sir Alec Cairncross of the Economic Section warned the Chancellor that the rate of expansion was unsustainable with a rise in demand of 4.5 per cent that was higher than the underlying growth rate. There would be a very large balance of payments deficit in 1964 and throughout 1965. Precisely how great it would be was unclear, but one estimate after another put the figure ever larger. By the end of June Cairncross and Sir William Armstrong were talking in terms of a deficit of at least £500m., and very likely more, a terrifyingly large total unknown previously in peacetime.[32]

The Treasury kept up a public façade of unflappability, along the complacent lines of *The Economist* which insisted that there were no signs of overheating and that Maudling need take no steps during that hot summer to keep demand in check.[33] On 18 June Callaghan called on Maudling in his room in the Commons. It was the last time that they met before the general election due to be held that October. Callaghan liked Maudling personally and warmed to the relaxed way in which he was greeted by the Chancellor, a whisky and soda at the ready. His message was a different matter. Maudling was adamant that the economy was not overheating, although there would be a deficit in the capital account shown in the balance of payments figures for the first quarter of the year, due to be published in July. There would probably be no rise in bank rate before the election although there might be a case for a large overseas loan from European countries after the election. William Armstrong, he told Callaghan, had not advised any further measures to strengthen the economy (a view certainly not confirmed in the Treasury papers in the Public Record Office). Callaghan raised the possibility of there being a joint statement between the two of them if there were a run on the pound in September, but Maudling, not surprisingly, felt this would not be practicable. Clearly there were likely to be problems about sterling. Privately he told Callaghan that he expected Labour to win the next election.[34]

Callaghan thus faced a prospect that was both exciting and disturbing. A Labour election which would place him in 11 Downing Street seemed highly probable. The Douglas-Home government showed all the symptoms of a struggling regime that had been in power far too long, while Labour under Harold Wilson seemed fresh and forward-looking. On the other hand, Callaghan would become Chancellor, if Labour won, with a most confusing arrangement within the governmental machine through the invention of the ill-defined DEA, and the likelihood of serious international financial difficulties, including very probably a run on the pound. If not the 'financial Dunkirk' of which Keynes had warned Labour in August 1945, it was still an extremely worrying prospect. As he relaxed on the Isle of Wight with Audrey and his children during a remarkably warm and sunny summer, he replenished his energies for a bruising election campaign and the grave inheritance that it might bring.

1. Benn, *Years of Hope*, 330 (10 May 1960).

2. For Balogh's condemnation of the government's industrial policy and absence of exchange controls, see Callaghan Papers, box 14.

3. This account is based on material ibid., box 6, and especially an interview with Professor Ian Little, and access to his private files, for which I am much indebted. They include the following papers: 'The Visit of Mr. Callaghan to Washington' and 'Background Notes to Some of the International Economic Problems' by Robert Hall, spring 1963; 'Devaluation' and 'Policies for Sterling' by Kit McMahon, 1962; 'Steady Growth and the Regulation of Total Demand' by Ian Little, 1962; 'An Incomes Policy for the Labour Party' by Michael Stewart, a paper for the Finance and Economic Subcommittee of the Labour Party, RD 333, Oct. 1962; 'Incomes Policy' by Dick Ross; 'Wage Drift and Wage Policy' and 'A Note on Incomes Policy and "Disregards" ' by John Corina, together with notes on planning, industrial policy, etc. Also see Sir Fred Catherwood, *At the Cutting Edge* (London, 1996), 77 ff.

4. Paper on devaluation by McMahon, 1962 (Little Papers).

5. L. J. Callaghan, 'The Opposition Chancellor's Point of View', *Works Management* (May 1962), 13.

6. L. J. Callaghan, 'Labour's Plan for Prosperity', *Statist*, 16 Feb. 1962.

7. Callaghan to Little, 10 Apr. 1963; Little to Callaghan, 11 Apr. 1963 (Little Papers).

8. Record of visit to the United States (Callaghan Papers, box 30). The present writer attended these sessions at Princeton and Columbia.

9. Record of conversation with Al Hayes, 27 May 1964 (Callaghan Papers, box 6).

10. Balogh to Callaghan, 7 Nov. 1962; Callaghan to Balogh, 13 Nov. 1962 (ibid.).

11. Gaitskell to Callaghan, 19 June 1962; Callaghan to Gaitskell, 29 June 1962; Gaitskell to Callaghan, 3 July 1962 (ibid.).

12. Peter Shore, *Leading the Left* (London, 1993), 61–2. Shore was head of the Labour Party Research Department from 1959 to 1964.

13. *Penarth Times*, 21 Sept. 1962; notes on Edmonton speech in Callaghan Papers, box 7.

14. *Parl. Deb.*, 5th ser., vol. 671, 1118 ff. (12 Feb. 1963).

15. Jenkins to Callaghan, 12 Feb. 1962 (Callaghan Papers, box 7); Callaghan's article, 'Labour's Plan for Prosperity', *Statist*, 16 Feb. 1962.

16. 'Witness Seminar: The Campaign for Democratic Socialism, 1960–64', *Contemporary Record*, 7/2 (autumn 1993), 382.

17. Ben Pimlott, *Harold Wilson* (London, 1992), 254 ff.

18. Brandon to George Brown, 10 Jan. 1963; Brown to Brandon, 15 Jan. 1963 (Bodleian, Brown Papers, 118).

19. Callaghan to Brown, 18 Jan. 1963 (ibid.).

20. George Thomas to Callaghan, 13 Feb. 1963 (Callaghan Papers, box 31); Callaghan to Neild, 6 Feb. 1963 (ibid., box 18).

21. Susan Crosland, *Tony Crosland* (London, 1982), 116.

22. Crossman, *Backbench Diaries*, 973 (8 Feb. 1963).

23. Pimlott, *Wilson*, 280.

24. *Time and Chance*, 153. A valuable source for the origins and later history of the DEA is the 'Witness Seminar' held at the Institute of Contemporary British History on 5 June 1996, in which Callaghan, Cairncross, Roll, Croham, McIntosh, Catherwood, Dell, and others took part under the chairmanship of Peter Jay. (I am much indebted to Nick Crowson and Virginia Preston for a transcript of this seminar.)

25. Crossman, *Backbench Diaries*, 1014–15 (17 July 1963); Patrick Gordon Walker, *Political Diaries, 1932–1971*, ed. Robert Pearce (London, 1991), 282 (19 Mar. 1963).

26. 'Co-operation between the Department of Economic Affairs and the Treasury': note by Sir Burke Trend, 16 Dec. 1964, C (64) 28 (PRO, CAB 119).

27. Douglas Jay, *Change and Fortune* (London, 1980), 166. 'There was less excuse in 1964 than in 1945', Jay observes.

28. *Guardian*, 1 Oct. 1962. Cf. Tony Benn, *Out of the Wilderness: Diaries, 1963–67*, ed. Ruth Winstone (London, 1987), 66 (2 Oct. 1963).

29. Home Policy Subcommittee, 11 Nov. 1963 ff. (Labour Party archives).

30. Ian Little to Callaghan, 14 Feb. 1963; Callaghan to Kaldor (Callaghan Papers, BLPES, box 4); Callaghan to D. G. Arbuthnot, 20 Feb. 1963 and Callaghan to Dr David Pitt, 21 Feb. 1963 (Callaghan Papers, box 14). Many trade union leaders were concerned over a wealth tax: see Frank Cousins's comment, 1 Oct. 1963 (Cousins Papers, MSS. 282, TBN 37).

31. Gordon Walker, *Political Diaries*, 286 (22 May 1963).

32. 'The Longer Range Economic Prospect': paper by Alec Cairncross, 23 June 1964; 'The Next Five Years': paper by Sir William Armstrong , 6 July 1964 (PRO, T 171/755). I have taken the phrase 'Keynesianism in one country' from Edmund Dell, *The Chancellors* (London, 1996), 289.

33. *The Economist*, 20 June 1964.

34. Note of a talk with Reginald Maudling, 18 June 1964 (Callaghan Papers, box 6).

10

INTO POWER

In the high summer of 1964, as the Wilsons relaxed in warm sunshine on the Scillies and the Callaghans did likewise on the Isle of Wight, commentators examined the political entrails to discover whether what Labour called 'thirteen wasted years' of Tory rule was coming to an end. Despite the government's long-running unpopularity dating from Selwyn Lloyd's 'pay pause' in July 1961, the evidence was not wholly convincing. In the calm of the 'silly season', with no speeches or campaigning to trouble the electors, the opinion polls showed signs of Labour's lead eroding. It drifted down to 5 per cent in Gallup; in NOP it slumped to the extent that on 13 September the Conservatives were shown as actually having a small lead of 1.6 per cent, admittedly well within the usual margin of error. Two days later, the Prime Minister, Douglas-Home, announced that the general election would take place on 15 October. Evidently it could well be a much closer-run thing than had appeared likely before the summer break.

In particular, there were still no signs before the election campaign began on 15 September that the economy was in serious trouble. The Maudling boom was still in full flow with powerful effects on the electors' pay packets. The general mood was one of affluence; unemployment and inflation were both remarkably low. In June the rate of unemployment had fallen to a mere 1.6 per cent while job vacancies stood at 368,000.[1] If anything, criticism was now focusing on a series of industrial strikes by postal workers, car component makers, and others, which were unhelpful to Labour's prospects. The Opposition, including Callaghan, seemed very restrained in making criticisms of the economy which might damage sterling—and, of course, create serious problems for an incoming Labour government, in 1964 as in 1929 and 1945 when the eventual outcome had been a devaluation each time. Callaghan wrote to Wilson on this aspect on 14 September.

> There is a tactical issue to be decided here that I am not fully clear about. My instinct is to tell people that the situation is extremely serious and that we cannot carry on with the current expansion without substantial changes. On the other hand, when Maudling and Home deny the seriousness of the situation, as I suppose they will, and we are unable to prove that what they say is true, we do not get much further. There is also the additional complication that the market researches seem to show that if people sniff economic trouble, there is a prospect that they will turn back to the Tories.[2]

But within the governmental machine, the mood was increasingly disturbed, as the consequences of Maudling's headlong and barely controlled expansion were becoming more alarming with every week that passed. Lord Cromer, the Governor of the Bank of England, wrote to the Treasury on 28 August stating that he had for some time had 'considerable misgivings about the direction in which our financial affairs are going'. He complained that he had asked Maudling to convey his misgivings to the Prime Minister but that nothing had been done. Sir William Armstrong had already spelt out his concern (probably with insufficient force)—'the balance of payments is very bad'. Other key officials, however, notably Douglas Allen, felt that Armstrong should have done more to restrain his Chancellor, and that he 'behaved weakly' in the spring and summer of 1964.[3]

Sir Alec Cairncross of the Economic Section spoke gloomily of a rising annual deficit. The figure of £500m. mentioned by Armstrong was steadily revised upwards. By 12 October, almost on the very eve of the general election, Cairncross was talking in terms of £600m. (a note in the margin by a Treasury official said 'higher'). The deficit was likely to continue into 1966 and beyond. The level of demand was unmanageably high, and an early rise in bank rate was inevitable. Cairncross concluded, 'The larger the debt we incur, the greater is bound to be the distrust of sterling and the danger of a flight from the pound.'[4] In fact, the eventual deficit was to be far worse than even Cairncross's gloomiest prediction. Armstrong was to welcome Callaghan to No. 11 on 16 October, four days later, with a figure of £800m.[5] By 14 September it was reported that Britain was likely to require either a large loan from the International Monetary Fund or perhaps a $500m. swap arrangement with the Americans. Callaghan wrote to Maudling, 'I am sure you have in mind the adverse effects that are bound to be felt by a new government if one of its earliest measures is to announce that it needs to borrow from abroad. It would start its life labouring under a disadvantage for which it was not responsible.' He asked Maudling for a statement, but the Chancellor gave a guarded and imprecise reply.[6]

In writing to Douglas-Home four days later, Maudling was more frank. 'The fact is of course that we are running a deficit at the moment of over £50m. a month and it is surprising that the reserves have not reflected this before now.' The Bank of England was approaching central banks in Europe and Canada to borrow $450m. along with a previous facility of $500m. from the USA which had hardly been used.[7] Douglas-Home of matchsticks fame, who knew very little of economics, had nothing to say on these matters. On 21 September, it was publicly announced that swap facilities had been agreed with the banks of Germany, France, Switzerland, Holland, Belgium, Canada, and, somewhat later, Italy.[8] The public, no better informed than the Prime Minister on the arcane details of the balance of payments, could nevertheless smell a financial crisis in the making, and the Opposition was unlikely to keep a vow of silence for long. When on 30 September it was announced that there was a £98m. fall in the balance of payments figures, a significant figure in those times, the prospect of serious economic trouble, affecting pay, jobs, savings, and the strength of the pound, became a central theme of party controversy.

Prior to the election, though, the shadow Chancellor could only guess at the full enormity of the undoubtedly serious situation that would confront him if Labour won. What he did know was that he would have to fight hard to retain his seat in Cardiff South-East; after all his majority of only 868 in 1959 had made it distinctly marginal. He had actually been approached by the Swansea Labour agent to see whether he might prefer to fight rock-solid Swansea East instead when its veteran member, Dai Mort, died. Labour had put in considerable efforts since then, both over ensuring the registration of voters in newer housing estates such as in Llanrumney, and in working on postal voters, a significant element in a large urban seat. For the first time, Labour had a full-time paid agent, Maldwyn Davies.[9] The Welsh Labour Party, and its secretary Cliff Prothero, had targeted Cardiff South-East for special assistance, and during the campaign many workers were brought in from rock-solid valleys seats where Labour were so impregnable that a campaign was virtually redundant. Many young students worked for the Labour cause in Cardiff South-East, including at least three future MPs, Rhodri Morgan, Alun Michael, and the president of the Cardiff University students' union, Neil Kinnock. Callaghan also had the benefit of an enthusiastic and vigorous young organizer, Paddy Kitson.

Another powerful personal factor was the presence as party secretary of Jack Brooks of the Transport Workers, a former plasterer from Splott and one-time amateur boxer.[10] A local councillor, Brooks became Callaghan's *doppelgänger*, an invaluable minder of the shop in his constituency, a kind of Cardiff Jim Farley to take care of the machine, sidetrack dissenters on the Management Committee, and provide an early warning system for Jim. If urgent messages had to be conveyed to Callaghan, this was done via Brooks's house in Janet Street, Splott. For over thirty years from 1962 when their association effectively began, Jack Brooks was a quite indispensable and loyal lieutenant, an essential figure in Callaghan's political career. Each admired the qualities of the other and their relationship was always a very good one, despite Brooks's former reputation as a Bevanite. When Callaghan fell from power in 1979 his farewell honours list was to include a peerage for the future Lord Brooks of Tremorfa.

If Jack Brooks was one personal asset, another was Callaghan's Conservative opponent.[11] This was a surprising choice indeed. Since the defeat of Callaghan would have been so rich a prize for the Cardiff Conservatives, it might have been assumed that they would adopt an experienced, skilful, and politically adept person to be their candidate to confront a sitting MP generally agreed to be a total professional. In fact, they chose someone with none of these qualities, the wholly inexperienced captain of the England cricket team, Ted Dexter. He was not, of course, Welsh and in fact had been born in Milan. He had no political background and spent the summer of 1964 captaining the England cricket team against the Australians (not very successfully since the latter retained the Ashes).

His selection to fight Cardiff South-East owed a great deal to the influence of G. V. Wynne-Jones, the sports commentator, now the Tory agent in the constituency, and also to the Glamorgan cricket captain Wilfred Wooller, a famous rugby player as well in his youth, and an active right-wing Conservative. When Howard Davies, the Conservative chief agent for Wales, was asked over a drink by two university lecturers, one from Essex, one from Swansea, engaged on the Nuffield election study why on earth Dexter had been selected, he replied, 'To appeal to the West Indian vote.' Even this answer is improbable since the voters of West Indian origin in the Cardiff Bay area were very few; black or brown electors in Bute Town and Tiger Bay tended to be Arabs or Somalis, or perhaps west African. Cardiff in any case was hardly in the same category as Manchester or Sheffield as a stronghold of cricket, even though Glamorgan played some of their home games in the county cricket championship there. For the earthy democracy of Splott, Adamsdown, and Bute Town, an upper-class sportsman from Radley and Cambridge University (known to cricket journalists as 'the lord Edward') was the most inappropriate candidate that could have been imagined. Such people often fought hopeless Labour-held seats in the valleys to gain experience prior to capturing a safe middle-class stronghold in areas such as the Surrey stockbroker belt. But in a potentially winnable seat such as Cardiff South-East, the choice was hardly comprehensible. Dexter was a pleasant, unassuming man, but as a candidate he gave the wily and experienced Callaghan a virtual walkover.

The campaign began on 12 September with a mass rally at Wembley Arena, and a televised presentation of the Labour election manifesto, chaired by the youthful Wedgwood Benn and including Callaghan, Crossman, Michael Stewart, and Gerald Gardiner. Wedgwood Benn pronounced it to be 'dull, earnest—and good'.[12] Callaghan had been on the committee drawing up the manifesto and, according to Wedgwood Benn, woke up at night in a panic remembering that neither Scotland nor Wales received a mention in it.[13] He was to make sure that the omissions were put right. The section on the economy highlighted the proposed Ministry of Economic Affairs which would draw up a national economic plan, but also specified Callaghan's side of things via price controls and the reform of taxation. Callaghan thereafter was a leading figure in Labour's national campaign. He and Wilson waged fierce attacks on the government when worrying trade figures were announced on 30 September, followed by other gloomy financial indicators. Callaghan accused Maudling of lurching into a crisis only to be rescued by foreign banks; Labour's previous caution in referring to the economy was cast aside. There was much campaign rhetoric, which the economic indicators appeared to support, of Britain being caught up in a low-growth, low-productivity economic cycle under Tory government. Callaghan also chaired Labour's fourth television broadcast, appearing along with Gordon Walker, Denis Healey, and Ray Gunter in a question and answer session held in a 'coffee meeting' in the house of a Labour councillor in Wood Green who lived conveniently near the Alexandra Palace transmitter. The questioners were deliberately of various political persuasions, though the image-makers in the party were worried at projecting a message of economic decline against the well-stocked bookshelves of the Murphys' comfortable sitting room.

In addition, of course, even with Dexter as his opponent (whom he ignored throughout the campaign and only met briefly at the declaration of the poll), Callaghan had to pay full attention to Cardiff South-East to ensure that there would be no slips this time. He spent much time in all parts of the constituency, strolling amiably through its distinct and variegated areas—the 'young marrieds' on the housing estates at Llanrumney and Rumney, the working-class core of Splott and traditionally Irish Adamsdown, the remaining dockside population of picaresque Bute Town currently famous as the home of the vocalist Shirley Bassey, the professional middle-class residents alongside the lake in Roath in the central area, the senior citizens enjoying the sea air on the promenade in Penarth.

His speeches focused on the local application of national themes. He strongly endorsed proposals for the enfranchisement of leasehold, a historically familiar grievance in Cardiff and the subject of a private member's bill by Callaghan's colleague George Thomas. He defended Cardiff's docks against the potential competition from the modernized Portbury facility in Bristol across the Severn. On steel nationalization, a theme on which the Conservatives aimed to put Labour on the defensive, he claimed that it would be beneficial for the ailing East Moors steel works in his constituency. In any event, many of its workforce had now found employment in the brand-new giant RTB/Spencer works at nearby Llanwern. Callaghan's private view that steel nationalization was a distraction that a Labour chancellor could well do without was suppressed. He had indeed spent much time on these and other local matters of interest to Cardiffians for some years past. Somewhat unexpectedly, he supported other south-east Wales spokesmen, Labour and Conservative, who urged that the University of Wales be defederalized and Cardiff's university college in Cathays Park given independent university status. This was a view he was later to reverse as president of the University College of Swansea in the later 1980s, when he strongly defended the central planning mechanisms of the national university. He also called for university status for the Cardiff College of Advanced Technology; in fact, it was to become a constituent college of the federal national university in 1968.

On a broader Welsh theme, Callaghan also spoke out strongly on behalf of a secretary of state for Wales. This had unexpectedly appeared on Labour's election manifesto for the first time in 1959; James Griffiths had persuaded Hugh Gaitskell of its desirability and also its compatibility with Labour's schemes of nationwide economic planning. Callaghan had previously shown little sympathy with the idea, which he regarded as a sop to Welsh nationalism. But he seems to have changed his view in the later 1950s after observing how the Scottish Office was able to promote the idea of a Forth bridge without there being any comparable pressure on behalf of a Severn bridge for south Wales. He spoke out strongly in the campaign for a Welsh secretaryship without being very specific on its powers and whether it would be little more than a Welsh-based branch office carrying out directives emanating from Whitehall. In Cardiff and elsewhere, he attacked the Conservatives on their record of economic competence, and for social failures over old-age pensions, housing, and education. When asked how Labour would pay for its increased social expenditure, like Wilson and Brown he replied that it would come from increased growth in the economy, not from higher taxes. A growth rate of 4 per cent would generate an additional £300m. a year.[14] Meanwhile, Dexter's campaign was something of a nightmare; in working-class Splott he chose to pronounce on, of all topics, the public schools. There were Tory murmurings that Labour-voting households were identified by grubby lace curtains and unwashed milk bottles on the doorstep. This did not go down well. One ray of light for Dexter was a message of endorsement from the Yorkshire and England fast bowler Freddie Trueman.

Labour's campaign, directed personally by Wilson himself, seemed to pick up momentum as a generally quiet campaign got under way. The Conservatives found themselves increasingly on the defensive, especially as gloomy tidings about the balance of payments sank in. George Brown proclaimed that the country was 'lurching towards the biggest economic crisis since the war'. The Gallup poll showed Labour consistently well in the lead; NOP showed its original findings of a Conservative lead steadily eroding. On the eve of the poll it showed Labour with a lead of 3.1 per cent. Commentators expected Labour to win with a comfortable majority though certainly not a landslide.

But when the results came through on the night of 15–16 October, it was clear that the outcome would be close. Labour showed up strongly in early urban returns. One of them was in Cardiff South-East which showed a swing to Labour of nearly 7 per cent with Callaghan's majority rising to 7,841 over Dexter in a straight fight. There had been a high poll of 80 per cent, which was 2.8 per cent higher than the national turnout. Labour's poll of 30,129 included for the first time Jim and Audrey Callaghan since they now had a flat in Cardiff. There was jubilant celebration in front of Cardiff City Hall, several choruses of the campaign song 'Let's go with Labour', and a brief champagne and (mainly) beer celebration with party workers in the constituency. In fact, Labour performed strongly in all the south Wales urban seats, with a large swing also in George Thomas's Cardiff West constituency and in Tory-held Cardiff North, and regaining Swansea West from the Conservatives. In a television interview in the Cardiff studio by the BBC's election analyst shortly afterwards, Callaghan was genial and relaxed, looking almost sun-tanned in a cream lightweight suit. He insisted that Labour had in no way tried to conceal its plans for steel nationalization. Meanwhile poor Dexter, familiar with media attention on the cricket field, seemed shell-shocked when he entered the studio, almost in tears.

But the prospects for Labour overall were less certain. An early projection of an overall majority of 30 was revised downwards as rural seats on the Friday stayed stubbornly Conservative. Just after 2.30 p.m. Labour's holding the mainly rural Welsh constituency of Brecon and Radnor assured them of a bare majority. The final result was Labour 317, the Conservatives 304 and the Liberals 9, a majority of only four. What had happened was not that the Labour vote had gone up but that the Conservative total had fallen by 6 per cent, much of it to the Liberals who polled 3 million votes in all. Butler and Stokes were later to emphasize the demographic foundation of Labour's victory, based on 'Old Labour' family backgrounds. Had the electorate of 1964 been that of 1959 the Conservatives would almost certainly have retained power. The margin could scarcely have been closer, but, as George Brown defiantly pronounced, one was enough.

Callaghan had stayed in Cardiff on the Friday morning while the outcome was still uncertain, recovering from his election exertions. During that period, he was urgently sought after by Peter Jay—his son-in-law, but operating here as private secretary to the joint permanent secretary to the Treasury, William Armstrong. In the early afternoon a telephone call from Jay did reach him telling him that Harold Wilson, the new Prime Minister, was waiting impatiently at No. 10. Callaghan hastened to get to Paddington by train (leaving campaign workers on the platform of Cardiff station with champagne glasses in their hands, according to his own account)[15] and then to Downing Street. Here Harold Wilson briskly asked him where he had been all morning and told him he was to be Chancellor of the Exchequer. It was the climax of a remarkably consistent and unfaltering political ascent since he had entered parliament in 1945. A shoal of congratulatory letters followed: those writing from Africa included both Dr Hastings Banda and a surprisingly genial Sir Roy Welensky.[16] But Callaghan well knew the massive challenges he faced in his new role. Much of the success or otherwise of the Labour government, recapturing power after years in the wilderness, would rest on his efforts. A few moments later, as Callaghan tried to come to terms emotionally with the dimensions of his new public role, he walked through the connecting door to No. 11, for immediate crisis talks with Ian Bancroft, his private secretary at the Treasury, and the permanent secretary, Sir William Armstrong. A new era and a new ordeal had begun.

1. *The Economist*, 27 June 1964.
2. Callaghan to Wilson, 14 Sept. 1964 (Callaghan Papers, box 14).

3. Lord Cromer to D. J. Mitchell, Treasury, 18 June 1964; 'The Next Five Years', memo by Sir William Armstrong, 6 July 1964 (PRO, T171/755); Roy Jenkins, *A Life at the Centre* (1991), 291, citing Allen's view in 1970.

4. 'The Economic Situation', draft paper by Cairncross, 12 Oct. 1964 (PRO T171/755).

5. 'General Briefing for the Chancellor', Sir William Armstrong, 16 Oct. 1964 (T171/758)

6. Callaghan to Maudling, 14 Sept. 1964; Maudling to Callaghan, 15 Sept. 1964 (T171/755).

7. Maudling to Douglas-Home, 18 Sept. 1964 (ibid.).

8. Memo, Sir Denis Ricketts to Sir William Armstrong, 18 Sept. 1964 (ibid.).

9. Callaghan to Cliff Prothero, 16 Oct. 1959 (Callaghan Papers, box 15); Callaghan to Harry Sherman, 19 Apr. 1961 (ibid.).

10. Interview with Lord Brooks of Tremorfa, 18 Oct. 1995.

11. This treatment of the Cardiff South-East contest is based on my own work as BBC (Wales) political correspondent in elections, 1964–79.

12. Benn, *Out of the Wilderness*, 140 (11 Sept. 1964).

13. Ibid. 138 (8 Sept. 1964).

14. *Western Mail*, 14–15 Oct. 1964.

15. 'Witness Seminar' on the DEA, 5 June 1996.

16. Material in Callaghan Papers, box 31.

PART TWO

1964–1976

11

BAPTISM OF FIRE

'WE greet the Chancellor with a set of briefs (numbered G.B. (64) 1–62) about the main issues of financial and economic policy.' Thus did Sir William Armstrong and Ian Bancroft welcome Callaghan to No. 11 in the early evening of Friday, 16 October 1964.[1] The briefs consisted of around 500 sheets of carefully tabulated material, arranged in forty-nine sections. The message they conveyed was uniformly grim. It formed the backdrop to Callaghan's traumatic public experiences over the next three years. The deficit that Maudling had left the new Chancellor had been steadily revised upwards in recent weeks and was estimated as being as much as £800m. It was believed that the balance of payments would continue in deficit until at least the second half of 1966. No doubt in the light of the colossal growth of the borrowing requirement in the 1990s, the public indebtedness of thirty years earlier might seem modest enough, but in the 1960s such figures as these were invested with an air of imminent doom. The new Chancellor would also have to 'get a grip of public expenditure', with defence expenditure forecast to be £2,140.7m. in 1965–6, and expensive new commitments in civil expenditure such as the Anglo-French transatlantic airliner Concord (the British still omitted the final French 'e' at this stage). Severe cuts in public expenditure and higher taxes to restrict domestic demand were felt to be inevitable. There would also be threats to sterling's role as a world reserve currency, which would mean a range of measures yet to be decided to bolster the exchange rate of the pound.

Even had Maudling not left this difficult legacy, and done so with such remarkable casualness, any new chancellor in October 1964—particularly a Labour one likely to face threats from foreign speculators—would have had a difficult inheritance. The boom years of the 1950s, when British exports flourished in easy markets and import prices fell, were over. Britain's manufacturing performance and productivity were still respectable in absolute terms, but clearly falling behind that of competitor countries such as Germany and France, quite apart from the astonishing growth of Japan. With an above-average inflation rate at home, despite the deflationary policies of Selwyn Lloyd in 1961–2, the outcome was frequent balance of payments deficits which had endured for some years, quite apart from the damaging consequences of Maudling's 'dash for growth'. Labour's answer to these problems while in opposition had been to offer a kind of 'supply-side' approach, which emphasized the need for improved long-term investment, the retraining of labour and the revitalizing of management, and dealing with the social and economic roots of domestic equality. But these would manifestly take some years to show results. Pending that transformation, Labour's approach was for a balanced growth, steering a discreet course between the twin dangers of a recession and over-rapid growth leading to a surge in imports and a balance of payments crisis. Much had been made of the need for a stable economic environment in place of Tory 'stop-go'. But Labour's own macro-economic diagnosis did not differ fundamentally from that of the outgoing Conservatives, namely that the need was for higher and sustained growth. Neither embraced the view of later post-Keynesian economic commentators (including Callaghan's son-in-law Peter Jay) that the real British problem was not growth but inflation, or rather the inability to sustain stable prices with high levels of employment. The main policy that Labour appeared to offer was the panacea of 'planning', with the proposed National Economic Plan, to set the course of the economy over the next five or six years as its centrepiece.

In terms of the domestic economy, Harold Wilson and his colleagues could reasonably foresee a brighter future. Some of the problems that would bedevil the economy in later years were not serious at this period. Inflation was not yet seen as one of Callaghan's immediate problems: it was to average a little over 2 per cent in his three years at the Treasury. Nor was unemployment (1.7 per cent in October 1964) a great worry at this time, although always a sensitive issue in talks with the TUC when an incomes policy was discussed. Any increase at all was a matter of concern.

What caused the underlying unease abroad—especially in the United States where Treasury officials were consistently pessimistic over the prospects of the British economy—was Britain's external position. Callaghan was to tell the Cabinet in July 1965 of 'a serious lack of confidence overseas in the future of the country. We were continuing to live on borrowings and this situation could not be corrected without a slowing down in the rate of growth in the economy.'[2] Foreign markets and speculators noted the growth of Britain's liquid debts, dating from Maudling's last phase. Indeed it has been argued that the incoming Labour ministers added to the problem by underlining the burden of their inherited deficit.[3] This caused especial alarm in the United States, although in fact the US administration added to the problem by putting pressure on Britain to maintain its defence commitment around the world, and notably east of Suez. More fundamentally, there was the well-established phenomenon of an ageing nation living beyond its means, relying on its borrowings, and playing out great-power pretensions which had largely been invalidated since 1945. The problems were compounded by the constant difficulty of Britain trying to maintain the pound as a world reserve currency. Although this was not immediately questioned by the new Labour government, nor by Callaghan himself, it clearly made Britain vulnerable to threats to its reserves through international speculation. Economists of historical disposition argued that, with the disintegration of the old empire and the financial dominance of the United States, the very concept of sterling as a reserve currency, of large but vulnerable sterling balances and a 'sterling area', was dangerously out of date. Roy Jenkins, almost alone of front-rank Labour politicians, had advanced this view also in *The Labour Case* (1959). The argument focused attention above all on the exchange rate of the pound. Ever since the financial crisis of 1931, the pound had been declining steadily in relation to the dollar. Devaluation had been discussed—though instantly rejected—by Treasury officials prior to the 1964 election. But clearly the issue would cast its shadow over any incoming administration in October 1964.

Callaghan contemplated these problems in October 1964 from the vantage point of the Treasury. It was an agency of government which Labour had long tended to view with suspicion. One aspect of the move that was not wholly acceptable, it seemed, was the domestic. Audrey Callaghan was not impressed with No. 11 Downing Street, which she found 'rambling' as compared with 'our most convenient modern house'.[4] As regards his new department, Callaghan himself was old enough to recall the trauma of 1931 and a 'bankers' ramp' with all that meant for Labour's folk memories. Many of these fears had been revived in the last years of Conservative government, with the Treasury felt to be the agent of 'stop-go' short-termism, and hostile to policies of economic growth which might add to the level of public expenditure. In addition, Lord Cromer, the Governor of the nationalized Bank of England since 1961, was seen as a right-wing reactionary in Labour circles, in the direct line of descent from Montagu Norman. Indeed, in at least one respect, Cromer was to emerge as worse than Norman since he made his criticisms of the Labour government very public in a number of speeches. Crossman described him to the Prime Minister in February 1965 as no more than 'a one-man May Committee' (a reference to the Economy Committee whose report of July 1931 indirectly led to the downfall of MacDonald's Labour government) and asked that he be 'shut up'.[5] Callaghan, Brown, and other ministers shared his view.

The new Chancellor had somehow to fight free from these potential shackles. He shared to the full the view that Labour developed after the 1959 election that new planning instruments must be devised to provide a long-term approach to economic management. On the other hand, the proposed Department of Economic Affairs might create more difficulties than it solved, especially with George Brown in charge of it, and as shadow Chancellor Callaghan was naturally anxious that his own role should not be neutered or diminished in authority simply to provide a solution to a political balancing act for Harold Wilson. His view from the start was that the Treasury should be reformed and revitalized, not undermined.

Even with the new experiment of the DEA coming into being, with such powerful figures as Sir Eric Roll and Donald MacDougall running it, the Chancellor still inherited the premier department of government, of whose historical centrality he was very well aware. In parliament, he had two able ministers in support—Jack Diamond, a former accountant who became Financial Secretary to the Treasury, and Neill MacDermott, an Irish barrister knowledgeable on legal complexities. They remained Callaghan's essential ministerial team for almost two years, the Chancellor successfully resisting a possible move of Diamond elsewhere in the government. In the summer of 1967, however, MacDermott was somewhat extraordinarily to be removed from government after security rumours from within MI5 surrounding his (or rather his wife's) links with eastern Europe. He had himself once worked for MI5 as a colleague of Philby. It was alleged that his wife had been the mistress of Russian agents in the 1950s, and that he himself was a possible security risk. His promising political career (he was now Solicitor-General) came to an abrupt end.[6]

His civil service advisers in the Treasury gave Callaghan an immensely powerful armoury. He may have viewed them with some initial suspicion on class or ideological grounds, but their intellectual power and sheer weight in the making of policy added enormously to the Chancellor's authority. Sir William Armstrong, Permanent Secretary, was without doubt the dominant intellectual force in the making of economic policy. He was strongly opposed to the devaluation of sterling. It is very possible that the more mercurial 'Otto' Clarke, over whom amongst others Armstrong was promoted as Permanent Secretary in July 1962, and who had strongly endorsed devaluation in 1949, might have taken a different view. To Armstrong, Callaghan was inescapably bound, even if (in Sir Alec Cairncross's view) he found the introverted Armstrong unduly inclined to keep his own counsel at times. He and the Permanent Secretary developed a good working relationship, however. This was seen in the way they collaborated in 1966–7 in the decision to transfer the Royal Mint to Llantristant, near Cardiff. Callaghan's successful liaison with Armstrong included a ticket to the Wales–England rugby international at Cardiff Arms Park which, despite the heavy rain and an English defeat, the Permament Secretary much enjoyed.[7] His presence alone would ensure that the Treasury would be dislodged from its central role in government only with difficulty.

The Chancellor's private secretary until the summer of 1966 was Ian Bancroft. He was an influential and liberal-minded Treasury figure, initially appointed in the later Maudling period. The Chancellor worked closely and well with him also, as he did with Bancroft's successor Peter Baldwin. Bancroft in his turn developed a strong relationship with Callaghan who impressed him by his hard work (far more noticeable than in the case of Reginald Maudling) and his open-minded willingness to learn. He admitted that he was not a specialist economist and was fully prepared to ask questions of his advisers, which Bancroft saw as a sign of strength not of weakness. He went through his 'boxes' in the Treasury each morning with Bancroft beside him. On balance, his secretary felt that he slipped into his new role with remarkable ease. He was not easily overawed by the tasks confronting him. 'Robust' was his officials' description of him.[8]

On the other hand, the exclusion of senior civil servants from key ministerial meetings testified to some abiding suspicion of the role of Treasury advisers. This was acknowledged, and much resented, in some official circles. Sir Denis Rickett for one protested at his exclusion, but Callaghan gave no ground. On one memorable occasion, according to Cairncross, he asked Rickett, with some exasperation, precisely what it would require for him ever to vote Labour. Sir Eric Roll, now permanent under-secretary at George Brown's DEA, was necessarily at some remove from Treasury decision-making. On the other hand, one much more junior Treasury adviser had far more access to the Chancellor, namely Peter Jay, his son-in-law, whose influence was always important.

A somewhat different relationship existed with the Economic Section of the Cabinet, headed since 1961 by Sir Alec Cairncross, a shrewd Glaswegian of broadly Fabian outlook. After a difficult start, when it seemed that Cairncross was being shunted into the Washington embassy instead, he and Callaghan enjoyed a good, even friendly, working relationship. Congenial Labour-inclined advisers were inserted, of whom the most important was Robert Neild. Callaghan retrospectively felt Neild to have been his closest adviser. On the other hand, the Economic Section stood at some distance from the Treasury. To the new Chancellor's surprise, they told him that they had seldom met Maudling during his period at the Treasury.[9] Long periods would go by without Callaghan meeting Cairncross or his colleagues either, but in time the relationship became much closer. In particular, the views of the Economic Section and of Cairncross himself were to have a decisive impact on Callaghan in determining the timing of devaluation in November 1967, and the fiscal measures that would accompany it. Significantly, many of the key personnel of Callaghan's Oxford group in the 1961–4 period were not used in the Treasury, although some of them turned up amongst the battalion of Oxbridge economists who worked in George Brown's DEA.

However, two advisers of much personal weight did come in, both of them favoured by Harold Wilson. They were the famous Hungarian economists ('Buda' and 'Pest' in the media) Thomas Balogh and Nicky Kaldor. Balogh was not a favourite of Callaghan's. He had been pestering him on various topics from Malta to the exchange rate for some years. The civil servants found him talkative, intrusive, and disruptive; one of them summed him up as 'Wilson's spy'. Not surprisingly, Balogh was a particular intimate of Richard Crossman, another of Wilson's entourage. Armstrong found himself having to arrange extra meetings simply to placate Balogh; he is said to have observed, 'other people have strikes, we have meetings'.[10] To Callaghan, some observers felt, he was essentially a nuisance. But he was also a recognizably socialist gadfly with a strong relationship with the Prime Minister. Nicky Kaldor, however, who had been in Callaghan's private group from 1962, was far more acceptable, even if as verbose as Balogh. Callaghan was loyal in defending Kaldor against attacks in the press and amongst right-wing Tory MPs, which threw in his Hungarian origins ('miserable chauvinism' was Callaghan's private view)[11] as well as his influence on public taxation. Callaghan took the unusual course of writing to *The Times* in December 1964 asking that newspaper to focus its attacks on him rather than criticize an adviser like Kaldor. The Chancellor's budgets owed much to Kaldor. He was much influenced by him in the introduction of corporation and capital gains taxes in his 1965 budget as well as in, less fortunately, the devising of selective employment tax in 1966. Only on the supreme issue of devaluation of the pound (which Kaldor favoured) did Callaghan reject his views totally.

The Treasury, were it to stand alone, was powerful and imposing as an instrument of policy-making in October 1964. But it did not stand alone. As a result of Labour's election campaign and manifesto, there were two major departmental novelties. The first, the Ministry of Technology, was the main practical attempt to implement Harold Wilson's pre-campaign rhetoric about science and the 'white heat of technology'. Its head, surprisingly, was Frank Cousins, the general secretary of the Transport Workers, who shortly became MP for Nuneaton, with such varied scientific advisers as C. P. Snow and Professor Patrick Blackett FRS to back him up. Cousins and Callaghan were hardly blood brothers; Cousins was a figure on the left and a leading figure in the Campaign for Nuclear Disarmament. He never regarded Callaghan with overwhelming enthusiasm. In addition he had enjoyed a close relationship with Callaghan's political rival George Brown, a TGWU nominee.[12] On the other hand, he and the Chancellor had a perfectly reasonable working relationship, until talk of an incomes policy developed at the start of 1966. It was the equally combustible George Brown who had more difficulty with the new Ministry, as with almost everybody else.

On the other hand, the creation of a new major department for George Brown, the Department of Economic Affairs, was a constant thorn in the Chancellor's flesh from the start. Many authoritative figures, notably Douglas Jay, had considered from the start that its dualism with the Treasury was a recipe for disaster. He cited the confusions that had arisen in September 1947 when Hugh Dalton was still Chancellor and Stafford Cripps headed the temporary Ministry for Economic Affairs. Alec Cairncross thought the new department was based on a fundamental misunderstanding of French-style planning; in fact, planning in France was prepared within the French Treasury not in a commissariat. Callaghan himself had become increasingly suspicious of the idea of a DEA, since the precise boundary between its remit and that of the Treasury remained so unclear. Indeed Harold Wilson almost wilfully left matters vague so that neither Callaghan nor Brown could become an overmighty challenger to the throne. Long-term planning was hardly the specialism of a premier who 'flew by the seat of his pants'. A crude popular stereotype existed of an inflationary DEA and a deflationary Treasury, an accelerator and brake in perpetual conflict. Callaghan himself spoke of the false image of a 'musty old Treasury always putting a dampener on what was at hand'. 'Creative tension' was somehow to emerge as the outcome. It would have been an administrative mess whatever the personalities. But matters were made much worse by the DEA's being led by the ever forceful George

Brown, a gifted but impulsive figure, and a former trade unionist like Callaghan himself. Within the Treasury, the initials DEA were said to stand for 'Department of Extraordinary Aggression'.

From the start, there were clashes between the two key ministers, including in Cabinet where Callaghan found it difficult to impose himself on colleagues. As Sir Alec Cairncross privately observed, Brown was 'a hell for leather character';[13] not infrequently he was drunk. The new Chancellor found himself on occasion shouted down in full Cabinet. On the other hand, Callaghan, who had stood up combatively to Shinwell or Bevan in the past, was no shrinking violet himself, and he began to respond in kind. By early 1965 civil servants noted that in the frequent rows between these two members of Labour's 'big three' it was Callaghan who was often the aggressor, Brown the more ready to withdraw or even apologize. On balance, however, Bancroft felt that Callaghan was highly successful in keeping his temper and composure when Brown ranted over the telephone, and gradually emerged as much the more effective of the two.[14]

Clearly something had to be done. The broad premiss that the Treasury would deal with the short term and the DEA with the long term was vague to the point of total absurdity. With the gravity of the national situation, the economy could hardly be left to the conflicting pressures of the Chancellor and the Minister of Economic Affairs, with the Prime Minister, himself a trained economist after all, all too prone to put his oar in as well. Lloyd George had observed that you could not govern with a sanhedrin. In economic policy, a troika was (to adapt a phrase in another context from Princess Diana) 'a bit crowded'. Weary sessions were held in the first few weeks of the administration between William Armstrong on behalf of the Treasury and Sir Eric Roll for the DEA, with the secretary of the Cabinet, Burke Trend, holding the ring. Turf wars of all kinds emerged. On occasion, Callaghan and Brown intervened personally with forceful, if often divergent, views.

There was a difficult meeting in Sir Lawrence Helsby's room on 2 November, with Armstrong and Richard ('Otto') Clarke of the Treasury and Roll and MacDougall of DEA present.[15] MacDougall offered the view here that the Treasury's main interest was in the 'vertical' division of public sector outlay, while the DEA was interested in the 'horizontal' division of expenditure between various categories. But this did not remove the difficulty. It was noted that public sector expenditure was hardly a discrete area of policy. There was 'a spectrum from those of almost exclusive Treasury concern (e.g. Pensions, forces pay etc.) to those of prime DEA interest (nuclear power, public investment and construction industry etc. . . .)'. The Treasury supply divisions were not engaged in considering public sector expediture, so it was recorded, from the point of view of 'old fashioned financial criteria' but from that of broad economic criteria. A sceptical Callaghan privately underlined the words 'old fashioned' and added two bold exclamation marks in the margin.[16]

The Treasury drew up a draft agreement on 2 December, but even that required further extensive rewriting.[17] Finally on 16 December, when the government had been in office for two months grappling with horrific economic crises, a final version of the agreement was drawn up.[18] Its formal author was Peter Jay who supplied the historically respectable term 'concordat' for the deal. The Treasury's functions were said to focus on the management of the civil service and other public services, public sector expenditure, and home and overseas finance and monetary policy. The DEA would formulate a plan for economic development including forecasting and modelling; supervising its implementation; and developing machinery for questions of external economic policy. The DEA would be 'primarily responsible for the long-term aspects' and the 'Treasury for the short-term'; the DEA would be primarily concerned with resources, the Treasury with finance. There would be 'a network of mutual information and consultation'. The word 'primary' in relation to both departments did not, however, mean 'only' or 'exclusive'. The short term did not exclude the long term and vice versa.

Yet, for all the best endeavours of very able men like Trend and Armstrong, it is difficult to imagine a document that was more likely to lead to confusion and administrative deadlock. It was, in fact, a total mess. Since the Treasury retained control of such essential areas as exchange rate policy and taxation, it was difficult to see precisely how the DEA could possibly formulate economic planning in the long term. The confusion and the shouting continued throughout 1965. Nigel Lawson, then a journalist in the *Financial Times*, spoke of bitter battles between Callaghan and Brown, although the Chancellor himself chose to deny it. In practice, the difficulties confronting the new DEA from the start and the established position of the Treasury, along with the nature of the external financial crisis that arose in 1965–6, meant that it was Callaghan's authority which tended to grow. He had, after all, the immense weight behind him of William Armstrong, always intellectually dominant, a workaholic always on the job since his flat was very near the Treasury. Sir Eric Roll, by contrast, was only seldom in evidence in the office of the DEA. The famous concordat proved to be a defunct document eighteen months later as the DEA crumbled into desuetude. But the problems the position created for a harassed and pressurized Chancellor over a long and difficult period were undeniable—and certainly avoidable. For a government supposedly dedicated to modernizing and a streamlined system of decision-making, it was the worst possible start. Labour did not repeat it in 1997.

The tone of Labour's economic policy was set from the very start by a key meeting on its first day in office. At 11 a.m. on Saturday, 17 October, there met at No. 10 Wilson, Brown, and Callaghan, along with Armstrong and Helsby for the Treasury, and MacDougall and Eric Roll for the DEA. It was agreed, almost without discussion, to endorse the Prime Minister's insistence that devaluation of the pound was not an option and the government would not pursue it. The very word 'devaluation' does not appear in the minutes of the meeting. Civil servants in effect removed it from their policy agendas, no papers were circulated on the topic, and there was no discussion of the topic again until July 1966. Officials who even hinted at the possibility were rebuked, their memoranda censored. The meeting on 17 October briskly got on to other topics—the control of imports, reducing the level of demand, determining priorities for public expenditure. A controlled deflation policy was to be prepared, without causing social damage or impairing Britain's ability to borrow. A later meeting of Wilson, Callaghan, and Brown alone with no officials present at 6 p.m. that day confirmed the strategy.[19]

It was a fateful decision which has been hotly debated since. There were many in government at the time—for instance Kaldor and Neild—who felt that they should have seized the moment to devalue immediately and thus capture the initiative. Donald MacDougall considered the rejection of devaluation a fundamental error. It has become a litany among later commentators that this initial decision in effect doomed the Wilson government's economic standing from the start. Edmund Dell's scathing account of Callaghan's (and every other) chancellorship makes the failure to devalue the core of his argument. But this view underestimates many features of the position in October 1964. The majority of economists at the time were firmly against devaluation. So were Armstrong and the Governor of the Bank of England, Cromer. It was strongly argued that devaluing the pound would harm the balance of payments by raising the cost of imports and have an adverse effect on domestic prices. Douglas Jay, the President of the Board of Trade, was a distinguished economist himself who had been closely involved in the devaluation of 1949. He felt that repeating that decision now would lead to the danger of a competitive devaluation by other currencies while an outflow of capital could have been dealt with by normal exchange controls. He also felt it would generate cynicism amongst world opinion in view of the tone of the past election campaign.[20]

Callaghan himself felt that it was in part a moral issue. Britain had obligations of trust to overseas holders of sterling, many of whom were third-world countries (Malaysia, for instance) in the early stages of economic development. There was also the effect on world trade and on American opinion which was vehemently against a devaluation of sterling which might well lead to further pressure on the dollar. For an Atlanticist like Callaghan who placed reliance on American friends like Al Hayes or Bob Roosa with whom he had recently discussed the position of sterling, this was a determining factor. Harold Wilson himself responded to these economic arguments. He had been a reluctant devaluer in 1949 and followed Thomas Balogh in believing that the problems of the economy were 'real' issues of production and supply rather than a question of market measures. It was a view he had taken long ago in his time as President of the Board of Trade. But for him—and perhaps for all his Cabinet—the overriding element was political. For an incoming Labour government to be saddled from the start with the stigma of devaluation, as MacDonald's had indirectly been in 1931 (in fact it had been the National Government that had devalued then) and Attlee and Cripps had been in 1949, would have been political suicide. It would have destroyed the government's credibility in the world at a stroke. It is, therefore, not merely unsurprising but defensible that Callaghan and others should have tried to avoid devaluation almost at all costs when they took office. To argue otherwise is to argue from hindsight, and from a distinctly more comfortable position than that in which ministers found themselves during the actual crisis in October 1964. It is noticeable that Edmund Dell's severe critique underplays this political aspect: then and later, Callaghan and leading civil servants considered Dell 'a political innocent'. The position on sterling was held then and perhaps rightly so. Whether it should have continued to be held after July 1966 is another matter. William Armstrong did at least come to concede that devaluation might be inevitable some day. In 1965 he secretly prepared a 'War Book' for policy on sterling should it come about. The authors were a secret 'FU' committee: FU stood for 'Forever Unmentionable'.

Nevertheless, with immediate pressure on the pound and heavy selling on Continental markets, the Chancellor had to take immediate action. He told a relieved Douglas Dillon, the US Secretary to the Treasury, on 19 October that the pound would not be devalued,[21] but clearly something had to be done promptly. The government ruled out import controls (which some ministers favoured) as too destructive, but on 26 October

Brown announced, with Callaghan in attendance, that there would be a 15 per cent surcharge on all foreign imports.[22] This caused a massive outcry, notably from other European countries including Britain's partners in EFTA who felt betrayed. Douglas Jay, never a lover of Continentals, found himself having to defend Britain's action at the EFTA meeting at Geneva on 18–21 November. In the interim, the French, 'in an act of pure hypocrisy and dishonesty', had been stirring up European opinion against the perfidious British.[23] Jay's partner at Geneva was Patrick Gordon Walker, the Foreign Secretary, whose own standing had been much weakened by his having lost his seat at Smethwick in the general election. Facing a threat of retaliatory action from EFTA which might well lead to trade difficulties for Commonwealth countries, Gordon Walker reported to the Cabinet on 24 November that Britain had been forced to concede that it would reduce and finally abolish the import surcharge within a short space of time.[24] The entire episode did not improve the government's shaky position. For ministers like Callaghan it may have confirmed a long-held view that, while the Europeans were unpredictable and liable to spread doubts about the strength of the pound, only the Americans could be relied upon for help in a crisis.

Apart from the import surcharge, Callaghan had the more fundamental task of preparing an emergency budget to try to deal with the crisis and stop the run on the reserves. He proposed an initial package of £217m.–£238m. of cuts in public expenditure, to which might be added others in defence and railway closures. Prescription charges would have to remain for the time being.[25] On the other hand, the government had inherited a clutch of spending commitments from the election for pensions, schools, and other matters, while Callaghan had to modify a proposal to defer national insurance benefit payments following a protest from the popular Pensions Secretary, the Scot Margaret Herbison.[26] At a meeting with Wilson late on 27 October, Callaghan outlined the broad problem. There was a need to reduce purchasing power by up to £340m., over half being due to countering the inflationary effect of the import surcharge. Taxes would have to be raised. Wilson suggested a *6d.* increase in income tax, along with an increase in surtax, higher profits tax, and other measures. Extraordinarily, he suggested that Callaghan should seek Cabinet approval for additional revenue of £300m. without indicating at that stage precisely how it would be raised, which is what happened.[27] Callaghan himself added a point, not included in the official record of his meeting with the Prime Minister, that the import surcharge should run only to August 1965 and be subject to renewal thereafter.[28]

Callaghan's budget statement on 11 November was a tense affair. Alec Cairncross felt he 'delivered it well except perhaps that he seemed at times almost too anxious to illustrate his point and get it across'.[29] It received much praise from colleagues, including from the former Scottish Secretary Arthur Woodburn, who felt it was the most impressive for 'clarity, competence and good manners' that he had heard since 1939.[30] But the important point was the content and how the markets responded to it. Callaghan's statement began with critical comments about his inheritance from the Tories but that was of purely historical and partisan interest after all. What the market noticed was the new taxes and social expenditure, at a time when a large balance of payments deficit had been announced. The taxes would include *6d.* on the standard rate of income tax and another *6d.* on petrol and diesel fuel. The imposition of a new capital gains tax and corporation tax was announced (Douglas Jay criticized the latter as being an unnecessary and cumbersome replacement of the existing profits tax). On the other hand, as a sign of Labour's radical credentials there would be increases in pensions, national insurance benefits, and national assistance rates. One benefit perhaps drawn from Callaghan's own experience was an improvement in the meagre widows' benefits.

On balance the budget was mildly deflationary. But that was not how the markets saw it, either genuinely or wilfully. The new taxes, especially the corporation tax, spelt out in vague enough terms, were seen as a new destabilizing charge on business and enterprise. The new social expenditure of £345m. a year increase on pensions and benefits was felt to be irresponsible at a time which above all called for restraint. The international financial community saw in it a signal that the government was failing to recognize the seriousness of the situation, just as an earlier Labour government had failed in 1931. In the words of William Davis of the *Guardian*, not an unfriendly observer, the budget was felt to be 'a costly blunder'.[31] It was followed by a huge wave of selling of sterling. On 20 November it emerged that there was massive loss in the gold and foreign exchange reserves, a hefty fall in industrial share prices and in the value of gilt-edged, and open talk of a devaluation of the pound. In the view of *The Times*, 'It was the worst day of the post-election slide.'[32]

At a meeting on the evening of 17 November, Wilson and Callaghan had agreed that, if at all possible, they should try to avoid a rise in bank rate which could 'conflict with the government's policy objectives'. Despite complaints from Cromer, Wilson sent a message to President Johnson in Washington suggesting that the United States as well as Britain had an interest in the raising of interest rates, and appealing instead for 'substantial and early help' from America.[33] But none was forthcoming, and a meeting of ministers at Chequers on the afternoon of Saturday, 21 November, agreed that bank rate would rise by 2 per cent to 7 per cent at 10 a.m. on Monday, the 23rd. Perhaps unwisely, the agreed statement went on to say that 'It might be possible to couple the undeniably deflationary effect of the Bank Rate increase with a measure of "selective inflation" in certain areas of the economy and regions of the country where there was slack to take up'.[34]

Even after bank rate was raised on 23 November, however, sterling remained under heavy pressure. The following day Cromer, the Governor of the Bank of England, and Leslie O'Brien, his deputy, met Callaghan at 5.30 p.m. to report a loss of $211m. on the day. Cromer took the opportunity to promote his own agenda and to suggest 'the deferment of what foreign opinion would regard as the more doctrinal [*sic*] elements in the Government's legislative programme'.[35] Late that evening, Wilson and Callaghan had a tense meeting with Cromer and O'Brien which went on until 11.30 p.m.[36] Cromer declared that Britain faced a huge crisis of confidence and called for a credit squeeze and a major deflation. As an extra, he called for the nationalization of steel to be withdrawn. Wilson responded with considerable force, concluding his remarks by threatening to float the pound and to call an immediate general election on a broad 'who governs Britain?' theme. As the Prime Minister phrased it, they would have to 'consider seeking a mandate for devaluation'. Cromer retorted that 'to go to the country on that issue would mean putting Party before Country', but he was reportedly taken aback. In practice, it gave the government a little more breathing space. But the pressure on sterling continued relentlessly. This was very much the kind of early crisis that Callaghan and others had feared might confront any new Labour government and which he had spent some time in America trying to anticipate. But it was on a more serious scale than in his worst forebodings.

As the selling of sterling went on apace on 25 November, the US connection finally began to pay dividends for the beleaguered British government. Remarkably, Henry 'Joe' Fowler, the US Treasury Secretary, was to tell President Lyndon Johnson some months later that Callaghan had privately shown his predecessor, Douglas Dillon, the terms of his budget shortly before presenting it to the House of Commons.[37] By adroit crisis diplomacy, a massive package of international aid amounting to $3,000m. was rapidly assembled by Cromer and O'Brien, with Al Hayes, president of the Federal Reserve Bank of New York, the pivotal figure. A significant amount, $500m., came from American sources, with German and ten other central banks, along with the Bank of International Settlements, supplying the rest. It was seven days that had shaken sterling, and Labour's confidence in general. *The Economist*, in historical vein, commented that 'the Labour government had gone to Canossa'.[38] It was in hock to the world. Callaghan explained to the Cabinet and to parliament that the aid package did not mean that further difficult choices could be avoided, and that a thorough review of public expenditure in all areas would be undertaken. *The Times* reported that he seemed 'much less smooth and relaxed than he has so far been as Chancellor'.[39]

With this package of credits, the immediate crisis now appeared to be over. Al Hayes rang through from New York to say that United Kingdom policies were now on the right lines.[40] He and Bob Roosa publicly endorsed the wisdom of not having any realignment of currencies. Sterling kept its existing rate, or even gained in strength above the $2.80 level for a time. This continued to be the case until the new year. At home, the stock exchange was somewhat stronger although there were some jittery periods throughout December. Callaghan had to give some hostages to fortune in the interim to placate the markets. In a statement of 'clarification', he assured them on 8 December that there would be a generous view taken of exemptions to capital gains tax.[41] He made clear that the politically sensitive area of owner-occupied houses was never intended to be included. Corporation tax might be no more than 35 per cent. On 15 December he announced the public burial of any idea of a wealth tax, an idea which he had himself floated at the party conference in 1963 despite Harold Wilson's disapproval.[42] On 2–3 December, accompanied by Tony Crosland, Callaghan had had a potentially very difficult time at his first meeting of the OECD. He had to defend the imposition of the import surcharge in face of overseas 'uproar', and to justify the social expenditure proposed in his budget. More positively, he outlined new measures to stimulate exports and reduce the anticipated surge in imports. Any speculative attacks of sterling could now be warded off through use of the reserves.[43] In fact, his speech was well received and the Chancellor's somewhat battered standing appeared to improve. Cromer, sending lengthy messages to the Chancellor on his dictaphone, relentlessly added to the gloom. He sent an emergency message to Wilson on 21 December saying that 'the financial and economic situation is deteriorating' and talking of 'the demoralisation of the security markets'. At a meeting with Wilson and Callaghan on 23 December, he listed a number of countries, Burma, Libya, and Jordan among them, where there was heavy selling of sterling. Wilson managed to persuade him to keep calm for the moment. He declined the view that he should give an emergency prime ministerial broadcast on television. The Prime Minister and Chancellor proposed that the end of month losses from the reserves could be given as £8m., rather than the real total of £115m., by deleting £107m. financed by borrowing.[44] This seemed to do the trick. By the new year, the threat to the pound seemed over, at least for the moment, and the government and the Chancellor could look forward to somewhat more tranquil times. The *Financial Times* could speak of exports picking up and confidence returning.[45]

It had, however, been a traumatic baptism of fire, even worse than an incoming Labour Chancellor could have anticipated. The import surcharge, precipitately pushed ahead by Brown over the hesitations of Gordon Walker, Jay, and others, was a public relations disaster. Callaghan's budget had been badly received. At the end of the month, Britain was forced to take the option of deferring its end-year payments on North American loans, amounting to £62m. in interest and principal.[46] The government, with a majority of only two, and Gordon Walker, the Foreign Secretary, facing a difficult by-election at Leyton (which, in fact, he was to lose), seemed in a precarious state, surviving rather than governing.

The pressures on the Chancellor, normally so confident and articulate, had taken their toll. On 5 December he travelled down by train to south Wales with a fellow Welsh MP, Desmond Donnelly, an erratic and gossipy colleague.[47] Donnelly found the Chancellor apparently tired, listless, and preoccupied. To make matters worse there had been some confusion in booking his train ticket. Callaghan, he reported, whispered that he had been through hell. He quoted a letter in *The Times* that 'all Chancellors leave either in disgrace or get out in time'. Callaghan commented, 'I have begun in disgrace.' The Chancellor went on that he was now saying his prayers for the first time in years. He was operating far beyond his depth, the paperwork was killing, and the strain of the responsibility appalling. 'He shocked me at the end', wrote Donnelly, 'by saying that he was going to tell Harold that he could only do the job for 18 months. Defeat begins in the heart, I'm afraid.'

There is little doubt that Callaghan's self-confidence was for a while at a low ebb; it would have been surprising if this were not so. Derek Mitchell, the Prime Minister's personal secretary, wrote to Wilson thoughtfully suggesting that he might see a warm letter from Bob Roosa of the US Treasury which strongly praised Callaghan's speech to the Group of Ten in Paris. Roosa described Callaghan's speech as 'the clearest and straightest we have ever had from a Chancellor or at any rate UK spokesman'. He expressed his confidence that the British economy had 'bottomed out' and that an upward movement in sterling and the reserves would shortly follow. Mitchell showed this to Wilson and suggested that, 'in view of what we know of the Chancellor's morale, it might be a kindly gesture if you were to take Bob Roosa's letter as a cue for a manuscript note to the Chancellor designed to raise his morale and wish him a good rest over Christmas'. Ian Bancroft added that the reception of Callaghan's statement in Paris was 'extremely good'.[48]

It was a traumatic time at the Treasury, and it would certainly not be the last. Even so, the initial storm had been weathered. Callaghan was shaken but not broken. Indeed he emerged in the more tranquil period in early 1965 toughened by the experience. It had been a difficult episode, but he had found his feet. He also showed himself a fast learner. In particular, he had discovered a good deal about international aspects of finance, liquidity, and indebtedness, a highly technical area which he was to make his own.[49] The extent to which the lessons had been absorbed would now be shown.

Callaghan returned from his Christmas break in more typically confident and energetic vein. He wrote to Wilson on 12 January suggesting a range of options if sterling proved slow to recover.[50] In addition to gaining an extension of the $3 bn. credit down to the end of 1965 to convince speculators, other possibilities included a further IMF credit, calling up the overseas investments holdings of UK residents (amounting to £3,000m.), the sale of non-sterling portfolio investments, possible restrictions on the export of capital, and pressure on the Germans to pay more for the support costs of the British army on the Rhine. In fact, although there was a continued slow drain on the reserves, the pound remained robust and it was a far more gentle spring for the economy after the storms of the autumn. Douglas Dillon, the US Secretary to the Treasury, gave cheer to the stock exchange in early February by declaring that the British financial crisis was over. Callaghan added to the better atmosphere by hinting that the import surcharge might shortly come to an end; in fact, it was to be cut to 10 per cent in the April budget, but lingered on until November 1966.[51] A continuing thorn in the ministerial flesh was the series of independent pronouncements by the Governor of the Bank of England, Cromer, calling for further swingeing cuts in public expenditure. This led to furious protests from George Brown, Crossman, and Balogh and calls for Wilson to discipline him. Callaghan himself was more measured. He summoned Cromer to tell him that 'he is making my task more difficult by these excursions into the policy field so close to the Budget and at a time when I am trying with some success to secure an orderly development of the national finances'.[52] But the affair passed over, with even Nigel Lawson in the *Financial Times* criticizing the Governor for going considerably beyond the normal bounds of independence allowed in his office.[53]

The spring was taken up with preparations for the April budget. This was a far more measured process than the emergency budget of October, with the Chancellor now under less pressure. Abroad, sterling was more stable, though still somewhat shaky; at home, relations between Callaghan and George Brown, and their two rival departments, had appeared to settle down, even if only on the basis of an armed truce. It was Brown who seemed to be facing most of the pressure now as he laboured intensively with the unions and employers' organizations to produce a credible National Plan, following the publication of the Declaration of Intent before Christmas. Conversely, like all Chancellors Callaghan had to withstand pressure from other ministers anxious for concessions, notably from Richard Crossman, concerned for aid to building societies to boost the private housing market. But Callaghan now seemed to have recovered his previous buoyancy and equanimity. Alec Cairncross depicts him on 5 April, on the eve of his budget speech, as 'in good form and free from any anxiety now that major decisions lay behind him. He prophesied that next April we would all be sitting there agreeing that we had done the right thing. We wouldn't devalue, there would be no recession, and things would come out to our satisfaction.' When Nicky Kaldor questioned the public response to all the new taxes, the Chancellor responded in jocular vein. 'Well, we haven't had a revolution yet! And if we do, I'll see to it that you get pushed to the front of the crowd.'[54]

The budget speech on 6 April was a major event. Its transit from No. 11 to the Commons included one novelty: the Chancellor carried it in a newly made blue box instead of the historic battered old box used by chancellors since Gladstone in 1860. Callaghan spoke soberly but effectively for two and a half hours. Cairncross thought him to be 'stumbling a little at the beginning, but showing more self-confidence than in November'.[55] He received warm congratulations from two senior Welsh colleagues. George Thomas, who addressed him as 'My dear Leonard' as befitted a comrade from 1945, thought his speech 'excellent. . . . It is marvellous to see you climb to the top.'[56] Jim Griffiths, the veteran Welsh Secretary, thought it 'a magnificent achievement. . . . I was very proud of you as a Welsh colleague.' Callaghan replied a few days later, with evident genuineness, 'As you know I feel my roots are deeper in Wales now than anywhere else, and I am always glad I came in 1943 to the Cardiff Selection Conference'. Another Cabinet colleague, Lord Longford, who referred to

Callaghan's supposed credentials as a practising Christian, thought the budget 'a classic' and 'the man behind it still more to be admired'.[57] Apart from these courtesies, Callaghan's budget was a major one in terms of its tax changes, 'probably the biggest of the century' in his own estimation in his memoirs. There were over fifty new proposals in all, admittedly some of the major ones including capital gains and corporation taxes anticipated in November. Corporation tax would not take effect, however, until April 1966. There would also be, as foreshadowed, another *6d.* on the standard rate of income tax. Other measures included sharp rises in duties on drink and tobacco and a higher licence duty on motor vehicles of all types. In all taxation would rise by £164m. in 1965–6 and by £217m. in 1966–7. Home demand would be reduced by £250m. Among major economies, the Chancellor's wish on financial grounds to scrap the TSR 2 strike reconnaissance aircraft had caused much *angst* in Cabinet. Here Denis Healey, the Defence Minister, also wanted to be rid of it but to substitute the American F/111A instead. In the end, Callaghan got his way and the ending of the TSR 2 was included in his 1965 budget speech.

There were apoplectic responses to the budget in some circles. Major-General Spears, chairman of the Institute of Directors, talked of socialist revolution and of the French guillotine of 1790. An inflamed City businessman denounced the budget as Marxist and spoke of fighting the new taxes on the beaches and the farms (and no doubt in the banks and the bars as well). There were complaints in the 'golden square mile' on the new restrictions on business entertaining. But the general response from markets, City, and press was a favourable one. Callaghan told a Paris colleague, 'it has certainly made the pound very much stronger. I think that those who were faint-hearted about the pound did not realise the tremendous reserves that exist overseas and which I should not hesitate to use.'[58] *The Economist*, approvingly, called it 'orthodox-Treasury-deflationary' rather than 'heretical-Labour-expansionary' and believed that it showed the Treasury had finally won its battle for ascendancy with the DEA.[59] A later decision on 6 June to reduce bank rate from 7 to 6 per cent also went down well. In this instance, a cautious Chancellor seems to have bowed to the demands of a more confident Lord Cromer, an interesting reversal of the usual roles. Sterling did not seem to suffer. *The Economist* noted that the City, which had been neurotically hostile to the new Labour government in October 1964, now seemed much more warmly disposed.[60] Industry, by contrast, showed something of the reverse. Leftish economists, like Nicholas Davenport writing in the *Spectator* at the time, complained that a Labour government was deliberately pursuing a deflationary and restrictive policy which comforted the *rentiers* in the City while it damaged the very industry which Labour was pledged to expand.

Politically, the Cabinet seemed happy with the budget. Wilson seemed far more confident in his Chancellor now. Left-wingers like Barbara Castle and the editors of the *New Statesman* rejoiced in the taxes on corporations and the rich in general, and in the cuts in defence spending. Callaghan and his government seemed to be turning the corner. Even the contentious issue of the nationalization of steel made headway. This was not a measure for which either Callaghan or Brown felt immense enthusiasm. The Chancellor (who had the ailing East Moors works in his constituency) disliked the idea of lavish compensation to the steel owners at a time of economic difficulty. However, as Chancellor, he was responsible, along with Fred Lee, the Minister of Power, for presenting the basis for the compensation package to the Cabinet. In the end, the principle of steel nationalization was scrambled through the Commons by a single-figure majority, even if the actual bill was later deferred to 1965–6. George Brown aided the cause with maximum-decibel pressure on two right-wing Labour dissentients, Woodrow Wyatt and Desmond Donnelly.[61]

The Chancellor was in a buoyant mood once again. The German newspaper *Die Zeit* wrote warmly about him as 'quiet, controlled and friendly'. He radiated warmth on television. It also designated him as the best-looking man in the Cabinet other than Anthony Greenwood.[62] Soon after he and the Prime Minister were given a cheerful interview by David Coleman on the Saturday TV sports programme on their way to the rugby league Challenge Cup Final at Wembley. Callaghan handled a potentially delicate moment (professional rugby league was not popular in rugby-union-playing south Wales) with his usual ineffable skill. He pointed out to the viewers that one of the star players on view, the Wigan winger Billy Boston, came from Tiger Bay in his own constituency. Harold Wilson declared that he had played both codes, rugby union and rugby league, in his time and greatly enjoyed both. Altogether, it was an episode for political connoisseurs.

Much of Callaghan's new confidence came from the consistent support he appeared to be enjoying from the United States, including from its genial Secretary to the Treasury, the Virginia banker and lawyer 'Joe' Fowler. Callaghan in fact felt his predecessor Douglas Dillon to be a 'bigger man' than Fowler, who was essentially 'a cautious lawyer', but they, too, worked well together. A new perspective on the Anglo-American relationship would be afforded on 29–30 June when Callaghan paid his first visit to Washington as a Cabinet minister. His programme would include not only meetings with Fowler and Robert MacNamara, the Defense Secretary, but also with President Lyndon Johnson himself in the White House. It was a difficult time. Apart from the perennial difficulties of the British economy, there were rumblings of disagreement between the British and US governments over Britain's defence commitments, not only in the Far East but even in Germany, while Harold Wilson's attempts to provide some kind of mediatory assistance in the growing bloody imbroglio in Vietnam had been badly received in the White House. Callaghan put it about publicly that he was going to Washington to discuss matters of international liquidity in general. However, Sir Patrick Dean told US government representatives that this was for public consumption only.[63] The real object was to discuss US financial support. 'It almost surely has to do with the state of the pound', McGeorge Bundy told Johnson.[64]

Callaghan's visit was preceded by briefings by Fowler, Bundy, and others which looked at the state of the British economy and finances in the most gloomy terms. He was seen basically as a suppliant, albeit a very important one. However weak an ally Britain was seen to be, its defence deployment east of Suez was regarded as crucially important for the US position in the Far East, while any talk of devaluing the pound would throw immense pressure on the dollar. Fowler's memorandum to Johnson on 28 June described Britain's financial position as 'so weak, its reserves so low, and its liquid debts so heavy that it has been plunging repeatedly into payments crises'.[65] Recent bad trade losses (£57m. in May) had triggered losses of nearly $200m. in the British reserves in three days. Yet the British public remained complacent and unaware of the problem. There remained levels of 6 per cent wage increases and 4.5 per cent price increases. The reserves were in parlous plight. Britain had external debts of more than $16 bn. at the end of May, including more than $8 bn. net in liquid sterling liabilities, whereas the official reserves and fairly realizable assets amounted to a mere $5.2 bn. 'The British have, for all practical purposes, exhausted their recourse to the International Monetary Fund and have been told by European officials that it would be politically impossible for them to extend further credit.' Further US credits were, therefore, inescapable although Fowler also urged that a long-term multilateral financing approach be adopted, covering three to four years, to buttress the UK reserves and ensure that sterling would not remain under threat. Bundy was more hawkish and also more circumspect. 'We should not make any deals with the British on the pound alone.' He added, 'none of us expects this kind of deal can be made with Callaghan. It will have to be a bargain at higher and broader level.'[66] He also murmured about the situation in Vietnam and the British attitude to it. Francis Bator, another presidential economist, was however more sympathetic: he sent Johnson newspaper material on the success achieved to date by the new National Board for Prices and Incomes set up by George Brown in April under the chairmanship of the former Tory minister Aubrey Jones.[67]

The briefing given to the White House prior to Callaghan's visit featured such issues as the prospects for equilibrium in the British balance of payments in 1966, proposed measures to check speculative attacks on the pound, and any measures contemplated to avoid showing a further substantial fall in the reserves. There should also be detailed questions about wage settlements and a credit squeeze. Callaghan was expected to want to set up arrangements to continue 'a very close special relationship' over Britain's financial position. The year 1966 was likely to show 'a touch-and-go race between progress in balance of payments improvement and the attrition of the remaining resources against the background of political controversy'.[68] In addition to this bleak scenario, there was a more practical matter. A memo to the president informed him that the name given as 'Callahan' had been misspelt.[69]

Callaghan arrived in New York from Ottawa, where he had had talks with Prime Minister Lester Pearson early on 28 June. He then plunged into meetings with Fowler and his advisers, followed by Gardner Ackley (chairman of the Council of Economic Advisers) and other financial representatives. With all of these, the talks appear to have been cordial and constructive. At 5.35 p.m. he met Johnson at the White House, via the south-west gate, and was driven to the diplomatic entrance. Bundy had suggested 'a brief meeting'. In fact, Callaghan and Johnson talked for an hour, following which the Chancellor held a brief press conference. He was accompanied by the British ambassador, Sir Patrick Dean, and by Sir William Armstrong on the British side; David Bruce, the US ambassador in London, was also present, along with Joe Fowler.[70] The conversation with Johnson turned out to be unfocused and rambling, although Callaghan much enjoyed first-hand exposure to Johnson's overpowering Texan personality. 'The president was in no mood to talk serious business', he recalled. Johnson, however, did confide that he 'hated bankers',[71] perhaps a legacy from his Populist heritage in eastern Texas. Other than Johnson's stream of anecdotes about how he dealt with businessmen and labour leaders, the main theme was Johnson's gratitude to British support for the US role in Vietnam. Significantly, he heaped praise on the Australian government which had gone so far as to send troops to fight in

Vietnam alongside American GIs. This enjoyable episode over, Callaghan and colleagues went off to enjoy a performance of *Fiddler on the Roof*. Perhaps he noted ruefully one of that musical's famous songs, 'If I were a rich man'.

Much controversy centred after Callaghan's visit on whether US aid to Britain had been linked with British support for American policies in Vietnam. Callaghan himself always strongly denied that any linkage had ever been brought up in discussions in which he was involved. Literally, this is wholly correct. Vietnam never appeared formally in such a context. Harold Wilson strongly denied it at the Labour Party conference in September—'Britain would never modify its foreign policy to buy help on sterling.'[72] He had turned down US requests to dispatch British troops on more than one occasion. He and Callaghan regarded the prospect of any British military involvement in Vietnam as unacceptable and quite different in its thrust from the British presence east of Suez in which they both still believed. In Washington, there were the hawkish views of McGeorge Bundy. He had told Johnson on 28 July that 'it makes no sense for us to rescue the Pound in a situation in which there is no British flag in Vietnam, and a threatened British thin-out in both east of Suez and in Germany. What I would like to say to [Burke] Trend myself is that a British Brigade in Vietnam would be worth a billion dollars at the moment of truth for Sterling.'[73] These, he said, were also the views of MacNamara and Dean Rusk, the Secretary of State. But such appalling frankness remained unstated and confidential. On the other hand, it was obvious that Vietnam lay in the background and that attempts to offer British mediation were, to put it mildly, subject to massive constraints.

Callaghan had a much more direct insight into linkage between economic and defence issues the following day when, in the most robust of his meetings, he had a lively exchange with MacNamara, the Secretary for Defense.[74] The latter fiercely denounced proposed naval and other defence cutbacks east of Suez. America would not be the world's policeman and take over Britain's proper role in South-East Asia where the USA was already over-committed. Callaghan hit back with some vigour. He reaffirmed his view that Britain was overstretched in defence terms with a higher proportion of GNP spent on defence than was the case in the United States, and criticized American short-sightedness. After these sharp exchanges, the discussion was more constructive and focused on practical ways in which the Americans could ease the cost of Britain's defence burden. But the linkage here between Britain's international role and the American perception of the balance of payments difficulty was manifest. It should, however, be noted that, for all MacNamara's protestations, the withdrawal from east of Suez did take place over the next few years, despite complaints from Singapore and Kuala Lumpur, not to mention Washington.

Callaghan returned from Washington in pensive mood. The sense of British frailty was overwhelming. But on balance, his visit to the United States had a positive effect, and American aid was duly forthcoming as he gratefully acknowledged to Fowler and others. With assistance from the US Federal Reserve, along with a loan from the IMF, further pressure on sterling that summer was repelled. The government was able to reaffirm that there would be no devaluation; exports, notably of aircraft and machinery, rose sharply; and the deficit on the balance of payments was being rapidly eroded, more quickly indeed than the Treasury had anticipated in October 1964. At the end of September, the spot rate for sterling rose above par for the first time for over five years, and the Bank of England took in large amounts of foreign exchange in the last quarter of the year. It was certainly a happier autumn than that of the previous year. *The Economist*, often critical, hailed Labour's first year for its success in eliminating the long-term capital deficit and for the marked rise in foreign confidence in Britain's Labour government.[75]

The Treasury, then, had come through its baptism of fire in fairly good order, it seemed, with the significant assistance of huge overseas credits. At home, by contrast, there was a picture of limited expansion and distinctly less growth than had been the case in the Maudling years. However, George Brown and the DEA could point to the achievement of the National Plan in September. Agreed after long negotiations, it proclaimed a target of 3.8 per cent a year, or a 25 per cent increase over the six-year period 1964–70.[76] George Brown's presence ensured that the plan would be launched with the maximum of bravura and panache. Sterling would be rescued by socialism. But most economists viewed it with considerable doubts. There appeared to be effective instruments for enforcing neither a wages policy nor price controls. The proposed huge increase in exports might lead as before to an overheating of the economy, and problems again with the balance of payments. A major DEA figure like Ronald McIntosh felt that the refusal to devalue doomed the proposed growth targets from the outset. At the Treasury, Callaghan publicly hailed it in a speech at St Austell on 11 September. But he and Armstrong tried in vain to restrain the DEA and deplored the over-optimism with which the plan was launched. In the very near future these doubts were to confirmed. But for the moment, the Chancellor could remain serene.

While managing the national finances had obviously been Callaghan's main commitment over the previous twelve months, he was of course in addition a powerful figure in the Cabinet and the party whose influence could be thrown in many other directions. By the summer of 1965, Harold Wilson's main energies seemed to be focused elsewhere than on the economy. To the dismay of Crossman, Marcia Williams, and others, his attention was directed towards the American involvement in Vietnam and the growing crisis in Rhodesia which resulted in the unilateral declaration of independence by Ian Smith's government there in late 1965. On both issues, Callaghan's influence was important.

Vietnam was an issue on which he did not speak out publicly in rebuke of American policy.[77] But he was a broadly moderating influence. Long before he visited North Vietnam in January 1973 on a Labour Party delegation,[78] he had concluded that American policy there was doomed to fail. In any case, more than most ministers, the Chancellor wanted to curtail British defence expenditure and commitments. He pressed successfully in the next twelve months for the British military and naval presence in South-East Asia to be withdrawn, even at the cost of annoying his old comrade Lee Kuan Yew. There could be no question of Vietnam being another Korea, as when Oliver Franks persuaded Attlee's Cabinet in July 1950 that the special relationship depended on an early dispatch of British battalions.[79]

Rhodesia concerned Callaghan much more directly. After the UDI on 11 November, he was heavily involved. Indeed, Crossman was startled on 9 December to hear the Chancellor say privately that more than a third of his time was being spent on the Rhodesian problem.[80] Several aspects of the crisis with the illegal Smith regime concerned Callaghan. The imposition of economic sanctions by Britain, and its resultant impact on the British economy, was obviously his problem. In Cabinet in November 1965, while supporting the government's policy of imposing sanctions, he expressed some anxiety that freezing the assets of the Bank of Rhodesia should not encourage withdrawals from the sterling balances held in London.[81] In addition, a major issue for Harold Wilson, whose personal prestige was to be laid on the line on Rhodesia as on no other question, was to enlist the indirect help of the Americans. Callaghan, with his sensitive links with Washington, was an important liaison here. In the event, something was achieved; the Americans were prepared to help the British by putting economic pressure on Salisbury in return for British acquiescence towards US policy on Hanoi. One post-imperial policy bolstered another.

More broadly, Callaghan's long expertise in African matters was also enlisted. In particular, his friendship with Kenneth Kaunda was drawn upon since the President of Zambia (Northern Rhodesia) was thought by Wilson to be a major factor in putting economic pressure on Ian Smith through a 'quick kill' policy of cutting off key exports such as copper. Callaghan tended to be critical of Wilson's diplomatic style. He felt that the Prime Minister combined an initial timidity, in ruling out from the start a show of military force which Callaghan himself would have been prepared to try, with an unreal rhetorical optimism about the impact of sanctions. When the Prime Minister spoke of an oil embargo causing the downfall of the Smith regime 'in weeks rather than months', the Chancellor saw the warning signs of hubris. By 12 January, however, when Wilson was in Lagos for the Commonwealth leaders' conference, he was more sanguine. The presence of British Javelin aircraft, he felt, would make the Rhodesian white settlers the more conscious of the risks they were taking.[82] In practice, though, for all the energy and determination with which Wilson tackled the problem, the opportunity for dislodging Ian Smith and reasserting British authority in central Africa was already slipping away, to haunt Wilson for the rest of his term.

The most direct involvement of Callaghan in wider policy, however, inevitably concerned economic matters. Throughout 1965 the government had concluded that a more effective instrument to curb domestic wage inflation was required than Aubrey Jones's Prices and Incomes Board which, after all, had no effective teeth. Ray Gunter, the Minister of Labour, championed this view. This theme had been pressed hard by US Treasury spokesmen when Callaghan went to Washington at the end of June. By the end of the year, left-wing critics in the Cabinet, notably Frank Cousins, the Minister of Technology, and Barbara Castle, were complaining that a wage freeze policy was being imposed on the sovereign British government by American pressure. Despite official denials, there is no doubt that the Johnson administration, not unreasonably, was seeking guarantees as to the conditions under which its massive new credits would be used. Callaghan found himself also under criticism from his old Inland Revenue boss Douglas Houghton, and more gently from other ministers of trade union background such as Jim Griffiths and Fred Lee.

However, on this issue, the old adversaries, Callaghan and Brown, were of one mind. Brown had reluctantly come to agree with the view that wages were rising far too fast at 8 per cent and kindling inflationary pressures. Sir Alec Cairncross has noted that incomes policy involved as fundamental a change of heart for George Brown as altering the exchange rate of sterling did for Callaghan.[83] Harold Wilson also had come round to accepting that wages should not rise more than increases in productivity and that statutory restraints were needed. Wilson managed to head off an immediate public revolt by the discontented Frank Cousins. 'If I would withhold any action he would be moving for an early election in March, after Jim had made a statement of Budgetary intentions in order to avoid the accusation that we were afraid to face a tough budget', Cousins noted.[84] For the moment a crisis was averted. But clearly it was another issue that Callaghan, the lifelong advocate of trade union voluntarism and unfettered collective bargaining, would bring up again, with controversial implications.

At the start of 1966 Callaghan's position seemed stronger than at any time since he had become Chancellor. The battle with the DEA was never-ending and never far from Callaghan's thoughts. He rebuked Cairncross and colleagues at the end of December over the purely cosmetic issue of whether *Economic Trends* should be published by the Economic Section or the DEA, always anxious to claim any possible credit.[85] On balance, though, the prestige of George Brown was somewhat on the wane. As a balancing factor in the Cabinet Callaghan welcomed the advent of Roy Jenkins, who had succeeded Frank Soskice as Home Secretary. Brown commented on the Chancellor in this connection, 'We'll have to watch him. He's too kind to these buggers.'[86]

With Harold Wilson, his relationship had clearly become closer if not exactly cordial, despite a host of differences on detail. Some time in 1965 Callaghan had sent Wilson a scrappy note, 'I feel that sometimes your constant job is to tell us how well we are doing (when we sometimes aren't) but the chap at the top is hardly ever told he is doing a good job—& he needs encouragement perhaps more than anyone else.' Wilson (who had just been with his Chancellor to a match at Cardiff Arms Park) responded, 'I see my job as a scrum half who can sometimes get the ball, hare off round the blind side of the scrum & go off diagonally to the far corner flag & generally open up the game.'[87] It is a vision which in rugby terms hardly bears close examination, but politically it clearly suggested a new intimacy between two of Labour's 'big three'. Although Callaghan was prone to talk to officials as though his presence at Treasury was merely transitory (he was widely believed to be hankering for the Foreign Office, now in the gentle hands of Michael Stewart), his position there seemed more assured than ever. On the other side of the House, Labour took encouragement from the somewhat brutal way in which Douglas-Home was removed as Tory leader and his replacement by (it was believed) the wooden and unappealing Edward Heath. In increasingly confident mood, Callaghan continued his unending task in shoring up the balance of payments and defending the pound.

Then on 27 January came an event which drove every other consideration from the politicians' minds. In the Hull North by-election, where Labour was defending a tiny majority of barely 1,000, there was a sensational result. Despite the intervention of an anti-Vietnam left-wing candidate, Richard Gott, Labour achieved a remarkable 4.5 per cent swing and their majority soared to 5,351. Shortly after, Harold Hayman, who held Labour's only seat in Cornwall, died, leaving the government with an overall majority of just one. A few weeks later, Harold Wilson called a general election, to be held on 31 March. He, Callaghan, and his colleagues now had the opportunity to transform British politics, to make Labour not just a movement of protest, but the natural party of government.

1. General briefing for the Chancellor, 16 Oct. 1964 (PRO, T 171/758); Cabinet Minutes, 19 Oct. 1964 (CAB 128/39). It should be noted that no Treasury (T) Papers were available to researchers for 1965 and 1966 down to the summer of 1997.

2. Cabinet Conclusions, 27 July 1965 (CAB 128/39 pt. 2).

3. Interview with Lord Bancroft.

4. *Western Mail*, 23 Oct. 1964. She noted that her husband had been working a sixteen-hour day since taking office a week earlier.

5. Crossman to Wilson, 16 Feb. 1965 (PREM 13/275).

6. Stephen Dorril and Robin Ramsay, *Smear!* (London, 1992), 158–9; obituary of MacDermott by David Leigh, *Guardian*, 26 Feb. 1996.

7. Lord Callaghan, MS notes on decimalization (in the author's possession).

8. Interview with Lord Bancroft.

9. Interview with Sir Alec Cairncross.

10. Alec Cairncross MS diary, 19 Oct. 1964. He added that the Chancellor had obviously 'no conception of what the Economic Section actually did'.

11. Note for the record, Callaghan Papers, box 24.

12. Interview with Jack Jones.

13. Interview with Sir Alec Cairncross.

14. Interview with Lord Bancroft.

15. Note for the record, Callaghan Papers, box 24.

16. Callaghan MS note, ? Dec. 1964 (Callaghan Papers, box 24).

17. Draft memo, 2 Dec. 1964, and memo from George Brown (ibid.).

18. Note by Secretary of the Cabinet on 'Co-operation between the Department of Economic Affairs and the Treasury', 16 Dec. 1964 (PRO, CAB 129/119). See generally Eric Roll, *Crowded Hours* (London, 1985) on the founding of the DEA.

19. Meeting of Economic Affairs Committee, MISC 1, 17 Oct. 1964 (PRO, CAB 130/202); notes in Callaghan Papers, box 24; information from Dr N. H. Dimsdale.

20. Donald MacDougall, *Don and Mandarin: Memoirs of an Economist* (London, 1987), 152; Jay, *Change and Fortune*, 297–8; Dell, *The Chancellors*, 304–46. In fairness, it should

be noted that Mr Dell is highly critical of virtually all post-war chancellors with the exception of Peter Thorneycroft.

21. Callaghan to Dillon, 19 Oct. 1964 (Callaghan Papers, box 24).

22. *The Times*, 27 Oct. 1964.

23. Jay, *Change and Fortune*, 308.

24. Cabinet Minutes, 24 Nov. 1964 (PRO, CAB 128/ 39).

25. Ibid. 28 Oct. 1964 (ibid.).

26. Ibid. 24 Nov. 1964 (ibid.).

27. Note of conversation between Wilson and Callaghan, 27 Oct. 1964 (PRO, PREM 13/33).

28. Note by Derek Mitchell (ibid.).

29. Cairncross MS diary, 16 Nov. 1964.

30. Arthur Woodburn to Callaghan, 11 Nov. 1964 (Callaghan Papers, box 17).

31. William Davis, *Three Years' Hard Labour* (London, 1968), 27.

32. *The Times*, 21 Nov. 1964.

33. Record of meeting of 17 Nov. 1964; Prime Minister's draft message to President Johnson, 18 Nov. (PREM 13/261).

34. Record of meeting of ministers, 21 Nov. 1964 (ibid.).

35. Record of meeting of Callaghan, Cromer, and Armstrong, 24 Nov. 1964 (PREM 13/261).

36. Record of meeting of Wilson, Callaghan, Cromer, and O'Brien, 24 Nov. 1964, 10.30 p.m. (ibid.).

37. Henry Fowler to President Lyndon Johnson, 30 Mar. 1965 (President Johnson Presidential Papers: confidential file, name file, BU, box 144, Lyndon B. Johnson Library, Austin, Tex.).

38. *The Economist*, 28 Nov. 1964. The historical reference is to the Holy Roman Emperor Henry IV standing in the snow at Canossa in 1077 to try to escape excommunication.

39. *The Times*, 27 Nov. 1964.

40. Callaghan note, 28 Dec. 1964 (Callaghan Papers, box 24).

41. *The Times*, 9 Dec. 1964.

42. Ibid. 16 Dec. 1964.

43. Callaghan MS note of OECD meeting (Callaghan Papers, box 24).

44. Cromer to Wilson, 21 Dec. 1964; meeting of Wilson, Callaghan, Cromer, and O'Brien, 23 Dec. 1964 (PREM 13/237).

45. *Financial Times*, 23 Dec. 1964.

46. *The Economist*, 26 Dec. 1964.

47. Desmond Donnelly, diary, 5 Dec. 1964 (National Library of Wales, Aberystwyth). One source has claimed that Callaghan burst into tears at this period on more than one occasion (Pimlott, *Harold Wilson*, 334, 353). The informant, 'a ministerial rival', is not named but may have been Edward Short.

48. Derek Mitchell to Prime Minister, 18 Dec. 1964, enclosing Ian Bancroft to Mitchell, 18 Dec. 1964, and Bob Roosa to Callaghan, 16 Dec. 1964 (PRO, PREM 13/65).

49. Interview with Peter Jay.

50. Callaghan to Wilson, 12 Jan. 1965 (Callaghan Papers, box 24).

51. *The Economist*, 6 Feb. 1965.

52. Note by Balogh, 16 Feb. 1965; Brown to Wilson, 16 Feb. 1965; Crossman to Wilson, 16 Feb. 1965; Callaghan to Wilson, 16 Feb. 1965 (PREM 13/275).

53. Nigel Lawson, 'Has the Governor Gone too Far?', *Financial Times*, 17 Feb. 1965.

54. Cairncross MS diary, 5 Apr. 1965. Cf. Budget Committee meetings (T171/804).

55. Ibid. 6 Apr. 1965.

56. George Thomas to 'Leonard' Callaghan, 7 Apr. 1965 (Callaghan Papers, box 17).

57. James Griffiths to Callaghan, 7 Apr. 1965 (ibid.); Callaghan to Griffiths, 11 Apr. 1965 (Griffiths Papers, National Library of Wales, C7/11); Longford to Callaghan, Apr. 1965 (Callaghan Papers, box 14).

58. Callaghan to Jacques Segard, 12 Apr. 1965 (ibid.).

59. *The Economist*, 17 Apr. 1965.

60. Ibid. 19 June 1965.

61. Callaghan/Lee memo C (65) 42, Cabinet Conclusions, 18 Mar. 1965 (CAB 128/39 pt. 2); Desmond Donnelly diary, 23 Mar., 5 May 1965.

62. Material in Callaghan Papers, box 17.

63. Memo of conversation between John Liddy and Sir Patrick Dean, 22 June 1965 (President Johnson Papers, NSF country file, box 208).

64. McGeorge Bundy memo for the President, 28 June 1965 (President Johnson's Appointment File, diary back-up, box 18).

65. Fowler memo for the President, 28 June 1965 (ibid.).

66. McGeorge Bundy memo for the President, 28 June 1965 (ibid.).

67. Francis Bator, memo for the President, 29 June 1965, enclosing cutting from *New York Times*, 29 June 1965 (ibid.).

68. Briefing for Chancellor Callaghan's visit and general position paper, 25 June 1965 (President Johnson Papers, NSF country file, box 208).

69. Fax from W. Thomas Johnson, assistant press secretary, White House (President Johnson Papers, WHCF name file C, box 21).

70. Chancellor Callaghan's schedule, Henry Fowler Papers, box 42 (Lyndon B. Johnson Library, Austin, Tex.).

71. Callaghan, *Time and Chance*, 188.

72. US embassy cable to State Department, 29 Sept. 1965 (President Johnson Papers, NSF country file, box 208).

73. McGeorge Bundy to Johnson, 28 July 1965 (President Johnson Papers, NSF country file, box 215).

74. MS note in Callaghan Papers, box 25.

75. *The Economist*, 6 Nov. 1965.

76. Callaghan, *Time and Chance*, 183–4. Peter Paterson, *Tired and Emotional: The Life of Lord George Brown* (London, 1993), 178–81 has a dramatic account of how the plan was finally drawn up, including Brown's having to hitch-hike with it to London and then leaving it behind in the car.

77. For an excellent account, see Pimlott, *Harold Wilson*, 366 ff.

78. Memo of visit in Callaghan Papers, uncatalogued.

79. See Morgan, *Labour in Power* (Oxford, 1984), 422–3.

80. Richard Crossman, *The Diaries of a Cabinet Minister*, ed. Janet Morgan, 3 vols. (London, 1979), i. 407 (9 Dec. 1965).

81. Cabinet Conclusions, 11 Nov. 1965 (CAB 128/39 pt. 2).

82. Cairncross MS diary, 12 Jan. 1966.

83. Interview with Sir Alec Cairncross.

84. Memo on 'Wages Policy' by Frank Cousins, 18 Jan. 1966 (University of Warwick Modern Records Centre, Cousins Papers, TBN 36).

85. Cairncross MS diary, 12 Dec. 1965.

86. Ibid. 25 Dec. 1965.

87. Callaghan to Wilson, n.d.; Wilson to Callaghan, n.d. (Callaghan Papers, uncatalogued).

12

BLOWN OFF COURSE

In the lead-up to the March 1966 general election, Labour's confidence was at its highest. Indeed, it was probably the one, fleeting period since 1945–6 that the British left felt itself to be in control. For a long period after the election of October 1964 Labour seemed on the defensive, buffeted about by economic storms, clinging on with a tiny minority of only four. This was reduced even further by the defeat of the Foreign Secretary, Patrick Gordon Walker, in the Leyton by-election in January 1965. Labour showed a steady decline in the opinion polls thereafter. Then the death of the Speaker, Harry Hylton-Foster, which meant the succession of his deputy, a Labour member, Dr Horace King, bade fair to destroy Harold Wilson's majority altogether. With miraculous skill, however, he found an available Liberal, Roderic Bowen, the little-known member for Cardiganshire, prepared to become deputy Speaker and thus preserve Labour's overall majority of three. Combined with apparently better economic tidings, the opinion polls showed Labour moving ahead from September. From then onwards, Labour showed a commanding lead in the polls. The reasons were not wholly clear, although one factor was the much greater popularity of Wilson with the voters compared with the new Tory leader, Edward Heath. When Wilson decided in early March to go to the country, the party's leaders, Callaghan very much included, were in good heart.

Harold Wilson dominated the campaign in almost presidential fashion. But Callaghan also played, inevitably, a central part, in public meetings, press conferences, and television and radio broadcasts. Indeed, he was a major player even before the election officially began. His 'little budget', carefully presented on 1 March 1966, St David's Day, as his constituents would note, was a fine electioneering occasion. The Welsh daffodil was prominent in the Chancellor's lapel. The nation's finances were said to be now greatly improved. He offered tax rebates for mortgage-holding home owners, skilfully linking them in his speech with a new tax on gambling, and declared that he did not see the need for a great increase in taxation in his spring budget. Labour's backbenchers cheered him to the echo. Crossman noted that the delivery of the statement was 'magnificently done with enormous parliamentary skill'. He added, 'On TV in the evening he was equally superb. He is an extremely interesting example of how important image is in modern politics.'[1]

The speech included a dramatic modernistic proposal that in 1971 Britain would convert to decimal coinage. This was a highly technical matter on which the Halsbury Committee had reported in 1963. However the report, in Callaghan's naval phraseology, 'lay becalmed' in his first few months in office, when there were problems enough with the existing currency. When he did apply his mind to the question in the summer of 1965, it became apparent that if there were to be a new decimal coinage minted, a new Royal Mint would have to be built, somewhere different from the old, hallowed, but cramped building on Tower Hill. However, Callaghan found in discussions with William Armstrong and Ian Bancroft that they were enthusiastic for change, as he was himself, and it was agreed with Wilson that the proposal should be included in the pre-election budget on 1 March. Wilson, according to Callaghan, responded simply, when the idea was put to him, 'Why not?' In a few seconds, a century and a half of argument about decimalization came to an end. The most remarkable feature of this episode is that so major and historic a long-term decision should have been decided effectively by the Prime Minister and Chancellor in secret conclave. There was only a very brief endorsement from the Cabinet on 24 February, but in this pre-election frenzy their colleagues would go along with almost anything.

So decimalization was announced to the public. The details were later finalized and approved by the Cabinet in November. It was agreed that the new coinage would come into use in February 1971. The consequences of the decision to divide the pound into 100 new pence instead of the traditional 240 pennies caused some controversy. In the course of time, the conservatively minded British were to lament the disappearance of the much-cherished 'tanner' (sixpence), 'bob' (shilling), florin, and half-crown. Even the halfpenny had its defenders, but Callaghan sternly told the head of the CBI that this modest little coin was 'nearing the end of its useful life'.[2] In March 1966, it simply made Labour appear modernizing and forward-looking. The halfpenny in your pocket would not be devalued. The hidden agenda that it might well speed on British membership of the European Common Market was noticed by relatively few.

If the 1 March budget was a harmonious event, it was followed by a brief, but highly significant, note of discord. The announcement of an election led to disturbance in the markets and pressure on the pound. There followed on 9 March a ferocious private clash late at night between Wilson and Lord Cromer, the Governor of the Bank of England, when the latter had called for interest rates to be raised perhaps by a full 2 per cent to 7 per cent. Anxious not to damage Labour's election campaign, Wilson refused point blank. In highly belligerent mood, he appeared to threaten Cromer with something close to dismissal. He told the Bank to keep out of politics and 'allow the civil power to hold a free election'. Sterling could best be protected by asking President Johnson to encourage the US Federal Reserve to intervene in the markets. Interestingly, Callaghan, who was also present and kept generally silent while the Prime Minister and the Governor traded blows, seems to have shared Cromer's views on the bank rate issue. He feared substantial losses of the reserves: 'for his part and leaving aside political considerations, he would feel happier with a rise in bank rate than without one'. Wilson, however, swept his Chancellor aside. A few days earlier, he had had a brisk correspondence with Callaghan over setting up a committee on monetary policy which Armstrong had said that Cromer opposed. In prime ministerial green ink, Wilson noted tersely, 'We can't let the Gov. walk all over us.' The meeting on 9 March ended, with bad temper all round, at half-past midnight.[3]

At a lively Cabinet a few hours later at 10 a.m., however, Callaghan took up Cromer's unpopular proposal—surprisingly so at a time of what Wilson called 'electionitis'—and suggested that they raise bank rate by 1 per cent. Wilson and Brown strongly resisted, and were backed by, amongst others, Mrs Castle and Jenkins. Colleagues ingeniously suggested that a rise in bank rate might be misinterpreted abroad as indicating that the economic position had deteriorated unduly. In the face of his colleagues' political preoccupations, Callaghan had to retreat with good grace, and bank rate stayed as it was. It was hardly surprising that the Wilson Cabinet was unwilling to raise interest rates on the very eve of a general election. But the underlying economic problems, especially those involving the exchange rate of the pound, were soon to suggest that it was Callaghan who had fundamentally the stronger case.[4]

During the campaign, it was Callaghan who fronted Labour's attack in many press conferences in London. He had to do so because George Brown again undertook an exhausting nationwide speaking tour which attracted publicity even if its effect on voting intentions was less clear. But, of course, Callaghan's frequent appearances in London and other parts of Britain testified to his total confidence in holding his once marginal seat of Cardiff South-East. After the demolition of poor Ted Dexter in 1964, Jack Brooks, Gordon Houlston, Ken Hutchings, and other party strategists in Cardiff felt there would be no problem. Canvassing could be left, in part, to swarms of eager university students, including a red-haired future leader of the party, the ex-student president Neil Kinnock, along with his girlfriend Glenys Parry. As before, the Labour approach had to be adapted to accommodate the varying ethos of the dockland, the slums of Splott, and the residential areas of Penarth on the seafront and Cyncoed in the centre of the city, but it was well equipped to do so. The Conservative candidate this time, Norman Lloyd-Edwards, a solicitor, was a far more professional performer than Dexter. Indeed he was a local city councillor and a member of the liberal Tory Bow Group. He was a courteous and cheerful man who was later to become Lord Lieutenant of South Glamorgan, and friendly with Callaghan himself.

He needed all his reserves of good humour since he clearly had no chance of success. Apart from the manifest national swing to Labour recorded in the opinion polls, the Conservatives suffered in Cardiff from the lingering effect of the leasehold reform issue and also from the Conservatives' pledge to develop a new port at Portbury on the Bristol side of the Channel, which did not go down well in Cardiff docklands. There was also a Liberal candidate, George Parsons, a local businessman of right-wing views, but his was obviously a forlorn hope. The polling on 31 March showed Callaghan easily home and dry. He gained a 3 per cent swing (as against a national average of 3.5 per cent), and had a majority of 10,837 over Lloyd Edwards, 21 per cent as compared to 15 per cent in 1964. Parsons lost his deposit. He was to do even worse in the 1970 election when he appeared as the representative of the National Front.

The election as a whole went Labour's way with equal ease. They showed a mastery only previously demonstrated in 1945 in the party's long history. Harold Wilson seemed more concerned by the presumed hostility of the BBC than by the opposition of the Tories. Labour won 363 seats against the Conservatives' 253 and the Liberals' 12, an overall majority of 97. Many middle-class seats were won for the first time, Oxford and Cambridge, Lancaster and York, an affluent borough like Hampstead. Brighton (Kemptown), Labour's first-ever seat in Sussex captured in 1964, was comfortably retained. Even remote rural seats like Caithness and Cardiganshire fell to Labour: in the latter, the Liberal member, Roderic Bowen, suffered from his decision to accept Wilson's offer of the deputy speakership. Labour's claim to be the natural governing party had apparently been triumphantly vindicated.

Then it was back to the crises of government. Callaghan remained at the Treasury, as anticipated, even though he had murmured to colleagues about the attractions of the Foreign Office, currently occupied by Michael Stewart after the resignation of Gordon Walker. There were Treasury problems in abundance now that the tumult and shouting of the hustings had died away. Callaghan remained deeply unhappy at the continuing tension with the DEA and appeared to be threatening possible resignation if something were not done. On the other hand, it was clear that the battle for primacy with the newly invented department had been won. The National Plan was not going anywhere, its forecasts of a 40 per cent increase in GNP by 1970 were being radically scaled down, and George Brown was increasingly and volubly discontented.

Another continuing issue was the need to cut back defence spending to help the balance of payments and make Britain's manifestly overstretched global role more realistic. Here again was a battle that the Treasury was beginning to win. Before the election, Denis Healey's defence white paper had included a ceiling of £2,000m. from 1970 onwards, at 1964 prices and pay scales. This sharp reduction was seen by the left-wing *New Statesman* to be a victory for Callaghan.[5] It included other items that might well be pared down in the light of later economic circumstances, for instance the F/111 aircraft. Here the burden was considerable with ten aircraft ordered already and a further forty to be ordered in April 1967. As regards the manpower costs of the services, British troops were being transferred from Aden to Bahrein, which sought protection against both the Shah of Iran and Saudi Arabia. On the other hand, the potentially dangerous confrontation in defence of Malaysia against Indonesia which had seen British troops in action in Borneo and Sarawak since 1963 was now resolved, with both Sarawak and North Borneo (Sabah) confirmed as parts of the federal state of Malaysia, and governed from Kuala Lumpur. For the moment, there was a reprieve for some major east of Suez commitments including the massive naval base of Singapore. But here, too, Callaghan, assisted by left-wing ministers such as Crossman and Barbara Castle, would keep the pressure up for retrenchment and withdrawal in the post-imperial age. The arguments over defence had cost the government the services of the Navy Minister, Christopher Mayhew, before the election. He had resigned on 22 February, after disagreement with Denis Healey over the scrapping of a proposed aircraft carrier, in favour of the shore-based F/111. Eventually he became a Liberal peer. But, for the Chancellor, economic factors transcended naval sentiment.

His main priority, though, was clearly the post-election budget to be introduced at the beginning of May. Here he had to act quickly. The overall situation with regard both to the balance of payments (where a deficit of £350m. was to be forecast for the calendar year) and to the gold and dollar reserves was still anything but secure. The country was still spending substantially more than it earned. More generally, Labour had to strive to hold a balance between achieving growth and defending the pound; so far, it was the latter objective that had clearly won out. Callaghan was anxious to take corrective action while preserving his bold pre-election pledge that swingeing increases in taxation were unnecessary. To that end, increases in income or purchase taxes, or unpopular rises in duties on drink or petrol, were ruled out. They would clearly affect the retail cost-of-living index. On the other hand, he had to find somewhere a potentially dynamic new tax which might stimulate the economy in the right direction as well as supplying revenue to balance the budget. A new betting tax, directed against what Labour politicians in nonconformist language termed 'the candy-floss economy', would achieve neither. In a rush, he turned to a bright idea from Nicky Kaldor, who next to Robert Neild was his major adviser, for a selective employment tax, a flat-rate tax on employers for each of their employees, but with a discrimination in favour of manufacturing industry over service employment. The idea was supposed to be to ease manpower shortages in manufacturing industry and encourage industries to be more economical in their use of labour, and Ray Gunter at the Ministry of Labour agreed to operate it. The tax was certainly novel and ingenious, and it appealed to Callaghan as an old Inland Revenue man.

His budget speech on 4 May was a polished and confident performance, and congratulations flowed in thick and fast. It was Callaghan's—and Labour's—high noon in public esteem. Richard Crossman thought the speech 'brilliantly successful' and Callaghan's later television broadcast 'superb'.[6] The contents were a different matter. From the outset, economists and many political observers across the spectrum thought the SET was a crude and insensitive weapon. It would unnecessarily penalize a range of service industries from construction to hotels and catering, and encourage manufacturing industry to be reliant on a wasteful subsidy on all its workers. Alec Cairncross and the Economic Section did not believe that an effective tax could be devised in so short a time.[7] Nor could it. Many anomalies arose, including protests from Wales and Scotland. In time, under pressure from the new Welsh Secretary, Cledwyn Hughes, a special regional employment premium (REP) had to be invented to provide assistance for the Celtic fringe. Douglas Jay, who had felt it would give him new problems at the Board of Trade, summed up later on: 'SET proved highly unpopular, annoyed the Co-ops and gave the Tories a free run of opposition.'[8] More generally, the tax was simply based on an invalid analysis. The British economy now was less and less dependent on its traditional manufacturing base. For decades it been reliant on its services to keep its balance of payments under control. Soon it emerged that SET, designed to raise £300m. of revenue, could not do so and the books were left unbalanced. The markets reacted badly and sterling began to slide again.

In late June 1966 the Labour government, fresh from a massive majority at the polls, with leading ministers such as Wilson, Callaghan, and Jenkins receiving strong public approval ratings, ought to have been in a commanding position. One apparent obstacle was removed with the retirement (agreed before the election) of Lord Cromer as Governor of the Bank. His successor Leslie O'Brien, a career banking professional from a humble background, was far more congenial to Callaghan and others. Wilson himself looked forward to a cheerful summer of public relations opportunities in 'swinging London', in which England hosted the World Cup, and the England football team under the captaincy of Bobby Moore of West Ham United had a fighting chance. In time, of course, England won the Cup; the fact that the defeated team in the final was West Germany added to popular rejoicing. It was a case of 'two world wars and one world cup' as English football hooligans were later to chant. Harold Wilson appeared on the balcony with Sir Alf Ramsey and the victorious English team. Success at the national game of football was, it was implied, an additional blessing of Labour in power.

But in fact an unexpected further deterioration in the economy that lasted until the middle of August plunged Wilson, Callaghan, and their colleagues into new difficulties. In effect, the re-elected Labour administration faced a huge crisis of confidence from which it never really recovered. For almost the next four years it was under constant pressure from rejuvenated Conservatives; perhaps not until the advent of Tony Blair as Labour's leader in 1994, following four successive heavy electoral defeats, did it really look like a potentially dominant party of government again. The mood was distinctly tetchy in the hot summer of June–July 1966. Left-wing MPs were angry over the government's endorsement of American atrocities in Vietnam; trade unionists were upset at an impending wage freeze policy in a Prices and Incomes Bill; cuts in public expenditure were causing unhappiness in all wings of the party. The economy, which governed all else, was showing new signs of frailty. Much harm was done by a seven-week strike of the nation's seamen which led to ships tied up and

1. Lord Callaghan's mother, Charlotte

2. Callaghan (*left*) in the Portsmouth Northern school football team, December 1928

3. Callaghan (*back row left*) with IRSF delegates, Scarborough, May 1936

4. Callaghan carried on his victorious supporters' shoulders, Cardiff City Hall, 25 July 1945

5. Jim and Audrey Callaghan, Ramsgate, 1947

Sentry: "Remember what Attlee said, THERE'LL BE WAR IF SOMEONE CHANCES HIS ARM TOO FAR!"

6. Callaghan's attack on Emanuel Shinwell's views on nationalization, 7 May 1948

7. Canvassing in Tiger Bay, Cardiff South-East, 1950 general election

8. With Harold Wilson at the Scarborough Labour Party conference, 27 September 1963

9. With President Lyndon B. Johnson in the Oval office at the White House, 29 June 1965

10. Enjoying a pint with Cardiff supporters, 1966 general election campaign

11. Callaghan driving to the House of Commons to make a statement on the devaluation of the pound, 20 November 1967

12. Callaghan at a Crime Prevention Campaign press conference, Home Office, 16 February 1968

13. Callaghan speaking to the crowd in Londonderry during his visit to Northern Ireland, 29 August 1969

14. Callaghan in a Cardiff bus with George Thomas MP, 1973

15 (*above*). Callaghan meets President Amin's son Mwanga after the release of Dennis Hills, Kampala, Uganda, August 1974

16 (*right*). First day as Prime Minister, 5 April 1976

17. At the Charing Cross Hotel farewell luncheon for Harold Wilson, 28 April 1976

18. With the Queen at Windsor Castle at the time of President Giscard d'Estaing's visit, 12 December 1977

19. Sailing across the Firth of Forth with Dr J. Dickson Mabon, and a young friend, 18 March 1978

20 (*above*). Presentation to Hugh Scanlon on his retirement at St Ermin's Hotel, London, 3 July 1978

21 (*right*). Sketch of Callaghan while addressing the TUC on 5 September 1978, by Ken Gill, General Secretary of TASS

22. The end of the Labour Party conference at Brighton, 7 October 1977: the Red Flag, being sung by Frank Allaun, Callaghan, Ron Hayward, and Joan Lestor

23. Callaghan and Margaret Thatcher at the state opening of Parliament, 1 November 1978

24. The 'winter of discontent': march by ambulancemen to the House of Commons, 22 January 1979

25. Callaghan leaving Cardiff station: 4.45 a.m. on 4 May 1979 after his defeat in the general election

26. Ships passing in the night: Callaghan and Tony Benn at party conference, Brighton, 2 October 1979

27. The Vail Foundation World Forum: Callaghan with Gerald Ford, Valèry Giscard d'Estaing, Helmut Schmidt, and Malcolm Fraser, in Colorado 1983

28. At Temple West Mews with his granddaughter Alice Jay, 1990

silent docks, with consequent damage to British trade, the balance of payments, and the prospects for sterling. Harold Wilson's assaults on Communist involvement and 'a tightly-knit group of politically motivated men' (he instanced Bert Ramelson), a rash response to the prompting of MI5, did not go down well. Several ministers, including Peter Shore, thought this maladroit. After a long and unreal silence, the taboo subject of devaluation of the pound, which Wilson and Callaghan both detested, was being publicly discussed in Whitehall.

In the first two weeks of July, the drain on the reserves and the attacks on sterling became unsustainable. While the Prime Minister announced his early departure to Moscow to continue his efforts at peacemaking in Vietnam, his position seemed to be crumbling all around him. There was turmoil in the markets, stock prices plummeted, and there was a rush to buy gold, always a sign of crisis. On 12 July the pound fell to its lowest point since November 1964. The government's response seemed indecisive, even panicky. Callaghan's paper for Cabinet on 12 July gave an alarming picture. The economy was in 'inflationary condition' with 'labour short, wages rising fast and more imports sucked in'. Far from the balance of payments improving, the deficit for 1966 and early 1967 would be substantial. Public expenditure was growing much too fast, while both the IMF drawing of September 1965 and the £3,385m. loan from the Swiss banks had somehow to be repaid by the end of 1967. The National Plan had looked to an increase in GNP of 40 per cent by the end of the decade. In fact, barely half that figure was likely to be achieved. On 14 July the Cabinet announced, belatedly, that bank rate would rise to 7 per cent.[9] Undisclosed further deflationary measures were promised on 20 July after the prime minister returned from Moscow, a visit which looked increasingly ill-timed. On 14 July also it was revealed that the trade deficit was nearly doubled from £28m. to £55m. in June as a result of the seamen's strike.[10]

Two further blows struck the government at this disastrous time. Frank Cousins, the Minister of Technology, resigned as a result of the introduction of a wages policy, to be succeeded by Anthony Wedgwood Benn. Then Labour lost a by-election at Carmarthen, a Plaid Cymru candidate being returned to parliament for the first time. The party was shaken to the core, and rumours were rife of storms and disputes in the government, with rumours of the resignation of Wilson, Callaghan, and (daily if not almost hourly) George Brown. Wilson flew off to Moscow on 16 July at the most parlous time, with further massive sales of sterling under way, and desperate measures taken by the Bank and its new Governor to prevent its going under completely.

Precisely what occurred at this period, including the three days that Wilson was away in Moscow, is open to much dispute. A good deal of it involves the role of Callaghan who was a pivotal figure both as the Chancellor trying to stem the flood, and as a leading player in the political drama in the Cabinet. Even central Whitehall figures like Alec Cairncross felt themselves on the sidelines, totally at a loss to know what was going on.

The premonitions of crisis had come as early as 1 July when Wilson, Brown, and Callaghan had a morning meeting to discuss long-range government strategy.[11] At this meeting Callaghan pushed Wilson hard (Brown said 'brutally') about his willingness to abandon the east of Suez defence commitment. Defence expenditure, indeed, was one of Callaghan's central preoccupations at this time. Earlier on 16 May he had written to Joe Fowler complaining of the cost of maintaining the British army on the Rhine. This ran to £90m. a year, of which it was felt the Germans should pay half. Callaghan suggested ironically that he would get sense out of the German Chancellor Erhardt only if he could persuade the Cabinet to withdraw a platoon a week.[12] Later on 1 July, Brown had a private talk with Callaghan over a glass of sherry. He told the Chancellor that, in view of the gravity of the economic situation, he now favoured applying for entry into the Common Market, to avoid a debilitating dependence on the United States to prop up sterling. Equally dramatically, he also now favoured the consequent devaluation of the pound, a strategy he had resisted as robustly as Callaghan since October 1964.

Callaghan was unenthusiastic about both propositions, but his view began to change as a result of a visit from Pompidou and Couve de Murville, the French Prime Minister and Foreign Minister, on 6 July. Both indicated a much more relaxed attitude to British entry into Europe than the French had previously shown, but suggested devaluation was a necessary preliminary, followed by a stiff deflation. Callaghan was shaken by their view, it seems, especially when it was followed by a forecast for the balance of payments deficit in 1966 'far worse than anything I had ever dreamed of'.[13] Originally expected to be around £100m. only, it now appeared that it could even reach £350m., a position as bad as that of 1965. There had, in effect, been no underlying improvement at all. Callaghan sent a paper to the Cabinet on 8 July conveying the gist of this serious message, but Wilson had it watered down for general consumption, the first of many serious prevarications on his part. The next morning the Sunday papers were full of grim prophecies on the economy. David Astor in the *Observer* openly advocated devaluation of the pound.

The situation became very much worse on 12–14 July, as has been seen. Wilson had a statement on raising bank rate disastrously delayed. Callaghan's own answer to a parliamentary question on 14 July, announcing only a restriction of credit and being vague on wider policies, suggested that the government had no clear strategy for the sterling crisis. Meanwhile he had had a meeting with the president of the CBI, Sir Maurice Laing, to discuss curbs on overseas investment.[14] The background to Callaghan's statement on 14 July was complex and confused. All the main actors in the drama were poised between action and inaction. Their positions changed almost hourly. Callaghan himself combined a wish to do something decisive before Wilson left for Moscow with a belief that only a limited deflationary package was necessary, combined with large cuts in defence. Brown, fearful for what was left of the National Plan, veered between strategic delay and anxiety to devalue before Wilson departed for Washington on the 28th. The Prime Minister oscillated unpredictably between the two. Callaghan was pressurized into making a half-cock generalized statement following meetings with Wilson and Brown, with Armstrong and the new Governor, O'Brien, also feeling that some kind of statement should be made to placate the markets. Both the timing and the content of the statement were hotly disputed. Callaghan insisted that any statement would have to cover defence retrenchment overseas as well as cutbacks at home. There followed 'a particularly stupid quarrel with George Brown' around midnight on 13 July: Brown, for reasons that are not clear, felt that Callaghan was trying to manœuvre him by advancing the date of the statement on cuts by a week. More likely he simply resented the fact of a meeting being held between Wilson and Callaghan behind his back. He called the unfortunate O'Brien at 1 a.m. to enlist his support. Callaghan finally rang up Brown at 8.30 a.m. on 14 July to confirm that he was now prepared to make a Commons statement on the economy that afternoon. Almost inevitably, this statement, made against the Chancellor's better judgement, the result of a political manœuvring rather than coherent policy-making, went down badly. It led to the flight from sterling intensifying, not least because many concluded that early devaluation was now on the agenda. Threats of immediate resignation by Brown resounded around Whitehall and Fleet Street.

The following day, 15 July, Brown had a row with Wilson instead, over the proposal that economy measures would be announced only on 20 July. He wanted an immediate devaluation, since he feared that a few days' delay would result in an incurable deterioration in the reserves. It would also, of course, nail down Wilson before he flew to Moscow. For the first time since becoming Chancellor, Callaghan's view on devaluation had begun to shift, not because of abusive and aggressive pressure from Brown but simply because of the facts of the situation. 'The run on sterling was so great at this time that I was coming to the conclusion that whatever we did, we would be forced off parity, because it would be wrong to run our reserves down to negligible proportions without any prospect of them coming back.' If Brown was now a devaluer by conviction, Callaghan appeared to be turning into one by default. As was well known, both his main advisers, Nicky Kaldor and Robert Neild, had been devaluers from the start of the government; Alec Cairncross and the Economic Section were veering the same way. Wilson, who alone stood firm against devaluation of any kind, seemed to be faced with an alliance between Brown and Callaghan to force his hand.

The atmosphere between the key ministers had deteriorated to glacial levels by the time Wilson left for Moscow at 10 a.m. on the morning of the 16th. The Prime Minister was later to tell Barbara Castle of his suspicions of a plot being hatched between, amongst others, Jenkins, Callaghan, and perhaps Crossman and Crosland, at the highly unlikely location of a weekend party at the home of the wealthy society hostess Mrs Anne Fleming, the former mistress of Gaitskell and a close friend of Jenkins. In fact, Callaghan spent that weekend with his wife in Sussex at the home of his friend Gordon Denniss, Longbridge Farm. The circles frequented by Anne Fleming (and indeed Jenkins) were most unlikely to be ones in which Callaghan ever moved. The atmosphere was made distinctly worse by the extramural activities of George Wigg, Wilson's main bloodhound or mole. Ministerial discussions were totally confused. Harold Wilson was against devaluation and George Brown against deflation. Each of them refused to acknowledge that the two difficult options were inseparable. There were suggestions from Wilson that he might devalue immediately on his return from Washington but few could rely on his assurances at this point.

The three days that Wilson was away, up to his return from his abortive Moscow attempt at peacemaking on the late afternoon of 19 July, were a time of frenzied political rumour and of much speculation ever since. While in Moscow Wilson was to receive a telegram from Brown offering his resignation. In Westminster, there were active manœuvres to overthrow Wilson and promote Brown to the premiership. His supporters included Jenkins and Callaghan's friend Tony Crosland, along with influential young Midlands backbenchers such as Roy Hattersley and Brian Walden. Wilson felt sure there was 'a Birmingham conspiracy' of old

Gaitskellites, seeking revenge for the struggles of the 1950s.[15] At the same time, left-wing ministers such as Crossman, Barbara Castle, and Wedgwood Benn, allied to the ineffable George Wigg, were trying to shore up Wilson's position.

What does seem to be agreed is that, while always well placed to defend his own position, during the weekend of 16–17 July Callaghan joined no anti-Wilson 'conspiracy' of any kind, whether emanating from the comfortable home of Anne Fleming or anyone else. Indeed no evidence that he manœuvred against the Prime Minister or made any kind of bid for the premiership has ever been put forward, other than vague gossip. Wilson later said firmly that Callaghan 'was on the side of the angels that weekend'.[16] More seriously than these paranoid fears perhaps, Callaghan's brief emergence as a devaluer now disappeared. He turned sharply back to his previous view of devaluation as broadly harmful to the British economy, which was still the view of the majority of his Treasury advisers. In any case, devaluation and Wilson's leadership were so inextricably linked that to urge the former would be to advocate the dismissal of the premier. Callaghan and Brown had angry words that weekend; Wilson was told that they had 'quarrelled almost irretrievably'.[17] In effect, Callaghan had made his intermediate bargaining position one of residual strength. As Ben Pimlott rightly observes, he had saved the premier's bacon.[18] In the longer term, their relationship subtly shifted, to Callaghan's advantage.

The consequences were to be seen at what Callaghan called a 'ludicrous' Cabinet on the evening of 19 July after Wilson's return from Moscow (the discussions over Vietnam with Kosygin did not detain ministers who had more urgent priorities). In 1997 its conclusions were not released by the Cabinet Office. There had been frantic discussions beforehand to try to ensure some order in Cabinet business. Brown agreed for this occasion to withdraw his resignation. Crossman and other Wilson supporters agreed to suspend a proposal to float the pound. Callaghan said little in the discussion as Wilson proposed a package of cuts to be announced that day. In the end, there was a round-table discussion on devaluation and a formal vote. A large majority of seventeen, including Callaghan and Healey, voted against it, as against a minority of six in favour, Brown, Jenkins, and Crosland on the party right, Wedgwood Benn, Crossman, and Castle on the centre-left.[19] Callaghan told Wilson afterwards how strongly he disapproved of his habit of taking votes in Cabinet: ministers had been saying the same thing to prime ministers since the time of Gladstone.

On 20 July Wilson announced the government's package of measures. Journalists noted that George Brown was absent from the House when the statement was made. In fact, he had sent Wilson a formal letter of resignation which he later withdrew again. There would be no devaluation, but rather cuts of £500m. This was, said *The Economist*, 'perhaps the biggest deflationary package that any advanced industrial nation has imposed on itself since Keynesian economics began', the equivalent of a cut of 1.5 per cent of national income. Some felt it was needlessly severe, the result of disorder and panic. The proposals (which Callaghan had relayed to Joe Fowler in the US Treasury beforehand) ranged from higher postal charges to cuts in public investment and a 10 per cent surcharge on surtax. A cut in gross domestic product for next year and perhaps 1968 as well was inevitable. For the ordinary citizen, the bleakest feature would be a six-month total freeze on wage, salary, and dividend increases, with severe restraint for the six months after that. Another tiresome feature was a £50 limit on currency taken overseas for holidays.[20]

Perhaps with relief, Callaghan departed to Bonn to discuss international help. Here, in fact, he was greeted with enthusiasm by Blessing, president of the German Bundesbank, who felt that Britain was at last facing up to its difficulties and that he was prepared to put in $25m. on the markets to help steady the pound. More difficult were tough negotiations with Dr Dahlgrin, the German Finance Minister, about German help to meet the offset costs of BAOR. This amounted to £90m. whereas the German government could be persuaded to offer only £54m. Callaghan then threatened to withdraw 20,000 of the 60,000 United Kingdom servicemen from Germany. However, a face-saving compromise, inevitably setting up a committee, was reached in the end.[21]

The troubles of British internal politics continued to plague Callaghan. While in Bonn he heard that Brown had again sent in his resignation and again withdrawn it after a talk with Wilson. He also heard of an injudicious newspaper interview he had given William Davis of the *Guardian*, published on the 23rd. This hinted that the Chancellor was tired and fed up with his job and anxious to become Foreign Secretary. Neither of these intelligences helped the pound or the government. In the next days, however, the crisis appeared to ease. Callaghan met with a surprisingly warm reception from the European finance ministers, especially Michel Debré, the French minister, at The Hague on 25–6 July. The following day Joe Fowler, the US Secretary to the Treasury, visited London and reaffirmed his government's support for a British policy of cutbacks but no devaluation. Fowler disavowed statements by his colleague George Ball that a 10 or 12 per cent devaluation was desirable. 'It could start a chain reaction round the world and blow the whole place up', as he put it.[22] By the end of the month, with a blessed parliamentary recess at hand, the atmosphere, though still tense, had improved, with sterling pushed up to $2.70 with much help from the Bank of England and the US Federal Reserve.

The impact of the turbulence of July 1966 was long-lasting, for both the government and Prime Minster. Labour's authority was never the same. Wilson spoke of the Labour government being 'blown off course': it had rather seemed rudderless and in danger of being totally destroyed through a mixture of incompetence and misadventure. It was apparently going the way of the Attlee government in August 1947 with no powerful Cripps figure to shore it up. Both Brown and Wilson had seriously lost prestige and authority. Brown had seemed impulsive and uncontrollable, no man for a crisis. Wilson seemed devious, calculating, and inconsistent, driven more by paranoia than by policy priorities. He never quite recaptured his stature after that; indeed his fear of plots and intrigue increased and multiplied for the remainder of his somewhat tattered premiership, with Callaghan, Jenkins, and even the mild-mannered Michael Stewart thought to be intriguing against him. Callaghan, by contrast, even if he veered briefly towards devaluation on 13 July before veering back again two days later, emerged from the crisis somewhat stronger, more so than perhaps he deserved. He could present himself as a firm champion of deflation and an intermediate figure who stood somewhat detached from the mêlée of Wilsonites and old Gaitskellites. His long-held position as a member of the 'Keep Calm' group in the early 1950s, neither Gaitskellite nor Bevanite, stood him in good stead. While the Prime Minister was away in Moscow, Callaghan had behaved more honourably than most. He had declined to act as either the Brutus or the envious dagger-holding Casca. It meant that his prospects of sometime perhaps becoming the substitute Caesar figure himself were done no harm.

The consequences emerged in August. Wilson saw Callaghan privately on the evening of 10 August and told him that, at long last, George Brown's wish to move from the DEA had borne fruit. In a Cabinet reshuffle Brown, somewhat astonishingly perhaps in view of his undiplomatic style, would go to the Foreign Office, to prepare for Britain's application to join the European Common Market. Wilson telegraphed President Johnson, presenting it all as part of a master strategy of getting the best out of his team. 'You know George Brown. He will bring a new kind of robustness to the Foreign Office.'[23] In exchange, Michael Stewart would move from the Foreign Office to the DEA; he was a much milder figure and one totally congenial to the Chancellor. In effect the transition from Brown to Stewart meant that the DEA, heralded with such bravura, was an increasingly enfeebled department. Elsewhere, the left would be rewarded by Barbara Castle moving to Social Security and Crossman moving from Housing, where he had been something of a cross for Callaghan to bear, to lead the House of Commons. Callaghan would remain where he was, apparently stronger than ever.

The next day, however, serious doubts returned. The Chancellor had raised, with renewed vigour, the question of the impossible relationship, as he saw it, between the Treasury and the DEA at his long conversation with Wilson on the 10th. He had had two years of confusion and was not prepared for any more. His anger was intensified by the morning's newspapers which mentioned a press conference at which the normally diffident Stewart had talked of now being No. 3 in the Cabinet, presumably behind only Wilson and Brown and ahead of Callaghan. This led to a heated conversation between Callaghan and Wilson at No. 10.[24] The Prime Minister answered the point indirectly. In ample paranoid style, he referred to the many plots against him, mainly from former Gaitskellites. 'I trust George Wigg to find out the facts', Wilson observed, which can hardly have fortified Callaghan's confidence in the premier's judgement at that particular moment. In response, Callaghan told Wilson that many of his fears were fantasies, in particular the view that younger men like Jenkins or Crosland would or could displace him. 'That is not the way the party works', declared Callaghan, a view with which Wilson concurred.

Callaghan then told the premier 'that I thought he was seeing too much of the Hungarians. This was a conspiratorial theory of politics that I did not believe in.' Wilson went on to acquit Callaghan of any involvement in conspiracies himself, a view indeed fully endorsed by the available evidence though nevertheless faithfully reproduced by some commentators over the years. There was then some discussion over the precise order of precedence. One possibility was to bracket Callaghan and Stewart as equal third; in fact, Burke Trend, the Cabinet Secretary, had already been told to seat Callaghan next to the Prime Minister (possibly, Callaghan thought, to rid himself of the prospect of having the sometimes tiresome Crossman as an immediate neighbour in the Cabinet room). Callaghan and Wilson had another meeting later on 11 August, with the chief whip John Silkin also present. In the interim the premier had seen Stewart who had discovered that he was losing some of his key staff at the DEA, including the powerful figure of Sir Eric Roll. The outcome was that the mild-mannered Stewart was now threatening to resign himself. Callaghan left for a much-needed family holiday on the Isle of Wight in the morning. He told his office, if asked, to convey to the press the cricketing view 'that it did not matter what was the order of batting, so long as everybody made some runs'.[25]

Nevertheless, even if the head of the DEA were a veritable saint, there would still be a battle for priority with the Treasury. Stewart remained 'in violent mood' on the question of priority of status in Cabinet during August. On returning from holiday on 31 August, therefore, Callaghan had a private talk with him; he was an old friend with whom he had no personal problem.[26] He pressed on Stewart the view that the main problem in the economy was short-term pressure of demand. Without tackling this properly, a long-term national plan would not be a realistic one. Callaghan added that the original plan of George Brown had been prepared on the basis of fudged estimates about the balance of payments figures for 1970. No one in the Treasury believed they made sense. There was no prospect of the payments situation being so secure as to permit the level of growth that the plan envisaged. Stewart did not dissent.

Callaghan again raised the wider issue of his own future with the Prime Minister on 1 September. Wilson now felt that he could stay on at the Treasury until at least his next budget which was unlikely to be worse than a neutral one. The Chancellor was told he was 'one of the main pillars of the Government; it was simply not possible for him to go'. He knew very well that if Wilson fell under a bus, the party would make Callaghan leader. The latter recorded Wilson as adding, ' "Mind you I take good care not to go near a bus these days". Was it not the case that on nine occasions out of ten he had sided with me against George when there were differences. He thought my friends would tell me I ought to stay.' It was agreed that yet another concordat would be prepared, to try to define precisely, once and for all, what the demarcation lines would be between the Treasury and its upstart, though enfeebled, challenger.

Callaghan naturally took Wilson's view about remaining where he was. He had no option other than the wilderness at this time. But there was a significant consequence of these serpentine events, which left Brown, Stewart, and Callaghan all somewhat up in the air, a quarrelsome trio of crown princes, but which also left Wilson far more vulnerable than ever before. It was that Callaghan for the first time began to prepare his defences with a view to posing a future challenge for the leadership. Despite all the turmoil that ensured over the next few years, devaluation, *In Place of Strife*, and Labour's election defeat in 1970, Callaghan's position as prime challenger for the party leadership was a constant factor. The germ of what happened in April 1976 can be seen in these tense conversations—almost confrontations—between Callaghan and Wilson in August

1966. Callaghan told Wilson that he was 'now taking active steps to see that I had the advice of a group of friends. I was not going to be left in the innocent position I was in July when people were using my name for matters for which I had given no agreement.' This was a reference to rumours regarding the 17 July 'conspiracy' that Callaghan was the front-runner to replace Wilson while, as Brown was shuffled to one side, Roy Jenkins would emerge as the coming power. Wilson replied, gloomily, ' "I wish you would tell me how to make some friends: I have not got any". I forebore from giving the obvious retort', Callaghan observed. Wilson, seemingly isolated and paranoid, himself might have given the same unspoken response.

From this time onwards, the political balance in the government, and to some degree in the country, was different as Wilson manœuvred left-wingers like Castle, Crossman, and Greenwood, and right-wingers like Stewart, Jenkins, and Crosland, this way and that, with others like Fred Peart, Ted Short, Peter Shore, or Herbert Bowden additional pawns in his gambits. There was felt to be a potential vacancy at the top. If this ever materialized, Callaghan would ensure that he was well placed to compete, and perhaps to win. Callaghan took up the theme directly on 7 September with the Home Secretary, a younger coming man of well-known ambition.[27] Callaghan again refuted suggestions that he had been involved in a leadership conspiracy in July. Jenkins, who had been far from inactive himself at that time as a semi-detached Brown supporter, readily concurred. Using Wilson's well-worn analogy of accidentally falling under a bus, Callaghan stated, 'I would regard myself as in the running—at any rate for the next two or three years. If it turned out that way I would certainly see that he was given every chance to prove that he could become Leader in due course. He accepted this as a sensible possibility and we agreed to consult from time to time.' Precisely who Callaghan's 'friends' were with whom he built up this core of support is not wholly clear. No formal group was ever built up. But his Treasury colleague Jack Diamond, George Thomson, and his longer-term supporter Tony Crosland were three who were prominent. Another newer friend was Merlyn Rees, a Welshman who admired Callaghan's dexterity at the Treasury, especially in working out the technicalities of special drawing rights for long-term international loans.[28] He had started as Callaghan's PPS at the Treasury in 1964 but had then moved to work with Healey at Defence. Along with Crosland, DEA minister in 1964–5, he had in effect cast his lot with Callaghan. In 1967 the Chancellor was to have intimate talks with Rees about whether he should resign in the event of devaluation. To Brown, it seemed that Rees and Crosland were guilty of intrigue or treachery.

Callaghan continued to be a formidable figure on all issues that winter. At the October party conference at Brighton, he made an outstanding speech. Crossman, one of his admirers at this period, commented that 'he raised all the issues which were in the delegates' minds and answered them with magnificent clarity and frankness, making far the best speech of the Conference and pummelling the audience with answers'.[29] Indeed, if one looks at the pattern of Labour Party conferences in the entire 1964–70 period, Callaghan emerges as much the most consistently effectively front-line orator there. He continued to press ahead with key areas of policy, notably in preparing for the next stage of a statutory incomes policy on which he and Brown were allied.

One continuing crisis which gave Callaghan much leverage with Wilson was that of Rhodesia. Here the illegal Smith regime was as obdurate as ever, in the face of oil and other sanctions of doubtful effectiveness. Callaghan had favoured a show of military force at the outset, believing that Rhodesian commanders would remain loyal to the Queen. But he was now convinced that the opportunity for action of that kind had been lost, any surprise element had vanished, and the policy had to be that of the long haul. He used his connections with African leaders to spell out his objectives. At the Commonwealth prime ministers' conference in early September, he told Milton Obote of Uganda, Tom Mboya of Kenya, Joseph Murumbi (the Kenyan Foreign Minister), and Hastings Banda of Malawi of 'the catastrophic effect on the British economy of limited sanctions that would in my view bring us into head-on collision with South Africa. The Africans must know that there is no quick solution once force is ruled out, and in my view rightly ruled out.'[30]

Callaghan sat on the Cabinet's highly secret Rhodesia X Committee. Here on 31 August Wilson outlined the dangers of African leaders like Kenneth Kaunda either leaving the Commonwealth outright or else pushing economic sanctions against Britain itself if it failed to impose oil and other sanctions against South Africa and Portugal, both of whom were flouting Britain and dispatching oil to Rhodesia.[31] Wilson's characteristic compromise was to press for sanctions against Portugal, the lesser element in the equation, but not against South Africa, whose trade was too important for the United Kingdom. Callaghan strongly argued against this policy. Sanctions were already costing Britain £80m. a year at a time of much economic difficulty. The United Kingdom should persist with the present sanctions against Rhodesia. Indeed it should be making them more effective by helping Kenneth Kaunda of Zambia financially, to enable him to cut off trade with the Smith regime entirely. 'We should not be willing to shed blood: we had not done so in other African countries. It had been shed before we had been called in.' But Britain's economy could not withstand full-scale sanctions against Portugal and South Africa, whatever African nations like Sierra Leone (whose commitment was minute) might say. Callaghan was supported by every member of the Rhodesia X Committee, including somewhat surprisingly Crossman, and Wilson was left in a minority of one. In Cabinet, it was the same, Wilson's only supporter being predictably Barbara Castle. Callaghan, Houghton, Crossman, and Stewart all said that they considered her views on putting pressure on South Africa to be impractical.[32]

The crises drifted on that autumn until Wilson's summit talks with Ian Smith on HMS *Tiger*, off Gibraltar, in early December. Despite intense negotiations, the outcome was another impasse. On his return to Salisbury, Ian Smith promptly rejected any proposal for African majority rule as a precondition for independence. This failure, however, tended to redeem Wilson in the eyes of his colleagues for his determination and command of minute detail. When Barbara Castle made some private criticisms of Wilson's negotiating stance as being too full of concessions, Callaghan is reported as saying quietly to her, 'He *is* a Superman. I couldn't have done what he has done.'[33] After the traumas of the summer, the Prime Minister was still far from a spent force.

From the autumn of 1966, the government's entire world strategy began to change. It had come to office with a broadly Atlanticist approach. Wilson and Callaghan in particular felt an instinctive affinity with the United States as a special ally and financial benefactor in times of need. Europe was by contrast held somewhat at arm's length. EFTA was a loose-fitting arrangement, shaken to its foundations by the British unilaterally imposing an import surcharge at the very outset of Labour's term of office. Throughout the period down to the spring of 1966, the Common Market countries, the French above all, often seemed a negative factor, nagging Britain about the position of sterling as a reserve currency and its international liquidity problems, without doing much to help or to discourage speculators. Along with the Atlanticist tradition to which British Labour since the time of Ernest Bevin had broadly subscribed, there was the even longer commitment in terms of trade and political and economic development with the Commonwealth. Men like Callaghan had an instinctive historical and emotional commitment to the Commonwealth idea. They had been brought up as children of the empire. They had emerged in politics as champions of a multiracial partnership of free nations. As shadow Colonial Secretary, Callaghan had voiced this instinctive commitment on behalf of a united party. Even the left-wing Movement for Colonial Freedom could find little fault with his or the party's outlook.

But after July 1966, it became clear to a growing number of Labour figures that Britain's economic weakness meant that it must look elsewhere. There were limits to the Americans' willingness to provide assistance in a crisis, while in any case the packages of aid from September 1964, when the Conservatives were still in power, down to August 1966 had left the endemic problems of the British balance of payments and the vulnerability of its currency much as they were. Wilson's visit to meet President Johnson on 28 July 1966 had been accompanied by the same tidings of woe from Fowler, Dean Rusk, and others about the British economy as had preceded Callaghan's visit in June 1965.[34] The sterling crisis of July was still very far from over, and the market response to the economy proposals of 20 July had been only lukewarm, the US Treasury reported. Wilson's own political position was noted as having been shaky. Walt Rostow's background paper for President Johnson, prior to a visit by George Brown in February 1967, added that 'reports of a movement to put Callaghan in his place have been denied on all sides, but Callaghan did not get the Foreign Office as he desired when the Cabinet was reshuffled and relations between the two men do not appear to be close'.[35] It was accurate enough as a summary.

Johnson's reception for Wilson was fulsome to the point of self-parody. The British premier was treated to observations on Shakespeare, Nelson, and other historical eminences, and compared, barely credibly, with Winston Churchill. There was warm gratitude for British understanding of the American position in Vietnam. But the general drift of the discussions was that the British should do much better, and that maybe joining the more prosperous nations of western Europe in the Common Market was a better option. American analyses of Britain's financial strength, understandably, remained gloomy throughout Wilson's tenure of office. When he visited America again in February 1968, the New York Met baritone Robert Merrill was instructed to scrap plans to sing 'I got plenty of Nuthin'' and 'The Road to Mandalay' from his repertoire of songs to entertain the British Prime Minister.[36] After the devaluation of the pound and the retreat east of Suez, it was felt that these echoes of Gershwin and Kipling would strike the wrong note.

Callaghan had not been any kind of Euro-enthusiast in the 1960s, but along with Wilson he recognized the need for Britain's economic future to aim for a different and more secure course. He passed on to Wilson material about French attitudes gleaned from OECD meetings in Paris. The key, he told the Prime Minister, was obviously his relationship with de Gaulle, whose main concern was less the EEC as such than Europe's political independence from the United States.[37] Both Chancellor and Prime Minister were pragmatists on Europe as on most other issues, prepared to see how discussions would go. In addition, Wilson had in mind the fact that success in European negotiations would counter the drifting, rudderless character of British policy in economic matters, Rhodesia, Vietnam, and much else besides. George Brown had always been warmly pro-European and the main theme of his unexpected elevation to the Foreign Office was to pursue British membership. By the end of the year, Callaghan was telling the French Finance Minister, Michel Debré, that the political will to join the EEC existed in Britain, and that its economic policies could readily be co-ordinated with those of France. There was no question, however, that this would lead to sterling being devalued. Debré was apparently sympathetic. Callaghan noted in manuscript on the margin of the record of their meeting, 'Debré would like us in, if the General would let him.'[38]

Europe, then, became centre-stage for the Labour government, contrary to its previous expectations. Hopes rose sharply when Wilson and Brown had an apparently cordial meeting with President de Gaulle, the main stumbing-block to British entry four years earlier, at the Élysée Palace on 24 January 1967. Wilson then presented to his Cabinet a paper which proposed an early application for British membership, ideally in 1969 before the next general election. The British Cabinet, like the Labour movement as a whole, was divided over membership of what the party had in the past regarded as an ingrown capitalist club, hostile to ideas of socialist planning. Gaitskell had led the opposition to membership back in 1962. His conference speech cited Gallipoli, Vimy Ridge, and a thousand years of history. Callaghan had gone along with this insular line, although newsreels of the time show him not to be applauding this passage. Now, however, the Cabinet saw the political, and perhaps economic, advantages of a new shift of policy. Douglas Jay was the only vehement opponent of British entry, which he regarded, then as always, as financially catastrophic. Barbara Castle and Fred Peart were less outright opponents. The majority however went along, some of the younger people like Anthony Wedgwood Benn enthusiastically so with visions of technological co-operation on the Concord (or Concorde) model in mind. Callaghan himself, with his naval background and 'open sea' views, was sceptical, along with Crosland and Healey amongst others. But he was happy to endorse an attempt to enter the Market—that is, if the terms were right.

A fundamental problem was that membership of the Common Market almost certainly would imply devaluation of the pound and removal of its status as a reserve currency. The latter aspect would have brought much relief, not least to Callaghan himself. Devaluation, however, as we have seen, was vehemently opposed by Wilson and a clear majority of the Labour Cabinet, very much including Callaghan, as late as 20 July. Burke Trend, the Secretary of the Cabinet, had written to Wilson on 19 July firmly ruling out devaluation as a cure for Britain's economic ills. He compared it not with the removal of an aching tooth but with chopping someone's head off to cure a headache. It would also be a massive breach of faith with holders of sterling in the Commonwealth.[39] But devaluation was gaining in support as an idea from economists inside the administration as well as outside. William Armstrong made it clear in October that he was now a convert. Even Tommy Balogh, once violently opposed, felt that after the events of July it was unavoidable.[40] The issue was widely aired in the press. One personal tension that it caused was between Callaghan and his son-in-law Peter Jay. The latter threatened to resign from the Treasury over the failure to devalue in the aftermath of the events of July 1966, and actually wrote a letter to this effect to his father-in-law.[41] In April of the following year, however, he became financial editor of *The Times*.[42] Here he was to prove both a sympathetic observer of Callaghan's policies but also an advocate of devaluation, although one hostile to membership of the EEC. At any rate, with membership of the Common Market on the agenda, and free discussion in the press and Whitehall of the arguments for and against devaluation, the entire context of government policy had changed.

In the meantime, the government's fall in the opinion polls had been catastrophic. By-elections went uniformly badly, at the hands of Conservatives in England, and unexpectedly the Scottish and Welsh Nationalists in the Celtic nations. Local government elections were dismal throughout. In April 1967 the outcome was that Labour, traditionally strong in the localities, retained only three county councils, the traditional coal-mining counties of Durham, Glamorgan, and Monmouthshire. The Greater London Council, which had had a Labour majority of 64 : 36 in 1964, now showed a huge Tory majority of 82 : 18; Audrey Callaghan was among the casualties but became an alderman. The borough elections in May were almost as bad, with Labour losing heavily even in older industrial areas in the north-west and the Black Country. Only south Wales stayed firm. The government's success in handling negotiations in Europe and in at least forming a credible view on devaluation of the pound took place against a background of alarming political weakness.

For Callaghan himself, the winter and the spring of 1966–7 was a more tranquil time. The combination of international assistance and massive domestic deflation in July had steadied the markets. The Chancellor was inclined to believe that the situation with regard to the balance of payments and the markets was now under control. The worst was apparently over. In December it was recorded that the balance of payments had greatly improved in the third quarter of the year, with the deficit on the current and long-term capital account falling from £204m. in 1965 to £153m. Back in August he had told the Cabinet that there would be a 'sizeable' surplus on the balance of payments in the second half of 1967 and that the IMF agreed that the United Kingdom would be in the black for the year as a whole.[43] Callaghan was also in positive contact with Joe Fowler in Washington on many issues, especially in seeking to get international interest rates down, and perhaps raising a multi-billion international loan.

He could spend time on less anxious, though still important, matters like the relocation of the new Royal Mint. Various sites were investigated from Inverness to the West Country, and the lobbying was intense. Among other factors, over 1,500 new jobs could be created in a development area. Cledwyn Hughes fought for Wales, William Ross for Scotland, Fred Peart (member for Whitehaven) for Cumbria, Ted Short (Newcastle Central) for the north-east, Peter Shore (Stepney) for London. Crossman, chairman of the relevant committee, seemed determined to locate it anywhere other than where Callaghan wanted. Meanwhile Jack James, the deputy master of the Mint, reported that his staff did not want to move anywhere, or certainly not beyond the capital. Callaghan's own preference was for Llantrisant, only a few miles away from his own Cardiff. With the aid of Cledwyn Hughes at the Welsh Office the cause of the Welsh valleys was steadily advanced.[44]

The Chancellor's own general standing varied according to the vantage point of the observer. Some economists were less than impressed. Robert Neild was recorded as stating that 'in Cabinet he was weak and very much inclined to sit on the fence until he saw which way things were going'.[45] To a politician, however, this might have seemed a prudent course in most circumstances. Politically, his standing was still high, at a time when that of Michael Stewart was quiescent and that of George Brown at best unpredictable, at times almost in free fall. His colleagues probably felt Callaghan's authority in the government to be higher than at any other time since he took office. Crossman, assessing the key personnel on 27 March, thought him 'a big man and bit of a bully these days'. (The latter comment might seem a compliment from such a source.) Contrary to

Neild, Crossman felt Callaghan could collect support in Cabinet whenever he needed it. 'Roy Jenkins and Tony Crosland recognize their master in big Jim. He is the leader of the right wing in the Cabinet and with George Brown absent that has shifted the whole balance of Cabinet policy to the right.'[46] The leader of the left Crossman felt had inevitably to be himself, but he recognized his comparative weakness compared to Callaghan's strength and authority.

In his budget speech on 11 April 1967, Callaghan struck a confident note. He had no great novelties to reveal. *The Economist* scathingly attacked it as a 'non-event'. By contrast, Peter Jay in *The Times* felt it was remarkably innovative and a clear break with traditional Keynesian orthodoxy. Certainly it would appear that for the first time since the war a Chancellor was deliberately breaking with the commitment to full employment enshrined in the 1944 white paper, a basic component of the post-war consensus over two decades.[47] In a lengthy oration of an hour and three-quarters, the Chancellor seemed calm and authoritative. He pointed to recent healthy indicators about growth in the economy and the reduction of bank rate to 6 per cent in March. The note of confidence was irresistible. The speech reads well now although it is understandable that journalists who criticized it for its dullness of style failed to be enthused by a long and technical disquisition on the international monetary system. Callaghan made the platitudinous nature of the budget a virtue. Everything was under control. Turning to his maritime past, he declared, 'All seamen know the word of command—steady as she goes.' Harold Wilson was said by Crossman to be irritated that in preparing this budget, unlike the previous two, Callaghan had not consulted him at all.[48] The latter denied it. The press that weekend had been full of stories of Jim as the crown prince, leaving the Prime Minister seething in impotent rage. Very bad local election results followed, but it was Wilson who took all the blame.

It appeared, from the point of view of a long-beleaguered Chancellor, that the prospects for a period of economic stability were now better in the spring of 1967 than at any previous stage in his time at the Treasury. There were clear signs of growth, even if well below the level visualized in the heady days of the National Plan, now a defunct document. Callaghan had told Michel Debré that exports were running at a level of 11 per cent higher than a year ago: 'Britain's balance of payments had been effectively tackled.'[49] Whatever the outcome of the Common Market talks, devaluation of the pound seemed further away than for many months. Indeed, the budget was followed by a sharp rise in the parity of sterling, whch rose to the full rate of $2.80 for the first time since February 1966.[50] The

Chancellor, armed with a new strategy to attack the main problems, could surely now look forward to a more tranquil period, and to receiving his consequent reward in due time.

But it was not to be. At the end of April, he met Alec Cairncross and was startled to hear from those clipped Glaswegian tones, 'That's the end of the good news.'[51] Even if only of biblical man's hand dimensions, economic storm clouds were building up. At a time of apparent authority, James Callaghan found himself confronting a massive tempest in which he and the government were almost to be swept away. The central trauma of his entire political career was close at hand.

1. Crossman, *Cabinet Diaries*, i. 466 (1 Mar. 1966).

2. For discussions in the Cabinet, see Cabinet Conclusions, 24 Feb. 1966 (CAB 128/41 pt. 1) and 9 Nov. 1966 (CAB 128/41 pt. 2), and Callaghan's two Cabinet papers on 'Decimalization', C (66) 40, 24 Feb. 1966 (CAB 129/124 pt. 2) and 'Decimal Currency: Coinage', C (66) 148, 7 Nov. 1966 (CAB 129/127 pt. 1). Also relevant are Callaghan, 'Notes on Decimalization'; and letters from Callaghan to Sir Maurice Laing and Sir Stephen Brown, 13 June 1966–14 Feb. 1967 (University of Warwick Modern Records Centre, CBI Archives, Laing presidential papers, MSS 200/C/3/P1/13/1–3).

3. 'Note for the Record', 9 Mar. 1966, and note of meeting at 10 p.m. on 9 Mar. 1966 (PREM 13/851); Callaghan to Wilson, and Wilson's MS note, 21 Feb. 1966 (PREM 13/834).

4. Crossman, *Cabinet Diaries*, i. 475–6 (10 Mar. 1966); Cabinet Conclusions, 10 Mar. 1966, 10 a.m. (CAB 128/ 41 pt. 1).

5. *New Statesman*, 25 Feb. 1966.

6. Crossman, *Cabinet Diaries*, i. 511 (4 May 1966).

7. Cairncross MS diary, 13 Apr. 1966.

8. Callaghan's memo 'The Economic Situation', C (66) 103, 12 July 1966 (CAB 129/126 pt. 1); Cabinet Conclusions, 14 July 1966 (CAB 128/41 pt. 2).

9. Jay, *Change and Fortune*, 340.

10. *The Times*, 15 July 1966.

11. Callaghan memo on July 1966 crisis, 1 July 1966 (Callaghan Papers, box 25).

12. Callaghan to Fowler, 16 May 1966 (ibid.).

13. Callaghan memo, 6 July 1966.

14. *The Times*, 15 July 1966; *The Economist*, 23 July 1966; meeting of the Chancellor and the CBI, 12 July 1967 (CBI Archive, presidential papers, MSS 200/C3/P2/17/22–25).

15. Callaghan memo, 11 Aug. 1966.

16. Ibid.

17. Pimlott, *Harold Wilson*, 422.

18. Ibid.

19. Callaghan, *Time and Chance*, 199.

20. *The Economist*, 23 July 1966. The *Financial Times*, 21 July 1966 and subsequently, is an important source. Telephone conversation between Callaghan and Fowler, 20 July 1966, 3 p.m. (PREM 13/854).

21. Callaghan memo, 20 July 1966.

22. Ibid. 25–6 July 1966; record of Fowler's visit to the Treasury, 27 July 1966 (PREM 13/855).

23. Callaghan memo, 10 Aug. 1966; personal telegram, Wilson to Johnson, 11 Aug. 1966, T273/66 (PREM 13/855).

24. Callaghan memo, 11 Aug. 1966.

25. Ibid.

26. Ibid. 31 Aug. 1966. Stewart had been one of Callaghan's nominators in the leadership contest of Feb. 1963.

27. 'The July Conspiracy': Callaghan MS, 7 Sept. 1966 (Callaghan Papers, box 24).

28. Interview with Lord Merlyn-Rees.

29. Crossman, *Cabinet Diaries*, ii. 65 (5 October 1966).

30. Callaghan to Wilson, 9 Sept. 1966 (Callaghan Papers, box 24).

31. Callaghan memo, 31 Aug. 1966.

32. Barbara Castle, *The Castle Diaries, 1964–70* (London, 1984), 163–4 (1 Sept. 1966).

33. Ibid. 199 (5 Dec. 1966).

34. Background paper to Prime Minister Wilson's visit, 27 July 1966, PMW B–7; Dean Rusk memo for the President, 27 July 1966; Bill Moyers memo for the President, 29 July 1966 (President Lyndon Johnson presidential papers, NSF country file, box 216).

35. Walt W. Rostow memo for the President, Feb. 1967 (ibid.).

36. Background paper to Prime Minister Wilson's visit, Feb. 1968 (ibid.).

37. Callaghan to Wilson, 25 Nov. 1966 (Callaghan Papers, uncatalogued).

38. Meeting of Callaghan and Debré in Paris, 14 Dec. 1966 (PREM 13/826).

39. Burke Trend to Wilson, 19 July 1966 (PREM 13/854). Trend suggested instead a severe deflation which he admitted would lead to an increase of up to 500,000 in the total of unemployed.

40. Cairncross MS diary, 7 Oct. 1966.

41. Peter Jay to Callaghan, ? Aug. 1966.

42. John Grigg, *The History of the Times, 1966–1981* (London, 1992), 37.

43. Cabinet Conclusions, 10 Aug. 1966 (CAB 129/41 pt. 2).

44. Callaghan, 'Notes on Decimalization'.

45. Cairncross MS diary, 9 Feb. 1967.

46. Crossman, *Cabinet Diaries*, ii. 295 (27 Mar. 1967).

47. *The Economist*, 15 Apr. 1967; *The Times*, 12 Apr. 1967. Jay felt that the speech showed that the Chancellor had deliberately decided to allow unemployment to run on at its present level (about 500,000) and given priority to securing a £200m.–300m. balance of payments surplus. He had diverged from Balogh, MacDougall, Kaldor, and Neild who were all 'low unemployment men' on Keynesian lines.

48. Crossman, *Cabinet Diaries*, ii. 314 (16 Apr. 1967); interview with Lord Callaghan.

49. Record of meeting of Callaghan and Debré, Paris, 14 Dec. 1966 (PREM 13/826).

50. *The Economist*, 15 Apr. 1967.

51. Interview with Sir Alec Cairncross.

13

DEVALUATION AND DEPARTURE

Most later commentators have given the devaluation of the pound by the Labour government an air of inevitability. Indeed, surprise or disbelief have been expressed that this did not take place years earlier. That was not how the issue presented itself to many contemporaries. While the number of converts to the idea of devaluation of the pound had grown rapidly since the crises of July 1966, there were still many key economists who held to the view that on strict economic grounds the disadvantages of devaluation would outweigh the advantages. The supreme issue of the time, the balance of payments, appeared to be improving and it was hardly possible for ministers to underline the stronger prospects for British trade and at the same time argue that the outlook was so serious that exports required the sledgehammer assistance of devaluation. There would be always the difficult problem of timing and of ensuring that any decision to devalue would not immediately be nullified by other countries taking similar action to ensure that Britain did not gain any undue competitive advantage. Ministers like Douglas Jay argued that any constraints imposed by a decision not to devalue were a useful restriction on the possible growth of either inflation or unemployment—and certainly more acceptable than swingeing cuts which would do social damage. The great majority of Treasury advisers, from William Armstrong downwards, still argued against devaluation and so did Alec Cairncross and the Economic Section.

Callaghan himself needed no persuasion to respond, quite apart from political considerations such as the government's authority and credibility and the views of the United States. As has been noticed, he also felt that devaluation had moral implications and would constitute a kind of betrayal both towards British citizens in terms of their standard of living and towards holders of sterling in the developing world. He took this line vigorously in Cabinet down to October. The majority of his colleagues agreed with him, including particularly of course the Prime Minister who was even more vehemently committed to maintaining the exchange rate of the pound sterling than was his Chancellor. Callaghan argued that devaluation was unnecessary since the improvement in exports and the structural efficiencies being introduced in manufacturing industry would in themselves improve the balance of payments at least down to 1970. It was defeatism and a stream of denigration in the financial columns of the press, what Wilson called 'the sell Britain short brigade', that threatened the pound, not the weakness of the economy. He looked forward to a small surplus in 1967 and a large one in 1968.

It is certainly true that powerful ministers, including Brown, Crossman, and the two economically literate figures of Jenkins and Crosland, were now strong devaluers. Within the ranks of government more and more economists were coming to the view that devaluation was inescapable and even desirable as offering a new departure. This was the long-held view of Nicky Kaldor. He had been made so miserable at the start of the government at Callaghan's refusal to discuss the possible merits of devaluation that he had been distracted when driving his car, crashed, and ended up in hospital seriously injured.[1] Robert Neild, Callaghan's closest adviser, was another long-term advocate of devaluation, and Tommy Balogh, who always had the Prime Minister's ear, was a reluctant convert by now. Everyone in the DEA from Donald MacDougall downwards was totally committed to the cause. Nevertheless, it is important historically to realize the strength of support for not devaluing, and the powerful economic arguments that were advanced to this end, in order to appreciate the very real political and emotional difficulties that devaluation gave Jim Callaghan down to the very end.

For the moment, with the markets quiet and the economy growing steadily, there seemed no need to panic after the budget. The press may have thought it dull or even beneath contempt; world financial circles seemed to think that 'steady as she goes' was just what was needed. The Americans were particularly happy. In any case, Callaghan was anything but quiescent at this time. As Peter Jay had noted in his *Times* comments on the budget, the Chancellor was embarking on a subtly different tack, his so-called 'new strategy' first unveiled the previous December. This seemed to offer a distinct variant on the orthodox Keynesianism which had largely governed British economic policy-making since the time of Stafford Cripps, perhaps since Kingsley Wood's famous wartime budget of 1941. The presupposition behind the new policy was that curbing domestic demand and reining back public expenditure were the main needs of the moment. The former was guaranteed for a time with the incomes policy agreed with the TUC together with the stern deflationary measures announced by Wilson on 20 July. As for public expenditure, it had risen by one-sixth in real terms between 1963–4 and 1966–7, and was likely to rise still further in subsequent years. In order to try to keep it in hand, Callaghan was prepared to deviate from the Keynesian norm to which Labour instinctively subscribed and allow unemployment (standing at 515,000) to drift upwards slightly. A level of 2 per cent was acceptable, and, it could be argued, desirable in any case to allow greater flexibility in the labour market. It all depended on uncertain factors in the world outside, behaviour in foreign markets, and the course of international prices of oil and other key commodities. But for the time being in early May 1967 there was a period of apparent calm. The government's decision to relax hire purchase restrictions was taken as a signal of confidence. The Chancellor could sit tight and allow press chatter about devaluation to peter out.

The main controversy at this time focused not, for once, on the running of the economy but on Europe. Wilson and Brown were sufficiently encouraged by their tour of European capitals and their reception, even in Paris, to formulate a specific proposition that Britain should formally apply for membership. At a tense meeting at Chequers on 30 April, Wilson got the Cabinet to agree, by the narrow margin of 13 votes to 8, that Britain should make an unconditional bid.[2] The weight of those voting however varied a good deal. All the key ministers who were in some sense charged with running the economy—Wilson, Brown, Stewart, and Callaghan—were in favour of an application. Callaghan, always classed as a 'maybe' by the press, felt that the continuing uncertainties of the economy made an application inevitable, although he would defer judgement when and if the key issue of devaluation came up afterwards. Crossman records him making the observation on 30 April that if Labour were to devalue now, it would be the Tories who would reap the benefits in three or four years' time—in itself a remarkable admission in its way.[3] The Cabinet was divided in Crossman's view into ten unqualified supporters of application, six more doubtful who were veering Wilson's way (including Callaghan and indeed Crossman himself, along with the younger figure of Wedgwood Benn), and seven opponents, Fred Peart, Denis Healey, Barbara Castle, Willie Ross, Richard Marsh, Herbert Bowden, and Douglas Jay. Of these seven, Jay, the only trained economist amongst them, was the one root-and-branch opponent who would not countenance membership of the EEC under any circumstances. Industrialists in large numbers saw entry into the Market as a great opportunity, and so did a growing number of union leaders. In Whitehall, most key civil servants were warmly in favour, including Cairncross and the Economic Section.

It all came to nothing. On 16 May President de Gaulle once again vetoed Britain's application. He stated that Britain had not yet met the economic and financial conditions to make it an appropriate member. The unspoken view, as everybody knew, was that Britain would really be a kind of Trojan horse member, concealing the influence of the United States. De Gaulle's 'velvet veto' was generally seen as yet another political setback for Wilson's government. The Prime Minister's Walter Mitty-like insistence that the British bid was still on the table carried no great conviction. Callaghan viewed the rejection pragmatically, without tears. His European sympathies would not get any warmer as the years went by. He felt that there had been almost a hysteria about pro-Europeanism over recent months (as there had been over support for devaluation) and that now opinion would settle down in a cool and rational way to await events.

The Common Market rebuff did not shake sterling or the British economy. But other unforeseen issues certainly did. In early May *The Economist* was speaking of the robustness of the pound, a £52m. gain for the reserves in April, and a further cut in bank rate to 5.5 per cent.[4] But distant problems in the Middle East soon destroyed this optimism. In mid-May a new crisis broke out in the region. President Nasser of Egypt called for UN troops to be withdrawn from the Gaza strip and threatened to close the Straits of Tiran (or Aqaba) as an international waterway in pursuit of his country's hostility to Israel. Harold Wilson rapidly departed to Washington to try to promote action to secure free passage in the Straits and head off what looked a rerun of the Suez crisis of 1956. However on 5 June the so-called Six-Day War broke out between Israel and Egypt as a result of which the Israelis made massive territorial gains, including the whole of Jerusalem. Nasser then claimed that the USA and Britain had been providing assistance to Israel and the outcome was an oil embargo on Britain imposed by Iraq and Kuwait. The six-day war triggered off a six-month crisis for the economy which almost broke it and the Chancellor with it.

Callaghan was inevitably a key player in the Middle East crisis. In Cabinet, George Brown struck a belligerent pose at the outset and demanded that British vessels should be sent through the Straits to assert rights of passage in the most visible way. Wilson, with his strong personal links with Israel, appeared sympathetic. But Callaghan declared firmly against such John Bullish postures on both economic and strategic grounds.[5] He drew on his own experience of naval warfare to argue that it would be disastrous to put a British aircraft carrier into so confined an area as the Straits. Brown responded furiously and suggested that Callaghan might like to do his job. Patrick Gordon Walker recorded Callaghan as being 'pale with anger' at this point.[6] But Healey, the Defence Secretary, who had held talks with his chiefs of staff, also braved Brown's wrath and supported Callaghan. So did Crosland, Crossman, and Barbara Castle; the majority was clearly in favour of Callaghan's prudent line. Only Wilson, Brown, Stewart, Bowden, and Gunter wanted military action. Thereafter, Brown moved to a far more balanced position and he and Callaghan were as one in seeking assurances that the Suez Canal itself would remain open to British shipping.

Even if the Arab–Israeli war did not create any military alarms for the government, the economic effects were distinctly unpleasant. There was some flight from sterling, the oil embargo damaged the balance of payments to the tune of £20m. a month, and there were significant additional costs incurred at having to reroute oil tankers around the Cape of Good Hope. Prospects of a balance of payments surplus of any size in 1967 promptly disappeared, even though the Treasury felt the overall prospects for the economy were still quite encouraging. For instance, the trade figures for July were unexpectedly good, the first surplus for seven months.

The Cabinet continued to be divided over the social consequences of the government's campaign for cuts in public expenditure. Here Wilson and Callaghan were very much as one. There was vigorous discussion on proposals to link family allowances with child allowance: Callaghan felt that to do so would unfairly assist taxpayers without children. This was eventually resolved amicably. More contentious were proposals to hold down increases in pensions. The Social Services Secretary Peggy Herbison, a gentle Scot, protested over Callaghan's proposals which in fact would have increased pensions by 9*s*. (45p) a week. The Chancellor used his long-standing friendship with her to persuade her to stay. However, she remained discontented and resigned on the issue of family allowances instead.[7] On the other hand, the Chancellor's axe on public expenditure was distinctly selective. Barbara Castle, who as always had warm backing from Harold Wilson, managed to get away with a tiny cut in her £894m. transport budget. Callaghan himself, significantly, proved anything but an iron Chancellor on education, a theme which had attracted his keen sympathy since his youth. He led a campaign not to defer for some years the raising of the school-leaving age to 16, despite the opposition of Wilson and Crossman, both former Oxford dons. Callaghan's view was a simple egalitarian one which saw education as a key to social justice. In addition, he agreed at a private meeting to concede, in return for other public expenditure cuts, the £2m.–4m. for the Open University of the Air, championed by the Arts Minister, Jennie Lee,

Aneurin Bevan's widow and something of a favourite of the Prime Minister's. Callaghan's important role was to be recalled in July 1996 when the Open University, not before time perhaps, awarded him an honorary degree.[8] In the end, the summer vacation came without the draconian cuts that many had feared. The great bulk of the savings, £200m. on the estimated expediture for 1970–1, was in the area of defence, much of it east of Suez. One concession near home which gave the Chancellor much pleasure was an alloction of £140,000 to the Welsh Office during July for 13,000 acres from the Vaynol estate in Snowdonia to be purchased for the nation.

August was a relatively tranquil month for the economy, as the Callaghans for the first time spent a summer break in their prospective new home, not in the Isle of Wight but at the farm at Upper Clayhill, near Lewes in Sussex. The Treasury reported that exports were going reasonably well, the pound appeared to have survived the Six-Day War without undue alarms, and a surplus of some size was still expected in 1968. Modest measures of reflation such as with hire purchase terms were in the pipeline. When Callaghan returned to his Treasury desk in September, there was more good news. At long last, the battle with the DEA had been decided, overwhelmingly in favour of the Treasury. Michael Stewart, a retiring personality, had not made a great deal of impact. Callaghan commented, 'He cannot get on terms with the trades unionists. I am quite sure he does not know when to produce the bottle of whisky to put them at their ease. And he is too precise and pedantic in his discussions with industrialists. But they all respect him even though he does not persuade them.'[9] In personality, Stewart was the complete opposite of his rumbustious predecessor George Brown. With much relief, Callaghan heard on 9 September that the DEA would now be added to the remit of the Prime Minister. He and Wilson, especially friendly at this time, would share the chairmanship of NEDC, with lesser responsibilities given to Peter Shore, Secretary of State for Economic Affairs, and Fred Lee. Callaghan would also have effective charge of incomes policy. The Treasury had finally won the great interdepartmental gladiatorial contest. Edmund Dell recalled later that Harold Wilson's Thursday lunches with DEA ministers (of whom he was one) focused on political conspiracies rather than economic policy. From that time onwards, the demise of the DEA was inevitable. It was placed under Peter Shore later in 1967 and wound up almost unobserved in the course of the following two years. In another move, Douglas Jay, the most vehement opponent of entry into Europe, was removed from the Board of Trade, to be replaced by Callaghan's intimate Tony Crosland. Alec Cairncross concluded on 14 September that 'the Cabinet changes are unmistakably to the advantage of the Treasury'. He added, 'Not a breath about the Plan.'[10] Crossman was struck by the new dominance of Crosland and Shore in economic policy-making.[11] But the essential power clearly lay in the new alliance of convenience between the Prime Minister and the Chancellor, who held confidential meetings every Monday evening to plan and plot the way ahead.

It was only a few days, however, before the government, fresh from the ordeals of the Six-Day War and public expenditure battles, faced a still more damaging challenge. This time it came in industrial relations which for most of the year had been remarkably quiescent, despite slowly rising unemployment, with midsummer figures of 555,000 the highest since the 1930s. On 18 September, following endless local stoppages, major unofficial disputes broke out in the docks. The great ports of Liverpool, Manchester, Hull, and eventually London virtually closed down. The cause, following an inquiry into the docks by Lord Devlin, was the intended positive reform of the decasualization of dock labour, with which Callaghan himself, as a Cardiff MP, was fully familiar. But it followed a tangled web of labour tensions in dockland communities; the men refused requests from Frank Cousins, the Transport Workers' leader, that they should remain at work. Potential British exports piled up idly on quaysides.

There had been dock strikes before but at this particular time, with pressure on sterling always close at hand, the effect was appalling. After much delay, the government raised bank rate to 6 per cent in mid-October. However, the news of the October trade figures, which showed a massive deficit as a result of the docks strikes, was catastrophic in its effects. After years of holding the line against changes in the exchange rate and the value of the currency, the government was in headlong retreat in the face of forces it was no longer able to control. At this same unfortunate time, a report commissioned by the Common Market gave the European view that the pound could no longer be sustained as a reserve currency. The voters, too, were giving the thumbs down. The Conservatives gained two seats from Labour at by-elections in late September, with a colossal swing of 18 per cent at West Walthamstow. This was a largely working-class London constituency which had been Labour since the 1920s, even in the débâcle of 1931. Latterly the parliamentary seat of Labour's great Prime Minister Clem Attlee, its loss had symbolic impact.

There was a curiously measured approach leading up to the ultimate crisis. At the start of October, Labour's passions were engaged not by the dock strike, but by the party conference at Scarborough on 2–6 October. Here, while Wilson made a fresh and highly effective speech, Callaghan on 3 October made a quite outstanding one. Later he felt it was perhaps his best ever conference performance, delivered largely extempore. The troubles of recent months rolled back as he captivated his audience with great panache. He defended the government's economic record and successfully rebutted criticisms by Clive Jenkins over incomes policy. Several important unions including Tom Jackson's Post Office Workers changed their vote as a direct result of Callaghan's speech. *The Times* declared that his triumph was 'as complete as it could be'. He had 'set himself to teach the delegates the rudimentary economic facts of life, seen with all the clarity of which the Treasury was capable' and he had perfectly caught the mood of the delegates.[12] The syllogism that 'free for all' collective bargaining would mean inflation which would lead in turn to deflation, which would lead on to balance of payments difficulties and then higher unemployment, was accepted without demur by the delegates anxious to hail their champions after the traumas of the past. The *Guardian* thought his speech 'politically brilliant'.[13] The *Daily Telegraph* was to describe Callaghan as 'the man of the week' after his 'virtuoso performance', and concluded that he had manifestly supplanted George Brown as the heir apparent.[14] In the *Sunday Times*, James Margach saw the Chancellor as 'the Crown Prince' whose speech showed qualities of 'near-greatness'.[15]

Praise from the Tory press might be a two-edged weapon. But Callaghan's oration received acclaim equally from left-wing potential critics on his own side. Richard Crossman was deeply impressed, as seldom before. Callaghan had showed 'an extraordinary assuredness' and proved himself 'completely en rapport with the rank and file'.[16] Barbara Castle described the speech as 'a triumph'. She added, 'I can't help feeling the conference *wants* to be reassured. It certainly doesn't want the old splits.'[17] Frank Cousins, who had resigned from the government after falling out with Callaghan over incomes policy, and had earlier been a vehement opponent over nuclear disarmament, was another admirer of his skills. 'Jim Callaghan is a splendid platform performer, skilled in the art of answering points not raised and putting queries to people who are not going to be allowed to answer them. He is a *very satisfying* man and if he could ever break away from the Treasury grip could be quite a politician.' By contrast, George Brown (a TGWU nominee who had once been close to Cousins) was felt to have spoilt himself, combining assertiveness with inferiority complex. He had had an unseemly brawl with press photographers at Scarborough. In short, he was 'a drunken bum'.[18]

These plaudits for Callaghan are worth recalling at length here. Interestingly, they and his speech do not appear in his autobiography which focuses on high policy. They were not merely self-reinforcing Fleet Street gossip, but considered judgements along the whole political spectrum. They indicate the considerable political stature that Callaghan had managed to build up over the trials of the recent past. Whatever the economic future might hold, that essential political strength would endure, a crucial foundation which could never be eroded.

But it was the economy, not applause from Labour's conference delegates, which would dictate the Chancellor's immediate future. Here the news was appalling. By the end of October, there was a tidal wave of selling of sterling, By the beginning of November, the pound stood at a little above $2.78, its lowest level for fifteen years. All the support of the Bank could not prevent its slide. On 25 October Sir William Armstrong and Leslie O'Brien, Governor of the Bank of England, had already had an urgent meeting with Callaghan suggesting that an early devaluation must be considered. Callaghan was disquieted by this advice, and responded that he preferred to defer a decision until the spring.[19] He had in the meantime had a telegram from Joe Fowler in Washington outlining the prospect of further US credits amounting to another $100m. and indicating that the European central banks might offer more. Callaghan was told that the US Treasury 'clearly regarded our troubles as temporary and reflecting the state of world trade'.[20] Other options short of devaluation, therefore, still presented themselves.

Then in the late afternoon, Callaghan received a private handwritten letter from Alec Cairncross of the Economic Section.[21] He arranged that they should have a private meeting on the morning of 3 November, the first between the two since Callaghan had first gone to the Treasury.[22] Cairncross's message, conveyed in crisp, logical terms, was that the battle was over. The game was up. Sterling could no longer be held. Devaluation was unavoidable. It was the Chancellor's moral responsibility and public duty to act at the earliest moment. Cairncross's quiet Scots tones made his message all the more telling. The Chancellor was clearly devastated. From his conversation with Cairncross came the dénouement of the crisis, a pivotal event in the history of Britain as a major economic power, and the most shattering moment Callaghan was ever to experience in sixty years of public life.

Cairncross's blunt message spelt out the implications of what he had told Callaghan back in May, that he had now had all the good news. The fall in world production and trade had been to the huge disadvantage of the British economy. In the face of the Chancellor's questioning, he repeated that further borrowing abroad was no longer feasible. It was in fact the case that the Bank of International Settlements was about to provide a credit of $250m. but this was to refinance debts that were due for settling in December. Already over £1,500m. had been borrowed, there was a huge commitment of £1,100m. in the market for forward sterling and the danger that Britain's lines of credit would run out during November. 'We'd need a lot of money to wait till the spring.' It was understood between the two men that devaluation meant Callaghan would have to resign.

In more human terms, Cairncross asked the Chancellor if he was sleeping well. Callaghan replied that he was, and had slept well the previous night. 'He felt that if it did come to devaluation in the end he had at least the satisfaction of guiding the country for three years and would be able to look back on a great deal that had been accomplished over that time.' There was a sense of catharsis about Callaghan on that fateful morning. 'He gave no sign', reported Cairncross, 'of worry or perturbation. His demeanour was that of a man who has thought it through, come to a firm conclusion, and is incapable of being ruffled.' The meeting ended cordially, even affectionately. Cairncross then saw Kaldor who gave a more cynical interpretation. Callaghan had been unwilling to devalue because Wilson would saddle him with all the blame and his career would be at an end. 'He had to wait till HW himself would feel obliged to take the lead and identify himself with the change.' Cairncross felt this was 'too simpliste'.[23]

The next day, Saturday, 4 November, Callaghan had a meeting with O'Brien, the Governor, and then saw Wilson in private in No. 10. The government's confidence was now at a low ebb on all fronts. A by-election defeat at Hamilton inflicted by Mrs Ewing of the Scottish Nationalists showed that hostility amongst the voters was as great north of the border as in England and Wales. Callaghan reported on his conversation with Cairncross and on the accelerating flight from sterling. Now the Prime Minister also appeared to realize that the battle for the exchange rate had been irretrievably lost. A note in Callaghan's hand comments, 'He does not demur.' Wilson's memoirs appear to confirm this since he affirmed that devaluation would no longer face a 'political veto'.[24] Even so, Callaghan had yet to concede publicly, and perhaps in his own mind too, that devaluation was unavoidable.

It was a time of extreme strain for him. On Tuesday, 7 November, tired and tense, during the debate on the Queen's Speech he annoyed several backbenchers, including Michael Foot, John Mendelson, and James Dickens of the Tribunite left, by appearing to lend support to a speech given in Buenos Aires on 5 October by Leslie O'Brien, Governor of the Bank of England. There, the latter had argued the economic case for maintaining a pool of unemployment. The Chancellor seemed also to be endorsing the controversial views of Professor Frank Paish, who urged the need for a greater margin of unused capacity and had welcomed the 1967 budget as a signal of conversion. Callaghan's remark on the need for 'a somewhat larger margin of unemployment than we used to have', accurate though it undoubtedly was, seemed inappropriate in the extreme for a Labour chancellor, and a vote of censure was proposed at the PLP meeting on 21 November. A row with backbenchers was the last thing he needed at this critical period.[25]

Several days were now being taken up with desperate efforts to try to put together further loans from abroad, from the United States in particular. On Wednesday, 8 November, Callaghan saw William Armstrong and Denis Rickett at 9 a.m. at No. 11. There was discussion of possible assistance coming from Chancellor Kiesinger of West Germany, and of the fears expressed by Van Lennep, the chairman of the Monetary Committee of the Six, that a devaluation of the pound might trigger a further devaluation of other European currencies. He told Van Lennep at a meeting in the Treasury that afternoon at 3.15 p.m. that 'it was the view of the Government that the existing parity of sterling should be maintained. Certainly this was the strong conviction of both the Prime Minister and himself. The results of an authoritative independent analysis which had recently been made had confirmed him in his view. It had been shown that, if the effects of the closing of the Suez Canal and other temporary influences were left out of account, our position would have been satisfactory.' Van Lennep himself supported a British devaluation of 10–15 per cent. It was acknowledged that if the United Kingdom were to devalue it would remove a powerful argument against British entry into the Common Market.[26] The next day, bank rate rose to 6.5 per cent but in the markets sterling kept on being sold.

In the course of 9 November, a telegram was sent to Sir Patrick Dean in the Washington embassy to inquire whether further long-term US help was likely.[27] Wilson was anxious to have an early meeting with President Johnson, which might deal with cuts in defence commitments and the pressure he faced over Vietnam as well. But it was difficult to construct a 'cover story' which did not refer damagingly to sterling. On the morning of 10 November, Callaghan told Armstrong, Rickett, and O'Brien at the Treasury that he was prepared to go on borrowing. If there were to be devaluation, there would be strong pressure to withdraw British forces from Germany as well as from east of Suez.[28] However, Callaghan also wrote to Joe Fowler, the US Secretary of the Treasury, on the same day, 'I think we are getting to the end of the period when we can afford to carry on a hand to mouth basis.' He underlined the serious effect that floating the pound would have for world trade.[29] Even as late as the evening of Sunday, 12 November, Callaghan though was still clinging to the hope that he might get by without devaluing. He had a meeting with Wilson and Brown, the latter now favouring devaluation at an early date. The Treasury record was that Callaghan's inclination 'was still to stick to the existing parity or leave devaluation to the next budget'.[30]

The next day, 13 November, it was clear that the end of the road had been reached. Original proposals for a standby operation from the United States, Germany, Italy, and the IMF had been replaced by less helpful suggestions for a $2.4 bn. standby credit. The Americans, though 'hotly opposed to our devaluing', could go no further. Callaghan's note states, 'We met at 11.15 [p.m.] on 13 November after Guildhall and *decided finally*.'[31] This followed the Lord Mayor's banquet at the Guildhall, a meal which neither Prime Minister nor Chancellor can have much enjoyed. The latter told Tony Crosland, the President of the Board of Trade, that a devaluation to $2.40 was likely on 18 November. It might well be bolstered by major defence cuts including a withdrawal from the Far East by 1970 and cancelling the F/111 aircraft. Devaluation, he added, he regarded as 'a political catastrophe'.[32]

Preparations were now well under way for the massive deflationary measures that would have to accompany devaluation to make it work. This was anything but straightforward, mainly for political reasons. Alec Cairncross was not the only one to feel that it was undertaken in a haphazard way despite the 'War Book' the Treasury had prepared for the emergency. Callaghan himself felt the markets should have been closed. At midday on 14 November, Callaghan saw Armstrong and Cairncross at the Treasury; Armstrong insisted that Kaldor should not be called in. The Chancellor here accepted restrictions on hire purchase, credit squeezes, and even an 8 per cent bank rate, a rate hitherto unheard of except in wartime. But he resisted proposed rises in income tax or SET. Cairncross reported, 'When I tried to argue with him it was important to announce it all now because it wouldn't be possible later, he checked me by pointing out that this was a political judgement and he preferred to take these himself.' The Chancellor added, 'Professor Cairncross [the use of academic titles by Callaghan was always a sign of squalls] we have here a package of £450m. excluding income tax. Would you not consider that enough?'[33]

That evening, there was a ferocious Cabinet meeting. Callaghan for the first time informed his colleagues that a devaluation would take place on

18 November. That day the trade figures for October had been released. They showed a monthly deficit of £107m., easily the largest on record, much higher than the £74m. in January 1964, the previous highest total. He raced through the figures for the proposed economies in great haste which led to many protests from Roy Jenkins and others, with ministers trying desperately to add up the results on the backs of envelopes. The most ferocious reaction came from Denis Healey, whose Defence Department would inevitably bear the brunt. He asked Callaghan, according to Armstrong who was present, 'why anyone should trust him or believe his forecasts after all he has dragged the party through'.[34] Healey was still fearfully angry the next morning, and a placatory breakfast took place with George Brown, of all people, calming him down. Healey might have been even angrier had he realized that the proposed cuts of almost £500m. were not all, and that the accompanying measures were not yet divulged. At a meeting with Cairncross, Armstrong, and Kaldor on the 15th, however, Callaghan was reported as being 'in good humour and remarkably quick and alert'. An autumn budget including increases in fuel tax, betting tax, and perhaps taxes on dividends was outlined, with some reduction in the standard rate of income tax. This 'would not be unattractive, although any increases in personal taxation would lead to presentational problems'.[35] At this time of almost unremitting strain, there was one amiable social interlude, when Cyril Plant, now president of the Inland Revenue Staff Federation, joined the Chancellor in his room at the Treasury, along with the chairman of the Inland Revenue, the head of Customs and Excise, and the Chief Inspector of Taxes. It was the thirty-eighth anniversary to the day of Callaghan's appointment as a very young tax officer in Maidstone, and he was presented with a bound copy of the history of the Revenue and a copy of his certificate of qualification issued by the Civil Service Commission back in 1929. Plant slightly soured the mood of relaxation by inquiring whether the coming devaluation of sterling meant that Callaghan would not be around to celebrate the fortieth anniversary.[36]

As the threat to sterling continued, a disastrous episode occurred in the Commons on 16 November which made the crisis even worse. A backbencher, Robert Sheldon, an accountant by profession, chose to ask a question in the House about reports of the possibility of a $1,000m. loan being negotiated with foreign banks. Almost thirty years on, Sheldon professed himself unable to understand why he was not asked to withdraw his question.[37] What is even more difficult to understand is why he, a knowledgeable observer of the markets, chose to ask such an unbelievably insensitive question at such a time. Various efforts were made by John

Silkin, the Labour chief whip, to persuade the Speaker (the Labour member Dr Horace King) not to call the question but these failed in the face of what King saw as the constitutional proprieties. Pressure on Sheldon himself, it was felt, would be counter-productive. After discussions with Wilson as to how he might conceal that devaluation was going to take place without actually offering a direct lie, Callaghan stonewalled desperately in response to Sheldon's question. For a tense ten minutes, he repeated the formula that he had nothing to add or to subtract from his previous answers on the subject. He repeated this formula in response to a further difficult question from Stan Orme that devaluation would be preferable to swingeing deflationary cuts or mass unemployment. No direct denial was offered since the direct question was not put. He refused to make any comment on press rumours. 'I did not start the rumours and I do not propose to comment on them', he stated in reply to a question by the Tory shadow Chancellor Iain Macleod.

In parliamentary terms, colleagues thought Callaghan's refusal to answer skilfully done. But the fact that devaluation was implicitly brought up, and its inevitability not denied, had a catastrophic effect on the markets. Almost £1,500m. was lost in 24 hours as a result of the Bank's efforts to prop up the ailing pound. Sheldon's was said to have been the most expensive question in British parliamentary history. Crossman rounded furiously on Sheldon and his ally Joel Barnett when he saw them in the lobby that evening, but the news got out and the papers were now full of reports of Cabinet splits.[38] There were further heavy losses on Friday, 17 November, while Treasury advisers wrestled desperately to try to put together a coherent package of cuts. Even though his journey was delayed by heavy fog, Callaghan himself had to take the train to Cardiff that evening; no doubt he was delighted to free himself from his toils in Whitehall if only for a moment.[39]

On 18 November the devaluation of the pound to $2.40 was announced by Harold Wilson in a Prime Minister's broadcast at 6 p.m. A variety of deflationary cuts were to follow, including a rise in bank rate from 6.5 per cent to 8 per cent, hire purchase restrictions, an increase in corporation tax, and large cuts in public expenditure including £100m. off defence spending. It looked substantial, but in Cairncross's judgement 'fell short of what the occasion required', certainly when compared with successive deflationary packages introduced by Jenkins. The news caused shock waves, but not because of the effect of devaluation alone. Wilson's tone seemed inappropriate for the occasion, buoyant, almost chirpy. He may have been trying to reassure the archetypal 'housewife' that the internal value of the pound was not affected, but the symbolic impact of what he said went far beyond mere words. His phrase, popularly interpreted as 'the pound in your pocket is not being devalued', seemed barely credible, not only to professional economists but to ordinary citizens. It made Wilson appear evasive, even dishonest. To adapt Nye Bevan's famous observation on Selwyn Lloyd at the time of the Suez debate, Wilson was sounding the bugle of advance to cover his retreat. The Prime Minister's credibility sank still further. The dread phrase was to haunt him for the rest of his career. Callaghan, by contrast, sunk in deepest gloom at No. 11, came out almost unscathed in terms of public probity if not of competence.

Callaghan spelt out the gloomy news of the deflationary package to the Commons on the afternoon of 20 November.[40] Its purpose was to enable the United Kingdom to enjoy 'a lasting and substantial improvement' in its balance of payments. There would be cuts of over £400m. in the expected rate of growth of public expenditure (which meant that they would have no immediate effect, of course). He had recommended devaluation to the Cabinet 'with great personal regret'. Callaghan's visible sense of dismay gave him a haunted look. He spoke of 'a suspended sentence of execution'. His opposite number was Iain Macleod, who greatly liked Callaghan personally and had long been associated with him on colonial matters. He refrained from going for the Chancellor's jugular, although he accused him nevertheless of having 'devalued his word and betrayed his office'.[41] Other Tories were fiercer still. When Callaghan faced a critical question from Eric Heffer, a left-wing Labour backbencher, he replied pathetically, 'I need friends at the moment.'

However, when he came to wind up the debate on 22 November, he had recovered much of his self-confidence and pride.[42] He defended his long-term policies with much vigour and turned savagely on Tory critics. He condemned 'dubious people' such as Paul Chambers of ICI who had pursued 'sinister' policies damaging to the currency, and this cheered up Labour's backbenchers. However, his tone as a whole was almost elegiac. David Wood in *The Times* noted that it sounded like a swansong.[43] It was, in fact, a highly effective speech, far better than that of Wilson who seemed tired and embittered. Callaghan set aside a pile of detailed notes and spoke almost off the cuff in a consensual, moderate tone. 'There was something in the sombreness and gravity of his manner that profoundly impressed the House', wrote David Wood.[44] It confirmed Terence Lancaster's view in the *People* that Callaghan was 'the Tories' favourite Socialist'.[45] Crossman was deeply impressed. 'That was a marvellous speech, Jim, but it won't do you much good in the Cabinet.' 'I know,'

Callaghan replied, 'but it would [*sic*] not be for long.'[46] Everyone knew that he was about to resign. Kaldor claimed that Wilson had dissuaded him from resigning immediately and speaking in the debate on the backbenches, but in fact this was quite incorrect.

Britain's devaluation shook the world. The markets were in turmoil for a while, and watched sterling nervously until the precise terms of the international credit that would be forthcoming were known. There was a general sense that the package of cuts was inadequate and that the whole devaluation exercise had not been well handled. In the United States, the British devaluation was regarded with great alarm. Callaghan had made a point of not telling them until 5 p.m. in the evening after their markets had closed. Until as late as 14 November the Americans had tried every stratagem to keep devaluation of the pound at bay. President Johnson called a special meeting of the US Cabinet on Monday, 20 November, since 'the British move has the most serious consequences for the Administration', in Johnson's own words.[47] Cuts in the federal budget were essential to save the Great Society programme, already threatened by the war in Vietnam. Fowler stated that the United States must preserve the gold exchange standard and protect its political, military, and diplomatic positions abroad. 'We have only to read the story of Great Britain in the last five years to see the danger,' he said. He went on, 'We can see it in the sad last paragraph of Prime Minister Wilson's statement. It is now Britain first.'[48]

However a paper for the President on 'the Effects of the Devaluation of Sterling' on 24 November acknowledged that it was 'an unavoidable necessity.'[49] It was basically caused by Britain's inability to export on a scale necessary to finance its imports and other overseas payments, 'an old and chronic problem'. Britain had been trying for three years to eliminate its balance of payments problem. Although prices and costs had been very stable for eighteen months, the problem continued. The United States, though, would be directly affected as by far Britain's largest trading partner. British exports would rise while it was improbable that the foreign exchange cost of United Kingdom imports, mainly food, fuel, and basic materials, would be reduced. The devaluation of sterling had reduced the dollar equivalent of foreign private holdings by about $785m. There was an unpleasant feeling that, with sterling having been devalued, the dollar would be very much the next in the front line. The Dow Jones index slumped as a result.

Some political effort was put in by the administration to counter accusations, for instance from the New York *Daily News* columnist Eliot Janeway, that the British devaluation was the result of pressure from

Washington and from Secretary of Defense Robert MacNamara in particular to keep up its defence commitments in German, Aden, and the Far East.[50] The liberal Democrat Eugene McCarthy, a Senator from Minnesota, declared roundly that 'the British pound was worth more to the west than the British navy'.[51] Adapting Keynes, he said that America had stood by while its British ally 'suffered a financial Dunkirk'. On balance, the special relationship to which Callaghan was so strongly committed distinctly suffered from the entire episode. The advent of Nixon in place of Johnson as President in 1969 was to make matters somewhat worse.

Callaghan's personal position was now the cause of much speculation. At the time of devaluation, he had handed in his resignation to Wilson.[52] Devaluation was associated with him personally. It was his failure, and he should go. His wish was to leave the government entirely. Wilson, however, was anxious that he should stay. There seems to have been genuine cordiality between him and his beleaguered Chancellor at this time. They were both victims of devaluation and extreme adversity drove them together as triumph had seldom done. Callaghan was a major figure and his departure would tarnish the administration with failure perhaps ineradicably. Wilson might also well feel that a Callaghan lurking refreshed on the backbenches could be a dangerous potential challenger, somewhat on the lines that Michael Heseltine was to be to Mrs Thatcher in 1986–90. Callaghan's own friends, notably Merlyn Rees, worked hard on his morale also and urged him that he still had a major contribution to make.

The atmosphere was then soured by newspaper comment surrounding devaluation. Crossman had made some efforts to present it as a triumph for Wilson and a defeat for Callaghan. Ludicrously, he spread it abroad that Wilson emerged as the Churchill of the affair, and Callaghan as the Neville Chamberlain.[53] This view did not long survive Wilson's devaluation broadcast on television. Conversely, Peter Jay in an extremely well-informed piece in *The Times* on 23 November placed the blame solely on Wilson. Using a more distant historical analogy, he compared Callaghan to Wolsey and Wilson to Henry VIII at the time of the former's dismissal in 1530. 'Had I served my God as well as I served my king . . .'[54] (He did not add that Wolsey's fate was his early death after being dispatched to the Tower of London accused of high treason.) Callaghan, he claimed, had been let down by a master to whom he had been faithful. Jay attacked Wilson for stubbornly defending the rate of sterling in October 1964 and again in July 1966, and refusing to acknowledge that entry into Europe would inevitably lead to devaluation. He had repeatedly suppressed reports from financial advisers such as Kaldor and Neild in favour of devaluation and even destroyed all copies of one in 1966. Wilson was furious with Jay, who after all was Callaghan's son-in-law, and whose criticisms were all too accurate. He ensured that Jay was kept off the television programme *This Week* because his views were slanted.[55] The Sunday press, however, repeated accusations that Wilson had deliberately suppressed pro-devaluation advice from key Treasury personnel. Peregrine Worsthorne in the *Sunday Telegraph*, a maverick observer, chose to praise Callaghan for the way he had handled the crisis and underlined the 'peculiar bipartisan respect' for him in the House.[56] This sent alarm signals amongst some left-wing figures such as the veteran Emanuel Shinwell and Michael Foot who feared that in the turmoil right-wing Labour ministers might be tempted to replace Wilson with Callaghan.[57]

There were many possible scenarios, but much the most likely was Callaghan's being transferred to another major department. He stayed just long enough to negotiate with the IMF and the Group of Ten the terms for the standby credit of $1,400m. following devaluation. The severity of the Declaration of Intent, published as Callaghan left the Treasury, caused immense shock, with fears expressed that the British budget would now be decided not by the Chancellor of the Exchequer, but by Pierre-Paul Schweitzer of the IMF. Callaghan himself asked Wilson for the Education Department since this was an area in which he had long-standing and highly personal interest. But Wilson responded that this was too minor a position for such an important figure—in itself, an interesting comment on how Labour regarded the education portfolio. It might also lead to a difficult reshuffle of Cabinet posts and a political chain reaction thereafter. Wilson, in short, wanted to shore up Callaghan to the extent of eroding any impression that he was being dismissed or even demoted. On 30 November, it was announced that Callaghan and Roy Jenkins would exchange office. Jenkins, highly literate in economics if not exactly an economist, was welcomed in the press for his ability and articulateness. Callaghan went to the Home Office in his place.

The exchange was not as Callaghan had wished. His preferred successor was Tony Crosland, a long-standing rival of Jenkins's for key economic positions. Indeed, he had a private meeting with Jenkins to tell him that Wilson would not be appointing him as his successor.[58] But Wilson rejected this, in large measure perhaps because of Crosland's closeness to Callaghan, which would be politically awkward. Some politicians believed that Crosland blamed Callaghan for the decision and bore something of a grudge against him later. Jenkins, by contrast, had no closeness to Callaghan and indeed no personal regard for him either. Callaghan was disappointed by Wilson's decision, although the appointment as Foreign Secretary in 1976 when he chose Crosland, afforded him an opportunity to turn the tables as far as Jenkins was concerned. Like the Kennedys, he felt that getting even was always better than getting mad. Dejected and at a low ebb, he went back to his Sussex farm on 30 November to contemplate the joys of the Home Office and the tribulations of the recent past.

Callaghan's resignation and the entire way that devaluation was conducted have naturally given rise to immense discussion. Inevitably, the Wilson government comes out of it very badly, even when incidental and unexpected crises such as the Six-Day War and the dock strike are taken into account. The handling of the economy in November caused record and disastrous losses. The reserves had lost £200m. on one single day, 16 November. The balance of trade for November was horrendous, a deficit of £153m. following one of £107m. in October. Aided by the dock strikes, imports soared to a record level of £575m.[59] Even after devaluation the pound remained in sickly health and the longer-term implications of the terms for the standby credit when announced by Jenkins in 1968 sent shock waves through the country and especially the Labour Party.

There is, however, one moral issue to be disposed of first. In 1994, during the hearings of the Commons Treasury and Civil Service Select Committee, it was claimed that in handling the devaluation affair, whatever the aspect of competence, Callaghan had actually lied. This was alleged both by a Conservative Cabinet minister, William Waldegrave, and before the Scott Inquiry by the Secretary to the Cabinet, Sir Robin Butler. In the later Scott report Waldegrave was eventually to be criticized for breaching ministerial responsibility by misleading parliament over the arms to Iraq affair—though apparently without intending to do so. But Waldegrave had argued before the Treasury select committee that ministers had sometimes to lie to the House of Commons for reasons of state. 'That is what Lord Callaghan did about devaluation', he added.[60] He was at once fiercely challenged by Lord Callaghan who pursued him with great professional skill thereafter. Hurt that his probity should be challenged, Callaghan expressed astonishment that his replies to the Sheldon and Orme questions on 16 November 1967 could be construed as lying rather than simply declining to offer an answer, and took the matter up publicly with Waldegrave. His reply, on 9 March 1994, was that Callaghan's response in 1967 that he had nothing to add to or subtract from his previous statements, which clearly ruled out devaluation, amounted to a lie. Waldegrave hastened to add on 10 March that he believed nevertheless that his answers on that occasion were fully justified on patriotic grounds.[61]

Callaghan then wrote to the Prime Minister, John Major, for his view of what Waldegrave had said. Major (who enjoyed in any event a good private relationship with Callaghan) responded that Callaghan 'acted entirely properly throughout the devaluation episode' and confirmed that neither Heath nor Macleod had made any complaint at the time. Guardedly, he added that Callaghan could not 'altogether avoid saying something that was misleading even though he rightly tried to say as little as possible'.[62] To that extent, he lent Waldegrave modest protection. The press reaction was unanimously that Callaghan came well out of this controversy and that the Hansard record confirmed that he had not lied. A variety of commentators in *The Times*, including the former Conservative MP Sir Robert Rhodes James, endorsed Callaghan's interpretation of events.[63] Donald Macintyre in the *Independent* suggested that Waldegrave had picked on the wrong adversary in citing a heavyweight such as Callaghan. Macintyre wrote that Callaghan in 1967 'did not tell the whole truth by any means . . . *but he did not lie*'.[64] By comparison, Sir Stafford Cripps, that model of pious rectitude, had come nearer to lying in September 1949 when he declared that the government 'had not the slightest intention of devaluing the pound'. The *Times* correspondent, Philip Webster, delicately commented that that was 'over-egging the pudding'.[65] By comparison, Callaghan came out with scarcely a stain on his character. The pro-Labour *Guardian* headlined the story (wrongly) as an apology by Waldegrave[66] and there was hopeful speculation by Labour supporters that Waldegrave, who was in political trouble over the Arms to Iraq accusations, might have to resign from the government. In the circumstances, such a comment by a Conservative minister about a Labour predecessor need not have occasioned much debate or surprise. Waldegrave, albeit a Fellow of All Souls, had been an undergraduate in 1967 and had no claims to be an historian. When the same accusation was thrown at Callaghan by the Secretary of the Cabinet, Sir Robin Butler (a former civil service adviser of Callaghan's at the Treasury and a sailing companion of Peter Jay's), he escaped rebuke or even press attention. He did, however, write privately to Callaghan expressing apologies, after the event.

The semantics of whether Callaghan lied is not of significant interest. Sins of omission and of commission are not identical. It would be an extension of meaning to see a refusal to offer an answer as a lie, even though edicts by the Home Office in the 1990s held that silence could be taken as an admission of guilt in criminal cases. The point is worth labouring, rather, because of the broad confusion of the chronology in the minds, apparently, of several commentators. They correctly focused attention on many statements by Callaghan that he had no intention of devaluing—but these dated from the period up to the first week of November 1967. Until that period, devaluation was indeed something he sought to avoid at all costs. The essential point is that, as the evidence from the Treasury files shows, Callaghan was converted very late indeed, not in fact until the late evening of 13 November, five days before devaluation actually took place. That was much later than he should have been in the view of many colleagues and advisers such as Kaldor and Neild, and in the end Cairncross. Be that as it may, an essential component of the history of the crisis is that Callaghan did not merely feel that devaluation would be extremely harmful economically and politically (as did Wilson). Almost until the end he believed it could be averted by a combination of further foreign loans or standby credits, and by simply playing for time until the spring when the balance of trade might be much better, and not spoilt by dock strikes or wars in the Middle East. Callaghan had every ground for believing this was the American view also, conveyed to him until at least 12 November by Joe Fowler or his colleagues.

Until the start of September, after all, this kind of policy had worked, and the pound was apparently no more frail and the balance of payments no more disturbed than in the previous months since October 1964. Compared with the 'Canossa' of the first three months of the Wilson government, the situation was comparatively serene at this period. Callaghan's nine months from September 1966 until after the 1967 'steady as she goes' budget, sneered at in the financial press but welcomed in the markets, were the calmest period he had known, indeed calmer than most British chancellors have known in the troubled history of the British economy from Dalton in 1945 to Clarke fifty years on. To telescope the chronology, even through simple historical error, and to see devaluation as self-evidently inescapable right through the 1964–7 period, with no alternative strategy and no real arguments on the other side, distorts the complexity of the battle for the pound in these years and the historical and emotional context in which it was seen by the main actors in the drama.

Callaghan undoubtedly felt himself to be a great failure in the aftermath of his move to the Home Office on 29 November. The mood wore off in time, and by the spring, as will be seen, he had bounced back and was starting to enjoy himself at the Home Office. He wrote reflectively to Joe Fowler on 7 April 1968, 'I am sure I was right to go when I did; my successor speaks with a new authority I would not have had and he has matched the needs of the situation. What is just as important, he has got the majority of public opinion makers behind him.'[67] This generous judgement is surely accurate, although some supporters of devaluation might say that it evades the extent to which Jenkins's eventual success (much more evident in late 1969 than in the spring of 1968) was based on the kick-start to exports and growth lent by the delayed decision to devalue in Callaghan's time. Much of the press comment at the time was highly critical of his stewardship of the economy. Ian Trethowan, far less charitable than his *Times* colleague Peter Jay, saw his three years as Chancellor as a time of 'continuous brinkmanship' with the economy never really under control and the government never gaining international credibility after the chaos of its first few weeks—so much for Wilson's promise of a hundred days of dynamic and purposive action, Roosevelt-style. Trethowan, however, did add that a major reason for the failures of the Treasury lay in the interference of others, notably the Prime Minister himself and the blunder of the DEA.[68] William Davis in the *Guardian* was more charitable, but still saw the period with Callaghan in charge of the nation's finances as one of mistakes, notably his first budget.[69] *The Economist*, which had in fact often been complimentary since 1964, dismissed Callaghan as a disastrous Chancellor and was euphoric at the succession of Roy Jenkins whom it regarded as far more able.[70] Alec Cairncross, while admiring of Callaghan's style and political gifts, felt that he lacked intellectual confidence as Chancellor, and never really possessed full authority. This was a view shared emphatically by Edmund Dell, a sharp but highly knowledgeable critic, who felt that 'Jim was out of his depth' throughout.[71] Callaghan himself made little immediate attempt to depict his time as Chancellor as a success. He took time out in the last few days of his chancellorship in lugubrious reading of the events of Cripps's devaluation in September 1949 and what that did to Cripps's reputation.[72] Twenty-five years on, he was still inclined to dwell on the negative aspects of what he regarded as a relatively inglorious phase of his career.

With hindsight, however, it is doubtful whether his period as Chancellor should be looked at so negatively. Clearly, attempts at the time to write his political obituary, encouraged by certain elegiac passages in his Commons speech after devaluation, were as premature as the obituaries of Mark Twain. Even at the time, many contemporaries took a far more upbeat view of both the Chancellor and the politician. Alec Cairncross thought that, despite the delays, the policy might well prove right in the end. 'I can't believe we'll always be out of luck and this may prove to have been a good time to devalue provided trade now begins to expand. The foreigners, curiously enough, are far more impressed than the British press.' He felt that there was undue pessimism and defeatism from the self-flagellating British public. It was not such a disaster after all. Callaghan put up a 'very good showing' in the House after devaluation and had risen in popular esteem. In any event, 'the English [perhaps Sir Alec was phrasing this as a Scot, intended for a Welsh listener!] love their Dunkirks and Sir John Moores in retreat more than their victorious generals'.[73]

The basic problem of the British economy in the 1960s was that of the balance of payments. This resulted from changes in British trade, formerly directed to the sterling area, but now transformed by the expansion of continental Europe, both the EEC and EFTA, and the much greater competition in sterling area markets, notably from the Far East and the Pacific Rim. There were long-term problems which acutely complicated the situation. They included the vulnerability of sterling as a reserve currency, the overvaluing of the pound in terms of the level of demand at which it was intended to run the economy, along with basic supply-side problems of low productivity and an under-trained workforce, an unadaptable management, and a financial sector historically resistant to investing in industry and to backing long-term real growth rather than short-term dividend profit. Callaghan's period at least saw the end of sterling's being overvalued (even if against the government's fundamental wishes) while the Chancellor was beginning the process of bolstering up the reserves as well, notably through the devising of special drawing rights. His three years saw a steady if modest growth, without the stagflation of the Barber boom or the credit explosion of the Lawson expansion in later years. Unemployment remained low and inflation was not yet a dominant problem.

Without doubt, devaluation in 1967 was seen as a huge national defeat. It raised fundamental questions about Labour's competence in managing the economy, questions inherited from the MacDonald era and perhaps only resolved finally during the era of Tony Blair after 1994. And yet, for most British people, economically the 1960s continued to 'swing'. Psychologically, the pound in their pocket had not been devalued. Historians in later years were to bracket the Callaghan period as part of the affluent years—even a 'golden age', in a later book edited by Alec and Frances Cairncross, before the chronic inflation of the 1970s and the structural unemployment of the 1980s that resulted from it. Callaghan's tenure of the Treasury was hardly a triumph but neither was it as catastrophic as has often been represented. Britain in the 1960s managed to hoist up its growth rate from a level of only 58 per cent of the OECD in the 1950s, and there was an effort to retool, reinvest, and rethink. On the other hand, Britain's economic growth rate under Labour, as Tony Crosland was to lament subsequently, averaged only 2.3 per cent and actually lagged well behind that of the Lloyd–Maudling period of the Tories' so-called 'thirteen wasted years'.

On Callaghan's personal performance, the critics were much kinder. Even if he never seemed wholly in control of events, his achievements were striking enough. They were gained, after all, despite the administrative mess resulting from the creation of the DEA and George Brown's largely rhetorical National Plan. They withstood also the constant attention to cosmetics resulting from Wilson's own unique perspective of events and conduct of his office. Right down to the end, Wilson was interfering to prevent the satisfactory deflationary package needed for the success of devaluation. He even proposed a *6d.* cut in income tax, of all things, as part of his cuts in public expenditure and the restriction of demand.[74] Time and again he rejected (or even tore up) Treasury advice which offended his political perceptions. Whether or not Callaghan was appropriately cast as the Chamberlain of the government is debatable, although from most perspectives it looks quite unreasonable. But certainly Wilson was no Churchill. He never fought on any beaches, in 1967 any more than he had done during the war, when Callaghan was serving on the high seas and he was behind his desk in Whitehall.

Rather than being seen as a failure as Chancellor, Callaghan could well be seen—and, more to the point, was seen by many at the time—as an innovator. Lord Boothby, an old sparring television partner on *In the News*, told Callaghan he was the best chancellor since Lloyd George.[75] It is an odd judgement from an erratic source, but one sees what was meant.

First of all, in terms of public taxation Callaghan had been a radical reformer. His new taxes included capital gains tax, corporation tax, a new betting tax, selective employment tax, and the regional employment premium. Here, as an old Inland Revenue hand, he was inventive and open to ideas. Kaldor found him often, though not always, a willing pupil. These taxes varied in their effectiveness. SET was soon to be wound up, but capital gains tax (set at the low rate of 30 per cent) was a major reform, one of the innovations of the century even if the revenue it brought in declined over time. There were also impressive surveys and white papers on public expenditure and on the financing of the nationalized industries. The conversion to decimal coinage on a pound basis was a notable technical change that had, of course, the most visible impact on the purchasing power of every citizen in the realm. There was also the transfer of the Royal Mint out of London as part of industrial regional devolution—though it must be said that the choice of Llantrisant, a former mining community in south Glamorgan, rather than Cumbernauld new town in

Scotland testified to the greater clout in Cabinet of the member for Cardiff South-East than of Willie Ross, the Scottish Secretary, who was loud with his lamentations to Crossman.[76] Llantrisant proved less agreeable a move to some Mint employees (the popular argot described the town, parodying the Polo advertisement, as 'the hole with the mint') but it was a boost to the south Wales economy.

Apart from these domestic matters, Callaghan undoubtedly grew in stature in the international aspects of his role. He rose steadily in the esteem of both American and European finance ministers and experts in this often arcane area. He was innovative in looking at the weaknesses of sterling's role as a reserve currency, and in monetary co-operation with the Group of Ten. Complex issues of international liquidity and problems of indebtedness he was able both to absorb and to expound on countless occasions with masterly lucidity. Douglas Jay, a gifted Oxford economist himself, praised Callaghan as 'always doing a more difficult task much better than one expected'. His essential talent, Jay added, 'was for learning—learning quickly a new atmosphere, a new subject, a new technique'.[77] He showed real intellectual versatility in this area, and the interest continued in his concern with the recycling of debts and global liquidity in the 1980s and beyond.

By general consent, his greatest achievement, and one which led to his being seriously considered for the managing directorship of the IMF in 1973, was his role in the devising of special drawing rights (SDRs) with the IMF in 1965. As chairman of the Group of Ten finance ministers meeting in London on 17–18 July 1967, Callaghan acted as midwife and executant of a scheme worked out by a group of bankers, notably Otmar Emminger of the German Central Bank. In effect they were creating a new international asset by which the IMF drew up accounts in gold and national currencies rather than in dollars. This would eliminate doubts about whether the dollar was indeed as good as gold. It was pushed through by American pressure although there was much resistance by Michel Debré, the French Finance Minister, who pursued the traditional French line of demanding an international asset linked to gold. After he ceased to be Chancellor, Callaghan would pursue this theme, suggesting to Fowler in April 1968 that rather than raise the price of gold it would be better in the long run to demonetize it completely (an idea more likely to appeal to American westerners of Populist background than to an eastern banker like Fowler).[78] The special drawing rights were valuable in dealing with a perceived shortage of international liquidity, and in his memoirs Callaghan rightly took pride in their widespread use since their introduction in 1969. Here he emerged as a genuinely creative figure, one seen as such across the world. It reinforced the general view that there was much in his chancellorship which had bolstered, rather than undermined, his public standing.

Beyond this range of financial and economic issues, there is no question that Callaghan remained a formidable, front-line politician. He was anything but a broken reed after his resignation as Chancellor. Indeed, the next two and a half years of Wilson government were to see a steady stream of press stories, almost all wholly fanciful admittedly, that Callaghan was being launched, either by Labour supporters or on a cross-party basis, as the next prime minister. On occasion a putative Callaghan coalition was floated abroad. He himself had nothing to do with this speculation but at the very least it testified to his authority. In his own party, he remained a major force. Throughout his period as Chancellor, indeed, he had been careful not to cut himself off by immersion in the private world of the Treasury, but to keep his lines open to the party at all levels. To this end, he had regular meetings with friendly journalists, such as Alan Watkins, a columnist on the *Spectator* at that time, but a Labour supporter sympathetic to Callaghan's position.

In one very important respect Callaghan had strengthened his position within Labour's ranks. At the October 1967 party conference, in addition to making a remarkably effective conference speech, he was also elected to the key post of party treasurer. He defeated the left-wing candidate, Michael Foot, by the large margin of 4,312,000 to 2,025,000.[79] He remained treasurer until he took office as Prime Minister in April 1976.

The idea of the treasurership had first struck him at the 1966 conference, when he sensed that the NEC might become more hostile towards ministers, as had happened after the fall of the Attlee government in 1951. In addition Callaghan was well aware of the pivotal importance of the treasurer's role in the party hierarchy since the rivalry of Gaitskell and Bevan in the early 1950s, not to mention that of Morrison and Greenwood before the war. The outgoing treasurer, the steelworkers' official Dai Davies, was to become general secretary of BISAKTA in 1967 and there was no obvious trade union successor. Although, of course, a former trade union secretary himself, Callaghan had had little to do in building bridges with the unions hitherto, while the IRSF, of course, was a small, white-collar union of no political clout, and not affiliated to the Labour Party at all. Callaghan had friendly talks with Jack Cooper of the Municipal Workers, and Bill Carron of the Engineers, who then suggested a meeting with Frank Cousins, the Transport Workers' general secretary and, of course, a recent Cabinet colleague. He consulted Jack Jones, his deputy, who anticipated succeeding

Cousins in the TGWU himself, and also Harry Nicholas, who raised no objection, although being lukewarm. Callaghan then spoke to 'my foremost political friend', Merlyn Rees, and also had an approving nod from Harold Wilson himself.

After a meeting of the Economic Committee of the TUC, Callaghan then built up a network of support, Lewis Wright of the Textile Workers, Alf Allen of the Shop Workers' union USDAW, and Albert Martin of the National Union of Mineworkers. Sid Ford, the railwaymen's president, was enlisted for the cause, along with a group of close political supporters in the House—Merlyn Rees, George Thomson, Gregor MacKenzie (a somewhat eccentric Scot who acted as a kind of political minder to Callaghan for over a decade), Jack Diamond, and Reg Prentice. A series of trade unionists were engaged to lobby within the unions, with Reg Prentice approaching the building unions. Merlyn Rees, who had some flair for organization, led the lobbying amongst MPs, using the whips' constituency divisions as a base. Callaghan also spoke to several Cabinet colleagues in the course of February 1967—Denis Healey, Roy Jenkins, Dick Marsh, and Michael Stewart. He told them he was no longer going to stand for the constituency section of the NEC and advised them all not to stand also. All agreed, although Jenkins took some time to reach a view; in the end, he probably judged that his best target was the deputy leadership of the party as a springboard for the fuure. The trade union members on the NEC were at first hostile to so powerful a minister as Callaghan standing for the treasurership, and preferred one of their own, perhaps Joe Gormley of the NUM. But, with the mediation of Andy Cunningham, an old friend on the Municipal Workers and a major potentate in the north-east whose son Jack was later to serve as Callaghan's PPS, Callaghan prevailed on Gormley not to oppose him. A speech arranged by Carron at the Engineers' conference at Eastbourne secured the backing of that important union.[80] Callaghan's reported activities aroused alarm amongst the Labour left, and Michael Foot announced his candidature as the champion of dissent, especially over economic policies such as wage control. But Callaghan was already sewing up most of the major unions and, as has been seen, his victory over Foot was an overwhelming one in the end.

The entire exercise was a revelation of Callaghan's political skills and attention to detail, including the cultivation of key personalities. It gave him a new, powerful base within the party and strengthened his claim to be the crown prince should Wilson somehow disappear from the scene. Geoffrey Goodman, an influential newspaper correspondent over many years, felt that election to the Treasurership was 'a natural calculation' for

Callaghan at that time. With the inevitable jockeying for position in the party's leadership and Roy Jenkins (eight years younger) as a coming rival, this new move was 'sensible politics' as far as Callaghan was concerned.[81] It also for the first time built up a powerful alliance with the unions, whose spokesman Callaghan now to some degree became. This was to have the most important consequences for the future alignment of his career, from the battles over *In Place of Strife* all the way on to the premiership. Above all, it confirmed for every literate political observer that the rejected Chancellor was still a major political force. He had been downed, but he would bounce back. He had manifestly overtaken the erratic George Brown as Wilson's potential replacement. Only the rising power of Roy Jenkins, the new Chancellor, might stand in his way. In major respects, November 1967 was a humiliation and setback for Callaghan. He would be tarred for ever with the devaluation he had always opposed. On the other hand, Wilson's reputation was perhaps more dented than his own. It was the folly of the 'pound in your pocket' broadcast that provided the popular image of the devaluation of November 1967. Callaghan for the first time in his career had suffered a serious rebuff. His morale for the moment seemed shattered. But, like General MacArthur, he would return.

1. Crosland, *Tony Crosland* (London, 1982), 132.
2. Benn, *Out of the Wilderness*, 496 (30 Apr. 1967).
3. Crossman, *Cabinet Diaries*, ii. 336–7 (1 May 1967).
4. *The Economist*, 6 May 1967.
5. Callaghan MS memo, dictated 23–4 June 1967 (Callaghan Papers, box 24).
6. Gordon Walker, *Political Diaries*, 314–15 (23 May 1967).
7. Callaghan MS memo.
8. Ibid.
9. Ibid.
10. For the later stages of the DEA, the ICBH 'Witness Seminar' of June 1996 is most valuable. Also Cairncross MS diary, 14 Sept. 1967.
11. Crossman, *Cabinet Diaries*, ii. 466 (7 Sept. 1967).
12. *The Times*, 4 Oct. 1967.
13. *Guardian*, 4 Oct. 1967.
14. *Daily Telegraph*, 7 Oct. 1967.
15. *Sunday Times*, 8 Oct. 1967.
16. Crossman, *Cabinet Diaries*, ii. 503 (3 Oct. 1967).
17. Castle, *Castle Diaries, 1964–70*, 303 (3 Oct. 1967).
18. Cousins, notes on 1967 party conference (Cousins Papers, MSS. 282 TBN 16).
19. Cairncross MS diary, 2 Nov. 1967.
20. Ibid. 25 Oct. 1967.
21. Cairncross to Callaghan, 2 Nov. 1967 (Callaghan Papers, box 24).
22. Cairncross MS diary, 4 Nov. 1967; interview with Sir Alec Cairncross.
23. Cairncross MS diary, 4 Nov. 1967.

24. 'Note for the Record' by Peter Baldwin, 8 Nov. 1967 (Callaghan Papers, box 24); MS note by Callaghan on 'The Devaluation Crisis' (ibid.); Harold Wilson, *The Labour Government, 1964–70* (London, 1971), 570.

25. *Parl. Deb.*, 5th ser., vol. 753, 874–5 (7 Nov. 1967); Crossman, *Cabinet Diaries*, ii. 558–9 (7 Nov. 1967). I am grateful to Dr Tim Bale for helpful information on this episode.

26. 'Note for the Record', 8 Nov. 1967 (Callaghan Papers, box 24).

27. Memo to Washington embassy, 9 Nov. 1967 (FO telegram 11797, ibid.).

28. 'Note for the Record', 10 Nov. 1967 (ibid.).

29. Callaghan to Fowler, 10 Nov. 1967 (ibid.).

30. 'Note for the Record', 14 Nov. 1967 (ibid.).

31. MS note on 'Devaluation Crisis' (ibid.).

32. 'Note for the Record', 14 Nov. 1967 (ibid.).

33. Cairncross MS diary, 14 Nov. 1967.

34. Ibid. 15 Nov. 1967.

35. Ibid.

36. Cyril Plant, 'Prime Minister Callaghan', *Taxes* (Apr. 1976), 157.

37. *Parl. Deb.*, 5th ser., vol. 754, 632–5 (16 Nov. 1967); *Guardian*, 10 Mar. 1994.

38. Crossman, *Cabinet Diaries*, ii. 566–7 (16 Nov. 1967).

39. Cairncross diary, 17 Nov. 1967.

40. *Parl. Deb.*, 5th ser., vol. 754, 935–9 (20 Nov. 1967).

41. Shepherd, *Iain Macleod*, 452–3.

42. *Parl. Deb.*, 5th ser., vol. 754, 1433–41 (21 Nov. 1967).

43. *The Times*, 22 Nov. 1967.

44. Ibid.

45. *People*, 19 Nov. 1967.

46. Crossman, *Cabinet Diaries*, 587–8 (22 Nov. 1967).

47. Cabinet meeting, 20 Nov. 1967 (President Johnson Papers, Cabinet Papers, box 11).

48. Fowler's intervention, ibid.

49. Paper for the President, 'The Effects of the Devaluation of Sterling', 24 Nov. 1967 (Henry Fowler Papers, box 41 (UK)).

50. Materials ibid.

51. Ibid.

52. Callaghan to Wilson, 18 Nov. 1967 (Callaghan Papers, uncatalogued).

53. Crossman, *Cabinet Diaries*, ii. 569–70 (13 Nov. 1967).

54. *The Times*, 23 Nov. 1967; interview with Peter Jay.

55. *The Times*, 24 Nov. 1967.

56. *Sunday Telegraph*, 26 Nov. 1967.

57. *Financial Times*, 1 Dec. 1967.

58. Jenkins, *A Life at the Centre*, 214.

59. *The Economist*, 16 Dec. 1967.

60. Nolan inquiry, *Standards in Public Life* (Cm. 2850–II), qu. 1838; *The Times*, 10 Mar. 1994; *Guardian*, 9, 10 Mar. 1994; Callaghan to Waldegrave, 9, 16 Mar. 1994.

61. Waldegrave to Callaghan, 9, 10 Mar. 1994 (author's private possession).

62. Callaghan to Major, 10 Mar. 1994; Major to Callaghan, 10 Mar. 1994 (ibid.).

63. *The Times*, 10 Mar. 1994; Rhodes James to the author, 17 March 1994.

64. *Independent*, 10 Mar. 1994.

65. *The Times*, 10 Mar. 1967.

66. *Guardian*, 10 Mar. 1967 'Waldegrave says sorry to Callaghan'.

67. Callaghan to Fowler, 7 Apr. 1968 (Callaghan Papers, box 24).

68. *The Times*, 30 Nov. 1967.

69. *Guardian*, 30 Nov. 1967.

70. *The Economist*, 25 Nov., 2 Dec. 1967.

71. Cairncross interview and conversation with Edmund Dell; also Dell, *The Chancellors*, *passim*.

72. Cairncross MS diary, 21 Nov. 1967.

73. Ibid.

74. Ibid. 25 Nov. 1967.

75. Boothby to Callaghan, 14 June 1965 (Callaghan Papers, box 17).

76. Crossman, *Cabinet Diaries*, ii. 317 (18 Apr. 1967).

77. Jay, *Change and Fortune*, 336.

78. Callaghan to Fowler, 7 Apr. 1968 (Callaghan Papers, box 24).

79. *The Times*, 4 Oct. 1967.

80. Callaghan MS memo, dictated 23–4 Aug. 1967 (Callaghan Papers, box 24).

81. Interview with Geoffrey Goodman.

14

LAW, DISORDER, AND THE PERMISSIVE SOCIETY

'It is I who am the ruler of England', Sir William Joynson-Hicks had declared on being appointed Home Secretary by Stanley Baldwin in 1924. The Home Office has been regarded as one of the three great departments of state ever since the division of the functions of government between a Home and Foreign Secretary by George III. Indeed, it has always held a titular primacy: when R. A. Butler served at the Home Office in the late 1950s, he was widely known as 'the first Secretary'. It was increasingly expanded and professionalized in the late nineteenth century. Two powerful Scottish permanent under-secretaries, Sir Edward Troup (1908–22) and Sir John Anderson (1922–32) extended its central direction of the localities, notably in police matters; another Scottish under-secretary, Sir Alexander Maxwell (1938–48), continued the process during and after the Second World War. It retained its historic control over law and order, and the criminal justice system, while the growing social functions of the state had given the Home Office wider social responsibilities as well from the turn of the century, including liquor, gaming, drugs, immigration, and the treatment of children. It might well have appeared a more natural department of state for James Callaghan than the Treasury had ever been, given his interest both in welfare matters, and in the relationship between civil liberties and the operations of law and order. He had, as has been seen, been a highly effective parliamentary consultant for the Police Federation from 1955 to 1964, and many friends felt that, in terms of both historic prestige and its public order and social responsibilities, he would be thoroughly at home there after the traumas and crises of the Treasury.

On the other hand, the Home Office had the reputation of being something of a political graveyard. Although giants like Peel, Russell, and Palmerston had served there before moving on to the premiership, it had not carried quite the same political clout as either the Foreign Office, or more particularly the Treasury. Politicians who found themselves at the Home Office tended to miss out on the glittering prizes: Morrison or Butler were recent examples. The cases of Roy Jenkins and Willie Whitelaw might be added in the 1970s, although in fairness it was the events of 1970–2 rather than his impressive period at the Home Office in 1965–7 which ended Jenkins's hopes as a leadership contender. Only two prime ministers in the twentieth century had previously served as home secretary, Asquith and Churchill. Both had been highly successful in that office; indeed Churchill's brief spell there in 1910–11 had confirmed him as a notable social and penal reformer. But in each case, the gap between being home secretary and attaining the premiership was a considerable one. Asquith became Prime Minister in 1908 thirteen years after being Home Secretary and with his authority much reinforced by having been Chancellor. Churchill also became Chancellor many years after being Home Secretary, and of course his eventual promotion to the premiership, totally unpredictable until 9 May 1940, was wholly the product of wartime crisis.

Callaghan was well aware of this. He also knew of the pitfalls that the Home Office could bring a Labour Home Secretary, given the long-term suspicion of the powers of the police in industrial disputes and the insidious encroachment into civil liberties widely felt on the British left, especially the middle-class left. In so far as British working people felt an attachment to the system of law and order, it was through its being seen as a local, visible operation within the community. The image of the 'bobby on the beat', unarmed and a kind of local servant, on the pattern of Dixon of Dock Green or Jack Warner's other police icon in the film *The Blue Lamp*, was still potent. One authority has described the period down to the 1960s as 'the golden age of policing'.[1] Only in the 1960s did public attitudes change and the police lose much of their legitimacy and public acceptance. In many black communities, they probably never had it in the first place.

However, whatever the public view of the police and the criminal justice system, it was historically a benevolent one. The criminal justice system was viewed as more democratic and consensual than, for example, in France or the United States. Conversely, the Home Office was increasingly viewed as a potentially centralist and coercive organization, restricting liberties and trying to mould the police into a developing system of national control on the Continental pattern. Bodies such as the National Council of Civil Liberties and, later on, Amnesty International were invariable critics of the Home Office. Their membership always came in large measure from supporters of the Labour Party.

Callaghan was well aware of both the political limitations and the potential civil unpopularity of the Home Office when he moved there on 29 November. It served to intensify a mood of deep gloom and pessimism stemming from his Treasury experience, and especially from what he saw as the humiliation of bearing the stigma of devaluation. For weeks, perhaps months, he seemed less confident in high office, often sunk in gloom, frequently bad-tempered, and not handling matters with the aplomb he had shown throughout his career. Crossman, writing in 1969, retrospectively described Callaghan at this earlier period as 'psychologically out, clearly exhausted, nearly broken'.[2] It was at this time, in the days 10–17 December, that, as will be seen in the next chapter, the new Home Secretary was heavily involved, in alliance with George Brown, in the tense and tetchy Cabinet dispute over whether to resume arms sales to South Africa.

A curious example of this lack of his usual judgement came in a potentially disastrous episode on 20 February 1968 when Callaghan startled the House by announcing that the police had arrested not merely suspects but men responsible for murders committed in Fulham and Acton in London. He was saved by his Conservative opposite number, Quintin Hogg, who liked Callaghan very much personally and who pointed out gently that he actually meant alleged, not proven, criminals. The incident, embarrassing as it was, was set aside as a totally uncharacteristic lapse.[3]

Some of his friends and colleagues felt that Callaghan was allowing his depression after his time at the Treasury to dominate him unduly. One rather surprising rebuke came from Tom McCaffrey, a normally quiet Scot and former journalist whom Callaghan had taken on as his press secretary and who was to work closely with him for the rest of his time as a major politician. McCaffrey felt that Callaghan was showing himself to be too brusque and aggressive; after his experiences he was adopting what McCaffrey called an 'action man' approach more suitable for the Treasury than for his new department. For a politician of such immense talent, Callaghan should be doing better.[4] McCaffrey's comments were taken to heart, and Callaghan thereafter more than recovered his equanimity.

Indeed, he soon showed every sign not only of being in command but of enjoying himself, more than at any time since October 1964. Donald MacDougall, who had viewed Callaghan's torments as Chancellor with much sympathy, reported him as telling Maudling early on that the Home Office was 'much more fun than the Treasury'.[5] He used it as a springboard to help him bounce back. Sympathetic journalists such as John Cole of the *Guardian* and Alan Watkins of the *Observer* were used to develop his image as a strong minister. When the flats at Ronan Point collapsed in May 1968, following a gas explosion, Callaghan used his position as chairman of the Cabinet Emergency Committee to hijack the affair, which really concerned the Ministry of Housing rather than the Home Office. The Housing Minister, Anthony Greenwood, a more gentle character, found himself ridden over roughshod. Later in the year, the way in which Callaghan handled student and other protest, especially the massive anti-Vietnam demonstration in Grosvenor Square, completed his rehabilitation. A phase of extreme political tension, and difficult relations with Harold Wilson, over *In Place of Strife* in early 1969 was neutralized by a highly effective involvement in Northern Ireland. Eventually, the effect of his two and a half years at the Home Office was to build up his reputation still further as both an authoritative governmental minister and a front-line politician, 'a big man' in Crossman's habitual phrase. Against all expectations, he advanced his claims, more than he had ever done at the Treasury, to be Harold Wilson's crown prince and natural successor.

From the first day, Callaghan found working in the Home Office a very different experience from being at the Treasury. As he recalled later in a lecture to the Institute of Public Administration in 1982, in some ways it was easier, but in others much more frustrating.[6] The Home Office, more than any other government department, had and has its own arcane and somewhat inbred style. Callaghan confronted a group of officials, in some ways independent potentates as much as members of a team, who were 'constrained by hierarchy' (in his own words). The tone was stiff; it was no longer Nicky, Donald, or Alec but civil servants addressing each other formally, with the junior members present largely dismissed or ignored. In view of the colossal range of issues that were the remit of the Home Office, Callaghan found it much more difficult than at the Treasury to keep his finger on the pulse and have a general sense of the course of policy.

Perhaps as a result, he felt at first that he was much less well briefed by his officials and therefore somewhat more exposed in the Cabinet. Whereas there was a broad thematic unity about such matters as the balance of payments or the exchange rate of the pound, in the sombre ambience of the Home Office there seemed to be a myriad of different policies and initiatives, with the Home Secretary himself somewhat marginalized. He could spend long hours perhaps studying the files on an individual prisoner, without really getting close to understanding the rationale for the penal policies surrounding such cases. He complained that his officials were reluctant to engage in systematic long-term forward planning. It was not easy for him or them to adapt. Officials noted that he did not always approach the problem in the most genial of dispositions. He was a severe taskmaster, and fierce in reprimanding aides whom he felt had not prepared his papers in a sufficiently comprehensive or accurate way. In return, they sometimes felt that they had not the easiest of superiors. They might suggest policy initiatives to him (perhaps on Borstals or women prisoners) which he then ignored. On issues where he did not wish to take action, they felt that he seemed deliberately to temporize: this especially applied to Kenyan and Ugandan Asian would-be immigrants. In time, he came to adopt the habit of going through his departmental boxes with his officials late at night in the Commons, after the debates and divisions had left him tired and bad-tempered. His departure to the Sussex farm on Friday afternoons could generate a sense of relief amongst his officials, although the awkward problem of whether to disturb him there with official business remained. His permanent secretary, Philip Allen, recalled that he had more rows when Callaghan first went to the Home Office than with any other Home Secretary in his time.[7]

But, as his psychological strength and confidence returned, by perhaps March or April 1968, Callaghan was able to impose his style on his new department with powerful effect. It was a trade unionist's negotiating style, quite unfamiliar to the civil servants, and utterly different from the manner of Soskice or Jenkins before him, but it worked. Philip Allen, moved to the Home Office in 1966 during Roy Jenkins's time, was an exceptionally clear-headed official of equable disposition. He and Callaghan built up a good working relationship with much regard on both sides. Allen noted that, while Callaghan was in some respects less responsive than Jenkins, especially on libertarian issues such as gambling or censorship, in others he was the better performer of the two. He instanced in particular his relations with the police and his general approach to his civil servants, some of whom had found Jenkins's air of intellectual superiority hard to take. Allen gave his new minister the sound advice that he should decide where his particular interests lay, since he could not possibly be a master in all areas of policy. In practice, here as elsewhere, Callaghan was to be something of a generalist. Both his private secretary Brian Cubbon and his assistant Geoffrey de Deney thought him in many ways an outstanding minister, with a broad grasp of all the departmental issues, and with a rare capacity for leadership in the handling of student protest and in Northern Ireland. David Faulkner, not a whole-hearted admirer, felt that here he showed outstanding vision. Cubbon compared him with Churchill and also with Whitelaw in his capacity to take command and see matters through.[8]

Callaghan instituted a new practice of calling in a whole range of civil servants at once, to discover what the drift of Home Office policy really was. He would make a practice of starting with the most junior person present. One major problem that soon emerged was that the Home Secretary appeared, by the nature of his portfolio, to be more excluded from the stream of general government policy than a Chancellor had been. To counter this, Callaghan had a principal private secretary appointed to keep him briefed. With his initial secretary, Michael Moriarty, the Home Secretary felt some personal incompatibility, for reasons that are not altogether clear. Very early on therefore, in March 1968, he had Brian Cubbon appointed instead. Although the experiment was not a total success, Cubbon, until he moved posts in September 1969 to be replaced by David Faulkner, proved to be someone with whom Callaghan could commune on a wide range of issues, political as well as administrative.

The exigencies of party politics were never far away. The very breadth of issues with which a Home Secretary was concerned meant that there were always ample opportunities for storing up points of political credit. During crises such as that surrounding the Industrial Relations Bill in April–May 1969, political priorities became overwhelming. While he was always punctilious in keeping a distance between party and departmental concerns, Callaghan would on occasion use Cubbon and McCaffrey as a sounding-board in assessing his future. Otherwise, so far as was possible in the always unpredictable course of Home Office affairs, a kind of daily routine evolved. The usual pattern was that Callaghan would spend his mornings on party matters, and then come in every day to the Office to go through his parliamentary questions. They would be examined over a lunch of fish fingers, a gastronomic delicacy which Philip Allen himself always turned down.

By the end of Callaghan's time at the Home Office, the department seemed on balance more relaxed in style. This was thanks in large measure to Philip Allen, who helped make it a more effective and businesslike department than the secretive institution that had confronted Roy Jenkins when he succeeded Sir Frank Soskice in 1965. David Faulkner, a distinctly liberal and enlightened man who succeeded Cubbon as private secretary, was impressed by his chief's handling of the ending of capital punishment and Northern Ireland at that period, though much less so over immigration matters. A high degree of respect had been built up on both sides. On the other hand, in later life Callaghan seemed to retain rather more intimate and friendly social relations with his former advisers at the Treasury and particularly the Foreign Office than with his officials during his eventful years at the Home Office.

Callaghan had the assistance of a varied, but talented, team amongst his governmental assistants. As Minister of State he inherited a peer, Victor Collins, Lord Stonham, a businessman who had been briefly Labour MP for Taunton in 1945. Although a zealous penal reformer, Stonham was said not to enjoy Callaghan's total enthusiasm, and in October 1969 he was eventually replaced by Shirley Williams. She was a rising star of the centre-right who had served under Crosland at the Education Department and who was to be an important member of Callaghan's Cabinet in 1976–9. Since she was well known to be in Roy Jenkins's camp of supporters, Callaghan was somewhat wary of the ally of a political rival. Williams found herself sometimes excluded from departmental meetings, to her understandable annoyance. But in time she developed a distinctly cordial relationship with Callaghan, too. The under-secretaries were all talented people. Dick Taverne was moved very early on, in April 1968, to work with Jenkins at the Treasury. His colleague who stayed until that November was David Ennals, a former chairman of the United Nations Association with a strong interest in race relations. He had to take the full fury of the Home Office's policies on immigration that summer. Though he lost his marginal seat of Dover in 1970, he was later to be the Callaghan government's Minister of Health.

Callaghan's most congenial ministers, however, were two Welshmen, reflecting perhaps his growing involvement with the nation where his constituency was located. Elystan Morgan, who became under-secretary, was an able and articulate Welsh-speaking barrister. Crossman opposed his appointment because he had been a parliamentary candidate for Plaid Cymru as recently as the 1964 election. However, Morgan, whose qualities had been spelt out to Callaghan by Cledwyn Hughes, the Welsh Secretary, proved to be a strong appointment, not least for his expertise on Welsh and Scottish devolution, not an issue in which Callaghan himself took much initial interest. From November 1968 to the June 1970 election, Morgan's fellow under-secretary was Merlyn Rees who, as has been seen, had been an intimate of Callaghan's for some time.[9] A warm and unpretentious man, and in no sense a political threat to his master, Rees proved an admirable lieutenant, handling the Children's Bill with much sensitivity. He also proved to be a natural parliamentary tactician on whose judgement Callaghan could rely, and his campaign organizer when he became leader and Prime Minister in April 1976. Rees, Callaghan, and Tom McCaffrey were often in secret conclave. Rees himself became Home

Secretary in due time. From this time onwards, the Callaghans were the warmest of friends with Merlyn Rees of Cilfynydd and his Irish wife.

Callaghan's departmental responsibilities covered an immense range of issues. One aspect which somewhat overshadowed his work was the high reputation as a liberal reformer gained by his predecessor Roy Jenkins. The new Chancellor was never the warmest of Callaghan's admirers. He took legitimate pride in his libertarian approach as Home Secretary in 1965–7. Certainly, those two and a half years were marked by various crises of a kind almost all home secretaries encounter; in particular there was an alarming sequence of escapes from jail, including that of the spy George Blake. On the other hand, it was also a time when liberal opinion saw Britain becoming a more civilized society, freed from the shackles of Victorian puritanism. The censorship of plays and books was effectively ended; the Lord Chamberlain was put to flight and, with the aid of Roy Jenkins's Obscene Publications Bill of 1959, *Lady Chatterley* came into her own. Homosexuality was effectively decriminalized; abortion was officially legalized; the divorce laws were brought more into accord with the contemporary realities. Under Jenkins's predecessor Sir Frank Soskice, Sydney Silverman's private member's measure, the Murder (Abolition of Death) Penalty Bill, was finally carried through the Commons, 355 to 170, in December 1964, and Jenkins was thus the first Home Secretary not to have to decide whether to end anyone's life.

Callaghan had supported all these changes. On capital punishment in particular he had always been a vehement and enlightened supporter of abolition: as has been seen, he opposed the Attlee government's Criminal Justice Bill of 1948 on this point. Sydney Silverman's abolition bill had in fact been amended by the Lords so that it would only apply for five years. The Wilson government had, therefore, to decide whether take the politically risky step, some time before the next election, of making the abolition permanent. In the face of a Conservative vote of censure, the issue was brought forward on 16 December 1969, with Callaghan inevitably centrally involved. On the death penalty, he had declared that he would resign rather than order any further executions. His speech on the resolution for a permanent abolition was a very powerful one. On a free vote, the death penalty was finally erased from the law of the land by 343 votes to 185. Under Callaghan's regime, the rope had gone for ever. Nevertheless, it was immediately put about that he was instinctively far less tolerant and liberal than his predecessor. Jenkins spread this view himself; the chapter on this period in his memoirs is entitled, Kennedy-style, 'the liberal hour'.[10] Callaghan resented this view, and felt it reflected in part the way the chattering middle classes regarded his working-class roots (of course, Jenkins himself was a Welsh miner's son) and lack of a university education. There is no doubt that Callaghan approached the issues of the Home Office from a somewhat different political and moral perspective. His outlook and background were socially more conservative than those of Jenkins. There is no doubt, either, that he too proved to be a reformer, although of a different cast.

Social policies impinged heavily on the Home Office at that period. The whole span of family life and community development came within its remit. In particular, Callaghan had to deal with policies towards children. It was a new area for him as a minister, but one where he could receive valuable guidance from close at hand. Audrey Callaghan was now beginning an important connection with Great Ormond Street children's hospital. She gave up her role on the GLC to become chairman of the Board of Governors of Great Ormond Street from 1969 to 1983; thereafter she was to serve as chairman of the Board of Trustees. In any case, the problems of young people were something that had already caught Callaghan's attention as member for Cardiff South-East. In the deprived docklands areas, he had long noted the impact of unstable family and environmental backgrounds upon delinquency in young people.

Jenkins had begun work on this area. Callaghan completed it by publishing an important white paper, *Children in Trouble*, in May 1968 and passing the Children and Young Persons Act in 1969.[11] These followed the view of the Longford Committee in 1963–4 that the differences in handling young delinquents and children in care were unreal. To deal with the problem of the young offender, they proposed a form of intermediate treatment for young people aged between 14 and 17. The Act also laid down that children under 14 should not automatically be taken to court unless they were beyond parental control. Juvenile courts from now on could only make supervision or care orders. For older children, the approved schools would be integrated within a comprehensive system of residential establishments for children in the care of local authorities. The various types of institution for young people of deviant behaviour or otherwise in need of care, from remand homes to local authority homes and hostels, would be brought together as community homes.

The Children Act was felt to be an enlightened one by social workers and the professional services in general. Many Conservatives, however, criticized it for diminishing the custodial or other powers of the juvenile courts, and it was opposed in the Commons. The Magistrates' Association in particular fiercely criticized it, especially the provision that care orders should be the responsibility of social workers over whom the courts would have no power. On balance, however, the Act was felt to be a rational way forward. It was certainly a considerable legislative achievement for the new Home Secretary. The future, though, was to show the great range of wider issues relating to children that still had to be tackled—the problems of children in care, cases of child sexual abuse as in the Cleveland affair, and the lack of coherence in treating children as direct or indirect victims of crime.[12] The Home Office was to sponsor research by criminologists on all these issues later on, though not always to respond to their findings.

A wider question was whether the Home Office was a suitable department for handling children's issues at all. It had been amongst its prime responsibilities since the later nineteenth century. There were important measures like the 1908 Children's Act, while Churchill had devoted time and thought to the problems of the juvenile offender when at the Home Office in 1910. The reorganization of the department in 1913 had in effect set up a separate children's division.[13] Harold Wilson had laid down that the revamped and expanded Social Services Department, given to Crossman in 1968, should take over the Children's Department from the Home Office. But Callaghan resisted this, even though it had been recommended by the Seebohm Committee on the social services. Crossman and others naturally accused Callaghan of simply wanting to preserve his empire intact, and of thinking in terms solely of territorial rights. No doubt there was some element of this. On a personal basis, Callaghan and Crossman were seldom the closest of comrades.[14]

But there were more positive aspects as well. Callaghan also argued that the transfer of children's issues to the new ministry would produce overlapping and administrative confusion. There would be a lack of liaison, and perhaps conflict, between the local authorities and the juvenile courts without the interposition of the Home Office. He was much impressed here by the ideas of Derek Morrell, the head of the Children's Department, and Joan Cooper, its Chief Inspector. There was much force in Morrell's argument which favoured a continuous line of responsibility, 'from care to control' in the phrase of the time. This meant there would be a consistent framework within the Home Office for looking at difficulties surrounding children and young people, from the children's service at one end to, if need be, the justice system at the other. Callaghan sharply criticized Maudling's decision to complete the transfer of the Children's Department in 1971. In the meantime he and Crossman had reached a kind of informal political agreement that the transfer would not occur during Callaghan's tenure of the Home Office; nor did it.[15]

It was not just a matter of turf wars. Callaghan had an idealistic side in dealing with the issue of children in public policy. As a father and family man, it was an issue on which he felt deeply. He argued that policy towards children 'should measure up to the level of events'. In handling such difficult cases as that of the plausible mass child-murderer from Newcastle, Mary Bell, officials were struck by his rare fusion of clear-headedness and compassion. Callaghan felt that removing the issue of children's welfare from its remit would limit and somewhat dehumanize the work of the Home Office. It could be argued that the slowness with which the Home Office handled the issue of child victims down to the 1990s, including the way they were dealt with in prosecutions and court proceedings, tended to confirm his point of view. In the meantime, he remained active in the field of children's policy throughout his time as Home Secretary. He gave much encouragement to a Welsh backbench colleague in his efforts to reform the adoption laws. One other important initiative, a departmental committee on the adoption of children in 1969 led to a major report on this sensitive area three years later, with which Callaghan was closely identified.

A more familiar area of Home Office work for Callaghan was the handling of the police. Here he had the strong advantage—one which aroused much suspicion in the ranks of the libertarian left—of personal connections with the force, through his work as parliamentary consultant for the Police Federation 1955–64. He had a good working relationship with the Federation's officials, with several chief constables, and with his appointee as the Commissioner of the Metropolitan Police, Sir John Waldron. He inherited a major reorganization of the police forces by Roy Jenkins which had reduced the number of local forces from 117 to 49: it was a process of rationalization which had met, predictably, with some local resistance including from Callaghan's own Cardiff where it was argued that an independent police force was required for the ceremonial and public work of the capital city of Wales.

Callaghan's move to the Home Office was greeted with enthusiasm in police ranks, and on the personal side this seemed to be justified. In handling the difficulties that the authorities faced over the massive protests against American involvement in Vietnam, he appeared sympathetic without being illiberal. At the great confrontation between the anti-Vietnam marchers and the police in October 1968, Callaghan created an excellent impression by the way in which he visited the police after the main events were over, and by the fact that major violence and bloodshed were avoided. He had shown that a Labour government would not be weak in confronting potentially violent demonstrators. Indeed, with his bluff manner and the tall broad-shouldered physique of an ex-rugby lock forward, Callaghan looked like everyone's idea of what a police officer should be.

Even so, the pressures of the economy necessarily impinged on the police as on every other of the public services, and Callaghan found that his close relationship with the police was being shaken up. Police pay appeared to be lagging behind after the major boost given with the help of Callaghan's own services in 1960–1. The police were dissatisfied with the view taken of their pay by successive tribunals; Callaghan's view, as an old trade union negotiator, was that they had agreed to the arbitration procedure and that they should therefore accept its findings without dissent. There were also complaints about police recruitment, affected by public expenditure cuts after devaluation. As early as 13 February 1968 Callaghan had warned the Commons that police recruitment would be looked at 'on a much more scientific basis than it was in the past'. The government eventually decided that the service would not be allowed to expand by more than 1,200 in the next fifteen months.

A dossier of other complaints on these issues was compiled by the Police Federation and used against Callaghan in 1968–9.[16] They complained that numerals were being retained on police uniforms, to reassure the public in cases of harassment. Undermanning allowances to Liverpool and Birmingham were turned down. The Discipline Code was to include possible penal sanctions on policemen guilty of discrimination on grounds of race. Callaghan was also under attack for his strong defence of the abolition of the death penalty and his steadfast refusal to allow the police to carry firearms. The one-time Police Federation spokesman faced a mixed reception at the Federation's annual conferences, with some booing. At the May 1970 conference in Llandudno, Callaghan's one-time home, a motion of no confidence, focusing on the issue of policy pay, was passed. Brian Cubbon for one felt this showed that the Federation had not made the mental adjustment to the fact that Callaghan was now Home Secretary acting for the nation, and no longer their paid employee. He responded in forthright fashion. He both pointed out the way in which public perceptions were changing, notably over race and immigration, and also showed that if the projected new recruits were achieved in 1969, there would be 93,000 serving police officers, the largest number in British history.[17]

It is worth noting that many of the complaints against Callaghan by the police were the result of his deferring to points made by supporters of civil liberties. This should be kept in mind when Callaghan is claimed to be a particularly reactionary Home Secretary, far less libertarian than Roy Jenkins, his predecessor. In fact, throughout his career Callaghan was a doughty defender of civil rights against exaggerated powers of intrusion and surveillance, on the part of the police as well as the security services. One of his rare implicit protests against the Labour leadership in his retirement came when in January 1997 he attacked Michael Howard's Police Bill, supported by Jack Straw for Labour as well as by the Conservative government, which gave senior police officers much extended powers to issue warrants for police bugging or entering people's homes.[18] Here and elsewhere, libertarian Old Labour came to the rescue to redeem New Labour's incipient illiberalism.

A more difficult matter by far in connection with the police was that of internal corruption. In November 1969 *The Times* reported serious charges against three officers of the CID who were alleged to have demanded money from a criminal as a bribe to drop a prosecution. This report greatly alarmed the Commissioner of the Metropolitan Police, Sir John Waldron, and Callaghan was privately indignant that such an issue should have been given such prominent coverage in so important a newspaper. Nevertheless he eventually appointed an inquiry under Frank Williamson, an Inspector of Constabulary and former Chief Constable of Cumbria. Williamson promptly got to work but complained to Callaghan that he was being seriously obstructed in his inquiries by groups within the police service. The matter was still being cleared up when the Wilson government fell from office in June 1970. Soon afterwards, Williamson had to give up his inquiry, frustrated and angry. After much pressure from Callaghan, his successor at the Home Office, Reginald Maudling, appointed a new Police Commissioner, Sir Robert Mark, a brisk man whom Callaghan himself greatly admired. The outcome was a shake-up of the system, the CID being placed under the uniformed branch of the Metropolitan Police, and some police officers being dismissed for corrupt practices. On balance, given the sensitivity of the role of the police at a time of extreme public volatility on many fronts, Callaghan may be fairly deemed to come out of this quagmire with considerable credit, with the reputation of the police and of himself strengthened. Most unusually, he was believed to have considered appointing an outside figure as head of the Metropolitan Police at some point: his old union colleague Stanley Raymond, a tough character and recent sparring partner of Barbara Castle, was a possibility. However, Robert Mark would seem to have achieved the broad objectives Callaghan had in mind.

The other classic law-and-order issue for a Home Secretary was prisons. Inevitably Callaghan was heavily involved here, too. One of his responsibilities was carrying into effect Roy Jenkins's Criminal Justice Act of 1967, a measure designed to liberalize the treatment of prisoners in key respects. Naturally, he also took initiatives of his own, including the appointment of Sir William Pile as the director-general of prisons in 1969. Another responsibility, which he carried out faithfully, was setting up a Parole Board to see whether prisoners serving an eighteen-month sentence could be released after a minimum of twelve. His Board chairman was Lord Hunt, the Everest mountaineer; its other members included such penal reformers as 'C. H. Rolph' (C. R. Hewitt). Hunt, an energetic and unstuffy man (who was also a Labour supporter), gave a powerful lead to his Board. Callaghan records with pride in his memoirs that he accepted its recommendations to release 2,500 prisoners on licence within the next two years. Some civil servants, however, felt that he was not instinctively engaged in an area such as this; with the Parole Board he was the efficient manager rather than 'blazing a trail'.[19] On balance, though, his policy had some impact in reducing the prison population. Callaghan reacted as strongly as anyone to the sharp rise in offences of all kinds to over a million and a half in his time at the Home Office (of course, still far below the colossal numbers that erupted in the crime wave after 1980). But he still had genuine civilized doubts about the social effect of keeping offenders in prison. The great majority of offenders, particularly young offenders, were released only to re-offend, he noted. The sole effect of the supposed prison deterrent was simply to confirm them in their life of crime.

The whole range of prison reform attracted Callaghan's active attention, an area in which Victor Stonham's expertise was helpful. He worked to improve prison conditions and to reduce such disagreeable practices as 'slopping out'. He sought to improve prison officers' morale by reinforcing their promotion prospects. He noted the same restrictive attitude towards staff promotion as in the Inland Revenue in his youth, and the difficulty in combating it. A departmental inquiry was set up into the career prospects for internal prison staff, and the possibility of even prison governors being found from among their ranks. In a quite different area of prison life, Callaghan had to respond to aspects of security. This involved the release of the convicted spies Peter and Helen Kroger in 1969 in exchange for Gerald Brooke, and the release of Harry Houghton and Ethel Gee, of the Portland naval base spy ring, in 12 May 1970, shortly before Callaghan left the Home Office. Callaghan and MI5, however, which came within his departmental responsibilities, seem to have operated at arm's length from each other in this period.

The department was intent on improving conditions within prisons. But there was also the problem of making them more secure. The series of major escapes, the train robber Ronald Biggs, the spy George Blake, and the axe-man Frank Mitchell amongst others, during Roy Jenkins's time had led to an inquiry into prison security being conducted by Lord Mountbatten. He was an old associate of Callaghan's from his Admiralty days and naval connections generally. His report proposed that there should be a fourfold security classification of prison inmates. For Category A prisoners, the highest risk, a new maximum-security prison should be built at Albany on the Isle of Wight, near to that in Parkhurst. However, Mountbatten urged also that the regime in high-security gaols be liberalized and humanized. The new island fortress would be given the old Roman name 'Vectis' (an unpopular idea with a local bus company which bore this name). Callaghan had immediately to respond, both to consider Mountbatten's recommendations for a new prison, and also to try to persuade the prison service of the value of his more liberal proposals, such as that firearms should not be used by prison officers.

From the start, Callaghan took the closest of interest in the conditions in high-security prisons. He visited successively the maximum-security blocks of Durham, Leicester, Parkhurst, and Chelmsford prisons. In 1995, he was to criticize severely the rigid distinction drawn by Michael Howard between government policy and operational matters for which the inspector of prisons, Derek Lewis, was responsible (and sacked). Callaghan was very much a hands-on Home Secretary in terms of the detail of prison management. On one occasion, he got into a row over the redecoration of a wing at Wormwood Scrubs. The inmates of prisons were of much concern to him, too: he consulted Tom McCaffrey about the best approach to adopt in talking to prisoners. McCaffrey considered him far more effective than Jenkins in this respect, more human and direct, as he was when talking to constituents in Cardiff South-East. In Durham, he interrogated personally John McVicar, a prisoner convicted of murder.[20] This was one of his more difficult exercises in man-to-man communication, but it was not unsuccessful. There was much difficulty with the prisoners in some of these necessarily severe institutions. In early May 1968, Callaghan visited the Durham maximum-security wing where twenty men had rioted over a new work schedule. They refused to work in the workshop, to wear prison clothing, or to clean their wing. Amongst them were some of the most violent and desperate criminals in Britain. They also, however, had the enterprise to call the *Daily Mirror* to publicize their complaints. As for all home secretaries, it was a crisis for Callaghan; to right-wing critics it was the result of the liberal approach of soft-headed reformers like Mountbatten. Callaghan's approach was to reinforce the governor of Durham by dispatching Alan Bainton, a Home Office official and a former prison governor. He was able to persuade the prisoners that their grievances would be looked at properly and that there would be no reprisals if they surrendered peacefully. After some debate amongst themselves, the prisoners did so, and a potentially serious episode wound down quietly.

The Durham affair highlighted yet again the question of prison security. Mounbatten's report, as we have seen, had proposed segregating the high-security prisoners in one fortress-type prison which would be escape-proof. The Isle of Wight would house this British version of Alcatraz. But there was also a quite different scenario on offer. The Advisory Council on the Penal System, through a subcommittee chaired by the eminent Cambridge criminologist Professor Leon Radzinowicz (reporting in March 1968), advocated instead a policy of the dispersal of Category A prisoners into four separate institutions. After much thought and the experience of the Durham episode, Callaghan and his officials reached the view that it would be safer, as well as more civilized, to disperse the most dangerous prisoners in very small groups throughout the system rather than set up a Colditz-style armed prison with watch-towers and guard dogs. Scattering rather than concentrating the hardest of criminal cases would be most effective. In May 1968 the dispersal took place quietly, and Callaghan's remaining time at the Home Office was relatively trouble-free in this regard. Academics and experts, however, continued to debate the merits of Mountbatten versus Radzinowicz, while Mountbatten himself felt that his grand design for concentration rather than dispersal had been thwarted by Home Office permanent officials. Elsewhere, Callaghan turned instead to trying to establish a more civilized prison regime. At the conference of prison officers at Alderley Edge, Cheshire, in May 1968 he welcomed the innovation of the psychiatric prison at Grendon in Buckinghamshire, along with the prospect of four new Category B prisons, four new Category C prisons, and new remand centres, Borstals, and detention centre units over the next five years.[21]

The most imaginative experiment began in 1969 with the opening of a new prison at Coldingly in Surrey, to provide Category B prisoners with a kind of industrial regime with such installations as an engineering machine-shop to develop light manufacturing industry. There would be 'foremen' on the workshop floor rather than disciplinary officers and the prisoners would clock in and out as if they were in a factory. At the formal opening on 8 October 1969, Callaghan spoke with pride of this enlightened new approach.[22] He had enlisted the support of his ally Vic Feather of the TUC to deal with possible labour difficulties. It would, for instance, be possible for prisoners to become members of the TGWU and other unions prior to their discharge. The CBI were also very helpful. In the event, Coldingly proved a lone venture, partly because of the sheer volume of numbers in the prison population, partly because it fell victim to the economically depressed climate of the 1980s which meant overcrowding and staff shortages. Some investigators were now querying the value of such an innovation. Even so, Coldingly, which brought Callaghan's penal and industrial expertise together, was another example of how he could respond to the more liberal ideas of the time. As a prison reformer, again, his record was entirely respectable.

What brought Callaghan into the limelight, though, as Home Secretary, were not the traditional issues of law and order and the operations of the criminal justice system. The later 1960s proved to be a time of great social volatility, when hitherto disregarded tensions in British society were alarmingly revealed. These involved in particular race relations, political protest and student demonstrations of various kinds, and the general cultural and public order impact of 'permissiveness' as the lifestyles and outlook of young people showed a dramatic change. In a world utterly unfamiliar to people of his generation, an era when, according to Philip Larkin, sexual intercourse began, the ethos of 'sex, drugs and rock and roll' posed quite new challenges to the Home Office and tested the powers of its occupant to the full.

Race relations in the 1960s had become a potentially explosive cauldron of prejudice and hate.[23] There had been a rapid growth of immigration from Commonwealth countries throughout the 1950s, mainly from the West Indies with the economic difficulties there and the ease of cheap passage, but also increasingly from India and Pakistan as well. According to the census returns, in 1951 the numbers of Indians, Pakistanis, and West Indians had stood at 30,800, 5,000, and 15,300 respectively. Apart from a few ports such as Callaghan's own Cardiff, black or coloured people in Britain were few and far between. In many towns, only American servicemen or an occasional student provided an ethnic minority. Much the largest immigrant group was the Irish, which continued to rise.

By 1961, however, the census showed 81,400 Indians, 24,900 Pakistanis, and no fewer than 171,800 West Indians resident in Britain. The entire 'coloured' population had risen in ten years from 74,500 to 336,000. Many British cities, including London, Liverpool, Manchester, Bristol, and Cardiff, had large black communities concentrated usually in inner cities of poor housing and environmental deprivation. There were large Asian minorities in Birmingham, Leicester, and Luton, along with northern textile towns and cities such as Bradford and Leeds. The Milner Holland report in April 1968 was to detail the ghetto conditions existing in West Indian neighbourhoods like Notting Hill. Although the Afro-Caribbean and Asian communities were usually employed and comparatively peaceful, there had been disturbances to remind British people of the possible powder keg of racial tension that had manifested itself in so many American cities in the past. There was growing evidence of rampant prejudice and of discrimination in such areas as private housing and employment. Bodies such as the British National Party, and the re-emergent pre-war fascist leader Oswald Mosley, showed disturbing signs of activity in the old fascist stamping ground of London's East End. As a result, in 1962 the Macmillan government had passed the first significant Immigration Bill in British history. It severely restricted Commonwealth immigration through a voucher system. Those with passports not issued in Britain were obliged henceforth to obtain work permits to gain entry. It was a measure clearly designed to check the inflow of black immigrants, a response which the previous immigration of whites from Ireland, Canada, or Australia had never produced. It was vehemently opposed by the Labour Party at the time, headed by Hugh Gaitskell but with Callaghan joining the attack.

However, the issue continued to fester in political circles. Even though immigrant areas remained comparatively peaceful, right-wing publicists attacked the number already present (and the large families they were reproducing), the number of relatives or others who could slip through the net, and the cultural clash between local white and ethnic minority populations, especially in the Midlands. There was extreme racialist incitement in the Smethwick area of Birmingham, where the slogan flourished, 'If you want a nigger for your neighbour, vote Labour'. As a result, an extreme right-wing Conservative, Peter Griffiths, defeated Labour's Patrick Gordon Walker in the 1964 general election in a particularly distasteful campaign. Harold Wilson furiously attacked Griffiths in the Commons and urged that he be treated as 'a parliamentary leper'. However, some prominent Conservative politicians in 1967, Duncan Sandys and even more Enoch Powell, a Wolverhampton MP, called for 'a turning off of the tap'.

There was an additional issue now to inflame racist demagogues, but also to worry others not necessarily racially prejudiced. Tens of thousands of east African Asians, especially from Kenya, were now likely to flee to Britain in view of pressure exerted upon them from Jomo Kenyatta and other east African leaders.[24] These Asians had opted for British passports and citizenship, with the rights of free entry to Britain that this implied, instead of local nationality when Kenya, Uganda, and Tanzania gained their independence. This fanned the flames of racial discord in Britain. It was believed that 300,000 east African Asians might use their rights (or rather follow up the legal pledges given them by the British government at the time). The immigration issue was a key issue for the Home Office. Measures had been framed in the latter part of Roy Jenkins's time, both to restrict still further the potential flow of Commonwealth immigrants, and also to reinforce the civil and social rights of black or brown citizens already in Britain. An inconclusive paper had been sent to the Home Policy Committee in October 1967. However, no legislative bills had seen the light before Jenkins left for the Treasury. He regarded them as controversial. They also clashed, so officials believed, with his public image and personal conviction as a liberal crusader, sustained by advisers such as the barrister Anthony Lester. But the issue would not go away and needed some kind of government response. It was Callaghan, therefore, who was left to act and it was to plunge him into deep controversy.

As an individual, Callaghan could not possibly have been accused of racial prejudice. His constituency was a good example of long-term racial integration and partnership. The Docks Women section of the local party was largely Asian and African. He had many coloured friends in Cardiff including West Indians such as 'Chalky' White. He had had first-hand experience of racial issues during his wartime naval service. He had raised the case of a black employee of BOAC, Acte, who had suffered from racial discrimination after flying in the RAF as a rear gunner during the war. And, of course, he had been a progressive spokesman on colonial issues who enjoyed a good personal relationship with east African leaders such as Tom Mboya in Kenya, Milton Obote in Uganda, and President Julius Nyerere of Tanzania. It greatly angered him to be accused of racial prejudice by the chattering classes in the weeklies and the Sunday supplements, and even by Cabinet colleagues. Roy Jenkins told Crossman in February 1968 that Callaghan was the most reactionary Home Secretary on racial matters for years; he cited his opposition to the immigration of Kenyan Asians. It was an issue on which Crossman, a Midlands MP himself (as indeed was Jenkins), disagreed with Jenkins's view.[25]

However, Callaghan also felt that immigration was an issue to be handled in a way attuned to public opinion, rather than on the basis of abstract liberal political theory. He was unsentimental on the principle of restricting immigration into Britain. Civil servants felt that the issue of the passport rights of Kenyan Asians did not excite or offend him. It was a question of political and social management rather than striking moral postures. He was being pressed by Labour MPs and others in the Midlands to act urgently. In any case prudence would appear to dictate that some kind of control, whether in terms of health, skills, or criminality, was needed to regulate a possible endless flow of people from east Africa.

He took very rapid action on two fronts. A Race Relations Bill was introduced to produce harmonious race relations in the community. The Race Relations Board set up by Sir Frank Soskice in 1965 had exuded goodwill but had very few powers. Passed in the 1968 session, Callaghan's measure laid down that discrimination on grounds of race in employment, housing, or commerce would be unlawful.[26] A new Community Relations Commission would be set up, with regional conciliation committees, to investigate any complaints that arose. It had a positive effect without doubt and was in advance of public opinion. Callaghan had asked for bipartisan support in the House, but the Conservatives abstained, apart from a right-wing fringe who voted against. It was this decision (or, as he saw it, indecision) by his Opposition colleagues that provoked Enoch Powell's so-called 'rivers of blood' speech. But Callaghan's verdict in his memoirs is a fair one. 'It had an important educative effect but it was no more than an interim measure.'[27] Frank Cousins of the Transport Workers, who had taken a courageous lead in combating cases of racial discrimination in the trade union world, agreed to head the new Community Relations Commission set up under the Race Relations Act. But he later became depressed at his lack of effective powers and left after two years.[28] A further Act of 1975 went much further along the road in the enforcement of legal rights, and from then onwards pressure on discriminatory practices which undermined the rights of citizenship of blacks and other ethnic minorities was inexorable. Callaghan could claim to have played an honourable part in this process.

On the other aspect of immigration and race relations, by contrast, he took a much more conservative and restrictive line. As a result, he faced bitter attacks from liberal opinion and groups concerned with civil liberties. The Commonwealth Immigrants Bill was introduced in February 1968.[29] With the Conservative Opposition deciding not to oppose it, it received its second reading by 372 : 62. The minority consisted mainly of Labour MPs including Michael Foot and newer figures like Ben Whitaker (Hampstead) and Andrew Faulds, a Birmingham MP, but also some Scottish Nationalist and Plaid Cymru support, along with a small but distinguished group of liberal Conservatives headed by Ian Macleod and Sir Edward Boyle, and including Michael Heseltine, Nigel Fisher, David Howell, and Ian Gilmour. The third reading was carried by 145 to 31 on 28

February. This important bill, a major restrictive measure with potentially serious consequences for Kenyan Asian holders of British passports, had been rushed through with bipartisan support in less than a week.

Its main purposes were twofold. In the first place, clandestine immigration from the Commonwealth was to be severely restricted. The rights of dependent children of 16 and over to join a parent in Britain would be severely curtailed. Secondly, the entry of British passport holders from east Africa would be reduced to an extremely small total. There would be 1,500 vouchers only to heads of households; in effect this meant that up to 6,000–7,000 Asian immigrants a year would be allowed in, and no more. Some minor concessions were made in committee, notably that the period in which a Commonwealth citizen would be required to submit to examination by an immigration officer would be extended from 24 hours to 28 days. Entry was to be permitted only to British passport holders whose parents or grandparents were born in the United Kingdom (or else naturalized or registered as citizens). In effect, non-whites would effectively be kept out. The restrictions were tightened by the Immigration Appeals Act in 1969, which created an appeals system but also decreed that dependants seeking to join relatives should first obtain an entry permit. These would only be obtained from British High Commissioners in Commonwealth countries which could mean a lengthy, expensive, and perhaps fruitless journey for the people involved. These measures were to be reinforced by the Heath government's Act of 1971 which limited entry into Britain to Commonwealth citizens of 'patrial' status. Of course, other immigrants from India, Pakistan, and the West Indies continued to come in under the existing rules.

Callaghan was well aware at the time of the intense feelings that his Commonwealth Immigrants Bill aroused. He struck a defensive note in his second reading speech: 'Despite what some may say, I am not an unfeeling man nor am I unconscious of deep feeling when it is genuinely held by others.'[30] In Cabinet, his bill had been vehemently condemned by George Thomson, the Commonwealth Minister (and a close political ally of Callaghan, as it happened). Shirley Williams, later Minister of State at the Home Office, was another fierce critic. Barbara Castle, who would also have been strongly opposed to the bill, failed to resist in Cabinet on 21 February because she fell asleep![31] Crossman, her neighbour, failed to wake her perhaps out of compassion for a tired colleague, perhaps because he supported Callaghan's bill. Jenkins also expressed reservations although the practical effect of his proposed amendment would only have raised the number of vouchers from 1,500 to 2,000. But Wilson supported his Home Secretary as did the majority of the Cabinet.[32]

In the country, Callaghan was vehemently denounced as a reactionary pandering to racism. He felt angry that he had to carry the can when Jenkins and Soskice before him had ducked the issue. A clear policy was needed and he felt no embarrassment in enforcing one. Quite reasonably, he also pointed out that the critics failed to criticize Jomo Kenyatta and other east African heads of state who had been responsible for the problem in the first place. Kenyatta had flatly refused to discuss the matter with Malcolm MacDonald, the British roving High Commissioner in Africa. Callaghan attempted to have the Kenyan Asian issue put on the agenda of the next Commonwealth conference, but both the African nations and India resisted. No doubt moral protest was the easiest rhetorical line for them to pursue. Britain could claim to have put pressure on Kenyatta not to expel 40,000 Asians all at once, but to think again.

Still, the fact remained that a serious restriction of rights of entry to Britain for non-whites had been enacted by a Labour government dedicated to human equality; many wondered whether there would have been an outcry if the proposed Kenyan immigrants had been whites. The problem had arisen since, unexpectedly, a provision intended to offer Kenyan white settlers a legal departure route from Kenya to Britain some years back was taken up by Asians instead. There was also a clear breach of a solemn pledge to holders of British passports, while the difficulties that their entry might cause were never spelt out. The European Commission on Human Rights in 1970 condemned the British government's policy as racially discriminatory, but that of course had no effect. Several of his Home Office officials were dismayed at what they felt was a breach of faith. They noted that attempts to issue vouchers to would-be Kenyan or Ugandan Asian immigrants in 1968–70 were often met by the Home Secretary with delaying tactics such as endless and fruitless inquiries into the personal backgrounds of the individuals concerned. Probably no aspect of Callaghan's generally liberal regime at the Home Office aroused such strong opposition from Labour's natural supporters. In July he had a fierce confrontation with Oxford students in the front quad of Nuffield College, when there was some suggestion of physical violence. Characteristically, he chose to leave the college by the front entrance to confront his critics instead of avoiding trouble by using the back door as the college authorities suggested. Middle-class radicals were without doubt horrified. Equally, it is clear that the Labour MPs who conveyed the forebodings of their white inner-city constituents approved of the Home Secretary's measures and probable that they reflected the mass of public opinion.

By July, the political context had changed somewhat in a way that both indicated the potential of race relations to cause social and communal tension, but also somewhat let Labour off the hook, politically. Enoch Powell had been long waging a campaign of diatribe and innuendo against coloured Commonwealth immigrants. This was highly ironic since, as Minister of Health, he had significantly added to the number of Commonwealth immigrants working in the National Health Service, despite being warned about the possible social and cultural consequences by a fellow minister, Mervyn Pike, at the time. He made a series of speeches in Midlands towns like Walsall which inflamed racial prejudice. Finally, on 20 April in Birmingham, he made a speech far more inflammatory than any other he had made, full of anecdotal evidence, innuendo, and false statistics about the actual and anticipated rate of immigration into Britain.[33] Powell spoke of (unproven) cases of uncivilized behaviour and harassment of elderly white citizens, and of 'wide-eyed grinning piccaninnies'. He also seemed to anticipate, many thought even to incite, a racial bloodbath when he talked, in grandiloquent terms, of an ancient Roman who had spoken of the river Tiber 'foaming with much blood'. His listeners, perhaps less versed in Latin literature, may well have had the Birmingham canal system in mind for a similar terrifying experience. That led to demonstrations by Port of London dockers who marched on Westminster, chanting 'We want Enoch' and 'Maybe it's because I'm a Londoner'. They had an angry confrontation in the lobbies with the left-wing Jewish stalwart Ian Mikardo.[34] Although Powell met with some considerable support in the Tory grass roots, his party leadership, headed by Heath, Boyle, and Quintin Hogg, at once denounced his speech and he was dismissed from his position as Tory front-bench spokesman on defence. From that time on, Powell and the Tory leadership went their separate ways, until in February 1974 he was to emerge as an anti-European Ulster Unionist who urged the electors to vote Labour. Powell was a marked man for liberal-minded demonstrators all over the country, and much disorder attended his appearances on university campuses.

From Callaghan's point of view, Powell's antics were a valuable distraction. They enabled the government to appear, by contrast, sane and balanced, controlling the flow of immigrants in a disciplined way, securing decent conditions for immigrants who became citizens, and strongly repudiating Powell's irrational, almost hysterical racialism. For all that, many of Callaghan's friends and admirers did not feel that his handling of immigration in 1968 was at all his finest hour. To them, regarding black immigrants in terms of public management and party self-interest rather than of morality or Britain's cherished reputation as a liberal refuge ignored the central dimension of the problem.

In another area of race relations, by contrast, Callaghan could appear in his more accustomed colours as a reasonable liberal. South Africa was a particular target for all opponents of racial discrimination. Its entrenched apartheid policies offended the consciences of liberal-minded people, not least with the spectacle of the dignified black African leader Nelson Mandela in the early stages of a sentence of imprisonment on Robben Island that would last over a quarter of a century. A trade boycott of South African goods was organized and the Labour government had an embargo on arms sales. A particular flashpoint concerned sport, an area where an international boycott had a strong impact on a sport-mad South African populace. In the autumn of 1968, the MCC was due to send an English team to play in South Africa, but with craven judgement they initially omitted an African Coloured all-rounder, Basil d'Oliveira. He had been denied the opportunity to represent his country at home but now played with much distinction for Worcestershire and was a regular member of the England team. It was noted that, far from d'Oliveira having lost form on the field, he played in the last test at the Oval in 1968, against Australia, and actually scored a century. There was an immense outcry led by, amongst others, the bishop suffragan of Woolwich, the Revd David Sheppard, himself a former distinguished England batsman and a future bishop of Liverpool. The MCC tried to make amends by including d'Oliveira when one of the original team dropped out, but then Vorster, the South African Prime Minister, vetoed the team, stating that it was a team chosen for political reasons. The MCC then called the tour off.

In 1970 South Africa (who, incidentally, had never in their history played the West Indies, India, or Pakistan but confined their international matches to white countries) were due to visit England. By this time, it was hardly credible that the MCC, right-wing and politically simple-minded though they were, should think that such a tour was feasible after *l'affaire* d'Oliveira. Chief constables all over the country warned of mass demonstrations, disorder, and probable violence. There was a real possibility of cricket grounds like Lord's being invaded and the pitches damaged or dug up. Quintin Hogg, whose Marylebone constituency included Lord's, feared for the safety of his constituents in St John's Wood.

Callaghan acted here with an effective combination of subtlety and vigour. After communications to the MCC he summoned M. J. C. Allom, the chairman of the MCC, along with his secretary Billy Griffith, a former England wicket-keeper, to the Home Office and advised them of the dangers if the tour went ahead. While he left the final decision to them, and did not have the power to cancel the tour himself, he left them in no doubt about the likely serious consequences.[35] His emphasis throughout was on the threat of civil disorder rather than the evil of racialism in sport. Among other issues, the future of the Commonwealth Games, to be held in Edinburgh later that summer, would be in grave doubt. In these circumstances Allom and Griffith promptly saw to it that the South African tour was cancelled. In due course, aided by the Gleneagles Agreement on sporting contacts with South Africa decided while Callaghan was Prime Minister in 1977, the sports ban continued, and played a major part in swaying white South African opinion towards ending the era of apartheid. In the summer of 1994 a South African test team (still all white) played England at Lord's for the first time since 1965. Nelson Mandela, now president of a multiracial South Africa, sent a goodwill message and, but for a minor eye operation, might well have attended. Callaghan enjoyed it on television at his Sussex farm. And South Africa won the match.

In racial matters, as has been seen, Callaghan ran into stormy controversy. Other areas of policy proved to be scarcely less complex and demanding. Here, however, he was far more successful in building up a consensus and striking a reasonable balance commended by the nation. Student protest built up massively in the summer of 1968, fanned by violent events in France, at the Sorbonne and at Nanterre, and by university demonstrations and riots right across the United States. Television news brought the reality home to students in Britain. There was much talk of 'student power' on the model of 'black power' in the United States. They had no similar nationwide cause for protest, and their targets tended to be localized university-based institutions and officials. Instead of the Paris CRS or the state guards who shot down and killed American students at Kent State, British students confronted virtually undefended universities run by worried academics with nothing more terrifying as a defence force than the few elderly 'bulldogs' and white-tied academic proctors at Oxford.

There was, however, one powerful and highly understandable link between student protest in Britain and in America—the war in Vietnam. By 1968, the atrocities of that war, with American commanders threatening to bomb the Vietnamese 'back to the stone age', were arousing widespread disgust. It led to mass protest, which a variety of individuals and organizations joined. To the wide range of student and other protesters giving peaceful voice against the course of American policies in Vietnam were added Trotskyists and Maoists, headed by Tariq Ali, a former president of the Oxford Union, in the Vietnam Solidarity Committee. They were variously urged on by an underground left-wing journal, *Black Dwarf*; Marxist protesters like the Warwick University historian E. P. Thompson, who kept at a safe distance and never appeared at the point of conflict themselves; and a popular folk song (banned by the BBC), 'Street Fighting Man', by Mick Jagger of the pop group the Rolling Stones.

There were many violent demonstrations, the most serious outside the US embassy in Grosvenor Square. It was a major public order crisis which taxed all Callaghan's skills to the full. His instincts, of course, were totally at variance with the violence and mass (almost mob) protest of the anti-Vietnam movement. He dismissed Tariq Ali as 'a spoilt rich playboy'. On the other hand, he had a genuine libertarian commitment to free and independent protest and was anxious that proper opposition to the war in Vietnam should be expressed, as he himself had demonstrated about the civil war in Spain as a young man. The converse was the need to ensure not only that the police were able to defend buildings like the American embassy properly, but also that they were adequately protected themselves and did not suffer unduly as the innocent line of defence in a political confrontation which did not directly involve them at all. A disturbance in Grosvenor Square in July 1968, in which bottles and bricks were thrown and there were some police casualties, did not go well, since the police were not adequately prepared for it. Thereafter, Callaghan and the Police Commissioner worked out tactics in much detail.[36] The Home Secretary also conducted his own private inquiries with fringe groups and was able to distinguish between the broad mass of the demonstrators who were anxious only for a peaceful march and demonstration, and a small fringe of Maoists and students from the London School of Economics and elsewhere, anxious for a punch-up with the police.

It was announced that there would be a great march to the US embassy on Sunday, 27 October. It would be a huge affair of many thousands and real trouble could be expected. Callaghan persuaded the Cabinet that the march should be permitted—which drew upon him the scorn and censure of right-wing Tories like Sir Gerald Nabarro—but also made prudent preparations with police. A direct duplicate hand-line for the closed television circuit used by the police service was installed in the Home Office. On the other hand, some of the more excitable demands, such as that of Quintin Hogg that all the mainline London railway stations should be closed for the day, were wisely resisted.

Callaghan made a point of visibly supporting and associating with the police beforehand. He appeared with them early in the morning of 27 October, although keeping away on police advice during the demonstration.

He did, however, stroll, very deliberately, with Brian Cubbon and Tom McCaffrey, through the streets to be used by the demonstrators prior to the event. As matters worked out, the Vietnam march went astonishingly well from the Home Office point of view. Although 30,000 demonstrated in Hyde Park, only 5,000 or so went on to nearby Grosvenor Square, where there were prolonged confrontations with a strong line of thousands of police, but no serious violence or injuries. At the Home Office, Callaghan watched events with quiet satisfaction. In addition to his key civil servants, those with him, perhaps significantly for the political future, were especially close and trusted colleagues, namely Harold Lever, Merlyn Rees, and George Thomson. The march melted away with the police line holding firm, and Callaghan later went amongst them to convey his warm congratulations. It was generally felt to be a masterly keeping of the balance by the Home Secretary, vindicating his slogan of 'freedom under the law' (preferred by him to 'law and order').

From this time onwards, the tide of opinion turned. The demonstrations over Vietnam began to lose their potency as disillusion set in amongst the student radical bodies, whose attention span was in any case liable to be short. Student demagogues like David Adelstein lost their charisma; indeed, in the 1990s, one of them was to serve as the spokesman for the Association of University Teachers, the voice of the alleged instruments of 'repressive tolerance' in the 1960s. The Cabinet on 22 October offered Callaghan their warmest congratulations for his stand, not least in protecting civil liberties and keeping the troops away. 'Jim's real strength', commented Crossman, 'was that he wasn't rattled.' He added, typically, 'No doubt it has added even more to his strength, building him up as the only alternative to Harold Wilson.' But it was more than an achievement in party terms. Callaghan, many felt, had shown coolness, judgement, and moral courage in defusing a potential social crisis.[37] Brian Cubbon felt that it was at Grosvenor Square rather than in Northern Ireland a year later that the turning point in Jim Callaghan's career occurred.[38] It was here that he showed signs of greatness.

Callaghan's involvement with left-wing or student protest was far from over in October 1968. One consequence was that he had to take a stand over the entry into the country of radical student agitators from outside. Again he showed a cool head and a steady hand. He had prudently refused the entry of Daniel Cohn-Bendit, 'Danny the Red', at the time of the Grosvenor Square demonstration.The latter was, however, allowed in earlier to take part in a BBC television programme on European student leaders. Callaghan cheerfully defended himself on 13 June against Tory attacks on his decision to allow Cohn-Bendit to stay on in Britain for a further fourteen days. Jokingly, he proposed to teach Danny the Red the words of the socialist anthem, the Internationale, as he did not appear to be too sure of them.

More seriously, he allowed Rudi Dutschke, the German student radical who had been shot in the head in West Berlin in April 1968, entry into Britain. He renewed his residence permit for successive six-month periods, thus receiving the warm acclaim of Michael Foot and other champions of civil liberties.[39] The agreement was that Dutschke should convalesce and undertake not to embark on any political activity. He actually met the German radical and attempted to convert him to the constitutional, evolutionary ways of the British, though without success. Callaghan also was happy to allow Dutschke to be enrolled for a graduate course at Cambridge University, on the recommendation of Richard Lowenthal and Raymond Williams, and following a passionate plea by the eminent ecclesiastical historian and master of Selwyn College, Professor Owen Chadwick and a deputation of vice-chancellors, that he should not be deported.[40] In October 1970, however, Reginald Maudling, the new Conservative Home Secretary, rescinded Callaghan's decision and Dutschke was forced to leave. Callaghan strongly attacked this in the House as a breach of British traditions of 'political asylum' and queried privately whether Maudling had been apprised of the security papers that he had seen at the Home Office.[41] But it had no effect.

Apart from public activities like the Vietnam Committee and the affair of Rudi Dutschke, British universities were also caught up in much domestic protest during 1968–9. It was not surprising that there should be a tide of generational revolt at this time. This took many forms—the Vietnam protests in London, Scottish Nationalist demonstrations at Holy Loch against Polaris, Welsh Nationalist direct action on behalf of the Welsh language, and university campus revolts, 'demos', and 'sit-ins' across the land. Some of the new universities, Warwick, Essex, and East Anglia, were especially prominent. But there were also sit-ins in central university buildings in Oxford and Cambridge, and violent scenes at the London School of Economics where a highly regarded university porter suffered a heart attack and died, during riots in Houghton Street. What was striking was that this was a revolt by middle-class young people, products of the post-war 'baby boom' and consumer affluence, literate, articulate, and often academically seriously motivated. The incoherence of many of their aims and the irrelevance of some of their targets did not diminish the seriousness with which they were rightly regarded.

Callaghan strongly disapproved of this behaviour, but again tried successfully to keep a balance between peaceful protest and preserving order. He left it to universities to preserve their own campuses, unless they were physically unable to do so. In general, it worked very well and the tide of student protest had largely beaten itself out by the time of the June 1970 general election. There were however valuable political gains in the way that young people were regarded by the law and the authorities. A recognition of the more rapid maturity of the young led to the acceptance of the proposal of the Latey Commission to lower the voting age from 21 to 18 (a move which, incidentally, was expected to help Labour electorally). In universities, some antique restrictions were removed, disciplinary procedures overhauled beneficially, and student representation allowed on university courts, councils, senates, and committees. On many issues, including student welfare and housing, the facilities for overseas students, and (in the 1990s) the problems of student indebtedness, the results in university governance were nothing less than wholly beneficial. Conversely, the tunnel-visioned intemperance with which the student demonstrators pursued their sometimes trivial 'great causes', and the spectacle of universities apparently unable to manage themselves, did long-term damage. It led to a campaign against student unions by some elements in the Conservative Party, including John Patten at Cabinet level, down to the 1990s, and an unsympathetic attitude towards the financial difficulties in which grant-maintained students found themselves. More seriously, it also helped in a growing range of shackles being imposed on universities by governments and their effective agents, the higher education funding councils, which made serious inroads into academic freedom and university autonomy.[42]

For Callaghan the student demos were another unwelcome aspect of the mood of the times. This was widely known in the media as the era of 'permissiveness'. Roy Jenkins's liberal regime at the Home Office, ending censorship and decriminalizing homosexuality, was one response to it. But the mood amongst the young provoked more and more head-shaking as they proclaimed their belief in all manner of social experimentation—premarital sex, lesbian and male homosexual relationships and even marriages, the widespread use of 'soft' or other drugs. Time-honoured institutions appeared to be treated with contempt, as the student revolt on the campuses had shown. Moral conventions were flouted, the 'pill' widely used, and the ties of the family regarded with scorn. Youth revolt was manifested in certain obvious forms of lifestyle, in a culture symbolized by pop music of an increasingly emancipated kind (the Beatles by 1968 had turned from 'boy meets girl' folk ballads to psychedelic hymns to drug-taking as in *Sergeant Pepper*), by outré clothing based on shabby denim jeans or spectacularly brief miniskirts, by dirty long hair and a generally unkempt appearance, all of them indices of a generation in revolt. Their heroes could vary from the mysterious South American Maoist rebel Che Guevara, to the Californian philosopher of drug-induced mysticism Timothy Leary, to the veteran American Marxist guru Herbert Marcuse. At a more plebeian level, the Northern Ireland and Manchester United footballer (and alcoholic) George Best symbolized a more rebellious and ambiguous lifestyle than anything ever suggested by Stanley Matthews or other more modest sporting heroes in the past.

All this went far beyond other manifestations of youth revolt, such as the smoking, drinking, short-skirted 'flappers' of the 1920s. Libertarianism now seemed to be turning into anarchy with the gravest of social consequences. Things were falling apart, as in Yeats's poem on the 1916 Easter Rising, and a profound dissolution taking place. Callaghan, like almost everyone of his generation, did not like it at all. Although highly sympathetic to young people in general, he viewed most of the mood of permissiveness with dismay. His watchwords were order and accountability. He upheld democracy, not demonstrations. Throughout his career, he was a politician who valued hard evidence and practical, down-to-earth solutions. He was never one for glib slogans, especially those fashionable amongst the trendy middle class. 'Permissiveness', the word and the ethos, was pre-eminent among these in the later 1960s. Personally, he was well content with the ending of the Lord Chamberlain's powers of censorship, though he had a deep distaste of pornography. On one occasion he asked to see a pornographic volume that a Labour MP wanted to be published, and was deeply shocked. On libertarian grounds, he was content to have homosexuals immune from police harassment. He disapproved strongly of the kinds of persecution that sexual deviants had suffered from in the past, one being the Tory MP Ian Harvey, whose career was ruined thereby. In 1993 Callaghan was vehemently to oppose Lord Jakobovitz, the former chief rabbi, whose astonishingly harsh remarks about the gay community referred to genetic engineering and even the gas chamber, extraordinarily enough for a Jewish leader. Callaghan was never a vehicle for what *Private Eye* called the 'Inspector Knacker of the Yard' tendency, for all his links with the police. However, homosexuality in itself was something he disliked intensely. He allegedly had an unexpected first-hand display of it from his fellow Labour MP Tom Driberg, the crusader of the 'cottages'.

Callaghan believed in the family, in the domestic virtues. During his youth, the wife looked after the home and the husband stayed loyal and hard-working in his career, although he did recognize the forces of change, not least in the public career of Audrey Callaghan. The more vehement forms of feminism were only just emerging in 1967–70 with the publication of Germaine Greer's *Female Eunuch* in 1970 a sign of changing times in gender relations, which Callaghan broadly disliked. He did carry through Roy Jenkins's Gaming Bill designed to simplify betting operations. His old friend Stanley Raymond, comrade-in-arms in the New Entrants' movement of the IRSF long ago, was appointed to head the Gaming Board.[43] A strong man was needed here in an area where Mafia involvement was feared. But this legislation, too, went against the grain. Nor did the measures introduced to permit easy divorce appeal to him at all.

Above all, he strongly disapproved of drug-taking and looked with extreme disfavour at proposals to legalize it in any form. He hated the Timothy Leary philosophy of 'turn on, tune in, and drop out'. A defining moment, both for 'permissiveness' and for Callaghan's own career, came in January 1969 when the House of Commons considered the proposal made by the committee headed by Barbara Wootton to legalize the use of cannabis. It was a so-called 'soft drug' which, it has been estimated, was used by perhaps a third of university students in the early 1970s. Callaghan opposed the Wootton report and did so with much passion. He felt it was dangerous to treat cannabis in isolation from other drugs, especially in the present state of medical knowledge. After all, Roy Jenkins's own Dangerous Drugs Act was restrictive since it had given the police new powers to stop and search for cannabis and other drugs. To rising Conservative applause (but also much approval from trade union MPs on his own side) Callaghan strongly announced his wish 'to call a halt to the rising tide of permissiveness' which he called 'one of the most unlikeable words that has been invented in recent years'.[44]

It is not difficult to hear in Callaghan's solemn tones the silent majority fighting back. Opinion polls showed that greater public 'permissiveness' over sexual practice went alongside a tough attitude on drug-taking (as also on capital punishment). With terrifying statistics of the availability of drugs in America, British people wished to be preserved from Haight-Ashbury, psychedelic escapism and the throbbing message underlying the Beatles' *Sergeant Pepper* hit song 'Lucy in the Sky with Diamonds' (LSD). Even more, they wished their children to be preserved from them. After years of street violence, student upheaval, and moral relativism, of sex, drugs, and cultural experimentation, the older generation were saying enough was enough. Some of the changes in popular mores were to be of permanent effect. The 1960s left their lasting mark. Most of the last vestiges of repressive Victorian puritanism were expelled. In subsequent years, family breakdown and divorce went on apace, homosexuals and lesbians won a growing measure of legal and social tolerance, and premarital 'relationships' or 'partnerships' became almost the norm amongst the young. But other values, respectability, order, decency as traditionally understood, staged a recovery and Callaghan was their authentic representative voice. He believed private virtue and civic order to be indissolubly linked. His tones went ringing out over subsequent decades. When in 1995 a Labour front-bencher, Clare Short, appeared to be endorsing the legalization of cannabis (or at least questioning the effectiveness of present legislation), she was firmly rebuked by the party leadership. Drugs, so Tony Blair and his colleagues implied, were no part of a 'New Labour' vision of a settled face-to-face community and a 'stakeholder society'. Labour, they insisted, was truly the party of the family. In this they were playing again the cherished tunes of 'Old Labour' which Callaghan held most dear.

The abrupt governmental rejection of permissiveness and libertarianism associated with the youth counter-culture was a historic landmark in British social experience. Callaghan was its natural spokesman. By background and outlook, he embodied the traditional working-class virtues of thrift, hard work, and respectable artisan industry and craftsmanship. He took pride in his public stand against permissiveness and spoke with contempt in later years of the cynical, unrepresentative, and destructive view of the bourgeois chattering classes. His very language recalled the social gospel as he had learnt it from the good people of London Road chapel long ago. His Baptist upbringing, rejected in terms of his religious viewpoint, was powerful still in influencing his code of conduct. He worked in politics partly as the instrument of the historic nonconformist conscience, just as much as his self-consciously Methodist, teetotal, bachelor colleague in Cardiff, George Thomas. Callaghan felt that you did not need to be a do-gooder in order to do good. A man close to his sixtieth year, he felt attached to an older, more deferential social order. Youthful Britain appeared to be turning amoral. It was going wrong. On the other hand, he was still enough of an idealist to believe, in 1970 at least, that the old values would revive. The youthful sinners would repent (some of them at least), the prodigal sons and daughters would return, and the fatted calf be prepared in joyful celebration. There is no doubt at all, from the opinion polls and mass observation data of the period, that Callaghan's outlook was that of the vast majority of the British people at the time. Like him, they felt that protest and revolt by publicly subsidized young people had gone much too far. Someone had to take a stand against the forces of anarchy. It was, most people felt, hugely to Callaghan's public credit that he had done so.

Callaghan's activities at the Home Office ranged over some of the most profound aspects of human activity—the treatment of children, the operation of law and order, race relations, public protest and free expression, sexual and moral liberty, and the right or otherwise to indulge in experiments with drugs and other substances. The mix of responses he offered had its critics. In particular, his handling of the issue of coloured immigration lost him some admirers and seriously affected morale amongst constituency Labour activists, while perhaps gaining him wider support in the country as a whole. On the other hand, in penal reform, in striking a balance between protest and order, and in trying to discipline the excesses of the young (as many saw them), he was felt to have been an effective Home Secretary. In areas such as the handling of popular protests, he had demonstrated genuine powers of national leadership. He achieved the difficult feat of winning approval from supporters of civil liberties and champions of the police at one and the same time. He proved himself to be a determined, brave, and highly effective minister in a department which was not at first congenial to him. In his traditional Home Office activities, his prestige had risen immensely by early 1970 compared with his blanket of introspective gloom when he first went there. There were, however, important wider issues in this period, which had a dramatic impact on his own standing and on public discourse. In particular, industrial relations and the hitherto unnoticed area of Home Office responsibilities in Northern Ireland caught the public attention, and it is to those that we must now turn.

1. Robert Reiner, *The Politics of the Police* (London, 1985).
2. Crossman, *Cabinet Diaries*, iii. 404 (9 Mar. 1969).
3. *Parl. Deb.*, 5th ser., vol. 759, 240–1 (20 Feb. 1968); cf. Lord Hailsham, *A Sparrow's Flight* (London, 1990), 363.
4. Interviews with Sir Thomas McCaffrey and Lord Callaghan.
5. MacDougall, *Don and Mandarin*, 179.
6. Callaghan, 'Cumber and Variableness', in *The Home Office: Perspectives on Policy and Administration* (Royal Institute of Public Administration bicentenary lectures, 1982), 9 ff.
7. Interviews with David Faulkner and Lord Allen of Abbeydale.
8. Ibid.; interviews with Sir Brian Cubbon and Sir Geoffrey de Deney.
9. Interview with Lord Merlyn-Rees.
10. *The Times*, 9 Dec. 1969; Jenkins, *A Life at the Centre*, 199–213.
11. *Children in Trouble*, Cmnd. 3601 (Apr. 1968); material in Callaghan Papers, box 24.

For the wider background, see A. E. Bottoms, 'On the Decriminalization of English Juvenile Courts', in Roger Hood (ed.), *Crime, Criminology and Public Policy* (London, 1974), 319 ff.; and Terence Morris, *Crime and Criminal Justice since 1945* (Oxford, 1989), 113–20. On these and other aspects of social policy and criminology, I am much indebted to Roger Hood, David Faulkner, and my late wife Jane.

12. Cf. Jane Morgan and Lucia Zedner, *Child Victims* (Oxford, 1992), a project sponsored by the Home Office Research and Planning Unit.

13. Jill Pellew, *The Home Office, 1848–1914* (London, 1982), 80. For Winston Churchill's pioneering work on juveniles, see Leon Radzinowicz and Roger Hood, *A History of English Criminal Law*, v: *The Emergence of Penal Policy* (London, 1986), 770–5.

14. Crossman, *Cabinet Diaries*, 146 (19 July 1968). Crossman noted the seriousness of the threat: '[Jim] backs winning causes whereas I back losing causes like devolution.'

15. Ibid. 554 (9 July 1969).

16. Judge, *The First Fifty Years*, 132. Also see J. P. Martin and Gail Wilson, *The Police: A Study in Manpower* (London, 1969), 164–5.

17. Callaghan to Les Knowles, 15 Oct. 1970 (Callaghan Papers, box 14); speech at golden jubilee of Police Federation, Blackpool, 23 May 1969.

18. *Guardian*, 13 Jan. 1997.

19. *Time and Chance*, 247.

20. Interviews with Sir Thomas McCaffrey, Lord Allen of Abbeydale, and Sir Brian Cubbon.

21. On these matters, see Morris, *Crime and Criminal Justice*, 131–5; Advisory Council on the Penal System, 'The Regime for Long Term Prisoners in Conditions of Maximum Security' (HMSO, 1968); material in Callaghan Papers, box 24.

22. Callaghan Papers, Box 24.

23. See Colin Holmes, *John Bull's Island: Immigration and British Society, 1871–1971* (London, 1988) for a valuable overview.

24. Material in Callaghan Papers, box 24.

25. Crossman, *Cabinet Diaries*, ii. 666 (6 Feb. 1968).

26. *Parl. Deb.*, 5th ser., vol. 763, 53–67 (23 Apr. 1968).

27. *Time and Chance*, 269.

28. Geoffrey Goodman, *The Awkward Warrior* (London, 1979), 569–71.

29. *Parl. Deb.*, 5th ser., vol. 758, 659–64, 1241–58 (22, 27 Feb. 1968).

30. Ibid. 1252 (27 Feb. 1968).

31. Castle, *Castle Diaries, 1964–70*, 378–8 (22 Feb. 1968).

32. Material in Callaghan Papers, box 24.

33. *The Times*, 22 Apr. 1968. Cf. Paul Foot, *The Rise of Enoch Powell* (London, 1969), 115 ff.

34. *The Times*, 24, 27 Apr. 1968; Mikardo, *Backbencher* (London, 1988), 173.

35. Material in Callaghan Papers, box 24.

36. Ibid.

37. Crossman, *Cabinet Diaries*, iii. 241 (29 Oct. 1969).

38. Interview with Sir Brian Cubbon.

39. Michael Foot, cited in *Observer*, 29 Jan. 1969; Callaghan to Foot, 6 Dec. 1968, 22 Jan., 17 July 1969, 27 Jan. 1970 (Callaghan Papers, box 24).

40. Professor Owen Chadwick to Callaghan, 9 Jan. 1971 (Callaghan Papers, box 24).

41. Callaghan to Maudling, 20 Nov. 1970 (ibid.).

42. See a fuller treatment of this point in J. P. Carswell, *Government and the Universities in Britain: Programme and Performance, 1960–1980* (Cambridge, 1985).

43. *Parl. Deb.*, 5th ser., vol. 758, 1164–81 (13 Feb. 1968), Callaghan's first Commons speech as Home Secretary. Perhaps an added satisfaction from Raymond's appointment came from the fact that Raymond had quarrelled violently with Callaghan's old adversary Barbara Castle, when she was Transport Secretary and Raymond was head of British Rail. Raymond resigned, allegedly saying, 'I have never understood women. Perhaps that is my undoing.' *Castle Diaries, 1964–70*, 328 (21 Nov. 1967).

44. The Wootton Commission reported in July 1968 (Cmnd. 3263). For the taking of cannabis, see Arthur Marwick, *British Society since 1945* (London, 1990 edn.), 251–2. Also helpful is Kenneth Leech, *Youthquake: The Growth of a Counter-culture through Two Decades* (London, 1973).

15

TROUBLES, INDUSTRIAL AND IRISH

THE two years following Callaghan's resignation as Chancellor in November 1967 were a time of exceptional political turbulence. Political journalists had a field day, There was an endless stream of stories of government plots and conspiracies, a fashion encouraged by the paranoid fears of Harold Wilson himself and his use of rumour-mongers such as George Wigg. Some of the surviving published documents reinforce this sense of volatility. The Crossman diaries throughout are full of excitements of this kind; by contrast, those of Castle and Benn are more balanced if perhaps less fun to read. The diaries of Cecil King, the editor of the *Daily Mirror*, are more excitable still, with stories of coups and *putsches* involving on occasion bankers, high-ranking generals, and even members of the royal family. The truth is almost certainly more prosaic. Nevertheless, the Cabinet changes at the end of 1967, followed by others in early 1968, certainly destabilized the political balance in the Wilson administration. Of the original 'big three', Wilson himself was tarnished by devaluation and apparently his leadership was more vulnerable. Brown, although operating at the Foreign Office, had diminished his own reputation with his series of outbursts and threats of resignation, while Callaghan was, for the moment, in the shadows after leaving the Treasury.

The rising force was manifestly Roy Jenkins, the new Chancellor, but he was largely engaged in trying to turn the economy around after devaluation. In the first instance, this meant imposing an exceptionally severe dose of deflation to fulfil the terms agreed with the IMF. This was essential to prevent the competitive advantage Britain gained from devaluation being eaten up in higher costs at home. There was in fact a dangerous delay before Jenkins took what appeared to be the necessary deflationary action. His budget of March 1968 rained blows on industry and the consumer alike; in all, £923m. would be taken out of the economy. Yet the balance of payments continued to deteriorate, with exports slow to respond.

There was alarm that the pound, even after its recent devaluation, was not secure at its present exchange rate. Certainly it was constantly under threat from external speculative pressures, with vast sums spent to maintain the parity. If Jenkins represented the Labour right, the other rising force was the left-winger Barbara Castle, but she too had a major task ahead in attempting to resolve the morass that was British industrial relations. Throughout the whole of 1968 the government appeared tetchy and precarious, while by-election and local government results testified to a deep and growing unpopularity.

Even in his initial gloomy mood, Callaghan could not fail to be a major player in the Cabinet's internal manœuvres. Indeed, his being released from the toils of the Treasury gave him somewhat more freedom to act. Very early on, within a few days of leaving the Treasury, he was involved in two controversies, each of which caused Wilson much difficulty. The first arose from a proposal stemming from George Brown, and supported also by Denis Healey, Patrick Gordon Walker, and Ray Gunter, the Minister of Labour, for the renewing of arms sales to South Africa. A number of other ministers seemed to feel that their departments would avoid cuts if the national income could be boosted elsewhere. The principle, after all, had already been conceded in part. In February 1965, Denis Healey as Minister of Defence had agreed to provide four Wasp helicopters to South Africa partly to replace ones which had crashed, partly to equip frigates. They were regarded as an integral part of the anti-submarine equipment of frigates already supplied to South Africa as part of the Simonstown Agreement.[1] Callaghan himself, when asked about exports, joined in to support the calls for renewed arms sales. He pointed out that the arms were for external defence, not for the enforcement of apartheid at home. As so often his instinct was for practicalities, rather than striking abstract moral postures. His main concern lay in the need to fortify the economy after his devaluation, and this would certainly mean controversial decisions at home and abroad.

At a meeting of the 'Under Forty' club of MPs at St Stephen's Tavern on 10 December, he told them that, to turn the economy around, the government would have to change its stance on several issues. He itemized dropping the Industrial Expansion Bill, extending the wage freeze for another eighteen months, and rethinking the ban on arms sales to South Africa as a part of the stimulation of exports. According to one young Welsh MP, Donald Anderson, who was present, the discussion was relatively uncontentious; what caused trouble was a damaging press leak afterwards. At a venomous Cabinet on 15 December, however, when George

Brown was the central combatant, it emerged that the majority of ministers, including Wilson himself, mindful of the effect on Commonwealth opinion, wanted no change on arms sales to South Africa. In addition, almost 140 Labour MPs, encouraged it was believed by the chief whip John Silkin, signed a motion urging the government to maintain its arms embargo. At a Cabinet meeting on 18 December Callaghan and Gordon Walker then switched to support Wilson, after a strong speech by the Prime Minister, and this left George Brown exposed and isolated.[2] It was a moral and political triumph for Wilson of a kind relatively rare at this time, although it did not strengthen his hand for long.

In another fierce debate in January 1968 the range of proposed cuts in public expenditure following the devaluation of sterling aroused controversy in Cabinet. This was not surprising since hard decisions had to be taken, many of them difficult for any Labour government. One that led to angry exchanges concerned the proposed two-year delay in raising the school-leaving age to 16. This issue brought to the surface something of a class divide in the Cabinet. Jenkins and the Education Secretary, Gordon Walker, both of them Oxford-educated intellectuals, backed this proposal. By contrast, George Brown, Ray Gunter, and James Callaghan, usually seen as three working-class ministers by background, strongly condemned it as inegalitarian. Working-class children would have expectations unfairly deferred; if cuts had to be made, they should fall on the universities, patronized mainly by middle-class people. There might be economies in their scientific budgets or capital building programmes; student loans might even be visualized. Callaghan as Chancellor had rejected a proposal to defer the school-leaving age: there is no doubt that an assault on working-class education roused the strongest of personal feelings in him. Crossman produced counter-arguments, and the decision was carried by 11 votes to 10.[3] Lord Longford then resigned from the government. Of greater moment were the huge defence cuts, notably withdrawal from east of Suez in 1971. Callaghan went along with the majority here, consistent with his line as Chancellor. A by-product was the scrapping of the F/111 aircraft where he supported Denis Healey's efforts to retain it. Both of them, however, were defeated after a powerful intervention from Roy Jenkins.

As Callaghan's self-confidence returned, his reputation rose through his successful handling of major Home Office legislation (albeit controversial in the field of Commonwealth immigration). His standing in Cabinet, party, and country rose with it. By May Wilson's primacy was again in grave doubt. Rhodesia, Vietnam, and incomes policy all appeared to be running into the sands, with Callaghan's somewhat pyrrhic victory on race relations one of the few achievements. Press criticism of the beleaguered Prime Minister was unrelenting. On 9 May Cecil King ran a lurid press story of an open *putsch* against Wilson being imminent in view of a colossal impending financial crisis. The fact that King was a member of the Bank of England court gave his story some fleeting credence.[4]

The one major change in political personnel that spring had been the final and irrevocable resignation of George Brown from the government in March. This was over a relatively minor issue of decision-taking concerning the procedure followed in closing the London gold market during the so-called 'gold rush'. Had it not been closed, a second devaluation would have been highly likely. Brown's departure after so many cries of 'wolf' left Jenkins in an apparently clear position as Wilson's putative challenger in any leadership contest. There was now a distinctive group of mainly young 'Jenkinsites' such as Roy Hattersley, David Owen, David Marquand, Bill Rodgers, John Mackintosh, and Brian Walden pushing their champion's cause. Christopher Mayhew, a disaffected ex-minister, worked with Dick Taverne, Ivor Richard, and others in compiling a list of supporters. The Lloyd George Liberal supporters had done much the same in the autumn of 1916, in drawing up a list of firm backers prior to the overthrow of the then Prime Minister, Asquith. Jenkins himself made little secret of his ambitions: as a distinguished biographer of Asquith, he would have no doubt noted the historical precedent. Wilson himself viewed the noises off on behalf of Jenkins with some disdain, but he had for the moment lost the political initiative. He had no obvious figure to neutralize the threat from Jenkins. Crossman was too erratic and Barbara Castle, an impressive performer, ruled out on gender grounds and perhaps temperamental grounds as well.

The only possible alternative, one quite as unacceptable to Wilson as was Jenkins, was the restored figure at the Home Office, Jim Callaghan. There was talk of 'Callaghanites' engaged in plots to overthrow Wilson, but no serious evidence was ever produced either that such plots took place or indeed that the 'Callaghanites' as a collective group existed either. The only name ever mentioned seriously as a Callaghan promoter was the 70-year-old Douglas Houghton, his old boss at the Inland Revenue Staff Federation thirty years previously, who had now succeeded Shinwell as chairman of the parliamentary Labour Party. Nevertheless, Callaghan's name also came up in other contexts. Cecil King sometimes ran his name, along with that of Jenkins or even Healey, as a replacement for Wilson—with no encouragment from his nominees. Callaghan was sometimes mentioned also by centrist figures, or even by moderate Conservatives such as Iain Macleod, as the putative head of some kind of coalition government. Again, there is no evidence that Callaghan, while communicating to influential lobby correspondents like John Cole and Alan Watkins and to industrial reporters like Peter Jenkins of the *Guardian*, had anything to do with wild rumours of this kind. What is clear, however, is that individual Labour MPs, perhaps a dozen in all, from time to time approached Callaghan urging him to bid for the leadership. He never gave any of them any encouragement, not least because his chances of toppling Wilson at this stage were exceedingly thin. His personal relations with the Prime Minister were glacial, and there was little loyalty or even friendship on either side. The Prime Minister blankly refused to see Callaghan at No. 10 and the former resident of No. 11 felt hurt. Were there ever to be a leadership contest, Callaghan was increasingly well placed to be a significant participant.

What brought Callaghan right to the political forefront, however, and reduced his relations with Wilson to the lowest point ever, was what proved to be the dominant theme of domestic politics for the twelve months up to July 1969. This was the reform of industrial relations. Callaghan, of course, was an old union man, but in his early period as a Labour MP he was essentially a political figure rather than the voice of the unions. Things had fundamentally changed since his election as party treasurer with the votes of the major unions, in October 1967, and the implications of that new relationship continued to reverberate. He angered Wilson intensely in May 1968, when he made an unauthorized speech to the Firemen's Union at Nottingham. In this he appeared to promise that the incomes policy, or wage freeze, would shortly be brought to an end, in return for the continuing flow of funds from the unions to fill Labour's coffers. His underlying view was that incomes policies did not last. At the Cabinet on 30 May, Crossman made an attempt to extract an apology from Callaghan. But Wilson, as so often in his relations with Callaghan, seemed reluctant to widen the breach, especially with a powerful colleague whose stock was again rising. The Home Secretary robustly refused to apologize for anything and the issue subsided.[5]

Another sign of Callaghan's growing sensitivity for union views came that July, when for once he and George Brown made common cause. This was over the issue of the Labour Party secretaryship in succession to Len Williams. Wilson had encouraged Anthony Greenwood to resign from the Cabinet as Minister of Housing to fight for the party secretaryship. Greenwood, a pleasant but not very forceful man, was hesitant, but he did Wilson's bidding. In the decisive meeting of the National Executive on 24

July, Callaghan, Brown, and Alice Bacon launched a pre-arranged attack on the nomination of Greenwood and proposed instead Harry Nicholas, a senior trade unionist who was acting general secretary of the Transport Workers. After a vigorous debate, in which the chairman, Eirene White, changed her view and abstained, Nicholas defeated Greenwood by 14 votes to 12 to become general secretary of the Labour Party, a position he was to hold until 1972.[6] Greenwood, who had not sought the position anyhow, went on from one misfortune to another. In the spring of 1970 he left the Cabinet to become chairman-elect of the Commonwealth Development Corporation but then found that, after Labour's election defeat, Edward Heath declined to appoint him. Poor Greenwood, a popular and pleasant man who had given up his parliamentary seat, found himself thrust into unexpected poverty, scarcely able to afford his daughter's wedding reception.[7] From the purely political standpoint, however, there was much to justify Callaghan and Brown's stand. Greenwood had been generally thought an ineffective Minister of Housing, and Nicholas appeared a more appropriate choice as general secretary at the time. But the decisive factor was that Greenwood was widely felt to be Harold Wilson's creature and he was kept out for that reason above all. It did not improve the already tetchy relations between Wilson and his difficult Home Secretary.

But these were merely preliminary skirmishes in what blazed forth as a major war over the trade unions, with Callaghan a central combatant. Barbara Castle had become Secretary for Employment and Productivity in April 1968 determined to reform the system of industrial relations once and for all. As a left-wing socialist, she felt that in the context of a planned economy, industrial relations verged on the anarchic. Trade union power had grown and seemed almost above the law. In the 1940s and 1950s, powerful right-wing union potentates like Arthur Deakin, Will Lawther, and Tom Williamson had compelled the TUC to do the Labour leadership's bidding, but this was no longer the case. In the 1960s there was a new mood in trade unionism, indicated by a rash of unofficial strikes, in which power appeared to lie not in the national officers of unions but at the local, grass-roots level, shown by the dominant role of shop stewards in factories, in car manufacturing plants, and elsewhere.[8] New militant union leaders were emerging, along the pattern of Frank Cousins in the TGWU in the 1950s; the rise of the Scottish ex-Communist Lawrence Daly as general secretary of the National Union of Mineworkers, a traditionally moderate union since the days of the General Strike of 1926, was a portent. Even more formidable was Jack Jones, Frank Cousins's successor in 1969 as general secretary of the Transport Workers. He was an open advocate of decentralization and industrial devolution, with wage negotiation to take place essentially through local plant bargaining where the shop stewards would take the lead, coming together nationally in industrial delegates' conferences from time to time. The failure of the government's incomes policy to stick in 1968 was a sign of union power, or as some argued indiscipline. The same kind of shop-floor militancy, almost syndicalist in character, evidenced in France in the events of that year seemed to be paralleled in Britain.

There had been a royal commission inquiring into labour relations since 1965, under the chairmanship of Lord Donovan. When it reported in June 1968, it was a huge disappointment to Barbara Castle. Instead of proposing effective sanctions, legal or otherwise, upon unions which went their own way, Donovan's findings were swayed by two Labour academics, Hugh Clegg of the University of Warwick and Allan Flanders of Nuffield College, Oxford, in the direction of a purely voluntary reform of industrial relations on the shop floor. Only the economics writer Andrew Shonfield signed a minority report in favour of legal sanctions. The report noted, and largely approved of, the growing pattern of factory bargaining rather than national bargaining. Donovan took its stand, within this new framework of plant negotiation, on the traditional voluntarist position that there should be little state interference in the collective bargaining; such intervention as the report did support would operate on behalf of the workers, as in statutory protection against unfair dismissal.

Many leading Labour figures welcomed the general drift of Donovan; Callaghan, a former union official himself with a special insight into the trade union mind, did so strongly. He had the endorsement of such eminent Labour experts on industrial law as Professors Otto Kahn-Freund and Bill Wedderburn. This was almost the academic orthodoxy of the time, upheld by leading scholars such as Sir Henry Phelps Brown. The Cambridge historian Henry Pelling's essay on the trade unions and the law, published in an important volume of historical studies in 1968, emphasized the historic resistance of British union leaders, unlike those for example in Australia and New Zealand, to being involved with the process of the law, whether arbitration, legal liability, or the restriction of strikes.[9] George Woodcock, the TUC general secretary, who wanted to impose more central direction on individual unions, took a different view after serving on the Donovan Commission. But in early 1968 he moved to become head of the Commission on Industrial Relations. His successor was his deputy Vic Feather, a vigorous champion of Donovan with whom Woodcock himself had frequently clashed. Barbara Castle herself was greatly dismayed by the course of events. She regarded the whole Donovan exercise as a missed opportunity. The Commission, she complained, offered no philosophic view of industrial relations. Its report could not form the basis of a sensible industrial policy.[10] Recent strikes at Girling Brakes and in the steel industry confirmed her views about the dangers of indiscipline on the shop floor. She was supported in her views by Roy Jenkins, the Chancellor, who was convinced that the economy could not recover without an effective wages policy and machinery to enforce it. In any case, the political balance of the Cabinet meant that the two ministers were now bound in an unlikely alliance.

Mrs Castle thus set herself the task of framing far-reaching legislation that would both provide the unions with legal recognition and protection, and also ensure that industrial discipline would be imposed on them to avoid unofficial strikes, irresponsible wage demands, disruptions caused by inter-union disputes, and the other plagues characteristic of British labour relations at that time. She and her advisers, notably Bill McCarthy of Nuffield College, who had served on Donovan but had become convinced of the need for a major reform of industrial relations nevertheless, worked out a new white paper to embody these views, as the basis of future legislation. On a suggestion from her husband Ted, Mrs Castle adapted the title of a famous left-wing work by the legendary Nye Bevan fifteen years earlier. It appeared in November 1968 under the title *In Place of Strife*.

From that moment, the trade union issue consumed domestic political attention. Barbara Castle was intent on getting the proposals of *In Place of Strife* onto the statute book in the quickest possible time. Key figures were equally determined to oppose her. They included virtually every leading trade unionist of the land. But they had as allies significant political personalities, of whom the most imposing by far was the Home Secretary, James Callaghan. The clash of wills between Callaghan and Mrs Castle, the latter strongly backed by the Prime Minister, dictated high politics for much of 1969. The political and industrial fallout largely determined the gloomy course of British social and economic history throughout the 1970s.

On the last day of 1968, Barbara Castle sent a proposed draft white paper around to Cabinet colleagues.[11] It was the work of a committee of four—herself, Anthony Wedgwood Benn, Peter Shore, and her PPS Harold Walker. The first three of these had no first-hand knowledge of the trade union world, Callaghan pointed out. Walker, who did have a union background, was significantly the only one to have reservations. On the other hand, all four were broadly on the left and it is notable that Bevanites such as Barbara Castle and Harold Walker in the early 1950s had called for an incomes policy rather than allowing wages to be left to the vagaries of the free market. Mrs Castle declared that she wished to publish a white paper on 9 January, but Callaghan, Crossman, and others vehemently objected, stating that this would give the Cabinet the absurdly short time of a week in which to consider it, and that in effect it would make consultation with the TUC the purest formality. In the event, the white paper was published on 17 January instead, with the corollary that a bill would be introduced in the next session. The proposals in the white paper *In Place of Strife* were few in number but pregnant with significance. In part, it offered proposals congenial to the unions including the compulsory registration of unions and a Commission on Industrial Relations to spread good practices in all aspects of collective bargaining.

But uproar was caused in the union world by three other proposals—a 28-day enforced 'conciliation pause'; powers given to impose a settlement in inter-union disputes; and powers to impose a strike ballot. These would ultimately be backed by penal legal sanctions, including a detachment from earnings or other civil penalties. For the first time since 1927, a government—a Labour government—was proposing to interpose the force of the law into hitherto unfettered collective bargaining. For the TUC almost to a man and woman, this was the ultimate heresy, a betrayal of hard-won union freedoms going back to the mythical heroism of the Tolpuddle martyrs. The fact that almost all the applause came from the right-wing press intensified their fury. There the matter remained for another two months until after Harold Wilson returned from a major Commonwealth heads of government meeting in Nigeria.

From the outset, Callaghan had made very plain his fundamental hostility to legal controls and penal sanctions. Mrs Castle knew this perfectly well and, not surprisingly, took every step to try to exclude him from meetings to prepare the bill. For him, it was a matter of fundamental principle, though one reinforced by his personal links to key unions since his election as party treasurer. He welcomed Donovan as a safeguard for free collective bargaining and for industrial freedom. As a young trade union official, he had campaigned bitterly against the 1927 Trades Disputes Act which imposed penalties of a financial and legal kind on the trade unions, including the civil service unions. Its repeal in 1946, moved by Ernest Bevin the Foreign Secretary, was another Magna Carta for the union movement. Callaghan's view was that Barbara Castle and most of her associates were ill-informed about industrial relations, unlike a participant like himself, and oblivious to the intensity of the TUC's reaction. Politicians like Harold Wilson or Barbara Castle were deaf and blind to the nuances of the trade union world, the key importance of matters such as union rule-books, one of which Callaghan himself had drafted as a young man. Donovan had rightly endorsed a voluntary system; the only reform possible of the industrial system must necessarily come from the unions themselves. That, rather than the heavy-handed pressure of the courts, was the only way to control unofficial strikes. Legal penalties would make the temper of labour relations much worse, and make a successful attack on the balance of payments impossible. His new political relationship with the major unions since October 1967 added point to his views, but without doubt it was fundamentally a matter of deeply held conviction which he made plain to Wilson and Mrs Castle. It was not long before important allies emerged. In early March eighty-seven Labour MPs refused to support the white paper. But more significant elements were soon to declare their hand.

On 26 March 1969 one of the most remarkable meetings of Labour's National Executive ever held took place.[12] Here the Home Secretary publicly cast his vote in favour of helping to defeat Cabinet policy. Collective responsibility lay in ruins. A motion moved by Joe Gormley of the Miners which originally proposed that the NEC reject 'any legislation designed to give effect to all the proposals contained in the White Paper' was carried by 15 to 6. Callaghan, who had succeeded in having the word 'any' struck out, was ostentatiously amongst the majority; other ministers, Eirene White, Alice Bacon, and Fred Mulley, also failed to back the government's proposals, but Callaghan was by far the most important dissentient. In impotent anger, Barbara Castle then saw the resolution carried against her by 16 to 5, another minister, Jennie Lee, joining the revolt. It was an extraordinary public display of Cabinet division. Wilson, on the point of his visit to Lagos the next day, had a tense talk with Callaghan afterwards. The press was later primed with stories of the Prime Minister slapping his Home Secretary down and showing the smack of firm government, although this seems to be the reverse of what happened.[13] Jenkins, Healey, and others spoke of Callaghan's 'shabby' behaviour. Callaghan had a further talk with Wilson after a difficult Cabinet on 2 April. He wrote to the Prime Minister, 'The Party situation is serious in morale and policy. They are linked and confidence is low. . . . Can we make a fresh start and get PLP, Cabinet, Party and TUs together?'[14] Again there seemed to be no meeting of minds. To a background of mounting TUC opposition to the proposed Industrial Relations Bill, the essential fact was that a very senior government minister was challenging his Prime Minister's authority. He could drop the bill or sack the minister. Both strategies were impossible. The fight was on.

After a lull, the crisis reached a still more serious stage on 6 May. The chairman of the parliamentary Labour Party in effect denounced the industrial relations proposals and warned the government against causing a split with the TUC. This would have caused a stir in any circumstances. It was intensified because the chairman was none other than Douglas Houghton, Callaghan's old union colleague and mentor; Callaghan noted later that the two 'had talked two or three times about the matter'. In fact, Houghton, Callaghan, and Vic Feather were to form a decisive troika of opponents during the ensuing crisis. In Geoffrey Goodman's view, the key figure was Houghton, chairman of the party, a major trade unionist, and diligent unattributed leaker to the newspapers. He encouraged Callaghan to stand firm, secure in the knowledge that he had growing support in the parliamentary party. There were rumours that Jack Jones and Hugh Scanlon were putting pressure on the sixty to seventy TGWU- and AEU-sponsored MPs to oppose any government industrial legislation.[15] The press was full of stories of droves of Labour MPs announcing their endorsement of Callaghan's views and of some members of the Cabinet doing so also (Richard Marsh was one name much mentioned). Robert Mellish, the chief whip and a former London docker, was another open dissentient. This was the more remarkable since he had only just been appointed as a tough disciplinarian instead of the more lenient John Silkin. *The Times* now claimed that Wilson's departure as premier was 'imminent'.[16]

At a ferocious Cabinet meeting on 8 May, Callaghan's opposition was naked and unapologetic. Wilson urged that the bill was absolutely essential, and that Houghton, the PLP chairman, would have to be disciplined for openly opposing government policy. Somewhat unwisely, however, he elaborated on the constitutional challenge that he claimed Houghton had opened up. The Prime Minister was backed up by Michael Stewart and Roy Jenkins, but the constitutional aspect enabled Callaghan to suggest that they defer the bill until after further discussions with the TUC. He argued that the penal clauses were at best of marginal importance and were driving sections of the party to the limit of endurance and straining the loyalty of ministers to breaking point. In a dramatic scene, when Crossman declared that they must 'sink or swim together', Callaghan interposed 'sink or sink'. Crossman turned on him furiously for his defeatism. 'Why don't you go? Get out!'[17] Callaghan responded calmly that if his colleagues wanted him to leave the Cabinet he would do so. Wilson promptly offered some soothing words, and no one took up Callaghan's offer of resignation, such as it was. The Home Secretary moved on urbanely to raise the affairs of Northern Ireland. The Cabinet meeting was followed by press reports giving an almost verbatim account (not from Callaghan himself) of what had been said by ministers. There was also a weekend speech by Callaghan which raised the question of the leadership, albeit in a very indirect form. Further accusations of disloyalty resulted.

At 10 a.m. on 13 May, Callaghan was summoned to a private meeting with the Prime Minister.[18] Wilson mentioned here that all members of the so-called Inner Cabinet thought that Callaghan should resign. However he also praised his excellent work at the Home Office, including on Northern Ireland. After twenty minutes of fencing on both sides, Callaghan was told that he would no longer be a member of the Management Committee, as the Inner Cabinet was conventionally called, and that this would be released to the press. Callaghan returned to the Home Office, angry but still defiant. Amongst his advisers there was anxious debate. Brian Cubbon, his private secretary, felt reluctantly that he would have to resign, as did Tom McCaffrey after this public humiliation; Philip Allen, by contrast, took an unusually robust view and urged him to stay. Senior civil servants such as this appear not to have been disturbed by giving advice on an essentially party political issue. After this discussion, Callaghan felt convinced that he should stay, lest he otherwise play into the hands of his opponents, the advocates of the Industrial Relations Bill. He then drove with Audrey, who was off to America, to London airport. He did not tell her what had taken place that morning lest she think of cancelling her visit.

That afternoon, he appeared on the government front bench, despite the taunts of the Conservatives. His supporter and aide Gregor MacKenzie had urged him to make a point of being visible in the House during prime minister's question time. As luck would have it, Harold Lever left the chamber and Callaghan had perforce to sit next to the Prime Minister. But equally Callaghan was aware of waves of sympathy from behind him on the Labour benches, including encouraging cries from the aged Manny Shinwell, an old adversary. The day passed without further incident. Roy Jenkins, furious at Callaghan's behaviour which he saw as disloyal, was nevertheless compelled to admire his 'defiant dignity' as he thrust his way, head held high, along the crowded platform of Victoria station for a weekend on his Sussex farm.[19]

In fact, the political crisis as far as Callaghan was personally concerned was largely over. He had consulted Douglas Houghton about the substance of a proposed resignation speech perhaps in early June. His notes included points added by Houghton in red ink. But this speech remained a long way from being delivered. Wilson had had every opportunity to dismiss him. But the Prime Minister had been forced to conclude that Callaghan was too dangerous a figure, with far too much support in the party and the unions, for him to be removed in such a way. The exclusion from the Inner Cabinet, while a marginal loss of prestige, was in no way a major blow for Callaghan; it met only occasionally and its deliberations were never in the public eye. Barbara Castle still had to make progress with her bill. She spoke optimistically of a changed mood in the union movement. But this carried no conviction, not least because of the concessions she was forced to make, including the removal of the provision for secret ballots. Wilson primed the press repeatedly with stories of his imposing his authority, but it was obvious that the smack of firm government had been at most a fairly mild slap. Callaghan was thereafter out of the spotlight as events moved rapidly his way.

The unions were almost unanimous in opposing anything that resembled legal sanctions of financial penalties on trade union members. Vic Feather, the general secretary, had to defend himself for being apparently too mild in manner when meeting Wilson and Mrs Castle. Hugh Scanlon of the Engineers had a famous clash with Wilson at Downing Street, when the Prime Minister, according to Peter Jenkins's famous account, urged the trade union leader to take his tanks off the lawn of No. 10; he refused to be another Alexander Dubcek, a reference to the Czechoslovak leader recently forced out of power by the Red Army.[20] At a special congress held at Croydon on 5 June, the TUC's own proposals were carried by the huge majority of 7,908,000 votes to 846,000.[21] It rapidly became clear also that opposition in the parliamentary party was overwhelmingly strong. Unlike revolts on Vietnam or wages policy where the rebels almost all came from the party left, this issue found supporters right across the party spectrum, from Douglas Jay on the right to Ian Mikardo on the left. Members from the centre-right such as Eric Moonman or intellectuals such as John Mackintosh were openly engaged in moves to try to depose Wilson as leader. The turmoil, by implication, left Callaghan available as a rare unifying force. One after another Cabinet ministers, many of whom had hitherto remained silent, deserted Barbara Castle. Edward Short, Peter Shore, Roy Mason, Judith Hart, Cledwyn Hughes all backed away; Crossman, more vehemently, had already done so. The ship was sinking fast. In the end, the one real heavyweight ally that Wilson and Mrs Castle still had, the Chancellor, Roy Jenkins, also (in Peter Jenkins's phrase) 'slid elegantly on to the fence'.[22] He had to rescind statements in his budget that legislation on strikes would be forthcoming. On 17 June Bob Mellish told the

Cabinet that there were not the votes to pass the penal clauses. Wilson, in fact, was for the moment helpless, out of votes and out of touch.

Callaghan was mainly an observer by this stage. He had close contacts with several union leaders, notably Danny McGarvey of the Boilermakers and Joe Gormley of the Miners. At a Lancashire Miners' dinner on 13 June, Callaghan sat next to Vic Feather who spent the meal denouncing Mrs Castle in violent language. 'His language was frankly unprintable.'[23] He reported that he had already asked Wilson to dismiss her but the Prime Minister refused. At a Cabinet meeting on 16 June Wilson seemed finally to lose authority. He admitted that the existence of penal sanctions would not have stopped a current serious dispute in British Leyland, and he now proposed withdrawing the threat of financial penalties being imposed on individual striking trade unionists. Peter Shore, formerly a Wilson loyalist, turned on Barbara Castle for being over-emotional and strongly backed the TUC. Callaghan had no need now to be aggressive; his tactical position was so strong that he could well be magnanimous. In studiously moderate terms, he warned of the dangers of imposing fines on the unions instead of on individuals. He encouraged the Prime Minister to believe that, far from being in retreat, the government had won valuable ground, but the penal clauses were 'an exposed salient' on the front.[24] Wilson in response was almost plaintive; some thought him simply malicious. He turned not on Callaghan, whose opposition had after all been clear and consistent, but on Crossman and Jenkins for letting him down. He questioned whether he had the personal authority to conduct negotiations with the TUC alone. The Cabinet agreed that he had their confidence, but Crossman, Callaghan, and others indicated that they would not necessarily automatically endorse any settlement that resulted.

On 18 June, Wilson saw the TUC leaders with Mrs Castle his only Cabinet colleague present. They took up the lifeline offered by Vic Feather: following the hitherto obscure Bridlington Declaration of 1939, from now on the TUC would undertake to monitor industrial disputes themselves. They gave a 'solemn and binding undertaking'; hence the appearance in the press of Solomon Binding, a phantom figure who became a source of much merriment.[25] Wilson was sour and bitter when he reported to the Cabinet at 5 p.m. Callaghan struck an emollient note. 'I wanted to make it clear as one of the opponents of the clauses that I now felt we had a fighting chance of winning the next General Election and I would do everything in my power to ensure that we did.'[26]

George Thomas, the Welsh Secretary, showered Wilson with Methodistical compliments—'Hallelujah Harold' and 'Dare to be a

Daniel' were amongst his copious biblical rhetoric. In a letter later that day, he was even more effusive. 'I have never been more proud to serve under you. You kept your head when all around you were losing theirs. This is the most remarkable achievement in my lifetime. I was praying for you whilst the battle was on.... You have changed the course of our industrial history.' Thomas added that he had sent a message to Barbara Castle also, which began with the words, 'Oh! you beautiful doll!'[27] Her response to this is not recorded. Few others were as ecstatic. After Wilson had gone off to meet the press, a proposal by Judith Hart that they should give a dinner to Wilson and Mrs Castle not surprisingly fell flat, Fred Peart leading the negatives. Callaghan noted in his account of 30 June, 'Everyone is relieved; there is a great desire for unity.' Wilson, however, remained in a savage mood. He told his press secretary Trevor Lloyd Hughes that he would 'get everybody' for this betrayal. He told Richard Marsh that he was drawing up a 'charge sheet' of ministers who had engaged in tendentious press briefing. Callaghan, who had been almost sympathetic to Wilson's plight on 17–18 June, was unimpressed. 'He does show himself on these sort of occasions to be a spiteful, mean little man.' In later years, however, his disposition was to be more charitable towards his stricken leader.[28]

The crisis in the Cabinet and the Labour Party over *In Place of Strife* and its aftermath was a massive trauma for all concerned. Callaghan was in most respects the key player. His officials noted that it affected his behaviour in office. At odds with the Prime Minister and most of his leading colleagues, he became more withdrawn and secretive in his methods, not to mention more uncertain in temper. He chose to commune in private with a few trusties like Merlyn Rees, Douglas Houghton, and Tom McCaffrey. But he emerged from the carnage strong and having been proved sound in his judgement, though that won him few friends. The questions arise as to how he was able to inflict this remarkable defeat on his leader, and whether in fact his judgement was sound in the short and long term.

The question of how Callaghan managed to prevail over his Prime Minister is easily answered from most of the accounts that have appeared. They all suggest that Callaghan mounted some kind of conspiracy designed at overthrowing Wilson as leader. The published versions of the crisis by Barbara Castle, Crossman, Benn, and, of course, Wilson himself are all, to varying degrees, prejudiced against Callaghan. Benn is the most balanced, Castle understandably the most hostile towards the 'snake in the grass' at the Home Office.[29] There has been discussion of relations between the 'Jenkinsites' and the 'Callaghanites', contemplating a coup against Wilson, and focusing on the period 7–9 May. Callaghan's own perspective has never previously been revealed; his own memoirs skate rapidly over the entire debate on industrial relations which evidently he regarded as a painful episode not to be recalled at any great length. The most savage view of his behaviour came in three private letters from George Thomas, the Welsh Secretary, to Wilson, on 11 June and twice on 18 June. Thomas had been an old colleague and fellow Cardiff member of Callaghan's since 1945. The latter regarded George as a warm friend with whom he had fought shoulder to shoulder for many a stout cause. In reality, Thomas combined genuine Methodist benevolence with a certain sense of rivalry, which was to surface again in his volume of memoirs published after he had served as Speaker. He urged Wilson not to let Callaghan 'provoke' him: the latter would make mistakes through his over-confidence. After the agreement with the TUC, Thomas declared (turning to the Bible as usual), 'Our Judas Iscariot looked sick—all his intriguing will now look so shabby and tawdry.'[30]

In fact, evidence of a secret conspiracy by Callaghan to overthrow Wilson, as opposed to his open defiance in Cabinet and on the public platform, is impossible to unearth. The 'Jenkinsites' were certainly in evidence and happy to identify themselves—they included very able younger members like Taverne, Mackintosh, Marquand, Owen, Rodgers, Maclennan, and Hattersley, with some senior figures like Christopher Mayhew and Patrick Gordon Walker. It has been said that they urged the Callaghanites to come out into the open. But this was difficult to do since it was by no means clear that the latter actually existed. There were certainly colleagues whom Callaghan consulted with much regularity, including particularly his old mentor Douglas Houghton, Merlyn Rees, and his two PPSs, Roland Moyle and Gregor MacKenzie, but they certainly were not seen, and did not see themselves, as any kind of coherent group. Cabinet colleagues like George Thomson and Tony Crosland were even less open to this kind of identification.The main figures in the party manœuvres were Jenkins supporters, identified by Callaghan as 'the Mackintosh/Alan Lee Williams group of 1964/66 "intellectuals" '.[31] There was no similar group acting on Callaghan's behalf. The closest that he appears to have come to challenging Wilson was on 12 May 1969 when John Mackintosh, an able politics professor who was an ardent Jenkins supporter, saw the Home Secretary to discuss a possible change in the leadership. Callaghan, as on other occasions, agreed that Wilson claimed neither the affection nor the respect of many in the party. However he replied, as on other occasions, that 'the only time they could move was when they could show that a solid body of the Party were with them and that time had not arrived. I think he

[Mackintosh] seemed glad to get the advice, as I think he felt it was a forlorn hope.'[32]

That is about as far as any Callaghan involvement in a plot against Wilson went, then or later. Through his legal adviser Lord Goodman, he was able to obtain a retraction from David Astor of the *Observer* in August 1970 after extracts from Peter Jenkins's forthcoming book *The Battle of Downing Street*, published by Charles Knight later that year, made allegations that Callaghan had acted improperly in leaks to the press and in conducting general political intrigue. The publishers' solicitors offered some deletions from the text: they included the words 'malice' on page 82, 'double-dealing' on page 115, and 'back stabbing' on page 116, which conveys the general flavour. The *Observer* apologized to Callaghan; he in turn made sure that they paid the legal charges.[33] Then as always, Callaghan made very sure that he would be well positioned in the party and the movement if any challenge to Wilson were to occur in the future. More than most, he appreciated the fragility of the Prime Minister's position and his own residual support in the parliamentary party and the unions. For all his daring, he was almost unsackable. On the other hand, he neither encouraged nor instigated any direct challenge himself. In reality, he felt that his historic moment had passed with his resignation as Chancellor. Until Harold Wilson's private announcement to him at the end of 1975 that he was going to resign as premier, he regarded himself as no longer in the running as leader, but rather as a significant senior figure who would make the best use of being in second place.

Callaghan, in short, did not defeat Wilson because of any covert intrigue, but because he was far more in tune with the overwhelming wishes of the Labour movement on the issue of penal sanctions upon trade unionists. He played his role with immense skill, keeping his distance from the TUC, judging precisely when and how vigorously he could challenge his Cabinet colleagues to sack him. It was a risky strategy, variously considered 'shabby' and 'rough' by other colleagues, including Castle, Healey, and Hattersley. But it was also highly popular with the great majority in the party. It also reflected the view of the entire trade union movement. Len Murray felt that the whole episode demonstrated Callaghan's 'intuitive' understanding of industrial relations, whereas Barbara Castle and Wilson, who viewed the unions from the outside, had been 'ideological'. In the event, Wilson lost control of his parliamentary supporters, and his Cabinet; he could never remotely claim to have control over the unions. It was all a remarkable demolition of Crossman's thesis, outlined in a republication of Walter Bagehot's *English Constitution*, to the effect that Cabinet government had been replaced by prime ministerial government, and that the Cabinet was joining the House of Lords and the monarchy as 'dignified' rather than 'efficient' parts of the constitution.[34] It was a view publicized also by Professor Mackintosh, in a lengthy work on *The Cabinet*; he dated the rise of prime ministerial government from Lloyd George's ascendancy in 1916, a view with which many Lloyd George scholars disagreed. Callaghan's demonstration that, at a time of crisis, a senior figure could have more authority over the Cabinet than the prime minister himself emphatically disproved both authors.

But was Callaghan's view of policy towards the unions correct? He has been widely condemned by centrist and right-wing commentators as having given the unions free rein, and giving political impetus to developments that led to trade union muscle being irresponsibly exerted in the 1970s. He is seen as having become his own victim in the winter of discontent in 1978–9, and as having met with the fate he deserved. Callaghan himself appeared reluctantly to accede to this view in 1991. At a colloquium held in honour of Sir Alec Cairncross's 80th birthday in Glasgow, he declared that he had been in error in 1969 and that legislation, including penal sanctions, had been necessary after all. 'I would now like to recant but not wholly', he observed.[35]

But whether this represented or represents Callaghan's settled and final view is doubtful. After 1992 he was still insistent in discussions on the matter that Donovan was the right approach, and that legal interference with free collective bargaining would be both industrially and politically wrong.[36] It is useful to look at the terms of Mrs Castle's bill. Not merely was it unacceptable to the great majority of her party, including the members of the Cabinet, its threat to penalize individual trade union members would have vastly inflamed TUC opinion in 1969 and would have led to far wider industrial unrest. Its impracticality was insisted on by at least one prominent political commentator, Alan Watkins now of the *New Statesman*, who complained that among other things the government's bill gave excessive executive power to the minister, with no redress for the unions in the face of legal sanctions. A staunch figure on the Labour right like Philip Williams felt, perhaps reluctantly, that Mrs Castle's proposed penal sanctions were unworkable. The fate of the Heath government's sanctions in its prices and incomes policy in 1972 is suggestive: legislation was openly flouted and individual unionists such as the 'Pentonville five' became popular heroes and had to be bailed out on the advice of the Official Solicitor. A Tory government could not make penal sanctions stick, but even a Labour one with its historic union links would hardly have been more successful. Harold Wilson himself admitted at the time that penal sanctions would not have solved a major dispute like the unofficial strikes at British Leyland. With the structural change in the trade union movement in the 1970s, it is not credible that they would have stopped the 'winter of discontent' either. It is not easy to see Moss Evans or Clive Jenkins ending up in jail as latter-day Tolpuddle martyrs (though Jenkins was to end up in Tasmania for other reasons). Mrs Thatcher's Act of 1981 was deliberately conceived by Jim Prior as a moderate exercise, focusing on such issues as secret ballots and the ending of secondary picketing (really only a cause for concern after Arthur Scargill's flying pickets at Saltley coke depot in 1972). Mrs Thatcher herself had to make concessions to the unions on occasions thereafter, as when lightning strikes by miners in south Wales and elsewhere forced her into conceding a temporary subsidy.

What imposed a new discipline on the unions was rather the wage cuts, massive unemployment, and political impotence they endured from the 1979–81 period onwards, followed by the costly defeat of successive strikes culminating in that of the miners in 1985. Anti-trade union legislation which would have been impossible in the late 1960s was now all too easy to impose on the demoralized unions. Thereafter they were in no position to ward off further legislative blows; the sharp decline in their own membership in the later 1980s undermined them politically as well as industrially. In 1995–6 Tony Blair's 'New Labour' could freely dissociate the party from its previous close ties with the unions, almost marginalize them completely, a position which would have been totally untenable twenty years earlier.

Callaghan, then, could argue that Barbara Castle's actual proposals in 1969 were politically unacceptable and untimely. They would not work, would divide the movement, and lose the next election. But he offered almost nothing in return. He rejected the view reached by trade unionists such as Bill McCarthy and even the TUC general secretary George Woodcock, who had served on Donovan, that fundamental changes were needed. Better that they should be drafted by a sympathetic Labour government than by a hostile right-wing Tory administration (as, of course, happened after 1979). Even the reasonable proposal for proper strike ballots to be held was dismissed. In effect, he relied on the unions behaving as they had done under Deakin and Lawther, and reforming themselves, and on their leaders arousing the same kind of deference as men like Deakin had once done. Callaghan was a passionate defender of the unions, while admitting the need for change. At Mansfield on 4 May he had reaffirmed to the Nottinghamshire miners his abiding faith in the unions. 'I was told recently by someone skilled in public relations that it is unpopular to speak up for trade unionism in this country today. If that is true so much the worse for the future.'[37] The effect was that industrial relations and strikes were left to the TUC's voluntary package of 1969. Jack Jones has insisted that it did prove its effectiveness over time. Many inter-union disputes were resolved, while the TUC's power to expel obstructive or disobedient unions was a significant weapon. An expelled union risked the prospect of having its members poached by rival unions.[38] But to most observers of British industrial relations in the 1970s, the agreement of 1969 was a failure. Solomon Binding was a man of straw. The 1970s were punctuated by massive strikes, official as well as unofficial, especially in the time of the Heath government, and then again in Callaghan's *sturm und drang* in the winter of discontent of 1978–9. Even if penal sanctions were hard to frame or to make effective, the voluntary system failed totally. The social contract of 1974–6 had its manifest limits, with grave consequences for the stability of British society and institutions, and for the revival of the British economy. Merely rejecting penal sanctions was not enough. It probably imposed on the TUC general council an impossible task, and one which was properly the remit of government. The corporate relationship, negotiated in private conclave by union barons, seemed both ineffective and profoundly undemocratic.

The outcome of 1969 was to be an immense revulsion against trade union power. The public standing of men like Bevin and Citrine in the past was no more. Union leaders like Jack Jones and Hugh Scanlon seemed entirely happy to defy the elected government and the law of the land. No reform of Mrs Thatcher's was electorally more popular, including amongst trade unionists and their families who were after all consumers as well as producers, than her curbs on union power. In 1969 Callaghan achieved a great political victory. But it was a negative, short-term one, and damagingly so. It left unresolved all the fundamental issues. It failed to answer the challenge presented by Harold Wilson and Barbara Castle that the government needed a new injection of socialist energy and to break out of its cycle of labourist-corporatist dependency with the unions. Callaghan himself, for much of his career a politician of broad sympathies who could challenge conventional views, here showed himself unduly narrow, locked into a traditional alliance already showing signs of incipient decay. The outcome was the effective neutering of the unions as instruments of power and voices of the working class, perhaps for the rest of time.

Callaghan's stand on industrial relations in 1969 had plunged the government and its leader into immense division and unpopularity. Many commentators felt it was impossible for Labour to recover anything like its old strength and vitality to put up a respectable showing in the general election that was shortly to follow. But, in one of the many astonishing twists of his career, Callaghan was also largely the instrument of rescue. More than anyone else in public life, he suddenly looked like a commanding leader of immense capacity. In a way not true of any other minister at that particular time, he achieved a great executive success, revived the fortunes of the government and the Prime Minister, and reaffirmed what a powerfully effective figure Jim Callaghan in constructive mood could be.

This came in a totally different sphere of policy, one that had hitherto played very little part in the career of Callaghan himself or in the history of any Labour government, namely Northern Ireland. The island of Ireland had been partitioned by Lloyd George in his famous settlement with Arthur Griffith and Michael Collins of Sinn Féin in December 1921. This confirmed the effective division of the island created by the 1920 Government of Ireland Act. Thereafter, for forty years the six counties of Ulster, which remained in the United Kingdom, were ossified and marginalized. They were run by a Unionist Party which governed at Stormont and dominated Northern Irish representation at Westminster. It embodied the total domination of the Protestant majority (numbering a diminishing figure of perhaps 55 per cent of the population at the time). In local government, in employment, in housing, and in education, the Catholic minority was clearly discriminated against, which political gerrymandering by Unionist politicians merely intensified. The Royal Ulster Constabulary was regarded as the partisan instrument for enforcing the Protestant ascendancy, while the Special Constabulary, the paramilitary B Specials, were universally loathed by Ulster's Catholic community. Down to the mid-1960s, however, there was no change. Attlee took care not to intervene in Northern Irish matters in 1945–51, and neither did Wilson in 1964. There was very little pressure from the Dublin government, even though it was largely in the hands of the anti-partitionist Fianna Fáil, for any disturbance of the status quo. A rare reformist Unionist Prime Minister like Terence O'Neill was eventually to be swept aside in 1969 by his Unionist Party and their Orange Order allies. There was no significant attempt to remedy the manifest discrimination exercised against Roman Catholics in Ulster between 1920 and 1967. It was a denial of basic civil liberties as stark as that operated by white supremacists in the southern states of America, with the Orange Order as an only slightly more respectable version of the Ku-Klux-Klan.

Callaghan himself had visited Northern Ireland, as we have seen, in 1954, but he focused then almost entirely on the need for social and economic development. He was no expert on the arcane problems and centuries-old tribal hostilities of the province, dating from barely recalled episodes relating to Cromwell or King Billy. Ancestral folk memories could go back eight centuries to the regime of Strongbow under King Henry II. Neither Callaghan nor his party made any attempt to raise the question of political balance or constitutional reform. The Northern Ireland Labour Party, under David Bleakley, was in any case a minor player. A maverick figure like Harry Diamond, who attempted to appeal both to Nationalists and to dispossessed working-class Protestants, was politically an uncompromising republican. Ulster remained a little-regarded section of 'the other island', best left well alone. Only occasional eruptions and acts of violence by the IRA, the military wing of Sinn Féin, reminded people on the British mainland that Northern Ireland was part of their world too, unfinished political business and a potential powder keg.

Then from the autumn of 1967 the dormant state of Northern Ireland began to be transformed dramatically. The currents of change in Europe and North America in the 1960s, including the political upsurge of protesting young people, began to have its impact in Northern Ireland too. A major civil rights campaign began. A new constitutional party was formed to represent Catholic opinion, the SDLP led by Gerry Fitt. The reform movement was mainly peaceful at first, but tension soon arose. After a violent confrontation in Londonderry's Catholic Bogside area in October 1968, Wilson summoned the Prime Minister, Terence O'Neill, to London for talks, after which modest reforms were introduced. There were marches and demonstrations down to the summer of 1968 leading to violent reactions by Protestants as Catholics from Bogside or the Falls Road began to protest against their deprivations in terms of jobs, houses, and political power, and against the injustices of the instruments of law and order. The election of the youthful Bernadette Devlin in a by-election at Mid-Ulster lent encouragement to the Nationalist cause. There was renewed IRA activity, accompanied by explosions associated with the Ulster Volunteer Force, a secret Protestant body. The ruling Unionists appeared determined to stand firm. O'Neill was removed as prime minister in April 1969 for being too prepared to make concessions. His successor was James Chichester-Clarke, another Protestant landowner, and a politician of traditional outlook and limited ability.

It was all very much the business of the Home Office at this time. There had been no secretary for Ireland, of course, since the disastrous Hamar

Greenwood in 1922. Along with the Isle of Man and the Channel Islands, Northern Ireland formed the remit of a division of the department headed by Robin North, although one that had had remarkably little to do since the 1920s. Down to 1968 the most contentious area had been the constitutional problems of the Isle of Man. Ulster's affairs were filed away under the heading 'General'. When Callaghan went to the Home Office there were no policy briefings, and no boxes whatsoever on how to handle Northern Irish affairs. They were handed over to Stormont *en bloc*. But he had soon to take action, relying on his finely honed political skills and long political experience—what he called his 'political nose'. He had very little background in matters Irish other than his name. But as the Protestant son of an Irish Roman Catholic, he had at least some advantage. Consumed as he had been by controversies concerning race, political protest, drugs, and industrial relations, he found himself plunged, as British politicians had been since the days of Pitt, Peel, and Gladstone, in the bog of Irish politics, and he reacted with considerable effect, amounting to mastery.

The affairs of Northern Ireland came to crisis point in August 1969. There was mass violence in Belfast on 2 August 1969. It was followed by a far more serious event on 12–13 August in Londonderry.[39] Following the Apprentice Boys' march by local Unionists, to commemorate their success in resisting the exiled King James II in 1690, there was almost uncontrolled disorder in the Catholic areas of the city. The Bogside was under siege and there were fierce clashes between local Nationalists and the Royal Irish Constabulary. It generated further mass confrontations in Belfast on 14 August. More than 200 houses in the Catholic Falls Road were gutted; following clashes between the Catholic residents and their supporters and the RUC and the paramilitary B Specials, ten people were killed, including a 9-year-old boy who was asleep at the time, and over a hundred injured. In fighting in Armagh, a young Catholic man was killed. Law and order in Northern Ireland, an integral part of the United Kingdom, seemed in some areas to have broken down.

Callaghan acted with great energy. Relying on instinct as much as on settled understanding, he imposed his authority on the disorderly province in a way that deeply impressed his civil servants and the wider public. He held immediate strategy meetings with officials like Neil Cairncross and Robin North. His assistant private secretary Geoffrey de Deney later reflected on how 'he picked up the whole subject and made it his own'.[40] Furthermore, he did so immediately after returning to London from a particularly difficult and taxing conference of probation officers in the north of England. After the Belfast eruption on 2 August he had decided, while on holiday in Cornwall, to send in British troops to restore order. On 14 August, he dined with Crossman at Prunier's fish restaurant. In a genial conversation, the tensions over *In Place of Strife* already forgotten, he outlined his plans for sending in battalions of the army; in passing he emphasized the need to keep it a British operation, rather than involve the United Nations. According to Crossman, 'Jim was big and burly and happy'. He said, 'It's much more fun being Home Secretary than Chancellor. This is what I like doing, taking decisions.'[41] That evening, troops from the Prince of Wales's Own Yorkshire Regiment, under the command of General Freeland, marched over Craigavon bridge in Londonderry and took up positions around the city. British troops were on military duty on the streets of Ulster for the first time since 1921. On this occasion, they were greeted with enthusiasm by the Catholic population as a protective and politically impartial force, at least at first.

But Callaghan could see that Northern Ireland required a political rather than a military solution. There were two immediate issues to be dealt with. There were the various demands for reform (notably in the housing market) coming from the civil rights movement and the SDLP. And there was the problem of law enforcement, with authority currently divided between the army and the RUC, an overwhelmingly Protestant police force. Alongside them were the B Specials, also Protestant-run, with their ambiguous paramilitary status reminiscent of the 'Auxis' in years gone by. On 19 August, a high-powered meeting took place at Downing Street between Wilson, Callaghan, and Denis Healey, the Defence Secretary, with Chichester-Clark, Brian Faulkner, and other Stormont ministers. The outcome was the so-called Downing Street Declaration, the first of many to punctuate the history of Ireland between then and the mid-1990s.[42] It was a notable harbinger of change, the first Ulster had known for almost half a century. The British army would take over responsibility for law and order from the RUC which would be answerable to the general officer commanding. At the same time, Sir John Hunt would head an inquiry into the conduct of the RUC in recent troubles. The hated B Specials would be phased out. Reforms were promised with regard to local government boundaries, the franchise, and the allocation of houses, and a parliamentary commissioner would be appointed to consider grievances. It was hailed by the Catholics as a long overdue charter of freedom. In Pavlovian fashion, it was denounced by the Revd Ian Paisley as a surrender to the IRA.

Between 27 and 29 August, Callaghan paid his first visit to Northern Ireland as Home Secretary. He was accompanied by Lord Stonham,

Roland Moyle his PPS, key civil servants like Brian Cubbon, and the reassuring figure of Tom McCaffrey as his press officer (who paid special attention to briefing the *Financial Times*). It required all his skill and no little courage, especially in a walkabout accompanied by Gerry Fitt, in the Bogside area of Londonderry, where the atmosphere was still very tense after recent deaths. He had two meetings with the Northern Ireland government in Belfast. The first was to discuss the Cameron report on disturbances during the past winter and spring. At the second, the Unionists agreed to examine housing provision, job discrimination, unemployment, and economic development generally. A minister for community relations was proposed. He also met the police commanders; Wolseley, the Police Commissioner, told him of no-go areas for his force in Belfast and Londonderry. He also had an explosive meeting with the Revd Ian Paisley. When Callaghan suggested to him that we were all the children of God, Paisley exploded, 'No, we are all the children of Wrath!' But Callaghan, having confronted aggressive figures like Shinwell, George Brown, or Roy Welensky in the past, certainly had more than sufficient strength of personality to stand up to Paisley. The Unionist Protestant firebrand emerged from their meeting looking pale and shaken.

Callaghan was evidently in his element in this emergency situation, taking charge, giving instructions, imposing himself on the crisis. It was, he recalled, 'a most enviable position for any politician to be in', with parliament not in session, Cabinet colleagues scattered abroad, and Wilson himself immured on the Scillies, though giving every encouragement. Callaghan himself made an immense impression. 'Big Jim' appeared almost physically to tower over the Unionist politicians. He gave an air of a major-league performer showing the parish-pump locals how to run their affairs. When Chichester-Clark protested that Ulster matters were so complex that he did not know where to begin, Callaghan encouraged him physically by removing his own jacket and rolling up his shirt sleeves. As always, his touch was masterly with ordinary citizens. He won over a group of potentially aggressive Shankill Protestant housewives by persuading them to sing with him 'God save the Queen'.[43] The press coverage, orchestrated by McCaffrey, was intense and helpful. On his return, Callaghan wrote to Lord Mountbatten that the army was doing well but the Unionist government was 'inert'. He added, 'I am not overoptimistic about developments.'[44]

It was followed by a period of tranquillity throughout September. The troops maintained an air of calm. A so-called 'peace line' of corrugated iron and barbed wire was built in Belfast between the Protestant Shankill and the Catholic Falls Road. Lord Scarman inquired into the troubles of Londonderry; Lord Hunt (along with Robert Mark and the Chief Constable of Glasgow) investigated the operations of the RUC. His carefully argued report in early October that they should be kept unarmed just like London policemen brought much joy to the Catholic community. Callaghan then paid a second visit on 8–13 October.[45] He was not at his best physically since he travelled with a heavy cold and arrived somewhat deaf in one ear. Nevertheless, his second visit to troubled Ulster appeared to be quite as successful as his first. He spent most of the time with the Northern Ireland Cabinet of Chichester-Clarke. Important decisions were taken on law enforcement. It was confirmed that the RUC would be disarmed, and the B Specials disbanded. Sir Arthur Young, the City of London Police Commissioner, would take over as Inspector-General of the RUC. Callaghan had invited him down to Brighton, during the Labour Party conference, to persuade him to take on the job, which he did with masterly powers of human persuasion. A new part-time Ulster Defence Regiment would also be raised, to be placed under the command of General Freeland, the British commander. There were further proposals about investment grants, improved housing, and development of the economic infrastructure. Callaghan also visited the Bogside, and was again warmly greeted by its Catholic residents. On the other hand, a grim reminder of the recurrent violence came during his visit with disturbances in Belfast, the work of Protestant militants, as a result of which three people were killed including a police constable, PC Arbuckle. Brian Cubbon had to wake up the Home Secretary very early in the morning to tell him of this death, actually the work of Ulster loyalists. The British government was criticized in some Ulster circles for releasing the Hunt report at a weekend when large numbers of Protestant pubs and Orange clubs in Belfast were open and full of customers.

Nevertheless, the positive mood remained after Callaghan's visit. The new Ulster Defence Regiment was set up in November, initially 6,000 strong but later built up to 10,000. The differences between its ethos and that of the RUC, let alone the B Specials, was underlined, although it was noticeable that Catholics were very reluctant to enlist in the UDR either. Meanwhile, the British army remained generally popular among both communities. Fears that it might have been partial to the Protestants, a legacy of the army's supposed preferences during the so-called Curragh 'mutiny' just before the First World War, proved to be groundless. The detachment and professionalism of the British troops had clearly been greatly underestimated. A period of continued relative calm continued throughout the winter. Not until violence on the Ballymurphy housing estate in Belfast at Easter time 1970 did mass disorder threaten to return, leading to a vigorous response by General Freeland and the British troops.

In the way he handled the Northern Ireland problem in the summer, autumn, and winter of 1969–70, Callaghan appeared as little less than a great deliverer to supporters of civil rights in the province. He made the most positive imprint upon Irish affairs by any British politician since David Lloyd George's mercurial negotiations with Eamon de Valera in Downing Street in the summer of 1921. Callaghan had never seemed so commanding and so effective. He also showed a remarkable sensitivity to the needs of both Northern Irish communities. He appeared utterly impartial throughout. He had personal channels to a variety of Catholic trade union figures such as Paddy Devlin of the NILP and a reasonable relationship with Gerry Fitt, the leader of the SDLP, but he was also intimate with Protestants such as David Bleakley. The fact that Callaghan had two ministers in his department who were Welshmen, Merlyn Rees (whose wife was Irish) and Elystan Morgan, may have helped his understanding of the eternal aching soul of Celtic nationalism. Social progress and civil rights seemed to be on the move. Law and order appeared much improved, with the British troops popular in most quarters. The disappearance of the B Specials was especially acclaimed on all sides. The fundamental political and constitutional questions still remained to be tackled, and prospects of progress there were unpredictable and probably gloomy. Still, there was at least one experiment in power-sharing, the new Housing Executive which allocated thousands of houses objectively to Catholics and Protestants on the basis of housing need, and which still existed in the mid-1990s. For one of the very rare periods in the troubled history of modern Ireland, the years 1968–70—comparable perhaps to 1895–1905, the era of land purchase and the 'green revolution', of Yeats and Lady Gregory and Synge and the Abbey Theatre—were a time of genuine hope.

But, as Callaghan well knew, the fundamental communal tensions of Northern Ireland remained. There was still an essential deadlock between Protestant Unionists dedicated to maintaining their own ascendancy within the United Kingdom framework, and Catholic Nationalists seeking an end to partition and absorption within the republic to the south. These were long-term matters and susceptible to no simple settlement. He was well aware of the imperfect structure of government in Northern Ireland and how shaky the maintenance of order was when it was shared by the Home Office and the frail reed of the Stormont government. Callaghan began to encourage a process of forward planning for the longer-term future of Northern Ireland amongst his civil servants. He rebutted the view of some *bienpensant* officials that an expansion of the Northern Irish economy—a modern version of 'killing home rule by kindness'—would enable Britain to circumvent the essential political problem that lay beneath. The removal of Stormont entirely was something being contemplated long before the imposition of direct rule by Westminster in 1972. A political journalist was told privately by the Home Secretary that he wanted 'to do down the Unionists'. Callaghan floated the idea of some kind of additional minister of state being appointed (Wilson pointed out that the quota of these appointments was already used up): the prospect of Terence O'Neill, the former Stormont Prime Minister, being given a peerage to act as such a member of a British government was considered at one time.[46] Until a more permanent solution was found, the entire Northern Ireland situation might fall apart. Nor, as yet, had any particular steps been taken to involve the Dublin government. In 1969–70 the assumption still held that it was purely and simply a matter of internal British government and jurisdiction. Nor was the United States offered any kind of role at that time, although the financial assistance that republican sympathizers found in North America from Noraid and other groups was a cause of friction.

By the spring of 1970, there were signs that control in Ireland was beginning to drift away. The army was in action now in Belfast and Londonderry to deal with Catholic disorder. Its early popularity was evaporating. There was greater activity from Protestant militants, while the anti-papist rhetoric of the Revd Ian Paisley attracted a huge following. The Orange Order met with as much grass-roots endorsement amongst the workers in Harland & Woolf's shipyards in Belfast or in Short Brothers' aircraft plant, as it did amongst the farmers in backwoods Antrim and county Down. Its marching season every summer, to commemorate the dimly recalled events of the battle of the Boyne and the defiance of the Protestant Apprentice Boys of Londonderry three centuries earlier, threatened massive mob violence. More serious than any of these, perhaps, was the emergence in January 1970 of a new wing of the IRA, the Provisionals or 'Provos', Marxist in ideology and dedicated to the overthrow of British rule by the most violent means. Stores of arms were being built up in the Bogside and on the Falls Road.[47] From that summer, the ruthless terrorism of the IRA was to take Northern Ireland into a horrific new phase, one that spread, by means of explosions and assassinations, on to the British mainland from the early 1970s down to mid-1994 when a precarious ceasefire resulted after negotiations between John Major and

Albert Reynolds, the leaders of the governments in London and Dublin. This was to last less than two years and to end with massive IRA bomb explosions in London's dockland and then central Manchester. Callaghan, still intensely interested in Ireland, wrote in the *Evening Standard* then, a full quarter of a century after his own involvement, strongly endorsing the Declaration and welcoming the idea of a Northern Ireland assembly being restored after twenty-three years.[48] But the ending of the IRA ceasefire in early 1996 confirmed yet again the endless communal difficulties that marked Ireland's unhappy history.

Callaghan was well aware that peace in Ireland was showing signs of sliding away when he left the Home Office in June 1970. However he argued, as did his civil servants at the time, that it was in the subsequent period of Conservative government, when Northern Ireland was under the far more relaxed and less focused regime of Reginald Maudling, that the situation really deteriorated. It was then that mass internment and the use of the Diplock courts inflamed Catholic opinion, and new violence broke out between the IRA and the British troops. General Freeland and Sir Arthur Young were both to leave Northern Ireland in September 1970, which did not help.

Callaghan paid a further visit to Northern Ireland on 25–9 March 1971 when in Opposition. Maurice Hayes, a Catholic civil servant he met and not altogether a friendly witness, saw him then as 'a big man who was still interested in the progress of the reforms he had seen as his creation'.[49] In a major speech at the Ulster Hall, Callaghan called for a new impetus to be given to the economic regeneration of Northern Ireland and roundly condemned Unionist failures in the past.[50] He was less popular in the streets this time and was jostled in Protestant areas of Belfast. There were meetings with both Social Democrat leaders and Brian Faulkner, the new Unionist Prime Minister. He urged the Northern Irish Labour Party to build itself up. He also called for the idea of an All-Ireland Council to be discussed with Jack Lynch, the Irish premier. This idea was rejected by the Heath government, but was later to be a component of the Sunningdale Agreement of 1973 which included a Council of Ireland. The scheme was endorsed again by Mrs Thatcher in her Downing Street Agreement of 1985 with Dr Fitzgerald, the Irish premier. By then, involving the Dublin government directly in Ulster's affairs seemed inescapable. Robert Armstrong's seminal paper for the Thatcher Cabinet in 1984 pushed British government policy on to a higher strategic level in this respect.

Callaghan was deeply depressed at the failure of the Heath government to follow up his own initiatives in Northern Ireland. He wrote strongly to

Maudling in August 1971 criticizing the government for not opening up political talks in an Irish context alongside security arrangements.[51] He also condemned Maudling's decision to make the Ulster Defence Regiment full-time which would impair intercommunal relations by needlessly antagonizing Catholics.[52] There was also the calamitous decision to impose internment which inflamed the Catholic community still further. Then on 30 January 1972, 'Bloody Sunday', there was the horrific violence of Londonderry at which thirteen men and boys were shot and killed by British paratroopers. None of those killed had been shown to be engaged in any violent or criminal activity. As Professor Joseph Lee has sardonically observed, 'the professionals gave an amateur performance'.[53] It was an appalling indictment of how Maudling had sacrificed the initiative Callaghan had gained. He appeared detached, almost comatose, sleepwalking to disaster. Shortly after, Stormont was abolished, direct British rule was imposed on Northern Ireland, and the troubles of the island reached a new and dangerous stage.

These grave events, though, went far beyond Callaghan's activities in Northern Ireland. Indeed, by the time of 'Bloody Sunday' he was not even Northern Irish spokesman, having given way first to Harold Wilson himself and then to Merlyn Rees. He himself took manifest pride in his Irish policies, to the extent of writing one of his very rare books, *A House Divided* (1973), on the suggestion of his fellow MP Maurice Edelman and the publisher William Collins. It was a cogent, if inevitably selective, defence of his own policies. It contained fierce condemnation of the way Maudling had lost the initiative and allowed Northern Ireland to degenerate into violence. In few areas of his varied public career had James Callaghan taken such manifest pride, or shown so marked a gift of statesmanship. Officials in the Home Office, reflecting twenty-five years later on Callaghan's period when in charge of Northern Irish affairs, felt that his replacement by Maudling at such a critical moment was little less than a tragedy for Northern Ireland. At a time when the situation still appeared manageable, without the widespread violence of later years and with some feeling of cross-community hope in the province, a historic opportunity had been lost. With a combination of manifest fairness, executive decisiveness, and imaginative flair, Callaghan had come tantalizingly close to finding a constructive way for all the people of Northern Ireland. In the next quarter of a century, that window of opportunity was not to return.

In the context of British politics in 1969–70, Callaghan's Irish initiatives, dramatically covered in television newsreels and sympathetically presented in all the British press, had a galvanizing effect. At last Harold

Wilson had successes to show. At last Labour, divided, demoralized only a few months ago, was showing that it could win and provide vigorous, firm government. From his Cabinet colleagues, Callaghan had nothing but plaudits. Anthony Wedgwood Benn was full of genuine praise. Even Barbara Castle was generous in her verdict. 'Jim is doing his stuff magnificently on TV over Northern Ireland and so far—touch wood—our sureness of touch continues. It is Jim's ideal "scenario".' She felt that Harold Wilson was somewhat grudging in his praise.[54] However, Wilson was also to demonstrate his unreserved gratitude to Callaghan later on. Indeed, from that time onwards, a great rapprochement between the two often warring leaders took place. One sign of it was Callaghan's readmission to the Inner Cabinet (or Management Committee) during the autumn of 1969. The troubles over the unions were set aside, they each accepted the other's standing without rancour. Wilson was beginning a process of regarding Callaghan as his natural—and worthy—successor.

The period at the Home Office was indeed a tumultuous one for Callaghan. In 1969 in particular, the ups and downs of his career had been breath-taking. But in the two, very different, crises of that year, he had much reinforced his political standing. In the case of the unions, he did so by emphasizing his sensitivity to the views of all wings of the party, industrial and political. He emerged a stronger figure through rebellion and challenge, and an open confrontation with Harold Wilson. In Ireland, it was a collaborative role, colleagues watching with admiration as he showed executive flair and political decisiveness. He underlined his strength through consensus rather than through challenge. In Ireland, as on other occasions in his career, he was able to strike a genuine supra-political note, which commanded the support of Quintin Hogg and the Conservatives as well. The Commons responded to his call for a better way in Ireland, emphasizing the need for social and economic progress instead of being mired in ancient communal hostility. His call for an end to religious bigotry in the province also made a strong impression in Westminster (though probably much less so in Belfast). He referred movingly to his own religious and ethnic background. 'I remember how my parents regarded the Catholics', he recalled simply.[55] He seemed to have crossed the great divide between partisan politics and genuine statesmanship. Perhaps for the first time since Gladstone, a leading British politician had actually enhanced his reputation through his intervention in the immemorial troubles of Ireland.

By any test, it was an extraordinary transformation. At the end of 1969, the *Guardian* proclaimed Callaghan as 'Politician of the Year'. He had been dropped from the Inner Cabinet in May. 'Since then Sunny Jim has dragged Ulster back from disaster; saved Labour from the combined wrath of the Tories, the Lords and the Boundaries Commission; and banished the gallows.' One Cabinet minister had observed that 'The Irish shot Harold's fox', on which the *Guardian* commented, 'The hounds won't get another chance.'[56] Perhaps more remarkably, Richard Crossman sent Callaghan an unsolicited note at this time. Their relations had gone through all manner of vicissitudes during the year. In May Crossman's diaries are full of scorn and vituperation. He had shouted across the Cabinet table at his colleague, 'Get out! Get out!' Yet by 5 September, in response to some rather snobbish comments of disparagement by Jenkins, Crossman was describing Callaghan as 'a wonderful political personality, easily the most accomplished politician in the Labour Party'.[57] His note to Callaghan, written on Boxing Day 1969, is worth reproducing in full:

> 1969 has been an astonishing in and out, up and down year for you, but ending *up and up*. You were chiefly responsible (apart from my giving up being Leader and Harold giving the Opposition Front Bench a let-out by breaking off the talks) for scuppering Parliamentary Reform (House of Lords) as well as Barbara's I.R. Bill. For the second you nearly got the push in July though I always thought the bite could not actually follow the bark on this occasion. But then you were able to show yourself indispensable first on Boundary Commission and then (even more so) in Ulster. I can well understand you being depressed at Ulster's prospects, but no one can challenge the role you have played—a tremendous come back.[58]

Thus did one of his most severe colleagues regard Callaghan just as presidential candidate Bill Clinton was to view himself in 1992—not as a busted flush or a broken reed, but as the Comeback Kid.

1. C. A. Whitmore, Ministry of Defence, to Denis Healey, 2 Mar. 1971 (Callaghan Papers, box 4); letter by Healey to *The Times*, 9 Mar. 1971.

2. Information from Mr Donald Anderson MP; Crossman, *Cabinet Diaries*, ii. 607–8 (18 Dec. 1967). An excellent treatment is Tim Bale, ' "A Deplorable Episode?" South African Arms and the Statecraft of British Social Democracy', *Labour History Review* (forthcoming).

3. Crossman, *Cabinet Diaries*, 636–7 (5 Jan. 1968).

4. See Cecil King, *The Cecil King Diary, 1965–70* (London, 1972).

5. Crossman, *Cabinet Diaries*, iii. 92 (30 May 1968).

6. Labour Party, National Executive minutes, 24 July 1968.

7. Private information from Lady Greenwood; see the present writer's entry on Greenwood in *Dictionary of National Biography*, supplement, 1980–5 (Oxford, 1990), 170–2.

8. For valuable general discussions, see Henry Phelps Brown, *The Origins of Trade Union Power* (Oxford, 1983), and Robert Taylor, *The Trade Union Question in British Politics* (Oxford, 1993).

9. Henry Pelling, 'Trade Unions, Workers and the Law', in *Popular Politics and Society in Late Victorian Britain* (London, 1968), 62–81. Professor Pelling's conclusion was that the unions' tradition of 'collective laissez-faire' was no longer in touch with the realities of contemporary British society, ibid. 81.

10. Castle, *Fighting All the Way*, 413–14.

11. Callaghan, dictated memo, 25 May 1969 (Callaghan Papers); Crossman, *Cabinet Diaries*, iii. 312–13 (8 Jan. 1969).

12. Labour Party, National Executive minutes, 26 Mar. 1969; Joe Gormley, *Battered Cherub* (London, 1982), 73–4.

13. Callaghan memo, 25 May 1969. Harold Wilson's memoirs do not refer to this meeting and are generally brief on Callaghan's role at this time.

14. Callaghan to Wilson, 2 Apr. 1969; Wilson to Callaghan, 2 Apr. 1969 (Callaghan Papers, box 26).

15. Callaghan memo, 25 May 1969; interview with Geoffrey Goodman.

16. *The Times*, 2 May 1969.

17. Crossman, *Cabinet Diaries*, iii. 480 (8 May 1969); *Castle Diaries, 1964–70*, 647 (8 May 1969).

18. Callaghan memo, 25 May 1969.

19. Jenkins, *A Life at the Centre*, 288.

20. Peter Jenkins, *The Battle of Downing Street* (London, 1970), 140.

21. *The Times*, 6 June 1970.

22. Jenkins, *The Battle of Downing Street*, 153.

23. Callaghan memo, 30 June 1969 (Callaghan Papers).

24. Ibid.

25. *The Times*, 19 June 1969; Jenkins, *The Battle of Downing Street*, 157–8.

26. Callaghan memo, 30 June 1969.

27. Ibid.; George Thomas to Harold Wilson, 18 June 1969 (Callaghan Papers, uncatalogued).

28. Callaghan memo, 30 June 1969, with MS note added, 20 May 1986.

29. *Castle Diaries, 1964–70*, 647 (8 May 1969).

30. George Thomas to Harold Wilson, 11, 18, and 18 June 1969 (Callaghan Papers, uncatalogued).

31. Callaghan memo, 25 May 1969.

32. Ibid.

33. N. Stewart-Pearson (director Charles Knight publisher) to Coward, Chance & Co. (solicitors acting for Callaghan), 5 Aug. 1970, and other materials in Callaghan Papers, box 26.

34. Interview with Lord Murray of Epping Forest. For prime ministerial government, see Crossman's introduction to new edition of Walter Bagehot, *The English Constitution* (London, 1963), 51 ff., and John Mackintosh, *The British Cabinet* (London, 1962), 384 ff.

35. Frances Cairncross and Alec Cairncross (eds.), *The Legacy of the Golden Age: The 1960s and their Economic Consequences* (London, 1992), 75. Lord Callaghan mentioned the absence of 'Bevin-type leadership' amongst the unions in the 1960s and 1970s. 'He had reluctantly accepted the need to turn to the law in spite of his preference for self-discipline whenever possible. The rot had set in and things had gone too far.'

36. This view is based on conversations with Lord Callaghan between 1990 and 1997.

37. Labour Party news release, 4 May 1969 (Callaghan Papers, box 26).
38. Interview with Jack Jones.
39. *The Times*, 13–14 Aug. 1969.
40. Interview with Sir Geoffrey de Deney.
41. Crossman, *Cabinet Diaries*, iii. 619 (14 Aug. 1969).
42. The text and accompanying letter are printed in L. J. Callaghan, *A House Divided* (London, 1973), 189–92.
43. Interview with Sir Thomas McCaffrey.
44. Callaghan to Lord Mountbatten, 10 Sept. 1969 (Callaghan Papers, box 1A).
45. Communication from Lord Hunt of Llanfairwaterdine; *The Times*, 9–14 Oct. 1969; interview with Sir Brian Cubbon. Callaghan, *A House Divided*, has a graphic account.
46. Interview with Sir Geoffrey de Deney.
47. The *Evening Standard*, 23 Feb. 1995.
48. Kevin J. Kelley, *The Longest War: Northern Ireland and the IRA* (Westport, Conn., 1988 edn.), 124–39.
49. Maurice Hayes, *Minority Verdict* (Dublin, 1995), 102–3. Hayes's account of his meetings with Callaghan (in which Hayes claims to have been offered the leadership of the Northern Ireland Labour Party) is strongly disputed, and it seems most improbable: David W. Bleakley to Callaghan, 30 Dec. 1995, Callaghan to Bleakley, 9 Jan. 1996 (Callaghan Papers, private correspondence).
50. Text in Callaghan Papers, box 1A.
51. Callaghan telephone call to Maudling, 13 Aug. 1971 (Callaghan Papers, box 1B).
52. Callaghan to Maudling, 15 June 1971 (ibid.).
53. Joseph Lee, *Ireland, 1912–1985: Politics and Society* (Cambridge, 1989), 440. He points out that the subsequent Widgery inquiry failed to establish that any of the thirteen victims were armed.
54. Tony Benn, *Office without Power: Diaries, 1968–72* (London, 1988), 196–9 (19 Aug. 1969); *Castle Diaries, 1964–70*, 701, 704 (26–8 Aug., 4 Sept. 1969).
55. *Parl. Deb.*, 5th ser., vol. 788, 47–65 (13 Oct. 1969). The reference to his parents is in col. 62. He also noted that Protestant women in Belfast had called him 'a Fenian lover'.
56. *Guardian*, 27 Dec. 1969.
57. Crossman, *Cabinet Diaries*, iii. 628 (5 Sept. 1969).
58. Crossman to Callaghan, 26 Dec. 1969 (Callaghan Papers, uncatalogued).

16

OUT OF OFFICE

In the early months of 1970 Harold Wilson's Labour government moved from bleak house to great expectations. After three years of being in the doldrums, ever since being 'blown off course' in July 1966, it suddenly looked stronger and much more confident. For the first time since the last election, the polls began to move in Labour's favour. Ministers dared hope that victory, perhaps a quite substantial one, in the general election due some time during the next twelve months was now possible.

No doubt Callaghan had played some considerable part in this, especially through his evident success in restoring order and promoting reform in Northern Ireland. This had given the whole government, at low ebb until that point, a huge boost. But the minister most identified with the change in Labour's fortunes was the Chancellor of the Exchequer, Roy Jenkins. At long last, the 'hard slog' imposed on the nation since devaluation seemed to be paying off. There were several successive months of trade surpluses in the latter part of 1969, and at the end of the year the rare prize of a solid balance of payments surplus was revealed, to the tune of £286m.[1] The strength of the reserves enabled Britain to pay off outstanding debts to the IMF and the Bank of International Settlement ahead of schedule. The economic indicators continued to be cheerful down to April 1970. Bank rate was cut to 7.5 per cent on 5 March, the first such reduction for over a year. Britain continued to do significantly better than was laid down in the letter of intent to the IMF. A massive inflow of funds enabled almost £700m. of United Kingdom overseas debts to be paid off during 1969.[2] In March, for the seventh successive month, the gold and foreign exchange reserves went up, and the reserves as a whole rose despite further large debt repayments.[3]

Roy Jenkins's budget of 14 April was a prudent one. Somewhat on the lines of Stafford Cripps in 1950 (who actually forced Attlee into a somewhat premature election then) Jenkins refused the option of a popular electioneering budget. But the Cabinet agreed with his strategy, and in any case the budget contained a modest stimulus of £220m. to the economy. There was also a further cut in bank rate to 7 per cent. There remained anxiety at the sharp inflationary rise in wage levels: Solomon Binding was not doing his work at all. But the consequences would not be felt for quite some time. At this particular period, the Labour government contemplated a general election with confidence. Indeed, so buoyant was the mood that it was stated that almost all the 'Octobrists' who had wanted an election delayed until the autumn now demanded one at the earliest opportunity. They included Jenkins, Crossman, Crosland, Barbara Castle, and Stewart—Callaghan, characteristically, was keeping his options open. With the Conservatives under the apparently uninspiring leadership of Heath and with Powellite rumblings in the background threatening Tory unity, Labour felt certain that it could win.

The sources of party disaffection seemed less acute now. The TUC had come back into line after the burial of Barbara Castle's Industrial Relations Bill. Dissenters over the Vietnam War had at least the satisfaction that Lyndon Johnson had had to resign because of protest in America against his policies. The domestic threat of Welsh and Scottish nationalism appeared to be receding after the by-election shocks of 1967–8. In Wales, Plaid Cymru was declining in the polls after its remarkably strong showing in by-elections in Labour's bastions of Rhondda West and Caerphilly. The investiture of Charles as Prince of Wales at Caernarfon Castle in July 1969, an event attended by Callaghan as Home Secretary and orchestrated by George Thomas, the Secretary of State for Wales, had helped to suppress Welsh nationalist sentiment, and Plaid's showing in the opinion polls was almost back to its weak position of 1966. In Scotland, the Scottish Nationalists had been unable to wreak further damage on Labour since Mrs Ewing's by-election at Hamilton in 1967. A further by-election in Bute and South Ayrshire on 19 March saw Labour easily brushing the SNP aside. Secure in its Celtic strongholds and its old industrial heartland, therefore, Labour felt more at ease with itself.

Callaghan had made his own distinctive contribution to Labour's election prospects, in an episode that caused much constitutional debate. In general, like Harold Wilson himself, the Home Secretary had not been a constitutional innovator. Indeed his outlook seemed quite conservative. He had made only modest efforts to promote a bill to reform the composition of the House of Lords in 1968 and appeared almost to encourage critics to allow it to founder. He seemed positively thankful that it eventually had to be withdrawn, following a most effective guerrilla action by an unlikely pairing of critics, Michael Foot and Enoch Powell. The bill was dropped in April 1969. On the other hand, a good many commentators shared Callaghan's reservations to the full since the bill's main provision would have enabled the prime minister to nominate a significant number of life peers, in effect vastly increasingly prime ministerial patronage. There were objections to this in general terms, quite apart from the suspicions harboured about the particular manœuvres of Harold Wilson himself. Callaghan, whose relations with Wilson were glacial in April 1969 after the disputes over *In Place of Strife*, clearly viewed the defeat of a bill he was supposed to be in charge of with a marked absence of pain.[4]

He had no great enthusiasm either for government proposals for extending Welsh and Scottish devolution. They were essentially the product of SNP and Plaid Cymru successes in by-elections in 1967–8. These had terrified Labour officials in Scotland and Wales. The aged James Griffiths had been persuaded not to resign lest his 26,000 majority in Llanelli be under threat. Callaghan had come to accept, and indeed welcome, the creation of the Welsh Office in 1964;[5] he had a good relationship with successive Welsh secretaries, Jim Griffiths, Cledwyn Hughes, and (so he believed) George Thomas. The new department's administrative responsibilities expanded after the 1966 election into health and agriculture (to be followed in later years by education). As a Cardiff member whose closest friends included many Welshmen and some Scots, he devoted much attention when a Cabinet minister took measures to promote the economic and social fortunes of the Celtic nations. However, he viewed, as most Englishmen did, moves towards devolution as concessions to parochial nationalism, in conflict with the central power of Cabinet and parliament, as well as with socialist notions of planning. He and the conservative Patrick Gordon Walker resisted the transfer of health to the Welsh Office in 1969: Callaghan explicitly felt that he was speaking for the 'Anglicized Welsh' majority. However, Crossman managed to out-manœuvre them. When the Crowther Commission on the constitution (later the Kilbrandon Commission when Lord Crowther died) was appointed by Wilson in 1968, Callaghan was not immediately enthusiastic. No doubt like Harold Wilson himself he hoped the entire issue would go away and that the years taken up by Crowther's deliberations in Scotland and Wales would bury it for good. On the other hand, a discussion over dinner in September 1968 left Cledwyn Hughes, now the Agriculture Secretary, with the clear impression that Callaghan could get much more intellectually engaged in the question.[6] As the Crowther Commission got under way, his interest quickened, and he began to see something of John Mackintosh, an intellectual Scottish Labour MP who was an ardent devolutionist and constitutional reformer. One of his close advisers, Geoffrey de Deney, noted how, in characteristic fashion, Callaghan moved on from confronting an immediate practical problem resulting from the upsurge of nationalism in Scotland and Wales to long-term forward thinking on the constitutional structure in general. It was, Geoffrey de Deney felt, disappointing for him that Lord Crowther's replacement by Lord Kilbrandon made the commission a somewhat more 'pedestrian' operation.[7]

However, in 1969 an issue arose which saw Callaghan take a far more adventurous view of constitutional change, one which bore directly on the outcome of the next general election. The Boundary Commissioners had been sitting, and their proposals for altering the boundaries of parliamentary constituencies were of much strategic import. They provided the first changes of parliamentary boundaries since 1950. In the general election of that year, it was known that boundary changes had cost Labour many seats, perhaps up to sixty in all. It was part of Labour's folk memory that a needless display of legal rectitude by the then Home Secretary, Chuter Ede, had undermined the Attlee government. Indeed that election had seen Labour outperform the Conservative share of the poll by almost 3 per cent, but end up with an overall majority of only six. Boundary changes which favoured suburban and middle-class constituencies had had their effect. Wilson and Callaghan had been members of the Attlee government, and were determined that Labour would not make any such needless ritual sacrifice again.

When the Boundary Commissioners reported in April 1969, it was generally agreed that their proposals would be somewhat damaging to Labour. In all, they might cost the party up to twenty seats, in view of their rearranging English and Welsh boundaries in favour of growing middle-class areas; in Scotland, on the other hand, Labour might actually benefit.[8] Callaghan saw the importance of this from the start. He had lengthy private discussions with Harry Nicholas, Labour's general secretary, which confirmed that the likely consequences of redistribution might be harmful to the cause. The Home Secretary determined on pragmatic delay, untrammelled by principle. He took his stand on the impending findings of the Redcliffe-Maud Royal Commission on Local Government which was due to report by November on local government boundaries. It was not feasible, he argued, for parliamentary and local government boundaries to be considered separately. Instead, he proposed to offer only minor changes. The proposals relating to Greater London, which was not affected by Redcliffe-Maud, would go ahead. So would four exceptionally large constituencies where immediate action was needed—Billericay and

South-East Essex, the region around his native Portsmouth, Hitchin and South Bedfordshire, and the Cheadle area south of Manchester which covered over 100,000 electors as it stood. In practice, these were thought to favour Labour. The rest of the Boundary Commissioners' proposals would have to wait until after Redcliffe-Maud had been considered, in effect until after the election.[9]

This produced a good deal of cynicism from commentators who felt, and with reason, that this was a simple gerrymandering exercise by the Labour government. There was much anger from Conservatives who claimed that Callaghan was evading his statutory and legal obligations. In the Commons on 19 June, the Home Secretary was vehemently denounced. The most effective critic perhaps was John Boyd-Carpenter who declared that the Chancellor who had devalued the pound had now turned into the Home Secretary who had devalued parliament. It was, he asserted, simply a shabby and cynical manœuvre. 'He did the dirt on me and was very effective', an unabashed Callaghan later told Crossman.[10] The government's proposals went through, with inevitable massive Labour support, but were then rejected by the House of Lords, with its inbuilt Tory majority. Callaghan refused to take precipitate action. He was fortified by advice by the Attorney-General, Elwyn Jones, who pronounced that the Home Secretary had the statutory duty to lay the Boundary Commission's proposals before parliament, but no obligation to do anything about them thereafter. Orders could be laid before the House and the government could then use its parliamentary majority to ensure that they were not passed. Constitutional proprieties and partisan politics could thus be squared.

It was a viewpoint that was both technically correct and remarkably brazen. Barbara Castle worried about the 'political morality of it all'.[11] But, politically, she was right behind Callaghan's decision. Nothing could be done, she prudently felt, until Redcliffe-Maud was sorted out and that could take until 1972. Callaghan advised the Commons formally to note the Lords' contrary view but to take no further action. This view, of course, prevailed. In later years, Callaghan was embarrassed by the action he had taken over the electoral boundaries, and he was right to be so. It was a cynical partisan manœuvre, hard to square with the high public standards proclaimed before the Nolan Committee years later. At the time, though, he seemed as unembarrassed by the non-redistribution of constituencies as by the withholding of passports to Kenyan Asians. His civil servants felt that he saw it as a political, not a constitutional, matter and it would be handled accordingly. It certainly had the unanimous support of the

Cabinet, and Labour MPs in England and Wales greeted it with gratitude and relief.

Callaghan was also preparing for the election in his home base. He had carefully studied the effect of the Boundary Commission proposals on the Cardiff seats, which would henceforth be four in number. He had told Emrys Jones, the Welsh Labour agent, that the Commissioners 'have done just about as well for us in Cardiff as we could have expected'. Cardiff West, George Thomas's seat, would be the strongest for Labour, while Cardiff North, containing such suburban districts as Whitchurch and Rhiwbina, would clearly be Conservative. The new Cardiff Central seat was marginal but winnable (in fact, this seat was not to materialize in 1974).[12] However, his own Cardiff South-East, now renamed Cardiff South, would be safe enough. The urban district of Penarth, usually strongly Tory, would be removed into the Barry constituency of the Conservative Raymond Gower, while Callaghan's seat would be reinforced by Grangetown, a largely working-class ward transferred from the west. A Labour organizer told Ruth Sharpe, Callaghan's faithful secretary, that with the five wards of Grangetown, South, Splott, Adamsdown, and Roath, Cardiff South was 'healthy' with only Roath, a prosperous residential area in the centre of the city, likely to go the wrong way.[13] Even here there tended to be university lecturers and other likely Labour sympathizers. In the event, of course, there were to be no changes in Cardiff South because of Callaghan's delaying tactics in putting off the revision of boundaries.

In other ways, he took good care as always to ensure that his constituency machine was in good fighting trim. Jack Brooks, always a powerful presence, would be the agent this time. The party's finances were reasonably healthy. The indefinable element was that of morale. Rhodri Morgan, at the time a city planner who was to be elected to parliament for Cardiff West himself in 1987, told Callaghan that they were missing, in Cardiff as elsewhere, 'real drive from the party workers and supporters'. He added that 'I think all of us feel that, with honourable exceptions, what we have had has been competent bankers' government with insufficient Labour flavour to its style and achievement.'[14] People from valleys constituencies with their rock-solid Labour majorities were unwilling to come in to canvass as they had done in 1964. These views were probably quite representative of rank and file qualms, but they did not undermine the ministers' general confidence.

In the spring of 1970, Callaghan had the most tranquil period he had enjoyed since becoming Home Secretary. The great crises of the past—

race, student protest, the unions, Northern Ireland—had subsided. There were ominous rumblings from Northern Ireland where the Provisional IRA were threatening a campaign of violence. But by comparison with August 1969, the province was still relatively calm and orderly. He was able to persuade the MCC, as has been seen, to call off the impending South African tour which might well have led to grave disorder during the election campaign. On another issue, Callaghan took a more liberal line on immigration than that with which his critics associated him, when he refused to bar the entry of Colonel Ojukwo, the leader of the seceding Biafrans in the recent Nigerian civil war. This was in the face of protests from George Thomson, the Commonwealth Secretary, that it might imperil relations with the Nigerian government in Lagos. Callaghan took a robustly libertarian view here, which brought him the approval of former critics like Barbara Castle.[15] In fact, the Colonel was to flee to the Ivory Coast. In a curious twist, in due time the Nigerian head of government, General Gowon, was to enter Britain instead to enrol at the University of Warwick, more tranquil by far now after the excitements of 1968, as a mature student reading for a politics degree.

By this time, Callaghan was in a strong position politically. He had been back in the Inner Cabinet (or Management Committee) since the autumn and was a pivotal member of Labour's campaign team. His relations with Wilson continued to improve, even though the Prime Minister might still make waspish remarks behind his back and harbour suspicions of rumbling plots. The Cabinet reshuffle of the previous autumn had been helpful to Callaghan's position, too. The last rites had been concluded for George Brown's DEA, while Tony Crosland's new empire as Minister for Local Government and Regional Planning notably advanced one of Callaghan's main political allies. Also welcome was the advent of Harold Lever to the Cabinet in place of the left-winger Mrs Judith Hart, to strengthen Labour's handling of finance.

Throughout March, April, and May, Callaghan was active in building up the national organization through agents and regional organizers, and in shoring up relations with the unions who he persuaded as treasurer to step up their contributions to party funds. Crossman noted on 27 May that Callaghan was now in the inner group to run the election campaign, along with people like Peter Shore, Tommy Balogh again, and the public relations man Will Camp from British Steel. Crossman observed that he and Barbara Castle were excluded, no longer part of the personal entourage, and he felt somewhat out of things, or so he claimed.[16] Callaghan was also on the joint committee to draw up the election manifesto, along with

Shore, George Brown, Healey, Houghton, Wedgwood Benn, Ian Mikardo, Harry Nicholas, and others. The actual drafting of the manifesto would be in the hands of a group of four, Gwyn Morgan and Terry Pitt from Transport House, Peter Shore, and Tom McNally, the International Secretary, who was shortly to become an intimate long-term adviser of Callaghan's.

The opinion polls continued to go well and the local government elections in May were remarkably good for a governing party, though it was noticed that the Conservatives did well in southern England and much of the Midlands, along with new towns such as Harlow and Hemel Hempstead. *The Economist*, though, on 16 May felt certain that Heath and the Conservatives, with their unexpectedly right-wing Selsdon Park programme so much at variance with Labour's social corporatism, faced 'the apparent certainty of humiliating defeat'. Despite all the setbacks, Labour had become the natural party of government after all. It might well be 'Harold Wilson for ever and ever'.[17] With his habitual care, Wilson took soundings from all his ministers to ensure that they agreed with him over an election date. Callaghan was amongst the key figures who had now firmly swung to backing an early election, preferably in June.

One tactical consideration for Harold Wilson was the imminence of the football World Cup in Mexico.[18] It was at least possible that England, who had won the cup at Wembley in 1966, might appear in the final again, and the nation's football enthusiasts might be distracted from casting their votes for the people's party. The election date should ideally be before the final took place at the end of June. Crossman thought this a very minor consideration. This led Wilson to comment that he demonstrated his political limitations thereby. Callaghan, like Crossman a former rugby forward, but also a football follower who had spent weary hours in Ninian Park watching the usually disappointing fortunes of Cardiff City, did recognize the centrality of this aspect of popular culture. At the end of May, with a feeling of inevitability, Wilson announced that there would be a general election, voting to take place on 18 June. No one appeared to notice that this was Waterloo day.

In Cardiff South-East, Callaghan had every ground for confidence.[19] His opponent was again Norman Lloyd-Edwards, the Conservative local councillor and solicitor whom he had defeated comfortably in 1966. There were two other candidates, Richard Davies of Plaid Cymru who could hardly be a threat in so overwhelmingly Anglicized a constituency, and George Parsons, a company director and former Liberal candidate, who now stood for the National Front. No doubt, he hoped to exploit any racial tension that might result from the presence of a large black population along Bute Street, perhaps in reverse the kind of thinking that had led to the nomination of the cricketer Ted Dexter in 1964. The constituency as a whole was prosperous with few pockets of unemployment. The docks were busy, although there was continuing concern over the future of the aged East Moors steel works, which had been kept going with the help of government subsidy throughout the 1960s. But in general, Callaghan did not need to make a special effort to hold the seat in which he had been successful in seven previous contests. He could concentrate on the meetings, broadcasts, and especially press conferences of the national campaign.

The general election kicked off in magnificent warm and sunny weather with a large open-air meeting held before the main stand at Ninian Park football ground in Cardiff. The main speakers were Wilson and Callaghan, although there were also appearances from younger figures such as Ted Rowlands, the candidate for Bedwellty, the 28-year-old Neil Kinnock, and the film star Stanley Baker, of *Zulu* fame. The meeting went well enough. Yet those present (including the present writer) felt that the old snap and enthusiasm typical of Labour election rallies in south Wales over the years had been absent. Hecklers of Wilson were not being slapped down. There was a detectable sense of disillusion. Most attention focused on a cautionary note in Callaghan's own speech—'Our principal concern is the level of wage increases.'[20] Nevertheless, the campaign went on, in the same glorious weather, and Labour continued to feel confident. Benn and Crossman as diarists felt certain that victory must be theirs. (Jenkins, conversely, felt as Rab Butler had done in 1964 that the 'election might be slipping away from us'.) Heath's apparently plodding campaign, which concentrated on the rising cost of living, had according to *The Times* 'an air of incipient doom'.[21] This seems to have been peculiarly a contest when the political journalists, who travelled round together to meetings and press conferences, convinced each other that there could be only one result, a large Labour majority. The opinion polls told a similar story; the Labour lead at times appeared in double figures (12.3 per cent in the NOP), which would have meant a virtual wipe-out for the Conservatives in many parts of Britain, comparable to what was to happen in 1997.

Callaghan tried to raise the temperature with attacks on Enoch Powell's pronouncements on race. He was himself heckled by left-wing students from Reading University, which led to his expressing some reserve at the voting age being lowered to 18. But overall it was a low-key campaign, with no great enthusiasm. Labour's manifesto and speeches concentrated on being unprovocative and had little novelty. The national mood was not improved by the England football team being put out of the World Cup in Mexico. The decisive defeat, as luck would have it, was by West Germany, whom England had beaten in the final in 1966.

Then on 16 June, two days before polling, a more serious portent was announced. There was an unexpected balance of payments deficit of £13m. announced for May. It was the result of certain fortuitous elements such as the import of expensive jumbo jets (ironically, John Harris, Roy Jenkins's adviser, had suggested 11 June as the election date to ensure that it preceded the release of the trade figures). But suddenly Heath's flagging campaign seemed to be justified after all. Women voters were said to be flocking to support the bachelor Heath in unexpected numbers, mindful of price increases and uncertain prospects for family finances including house mortgages. Samuel Brittan in the *Financial Times* wrote that the balance of payments surplus had passed its peak. Output was sluggish and unemployment likely to rise.[22] There were one or two last-minute polls which suggested, almost unbelievably, that the Conservatives were in the lead after all.

When the results were announced on the night of 18–19 June, two things became apparent from the start. There was a strong and uniform Conservative swing throughout the country; in all, a 5 per cent swing from Labour compared with 1966 was the outcome. The Conservatives began to eat into Labour's total of seats and won back many of the marginal, middle-class constituencies like Oxford, Cambridge, Lancaster, and York captured by Labour in 1966. In the end, the result was 330 Conservatives, 288 Labour, 6 Liberals, and 1 Scottish Nationalist (in the Western Isles). The opinion pollsters, always slow to admit error in their sampling method, excused themselves with talk of a (very) last-minute swing to the Tories, but obviously many of the election polls must have been hopelessly wrong. Callaghan himself won Cardiff South-East without difficulty but with a majority reduced to 5,455, almost exactly half his majority in the previous election. His poll of 26,226 was just over 51 per cent. The Plaid Cymru and National Front candidates were not very significant, since both had lost their deposits, Parsons the National Front man abysmally so. Callaghan had suffered a swing of 5.1 per cent against him, more or less the national average. In Wales generally, Labour showed something of an ebb in support compared with the high tide of 1966 when they had won 32 seats, their best ever in the principality. In 1970, they ended up with 27. Carmarthen was won back from Plaid Cymru, but Cardiff North, Monmouth, Pembroke, and Conwy were lost to the Conservatives. As a sign of friction in the valleys, the octogenarian Marxist S. O. Davies held on to Merthyr Tydfil as an unofficial Labour candidate, defeating the Transport House nominee.

More significant than the results was the reason for them. The other striking feature was the low poll. It was only 72 per cent compared with 75.8 per cent in 1966 and 77.1 per cent in 1964. In Cardiff South-East it was higher than average, at 73 per cent. Labour voters in particular had voted with their feet and stayed away from the polls. Labour's vote in fact had fallen by no less than 930,000 since 1964. By contrast, Heath, who had rebuffed the racialist extremism of Powell, seemed a comparatively reassuring moderate figure, even though race factors may have helped an above-average swing in the West Midlands. The long years of party disillusion and frustration, over the economy, Vietnam, Rhodesia, strikes, and much besides, had their effect. It was not only Cardiff South-East which showed party workers less numerous and passion for the cause much diminished. Individual party membership had fallen from 830,000 in 1964 to 680,000 in 1970, according to the notoriously fictitious official figures issued from Transport House.

Many issues had taken their toll. Support for American bombing of North Vietnam was often cited as a factor that had disillusioned young voters and liberal idealists in general. Trade unionists were also more reluctant to rally round after the arguments over *In Place of Strife*. For many of them Pele and the Brazilian team victorious in the World Cup in Mexico were a far greater attraction than any British politicians. Callaghan, entrenched after the election as chairman of the NEC Home Policy Committee, wrote a memorandum for Transport House in August which emphasized the sharp fall in the poll, the lowest since the war. 'We have to try to restore a conviction in people that political activity is a valid and effective means of shaping the lives of ordinary men and women, and that politicians are people who can do it.'[23] It all meant a traumatic shift for the former Home Secretary, out of office and out of power at the age of 58. A turning point in his life had been unhappily confronted. As he went back to Upper Clayhill Farm in Sussex, he was sharply aware of being amongst what a harsh BBC television programme shown in 1971 was to call 'Yesterday's Men'.

James Callaghan's six years in government were not a period on which he looked back in later life with great pleasure or satisfaction.[24] It appeared like a series of crises, with endless outside difficulties combined with fractious relations with some of his colleagues and especially with Harold Wilson. At the Treasury he had been on the defensive for most of the time and had had to resign after giving way to what he regarded as the great personal defeat of the devaluation of the pound. At the Home Office, there were many difficult passages, especially on race relations, and the central Cabinet trauma over industrial relations. He had actually drafted a letter of resignation with the help of Douglas Houghton in 1969, but it remained undelivered.[25]

On the credit side, he had never given way, but had taken arms against his difficulties time and again. He had emerged from the Treasury still very much a major political player. Both his reputation and his image had been refurbished. At the Home Office most of the crises had resulted in his position in the party and perhaps the country becoming stronger, particularly so after what was generally felt to be his finest hour in Northern Ireland. He received ecstatic praise from his last Minister of State, Shirley Williams, a close colleague albeit one who had differed sharply with him on east African immigration and some other issues: 'It was an immense privilege to work with you. I have never encountered anyone with such grasp and judgement. I think you were quite brilliant.'[26] He had built up powerful new links with the unions and as treasurer was a pivotal figure in the affairs of the party at all levels. Of the 'big three' in 1964, George Brown was not merely out of the Cabinet but out of parliament, never to return, since he had been defeated in his marginal seat at Belper. A process of disillusion was setting in as a result of which Brown was to break his lifelong ties with the Labour Party. Harold Wilson himself had emerged with his reputation severely damaged. The election had taken the form of a personal plebiscite on the leader, as Leo Abse and others had complained. The resultant defeat could not be other than politically and personally weakening for Harold Wilson. Disputatious memoirs from Marcia Williams, Joe Haines, and others in his personal entourage after the election hardly helped. Roy Jenkins (Wilson's designated Foreign Secretary had Labour won in 1970) remained as a serious rival in any future leadership contest.

More generally, the six years of Labour government were felt by very few to have fulfilled the promise with which they began. There were individual achievements to delight liberal-minded intellectuals. The (then) left-wing editor of the *New Statesman*, Paul Johnson, rejoiced in the progress that had been achieved in making Britain a civilized nation. 'We no longer terrorise homosexuals. We do not force mothers to bring unwanted children into the world. We have made it much easier to end wrecked marriages. We have begun the true liberation of women. Children by and large get a better deal . . . We do not murder by the rope.'[27]

There were not, however, many votes in these issues at the time, however worthy any or all of them may have been. Most voters rather saw the failure to live up to the hopes of scientific and technological change outlined in 1964. The DEA of George Brown was on the scrap heap of history, along with the proposed reforms of land valuation, superannuation, the House of Lords, and much else besides. Above all, a government run by a trained economist and containing such powerful minds as Jenkins, Crosland, Healey, Jay, and Shore had been unable to transform the economy. Tony Crosland was blunt about the central economic failure. 'In 1970, unemployment was higher, inflation more rapid and the rate of growth slower than when the Conservatives left office in 1964.' The rate of growth, at 2.3 per cent per annum, had been much less than the 3.8 per cent the Conservatives had managed in 1958–64,[28] let alone the 4 per cent promised in the National Plan. It was hard to argue, even with Jenkins's remarkable success over the balance of payments, that the root causes of economic weakness had been cured. For one thing, the wage explosion of 1969–70, following the abject failure to reform the trade unions, had added seriously to cost inflation. Much more industrial trouble, observers felt sure, lay in store with dire consequences for the corporatist regime which Labour represented. Britain's role as a first-rank economic and manufacturing power was under serious threat, as thrusting efficient competitors like Germany, France, Japan, and the emergent nations of the Pacific Rim took bold leaps forward. Like the empire before it, the sterling area was being slowly dismantled.

It was to this problematic scenario that Callaghan had to attend after he had freed himself of the intense fatigue of the election and of high office. He might perhaps now subside into the background, a *passé* figure in a declining party approaching the normal retirement age and thus seeking an outlet for his abilities elsewhere. Or he might yet find his career taking a new turn, as it had done for many a senior politician previously, from Gladstone onwards. Callaghan, after all, was at 58 just the same age as Gladstone had been when he formed his first administration in 1868. Disraeli was nearly 70 when he began his major administration in 1874, while Churchill had remained Prime Minister until he was over 80. No one regarded Callaghan as any kind of veteran. The years of opposition would manifestly be years of transition. But there were many people who still believed that, even in this unpromising circumstance, Jim Callaghan's long march was far from over.

1. *The Economist*, 13 Dec. 1969.
2. *Financial Times*, 6 Mar. 1970.
3. Ibid. 3 Apr. 1970.
4. Crossman, *Cabinet Diaries*, iii. 440 (15 Apr. 1969).
5. Kenneth O. Morgan, *Rebirth of a Nation: Wales 1880–1980* (Oxford, 1981), 388.

6. Cledwyn Hughes diary, 4 Nov. 1970 (National Library of Wales, Aberystwyth, Lord Cledwyn Papers). I am indebted to Professor Charles Webster for information on the Welsh Office, and its relationship with health.

7. Interviews with Sir Brian Cubbon and Sir Geoffrey de Deney.

8. *Financial Times*, 18 July 1969, article by David Watt; material in Callaghan Papers, box 24.

9. *The Economist*, 18 Oct. 1969; material in Callaghan Papers, box 24.

10. *Parl. Deb.*, 5th ser., vol. 785, 729 ff.; Crossman, *Cabinet Diaries*, iii. 530–1 (19 June 1969).

11. *Castle Diaries*, 791 (14 Oct. 1969).

12. Callaghan to Emrys Jones, 23 Mar. 1967 (Callaghan Papers, box 15).

13. 'Ron' ? to Ruth Sharpe, 16 Mar. 1967 (ibid.).

14. Rhodri Morgan to Callaghan, 13 Mar. 1970 (ibid.).

15. *Castle Diaries, 1964–70*, 787 (16 Apr. 1970).

16. Crossman, *Cabinet Diaries*, iii. 927–8 (27 May 1970).

17. *The Economist*, 16 May 1970.

18. Crossman, *Cabinet Diaries*, iii. 846 (8 Mar. 1970).

19. This account is based on material accumulated by the author for election commentary for BBC (Wales) in 1970. The files will eventually be deposited in the National Library of Wales, Aberystwyth.

20. *The Times*, 4 June 1970.

21. Ibid. 18 June 1970. It is remarkable that this newspaper missed the significance of the latest move towards the Conservatives in the polls. For the opinions of some ministers, see Jenkins, *A Life at the Centre*, 300; Crossman, *Cabinet Diaries*, iii. 944–5 (14 June 1970), comparing the mood to Macmillan's 'never had it so good' election in 1959; *Castle Diaries, 1964–70*, 805; Benn, *Office without Power*, 292 (14 June 1970).

22. *Financial Times*, 17 June 1970; Jenkins, *A Life at the Centre*, 297.

23. Callaghan to Terry Pitt, 8 Aug. 1970 (Callaghan Papers, box 1B).

24. *Time and Chance*, 272 (referring specifically to the years 1968–9); conversations with Lord Callaghan.

25. Interview with Lord Houghton of Sowerby.

26. Shirley Williams to Callaghan, 3 July 1970 (Callaghan Papers, box 18); information from Baroness Williams.

27. *New Statesman*, 26 June 1970.

28. Anthony Crosland, *Socialism Now* (London, 1974), 18. He goes on to praise the increase in public spending, the redistribution of income, education, and housing, as successes for the government, but adds that there was 'little sign of a coherent overall egalitarian strategy', ibid. 19.

17

IN PLACE OF POWER

THE years that followed the general election of June 1970 brought an important change of rhythm and mood for Jim Callaghan. This was evident in his lifestyle as well as in his career. After years of fierce combat, in which friends would call him a 'streetfighter' and critics a 'bully', he entered upon a somewhat more mellow and reflective phase, which was to prove permanent.

This was most obviously apparent in his domestic and personal life. It meant, first, a change of home. The Callaghans' house in Blackheath had been let since 1964. After he left the Treasury in 1967, Callaghan and his family had stayed on for a few weeks in No. 11 Downing Street, pending the arrival of Roy Jenkins and his wife from Ladbroke Square. Then they lived for a short period in the private home of George Thomson, the Commonwealth Secretary, who had an official residence of his own. But a more permanent base was required, and Blackheath was no longer so suitable, bearing in mind the fact that Callaghan at 58 was approaching an age when retirement might be contemplated. In addition, with all three children married and in the process of having families of their own, the needs of a growing family of grandchildren made a different and more tranquil residence appropriate.

The change, however, was quite dramatic. The Callaghans moved from suburban London, where they had lived for over twenty years, to a substantial farm on the Sussex Weald. This arose from the suggestion of Gordon Denniss, a prominent chartered surveyor whose friendship with Callaghan had begun when they were both fire-watching during the London blitz in 1940. Subsequently, they had been neighbours in Blackheath. The friendship continued: Denniss's interests, as recorded in successive volumes of *Who's Who*, included not only farming and cricket but also 'political economy', perhaps a tribute to his links with a former Chancellor.

In 1967, Gordon Denniss persuaded Callaghan to take up a half share in Upper Clayhill Farm, about 4 miles from the medieval town of Lewes in east Sussex. Its 138 acres are set in gentle rolling country of much historical fascination and scenic charm. The opera at Glyndebourne is near by. Only an hour from London by train, it is also most conveniently placed for party conferences at Brighton, about 20 miles to the south. The main farmhouse is Elizabethan, built of red Sussex brick, with mullioned windows, but there is also a Georgian wing with sash windows, overlooking a most attractive garden. Inside there are exposed beams and a large Tudor fireplace. The bedrooms have pleasant views of the barns and nearby water meadows. The walls were adorned with prints and mementoes testifying to Callaghan's lifelong interests, particularly the navy but also his links with Cardiff and south Wales, and his interest in chess. One bedroom had also a charming print of Upper Clayhill in 1895, and a framed manuscript deed testifying to the farm's centuries-old antiquity. The dining room, in the Georgian wing, has an astonishing range of gifts and mementoes from world leaders since the 1960s, including a striking painting of the Russian landscape from Gromyko. This was to be home for the Callaghans henceforth. The purchase was completed in 1968, with the assistance of a loan from the Agricultural Mortgage Corporation. The house at Blackheath was sold, although the Callaghans also rented a small *pied-à-terre* at Carrick Court, Lambeth, from 1968 to 1976 as a London base near to Westminster.

In contrast to his busy urban life in the metropolis, Callaghan had long been attracted by the prospect of being a farmer. It afforded both rural tranquillity and the possibility of a creative, productive base of his own. Gordon Denniss further stoked up his enthusiasm. Life at Upper Clayhill Farm proved from the first to be deeply satisfying. While Audrey Callaghan could take pleasure in cultivating the gardens, Callaghan himself became increasingly expert in running the farm, and in time had the pleasure of winning prizes for the crops. Its agriculture was a mixed one, based on beef and barley. Callaghan was able to describe at length to an academic interviewer in 1974 the problems confronting beef farmers at a time of falling prices for livestock and rising costs for aminal feedstuffs.[1] In time the farm was to diversify further, into sheep farming and the cultivation of wheat and oats. Close co-operation with friendly neighbours helped with the arrangements for sheep grazing and the use of harvesters, while corn was to be marketed by Weald Granaries and sold by them on a co-operative basis. It seldom stayed in his barns for more than a day or two.

At one level, Callaghan of course became increasingly knowledgeable about agriculture and the problems of a rural economy. This added force to his fierce criticisms of the Common Agricultural Policy operated by the European Common Market. But, more profoundly, his new lifestyle as a farmer appeared to satisfy a basic need, including a deep love of the countryside. Even as Prime Minister he would be up and about the farm early in the morning, checking the security of fences and the well-being of his stock, keeping a daily rain check without fail for over a quarter of a century. He would rise in the dark of the small hours during the lambing season. Visiting the Callaghans in October 1970, Cledwyn Hughes, the former Minister of Agriculture, was struck during the evening, fortified by a meal of scrambled eggs, by his colleague's growing enthusiasm for his farm, especially for a new bull recently bought.[2] His devoted personal secretary Ruth Sharpe was somewhat alarmed at Callaghan's becoming a farmer, fearing that it might deflect him from his proper political ambitions. But the move was clearly beneficial. For the first time since he entered politics Callaghan had a major long-term hobby, an additional interest well away from Westminster. It added to a perceived sense of growing happiness and relaxation.

He could also find time now to indulge in other interests, the theatre and reading biographies. Lord Butler's *The Art of the Possible* was one which he particularly enjoyed. Retreat to the countryside, Lucullus-style, had been the choice for many senior British politicians over the years. Lloyd George had taken up horticulture at Churt and developed a famous strain of raspberries. Stanley Baldwin, actually the son of an industrial ironmaster in the West Midlands, had developed a kind of 'farmer George' image, based on the contemplation of pigs and an admiration for Mary Webb's novel *Precious Bane*, before he retreated to Bewdley. But for a leading Labour politician, recourse to farming was most unusual. Friendly observers thought it made Callaghan a warmer, more interesting, multidimensional personality. And the grandchildren all loved it.

In addition to the effects of life on the farm, Callaghan's health quite unexpectedly led to a sense of reassessment as well. Throughout an intensely strenuous and demanding political career at the highest level, he had never been seriously ill. After some traces of tuberculosis had been found when he joined the navy during the war, he had made a complete recovery. He had made lengthy journeys to Africa or the Far East on countless occasions without any ill effects. However at the start of January 1972 he went into Bart's hospital for a serious operation on his prostate which could have led to a cancerous growth. Fortunately the problem had been identified in good time, there was no malignancy, and the operation was a total success. An early visitor was Tony Benn who (in addition, no doubt, to conveying his good wishes) wanted Callaghan's view on the desirability of an early removal of Harry Nicholas as Labour's general secretary: he was soon to leave, replaced by Ron Hayward on Benn's casting vote (in preference to Gwyn Morgan whom Callaghan supported). One member of the medical team who was later to become the head of a Welsh university institution recalled Callaghan as an excellent, cheerful patient who did what he was told. As a good politician, he also seized the opportunity for a photo opportunity with some elderly patients before he left hospital.[3]

In the course of the year, a colleague like Benn detected some enduring signs of fatigue; on this occasion he helped his less competent senior colleague by sewing a button on his coat. Some journalists who talked to Callaghan some time after the operation found him in depressed mood, gloomily speculating that his political career might be over.[4] But in general he bounced back with much resilience, and re-emerged as a spry and physically vigorous 60-year-old. He gave up smoking entirely and, on entering the Foreign Office, was to give up drinking also. He also claimed to take comfort from the advice of his doctor, a Welsh-speaking practitioner from Aberaeron in Cardiganshire, that it would assist his recovery if he took as little exercise as possible. On the other hand, so serious an operation, bringing with it the first intimations of mortality, had its psychological impact on Callaghan as for many men his age. It added to a sense of perspective, of lowered tension in the face of the pressures of the political life. While he retained his keen sense of ambition, his operation made him more relaxed about what seemed the remote prospects of attaining the party leadership. Paradoxically it may also have made that goal the more likely.

It was not only health but also wealth that brought something of a changing lifestyle for Callaghan in the years of opposition after 1970. He had had no great sources of private income in 1964. The cottage in the Isle of Wight, which led to some *sub rosa* comment amongst party activists, was bought from a legacy bequeathed by Audrey's aunt. However, the purchase of a substantial farm on the Sussex Weald was a more visible sign of affluence, and the fact that Callaghan appeared by 1974 to be significantly more comfortably off than ten years earlier lent some personal controversy to a career hitherto largely free from accusations of a personal nature. He was far from alone amongst the fallen Labour leadership in facing this kind of attack. So did Healey and Jenkins amongst others, while

Harold Wilson's sudden surge of affluence, fortified by a huge advance of perhaps £250,000 from Weidenfeld & Nicolson along with serialization rights in the Sunday press, made him a constant target. By comparison with the use made by ex-Conservative Cabinet ministers in the 1980 and 1990s of the business opportunities open to them in privatized industries and the like, Callaghan's response to the prospects available was remarkably restrained. In later years, the Nolan Committee was to comment adversely on the semi-corrupt links between government office and subsequent directorships of privatized industries, merchant banks, and other perquisites of power. Callaghan himself appeared before Nolan and effectively added his voice to the criticisms.

His growing financial security was essentially the product of prudent investment and saving in insurance endowment policies and to a lesser degree in the stock market, an area in which he took a close personal interest. His Welsh parliamentary colleague Leo Abse, in a book written at this time, was to refer to Callaghan's being 'over-fascinated with money'. Abse linked this, in Freudian fashion, with his deprived childhood. Trade unionists noted that he liked 'dabbling' and he once startled Jack Jones by suggesting that his union might sell and then lease back Transport House. Certainly, like other people facing possible retirement, he took care to protect his personal and family finances, though hardly to the point of obsession. Later on, he was to set up a new personal limited company, 'Leaderwise', with investments in the Bank of Wales and other enterprises, but this was after his retirement as party leader.[5] In 1970 he still considered himself a front-line politician with conceivable, if remote, prospects of the highest office of all, and he made little effort to look for directorships or business connections. No doubt he found, as Roy Jenkins did, that City companies were less enthusiastic about taking on Labour ex-Chancellors, as compared with their Tory equivalents, even if like Reginald Maudling, Anthony Barber, or Norman Lamont they had been largely unsuccessful. Along with Lord Cobbold, former Governor of the Bank of England, he did take up one directorship, of the Italian National Bank in Siena. This was largely the result of his interest in European finance although of course it afforded occasional visits to that beautiful Tuscan hillside town. But what led to some press criticism was his friendship with one or two wealthy business associates, Sir Charles Forte, head of the hotel chain, who was a contributor to Conservative Party funds and who later made Callaghan a trustee, and more particularly Sir Julian Hodge, a business friend from Cardiff.

Julian Hodge, a man in his late sixties now, was that relatively rare phenomenon, a successful Welsh businessman, whose finance and investment house in Cardiff rivalled major institutions in the City of London. He was, equally unusually, a member of the Labour Party, and financed the party generously in meeting election expenses and other charges. In the 1966 general election, as a constituent he had contributed £500 to Callaghan's election campaign in Cardiff South-East (a fact which the party made sure did not become public knowledge) and also contributed a minibus to help with transporting Labour voters. In 1970, he provided assistance with printing and advised over poster sites.[6] But he was also a very liberal donor to good causes generally in south Wales, including medical foundations relating to cancer, and a benefactor of university education, notably financing chairs in business and accountancy in the University Colleges of Wales at Cardiff and later Aberystwyth. Callaghan was to arrange a series of Julian Hodge public lectures on banking or finance at the University College, Cardiff, to promote the Hodge foundation's work on cancer research. The first lecture in 1970 was by Leslie O'Brien, the Governor of the Bank of England, the second in 1971 by Pierre-Paul Schweitzer, managing director of the International Monetary Fund. Respectability could scarcely go further.

But controversy surfaced in 1972 when Callaghan accepted Hodge's invitation to serve on the board of directors of his new Commercial Bank of Wales.[7] He took 1,000 (later increased to 5,000) ordinary shares in consequence. The new bank had every air of respectability. Its directors included George Thomas, Callaghan's fellow Cardiff MP and a future Speaker; Sir Cennydd Treherne, the Lord Lieutenant of Glamorgan; Lord Harlech, recently ambassador to the United States; Alun Talfan Davies QC, an eminent barrister prominent in the political, educational, and media life of Wales; and Sir Goronwy Daniel, formerly head of the Welsh Office and now principal of the University College of Wales, Aberystwyth. There were also two directors of the First National Bank of Chicago, Homer J. Livingston and Gordon J. Sapstead. These were figures of the utmost probity. Few could cavil at Callaghan's justification that he had a genuine personal interest in banking in general as well as a political commitment to injecting new capital investment into the south Wales economy.

The criticisms followed two lines. There were Labour critics who felt, perhaps on doctrinaire grounds, that it was wrong for one of their leaders to accept offers for private financial gain from a millionaire capitalist. There was muffled criticism from his Cardiff constituency, which Callaghan described to George Thomas as 'impudent'. Alun Michael, a key party worker in Rhiwbina ward and in due time Callaghan's successor as member for the constituency, felt some anxiety and conveyed it to Callaghan on behalf of himself as well as others. Callaghan responded that the Commercial Bank of Wales channelled overseas investment into developing countries and could do the same for Wales. Also it was a regional bank which could harness savings for industrial development in the different areas of Britain. But he felt no obligation to have to explain his 'private actions'.[8] He remained a member of the Board of the Bank of Wales from 5 May 1972 until 4 March 1974, when he entered the government again as Foreign Secretary.

The Bank of Wales certainly had some success in assisting industrial expansion in south Wales. By 1975 it could claim a working profit of £532,000, despite the massive price inflation that followed the Arab oil embargo following the Yom Kippur War with Israel. But what formed the second, and perhaps more marginally damaging, line of attack was not the work of the Bank *per se* but its association with Julian Hodge. By 1972 he was undoubtedly a controversial figure in financial circles, almost as much so as another Labour sympathizer and contributor, Robert Maxwell. The Bank of Wales bore his personal stamp since he owned, by 1975, 255,940 of its 326,340 ordinary £1 shares. Of these 255,940 shares, 195,740 were deemed to be beneficial. At this very time, Hodge had attracted public odium for some of his other enterprises, in particular second mortgage schemes on apparently harsh terms and a pyramid-selling plan which many Labour MPs complained had brought ruin to their poorer constituents, many of them from ethnic minorities.

Callaghan had nothing to do with any of these Hodge ventures, but he suffered from guilt by association.[9] His relationship with Hodge, after all, was a close one. He took him with him to meetings of the IMF on more than one occasion, the first time to Rio de Janeiro when a visit to a luxurious yacht brought some comment. As party treasurer, he had discussions with Hodge in 1969 about raising funds for the party through the sale of 'Labour bonds'. In 1971 there were further talks about Hodge helping the party through a scheme for selling motor insurance through Hodge Motor Insurance Brokers Ltd. It aroused enthusiasm, remarkably, from Ian Mikardo but was resisted by the shopworkers' union, USDAW, the Federation of Insurance Trade Unions, and the Co-operative movement. Callaghan was to comment that he did not feel that Hodge 'sufficiently appreciates the degree of scepticism we would need to overcome in a scheme of this sort'.[10] There was also Labour criticism of the profits that Hodge himself would make out of these arrangements. Callaghan did put the scheme forward at the party conference in October 1971 but the reference back, moved by Alf Allen of USDAW, was carried by 4,358,000 to 1,642,000. The scheme therefore foundered.

Public criticisms of Hodge in the financial columns of the press inevitably tended to focus also on his friendship with Callaghan, and did the latter some temporary harm. It was said that Callaghan had been responsible for his knighthood in the 1970 honours list; in fact, he and George Thomas had vied for this role. He also had to rebut charges that he had suggested Hodge as a governor of the Bank of England. The magazine *Private Eye* conducted a persistent (and ultimately libellous) campaign against him in 1972. This expressed itself most forcefully in its 2 June issue, in an article entitled 'Julian and Jim', parodying the title of a recent French film, *Jules et Jim*.[11] It was not the first time that this satirical journal had had Callaghan in its sights. It did not actually offer any new evidence and its direct allegations (such as that Callaghan had bought his Sussex farm with money from Hodge) were all wrong. After the 1967 budget it had run a scurrilous story to the effect that Callaghan's proposal to extend relief to motor bicycles and three-wheeler cars was the result of his association with Hodge, who had a business connection with Robin Reliant three-wheelers. This accusation of corruption may have originated from gossip by *Private Eye* with a prominent Conservative journalist recently involved in legal action (and later to become a Cabinet minister), so Callaghan surmised.[12] At any rate, Callaghan's budget decision was solely the product of being warned by industrialists in Lancashire of the need to aid motor-cycle manufacture, and the inclusion of three-wheeler Reliants as well was quite fortuitous.

This episode died away, but the charges in 1972 took longer to deal with. It was believed that the Tory press had a lengthy dossier on the Callaghan–Hodge relationship which they would release at the time of the 1974 election; in fact, nothing materialized. Hodge contemplated a libel action against a radical Cardiff journal, *Rebecca*, in 1974 but the case fell through partly because Callaghan, who would have been a key witness, was Foreign Secretary at the time. In reality, the charges against Callaghan were insubstantial. His only crime, such as it was, was to know Hodge personally. Hodge himself has been described by a work of exposure as 'just a money-lender in a hurry who took advantage of the cheap money/few controls policy of the Heath years',[13] although it is doubtful whether the humble victims of his second mortgage policies would have been so charitable. A popular hostile description in Cardiff was 'the usurer of the valleys'.

The affair did Callaghan no fundamental damage, since he had nothing scandalous to hide. The Bank of Wales was a perfectly proper institution whose accounts were in the public domain. What it did show was the difficulty of creating an impeccable relationship between a major politician, particularly a Labour politician, and a leading financier. It might also, perhaps, reflect a vein of naivety on Callaghan's part. He welcomed support from Hodge's Bank of Wales for Welsh industrial development, just as he endorsed aid from Agha Abedi and the Bank of Commerce and Credit International in the 1980s for the wholly altruistic and public-spirited Commonwealth Scholarship scheme run via Cambridge University without taking sufficient account of the methods used by that Bank in building up its profits. On balance, in the early 1970s as throughout his career, Callaghan came out of the Hodge affair comparatively unblemished. Second mortgages were less troublesome to him than the slagheaps invested in by Marcia Falkender's brother were to Harold Wilson. Callaghan was not to be tarnished, as several Labour figures (among them some of his aides) were in the 1980s, by identification with, and employment by, the Maxwell empire with its record of the criminal deception of thousands of pensioners. Callaghan, however, was prudent in damage limitation exercises. Thus he was careful in his farewell honours list after his premiership ended in 1979 not to offer Hodge or indeed any financial associate a peerage. The lesson of Harold Wilson's notorious 'blue lavender paper' honours list of 1976 had been duly absorbed.

The other major personal episode in his life at this period was that, for the one and only time since 1945, he might have changed jobs. In 1973 he was seriously considered by the International Monetary Fund for the post of managing director in succession to Pierre-Paul Schweitzer. This new proposal came from the British Chancellor of the Exchequer, Anthony Barber, and was endorsed by Helmut Schmidt, shortly to be the West German Chancellor.[14] Callaghan was certainly tempted by the prospect of this change of scene. He had developed a strong interest in problems of international financial liquidity since his time at the Treasury. Of course, the very suggestion shows the high standing he had retained since that difficult period, not least for his ingenuity in devising international drawing rights in collaboration with the IMF in 1965. It would provide a new scenario and a total break with the political tensions of the past. But there were problems. Audrey Callaghan was not enthusiastic about living in Washington, away from the children and grandchildren, nor was Callaghan himself. Most important, he retained his zest for the political life at home, with still a real prospect of high office as the Conservative government of Edward Heath floundered in a variety of economic and industrial difficulties. Somewhat to his relief, his name was eventually vetoed by the French. Callaghan never regretted this outcome since he felt that he might have lost more than he would have gained by becoming attached to an international agency. Roy Jenkins was then approached by the IMF but refused to have his name put forward.[15] In the end, the Dutchman Johannes Witteveen was to be appointed instead. Thus Callaghan's one fleeting prospect of breaking free from the political life failed to materialize. There is much residual doubt as to whether he would have accepted the offer in any circumstances. It is, however, fascinating to speculate what role he might have played in 1976, when Britain had to engage in life-saving negotiations with Witteveen and the IMF, had he been not the occupant of 10 Downing Street but an international civil servant on the other side.

Callaghan, then, emerged in the early 1970s as a more mellow and relaxed politician, an affectionate grandfather, a genial host settled in an attractive farm, somewhat more comfortably off, recovered from a serious operation. Yet his ambition for the political life remained undimmed. His prospects of ever becoming leader seemed a relatively long shot. For one thing he was four years older than Wilson while there was the prospect of a challenge from still younger figures like Roy Jenkins and perhaps Denis Healey, apart from the unpredictable fortunes of Tony Benn. When Callaghan met Lord Avon (Anthony Eden) after the election, the former Conservative leader murmured that Callaghan's time at No. 10 would come in due course, but he himself rejected any possibility of it.[16] Talking to Cledwyn Hughes at home on 26 October 1970 he declared that he was 'not interested in the leadership unless Harold decided to retire or something extraordinary happened'. Time was against him. Hughes added that Callaghan said that 'Harold "hated" him. I said I doubted this; they had a very bad patch in '69 but "hate" was a strong word. He said Harold wanted Tony Benn as his successor.' Hughes demurred at this last suggestion—'too undergraduate and too unreliable' was his view, while there were also objections to Jenkins and Healey. Callaghan 'said he hoped his friends would tell him when they thought his prospects were finished. I said they would be poor friends who would encourage him if his chances were bad.'[17] Evidently his hopes were felt to be still alive.

For the moment, Callaghan retained a strong position in the party, a base for confronting any possible leadership crisis, while on the surface his relationship with Wilson did appear to be much improved. As shadow Home Secretary after the election, he was in the influential role of chairman of the National Executive's Home Policy Committee, and in effect supremo of the whole range of domestic social and economic policy. It was a role to which Tony Benn would succeed and use to much effect. In early 1971, Callaghan moved on to become spokesman on employment in succession to Barbara Castle. He was thus a prominent figure in leading the attack on the Heath government's Industrial Relations Act which entailed bringing in the kind of penal sanctions that had been resisted by him when proposed by Barbara Castle. Industrial relations, he declared, could not be run by 'barristers' courts, writs of contempt and the full panoply of the law'. Callaghan strongly attacked the government's approach as 'making for greater divisions on the shop floor'. In fact, the Industrial Relations Act proved to be virtually unenforceable, and a series of adverse decisions in the courts turned it into a near-fiasco. Labour rejoiced on 1 August 1972 when the 'Pentonville five', dockers' shop stewards sent to prison for picketing the Midland Cold Storage Company, were released on the authority of the House of Lords without having purged their contempt. There were tumultuous scenes outside the prison, a vivid demonstration of trade union power. On the other hand, since Callaghan now saw the ineffectiveness of the solemn and binding covenant of 1969 starkly revealed, he combined attacks on the Industrial Relations Act under Sir John Donaldson with an appeal for greater trade union voluntary discipline. The unions should operate proper procedures of collective bargaining, and avoid selfish and antisocial strikes that were much resented by the general public.[18] The potential dangers of the political victory he had achieved in 1969 were all too apparent.

Like other Labour leaders, too, he kept his distance prudently from the miners' strike of January–February 1972, the first national stoppage by the NUM since 1926. He sympathized with the miners' claim that they had slipped down the wages league and welcomed the considerable improvements to their pay that they gained following the Wilberforce arbitration. On the other hand, the alarming use of industrial force and the physical intimidation that accompanied the strike, especially through the secondary picketing employed by Arthur Scargill's 'flying pickets' at Saltley coke depot, was an unwelcome reminder of the difficulty that any government, Tory or Labour, faced in trying to restrain trade union power. Callaghan always argued strongly against the political strike but even lawful industrial strikes, conducted within the context of the Trades Disputes Act of 1906, had their alarming features too.[19]

He appeared to be moving somewhat to the left in his view of industrial policy at this time. It was remarkable to see a former Home Secretary defending the right of workers to resist the operation of 'bad laws', constitutionally passed through parliament. Some contemporaries speculated that he was repositioning himself in the light of new grass-roots radicalism in the party and the unions, perhaps with a leadership bid in mind. This shift to the left was the more emphatic, as will be seen in the next chapter, in his move to a much more sharply anti-European position on possible British entry into the Common Market. But in general for him, as for Labour leaders in general, this was a relatively unfocused and unattractive period, in which it seemed difficult for the party to define its objectives or its strategies effectively while in Opposition.

What was apparent was that the party was increasingly divided between right and left, the former focused on the parliamentary party, the latter on activists in the constituencies. This had happened on previous occasions in Opposition, after 1931 and after 1951. But the new 'hard' left of the early 1970s was more fundamentally radical than the parliamentary Bevanites, people like Foot, Crossman, and Barbara Castle, had ever been. They were in open alliance with a far more militant trade union movement of an almost apolitical or even anti-political kind. These new unions were far removed from Callaghan's youthful experience, with aggressive shop stewards rejecting any kind of wage restraint and urging more nationalization and central controls over the economy. There were alarming signs of the militant left in the constituencies and the unions taking the law into their own hands. There was much popular enthusiasm for the resistance of the Labour local councillors at Clay Cross in the Derbyshire coalfield in 1972 who refused to raise council house rents as required under the government's Housing Finance Act, and faced financial surcharges and possible imprisonment. Callaghan sombrely noted the popular support that they and the Pentonville five had generated among the Labour rank and file, but he did not challenge it either.

The various leftwards movements now found a remarkable charismatic leader in Tony Benn. He had changed not only his name (from Anthony Wedgwood Benn) but his entire political outlook. Previously a centrist and technocratic member of the Wilson Cabinet, pro-Europe, pro-NATO, and a supporter of Barbara Castle's Industrial Relations Bill, he underwent a political conversion following the 1970 election. In a Fabian tract, *The New Politics*, he concluded that Labour had lost because they pursued negative, right-wing policies which had disillusioned their supporters. Only a more emphatically socialist approach would return them to office. His embrace of left-wing policies went far beyond the relatively modest critique of the old Bevanites; indeed, his relations with senior figures of the Tribunite left such as Michael Foot were not very good.[20] As party chairman in 1972–3, he went much further than they in calling for a fundamental reappraisal of Labour's economic and international policies. In addition, through a 'Participation '72' campaign, he also pressed for a revamping of the constitution of the party to give grass-roots militants and enthusiasts far more influence on the leadership and policy-making procedures. It was not, however, until the founding of the Campaign for Labour Party Democracy in June 1973, with its populist campaigns on the reselection of MPs, drafting the party's election programme, the composition of the shadow Cabinet and the election of the leader, that the new grass-roots movement gained real momentum. The obvious targets were Labourist centre-right figures symbolized by Jim Callaghan. Inevitably, therefore, even though he and Benn had previously had a satisfactory working relationship without ever being close, he and Harold Wilson found themselves, as the old guard, under siege from powerful new forces of industrial, political, and generational revolt.

The political turmoil in the party reached fever pitch in April 1972 when Roy Jenkins resigned as deputy leader following fierce internal party battles over Europe. Jenkins's departure resulted from the decision to commit Labour to a referendum on membership after Britain formally joined the EEC on 1 January 1973. This decision, an idea of Benn's in the first instance, provided an inspired initiative by Harold Wilson in a bid to avoid a fundamental split in his party. It was backed by Callaghan despite his natural reluctance to challenge the primacy of parliament or interfere with the broad outlines of the constitutional system. However, he went along with the relatively anti-European majority of his colleagues. Tony Benn records the shadow Cabinet as endorsing a referendum by 8 votes to 6, the majority being Wilson, Callaghan, Foot, Benn, Mulley, Shore, Short, and Mellish, with the mainly pro-European group of Shirley Williams, Lever, Crosland, Houghton, Thomson, and Jenkins on the other side.[21] The parliamentary party mirrored these divisions. Wilson's proposal for a referendum on Europe was carried by only 129 to 96, with over 50 abstentions. Another development strongly influenced by feelings about Europe was the appointment of a new party general secretary in succession to Harry Nicholas on 29 March. After a long wrangle, and on the casting vote of the chairman, Tony Benn, the NEC appointed the leftish Ron Hayward at the expense of Gwyn Morgan, a Welsh and pro-European Transport House officer close to Callaghan and whom he strongly backed.

A major issue that now arose was that of electing the new deputy leader. It was in itself a job of only symbolic importance, one invented to gratify Herbert Morrison after the 1951 election. Contests for it had often involved trials of strength between the party's left and right wings, with the latter invariably triumphing. Callaghan refused to put his name forward in 1970 when Jenkins had become deputy leader. Now in 1972 he faced strong union pressure to enter the contest, especially from Jack Jones, the general secretary of the Transport Workers. Callaghan, however, was reluctant to intervene. Personally, of course, he was still recovering from his prostate operation. But a more important consideration was that he felt his role as party treasurer offered a stronger base, especially since he had defeated his left-wing challenger Norman Atkinson with some ease in successive elections. Callaghan took pride that he received solid constituency support as well as trade union backing. Some of the union leaders were less than enthused by his refusal to stand, however. It led to something of a rift with Jack Jones, never a particular admirer of his, which was not altogether resolved by the time of the next general election.[22]

In terms of long-term strategy, however, Callaghan's judgement was surely sound. Harold Wilson was showing increasing signs of strain after nearly a decade as leader, and his health had deteriorated. A serious stomach operation, with the resultant effect of medical drugs, did not help. The path to the succession, should the issue arise, was getting clearer. The new deputy secretary who emerged was Ted Short. He was a 'nonentity' in Callaghan's view,[23] but he defeated Michael Foot and Tony Crosland with some ease. However, his very success opened up new possibilities for Callaghan. No one thought of Short as a possible leader, while Roy Jenkins, the presumed heir-apparent, had now ruled himself out, perhaps for ever, by resigning. Healey and Crosland were not seriously in the running, while there remained the erratic meteor of Tony Benn, very talented but arousing the gravest doubts as to his political judgement. Callaghan was now more than simply treasurer of the party. His stature was illustrated by his moving the adoption of *Labour's Programme for Britain* at the Blackpool party conference in October 1972: he did so in an hour-long speech which severely overran its scheduled time. Since Denis Healey became shadow Chancellor in succession to the departed Jenkins, he also took on the imposing portfolio of shadow Foreign Secretary. For the first time perhaps since the general election, he had a real job to do and one that fully engaged his intellect and his enthusiasm. Even at the age of 60, with major changes in his lifestyle behind him, James Callaghan was still a coming man.

In the next year and a half the Heath government, never looking in command and sorely weakened at the outset by the death of Iain Macleod, fell into disarray. There was deadlock in Ireland, where Stormont had been wound up and the province placed under direct rule, with a massive rise in IRA violence in consequence. The trade unions appeared close to being ungovernable, with a series of major strikes and rising wage inflation. Barber's financial policies were calamitous, reminiscent of the Maudling spending spree of 1962–4, with 'stagflation', massive inflation and rapidly rising unemployment at one and the same time. The Heath government's woes culminated in the disastrous economic effects of the Six-Day War, the oil embargo, and a fourfold rise in world prices. The trade deficit, £196m. in August 1973, reached £270m. in November, worse than anything Labour had experienced. In January 1974 the deficit soared to a record £383m. Bank rate rose to 13 per cent, which was almost unprecedented for peacetime. Clearly even a Labour Opposition battered by internal divisions over economic policy and Europe was increasingly well placed to take over. At 61, Callaghan was now a key figure in its preparations for such an eventuality.

His authority was strengthened in early 1973 when he became party chairman, in succession to Tony Benn, a key role in what was likely to prove an election year. Here his role was to some degree a defensive one, to keep at bay Tony Benn's campaigns for more internal party democracy (as the left defined it) and more socialistic economic policies. On the former, Callaghan was strongly committed, as Gaitskell and he had been in 1960, to upholding the primacy of Labour's parliamentary representatives. They, after all, had been elected by the people at large, not just party caucuses or constituency management committees. He was strongly hostile to upsetting the balance in what Crossman had called the 'constitutional hybrid' of the Labour Party's institutions by building up either the role of the National Executive or that of the party conference as against the authority of members of parliament and their leader. But he recognized the difficult inheritance they had been left by the founding fathers. In notes after the 1970 election, he attacked the wrong-headedness of recent party conference decisions. 'Constitution is devised for permanent opposition and not preparation for Govt.', he noted.[24]

In June 1973, as party chairman, he also spelt out his concern about the changing attitude of the left-dominated National Executive towards the parliamentary party and a future Labour government. He gave four examples—encouragement to rebels against the Housing Finance Act, the NEC insistence that there should be no compensation to shareholders for the reacquisition of hived-off company assets, the ill-judged support for the day of industrial protest and stoppage which he regarded as just a political strike, and the proposed nationalization of the twenty-five leading companies by a future Labour government. He offered a vigorous pledge of endorsement to Wilson, 'a most popular leader' whose veto on the twenty-five companies issue was widely supported.[25]

As regards Benn's 'alternative' economic strategy, Callaghan sided strongly with Wilson in resisting the whole notion of the takeover of the twenty-five companies, which by extension embraced Benn's general strategy of a centralist economic policy based on planning agreements. When Tony Benn pointed out that Labour's election manifesto in 1935, under leaders such as Attlee and Morrison, proposed the mass nationalization of industry, banking, and credit, Callaghan was able to offer a personal riposte. He well recalled that election, and had taken an active part in it. The result had been a massive Labour defeat, and the party had ended up with only 150 seats. None the less, the proposal was supported by a 7 : 6 majority on 30 May at the NEC, the minority consisting of Callaghan, Healey, Foot, Shirley Williams, and two moderate trade union leaders, Walter Padley of USDAW and Sid Weighell of the NUR.[26] On the other hand, he continued to argue for a broad system of voluntarism in the industrial relations world. Collective bargaining should be based on loyalty and good faith. This was in the face of the views of his old IRSF ally Douglas Houghton, who had stood shoulder to shoulder with him in 1969 but who now felt that Labour was in the 'grip of 19th century trade unionism' and that the TUC was 'palpably weak'. He believed that 'once again the unions will lose us the election'.[27]

It was a curious period of phoney war inside the party, with militancy and inertia in combat. The steady decline of the 1980s was being foreshadowed. There was still an urge for power, but also an acute sense of profound and growing divisions within the party at all levels. There was also an awareness that Labour's social base had been narrowing with the decline of the old back-to-back working class based on heavy manufacturing and extractive industry. The party relied now to an undue extent on client votes in the public sector trade unions, including white-collar workers, and on local authority housing estates. Many of its strongholds were the oldest and least economically dynamic parts of Britain. To some degree, the apparent overwhelming power of the unions was a façade which concealed a basic structural erosion.

Nevetheless the party's high command had somehow to hang together. With Tony Benn, for instance, although Callaghan had fundamental policy differences which were to get more acute in future years, his personal relationship was still comparatively amiable. Benn reports a curious discussion on 16 May with Callaghan saying, 'My dear boy, I know what you've been going through over the last few days. This is what happens to every political figure as he breaks through to become a major figure and I want you know that I understand how you feel.' Benn records himself as feeling touched. 'I can't help liking Jim; he is so avuncular and agreeable.'[28] Wilson, by contrast, he thought paranoid. With his leader, Callaghan found that relations were still enigmatic. He still heard of Wilson making distinctly unfraternal observations about him in private. On the other hand, their policy positions were now virtually identical and they found themselves comrades-in-arms on the NEC and in the parliamentary party in keeping the left at bay and trying to make Labour a party that would appeal to the country at large and not an unrepresentative, left-wing minority within its own membership. In view of the alternatives, Wilson, now beginning to consider the various candidates for the succession when he stood down, probably in 1975 or 1976 at the latest, felt that Callaghan was really the only serious option. At times, he probably even liked him.

What was beyond question was that Wilson needed him, for his experience, his strength in the country, and his ability to keep the party together. He was able to finesse to keep much of the Benn alternative economic strategy out of any party manifesto. But on the two main issues of the day, Labour needed to find some kind of unifying position to keep its ranks in step in any future election. These were the role of the trade unions and attitudes towards the European Community. In each case, a formula was found in 1973. It was Callaghan, as the party chairman, who helped supply it in each case.

With regard to the unions, he had been heavily involved as chairman of the Home Policy Committee in discussions leading to the famous 'social contract' proclaimed by Harold Wilson during the election campaign in February 1974. This agreement had originated in the Labour/TUC Liaison Committee and was first unveiled in a joint policy document introduced by Vic Feather and Harold Wilson, *Economic Policy and the Cost of Living*, in January 1973. The dominant influence was probably Jack Jones. Labour and the TUC agreed here to seek 'a wide-ranging agreement' over inflation and the cost of living when Labour was back in government. In return, a Labour government would pursue social and economic policies congenial to the workers, or at any rate to the unions, on conciliation and arbitration procedures in industrial disputes, the redistribution of wealth, and progressive social policies such as higher pensions.

This was an attempt to give political flesh and blood to the skeletal agreement between the party and the unions sketched out during the crisis over *In Place of Strife* in 1969. It was corporatism in its most undiluted form. Callaghan himself had doubts about aspects of its effectiveness. In 1972 he told the Oxford industrial relations don Allan Flanders that he doubted the success of a 'tripartite incomes policy' and felt it better to rely on 'fiscal and monetary instruments'.[29] It was a somewhat uneven agreement. While a future Labour government laid down in detail its future programme, and in a way that perhaps compromised its role as voice for the entire nation, the union side of the bargain was distinctly unclear. There was no mention of incomes policy or even restraint, no reference to productivity, industrial efficiency, or economic modernization, little attention to the generation of wealth rather than its distribution. Even so, after the three-day week, the social contract represented a better way. In 1973–4, with the collapse of Heath's attempt to bring industrial disputes within the formal processes of the law and the national miners' strike that followed, a 'contract' with the unions was Labour's only strategic option if it hoped to win the next election. Jim Callaghan became its political embodiment. Indeed it was he who first publicized the phrase at the Blackpool party conference on 2 October 1972. There he declared that 'what Britain needs is a new Social Contract', Rousseau for the modern age, although in fact the term first appeared in Tony Benn's Fabian pamphlet *The New Politics*, in September 1970. It was to cast its long shadow over the rest of Callaghan's career and his subsequent reputation.

Over Europe, it was Callaghan, too, who produced the formula of 'renegotiation'. Under this, there would indeed be a referendum by the people but only after a sustained attempt by a future Labour government to negotiate to get better terms. The Social Contract and Renegotiation, redefining the parameters of national authority at home and abroad, were thus the twin pivots of Labour's claim for credibility before the electors and the nation. More than any living politician, Callaghan symbolized them both. On balance, of the two themes, it was Europe which loomed even more urgently than the issue of industrial relations as an area on which Labour must somehow patch up a coherent agreed policy. Thus it was that Callaghan's new standing, institutionalized in his role as party chairman, flowed naturally also from his position as shadow Foreign Secretary. Linking his past and his future, his old worldwide concerns as a young trade union official in the 1930s and as a serving officer in the Royal Navy with his future prospects as a Labour Foreign Secretary, internationalism was once again crucial for his career and his destiny.

1. Interview with Professor Anthony King in 'Talking Politics', printed in *Listener*, 15 Aug. 1974.

2. Cledwyn Hughes diary, 26 Oct. 1970 (Lord Cledwyn Papers).

3. Information from Vice-Chancellor Ian Cameron, 1995.

4. Benn, *Office without Power*, 435 (26 June 1972); interview with Geoffrey Goodman.

5. Material in Callaghan Papers, box 29; interview with Jack Jones; Leo Abse, *Private Member* (London, 1973), 245.

6. Hodge to Callaghan, 24 Mar. 1966 (enclosing £500 cheque), and other material in Callaghan Papers, box 2; Hodge to Callaghan, 9, 16 Apr. 1970 (ibid.).

7. This account is based on material on the accounts of the Commercial Bank of Wales, 1972–5, kindly sent me by Mr Gerald Rees, to whom I am indebted.

8. Interview with Mr Alun Michael MP; Callaghan to Alun Michael, 5 Dec. 1972 (Callaghan Papers, box 1A).

9. On these matters, see Dorrill and Ramsay, *Smear!*, 241–2.

10. Hodge to Callaghan, 16 Dec. 1969; Callaghan to Douglas Richards, 20 Jan. 1970 (Callaghan Papers, box 2).

11. Callaghan to Maitland Earl, 14 Nov. 1973 (Callaghan Papers, box 18); Callaghan to the editor of *Private Eye*, ? June 1972 (ibid., box 1A); *Private Eye*, 2 June 1972. A helpful general book is Timothy Sullivan, *Julian Hodge: A Biography* (London, 1981).

12. Callaghan memo, dictated 23–4 Aug. 1967 (Callaghan Papers).

13. Dorrill and Ramsay, *Smear!*, 13, 365–6 n. 13.

14. Callaghan, *Time and Chance*, 281.

15. Interview with Lord Jenkins of Hillhead.

16. Note in Callaghan Papers (uncatalogued).

17. Cledwyn Hughes diary, 26 Oct. 1970.

18. Speech of 17 May 1972 (Callaghan Papers, box 6); James Callaghan, 'The Way Forward for the Trade Unions', *AUEW Journal*, 1 (1971).

19. Material in Callaghan Papers, box 2.

20. See Michael Foot, 'Brother Tony', in *Loyalists and Loners* (London, 1986), 107 ff.

21. Benn, *Office without Power*, 421 (29 Mar. 1972).

22. Interviews with Jack Jones and Lord Callaghan.

23. Interview with Lord Callaghan.

24. Note in Callaghan Papers, box 2.

25. Tony Benn, *Against the Tide: Diaries, 1973–76* (London, 1989), 47–8 (28 June 1973).

26. Ibid. 42 (30 May 1973).

27. Houghton to Callaghan, 26 Sept. 1973; Callaghan to Houghton, 3 Jan. 1974 (Callaghan Papers, box 2).

28. Tony Benn, *Against the Tide*, 37 (16 May 1973).

29. Callaghan to Flanders, 26 Apr. 1972 (Callaghan Papers, box 1B).

18

EUROPE AND A WIDER WORLD

In the 1990s it became commonplace to regard the relationship with continental Europe as the dominant theme of British history in the second half of the twentieth century. Commentators of a pro-European outlook in particular pointed to the early challenge of the Schuman Plan in 1950; the decision to steer clear of the EEC after the Treaty of Rome and the creation of EFTA; the two unsuccessful bids to join the Common Market under first Conservative and then Labour governments in the 1960s; the eventual decision to join in 1973 followed by an approving vote in the referendum; and the subsequent long and anguished debate about the relationship with a centrally directed or even federal European union, in its monetary or political forms, for the remainder of the century. John Major in 1997 was even more harassed by party divisions over Europe than Hugh Gaitskell had been over thirty years previously. At the same time, it seemed obvious in retrospect that the alleged 'special relationship' with the Americans was increasingly one-sided and insignificant, especially after Suez; that the weakness of the pound was gradually undermining the sterling area; and that the Commonwealth by the mid-1960s had a largely symbolic and sentimental role. Europe, its opportunities and challenges to British sovereignty, therefore, clearly overshadowed every other issue.

That was certainly not how matters presented themselves to James Callaghan and most of his contemporaries in the 1960s and early 1970s. On the contrary, after the 1970 general election, he would have seen British economic revival, policy towards the trade unions, or the prospects for détente or controlled arms limitation as being quite as crucial as the prospect of Britain's becoming, as the jargon of the day put it, 'a part of Europe'. He had viewed the rebuff of Britain's application by President de Gaulle in 1967 without any great sense of loss. His stance thereafter was cool and detached, as was the case with other major Labour figures such as Denis Healey or Tony Crosland. He was neither a Euro-enthusiast nor a Europhobe. He could best be described as a Eurosceptic, without the implications attached to that term in the 1990s. He had told Michael Stewart that he did not regard the economic case for joining Europe as a strong one; the more compelling argument was also the more intangible one, namely the degree of added political influence that Britain might acquire if it merged in some form into a more unified western Europe.[1]

His world stance was Atlanticist rather than European. His experiences in government, his close links with the US Treasury and Federal Reserve during the fight to save the exchange rate in the 1960s, had confirmed a view that, when Britain was truly in crisis, the Americans would help it out. In any case, by political outlook, legal conventions, and ties of culture and sentiment, Britain had a more natural affinity to the United States than to the motley array of European nations, many of whom had traditions of political unreliability and instability. France, Douglas Jay had written, lurched 'between Bonapartism and anarchy'. Callaghan was also a natural Commonwealth man, even before he served as shadow colonial spokesman. His naval background and childhood in Portsmouth, his wartime service and attachment to Indian independence, his relationships with Commonwealth leaders, white, black, and brown, made the world-wide network of links that resulted central to his view of the world. Like Churchill, he saw Britain's world role as consisting of three concentric rings, the North Atlantic alliance, the Commonwealth, and a relationship with western Europe, but the last of these was also last in importance.

He was not enthusiastic when the Heath government took up the question of British membership of the EEC in 1971. Contemporaries were well aware that, this time, a successful application was far more likely, partly because of the passionate commitment of Heath himself, partly because the replacement of de Gaulle by Georges Pompidou had produced a French president instinctively more sympathetic to British sentiments and less obsessively fearful of Europe being undermined from within by the Anglo-Saxons. Callaghan also felt that all the causes for apprehension about the economic implications of membership of the EEC remained as before—the hated Common Agricultural Policy which would supplant a century-old British tradition of free trade and the post-war system of deficiency payments to British farmers, of whom he was now one; the unfair budget contribution demanded of the United Kingdom; the possible effect on the international role of sterling; the threat to the commercial freedom offered to Commonwealth nations, not only thriving ones like Australia but much poorer ones like Malaysia or Botswana; the weakened prospects for an effective British regional policy via the IDCs to assist more marginal areas such as Wales. Edward Heath seemed likely to sweep all these objections aside and march headlong into membership of the EEC at virtually any cost. His main argument was the commercial and industrial one which had largely won over the CBI and the manufacturing and banking communities. The underlying assumption lay in the benefits of sheer size and the economies of scale. Heath was, in Callaghan's view, basing his cause on the unproven and probably dangerous economic argument which he himself flatly contradicted.

The scepticism of Labour towards the Common Market was very apparent in 1971, and indeed was part of the leftwards movement in the party after the 1970 election. However, campaigns for mass nationalization and planning agreements, a renunciation of nuclear weapons, and removal of British troops from Northern Ireland were spearheaded by Tony Benn and the left. By contrast, over Europe Callaghan, usually regarded as a cautious, centre-right politician, surprised many by taking the lead himself. In 1971–2 he was one of the foremost campaigners against rushing into Europe, acclaimed as such by anti-marketeers from Douglas Jay on the right to Tony Benn on the left. Clearly, there were tactical factors of internal party positioning in all this as Harold Wilson's air of fallibility opened up again the prospect of a changing balance in the party and perhaps a challenge to the leadership. But it was also a reflection of Callaghan's long-held and principled suspicion of the pro-European case. At the very most he regarded the argument as unproven.

The degree of his opposition emerged with startling effect in the relatively humble location of Bitterne Park School in Southampton on 25 May 1971.[2] Here Callaghan launched a fierce attack on the government's approach to Europe in words which made it appear unlikely that any acceptable terms could ever in his view be found. He called for a long-term and informed national debate, and demanded a proper timetable from the government in which this momentous issue could be discussed. President Pompidou, he complained, wanted the language and global stance of the EEC determined by what he called a 'French continental-European approach'. This would mean 'a complete rupture of our identity'. Heath's dogmatic negotiating style meant that it was improbable that Britain could renegotiate the terms of entry once inside, over the Common Agricultural Policy or the import of cheap Commonwealth foodstuffs. He particularly attacked Pompidou's vision of a European economic and monetary union which would be potentially disastrous. It would impact upon the British exchange rate and perhaps lead to unemployment. It would affect the reserve role of sterling and its orderly rundown. Politically it would mean-breaking with old friends in the Commonwealth and the United States: 'the very words a European Europe give an aroma of continental claustrophobia.'

Perhaps the part of Callaghan's attack that caused most comment, though, was not his discussion of economic or political-legal issues but a passage in defence of the English language. Pompidou had commented in passing, during a *Panorama* programme on television, about the desirability of having French as the language of Europe. This followed an interview in *Le Soir* in which he had dismissed English as the language of the United States. Callaghan responded in robust populist style:

> Millions of people in Britain have been surprised to hear that the language of Chaucer, Shakespeare and Milton must in future be regarded as an American import from which we must protect ourselves if we are to build a new Europe. We can agree that the French own the supreme prose literature in Europe [a debatable proposition in itself]. But if we are to prove our Europeanism by accepting that French is the dominant language in the Community, then the answer is quite clear and I will say it in French to prevent any misunderstanding: 'Non, merci beaucoup.'

This uncharacteristically dogmatic and chauvinist speech caused a minor sensation. Supporters of entry into Europe felt that Callaghan was pandering to cheap insular prejudice and that the alleged threat to the 'language of Chaucer' was fictitious. It was not his finest hour, and his memoirs do not mention it. Nor was it an aspect of the Europe case to which he returned. However, for the rest of the year and in early 1972 he continued to be a vocal opponent of British entry and a critic of the EEC. He told Jack Jones, the Transport Workers' general secretary, on 29 June 1971 that they had three supreme objectives—to beat Heath, to keep the party united, and 'to stop us going into the Common Market'. He suggested that they propose a timetable at the National Executive meeting on 28 July to achieve this last objective.[3] He continued to deploy a range of arguments, mainly economic, in speeches during the autumn. He was helped in this by several like-minded correspondents. Peter Jay, an opponent of entry like his father, forwarded statistics which showed that only 21.8 per cent of British exports in 1970 went to EEC countries, while 23.2 per cent went to developing countries, many of them in the Commonwealth.[4] Mark Arnold-Forster of the *Guardian* argued that the Common Agricultural Policy meant a huge subsidy to French and other farmers, which meant that British industry would have to earn a surplus of at least £500m. to pay for it. He also attacked the injustice to British regions such as Scotland and Wales, the 'administrative mess' of the Brussels bureaucracy, and the imposition of valued added tax, 'a Tory tax through and through'. The Common Market as it stood was 'a capitalists' paradise'.[5]

Callaghan's basic premiss was that the Common Market was an inward-looking, parochial, protectionist grouping inappropriate for the 1970s with the Bretton Woods system now in process of breaking up. The EEC, he declared, was 'a concept of the 50s'. He added, 'There is a common purse into which the British housewife will pay for the privilege of supporting the French farmer. It is an outworn, out of date policy designed for the days when bigger was better.' In the Commons, using his newly acquired expertise as a working farmer, he attacked the huge increase in food prices, the price Britain would pay for ending long-standing trading preferences with the Commonwealth. As for the tariff reductions to EEC markets, the latter took only 22 per cent of total world trade in any case. A world, not a regional, answer was needed to the problems of the global economy and trade. In 'boyhood of Raleigh' sentiments redolent of his upbringing, he declared, 'For centuries we have looked towards the open sea and the world beyond, and we will continue to do so.'[6]

On another occasion, he declared that the Treaty of Rome existed simply to foster the needs of French agriculture and German industry. When told that European socialist parties and trade unions wanted Britain in, he countered, 'What suits them may not suit us.' As against possible additional exports to Europe, there were the incalculable effects of the free movement of capital on the balance of payments, of the higher cost of European-produced food, of the loss of Commonwealth and EFTA preferences in trade, and the higher cost of European imports in general. 'So it is a gamble—an act of faith.'[7] At the party conference in October 1971, he joined trade union leaders like Jack Jones and Hugh Scanlon of the Engineers in root and branch assaults on the Common Market. Tony Benn was in the chair, the mood of the delegates was strongly opposed to entry, and Roy Jenkins prudently did not intervene for fear of a hostile reception.[8]

Callaghan's opposition to entry, while couched at times in appeals to old-fashioned insular prejudice as in the 'language of Chaucer' speech, was the product of a genuine concern. Membership of the EEC as it currently existed offended both his economic judgement and his sense of history. He rebelled against it both as a pragmatist and as a patriot. On the other hand, in the course of 1972 he quickly recognized that it was not merely a matter of taking a stand on principle in a way that would unite the party, but also one of formulating appropriate tactics in the light of the near certainty that Heath's application would succeed where those of Macmillan and

Wilson had failed. Callaghan thus backed Benn's original proposal for a referendum on membership after Britain had joined. It had become a tactical necessity which Wilson also endorsed. As has been seen, the shadow Cabinet narrowly endorsed it by eight votes to six. Callaghan now had succeeded Denis Healey as foreign affairs spokesman for the party, which also imposed a level of restraint upon him. For one thing, some of his closer political friends, such as Harold Lever, George Thomson, or Cledwyn Hughes, were convinced supporters of British entry. It was clearly an issue that evoked strong feelings beyond the immediate personal entourage that surrounded Roy Jenkins. In the decisive Commons vote on 28 October 1972, Heath's proposal for British membership was comfortably carried, by 356 votes to 244. The Labour Party was seriously split. No less than 69 Labour pro-marketeers voted with the government and another 20 abstained. Wilson's speech on the final day of the six-day debate was restrained. Douglas Hurd thought it 'soporific . . . well below the level of events'. Tony Benn apparently thought it implied that, if Labour were returned at the next election, membership of the European Community would be regarded as a *fait accompli*.[9]

Callaghan himself, never one to burn too many boats or cross a superabundance of Rubicons, was also careful not to let his opposition to Europe carry him too far. From 1 January 1973 British membership of the EEC was a political and constitutional fact. Hence his insistence on the formula of 'renegotiating' the terms of entry in a future Labour administration, with a referendum to follow giving the people the right to decide. That would preserve Labour's principled opposition and ensure party unity. It also made it the more unlikely that British withdrawal from the EEC would in fact take place. However unenthusiastic, grudging, and insular it felt, Britain was in and was likely to stay in. In 1974 Callaghan was to tell the German Chancellor Helmut Schmidt, on the eve of his renegotiation marathon in Brussels and Luxembourg, that he was 'negotiating to succeed'.[10] That cast of mind was already implicit in the period of opposition two years earlier. Facts were facts. He would fight for a losing cause but not a lost one.

As shadow Foreign Secretary, however, Callaghan had a wide variety of other issues to consider beyond membership of the EEC. He did so in a way that suggested a political as well as a personal renewal. When he succeeded Roy Jenkins as foreign policy spokesman in April 1972 there was critical comment from those who felt that perhaps Healey, Jenkins, or even Crosland might prove a figure of greater stature and breadth of international vision. In fact, Callaghan made a considerable impression from the start in his new role. He could, indeed, be claimed to be Labour's best possible representative in this key area with his long-standing interest in foreign affairs going back to the war years, his activities in the 1945 parliament, his role at Strasbourg, his strong links with the United States, and his personal ties to African and Asian political leaders dating from his time as colonial policy spokesman. He also had experience of work in the Socialist International and a variety of third-world movements and organizations, while his experience as Chancellor had given him a broad insight into the economic, commercial, and monetary aspects of world affairs. He felt thoroughly at home in his new role and promptly established his international credibility after the rather inbred period of opposition after the 1970 election.With his zest for overseas travel, he clearly enjoyed his new role and put it to good use. Naturally, in a variety of areas, especially in Vietnam and the third world generally, he was likely to face a good deal of left-wing flak from socialist comrades concerned with colonial liberation and international nuclear disarmament. It was the role of his able young PPS Dr Jack Cunningham to act as his eyes and ears in this regard. But, more than any other possible foreign affairs spokesman, Callaghan as party treasurer, forthcoming party chairman, and wise old bird who could hold his own in party infighting was well placed to cope.

He was much assisted in his new role by the enlistment of the services of Tom McNally. He was a bright young Lancastrian of only 29 who once worked for the Fabians and had served since 1969 in the International Section of the Labour Party in Transport House. He at once struck up a rapport with Callaghan, perhaps more so than with Denis Healey who he considered had made much less use of him.[11] He was also wise enough to discount Callaghan's initial characteristic disclaimer to know much about foreign affairs. On the contrary, McNally recognized that, with his wide range of contacts with African and other third-world leaders and his first-hand knowledge of Russia and eastern Europe, his man was unusually well equipped for the role. He also was comforted by the fact that Callaghan appeared genuinely interested in foreign affairs issues for their own sake and not as a stepping stone to other, perhaps higher, things. On the contrary, he was struck by Callaghan's mellow, detached viewpoint. He once confided to McNally that he did not 'ache' to become prime minister as he had done in the 1960s. The result was that McNally became perhaps Callaghan's closest associate, working with him as political adviser when he served as Foreign Secretary in 1974–6 and again when he was Prime Minister in 1976–9. Throughout Callaghan gave him his head to follow up leads and ideas on a wide variety of issues. He poured forth not only short-term tactical advice or ideas on self-promotion or projection, but also long-range strategical thoughts on issues ranging from arms limitation to Scottish devolution. Unlike Harold Wilson's closest advisers who focused on leaks and moles, plots and threats to the leader's position, McNally, like Bernard Donoughue and other key advisers after 1976, took a higher ground of policy debate, at the point where tactical and strategic issues intersected. It made him a key player in Callaghan's rise to supreme office and probably made his master thereby a more enduringly successful political leader.

McNally's advice was to be important not only on issues but on personnel. One question that eventually arose was who was to be Callaghan's deputy voice in the Lords when he became Foreign Secretary in March 1974. Europe was the essential litmus paper. A violent anti-marketeer would not be helpful, but neither would someone who was passionately pro-EEC. As a result McNally persuaded Callaghan not to choose the recently ennobled Eirene White who was thought too much of a European. Instead, he turned elsewhere amongst former Welsh members and alighted on Goronwy Roberts, formerly a junior minister at the Welsh Office and hitherto associated largely with the economic and cultural affairs of the principality. A cultured and sympathetic man, Roberts was a fluent and patriotic Welsh-speaker. He had also borne the scars of serving at the Foreign Office under George Brown. He was defeated by a Plaid Cymru candidate in his Caernarfon seat in February 1974. On McNally's advice, Callaghan promptly arranged Roberts's peerage (when he became Lord Goronwy-Roberts) and in forty-eight hours he was off from the mist and damp of Snowdonia to the colour and warmth of Bali. He served in this capacity throughout the five years of Labour government.

As shadow Foreign Secretary, Callaghan had necessarily to spend time with and on the NEC, which indeed he chaired himself in 1973–4 as party chairman. But there were also ample opportunities to see world problems and leaders at first hand. An early visit was to renew his acquaintance with the Soviet Union, where the tranquillity of détente was constantly vulnerable as Russian arms policy fluctuated. There was also the important new initiative of the *Ostpolitik* launched by the German Socialist Chancellor Willy Brandt, himself a friend of Callaghan's. In August 1972 he travelled with Tom McNally to Moscow where he met Shitikov, president of the Supreme Soviet. In addition to Anglo-Soviet trade, a key item on their agenda was Russian interest in an early conference to discuss European security.[12] The germ of the 1975 Helsinki accord was thus emerging.

In July 1973 he went a second time to eastern Europe. He flew with McNally and also Ron Hayward, the new Labour Party general secretary who had succeeded Harry Nicholas, to Hungary, Bulgaria, and Romania.[13] In Bulgaria he talked to Zhivkov, its head of state, again to discuss a European security conference, along with trade and economic co-operation. In Romania he had a 'cordial' talk with President Ceauşescu In later years, the links with this abhorrent dictator proved to be embarrassing. In 1973, by contrast, he appeared as a useful critic of the Soviet empire from within who sought wider cultural links and trade with Britain. There was a constructive discussion over Romanian exports to the United Kingdom and a possible end of quota restrictions. Callaghan cannot reasonably be condemned for entering into discussions with a dictator as offensive as Ceauşescu. He might have replied to criticism as Lloyd George did to King George V in 1922 when he complained that he was likely to meet Lenin and Trotsky at the Genoa conference. 'A little while ago I had to shake hands with Sami Bey, a ruffian who was missing the whole of one day and finally traced to a sodomy house in the East End. He was the representative of Mustapha Kemal, a man who I understand has grown tired of affairs with women and has lately taken up unnatural sexual intercourse. I must confess I do not think there is very much to choose between these persons whom I am forced to meet from time to time in Your Majesty's service.'[14] Callaghan, like Lloyd George, had to accept an imperfect world as it was. In 1922, George V, it was recorded, merely 'roared with laughter'.

A particularly influential visit was that in January 1973, to North and South Vietnam and also Laos, undertaken with Tom McNally and also Ian Mikardo representing the NEC.[15] This was not an altogether smooth episode at first. Mikardo, left-wing and opinionated, was never a favourite of Callaghan, for all their common Portsmouth antecedents. He found his colleague's sharp public comments about the situation in South Vietnam unhelpful. He had to administer a private rebuke, and threaten to return to Britain immediately. Mikardo reluctantly agreed to tone down his remarks and thereafter the visit went much more smoothly in terms of personalities.

In other respects, the visit was anything but smooth. They were delayed by a faulty aircraft in Saigon, while there was also a delay in obtaining a visa to reach Hanoi, the capital of North Vietnam. The American Secretary of State Henry Kissinger had negotiated a ceasefire a few weeks before the British Labour group arrived, but it manifestly was not being observed. Callaghan was greatly struck by what he heard and saw in South-East Asia. In Saigon, he met South Vietnam's President Thieu whose bland account of civic freedoms in his country was flatly contradicted by other evidence. *En route* for Hanoi, they flew into Laos, a supposedly neutral country which had been ravaged by both sides. Hanoi appeared totally shattered, with war continuing with the South even though hostilities with the Americans were formally over. Callaghan and Mikardo met Pham Van Dong, the premier of North Vietnam, whose confidence in ultimate victory appeared ironic amidst the physical devastation and carnage around him.

Callaghan had long been sceptical about American claims in Vietnam, and his main abiding impression seems to have been the political corruption and general feebleness of the South. In talks with McNally after they returned at the start of March, he suggested that a new US aid initiative would help the ceasefire to stick.[16] The Americans' desire for a permanent peace in the region was beyond question. 'Looking ahead it is possible that they are ready to leave South East Asia altogether, except for Thailand.' He was inclined to give South Vietnam perhaps two more years in its present condition. Its régime, however, was thoroughly flawed and corrupt. He agreed with Mikardo that the North Vietnamese were happy to stop fighting against the Americans because they were certain that political victory would be theirs in the end.

The other significant visit he undertook was in January and February 1974 when he went to the Middle East.[17] Labour had a traditional attachment to Israel, very fiercely so in the case of Harold Wilson himself. It was important for its foreign spokesmen both to reaffirm this to the Israeli leaders, representative as they were of the Labour Party, and also to build bridges to the Arabs. Callaghan was well equipped to do this. Since the 1940s he had taken a relatively balanced view on the Israel–Palestinian issue. He was neither emotionally pro-Israeli as Wilson was, nor dogmatically anti-Zionist and pro-Palestinian like George Brown. It was well known that an Israeli Labour leader like David Ben Gurion always refused to meet Brown in person, whereas Callaghan's personal relations with the Israeli Labour Party were perfectly good. In the Middle East, the situation was still extremely tense following the Six-Day War. Wilson and Callaghan had met other leaders of the Socialist International—Mitterrand, Brandt, Nenni, den Uyl of the Netherlands, Soares of Portugal, Palme of Sweden, Mintoff of Malta, and Golda Meir from Israel—at the Churchill Hotel in London on 11 November 1973, to discuss the implications of the Yom Kippur War for both the Middle East and Europe.[18]

The main impact during Callaghan's visit to the Middle East came from a personal meeting he had with President Sadat of Egypt in Cairo on 2

February. In an amiable conversation, Sadat assured the Labour spokesman that he wanted a permanent peace with Israel, despite the recent war. His main criticisms appeared to be directed against King Hussein of Jordan rather than against the Israelis. Callaghan felt his criticisms in this respect to be exaggerated and unfair. Sadat assured Callaghan of his desire formally to recognize Israeli and safeguard its territorial integrity. The Palestinian Arabs should be allowed to establish themselves on the West Bank and the Gaza strip with a corridor to be created between the two areas. Callaghan passed on to Golda Meir President Sadat's earnest wish for a formal meeting of the two Middle East states, which had been locked in battle in 1949, 1956, 1967, and 1973, and to make a fresh start.

The links he established with President Sadat were important for Callaghan, and indeed the international community. He was used by President Carter as a source of wise counsel and first-hand information thereafter. The President respected Callaghan as a fount of wisdom on the area; Henry Kissinger was to be equally responsive during Callaghan's time as Foreign Secretary in 1974–6. The visit, allied to his previous visit to the Middle East and the Labour Party's long ties to the Israeli Labour government, made Callaghan's insights into security and developmental issues in the region more than usually valuable. They were to help Anglo-American responses to some degree down to the period of the Camp David peace talks in 1978. By this time the Labour government had been replaced in Israel by a new Likud administration under Menachem Begin, for whom Callaghan had a lower regard.

In this and other ways, Callaghan's insight into international affairs was much reinforced. In eastern Europe, the Far East, and the Middle East, he added to his fund of knowledge and observation at first hand. He was always a quick learner. All this fortified his view that the major dynamics of world events lay beyond the narrow internal affairs of Europe, important though they would be for a forthcoming Labour government. At a time of détente, a Labour Britain could once again act, as in the past, as honest broker in key areas. Callaghan himself, with his bargaining style and trade union negotiator's background, could play this part to perfection. Above all, these years reinforced his view of the supreme importance of the alliance between Britain and the United States, a belief to be cemented shortly by his close personal relationship with Dr Henry Kissinger. The Heath years had been notable for their extreme coolness between the two governments. The Prime Minister took every opportunity to play down the 'special relationship'. During the Yom Kippur War, he appeared to delight in aligning himself with his European partners rather than with the Americans, whom he regarded as uncritically and even disreputably pro-Israeli. Heath's enthusiasms were almost entirely focused upon Europe—Kissinger felt that his foreign policy was 'horrible' in this respect[19]—while the Nixon administration made limited efforts to rebuild even the formal relationship that existed between President Johnson and Harold Wilson. Of course, by 1973 the all-consuming fire of Watergate was in any case beginning to undermine what effective diplomatic leadership Nixon could offer.

The other abiding interest for Callaghan lay in the new possibilities for international détente and limited disarmament. This of course involved Britain's own independent nuclear deterrent. Through the hugely expensive 'Chevaline' programme, it was based on the ageing Polaris missile system, which was deeply controversial. The prospects for a European security conference were now more hopeful. Callaghan noted changing strategic perceptions in the Kremlin; eastern and western European anxiety for strategic arms limitation; the diplomatic impact of Willy Brandt's *Ostpolitik*; and the Americans' concern to reduce their worldwide obligations after the catastrophe of Vietnam. When Callaghan became Foreign Secretary and even more as Prime Minister, he was therefore to devote himself quite single-mindedly to the relatively unfamiliar issues of international security and arms limitation. It was a most difficult, technical area but, with his usual capacity for acquiring new information and insights, he made himself authoritative in it. Away from the neo-Marxist or quasi-pacifist postures struck by some members of the Labour National Executive, there was real scope for a multi-role Britain playing its own distinctive part in the search for peace.

But when he reached Israel in February 1974, Callaghan's talks with Mrs Meir coincided with the announcement of a general election in the United Kingdom. He had to make a quick return. The endless crises of the Heath government reached their climax with the trauma of another national miners' strike. Once again the NUM, fortified by their victory in 1972 and with an executive that had moved to the left even since then, appeared determined to hold out for victory. After much tense discussion in the Cabinet, when many ministers told Heath that an early appeal to the electors would bring victory on a 'who governs Britain?' slogan, Heath eventually decided to hold the election on 28 February. Labour had not been unduly confident beforehand, given its own divisions between left and right over economic, industrial, defence, and European policy. Callaghan had, as party chairman, been much involved in preparations beforehand, in drawing up policy statements and the manifesto. Here, Wilson, with

Callaghan's backing, had managed to tone down the more radical aspects considerably, particularly in eliminating Benn's aim of nationalizing twenty-five major companies and imposing state planning controls upon the economy in general. At the same time, Callaghan was also much pre-occupied in discussions about a possible move of party headquarters from Transport House to Walworth Road, near the Elephant and Castle. It was a change he viewed without much enthusiasm.[20]

Immediately on his return, Callaghan plunged into the fray. He gave Labour's first television election broadcast. McNally had advised him beforehand that inflation was proving to be the main concern of the electors, judging from the private opinion polls conducted for the party by Bob Worcester. Harold Wilson had much success in pointing out concealed price increases during the high inflation that had marked the Heath years: in February 1974 inflation stood at 15 per cent. Callaghan, McNally suggested, should focus on three issues above all—petrol price increases ('the government has stood up to the miners and sold out to the Sheikhs'), Labour's ability to arrive at an early settlement with the miners, and control of prices along with arbitration and conciliation services to moderate wage demands. He should also emphasize that Labour would reduce considerably the costs of entering the EEC.[21] The broadcast was regarded by Harold Wilson as a great success and it helped to strengthen his view that only under Callaghan would the party be in safe hands.

Between 20 and 25 February Callaghan embarked on a vigorous speaking tour, taking in Northampton, Peterborough, Leicester, Swadlincote, Cardiff, Manchester, Blackburn, Nelson, Stretford, Chorley, and Bolton.[22] He was generally well received. Overall, it was a reasonably quiet if tense campaign, since the miners had suspended strike operations during the election in order not to harm Labour's chances. In all his speeches, Callaghan particularly emphasized Labour's ability to avoid industrial conflict. 'Fixing wages by law means tension, unfairness and strikes.' He defended the proposed Advisory and Conciliation Service, and also made as much as he could of the social contract.[23] By contrast, Heath was identified with confrontation, power cuts, and the three-day week. Throughout the election, there was a detectable sense of anxiety and of social polarization. This was to be confirmed on polling day when there was a poll of 78.8 per cent, six points up on 1970 and the highest turnout since 1951.

In Cardiff South-East, Callaghan again felt pretty safe, especially as the boundary changes delayed by him as Home Secretary in 1969 were now in operation, and making his constituency somewhat more secure for Labour.[24] Working-class Grangetown was in but Penarth was out, transferred to swell the Tory majority in the Barry constituency. His Conservative opponent was a somewhat unusual character, a right-wing Ukrainian émigré, Stefan Terleski, a naturalized Briton who had become a local hotelier. There were two rival Liberals, Chris Bailey (Independent), who had fought the seat before, and B. Christon (official Liberal), and also a Plaid Cymru candidate, Keith Bush. The large housing estate at Llanrumney was a particular prize for Labour, it was believed, and much canvassing effort was devoted to it. Economically, the city showed signs of weakness. The wet docks and dry docks were still operating, though less vigorously so than in the 1960s, while East Moors steel works was as frail as ever. In the event, Callaghan's majority of 7,146 was a modest improvement on that of 1970, adding up to a swing of about 3 per cent. Terleski's vote showed a drop of 9 per cent from that of Lloyd-Edwards in the previous election. However, the combined Liberal vote, at 6,778, was surprisingly large and this provided a clue to the election result at large. Labour showed a small number of gains, but with 301 seats they were only slightly ahead of the Conservatives' 297. Their share of the poll actually fell from 43.1 per cent in 1970 to 37.2 per cent and their poll fell by over half a million. The Conservatives polled 37.9 per cent, with 220,000 more votes than Labour. What proved decisive was the much stronger showing of the Liberals, whose small tally of 14 seats masked a dramatic surge in support from 7.5 per cent of the poll in 1970 to 19.3 per cent in February 1974, with over 6 million votes. It was Liberal intervention rather than Labour's challenge which had proved decisive in showing a sufficent swing away from the Conservatives (under 2 per cent) to force them into second place.

There followed a tense period of party manœuvring.[25] Heath saw Jeremy Thorpe, the Liberal leader, privately to propose a coalition, but messages from Liberals all over the country deterred Thorpe from any thought of acceptance. Heath's position was really unsustainable. He had little realistic prospect of commanding a majority in the Commons. There were eleven Ulster Unionists in three different groups but their loyalty was no longer assured after the abolition of Stormont, which had angered them deeply. They were allied in the United Ulster Unionist Coalition and were all committed to the destruction of the Sunningdale Agreement, which clearly Heath could never accept. In addition to these habitual Irish difficulties, there had been strains in Tory ranks during the campaign; Enoch Powell actually suggested that the voters should back Labour as the more reliable in their attitudes towards the Common Market. On the Labour side, Callaghan rather than Wilson took command during this tense interlude. The older man by four years, he seemed physically and mentally the more vigorous of the two, almost relaxed after his various personal transformations since 1970. In a remarkable display of the new balance of power amongst Labour's leaders, he persuaded (or told) Wilson and fellow shadow Cabinet members to make no communication of any kind to the media.[26] An announcement that Wilson would make a post-election statement was abruptly cancelled and the television cameras sent packing. Quoting a famous if sinister phrase from American politics, Callaghan declared that Heath should be 'left hanging slowly, slowly in the wind'. The strategy, highly appropriate for a hung parliament, certainly worked. On 4 March it was announced that Heath had given up the attempt to form a government and resigned.

For the third time, Harold Wilson, physically and emotionally weary and almost against his will, became Prime Minister. At his side as senior lieutenant was James Callaghan, the new Foreign Secretary and generally felt to be the decisive force. Even though Roy Jenkins returned to the government, reluctantly returning to the Home Office, his moment had passed with his resignation over a European referendum in 1972. Younger men like Tony Crosland were content to bide their time in March 1974 as again in April 1976. Their friends noted that Callaghan was after all a man well into his sixties who had recently suffered a prostate operation.[27] But the cards had fallen in the older man's favour throughout. During years of internal party turmoil, he had kept his head. He had maintained a balanced position on Europe and domestic policy throughout the difficult opposition years. His prospects of getting further, unlike those of Jenkins, had depended on Labour winning the next general election. Against all the odds, almost against its own will, it had done so. As he entered the spacious surroundings of the Foreign Office's apartments in Carlton Gardens, Callaghan could well feel that, in a world full of surprises, his kaleidoscopic career was starting all over again.

1. Callaghan to Michael Stewart, 31 Oct. 1969 (Callaghan Papers, uncatalogued).
2. News release in Callaghan Papers, box 1B.
3. Callaghan to Jack Jones, 29 June 1971 (ibid., box 7).
4. Peter Jay to Callaghan, 1971 (ibid.).
5. Mark Arnold-Foster to Callaghan, 2 June 1971, and notes for speech (ibid.). The *Guardian* itself was strongly pro-Common Market.
6. Notes in Callaghan Papers (ibid.).
7. Ibid.
8. Benn, *Office without Power*, 454–5 (4 Oct. 1972).
9. Cited in John Campbell, *Edward Heath* (London, 1993), 403.
10. Interview with Mr Helmut Schmidt.
11. Interview with Mr Tom McNally.

12. Notes on visit in Callaghan Papers, box 7.

13. Ibid.

14. Lord Beaverbrook, *The Decline and Fall of Lloyd George* (London, 1963), 135–6.

15. Notes on visit in Callaghan Papers, box 25. Ian Mikardo does not mention this visit in his autobiography *Backbencher*, but he does refer to an earlier trip to South Vietnam in 1954 in the company of some other Labour left-wingers.

16. Callaghan to McNally, 6 Mar. 1973 (Callaghan Papers, box 7).

17. Notes of visit, ibid.

18. Record of meeting, ibid.

19. Interview with Dr Henry Kissinger.

20. Callaghan to Ron Hayward, 23 Nov. 1973. Callaghan considered Walworth Road unsuitable, 'too far from the House and too difficult to get to' (Callaghan Papers, box 1B).

21. Memo from McNally for Callaghan, 12 Feb. 1974, and other material (ibid., box 2).

22. Ibid.

23. Ibid.

24. This discussion is based on material on the 1974 elections accumulated by the author as BBC (Wales) political analyst, and on the *Western Mail*.

25. Campbell, *Edward Heath*, 611–19 has a good account of this period.

26. Interviews with Lord Callaghan and Lord Merlyn-Rees.

27. Dick Leonard to Crosland, 1 June 1976 (London School of Economics Library, Crosland Papers, 6/4).

19

NEGOTIATING TO SUCCEED

THE new Wilson government which had defied the prophecies and returned to office in March 1974 was anything but a fresh-faced, untried administration. On the contrary, its major personalities were all too familiar to the electors. Wilson, Callaghan, Healey (Chancellor of the Exchequer), Jenkins (who wanted the Treasury but returned reluctantly to the Home Office), Tony Crosland (Environment), Barbara Castle (Social Services), and Tony Benn (Trade and Industry) had all been mainstays of the Labour governments of the 1960s. But there nevertheless were important changes, some obvious, some more subtle. There was impressive new blood, notably Shirley Williams who entered the Cabinet for the first time. Callaghan's friend and ally Merlyn Rees also became a Cabinet minister as Labour's first incumbent of the newly created Northern Ireland Department. There was also a more notable newcomer, Michael Foot, who forsook a lifetime of protest and opposition to enter the Cabinet for the first time at the age of 61 as Secretary for Employment. His primary task at first was to reach a settlement with the miners who were still on national strike; there could be little doubt as to what the outcome could be.

Within the highest levels of the Cabinet, there was a less visible transformation. Harold Wilson was manifestly less vigorous than in 1964 and perhaps generally less healthy. He announced his wish to play a more withdrawn role than in his personal leadership in 1964–70 which had proved so bruising and wearing for him and his reputation. He proposed, using his favoured footballing analogy, to act as 'a deep-lying centre half' like Herbie Roberts, the 'stopper' of the famous Arsenal team in his younger days, rather than as a goal-scoring centre-forward.[1] The emphasis would be on the government as a team rather than a solar system revolving around one brilliant individual. This directly affected Callaghan's role in the Cabinet. Roy Jenkins has suggested that Wilson's hope was that Callaghan could be moved to handle Industrial Relations, leaving the Treasury for Jenkins himself, but it was hardly likely that Callaghan could be persuaded to retreat from the Foreign Office portfolio which he obviously enjoyed.[2] In fact, apart from holding a key post, Callaghan clearly became Wilson's most intimate adviser on all issues. Indeed, as the Prime Minister's energies showed signs of running down, even his famous memory no longer so reliable, Callaghan emerged as all-purpose operator to fill any gaps and give direction to the government. He was almost an alternative prime minister. Wilson generally gave him a free hand in foreign affairs: the premier's international interests were largely confined to South Africa and Israel on which he regularly asked Callaghan for information. The latter's relations with his leader were now restored to the harmony of 1964–6. There was no question of rivalry between the two senior figures; Wilson was happily reconciled to Callaghan's succeeding him in due time, to be announced by him. At the press conference after the Dublin summit on 12 March 1975 Wilson, with every appearance of cordiality, was to proclaim that 'Jim and I are a complete partnership. We pass the ball to each other. Britain has a literate Prime Minister and a numerate Foreign Secretary.'[3] It was a far cry from the apparently terminal animosity of 1969, but five years were indeed a very long time in politics.

There was a visible sign of the close relationship between Harold Wilson and Jim Callaghan. Every Friday morning, Callaghan would stroll over from the Foreign Office to 10 Downing Street and have an open-ended private talk with Wilson about the state of the party and the nation. Occasionally the chief whip, Bob Mellish, would also be present.[4] Callaghan's role in these discussions, which he increasingly came to dominate, was to provide some kind of strategic overview, and even more advice on how to keep the party united. He looked on the political scene with controlled detachment, ambition (for the moment) on the back burner. Indirectly, he supplied a kind of leadership which Wilson himself seemed less anxious to provide.

The mores of the Foreign Office, like those of the Treasury and the Home Office, confronted Callaghan with a new challenge. His attachment to the Treasury had grown since his leaving it. The Home Office, too, in the persons of such as Philip Allen, Brian Cubbon, and David Faulkner, had had increasing attraction for him, for its humane attention to individual liberties as much as for its efficiency. The Foreign Office, the most traditional department of them all, was harder to take. He seemed anxious at first to emphasize the distance between himself and his new department. A fortuitous sign of it appeared when Callaghan and Audrey did not actually move into the Foreign Office residence in 2 Carlton Gardens as was traditional, and as his predecessor Alec Douglas-Home had done. This, however, was the result not of fragile confidence but of a fragile roof which, as Lady Douglas-Home had told the Callaghans, needed major repairs since there was a constant leak which required the strategic placing of buckets in rainy weather.[5] The Callaghans stayed on their London *pied-à-terre* in Carrick Court in nearby Lambeth.

But the personnel no less than the physical structure of the Foreign Office caused some initial concern, too. It seemed to him socially superior and liable to swallow a Labour minister whole as it had done with figures such as Morrison or Stewart in the past. Callaghan, still sharply conscious of his unprivileged background in working-class Portsmouth and his lack of a university training, did not react warmly at first to products of Eton and Winchester offering political bromides or telling him how to talk to foreigners. One of his early responses was to launch an internal inquiry into the social and educational background of Foreign Office recruits. The patrician mandarin 'Nico' Henderson, ambassador to Bonn and then to Paris, whose wife had a penchant for *haute cuisine* and putting on fashion shows in the Paris embassy, represented much that Callaghan disliked in life.[6] It was somewhat reminiscent of Nehru's remark to J. K. Galbraith, when the latter was ambassador to India, that Duncan Sandys reminded him of the kind of Englishman who used to put him in jail. Henderson himself found Callaghan at first grim-visaged, with little of the 'light-hearted banter' to which he had become accustomed at the Foreign Office. Things soon thawed out, however, and before long he had struck up an excellent relationship with his new colleagues, and welded them into a highly effective team who eased his own duties considerably. Indeed, he was later to tell Nigel Lawson that the Foreign Office proved to be a 'doddle' compared with the demands of the posts he had held previously.[7] He was especially impressed by the skilful work of the Foreign Office negotiating team in the lengthy and highly technical negotiations at Brussels to amend Britain's terms of entry into the European Community. Among those who particularly impressed him was Michael Alexander, his private secretary in 1974 and a key member of his delegation; Callaghan had an indirect relationship with him already through his interest in chess since his father C. H. O'D. Alexander was a famous British chess champion. Michael Alexander was later to play a major role in preparing the Helsinki accord with the Soviet Union.

Callaghan also formed a strong relationship with his first permanent secretary, Sir Thomas Brimelow, a specialist in eastern Europe, and then with his successor Sir Michael Palliser (previously ambassador to Brussels); with his principal private secretary Sir Anthony Acland (who had previously served under Sir Alec Douglas-Home); and with both his advisers on eastern Europe and east–west relations, Sir Julian Bullard and his successor Sir Bryan Cartledge, later to be his foreign affairs adviser in 10 Downing Street. Another congenial diplomatic figure was Ewen Fergusson, a former international rugby forward for Scotland, a link of a kind with Callaghan himself. When Anthony Acland moved on in 1975 Callaghan ensured that Fergusson was uprooted from Brussels to take Acland's place as principal private secretary. He was also effective, as in previous departments, in drawing out the whole range of ability within Foreign Office ranks and was highly successful in getting the ideas of bright young men. A close observer, however, noticed that he was somewhat less at ease in addressing bright young women in the department.[8] Like most men of his generation, Callaghan felt himself slightly at a loss in conversing with female professional high flyers. His Foreign Policy officials were always wary of his temper, and he could be brutal in the extreme. When his private secretary Stephen Barrett was thought to have mishandled a key briefing paper, he was rapidly transferred elsewhere. In general, however, his personal relations within the Foreign Office were very good, and he was highly regarded there. Colleagues like Julian Bullard and Bryan Cartledge could look back on this period with great affection and regard Callaghan as a quite excellent Foreign Secretary. Among other positive qualities, Bullard regarded him as very human with 'a natural gift for gracious comment'.[9] But inevitably building up the relationship took a little time.

To help him, he had the energetic and influential figure of Tom McNally. One of his ministerial support was carefully chosen. His two ministers of state were David Ennals, who had been with him in the Home Office and who was invariably bound to Callaghan as his guiding light. The other was the rising figure of Roy Hattersley. Until recently a close follower of Roy Jenkins, he had broken with his leader over his decision to resign over a referendum on Europe, and incurred some odium from right-wingers as a result. Hattersley was a strong pro-European who was told by Wilson, on his appointment, that he would have primary responsibility for renegotiating the terms of British membership of the European Common Market. Strangely he told Hattersley that Callaghan would be '*nominally* in charge'; equally strangely, Hattersley's memoirs carry no suggestion of disbelief.[10] At any rate, his new role as a Minister of State strongly suggested what the outcome of any renegotiations would be.

On the other hand, Callaghan had as his under-secretary Joan Lestor, a Tribunite and anti-marketeer but also a figure of genial disposition popular throughout the party. Callaghan claimed to regard her as his private voice of conscience, somewhat in the way that Wilson felt about Barbara Castle, but she had much less direct impact on his decisions than other members of the team. Callaghan was always wary of the emotionalism of the Tribunite tendency. Lestor was to be replaced later on by Ted Rowlands, member for Merthyr Tydfil, a trained historian (of late seventeenth-century Wales) who published in scholarly journals. He brought a valuable historical perspective to the tricky out-of-the-way problems with which Callaghan asked him to deal, notably Belize and especially the Falklands and their relationship to Argentina. In the Lords, the spokesman, as noted, was to be the newly ennobled Lord Goronwy-Roberts rather than the more passionately pro-European Eirene White. Callaghan was content to have Welshmen around him. Another PPS by 1976 was John Grant, a former industrial correspondent who was later to join the Social Democrats in 1981.

There was a division of area responsibilities between them all. Ennals dealt with the Middle East, the United Nations, and aid programmes; Hattersley with Europe, east–west relations, North America, and defence; Goronwy-Roberts with South-East Asia, the Far East, and the Commonwealth; and Joan Lestor with Africa, Latin America, and the Caribbean.[11] They were a sound team, and made to feel they had a collective identity by regular meetings with the Foreign Secretary. One that Callaghan records at some length is that of 28 October 1975, when he, Ennals, Goronwy-Roberts, Rowlands, and Grant listened to a report from Roy Hattersley on the state of the so-called 'cod war' with Iceland.[12] Equally they had to defend each other against frequent criticisms from the left-dominated International Committee of the NEC on such matters as Chile and South Africa. Its combative chairman Ian Mikardo, never one of Callaghan's favourite politicians, was felt to be particularly tiresome.[13]

There was an immense variety of themes across the world, ranging from a European security conference to local problems such as Rhodesia or Belize calling for Callaghan's attention. He was to say in later life that his general role as Foreign Secretary was essentially reactive, although this seems to underplay the major creative input he was able to offer in areas such as the Middle East, Cyprus, or Portugal. Certainly, Britain's international bargaining power had visibly diminished even since 1964; devaluation and the various ailments of the British economy in the recent years had taken this further. The sterling area had gone. The Commonwealth had continued to decline as any kind of cohesive force with the withdrawal from east of Suez in 1971 and even more as a result of Britain's entry into

Europe. Rhodesia had been a Commonwealth failure as well as a British one. Meanwhile the relationship with the United States had largely stagnated in the Heath years, with their sole emphasis on entry into the Common Market. However, Britain still retained a significant position in world affairs. Callaghan would try to impose himself on all these problems and had clear views on most of them, including some long-dormant areas such as Anglo-Soviet relations which he was anxious to revive.

He spelt out his priorities to Nicholas Henderson on 24 March. He intended to 'put more muscle' into the United Nations, to place prime importance on the Atlantic alliance, and to have closer relations with the Commonwealth.[14] He favoured global rather than regional solutions to international problems and in this he regarded the alliance with the United States as quite vital. It was certainly a different note from that struck by Heath in 1970–4. In varying degrees, he succeeded in generating new energy in all these areas, both as Foreign Secretary and again as Prime Minister. But, of course, he recognized that Britain was largely an experienced counsellor rather than the leading player in most of the critical areas of the world, and that its national initiatives must be accordingly limited.

In one supreme area, however, he had to take action immediately. This was in Britain's renegotiating of the terms of entry into Europe. He was greeted at the Foreign Office on 4 March 1974 with a letter from George Thomson, a former Cabinet colleague about to leave Westminster to become a European Commissioner. He told Callaghan that there was a prospect of real movement on issues such as the Common Agricultural Policy and the community budget, and that the Germans would be supportive, but that any renegotiations must begin from the premiss that Britain would remain a member of the European Community.[15] This was not how the new Foreign Secretary saw things at all. From the start, Callaghan emphasized his coolness about the whole European project, and his intention of dissecting it in its fundamentals. Wilson was of like mind, although Bernard Donoughue was later to conclude that, whereas Wilson's suspicion of Europe was fundamental, based in part on sentimentality towards the Commonwealth on issues such as New Zealand butter and cheese, Callaghan was less rigid and a genuine internationalist towards the European no less than the Atlantic community.[16]

But Callaghan began in characteristically aggressive style. He told Nicholas Henderson at Bonn that he was 'an agnostic' on the European issue other than in certain specific areas of economic collaboration.[17] This would be made transparently clear to his advisers. At the start of his period in the Foreign Office, he called a meeting of Foreign Office mandarins to him and gave each of them a copy of the Labour Party manifesto which he told them to read if they had not already done so. In this, he consciously emulated an earlier ex-trade unionist Foreign Secretary, Arthur Henderson, when he presented the Labour Party policy statement, *Labour and the Nation*, to Foreign Office dignitaries in 1929. When officials questioned the government's views on the Optional Clause, Henderson had asked Dalton impatiently, 'Don't these chaps know what our policy is?'[18] Callaghan operated in similar fashion. He bridled when Michael Palliser appeared to suggest that any negotiations must assume that British membership of the EEC be taken as given. The most that could be hoped for, Palliser seemed to suggest, was that details such as the British contribution to the community budget might be revised. Callaghan dismissed this out of hand. That was not how he proposed to handle matters. He was aiming for fundamental renegotiations which would involve a change in the Treaty of Accession. He was neither negotiating to remain in nor to withdraw. His aim was to 'return to a more traditional and pragmatic British policy' and the Foreign Office, for all its ingrained pro-Europeanism, would have to accept that this was the approach of the new Labour government.[19]

He dealt in equally severe fashion with doubts expressed by Michael Butler, assistant under-secretary responsible for EC affairs, on the plane to Brussels for the first of many visits. When Butler made comments to the effect that he did not know how 'his friends in Brussels' would react to the British proposals, Callaghan referred him again to the Labour Party manifesto. He added sharply that if Butler felt like that he might as well return home immediately.[20] Similarly, he rejected out of hand Henderson's suggestion that the Germans might be more supportive on the various British demands if Britain in turn showed a more cordial attitude to German aspirations for a more integrated Europe, political as well as economic.[21] His own officials could be suitably cowed by this browbeating. What was more debatable by far was whether Pompidou, Brandt, and other European heads of government would be equally amenable.

From the start, Callaghan took a forceful, even belligerent line. He was reported as being unhappy with the German approach after an Anglo-German meeting at Königswinter, even though the bulk of the Germans there, such as Willy Brandt and Helmut Schmidt, were fellow Social Democrats. Schmidt felt that Callaghan was distinctly lukewarm, and that Denis Healey had a rather better understanding of the strategic necessities both for Britain and for Europe. In addition, Healey, who had had wide contacts since his time at the International Section in Transport House, spoke several European languages.[22]

Whether Callaghan actually felt so negative after the Anglo-German exchanges at Königswinter is more doubtful. He certainly had disagreements with Walter Scheel, the FDP Foreign Minister, on agricultural and other issues. But he struck up an excellent relationship with Helmut Schmidt, who struck him as both immensely able and basically supportive. In a short time, the whole membership of the German government was to change in a way helpful to the British.[23] Willy Brandt, who was not in good health and had political difficulties relating to his private life, had soon to resign as Chancellor when an East German spy was found working in his private office. Helmut Schmidt took his place. He was to be perhaps the dominant intellectual influence on Callaghan's perceptions of international relations for the next five years. Scheel, too, gave way shortly as Foreign Minister to another Free Democrat, Hans-Dietrich Genscher; he appeared to be as Eurosceptic as Callaghan himself. With potential support from so vital a component of the European Community as Germany, with the Benelux countries always favourable to British entry and the Italians generally amiable, the difficulties that were expected to be posed by the French did not seem so insurmountable. Even they were less intransigent under Pompidou. In fact, the French President died unexpectedly on 2 April and the transition to Giscard d'Estaing as President, a relaxed figure, almost an Anglophile, and with at least a fine command of spoken English, was another favourable omen.

The issue of renegotiation was a fundamental one for the fortunes or survival of the Labour government, and it affected the administration's conduct of policy at the highest level. Two Cabinet committees were set up. The European Strategy Committee would consider wider implications and would be chaired by the Prime Minister, Harold Wilson, himself. Beneath this, there would be the committee to deal with tactical issues and monitor the details of the renegotiation, the so-called EQS Committee, chaired by Callaghan. Two ministers would assist him in Brussels—Roy Hattersley, junior minister at the Foreign Office, and Peter Shore, Secretary for Trade and Industry. This pair aptly illustrated the total polarization that existed in the Wilson government, since while Hattersley was a strong (though not fanatical) supporter of EC membership, Shore was a vehement opponent on English nationalist grounds, similar in outlook to the vigorous Europhobia of Douglas Jay. Callaghan viewed with some regret the presence of two colleagues with such antithetical views. But he was well aware of the domestic aspects of his renegotiation at every turn, and the extreme delicacy as well as tactical skill he would have to demonstrate in order to carry the Cabinet with him. In short, he had become the decisive figure in Labour's survival in office, even more so than the Chancellor, Denis Healey, who had to deal with a massive legacy of indebtedness somewhat as Callaghan himself had had to do in 1964. The Foreign Secretary was pivotal to party unity and Harold Wilson well knew it. He had told Callaghan at the outset that on most issues, except for a few areas such as relations with Israel and Anglo-Soviet contacts, he would be given a free hand,[24] and this certainly applied to Europe.

On 1 April in the first session of the renegotiation at Luxembourg, Callaghan sailed into the attack with a vehemence that surprised and offended most of the Continentals present. His audience now represented eight nations. The original six had increased to eight in the early 1970s, with the adherence of Denmark and—very significantly for Britain—the Republic of Ireland which had its own distinctive approach on agricultural and other matters. Callaghan's boldness was a calculated approach, intended to show detachment instead of adopting a suppliant attitude. He had rejected the original Foreign Office draft and had rewritten it himself, injecting a much more belligerent tone. It was also a case of holding something in reserve. He offered Henderson the analogy of the tactics of the Welsh rugby team, highly successful at this time, in keeping something back until the last fifteen minutes of a game when victory would finally be secured.[25]

His speech, printed as a government white paper, attacked the European Community at most points, and brought the heads of government down to earth. The proposal for a European monetary union with fixed parities by 1980 was 'overambitious'. The idea of a political 'European Union' by 1980 was 'unrealistic'. The Common Agricultural Policy was quite unacceptable with the high costs that it would involve for a nation like Britain. Trade with the developing nations of the Commonwealth would have to be given a high priority. The Community budget would have to be substantially revamped. Britain would have a likely 16.5 per cent share of gross national product at the end of the transition period, but would be paying a 19 per cent contribution to the budget.[26] It might be noted that in all these points Callaghan was prophetic in his analysis. In 1997 a European monetary union was perhaps less than two years off and the idea was productive of intense controversy, not only in Britain. The British contribution to the Community budget continued to plague British governments long after Callaghan's time in government, and only in the Fontainebleau summit in 1984 did Mrs Thatcher and Chancellor Helmut Kohl reach an agreement on this vexed issue which laid it finally to rest. Britain was to gain a 66 per cent annual rebate on the gap between its VAT contribution to Europe and EC expenditure in Britain. On the other hand, Mrs Thatcher's compensatory diplomatic stance, pushing on for a European Single Market, went much further than Callaghan in 1975 (or many Conservatives in the 1990s) was prepared to go.

Callaghan's blunt speech at Luxembourg was badly received in the capitals of Europe, in Paris and Rome particularly. Callaghan, it was felt, had created a sense of isolation between Britain and the rest, a kind of 'us' and 'them' approach, and his tone had been insensitive on longer-term aspirations for a political and monetary union. It was claimed that the speech had spread 'a shadow of gloom over Brussels' and that he had presented the choice facing Britain in needlessly harsh terms. Even the Anglophile Dutch were critical; their President complained that he had not been paid a courtesy visit by the British Foreign Secretary.[27] Only the Germans were more measured. Brandt and Schmidt noted that the brusque style of the initial negotiating speech was largely intended for Eurosceptics within the Labour Party at home. They also were socialist enough to recognize the British Foreign Secretary's background as a trade union negotiator, which meant putting your cards on the table initially in the most forceful way and moving towards an accommodation later. Callaghan largely ignored Continental reactions but he did have to deny a hostile report in *Le Monde* which claimed that he believed Britain's withdrawal from the EC was 'inevitable'.[28]

He left Luxembourg on 2 April, leaving the British case to be variously and antithetically deployed by Hattersley and Shore, so far as this was remotely possible. In the Commons, he vigorously defended his 'rougher style' of diplomacy when criticized by Douglas-Home for the Conservatives. He claimed that the entire situation fully justified Labour's decision to have a referendum in due course and said that the decision should have been put to the British electors in the first place.[29] Anti-Europeans on the Labour benches took heart from his words and even more from his tone. On balance, Callaghan emerged from the debate as anything but an ardent European. He appeared rather as an unreconstructed Atlanticist who believed in the special relationship with the Americans, and also retained a powerful kinship with the old and new members of the Commonwealth. But his Luxembourg performance certainly had a powerful impact, perhaps bracing, perhaps quite alarming. Commentators noted that it was an event that had taken place on All Fools' Day.

In fact, the lengthy grind of renegotiation that followed until the Dublin Castle conference in March 1975 was inevitably far lower key. The total deadlock suggested by the Luxembourg speech never materialized. The mere fact of constant association with the leaders and foreign ministers of the various European governments in itself made for an organic growth of relationships. On 13 May, Callaghan had a lengthy meeting with François Ortoli, the chairman of the European Commission, and set out what seemed to him the main areas of difficulty. There were four primary issues—the Community budget, the Common Agricultural Plan, greater access for the products of Commonwealth countries notably sugar, and a guarantee that British policies of regional development within the United Kingdom would not be disturbed. Of these, the first, the scale of British contributions to the Community budget and the resultant return from the budget, was felt to be the most significant. Ortoli, by all accounts, was conciliatory and responded that the Community would be able to make adjustments on all these points. There were, however, major problems, not least the political fact that any adjustment to the British budgetary contribution might well result in Germany, the largest net contributor, paying even more, which Helmut Schmidt and his Social Democrats would strongly resist.[30]

Nevertheless, it is significant that the main focus was on the arithmetical detail of the budgetary contribution. This would clearly afford a great deal of scope for bargaining and indeed for creative accounting on all sides. A theme of fundamental principle such as the Common Agricultural Plan was, implicitly, regarded as too central to be seriously challenged at this stage. To do so would hardly be consistent with what Callaghan told Ron Hayward, that the Labour Party was adopting a posture of 'negotiating for success'. The longer the talks went on, the greater likelihood of a positive outcome. As early as 31 May, Peter Shore, amongst the most opposed to joining the Community of all government ministers, complained to Callaghan that his latest speech at Luxembourg 'gives an impression of weakness and retreat from the strong opening position in April. I think it will come as a shock to many in the House and in the country.'[31] On the same day, Tony Benn noted that Callaghan had sent a draft of his speech to other EEC governments without allowing for amendments from Cabinet colleagues. 'Put simply he had sold out on the central question of British sovereignty and appears to think that the industrial and regional policy aspects are not worth emphasising as major points for renegotiation.'[32] Among other factors, Callaghan was no doubt content that the unknown might of Brussels could perhaps be wheeled in to help frustrate some of what he regarded as the wilder excesses of Benn's 'alternative economic strategy' with its massive directive powers over British industry.

In the summer of 1974, the talks at Brussels stagnated to some extent and Callaghan himself somewhat withdrew from direct involvement in them. He had many other claims on his time at this period. The National Executive, with its left-wing majority, was pushing him hard on arms shipments to the right-wing dictatorship in Chile. More important, there was a massive crisis in the Mediterranean over Cyprus when Greeks and Turks came into violent conflict in late July and August, as will be seen in the next chapter. Apart from the security dangers in the region that this involved, it also meant dispute between the British and American governments which taxed Callaghan's skills and energies to the utmost. At the start of August he was in Helsinki for the CSCE conference on east–west security and détente; a few days later he was in Uganda arranging the release of Dennis Hills from apparently likely execution by President Amin. He was certainly kept on the move.

But the main factor to deflect him from the bog of the Brussels negotiations was something even more fundamental—the calling of a second general election. This had long been anticipated. Harold Wilson's minority government had only got thus far through the miscellaneous nature of the Commons with various Liberals, Nationalists, Unionists, and Independents of different kinds creating a fluid situation, and the Conservatives under the somewhat beleaguered leadership of Edward Heath reluctant to precipitate a crisis. The past few months had gone better than many expected. Although there was continuing trouble in Northern Ireland where a state of emergency had been declared, the economy was showing some signs of recovery, industrial relations were much more tranquil with the social contract showing signs of effectiveness, and Labour moved ahead strongly in the polls. Healey's mini-budget of July was mildly reflationary and added £900m. to consumers' purchasing power, pointing the way to an early election.[33]

Some ministers such as Foot and Crosland were believed to have wanted an election as early as June, but Callaghan was amongst the majority who counselled delay. When Wilson called an election for 10 October, however, all ministers were in agreement. A feature much trumpeted in the press, after selective briefing by 10 Downing Street, was that the manifesto was a relatively moderate one, Wilson and Callaghan having watered down almost to disappearing point Benn's proposals for planning directives and nationalization by statutory instrument.

The second general election within six months was a very quiet, indeed uninspiring affair and little that was new emerged. As always, Callaghan was a major player in press conferences and on the air, fortified by sage advice from McNally and others. His own position in Cardiff South-East was hardly in doubt. He faced Stefan Terleski again as his major opponent, with Christopher Bailey (Liberal), Keith Bush (Plaid Cymru), and a Marxist-Leninist also in the field. Labour had no qualms here and the question really was whether Labour would this time win an overall majority to be able to command the next parliament. In the event, the results were disappointing for Wilson and his colleagues since they almost repeated the previous statemate. The Conservatives slipped somewhat further to 277 seats and only 35.8 per cent of the poll to Labour's 39.2 per cent. Both the main parties lost votes, but Labour's total of 11,457,079 was nearly a million higher than that of the Tories. This led to almost deafening calls for Heath's resignation as party leader now that he had lost three elections out of four. But Labour's total of 319 seats meant only a majority of three, and the swing to Labour at less than 1 per cent was negligible.

In Cardiff South-East, Callaghan won easily with the swing to Labour at 4.7 per cent well above the national average. He received 21,074 votes (52 per cent) as against Terleski's 10,356. The Liberals were a poor third, Plaid Cymru polled only 2.4 per cent, while the Marxist-Leninist total of votes, at 75 (0.2 per cent), was of Screaming Lord Sutch dimensions. It was an unremarkable contest in Cardiff South-East. Elsewhere in Wales, the Plaid Cymru tally of seats rose to 3 with Gwynfor Evans recapturing Carmarthen. But with the tiniest of majorities, even smaller than in the 1950–1 parliament, the Labour government and whoever headed it were in for a hard slog.

It did at least mean that Callaghan could now throw himself into bringing the European renegotiating process to a conclusion. If Harold Wilson emerged from the election campaign tired, dispirited, and almost disappointed that he had won,[34] Callaghan returned to the Foreign Office full of vigour. In his sixty-third year, he had not lost his appetite for government, nor his ambition for further advance. That autumn, the renegotiations in Brussels resumed with full momentum. They were punctuated, inevitably, by the numerous overseas visits that the British Foreign Secretary had to undertake. He was in the Persian Gulf in late November and in southern Africa to deal with the problem of Rhodesia in January. There were also other international gatherings, but meetings such as these tended to reinforce the collegial relationship beginning to build up between Wilson and Callaghan with Schmidt, Giscard, and other foreign heads of government. They were, therefore, indirectly helpful in the EC renegotiations.

The new impetus was heralded by the Labour Party conference, postponed until 30 November because of the intervening general election.

Here, Helmut Schmidt was invited to speak at Callaghan's personal suggestion. He did so brilliantly, with wit and wisdom. In faultless English, he appealed to the spirit of socialist solidarity with Continental comrades and made a considerable impression. Barbara Castle, an ardent anti-marketeer who already felt that Callaghan had betrayed the United Kingdom bargaining position, thought Schmidt's performance 'masterly'. She noted his sense of command. More personally, 'I thought how handsome and relaxed he looked.'[35] There was a growing sense that the outcome of the renegotiations was following an inevitable course. The German Chancellor was clearly an ally, if a tough-minded one. He got Callaghan and Wilson to offer a pledge that, if negotiations with the Community on budget contributions went satisfactorily, they would make a positive recommendation to parliament that Britain should stay in. The other key player was the new French President, Valéry Giscard d'Estaing, who had recently defeated the socialist François Mitterrand, even if narrowly. Callaghan had had private talks with him and his Foreign Minister Sauvargnargues at the Élysée Palace on 19 November in which the tone of the discussions was good. Callaghan reaffirmed that he was indeed 'negotiating for success'.[36]

On 5 December there was an important meeting at the Élysée between Wilson, Callaghan, and President Giscard and his Foreign Minister. Here Giscard showed himself distinctly more flexible than Pompidou, let alone de Gaulle, had been before him. He emphasized his desire for Britain to remain a member of the Community, explored the possibilities of reducing Britain's budget contribution in the transitional period, and affirmed his view that the Community should continue to take decisions by broad consensus rather than by majority vote, which was of course very much Britain's position also.[37] There followed a heads of government summit on 9 December in Paris, with Giscard in the chair. Harold Wilson was not in the best of health here—indeed his growing fatigue was becoming more evident, following a heart tremor—and more of the work fell on Callaghan, a burden he was happy enough to take up. Again there was a sense of the tide turning in favour of a successful outcome. The Agricultural Plan was virtually set on one side. The sugar quota was now resolved, with the United Kingdom offered a saving on the threshold price and the production quota increased to 1.1m. tons which was important for West Indian producers.[38] Wilson emphasized again the case of New Zealand, one particularly dear to him, on which most of the Continentals were non-commital. The main issue, yet again, was the scale of the British budgetary contribution. Here the Foreign Office had produced an alternative formulation which cleverly linked Britain's needs with the EC's broad position that the various national economies should move towards convergence before any form of monetary union could be considered. The final formula that 'a correcting mechanism of a general application' be worked out was entirely satisfactory to the British representatives. One important issue was settled for good. It was agreed that a European regional fund would be created to lend assistance to hard-hit areas such as those suffering from industrial decline. This would be of particular benefit to areas such as the Welsh valleys and the industrial areas of Scotland, Merseyside, and the north-east.[39]

What was more important than the substance of this meeting was the tone. It was friendly, informal, collegiate. Giscard and Schmidt emphasized their strong support for British membership; the agreement of the Benelux countries and Italy could be assumed. There was also an attempt to move away from more grandiose or abstract formulations of possible future forms of union towards a more practical, step-by-step approach, more consonant with British empiricism. At the intergovernmental level, things were going well.

The more critical aspect of renegotiation now was to keep the Cabinet and the party together at home. A decisive meeting of the Cabinet on 12 December saw divergences of opinion, fierce at times even though Callaghan's memoirs describe this meeting as 'temperate'.[40] Wilson spelt out the terms of the communiqué of the Paris summit; a rich miscellany of opinions then followed. Michael Foot, backed up by Tony Benn and Barbara Castle, spoke of his alarm at the concessions over parliamentary sovereignty and the talk of political and monetary union in due time. These were things which had never been discussed in Cabinet, let alone approved there. Wilson, generally agreed to be somewhat vague and garrulous in his presentation, was not very effective, but Shirley Williams and Harold Lever, both pro-marketeers, gave him support. The atmosphere became more heated after a ferocious intervention by Peter Shore who spoke of his shock at the relaxation of the power of veto, which struck at the heart of British national sovereignty. Wilson then got angry and emphasized his own long record of international negotiations, going back to his visit to Moscow in the late 1940s when he was at the Board of Trade. 'I resent the suggestions that Jim and I are little innocents abroad.' The disagreements remained in the air as the Cabinet moved on to other topics.[41]

The year ended with Tony Benn sending a new year message to his Bristol constituents saying that he would continue to oppose British membership. This caused another row with the Prime Minister who had taken to slapping down Benn's interventions in Cabinet. Wilson told him that his message was not in accord with the Cabinet's resolution on 14 December. Benn, somewhat disingenuously perhaps, argued that in sending his message he was acting not as a Cabinet minister but as a member of the National Executive. It could be argued that Callaghan's behaviour over trade union legislation in 1969 had not been so very different. The episode ended with Wilson angrily instructing Benn and all other members of his Cabinet to desist from sending individual messages or communications, and to observe the established conventions of collective responsibility.[42]

In January and February 1975, Wilson and Callaghan both continued a process of softening up Labour Party and TUC opinion; Wilson, for instance, had a special session with the Labour mayors. Callaghan also had an important series of supportive meetings with Henry Kissinger, the US Secretary of State, who was a particularly close associate. Neither man was 'passionate' about British membership of the EC in Kissinger's later recollection, but the Secretary of State was broadly in favour of British membership for diplomatic reasons. He recognized it as a matter for national decision by the United Kingdom; either way, he assured Callaghan that relations with the United States would remain close and cordial.[43] Callaghan's paper to Cabinet colleagues, the Second Tactical Plan on Renegotiation in February 1975, met with strong criticism from Peter Shore. He felt that it fell short of the Foreign Secretary's previous declarations.[44] His criticisms, which Michael Foot was to support in Cabinet, were sidelined rather than answered.

The issue was finally resolved at another summit meeting in Dublin on 10–12 March 1975. Wilson represented this conference as a 'make-or-break' occasion, although by this stage it was increasingly difficult to imagine British withdrawal. Since progress had been made on most other issues, the discussions focused on the two remaining areas of disagreement. One was Commonwealth dairy products, notably cheese and butter from New Zealand. This was important not only for New Zealand farmers but also for British consumers; it was proposed to import up to 140,000 tons of New Zealand butter alone up to 1982. A valuable ally whom Callaghan had enlisted was Genscher, the German Foreign Minister, who took a less dogmatically 'communitaire' view than some other national representatives. On 11 March, with the aid of den Uyl and Jorgensen, the prime ministers of the Netherlands and Denmark respectively, both of them major exporters of dairy products, a concessionary form of entry for New Zealand produce was duly worked out.

There remained the ever difficult issue of the budget. When a compromise was suggested by the president of the Commission, there was stern opposition, somewhat unexpectedly, from Helmut Schmidt, who pointed out that Germany was the largest net contributor and could not possibly go any higher. Callaghan himself then made a highly effective speech on 11 March even if it largely repeated points made many times over. The outcome he proposed was that the broad principles underlying the budget and taxation system of the Community remain undisturbed, but that Britain be merely repaid on the basis of its comparative GNP. Helmut Schmidt at once proved totally conciliatory. Agreement was rapidly reached on the basis that 250m. units of account (amounting to £125m. in a year) would be a maximum refund for any country paying a disproportionate amount in its share of the budget. There was an immediate sense that the knot had been cut and final agreement reached. The negotiations had been dragging for almost a year and no one felt that any more talks would be necessary or helpful.[45]

Wilson and Callaghan gave an upbeat presentation at the final press conference in Dublin. It was probably a more euphoric message than the facts warranted, but the sense of achievement was nevertheless justifiable. In addition to spelling out how harmonious a team he and Callaghan had been, Wilson explained the agreement on the community budget as a great negotiating success. (In fact, the proviso about Britain's share of the Community GDP exceeding its share of budget contributions related only to cases where it was in balance of payments deficit, an important point on which Callaghan had disagreed privately with Wilson.) There was also progress on New Zealand cheese and on steel production. Wilson announced that he believed that renegotiation had been a success and that he would now recommend the terms to parliament, with the corollary that Britain would remain a member of the Community. Callaghan took an identical line. He declared that he could with conscience support the revised terms. The main anxieties he regarded as being about the 'theology' of the Common Market (which was why colleagues like Schmidt felt he had no visionary sense about Europe). On the practicalities, the British should be content.[46]

It now remained for the Cabinet to give its view. On 17–18 March there was a marathon discussion, led off by a lengthy and balanced report by Callaghan. The views that were expressed followed to some degree predictable lines, with Tony Benn being eloquent on the dismemberment of parliamentary democracy as he saw it through the sacrifice of British sovereignty. He also attacked Wilson and Callaghan on industrial and regional policy and condemned the EEC as a capitalists' club.[47] But there had been an important sea change in the collective view, and it was Callaghan rather than Wilson who had been the crucial agent in it. He wound up his contribution to the discussion with a powerful general apologia. He declared himself an unashamed Atlanticist but they now lived in a regional world from which Britain could not be excluded. Détente with the Soviet Union would, if anything, be helped if Britain were able to exert its influence in a regional organization. He also pointed out that four of the EC countries—Germany, Denmark, Holland, and the Republic of Ireland—had governments with socialist representation in them (he could have added Luxembourg). Britain would make a fifth. He frankly admitted that he had changed his mind, and cited Benjamin Franklin's views on a new constitution for the American colonists as a distinguished precedent.

Journalists beforehand had speculated that the Cabinet was about evenly divided 11 : 11 (with Callaghan assumed to be 'pro'), leaving Wilson with the decisive casting vote. But that was not how things worked out. In a coffee break, Callaghan had taken the important initiative of asking potential opponents if they wished to register formally as dissenters against the Cabinet's view. Not all of them did. In the end, the Cabinet endorsed the terms and thereby continued British membership of the Community by 16 votes to 7. The seven dissentients were Mrs Castle, Benn, Foot, and Shore (the hard core of the opposition) along with the less influential figures of John Silkin, Willie Ross, and Eric Varley. The last-named had been heavily pressed by Gerald Kaufman and Marcia Falkender from Wilson's entourage and vaguely specified energy issues, but he was not intending to campaign. The majority was swollen significantly by five ministers in effect switching from potential 'no' to 'yes' votes—Merlyn Rees, John Morris (Secretary for Wales), and Fred Peart (Agriculture), along with Lord Shepherd and Reg Prentice. The first three at least were directly influenced by Callaghan personally. Merlyn Rees was a very close ally, and John Morris a fellow Welsh member; Fred Peart was another long-term associate. Along with somewhat uncommitted ministers such as Denis Healey and Tony Crosland who tended to regard the remaining difficulties as matters of detail only, there was a majority of more than two to one in favour. Even though Labour MPs were marginally balanced in favour of the anti-marketeers, the domestic battle, like the international, appeared to have been won.[48]

In the Commons debate on the European renegotiation on 9 April, Callaghan spoke both as Foreign and Commonwealth Secretary. Indeed, the latter aspect predominated in what he had to say. With unusual frankness, he confessed that he had changed his mind since Labour's policy statement on Europe in 1972. He laid emphasis on the fact that all the Commonwealth countries, not merely the older dominions, but also the seven African states he had visited during the Christmas recess, now favoured British membership of the EEC. An important new direction he mentioned was the Lomé convention for aid to African, Caribbean, and Pacific Commonwealth nations which, he argued, showed the European Community in a positive new light. He also welcomed the abandonment of the insistence, to which Heath had meekly agreed, that Britain give up its open seas approach. He paid especial tribute to the role of a socialist comrade, Helmut Schmidt. The majority of Labour MPs went along cheerfully enough with the Foreign Secretary's change of mind.[49]

It now remained to conduct the referendum on British membership which was to take place on 5 June. From the start it was evident that it could go only one way. As agreed, ministers campaigned on opposite sides. Roy Jenkins, Shirley Williams, and some pro-marketeers happily appeared on 'yes' platforms with political opponents such as Ted Heath and David Steel; indeed, Roy Jenkins for one found that his own innate centrism was reinforced thereby. Equally Barbara Castle, Michael Foot, Tony Benn, and Peter Shore were active in cross-party 'no' activities, usually appearing on platforms with right-wing Tory MPs such as Enoch Powell, apart from Labour colleagues ranging from Douglas Jay on the right to Arthur Scargill on the furthest left. Callaghan was charged by Wilson with organizing the ministerial support for the 'yes' campaign, the meetings, broadcasts, and press conferences that ministers would attend. He insisted, in a letter to the party secretary Ron Hayward, a traditional leftish anti-marketeer, that the government white paper, *The Common Market Negotiations*, be circulated to delegates to a special party conference on the issue, alongside Transport House's own generally hostile paper.[50]

But he himself played very little part in the campaign, confining himself to three speeches and some incidental comments. He disliked referendums as an exercise in any case, apart from his general coolness towards Europe as a concept. His general view was that, in a changed world, getting out of the Common Market would be worse than staying in. 'We can look after ourselves in the Common Market', was his nationalist conclusion.[51] He told Will Howie, a government whip, on 15 May that 'I think things are going pretty well at the moment and as regards those of us who are not convinced Europeans we have to ensure that the E.E.C. remains firmly based in the Atlantic alliance and is outward looking.'[52] The vote on 5 June was a very large majority for the 'yes' campaign, with a two-to-one of roughly 17 million to 8 million. Even in Scotland, where there was nationalist opposition to membership, the 'yes' vote was 58.5 per cent. Of all the United Kingdom counties, the 'noes' carried only Shetland and the Western Isles. It was an unsatisfactory exercise in many ways. The two sides of the argument were hardly presented in a equal fashion despite government funding for both campaigns. More deep-rooted British scepticism about the power of Brussels and the changing development of the EEC towards a more federal system in the future remained in full measure. Even in the mid-1990s, British reluctance to involve itself more fully in Europe continued to provide friction, especially within the Conservative Party where the former Prime Minister Lady Thatcher, herself a very cool supporter of EEC membership in 1975, fanned flames of right-wing dissent. In 1996 some right-wing Conservatives were to endorse Sir James Goldsmith's campaign for a referendum on a federal Europe. A few prominent Conservatives, notably Norman Lamont, actually called for British withdrawal from the EC altogether. Still, the issue of entry was settled for any foreseeable future in 1975. Callaghan wrote to a former fellow south Wales MP, the ex-miner Harold Finch, on 12 June, after it was all over, 'I cannot pretend that I am sorry the referendum is over: the atmosphere was so different from an ordinary Election campaign, but the result was very satisfactory.'[53]

Most accounts of the conclusion of Labour's discussions on Europe claim it as a great victory for Harold Wilson, and rightly so. He had kept his party together with masterly skill, and in the end reached a clear-cut decision by the people while keeping his party intact. From then on, Europe was not a major point of friction within the Labour Party even though the left-wing movement associated with Tony Benn in the early 1980s demanded that Britain withdraw from the Community. The 1983 manifesto included that with many other left-wing demands, but it was perhaps largely symbolic at that time. Neil Kinnock, John Smith, and especially Tony Blair were able to lead their party towards a much more positive view of Europe. They could argue that, especially through the Social Chapter, membership of the Community was an effective route for pursuing the ideas of social justice and economic planning in which the Labour Party had always believed. Harold Wilson's own tactical finessing in 1974–5 was a major factor in this change, his last notable contribution to his party and his nation.

But in some ways Callaghan, equally Eurosceptic at first, made an even larger contribution. He, after all, had to conduct the detail of the negotiations with other European representatives, and he did so with exemplary patience and skill. As in a rugby international, there was a tough opening period but the match had then settled down. By setting the Agricultural Policy to one side and focusing on the financial detail of the British contribution to the budget, Callaghan had ensured that the talks would have some continuity and momentum. It also enabled agreement on other key issues, such as Commonwealth produce of various kinds, regional policy, and quotas for steel production, to be the more easily arrived at. Many contemporaries felt that the renegotiation process was cosmetic, and that in many ways the long-drawn-out process of talks and heads of governments was a kind of charade designed to reassure opinion at home. Certainly, Callaghan and Wilson were well aware of the deep divisions in British opinion and especially within their own party. Without carrying the nation with them, they could not hope to remain an effective part of Europe.

But it would be unfair and trivializing to regard the negotiations as unnecessary or even a farce. Sir Julian Bullard for one thought the discussions were very serious.[54] There were important concessions won on issues such as Commonwealth produce which made the package much more acceptable both to Britain and to its Commonwealth partners. German sceptics of the British approach to renegotiation perhaps did not realize the profound political and emotional import of an issue such as New Zealand butter and lamb exports. They perhaps did not appreciate either the significance of some of the terms won for poorer nations in the Commonwealth, such as sugar for the lesser West Indian islands. For a small nation like Botswana, the protection it gained through the entry of its beef exports to the European Community was absolutely vital to its economic well-being and Callaghan remained an honoured figure in that small country thereafter. When the principal of the University of Wales, Swansea, visited Botswana in the early 1990s on an academic mission it was valuable to him that Lord Callaghan, the saviour of Botswana beef, was the president of his institution.[55] A development like the Community regional fund was also immensely helpful in the internal economic planning of the United Kingdom itself, and another important gain.

The terms won were very far from perfect. The Agricultural Plan remained as a huge, if immovable, source of contention. The arrangement on the budget contributions would only last for a period and would need renegotiation again in the future. The issue was to generate much bad temper when Mrs Thatcher handled European arrangements in the early period of her administration in 1979–82. It was at Dublin at the end of 1980 that she seemed close to opening up again the whole question of British membership, and only after anxious discussion was a solution finally patched up in the following two years. The relations of the *Dame de Fer* with Schmidt and Giscard at that time were as bad as Callaghan's had been good. The future development of the Community towards a more integrated form remained a source for passionate argument in Britain itself, especially with moves towards a European monetary union, heralded by the ERM, the exchange mechanism begun in March 1979 which Britain temporarily joined in 1986. There were interminable arguments about foodstuffs such as lamb, fish, and especially beef. In 1996 Europhobia in the tabloid press reached new heights of virulence over diseased British beef. But these issues lay in the future. For the moment, Callaghan had won a major interim settlement. More than that, the very tone of the discussions and the new kinds of European relationships that were built up made the British attitude towards Europe the more constructive and tolerant. By any test, the adherence of Britain to the European Community in 1975 was a major landmark in the history of national self-perception and relations with the outside world. It confirmed a break with centuries-old traditions of insularity, dating from memories of the Armada to sentiment over the battle of Britain and the retreat from Dunkirk in 1940. Britain and Europe had come to terms one with another. Founded on the more genuinely pioneering work of the Conservatives Macmillan and Heath, this historic achievement must be regarded as one of the supreme moments of James Callaghan's career.

Now that British membership of the Community was confirmed, however, a variety of difficult issues remained in the evolving relationship of member states, and Callaghan had to deal with them seriatim for the rest of his time at the Foreign Office. Proposals for a future monetary union were imprecise at this stage, although the idea of an exchange mechanism was under discussion even in 1975–6. There were many problems here for Britain including the new position of the pound as a floating currency, which had proved beneficial since 1972, and the difficulties of joining any system which might appear to be directed against the dollar. Another problem that arose came directly from British membership of the Community, namely direct elections to the European parliament. Callaghan and Wilson fully accepted this provision, although without immense enthusiasm, while the method of election, particularly the drawing up of the Euro-constituencies and whether Continental forms of proportional representation might be favoured in the voting system, remained to be debated. At a Rome summit in December 1975 Wilson and Callaghan refused to fix any date for community-wide elections to the

European parliament and there the matter rested for the remainder of Wilson's premiership.[56]

In December 1975 a more direct issue arose in connection with the conference on International Economic Co-operation, the 'Group of Seven' so-called, at Rambouillet near Paris. On behalf of the United Kingdom Callaghan objected to proposals that Britain should be represented only as a part of the EEC delegation. On the contrary, as Europe's only oil-producing state, Britain should be represented in its own right. Callaghan had a point here since he wished to make his own independent proposals for the stabilization of international oil prices. By 1980 Britain would be producing 90 per cent of Europe's oil. In the end, after some bad temper all round, it was agreed that Callaghan should offer separate 'statements or remarks' (as Harold Wilson put it) as well as appearing as part of the EEC representation. The result was a very brief speech in which he called for a floor price for oil which would protect Britain's immense investment in the North Sea.[57] *The Times* wrote of 'Harmony Restored'.

But there continued to be problems. The French complained that Callaghan's 'additional comments' on 16 December, after the Rambouillet conference was over, went beyond the Europeans' agreed position. On that day, after a difficult air journey when his plane was delayed by fog, he had spoken in Paris of the need for a minimum price for oil as 'an essential ingredient' for any European energy policy. The Italians smoothed this over as 'a storm in a teacup' (a phrase which must have gained something in translation). John Dickie, the diplomatic correspondent of the *Daily Mail*, weighed in with a vigorous attack on Callaghan's negotiating style. In the end, on 19 December the other seven members of the EEC announced that they agreed with Britain rather than France, and the International Energy Agency duly recommended a floor price of $7 a barrel for oil imports.[58] Another Euro-crisis had been smoothed over. On the other hand, in the broad areas of political co-operation which Callaghan had always regarded as the main rationale of British membership of the EEC, his continuing positive links with other European foreign ministers and heads of government were a fruitful sign of the benefits to be gained from Britain's new role.

It was not only through the European Community that Britain became enmeshed in European affairs in Callaghan's time at the Foreign Office. International conferences such as Rambouillet of course went far wider than EC business and included the United States, Canada, Japan, and other major players. One interlude in the early part of 1975 concerned a dispute with Iceland, the so-called 'cod war' which followed Iceland's declaration of a 50-mile exclusion zone around its complicated coastline. When British trawlers fished in Icelandic waters, the warp of some vessels was cut, and the Royal Navy was called upon to interpose destroyers between the British trawlers and Icelandic craft. Callaghan, however, for all his naval antecedents, wisely left this issue to Roy Hattersley, MP for the land-locked constituency of Birmingham, Sparkbrook. He was variously dispatched to Reykjavik to try to find a compromise, and to Grimsby and Hull to handle furious protests from the fishermen and their MPs, one of whom was Tony Crosland and another, rather more belligerent, John Prescott.[59] A war between Britain and diminutive Iceland was hardly a possibility and in the end the issue petered out. At the end of December, when the Icelanders apparently deliberately damaged a British naval vessel, HMS *Andromeda*, Callaghan complained to Kissinger about Iceland's attitude but in effect Goliath chose to let David get away with it.

A more significant, and indeed constructive, area of European policy came in connection with the revolution in Portugal in 1975. In this case, a focus for European contacts and collaboration was the Socialist International, which Wilson and Callaghan regarded as an important forum for discussion, Wilson especially so. It was a survival of the world-wide appeal of the socialist movement before 1914, before the International was fundamentally split into two (or for a time three) rival bodies by the Russian revolution of 1917. It included politicians of the highest eminence and deliberated on issues of fundamental importance. It had, of course, been one channel through which European views on British membership of the Common Market had been transmitted. Callaghan noted as 'a fascinating exchange' a meeting of the International on 18–19 January 1976 when there was a lengthy discussion on the relationships between the Social Democratic and Communist parties of western Europe. François Mitterrand, with much subtlety, defended his policy of tactical alliance with the French Communist Party as vital for improving the condition of the French working class and redressing the social imbalance of the de Gaulle–Pompidou years. His view was vigorously rebutted by Helmut Schmidt, less fiercely by Harold Wilson.[60]

A far more urgent case which concerned the Socialist International was that of Portugal. In 1968 the long-term dictator Dr Salazar had at last died. He was succeeded by another right-wing dictator, Caetano, and the country had plunged into a period of much instability with lengthy colonial wars in progress against nationalist guerrillas in Mozambique and Angola. On 25 April 1974, shortly after Callaghan became Foreign Secretary, there had been a coup in Lisbon as a result of which a new regime headed by a junta of seven army officers was installed.[61] However, it rapidly emerged that this new regime was largely Marxist. The likelihood was that Portugal, a major nation in the west of Europe, would proceed from fascism to communism with no democratic interlude. The key figure, in the estimation of Callaghan and others, was the Portuguese Socialist leader Mario Soares, a courageous man who had kept the ideal of social democracy alive during the years of fascist dictatorship but who was equally anathema to Portuguese Marxists. By 1975 he had become the Foreign Minister of the frail new régime in Lisbon. The Labour Party and the TUC were asked to do what they could to build up political support—Tom McNally was especially active in this area. On the other hand, left-wing elements were hostile to Soares for his anti-communism. Tony Benn, barely credibly, compared the Communist infiltration of the army in Portugal to the activities of the Levellers in the Cromwellian army at the time of the 1647 Putney debates.[62] But clearly something more tangible was required if democracy in Portugal was to have any chance of flourishing.

On 2 August, the day after the Helsinki CSCE conference, a major meeting of socialist heads of governments was held in Stockholm, under the chairmanship of Olof Palme, the Social Democrat premier of Sweden. It was a remarkable galaxy of talent. Those present included Harold Wilson and James Callaghan from Britain, Willy Brandt and Helmut Schmidt from West Germany, François Mitterrand from France, Bettino Craxi from Italy, Joop den Uyl from the Netherlands, Bruno Kreisky from Austria, Yitzhak Rabin from Israel, and Mario Soares from Portugal. The main item on the agenda was how to protect the Social Democratic movement in Portugal. Palme himself took a robust line on the need to protect comrades in Portugal from being suppressed by either fascism or communism. It was agreed unanimously that the European socialist parties would pursue a variety of methods, including military assistance, to ensure that this did not happen.[63] Thereafter, inevitably, the initiative was taken by national parties. Helmut Schmidt was especially helpful towards the Portuguese, but so, to an even greater degree, was the British Labour government. Callaghan had a high regard for Soares and kept in constant personal touch with him. On this important issue, he was at odds with Henry Kissinger. The latter felt that Portuguese democracy could not be saved and argued, curiously, that if the country went Communist the result would be such chaos that it 'would vaccinate the rest of Europe'.[64] Callaghan took a quite contrary view. Among other things, he well recalled his visit to Czechoslovakia in 1946 and how a Communist coup had extinguished democracy there less than two years later.

The full story of the support that the British Labour government offered the Portuguese Social Democrats, including covert military assistance in dropping supplies, has yet to be told. Even when the relevant public records become available in 2006–7, it may be doubted whether the complete truth will be revealed. There is no doubt, however, that Callaghan regarded sustaining the frail shoots of Portuguese democracy as a vital priority. Subsequently he was to regard this as one of the major achievements of his foreign secretaryship. In the spring of 1975 the first democratic elections for the Portuguese National Assembly saw the Socialists come top of the poll, while the Communists ended up at the bottom. But the stability of the entire democratic process there remained uncertain, especially with the ambiguous role of the army. Callaghan had private discussions with Antunes, a general who was the new Foreign Minister and was also a socialist, on the prospects for a pluralist democracy in Portugal. More important, he and Harold Wilson raised the topic directly with Brezhnev at the CSCE conference at Helsinki on 1 August, the day before the Socialist International meeting in Stockholm. The Soviet President had previously denied that there was any Russian involvement in the internal politics of Portugal. However, Wilson and Callaghan told him that they regarded it as a major test of détente and of the improved relations between Britain and Russia that had emerged in the past few months. Callaghan sent a memorandum to the Soviet leader subsequently on the supply of arms to Portugal.[65] Thereafter, the tension in Portugal subsided. The Prime Minister Gonçalves had to resign in early 1976, and Mario Soares himself eventually emerged as head of the first constitutional government in Portugal, a coalition albeit one without an overall majority. Although the state of Portuguese democracy remained precarious for some years, the legacies of military rule were gradually dismantled, and in 1986 Portugal, as a far more settled constitutional state, was to be admitted as a member of the EEC.

The case of post-revolution Portugal is an important one in many ways. It showed the importance of the Socialist International as an ancient body with some clout in building up international solidarity. It showed how the warmer Anglo-Soviet relationship could be mobilized in the light of the new international agreement at Helsinki. But it also shows the potential influence of a British Labour government in a major international flashpoint. The survival of democracy in Portugal was of concern far beyond that country. Spain had made its own transition to democracy in 1974 while Greece in that year had just thrown off the shackles of the bloody dictatorship of the colonels and had re-embraced democracy of a kind. All these traditionally unstable countries could have lurched into either fascism or communism, with possible civil war or the kind of political and regional anarchy that followed the breakup of Yugoslavia in the 1990s. None did, and all became members of the EC in due time. Against the odds, Portugal was not another Bosnia. Its democracy survived, and its socialist leaders were central to its survival. James Callaghan, as the British Foreign Secretary as again when Prime Minister, was one significant cause of its success. He had fought to sustain Soares in the face of Marxisant groups in the Labour Party who hated Soares for his devout anti-communism, and elements in the US State Department who would do nothing to help Soares since they believed that all Portuguese anti-fascists must be in effect Communists. It was not the least distinguished phase of his career.

In the two years he served in the Foreign Office, Callaghan, his party, and his country acquired a new European dimension. The national perspective gradually began to change. Callaghan was representative of a nation that viewed a merger with alien and unfamiliar continental regimes as unattractive in itself but a necessity forced upon it by change in the modern world. He had helped the transition massively, as had Harold Wilson, by undertaking a process of renegotiation, however qualified, which made the change acceptable to mass British opinion. At the same time, he had emphasized the need for this new Europe to have an Atlantic dimension and for it to pay due heed to the commercial and other rights of the Commonwealth, old and new. When he first went to the Foreign Office, he showed a high degree of Euroscepticism. He had bluntly told his Foreign Office adviser, Michael Butler, in 1974, 'You believe in Europe and I don't.'[66] Since those early days, he had undergone a process of partial re-education and conversion, but so to some degree had the European Community itself. It was a remarkable process of relatively painless transformation, one pregnant with immense implications for the future of the United Kingdom, its polity and culture. And throughout it all the Labour Party had remained intact. By the end of the year the great trauma over the referendum was largely forgotten. It was an immense landmark in Callaghan's career, another signal of his transition from domestic party politician to international statesman.

1. Harold Wilson, *Final Term: The Labour Government, 1974–1976* (London, 1979), 17.
2. Jenkins, *A Life at the Centre*, 371.
3. *The Times*, 13 Mar. 1975; material in Callaghan Papers (uncatalogued).
4. Interviews with Lord Callaghan and Tom McNally.
5. Callaghan, *Time and Chance*, 295.

6. Information from Sir Reginald Hibbert. Cf. John Kenneth Galbraith, *Ambassador's Journal* (London, 1969), 385 (19 June 1962).

7. Nigel Lawson, *The View from No. 11* (London, 1992), 124, quoting a conversation with Callaghan on a Remembrance Day early in Lawson's time as Chancellor.

8. Private information.

9. Interviews with Sir Julian Bullard and Sir Bryan Cartledge.

10. Roy Hattersley, *Who Goes Home?* (London, 1995), 128.

11. Memo in Callaghan Papers, box 22.

12. Material ibid. (uncatalogued).

13. Paper by Callaghan, 14 Oct. 1975 (ibid., box 22).

14. Nicholas Henderson, *Mandarin: The diaries of Nicholas Henderson* (London, 1994), 59 (24 Mar. 1974).

15. Thomson to Callaghan, 4 Mar. 1974 (Callaghan Papers, box 22).

16. Bernard Donoughue, 'Harold Wilson and the Renegotiation of the Terms of Membership, 1974–5: A Witness Account', in Brian Brivati and Harriet Jones (eds.), *From Reconstruction to Integration: Britain and Europe since 1945* (Leicester, 1993), 191 ff.; interview with Lord Donoughue.

17. Henderson, *Mandarin*, 59.

18. F. M. Leventhal, *Arthur Henderson* (Manchester, 1989), 145.

19. Henderson, *Mandarin*, 63.

20. Interview with Tom McNally.

21. Henderson, *Mandarin*, 64–5.

22. Interview with Helmut Schmidt.

23. Material in Callaghan Papers (uncatalogued).

24. Interview with Lord Callaghan.

25. Henderson, *Mandarin*, 62.

26. *The Times*, 2 Apr. 1974; see the government white paper *Renegotiation of the Terms of Entry into the EEC*, Cmnd. 5593 (1974).

27. *The Times*, 2–3 Apr. 1974.

28. Ibid. 5 Apr. 1974.

29. Ibid. 3 Apr. 1974; *Parl. Deb.*, 5th ser., vol. 871, 1257 ff.

30. Material in Callaghan Papers (uncatalogued).

31. Shore to Callaghan, 31 May 1974 (ibid., box 25).

32. Benn, *Office without Power*, 163 (31 May 1974).

33. *The Economist*, 27 July 1974.

34. Pimlott, *Harold Wilson*, 647–9.

35. Castle, *Castle Diaries, 1974–76*, 241 (30 Nov. 1974).

36. Material in Callaghan Papers (uncatalogued).

37. Ibid.; *Time and Chance*, 312–15.

38. Cabinet Conclusions, 17 Oct. 1974 (C (74) 38th).

39. Material in Callaghan Papers (uncatalogued).

40. *Time and Chance*, 318.

41. *Castle Diaries, 1974–76*, 248–50 (12 Dec. 1974).

42. Material in Callaghan Papers (uncatalogued).

43. Ibid.; interview with Dr Henry Kissinger, 26 Oct. 1993.

44. Material in Callaghan Papers (uncatalogued).

45. Ibid.

46. Ibid.; *The Times*, 13 Mar. 1975.

47. *Castle Diaries, 1974–76*, 340–1 (17 Mar. 1975). Benn's published diaries give a rather briefer and less revealing account.

48. Donoughue, 'Harold Wilson and the Renegotiation of the Terms of Membership'; interviews with Lords Callaghan and Merlyn-Rees.

49. *Parl. Deb.*, 5th ser., vol. 889, 1354–66 (9 Apr. 1975).

50. Material in Callaghan Papers (uncatalogued); Callaghan to Ron Hayward, 15 Apr. 1975 (ibid., box 7).

51. Callaghan to Ted Leadbitter MP, 27 Mar. 1975 (ibid.).

52. Callaghan to Will Howie, 15 May 1975 (ibid.).

53. Callaghan to Harold Finch, 12 June 1975 (ibid.).

54. Interview with Sir Julian Bullard.

55. Information from Professor Brian Clarkson.

56. Material in Callaghan Papers (uncatalogued).

57. *The Times*, 6, 11 Nov., 3, 4 Dec. 1975.

58. Ibid. 4, 19, 20 Dec. 1975; Henderson, *Mandarin*, 96–9 (20 Dec. 1975).

59. Hattersley, *Who Goes Home?*, 142–6, a light-hearted account.

60. Materials in Callaghan Papers (uncatalogued).

61. For a dramatic account of these events, see Ben Pimlott, *Frustrate their Knavish Tricks* (London, 1994), 243–72.

62. Benn, *Office without Power*, 315 (11 Feb. 1975).

63. Material in Callaghan Papers (uncatalogued); private information.

64. Interviews with Lord Callaghan and Dr Henry Kissinger.

65. Material in Callaghan Papers (uncatalogued).

66. Interview with Sir Brian Cubbon.

20

KISSINGER AND THE COMMONWEALTH

WHEN Callaghan became Foreign Secretary in March 1974 he told Nicholas Henderson that his two great priorities were the Atlantic alliance and relations with the Commonwealth. In both areas he played an active and in some ways creative role during his time at the Foreign Office. To some degree he improved relationships after a difficult period characterized by what he felt was Heath's fixation with Europe at the expense of other imperatives. Callaghan remained, as he had been ever since the Second World War, a very strong Atlanticist and supporter of NATO and the western alliance. He had maintained this stance during the savage intra-party battles on nuclear weapons and NATO strategy in 1958–60, when he had been as zealous as Hugh Gaitskell on behalf of what he regarded as the linchpin of Labour's international policy since the time of Bevin. Callaghan had also been an advocate of the closest relationship with the United States while at the Treasury. He had, so he believed, turned his close contacts with leading American banking figures like Al Hayes and David Rockefeller, and Treasury personnel such as Secretary Fowler and Bob Roosa, to good effect in trying to protect the pound in the mid-1960s. In a radio interview in 1993, he insisted on the existence of the 'special relationship' between Britain and the United States. On that occasion he defined it in terms of the historical and cultural ties between the two countries and their 'common approach' as evidenced in two world wars.[1] But it is clear that more practical aspects such as joint defence, regional security, intelligence, and, especially, economic and financial collaboration loomed even larger.

It had concerned him, and indeed Harold Wilson also, that the Anglo-American relationship had so deteriorated during the Heath years. It reached its lowest point during the Six-Day War when Heath positively opposed Britain's helping US air operations on behalf of Israel in its conflict with Egypt and other Arab states. By contrast, Callaghan told Tom McNally that he felt it was his 'responsibility' to get on with US secretaries of state. His own period at the Foreign Office, therefore, represented a purposive attempt to turn the clock back to more harmonious times, under both Labour and Tory governments. To a degree that has since often been underestimated, he was successful. In one sense, this might have seemed surprising. The earlier warmer relationships with the Americans enjoyed by Labour governments had been with Democratic governments, those of Truman after 1945 and Johnson after 1964 which might have seemed more ideologically congenial to the Labour Party. There were those who believed the same about the Clinton–Blair relationship in 1996–7. In 1974, by contrast, the Republicans were in power, and had been since 1969. Yet in fact, Callaghan was to get on somewhat better with them and build up a more enduring relationship.

When Labour came to power in March 1974, Richard Nixon was still at the White House, after a period in office marked by a growing distancing from Britain and indeed Europe generally. The main emphasis of US policy was on the Far East and in particular trying to clear up the mess in Vietnam. There was the corollary of improving relations with Communist China which the USA still refused formally to recognize. Callaghan and Wilson went to Washington as early as 26 June 1974 for a SEAC conference and for private meetings with Nixon and Kissinger. It was a friendly discussion mainly concerned with the prospects for détente and arms limitation. Callaghan pressed the need here for a test ban and non-proliferation treaty in view of the spread of nuclear weapons manufacture, most recently to India. It was a theme he was to pursue consistently over the next four years. Nixon was amiable and promised that nothing would be done on strategic arms limitation that would be harmful to British interests or to the viability of a British independent nuclear deterrent.[2] He gave a *tour d'horizon* of the international scene that deeply impressed the British. But Callaghan's connection with him was very brief, because the growing Watergate crisis was to blow him away. Nixon resigned on 8 August and was replaced by his vice-president, Gerald Ford.

The relationship between Callaghan and Ford was an excellent one from the start, marked by a good deal of personal warmth on each side. They had a long first meeting in Washington on 24 September, when Callaghan was attending the UN General Assembly. They discussed broad aspects of US–European relations. Their conversation was sufficiently lengthy and cordial for the White House press secretary to have to deny, somewhat ludicrously, that Ford was sympathetic to a Labour victory in the forthcoming general election.[3] In a later telephone conversation with Harold Wilson on 11 October, Ford spoke most warmly of this discussion. 'I really enjoyed the meeting with Mr. Callaghan about a couple of weeks ago. . . . He is a very impressive fellow and I know that he and Henry [Kissinger] get on really well.'[4] This friendly relationship continued right until Ford left office in January 1977 after his election defeat at the hands of Jimmy Carter. Callaghan was to find his contacts with the American President a particular comfort during the saga of the IMF negotiations in autumn of 1976, although it is right to add that their friendship did not produce the practical and immediate financial assistance for which the British premier hoped. The US Treasury Minister William Simon, a highly conservative Wall Street bond dealer, was distinctly less sympathetic than his President. Ford fell from office thereafter but his personal ties with Callaghan (and, indeed, the warm relationship between Mrs Betty Ford and Audrey Callaghan as well) continued long after both had retired. A remarkable group of senior statesmen was formed, to meet annually in Vail, Colorado, varied at times by cruises on an ocean-going yacht along the coast of Alaska or from Kiev to the Black Sea and the Crimea. This 'Vail Group', which included at various times Helmut Schmidt, Valéry Giscard d'Estaing, Malcolm Fraser of Australia, and other former heads of government, was a fascinating association which enlivened Callaghan's busy retirement.

But the relationship that was particularly noted, included, as we have seen, by Gerald Ford, was the friendship that blossomed between Callaghan and his opposite number, the Secretary of State Dr Henry Kissinger. They were indeed very different in background and personality. Callaghan was a union official from a disadvantaged home who had then turned full-time career politician. He had done nothing else for thirty years. Kissinger, on the other hand, was a brilliant German Jewish émigré who had been for years a university professor at Harvard in the government department, teaching and researching on international relations and strategy. His first major book had been on the policy of an earlier British Foreign Secretary, Lord Castlereagh, who occupied that position during and after the end of the Napoleonic Wars from 1812 to 1822, and whose *realpolitik* Kissinger admired. While at Harvard, he was thought to be possibly a Democrat in sympathy. His distinguished book *Nuclear Weapons and Foreign Policy* (1957) impressed the administration and he acted as part-time foreign policy adviser to Presidents John F. Kennedy and Lyndon B. Johnson. He had no particular regard for Nixon and had declined to be a part of his campaign team in 1968. His closest associate in the Republican

Party was the ex-Governor of New York Nelson Rockefeller, one of Nixon's long-standing opponents.[5] Quite unexpectedly, however, he had been asked to join the Nixon administration after the Republican victory in 1968. He served in the key role of head of the National Security Council. In effect, this eminent professor from the Democratic redoubt in Harvard Yard, home to the Galbraiths and Schlesingers, became the chief foreign policy adviser to the deeply controversial Republican president.

He was especially active in shuttle diplomacy to promote a ceasefire in Vietman, though he also attracted widespread notoriety after Nixon's bloody intervention in Cambodia in 1970. He was always a suspect figure in liberal circles in America. The President had finally made him Secretary of State at the start of 1973. He had subsequently played the most active role in a variety of regional crises, in South-East Asia, in the Middle East, and in arms limitation talks with the Soviet Union. He displayed a remarkable capacity for survival after Watergate and remained as Secretary of State under Gerald Ford. By the time he left the State Department in January 1977 he had extended his interests to international economic matters, notably the world's energy supplies, to complement his expertise on strategy and regional security.[6] Throughout it all, he continued to reflect his origins as mittel-Europa academic and intellectual, rather than politician or career diplomat. His was a reflective, deeply subtle, totally unsentimental mind. He was as conceptually organized an international politician as Callaghan was pragmatic and unideological.

Nevertheless from the very start, the two struck up an excellent relationship, one that became in time a bond of much affection. Kissinger, if not exactly an Anglophile, had a high regard for the alliance with the United Kingdom and believed in at least some kind of special relationship, as he was to spell out later in the journal *International Affairs* in 1982.[7] As he recalled there, his regard for the quality of the personnel of the British Foreign Office was such that he used them, rather than State Department advisers, to play key roles, including the drafting of documents, in bilateral negotiations between the United States and the Soviet Union. To some degree, he needed Britain as an ally because the United States in 1974 felt it needed allies in general. There was a new sense of vulnerability in that previously all-powerful nation on many fronts. Vietnam had proved a military catastrophe which had left Americans seeming to affront what the revolutionaries of 1776 had called 'the decent opinion of mankind'. It had caused a huge rift in domestic opinion and forced an American president from office. The military strength of the Soviet Union, in long- and intermediate-range missiles as well as in conventional arms, continued to grow.

The American economy was also experiencing unpleasant and unfamiliar difficulties, as the inflation of the dollar priced US goods out of world markets. In 1971 the United States experienced its first trade deficit of the century. Its European allies had long protested at having to accept inflated US dollars in order, indirectly, to finance an unwinnable and inhuman war in Vietnam. With political tensions and racial troubles at home, the United States needed affection and reassurance in the world, at a time when the European powers were grouping together inwardly in their Common Market. Callaghan was only one major European observer who felt deep alarm that the United States might at some stage pull out of its European commitments and leave the continent inadequately defended against a buoyant Soviet Union. Great Britain, therefore, appeared a traditional, reassuring, and intimate power, even if one in decline in terms of resources, with influence in key areas such as the Middle East and southern Africa, whom the United States of America still needed.

But Callaghan individually fulfilled many an American's requirements at this time, as a devoted, though not uncritical, Atlanticist. What is more, Kissinger liked him personally very much.[8] He found Callaghan friendly and unstuffy, and admired his directness and honesty. When he had a very early meeting with the new Foreign Secretary in March 1974, he recorded in his memoirs that Callaghan 'told his subordinates in my presence that he wanted an end put to the mutual needling'.[9] He also liked Callaghan's ability to respect confidentiality and to create an atmosphere of openness and trust. But there was more to it than that. Callaghan appeared to provide a considerable fount of wisdom with his long knowledge of critical areas of the world over three decades and his capacity for shrewd analysis of them. Like his American counterpart, he was above all else a realist, though not immune to flights of idealism. Kissinger's shuttle diplomacy in the Middle East in 1974 drew heavily on both Callaghan's personal knowledge of the Israeli political scene and his good relationship with both President Sadat of Egypt and King Hussein of Jordan. He particularly recognized Callaghan's great expertise in Africa and they worked closely together in trying to work out a new initiative in Rhodesia. Of course, Callaghan's renegotiation of the Common Market terms was to give him awareness of European power politics as well.

In short, Kissinger came to regard Callaghan as an experienced hand, a wise old bird, with whom he could commune in freedom and friendship. Soon private meetings of the two were regular events, usually in London when Kissinger was passing through to one of the world's trouble spots. There were dinner and other social gatherings. The press noted the new warmth of the relationship between the two foreign ministers. In February 1975 there was what the press called an 'extraordinary comedy double-act' at Heathrow airport. It reached a remarkable level on 6 March when Kissinger made a special flight to Cardiff to be present at the granting of the freedom of the city to Callaghan, as also to his fellow Cardiff MP George Thomas. He noted the genuine unforced pleasure that Callaghan derived from contact with his Welsh friends, colleagues, and constituents. He also enjoyed music from the harp, a hitherto unfamiliar instrument. The event was spoilt neither by a strike by Cardiff's electricians which closed down the public address system nor by some feeling from George Thomas (as conveyed in his memoirs) that he was being upstaged. At the City Hall, Kissinger spoke to the Cardiff audience of the qualities of 'my friend and partner Jim. . . . A citizen of the world . . . a friend on whose word one can always rely.' He compared him with Ernest Bevin in trying to link practical solutions with 'some deeper human value'. Callaghan replied simply, 'This is the greatest day of my life.'[10]

The close relationship between the two was reflected at the time Kissinger had to leave the State Department in January 1977 following the Democrats' victory in the presidential election. He wrote then to Callaghan with considerable warmth, describing him as 'by turn conceptual thinker, an innovator, a negotiator, a critic when need be . . . and always a leader and friend'.[11] He admired the fact that Callaghan had played an active and fruitful role in world affairs despite his manifold problems at home. Callaghan in return praised Kissinger as one of the greatest of American secretaries of state. He took pride in the fact that they had nurtured the special relationship which was 'unique and of supreme importance'.[12] The friendship between the two continued long after Kissinger ceased to be Secretary of State in 1977 and Callaghan retired from front-line politics in 1980. In subsequent years, Kissinger's visits to London would invariably include a get-together with Jim and Audrey, and he would also attend the Ford gatherings at Vail, Colorado, from time to time. The official diplomatic contacts that began in March 1974 led to a lifelong friendship.

But these social and personal aspects apart, the Anglo-American relationship had to be tested in the fires of specific policy issues and international crises. Here, for all the huge change in the personal chemistry produced by the Callaghan–Kissinger relationship, there were in fact several difficult passages. One has already been discussed—the implications of the 1974 revolution in Portugal, an event whose imminence had escaped the CIA. Kissinger and the American government were distinctly wary of

Callaghan's policy of giving moral and other aid to Soares and the Portuguese Social Democrats. They were almost inclined to believe it might be objectively better to let the country go Communist and prevent the contagion from spreading thereafter. Callaghan believed that Portugal could be saved for democracy and that indeed it was vital that it was, given its strategic position in western Europe. Events were to suggest that Callaghan's appreciation was the shrewder of the two.

Another area of disagreement was the hitherto little-regarded small British colony of Belize, formerly British Honduras, in the Caribbean. This, along with the Falklands and similar obscure parts of the globe, had been mentioned to Ted Rowlands when he took up his role under Callaghan to keep an eye on possible future flashpoints. Its historic ties with Britain were of long standing. Its logwood industry had been an imperial resource since the wars against Louis XIV, and it had been a British colony since 1864. Although it had become self-governing in 1964, British troops were still stationed there. Belize was, in fact, claimed by the militarist dictatorship which governed neighbouring Guatemala, much to the understandable alarm of the local population.

Kissinger took the traditional neo-imperial American viewpoint, most stridently shown during Theodore Roosevelt's presidency of 1901–9 ('I took Panama'), of regarding Central America as its own private preserve, where the US marines could be deployed without foreign interference and local puppet regimes manipulated at will. This policy had been followed by Presidents Harding and Coolidge even during the so-called isolationism of the 1920s. Guatemala had been a particular concern of the USA over the years, from the standpoint both of national security and of the economic exploitation of its agricultural produce, notably fruit, sugar, and coffee. There was the notorious centrality of United Fruit in the politics as well as the economics of the country. In the years of the Eisenhower presidency alarm had been caused by Soviet arms shipments which led to fears that Guatemala might be going Communist, a Cuba before its time. This had led the CIA to launch a coup to overthrow the vaguely liberal government of President Arbenz Guzman in 1954, and to install instead a right-wing regime of much repressiveness and brutality even by the standards of Central America. Protests at the UN were ignored, and United Fruit (in which key members of the Eisenhower administration, including the Dulles family, had a direct financial stake) continued its socially exploitative and environmentally damaging practices undisturbed.[13]

Things had scarcely improved in Guatemala by the 1970s. Nevertheless, over lunch with Callaghan on 13 December 1975 Kissinger inquired whether some kind of peaceful handover of Belize to Guatemala was feasible. Callaghan replied bluntly that this was 'impossible'.[14] He was no more likely to shift on Belize than he was on Gibraltar or the Falklands. He continued to resist US suggestions on the point and indeed sent British military force to the area to warn the Guatemala government off. British troops there were put on a war footing, and the support of Prime Minister Pierre Trudeau of Canada was enlisted to have British Phantom fighters land in St John's, Newfoundland, to refuel. The Phantoms very soon landed in Belize and conducted patrolling exercises in the Caribbean area in 1976–7.[15] In due course, the Guatemala government retreated from an apparent confrontation. Even in Central America, therefore, Callaghan was not going to surrender meekly in face of US disapproval.

But much the most difficult episode to generate Anglo-US tension came very early on in Callaghan's time as Foreign Secretary. It arose in July–September 1974 over Cyprus. The recurrence of the timeless hostility between the Turks and the Greeks in that divided island provided an action replay of the difficult issues of the fight for 'enosis' (union) with Greece and the subsequent granting of independence in the late 1950s. The personnel, indeed, were somewhat the same, since the president of Cyprus was Archbishop Makarios, a key player in the 1950s who had spent some time as a resident of a British jail in the Seychelles. In addition, differences over Cyprus led to the sharpest tensions between London and Washington since the time of Suez—which, indeed, raised some of the same issues both for the two governments and also for the authority of the United Nations.

The Greeks and the Turks were historic enemies. Britain had a tradition of defending Greek independence against the Turkish yoke since the days of Byron and the battle of Navarino. Greece and Turkey had often been at odds in the eastern Mediterranean, over Crete and lesser islands. The two countries had gone to war in 1912–13 and, more seriously, in 1921–2 when Lloyd George had fanned the flames of Greek nationalism. Matters in Cyprus reached a crisis in the 1950s when the Cypriot Greeks launched their campaign for enosis. In the end, the settlement of 1960 gave Cyprus independence, but left Greece, Turkey, and Britain as the guarantors of the island under a Treaty of Guarantee. It left a smouldering bitterness between the Greek majority and the Turkish minority in Cyprus and on several occasions a Turkish invasion to enforce some kind of partition had been threatened. In July 1974 Cyprus exploded into violence again. The regime of Archbishop Makarios, its president, had been attacked by Greek nationalists who resented his abandoning the aim of enosis, his disavowal of the EOKA terrorists, and his attempts to establish a better relationship with the Turkish minority. Quite unexpectedly—it seems that not even the CIA had engineered or even anticipated it—a coup took place in Cyprus on 15 July. Makarios was overthrown and was at first believed to have been killed. A new, violently nationalist regime was set up in Nicosia, led by a former EOKA terrorist of unsavoury reputation, Nicos Sampson.

This demanded urgent action from the British Foreign Secretary. Here was a Commonwealth country in crisis. Apart from Britain's role as a guarantor of the settlement in Cyprus, there were 5,000 British servicemen (not in fact a fighting force) on the bases on the island, as well as 12,000 dependants who needed to be protected. On 17 July the Turkish Prime Minister, Ecevit, came to London for talks with Wilson, Callaghan, and Roy Mason, the Defence Secretary.[16] Ecevit declared bluntly that he could no longer regard the Greeks as any kind of guarantors of the security and integrity of Cyprus and asked that British bases be used to assist a Turkish invasion to protect the minority community on the island. The British government inevitably refused and urged the Turks not to take unilateral military action which might turn Cyprus into a bloodbath. They assured the Turkish premier that Britain would not recognize the Sampson regime in Cyprus and would try to promote its downfall. Callaghan acknowledged that the Cypriot Turks had justifiable grievances that needed redress. But Ecevit went back to Ankara with Turkish intentions still unclear.

At this stage, Anglo-American diplomacy came into play. Joe Sisco, Kissinger's assistant under-secretary of state, saw Callaghan in London on 18 July when he was pressed on the urgency of an agreed Anglo-American response to try to keep the peace. The next day, Callaghan spelt out for Kissinger the components of what he felt such a response should be. The legitimacy of the presidency of Archbishop Makarios should be asserted. Every effort should be made to ensure that the Sampson regime was overthrown. A new constitutional basis must be worked out for Cyprus, and the USA must exert 'very great pressure' on the government in Athens to make them amenable.[17] Callaghan then had urgent talks with both the Greek and Turkish ambassadors in London and demanded that both governments turn away from military action and meet with the British to guarantee the territorial integrity of Cyprus. Both refused. The Turks mobilized their fleet and early on 20 July landed forces in Cyprus. The Greeks immediately threatened to declare war on Turkey and impose forcibly the union of Cyprus with Greece. On the 21st the Turks started to bomb Greek Cypriot positions; in return the Greeks began to assemble warships to transport their forces to the island to defend their compat riots.

This led to a very difficult period of strain in relations between Washington and London and, for once, between Callaghan and Kissinger personally. Many in London believed that the United States had orchestrated the Turkish invasion, and Kissinger's own role was highly dubious. Callaghan was anxious for immediate Anglo-American action, under the auspices of the UN preferably, to restore the Makarios government in Nicosia and to deter the Turks from continuing aggression which was contrary to the UN Charter. But Kissinger viewed this with alarm. He recorded in his memoirs his view that the US government should do nothing; Joe Sisco's mission to Europe had this very purpose in mind.[18] The regime of the Greek colonels was on the point of collapse anyway and the USA did not wish to be seen as the agents of their downfall. On the other hand, any policy of resisting a Turkish invasion would have many dangers. It would appear to be favouring the hated Greek junta. It would be regarded as a hostile act by the government in Ankara, which was regarded as a valuable buffer between NATO and the Soviet Union and which had permitted US military bases and nuclear missile installations on Turkish soil. In addition to not wishing to offend the Turks, Kissinger was also mindful of Muslim opinion generally in the Middle East, so delicately poised at this moment.[19] The impact on the Arab–Israeli situation there would be far more serious than antagonizing the Greek government, let alone the Greek ethnic vote in the United States. In effect, Kissinger's stance was one of 'neutrality in favour of the Turks', just as Bevin in 1948 had been 'neutral against the Jews'. There was a more direct reason for Kissinger being unwilling to take decisive action. The Congressional hearings on the Watergate break-in were reaching a climax in Washington and the authority of President Nixon and his administration was rapidly eroding. Kissinger's involvement in political turmoil at home meant that he could communicate with Callaghan only at long range at this time, and misunderstandings between the two rapidly multiplied.

On a hectic Sunday, 21 July 1974, violence escalated all over Cyprus and both the Greek and Turkish governments appeared on the brink of war. A resolution in the United Nations called for an immediate ceasefire and Kissinger and Callaghan engaged in frantic diplomacy all day to implement it.[20] The Foreign Office files for 1974 (not due to be released to historians until 2005) show that Callaghan spoke no less than seven times to Kissinger that day, as well as twice to Kypraios, twice to Ecevit, and once to the French Foreign Minister, Jean Sauvargnargues. In these discussions, Callaghan proposed a three-power meeting to create a new settlement, to be held in Vienna on the 22nd. Throughout there is an impression of the British government trying to urge the Americans into immediate action. At 4.55 p.m. Kissinger infuriated Callaghan by apparently proposing that a ceasefire be delayed, largely because a coup in Athens appeared to be imminent which would install a leftish Greek government more sympathetic to the Soviet Union. Cyprus itself was in chaos with the flight of thousands of Greek Cypriots from the path of the Turkish troops. Britain had to use some of its military strength to give protection to dependent British citizens wishing to leave the island. In the end, Kissinger agreed to put the maximum of pressure on the Turkish government and threatened to remove nuclear weapons from Turkish soil. The Ecevit government climbed down at the last moment. The Greeks had already agreed to meet in Vienna for talks. A ceasefire was arranged, to take effect at 2 p.m. on 22 July.

The following day, a new twist occurred. The colonels' regime in Athens was overthrown in a bloodless coup, and a relatively liberal prime minister, Karamanlis, took over, with Mavros as his Foreign Minister. They symbolized the restoration of Greek democracy. In Cyprus the ephemeral Sampson government was also removed and a respected civilian, Clerides, became acting head. Both events much improved the atmosphere. There were many alarms, and prospects of conflict between the Turks in Cyprus and the United Nations forces stationed there, perhaps with the British forces dragged in too. But the Cyprus crisis was now in diplomatic rather than military mode. On 25 July, meetings began, not now in Vienna but in the Palais des Nations in Geneva, between the Greek representative and the Turkish Foreign Minister Gunes, with Callaghan keeping the ring.

The negotiations at Geneva dragged on for the next three weeks. The Turks intransigently insisted on scrapping the settlement of 1960 and enforcing a partition of Cyprus to separate the two communities. The Greeks insisted that this was incompatible with the sovereignty of Cyprus as an integrated independent state and urged that the two communities work out arrangements on an internal basis. Callaghan reported wearily to the Commons on 31 July. *The Times* reported him as 'looking in much need of sleep after many days and nights of almost non-stop negotiation'.[21] The burden of his message was that there was no progress and that peace in Cyprus was fragile. He announced his pride in the work of the British troops in preserving some kind of stability and links with the outside world there, and was congratulated by Douglas-Home, the Conservative spokesman, for his labours.

But the real problem lay not so much in the predictable deadlock between the Greeks and the Turks, but in the continuing lack of accord between Britain and the United States. Callaghan was anxious that British troops in Cyprus should be significantly reinforced and also that the UN should be enlisted to ensure that any agreement was duly observed by both sides. Kissinger was most alarmed at this approach. He wished to see neither possible British military involvement nor the UN getting further embroiled. Callaghan urged him to put pressure on the Turks. In effect, Kissinger refused to do so. The prospects of an effective response weakened still further on 8 August when President Nixon finally decided to step down following the climactic developments in the Watergate affair. As Gerald Ford succeeded him, there was for a time a near vacuum in US foreign policy.

On 11 August Callaghan and Kissinger had sharp intercontinental exchanges.[22] The Secretary of State declared his opposition to what he regarded as British belligerence. He opposed the idea of British troops being placed under UN auspices to help deter the Turks. He expressed puzzlement about Callaghan's negotiating aims at the Geneva conference. There was talk of Kissinger referring to his colleague, the British Foreign Secretary, as a 'boy scout'.[23] Callaghan, in a brisk discussion with the Assistant Secretary of State, Arthur Hartman, rejoined that, in his inactivity, Kissinger 'was not facing up to the real problem'. He wondered what Kissinger would do if the Turks used further force to strike out from their bridgehead in the east of Cyprus. There was also the protection of 12,000 British dependants to consider. It was widely believed in London that the Americans were encouraging the Turks in their intransigence. Dr John Cunningham, Callaghan's PPS who attended the Geneva sessions with him, was one of many who were convinced that the Americans were deliberately sabotaging the conference.[24]

With the Americans so reluctant to act, or do more than urge the Turks verbally to take no further military action, the Geneva conference was running into the sand. The final blow for British efforts came when it emerged that, despite a robust attitude by Dr Kurt Waldheim, the UN Secretary-General, UN forces in Cyprus would do nothing to resist any further Turkish advance. The Geneva conference broke up amidst mutual threats from Athens and Ankara on 12 August. The Turkish forces in Cyprus proceeded to break the ceasefire and fighting on the island began in earnest again. Meandering negotiations continued between the two sides. In the event, the US Congress proved more resolute than Kissinger, and the House of Representatives resolved by 307 votes to 90 to cut off military aid to Turkey forthwith, despite the Secretary of State's vehement opposition. In the course of September, by which time Callaghan was himself increasingly deflected by the British election campaign, fighting stopped in Cyprus. Under the presidency again of Archbishop Makarios (who had miraculously escaped after the Nicos Sampson coup and had been protected in a British base thereafter), Cyprus moved towards a more peaceful condition, but this time with the island partitioned with a third of its territory ruled by the Turkish minority under their leader Raoul Denktash. It was an uneasy settlement with many countries refusing to accept the partition of Cyprus or the existence of Turkish northern Cyprus. Nevertheless, there matters remained down to the mid-1990s, with the two communities unreconciled. There was a continuing legacy of hostility between the almost equally unstable governments of Athens and Ankara which almost any stray island under territorial dispute in the eastern Mediterranean was liable to ignite. In 1996–7 there was renewed violence between Greek and Turkish Cypriots which threatened the stability of the region once again.

Cyprus was a highly unsatisfactory episode in the Anglo-American diplomacy at this period. Callaghan, whose later attitude was remarkably forbearing, was in an interview much later to recognize it as a major hiatus. Kissinger himself deeply resented the criticism his policies had attracted, not only in London but throughout Europe. He felt 'sore', Callaghan recorded.[25] The arms embargo passed by the US Congress was in Kissinger's view 'heavy-handed'.[26] He argued that any posture of threatening the Turks had been a mistake since it had only fuelled Greek nationalism. But, of course, he had wider strategic reasons for wishing to minimize the pressure he was prepared to put on the Turks. Callaghan himself felt that a major opportunity had been lost by the failure to back up diplomacy by force, especially American force. Turkish aggression had been rewarded and a constitutional settlement overthrown unilaterally by *realpolitik* from Ankara, backed up by the Pentagon. Reluctantly he was forced to accept the view of Denktash, the Turkish Cypriot leader, that only 'a geographical separation' of the two communities, in a 'bi-regional federation', could bring any prospect of lasting peace.[27] This was more or less what emerged in the twenty-two years from 1974.

On the other hand, Callaghan could reasonably argue that, with no prospect of military support from either the USA or the UN, there were sharp limits to what Britain could do other than protect its own nationals in Cyprus. At the very least, another Suez, this time perhaps with no allies at all, had been averted. Cyprus was, like Northern Ireland, a historically intractable problem and in the circumstances Callaghan had hardly any further cards to play. In any case, it can fairly be argued that the events of early August 1974 were highly unusual since Watergate and the resignation of Nixon seriously deflected the diplomatic energies of the US state. No previous American president had resigned midway through his term of office. Kissinger, on the other hand, argued that the Turks would have taken military action at that time whatever policy the USA had followed. On balance, Callaghan's reputation as Foreign Secretary was not shaken unduly by the Cyprus imbroglio. He did not face serious criticism from his Cabinet colleagues; a passionately pro-Greek minister like Barbara Castle recognized that Callaghan had at least genuinely tried to curb Turkish aggression and that Britain could hardly plunge into a full-scale war in the eastern Mediterranean. Peter Shore's belligerent cry that Britain should fight to defend democracy did not meet with much backing.[28] The Cyprus episode showed the limits to Anglo-US co-operation even at this time, and illustrated the different perspectives that even Callaghan and Kissinger, normally so close, could bring to bear. In effect, Cyprus was given up as a bad job, and swept to one side in the relations between Britain and America. Over the next twenty-two years, it was not to re-emerge.

In all other areas, from the Common Market to Rhodesia, the new closeness between London and Washington achieved positive results. This was especially apparent in what Kissinger himself regarded as the key area of global concern at the time, namely international security and the preservation of détente with the Soviet Union. Throughout the European continent, there had been a mood of growing relaxation in the early 1970s. The *Ostpolitik* championed by Chancellor Willy Brandt in West Germany notably lessened international tension. There was a great-power guarantee of the territorial boundaries laid down at Yalta in 1945, agreement on access to West Berlin, the mutual recognition of East and West Germany. This coincided with a growing campaign from the Soviet Union for détente with President Brezhnev simultaneously pressing for strategic arms limitation, a recognition of existing boundaries, and technological assistance from the west. A Conference on Security and Co-operation in Europe had been launched in 1973, not confined to Europe, however, but also with the participation of the United States and Canada. When Callaghan went to the Foreign Office in March 1974 these discussions had been dragging on and the British government was anxious to give them new impetus.

Callaghan took a keen interest in Anglo-Soviet relations; after all, his own first-hand knowledge of the Soviet Union went back nearly thirty years. He himself was convinced of the genuineness of the new mood of détente as evidenced in the more relaxed international posture of

Brezhnev and the Soviet Union. He had heard of support for it from such expected advocates as Ponomarev and the head of the KGB, Andropov. When Julian Bullard presented him in April 1974 with a Foreign Office memorandum which spelt out, in traditional terms, the constant threat from the Russians, militarily as well as ideologically, Callaghan in effect responded that he did not agree.[29] This provided the theme of many of his lengthy sessions with Henry Kissinger at Carlton Gardens and elsewhere. He believed, and with good reason, that the arms burden alone was making a long period of détente a necessity for the Soviet Union. It had half the gross national product of the United States, but its arms expenditure was greater. Callaghan told the Socialist International that there was a changing relationship between the Russians and the Americans. The Soviet Union was anxious for American technology. At the same time it saw the United States, along with western Europe, as large markets able to absorb raw materials and energy with which the Russians hoped to pay for western technology. Callaghan's rough notes of 1975 read: 'U.S.S.R. interest in detente is so great that she will back down on confrontation unless a vital interest is threatened.'[30]

Along with his Foreign Office advisers such as Sir Thomas Brimelow, Callaghan identified a dual approach in Soviet policy and attitudes. In the realm of party ideology, there would continue to be a philosophy of struggle, of trying to take up opportunities offered by social dislocation (such as the rundown of heavy industry) and weaknesses in the economies of the capitalist powers. But in the realm of inter-state relations, the Marxian dialectic had long ceased to apply. Soviet strategy was one of détente, the relaxation of trade, the expansion of trade credits, and a policy of moving away from confrontation and towards the building up of contacts at all levels. He worked to persuade Henry Kissinger of the validity of this interpretation, and with some fair success.

The Labour government, Wilson no less than Callaghan, believed that Britain had its own role to play in building up détente and giving reality to the CSCE negotiations on security. Both the Labour leaders had a long tradition of concern for eastern Europe. Wilson himself had had constructive contacts with the Russians, especially in the commercial area, since his time as Overseas Trade Secretary in 1946. He had kept up a series of contacts and visits to the Soviet Union in the 1950s (thereby, according to Peter Wright and others, arousing the interest of MI5).[31] Mikoyan had been a particular intimate of his. Callaghan's own experience had been somewhat wider, involving his particular concern with Africa and Commonwealth relations in general, but he retained his concern for better relations with Russia and a warm sympathy for its people since his visit to Moscow in the winter of 1945–6. He also enjoyed a good personal relationship with the long-standing Soviet Foreign Minister Andrei Gromyko, in some ways a somewhat similar figure with his direct, forceful manner, and his strict professionalism. He also dealt effectively with the Soviet ambassador, whose lengthy monologues were once interrupted by the Foreign Secretary with the comment that he was talking total nonsense.

Callaghan firmly believed that Anglo-Soviet relations could be made more cordial and fruitful, after the frigidity that had following the expulsion of a large array of alleged Soviet spies by Heath and Douglas-Home in 1971. Wilson and Callaghan had a very successful visit to Moscow in February 1975 at which they had lengthy discussions over the whole range of political and economic issues with Brezhnev and Kosygin. Perhaps a little surprisingly, part of Callaghan's preparation included private talks with his Tory predecessor at the Foreign Office, Douglas-Home, about Anglo-Soviet relations and the prospects for British trade.[32] The visit was an instructive occasion. Sir Julian Bullard, who was present, noted that Wilson concentrated almost entirely on trade aspects, including the prospect of £1,000m. of credits. He also kept asking embarrassing questions about the health and whereabouts of his old friend Mikoyan. Sir John Hunt noted his obsessive fear of surveillance there, whether by the KGB or MI5. Callaghan, by contrast, led for the British side on all other aspects of Anglo-Soviet relationships and showed a considerable mastery of all of them. He largely dominated the British deputation and helped draft the final communiqué. In addition to noting the growth of commercial, professional, and cultural contacts, there was much discussion of European security. Here, Callaghan pointed out the linkage that could be made between stability in continental Europe and a Soviet withdrawal from international subversion, including particularly Portugal. The priority to be given to allowing Portuguese democracy to flourish was often emphasized in talks on the lead up to a CSCE agreement. Callaghan also had a long discussion with Gromyko about the form and timing of a CSCE summit, and raised directly the question of human rights in the Soviet Union. Gromyko responded in measured terms and proved helpful in drafting the final communiqué.

This Moscow visit, the first by a British prime minister since Wilson had gone there in July 1966, was regarded by the Soviet leadership as a major preliminary to the CSCE summit on European security which was arranged to be held at Helsinki on 1 August. Much of the preliminary detailed work for it was done by the British Foreign Office, notably by Callaghan's assistant Michael Alexander. One useful intermediary, whatever his other shortcomings, was President Ceauşescu of Romania who helped prod the Soviet Union towards the Helsinki summit.[33] It was a meeting that aroused much enthusiasm in Germany and France. Despite some American misgivings, the CSCE agreement was duly signed. It provided the guarantees that Brezhnev sought on the post-1945 frontiers in eastern Europe. They were given *de facto* recognition while there was also the juridical recognition of Soviet sovereignty. On the other hand, the Soviet Union agreed to open up communications and provide greater protection for human rights and thereby some kind of yardstick by which its future evolution could be measured. This did not work out in the way that Brezhnev anticipated. The unexpected outcome was in fact to be the steady flowering of Soviet dissidence and the rapid opening up of a previously closed society that led to such dramatic changes under Gorbachev from 1985.

The Americans remained somewhat suspicious of Helsinki, Kissinger perhaps less so than some others. However, Callaghan regarded the Helsinki accord as a notable step forward in international détente. Subsequently he was to see it as an important precursor of Perestroika. On a more personal level, he had struck up a good working relationship with Brezhnev and confirmed his effective association with Gromyko. In the immediate future, the Russians had privately agreed to stop any subversion in Portugal which had most important and positive consequences.

Thereafter, Callaghan and the Foreign Office worked on improving relations with the Russians in a variety of areas. There were new trading links. There was also the Anglo-Soviet Round Table of businessmen, scientists, academics, and others, which was to hold its first meeting in Chatham House in the course of that year. This was an idea of Callaghan's proposed at the meeting in Moscow: its model was the annual Anglo-German sessions at Königswinter. Callaghan's final major commitment as Foreign Secretary was to come in three days of further talks with Gromyko in London in March 1976.[34] Among other things, the British Foreign Secretary here presented Gromyko with a list of individuals, including known dissidents and Jews, to whom exit permits might be given in order to reunite families. There was some evidence of movement on that front in subsequent months. Again, the importance of Anglo-Soviet relations came across clearly. Equally clearly, Britain engaged in these various discussions as the totally committed ally of the United States and a pivotal member of NATO. Callaghan's talks with Gromyko covered areas he had previously discussed in detail with Kissinger, for instance in a commitment not to try to interfere in or destabilize Yugoslavia after the departure of Tito. In addition, Callaghan embarked on much technical work to promote American ideas on further strategic arms limitation to reduce the apparent menace of Soviet medium-range ballistic missiles in Europe, the so-called SALT II treaty. He rapidly became a master of the arcane complexities of defence issues. The problems of measuring the capability of the heavier Soviet missiles against the lighter but more numerous American missiles was a difficult one, but some progress was made, and this progress continued under the Carter administration from 1977. In the lightening atmosphere of the international scene in the mid-1970s, British initiative was a factor of some weight, and a key area in which Anglo-American collaboration was fruitful.

Equally in the Middle East, Britain and America worked closely together. The main initiative here manifestly lay with Kissinger who spent much time and effort in 1974–5 trying to stabilize the situation after the Yom Kippur War. Equally it was an area in which he welcomed and respected Callaghan's strategic advice, and acute knowledge of the outlooks of both the Egyptian and Israeli governments. Callaghan spoke warmly to Kissinger of the efforts of President Sadat of Egypt to try to assist in the Palestinian problem, the very core of the Middle East dilemma. 'I formed a very favourable impression of President Sadat. He struck me as a man who would stick to his word.'[35] In addition, he had been the first Arab leader publicly to declare his willingness to recognize Israel. He advised Kissinger to put some pressure on the Israelis to test out Arab intentions; the wide range of divisions in the 'frenetic' Cabinet of Golda Meir, Israel's Labour Prime Minister, was a factor here.[36] Of course, several of its key figures, Moshe Dayan, Yitzhak Rabin, and Shimon Peres, were known to Callaghan personally, not least through the Socialist International.

At the same time, Callaghan was able to develop Britain's own particular position in the area. On 24–9 November 1975 he went on a useful visit to the Gulf area, visiting Saudi Arabia, Kuwait, Bahrein, Oman, the United Arab Emirates, and Qatar.[37] Here he proved an affable and persuasive salesman, and various agreements were signed for the exchange of technical experts and for joint agricultural and industrial projects. There were also discussions of economic development by Britain in southern Oman (a country where Britain was the most influential foreign power), and of building a new 'instant port' and extensions to King Faisal University in Saudi Arabia. In later years, the British presence was to be important in developing higher education in Oman, and in research in the earth sciences.

In the United Arab Emirates, which he was the first British Foreign Secretary ever to visit, Callaghan emphasized Britain's strong economic and security interest in the area. But it was noticeable that he always took care also to praise the efforts of Henry Kissinger in preserving regional peace and security. The visit to the Gulf states was one of Callaghan's most successful. The stay in Oman was particularly pleasant: Callaghan especially enjoyed himself when given a tour by Sultan Qaboos of local herds of Jersey cattle.[38] He minuted Harold Wilson that such a visit by a British foreign secretary was 'long overdue'. He noted, 'I found enormous goodwill and frank reproach that we have been slow to exploit our relationship since U.K. military withdrawal in '71.'[39] He also heard of complaint, in Saudi Arabia and Kuwait in particular, of British commercial shortcomings, slackness in meeting delivery dates, and the absence of high-level salesmen and representatives. Again it was a new initiative in a somewhat neglected area.

His final involvement with the Gulf region as Foreign Secretary came in March 1976 when he went to Iran. It was, he told a local newspaper, the *Kayhan International*, 'the single most important country from our point of view outside the west'.[40] The outcome was an extension of trade with that thriving country. On the other hand, Callaghan visited Iran in the wake of a serious British economic downturn in the winter of 1975–6, and an important purpose was to confirm a further $400m. tranche of a $1.2 bn. standby credit facility from the Shah. The political image-building of the Shahanshah, who was admitted to be anything but libertarian in his view of civil rights, was effective and his downfall was not at that period anticipated. Nor was it when David Owen went to Iran nearly two years later.[41] Callaghan spent much time rebutting talk of the weakness of the British economy and 'the impending physical and moral collapse of the west'.[42] He pointed out to that oil-rich country that Britain itself would be self-sufficient in oil in 1980. A local reporter, in commenting favourably on his visit, noted that he looked 'in much better shape than during our previous meeting in London over two years ago'.[43]

In all these areas, east–west relations, the Middle East, the broad range of Anglo-American diplomacy, Callaghan was pursuing the traditional path of British foreign secretaries since the war. But he had a dual responsibility, one that he took equally seriously. His full title was, after all, that of Foreign and Commonwealth Secretary, since the two departments had been merged by Harold Wilson in October 1968. The Commonwealth relationship was one to which Callaghan was passionately committed. He had laboured hard and long on behalf of New Zealand butter, Jamaican sugar, Ghanaian cocoa, and Botswana beef in the renegotiation of British membership of the EEC. Indeed, he felt that his role as Commonwealth Secretary during those talks was quite as significant as his position as Foreign Secretary. Beyond that, his roots in the Commonwealth, old and new, were profound since his time as shadow colonial spokesman in the late 1950s. Even in the changed circumstances of the 1970s when the sterling area had effectively wound up and the Commonwealth relationship appeared more symbolic than substantial, there were important areas where Callaghan could attempt new initiatives, and where his close relationship with the United States would be brought fruitfully to bear.

As always, many of his concerns originated in Africa. Here his long association with senior Commonwealth leaders like Kenneth Kaunda in Zambia and Julius Nyerere in Tanzania was valuable. Africa loomed large in Commonwealth leaders' conferences, over which Harold Wilson presided, and often caused difficulty. The continuing impasse in Rhodesia was a frequent source of complaint. So, from time to time, were relations with South Africa. There was criticism from black African states (echoed on the International Committee of the Labour Party's National Executive)[44] of the undue closeness of the defence relationship with South Africa. There was some criticism of the honouring of long-term arms contracts with the Vorster government, and even more of British naval manœuvres based on Simonstown. There were suggestions that Britain might withdraw from the Simonstown base altogether: Callaghan had prevented the navy visiting it in 1974. More positively, he immediately restored the embargo on arms sales which had been scrapped by the Conservatives in 1970. He also joined with other Commonwealth leaders in trying to co-ordinate the embargo on sporting and other contacts with the South African regime. British sporting contacts with that country were winding up after a disturbed rugby tour by the Springboks to Britain in the autumn of 1970, but New Zealand had subsequently sent an All Black tour and the issue continued to reverberate with the Commonwealth Games threatened by boycotts. Callaghan had considerable moral credit after his success in blocking the MCC cricket tour to South Africa when Home Secretary. His work in this area played its part in the achievement of the Gleneagles Agreement on a total sporting and other boycott during his premiership in 1977.

A more spectacular aspect of his Commonwealth role came in east Africa. This was a part of the world he knew well over many years. He paid a successful visit to Tanzania in January 1975 where he held talks with President Nyerere, an old friend. An important outcome was a proposed £2.5m. loan to enable Tanzania to buy British goods.[45] But the real stir was occasioned by a visit to Uganda and Zaïre in July 1975. Discussions with the unpredictable dictator President Idi Amin on economic and security issues would in any case have been hard to assess. But the atmosphere was worsened by the arrest of Dennis Hills, a British lecturer in Uganda, in April 1975. He was charged with treason for rashly writing a seditious work on the Ugandan government, an unpublished manuscript entitled *The White Pumpkin*. He was then convicted and sentenced to death. His execution was announced for 23 June. An appeal for clemency from the Queen was turned down. After intense Foreign Office pressure, President Amin was persuaded first to allow a stay of execution, but on condition that Callaghan visited his country to discuss Ugandan demands. With some mediation from President Mobutu of Zaïre, it was then agreed to release Hills while Callaghan was in the country.

There was still work for Callaghan to do when he reached the Uganda capital, Kampala, but on 9 July, in melodramatic circumstances, Hills was brought to Amin's headquarters and set free before the British Foreign Secretary. Like Beethoven's Fidelio, he emerged from his confinement 'blinking, shaken and dazed', according to Callaghan, and at first unaware who the British Foreign Secretary was.[46] Callaghan appears to have handled this episode masterfully. He interrupted Amin who was on the point of a long and politically charged oration, and dealt equably with pointed comment about Ugandan holders of British passports. Hills was promptly invited to a meal of steak and champagne (with the normally teetotal Foreign Secretary having a glass too). Hills wrote appreciatively of Callaghan's 'avuncular manner' and how he conveyed news that Hills especially wanted to hear, namely the latest test match cricket scores.[47] The Uganda visit required some courage as well as humanity from the British Foreign Secretary. His speech at Kampala was praised as 'a masterful performance', and was hailed as such by diplomatic missions there.[48] Hundreds of apprehensive British residents came to hear him and be reassured. A fellow Labour MP, Ray Fletcher, wrote to Callaghan, 'You've always been big in my eyes. After this, you're a damned sight bigger. Nobody could have handled it more splendidly.'[49] Barbara Castle congratulated Callaghan warmly on his success, but wondered sardonically why he could not have timed it for the day of the Woolwich by-election.[50]

The most constant preoccupation of the British government with Africa, as it had been since 1964, was Rhodesia. Callaghan had returned to this most difficult of questions during his period as shadow foreign affairs spokesman from 1972. He made a major speech on economic sanctions on 9 November 1972 and expressed support for the findings of the Pearce Commission—subject to their being acceptable to African opinion which soon proved not to be the case at all. He was also in touch with various key figures including Judy Todd and Sir Roy Welensky on aspects of the situation in Rhodesia. Hopes for a solution were not high. He told Sir Alec Douglas-Home, the Foreign Secretary, 'I fear you are being optimistic about hoping for a settlement with Smith and his regime. I very much doubt whether you can get it.' Douglas-Home, in effect, agreed.[51] As Foreign Secretary himself, however, working in close association with Kissinger, Callaghan attempted a series of new initiatives. The main new elements were the signs of growing isolation and weakness from the Ian Smith regime in Salisbury, and the wish of the South African government to try to resolve the impasse through a gradual move towards constitutional government based ultimately on majority rule. Callaghan well knew how far apart the various groups were and was careful not to build up expectations beforehand.

However, he set off for a ten-day visit to southern Africa on New Year's Eve 1974, bound for Zambia, South Africa, Botswana, Malawi, Tanzania, Kenya, and Nigeria.[52] At one time he actually visited five countries in two days. He took the opportunity to seek the views of each of them on British membership of the European Community. Each of them approved, with the aid and development programmes from Europe foreshadowed in the Lomé convention a major priority for them all. From the standpoint of the Rhodesian impasse, Callaghan's visit was clearly regarded as an important initiative, by both black African countries and the Republic of South Africa. It was the first high-level visit to the area by a British Cabinet minister since Macmillan's 'wind of change' speech in South Africa in 1960 and Callaghan's own first visit there for ten years.

He began with a successful meeting with President Kenneth Kaunda in Lusaka, but a serious blow then followed when the Ian Smith government prevented a six-man ANC delegation from flying to Salisbury to meet Callaghan. The most important part of his visit came in South Africa which included a private meeting with President Vorster in Port Elizabeth. Their talks were described as 'businesslike and frank' which indicated that not much headway had been made.[53] Callaghan urged that Vorster put pressure on the Smith government to effect a ceasefire against African guerrilla movements and then attend a conference with the British government. He also told Vorster that South African paramilitary police should be withdrawn from interfering in Rhodesia. There was also talk on Britain's wish to end the agreement on the Simonstown naval base. The South African press was enthusiastic about the meeting. British journalists noted that Callaghan emerged 'poker-faced' and that he declined Vorster's invitation for a joint press conference.[54] On arrival in Tanzania for talks with President Nyerere, he urged the assembled journalists, 'Don't let's get too euphoric yet.'[55]

In subsequent discussions with President Jomo Kenyatta of Kenya in Mombasa and with General Gowon in Lagos, Callaghan continued to emphasize caution and to spell out the difficulties that lay ahead in trying to get the release of detainees and the end of violence. He affirmed that the British government, more emphatically than its Tory predecessor, saw Rhodesian independence and black African majority rule as inseparable. He spoke of a new peace initiative which would involve a meeting with ANC leaders in Salisbury. He believed that a settlement would be reached in Rhodesia 'within this decade'. Ian Smith he likened to a man trapped on an ice floe with ice cracking all around him.[56] But it would all take time.

On a personal basis Callaghan's tour went down well and reinforced his image as a major world statesman. *The Times* wrote genially of the fast pace he set and the problems of being 'hot on the trail of the elusive Big Jim'.[57] There were important gains in the new confidence instilled in Commonwealth leaders, especially the key figure of President Nyerere, after doubts that had been expressed over Labour's commitment to black African rule. The links with South Africa were clearly useful too, although much depended on whether any agreements negotiated between its representatives and the Smith government could be implemented. But there was really little efffective progress to record. After Callaghan's cautious and careful statement to the Commons on his return on 14 January, *The Times* correctly observed that 'Peace in Rhodesia is still far off'.[58] Callaghan's inability to see ANC leaders was recognized as a serious blow. Ian Smith in Salisbury dourly refused to take up any opportunities to meet with British representatives, and complained that Callaghan had not communicated any proposals for a constitutional conference to him. He concluded sourly that Callaghan's visit had 'hampered the chances of an agreement rather than enhanced them'.[59]

Throughout 1975 British and American representatives made fitful efforts to make progress in Rhodesia, notably over the possible release of ANC detainees. Callaghan himself maintained indirect unofficial links with Nkomo, Mugabe, and other nationalist leaders. He saw the less radical black spokesman Bishop Abel Muzorewa in August 1975 about the impasse on any constitutional conference.[60] At the same time, he was criticized by left-wing members of the party National Executive for entering into any dialogue with the South African government or the Smith regime. They would probably have been more displeased had they known that he was also in regular contact with his old *bête noire*, Sir Roy Welensky, about the prospects for Anglo-Rhodesian talks.[61]

There appeared to be an opening of a kind in February 1976 when Callaghan was told by his former shadow Cabinet colleague Lord Robens of new prospects for talks between Ian Smith and the nationalist leader Joshua Nkomo. Lord Greenhill was sent to Salisbury on a secret mission and he reported that Smith was now prepared to consider British arbitration in Rhodesia, and that he now anticipated black majority rule, though not before three years.[62] Callaghan received through her secretary Sir Martin Charteris, the personal backing of the Queen for a new diplomatic initiative even though she recognized that it might prove 'ineffective'.[63] He then sent a message to Ian Smith stating that Britain would be prepared to use its good offices if he would commit himself publicly to endorsing the principle of black majority rule and to calling elections within eighteen months to ten years. The gist of this was conveyed to parliament on 22 March and received all-party endorsement. But in Rhodesia itself private talks between Ian Smith and Joshua Nkomo broke down, and the impasse remained. There was to be further impetus when Callaghan was premier, in a much firmer Anglo-American context this time, but in general the most serious problem affecting the Commonwealth remained incapable of resolution.

When the need arose in Commonwealth affairs, Callaghan could strike a robustly patriotic note. Thus it was over Belize, in the face of American murmurs of dissent, and over the status of Gibraltar despite the long-running complaints of the Spanish government. Over Hong Kong, due to revert to Chinese rule in 1997, there were no new developments at this period.

A very different issue which saw the Foreign Secretary in action concerned the Falkland Islands. At the time, it attracted very little attention. Callaghan himself had sarcastically asked in Cabinet, back in March 1968, whether 'the Falkland Islands were any use to us'.[64] Here was a tiny far-away colony in the South Atlantic with a population of a mere 1,850, largely sheep farmers, of which the British public knew nothing, other perhaps than its attractive postage stamps depicting marine life. The long-running Argentine claim to Las Malvinas, dating from Britain's expulsion of the Argentine presence on the Falklands in 1833, became a public issue during

Callaghan's tenure of the Foreign Office. Following a meeting with Vignes, the Argentine Foreign Minister, on 21 September 1974 in New York, on the 25th he saw Robledo, the Argentine ambassador, on the Falklands issue. He affirmed the Falklands' sovereign desire to remain British, but opened up the possibility of joint Anglo-Argentine development of the oil reserves, especially after Professor Griffiths's report on oil deposits in the region.[65] This was pursued with the Argentine government by the author of an Economic Survey of the Antarctic, Lord Shackleton, son of the celebrated explorer, and until recently Labour leader in the House of Lords. He was asked by the British government to prepare another report, on the economic prospects for the Falklands, which he completed in early 1976. Callaghan had taken the precaution to obtain Kissinger's goodwill on the Falklands issue. On 13 December 1975, the US Secretary of State assured him, 'We shall do nothing to embarrass you.'[66]

The issue continued to fester throughout 1975 as Argentina continued to make forceful noises about pursuing their territorial claim, backed up possibly by naval manœuvres in the South Atlantic. On 14 May Callaghan sent Harold Wilson a seventeen-page report on the Falklands issue and the general stance that Britain adopted towards Argentina's claim.[67] This continued to be one that emphasized potential joint collaboration in the energy and environmental spheres. There were suggestions that the idea of some kind of condominium with the Argentine government, as explored by the Heath government, might be considered, although it was recognized that the Falkland Islanders themselves were not enthusiastic. But a tougher approach was required also, to back up Britain's diplomatic stand. Callaghan told Wilson how vital it was that the Argentine never be misled into believing that Britain would not act in repelling any future invasion. After consulting Roy Mason, the Defence Minister, it was agreed that the British ship HMS *Endurance* should be retained in Falklands waters for 1976–7, with an additional earmarked charge added to the defence budget.[68] Callaghan refused to make any commitment to withdraw the vessel thereafter. He also took steps to have an up-to-date assessment of Argentine military and naval deployment, and to have information of possible harassment of British or other shipping or tampering with Falklands air communications. In reply to threatening noises made by Vignes, the Argentine Foreign Minister, it was made transparently clear that no Argentine occupation of any part of the Falklands or surrounding areas such as South Georgia would be tolerated. There was, however, some minor difficulty over Argentine proposals (or threats) to set up the token presence of a scientific station on the uninhabited frozen rock of Southern Thule, one of the south Sandwich Islands some 1,200 kilometres south-east of the Falklands. This was indeed to happen in December 1976 even though it was kept concealed from public knowledge for the next two years.

Callaghan's strategy in the Falklands was a dual one. He sought co-operation where possible with the Argentine though well aware of the volatility of the military junta in Buenos Aires. More provocative measures such as building a runway for RAF fighters in Port Stanley were not adopted. At the same time, Britain's willingness to defend the Falklands was made transparently plain. It was symbolized by the *Endurance* sailing in Falkland waters flying the white ensign. Even if it was not a fighting ship, its symbolic importance was considerable. In 1976 it was strengthened by Wasp helicopters and air-to-sea missiles. Attempts by the Minister of Defence to withdraw it from service were resisted. The issue continued to fester during Callaghan's subsequent period as Prime Minister, as will be seen below, and his junior minister Ted Rowlands was dispatched first to Port Stanley and then to Buenos Aires to take the prospects of some kind of international agreement forward. But, throughout, the Buenos Aires government was left in no doubt by Callaghan about British intentions to keep a British naval presence in Falklands waters. When the Thatcher government reversed this policy and withdrew HMS *Endurance* from the South Atlantic, despite protests from Callaghan in the Commons, in early 1982, the occupation of the islands soon followed and war with Argentina broke out that April. Mrs Thatcher claimed a famous victory and invited the nation to 'rejoice' over the recapture of South Georgia. The victorious Falklands War played a major part in her election triumph in 1983. At the time, however, and in his evidence before the Franks Committee of Inquiry into the origins of the Falklands War, Callaghan could justifiably claim that he had not had to fight to defend the Falklands. His flexible diplomatic and naval policy, as both Foreign Secretary and Prime Minister, had meant that the issue had simply not arisen.[69]

Throughout these manifold international problems, Callaghan had always kept a watchful eye on developments on the party scene at home. He had been noted by Foreign Office officials as being particularly zealous on this front, certainly far more so than predecessors, such as Douglas-Home or Michael Stewart. He spent his mornings if possible in domestic discussions, and much of the afternoon in the Commons when in London. One novelty of his was creating a Joint Group with the TUC International Committee, headed by Jack Jones. Callaghan saw this as a way of keeping the unions well informed. It was also fulfilling the social contract and met regularly. He also pursued the difficult task of keeping up links with the International Subcommittee of the National Executive. This was, he found, an exceptionally tiresome body presided over by the veteran Ian Mikardo, a stubborn and over-active left-winger. He found the presence of far left-wing figures such as Joan Maynard MP and Alex Kitson made meetings with the subcommittee of little value, and he sometimes kept away, as they complained to McNally.[70] There were constant bickerings over Europe, Cyprus, arms to Chile, negotiations in Rhodesia, or relations with Indonesia, such as over East Timor. Callaghan objected to the 'pernickety, sour and ungenerous' nature of Mikardo's reports on international issues. He complained that changes of policy as over Simonstown or Chile were not acknowledged, and commented that 'Ministers cannot be expected to follow robot-like every resolution that is passed at the International Committee'.[71] The representative of the Israeli Labour Party in Europe, Yoram Peri, complained that Mikardo was deliberately trying to antagonize the other European parties in the Socialist International. Callaghan told McNally, 'I agree. You should stick close to Mikardo and see him regularly. We may need to alter the composition of our Delegation.'[72]

These local difficulties, however, were part of the general grass-roots swing towards the left visible in the constituency parties and some unions at this time. They did not affect Callaghan's wider standing in domestic party politics. On the contrary, his period as Foreign Secretary, from broad issues like the European renegotiation or détente with Russia to particular episodes like the release of Dennis Hills in Uganda, had strengthened his reputation as the Cabinet's strong man and Wilson's most likely successor. He had solidly defended the Prime Minister during numerous other issues that winter, including the sale of Chrysler, defence cuts, and renewed violence in Northern Ireland.

Then on 16 March the political scene was transformed. To the stupefaction of his colleagues, and in circumstances that have generated much speculation ever since, Harold Wilson announced that he was going to resign as Prime Minister. The Cabinet was stunned at the news. Barbara Castle was near to tears.[73] Callaghan, however, was less shaken. He made a short, graceful speech of appreciation of Wilson's long services which lightened the atmosphere. He had heard around Christmas that Wilson was intending to resign in March after completing eight years as Prime Minister. How early Callaghan heard is a matter of some dispute, but there is no doubt that he knew some months earlier. Harold Lever was his informant, and used the occasion to urge Callaghan, whose leadership bid he had endorsed back in 1963, this time to fight and win. Callaghan could hardly take the matter further at that point, although he did discuss matters with Merlyn Rees, who echoed Lever's view. But evidently he was prepared psychologically for a leadership contest as none of the other possible claimants, Jenkins, Foot, Benn, Healey, or Crosland, could have been. After years of difficulty and frequent disappointment, the supreme opportunity of his career had suddenly presented himself. His 64th birthday took place a few days later, on 27 March. Nevertheless, at an age when most men were comfortably settled in retirement, his career was transformed and he himself rejuvenated. The top of Disraeli's famous greasy pole beckoned. Against the odds, life could begin all over again.

1. Transcript of interview of Lord Callaghan with Peter Hennessy, BBC Radio 4, Analysis Programme, *Moneybags and Brains* (by kind permission of Professor Hennessy).

2. Material in Callaghan Papers (uncatalogued).

3. Statement for White House press secretary, 'President's Meeting with UK Foreign Minister Callaghan, September 24 1974', White House Central Files, Edward J. Savage files, box 3 (Gerald R. Ford Library, Ann Arbor).

4. Telephone conversation between Ford and Wilson, 11 Oct. 1974 (Callaghan Papers, box 25).

5. Rowland Evans, Jr., and Robert D. Novak, *Nixon in the White House* (New York, 1972 edn.), 19.

6. Roger Morris, *Uncertain Greatness: Henry Kissinger and American Foreign Policy* (London, 1977 edn.), 289.

7. Henry Kissinger, 'Reflections on a Partnership: British and American Attitudes to Postwar Foreign Policy', *International Affairs*, 58/4 (1982).

8. Interview with Dr Henry Kissinger, 26 Oct. 1993.

9. Henry Kissinger, *Years of Upheaval* (Boston, 1982), 933.

10. *Western Mail*, 7 Mar. 1975.

11. Kissinger to Callaghan, 14 Jan. 1977 (Callaghan Papers, box 13).

12. Callaghan to Kissinger, 23 Jan. 1977 (ibid.).

13. Stephen E. Ambrose, *Eisenhower the President, ii: 1952–1969* (London, 1984), 192–7.

14. Material in Callaghan Papers (uncatalogued).

15. Interview with Lord Callaghan.

16. Material in Callaghan Papers (uncatalogued).

17. Ibid.

18. Kissinger, *Years of Upheaval*, 189–92.

19. Material in Callaghan Papers (uncatalogued).

20. There is a complete chronology of events on this day in Callaghan, *Time and Chance*, 344–6.

21. *Parl. Deb.*, 5th ser., vol. 878, 796–801 (31 July 1974); *The Times*, 1 Aug. 1974. Callaghan's evident fatigue was acknowledged courteously and sympathetically by the Opposition spokesman, Sir Alec Douglas-Home.

22. Material in Callaghan Papers (uncatalogued)

23. Interview with Lord Callaghan; Dr Kissinger did not recall this when I interviewed him on 26 Oct. 1993.

24. Material in Callaghan Papers (uncatalogued) and record of meeting between Callaghan and Hartman, Geneva, 11 Aug. 1974 (ibid., box 25); interview with Dr Jack Cunningham.

25. Material in Callaghan Papers (uncatalogued).

26. Kissinger, *Years of Upheaval*, 192.

27. Memo by Callaghan, ? Sept. 1974 (Callaghan Papers, box 25).

28. Benn, *Office without Power*, 200 (18 July 1974). Benn comments, 'This put Jim on the defensive.'

29. Interview with Sir Julian Bullard.

30. Notes of speech to Socialist International, ? 1975 or 1976 (Callaghan Papers, uncatalogued).

31. Pimlott, *Harold Wilson*, 698–9. Wilson's mission to Moscow, which allegedly brought suggestions of a British sale of fighter planes to the Soviet Union, apparently attracted the interest of the security services and the disapproval of Ernest Bevin.

32. Material in Callaghan Papers (uncatalogued); interview with Sir Julian Bullard; D. R. Thorpe, *Alec Douglas-Home* (London, 1996), 441.

33. Interview with Lord Callaghan.

34. Material in Callaghan Papers (uncatalogued).

35. Callaghan to Kissinger, 7 Feb. 1974 (Callaghan Papers, box 25).

36. Callaghan memo (ibid.).

37. Record of visit ibid.; *The Times*, 24 Nov.–1 Dec. 1975.

38. *The Times*, 29 Nov. 1975.

39. Material in Callaghan Papers (uncatalogued).

40. Material in Callaghan Papers, box 7.

41. David Owen, *Time to Declare* (London, 1991), 322–3.

42. Material in Callaghan Papers, box 7; *Financial Times*, 8–9 Mar. 1976.

43. The reporter for *Kayhan International* (Callaghan Papers, box 7).

44. Material ibid., box 22.

45. Ibid.

46. Ibid.

47. Dennis Hills, *Tyrants and Mountains* (London, 1994), 219–20.

48. Jim Hennessey to Callaghan, 18 July 1975 (Callaghan Papers, box 25).

49. Ray Fletcher MP to Callaghan, 'Thursday' [July 1975] (ibid.).

50. Castle, *Castle Diaries, 1974–76*, 458 (11 July 1975).

51. Callaghan to Douglas-Home, 12 Apr. 1973; Douglas-Home to Callaghan, 13 Apr. 1973; and other correspondence (Callaghan Papers, box 4).

52. Material in Callaghan Papers, box 22; *The Times*, 1–11 Jan. 1975.

53. *The Times*, 6 Jan. 1975.

54. *Daily Telegraph*, 9 Jan. 1975.

55. *The Times*, 7 Jan. 1975.

56. Ibid. 11 Jan. 1975; *Guardian*, 9 Jan. 1975.

57. *The Times*, 8 Jan. 1975.

58. Ibid. 15 Jan. 1975.

59. Ibid. 16, 18 Jan. 1975.

60. Material in Callaghan Papers, box 25.

61. Welensky Papers, 739/4. I have only seen the catalogue for these materials, which are barred to historians under the thirty-year rule.

62. Material in Callaghan Papers (uncatalogued).

63. Ibid.

64. *Castle Diaries, 1964–70*, 413 (28 Mar. 1968).

65. Material in Callaghan Papers (uncatalogued).

66. Ibid.

67. Ibid. See Callaghan's speech during the Falklands debate, *Parl. Deb.*, 6th ser., vol. 21, 971–6 (7 Apr. 1982).

68. Material in Callaghan Papers (uncatalogued).

69. *Parl. Deb.*, 6th ser., vol. 27, 482 (8 July 1982). For Callaghan's protest to Mrs Thatcher over the withdrawal of *Endurance*, see *Parl. Deb.*, 6th ser., vol. 21, 856 (9 Feb. 1982).

70. Mikardo memo for NEC, 1975 (Callaghan Papers, box 22).

71. Paper by Callaghan for NEC, 14 Oct. 1975 (ibid.).

72. McNally to Callaghan, 13 Jan. 1975, and Callaghan minute (ibid.).

73. *Castle Diaries, 1974–76*, 689 (16 Mar. 1976). Although no other Cabinet minister seems to have been told by Wilson, some leading trade union figures claim to have been, notably Jack Jones and Len Murray: interview with Jack Jones by the author, 15 Feb. 1996; interview with Len Murray by Geoffrey Goodman, 10 Feb. 1987, on television programme *The 20th Century Remembered* (transcript in Callaghan Papers, British Library of Political and Economic Science, box 7).

PART THREE

1976–

21

INTO NUMBER TEN

THE Labour leadership contest in March–April 1976 was a unique occasion. It was the first time that the party had selected its leader while in office. It was also the last but one time that the leader was to be elected exclusively by the Labour MPs, prior to the electoral college invented in 1981 and the membership ballot instituted in 1994. It was, therefore, the responsibility of Cledwyn Hughes, the chairman of the parliamentary Labour Party, to devise the rules and procedure of the election process that was to follow. Three candidates were nominated almost as soon as the PLP meeting on the evening of 16 March to draw up the electoral arrangements was complete. These were James Callaghan (who was nominated by Merlyn Rees), Michael Foot, and Roy Jenkins. Of these three, Foot was the standard-bearer of the left, pending a decision by Tony Benn on whether to stand. Given the general political complexion of the PLP, it was unlikely that a leftish candidate would command a majority amongst MPs. To promote his candidature, Roy Jenkins had a devoted, but small, group of right-wing, pro-European followers. It was generally assumed that, while he was acknowledged as a heavyweight figure, his moment had really passed in 1972 when he resigned as deputy leader over the European referendum issue.

Callaghan, in the view of most observers, was the candidate much the most likely to succeed. Since there would be an exhaustive ballot procedure, his candidature would not be unduly harmed by the emergence of two other candidates, both of them from the centre-right also, namely Denis Healey, the Chancellor of the Exchequer, and Tony Crosland, Secretary of the Environment and, like Healey, a major Labour intellectual. In addition, after discussion with family and friends, Tony Benn also decided to enter the contest. But from the outset of the campaign, a Callaghan victory was generally anticipated by friends and foes alike. The general strategy of the others, especially those on the left, was one of 'stopping Jim' if they could.[1]

He himself confirmed this expectation by behaving in a detached, quasi-presidential fashion during the brief election campaign. Alone of the five candidates, he seemed to the general public merely to continue in high-profile work as a leading member of the government and Harold Wilson's most experienced colleague. At 64 he was the oldest candidate (just—Foot was nearly 63), but by no means a veteran. He was a thoroughly familiar figure to the electorate at large, and behaved as such. Thus he offered no campaign platform and gave no interviews.[2] Alone of the six candidates, he declined to appear in a *Panorama* television programme prior to the ballot; naturally, he was concluding that exposure here would, as it were, drag him down to the same mundane level as the others. He had also the perfectly good reason that his work as Foreign Secretary was extremely time-consuming, especially the renewed contacts over the situation in Rhodesia and his talks with the Soviet Foreign Minister Gromyko over Anglo-Soviet trade and détente. Further, there was the difficult position in Angola where the Soviet Union was assisting the Frelimo guerrilla movement. He did, however, intervene in a much more controversial area on 24 March, close to the end of the poll, when, in the National Executive, he spoke out against a motion of Ian Mikardo, supported by Foot and the left generally, in favour of the reselection of Labour candidates. He also referred more directly than before to the dangers of 'entryism', the infiltration of constituency Labour parties, especially in inner-city regions of declining population, by extreme left-wing groups such as Militant Tendency.[3]

But in general it was a very quiet, good-natured campaign without personal attacks of any kind. The farewell dinner in honour of Harold Wilson for Cabinet ministers and spouses on 21 March was a thoroughly pleasant, almost sentimental affair. Wilson himself carefully arranged the dinner seating to mirror the arrangements in Cabinet meetings 'so that nobody could read anything into anything'. There was much genial banter between the candidates. Callaghan, according to Benn, was friendly and cheerful. He told him, undoubtedly correctly, that he had given up hope of the leadership long ago, but 'now I am really fighting to win'.[4]

In fact, his campaign was the most professionally organized of them all.[5] He had already drafted the Northern Irish Secretary, his close friend Merlyn Rees, as his campaign manager, though this promised to be something of a titular role. He had the support of other Cabinet ministers as well, notably Harold Lever, Fred Peart, and the Welsh Secretary John Morris, along with the Attorney-General Sam Silkin. He also had support at the junior minister level including two up-and-coming younger men,

John Smith, one of Callaghan's particular protégés and a future leader of the party, and Roy Hattersley. The latter, a strong pro-marketeer, had broken with Jenkins when the latter resigned as deputy leader. It was assumed that he might work for his mentor and close associate Tony Crosland, but Hattersley told him that he was going to support Callaghan as the man most likely to provide strong and effective leadership. To this, according to Hattersley, Crosland replied with an earthy two-word dismissal.[6]

Callaghan's organizer amongst rank and file MPs, and the master-mind of his overall campaign, was Dr Jack Cunningham. He was Callaghan's PPS, serving in this capacity since 1972 during his master's time as shadow Foreign Secretary and again when he was in the Foreign Office. An able young member who had briefly been a university teacher, he was the son of Andrew Cunningham, a Labour potentate in the north-east with whom Callaghan had been friendly. Another key figure was Gregor MacKenzie, the somewhat eccentric but persuasive Glaswegian who had been Callaghan's faithful ally and confidant since the mid-1960s. As his PPS from 1965 to 1970 he had worked hard to bolster Callaghan's prestige during such difficult passages as the resignation from the Treasury after devaluation in late 1967 and the arguments over *In Place of Strife* in the summer of 1969. Without the efforts of MacKenzie, so Tam Dalyell has argued, along with other loyal members of his 'Praetorian Guard', such as Jack Cunningham, Roland Moyle (Minister for Northern Ireland), and Roger Stott (member for Westhoughton), later to become the Prime Minister's PPS, Callaghan would not have had the standing amongst the Labour MPs to have become Prime Minister.[7]

Cunningham applied himself to the task of running Callaghan's leadership campaign with subtlety and skill. He operated on two levels, by forming an open group and a covert group, neither knowing much about the other. There was also close attention to regional groupings.[8] Cunningham assembled a visible, front-line campaign team to promote Callaghan's candidature, including MacKenzie, Moyle, Tom Urwin, James Wellbeloved, John Golding, Patrick Duffy, Ray Carter, John Smith, Dr Edmund Marshall, Ted Rowlands, Frank White, and Mike Thomas.[9] If many of these were hardly household names, and less glamorous than some of the Jenkinsites, they were representative of the centre-right mainstream of the parliamentary party (a few, such as Wellbeloved and Thomas, were later to join the SDP in 1981); several of them, such as Urwin or Golding, had valuable links with the unions. There was also a second group of supporters who worked in the background to promote Callaghan, including

Hattersley, Don Concannon, John Grant, Leo Abse, Jack Dormand, Donald Coleman, Ronald Brown (brother of George), Harry Ewing, Ted Graham, Jim Johnson, Eric Moonman, John Horam, Peter Hardy, Mark Hughes, George Grant. They were materially assisted by the services of Tom McNally and Tom McCaffrey of Callaghan's personal entourage of advisers, and found a sympathizer, so some surmised, in Dr Bernard Donoughue, the head of Harold Wilson's Policy Unit, and technically a civil servant. He had sided with Joe Haines in criticizing the role of Marcia Falkender. It was noted that Harold Wilson had come to think that Donoughue was not wholly trustworthy, and was guilty of the crime of 'leaks' to the press[10]—a sphere in which he was very far from the only suspect in the feverish climate of the Wilson era.

Much effort was devoted by the team to targeting specific groups of MPs. Thus Patrick Duffy, member for Sheffield, Attercliffe, was assigned the task of firming up support amongst Yorkshire MPs. He reported to Callaghan on 'Wednesday night' that he had 10 supporters among them, Foot 11, Benn 2, Healey 5, Jenkins 4, and Crosland 1 with three 'don't knows'. In addition, 4 of the 5 Healey supporters, 3 of the 4 Jenkins supporters, and the lone Crosland supporter had promised to support Callaghan on any second ballot, making a potential total of 18 out of 36 so far guaranteed. Duffy felt 'immensely encouraged' and believed that Yorkshire was very representative of the party as a whole.[11]

Other important groups were the union-sponsored MPs. Callaghan, with his friendship with its general secretary David Basnett, expected to gain the votes of all the General and Municipal Workers' MPs, along with a narrow majority of those sponsored by the National Union of Mineworkers. The Transport Workers, on the other hand, were expected to support Foot and the left. Another important group was the Celtic fringe. Callaghan expected to be strong here. The faithful Gregor MacKenzie worked on the Scottish members (41 in all), along with allies such as John Smith and Harry Ewing, while many of his fellow Welsh members (23 in number) also seemed likely to back Callaghan with the help of such supporters as John Morris, Brynmor John, Ted Rowlands, Donald Coleman, and Leo Abse. This was in contrast to the leadership in 1963 when Callaghan had met with scant support amongst his Welsh colleagues. George Thomas, his fellow Cardiff MP but now Speaker of the House, told Cledwyn Hughes of his ardent hope that his colleague of thirty years' standing would be elected, although Thomas's later memoirs suggest somewhat diminished enthusiasm.[12] Cledwyn Hughes, himself a much respected chairman, was another Callaghan supporter. The candidate was reported on 23 March as being 'in good form' although Audrey Callaghan said she would be glad for the election to be over.[13]

A number of meetings amongst MPs was arranged. In all, sixteen campaign meetings were held in the period up to the second ballot on 1 April. A total of nineteen core supporters attended up to the first ballot; they were joined by six others up to the second ballot, including the former Jenkinsites John Horam, Robert Maclennan, and Dickson Mabon.[14] Callaghan had anticipated that, with his strong reputation over the years, he would lead on the first ballot and was much put out when he did not do so. Cunningham, however, had worked out that there would be three ballots in all, with Foot leading on the first ballot, Callaghan leading on the second ballot, and winning comfortably on the third, which is precisely how matters turned out. Both Cunningham and Roger Stott were totally confident from the start that their man would win.[15] The essential strategic objective in the first ballot was for Callaghan to come in a good second, so as to pick up other centre-right votes on future ballots.

On 25 March it emerged that this had been duly achieved. Foot headed the poll with a remarkably high vote of 90. Callaghan was second with 84 (he had done 'less well than he expected' wrote Benn in his diary).[16] Jenkins polled 56, his maximum possible. Benn polled 37 and promptly announced his withdrawal in favour of Michael Foot. Healey polled only 30 but surprisingly decided to stay in the contest. Tony Crosland polled just 17 and also withdrew. Callaghan was now in a strong position, since he was likely to pick up almost all the 73 votes cast together for Jenkins and Crosland. Indeed, immediately after the result was known, he had messages from John Horam, David Marquand, Robert Maclennan, Giles Radice, and other Jenkins followers pledging their support for Callaghan[17] as both a plausible leader and also the one man capable of defeating Foot and the left. Dickson Mabon, a Scots MP hopeful for the Scottish Office, switched from the Jenkins to the Callaghan campaign team, as did Robert Maclennan. Joel Barnett observed that 'Jim is home and dry.'[18]

The second ballot confirmed Callaghan's strength. It was announced on 30 March that he headed the poll with 141 votes, as against Foot's 133 and Healey's 38. The press felt that Callaghan had polled slightly below his full potential strength.[19] Nevertheless it was acknowledged that almost all of Healey's 38 would go his way. On the third ballot, this was clearly demonstrated. Callaghan finally obtained 176 votes to Foot's 137. Two of the 315 ballots had not been returned, one of them presumably being that of the absentee fugitive John Stonehouse. Callaghan had therefore won 34 of the

38 Healey votes, losing only one or two natural supporters such as Douglas Jay who supported Foot because of their mutual hostility to Britain's membership of the European Community.[20] Foot also attracted one or two right-wing mavericks such as Brian Walden for his being 'a man of principle'. But Jim Callaghan had, at the last, won the party leadership and would now become prime minister. He had done so on the strength of the broad mass of the centre and right of the party, though with 'soft left' support as well, not least in Wales.

Peter Kellner's contemporary analysis of his 141 votes on the second ballot, produced for the *New Statesman*, is the fullest account of the distribution of his support in general.[21] He had won, according to Kellner's statistics, 4 votes from the Tribune group, 26 from the non-Tribune left, 47 from the party centre, and 64 from the generally pro-market right. He had picked up almost all the Jenkins vote on the second ballot, but his support from the centre and left had been more or less identical in the first and second rounds. Kellner confirmed Callaghan's strength among important union groups such as GMWU and NUM members; another important statistic was that he won 105 votes from English MPs and 36 from the Scots and the Welsh. It was a perfect model of traditional Labour, and the kind of industrial/regional solidarity which Callaghan as a politician embodied. By contrast, the left's strength was less than overwhelming, and Michael Foot (who conceded defeat with characteristic grace) perhaps did slightly less well in the end than his supporters might have hoped.

The result was announced at lunchtime on 5 April. It was given to Callaghan, who was waiting in his room in the Commons, by the chairman of the parliamentary party, Cledwyn Hughes.[22] First of all, Hughes saw the outgoing premier, Harold Wilson, who commented that Callaghan had done slightly better in the vote than he thought he would. He stated that he had voted for Callaghan himself, though Hughes wondered whether this applied to the first two, as opposed to the third, ballots. Then Cledwyn Hughes told Callaghan the news.

> He was much moved and said he felt the sense of responsibility. 'Prime Minister of Great Britain' he said. 'You will do it well' I said. 'And I never went to a University' he said. 'You are in good company' I replied. 'The two greatest Prime Ministers of the century did not go to University—Lloyd George and Churchill.' We laughed.

Hughes offered sage advice to the effect that the new administration must be recognizably his, and Callaghan concurred. 'It must be Callaghan Mark 1 and not Wilson Mark 2.' A special meeting of the parliamentary

Labour Party followed at 4 p.m. in Room 14 in the Commons. Callaghan spoke for about ten minutes and 'was loudly cheered when he sat down'.[23] Tony Benn described his speech as 'very emotional', replete with references to 'Human values'. Callaghan, however, also warned about steering clear of soft options and the world not owing Britain a living. On this Benn commented, 'It was the older man speaking, the party fixer with the block vote and the Praetorian Guard of the trade unions behind him.'[24] Michael Foot spoke in generous terms and there was much talk of unifying the party after the contest. However, it was noted that when a standing ovation followed for Harold Wilson two left-wing irreconcilables, Eric Heffer and Ian Mikardo, remained seated. Wilson whispered to Cledwyn Hughes, 'Remember to tell the lobby I had a standing ovation.'[25]

The way in which Callaghan conducted and won the leadership contest helped to cement his position from the outset. The contest was seen to be harmonious and free from personal acrimony. Callaghan was somewhat surprised years later in 1982 to read in Susan Crosland's biography of her late husband that there was some ill feeling on Crosland's part. It was, she recorded, directed towards people like Roy Hattersley rather than Callaghan, though it is certainly the case that relations between Callaghan and Crosland were less intimate in 1976 than they had been years earlier, perhaps ever since Jenkins rather than Crosland followed Callaghan as Chancellor in November 1967. Callaghan consulted Jack Cunningham, via Lord Merlyn-Rees, on reading the Crosland biography, and was assured that there was no cause for any 'aggro'. Cunningham concluded, quite accurately, 'The whole tenor of the campaign was to keep calm, avoid rows and wait for the victory we knew would be yours.'[26] There was some sourness at the time among Crosland supporters about the 'Callaghanites', although Dick Leonard was to conclude that they were really not a distinctive grouping at all, but rather made up 'of the least imaginative members of the PLP plus those with a sharp eye for the main chance'.[27]

This was not a charitable verdict. It might have been fairer to see Callaghan as the natural unifying candidate in April 1976, more so than either Foot on the left or Jenkins on the pro-market right, more personally approachable than Healey and with more weight than Crosland. The verdict in *The Times* at the start of the campaign that Callaghan was Wilson's 'only conceivable successor' was not unreasonable.[28] There was high regard for him, if not exactly affection; those, and they were many, who had come to distrust Harold Wilson's style of leadership looked forward to a change. Douglas Jay, who had not voted for his family relation because of their differences over the Common Market, wrote to

Callaghan, 'I happen to agree with you that what the country needs is a moral change more than any new economic policy.'[29] Tony Benn, though wary of the consequences, observed that 'Jim is a human guy'.[30]

The leadership contest was well received across the party spectrum. Apart from some centrist organs which had favoured Roy Jenkins, there was broad press support. *The Times* had described Callaghan after the second ballot as 'a man the nation would trust'. Perhaps less acceptably to the left, it cited his service in the navy and his representation of the Police Federation as testimony to his innate patriotism.[31] After his election, the paper's reporter hailed him as a man 'thoroughly at ease' at the Foreign Office and cited his friendship with Kissinger and his attachment to the Atlantic alliance.[32] The leading article observed, 'The nation is behind him'. Generally there was a view that the end of an era might be approaching. One of the last senior champions for post-war consensus and corporate harmony had been given his chance, at a time of growing polarization between a militant left and a revisionist right. Callaghan's election was perhaps an index that the centre could hold after all.

A critical, but shrewd, analysis of the new Prime Minister came from David Watt in the *Financial Times*.[33] Callaghan was praised as a supreme politician, a highly capable negotiator and conciliator, and a good salesman for Britain. However, it was argued that he was also 'weak on policy' when the conciliator's arts failed, and that there was a 'streak of insecurity' in his character (by which was probably meant that he had the humblest social origins since Ramsay MacDonald and Lloyd George). He had relatively few allies, Watt argued. He was 'a cat that walked by himself'—a comment often made about Healey and Crosland as well. He might 'feel the disadvantages of being a man without an ideology'. Callaghan himself would have put it differently but would have seen pragmatism and realism as major virtues that were central to his political persona.

In addition to being generally well received in Labour circles (other than the far left) and in the press and media, Callaghan was also somewhat startled by the warmth of his reception in the House of Commons amongst Conservative members.[34] He was, indeed, well respected amongst his opponents, even if they acknowledged and feared his political skills. Thirty years of political jousting had not left many scars. Callaghan received warm letters of congratulation from Lord Hailsham, Geoffrey Rippon, William Whitelaw, and Selwyn Lloyd. Reginald Maudling wrote that Callaghan had the gift of understanding 'what ordinary people want and think'.[35] Other congratulatory messages came from Cardinal Basil Hume and the Prince of Wales, writing while at sea, who expressed his pleasure that a Welsh MP was now the prime minister.[36] A more unusual tribute came from the far-right pro-Ian Smith Tory MP Patrick Wall, who sent his regards, commenting that 'we need a patriot at No. 10'. Many other members of the public sent warm congratulations, among them old school friends from Portsmouth and the Welsh TV weather forecaster Trevor Davies, popularly known as 'Trevor the Weather', who sent a meteorological benediction to 'Sunny Jim'.[37]

Callaghan had now to turn immediately to the task of the premiership, putting his stamp on his administration from the outset to show that it was indeed a 'Callaghan Mark 1' rather than a 'Wilson Mark 2' government. Cabinet-making presented some major decisions. The decisiveness with which he now acted confirmed the view of Healey and others of his stature for the new tasks in hand.[38] It had already been agreed with Healey that he must remain at the Treasury: for one thing, he was on the point of introducing another budget, one that would peg wage increases to no more than 3 per cent, which would test union support to the full. Callaghan recorded in a brief diary entry that on 31 March he had a discussion with Healey about the future. 'Told him he cd. have F.C.O. [Foreign and Commonwealth Office]. Thinks I must offer F.C.O. to Roy. M. Foot will be fiercely opposed to this & thinks Peter Shore shd. have it.'[39] Three months later, Callaghan was to have a private talk with his Chancellor on 20 July. 'Doesn't want to spend rest of his life at the Treasury. Will do 18 months if that is what I want. Chancellor shd. control Public Finance. Otherwise he loses connection with Industrial Strategy.'[40]

There were three main changes on which commentators were to seize. One concerned the Foreign Office. Roy Jenkins had been promised by Wilson before the leadership contest the succession to the presidency of the European Commission, but he would have forgone this if he could now move to the Foreign Office in succession to the new Prime Minister.[41] In fact, Callaghan at once made it plain that it was to Brussels rather than to Carlton Gardens that he must go. Jenkins with his passion for Europe and his right-wing stance on most issues, he judged, would be a divisive force in the party. This was Callaghan's view quite apart from pressure from Michael Foot and the left.[42] Instead, to some surprise, he appointed Tony Crosland. There had been anxious discussions amongst Crosland's friends as to what he should now do. Dick Leonard pointed out that his leadership ambitions still had validity now that Labour was led by a man 'rising 65 who has already had a prostate operation'.[43] There was some talk of Crosland's being offered the Home Office or even Northern Ireland (which Crosland had told his wife he would refuse) if Merlyn Rees were to be moved as a reward for his skilful campaign management.[44] In the event, Crosland, Jenkins's old colleague, vaulted over a rival who appeared to have been well ahead of him in the late 1960s. Callaghan always admired Crosland's intellectual powers, if not always his personal sensitivity, and felt confident of having a kindred spirit at the Foreign and Commonwealth Office. In the event, Crosland and Henry Kissinger were to strike up a good relationship, if not as intimate as that between Kissinger and Callaghan.[45] As Crosland's deputy there would be appointed in September the lesser-known figure of David Owen, a young medical doctor of much ability and executive decisiveness whom even then Callaghan apparently considered as a possible Foreign Secretary.[46] Along with Roy Hattersley and John Smith he was considered one of a trio of rising stars who at some future stage might be groomed for the leadership.

Another important development was Michael Foot moving from the Department of Labour and Employment to becoming leader of the House. Foot and Callaghan had never been intimate in the past,[47] but their partnership now was vital for the survival of the precarious Labour government. Foot would be the talisman of the social contract with the unions and also the tactician who would ensure that, in a singularly fluid House of Commons, the government would maintain its majority. In the event, Foot was to display the utmost loyalty to both his Prime Minister and Cabinet colleagues. His alliance with both Callaghan and Denis Healey, along with his continuing emotional hold over the leftish rank and file, were keys to the government's remaining in office for so long. Callaghan had hoped that Foot might stay on at Employment to cement further relations with the unions. But Foot, somewhat surprisingly, wanted the leadership of the House and, as one who won nearly two-thirds of the Tribune group vote, he had a strong bargaining position. He also exacted another important concession, namely that Albert Booth, from the Tribune group and his deputy at Employment, should succeed him there to maintain close relations with the unions. As has been seen, Foot also added his powerful voice to those hostile to Roy Jenkins moving to the Foreign Office.[48]

However, Foot was unsuccessful in another important decision. He had fought hard to persuade Callaghan that 'Barbara should *not* go'.[49] There were others who wanted her to stay also, including Jack Cunningham. Several meetings of Mrs Castle with Callaghan followed. However, after taking his time, Callaghan had a difficult but decisive meeting with her on the morning of 8 April. To her intense dismay, she was told that she was being removed from the administration. Callaghan told her that at 65 she was too old for the profile of his government (she noted that he and Foot were scarcely younger themselves).[50] There were three other unspoken elements in the equation also. First she had allowed herself to be embroiled in bitter disputes as Secretary for Health and Social Security over both doctors' pay and the issue of abolishing 'pay beds' in NHS hospitals. Secondly, she was thought to be intransigently and dogmatically anti-European. And thirdly she had no affection for Callaghan himself—this was hardly surprising since he had wrecked her cherished reform of industrial relations following *In Place of Strife* in 1969. She accepted the effective end of her career as a mainstream politician, which many thought might have made her Britain's first woman prime minister in due time, with public dignity and much sadness from colleagues, but also with much privately expressed bitterness which offended some erstwhile admirers. Her memoirs suggest she felt that, while Michael Foot had certainly defended her, he had, for all their long Bevanite and Tribunite associations (and indeed an affectionate youthful relationship in the 1930s), not been forceful enough.

She remained a biting critic of Callaghan from that time on, not least in her memoirs in 1993. To the general public, her removal confirmed a sense that the left was being significantly weakened. This contrasted with Wilson's careful juggling and balancing manœuvres over the years which had always ensured that a Jenkins would be balanced by a Castle, a Stewart by a Crossman, and similar equilibrist feats. Wilson had an old loyalty to the Bevanite past; Callaghan had none whatsoever. With a Callaghan loyalist, David Ennals, who had served at the Foreign Office in 1974–6, succeeding Barbara Castle at Health, Shirley Williams being elevated to Paymaster-General as well as Secretary for Prices and Consumer Protection, and the far-right Edmund Dell entering the Cabinet at Trade and Industry in succession to Peter Shore (who moved to Environment in succession to Crosland), the rightwards tendency was confirmed. Bob Mellish and Willie Ross left the government, the latter being succeeded at the Scottish Office by another centrist sympathetic to Callaghan, Bruce Millan.

It might be noted at this point that the move to the right was to be confirmed on 8 September, after Callaghan had been Prime Minister for five months. On that day, Roy Jenkins finally left the Home Office to take up the presidency of the European Commission in Brussels. The Prime Minister, it transpired, had some time on his hands since a projected visit to Canada had to be postponed by Prime Minister Trudeau because of prairie fires in the west.[51] Callaghan thus devoted himself to the higher strategy of a reshuffle which further emphasized the changes since the Wilson era. Jenkins was to be succeeded at the Home Office by Callaghan's great friend and ally Merlyn Rees. Shirley Williams advanced further to become Education Secretary; she followed Fred Mulley who went to Defence in succession to Roy Mason who in turn moved to Northern Ireland in succession to Merlyn Rees. While the Tribune group figure of John Silkin moved to Agriculture (Fred Peart moving on to the Lords), other right-wing younger figures to progress were Roy Hattersley who followed Shirley Williams at Prices and Consumer Protection, and William Rodgers who became Minister of Transport after lengthy periods as Minister of State, while as has been seen David Owen became Minister of State at the Foreign Office under Crosland. At close hand, to act as the Prime Minister's eyes and ears in the House, Dr Jack Cunningham moved to be Tony Benn's junior minister at Energy. He had to rebut press comment that he was moving there in order to serve as Callaghan's spy on a left-wing dissident. In fact, Callaghan had first suggested that he move to Trade and Industry, but Cunningham preferred to move to Energy where he would be broadcasting good news about North Sea oil rather than bad news about wages and perhaps strikes.[52] Roger Stott, one of Callaghan's stalwart Praetorian Guard in the leadership campaign who was not associated with any backbench group, right-wing or left-wing, succeeded Cunningham as PPS and remained in that sensitive post until the fall of the government.[53] A Lancastrian, a former merchant seaman and trade union official with a strong interest in cricket apart from his constituency commitment to Wigan rugby league club, he was evidently the kind of cheerful, down-to-earth man that Callaghan liked to have about him. Like Jack Cunningham before him, he developed a warm personal attachment to his leader whom he regarded as tough but also very human. He thought of him as 'a second father'.

Other than the interposition of death or other misfortune, this was evidently the kind of administration that Callaghan hoped would soldier on and eventually grasp the political initiative over the months and perhaps years to come. Of 23 members of the Cabinet, only 6 (Foot, Benn, Booth, Silkin, Shore, and later Stan Orme) could reasonably be claimed to be in any sense on the left, and they were not at all a cohesive group. Indeed, Foot and Benn soon developed a strong mutual antagonism while in some ways Shore, an English nationalist, was on the right. It was a solidly centre-right Cabinet in which Tony Benn was effectively isolated and neutralized. On the other hand, the fact that Benn for a considerable time appeared to have a much better relationship with Callaghan than he had done of late with Wilson (for one thing Callaghan treated him with more courtesy and much less sarcasm in Cabinet)[54] suggested that it was likely to be a harmonious one, not riven by faction. It was also, with figures like Healey, Crosland, Shore, Williams, Lever, and Dell, one of the more intellectually gifted. A question posed against one Cabinet minister of alleged homosexual tendencies, 'probably quiescent', was evidently ignored.

Meanwhile, there had been some changes of significance in the junior appointments back in April. The most cantankerous event had been the dismissal of Alex Lyons as junior minister at the Home Office, apparently because of the disapproval of Roy Jenkins rather than for ideological reasons. Jenkins, to his annoyance, found himself landed with Brynmor John, member for Pontypridd and one of Callaghan's Welsh cronies, as his deputy instead.[55] There were also some important non-events involving figures on the left. Tony Benn had suggested a variety of names to Callaghan for consideration, including Joe Ashton (his campaign manager), Norman Atkinson, Jeremy Bray, James Lamond, Michael Meacher, and Brian Sedgemoor, but with very little success.[56] Eric Heffer, who had resigned from the Wilson government, stayed out. Norman Atkinson, another far-left representative, declined the offer of a junior post. The youthful Neil Kinnock turned down the opportunity to serve under Roy Hattersley at Prices and Consumer Protection. He wanted to join Tony Benn at Energy instead. This might have made sense since Kinnock represented Bedwellty, an old mining constituency in Gwent. But since the purpose was to detach him from the left, not consolidate his role as a Bennite evangelist, the proposal fell through. So did, perhaps mercifully, a later projected move of Kinnock, a noted anti-devolutionist at that time, to the Northern Ireland department.[57] Anyhow, Callaghan was not the man to let anyone, let alone a 33-year-old neophyte, dictate to him the composition of his government. The effect was to confirm that it was a distinctly senior administration at first. None of the class of 1970—men like Kinnock, Gerald Kaufman, John Smith, or Jack Cunningham, all destined to play major roles in the party in future years—was given a significant role at first.

From the start, it was obvious that the new Callaghan government would face problems, both economic and political, on a massive scale. On 2 April, between the second and final ballots for the party leadership, the Bank of England announced that March had seen the largest ever fall of the reserves in a single month, amounting to the staggering total of £598m. The pound had fallen likewise to a new low level of $1.87, almost a full dollar below its exchange rate when Callaghan went to the Treasury in

October 1964.[58] On the political front, the government's majority, already virtually invisible, vanished entirely on 7 April, on Callaghan's first full day as Prime Minister. The eccentric and fraudulent John Stonehouse formally resigned the Labour whip to which he had not paid any attention in any case since his flight overseas. Then Brian O'Malley, Barbara Castle's popular deputy at Social Security, unexpectedly died. That left Callaghan in a minority of two, with 314 Labour members as against 316 for all other parties. He never experienced anything other than minority government from that moment on. He thus faced from the very outset both the perennial economic difficulties that had plagued Labour governments for over a decade and also new tests of his parliamentary management skills. Some visualized that the new Prime Minister might follow the Derby–Disraeli government of 1852 and that of MacDonald in 1924 in not seeing out a single year in office.

But the new Prime Minister was a resolute and determined man. He had waited for decades for this opportunity that had come to him so unexpectedly. He also felt, with reason, that he was unusually equipped for the challenges that lay ahead. No other prime minister, after all, had gone to No. 10 with a background of all the three other main portfolios, the Treasury, the Home Office, and finally the Foreign Office. He claimed to have had successes to record in all three, and a wide international reputation for statesmanship over and above his domestic role. He was anxious to show that his premiership could bring about a new mood. It was necessary, as he later put it, to 'redeem the tawdriness' of the Wilson regime,[59] an atmosphere confirmed in May by Wilson's farewell honours list, after which some individuals ended up either as guilt-ridden suicides or in jail. Callaghan made sure, for instance, that his private office, including figures like Jenny Jeger who looked after his political correspondence, was financed not from the public purse but from party sources, more particularly the unions and the Co-op. He immediately persuaded David Basnett of the Municipal Workers to provide a cheque for £10,000.[60] Callaghan was anxious, too, to prove that his government was not merely an interlude, a footnote to history, but an administration that existed in its own right and put its own stamp on the domestic and international fortunes of his country. 'It must be a Callaghan Government', he was told by his private aides. A man with a profound sense of history, he hoped to respond to historic opportunities by offering social cohesion and international leadership.

Above all, he sought to show that his advent to the premiership at the age of 64 was not just an addendum, a last phase of post-1945 consensus, playing again the old tunes of Beveridge and Keynes, pursuing the old mission of Attlee and Bevin, before new movements of change engulfed them all. A Callaghan government, amidst all the difficulties that confronted it, could mark the beginning of something as well. This particular pilot would not easily be dropped, let alone knifed. Even in an era of minority government, perhaps of office without power, the confident watchword would still be 'Steady as she goes'.

1. Benn, *Office without Power*, 536 (16 Mar. 1976). Benn attributes this outlook to Barbara Castle and calls it 'a typical defeatist view'.

2. Charles Curran to Tony Crosland, 23 Mar. 1976 (London School of Political and Economic Science, Crosland Papers, 6/4).

3. Labour Party, NEC minutes, 24 Mar. 1974; *The Times*, 25 Mar. 1976.

4. *Office without Power*, 543 (22 Mar. 1976).

5. Material in Callaghan Papers, box 17.

6. Hattersley, *Who Goes Home?*, 162.

7. Tam Dalyell, obituary of Gregor MacKenzie, *Independent*, 6 May 1992.

8. Interview with Dr Cunningham MP.

9. Material in Callaghan Papers, box 17.

10. Callaghan diary, 31 Mar. 1976 (ibid.).

11. A. E. P. Duffy to Callaghan, 'Wed. night' [Mar. 1976] (ibid., box 17).

12. Cledwyn Hughes diary, 23 Mar. 1976; cf. Thomas, *Mr Speaker* (London, 1985), 144.

13. Cledwyn Hughes diary, 23 Mar. 1976.

14. Roger Darlington to Callaghan, 1 Apr. 1976 (Callaghan Papers, box 19).

15. Interviews with Dr Jack Cunningham MP and Mr Roger Stott MP.

16. *Office without Power*, 544 (25 Mar. 1976).

17. Letters in Callaghan Papers, box 17. David Owen voted for Denis Healey on the second ballot and Callaghan only on the third. Cf. Owen, *Time to Declare*, 239. Dr Owen says that any remarks he made to Barbara Castle about his possibly supporting Michael Foot in the final ballot were 'purely tactical'.

18. Cledwyn Hughes diary, 25 Mar. 1976.

19. *The Times*, 31 Mar. 1976.

20. Interview with Douglas Jay.

21. Peter Kellner article in *New Statesman*, 9 Apr. 1976.

22. Cledwyn Hughes diary, 5 Apr. 1976.

23. Ibid.

24. *Office without Power*, 553 (5 Apr. 1976).

25. Cledwyn Hughes diary, 5 Apr. 1976.

26. Dr Jack Cunningham to Callaghan, 2 Apr. 1982 (Callaghan Papers, box 19).

27. Dick Leonard (of *The Economist*), memo to Crosland, 1 June 1976 (Crosland Papers, 6/4).

28. *The Times*, 17 Mar. 1976.

29. Douglas Jay to Callaghan, 5 Apr. 1976 (Callaghan Papers, uncatalogued).

30. *Office without Power*, 553 (5 Apr. 1976).

31. *The Times*, 31 Mar. 1976.

32. Ibid. 6 Apr. 1976: column by its diplomatic correspondent, David Spanier.

33. David Watt, 'Steady as We Go—at Least for Now', *Financial Times*, 6 Apr. 1976.
34. *The Times*, 7 Apr. 1976.
35. Letters from all of these in Callaghan Papers, uncatalogued.
36. Ibid.
37. Ibid.
38. Denis Healey, *The Time of my Life* (London, 1989), 447.
39. Callaghan diary, 31 Mar. 1976 (Callaghan Papers, box 19).
40. Memo of conversation with Healey, 20 July 1976 (ibid.).
41. Jenkins, *A Life at the Centre*, 441–3. Jenkins's account of Callaghan, whom he saw as 'a bit of a bully', is not cordial, but he much preferred him to Foot.
42. Callaghan diary, 6 Apr. 1976 (Callaghan Papers, box 19).
43. Leonard memo, 1 June 1976 (Crosland Papers, 6/4).
44. Notes by Susan Crosland (ibid.).
45. Letters from Kissinger to Callaghan and Crosland (ibid. 5/14).
46. Interview with Lord Callaghan.
47. Interview with Michael Foot.
48. Callaghan diary, 3 Apr. 1976 (Callaghan Papers, box 19).
49. Ibid. 5 Apr. 1976.
50. *Castle Diaries, 1974–76*, 725 (8 Apr. 1976). The meeting ended with a reluctant kiss.
51. Hattersley, *Who Goes Home?*, 163.
52. Interview with Dr Jack Cunningham MP.
53. Interview with Roger Stott MP.
54. Interview with Lord Merlyn-Rees; also cf. Benn, *Office without Power*, 556–9 (12–14 Apr. 1976).
55. Jenkins, *A Life at the Centre*, 443. Jenkins also seems to have disapproved of his secretary (and later wife) Clare Short for helping to create a 'bunker of suspicion'. He is critical of Callaghan's methods in this episode.
56. Benn to Callaghan, 8 Apr. 1976 (Callaghan Papers, box 19).
57. Hattersley, *Who Goes Home?*, 163–4; notes on possible reshuffles in Callaghan Papers, box 19; information from Rt. Hon. Neil Kinnock.
58. *The Times*, 3 Apr. 1976.
59. Interview with Lord Callaghan.
60. Interviews with Dr Jack Cunningham MP and Roger Stott MP.

22

PRIME MINISTERIAL STYLE

'If action and inaction seem equally valid, then act.' This perhaps unlikely precept, announced in a Hubert Humphrey memorial lecture on 'The Political Leader' at the University of Minnesota in 1982, embodied James Callaghan's philosophy of the prime ministerial role.[1] He was sometimes dismissed by commentators as a cautious fixer rather than one to take charge of events, condemned by critics as various as the diplomat Nicholas Henderson and the Tory politician Norman Tebbitt as hesitant and indecisive. Tony Blair once accused his predecessor of failing to take decisions; business went 'through umpteen committees which meant things never got done at all'.[2] But Callaghan did believe in a doctrine of leadership and sought to put it into effect as Prime Minister. In his Hubert Humphrey lecture he made a distinction between different types of leadership, somewhat as Max Weber had done in his analysis of 'charismatic leadership' long before. Callaghan spoke of 'visionary' leaders (such as Gandhi), 'inspirational' leaders (Churchill, Roosevelt, and 'my own fellow countryman [*sic*] David Lloyd George'), and 'consensus' leaders, amongst whom he classified himself. But while he emphasized the need to take a broad global view of a leader's role and stressed the reciprocal relationship between leader and led, he felt it essential for a political leader to seize the initiative and provide an active and engaged sense of direction, from both the strategic and moral point of view. The fact that his three years of premiership were constrained by the absence of a Commons majority and the need to conciliate various small minority groupings did not change his ultimate approach.

This was the kind of role he undertook from the outset as Prime Minister. He acted with a decisiveness and vigour which not only belied his 64 years, but surprised many observers of his previous career. He attended to every detail, including that of his own physical well-being: as he had done during his time as Foreign Secretary, he gave up alcohol entirely, and took care to conserve his energy through regular short catnaps during the day, a practice dating from his time in the navy. He worked in an intense and concentrated fashion all his own, often taking important papers home with him, perhaps to read in his study or even in bed, in a private, almost introverted way. His style was to hear all the arguments and not rush in recklessly to reach an early conclusion. Without doubt, he made a more enduring and positive mark as premier than he had ever done at the Treasury, Home Office, or Foreign Office. He is an unusual case of a leading British twentieth-century politician who left No. 10 not discredited as premiers before him from Asquith to Wilson had been, but with his public reputation significantly enhanced. Yet he did so not as a remote and domineering personality in the mould of Margaret Thatcher, but as the generally trusted leader of a team.

Callaghan's standing as Prime Minister, of course, was derived largely from the way he conducted himself in the supreme office. But it was, at least initially, based on the simple fact that he was not Harold Wilson. His predecessor, while widely admired as a wily tactician of legendary capacity for survival who had actually won four elections out of five, had fallen in public esteem by the time he left office. Civil servants found him increasingly unimpressive as a leader, forgetful and erratic in carrying out decisions. One cause appeared to be his consumption of brandy which made him less effective after lunch. Callaghan, by contrast, imposed a firm grip on the agencies of government from the very start. The decline in Wilson's reputation was to continue long after he retired, probably to an excessive degree. But, judging from some of the obituaries, it may be questioned whether the appearance of distinguished biographies in the early 1990s produced a significant process of rehabilitation.

By April 1976, Wilson was widely attacked not so much for policy failures, or the substance of his regime, but rather for his style. To the general public, he seemed almost a paranoid figure, obsessed with 'leaks' and 'moles', engaged in witch-hunts against the press or the BBC or unnamed adversaries in MI5. His public standing had never really recovered since his unfortunate television broadcast to the nation immediately after devaluation of the pound in November 1967 when he assured the voters that the pound in their pocket had not been devalued. He was never wholly credible again. It was Wilson's equivalent of Stanley Baldwin's 'appalling frankness' speech about rearmament in the 1930s which led to Winston Churchill's celebrated index entry in his war memoirs, 'Baldwin, Stanley, puts party before country'. On a personal basis, Cabinet colleagues and civil service advisers almost universally felt that, while Wilson was personally a kindly and generous man of great talent, the devious way in which he ran his administration undermined a sense of trust. This was also widely believed by Commonwealth leaders such as Lee Kuan Yew.

Callaghan, by contrast, a bluff and far more direct figure, seemed in this key respect to be a great improvement. Voters could identify with his prejudices, hesitations, and very English pragmatism. He was a severe taskmaster and could be fierce towards civil servants, especially when they appeared sloppy or ill-prepared. On one occasion in Karachi he reacted furiously when the British ambassador to Pakistan seemed to him inadequately briefed, and walked out of a dinner in the embassy in disgust. It was also thought that he could be uneasy at first with new appointments: some felt that Bryan Cartledge suffered a little in this respect. Even so, there was hardly one minister or civil servant amongst those who served under both premiers who did not feel a breath of fresh air and a cleaning out of Augean stables when Jim Callaghan entered No. 10. There was a more genuine sense of collective participation and collaborative endeavour on the part of the administration as a whole, and far more sense of loyalty. In particular, there was nothing resembling the Wilson 'kitchen cabinet' which had met with widespread disapproval, especially with the publication of volumes of memoirs by Marcia Williams, Lady Falkender, by Wilson's press secretary Joe Haines, and others. This had been a growing impediment to Cabinet cohesion. The personal entourage of Wilson was felt to be acting in at best a quasi-constitutional way, promoting its own prime ministerial agenda and instilling a kind of bunker mentality in Wilson himself. The penumbral role of George Wigg, as a kind of personal bloodhound for the Prime Minister sniffing out plots and leaks, had not been conducive to a happy atmosphere either.

Callaghan's premiership had nothing remotely like this. He had not got on badly with members of the Wilson entourage. Indeed in the case of Marcia Falkender he had a good working relationship. It had been Callaghan who first enlisted her to work for the Labour Party after he met her at a student political meeting at the end of the 1950s. (As noted earlier, when asked what her particular merits were, he replied good-humouredly, and not unreasonably perhaps, that she had 'beautiful blue eyes'.) There was some complaint about the kind of machine politician the new Prime Minister had tended to attract: Gregor MacKenzie and Roland Moyle were sometimes a target of criticism in this respect, especially from ministerial victims like Gerry Fowler. But his own group of personal advisers, notably Tom McNally and Tom McCaffrey who followed Joe Haines as press secretary, played a more orthodox and visible role than their predecessors and aroused no such antagonism. Comparatively speaking, a new era of open government seemed to begin on 6 April 1976 and so it was to remain. It should be added that Harold Wilson, who gradually diverted his energies to writing volumes of political reminiscences and a series of television programmes on previous prime ministers, made no difficulties of any kind for his successor. Unlike Lady Thatcher after 1990 he never claimed to be any kind of back-seat driver. Three weeks after Callaghan had taken office, Wilson wrote warmly to him accepting an invitation to Sunday lunch with the Callaghans. 'I am, naturally, watching and approving the course of events and the attacks made on the problems. A good start.'[3]

Callaghan inherited the formal structure of government that had operated under Harold Wilson in 1974–6, and indeed basically under Edward Heath in the 1970–4 Conservative administration. The essential governmental machinery consisted of the Cabinet Office, under its secretary Sir John Hunt, and the prime minister's private office, under the direction of Sir Kenneth Stowe. Between the two, so Bernard Donoughue believed, there was a dualism, almost a kind of discreet rivalry, which gave Whitehall observers (and connoisseurs of the TV series *Yes Minister*) some private amusement.[4]

The Cabinet Office, since its foundation under Sir Maurice Hankey and Thomas Jones when Lloyd George first became premier in December 1916, had a broad set function of servicing the Cabinet and its attendant committees. But it also had from its early years an agenda which included policy-making, although this varied according to the outlook and personality of the Secretary. Sir John Hunt, who had already served under Edward Heath and Harold Wilson since 1973, was among the more vigorous exponents of this tradition. He had some years earlier chaired a working party on rail transport during Barbara Castle's time at the Transport Ministry and continued to show an interest in policy-making. A firm Roman Catholic whose wife was the sister of Cardinal Basil Hume, he had a viewpoint of his own. His style as Cabinet Secretary appeared different from that of his subtle predecessor Burke Trend. He was a manager not a mandarin, more forceful and with more evident ambition to be active executively, especially on the economic side. Callaghan encouraged him in this. One early instance was the way in which Hunt suggested the agendas for the Prime Minister's various meetings with departmental ministers. Thus on 15 July 1976 his brief for Callaghan's projected meeting with Peter Shore listed such potentially controversial topics as housing finance (including a possible move away from a general subsidy), housing's share of public expenditure, the role of building societies, possible governmental devolution in England, the inner cities, and local government finance: he noted that the Layfield Committee had recommended a 'local income tax'. He observed that Shore 'does not always give the impression of being a happy man at the DOE and that his strength lay in intellectual argument rather than executive decision-making in a department of 70,000 people'.[5] He also offered views on Cabinet-making. In July 1976 he offered the view that if Merlyn Rees were to be moved to the Home Office in succession to Roy Jenkins, the Northern Ireland Office might conceivably go to a peer.[6]

The Cabinet Secretary naturally took a keen interest in the machinery of government. Early in 1977 Hunt was proposing to Callaghan a scheme agreed between himself and Sir Douglas Allen for dividing up the Treasury into a Ministry of Finance, and a bureau of the budget covering public expenditure and manpower. The Chancellor would focus on taxation, customs and excise, the mint, and national savings.[7] Callaghan appeared to have some sympathy with this idea and might well have tried to implement something like it had he won the 1979 election, with Denis Healey being moved to the Foreign Office. But, perhaps because it was too reminiscent of former troubles with George Brown and the DEA, nothing resulted. On a different tack, Hunt offered Callaghan in 1977 his candid views on the effectiveness of the various Cabinet committee chairmen. Healey was 'outstanding' and rarely lost the thread of an argument. Merlyn Rees was at best average and did not give a clear enough lead. David Owen was brisk but could be impatient. Shirley Williams was good but could be overrun when the going got rough. Michael Foot relied unduly on his brief. Altogether, Hunt's view of his role was more than merely functional. Tony Benn claimed to see in his operations a potential danger, especially in the way that he appeared to use Berrill and the CPRS as an arm of central government. In practice, Hunt's effective influence upon policy-making was episodic, although Donoughue noted approvingly that he acted as a 'very positive' chairman of a Cabinet committee on unemployment in 1978.[8]

Hunt's main role was to service and support the Prime Minister, although of course he served ministers in general. At various times, but particularly in 1977, he and Callaghan actually contemplated the idea of a prime minister's department to provide the fullest range of information and authority for No. 10. This was a proposal considered at times by Wilson, Heath, and Mrs Thatcher as well. However, Callaghan concluded, surely correctly, that it was unnecessary since 'all the levers of power' were fully at his disposal in any case.[9] The Policy Unit almost fulfilled this role. More generally the idea might revive old memories of Lloyd George's Garden Suburb of ill repute in 1918–22, and thereby make the Prime Minister appear unduly presidential. Hunt approved of the collective way in which Callaghan ran his government and got on well with him personally. He was much impressed by the Prime Minister's ability to focus on selected key issues. He did not, however, operate in Downing Street itself and was, therefore, somewhat distanced from the epicentre of decision-making in contrast to the private office under Stowe who operated in the very next room to the Prime Minister. For this, and perhaps other reasons, Hunt for all his energy and air of self-confidence was not felt by some observers to exude quite the same authority under Callaghan's premiership that he had done under Wilson in 1974–6, or Robert Armstrong was to do under Mrs Thatcher. On the other hand, the calm way in which he handled security and other matters helped to restore equilibrium in the central administration after the near-paranoia of the Wilson years.

The private office consisted of civil servants on secondment who ensured that the Prime Minister was properly briefed and generally sorted out the details of his day-to-day activities. Under Callaghan the somewhat overpowering personality of Robert Armstrong gave way to the more unassuming and congenial figure of Kenneth Stowe. Somewhat unusually, his previous experience had mainly been in the DHSS rather than in the Cabinet Office. He and the Prime Minister struck up from the first an excellent and enduring relationship; Callaghan particularly appreciated his sensitive awareness of the political context in which policy decisions were taken. It was Stowe who proposed on 28 April 1976 that Callaghan might involve himself more directly in relations with his ministers than Harold Wilson had done. The implication was that the former Prime Minister had been unduly detached and remote.[11] Callaghan, he suggested, might ask his ministers for short reports on departmental matters, as a way of informing himself (and, no doubt, keeping ministers on their toes). He might also suggest individual initiatives in policy 'in the context of regular and thorough consultations with them about their stewardship'. Following Stowe's initiative, the first such meeting was held with Fred Mulley, Secretary for Education, on 21 May, with meetings with Tony Benn (Energy), Bruce Millan (Scotland), Peter Shore (Environment), and David Ennals (Health and Social Security) to follow shortly. Thereafter, Stowe's quiet and judicious presence was a major factor in almost all aspects of government policy, domestic and overseas, from the attempts to frame a wages policy to relations with European colleagues such as

Schmidt and Giscard d'Estaing. He was also a crucial figure in the party negotiations that led to the Lib–Lab pact in March 1977. His strong relationship with the Prime Minister was founded on a high level of trust and mutual regard. It is a testimony to the impartiality of the British civil service tradition that Stowe was apparently to enjoy an equally cordial relationship with Mrs Thatcher.[12]

The other members of the private office were of equally high calibre. They included secretaries seconded from the Treasury. Of these Nigel Wicks was regarded by the Prime Minister as exceptionally able. He had the additional merit that he was never overawed by Treasury mandarins, since from 1968 to 1975 he had been one himself, following long experience of the petroleum industry. He also went far beyond the Treasury brief on occasion, for instance in giving examples of the populist style of Mrs Thatcher's campaigning rhetoric.[13] Wicks was succeeded in 1978 by another Treasury man, Tim Lankester. There were also two former ambassadors, not of course members of the home civil service, to advise on foreign affairs. Patrick Wright, a career diplomat and authority on the Middle East, had been Callaghan's private secretary at the Foreign Office and was in due time to become head of the diplomatic service. His successor, Bryan Cartledge, a future ambassador to Moscow, was an adviser on eastern Europe in particular, who was to accompany the Prime Minister on several overseas visits.[14] He developed a very high regard for Callaghan's diplomatic skills and sense of statesmanship. He admired his expertise in east–west relations and his idealistic commitment to the third world. His one serious error, so Cartledge believed, and one from which Kenneth Stowe might have dissuaded him, was the appointment of his son-in-law Peter Jay as ambassador to the United States. At a more routine level, David Holt kept the Prime Minister's diary, and Philip Wood assisted with the preparations for question time in the House.

Beneath this formal level of interacting Cabinet and private offices, there was a second level of advisers. This consisted of two institutions, one more important and more intimate with the Prime Minister than the other. The more tangential body was the Central Policy Review Staff, popularly known as the Think Tank. It had been set up by Edward Heath under the chairmanship of Lord Rothschild. Under Callaghan it was headed by Kenneth Berrill, formerly chief economic adviser to the Treasury, with Dick Ross as his deputy (Gordon Downey replacing Ross in 1978).[15] Its personnel included a very able younger woman member, Tessa Blackstone, whose particular specialism at that time was overseas development, although she was also to be involved in education.

Callaghan defined the CPRS's role as fourfold—'to think the unthinkable, to give a global picture through assessments in the round, to fulfil particular assignments in problem areas, and to inject a new angle in agreed interdepartmental papers'.[16] The last two were held to be of most importance. Its role, therefore, was broadly strategic, even visionary. How this worked in practice was another matter, and Callaghan tended to use the CPRS less than Heath had done in a wide-ranging capacity. The CPRS, however, could be very useful to the Prime Minister. He could use it to point out weakness in ministerial papers and to alert him to problems in advance. The CPRS was also involved on occasion in high policy, as when there was a complex discussion on long-haul aircraft in 1977 and some pressure on British Airways to develop a relationship with British Aerospace rather than with Boeing. Tony Benn's 'alternative economic strategy' during the IMF crisis in late 1976 was also grist for the Think Tank's mill. Tessa Blackstone was used in the important role of following up the famous Ruskin speech on educational reform in October of that year.[17]

The CPRS, however, was detached and episodic in its impact on Callaghan's policy. By contrast, his Policy Unit was more ideological and constant in its involvement. One clear instance of the different roles of the two came in the summer of 1978 when the merger of the tax and benefit systems, as a result of the start of child benefits (which Callaghan had originally opposed when Barbara Castle put it forward), brought the theme of the 'family' into sharp political focus. This was a subject which naturally appealed to the Prime Minister himself. However, while the CPRS was engaged on a somewhat theoretical exercise in looking at family structure, gender relationships, and matters of that kind, the Policy Unit had the practical task of relating the theme of the family to aspects of government policy from education to vandalism and crime. It also encouraged the Prime Minister himself to pronounce on the topic. This he did with relish, notably in a widely reported speech to the General Assembly of the Church of Scotland (22 May 1978) in which he extolled the importance of 'a sound and sure family life'.[18]

Callaghan inherited the Policy Unit from Harold Wilson in 1974. It was perhaps the latter's most important constitutional innovation. The Unit's capacity to range over the whole spectrum of domestic policy, from exchange rates to Scottish and Welsh devolution, made it little short of a prime minister's department, his private fount of ideas. To a degree political scientists have yet fully to take on board, it marked a revolution in government. Its head, Thomas Cromwell to Callaghan's Henry VIII so to speak, was an ex-academic, with an interest in both financial and educational policy (and also in football), Dr Bernard Donoughue, formerly a politics lecturer at the London School of Economics. It was perhaps unusual for him to be retained in post by the succeeding prime minister. But Donoughue, in fact, was beginning to detach himself from Harold Wilson during the leadership contest in March–April 1976. It is significant that he was invited to attend the drinks party for Callaghan's triumphant campaign team after the contest was over.[19] Although he had no expectations of continuing in government, he played a strong and creative role for the remainder of Labour's term in office. He found Callaghan somewhat more formal than Wilson in their working relationship but, if anything, even more formidable in his intellectual power and executive decisiveness.[20] The fact that both he and Callaghan shared a working-class background and a pragmatic outlook on life made the bond between them closer still. Donoughue told Cledwyn Hughes in 23 July that 'he very much enjoys working for Callaghan and is much impressed by his style—thoughtful and relaxed'.[21] He enlisted a powerful and gifted team in his Unit, and they poured out advice and policy positions for the Prime Minister over the next three years. These started with Donoughue's own important memorandum on 'Themes and Initiatives' (PU 175) on 16 April 1976. This outlined the need for new policy initiatives from the Prime Minister on such issues as home ownership for council tenants, schools curricula, and voluntary social service, under the heading of 'Social Responsibility and Social Cohesion'.[22] In some ways, the Policy Unit under Bernard Donoughue anticipated the keynotes of Tony Blair's 'New Labour' philosophy of communal citizenship in the mid-1990s.

His team, many of its members being university teachers, was remarkably young and dynamic. They included, as full-time or part-time personnel, Andrew Graham, a 33-year-old Fellow in economics at Balliol, Oxford, who worked on macro-economic issues, especially incomes policy and balance of payments and energy policy; Richard Smethurst, a 35-year-old macro-economist who worked briefly on monetary policy, a Fellow of Worcester College, Oxford; David Gowland, a 27-year-old economist from the University of York; and Gavyn Davies, only 26, an exceptionally able statistician and econometrician, also from Balliol College, Oxford, for whom Callaghan had a particularly high regard and whom he encouraged to give advice on the whole range of economic policy options. This group, reminiscent of the Oxbridge group who had advised Callaghan in the Nuffield seminars when he was shadow Chancellor in the early 1960s, could deal confidently and on a basis of intellectual equality with the Treasury's advisers at any level. In addition, there were the 30-year-old

David Piachaud, a lecturer at the London School of Economics who specialized in social policy, health, and consumer affairs; Richard Graham, a manager from British Airways; Catherine Carmichael, a lecturer in social administration at Glasgow University; James Corr, from the World Bank, whose responsibilities, rather strangely, covered both trade union matters and Scottish devolution; Richard Kirwan from the Centre for Environmental Studies, a housing expert; and Elizabeth Arnott from the Transport House research staff. In 1977 they were joined on a full-time basis by David Lipsey, a 28-year-old Oxford graduate who had been special adviser to Tony Crosland for the past five years and whose remit covered, among other things, election strategy.[23]

There are several points of interest about these individuals. Among other things, they dispel the canard sometimes promoted that Callaghan was ill at ease with intellectuals or academics, especially those from an Oxford background. Evidence of his insecurity was sometimes cited. An Oxford-educated Labour member (said to be Bryan Gould) Callaghan allegedly turned down as a Minister for the Arts on the grounds that 'he makes me feel as if I had just come down from the trees'. Certainly he was often needlessly oversensitive to apparent slights or to being patronized. But it was pretentiousness not professionalism to which he objected. The personnel of his Policy Unit suggests both his high regard for specialist expertise, and the respect and loyalty that his advisers, mostly Oxford-trained from Bernard Donoughue down, felt in turn for him. After the uneasy atmosphere of the Wilson period of leadership, Callaghan's premiership seemed for many to enshrine, in a term applied to American politics, the rule of 'the best and the brightest'. On the other hand, some aides felt that it had been something of a weakness in his earlier periods in office, notably at the Treasury and the Home Office, that he had allowed himself to be surrounded only by mundane politicians like Gregor MacKenzie or Roland Moyle. The absence of powerful intellectual advisers then, they believed, had led to his being unduly swayed by his civil servants, in contrast to his marked confidence and stature as Prime Minister. Nevertheless, with advisers like Neild and Kaldor at the Treasury for instance, Callaghan had hardly lacked intellectually high-powered officials earlier in his career.

By the time Callaghan had become premier, the Policy Unit was established. Its relationship with the Cabinet Office and the central governmental committee apparatus was comfortably negotiated. On occasion its perceptions could come into conflict with those of the CPRS. Thus in December 1976–January 1977 there was a revealing argument between

Berrill and Donoughue about the Policy Unit's draft programme for National Recovery. Berrill felt this was too much addressed to the government's own supporters, and was too wide-ranging. It should focus on a few particular themes such as North Sea oil, industrial regeneration, and education. The Policy Unit, however, saw no difficulty in appealing mainly to Labour supporters. Gavyn Davies felt that the National Recovery programme's hopes for economic revival were perfectly justified, while Bernard Donoughue expressed surprise that the Think Tank was so devastatingly critical and negative.[24] On balance, it was the Policy Unit's more political stance that carried the day. In any case, differences of view like this were a part of constructive government rather than a sign of an innate structural conflict between the two bodies. Callaghan welcomed creative tension within the ranks of his advisers, even if he never followed Franklin Roosevelt's approach of encouraging antithetical viewpoints from ideologically opposed groups and then 'weaving the two together'. The New Deal was not an administrative paradigm for the British government. Nor was Callaghan-style creative tension a continuation of the Wilson approach of divide and rule.

The Policy Unit was an ideas machine of much potentiality. It was, for example, a frequent critic of the Treasury. It was under Callaghan that it came into its own. He used it with particular effect during the IMF crisis in November–December 1976 when it supplied much material designed to isolate Tony Benn and explode the credibility of his 'alternative economic strategy'.[25] This was satisfactorily achieved, although with some difficulty, for example in the light of Benn's subtle advocacy of the cause of import controls which was attractive to many not on the left.

Beyond this, Donoughue and his colleagues supplied a steady stream of papers on key issues, detailed and strategic. In June 1977, for instance, there were proposals on broad government economic strategy with an eye to the next general election.[26] At the same time, ways were suggested to deliver material benefits to Labour voters and neutralize the appeal of Mrs Thatcher ('Selsdon Woman').[27] In July 1977, attention was urged to reclaim the support of women voters for Labour.[28] In September there followed proposals for a £3 bn. reflation in 1978–9.[29] A year later, the Unit proposed a new range of initiatives with a view to a forthcoming election, notably the NHS (especially the hospital service), unemployment and technical change, law and order, and 'democratizing society', relating to such matters as industrial democracy, the running of schools, and a tenants' charter in housing. Callaghan responded very positively to all of them, especially the last, which he chose to redefine as 'citizens' rights, responsibilities and participation'.[30] In the course of the election campaign in April 1979 the Policy Unit was fertile with ideas for Labour to capture the political initiative and point out the inadequacies of Thatcherism.[31] Donoughue was encouraged by Callaghan to send in memoranda on all feasible topics, and felt that in general they landed on fertile ground. Only in the first three months of 1979, when the Prime Minister was tired and dispirited after the disappointments of the 'winter of discontent', was it felt that the Policy Unit was no longer able to influence his mind and outlook.

There was a final level of governmental machinery. This was the most intimate of all. It consisted of the Political Office and the press office, headed respectively by Callaghan's trusted aides Tom McNally and Tom McCaffrey. McNally had impressed Callaghan immensely both with his sensitive awareness of the balance of factors within the Labour Party and the trade union movement, and with his wide understanding of international issues, during the time that Callaghan was Foreign Secretary. With his master now in No. 10, McNally fulfilled all this role and much more besides, both as a liaison with the troublesome NEC and the unpredictable trade union movement, and as a generator of ideas on any topic that interested him, domestic or external.[32] On issues ranging from European monetary union or Rhodesia to the pact with the Liberal Party, McNally offered a stimulating stream of ideas, always tailored to the practical needs of leading the Labour Party as well as governing the country.

There appears not to have been any particular difficulty in the Political Office liaising with the Policy Unit or intruding into the more formal machinery of the civil service. McNally sought an early meeting with Sir Douglas Allen (head of the civil service), Kenneth Stowe, and Bernard Donoughue, to find a flexible formula through which the political advisers could participate in the planning of future programmes.[33] This proceeded satisfactorily, though McNally had to raise with Stowe on 21 September 1976 civil service objections to the appointment of David Hill, his long-standing adviser, as formal private adviser to Roy Hattersley who had just joined the Cabinet.[34] But these boundary difficulties were invariably resolved harmoniously and turf wars were almost non-existent. Callaghan had the highest regard for McNally's ability right down to the election campaign in 1979, by which time the latter had become Labour candidate for Stockport South. He for his part admired Callaghan's strategic judgement, his ability to absorb new, technical information on matters relating to economic or defence policy, and his general methods of running his administration. It was McNally who saw Callaghan at his most intimate, his period of high political finesse during the IMF crisis, his indecision over calling an election in August 1978 (when McNally himself was left in the dark like everyone else), and the final phase of near-despair during the winter of discontent. He also got used to Callaghan's routine in Downing Street (where he and Audrey lived, in contrast to Harold Wilson who had commuted from Lord North Street)—the early start, the short catnaps, the teetotal approach to hospitality, and the zest for foreign travel. As troubleshooter, lively ideas man, and friendly companion, McNally was unique.

In the closest touch with McNally was Tom McCaffrey, Callaghan's press officer as he had been at the Home and Foreign Offices. In contrast to his predecessor Joe Haines, McCaffrey kept a lower profile and concentrated on working on relations with journalists and the lobby generally.[35] Almost without exception he conducted his duties to Callaghan's total satisfaction, while the press liked him because he did not mislead them. A rare cause for complaint came at the sensitive moment of Peter Jay's nomination for the Washington embassy, when McCaffrey appeared to make disparaging noises about the snobbish demeanour of the present incumbent, Sir Peter Ramsbotham. Like McNally he saw Callaghan at close hand and much admired him, including on a human basis: one instance was when the British Prime Minister was called upon for marital advice by Pierre Trudeau, the premier of Canada, whose young wife was involved with a member of a rock group. Like McNally too, he remained unaware of Callaghan's decision about a possible autumn election in 1978 and found himself in some difficulty with journalists who had been briefed by others that an election was inevitable. McCaffrey and McNally invariably worked in unison and formed similar general views. One rare episode when their judgements did not coincide was over the press conference that followed Callaghan's return from the Guadeloupe summit in January 1979.[36] This event, with its resultant headlines of 'Crisis, what crisis?', was a sign of tired leadership and an administration heading for a fall. One intriguing episode was that Callaghan was advised by Geoffrey Goodman to take on a prominent and forceful pro-Labour journalist from Yorkshire as his press adviser. In fact, Hugh Cudlipp was to be chosen instead and it was Mrs Thatcher who enlisted the services of Bernard Ingham.[37]

Backed by this formidable range of advisers and administrative machinery, Callaghan handled his Cabinet with confidence but also consideration. He was well liked by them all. David Owen was to note his particularly sympathetic, human response when Owen's young son fell dangerously ill soon after he became Foreign Secretary.[38] Many difficult moments were defused by straightforwardness and good humour; the relationship with Tony Benn was far more amiable than might have been imagined, at least until the final months of trade union militancy and near anarchy. Callaghan had to give him stern warnings early on of the need to observe collective responsibility and had no patience with his minister's tortuous attempts to differentiate between speeches he made as a Cabinet minister and those he made as a member of the National Executive.[39] Callaghan emphasized that the general public took an integrated view of Tony Benn and regarded him as one and indivisible. Even though Benn contrived to the end to give the impression to his left-wing followers that he was both a member and an opponent of the Cabinet at the same time ('semi-detached' was the popular journalists' adjective for his posture), the Prime Minister kept him in line with more success than Wilson had been able to do.

Otherwise personal harmony and even loyalty prevailed. One Cabinet minister found the Prime Minister supportive when the tabloids tried to pursue him over an extramarital affair of potentially scandalous import; another, suspected of homosexual proclivities, was also left undisturbed. A close aide felt that Callaghan was immensely supportive to him while he was undergoing a particularly painful breakup of his marriage.[40] There were good precedents for this tolerance and compassion. It could even be said to reflect 'Victorian values' in contrast, say, to the stern puritanism of Clement Attlee. Even the virtuous Mr Gladstone, after all, had for long turned a blind eye to the liaison of Charles Stewart Parnell with Kitty O'Shea.

Callaghan felt in total command from the outset. On a personal basis, he felt secure living in No. 10, instead of being a non-resident as he had been at the Foreign Office. Audrey Callaghan found the house alarmingly large and the kitchen arrangements less convenient than on the farm. But as always she was an immense support for her husband. Cledwyn Hughes wrote in March 1977, 'I have always liked her; she is pleasant, even tempered, and a real help to Jim.'[41] No. 10 had the merit of being relatively close to Great Ormond Street children's hospital with which she was now most heavily and fruitfully involved as chairman of the Board of Governors. It was a crisis for the Prime Minister if any misfortune overtook his wife. He was deeply anxious when she had a minor car accident when leaving Downing Street in February 1977 after which hospital treatment was required. When he visited her there afterwards, he was falsely accused in the press of dodging an awkward Cabinet. In early 1978 she was mildly unwell and this again caused the prime minister some worry. But generally the family context was deeply reassuring. The children and grandchildren were frequent visitors. Michael Callaghan, now a senior manager in Ford Motors, found it fascinating to compare his business experience with the conduct of industrial policy as seen from Downing Street.[42]

On the political front, Callaghan felt relaxed and confident. After all, he had held all the key portfolios and had known other key departments either under Attlee or as Opposition spokesman. His background in this sense, ranging from the Dock Labour Scheme to the affairs of central Africa, was exceptionally well informed. He felt he knew the idiosyncrasies of every major department. In particular, he retained both respect for and suspicion of the Treasury, knowing how their refusal to consider the political context had brought difficulties for him during his time as Chancellor. His civil service aides, however, believed that he never showed the innate suspicion of the Treasury felt by Harold Wilson and such advisers as Joe Haines. In addition, as Governor of the Bank of England, Callaghan had the much more congenial figure of Gordon Richardson, instead of the imperious Lord Cromer whom he had considered a constant irritant during his own time at the Treasury. His deputy was an old friend, Kit McMahon, a member of the Nuffield group of advisers back in 1962–3. While Callaghan had particularly close friends in Merlyn Rees and Harold Lever, he did not play favourites in the Cabinet, and preferred a dialogue with colleagues as a whole rather than one-to-one mediation with individuals. He offered equal opportunity to younger ministers such as Shirley Williams, Roy Hattersley, and John Smith to participate in full in Cabinet deliberations. He usually chose not to give a view before asking for contributions to discussion in Cabinet, but summed up with both skill and fairness. As chairman he was lucid and concise, and he expected his ministers to be the same. Like other prime ministers from Attlee to Thatcher, he asked for Cabinet submissions to be brief.[43] On the other hand, like all experienced politicians, he could divert a discussion his way. Thus when William Rodgers wanted to introduce compulsory seatbelts, the Prime Minister managed to get a discussion on the issue delayed until just before lunch. He himself was opposed to compulsion on populist grounds. Rodgers's proposal nevertheless was supported by the majority, David Owen speaking vigorously in its favour. Callaghan then handed it over to the leader of the House, Michael Foot, who opposed compulsory seatbelts on libertarian grounds, and the chief whip, Michael Cocks, another opponent, and the proposal got no further.[44]

On balance, in major setpiece discussions, particularly during the IMF crisis but on many other issues including wages policy or the British nuclear deterrent, Callaghan's government was remarkable for its demonstration of the full potentialities of collective responsibility on the classic lines of Cabinet government. Richard Crossman's diagnosis that 'Prime Ministerial government' had become the norm, the view advanced in his famous introduction to the new edition of Bagehot's *The English Constitution*, was shown to be, at least in this instance, quite misconceived. Indeed Crossman had reluctantly come to disavow his own thesis after his own experience of being in Cabinet from 1964 and Harold Wilson's apparent lack of a sense of strategy thereafter. But, of course, as with all prime ministers from the Younger Pitt onwards, the style varied, as did the circumstances. Callaghan's broad-based Cabinet, with a tiny or no parliamentary majority, was to give way to Margaret Thatcher's virtual autocracy, based on landslide majorities, in which on occasion she appeared to dissociate herself from the decisions of her own Cabinet, as over the EMS. John Major, with whom Callaghan had a good relationship, reverted from 1990 to something more like the collective style of his Labour predecessor. After 1992, indeed, he came to emulate him not only in method but in his vanishing parliamentary majority.

Callaghan dominated his Cabinet more completely than Wilson did, at least in 1974–6, for all his alleged insecurity as a non-graduate from a humble social background. He was helped in this by sheer chance or misfortune. The removal of Roy Jenkins to take up the presidency of the European Commission in Brussels, followed soon after by the untimely death of Tony Crosland, meant that two of the major heavyweights of British public life were removed, and succeeded by younger and less illustrious ministers. The sacking of Barbara Castle at the outset had removed another possible source of alternative power. Tony Benn, by contrast, never enjoyed anything like the same stature within the Cabinet that he did amongst the left-wing activitists in the constituency parties and many of the trade unions.

The two key ministers, without doubt, were Michael Foot and Denis Healey. Foot, newly ensconced as leader of the House and effectively deputy prime minister, was essential to Callaghan as his link to the left, especially in the trade union movement. The Prime Minister would make a particular point of consulting Foot in private on all key issues well in advance to ensure that they were of like mind.[45] In the handling of wages policy and industrial relations generally, this was of central importance to the government's fortunes. Callaghan ensured that Foot attended all meetings and dinners with the TUC's 'Neddy Six'. He entrusted him with key negotiations in the framing of the Lib–Lab pact. He also encouraged him to participate in Cabinet discussions where Foot, a passionate tribune on the public platform, sometimes appeared unduly modest or reticent. In return, Foot, while never an intimate of the Prime Minister (he and Jill Foot never once visited him on the Sussex farm, for instance), was totally and unambiguously loyal. Bevan's disciple, he fought shoulder to shoulder with his ex-Gaitskellite colleague, right down to the final defeat over devolution in March 1979. His view was a decisive factor in dissuading Callaghan from holding a general election in the autumn of 1978.[46]

The other major figure was Denis Healey, the Chancellor of the Exchequer. The course of events ensured that economic problems would dominate the government's fortunes henceforth; from the summer of 1976 this meant that the Prime Minister himself was totally involved in economic policy-making, despite his initial wish to concentrate on foreign affairs. There were some who believed that the Prime Minister, rather than the Chancellor, was truly in charge of running the economy. Nevertheless, Callaghan and Healey, old colleagues though not exactly close friends, formed a powerful alliance together, and Callaghan backed up his Chancellor through thick and thin. There was a period at the height of the IMF crisis when it appeared that a major rift over policy was occurring, and there was some inaccurate journalists' talk of Healey being removed from the Treasury. There were further disagreements when Callaghan insisted that the Chancellor limit the concessions on public expenditure to be made as a condition in the letter of intent to be signed prior to receiving the massive loan from the IMF.[47]

But thereafter the two men were as one in coping with economic challenges, including the final, vain attempt to impose a pay norm of no more than 5 per cent upon the recalcitrant unions. They had a high regard for each other. Callaghan had great respect for Healey's intellectual powers (a view shared by Healey himself) and recognized that by 1976 his command over the Treasury was a strong one. In the event, Healey was to stay on as Chancellor for the full five years, perhaps two more than Callaghan himself felt was desirable for anyone. By 1978 Cledwyn Hughes felt strongly that Callaghan regarded Healey as his likely successor, or rather as his desired successor, as Wilson had felt about Callaghan himself in 1974–6.[48] Hughes gave Healey the good advice that he should spend more time in the Commons cultivating friends. For his part, Healey felt Callaghan to be a decisive, clear-headed, courageous leader,[49] whose political dexterity could cover up the consequences of his own occasional blunderbuss politics in handling friends and foes alike. In his memoirs he was to describe Callaghan as the best prime minister since Attlee.[50] Healey and Callaghan formed a powerful alliance, as indeed did Healey and Foot in their turn, particularly in negotiations with the trade unions. Had Labour won the 1979 election, Healey would have moved to the Foreign Office.

Callaghan encouraged his ministers to use their own initiative and to act as independent and trusted advisers. But that did not preclude him from trying to find policy areas in which he could pursue a line of his own, either as a stimulus or goad to ministers, or else as a forerunner of general Cabinet strategy. Tom McNally, Kenneth Stowe, and Bernard Donoughue and his Policy Unit colleagues were all active in suggesting areas where this kind of prime ministerial initiative could most effectively be exercised. Donoughue had taken the lead in Callaghan's first few days as premier, as has been noted. He proposed such themes as the sale of council housing and teaching standards in the schools as areas where Callaghan could assert himself. Tom McNally offered a not totally dissimilar list of priorities comprising the sale of council housing again, Northern Ireland (with an emphasis on social and economic progress), the social services, Scottish government, and education.[51] Callaghan responded to these with varying degrees of enthusiasm. Northern Ireland, for instance, was unfruitful territory, and the transition from Merlyn Rees to Roy Mason as Secretary for the province in September 1976 meant in practice an emphasis on hard-line law and order policies rather than an attempt to find a political consensus. In any case, with provisional Sinn Féin heavily involved in a campaign of murder and bombings, that was scarcely possible. There seemed to be no durable political settlement on the horizon. All Callaghan could hope for was to keep channels open as Oliver Wright had done for him in 1969–70 when British representative to the Stormont regime. Nor did Scottish government seem a promising area for a prime minister always cool on the possibility of Celtic devolution. On the sale of council houses, Callaghan recognized that here, like comprehensive education, was a traditional Labour shibboleth where public opinion, including working-class opinion, was changing. But he felt unable to promote a change of policy here and Labour's policy of maintaining a public housing stock remained intact. Labour publicists like Joe Haines were to lament, with some reason, that this failure left the way open to one of the more popular aspects of Thatcherism.

One particular theme, however, that he did make his own, and on which his personal authority was stamped, was education. In his ministerial meeting with Fred Mulley on 21 May Callaghan spelt out his long-standing concern with standards of teaching in the schools, the content of the curricula in different subjects, the promotion of science and technology, and the need for ensuring basic standards of literacy and numeracy amongst schoolchildren.[52] Earlier in the decade it was the political right which had taken up this issue. There had been 'Black Papers' from Baroness Cox and others since 1969, and proto-Thatcherite educational pressure groups that owed much to London experience, notably in the North London Polytechnic and the William Tyndale school. But Callaghan rightly felt that educational standards were, if anything, of even more concern to his own supporters since it was they above all whose children went to the maintained state schools. Now was the time for Labour to hit back. Although it caused much concern amongst officials in the Education Department, therefore, the Prime Minister began to assemble his thoughts for a major pronouncement on education. He enlisted the help of Bernard Donoughue of the Policy Unit, and later of Tessa Blackstone of the Think Tank, in its implementation. The outcome was the famous Ruskin College speech of 16 October 1976, much of which was written by Donoughue.[53] In the long term it inaugurated a 'great debate' on standards in public education which was still in full swing in the mid-1990s. It encouraged Labour to adopt a less doctrinaire approach towards state schools, and to consider aspects of high professional standards and quality controls. It was also perhaps the best example of the Prime Minister independently pursuing his own agenda and initiative, more openly than Macmillan or Wilson, more selectively than Heath or Thatcher. It was Jim Callaghan's version of prime ministerial government in action.

On this and other occasions, Callaghan was anxious to articulate his government's philosophy by means of an overarching theme. In the Ruskin speech it was public standards, related to social cohesion and responsibility by a citizenry in charge of its own destiny, aware both of its rights and of its duties and social obligations to others. On other occasions, it was the need for a more equal society on which Callaghan focused his attention, especially in speeches which concentrated on the reform of the social services, for instance in regard to child allowances or pension arrangements in promoting a fairer society.[54] At other times, it was more decentralized society which he emphasized, although this was not perhaps a theme embraced quite so enthusiastically. But certainly Callaghan was one of the more philosophical prime ministers, anxious to have it seen that his government stood for perceived values and that theory and practice went hand in hand. Honesty and integrity were particular themes of his speeches. By comparison with the manœuvrings of the Wilson years, let alone the sleaze and scandal which gave rise to the Nolan Committee in

1994, his administration appeared to embody them. Callaghan made a strong impression when he appeared before that committee as the champion of higher standards of conducting public life, standards which his own government could reasonably be claimed to embody.

Sociological themes were also a part of the prime ministerial attempt to seize the political initiative by taking the moral high ground. The values of neighbourhood and particularly of the family were also themes which he emphasized and of which, by character and inclination, this singularly 'unpermissive' ex-Home Secretary seemed a most appropriate champion. His views, like those of many of his advisers (not to mention the vast majority of Labour voters), were in this area traditional and conventional. He was perhaps the first major politician to realize the wider political significance of merging the tax and benefit scheme, with the introduction of child benefit in 1978. His speeches now emphasized the 'family budget' as well as recognizing the power of the family, including especially the middle-class family, as a political and social pressure group. Enlisting a variety of Christian organizations in his support, he called for children to have 'a proper upbringing and a proper sense of values'. He urged parents 'to face up to their responsibility', for instance in ensuring decent day-care for their children when mothers went out to work. In his public pronouncements the silent majority seemed to find a clarion voice, while Mrs Thatcher, for the moment, seemed to be wrong-footed.

The other obvious theme of prime ministerial initiatives was that of law and order, one that came most naturally to the former spokesman for the Police Federation. He criticized the Labour Home Policy Committee in November 1977 for its comparative neglect of the problems of violence and vandalism, felt most acutely in working-class communities such as inner cities. In this he found an unexpected ally in the left-wing Liverpool member Eric Heffer. Back in September 1974 Callaghan had told the Cabinet, 'I am rather in favour of dealing with teenage hooliganism', to which Denis Healey gave a loud 'hear! hear!'[55] The Labour Party had long seemed unduly concerned with criminology rather than with crime. It placed emphasis on the social circumstances which allegedly promoted crime and which might effectively condone the actions of the criminal, rather than on the needs and rights of victims, often the least powerful and articulate members of society. The Policy Unit tried repeatedly to get Labour Party pronouncements to place more emphasis on crime and law and order issues generally, but with limited success at this period. It took the emergence of Tony Blair's leadership in 1994 to get a complete shift in attitudes—some felt to a wholly excessive degree when Jack Straw condemned street beggars whose presence offended respectable citizens and Tony Blair called, in American terms, for 'zero tolerance' towards them. Callaghan at least had an instinctive sense for what the public, including the working-class public, sought from their politicians, and how it should be expressed. He deplored a tendency in Labour ranks to discuss human and civil rights in terms of specific groups and organizations, often highly mobilized, rather than focus them in terms of the ordinary citizen, what Roosevelt called the forgotten man at the base of the economic pyramid. Callaghan wanted the forgotten man (and woman) to be restored and celebrated. Instead, to his dismay, self-interested bodies including many trade unions offered an individualistic approach that conflicted with the social cohesion and community self-discipline on which traditional British social democracy, from Keir Hardie to Jim Callaghan, fundamentally rested.

Apart from intervening at a general, philosophical, or moral level, Callaghan also intervened on a mass of individual policy themes without disturbing the general collective stance of his administration. He appreciated the space and perspective that the premiership, shorn of departmental policy responsibilities, provided. There were a variety of issues in which he took a close personal interest. One was the financing of the National Health Service. In 1977 and 1978 he intervened personally to ensure that extra expenditure was diverted to the Health Service, especially the hospital service, even at a time of public spending cuts after the IMF crisis. He compelled David Ennals, the Minister for Health and Social Security and one of the less forceful members of the Cabinet, to ensure that extra funding went to patient care rather than to the coffers of the Health Service unions.[56] The NHS, including especially the hospital service, became a priority on which he focused in 1978–9 as an election drew nearer.

Personal tax reform was another of his pet areas, drawing not only on his experience as Chancellor but on his even longer experience as a member of the Inland Revenue back in the 1930s. One remarkable aspect of prime ministerial involvement came with the question of the purchase and sale of aircraft. Callaghan became deeply implicated in this, not just as a matter of the operational policy of British Airways but as an aspect of Anglo-American relations. He immersed himself in the detail of aircraft sale and purchase in a way that astonished Bernard Donoughue and the CPRS alike. As he explained to the Commons during the Westland helicopters debate in January 1986, he was anxious that Boeing wanted 'to suck the technology out of British Aerospace and reduce its role to that of a sub-contractor'. He was also anxious about opposition in the US Congress to the use of export credits guarantees by the British government to support the sale of Rolls-Royce engines to American companies and took a robust stand in defence of British interests. He took Kenneth Berrill of the CPRS, who was chairman of the relevant interdepartmental committee, with him to Washington to discuss matters with Boeing and also with appropriate members of the US administration. The Rolls-Royce issue he took up personally with President Carter himself.[57] He also startled Norman Tebbitt, a right-wing Conservative MP who had begun life as an airline pilot, by engaging him in intimate private conversations about the details of the aerospace manufacturing industry. Tebbitt consulted his party leader about the proprieties here. Mrs Thatcher replied, 'Norman, if the prime minister wishes to speak to you, of course you must.'[58] In the event, British Aerospace, a major player in this episode, was to collaborate with the French in their airbus scheme, while Rolls-Royce co-operated with Boeing and British Airways finally chose the latter as the manufacturer of its new planes. Everybody got what they wanted. The whole affair was a remarkable case of sustained prime ministerial intervention.

In addition, Callaghan had ample scope for pressing his own policies since he was in effect in charge of foreign policy, however punctilious he was to lend moral and other support to the youthful David Owen when he succeeded Crosland at the Foreign Office in January 1977. This gave Callaghan a wide range of cards to play on many matters. They included international economic co-operation to promote recovery and liquidity, policy towards Rhodesia (where Tony Crosland tended to defer to him during his brief time as Foreign Secretary), and especially matters of defence including the future course of British nuclear policy and the prospects of a successor deterrent to replace the ageing Polaris missile system. Callaghan acted with real authority in all these areas. In addition, he undoubtedly felt that his personal links with President Ford and Dr Kissinger in the United States, until their defeat in the November 1976 presidential election, gave him extra leverage. Even more did he feel this about his strong bonds of comradeship with Chancellor Helmut Schmidt of West Germany. Like all prime ministers since 1973, he was constrained by the impact on British sovereignty of membership of the European Union. On the other hand, the fact that in 1976 the implications of membership were so uncertain and fluid perhaps gave the Prime Minister, especially as the former Foreign Secretary who had renegotiated the terms of entry, more authority in domestic politics as an interpreter of the new relationship. In the IMF crisis in November–December 1976 many Cabinet colleagues, among them Tony Benn and Edmund Dell, felt that the Prime

Minister was pursuing his own, externally directed policy by using his links with Ford and Schmidt in order to bypass the IMF to direct attention to his own favoured project of funding the sterling balances.[59] As events turned out, Callaghan's expectations were to be disappointed, even by Schmidt, and this venture into personal diplomacy was jettisoned in favour of a collective Cabinet approach. The Treasury and the Bank of England were strongly opposed. On the other hand, Callaghan's initiatives helped ensure that, with American assistance, the problem of the sterling balances was settled satisfactorily in the end.

Finally, it was in domestic economic policy that Callaghan often intervened on a personal basis. He was driven to do so after what he saw as the disastrous failures of the Heath government. From the summer of 1976, when the wages bargain with the TUC had to be renegotiated, he found himself increasingly embroiled in economic policy and often effectively in charge of it, however close his relationship with Denis Healey. His unique relationships with Len Murray of the TUC and key union leaders such as David Basnett or Tom Jackson added to his authority here. Jack Jones of the Transport Workers was more wary, but he too felt that the Prime Minister was a more sympathetic figure than his Chancellor, Denis Healey, and more committed to party unity.

At key moments, Callaghan often pursued his own course. The most remarkable instance of this, perhaps the most spectacular instance of any aspect of governmental policy between 1976 and 1979, was when he led the move away from traditional Keynesian policies and towards a modified monetarism in his speech to the Labour Party conference at Blackpool in September 1976.[60] Callaghan declared here that traditional pump-priming methods through deficit financing and public spending were no longer effective. Britain, he declared to the startled delegates, most of whom were trade unionists, could no longer spend its way out of a recession. That option no longer existed and another way must be found.

It was a bold declaration of intent to make a fresh start, and took the trade unions and the party aback. Callaghan saw it as a rejection of 'glib solutions'. Whether it was prudent or indeed wholly credible as a long-term policy is another matter. Many saw it as the Prime Minister embracing monetarism and, in effect, surrendering the ideological initiative to the Tories. It came as a surprise to Denis Healey who was not impressed by its thrust and later expressed himself pungently on the point.[61] It was largely the result of a last-minute telephone conversation between Callaghan and his economic son-in-law Peter Jay, a long-standing critic in the press of orthodox Keynesianism and an apostle of monetary discipline and cash limits.[62] How rigorous a break with traditional Keynesian ideas Callaghan meant this speech to be is open to debate. He himself was to reject some of the more apocalyptic interpretations of it later on, such as that it was an anticipation of the views of Milton Friedman and the Chicago monetarist school. He regarded himself as still a Keynesian but one who recognized the limits of the ideas of the master,[63] who after all had worked out his theories no less than forty years earlier. His speech was intended to focus on the particular problem confronting discussions with the IMF rather than suggest a general recasting of British economic management. It brought enthusiastic praise from one right-wing Labour economist, Lord Vaizey, who praised his 'GREAT speech at Blackpool'.[64] But the view of this recently ennobled peer, a beneficiary of Harold Wilson's final honours list, was a minority one at the time.

But the speech also caused political and industrial difficulties for him. The discussions with the unions on wage norms were made the more difficult, quite apart from the virtual ungovernability of some of the major unions such as NUPE. Prime ministerial appeals for wage restraint were met with bitter complaints by workers in the Health Service or local government who felt that they had borne the brunt of severe retrenchment in public expenditure from 1976. Callaghan's conference speech then suggested, perhaps, the dangers as well as the potentialities of prime ministerial policy initiatives. On balance, though, Callaghan seized his opportunities for individual action shrewdly, at least down to September 1978, and in a way that strengthened both his administration and his personal authority. In the 'winter of discontent', by contrast, a series of errors led both into an irreversible phase of decline.

In his views of the system of governance more generally, Callaghan reflected current orthodoxy and was relatively conservative. There was no need to change matters fundamentally since he had all the levers of power at his disposal and his authority was effectively untrammelled. That did not mean that he could not be innovative. The most notable instance of this was to be the 'seminar' on economic policy spearheaded by Harold Lever in 1977–8. Chaired by the Prime Minister, it included the Chancellor of the Exchequer, the Foreign Secretary, the Governor and Deputy Governor of the Bank of England, Bernard Donoughue, Sir John Hunt, Kenneth Berrill, Kenneth Stowe, and a few others, and took a broad overview of fiscal and monetary policy, especially in relation to that of other countries. Callaghan felt the Treasury was constrained by seeing matters in terms of day-to-day management. The seminar met on 5 July 1977 to discuss the reserves and interest rates; on 20 October 1977 to look at inflows of foreign currency which were endangering the Chancellor's M3 monetary targets; on 6 March 1978 to consider the 'dollar initiative' (Harold Lever wanted the dollar to be a new reserve currency); and on 7 November 1978 to examine monetary policy including a new target range for M3, the broad money supply.[65] It may be taken as an important additional forum for considering modifications of Keynesian policies. In a Fabian inquiry in 1980 Gavyn Davies was to criticize it sharply for bypassing the Cabinet and making collective responsibility 'a sham'. But this is surely an error. The seminar was merely that—a forum for discussion of long-term issues in an informal way, not an instrument for any kind of decision-making. It could well be argued that it brought ministers in to debate matters that would otherwise be discussed in secrecy with the Governor and officials of the Bank of England. They could not be discussed in full Cabinet—for one thing, it was believed that some ministers might immediately leak them to MPs or journalists. The seminar was just simply an occasional medium for stimulating discussion—Callaghan notes in his memoirs that fourteen meetings only were held in 1977–8, and his notes confirm the point—rather than any attempt to bypass the formal machinery for the conduct of economic and fiscal policy. It also enabled the Prime Minister to receive information and advice from key figures like Gordon Richardson and Kit McMahon, the Governor and Deputy Governor of the Bank of England, at first hand rather than have it mediated through the Treasury whose secretive approach the Prime Minister knew and resented.[66]

Otherwise, Callaghan, like Clement Attlee before him, did not leave a legacy of constitutional innovation. Harold Wilson did attempt reforms of the civil service and the House of Lords but they yielded little; the first national referendum conducted in 1975 was his one remarkably successful novelty. (On balance Labour's most adventurous prime minister in this regard may be considered to be Ramsay MacDonald, even if some of his innovations were forced on him by financial catastrophe in 1931.) Callaghan felt that the civil service worked well and efficiently and was a model for other nations. There was no need to tamper with it. The 'elephantine' Civil Service Department (to use Bernard Donoughue's term)[67] was left alone and it was to be Mrs Thatcher who abolished it in 1981. The other reforms proposed by the Fulton Committee in the 1960s were left dormant. A major criticism offered by Labour of the civil service machine was that it was ideologically biased in favour of continuity and that Labour's own advisers were left on the outside. However, with McNally and his Political Office and Donoughue and the Policy Unit, Callaghan felt that he had ample sources of appropriate party advice, while others could be brought in by ministers as Roy Hattersley had enlisted the aid of David Hill.

On balance, Callaghan took a stern and purist view as all prime ministers, other than Lloyd George and perhaps Churchill, had done before him, that political advisers and career civil servants should be kept in separate compartments. He strongly disapproved of the later policy of Mrs Thatcher which appeared to blur the line and to suck diplomats like Sir Anthony Parsons and Sir Crispin Tickell or civil service advisers such as Charles Powell into her personal political machine. Like all his Labour predecessors and most of his Cabinet colleagues (Tony Benn, the apostle of open government, being a conspicuous and vocal exception) Callaghan felt that the civil service should be left alone. It should stay unpoliticized, confidential, and non-partisan. As a senior figure in 1996 he was to speak out robustly in support of his former private secretary at the Treasury, Lord Bancroft, in condemning the 'letting out' of civil service posts on an agency basis. On other areas, he was equally cautious. The reform of local government had been undertaken by the Heath government in 1972–3 and Callaghan, while he disapproved of some aspects of it, saw no reason to tamper with so recent a structure. On Scottish and Welsh devolution, he felt that changes in this direction were a necessary evil, to placate the Scottish Nationalists and Plaid Cymru members in the House on whose support he partly depended, rather than something constitutionally desirable. He ploughed the sands of Celtic devolution in the later 1970s without enthusiasm or great commitment.

The House of Lords he also left on one side, mindful, as he told Douglas Houghton, of how he had burnt his fingers on the issue when Wilson proposed to reform its composition in 1968.[68] The fact that it often intervened inconveniently for his minority government, for instance rejecting government schemes for further nationalization or planning agreements, did not cause him undue pain. In the 1979 election manifesto he made sure that proposals by Eric Heffer for abolishing the upper house or, alternatively, making it an elective body, with the hereditary peers abolished, were cut out. Of the upper house in general he had a low opinion. He quoted Macmillan with approval as someone who had refused a peerage (of course, Macmillan later changed his mind and became Lord Stockton) and cited the former Conservative premier as someone who spoke with contempt of appearing in a minor provincial music hall after 'treading the boards at Drury Lane'. He told Cledwyn Hughes in February 1978 that he would not take a peerage after he retired. He would prefer to commute from his farm to take seminars in Sussex University and thus have the company of intelligent young people 'and not the old fogies who frequented the Lords'.[69] When he did in fact become a peer years later in 1987 it was simply to remain to some degree active in front-line politics. He had no particular admiration for the upper house even if no wish either to reform or modernize it. Again it was not until the mid-1990s that Labour was to make constitutional change a policy priority. Tony Blair was now personally committed to reforming the House of Lords, along with Scottish and Welsh devolution (on a PR basis) and a bill of rights. But over the years, compared with the handling of the Lords by the Liberals Asquith and Lloyd George, or even the Conservative Harold Macmillan, Labour governments have been restrained as constitutional innovators.

In one important area, Callaghan was highly traditionalist. He fully conformed to the pattern of the monarch's having generally better relations with Labour prime ministers than with Conservative ones. With Edward Heath, the relations of Queen Elizabeth were 'correct but cool'.[70] In terms of laying on compliments with a trowel for his sovereign (or, indeed, any woman) Heath fell a long way short of Disraeli. The Queen did not warm to Heath's somewhat glacial personality and disapproved of his coolness towards the Commonwealth as opposed to his obsessive enthusiasm for Europe. With Mrs Thatcher later on, the relationship, according to most accounts, was relatively frosty, with the Commonwealth again an area of indirect conflict, including the issue of sanctions on South Africa. The British right wing did not enjoy their Queen sharing a Christmas Day broadcast with Mrs Indira Gandhi.[71] By contrast, the Queen got on well with Harold Wilson whom she found human and amusing, in a gossipy way; the *New Statesman* once described him as 'the working man's Melbourne'. Callaghan also had an excellent relationship with the Queen whom he not only respected as monarch but greatly liked as a person. They got on well enough for the Prime Minister to compliment his sovereign on occasion for her dress sense. On Commonwealth and other matters, they were clearly of one mind. He derived personal pleasure from leading the national celebrations of the monarch's silver jubilee in 1977. This led to a lengthy discussion in the Cabinet about an appropriate form of present to the Queen. Shirley Williams proposed a saddle, Tony Benn a vase carved in coal by a Polish miner, and Lord Elwyn-Jones a Welsh clock. In the end, the Prime Minister authorized Audrey to buy a silver coffee-pot. The weekly royal audiences were genial and relaxed, with conversation ranging easily over a variety of topics, political and personal. The Queen was quick to offer her moral support on difficult occasions such as in the renewal of talks with Ian Smith to try to find a settlement in Rhodesia. By contrast, the Duke of Edinburgh, despite the shared naval background which Callaghan respected, had come to be regarded as a somewhat loose cannon, sometimes tactless and maladroit in giving his (usually reactionary) opinions on public issues.[72]

One of the areas to which Callaghan devoted some attention was in trying to find a meaningful role for the Prince of Wales. Indeed, as a Cardiff MP, Callaghan had already had a good deal of contact with Prince Charles on various Welsh public occasions; the Prince, for instance, became in 1977 chancellor of the University of Wales from which the Prime Minister had the previous year received an honorary degree and whose gatherings he often attended. They were to be thrown together much more in the future when Callaghan became president of the University College of Swansea (renamed in 1994 the University of Wales, Swansea). During his premiership, Callaghan devoted some effort to trying to find Charles 'a proper job', as the phrase went, and tried to instruct him in the processes of government. The Prince attended NEDO, toured 10 Downing Street, and on one occasion attended a meeting of the Cabinet. Callaghan also tried to interest the Prince in the activities of the private office, notably in the preparations for prime minister's question time. Mrs Thatcher was startled, and perhaps angered, when he turned up for this gladiatorial event in the House with relatively little warning. The relationship of the premier to the young Prince was avuncular and usually amiable. But it was also 'widely believed', as the royal biographer, Jonathan Dimbleby, correctly writes, that Callaghan was disappointed by the relative lack of interest the Prince took in political affairs, as compared to his various private enthusiasms for classical architecture, holistic religions, correct English, and organic farming. One important civil service aide, otherwise discreet, sharply criticized the Prince in private as 'an arrogant young man' in offering a disdainful lack of response to Callaghan's efforts to give him a meaningful training in public affairs. Apparently Prince Charles cited the view of Lord Home that his public duties as Prince of Wales were quite taxing enough without his having to involve himself in time-consuming administrative work. Possible membership of the Commonwealth Development Corporation met with the same negative and complacent attitude.

When the marriage of the Prince and Princess Diana came to an effective end in the mid-1990s, Callaghan was foremost amongst those asking for an early divorce so that the private breakdown of a marriage did not lead to a public debate on the future of the monarchy.[73] He did not want a historic institution put in jeopardy by the wayward behaviour of the heir to the throne and his glamorous but capricious wife. As Prime Minister, he set his face against attempts to weaken the authority or prestige of the Crown. Pressure from some in the Labour Party, notably Tony Benn, for the Civil List to be cut down if not abolished, and the Queen to lose her immunity to taxation on her vast income, was stoutly resisted, as it had been by Wilson before him. Like all Labour leaders since the time of Keir Hardie (who had famously derided the birth of the future Edward VIII at the time of a Welsh mining disaster),[74] Jim Callaghan was no constitutional radical and no republican.

The other aspects of the prime ministerial role, apart from his leadership of the Cabinet and the governmental machine, lay in his activities as party leader and as communicator and image-maker with the general public. With the party, as will be seen, Callaghan had constant difficulty. As Prime Minister he was uniquely preoccupied in devising ways of keeping the parliamentary party, the National Executive, the Cabinet, Transport House, and the unions in some kind of harmony, or, in the cliché of the time, singing from the same hymn sheet. In handling the PLP, for all the revolts that occurred on a variety of issues, he was remarkably effective. As he always had done, he spent much time in the Commons tearoom, hobnobbing with Labour backbenchers, soliciting their views, and taking a keen and genuine interest in their personal circumstances and problems. He spent more time with Welsh members than he had tended to do in the past: with Welshmen like Ted Rowlands, Brynmor Jones, Alan Williams, and Donald Coleman occupying key middle-ranking posts in the administration, there was talk of a Welsh 'Taffia' emerging as under Lloyd George. Unlike many prime ministers, he regularly lunched in the Commons dining-room, choosing his dining companions at random amongst Labour backbenchers. They mostly felt that they knew him and many had affectionate tales to tell afterwards.

The National Executive was far less amenable. Even for one of his prestige and dominance, especially since his links with the unions after his election as party treasurer in 1967, he had endless trouble as the NEC marched resolutely and almost unthinkingly to the left. Tom McNally's account of meetings with the NEC/TUC Liaison Committee, and of sessions of the National Executive from his first meeting with Geoff Bish and David Lea, of Transport House and the TUC respectively, from 11 May 1976 onwards, were a saga of the party's representatives failing to recognize the economic difficulties confronting the nation, ignoring the pressure of inflation, and pushing on with ever more costly social and economic projects. Callaghan had to rebut some of the immediate proposals, such as a 'generous' child benefit scheme to be introduced early in 1977. He minuted

McNally, 'Can you find some "costless" social projects? e.g. What about B.D.'s paper on selling council houses?' McNally replied that almost all the proposals would mean public expenditure, other than 'in the industrial democracy and machinery of government field'.[75] The Chancellor was quick to observe that a combination of labour subsidies and training programmes, the planning agreements with 100 leading companies, funding for the National Enterprise Board, a ceiling for the penetration of imports, a commitment to 150m. tons of coal output by the mid-1980s, a wealth tax, a proposal for half of average earnings for retirement pensions for married couples, higher child allowances, and community ownership of rented property would all cost much money at a time of severe economic difficulties. There was also a failure to acknowledge that these would mean swingeing tax increases at a time when working people had suffered cuts in their living standards for two to three years. Higher public expenditure in any case would compete with the vital demands of exports and industrial investment.[76] On a later occasion, Gavyn Davies pointed out the dangers of Labour's increases in public spending. Whereas the Tories planned a decrease of 2.7 per cent, Labour had increased it by 8.6 per cent, and indeed three times faster than gross national product.[77]

Callaghan fully endorsed all these criticisms, and various arguments with the NEC resulted. The belief of members of the National Executive that the government was deliberately marginalizing them raised the temperature still further. Barbara Castle was often an embittered critic in these meetings. Her proposal on 24 September to condemn the government for its spending cuts was tied 14 : 14, with Michael Foot and (under orders) Tony Benn supporting the government's view. Only the casting vote of the chairman of the NEC, Tom Bradley, prevented a conflict between party and government. McNally reported that the bitterness of Barbara Castle's 'attempt to make personal political capital' had alienated even some on the left but this kind of tension continued for the rest of Callaghan's premiership.[78] Her dogmatic, self-absorbed style annoyed some of her former admirers. On the other hand, she could very reasonably respond that she was speaking out in defence of the policies in Labour's 1974 election manifestos, whereas Callaghan and his aides were casting them aside.

As the swing to the left in the constituency parties and many of the unions went on, Callaghan's difficulties in keeping a hold over his party were compounded. This was sharply reflected in his problem in controlling the parliamentary party during the IMF talks in December 1976. The greatest machine operator of his time, he found that a newly radicalized, if diminished, party rejected the government's calls for moderation and consensus. The IMF crisis did not end the arguments since a feeling that at least Callaghan had averted a crisis of 1931 proportions was balanced by anger at the spending cuts and growing unemployment that followed. Demands for a siege economy continued unabated. On one issue after another, proposals by the Prime Minister, the Chancellor, and the great majority of the Cabinet for wage restraint, economic caution, and an end to proposals that, as Harold Lever put it, 'merely alarm business opinion at home and abroad' were rebuffed.[79] A typical episode was the presentation of a Liaison Committee document on July 1977. McNally reported the Policy Unit's view that it contained 'no serious discussion of inflation'.[80] On the other side, left-wing figures on the NEC such as Mikardo, Frank Allaun, and Joan Maynard, abetted by younger figures such as Neil Kinnock and Denis Skinner, and by union leaders such as Clive Jenkins of ASTMS and Alan Fisher of NUPE, pressed on with their own agenda—more socialism, a planned if not a siege economy, the nationalization of banks and insurance companies, the conscription of private funds and a wealth tax, minimal ties with Europe, and an end to the British nuclear deterrent. Tom McNally was to describe the Executive as dominated by ideologues. In Transport House, the national agent, Reg Underhill, was tired and dispirited. The general secretary, Ron Hayward, a leftish figure, was 'obsessed with pelf and peace', while key organizers like Geoff Bish and Jenny Little were mainly anxious to work with the left.[81]

It was clear, long before Callaghan fell from office in May 1979, that a sea change was occurring in the labour movement. The consensual ethos for which Callaghan had always stood—the famous 'broad church' view of the Labour Party—was, for the moment at least, in total abeyance. Callaghan had two choices. One was to engage in an all-out confrontation with the party left, in effect fight in a civil war more brutal even than that between Gaitskellites and Bevanites in the early 1950s, to purge the left of its influence. One signal of this would have been to act on the Underhill report on 'entryism' in the constituency parties by Trotskyist elements, Militant Tendency, and others on the furthest left fringe. Even had Callaghan been younger than his mid-sixties, it is unlikely that he would have been able to deflect himself from his wider role as Prime Minister. Nor did Healey, Crosland, Foot, or other key ministers show any sign of wanting him to do so. In any case, in the current mood of the party, any such attempt would certainly have failed. The other course was to soldier on, appealing to the mass public and the community at large over the heads of unrepresentative and doctrinaire constituency activists as a national leader, symbolizing the unity of the nation as a whole, and this is what Callaghan by instinct and by ideology attempted to do.

Here he was on much stronger ground. One opinion poll after another throughout the period 1976–9 showed that his reputation was high and often rising with the general public. His standing as Prime Minister went up as that of Labour as the party preference of the voters steadily went down. Down to May 1979, his standing with the voters was far higher than that of Margaret Thatcher, the Opposition leader, though gender prejudice may have contributed to the poor ratings that she achieved prior to entering No. 10. Some of his advisers in the 1979 election campaign pressed hard for a televised presidential-style debate with her, convinced that this would result in an overwhelming triumph for their man which would snatch an improbable last-minute Labour victory. He dominated her with some ease at prime minister's question time, aided by more than a trace of patronizing contempt shown by male backbenchers for a 'handbag swinging' (or even menopausal) female opponent. Hugo Young has criticized Callaghan's approach to Margaret Thatcher as offensive and 'extraordinarily condescending'.[82] But the premier was equally effective in handling male critics. Nigel Lawson had been an effective and sometimes damaging interrogator of Harold Wilson during prime minister's question time. Callaghan proved 'very much harder to deal with' and Lawson then gave up.[83] On television and in public appearances, Callaghan appeared as a genial and relaxed figure, avuncular, reassuring, embodying the old values of neighbourhood, family, and an orderly and law-abiding society. He became skilled in combating the probing of television interviewers, even those as robust as Robin Day, with whom he had some passages of arms. Usually his appearances on *Panorama*, *The World at Ten*, and similar programmes went well and strengthened his appeal with the electors. One or two Cabinet colleagues, however, felt that in television interviews he would appear too 'grumpy'.[84] Off camera, he could be sharper still. Overall, however, his public image was a strong one. Willie Whitelaw and other Tory leaders feared that a Labour victory in the next general election might see Callaghan build up a personal hegemony of a formidable and perhaps unbeatable kind.

More generally, he was a patriot of an old-fashioned type, whether in his attitude to British institutions or to British possessions such as Gibraltar or the Falklands. His naval background undoubtedly played a part in this, too. He felt thoroughly at home during the royal jubilee in 1977. Invariably, he offered an imperturbable image of British sang-froid and common sense. But this was not always in conformity with reality. Journalists and associates could find him in private to be alarmingly bad-tempered, when the public image of 'Sunny Jim' gave way to thunderous outbursts. One leading television journalist, trying to arrange an interview, even alleged that he had his professional future threatened as a result. One journalist on a quality Sunday newspaper was deeply hostile, using terms like 'thug', and 'bully' and speculating that Callaghan would have been at home in Nazi Germany.[85] But these cases were not typical and most members of the press usually found him amiable and considerate.

Some of these temperamental vagaries, anyhow, must have been the result of the extreme pressures to which any prime minister was subjected. Many others found the Prime Minister reassuring in his approachability and humanity. This was particularly the viewpoint of his constituents and party associates in Cardiff and in Wales in general, which he came to embrace as never before. In the past, he had tended to be seen in Wales as essentially an English spokesman for the Anglicized south-east. This, however, may have reflected the historic social and political divide between Welsh and Anglicized Wales: somewhat similar charges were later made against Neil Kinnock, undoubtedly a proud Welshman with a Welsh-speaking wife, but a man from the Gwent border country nevertheless. Callaghan sometimes attended the national eisteddfod and, as a working farmer, hugely enjoyed the Royal Welsh Show each July. As an old player himself, he made good use of the great success of the Welsh rugby team during his years as premier. The 'triple crown' team of 1978 was invited to 10 Downing Street for a reception, which was a highly popular move.[86] On balance, Callaghan offered a good public front for the British people. He was an excellent communicator in parliament and on the platform, and offered a solid, honest façade after the tensions of the Wilson era. As noted, he won widespread respect from overseas associates as well, in the United States and the Commonwealth, but also increasingly in Europe. Callaghan as Prime Minister was a highly effective image-maker, but he was the more successful because the image seemed to conform to the reality. He was amongst the most credible of populists.

James Callaghan's premiership offered a supreme challenge. It was one that he took up with aplomb and general success. He enjoyed a credibility and standing throughout his time as premier, even during the last difficult phase of the 'winter of discontent', which he had never enjoyed in public office before. He appeared to have made the transition successfully from party politician and machine operator to national and international statesman, and the reputation stuck thereafter. In many ways, perhaps, the premiership was the most appropriate position for his particular combination of talents. His main skills had always lain in strategic or global decision-making rather than the technical details of departmental policy. He had not, in that sense, ever been a willing technocrat, nor had he led Labour initiatives in individual areas of policy. As Prime Minister, he could stand back and reflect, and weigh up the options in a mood of some serenity and confidence. He felt himself to be, as Attlee had not, significantly more than *primus inter pares* in the administration. He noted how he appeared to have more time on his hands in No. 10, to stand back, to think, and to lead. The Cabinet Secretary admired his capacity to concentrate on a few salient issues such as pay policy or SALT II. He could leave the practicalities of implementing government policy to others, and remain himself detached and above the mêlée. He was a slow, deliberate reader of Cabinet papers. Bernard Donoughue noted how his style was to pace himself, to take his time and assess a problem in all its aspects, rather than hurl himself into the minutiae of individual areas as Harold Wilson, an intellectually more agile premier, tended to do.[87]

It was a sober, measured style, but one that brought some reassurance to a party and nation sorely tried by the disturbing pressures of the 1970s, the financial crisis brought about by the fourfold rise in the price of oil, the rising unemployment and spiralling inflation, the tension in labour relations, and the growing signs of violence in social, neighbourhood, and family life. The 1970s were a troubled, anguished time for the British people. It is not surprising that this decade has received the somewhat dubious accolade of being 'the golden age of criminology'.[88] It threw up class, ethnic, generational, and eventually gender tensions on a scale hitherto unparalleled in British history. From mass picketing to football hooligans to battered wives cowering in women's refuges, there were mounting signs of a far more violent society than in the immediate post-war years. In the Thatcher period, the indices for crime were to become far worse. It was perhaps as well in all this turmoil that Britain produced a prime minister as measured and urbane in style as James Callaghan. Two decades on, Blairite image-makers like Peter Mandelson would regard him as a dated figure, the epitome of 'Old Labour' rooted in the working class and the links with the unions.[89] For many contemporaries in the late 1970s, that was just what a troubled nation required. One Labour veteran, at least, was well pleased, and his view perhaps was not unrepresentative. Lord Noel-Baker told him in October 1977 that 'Lots of people, Liberals, Conservatives, journalists, say to me that you have become a great prime minister. So you have. Carry on!'[90]

1. L. J. Callaghan, *The Political Leader*, with a foreword by Senator Walter Mondale (Minneapolis, 1982), 21. Other observations of his on these themes appear in 'James Callaghan: The Stateman as CEO', an interview by Alan M. Webber, *Harvard Business Review* (Nov.–Dec. 1986), 106–12.

2. Information from Sir Reginald Hibbert; Norman Tebbitt, *Upwardly Mobile* (London, 1989), 196—'given time and excuse he would always prevaricate'; interview with Tony Blair, *New Statesman*, 5 July 1996.

3. Wilson to Callaghan, 27 Apr. 1976 (Callaghan Papers, uncatalogued).

4. Bernard Donoughue, *Prime Minister* (London, 1988), 30.

5. Hunt to Callaghan, 15 July 1976 (Callaghan Papers, box 22).

6. Hunt memo, 2 July 1976 (ibid. box 19).

7. Hunt memos, 16 Dec. 1976, 6 Jan. 1977 (ibid., box 19). At a later discussion between Callaghan and Lord Armstrong, 26 Oct. 1977 (ibid., box 19), it was agreed that the idea was impractical.

8. Memo, ? 1977 (Callaghan Papers, box 19); Tony Benn, *Conflicts of Interest: Diaries, 1977–80* (London, 1990), 172 (21 June 1977); Donoughue, *Prime Minister*, 146.

9. Lord Hunt, 'Cabinet Government in the Mid to Late 1970s', *Contemporary Record*, 8/3 (winter 1994), 467 ff.

10. On this, see John Turner, *Lloyd George's Secretariat* (Cambridge, 1980).

11. Stowe memo, 'Initiatives', 28 Apr. 1976 (Callaghan Papers, box 19).

12. Interview with Sir Kenneth Stowe; Prime Minister's diary (ibid., box 35).

13. Interview with Lord Callaghan; memo by Nigel Wicks (ibid.).

14. Interview with Sir Bryan Cartledge.

15. See Tessa Blackstone and William Plowden, *Inside the Think Tank: Advising the Cabinet, 1971–1983* (London, 1988).

16. Ibid. 56–7.

17. Tessa Blackstone, 'Education for 16- to 19-Year-Olds: Some Proposals for Change', in M. Williams, R. Daugherty, and F. Banks (eds.), *Continuing the Education Debate* (London, 1992), 86.

18. Donoughue minute on 'The Family', 9 June 1978 (private papers); *Sunday Times*, 28 May 1978, supplement on 'The Family'.

19. Material in Callaghan Papers.

20. Interview with Lord Donoughue.

21. Cledwyn Hughes diary, 23 July 1976.

22. Donoughue paper, 'Themes and Initiatives' (PU 175), 16 Apr. 1976 (Callaghan Papers, box 19).

23. Material ibid.; Donoughue, *Prime Minister*, 21.

24. Berrill to Donoughue, 15 Dec. 1976; Donoughue to Berrill, 17 Dec. 1976; Berrill to Donoughue, 24 Dec. 1976; Gavyn Davies note to the Prime Minister, 11 Jan. 1977 (Callaghan Papers, box 9).

25. e.g. 'Mr. Benn's Paper on Import Controls' (PU 236), 26 Nov. 1976 (ibid., box 13). Donoughue comments that Benn 'offers a bogus choice between a caricature of the IMF route and an unrealistically rosy alternative strategy'. He went on that 'Benn seems to think that the EEC would be willing to allow us to impose controls and then lend us money. This is most unlikely.'

26. Gavyn Davies, 'The Medium Term Asessment', 17 June 1977 (PU 284) (Callaghan

Papers, box 9). This paper concluded that the government should bring forward reflation as soon as possible and delay the election for as long as possible.

27. Donoughue memo, 'Thoughts on the Government's Future Strategy' (PU 281), 2 June 1977 (private papers).

28. Donoughue memo, 6 July 1977 (PU 289) (ibid.). This was in part an argument for the early implementation of child benefit paid direct to mothers.

29. Donoughue memo, 9 and 26 Sept. 1977 (PU 303, 306) (ibid.).

30. Donoughue memo, 'Themes and Initiatives' (PU 390), 14 Sept. 1978; Donoughue to Callaghan, 19 Sept. 1978 (private papers).

31. Donoughue memo, 'Last Three Days'. ? May 1979 (ibid., box 23).

32. Interview with Tom McNally.

33. Minute from McNally, 26 Apr. 1976 (Callaghan Papers, box 22).

34. McNally to Stowe, 21 Sept. 1976 (ibid.).

35. Interview with Sir Tom McCaffrey; Donoughue, *Prime Minister*, 25.

36. Interviews with Tom McNally and Sir Tom McCaffrey.

37. Robert Harris, *Good and Faithful Servant* (London, 1990), 67.

38. Owen, *Time to Declare*, 323.

39. Benn, *Office without Power*, 557 (12 Apr. 1976).

40. Private information.

41. Cledwyn Hughes diary, 31 March 1977.

42. Interview with Michael Callaghan.

43. Callaghan memo to ministers (Callaghan Papers, box 19).

44. Interview with Lord Rodgers.

45. Interview with Michael Foot.

46. Material in Callaghan Papers, box 19; interview with Roy Hattersley.

47. See memos on this by the Policy Unit, Callaghan Papers, box 13.

48. Cledwyn Hughes diary, 23 Feb. 1978.

49. Interview with Lord Healey

50. Healey, *The Time of my Life*, 447 ff.

51. See n. 22 above; McNally memo, 30 Apr. 1976 (Callaghan Papers, box 22).

52. Callaghan, *Time and Chance*, 409.

53. Various drafts in the Callaghan Papers. It was printed in *Education*, 22 Oct. 1976, in full. Blackstone, 'Education for 16- to 19-Year-Olds', says that civil servants, HM inspectors, and others were 'not too happy with Jim's splendid initiative'.

54. This theme appeared in Callaghan's first television broadcast as Prime Minister. The Policy Unit was anxious to distinguish between this approach and 'Thatcherism' and advocated a policy of 'tough honesty' which combined an emphasis on responsibility with a philosophy of reform and compassion for the disadvantaged (Donoughue memo, PU 175, Callaghan Papers, box 19).

55. *Castle Diaries, 1974–76*, 182 (16 Sept. 1974); Callaghan speech to WRVS, 25 Apr. 1978; Callaghan note on Home Policy Committee Papers, 2 Nov. 1977 (Callaghan Papers, box 23).

56. Donoughue, *Prime Minister*, 114.

57. Blackstone and Plowden, *Inside the Think Tank*, 141; interview with Lord Donoughue; see Callaghan's speech in Westland debate, *Parl. Deb.*, 6th ser., vol. 89, 1110–11 (15 Jan. 1986).

58. Tebbitt, *Upwardly Mobile*, 196.

59. Cf. Kathy Burk and Alec Cairncross, 'Goodbye Great Britain' (London, 1992), 91–4.

60. *Financial Times*, 29 Sept. 1976.

61. Interview with Lord Healey. The word 'crap' was used.

62. 'Message for Philip Wood from Mrs Jay', 25 Sept. 1976 (private papers).

63. Interviews with Lord Callaghan and Peter Jay.

64. Lord Vaizey to Callaghan, 1 Oct. 1976 (Callaghan Papers, box 9).

65. Donoughue memo (PU 287), 4 July 1977; Donoughue memo, 'The Economic Seminar' (PU 309), 14 Oct. 1977; Donoughue memo, 'The Dollar Initiative' (PU 364), 3 Mar. 1978 and Gavyn Davies's paper on 'The Dollar Seminar', ? 1978; and Donoughue memo (PU 397), 7 Nov. 1978 (private papers).

66. *Time and Chance*, 476; for Gavyn Davies's criticisms, see Peter Hennessy, *Cabinet* (Oxford, 1986), 92.

67. Donoughue, *Prime Minister*, 27.

68. Callaghan to Houghton, 20 May 1977 (Callaghan Papers, box 9).

69. Cledwyn Hughes diary, 9 Feb. 1978.

70. Campbell, *Edward Hearth*, 493–4.

71. Hugo Young, *One of Us* (London, 1989), 498 ff.

72. Note of a conversation with Michael Adeane, 27 May 1969 (Callaghan Papers, uncatalogued). For an interesting discussion of Callaghan's relations with the Queen, see Ben Pimlott, *The Queen* (London, 1996), 433–5.

73. Jonathan Dimbleby, *The Prince of Wales* (London, 1994), 229; Lord Callaghan, article in *Evening Standard*, Nov. 1995.

74. Kenneth O. Morgan, *Keir Hardie, Radical and Socialist* (London, 1974), 71.

75. McNally to Callaghan and Callaghan note, 11 May 1976 (Callaghan Papers, box 9).

76. K. Couzens (private secretary to the Chancellor) to Callaghan, 21 May 1976 (ibid.).

77. Gavyn Davies, 'Public Expenditure: Conservative and Labour Plans', 22 Nov. 1976 (Callaghan Papers, box 13).

78. *Financial Times*, 25 Sept. 1976; McNally to Callaghan, 15 Sept. 1976 (Callaghan Papers, box 17).

79. Memo from Harold Lever, 9 June 1976 (Callaghan Papers, box 9).

80. McNally to Callaghan, 22 July 1977 (ibid.).

81. McCaffrey memo, 24 June 1977 (Callaghan Papers, box 19).

82. *The Scotsman* survey, just before polling day in May 1979, showed Callaghan with a rating of 46% and Mrs Thatcher with one of 33%. However, Mrs Thatcher led amongst women voters. Also see Young, *One of Us*, 123. Cf. Margaret Thatcher, *The Path to Power* (London, 1995), 313, that Callaghan's manner towards her was 'patronizing and made it hard for me to advance serious criticism of Government policy without appearing to nag'. She had her revenge by never inviting him back to Chequers, whereas John Major invited him early on to an informal buffet lunch when he was shown his window in the Long Gallery. Callaghan commented, 'I had never seen it because Mrs Thatcher never asked me back here' (*The Times*, 18 Mar. 1991).

83. Lawson, *The View from No.11*, 12.

84. Private information.

85. Private information.

86. Prime Minister's diary, 1978 (Callaghan Papers, box 35); information from Mr Ray Gravell, former centre three-quarter in the Welsh team.

87. Interview with Lord Hunt of Tanworth; Donoughue, *Prime Minister*, 12.

88. Paul Rock (ed.), *A History of British Criminology* (Oxford, 1988), 61–2.

89. Peter Mandelson and Roger Liddle, *The Blair Revolution* (London, 1996).

90. Lord Noel-Baker to Callaghan, 7 Oct. 1977 (Callaghan Papers, box 9).

23

BRITAIN IN HOCK

WHEN he returned from the Palace as Prime Minister on the evening of 5 April 1976, Callaghan's intention was to focus more on international affairs. He did not mean to be bogged down in management of the economy, which he would leave to Denis Healey. This fond hope did not last twenty-four hours. In the course of 6 April, his first day at No. 10, he was told by Gavyn Davies of the Policy Unit that sterling, which stood at an exchange rate of $1.86 and falling, was thought to be so vulnerable that another devaluation of perhaps 10 or 15 per cent was felt by holders of sterling to be likely. A further severe jolt came with his first official meeting with Denis Healey, the Chancellor, at 10.30 on the morning of 12 April. 'I was astonished when I saw D.H. He said that Bank had spent $2 bn. in supporting sterling since 1 Jan. 1976.'[1] An immense international loan, probably from the IMF, seemed inevitable.

The new Prime Minister, therefore, like his three Labour predecessors, MacDonald, Attlee, and Wilson, found himself almost from the outset engaged in the unending task of shoring up the British economy and trying to promote recovery. He cannot have been surprised. There had been massive financial problems confronting the Wilson government in the winter of 1975–6. Wilson found himself facing, according to his own account, the most profound and complex range of difficulties he ever experienced in nearly eight years as Prime Minister.[2] Callaghan himself had been a frequently pessimistic Cabinet commentator during these events. He once passed a wry note to Tony Crosland welcoming some astringent observations by the latter: he himself had too often been 'a solo Cassandra'.[3] Barbara Castle and Tony Benn recorded him as having told the Cabinet in the autumn of 1974 that, while shaving in the morning, he felt that, were he a young man, he would emigrate (back in the late 1950s, indeed, he had spoken of the attractions of emigration to Rhodesia). Then, over breakfast, the mood would wear off because he could not think of any other country he would prefer to go to. In 1985 Callaghan was to tell the *Times* journalist Peter Hennessy that the remark was meant to be a joke.[4] But the laughter in that sombre group of ministers must have been distinctly muted. At all events, in April 1976 the new Prime Minister would have to set aside gloomy contemplation of his sea of troubles for something more positive.

The roots of the problems of the ailing British economy went back many decades, indeed to the late Victorian era. But his more immediate difficulties, of course, arose from the legacy of the preceding Conservative and Labour governments of Edward Heath and Harold Wilson. The years since 1970 had indeed been progressively more difficult and economic management in disarray. It must have given Callaghan some ironic amusement, after his own traumatic experiences at the Treasury in 1964–7, to hear academic economists such as Sir Alec Cairncross, often sharp critics at the time, refer in later years to the British economy in the 1960s as marking 'a golden age'.

The Heath government fell from power in March 1974 amidst circumstances of extreme economic crisis. To some degree the causes lay in world conditions which were quite beyond the control of any British government—the explosion of the world economy, the raging inflation that followed the Yom Kippur War in October 1973, and the consequent fourfold rise in the price of oil. However, these outside pressures affected Britain more acutely than most industrial nations because they were superimposed on a country whose economy had been under pressure for most of the post-war period and where there was the new phenomenon of 'stagflation', with rising unemployment and spiralling inflation at one and the same time.

In the Heath years, the economy was under the direction of Anthony Barber as Chancellor. He was a stop-gap appointment of limited experience in high office who took over when Iain Macleod unexpectedly died within a few weeks of the Conservatives' election victory. Barber left political life for the City when the Conservatives were defeated in the February 1974 general election. From the outset, his Prime Minister seemed to regard him as a lightweight. His policies were uniformly unsuccessful. Edmund Dell, not unreasonably, classified him as being, in a poor field, the worst Chancellor since the war. The first phase of Barber's regime down to mid-1972 was marked by a period of rapid expansion in industrial and manufacturing output, but coinciding with a deterioration of the current account. There followed a crisis for sterling which led to the floating of the pound in June 1972 and a sharp fall in its value, far below the level of

$2.40 fixed by Callaghan's devaluation five years earlier. At home, there was rising wage inflation with the failure of the government's attempts to impose a wages policy by statutory means. The second phase of the so-called 'Barber boom' was conspicuous for a failure to control spiralling inflation. Even before the Yom Kippur War demolished all earlier projections, union-inspired pressure to raise wage levels together with the effects of the depreciation of the pound was pushing inflation well into double figures. By the end of 1974 it was to be over 20 per cent and rising. Monetary growth in the latter phase of the Barber period at the Treasury was to reach 25 per cent and to fuel thereby pressure by monetarist-minded economists for a determined attempt to control M3, the basic money supply. At the same time, output was stagnating. With price instability and rising unemployment, the unfamiliar and disturbing spectacle of 'stagflation' had emerged. The Heath government ended up with the three-day week, candles spluttering on the Commons dispatch box. It was forced out of office amidst a long-running national miners' strike. It left as its legacy an economy in a state of endemic crisis.

The new Wilson government, taking office in March 1974, attempted with limited success to grapple with these problems. It launched a more determined attack on public expenditure, which was almost out of control, by introducing a novel policy of cash limits in place of a programme based on volume factors, adjusted upwards for inflation.[5] By 1977 this had led to a sharp and almost unprecedented fall in public expenditure, to a degree not projected in Treasury forecasts, but naturally it took time to have its effect. However, by the time that Callaghan became Prime Minister, an effective freeze on public expenditure had been announced. There was also a desperate attempt to reach some kind of agreement with the TUC to deal with domestic wage cost inflation. By 1975 it was approaching 25 per cent, a level hitherto associated with the economies of South America. This led American politicians to observe, with absurd exaggeration, that Britain was proving to be 'as ungovernable as Chile'. After negotiation between government ministers, principally Michael Foot and the Chancellor, with a TUC group headed by Jack Jones of the Transport Workers, a flat-rate wage increase limit of £6 a week was agreed in July 1975 for all workers earning less than £8,000 a year. This severe, if voluntary, incomes policy led to the level of wage increases falling spectacularly in the next two years, until inflation was back in single figures by the start of 1978. Nevertheless, external pressure on sterling remained intense and the overall weaknesses of an economy in deficit were impossible to conceal. After intense difficulties the Chancellor, Denis Healey, approached the IMF in

November 1975 for additional special drawing rights and a massive new standby credit. The first tranches of these, amounting together to over $1,800m., were negotiated in January 1976, with more to follow. Only then did the Treasury feel that any respite might have been gained, with the prospect of some gentle reflation to revive the economy.

Nevertheless, it was clear from the outset that Callaghan's administration would be struggling against a familiar background of economic pressure. Here he would face the problems he had encountered as Chancellor a decade earlier—the balance of payments and the fragility of sterling. But there were also two other perils that had not troubled him so much in the 1960s—rising unemployment and almost uncontrollable price inflation. The interaction of these themes made his task now even more complex than it had been a decade earlier.The specifics of policy, of course, were dealt with by the Chancellor, Denis Healey, with Michael Foot attending to the overall strategy of handling wage negotiations with the TUC. Healey's budget on 6 April, Callaghan's second day in office, had been cautiously welcomed by the markets for laying down the principle of 3 per cent pay increases, but it had made no significant proposals about cutting public expenditure. It was evidently an interim statement, dependent on further negotiations with the unions during the summer. Callaghan, however, had his own particular viewpoint to bring to bear in the conduct of economic policy and he rapidly became a dominant figure thereafter.

First of all, as a former Chancellor, he had a high regard for the quality of the Treasury's key personnel, with many of whom he had worked closely between 1964 and 1967. But he also took a disenchanted view of the Treasury's methods, the reliability of its forecasts, the context in which its policy proposals were framed, and the posture it tended to adopt in negotiating with outside bodies such as the IMF. Callaghan's view was that a more robust stance should be adopted: he had, after all, had ample experience of the weaknesses of timidity back in the 1960s. Along with some suspicion of the Treasury, he was measured, too, in his attitude to advice forthcoming from the Bank of England, although recognizing that Gordon Richardson was an altogether more co-operative and congenial governor than Lord Cromer had been back in 1964.

On the domestic front, he attached supreme importance to a voluntary agreement being reached with the TUC on future wage norms. He felt, too, that since he was, almost uniquely in his Cabinet, a former national union official, he had more understanding of the subtleties of this area than senior colleagues who lacked this background. He made a point of having regular monthly meetings, sometimes dinners, with Len Murray and his colleagues on the TUC's 'Neddy Six', accompanied by Healey and Foot. And finally the stamp of his experiences as Foreign Secretary in 1974–6 was powerful upon him. The close relationship he had built up especially with Helmut Schmidt, and his intimacy with Ford, Kissinger, and the US administration, left him with a conviction that he had other allies to whom he could turn, as alternatives to giving the IMF its pounds of flesh. He also felt that Britain's overseas allies understood more clearly than most ministers or Treasury officials at home the impact of the role of sterling as an international currency, and the particular kind of vulnerability for the reserves conveyed by the existence of massive and growing sterling balances. He told his Chancellor on 4 June that he wanted 'to get rid of the incubus of sterling as a reserve currency. Denis agreed.' This more global view was to be reinforced by his attendance at the otherwise unremarkable second world economic summit, held in Puerto Rico at the end of June.[6]

In short, Callaghan believed with some reason that he benefited from a particular insight derived from his unique background of having held all the major offices of state. Nobody else in Westminster or Whitehall had his wealth of experience. As Chancellor, he had come to understand the outlook of the Treasury and the international vulnerability of sterling. As Home Secretary, he had helped to set out the parameters that would govern an effective working relationship between the government and the unions. As Foreign Secretary he had seen at first hand the links between the British economy and its effective international influence, in Europe and in North America. It gave him a particular kind of confidence and determination in the crisis that lay ahead.

The spring and summer of 1976 were a tense, but in the end not unproductive, period. Many thought the government would not last out the year. There were major parliamentary difficulties, mainly resulting from the legacy that Callaghan inherited from the Wilson period and its pact with the unions. This included what turned out to be the last significant phase of nationalization in British history, with the proposed taking of the aircraft and shipbuilding industries into public ownership as agreed with the TUC. As leader of the House, Michael Foot was compelled to introduce the guillotine for both of these, along with other measures including the Dock Labour Scheme, the phasing out of private 'pay beds' in NHS hospitals, and the abolition of tied cottages. The Speaker, George Thomas, deeply angered government ministers when he added to their embarrassment by declaring the measure to nationalize aircraft and shipbuilding to be 'a hybrid' between public and private bills. On 27 May, when

Callaghan had been premier for barely six weeks, there was a massive parliamentary crisis as a result, which saw the nationalization proposals carried by the narrowest possible margin, 304 to 303. The government saved the day by sending through the Aye lobby an MP whom the Opposition knew to be paired. Tony Benn admitted that 'the fact is we cheated'.[7] To some extent public attention was diverted by some distinctly non-parliamentary behaviour by Opposition members, notably Michael Heseltine who caused some notoriety for himself by flamboyantly brandishing the Speaker's mace much as the future fascist, John Beckett, had done in the past. The nationalization measures caused immense difficulty for the government, first in the Commons, where they were criticized by some of their own backbenchers such as Brian Walden and John Mackintosh, and then in the Lords. Eventually British Aerospace and British Shipbuilders came into being in 1977, along with BNOC for Britain's oil resources. But it was transparently clear that many, perhaps most, ministers had little enthusiasm for them, and regarded them as a costly distraction from the real economic problems confronting the nation.

The new Prime Minister subordinated all else to 'getting the economy right'. His government operated against a background of constant crises for sterling which in early June fell to $1.70, and difficult discussions with the European central banks, the US Federal Reserve, and the IMF over new standby credits. On 7 June, a huge standby credit of $5.3 bn. was announced, coming variously from the Federal Reserve and the US Treasury, the central banks of Germany, Japan, Canada, France, and Switzerland, and the Bank of International Settlements. The purpose was to allow the British government time for its policies to have effect. But further measures, involving swingeing cuts in public expenditure, were also understood to be imminent. Domestically, the government was largely preoccupied with discussions with the TUC, headed by its general secretary Len Murray and dominated by Jack Jones, to reach an agreement on wage restraint. At the same time, the Cabinet was attempting to reach agreement on an effective programme of stringent cuts in public expenditure. There was a constant air of crisis and some commentators wondered whether so apparently weak a government would survive even to the summer recess.

In fact, that summer saw some evidence of success in key directions, both in negotiations with the TUC over wages policy and over public expenditure. On 28 April in a telephone conversation with Chancellor Helmut Schmidt, Callaghan was able to speak with confidence on the progress made in negotiations with the unions.[8] Like all their conversations, this one was marked by the easy, unspoken intimacy of two social democratic leaders instinctively aware of the movements they led and the traditions they inherited. Indeed, Callaghan's relationship with Schmidt during his premiership appears from the record almost closer than that with any of his Cabinet colleagues, except perhaps Merlyn Rees. The unions, he told Schmidt, had 'responded positively' to Denis Healey's proposals for a package of 3 per cent plus tax concessions; an ultimate settlement of less than 5 per cent would probably follow, to be ratified by a special conference of the TUC in mid-June. This would mean a cut in the real standard of living for the second year running. 'This I think is the important and disciplinary element.' Schmidt was warmly encouraging and mentioned in confidence that all the major German unions had settled for amounts ranging from 5.2 per cent to 5.4 per cent in 1976 which would mean a cut in the living standards of German workers also; Callaghan, he said, could use the German figures for his domestic purposes. The British Prime Minister added that, being so new in office, he felt he could push the British union leaders somewhat harder for the moment; 'I must say that our trade union leaders, Jack Jones and co. have been wonderfully good', he added and hoped that Schmidt could say something positive about them later on. 'If you, Helmut . . . in any speech later on when we have concluded the agreement could pay some tribute to the much-derided British trade union leaders, that could have a psychological effect, you know.' Callaghan felt that, with a majority over the Conservatives of 40, he could stay in office for perhaps another two years. The calm way in which Labour had conducted its leadership election had added to its prestige and given it a fresh boost of support in the country. He spoke to Giscard d'Estaing in much the same terms, though more briefly, later that evening.[9] He reaffirmed to the French President that he expected to reach an agreement with the unions of around 5 per cent 'or perhaps something under' for the next twelve months, with the increase in price levels likely to be around 7 per cent. The British government was going to be firm. 'Sometimes when you're new you can be a little tougher than when you've been there for some time.'

On 13 May, in another telephone conversation with Schmidt, Callaghan was in buoyant mood.[10] 'Denis and all the rest of the lads' had pulled it off. A settlement with the unions on wage claims had been reached. Even the miners, 'who were the touchy ones', had voted to back it by 13 to 11. Schmidt endorsed this enthusiastically and the discussion moved on to the tactics to be adopted at the Puerto Rico economic summit. Callaghan mentioned in passing that, unlike the Queen and Crosland, the Foreign Secretary, he would not be visiting America for the bicentennial celebrations. 'My enthusiasm is a little muted about going to the United States in present circumstances', he added, giving the pre-election uncertainty there and the sense of interregnum in US politics as one reason.

The agreement with the unions was hailed by the labour movement as a 'Social Contract Mark II'. It was overwhelmingly endorsed at a specially convened TUC on 16 June 1976 by 9,262,000 to 531,000.[11] It had included some last-minute concessions by the government which effectively made the limit 5 per cent with some income tax concessions thrown in. Jack Jones believed that agreement was reached in large measure because of the influence of the Prime Minister and his special knowledge of the trade unions.[12] It marked something of a watershed in party terms. Whereas the new social contract was referred back by the left-dominated National Executive by 11 to 8, it was endorsed by the TUC General Council by 20 to 3. Tom McNally was enthusiastic about what had been achieved, and anxious for an effective public relations presentation of the new agreement. 'The last four months have seen a remarkable change in internal Party politics. For the first time in recent years there is a split between the Tribune Left and the large trade unions. We should take all possible steps to avoid them driving them back together.' Callaghan scribbled on this letter, 'Quite right!'[13]

However the prospects for the new social contract remained uncertain, in large measure because of the other main prong of the government's domestic approach, the search for an agreement over major cuts in public expenditure. The TUC Economic Committee voiced its concern here. It had already swallowed a wage freeze. Now it was being asked to accept long-term deflation and growing unemployment as well. Len Murray was anxious that cuts in public expenditure would slacken recovery; a loyalist like David Basnett was concerned that his members had already had a cut in real wages for two successive years. Frank Chapple of the Electricians wanted cuts not in essential services but in what he called 'esoteric public spending', which he did not define.[14] On the other hand, the expectation was that the government would in the end be supported; no one, after all, could face the prospective terrors of a Thatcher administration. The Cabinet had long and difficult discussions in early July, and word of its deliberations spread throughout Westminster, even though Callaghan's government seems to have been far less leaky than any of Wilson's. The parliamentary party, whose chairman Cledwyn Hughes had been carefully briefed by Callaghan on the public expenditure debate, was reported to be in irritable and argumentative mood. 'The strain of late nights, no pairing and uncertainty as to when the House will rise makes this inevitable.'[15]

The Cabinet was known to be deeply divided about public expenditure cuts. Callaghan handled the matter by pursuing the same kind of exhaustive, almost open-ended strategy he followed during the IMF negotiations in December, as session followed session. The same pattern of three broad groupings, indeed, emerged during the discussions as appeared so starkly during the IMF crisis at the end of the year. There were the Treasury team of Healey and Joel Barnett, a broadly left-wing group headed by Benn and Foot, and a group of Keynesian dissenters led by Crosland and Harold Lever, whom the Policy Unit tended to support. The latter two contended with the Treasury ministers, from their radically opposed standpoints. Callaghan kept himself in reserve, as an arbitrator, although it was generally understood that in the end he would support his Chancellor, as would a group of uncommitted ministers such as Merlyn Rees, Fred Mulley, David Ennals, and John Morris, in various respects bound to the Prime Minister himself.

Seven Cabinets were then held between 6 and 21 July, culminating with two on the latter day.[16] A Cabinet being held on Monday was felt to denote a particular sense of crisis. On 6 July the Cabinet devoted time to considering (though in the end effectively rejecting) Tony Benn's proposed 'alternative strategy' based on import cuts. This won some support from Foot, Booth, Ennals, and other ministers. But it emerged that the majority did regard cuts as to some degree unavoidable. After bilateral meetings between Healey and individual ministers, notably Peter Shore who controlled huge local authority budgets at Environment, and Shirley Williams who administered food subsidies (costing over £500m. in 1974), an eventual programme of around £1 bn. of cuts was announced by Healey, to which a further £1 bn. would be added through a surcharge on employers' national insurance contributions. Thus £2 bn., it was claimed, would be trimmed off the PSBR for 1977–8. Healey announced the Cabinet's decisions on 22 July. He affirmed that the money supply in the following year would be no more than 12 per cent and that no increase in the money supply would be allowed to fuel inflation the following year. The impact was, some felt, weakened because no target figures were announced.[17]

Yet there was an air of some relief and a hope that perhaps enough had been done to avoid further recourse to foreign creditors, beyond the $5 bn. standby negotiated in June. It had been a tough episode. But Bernard Donoughue, who had argued strongly against swingeing spending cuts which would raise unemployment and negate the government's economic strategy, felt that the Prime Minister's personal prestige had been notably enhanced. His handling of the economic debate that July was 'superior to anything I had observed earlier'. The Prime Minister's guile and patience in wearing dissenting ministers down was particularly admired. 'Ministers have discussed the cuts so often, they come to think they have agreed them', the Prime Minister confided.[18] More brutally, Tony Benn was forced into line after he pleaded to Callaghan on 26 July that he must consult the views of constituency activitists in Bristol.[19] After discussions with left-wing colleagues such as Mikardo, Heffer, and Joan Maynard, he remained in the government. At the Labour Party National Executive, the Social Contract Mark II was endorsed 13 : 7, Benn being absent from the meeting. A motion supported by Ian Mikardo and Barbara Castle to throw out the public expenditure cuts also went the government's way, narrowly, by 13 to 11, with Jack Jones and Hugh Scanlon speaking strongly against it.[20] There were no other party rebels to contend with for the moment. The party seemed exhausted, all passion spent. On 5 August, the Callaghans went off for a brief holiday on the farm in Ringmer, hopeful that the cuts would satisfy the markets and that the long-running economic crisis might now slide away. Cledwyn Hughes, a prescient observer, was unconvinced. 'Jim and Denis have the very devil of a job. We have now survived until after the Recess and in these times that is an achievement.'[21]

In fact, the crisis was only just beginning. It was anything but a restful summer break. Sterling remained steady at around $1.77 in August but then became shaky again as it plunged towards the record low level of $1.70 during September, while the reserves continued to drain away. Commentators concluded that the expenditure cuts were simply not enough and that the broader endemic weaknesses of the British economy were untouched. Even the superb summer weather brought its problems, as Callaghan saw at first hand in the parched grassland and light crop yields of his Sussex farm. An unprecedented drought led to fears that some industries would have to adopt a three-day week. Indeed the Prime Minister had to return to London on 24 August to attend a meeting of GEN 33 to discuss the Mediterranean aridity of the climate. After this Denis Howell, a football referee who served as Minister of Sport, achieved fame as the Minister for Drought, to re-emerge in 1979 as Minister for Snow.[22]

There seemed no end to the nation's troubles. Callaghan spent 4–5 September staying with the Queen at Balmoral. Simultaneously, there were wildcat strikes in the car industry at British Leyland, and then on 9 September a national seamen's strike began. It was well recalled that it had been the National Union of Seamen that blew the Wilson government so violently off course in June 1966. The following day Callaghan took time off to reshuffle his Cabinet, as has been seen. Hattersley and Rodgers entered the Cabinet, and Merlyn Rees and Shirley Wiliams were promoted, with Stan Orme brought in as a left-winger at Social Security. On 11 September the Callaghans flew to Calgary in western Canada, for a week's holiday arranged by Prime Minister Trudeau, and travelled most of the length of that vast country from Banff National Park in the west to Nova Scotia in the east.[23] There were pleasant diversions such as the opening of the James Callaghan Trail in Newfoundland. But it was not much of a break from the nation's worries. He was constantly pursued by grave news about the pound, the full import of which greeted him on his return to Heathrow on 19 September. The Prime Minister's nerve and statesmanship now faced their most critical test.

From the first week of September, the pound had been under growing pressure and so was the government. Denis Healey in his memoirs refers to the last four months of 1976 as 'the worst of my life'.[24] The economic indicators were now all depressing. The current account showed a deterioration, prices were rising, and inflation still stood at 14 per cent. On 10 September, Denis Healey had to raise minimum lending rate to the almost unprecedented level of 13 per cent. At the same time, the Bank of England, which had spent up to $150m. in one intervention to sustain the pound, was instructed to go no further in spending from the reserves. A central consideration for Callaghan was that unlimited drawing on the reserves would leave Britain unable to meet its obligations in paying back its standby loan from the IMF. Great Britain would have been technically bankrupt.

The pound now seemed almost in free fall, as it plunged down by a rate of almost a cent a day. A further intervention by the Bank, to the tune of $100m., had no discernible effect on international market confidence. On 27 September trading in sterling saw it reach the alarming level of only $1.63 and a further, and a much more decisive, recourse to the IMF was now generally anticipated. Indeed, on 9 September, prior to Callaghan's departure for Canada, the Cabinet Economic Strategy Committee had agreed to make a new application to the IMF but also to defer an announcement for some weeks.[25] Even more cheerful events such as the settlement of the seamen's strike on 22 September seemed to have no positive impact.

The worst time of all was on 27–8 September. As ill luck would have it, the Labour Party annual conference at Blackpool took place precisely when the Chancellor was due to leave for a Commonwealth finance ministers' conference at Hong Kong, to be followed by a meeting of the IMF at Manila at which Britain's application for a long-term loan would be considered. In one of the most damaging episodes of the decade, Healey and the Governor of the Bank of England, Gordon Richardson, were at Heathrow airport, when news came of an even more horrendous fall in the pound, and a new low level of $1.50 seemed in prospect. There was panic in the stock market and on the exchanges. Confronted with this news, Healey decided that being out of contact with Britain on a lengthy flight for seventeen hours would be far too risky.[26] He and Richardson thus promptly returned to the Treasury in a highly publicized and deeply embarrassing retreat, comparable, some felt, to Napoleon's departure from Moscow. It was announced formally that Britain was making a huge application for a loan from the IMF. On 29 September it was made public that the sum requested or demanded was no less than $3.9 billion, much the largest sum for which the IMF had ever been approached. The same day the Ford workers, with an exquisite sense of timing and no discernible objection from their leaders, decided to go on strike.

The next day, 30 September, Healey, after some discussion with Callaghan, went up to Blackpool. By the ludicrous conference rules, he was allowed here only a five-minute intervention as an ordinary delegate since he was no longer on the National Executive. He gave a brief, pungent exposition of the case for an incomes policy, public expenditure cuts, and recourse to the IMF. The idea of a socialist siege economy was condemned: it would lead to a world trade war, a Tory government, and mass unemployment. He returned to his seat giving a kind of Muhammad Ali clasped salute but he sat down with the vigorous boos of the left-wing delegates, hardly any of whom showed the least understanding of the economic complexities, ringing in his ears. Benn bitterly wrote in his diary that his speech was a disaster, 'vulgar and abusive'.[27] Healey was a tough, strong man, physically and morally. But he was for a time close to being broken by the strain. 'For the first and last time in my life, for about twelve hours I was close to demoralisation.'[28]

It was inevitably the Chancellor who bore the brunt of these events and on whom an unforgiving spotlight invariably fell. But the Prime Minister had his own perspective, too. He had agreed with Healey that he should return to the Treasury instead of flying to the Far East, although after some hesitation on his part. Some argued that the evidence of retreat would merely heighten the crisis for the pound. Callaghan at first counselled against Healey's coming up to Blackpool to speak to the party conference, but changed his mind. In view of the unyielding left-wing cast of mind of most of the delegates, he might have felt later that it would have been better if second thoughts had not prevailed and that Healey had stayed in London. The mood at Blackpool was of blank opposition to wage restraint, cuts in public expenditure, or other measures to try to restore international confidence. Cledwyn Hughes was only one of many who felt that the Blackpool conference was 'an almost unmitigated disaster'.[29]

Callaghan, however, determined to seize the initiative from the left and to spell out the facts of economic life as he saw them. But he did so in a highly individual way, altering his speech due to be delivered to the party conference on 28 September at the last moment as the latest alarming facts of the pressure on sterling reached him. While his speech, as always, was heavily influenced by the Policy Unit, notably by Donoughue and Gavyn Davies, with political aspects adapted by McNally and the Political Office, he also consulted widely with others.[30] The full range of his contacts at this time is not clear, but the vital one was evidently Peter Jay, his son-in-law, and also a close political intimate who was being considered at this time for being made a kind of political adviser at No. 10 on the lines of Sarah Hogg under John Major in 1994. His wife Margaret acted as a conduit of information. Callaghan was seeking a clinching line of argument to justify a break with the free-spending, public pump-priming on orthodox Keynesian lines which had determined government policies, Conservative as well as Labour, for the last thirty years. In a telephone conversation on 25 September, later confirmed by teletext, Peter Jay supplied one. It was his dictated formulation, confirmed in a further telephone conversation on the evening of 27 September, that provided the substance of Callaghan's remarkable statement to a disbelieving party conference the following afternoon.

The speech began on reasonably consensual lines—the value of close relations with the unions, the co-operative approach to industrial relations, and the prospect of extending industrial democracy following the Bullock report which was shortly expected. But he then went on to detail the fundamental weaknesses of the economic and social structure as he saw it. 'I did not become a member of our party to propound shallow analyses and false remedies for fundamental economic and social problems.' (Here he departed from his script which read 'I did not become a Socialist'.) Britain's problems, he declared, were caused 'by paying ourselves more than the value of what we produce'. He went on, in words to be quoted on innumerable occasions thereafter:

> We used to think that you could just spend your way out of a recession and increase employment by cutting taxes and boosting Government spending. I tell you in all candour that that option no longer exists and that insofar as it ever did exist, it worked by injecting inflation into the economy. And each time that happened the average level of unemployment has risen. Higher inflation, followed by higher unemployment. That is the history of the last twenty years.

After that shock passage, received in almost stunned silence by his audience, he went on to justify the government's industrial strategy, emphasizing that 'there are no soft options', before moving on to other, less dangerous themes relating to Irish, Rhodesian, and eastern European affairs. A routine condemnation of racial discrimination produced the first heartfelt applause of the speech. He concluded with a daring, and many felt courageous, warning of the dangers of entryism into constituency parties and the need for the kind of close relationship between government and national executive that already existed between government and TUC. He invited the NEC to join in working out the government's programme. 'We began as a party of protest. We must never lose that. But we are more. We are now a party of Government.'

This remarkable speech went down badly with the majority at Blackpool. The left-wing tide was in full flood. NEC comrades such as Eric Heffer, Norman Atkinson, Frank Allaun, Joan Maynard, and several of the union representatives would have had scant interest in sitting down with government ministers in working out the details of policy. Norman Atkinson had a public and widely noticed clash privately in the Commons with his Prime Minister whom he accused of seeking to form a coalition with the Tories. Cledwyn Hughes felt the conference was awful. 'So many of the speeches were abrasively hostile to the government at a time when it is fighting for its life. The P.M. made a good, solid, honest speech and it was maddening to see NEC members, including some Ministers on the platform, sitting on their hands when he finished. These people do not represent the Labour voter. It shows again a fundamental division in the Party—an unbridgeable gulf if we really face up to it. The Conference is best forgotten, but I doubt if the public will forget it.'[31]

But it was, of course, to the general public that Callaghan was really speaking. Here the impact of his speech is debatable. It has commonly been taken as the start of monetarism being accepted as a pillar of government policy, a breach with traditional Keynesianism, with inflation rather than unemployment being identified as the central scourge of the economy. Edmund Dell, a Cabinet minister who warmly backed the Treasury's approach at this time, regarded Callaghan's speech as almost unremarkable, merely a summary of what he and other economics ministers had been saying for the past two years.[32] Whether this is what Callaghan himself intended is more doubtful. His speech was undoubtedly intended to generate a shock effect, to encapsulate an economically conservative message that the nation should not go on spending what it did not earn and should no longer regard uncontrolled public spending, backed from time to time by foreign creditors, as the recipe for prosperity.

On the other hand, the Prime Minister had not really rejected the full doctrine of Keynesianism either: his message was really intended as an attempt to update it rather than reject it entirely. Denis Healey, an independent-minded free spirit in the economic sphere, was, and remained, sceptical of its thrust. He had not known of Callaghan's speech in detail before it was delivered and felt it was misleading. 'Never have speeches written by your son-in-law' was one conclusion that he drew.[33] Certainly Callaghan's stance during the IMF negotiations, which was one of attempting to moderate the more severe deflationary policies suggested by the Treasury, perhaps to bypass a more fundamental restructuring of the economy by obtaining assistance from the Americans and Germans, and to deflect attention to the wider issue of the sterling balances, was not altogether in line with his Blackpool speech. Probably the speech caused more excitement than it need have done, especially amongst economists relatively oblivious of the political context in which it was made. It was more an episode of political than of economic significance, a clear statement by a Prime Minister exasperated by left-wing extremism and economic illiteracy amongst his Labour comrades that they must face up to reality, and that the embattled Prime Minister would show them how it would be done. Whether he needed to do so by raising the entire Keynesian–monetarist argument in this way and giving a hostage to Tory fortunes is another matter.

The Blackpool speech heralded a phase in which the Prime Minister emerged as an active and constant interventionist in high economic policy. He approached the coming of the IMF negotiations in determined mood. As a very senior Labour figure, he was anxious not to repeat the follies of the past. As he often put it to Cabinet colleagues, he was intent on avoiding another 1931. He would not be dictated to by foreign bankers, and their allies in the Treasury. And he would not pursue policies that he could not carry in his Cabinet and in the Labour movement at large. This meant two things above all. He would not be forced by the IMF into cuts of far greater severity than were required. It was well known that Johannes Witteveen, the Dutchman who had become managing director of the IMF when Callaghan's candidature fell through, and a sympathetic figure, was being pressurized by Simon of the US Treasury into demanding far more stringent cuts and a far more intrusive control by the IMF over the conduct of the British economy. Secondly, the management of the British Cabinet, and obtaining a consensus which could be defended to the TUC and the parliamentary party, was a vital consideration, however lengthy the debates amongst ministers might be. In each case, this meant that Callaghan was always pursuing his own version of 'an alternative economic strategy'. This was partly to outflank the strategic options presented by Tony Benn which almost the entire Cabinet regarded as economically incredible apart from some residual sympathy with import controls.

This policy meant exploiting to the full his close relations with the Americans and with Chancellor Schmidt, to try to avoid being cornered by the IMF. On 29 September, the day after his Blackpool speech, he was in telephone conversation with President Ford. He told him that the pound was now seriously undervalued, and this made an incomes policy much harder to achieve. He asked Ford for urgent help in obtaining a standby loan from the IMF but also aid in supporting the sterling balances against premature withdrawals, notably by Arab governments. Ford expressed sympathy on both fronts and reaffirmed that his relationship with Callaghan was 'an excellent one'.[34] Kissinger, it was well known, was highly supportive, while Callaghan also derived personal pleasure from the sympathy of George Meany of AFL-CIO, the American trade union organization, although the value of this hardly justifies the attention it has sometimes received.[35] More serious was the rigidity of the attitude of the US Treasury Secretary Walter Simon, a wealthy bond dealer on Wall Street, and of Arthur Burns of the US Federal Reserve. There was no emollient Joe Fowler or Bob Roosa this time around. And, of course, there was a presidential election only a month away in which it was widely expected that Ford's Republican administration would be removed from office. In similar vein Callaghan spoke to Helmut Schmidt on 2 October asking that Germany try to persuade the IMF to provide Britain with a long-term loan but 'on the basis of existing policies'. An urgent meeting with Schmidt was arranged at Chequers on the evening of Sunday, 10 October, and here Callaghan pressed again upon a highly sympathetic Chancellor the need for urgent help. A scheme was proposed by Schmidt of possible German intervention to assist with the problem of the sterling balances by withdrawing some of Germany's dollar reserves which in any case were being currently used to support the US budget deficit, although this would clearly depend on US collaboration.[36]

Harmonizing Callaghan's personal style of economic diplomacy with the procedures and policies of the Treasury was not altogether easy. The aftermath of the Blackpool conference led to a period of some strain between the Prime Minister and the Chancellor of the Exchequer, Denis

Healey, for the only time. With his well-developed scepticism of Treasury analysis and information, Callaghan was anxious to avoid excessively severe measures before the talks with the IMF had even begun. Thus when Healey asked Callaghan on 6 October for support in raising minimum lending rate by a further two points to the stratospheric level of 15 per cent, Callaghan at first refused. He declared that it would set back economic recovery and that he would not support the Chancellor in the Cabinet; Healey, in gloomy discussion with Edmund Dell, contemplated the prospect of resignation. Some of the Tory press were touting Dell as his successor. The following day, however, Kenneth Stowe passed the word on that Callaghan, having established the strength of the Chancellor's convictions on the point, would indeed support him.[37]

The 15 per cent rate afforded Mrs Thatcher the opportunity of making her best speech yet on the economy on 10 October. But it also had some alleviating effects, not least in assisting the government in the sale of gilts. The Prime Minister continued to be wary of submitting in supine fashion to whatever extreme PSBR cuts the IMF representatives, and the national finance ministers behind them, felt they could demand. There were limits to the pound of flesh, and the relationship between 10 Downing Street and the Treasury remained wary. On one occasion Healey had to rebuke the Prime Minister for apparently expressing scepticism about the judgement of Gordon Richardson, the Governor of the Bank of England.[38] On the other hand, in public and in Cabinet there is no doubt that he lent the maximum of support and moral strength to his Chancellor. On 12 October, Cledwyn Hughes recorded Callaghan as 'relaxed and looking well'. He said 'Denis was bearing a very heavy burden and he was doing his best to sustain him. He had been through it himself and knew what it was like.'[39]

As soon as the House returned from the recess, public attention was dominated by the negotiations with the IMF. But, of course, Callaghan as Prime Minister had the usual immense range of commitments and priorities. The rest of the world did not come to a halt while Britain was trying to cope with the problems of the ailing pound and the reserves. Thus, at around the time of the Blackpool conference, a new surge in negotiations with the Smith regime took place, with Henry Kissinger active in this area. On 24 September Ian Smith announced, after much South African pressure, his willingness to accept a black African majority regime within two years. Callaghan was much involved at this time in discussions both with Kissinger, and with President Kaunda of Zambia to ensure that Smith did not 'wriggle out of' this pledge.[40] International issues from détente to the Falklands also diverted the Prime Minister from his contemplation of

Britain's economic difficulties and no doubt were the more welcome on that score. At home the government was mired with Mrs Ewing and Gwynfor Evans in the bog of Celtic devolution. There were the usual atrocities in Northern Ireland where Roy Mason was embarked on a Strafford-like policy of 'thorough'.

The initiative that most captured public attention, though, as has been noted, was the Ruskin College speech on 16 October about educational standards.[41] This was seen as a notable personal intervention by the Prime Minister to start up a 'great debate' on education, and to seize the initiative from the Tories on this issue. It was one of the initial themes proposed by Donoughue and the Policy Unit which had particularly captured Callaghan's imagination. As early as 13 May Donoughue had written a memorandum emphasizing the new theme of quality in education, including basic standards and teaching methods in schools, and education as a preparation for work and adult life. It was said to be an area in which the DES was 'traditionally reluctant to commit itself', preferring instead to leave matters to the local authorities and the teaching unions.[42] It chimed in with one of his most long-standing concerns, and he took it up with an early meeting with Fred Mulley, the then Education Minister, back in May.

The Ruskin speech was an attempt to divert the educational debate away from sectarian arguments about selection and comprehensivization to a more fundamental level of concern about educational standards. He hoped to break away from clichéd dialogue on 'educational freedom versus State control'. This was a theme that appealed both to Callaghan and to Donoughue, both of them aspiring products of state schools and a working-class background. In his Ruskin speech, the Prime Minister expressed concern about the standards of literacy and numeracy in schools, the reluctance of school pupils to opt for science and technology, and the alleged shortcomings of 'new informal methods of teaching'. He asked for inquiry into such matters as the case for a core curriculum of basic knowledge in schools, a standardized system of pupil assessment, the methods and aims of teaching including 'informal instruction', the role of the inspectorate in examining the competence of teachers, the examination system especially at the post-16 level, and the management of schools, bringing together the local authorities, parents, and teachers. Characteristically, he spoke too of the importance of carrying the teachers with them in introducing changes; he was to criticize the Thatcher government for failing to do so. One political consequence was a decision to move Fred Mulley from Education, where he had shown alarm at the prospect of sweeping reform—'Fred rather blanched'. In September he was moved to Defence and replaced by the younger figure of Shirley Williams. However, officials in the department under her regime appeared anxious to water down the course of educational reform. Callaghan thus wrote forcefully to the new Education Secretary on 20 October urging her department to produce a rewrite of a green paper before the end of the year to set these issues out for public discussion and debate.[43] A series of regional conferences were to be called to chart the way forward.

The immediate effect was not dramatic. Tessa Blackstone, of the Think Tank, found that officials in the department continued to be resistant to new inquiry.[44] The teachers' unions were largely hostile towards proposals which they believed shed doubt on the competence of their profession. Max Morris, a former president, attacked the regional conferences as 'a shoddy public relations gimmick' and called instead for more resources for educational budgets. The Labour left regarded insistence on standards and quality control as reactionary, a traditionalist's diversion away from the social engineering which a non-selective state system of schooling should embody. Tony Benn was horrified by what he saw as a right-wing attack on the comprehensives. His wife believed it to embody an attack on the ' "lefties" who are teaching the social sciences'. But amongst the general public Callaghan's speech struck a powerful chord. At the time, the Great Debate never got off the ground. Even so, the Ruskin address proved to be a landmark in educational reform. In subsequent years, a national curriculum, a system of assessment, and a new emphasis on the professional skills and development of the teachers all came into effect, admittedly in a much more confrontational atmosphere than Callaghan himself would have wanted. In October 1996, in a major speech in London University twenty years on, he could reflect on how the concerns of his Ruskin speech had become almost conventional as themes for public debate, even if the problems of education 'were more urgent than they were twenty years ago'.[45] David Blunkett and Tony Blair's New Labour were as anxious to reassure parents about standards, skills, and school discipline as were the Conservatives. The Ruskin speech, which embodied personal commitment with practical knowledge, saw Callaghan at his far-sighted best. It was the more regrettable to him that overwhelming economic difficulties prevented him from following it up at the time.

It was, inevitably, the negotiations with the IMF and the Cabinet discussions that resulted that preoccupied Prime Minister and colleagues from mid-October in 1976 to the end of the year. Manifestly, it is a central crisis in post-war British economic and international history. For a comparatively recent episode, it is one for which a surprising amount of source material is already available, despite the restrictions of the thirty-year rule on the public records. At the same time, it still has many uncertain or unclear areas. The most important of these relate to the role of the Prime Minister, despite his own very lucid twenty-page narrative in his autobiography. Valuable existing accounts tend inevitably to be influenced by the material, especially the oral evidence, available.[46] They tend to rely on the diaries of and information from Edmund Dell and Tony Benn, neither of them central to the main crisis. There is less firm evidence from Denis Healey and nothing at all from the Prime Minister, other than his published autobiography. Yet without an understanding of his key role, the full significance of the IMF crisis cannot really be appreciated.

The IMF negotiating team, headed by an Englishman, Alan Whittome, as it happened, arrived in Britain on 1 November. But Callaghan had been active throughout the preceding three weeks attempting to pursue an alternative strategy to make any terms won from the IMF both less onerous and more politically acceptable to the Labour Party and the unions. This focused, as has been seen, on the international rather than the internal aspects of the British economy and in particular in trying to get American and European support in eliminating the sterling balances. He proclaimed this policy to the world on 25 October on an interview on the BBC television programme *Panorama*. Eliminating the role of sterling as a reserve currency would be more valuable than an IMF loan, and in addition make the terms for receiving such a loan more acceptable to Britain.[47] He spoke against a background of another attack on sterling. After two weeks of reasonable stability, it fell sharply on 25 October in the light of an article in the *Sunday Times* purportedly revealing the terms of a massive IMF standby, and it declined to a rate of $1.53 on 28 October. However, in spite of personal goodwill there was little that President Ford, deep in a difficult presidential election campaign, could do to help. His electoral defeat on 4 November at the hands of the Democratic candidate Jimmy Carter appeared to nullify hopes of help from that quarter. Callaghan on balance seems to have been disappointed by the Republican defeat. He had told Ford on 29 September that he felt he 'would come through at the finish'.[48] While he had built up a position of unusual trust and intimacy with Ford and Kissinger, the new figures of Jimmy Carter and his so far unknown Secretary of State (it turned out to be the Anglophile and doveish Cyrus Vance in the end) were unknown quantities. But the electoral facts were inexorable.

That left the apparently firm rock of Helmut Schmidt, whom he repeatedly pressed for help with the question of the sterling balances. To Callaghan's mind, this was a central issue which had been a drag on the national finances since the late 1940s, and a major cause of the weakness of sterling. A long-term solution on the funding of the balances was, in his view, essential. The German Chancellor, though, subsequently disavowed having given Britain any pledges. It was, he felt, 'not credible' although he added that he did not in fact feel that the British problems were all that dire in 1976 given the massive inflation in oil prices all round.[49] There was also the question of whether pledges from the German Chancellor on their own had great validity. He had to defer on such matters to the ultimate authority of the Bundesbank, which was unlikely to be forthcoming. Karl-Otto Pohl commented later (probably in jaundiced terms) that 'Schmidt always made promises of that kind at that time, committing the reserves of the Bundesbank to people like Callaghan' when he had not the lawful authority to do so.[50] In practice, Schmidt (who, after all, faced his own federal election contest in December) had to assure the US Treasury that no unilateral assistance from Germany to Britain was likely to be forthcoming. However, it is also probable that his moral support on behalf of the Callaghan government was a positive factor weighing in the mind of the IMF negotiating team.

The events of October confirmed his view that a more positive negotiating philosophy was required than appeared to be forthcoming from the Treasury, which he felt was too supine. According to the latter's memoirs, he accused Edmund Dell, a lone Healey supporter in the Cabinet, of political naivety in failing to take into account the effect of the kind of cuts the IMF appeared to be suggesting on the trade unions, and thereby on the prospects of an incomes policy and employment.[51] Hitherto Callaghan had been remarkably successful in holding on to TUC support, with Jack Jones and Hugh Scanlon being consistently helpful on the NEC/TUC Liaison Committee. Callaghan also had a long talk with Cledwyn Hughes, chairman of the parliamentary party, on 4 November. He told him that the government was determined to carry out the programme to which it was committed but inquired as to how further cuts following the IMF talks would be received—'if they had to be made'. Hughes told him that the PLP was likely to be difficult and that a 'balanced package' should be sought, including import controls.[52] The party's mood was made the more gloomy by disastrous by-election results on 5 November including a heavy defeat in the old Cumbrian stronghold of Workington, following the elevation of Fred Peart to the House of Lords. This made the Callaghan government appear even more of a minority, lame-duck administration.

November was spent in skirmishing between the Treasury and the IMF teams on the terms of a major loan. The full negotiating team of the IMF did not get to grips with the Treasury until 10 November. It was widely believed that the British government, and particularly the Prime Minister, were deliberately allowing the IMF negotiators to hang around in London so as to convince the Labour Party and the world that the British government did not intend to crawl or grovel before their foreign paymasters.[53] The IMF came out with an initial proposal of £3 bn. of cuts in the PSBR for 1977–8 and of £4 bn. for 1978–9. In return Callaghan insisted that anything more severe than £2 bn. for 1977–8 was politically and economically impossible. But there was evidently a diversity of views on both sides and scope for bargaining. Callaghan himself had not despaired of obtaining overseas help which might avoid the dilemma entirely.

On 16 November he tried again with President Ford, notwithstanding the latter's election defeat. Harold Lever, the Chancellor of the Duchy and a generally close Callaghan ally, was sent to Washington on 16 November to pursue again the prospect of US assistance for funding the sterling balances. It was a strictly Prime Ministerial initiative, since Healey does not seem to have been consulted about Lever's visit. Kissinger was to speculate that the Prime Minister and Lever were the only members of the British Cabinet in favour of what he was proposing, and in due course Lever admitted that this was so. Callaghan told the President, prior to his seeing Harold Lever, that 'We are in danger of getting into a downward deflationary spiral and monetary measures alone, with severe deflation, could have the most serious consequences for us.' Lever, he assured Ford, was 'not in Washington to negotiate, he's not seeing the I.M.F. or anything like that'. Rather, he would talk to the President about 'our ideas on the sterling balances and that sort of thing'. Callaghan wished to focus not so much on the IMF talks with Denis Healey, 'the Chancellor—you remember him?'—but on trying to 'get a break out in a different direction'. The precarious position of the sterling balances had resulted in the currency being pulled down repeatedly after a floor appeared to have been set. Dealing with them would not cost anybody very much and would be helpful to the western economies in general—for instance, Giscard was said to be worried about the impact on the franc of the problems of the pound. Various personal courtesies followed about Betty Ford's health and what Ford himself would do up to and beyond 20 January when he would leave office. Gratification was expressed on both sides on 'the very wonderful relationship' between the two of them, Schimidt, and Giscard d'Estaing.[54]

However, his subsequent talks with Harold Lever about a possible 'safety net' for the sterling balances produced little of immediate use other than goodwill. Simon and Yeo of the Treasury were adamant that any arrangement for the sterling balances must be a consequence of an agreement with the IMF, not a substitute for it. A talk with Henry Kissinger produced some further goodwill but then some confusion as to whether Lever had got US agreement for a deal on the sterling balances, and if so what the precise timing would be. The consequence was a muddled one. There was no specific US help in the short term at all, and the talks with the IMF went on as though Lever's visit to Washington had never taken place.[55] At a private meeting between Schmidt and Ralf Dahrendorf, director of the LSE and a Labour supporter, in Hamburg on 29 November, Schmidt reported that Ford was now 'very tough' on Britain's problems. His own sympathies were now distinctly qualified: he condemned the British government for spending money to nationalize shipbuilding, when he himself did not have enough to equip Bremerhaven.[56] On the other hand, an American agreement to resolve the issue of the sterling balances had somehow emerged from the maelstrom of argument between Ford, Kissinger, and the US Treasury and, after the IMF and the British government had reached agreement, the old and thorny issue of sterling as a reserve currency was finally to be resolved. Callaghan's external strategy to that extent was successful but only after he had no alternative left in the IMF negotiations other than giving the Treasury approach his backing.

The Cabinet began prolonged consideration of the IMF terms on 23 November. They were to go on, exhaustively and exhaustingly, until final agreement was reached on both dimensions of the loan and the terms of the letter of intent to be signed for the IMF. The initial stance of the IMF team was a tough one, namely a cut in the PSBR of 1977–8 of £3 bn., and of £4 bn. in 1978–9. This represented cuts of between 6 and 8 per cent of public expenditure. The British Cabinet was almost unanimously opposed to proposals of such severity.[57] There were, as there had been in June, four major groups of ministers. The left, headed by Benn but also tending to include Foot, Silkin, Shore, Booth, and Orme, were opposed to the cuts and favoured an alternative approach, headed by import controls. Secondly, there was a strong social democratic group of Keynesian expansionists, headed by Tony Crosland, the Foreign Secretary, but also including Lever, Shirley Williams, Hattersley, Mulley, and Rodgers, who felt that expansion could not be imperilled, or good relations with the TUC ruptured, and that the IMF should be presented with a tough stance including the possible withdrawal of British troops from Germany. There was the beleaguered Treasury team of Healey and Joel Barnett, supported only in the first instance by Edmund Dell and Reg Prentice, a right-wing member of the Cabinet who soon joined the Tories and later served under Mrs Thatcher. And there was the Prime Minister, to whom were attached on largely personal grounds a number of ministers, mainly Celts such as Lord Elwyn-Jones, Merlyn Rees, Bruce Millan, and John Morris, but also including Fred Peart.

At the initial Cabinet meeting on 23 November, the Treasury team had very little support, though Callaghan himself offered no direct view and merely summed up. There was talk of possible resignations, even of Denis Healey whose reputation had never seemed more tenuous. Callaghan told Cledwyn Hughes on 25 November, 'The Cabinet are united on one thing at present, namely that the three possible solutions would be equally unpleasant. I asked him if he thought there would be any resignation. It was not possible at this time to predict this but on the whole he thought not. He is preoccupied.'[58] The Prime Minister's position was a complicated one. In some measure, he was genuinely uncertain how to proceed and deliberately left all options open in Cabinet discussion as a result. In the first place, he was anxious as has been noted already not to give way to Treasury defeatism. His Policy Unit urged on him a broadly Croslandite viewpoint. On 5 November Donoughue wrote that there was 'no economic justification for deflation now' while higher taxes would be 'even worse than public expenditure cuts'. Deflation was 'an entirely inappropriate response to our current problems'.[59] On 16 November the Policy Unit argued that the projected cuts in PSBR should be resisted, and that the best political and least deflationary solution would be a net cut of £1 bn., including from defence.[60] After the Cabinet meeting on 25 November, Donoughue minuted Callaghan that it was striking how broad-ranging the opposition in the Cabinet was—'15 ministers at a rough count'—to the Treasury's proposals, not only from the left but also the 'tough' right-wingers like Hattersley and Rodgers. If the Treasury's proposals went through, there would be an adverse response from the PLP and the trade unions, the social contract would founder, there would be higher unemployment which would make the Benn 'alternative strategy' seem more attractive and even inevitable. On the other hand, major cuts in PSBR were undoubtedly needed, and the Policy Unit offered new cuts of £2.5 bn. in 1977–8 and £1 bn. in 1978–9. This would cut PSBR by over £3 bn. in the period 1977–9 through such measures as Treasury cuts, the sale of Burmah oil shares, and a limited import deposit scheme.[60]

Callaghan's own mind seems to have moved in much the same direction, with the crucial addition that ultimately he must somehow back up his

Chancellor or risk the immediate collapse of his government. Just as he proceeded in a skilful, Socratic way in Cabinet, keeping his own position in reserve, so he operated now in an indirect fashion also. By eliminating the undesirable, the desirable might effectively emerge. The undesirables were what Bernard Donoughue and Gavyn Davies had called 'the suicidal extremism of the Treasury and the protectionist extremism of Mr. Benn'.[62] It was the latter which presented the easier target. All ministers were encouraged to send in their submissions on what should be done, and fourteen did so.

But before the Cabinet met on the morning of 1 December, Callaghan had been engaged in key personal negotiations on his own account. After discussions with Ford and others in Washington, Johannes Witteveen of the IMF came to London and had a private meeting with Callaghan, known to Healey but attended otherwise only by Kenneth Stowe. It was the first time he had negotiated with the Prime Minister, rather than the Treasury team, face to face. The chronology is not altogether clear at this point, but clearly their meetings were kept totally secret (the Prime Minister's diary for November–December 1976 does not record in so many words that they ever took place). The timing suggested in subsequent accounts is that Callaghan and Witteveen met in the early morning of 1 December, perhaps around 8.45 a.m. with the Cabinet meeting delayed in consequence.

What is generally agreed is that these Callaghan–Witteveen exchanges were blunt and acrimonious. Witteveen insisted on huge immediate public expenditure cuts for 1977–8, and 1978–9. Callaghan refused to go much above £2 bn. for 1977–8, where Witteveen demanded £3 bn. He turned savagely on Witteveen, accusing him of being oblivious of the impact of mass unemployment on the British economy and of imperilling the future of British democracy itself. There was a tense and confrontational series of exchanges, in which Witteveen at various times threatened to leave London for New York, and Callaghan appeared to be close to dispatching him on his way. But as the tumult and the shouting died, a compromise began to emerge. It was certainly closer to Callaghan's position than to the IMF's starting offer, with proposed £2.5 bn. cuts over the two years 1977–9. The Policy Unit offered the alternative of £3 bn. cuts of which £1 bn. would be a major new investment programme. Witteveen returned to Washington by Concorde to host a cocktail party, the reason for his temporary departure not revealed. There were further sharp exchanges to come between Witteveen and Whittome and British government representatives, but something of a breakthrough had been achieved. Callaghan could address his Cabinet colleagues in the knowledge that he had managed to obtain less severe terms which could almost be presented as a diplomatic triumph.[63] It could be claimed in time that another 1931 had been averted.

It now remained to construct an agreed response from his Cabinet. At the key meeting on 1 December papers from Benn, Shore, and Crosland dealing with Benn's alternative strategy, so called, were discussed first at much length.[64] In fact, Benn's paper was demolished as Callaghan had long intended. He had no back-up from the Treasury, while Donoughue in the Policy Unit had been deliberately used by Callaghan to shred Benn's proposals as unreasoning protectionism. Non-economics ministers like Shirley Williams, Rodgers, and Peart joined in the attack. Benn in his diary does not seem to appreciate how cataclysmically he had been routed, and his case substantially collapsed from that time on. Peter Shore, with a more measured call for protectionism, got a somewhat better hearing, but he too hardly won over the majority. The third 'gladiator in the ring', as Benn called him, was Crosland who grandly announced that his case was much stronger than that of either Benn or Shore. He argued that the only reason for cuts was the confidence of international financiers. He outlined the case for import deposits and no further cuts, which might have some appeal to the Benn group also. However, it emerged that some of his key potential supporters, notably Lever and Shirley Williams, were unsympathetic.

That evening Benn tried to undertake the complicated task of working out the position of the various groups in the Cabinet. He made it Healey 8, Callaghan 3, Crosland 7, and Benn 6.[65] But this severely underestimated the residual strength of the Treasury. The decisive fact of all was that Callaghan, after much pondering, had decided irrevocably to throw his weight behind Healey since none of the alternatives had substance. Despite a belief by Michael Foot that he might finally come out against his Chancellor, he had come round to the view that a modified IMF loan would be the appropriate long-term solution. He agreed with Healey's view that they should be practical and avoid raising unrealistic expectations, as had happened with George Brown's National Plan a decade earlier. He had had an important private discussion with Crosland on 30 November, on the flight back from a European Finance Ministers' meeting in the Netherlands, telling him that he would be backing Healey. In effect he was pressing Crosland, with whom he had long ties of political association, to do the same. With Callaghan would inevitably go Lever, Elwyn-Jones, Peart, Rees, Mulley, Varley, Mason, and Morris, thus guaranteeing a clear majority. Williams and Ennals were won over with concessions on the education and health budgets. Against his inclinations and economic convictions, Crosland, left with the youthful Roy Hattersley as his only supporter, had to concede defeat. Hattersley was indeed the last dissident to be rounded up. Of him, Callaghan had remarked clinically, 'He'll be all right. . . . I appointed him to my Cabinet.' And so he was.[66]

At the Cabinet on 2 December Healey spelt out the problem with brutal clarity. Unless PSBR was cut from the forecast of £10.2m., the IMF would not lend and Britain could no longer borrow abroad. He proposed some scaled-down cuts which he now had reason to believe the IMF would accept, namely £1 bn. in the PSBR for 1977–8, plus a further £500m. sale of BP shares acquired from Burmah Oil, and another reduction of £1.5 bn. for 1978–9. Now for the first time Callaghan showed his hand and declared his unambiguous support for his Chancellor.[67] He had already prepared his ground at close hand. Jack Jones and Len Murray for the TUC, while warning of the serious consequences of more cuts and unemployment, had urged that everything be done to keep a Labour government in office. The social contract would somehow hold, they assured him. Callaghan's declaration of support for Healey was backed, as pre-arranged, by a similar statement by Michael Foot, the essential linchpin in relations between the government and the unions. In the end, it was agreed that the IMF would be offered £1 bn. in cuts and a further £500m. from BP shares, while the argument over import deposits would be 'tested out'. Benn, and less resolutely Shore, Booth, Silkin, and Orme, were still opposed, but the overwhelming view, endorsed, however reluctantly, by 18 ministers out of 23, was in favour. Callaghan told Helmut Schmidt the following day that the meeting had been 'long and difficult', and that there was a half billion difference between the IMF position and that of the Cabinet. 'There is not a cat-in-hell's of moving an inch from this.' Still, the Cabinet had finally decided. There were two episodes of a highly personal kind both involving the Prime Minister. At one stage he read out the transcript of part of a largely bland telephone conversation with President Ford. And he took stern issue with Tony Benn on whether another 1931 was in the making; Benn's father, Lord Stansgate, had been in MacDonald's Cabinet at that fateful time. Callaghan's entire strategy had been to avert another 1931 and he felt confident, as someone who remembered that distant time, that he would do so.[68] He could have added, had he wished, that Lord Stansgate had been amongst the majority voting for cuts in unemployment benefit back in 1931.

The issue was by no means resolved with the Cabinet verdict. Callaghan had told President Ford on 2 December, after the Cabinet had met, that he was 'not sanguine' and was indeed unsure whether 'I can keep all the Cabinet on board even yet.' A gap of £0.5 bn. still existed between the IMF's demand for cuts and the British Cabinet's final offer. There was a tense meeting between Healey and the IMF team on 3 December. When the latter called for cuts of £1.5 bn. in 1977–8 and of £3 bn. in 1978—9, 'the Chancellor said that Dr. Witteveen could take a running jump'. He told Whittome boldly that if the IMF forced Labour from office they would call a general election. Callaghan noted privately, 'Denis had no authority to say this—but I did not object in the circumstances.'[69]

But in fact the IMF team stepped back and discussions with them rapidly reached a settlement thereafter. Much of the devil was in the detail, and the cuts to be made in individual budgets were a sensitive area. On 7 December the Cabinet had anguished discussions about how to achieve the £1 bn. of cuts sought: at one stage only £954m. had been agreed. Benn observed that he did not see why the IMF should be so impressed with the sale of BP shares ('Nor more did I', observed the Prime Minister). Callaghan at this point lost his temper (deliberately so, thought Joel Barnett), stating that they would present a package to the PLP and to the Commons and that any dissenting ministers could hand in their resignations. Foot and Shore led those who smoothed things over.[70]

There was in the end an inevitable decision to accept the terms proposed, with defence bearing a large share of the cutbacks to be made. The parliamentary party had also to be squared. Callaghan had told Cledwyn Hughes on 6 December that the PLP must meet to endorse the Cabinet's conclusions on the evening of 15 December immediately after Healey's statement to the House. 'If the PLP did not support the package he would step down and a new leader would be needed. He would stay pending the election. I was taken aback and said I would speak to him later on.' Hughes pointed out the difficulties of a procedural kind and 'advised him not to talk about going out'. He added. 'He is under considerable strain and sensitive, which is understandable. I also detect a coolness between P.M. and Denis.' Callaghan also had a major meeting with Michael Cocks, Walter Harrison, and the other government whips on 8 December at 11.20 a.m. 'The question', he told them, 'was whether Government and the Party were going to hold together.' The whips wisely urged that any agreed economic package must avoid elements that would require legislation, in the present jumpy state of party loyalties. In the end Callaghan agreed with Hughes on 9 December, over the phone, that there would not be a formal motion and vote at the parliamentary party meeting 'which relieved me'. There would be a debate opened by Healey with Callaghan himself winding up.[71]

On 14 December the Cabinet considered the final stage in the form of the letter of intent. Crosland pointed out that a safety net for sterling and import deposits were not mentioned and Callaghan confessed he was disappointed on these two areas. He felt on the verge of being 'anti-American'. There was some private tension between Prime Minister and Chancellor on the issue, with Callaghan insisting on some further concessions and his Policy Unit complaining that the Treasury had conspired to deny them sight of the document in advance.[72] Concern was expressed by Shore and others on the future level of unemployment. On 15 December Healey announced to a hushed but not hostile House of Commons the terms of the IMF loan of £3.9m. A meeting of the parliamentary party on the following day went remarkably smoothly. Healey's initial statement led to some tension (Benn privately described his claim that it was endorsed by a united Cabinet as 'a bloody lie'). But Callaghan wound up almost serenely 'with great relaxation'.[73] He called for support from the unions, the party, the Tribune group, and the Manifesto group. He took the high ground as well. But the worst case scenario had been averted. There had after all been no 1931. Social benefits had been protected. In 1931 they had been the first target for attack. Critics were subdued. On the whole it was felt that the outcome was much less calamitous than could have been expected.

Almost all commentators agree that the IMF crisis was a great test for Callaghan. It is also the almost unanimous view that he handled it with immense patience and political skill. The only major critic is Edmund Dell who regarded the Cabinet discussions as a 'shambles' which held matters up for weeks while the IMF was waiting for urgent answers to real economic issues. But this seems to ignore the political context in which Callaghan and ministers were operating. Sir John Hunt, the former Cabinet Secretary, rebutted Dell by pointing out the immense range of opinion in the Cabinet and the essential need for Callaghan somehow to find a consensus.[74] After all, it was not only a matter of satisfying the IMF. It was a matter of keeping government and party together. This Callaghan did supremely well. Every member of the Cabinet felt that every point of view had been given ample opportunity and that a mood of fairness and free expression prevailed (even Benn, who might well have felt he had been roughly dealt with on 1 December, seems to have adhered to this view). The National Executive had been difficult and bad-tempered throughout, with Allaun, Heffer, and Atkinson especially critical. On one ironic occasion, the joint meeting of the NEC and the Cabinet on 19 October, Eric Heffer, a short-fused member of the Executive, attacked

Denis Healey for 'always wanting to introduce a sour note' which was 'totally unnecessary'. The left on the NEC, aided and abetted by an understandably embittered Barbara Castle, constantly urged that the IMF be defied and that the government pursue its own priorities—the public ownership of the docks was one mentioned. But in the end, the left lacked firepower where it mattered and its criticisms were left on one side.[75]

Of the political success which attended Callaghan's methods of operation and the impact on his prestige as leader there can be no doubt. Tom McNally felt that it was a great single-handed achievement. The Prime Minister, in office for only six months, had faced out Britain's creditors, using his international contacts to the full, and had persuaded or compelled them to find a compromise. On the economic significance of his victory, however, there has been much more argument. Some have seen the IMF as a humiliation, and Britain as being in hock, unable to run its own economy, and a permanent, impotent debtor. This was not how many contemporaries saw matters. Donoughue could fairly claim that the eventual cuts sustained were far less rigorous than those proposed in the IMF's original scenario, and that the impact on the economy was far less deflationary than had at first appeared.[76] Indeed, the point might be reinforced by stating that the cuts were far more severe than they ever need have been. Callaghan's suspicions of the erratic or false nature of Treasury forecasting were amply justified. The PSBR proved to be far less in 1977–8 and 1978–9 than had been forecast: after the imposition of cash limits on departments, it was only £8.5 bn. in 1976–7 rather than the £10.5 bn. prophesied by the Treasury. With diminished budgets in consequence, the cuts were much more savage than was justified. The government was able to eliminate its current account deficit in 1977 before the IMF loan even took effect. The Treasury's methodology was as unsound in 1976 as in 1967, but at least even more ferocious and needless economies were averted.

Callaghan's own strategy of international diplomacy and an emphasis on the sterling balances has been widely criticized. Healey did not believe in it. Later commentators referred to Callaghan's 'obsession' with the sterling balances, and regarded it as tangential to the main issues of the IMF negotiations.[77] For all that, Callaghan did win his point here, too, even if a shade after the event, and felt that a victory crucial to the future of sterling had been gained. The Americans kept their promise, hard won in the Lever visit, to provide a safety net for the sterling balances. Helmut Schmidt continued to use his good offices on Britain's behalf. Callaghan, in thanking Schmidt on 15 December for his moral support and the Bundesbank's $350m. standby credit, had the additional personal pleasure of congratulating him on his (narrow) re-election as Chancellor. The social democratic axis in Europe would continue.[78] On 29 December, the Prime Minister told Healey of his pleasure at the progress made over the twin problems of a safety net for sterling and the problem of future sterling inflows. He suggested that existing official holders of sterling be offered dollar-denominated medium-term bonds on market-related terms.[79] Negotiations began with the central banks and the IMF in the new year. On 11 January Healey announced the fulfilment of Callaghan's long-held objective, namely the running down of sterling as a reserve currency, with protective swap facilities if there were a run on the pound. On 8 February the agreement came into force and an age-old problem was finally removed.[80] Apart from winning this crucial point, Callaghan's strategy of working with the Americans and Chancellor Schmidt had its incidental psychological impact on the IMF negotiators also and helped strengthen the bargaining hand of the British team.

Callaghan, therefore, ended the year in surprisingly good heart. He had come through a crisis as severe as the devaluation in November 1967 but on this occasion was the stronger for it. On 21 December, Cledwyn Hughes found him in reflective mood, 'tired but relieved. . . . He thought the period before devaluation when he was Chancellor was more worrying. I suggested that this last period was more crucial for the Party and the country, and he agreed. . . . Jim said he was looking forward to Xmas at Chequers with all his family.' Benn then had an amiable talk with Callaghan. 'Jim was friendly and I felt things were relaxing a bit.' He took pleasure in the fact that Callaghan for the first time in a conversation used the word 'capitalism'. The Prime Minister unwound some more, despite his principled teetotalism, at drinks parties with the Transport House staff and with Cabinet ministers.[81] He had achieved a political triumph as notable in its way as Wilson's in maintaining party unity over Europe. And he had indeed avoided another 1931, even another 1967.

Many commentators had taken an almost apocalyptic view of impending doom: a writer as perceptive as Peter Jay had written in *The Times* of the combination of economic troubles and trade union pressures producing an inexorable cycle of 'rampant inflation, falling employment, industrial decay, administrative breakdown, social and political chaos'. The outcome would be a political revolution that would lead either to a self-perpetuating left-wing oligarchy or a 'strong man of the right' (not, apparently, a strong woman) taking control. Twenty years on, he admitted that his judgement had been proved mistaken and that Callaghan's political analysis had been shrewder than his own.[82] Instead of the IMF crisis being a slough of despond, it proved to be a springboard for advance. A Labour victory in the next general election was once again conceivable. Callaghan's premiership now moved on to a more positive and forward-looking phase.

1. Material in Callaghan Papers (uncatalogued).

2. Wilson, *Final Term*, 200.

3. Callaghan to Crosland, Cabinet note, n.d. (Crosland Papers, 5/25).

4. Castle, *Castle Diaries, 1974–76*, 221 (17 Nov. 1974); Benn, *Against the Tide*, 266; Hennessy, *Cabinet*, 84.

5. For the economic problems of these years, see Michael Artis and David Cobham (eds.), *Labour's Economic Policies, 1974–79* (Manchester, 1991), and Michael Stewart, *The Jekyll and Hyde Years* (London, 1977), chs. 5 and 6.

6. Material in Callaghan Papers (uncatalogued); for Puerto Rico, record ibid. (box 21A).

7. Benn, *Against the Tide*, 572 (27 May 1976).

8. Record of telephone conversation between Callaghan and Schmidt, 28 Apr. 1976, T10A/C76 (Callaghan Papers, box 33).

9. Record of telephone conversation between Callaghan and Giscard d'Estaing, 28 Apr. 1976 (ibid.).

10. Record of telephone conversation between Callaghan and Schmidt, 13 May 1976, T19C/76 (ibid.).

11. *The Times*, 17 June 1976; Jack Jones, *Union Man* (London, 1986), 305–8.

12. Jones, *Union Man*, 307.

13. McNally to Callaghan, 25 June 1976 (Callaghan Papers, box 9).

14. McNally note on Callaghan's meeting with TUC Economic Committee, 14 July 1976 (ibid., box 13).

15. Cledwyn Hughes diary, 8 July 1976.

16. Materials in Callaghan Papers (uncatalogued); Benn, *Against the Tide*, 591–600; Edmund Dell, *A Hard Pounding: Politics and Economic Crisis, 1974–6* (London, 1991), 228–30.

17. Dell, *A Hard Pounding*, 230–1.

18. Donoughue memo, 'Public Expenditure Cuts' (PU 194), July 1976 (private papers); Donoughue, *Prime Minister*, 91.

19. Benn, *Against the Tide*, 602–4 (26–8 July 1976).

20. *The Times*, 29 July 1976.

21. Cledwyn Hughes diary, 2 Aug. 1976.

22. Prime Minister's diary, 1976 (Callaghan Papers, box 35).

23. Ibid.

24. Healey, *The Time of my Life*, 428.

25. Material in Callaghan Papers (uncatalogued).

26. Healey, *The Time of my Life*, 429; *Financial Times*, 29 Sept. 1976.

27. *The Times*, 1 Oct. 1976; Benn, *Against the Tide*, 616 (30 Sept. 1976).

28. Healey, *The Time of my Life*, 429.

29. Cledwyn Hughes diary, 30 Sept. 1976.

30. Interviews with Lord Callaghan, Peter Jay, Lord Donoughue, and Tom

McNally. For the speech, see *The Times*, 29 Sept. 1976. There are various versions in the Callaghan Papers. I have greatly benefited from BBC video material of the 1976 party conference kindly given me by Kirsty White.

31. Cledwyn Hughes diary, 30 Sept. 1976.

32. Dell, *A Hard Pounding*, 237.

33. Interview with Lord Healey.

34. Telephone conversation of Callaghan and President Ford, 29 Sept. 1976, T85C/76 (Callaghan Papers, box 33); Callaghan, *Time and Chance*, 429–30.

35. Burk and Cairncross, *'Goodbye Great Britain'*, 62–3.

36. Callaghan to Schmidt, 2 Oct. 1976, T88C/76, and Callaghan to Schmidt, 6 Oct. 1976, T90C/76 (Callaghan Papers, box 33).

37. Prime Minister's diary, 1976 (ibid., box 35); Burk and Cairncross, *'Goodbye Great Britain'*, 64–5.

38. Healey, *The Time of my Life*, 430–1.

39. Healey interview; Cledwyn Hughes diary, 12 Oct. 1976.

40. Telephone conversation of Callaghan and President Kaunda, 25 Sept. 1976, T81C/76 (Callaghan Papers, box 33).

41. Printed in *Education*, 22 Oct. 1976; interview with Lord Donoughue.

42. Donoughue memo on education (PU 183), 13 May 1976 (private papers).

43. Callaghan to Shirley Williams, 20 Oct. 1976, M72c 76 (Callaghan Papers, box 32); Michael Barber, 'New Labour, 20 Years on', *Times Educational Supplement*, 11 Oct. 1996; *New Statesman*, 18 Oct. 1996.

44. Blackstone, 'Education for 16- to 19-year-Olds', 86.

45. Benn, *Against the Tide*, 626–7 (14, 18 Oct. 1976); *Guardian*, 16 Oct. 1996.

46. Burk and Cairncross, *'Goodbye Great Britain'. The 1976 IMF Crisis*, an unfortunate title for an excellent book.

47. Transcript of *Panorama* interview (Callaghan Papers, box 5).

48. Callaghan telephone conversation with Ford, 29 Sept. 1976 (ibid., box 33). For the *Sunday Times* article [by Malcolm Rutherford], see Callaghan's remarks to Labour/TUC Liaison Committee, 25 Oct. 1976 (Callaghan Papers, box 9).

49. Interview with Helmut Schmidt.

50. Burk and Cairncross, *'Goodbye Great Britain'*, 66. The authors point out that Pohl and Schmidt had fallen out at the time of Schmidt's resignation in 1982 and he was more dismissive in this interview than he might have been in 1976.

51. Dell, *A Hard Pounding*, 241; Joel Barnett, *Inside the Treasury* (London, 1982), 102.

52. Cledwyn Hughes diary, 4 Nov. 1976.

53. Burk and Cairncross, *'Goodbye Great Britain'*, 70 ff., lay stress on divisions in the British Treasury team on strategic objectives.

54. Telephone conversation of Callaghan and Ford, 16 Nov. 1976, T106AC/76 (Callaghan Papers, box 33).

55. Ibid. See Burk and Cairncross, *'Goodbye Great Britain'*, 76–81, for an excellent account based in part on interview material from the late Lord Lever.

56. Donoughue to Callaghan, 30 Nov. 1976 (private papers).

57. In preparing this account, I have benefited greatly from interviews with Lord Callaghan, Lord Healey, Michael Foot, Lord Merlyn-Rees, Lord Rodgers, Roy Hattersley, and others.

58. Cledwyn Hughes diary, 25 Nov. 1976.

59. 'The I.M.F. Negotiations' (PU/229), 5 Nov. 1976 (Callaghan Papers, box 13).

60. 'The I.M.F. Negotiations' (PU/230), 16 Nov. 1976 (ibid.).

61. 'The I.M.F. Negotiations: A Compromise Package' (PU 235/GD [Gavyn Davies]), 25 Nov. 1976 (ibid.); Donoughue to Healey, 26 Nov. 1976 (private papers) in which Healey is told of Callaghan's sympathy with the Policy Unit's views.

62. 'The I.M.F. Negotiations' (PU/230), loc. cit.

63. Interview with Sir Kenneth Stowe; Burk and Cairncross, *'Goodbye Great Britain'*, 92–6.

64. Material in Callaghan Papers (uncatalogued); Benn, *Against the Tide*, 661–9 (1 Dec. 1976), a remarkably good-humoured account.

65. Burk and Cairncross, *'Goodbye Great Britain'*, 99.

66. Healey to Callaghan, 22 Oct. 1976 (Callaghan Papers, box 13); Crosland, *Tony Crosland*, 379–80; Hattersley, *Who Goes Home?*, 176.

67. Material in Callaghan Papers (uncatalogued).

68. Note of Healey–Benn meeting, 9 Nov. 1977; McNally to Callaghan, 11 Nov. 1977; Donoughue to Callaghan, 11 Nov. 1977; joint paper on North Sea oil and materials on press conference (Callaghan Papers, box 17); Benn, *Against the Tide*, 672–3, 677–8 (2 Dec. 1976).

69. Callaghan to Ford, 2 Dec. 1976 (Gerald R. Ford Library, Ann Arbor, Kissinger/Sowcroft parallel file); material on discussions with IMF in Callaghan Papers (uncatalogued); telephone conversation of Callaghan and Schmidt, 2 Dec. 1976 (Callaghan Papers, box 33).

70. Material in Callaghan Papers (uncatalogued); Barnett, *Inside the Treasury*, 105–6; Healey, *The Time of my Life*, 432.

71. Record of Callaghan's meeting with the whips, 8 Dec. 1976 (Callaghan Papers, box 13); Prime Minister's diary, 1976 (ibid., box 35); Cledwyn Hughes diary, 6 and 9 Dec. 1976.

72. Donoughue, *Prime Minister*, 99–100. Callaghan was briefly incapacitated with an attack of bronchitis on 10–11 Dec. but stayed on in the flat at No. 10 working on his papers (Prime Minister's diary, 1976, Callaghan Papers, box 35).

73. Benn, *Against the Tide*, 689–90 (16 Dec. 1976).

74. Edmund Dell and Lord Hunt of Tanworth, 'The Failings of Cabinet Government in the Mid to Late 1970s', *Contemporary Record*, 8/3 (winter 1994), 453–72.

75. Record of NEC/Cabinet meeting, 19 Oct. 1976 (Callaghan Papers, box 17).

76. Donoughue, *Prime Minister*, 98–9. When I interviewed Lord Donoughue nineteen years after these events (26 Apr. 1995) he strongly maintained this view.

77. Healey interview; Burk and Cairncross, *'Goodbye Great Britain'*, 82.

78. Callaghan to Schmidt, 16 Dec. 1976, T127AC/76 (Callaghan Papers, box 33).

79. Callaghan to Healey, 29 Dec. 1976, M95C/76 (ibid., box 32).

80. Burk and Cairncross, *'Goodbye great Britain'*, 122–4. It should be added that Edmund Dell's consistently critical account in *The Chancellors*, 437–8, argues that the sterling balances agreement was 'totally unnecessary once the government was seen to be conducting a responsible economic policy'. But since the balances had been part of the problem, it seems unreasonable not to see them as part of the solution.

81. Cledwyn Hughes diary, 21 Dec. 1976; Benn, *Against the Tide*, 691 (21 Dec. 1976); Prime Minister's diary, 1976 (Callaghan Papers, box 35).

82. Peter Jay, ' "Success" Founded on Political Indifference', *Observer*, 29 Sept. 1996.

24

A SUCCESSFUL GOVERNMENT

THE Callaghan government has been a victim of disinformation. It has not exactly been written out of history as the Heath administration commonly was by supporters of Mrs Thatcher and hammers of the 'one-nation' 'wets' in the 1980s. It has rather been misrepresented by being recalled solely in terms of the initial crisis of the IMF negotiations and the culminating *Götterdämmerung* of the winter of discontent. This is less than half the story. Most of it has still to be written.

Historians should, of course, give due attention to the Cabinet's divisions in the autumn of 1976. They should emphasize also the industrial and political collapse that saw the Callaghan government almost humiliatingly thrust from power. But stories have a middle as well as a beginning and an end. The administration was to last in all three years and one month. For twenty of those thirty-seven months, more than half its length, from January 1977 to September 1978 the government showed many signs of being politically and economically successful. It was far from being simply an interlude. This appeared to be the most thriving period that Britain had known since the heyday of Harold Macmillan in the later 1950s. The Opposition under Mrs Thatcher seemed relatively ineffective. The year 1977 in particular was an *annus mirabilis*, with Callaghan's presidency of the European Community and successful chairing of the Commonwealth prime ministers' and NATO meetings, and the economic summit in London, along with ample photo-opportunities during the royal jubilee. James Callaghan achieved an authority as Prime Minister that astonished many close observers of his long career. Labour showed real signs of being not just in office but in power.

It is important, therefore, to avoid the kind of reductionism of some later accounts and to give proper weight to the effective record of the Callaghan government for most of its time in office. Historians of the Social Democrats after 1981 have, perhaps understandably, been remiss in not giving a properly balanced account of the Callaghan years,[1] as they appeared to contemporaries at the time and as they relate to the broader history of *fin de siècle* Britain. They were only in part a time of crisis and decline. They were also, to borrow from early American history, an 'era of good feelings' and a credible advertisement for Labour as a party of government. Some evangelists for New Labour in the 1990s, who wrote off the late 1970s as the death-pangs of an old corporatist order, failed to acknowledge that it was then that many of their party's social and economic policies were modernized and redefined.

The basis of the recovery in the government's fortunes lay in the great improvement in the economy once the IMF crisis was safely negotiated. The new year opened with news on 1 January that the pound was enjoying better health. It had risen to $1.70, thirteen points above its lowest point in relation to a basket of other currencies in late October. Tony Benn, as Minister for Energy, brought the glad tidings that the flow of oil from the North Sea was going on apace, with exports of top-quality crude increasing rapidly and huge potential savings on the balance of payments (£2,000m. was the figure commonly quoted).[2] By 1980 Britain, uniquely among all the western powers, would be self-sufficient in oil. The announcement by Denis Healey on 11 January of the agreement with the IMF and central banks to 'achieve an orderly reduction in the role of sterling as a reserve currency' was enthusiastically received in international money markets, as was a $1.5 bn. loan with European banks negotiated by the Bank of England to achieve this rundown. As Callaghan had prophesied, removing this crucial aspect of the vulnerability of sterling and ending the exposed position of the sterling balances had a strong impact on the national finances. There were massive inflows of foreign capital, both into sterling and into gilt-edged securities, amounting to $2 bn. for the month of January. On 28 January, minimum lending rate was cut by 1 per cent to 12.25 per cent, the biggest cut since the old bank rate was changed in 1972. This was only the start; twelve months later it was to stand at 8.5 per cent.[3] Small businesses and mortgaged home owners, the vulnerable vanguard of the beleaguered suburban middle class, rejoiced. At last Britain was hearing some good economic news with every expectation that it would last.

As the economy improved, so did the standing of the Prime Minister, even if his party continued to show up badly in the opinion polls. Journalists had been generally negative towards his performance until the completion of the talks with the IMF in early December. They were wont to compare his apparently brief administration with those of Douglas-

Home in 1963–4, or even of the lachrymose and hapless Lord Goderich in 1827–8. They now suddenly discovered all manner of positive qualities in the leader. David Watt wrote in the *Financial Times* of how Callaghan was proving a 'much more effective Prime Minister than most people had believed possible'. His temper was 'peppery to say the least', but his 'nerve and sense of purpose have been admirable'.[4] Even if his party lagged 15 per cent behind the Conservatives in the polls, a clear majority of the British people expressed their confidence that the Prime Minister was doing a good job. His approval rating far outstripped that of the still uncertain leader of the Opposition, Margaret Thatcher. Whereas Callaghan ran a powerful-looking team, she was still hemmed in by survivors of the old Heath administration—Whitelaw, Carrington, Prior, Pym, Gilmour, and Walker. Also, in a country like Britain (unlike, say, Norway or Iceland), being female did not help her political ratings.

Throughout the spring and summer of 1977, the British economy continued to do astonishingly well. The pound, now a petro-currency, strengthened week by week to reach $1.80 and then $1.90 later in the year; the reserves more than doubled from $4 bn. at the end of December to $7.2 bn. at the end of January and to more than $9 bn. at the end of April.[5] The markets grew stronger and the City more relaxed. More important, the real economy was growing too. Douglas Jay has, quite reasonably, written of the British economic performance between 1977 and 1979 that 'this is one of the few examples of any Western government in the seventies reducing both inflationary pressures and unemployment at the same time'.[6] Denis Healey's budget of March 1977 introduced some relaxation and £2.3 bn. of tax cuts, although the TUC attacked it for linking £1m. of these cuts to a tough pay restraint policy, and for failing to attack unemployment. In effect the citizen was being given back in purchasing power what the Treasury had tried to take away through its massive miscalculation of the Public Sector Borrowing Requirement. However, the markets reacted favourably, and interest rates could safely be cut to 9.5 per cent as gilts hit a four-year peak. Inflation remained in double figures but, with continued pay restraint, could soon be expected to fall. Callaghan told Schmidt it was the darkest hour before the dawn.[7]

Later on, it emerged that the deflation imposed was more severe than was justified because of the quite inaccurate forecasts offered by the Treasury. But the government were victims of convention and civil service misinformation or even disinformation like everyone else at the time. No one had the capacity to offer more authoritative statistics. Still, for the first time for well over a decade, Britain appeared the master of its own economic fate. After the trauma of the IMF negotiations, Healey needed only to draw half the IMF loan offered, and none of the standby credit from central banks after August 1977. The time for freedom from IMF control—what the Chancellor in his Yorkshire vernacular called 'Sod off day'[8]—was coming more rapidly than anyone might have anticipated in the bleak autumn of 1976.

In these distinctly more cheerful circumstances, Callaghan could withdraw from his intense involvement with economic management and leave the conduct of affairs to his Chancellor. But there were areas in which he could take the lead himself, notably in promoting a forward-looking industrial strategy. This had a number of key aspects, both enabling and restrictive. There was the plan for greater industrial democracy through some form of worker participation. There was the continuing need for severe pay restraint on the part of the unions. And there was the wider issue of industrial regeneration to stimulate productive efficiency in the light of the disappointing performance by British industry in 1974–6. Callaghan was personally identified with all these policies, as a goad to the Treasury as much as to both sides of industry. His role, not least as chief communicator, was a highly visible one. His new stance was illustrated by his chairing a meeting of the National Economic Development Council in February and his leading a detailed review of industrial strategy over subsequent weeks.[9]

The first part of the new industrial policy, the move to greater industrial democracy, proved, however, to be abortive. In February 1977 the Committee of Inquiry into Industrial Democracy, chaired by the eminent Oxford historian Alan Bullock, the biographer of Ernest Bevin (and also of Hitler), issued its report. The members of his committee included Jack Jones, general secretary of the Transport Workers, and a strong advocate of worker participation and greater decentralization in industrial management and labour relations, an outlook that reflected his quasi-syndicalist background in Merseyside industry. Others on the committee included David Lea, head of the TUC Economic Department, Clive Jenkins of ASTMS, and the Labour law academic Lord Wedderburn, along with three employers' representatives of whom perhaps the most powerful was Jack Callard, chairman of ICI. The committee was divided, but the majority report clearly favoured an equal number of trade union and shareholders' representatives on the boards of private companies with over 2,000 employees, with a few independents to hold the balance.

Callaghan had gone along strongly with Jack Jones's view of workers' participation on the management board.[10] He was strongly influenced by

Helmut Schmidt's passionate endorsement of German co-determination, deeply rooted in German industrial history over many decades. Callaghan's natural stance was to try to move on from a purely adversarial system of industrial relations to what would in the 1990s be called by 'New Labour' a system of stakeholding with mutual rights and obligations. He arranged and attended a meeting held in Germany between the members of the Bullock Committee and Helmut Schmidt and other key German figures. The German Chancellor argued strongly that Britain's confrontational system, allied to time-worn and inbred patronage methods operated by British management, was fundamentally harmful to the United Kingdom's industrial performance. It was a major reason why the German economy was so much more successful. He poured scorn on the idea that worker directors would harm the flow of private investment, with copious examples from German industrial experience. He attached much hope, as he was to affirm to the present writer eighteen years later, to creating an industrial transformation in Britain which would strengthen its international standing also. Callaghan, as a former trade union official who understood the problems and the psychology of industrial relations at first hand, was the man to achieve it.[11]

The Bullock report was not an extreme document. The Policy Unit correctly pointed out that it argued for a gradual approach. There would be a right to industrial democracy, but no executive order to impose it. The TUC general secretary Len Murray, an enthusiast now both for German co-determination and Swedish social market policies, was a warm supporter.[12] But, like all attempts to reform management–labour relations in British industry, it fell on stony ground. The managers were almost to a man resistant to workers' representatives being elected to their boards of directors. The CBI led a strong outcry against it. It would let loose unpredictable trade unionists into the closed world of the boardroom. The fact that the Bullock proposals would apply only to larger companies where a high degree of union involvement already existed was ignored. Some right-wing journalists, like the newly converted figure of Paul Johnson, a former editor of the *New Statesman*, denounced the influence of the Transport Workers' leader, who was described variously as the most powerful man in Britain and the 'Emperor Jones', echoing a famous American black musical. Amongst the unions, there was resistance across the spectrum to the idea of workers becoming bosses and their historic role thereby being compromised. Jack Jones and David Lea had tended to underestimate the degree of opposition in other unions. Relatively right-wing unions like the Engineers and the General and Municipal Workers joined the miners and the massed forces of the left in denouncing Bullock (a name which was paraphrased in less genteel nomenclature).

Some ministers, notably Edmund Dell, strongly resisted change. Others noted the commercial fiascos that had resulted from recent workers' co-operatives launched by Tony Benn during his time at Trade and Industry, such as Meriden motor cycles, the Fisher-Bendix plant (which, incomprehensibly, produced orange juice as well as car radiators) at Kirby, and the *Scottish Daily News* in Glasgow. They were derided as 'Benn's follies', financial disasters one and all. The Bullock report was offloaded to a Cabinet committee which included both Dell and Shirley Williams, both of them felt to be unsympathetic to its message. Shirley Williams chaired this committee as Paymaster-General. While she hailed the virtues of industrial democracy in her later book *Politics is for People*, she disliked the elements of union power enshrined in Bullock. Her preference was for workers' representatives on boards of directors to be elected directly rather than have the unions claim to represent them. Her committee produced a modest white paper, and it was never heard of again.[13] Industrial relations continued their negative, adversarial pattern. Callaghan's hopes of breaking through the barriers of class and economic power which held back British industrial performance were doomed to disappointment.

Elsewhere, however, the industrial strategy showed some real signs of progress. Despite all pressures and complaints, the policy of pay restraint agreed with the TUC in the summer of 1976, before the IMF crisis broke, held firm for the moment, even though the TUC had voted for a 'planned and orderly' return to free collective bargaining after the summer of 1977. Callaghan and Healey, backed solidly by Foot, urged the vital need for a third year of pay restraint. Callaghan had made a particular point of giving assurances to Jack Jones about a continuing social contract soon after becoming Prime Minister.[14] In return for their moderation, the TUC accepted the government's side of the bargain that the social contract implied, including social benefits and the public ownership of aircraft and shipbuilding. The Advisory and Conciliation Service (ACAS), a central part of the social contract negotiated by Michael Foot when he was at Employment, was already in place. Under the chairmanship of Jim Mortimer, a former trade unionist of left-wing background, it was already achieving a high degree of authority in handling potential labour disputes. There were also attacks on the unemployment problem such as temporary employment subsidies, job creation schemes, and measures to improve industrial training and retraining. Jack Jones later accepted that the TUC in effect obtained everything it could reasonably want in return for pay restraint. As the pound strengthened, the current account steadily improved and the deficit was whittled away. April was an especially good month with the trade surplus being £111m., the strongest performance since October 1971. Crude oil exports were doubled.[15] Britain was manifestly benefiting now from North Sea oil, where BNOC was presiding over the production of 550,000 barrels a day, amounting to close to a third of Britain's needs. By 1980, as Tony Benn affirmed, Britain would be self-sufficient, with production of about 20m. tonnes of oil a year.[16] It would be its own master, free from thraldom to Arab sheikhs in OPEC. The country was also virtually self-sufficient in gas supplies, with 97 per cent of its needs also coming from the beneficent reserves of the North Sea.

If the economic prospects were improving, however, the government's political fortunes were anything but secure. Since the start of Callaghan's period it had been a minority government. By the start of 1977, following adverse by-election results, its original tally of 319 seats (out of a House of 634, excluding the Speaker) had been whittled down to 314. There had been another unexpected loss in early December. Reg Prentice, a former member of Callaghan's Cabinet who had faced violent left-wing opposition in his Newham constituency in London and who had been supported there by Roy Jenkins, Shirley Williams, and others, announced his disillusion with Labour. He would no longer support the government. There followed a fierce public exchange of letters with Callaghan.[17] In due time, as noted above, Prentice was to become a Conservative MP and to serve for a period in Mrs Thatcher's government.

Meanwhile, the government's policy of pay restraint, cuts in public expenditure which added to unemployment, and a monetary policy of cash limits aroused immense anger in Labour ranks, relieved although they may have been that the IMF crisis had not led to Armageddon. Meetings of the Cabinet and the Liaison Committee were invariably tense and bad-tempered affairs. Left-wing Executive members led the attack on the government's reactionary policies as they saw them and called for more socialism. They found a frequent ally in Barbara Castle, a bitter critic who had many fierce clashes with Callaghan himself. In the House, the government had no secure majority at all, and was reduced to bartering for votes with miscellaneous groups of Welsh and Scottish Nationalists and occasional Ulster representatives such as Gerry Fitt of the SDLP. His colleague Frank Maguire, 'Independent Republican' and licensed publican, in effect a supporter of Sinn Féin, was regarded as hostile and in any case seldom turned up at Westminster.

The government now suffered a series of parliamentary defeats on industrial and economic policy. Measures to nationalize the aircraft and shipbuilding industries were making slow progress and facing delay in the House of Lords, which again became a target of Labour attack. There was also trouble on aspects of the Welsh and Scottish Devolution Bill which was now beginning its weary crawl through the Commons under the direction of Michael Foot. On 8 February the government met with defeat on a Reduction of Redundancy Rebates Bill (by a ludicrous mix-up over pairing, Callaghan's own vote for the government was not recorded), and there was a 29-vote defeat over the guillotine on the Devolution Bill on 24 February.[19] The Labour whips, headed by Michael Cocks, did their best: the deputy whip, Walter Harrison, was to become a Westminster legend in these years for his dextrous mixture of persuasion and coercion in getting his flock to support the government in the lobbies.[20] But the Labour ranks were often exhausted beyond normal levels of endurance by long hours and late nights in the House, and unmollified by the pleasures of Annie's Bar, which saw its halcyon period at this time. They were hard to keep under control. Solid trade unionists, especially in the public sector, were discontented by a policy which had seen their members' living standards actually fall for two years running. In fact, the government's record in the lobbies was appalling throughout the Callaghan period. In all, the government was to be defeated on no less than 42 occasions in the five years 1974–9, more than 30 of them under Callaghan's premiership, though never on a formal vote of confidence until the very end. On this basis, the government was simply unable to govern.

A serious personal blow also came at this time. Tony Crosland, the Foreign Secretary, unexpectedly fell ill and died on 19 February. It was an immense personal loss for Callaghan and a tragedy for devoted social democrats for whom Crosland had been philosopher and inspiration for twenty years and more. After some consideration, Callaghan startled the political world by replacing him with his youthful deputy, the 38-year-old David Owen, much the youngest Foreign Secretary since Anthony Eden in 1935. It was a calculated blow on behalf of youth by a premier anxious that his team should not appear stale. Callaghan had long formed a high opinion of Owen as a possible leader in the making, and Owen soon showed his capacity as a strong, if sometimes domineering, minister.[21] He struck up a good relationship with his American counterpart, Cyrus Vance. But Crosland's death manifestly weakened a floundering government still further at a most difficult time. Rock bottom was reached on a threatened adjournment debate on 17 March which Mrs Thatcher promised to regard as a motion of confidence. Callaghan, who had been away on a visit to see President Carter in Washington and had then flown on to Ottawa on 10–13 March, was told at 9 p.m. that evening that the government could not win since all the other groups in the House would be arrayed against it.[22] In the end, ministers had to take the humiliating course of advising Labour members to abstain. The Tory motion was carried by 293 votes to none.

Yet salvation was at hand. Talks with the Scottish Nationalists had been inconclusive, although their commitment to devolution meant that on votes of confidence they were likely to support the government. Plaid Cymru were somewhat firmer, perhaps a reflection of the radical Welsh political ethos, but they numbered only three MPs. Of these three, Dafydd Wigley was in effect a social democrat; Dafydd Elis Thomas was distinctly on the left; Gwynfor Evans, their long-term leader, was a green-minded rural nonconformist pacifist who hated centralization. It was as though a party consisted of Roy Jenkins, Tony Benn, and Jonathon Porritt. This variegated trio were a frail reed on which to rely.

There were some hopes of a liaison with the traditionally conservative Ulster Unionists, a miscellaneous group under the effective leadership of Enoch Powell, one of the wilder cards on the political scene. Powell urged the need for greater Northern Irish representation at Westminster, and had talks with Michael Foot, via Roy Mason the Northern Irish Secretary, about a possible Speaker's Conference on the issue.[23] There was also murmuring on the desirability of an oil pipeline to link Ulster with the British mainland.

However, the intractable problems of Ulster politics made any progress on this front speculative. One stumbling block was the future impact of direct elections to the European Assembly, where the generally pro-Labour SDLP under Gerry Fitt demanded some form of proportional representation, preferably the single transferable vote, to enhance Catholic/Nationalist representation.[24] Callaghan had a private meeting with James Molyneaux and the variegated group of ten who made up Ulster Unionist representation in the Commons at 5.30 p.m. on 16 March (after which he had dinner with the Apostolic Delegate, at Wimbledon).[25] There were further talks with Roy Mason, while Foot and McNally had private discussions with the Unionists about either a Speaker's Conference on Ulster's parliamentary representation or the reform of local government in Northern Ireland. Kenneth Stowe of the prime minister's office was another active go-between. But nothing concrete seemed to emerge. Enoch Powell and James Molyneaux were both prepared to do a deal with Labour. By 1979 Labour had agreed to Enoch Powell's demand for extra seats for Northern Ireland, to the fury of the SDLP. But now the majority of the Unionists, fearful of security considerations as the Provisional Sinn Féin continued a long and accelerating series of bloody atrocities directed upon the civil population, would not budge.[26] Offence was taken at a remark by Mason that Ulster was 'a one-party state'. Kenneth Stowe, Callaghan's private secretary who was much involved in these discussions, urged the Prime Minister that Foot should see Gerry Fitt of the SDLP, an emotional man who became very angry if he felt he was being taken for granted.[27] Northern Ireland, as usual, was irreconcilable. Yet something had to be done immediately since Mrs Thatcher was to move a vote of no confidence in the government on 23 March.

However, the other element in the political complexities was the Liberals. Here there was genuine hope. They numbered thirteen members of parliament and were under the shrewd tactical leadership of David Steel. Still under 40, he had nevertheless been in the House for twelve years. He had only recently succeeded the discredited Jeremy Thorpe as party leader and was ambitious to make a name. The Liberals were anxious to find a way to increase their influence on key aspects of policy; like the government, they had no particular wish for a general election. There had been unofficial overtures to the government (later disavowed) in February by the independent-minded and distinctly bulky Liberal member for Rochdale, Cyril Smith, once a Labour activist himself. There were also important figures in Labour's ranks who had good personal relations with the Liberals. Several of them were Celts, amongst them Cledwyn Hughes, a friend of such leading Liberals as Emlyn Hooson (Montgomeryshire), a fellow graduate of the University College of Wales, Aberystwyth.[28] There were also members of the Cabinet, such as Shirley Williams and Bill Rodgers, friendly with the Liberals. An important letter was written to Callaghan on 17 March by Cledwyn Hughes, conveying David Steel's wish for his party to be consulted 'on broad policy issues and on legislation'. Steel confirmed that he much preferred Callaghan's leadership to a Tory election victory, and he believed that Labour had a chance of winning in late 1978 to 1979. 'As a new Leader and a young man he felt it would be impertinent for him to approach you and he was glad, therefore, to have the opportunity of giving me these views.'[29]

On the late evening of 17 March, after the adjournment motion had been carried by 293 votes (including the Liberals) to none, Callaghan instructed the whips, Michael Foot and Cledwyn Hughes, to establish formal contact with David Steel; they reported to him at 11.30 a.m. on Friday, 18 March, along with Roy Mason, the Northern Irish Secretary.[30] Extensive soundings followed during the weekend. One important episode was a phone call to William Rodgers from Peter Jenkins of the *Guardian*. Rodgers then phoned David Steel and eventually the Prime Minister (unusually), late on Sunday evening. The message that Rodgers conveyed was that there was agreement between Labour and the Liberals on every issue other than the adoption of PR in the European elections. The decisive contact, clearly, would be that between Callaghan and the youthful leader of the Liberals, David Steel. There was indeed a kind of personal link between them. Callaghan had stayed with Mrs Steel's parents during his visit to Sierra Leone in 1946.

The first manœuvres were unpromising. Steel's initial letter to Callaghan setting out the Liberals' terms infuriated the Prime Minister, who flung it angrily on the floor. Tom McCaffrey and Kenneth Stowe, the only others present, retrieved the letter and persuaded the premier to calm down. Thereafter the outlines of a political pact emerged in the course of that afternoon. There was even a suggestion that Steel himself might at some stage become a Cabinet minister.[31] Callaghan saw Steel alone at 6 p.m. on Monday, 21 March (on returning from his regular haircut appointment at Simpson's in the Strand). The meeting was friendly; Callaghan, much the older man, was warm, almost paternal, towards the boyish Liberal leader. This was followed up by meetings with Foot and Steel at 12.30 p.m. and again at 6 p.m. the next day, followed by another meeting of Callaghan with Steel and his deputy John Pardoe at 7.45 p.m. Even though he and Pardoe were hardly blood brothers, Steel announced that he could carry his small force with him, and the famous Lib–Lab pact came into being.[32]

It contained four main proposals. There would be a consultative committee between the two parties to which any major departmental bill would be referred. There would be regular meetings between the Chancellor and the Liberal economic spokesman John Pardoe. On policy there was agreement on direct elections to the European Parliament, with a free vote on the voting system (though the Liberals wanted PR, and were to 'reaffirm their strong conviction' on its behalf), and a commitment to inject momentum into the flagging cause of Welsh and Scottish devolution, with two separate measures to replace the original bill. A Liberal demand that there should be no further nationalization proposals was set on one side. Subject to these conditions, the Liberals would vote to ensure that the government would not fall in the House of Commons, while keeping their options open on matters of detail.[33]

At midday on the 23rd, the day of the motion of confidence, an emergency meeting of the Cabinet was held. Callaghan, according to Benn, was very flushed, Michael Foot white and drawn. For all the tension of the occasion, however, Callaghan appears to have imposed his authority with remarkable effect. Kenneth Stowe later regarded his as 'a virtuoso performance', comparable to his handling of the Cabinet meetings during the IMF talks.[34] The Prime Minister told his colleagues of the pact with the Liberals. There was no alternative since the vote of confidence would otherwise be lost. A general election had been pencilled in for 5 May. Tony Benn was furious in his opposition, not least because he believed he had been fundamentally misled by Michael Foot; their relationship deteriorated substantially from that time on. But the pact was supported by Healey (who said that a deal with 'Nats and nutters' was the only alternative), Shirley Williams, Mulley, Hattersley, Booth (a left-winger influenced by Foot), Mason, Owen, Elwyn-Jones, Rees, Varley, Dell, Morris, Rodgers, Silkin, Ennals, Lever, and Peart. In the end the Cabinet endorsed the pact by 20 to 4 (Shore, Orme, Benn, and, rather surprisingly, Millan, the centrist Scottish Secretary). Benn then had a strong exchange with Callaghan. His signature had appeared on a left-wing letter organized by Eric Heffer, which denounced any deal with the Liberals as a betrayal of socialist principles. Callaghan responded bluntly that, if Benn signed the letter, he would be dismissed. After earnest discussions with Heffer, Foot, and his wife Caroline, Benn then withdrew his signature, and stayed, against his convictions, in the government.[35] In the event, the government survived the vote of confidence with some ease. The motion of no confidence was defeated by 322 votes to 298, with all thirteen Liberals voting for the government, and three Ulster Unionists, including Enoch Powell, abstaining. The Callaghan administration's lease of life was substantially extended.

The Lib–Lab pact was the essential political corollary to the recent economic success. In July, Steel was to confirm that it would be renewed by the Liberals for the whole of the next parliamentary session. In all, it lasted from March 1977 to August 1978 when the Liberals, by now much divided in counsels, decided to bring it to an end. However evocative of smoke-filled rooms the pact had been, it was an event of considerable political significance. It enabled the Labour government to remain in power with a reasonable expectation of life. It could probably call an election at a moment favourable to the government rather than being harried out of office in the wake of a untidy revolt by miscellaneous backbench fragments. In late June Bernard Donoughue analysed on behalf of the Policy Unit the new situation that had opened up. He wrote to the Prime Minister on 23 June, following further by-election setbacks including the loss of Ashfield, a solid Labour seat in the East Midlands, on 29 April with a 20.9 per cent swing to the Conservatives after David Marquand's departure to Brussels. That meant that the government could count on a tally of 323 votes—310 Labour (including Gerry Fitt but excluding the Nationalist Frank Maguire and Reg Prentice) and 13 Liberals. He might reasonably have included the 3 Plaid Cymru members as well. The Opposition at best could manage 310 (including all the SNP but excluding Maguire). That meant the government was virtually assured of surviving until the end of that parliament. There was now a real prospect of having time to wait for the effects of economic recovery, including a fall in prices and higher take-home pay, to show themselves. Public expenditure could be increased, reflation would boost the economy through higher purchasing power, and the fruits of recovery could be redistributed in the inner cities, and amongst the poor and unemployed. The Lib–Lab pact had created a moment of opportunity.[36]

That was not, of course, how everyone saw it. The Conservatives, naturally, denounced it as a cynical fix, devoid of principle, to keep the government lurching on in office though not in power. The Liberals themselves had divided counsels, with a broad spread of ideological opinion in the party and disappointment that they had not been able to impose PR in the European elections. On the Labour left, there was deep anger. Eric Heffer was foremost in circulating letters of protest and leading movements of dissent which continued reverberating until the summer, with (it was believed) the covert sympathy of Ron Hayward, Geoff Bish, and others in Transport House.[37] Tony Benn regarded it as a great betrayal.[38] Nor did all aspects of the pact develop straightforwardly. While most meetings of ministers with their Liberal counterparts were friendly and civilized, the high-decibel encounters of Denis Healey with John Pardoe, two highly combustible characters, reverberated down the corridors of Westminster. Joel Barnett had to sweep up the mess.[39]

But the pact stuck. Much was owed to the good relationship between Callaghan himself and Steel; the latter considered the Prime Minister to be 'first and foremost a patriot'.[40] Apart from personal courtesies, there can be little doubt that the main advantage of the pact lay strongly with the Labour government. Callaghan had given very little away: powers of consultation and co-operation did not amount to a veto. PR on European elections had been set on one side for the moment, although it remained a continuing difficulty: on 7 June Steel urged Callaghan in vain that the government should make a positive recommendation in favour of PR rather than leave it to a free vote.[41] Otherwise, the government's essential industrial and economic strategy could proceed as before. The one exception was the Local Authority Works Bill, the government's 'last piece of doctrinaire legislation' according to *The Economist*,[42] about which Callaghan had no positive feelings anyway. David had given Goliath a lifeline. The big battalions would continue undeterred, their parliamentary flank secured for as long as anyone could foresee.

One delicate issue which could have caused difficulty was allowed to remain dormant. This was the homosexual relationship of the former Liberal leader Jeremy Thorpe with Norman Scott. Harold Wilson had allowed himself to be implicated in what he regarded as a matter of security involving South African 'dirty tricks' against Thorpe; in February or March 1976 he apparently obtained from Barbara Castle, then at Social Security, the file on Scott's employment by Thorpe some fifteen years earlier. There were many rumours in Westminster about the affair (legal action against Thorpe was probable and David Steel and his party profoundly hoped that it would take place after the next general election). But the connection with Harold Wilson (and also Marcia Williams) remained hidden from public gaze, while in any case Callaghan himself had not even the remotest involvement in the curious behaviour of his former leader.[43]

In return the Liberals had gained minor concessions on a European assembly and devolution. Otherwise they had only the seductive whiff of marginal participation of government to console them after sixty-two years of isolation, apart from wartime and briefly in 1931–2. But there was the prospect of some form of extended Lib–Lab collaboration as in the 1906 parliament, albeit with a totally different balance of power, for which scholar-publicists like David Marquand had long called. Indeed, Marquand's massive and distinguished biography of Ramsay MacDonald which appeared in February 1977 was widely taken as an argument for the Progressive alliance on pre-1914 lines to be disinterred—probably correctly since Marquand was to move on to the SDP and the Liberal Democrats before joining Tony Blair's 'progressive' New Labour again in 1994. Politicians like Shirley Williams and William Rodgers who became Liberal Democrats in the later 1980s looked back to the Lib–Lab pact of 1977–8 as a creative and successful period of stable government that provided them with respectable political ancestry. Whether the pact implied the seeds of an SDP in the making, though, is highly debatable. What it did was to renew Old Labour and give it a credibility it had lacked since the election of 1966.

Fortified by the pact and continuing positive news in the financial columns of the newspapers, the government entered upon a cheerful and almost buoyant summer. Callaghan's own prestige at home and abroad rose substantially. His political troubles behind him, he looked and sounded like a statesman. There was only one incidental problem that troubled him. This was a very odd case, when he was attacked for nepotism and patronage in making his son-in-law Peter Jay ambassador to the United States in May 1977. This was, for once, not handled too well by the usually infallible Tom McCaffrey in the press office who let slip remarks to the effect that Sir Peter Ramsbotham, the present man in Washington, was a snobbish, effete fuddy-duddy. The *Evening Standard* ran the ineffable headline, 'Snob Envoy Had to Go'.[44] Callaghan had to intervene directly both to affirm his faith in Ramsbotham's qualities and also to defend McCaffrey's integrity as a public servant. Callaghan had the highest opinion of Peter Jay's abilities. He had previously considered him for a transfer from the world of the media to a political post, either as political adviser at 10 Downing Street, or indeed as a kind of economic adviser in the Washington embassy around the turn of the year. A proposal that he should 'join the team' as economic adviser had been made during the Christmas period, but Jay declined.[45] As has been seen, Callaghan's famous speech to the Labour Party conference on 28 September 1976 contained a key passage written privately by Jay himself.

However, the idea that he should actually become ambassador in Washington came from the new youthful Foreign Secretary David Owen, who was also a good friend and occasional sailing companion. Jay was summoned to the Foreign Office during April and, to his astonishment, offered the new post. Owen pressed Callaghan (who at first turned the idea down), in a handwritten note as early as 17 March when Owen himself had been at the Foreign Office for less than a month. Jay would be 'an impressive new appointment' and the Prime Minister need not be worried by accusations because the new ambassador was married to his daughter Margaret.[46]

Callaghan himself gave it much thought and discussed the proposal with President Carter on 6 May. He was warned against it by the Cabinet Office. In addition to laying himself open to charges of nepotism, there were doubts whether Peter Jay, whose background lay in the individual enterprise of journalism, had the managerial capacity to run a large embassy. But eventually Callaghan went along with the appointment, not least because of the crucial economic aspect of the Anglo-American relationship where Peter Jay's expertise would be invaluable. Jay himself had also to consider the matter, and talked it over with his head at London Weekend Television, John Freeman, a former parliamentary colleague of

Callaghan's and a one-time ambassador to Washington himself. Margaret Jay was not wholly enthusiastic, in part because of the disruption to the children's schooling.[47] But in the end Jay agreed to accept. Owen then announced the appointment to the diplomatic correspondents of the press on 11 May where it had a hostile reception. The charge of nepotism was thrown freely at Callaghan. American journalists came up with jibes such as 'The son-in-law also rises'. There were vicious attacks from some Labour MPs against both Callaghan and Owen, the latter shortly to be devastated by a very serious illness to his young son. But it passed by and in fact Peter Jay was to prove a capable and unusually numerate ambassador with his skill in economic matters supplemented by much political artistry in handling the Washington political and press Mafia.

Callaghan's summer was a cheerful one, the best he had known for many years. It was crowned by a highly successful hosting of a visit from the new US President Jimmy Carter on 5–7 May. This was followed by the Third World Economic Summit chaired by Callaghan and held in 10 Downing Street on 7–9 May with the heads of government of the United States, France, Germany, Italy, Canada, and Japan represented, and then by a meeting of the North Atlantic Council at Lancaster House on 10 May.[48] All these events were highly successful. As will be seen in the next chapter, Callaghan had already taken pains to cultivate the new American President, notably in a visit to Washington in March and in many subsequent communications. His first appearance in Britain was a most congenial occasion. The highlight was a visit by President and Prime Minister to Durham and the north-east. The President, a warm admirer of the poetry of Dylan Thomas (on whose behalf he successfully pressed the cause of a commemorative plaque in Westminster Abbey), had, it was believed, originally wanted to visit south Wales. But this was deemed to be unacceptable, perhaps because of bias shown by a prime minister who held a Welsh seat.

Carter's visit to Newcastle in brilliantly sunny weather proved to be a huge success.[49] He received the freedom of the city: the Mayor told him that, born a Georgian, Carter had become a Geordie. On the way to Newcastle, Callaghan instructed the President in the famous Newcastle United football cry, 'Hawa' the Lads!' and this went down exceptionally well in the vast Geordie gathering. The merry refrain of the 'Blaydon Races' was omnipresent. Callaghan presented him with a volume of autobiography by that fine old representative of the Durham mining community Jack Lawson, a member of Attlee's Cabinet for a time when Callaghan had first entered parliament, and this was evidently read on the flight home. Carter indeed had plenty of varied reading matter for his return journey since Tony Benn, who was unable to meet him, gave him an inscribed pamphlet he himself had written on the seventeenth-century Levellers and their contribution to democracy. He hoped that it might help the President to reach correct conclusions on current events, including on nuclear policy.[50]

The Downing Street summit was an even more effective event for the Prime Minister, the chairman and genial host, with ample photo opportunities. It was said that the French were angry with the press attention for Callaghan and the suggestion that an English-based summit, conducted in the English language, had been more effective than one held on French soil.[51] There was a general feeling that it had been very productive, more so than its predecessors at Rambouillet or Puerto Rico. In particular, Callaghan seized the opportunity himself of pressing the cause, dear to his heart, of international action to promote economic expansion in the west. Each major government committed itself to specific targets for the stimulation of growth and an attack on unemployment, without lapsing into protectionism. There was also a firmer commitment to assist aid levels and loan programmes for the development of the third world.[52] Potential storms, usually arising from the lack of compatibility of Schmidt and Carter over nuclear fuel policy and other issues, had all been happily averted.

After this series of major events, the summer continued to go well. There were no gloomy financial headlines, and no threat to sterling now that the decision over the sterling balances had been resolved. In fact, the attractiveness of sterling now that the economy was improving meant that the balances stayed distinctly higher than had been anticipated that summer and autumn. But this did not cause any international concern.[53] On the political front, discussions with the National Executive continued to be often unpleasant, notably when in late May the report of Reg Underhill, the former national agent, showed clear evidence of Trotskyist 'entryism', notably by Militant Tendency, into local constituency parties. On this occasion Michael Foot led the cry that there should be no witch-hunt, adding that there had always been Marxists in the Labour Party and citing the historic judgement of Clement Attlee to this effect.[54] No action, therefore, was taken against left-wing infiltration. A scourge remained for Callaghan, Foot, and the rest of the leadership in future years. At the parliamentary level, things were now much quieter. The pact with the Liberals was renewed for another year, and the recess was reached in a tranquil mood. The Prime Minister could enjoy a variety of events to celebrate the Queen's silver jubilee as a monarch. One that had a particular emotional poignancy for him was attendance at his native city of Portsmouth on the royal yacht *Britannia* on 27 June to witness the naval review at Spithead. Sixty-five years earlier his father had been a rigger aboard the royal yacht of the day, the *Victoria and Albert*, when King George V had presided.[55] Then the Prime Minister retired to Ringmer for a somewhat fragmented leisure period punctuated by a variety of visits from foreign dignitaries including Dr Kurt Waldheim and Cyrus Vance, the US Secretary of State.

That summer, the economic recovery seemed to go on and on. Sterling continued to rise to over $1.80. Indeed the government was shortly to take action to prevent its rising still further and thereby harming the performance of British exports. The Bank of England sold sterling for dollars in large quantities, but the pound continued to rise to $1.90 and beyond. In November Healey decided to allow it to float for a time, to avoid a possible rise in interest rates. The reserves reached a record level of $14.85 bn. by mid-September with a steady increase in demand for the pound. The very rapid inflow of sterling, indeed, caused some anxiety in the Policy Unit. Bernard Donoughue argued the case for lowering interest rates to slow it down; Gavyn Davies suggested a cap of around $1.75 on the value of the pound. Donoughue pointed out that, despite the government's intended policy of winding up sterling's role as a reserve currency, the sterling balances had actually risen by no less than $2 bn. since the start of the year, and the IMF became more concerned.[56] Shares on the stock exchange reached an unprecedentedly high level on 14 September, with the *FT* 30-share index standing at 592.2. This was 5.6 per cent higher than the previous record in May 1972 at the height of the unstable Barber boom. The balance of payments was steadier than for a decade. It moved from a deficit of £511m. in the third quarter of 1976 to a surplus of £483m. in the third quarter of 1977. August saw the largest ever surplus in one month at £316m.[57] The current account was in surplus for five months running from August to December. In January, it was announced that Britain had had a trade surplus for the year 1977, the first that decade.[58]

These abstract statistics were being translated now into terms that the ordinary citizen could appreciate. As opinion polls showed, what a later generation would call a 'feel-good factor' was at work. Interest on home loans, once in double figures, went down to 8.5 per cent in January. With the assistance of the Price Commission, prices were now manifestly falling, as they had not done for some years. Inflation in January 1978 was in single figures; the RPI showed that at 9.9 per cent it was at its lowest since the price explosion of October 1973 in the days of the Heath government. The Chancellor's autumn budget in October offered also a major reflation of £1 bn. in the current year and £2.2 bn. in the next. Increases in tax allowances and rise in public spending amounted to 'a considerable recovery in real take-home pay and personal consumption' for 1978, according to the *Financial Times*.[59] The Policy Unit, which had been arguing the case for a £3 bn. reflationary package, noted that higher tax allowances would be more advantageous for the poorly paid as well as being popular with higher income groups which had 'suffered a massive reduction in their living standards in the past two years'.[60] The ordinary citizen found himself with higher take-home pay, lower prices, and falling unemployment—an almost unbeatable recipe. Not surprisingly, for the first time the government found the opinion polls at long last beginning to move its way. In December 1977 there was actually a Labour lead of 0.5 per cent recorded, although things began to slip again in the new year. Even so, there were reasonable grounds for believing that the Prime Minister could now consider possible dates for a general election.

The economy at this time was benefiting from more cheerful global circumstances, Britain's recovery being in some measure part of a worldwide economic revival in the major industrial nations. But it was also benefiting from a more flexible course of policy. The economic seminars chaired by the Prime Minister were in full swing that autumn and ranged over a variety of central issues. Callaghan himself noted three excellent meetings on 28 October, 22 November, and 8 December: 'Harold Lever wrote a series of perceptive commentaries on Interest Rates, the Gilt-Edged Market, the decline of the dollar (and the need for a co-operative money system) in which I agreed with him.'[61] Denis Healey believed that these meetings stemmed in part from the Prime Minister's long-developed sense of distrust about the Treasury and its philosophy, but he felt that they nevertheless were helpful in keeping No. 10 and the Treasury in close touch. Callaghan himelf felt they offered a forum to discuss the future of sterling in the longer term beyond the Chancellor's preoccupation with day-to-day management. At the top at any rate, there was harmony in economic management.[62]

At all points the role of the Prime Minister was central. SuperJim seemed to be replacing the legendary SuperMac. Like his Tory predecessor, he was enjoying the job as well as apparently doing it well. He had been the key figure at the start of the summer in negotiating with the TUC Economic Committee for a continuance of pay restraint. This time it was much more difficult than in 1975 or 1976, with Congress having urged the return to free collective bargaining. The TUC Committee as a whole was almost intractable, consisting as it did of a wide variety of members including irreconcilable left-wingers such as Alan Fisher of NUPE. On the other hand, more common sense was likely to come from Len Murray, the pragmatic TUC general secretary, as well as the trade union members of NEDC. They included the two major figures of Jack Jones and Hugh Scanlon, both close to retirement, along with other moderate figures such as Alf Allen of the Shopworkers, David Basnett, and Geoffrey Drain. They persuaded the TUC Committee to issue a remarkably moderate statement on 19 July, which called for the avoidance of a pay explosion and emphasized the adverse consequences for inflation if pay increases went above 10 per cent. In the circumstances this was quite as much as the government could have hoped for.[63] Meanwhile, possible compromises were being floated. Gavyn Davies of the Policy Unit suggested the indexation of wage claims to meet the acknowledged recent drop in take-home pay. Relating wages to the domestic price index rather than the RPI would, he argued, be much safer and less potentially inflationary. It would be less affected by the global economy.[64] At the 1977 TUC annual congress at Blackpool at the start of September the Economic Committee's pronouncement of 19 July in favour of a renewal of the 'twelve-month rule' on pay claims was endorsed by nearly 3 million votes. Even though free collective bargaining was also reaffirmed, an essential component of the fight against inflation and on behalf of economic recovery had been achieved once again.

There was much debate amongst advisers at this point as to what economic and, ultimately, political conclusions the Prime Minister should draw. In general, the Think Tank tended to be cautious, even pessimistic, the Policy Unit, with its sharper political antennae, more optimistic. On 17 June 1977, Gavyn Davies was able to point to several positive aspects of the development of the economy which left room for much net fiscal reflation over coming months and years. He outlined the prospect of successive reflationary budgets with income tax basic rate being reduced to even 15 per cent by 1982, a heady scenario indeed.[65] Bernard Donoughue outlined the case for successive boostings of public spending and cuts in interest rate. It was generally agreed that the general election should be deferred for at least a year. But some time in late 1978 or early 1979 there would be a 'window' when unemployment was falling, the balance of payments was in surplus, inflation was steady, and take-home pay was rising.[66]

Callaghan himself hammered these points home in a series of major addresses to Labour audiences that summer. At an all-Wales rally in Aberystwyth, he went on to outline the more fundamental values for which a social democratic party and movement should strive—democracy (political and industrial), control of size, production for need not for profit, community care for all, neighbourliness, and a new basis for international relations.[67] Throughout that autumn and winter he struck an increasingly confident note. In an interview with Gordon Clough on BBC radio's *The World this Weekend* he described the components of the economic recovery that had continued throughout 1977. It was, he declared confidently, 'the year in which the pendulum has swung our way'.[68]

One fundamental aspect of the growing economic prosperity the Prime Minister somewhat skated over. This was the growing revenue coming in from North Sea oil. This was a massive potential benefit which could add £3–4 bn. to GNP in 1980 and up to £5 bn. in 1985, a huge source of revenue and a vast saving in foreign currency. A major, if predictable, difference of view on this emerged in Cabinet. Denis Healey urged that the oil revenues be used for long-term investment and paying off liabilities; Tony Benn argued the case for national development on behalf of social priorities. A meeting on 9 November 1977, attended by Healey and Derek Scott for the Treasury, and Benn and Frances Morrell for the Energy Department, produced total deadlock. Healey wanted the oil revenue used for tax cuts and debt repayment, Benn wanted to rebuild the manufacturing base. Callaghan decided to handle this in a remarkably Rooseveltian way, by trying to 'weave the two together'. Here was the Prime Minister in presidential mode, as supreme mediator, as FDR had been over tariffs or public works in 1933. Callaghan now asked Healey and Benn to produce a joint paper on the likely extent of the oil revenues and their possible beneficial uses. In strictly impartial terms, he also minuted Tom McNally, 'Please tell Mr. Healey and Mr. Benn that they are both trying to do too much too soon.' Bernard Donoughue, meanwhile, was trying to propose a compromise, not least because of a fear that Benn might otherwise go public and make known his own 'socialist' views.

All this was not without its entertaining aspects, but the outcome was fortunate from Callaghan's point of view. A joint paper signed by Healey and Benn and presented to the Liaison Committee on 21 November merely listed the possible options—overseas investment, foreign debt repayment, and tax reductions on Healey's side, the public services and social infrastructure, investment in manfacturing industry and energy resources on Benn's. It may be suspected that a majority of Labour supporters, many of them far from being on the left, would have taken Benn's side in this dialogue. But, given the balance of power in the Callaghan administration, there could only be one winner. On 16 February 1978, the Cabinet took the view, by a large majority which included Michael Foot, that oil revenue should be absorbed into general revenue and used for general Treasury purposes, which might include capital investment, debt redemption, or perhaps tax cuts.[69] Economics ministers like Harold Lever and Joel Barnett shredded Benn's proposals, for which there was much support in the party in the country. It was another defeat for the Tony Benn 'alternative strategy', a further victory for the Callaghan brand of centrism, as opposed to more interventionist forms of socialism.

In the first part of 1978 the good news continued, although less consistently than in 1977. The focal point of Healey's April budget was a programme of £2 bn. in tax cuts to regenerate a growth of 3 per cent in the economy. This went through although only narrowly. A sum of £1 bn. was repaid to the IMF; Britain had already agreed not to draw on its full entitlement of credits. On 16 June, in one of the last manifestations of the Lib–Lab pact, the Liberals supported the government in their 287 : 282 victory, by backing a package which included a 2.5 per cent surcharge on employers' national insurance contributions to finance a cut in the standard rate of income tax.[70] On the other hand, to counter possible overheating, the minimum lending rate was increased to 7 per cent. On 5 May it went up to 8.75 per cent after strong international pressure on interest rates. There was a deficit on the current account of £170m. in March. But it was followed by a large surplus of £336m. in April,[71] and further surpluses in May and June. The fall in prices was now very evident to the ordinary consumer. Callaghan told the Commons on 6 June that a level of 7 to 8 per cent inflation should be sustained for some time before falling again. There were many signs of a growth in consumer spending and much buoyancy in house purchase, that popular icon of private affluence, cheap credit, and upward mobility, despite rises in interest rates. Old Labour Britain had never had it so good.

Most of the political cards now seemed in the government's hands. They had had a long fifteen-month run of remarkably good news, free from the banana skins that seemed so regularly to disturb the various Harold Wilson governments. The government seemed competent, honest, and scandal-free. No spy stories or slag mountains now to dent its prestige. The opinion polls, though volatile, offered much better reading with Tories and Labour within range of each other. In a potentially tricky by-election in Scotland on 2 June, in Hamilton, the scene of a famous Scottish Nationalist victory back in 1967, the Labour candidate easily defeated the SNP representative.

The Prime Minister himself regularly scored well in pollings of the voters, easily surpassing Mrs Thatcher every time. His television and radio interviews struck the right balance between prudence and optimism. Cledwyn Hughes noted the Prime Minister's high reputation in all quarters. On 23 February 1978 Denis Healey was conveying 'high praise of Jim Callaghan with whom he gets on well'.[72] On 2 March he was having a friendly lunch with Tony Benn, with whom he had an ancestral bond in view of their common nonconformist background, and for whose father he had a strong regard. 'He praised Jim Callaghan, comparing him favourably with Harold Wilson. Everyone is praising Jim. I hope it does not go to his head.'[73] Others on the Labour side entertained the same hopes and fears after it was reported (in fact, totally misreported) that Peter Jay, the new ambassador in Washington, had compared his father-in-law the Prime Minister to none less than Moses. Mrs Thatcher, in a laboured joke provided for her by Sir Ronald Millar, responded in her speech to the Conservative Party Conference by urging Moses to 'keep taking the tablets'. (According to Alan Watkins, she herself would have preferred the more entertaining, though perhaps more *risqué*, joke, 'Keep taking the pill'.[74])

In fact, the Moses story was misunderstood and actually makes the reverse point. Callaghan was the last person to allow economic good news and political omens to go to his head. In conversation with Peter Jay in a walk along the South downs at Firle Beacon, the Prime Minister had indeed compared himself to Moses, but as a leader who set changes in train but might yet fail to see the promised land.[75] He well knew that the prospects for the longer term were still uncertain. On the surface, it might have seemed in the cheerful summer of 1978 as though things were moving his way, economically and politically, and that it was simply a matter of choosing the most suitable time for the next election for the reward to be his. In fact, there were many difficulties. The experience of being the head of a minority government was a constant strain, despite the bolstering effect of the Lib–Lab pact. Parliamentary embarrassments continued. As late as May 1978 there were two defeats on the committee stage of the Finance Bill. In the first, on 9 May, the government failed to carry its provisions on income tax, when the Ulster Unionists voted with the Conservatives to cut the basic rate of income tax by 1 per cent. On 11 May it was the Scottish Nationalists in this variegated Commons who joined in defeating the government over the level of higher tax rates being raised to £8,000.[76]

One difficulty here was the renewed tension that developed between the Prime Minister and his old Cardiff comrade, the Speaker, George Thomas. There were many points of friction between the two. This was reflected in 1985 in Thomas's memoirs (when he had become Lord Tonypandy) in which harsh observations are made about Callaghan, Foot, and Cledwyn Hughes amongst others, and some constitutionally improper revelations made about confidential discussions behind the Speaker's chair. The tension between Speaker and government ministers had begun early on, in 1976. Thomas had declared the government's Aircraft and Shipbuilding Bill to be a hybrid measure which thus required special parliamentary procedure. The Speaker believed that Callaghan 'never forgave him' after that.[77] Callaghan later took fierce issue with the Speaker's decision on Standing Order 9 (in relationship to British Leyland) on 1 March and called out loudly 'Bad! Bad!' He wrote privately, 'Not even our friendship can prevent me from saying that your S.O.9 decision was bad and should never have been given.' In effect, Callaghan had been compelled, so he felt, to make a statement before he had had enough time to consider the matter. 'I've often heard Speakers recognise that Govts. have rights too—not to be hurried when important issues are at stake—for which they carry the responsibility not the House.'[78] In November 1977 Callaghan complained that while it had been agreed that the Prime Minister should answer in the House questions which 'raise wider and important issues', indirect questions to him had increased and multiplied.[79] There was some sign of coolness between the clerk of the house and the government whips.[80] Relations were later patched up somewhat, but many ministers felt that 'Brother George' in the Speaker's chair had become another cross they had to bear.

The Prime Minister, however, had political troubles of a more basic kind. Despite sniping from left-wingers on the National Executive, the party conference of 1977 was a more serene affair with the government's economic policy given a somewhat grudging endorsement, pay restraint and all. Barbara Castle, somewhat unexpectedly, made a helpful and conciliatory speech. The Prime Minister was in relative control. Tony Benn noted that, while his speech contained 'the old economic nonsense', he got a standing ovation.[81] It was perhaps the last occasion in Labour Party history when the old trade union barons were still comfortably in charge of the conference and supportive of the leadership. A particular influence at this time was David Basnett of the Municipal Workers. He told Tony Benn on 28 September of his long friendship with Callaghan, whom he described (wrongly) as Labour's first working-class leader. Benn responded in similar vein: 'I get on with him extremely well. I much prefer him to Harold.'[82] Among other things, this conversation suggests that it would have been unwise for the Prime Minister to give the impression of taking the proud and hypersensitive David Basnett too casually.

But these genial sentiments could not conceal the growing rift throughout this period between grass-roots hard-left constituency activists and a moderate leadership. The decision not to open the Pandora's box of the Underhill report on 'entryism' was a sign of the potential conflict that lay within. Callaghan had ample experience of it in his own Cardiff constituency where Militant or other Trotskyist spokesmen such as Andrew Price and Terry Burns continued their attacks on him, which all Jack Brooks's watchfulness was needed to repel. The importance of left-wing MPs critical of the goverment was likely to be more damaging now that the Liberals, after much heart-searching, had decided to end the eighteen-month pact at the end of the summer of 1978. John Pardoe and others of their members had never been enthusiastic. The final straw was the failure to have proportional representation made the basis of the European Assembly elections in 1979. On the other hand, Callaghan had continued to confide in Steel and to treat the younger man with kindness and apparent consideration. They had, for instance, held discussions on possible election dates, which Steel believed would result in an autumn general election in 1978.[83]

There was even more potential trouble from the unions. Grass-roots protests against pay restraint, voiced by shop stewards in the car industry and by public sector workers, were growing. The prospect of firm leadership to hold them in check was doubtful with the simultaneous retirement of the two giants of the left, Jack Jones and Hugh Scanlon. The succession to Jack Jones of Moss Evans, a wordy Welshman who resisted attempts for the Transport Workers' executive to impose central control on branch activists, was worrying to the Labour leaders. Still, on the whole, the TUC guidelines and moderation prevailed during the winter and there were no damaging strikes.

One alarming exception was a strike by the Union of Fire Brigades which had put in a claim for a pay rise of 30 per cent and a forty-two-hour working week. Callaghan took charge of events personally. He had a tense meeting with Terry Parry, the general secretary, and the rest of his union executive, on 29 November. Here he pointed out the need to fight inflation; a settlement for the firemen could not be isolated from pay rises and comparability formulae for other workers. He urged that the firemen negotiate with the local authorities on the old formula with 'a specially guaranteed position' for the FBU.[84] The discussion ended with Callaghan's blank observation, 'Your strike will not win. You cannot be allowed to succeed.' Peter Rockley, an FBU executive member, commented on this episode, 'He certainly was the most determined person I had ever met.' The Prime Minister declared, according to Rockley, 'I stand or fall [*sic*] that no one will beat the 10 per cent this year.' As they left, one delegate noted the design of the letters 'J.C.' on the stripe of his suit (in fact a gift from a Yorkshire manufacturer, Moxon's). Did the letters mean 'James Callaghan'? No, responded a Derbyshire delegate, 'Jesus Christ'.[85] The firemen's strike went on until the end of January. The government, with memories of the Heath government in mind, refrained from having a state of emergency but sought to break the strike by the use of 20,000 troops as firemen and the use of 'green goddess' emergency fire engines.[86] In the end the firemen went back to work at the end of January with the forty-two-hour week achieved but not the pay increase they had demanded. On a snowy day in Bridlington, Terry Parry faced firemen chanting 'no surrender' who then punched and injured him.[87] But, thanks in large measure to the Prime Minister personally, the government's thin red line on pay restraint had just about held.

Throughout this period, the Callaghan government, which rested on maintaining a close relationship with the unions, faced the dilemma that these unions were increasingly an object of unpopularity and even fear. The great strikes (many unofficial) and almost uncontrolled pay claims of the period from 1970 to 1975 had seeped into the popular consciousness, despite the efforts of Jack Jones and others to achieve restraint thereafter. Strikes seemed more aggressive and socially irresponsible. The ability of hitherto little-regarded groups of workers, such as the water workers for instance, to use industrial muscle to promote their economic objectives caused much anxiety. Secondary picketing in particular had appeared as a new terror since Arthur Scargill's flying pickets in 1972. The public mood changed as a result.

One defining event of this period was the Grunwick strike in the summer of 1977. This arose in the Grunwick Film Processing Laboratories in north London, when an Anglo-Indian entrepreneur, George Ward, refused to allow his largely Asian and female workforce to join the white-collar union APEX. A mass picket developed with strong TUC support. The unions involved in the Grunwick dispute had the most powerful of cases. What Ward was doing was inequitable if not openly illegal. The workforce were only claiming standard rights of union membership and representation. The unions and union leaders involved, Roy Grantham of APEX and Tom Jackson of the Postal Workers, were impeccably moderate. The three government ministers who joined pickets outside the Grunwick works, Shirley Williams, Fred Mulley, and Denis Howell, were regarded as being on Labour's right wing. Yet in the end what lodged in the popular consciousness was not the legal niceties or considerations of social or moral justice, but the extreme violence with which the mass picketing of Grunwick was attended. There were attacks on Grunwick vehicles and on the police. Trotskyist and other left-wing groups not related to the Grunwick company in any way joined in mob action. A young policeman, lying in the road in a pool of blood, made bad news in the press. George Ward's brand of industrial tyranny escaped unscathed. Grunwick became not a fight for workers' rights but a symbol of mob rule and the uncontrolled threat from trade union power.

Similarly, the public took notice when Sam Silkin, the Attorney-General, declined to take any action when the Union of Postal Workers illegally refused in a week of action to handle mail for South Africa. The unions seemed above the law and to be treated as such by the government's law officer. They, like employers, governments, and monarchs in the past, had apparently ignored Sir Edward Coke's famous dictum in the reign of James I, 'Be you ever so great, the law is above you.' Silkin himself in the case of *Gouriet* v. *Union of Post Office Workers* was strongly criticized to this effect from the bench by the Lord Chief Justice, Lord Denning.

The Callaghan government, therefore, entered a crucial period in the summer of 1978. It faced potential trouble from the unions, from their residual supra-legal power and more immediately their pressure to end curbs on pay. For his part, the Prime Minister insisted that a fourth year of pay restraint, modified in specific directions but overall conforming to a fixed norm, was essential. In private conversations with officials in early 1978 he was talking in terms of a 5 per cent pay norm for 1978–9, half of that agreed with the TUC in July 1977. Healey believed that something more flexible, such as a 'single figure' norm which with wage drift would have meant around 10 per cent, was greatly preferable. Hardly anyone believed that the TUC would accept it. Len Murray believed it was all the result of the Prime Minister's giving in to his 'pretensions to intellectualism' rather than relying on his gut instinct about the unions as he had done in the past.[88] Yet in the summer of 1978 it seemed as if the Prime Minister was about to make a public declaration and to make a further stringent limitation of wage increases a pivot of his policy. It seemed a high-risk strategy.

On the other hand, his position was now a relatively strong one. He was the master of a successful Cabinet which had presided over a lengthy period of economic success. The political prospects were looking much more hopeful, and the Tories were still uncertain. Mrs Thatcher was making little impact so far as Opposition leader. In a potentially difficult debate on pay policy on 25 July, Callaghan tore into her on a variety of issues, including her views on an incomes policy, devolution, and immigration, which he claimed were the product of racial prejudice. Mrs Thatcher's reply, according to the *Financial Times* whose reporter was sympathetic to Callaghan, was 'nervous and faltering'. No Iron Maiden here.[89] Later on he was to launch a pre-emptive strike on the young Winston Churchill when he ventured to raise the issue of the coal industry. The Prime Minister countered with an aggressive and carefully considered attack on his grandfather's sending in the troops to Tonypandy. He condemned the Churchills' 'family vendetta against the miners'.[90] Historians queued up to intervene in *The Times* correspondence columns, most of them supportive of Callaghan's view. As a personality, he commanded the House and, many believed, commanded the country. There was another important dimension. Since April 1976 he had added substantially to his reputation by his apparent statesmanship in international affairs, foreign and colonial, as no prime minister had done since Macmillan's heyday. At home and abroad, his stature had grown. As he returned to Cardiff in warm sunshine in early August, to enjoy the 'blue riband' choral competition at the national eisteddfod, held that year in Sophia Gardens, he might feel that the electoral prize, too, was there for the winning.

1. e.g. Ivor Crewe and Anthony King, *SDP: The Birth, Life and Death of the Social Democratic Party* (Oxford, 1995), ch. 1.
2. *The Times*, 31 Dec. 1976.
3. *Financial Times*, 29 Jan. 1977.
4. Ibid., 10 Jan. 1977.
5. Ibid. 1 Apr. 1977; Kingsley Jones to Nigel Wicks, 8 Feb. 1977 (Callaghan Papers, box 9).
6. Douglas Jay, *Sterling: A Plea for Moderation* (London, 1985), 162.
7. Telephone conversation between Callaghan and Schmidt, 16 Mar. 1977, T59A/77 (Callaghan Papers, box 33).
8. Healey, *The Time of my Life*, 433.
9. *Financial Times*, 13 Jan. 1977.
10. Jones, *Union Man*, 314; interview with Jack Jones.
11. Jones, *Union Man*, 314; interview with Helmut Schmidt.
12. Donoughue memo, 'Meeting with Lord Bullock' (PU 223), 26 Oct. 1976; Donoughue memo, 'Industrial Democracy' (PU 243), 21 Dec. 1976 (private papers). Interview with Lord Murray of Epping Forest.
13. Jones, *Union Man*, 314–15; information from Lord Bullock and Lady Williams; cf. Shirley Williams, *Politics is for People* (London, 1981), 126 ff., where she draws a distinction between a consultative form of workers' representation in industrial management and the statutory form advocated by Bullock.

14. Interviews with Jack Jones and Lord Callaghan.
15. *Financial Times*, 14 May 1977.
16. Kingsley Jones to Nigel Wicks, 8 Feb. 1977 (Callaghan Papers, box 9).
17. Prentice to Callaghan, Callaghan to Prentice, 16 Dec. 1976 (ibid., uncatalogued).
18. Material in Callaghan Papers, box 9.
19. *Financial Times*, 9, 24 Feb. 1977.
20. *Observer*, 28 Jan. 1996.
21. Interview with Lord Callaghan; and Owen, *Time to Declare*, 256.
22. McNally memo on Mar. 1977 political crisis, ? Apr. 1977 (Callaghan Papers, box 10); Prime Minister's diary, 1977 (ibid., box 35).
23. McNally memo (ibid., box 19).
24. Roy Mason to Callaghan, 23 Mar. 1977 (ibid.).
25. McNally to Callaghan, 23 Mar. 1977 (ibid.); Prime Minister's diary (ibid., box 35).
26. McNally to Callaghan, 23 Mar. 1977 (ibid., box 10).
27. Kenneth Stowe to Callaghan, 18 Mar. 1977 (two letters, ibid., box 19).
28. Information from Lord Cledwyn of Penrhos.
29. Cledwyn Hughes to Callaghan, 17 Mar. 1977 (Callaghan Papers, box 19).
30. McNally memo and Prime Minister's diary, 1977 (ibid., box 35).
31. David Steel, *Against Goliath* (London, 1989), 166–7; Lord Callaghan has confirmed this to me.
32. Prime Minister's diary, 1977 (Callaghan Papers, box 35); *The Times*, 24 Mar. 1977.
33. Text in Callaghan, *Time and Chance*, 456–7.
34. Benn, *Conflicts of Interest*, 86 (23 Mar. 1977); interview with Sir Kenneth Stowe.
35. Benn, *Conflicts of Interest*, 85–95 (23–5 Mar. 1977).
36. Donoughue memo, 'The Government's Strategy' (PU 289), 23 June 1977 (Callaghan Papers, box 9).
37. McNally to Callaghan, 23 Mar. 1977 (ibid., box 10).
38. Benn, *Conflicts of Interest*, 87 (23 Mar. 1977).
39. Healey, *The Time of my Life*, 403, refers (presumably metaphorically) to picking up broken crockery.
40. Steel, *Against Goliath*, 167.
41. Stowe to Hunt, 8 June 1977 (private papers).
42. *The Economist*, 26 Mar. 1977.
43 MS memo by ? on 'The Jeremy Thorpe/Norman Scott Affair', 19 Oct. 1977 (private papers).
44. Interviews with Sir Thomas McCaffrey and Peter Jay; Owen, *Time to Declare*, 322.
45. Peter Jay to Callaghan [addressed 'Dear Grandad'], 10 Jan. 1977 (Callaghan Papers, uncatalogued); interview with Peter Jay.
46. Owen to Callaghan, 17 Mar. 1977 (Callaghan Papers, uncatalogued).
47. Interview with Peter Jay.
48. Prime Minister's diary, 1977 (Callaghan Papers, box 35).
49. *The Times*, 8 May 1977.
50. Callaghan, *Time and Chance*, 482; Benn, *Conflicts of Interest*, 128 (9 May 1977). Jack Lawson's autobiography, *A Man's Life* (London, 1944), was one Callaghan had read around the time of his election to parliament. For Benn's views on the Levellers, see Tony Benn, *Arguments for Socialism*, ed. Chris Mullins (London, 1980), 29–33. He

regularly took part in the annual demonstration each May in Burford, Oxfordshire, to celebrate the Levellers besieged in Burford Church by Cromwell's troops.

51. Benn, *Conflicts of Interest*, 130 (9 May 1977), citing David Owen.

52. Material in Callaghan Papers (uncatalogued) and *Time and Chance*, 484–5.

53. Burk and Cairncross, '*Goodbye Great Britain*', 125–6.

54. Benn, *Conflicts of Interest*, 150–1 (25 May 1977).

55. Callaghan, *Time and Chance*, 461.

56. Memos by Donoughue, 1 July 1977 and 14 Sept. 1977 (PU 285 and 304); memo by Davies, 27 July 1977 (PU 296) (Callaghan Papers, box 9).

57. *Financial Times*, 15 Sept. 1977; *The Economist*, 17 Sept. 1977.

58. Ibid. 17 Jan. 1978.

59. *Financial Times*, 27 Oct. 1977.

60. Donoughue memo for the Prime Minister (PU 306), 26 Sept. 1977 (Callaghan Papers, box 9).

61. Material in Callaghan Papers (uncatalogued).

62. Healey, *The Time of my Life*, 450.

63. *The Times*, 20 July 1977; obituary of Geoffrey Drain, *Guardian*, 7 Apr. 1993.

64. Gavyn Davies to Stowe, 'Pay Policy—an Alternative' (PU 274), 20 May 1977 (private papers).

65. Memo by Gavyn Davies, 'The Medium Term Assessment' (PU 284), 17 June 1977 (Callaghan Papers, box 9).

66. Donoughue memos, 23 June, 6 July 1977 (PU 289) (Callaghan Papers, box 9).

67. Speech text in Callaghan Papers; *The Times*, 4 July 1977.

68. Text of interview in Callaghan Papers, box 12.

69. Benn, *Conflicts of Interest*, 280–1 (16 Feb. 1978).

70. The Liberals were 'incensed' on this point, as is mentioned in Kenneth Stowe to Callaghan, 13 June 1978 (Callaghan Papers, uncatalogued).

71. *Financial Times*, 16 May 1978.

72. Cledwyn Hughes diary, 23 Feb. 1978.

73. Ibid. 2 Mar. 1978.

74. Alan Watkins, *A Conservative Coup* (London, 2nd edn., 1992), 36.

75. Interview with Peter Jay. See letters by Michael Cockerill and Peter Jay in *Spectator*, 9 and 16 May 1992.

76. *The Times*, 10, 12 May 1978.

77. Thomas, *Mr Speaker*, 149.

78. Callaghan to George Thomas, 1 and 8 Mar. 1977 (Lord Tonypandy Papers, National Library of Wales, Aberystwyth, file 126).

79. Draft ruling for Mr Speaker, 1 Nov. 1977 (Tonypandy Papers, file 130).

80. R. D. Barlas to the Speaker, 25 Oct. 1977 (ibid.).

81. Benn, *Conflicts of Interest*, 225 (4 Oct. 1977).

82. Ibid. 219 (28 Sept. 1977).

83. Steel, *Against Goliath*, 175.

84. Record of meeting with executive of Fire Brigades Union, 29 Nov. 1977 (Callaghan Papers, box 9).

85. Victor Bailey (ed.), *Forged in Fire: The History of the Fire Brigades Union* (London, 1992), 253, 420.

86. Keith Jeffery and Peter Hennessy, *States of Emergency* (London, 1983), 241–2.

87. Bailey, *Forged in Fire*, 422. The battered Parry commented afterwards, 'Just think what they would have done to the employers!'

88. Interviews with Lord Healey and Lord Murray of Epping Forest.

89. *Parl. Deb.*, 5th ser., vol. 954, 1379–93 (25 July 1978); *Financial Times*, 26 July 1978. In the vote, the Opposition amendment was lost by 304 to 287, but the motion endorsing government policy was carried by a reduced majority of 296 to 281, with a few Labour left-wingers such as Dennis Skinner, Arthur Lewis, and Arthur Latham abstaining. The Scottish Nationalists and Ulster Unionists voted with the Conservatives; Plaid Cymru abstained; the Liberals and Gerry Fitt of the SDLP voted with the government even though the speech of John Pardoe for the Liberals was generally critical of government policy.

90. On 30 Nov. 1978.

25

INTERNATIONAL HONEST BROKER

ONCE the IMF negotiations had been wound up, James Callaghan turned to his original mission as Prime Minister. This was to focus more on international affairs. Most British Prime Ministers since the war have fancied their skills as global statesmen; for many it had been a welcome release from burdens on the domestic scene. But Callaghan had more justification than most in feeling that he had a special expertise. Foreign affairs, after all, had provided a major thrust of his political career and outlook ever since his wartime experience and his early activities as a backbencher. His time at the Treasury and chairmanship of the Group of Seven had reinforced the international dimension of his view of economic policy-making, while his two years at the Foreign Office had hitherto been the most congenial period of all his time in office. His object now was to devote his long experience of world problems, of Africa, the Middle and Far East, Europe, and the North Atlantic alliance in particular, to maintain momentum in international diplomacy. In particular, he was focused on peacemaking in Rhodesia and the Middle East, on strengthening relations between the western heads of government, and especially on continuing to promote détente with the Soviet Union (and indirectly with China) and the process of strategic arms limitation, already under way. As events turned out, of course, he was inextricably absorbed with Britain's economic problems, his main immediate priority until the conclusion of the IMF negotiations at the end of 1976. But thereafter he threw himself increasingly into international matters. Here he emerged with a stature and authority which surprised many observers of his previous career.

Both the domestic and the international scene had moved on somewhat from what Callaghan had known while at the Foreign Office. In home politics, there was the totally unexpected loss of Tony Crosland in February 1977 and his replacement by the 38-year-old David Owen. Callaghan had a very high opinion of the talents of his new Foreign Secretary with whom his political relationship was excellent. He handled Owen with sensitivity and defended him loyally. He was anxious to give him his head in developing policies of his own, and Owen certainly did so, most notably in pursuing the Anglo-American initiative in Rhodesia. Nevertheless, it was inevitable that, given his seniority and background, Callaghan's domination of the conduct of foreign policy should become the more apparent with the change of Foreign Secretary. In particular, he emerged with the greater authority in high-level summitry with other western leaders in trying to take further the policy of détente with the Soviet Union and arms limitation which gave an apparently more hopeful tone to international relations in the mid-1970s. One central issue of British foreign policy, membership of the European Community, had been settled during Callaghan's tenure at the Foreign Office, as a result of the 1975 referendum. But there was much unfinished business to take forward, especially in the Middle East and in southern Africa, and the next stage of strategic arms limitation was reaching a much more critical phase in the aftermath of the Helsinki Agreement of 1975. Here Callaghan had his own thoughts, and his own unique nexus of strategic alliances with heads of state in NATO and the British Commonwealth.

The major change that affected British approaches to foreign policy stemmed from the 1976 American presidential election. This removed the familiar team of President Gerald Ford and Dr Henry Kissinger, with whom Callaghan and the British had worked so well for the best part of three years. The unavailing economic diplomacy with Washington during the IMF talks in October–November was the last hurrah of this relationship. The Americans' help in eventually removing the problem of the sterling balances showed its continuing potential; the dashing of Callaghan's possible hopes that US assistance might avert recourse to an IMF loan altogether illustrated its limits, quite apart from the intrusion of a presidential election campaign that autumn.

President Jimmy Carter was a new and unknown phenomenon. Callaghan from the outset strove to reach out to the new Democratic President, and with much success. He had a long telephone conversation with him as early as 13 January 1977 when Carter, still Governor of Georgia, had yet to be inaugurated as president. In this, Callaghan emphasized his lifelong commitment to the American alliance and suggested an early meeting. It was decided that Callaghan and his Foreign Secretary (still Crosland at that time) should pay an early visit to the United States, and that the new Vice-President, Walter Mondale, should visit London in March. The initial talks in Washington, which Callaghan visited very early in the new President's administration on 10–12 March 1977, proved to be cordial.[1] The British Prime Minister and the new President shared both a common naval background (Carter had served in the US navy during the Second World War) and an upbringing in the Baptist faith. Callaghan believed, with some justification, that the new administration would prove friendly to the United Kingdom, not least since the new Secretary of State, Cyrus Vance, was a noted Anglophile. The new US ambassador in London, Kingman Brewster, a former president of Yale, originated from the classic mid-Atlantic world of the Ivy League, the English-Speaking Union, and Ditchley Park. Further, Callaghan conceived a strong admiration for Carter's ability as well as his human qualities. He told a somewhat sceptical Helmut Schmidt in March 1977 that the new President had an 'ordered, well-stocked mind' and was 'quite a formidable person to deal with'. At the same time he was, in Callaghan's view, 'straightforward, without too much artifice' and tried to deal with people in 'a straight and level way'.[2] This directness proved helpful later when Callaghan robustly defended the interests of the British aircraft industry in talks with the President, both in asserting the right of Concorde to land in New York, and in backing the use of export credit guarantees to support the sale of Rolls-Royce engines to American aircraft companies. On both issues, he broadly won his point without rancour or resentment coming from the President.

Callaghan never felt quite the same degree of warmth towards Carter that he did towards Gerald Ford: the somewhat reserved nature of Carter's personality and his technocratic outlook may have had something to do with that. But he built up a strong personal link with the new Democratic President too, and gave new life to the somewhat shadowy 'special relationship' beloved of the Foreign Office mandarins. It was also believed on the American side that the relative closeness between Carter and Callaghan served to strengthen the influence in the new administration of Brzezinski, the President's special adviser on national security and a hawkish figure in cold-war diplomacy, as against the much more doveish Secretary of State Cy Vance. As it happened (perhaps illustrating the traditional animosity between Germans and Poles which even Karl Marx had once shared) Schmidt cordially disliked Brzezinski. This may have strengthened the latter's position still further in Carter's eyes.

In general terms, Callaghan sensed that Carter was not immediately at home in foreign affairs. He knew little of Europe and was well aware of his inexperience. On many areas he turned naturally for a second opinion to the wise and knowledgeable head of state in the United Kingdom.

Callaghan, for his part, as he freely confessed later on, 'cultivated' Carter[3] and turned to him for support in areas of mutual concern. He could use leverage by the Americans in putting pressure on the European powers in trying to promote world economic recovery in the lead-up to the Bonn economic summit in 1978. When Callaghan complained that Schmidt and the Germans were being too cautious and too inclined to emphasize the need for monetary stability, he and Carter made common cause. Another useful area of common ground lay in Carter's willingness to support the British in assisting transatlantic crossings by Concorde, the Anglo-French super-airliner which faced hostility from both transportation and environmentalist groups in the United States.

At the same time, Callaghan's closest relationship was still with his fellow European Social Democrat Helmut Schmidt. With Giscard d'Estaing of France his personal dealings were invariably friendly: Nicholas Henderson was much impressed by Callaghan's 'masterful' handling of the French President at Chequers in December 1977. The formal Frenchman rapidly thawed when confronted by a bluff and genial British Prime Minister in a bright blue pullover. They probably achieved a closer rapport at this time than any heads of the British and French governments have managed since the end of the Second World War, with the exception of the Heath–Pompidou relationship. It was underlined by the close interaction of the prime minister's private office under Kenneth Stowe with that of his French opposite number, Jean François-Poncet.[4] At times, Callaghan, Giscard, and Schmidt could form a powerful troika. This was especially apparent in their collaboration on a European airbus project in 1978 in the face of a perceived threat from the US Boeing company to British and European aerospace technology. On the other hand, his relationship with the French President had its limits. Giscard in general felt Callaghan to be too insular and insufficiently 'communitaire'; Callaghan for his part believed Giscard to be too inclined to give way to the French weakness for 'unanchored political speculation'.[5]

With Helmut Schmidt, however, the relationship remained strong, despite sharp differences over international monetary policy and particularly over European monetary union. Throughout his time as Prime Minister, he unburdened himself to his German comrade as to no other world leader. They had nine private sessions of meetings in Britain or in Germany during Callaghan's three years of premiership, quite apart from many other meetings at international gatherings across the world.[6] Schmidt was liable to sink into periods of Teutonic gloom but Callaghan usually had the skill to persuade him to unwind and collaborate. This was especially the case in getting him to build bridges with President Carter with whom, as will be seen, he had many difficult passages. In fact, Schmidt never lost his lack of regard, amounting to something near contempt, for Carter's erratic and sometimes treacherous behaviour as he saw it, on issues including variously nuclear fuel policy, the neutron bomb, the Americans' failure to stabilize their economy or currency, or the handling of human rights issues. As noted above, he also much disliked the Polish-American Brzezinski. Worse was to follow after Callaghan left office with fierce US–European disputes over the Russian invasion of Afghanistan and the American boycott of the Moscow Olympics in 1980. Schmidt in his memoirs recorded his view of Carter as 'fickle'. Fifteen years later, stronger adjectives came to mind. He told the present writer in 1994 that he had no regard for Carter either as a politician or a person.[7] He looked back nostalgically to the much more reliable methods of Ford and Kissinger.

Even so, Callaghan, with his strong links with both Schmidt and Carter, was able to generate sufficient trust and co-operation at successive summits to prevent western diplomacy falling into a vacuum in the face of destabilizing Soviet defence and political initiatives. At no time was his personal bond with Schmidt less than a strong one. It operated on matters of human and personal detail—the good relationship between Frau Schmidt, a botanist, and the garden-loving Audrey Callaghan, or Callaghan's assistance in getting his friend Henry Moore to provide a sculpture for the refurbishment of the German Chancellery in Bonn. Schmidt persuaded the British premier to write a contribution for a volume of essays to mark Willy Brandt's 65th birthday. Callaghan wrote here a strong piece on 'Democratic Socialism and the Rebirth of Britain'. The Callaghan–Schmidt axis reached a new level of intimacy during two alarming crises. Callaghan provided important technical assistance when Schmidt was confronted with the crisis of the kidnapping of a German industrialist by the Baader-Meinhof terrorists. In October 1977, there was the hijacking of a German Lufthansa airliner by an Arab terrorist group at Dubai. With the aid of the SAS and British anti-terrorist technology, a dramatic rescue was achieved at Mogadishu airport in Somalia. The lengthy personal communications between the British and German leaders is testimony to their closeness.[8] With their common ideological background, Schmidt saw his alliance with Callaghan as a stabilizing force in international affairs, and much regretted his departure in May 1979. Like most other European leaders, he reacted to the succession of the strident and confrontational Mrs Thatcher with dismay.

An important part of Callaghan's international diplomacy concerned the affairs of the Commonwealth. Here there remained much unfinished business. The entry of Britain into the European Common Market was, of course, a sign of a major realignment, but on a variety of levels the Commonwealth was still an important forum in which specific initiatives could be pursued. The meeting of the Commonwealth prime ministers at the Gleneagles Hotel in Perthshire in June 1977 was one such opportunity. Callaghan here won warm praise as 'a friendly chairman' in the view of Lee Kuan Yew of Singapore, less intellectually agile than Harold Wilson but more trustworthy. He was not only a friendly chairman but a remarkably relaxed one. He came in late for one session he was due to chair because he wished to see one of his favourite television programmes—The Muppets.[9] The Gleneagles Agreement banned all sporting contacts with South Africa, reinforcing a Commonwealth policy of trade sanctions in reaction to the policy of apartheid. It was a major step forward which played its eventual part in undermining the racialist policies of the Nationalist regime from within. This would have prevented such embarrassments as the British Lions rugby tour of South Africa in 1974 which took place despite the opposition of Wilson and of Callaghan, then Foreign Secretary. The rugby authorities, with their strongly right-wing cast of mind, proved less receptive than the MCC had been in cancelling their cricket tour to South Africa in 1970.

Callaghan also took much interest in problems of third-world aid, issues which he had addressed when Foreign Secretary both at the United Nations and in preparing for the UNCTAD conference in Nairobi. This was a major theme of several of Callaghan's international visits, notably that to India in January 1978. This was a highly congenial occasion with Callaghan warmly received as a survivor of the historic Attlee government that had granted independence to the Indian people. He himself had a powerful faith in the role of India and strong relationships both with the Prime Minister Morarji Desai and the Congress leader Mrs Indira Gandhi. He took up the theme of subcontinental regional planning and attempted to promote collaboration between the governments of India and Bangla Desh in joint development of the Ganges and Brahmaputra basins.[10] Elsewhere, he discussed with Prime Minister Trudeau of Canada, a good friend also, third-world aid programmes along the lines of the future Brandt report.

As always his strong links with African leaders such as Kenneth Kaunda and Julius Nyerere were a powerful factor. Lee Kuan Yew, for one, felt that the British Prime Minister's strength lay in Africa and that he was less at home in Asian matters. He was surprised when Callaghan pressed him for information about Japan at the Gleneagles conference.[11] However, this might reflect rather the British Prime Minister's genuine open-mindedness and willingness to learn, free from the Singapore leader's distinctive brand of dogmatic omniscience. On balance, again, Commonwealth leaders were to feel that the transition from Callaghan to Mrs Thatcher was unfortunate, especially in connection with sanctions on South Africa. It was widely believed that this view was shared by Queen Elizabeth herself.

There were other Commonwealth problems that the British government pursued on its own, such as the status of Gibraltar. (Here Callaghan enjoined David Owen, prior to a meeting with Spanish representatives, always to remember that British sovereignty was non-negotiable.)[12] Hong Kong was left dormant; a visit of David Owen to Beijing planned for April 1979 was overtaken by the fall of the British government. One recurring difficulty was the dispute with the Argentine government over the Falklands. Callaghan heard of new threats of invasion from Buenos Aires in the autumn of 1977 and pursued a policy of watchful defence. A dual policy was pursued.[13] On 13 December talks were begun with Argentine government representatives, the British spokesman being Ted Rowlands, junior minister at the Foreign Office. But his hand was strengthened by a naval presence in the South Atlantic. Despite the views of the Ministry of Defence, HMS *Endurance* remained in Falklands waters, with special funding added to the defence estimates, while there was distant deployment of frigates in the South Atlantic away from the Falklands and the threat of the further deployment of a nuclear-powered submarine. Rules of engagement were worked out to authorize a challenge to Argentine vessels coming within 50 miles of the Falklands, while legal advice was sought on the possibility of a 25-mile exclusion zone around the islands. Callaghan and David Owen made sure that intelligence of these measures was relayed to Buenos Aires. Maurice Oldfield, head of MI6, ensured that the Argentines knew of the hunter-killer submarine lurking in Falkland waters. The implication was that Britain would respond appropriately to any armed attack, but was also prepared to discuss areas of economic collaboration while steering clear of the juridical and legal aspects of British sovereignty. At any rate, no Argentine action followed; the naval threat to the Malvinas petered out. The Callaghan policy of indirect and essentially symbolic deterrence in the Falklands succeeded while the Thatcher policy of casual withdrawal in 1981–2 was to lead to war with Argentina, and a major international crisis.

Much the biggest Commonwealth problem was that of Rhodesia. No headway had been made in Callaghan's two years as Foreign Secretary, and Ian Smith remained head of the illegal government in Salisbury amidst growing international pressure and much internal guerrilla violence. The Callaghan government was to see a variety of initiatives taken to try to achieve a breakthrough on the basis of black African majority rule in the near future. There was a hectic attempt at mediation by Dr Kissinger in the summer and early autumn of 1976,[14] much on the lines of his summit diplomacy previously in Vietnam and the Middle East. Kissinger, as contemporaries wryly observed, 'had discovered Africa'. This reflected in particular the Americans' concern over possible Soviet infiltration in southern Africa, following the effect of the Portuguese revolution of 1975 on the former Portuguese colonies. This led first to Mozambique, which had a long frontier with Rhodesia, falling under the control of the left-wing Frelimo under its new President Machel. There followed civil war in Angola, with a likely victory for the Marxist MPLA, with Russian and Cuban aid. After the Kissinger initiative failed, there followed in 1977–8 an energetic pursuit by David Owen of an Anglo-American strategy to bring about an early constitutional settlement in Rhodesia. This would include, for the first time since 1968, direct negotiations with Ian Smith as well as with all the main African leaders. It was an initiative that finally stalled in the autumn of 1978 when attempts to bring about all-party talks in a conference at Lancaster House broke down on the obstacle of Ian Smith's continuing intransigence. But there is evidence to suggest that the final collapse of the Salisbury government after free elections in 1979 and the emergence of Zimbabwe under black African rule later that year was materially hastened.

The Prime Minister was content to let first Crosland and then Owen take the lead in Rhodesia. But of course he had his own background of expertise going back twenty years and his own particular perspectives. The Kissinger phase of the manœuvres in Rhodesia intimately reflected the close personal ties of Callaghan and the US Secretary of State. Their approaches were similar although Kissinger tended to emphasize more strongly the importance of Cuban involvement in Angola.[15] They met as early as 26 May 1976 in London when Callaghan gave his views on Kissinger's planned forthcoming talks with Dr Vorster, the South African premier. The object, as far as Vorster was concerned, was to create a kind of interim regime in which whites as well as blacks would have a part, with Britain underpinning this temporary settlement. Callaghan had his doubts. He told Kissinger on 5 August that Britain could 'not be tarred with the South African brush, especially with a Commonwealth conference coming along in London in 1977'. His view was that the plan should be presented not as a joint South African/American/British one but as 'a Kissinger plan which we would assist as best we could'.[16] However, he had already obtained the goodwill of Schmidt and Giscard d'Estaing, and suggested that Kissinger approach first Nyerere and Kaunda, and then President Machel of Mozambique. Everything, however, would depend on South Africa accepting what emerged and then ensuring Ian Smith's acceptance of it.

On 19 September, after visits to Dar es Salaam, Lusaka, and Pretoria, Kissinger met Ian Smith for a talk of eight hours. During the last four they were joined by Vorster; Anglo-American proposals were put forward. The views of Callaghan, on a visit to Canada at the time, were conveyed directly to Kissinger: the authority of the Foreign Secretary, Tony Crosland, in Rhodesian affairs was felt to be rather more frail. Five days later, in circumstances which still appear mysterious, Ian Smith agreed to them. The main thrust of them was that Rhodesia would accept black majority rule within two years. An interim government of a Council of State, half black, half white, alongside a mainly black Council of Ministers and First Minister, would be installed. Callaghan was attacked by Reginald Maudling for the Conservatives in the Commons for abdicating responsibility to the Americans.[17] This ignored the fact that Kissinger's diplomacy could have led to an apparent breakthrough in the previously intransigent approach of Ian Smith who was now committed to African majority rule in the near future. But the African Patriotic Front, headed by Joshua Nkomo and Robert Mugabe, refused to accept a plan which they themselves had played no part in negotiating. A conference at Geneva in October–December 1976 between the various Rhodesian parties, black and white, under the chairmanship of Ivor Richard, the British Minister to the UN, led nowhere. A visit to Salisbury by Richard when he presented Ian Smith with fresh proposals failed to elicit any agreement. The Democratic victory in the American presidential election meant a fresh start. Kissinger's African adventure as a born-again David Livingstone had failed.

When David Owen energetically took up the cudgels on behalf of a Rhodesian settlement in April 1977 Callaghan was an important background presence throughout. He ensured that this time all groups of African opinion would be brought into the negotiations. The Prime Minister's position was one of some vulnerability. Even before Owen had become Foreign Secretary, he had to deal with African complaints that he himself was a drag on the wheel in progress in resolving the Rhodesian impasse. In particular, he had to defend himself against Kenneth Kaunda's 'hurtful allegation' that he had connived in the breach of oil sanctions against Rhodesia while he was Foreign Secretary.[18] The whole issue of the breaking of sanctions had assumed much sensitivity after the publication of the Bingham report. Kaunda continued to complain and in the end Callaghan had to undertake a special flight, in the company of David Owen and Bryan Cartledge, his special adviser on foreign affairs, to Kano airport in Nigeria on 22–3 September 1978, to meet the Zambian president and reassure him of the righteousness of Britain's motives in approaching the Rhodesian issue. The Prime Minister and Cartledge picked out Kano almost randomly on the map of Africa as a convenient rendezvous with Kaunda: Callaghan knew Kano from his Nigerian visit back in 1946. What he had become convinced of over many issues was the inability of Britain alone to enforce a Rhodesian settlement. He thus ensured an early meeting of Owen with President Carter and Cyrus Vance to take the dormant Anglo-American initiative further. He used his personal links with Kaunda and Nyerere to set up meetings with the British Foreign Secretary in August and September 1977 and viewed with satisfaction their acceptance of the eventual white paper.[19] This embodied the main thrust of the Owen–Vance initiative. It laid down that there would be a ceasefire, and an interval of up to six months during which there would be fair elections under the supervision of the United Nations. A resident governor would temporarily exercise legislative and executive powers and also assume control of the Rhodesian armed forces. Field Marshal Lord Carver was Owen's chosen candidate to fulfil this role.

There followed the immensely difficult and complex task of getting the various black nationalist groups, led variously by Joshua Nkomo and Robert Mugabe of the left-wing Patriotic Front, the distinctly accommodating Bishop Abel Muzorewa, and the Revd Ndabaningi Sithole, to accept the details of a negotiated settlement involving a constitution for an independent Rhodesia-Zimbabwe, a ceasefire, and a transitional administration under Lord Carver. Several African states already felt that Britain had moved too far in being sympathetic to the wishes of Ian Smith and his followers. There were important elements in the Labour Party which took this view, as Tom McNally warned the Prime Minister.[20] Conversely, Smith himself seemed averse to accepting any interim arrangement which would not be under European control. The Cabinet rebuffed Owen's scheme for a Commonwealth force to be sent to Rhodesia to monitor the ceasefire. Another danger was that there was a real prospect of the

Americans not being able to deliver on their side of the agreement, and of Britain being left on its own imposing sanctions on South Africa as well as Rhodesia with consequent damage to British trade and investment.[21]

An internal agreement was signed in Rhodesia in March 1978 between Smith, Muzorewa, and Sithole, the less militant of the African leaders, but with the significant absence of both Joshua Nkomo and Robert Mugabe whose guerrillas continued to take up arms against the Salisbury government. Meanwhile the South African government played a complex and devious role in continuing both to try to promote a half-settlement and to maintain the internal defences of the Rhodesian white regime.

Callaghan himself continued to be prominent in Rhodesian affairs. In particular, he was again the target of criticisms from the front-line African states, notably Kenneth Kaunda, of his being insufficiently strenuous in trying to overthrow the Smith regime. He himself commented to the Danish Prime Minister, Anker Jorgensen, who himself had attempted some diplomatic initiatives in southern Africa, that 'I get a bit sick and tired of it'.[22] Ian Smith was 'the most slippery customer' who felt that he must win in the end. Finally, he suspected that an inevitable deadlock had been reached. He sent his old colleague Cledwyn Hughes, chairman of the PLP and a former Colonial Office minister, out to Rhodesia to meet Ian Smith and assess the prospects of convening an effective all-party conference in London. Hughes reported that such a conference was doomed to failure. At their first meeting, Ian Smith told him brusquely, 'You needn't try on your Welsh charm with me.'[23] The Anglo-American initiative, therefore, went no further. The subsequent phase of Rhodesia's sorry history, which resulted in April 1979 in Ian Smith stepping down in favour of a right-wing African government headed by Bishop Muzorewa, after a quite unrepresentative general election, owed little or nothing to pressure from the British government.

Rhodesia, then, frustrated Callaghan as it had frustrated Wilson and Heath before him. But he had had few illusions as to the prospects of success, and was not optimistic of Owen's diplomacy achieving a breakthrough. He told Nyerere and Kaunda in early 1978 of his concern that neither Nkomo nor Mugabe was prepared to endorse the Anglo-American proposals.[24] They wanted neither a UN force to monitor the agreements, nor a resident commissioner as commander of the Rhodesian armed forces. 'They still wanted a measure of control over the transitional period which will not be compatible with free and fair elections.' In effect, as he told Kenneth Kaunda, the major African leaders wished to pick and choose, to negotiate those elements of the package that were acceptable to them and to ignore the rest.[25] Morarji Desai of India was told that persistent division among the various African groups was merely reinforcing the position of Ian Smith.[26] The fact that the proposed round-table conference in London never materialized did not surprise Callaghan. Apart from the still unbridgeable gulf between Smith and most of the African parties, there were enormous divisions between the Africans themselves. In the Patriotic Front, Robert Mugabe, a militant Marxist who operated from guerrilla bases in Mozambique, and Joshua Nkomo of the ANC, whose bases were in Zambia, were rivals rather than collaborators.

Callaghan continued to take an interest in Rhodesia even after he ceased to be Prime Minister. A meeting with Bishop Muzorewa on 13 July 1979 saw him expressing concern at Ian Smith's continuing role in the Rhodesian government and his belief that the Muzorewa government would not receive international recognition. Labour would continue to endorse sanctions against the Salisbury government. For his part, the Bishop accused the Labour Party of being hostile and the meeting went badly with accusations of dishonesty on both sides. Callaghan told the High Commissioner, Miss Chibesakunda, a few days later, that 'until Nkomo and Mugabe state their conditions for peace, Muzorewa will go on gaining strength'. Mrs Thatcher would have to take a very different line in the forthcoming Commonwealth prime ministers' meeting at Lusaka. The best outcome, he believed, was for Joshua Nkomo to become president of Rhodesia-Zimbabwe.[27]

In these circumstances, with limited direct progress, he was mainly concerned with the indirect aspects of the Rhodesian impasse. He sought to ensure that diplomatic negotiations with South Africa did not alienate the black African states who were Britain's essential allies, and that African entanglements with the United States did not complicate the prospects of effective Anglo-American action elsewhere. On the other hand, the course of events in 1977–8 played their part in bringing black African parties in Rhodesia together more effectively, from which Robert Mugabe would emerge as the most powerful influence—to the surprise of McNally and others who felt certain that 'the winner' would be Joshua Nkomo.[28] It also played its part in destabilizing Ian Smith and helping to discourage Pretoria from assisting in a dangerous and uncontrolled military action alongside its own borders. The Anglo-American plan of Owen and Vance marked a partial breakthrough in its time, and indeed was in many ways the precursor of the eventual settlement reached at Lusaka in December 1979. Above all, and with much difficulty, the front-line African states had been kept on board. Cyrus Vance was later to pay tribute to the work of the Labour government in helping towards a final solution of the Rhodesian impasse. 'For this credit must go to David Owen and Jim Callaghan.'[29] The Prime Minister had managed to avoid having responsibility imposed on him either for the manœuvres by which Ian Smith clung to power or for enforcing an unstable settlement which could lead to anarchy. For him, therefore, the outcome could have been very much worse.

In Rhodesia, the Prime Minister's involvement was episodic and circumscribed. In higher matters, he was deeply engaged. In particular, he was a leading player in the attempt to form a coherent western view on détente and strategic matters throughout the period, and in trying to give momentum to a somewhat indecisive phase of American foreign policy. Freed from the incubus of the IMF talks, he threw himself in the spring of 1977 into trying to bring the different western perspectives into line in the lead-up to the Downing Street summit. This was a difficult task, especially with the constant friction between President Carter and Chancellor Schmidt. A whole series of issues were involved, each of them tending to intensify Schmidt's impatience and anger with the new American administration.

Several of them came to the boil in the international exchanges leading to the Group of Seven economic summit to be held in London and chaired by Callaghan in May 1977. Carter's style, untuned to the subtleties of international diplomacy, was to be direct and precise, with the objective of arriving rapidly at agreed solutions. Schmidt thought this method both offensive and in key areas dishonest, as well as oblivious to the nuances of national priorities outside the American hemisphere. He reacted with fury when Carter somewhat maladroitly raised the issue of nuclear fuel policy in his first few weeks in office and used American influence to cancel German and French plans for exporting nuclear reactors to Brazil and Pakistan, deals for which the contracts had already been signed. Schmidt commented that the more Carter sent envoys around the world 'and makes the Russians and other people make remarks towards me, the more stubbornly this Government will have to react because we cannot tear up a contract which we have put our signature to'.[30] There was also difficulty with Carter's insistence that the Group of Seven discuss the issue of worldwide nuclear proliferation, when both Callaghan and Schmidt both felt that discussions among the Four—America, Britain, Germany, and France—would be a more appropriate forum. Carter also chided the German and French governments about the need for further reflation to stimulate effective world demand. To this Schmidt commented, 'I will certainly never give in to public pressure or to summitry pressure which I can afterwards then read in the *New York Times*.'[31] There was further difficulty about American ideas on weaponry, in particular the AWACS plan and the contrary commitment to Nimrod aircraft which the British government was tending to favour since it covered Britain's maritime needs. Here again Schmidt was belligerent and stubborn. 'This AWACS thing is one of several examples in which the new American administration will have to learn that co-operation is not a one-way road.' He added, 'I'm not eager on selling weapons but I become rather difficult if somebody tries to cheat. I feel to be mislead [*sic*].'[32] It was a tribute to the diplomatic skills of the British Prime Minister that Schmidt turned up at the Downing Street summit in a reasonably equable mood although there was an underlying sense of strain.

Compared with these intercontinental issues of high politics, the other possible area of tension prior to the Downing Street summit was relatively minor although it caused Callaghan some personal embarrassment. The European Community urged that its new President should also be present at the Group of Seven economic summit; the exclusion of Ortoli from the Puerto Rico conference had caused offence. Since the European President was none other than Callaghan's former Cabinet colleague and erstwhile political rival, Roy Jenkins, this had obvious points of difficulty. Perhaps surprisingly, Giscard d'Estaing, the French President, was strongly opposed to Jenkins's attendance; the British were not alone in having a highly developed sense of national sovereignty. In fact, Callaghan applied all reasonable pressure to ensure that Jenkins would be able to be present at Downing Street and a compromise was reached by which, in effect, he attended half the summit meetings. In fact, he then attended the 1978 economic summit in Bonn as of right and the issue never emerged again.[33] Callaghan's own key role in this process deserves some recognition, perhaps more than it receives in Jenkins's memoirs.

The outcome of the Downing Street summit was apparently highly satisfactory. As has been noted, it also brought much acclaim for Callaghan's personal adeptness as chairman, at a time when the revival of the British economy was already enhancing the nation's prestige. It was a natural forum for the well-honed bargaining skills of an old trade union leader. Carter himself expressed enthusiasm for the informal and natural way in which the seven heads of government conducted their meetings. Schmidt was mollified by an American apology over the nuclear fuel issue, and it was agreed that he should visit Washington in the near future. A Nuclear Energy Group was set up under French chairmanship to monitor developments in that area. In a telephone conversation with Callaghan on 20

May, mainly intended to pick the British Prime Minister's brain on resolving the complex difficulties of the Middle East, Carter lavished praise on Britain and his host.[34]

Relations between the American President and his European colleagues continued, however, to generate tension and argument, which stretched Callaghan's powers as honest broker to the full. This was seen in a series of crises throughout the period from the autumn of 1977 to the heads of government meeting at Guadeloupe in January 1979. What caused most dispute were the related issues of international détente and a controlled arms limitation. Here the perceptions of the Americans and of the Germans, with their acutely sensitive location in central Europe, continued to diverge. Carter wanted to move on from the interim agreement on SALT II, begun as long ago as 1972 under President Nixon, to cover nuclear strategic weapons. Schmidt, backed up on many occasions by Giscard, was anxious to parallel any moves on strategic weapons with an agreement on medium- and short-term nuclear weapons as well. Otherwise, he argued that implementing SALT II would leave a clear disparity in nuclear and conventional weapons in Europe in the Russians' favour. He was fiercely critical of the Americans' perception of strategic needs, which he regarded as heavily influenced by the views of Brzezinski who took little account of European priorities.[35] Schmidt came close to urging that the Americans were merely looking after their own interests, focusing on long-range rather than intermediate-range weaponry, because the latter held no strategic threat for the people or the territory of the United States. His criticism of American policy was to become all the more strident in 1979 when the Russians developed the far more mobile SS 20s with their obvious threat to the people of West Germany.

The dispute over détente and disarmament was prolonged and tense. It invariably ranged the Americans on one side and the Germans and French on the other, with Callaghan striving to build bridges between them. Shortly after the Downing Street summit, on 30 June 1977, Callaghan wrote President Carter a highly personal letter in which he set out the criticisms voiced by both Giscard and Schmidt about Carter's policy on détente. Schmidt had gone as far as stating that Carter had jeopardized his prospects of getting more Germans out of Soviet-controlled territory. Callaghan wrote:

> I confess I do not fully understand the reasons that led Giscard and Helmut to work themselves into such a state. If I thought it was a passing mood I would not put this on paper, but yesterday [a European Council heads of state and government meeting in London] the atmosphere and the language was worse than I have

ever known. . . . Helmut is the man you must win back. Giscard will always go his own way but Helmut is a strong Atlanticist, moody and tempestuous, but basically on the side of the angels. If I may say so to you, I think it is vital that you give the impression of listening carefully to his views, of weighing them and of seeking agreement wherever you can. I urge you most strongly to give him your fullest attention. He is not the sort of man who is impressed by courtesies or parades. He will want to feel that he is able to meet you as an equal and to thrash problems out with you because Germany is a great nation.

Schmidt, he added, had some fears of German internal stability and also was concerned that 'the German economic miracle is not shining so brightly just now'. It was vital that, in Schmidt's forthcoming visit to Washington, Carter should find common ground with him on both détente and nuclear proliferation. He should also make Schmidt feel 'he has your confidence and understanding'. The letter ended, in half-diffidence, with the hope that Carter would accept it in the spirit that it was written. The President's handwritten response was brief and almost offhand. He felt that there was no inherent problem other than the issue of nuclear proliferation and assured Callaghan that he would do his best to alleviate Schmidt's concerns.[36] Confronted with a brisk note like this, Callaghan yearned somewhat for the much fuller communications he used to receive from Gerry Ford.

In fact, the differences on defence continued to cause inter-allied strain. Carter seemed to keep his distance from the Continental leaders and was markedly reluctant to embark on another international summit such as that at Downing Street. He and Schmidt viewed their separate approaches to Brezhnev over détente and security with great suspicion. This was intensified by a furious row that broke out over the 'neutron bombs', otherwise known as ERW (enhanced radiation weapons). These were short-range nuclear launchers to be deployed in central Europe and therefore of somewhat indirect interest to Britain. Carter now proposed to embark on the production of this terrible weapon, one that destroyed human beings while leaving tanks and buildings intact. Schmidt, who considered himself an expert on deterrence matters as a former Minister of Defence and the author of two books on the topic, had grave doubts as to the need for such a weapon. But he reluctantly agreed to accept its installation on German soil despite passionate protests from the anti-nuclear movement.[37] Callaghan, who confessed that he faced 'flak' on the issue at home, was also prepared to endorse the neutron bomb, perhaps because Britain already had its own nuclear weapons arsenal. Then, to Schmidt's fury, Carter changed tack and abandoned the neutron bomb project in early 1978 in the face of domestic Congressional opposition. The German Chancellor felt deeply let down and said so. Relations with Carter became more glacial still.

The British government's Nuclear Defence Policy Group, consisting of Callaghan, Owen, Healey, and Mulley, along with Sir John Hunt and Sir Clive Rose, considered matters at a secret meeting on 3 April 1978. It was agreed here to back the American decision not to go ahead with the neutron bomb. But it was also recognized that 'the Americans would have a problem in explaining their change in position to the Germans. We all said that it was the United States administration who had shown considerable incompetence in their handling of the issue.'[38] On nuclear policy generally, Callaghan felt rather less vulnerable than did Schmidt to domestic opposition, although it is noticeable that the neutron bomb controversy, taken together with the British agreement to the stationing of more nuclear-capable long-range aircraft in Britain (making a total of 156 in all), also produced anti-nuclear protest. By the end of Callaghan's premiership, the Campaign for Nuclear Disarmament, in the shadows since 1962, was again a potent force of protest and dissent.

The main theme of Callaghan's view of détente in the course of 1978 was to try to find common ground between the US and continental European positions. He applied himself to this arcane and highly technical area with the same impressive mix of political commitment and intellectual power that he had earlier demonstrated on economic matters. One particular aspect on which he worked closely with Carter was in joint approaches to Brezhnev about nuclear stockpiling and verification.[39] He had ensured that Britain was associated with a joint American and Russian working group considering a possible nuclear test ban treaty. Britain itself promoted the idea of a five-year ban covering all nuclear explosions.

But the main British concern over arms limitation was to try to define the so-called 'Grey Areas' with more precision. These would include all the nuclear delivery systems not covered in SALT negotiations, but could not be decoupled from the overall balance of weaponry. A Grey Area was difficult to define. In practice it tended to mean a catch-all of a vast range of intermediate- and short-range weapons, including US aircraft based on Europe and aircraft carriers potentially directed at the Russians; Russian missiles including the SS 20s and 'backfire bombers'; and the French nuclear submarines. These might form the basis of a SALT III agreement to follow on swiftly from SALT II.[40] Eventually it was this 'Grey Area' notion, on which the British expended much ingenuity and effort, which was to form a major basis for the next stage of western summitry agreed after prolonged argument. It was accepted that a meeting should take place of the four heads of government, rather than the seven of economic summitry. This would clearly place the emphasis on defence rather than economic issues. After much discussion, it was agreed that the meeting should be held in the West Indies, not in British Barbados nor in French Martinique but in another French Caribbean possession, the island of Guadeloupe, which Giscard assured his colleagues was an especially private location, easily defended against inquisitive journalists.[41] This would take place in early January 1979.

The work done by British officials and scientists supplied a good deal of the technical data about the 'Grey Areas'. But it also posed a major problem for the British Labour government. For Britain's own nuclear weapons were a part of that Grey Area, by most definitions. The independent British nuclear deterrent, as it was known, had been a source of contention since the late 1950s, and the anti-nuclear movement was again developing momentum. The British government maintained the so-called Chevaline project for improving the Polaris missile system (originally known as Super Antelope in 1967 when Tony Benn was involved as Minister of Technology) throughout the 1970s. The decision to continue with the Chevaline programme had been a very early episode in Harold Wilson's new administration in March 1974. A committee consisting of Wilson, Callaghan, Jenkins, Healey, and Roy Mason, the then Defence Secretary, endorsed Chevaline in secret session and presented it to the Cabinet as an enhancement of the Polaris system at a cost of some £250m. There was apparently little objection at the time. But it had proved to be horrendously expensive, running to over £200m. by mid-1976, four times more costly than originally visualized. Callaghan was later to argue to Sir Robert Armstrong that a project like Chevaline was so costly and the work so near to completion that it would have been 'idiotic' to discontinue it.[42] But even this meant leaving the original dilemma of British nuclear weapons policy unresolved. The Polaris submarines whose missiles had provided Britain's nuclear shield since the early 1960s were ageing and in urgent need of replacement.

Finding a viable and affordable system had been one of Callaghan's priorities since the start of 1978. He set up two important working parties, one to study delivery systems chaired by Professor Ronald Mason, chief scientific adviser of the Minister of Defence, and one on the political and military aspects chaired by Sir Anthony Duff of the Foreign Office. The question never seems to have come once to full Cabinet in 1977–8, no doubt because the ministers included such ardent nuclear disarmers as Michael

Foot and Tony Benn. The Cabinet's group on Nuclear Defence Policy was a body whose existence was kept totally secret, as with all British nuclear policy-making since GEN 163 under Attlee in 1947. It was to consider whether Polaris should be replaced by Trident submarines and C4 missiles. There might be a suitable *quid pro quo* for the Americans who would supply them, perhaps in the stationing of US missiles on British soil. This last point, with special reference to Cruise and Pershing II missiles, had already been foreshadowed in correspondence between Fred Mulley, the British Defence Minister, and Harold Brown, his US counterpart, in May 1977.[43] But clearly, in the complex state of disarmament and security discussions, the replacement of the British nuclear deterrent was intertwined with the wider question of whether the entire British system should be scrapped as part of a SALT III treaty in due time. This would provide much grist for the British mill when the heads of government duly assembled in tropical Guadeloupe.

On defence matters, Callaghan was in an intermediate, honest-broker position, trying to reconcile American and German positions on strategic arms limitations and security in Europe. At times, he would seem to be echoing Schmidt's litany of complaints about American insensitivity and recklessness. On economic matters, by contrast, he was frequently allied with the Americans in urging the French and Germans to take a more expansive view of economic recovery. The tone of the Downing Street summit in May 1977 had been forward-looking and collaborative, if general in tone. There were targets for economic growth, projections for more jobs, a boost to international trade, and international pledges on energy conservation and aid to the developing world.[44] But in 1978, as world economic growth began to slow down markedly, other than in the Pacific Rim countries, Callaghan began to take a more specific line. On one key aspect of international economic policy-making, he agreed with Schmidt who felt that Carter's casualness in economic policy was a major threat to European economic prospects, especially the weakness of the dollar and the inability of the administration to cut significantly the US budget deficit. On the other hand, he told Carter on 17 April 1978 of his concern at Europe tending to go it alone on economic as well as defence matters: the currency 'snake' had a built-in tendency to leave the dollar out of account. He found Schmidt, after a lengthy meeting in Bonn, 'pessimistic, almost fatalistic' on world economic problems. He saw no prospect of economic recovery in Germany or anywhere else, and was gloomy in the extreme about the Bonn summit meeting. He believed, however, that Schmidt would respond to a 'carefully worked out plan' for phased international recovery. He urged Carter again to go to special lengths to discover precisely what Schmidt's own thoughts were, given the fact that he headed a coalition government with the FDP and the independent role of the German Bundesbank.[45] Callaghan's drafts on future economic recovery, focusing on growth, long-term capital flows including aid, energy, trade, and currency stability, formed the basis of meetings he had with Carter in Washington in March.[46]

The British and American governments thus found themselves of the same mind in the lead-up to the Bonn economic summit in July 1978 in urging Schmidt and the other Europeans to promote a global strategy for economic recovery rather than insisting on the primacy of monetary 'stability'. At Bonn, Callaghan's proposal for a 'locomotive' strategy for world economic recovery, involving a general reflation led by Germany and Japan, was strongly backed by President Carter.[47] The Germans were less enamoured of the drift of the Bonn summit and called for a European initiative to restore monetary stability which later led to the idea of the EMS. Here again the western leaders ended in some disarray, and here too was further material for the already cluttered agenda for Guadeloupe.

Not all Callaghan's dealings with the US government, however, were concerned with trying to forge a coherent western view on defence, security, and economic matters. There was also a more private aspect, stemming from the British Prime Minister's special fund of expertise. Carter was anxious to act as a troubleshooter in difficult strategic areas, to promote a more stable world. In the general area of relations with the Soviet Union, there was perhaps not much to show in the end. Indeed, Carter's presidency ended alarmingly, almost humiliatingly, with new signs of Soviet defence deployment with the SS 20s, the invasion of Afghanistan, and the crisis over the hostages in Iran. Overall, the United States was felt to have lost ground in global relations. On the other hand, in specific regional crises, there were American successes. In 1979 the formal US recognition of Communist China was an immense landmark.

Perhaps the most striking accord between warring combatants came in the Middle East. Here Callaghan played his part in achieving success for American diplomacy. Carter had great respect for the British Prime Minister's fund of knowledge and experience of both the Egyptian and Israeli positions, and his personal contacts with President Sadat and also with Mrs Meir and the Israeli Labour Cabinet. By 1977 Israel was ruled by the right-wing Likud Party under the premiership of Menachem Begin, a former terrorist of hard-line outlook. Nevertheless, Carter turned to Callaghan for guidance on how to promote an accord. He found Begin somewhat more baffling a personality than his Arab counterparts and felt that the British Prime Minister had a deeper understanding of him.[48] Callaghan was thus to act as an important conduit of communication with Washington as various Middle East leaders, Begin, Sadat, Hussein, and others, winged their way across the Atlantic.

Callaghan had an important meeting with Begin at Chequers on 3–4 December 1977. Although he had been repelled in earlier years by Begin's right-wing nationalist views, the tone of their meetings now was far more cordial. They ranged over a variety of issues including British plans to supply Israel with North Sea oil and collaboration over the plight of Soviet Jews. But the main focus was on a series of forthcoming parallel secret talks in Cairo between Israeli and Arab representatives, one series focusing on security, the other on political aspects.[49] These talks were discussed again at Chequers on 20 December where Begin explained his plan for a partial withdrawal of Israeli forces from Sinai, and a demilitarized zone coming into being over a phased period. Callaghan's response was to welcome Begin's 'remarkable and imaginative' plan for Arab self-government on the West Bank, but he urged him to make more concessions to satisfy President Sadat on the security aspect.[50]

At the same time, he was in touch with Sadat too on the prospects for self-determination for the West Bank settlements coming in an evolutionary way. The Egyptian President urged Callaghan that Britain should use its influence in counselling moderation amongst the Israelis on the West Bank and in the Gaza strip. On his way back from India, Pakistan, and Bangla Desh, Callaghan saw Sadat in Cairo on 14 January 1978. In his subsequent communications with Carter, Callaghan passed on Sadat's 'emotional' feelings about the West Bank settlements. In return he suggested that the Israelis formulate a Declaration of Principles based on Carter's formulation on Palestinian rights, which should be presented immediately. His other main point was the need to bring King Hussein of Jordan into the discussions as soon as was feasible, since a link between Jordan and the West Bank would be a way of promoting security. Callaghan added that he hoped in the long term for an Israeli-Jordanian federation.[51] Carter evidently believed that Callaghan's involvement with both sides at this stage was an important factor in injecting momentum and trust into discussions about security arrangements for the West Bank, and therefore something of a diplomatic breakthrough. He cheerfully thanked Callaghan on his return for 'sorting out' the Middle East problem for him.[52]

In the course of 1978, American mediation brought the two sides closer together. The outcome was the Camp David Agreement of September which Begin related in detail to Callaghan on his way home to Israel on 22 September.[53] The effect was dramatic, with Egypt regaining Sinai and recognizing the state of Israel. The ingrained Arab coalition against Israel which had led to war in 1948, 1956, 1967, and 1973, and brought the world economy to the edge of catastrophe, suddenly collapsed. So, too, did Soviet involvement in the affairs of Egypt. Indeed, the most striking feature of the Camp David accords was that the Soviet Union was left on one side. It was an American achievement above all, much assisted by the courage of President Sadat who developed personal links with Israel that were later to cost him his life at the hands of an Arab assassin. But Callaghan's intervention at a key phase, especially in reconciling different perceptions of the potential for a secure settlement on the West Bank and in placing the whole Middle East question in a broader international context, was one of the more significant international initiatives in his career. He was not the least of the peacemakers.

These years of tension and international complexity had their effect on the Prime Minister's conduct of affairs at many levels. One consequence, especially of the course of Anglo-Soviet relations at this stage, was Callaghan's involvement with matters of security. The relevant government agencies were MI5, directed by the Home Office, and MI6, run by the Foreign Office. Espionage was not something that he brooded on as centrally or obsessively as Wilson. His own experience of naval intelligence during the war made him, so he felt, 'more level-headed' than Wilson in handling it. Relations with the Russians were much calmer than under the Heath government, when there was a mass expulsion of Russian spies, real or alleged, from Britain in 1971. Callaghan and Gromyko were old sparring partners. Nevertheless, there were important features of the security and intelligence arrangements with which the Prime Minister had to deal, relating to the past as well as the present.[54] As regards past security operations, he inherited the frenetic climate of the Wilson period with the then Prime Minister convinced that he was under surveillance himself from MI5 and that this extended to the bugging of No. 10 itself. Officials in MI5, so it was believed, thought that the Prime Minister along with Lady Falkender, Joseph Kagan, and others was running a kind of Communist cell, originally deriving from the Prime Minister's links with eastern Europe as a government minister in the late 1940s. Harold Wilson had had a difficult and somewhat unsatisfactory meeting in 1975 with Sir Michael Hanley, the head of MI5 and a man with no great private regard for his Prime Minister, to discuss these allegations. All this was later to lead to the sensations of the book *Spycatcher*, by Peter Wright. In addition,

Chapman Pincher and other enterprising journalists produced a stream of revelations about the operations of MI6, and its director Maurice Oldfield, in covert investigation of the former Prime Minister. There was also the sensational allegation that Roger Hollis, the former head of MI5, had himself been a Soviet agent: a private inquiry later by Burke Trend was to clear him. Another story was that Victor Rothschild, the head of the Policy Unit during the Heath government, was a spy. He had to explain himself to Callaghan over a glass of champagne.

Callaghan tried to grapple with all these rumours, none of which impinged on any aspect of his own reputation. No one ever needed to bug him. He also did what he could to prevent the bugging of others. Thus as Home Secretary he forbade MI5 from engaging in the surveillance of certain prominent trade union leaders and dismissed with derision the idea that they were in any way security risks. However, following pressure in some newspapers, voiced by Mrs Thatcher, he set up a confidential internal inquiry into security and surveillance matters in June–August 1977. It was under the chairmanship of Sir John Hunt, Secretary of the Cabinet. Colourful revelations emerged from its inquiries. Apparently, Harold Wilson had believed that a hole in the wall of the Cabinet room behind a portrait of Mr Gladstone contained a listening device. He had had a firm called Argon Ltd., run by one who was mixed up with South African intelligence, to check the relevant light fittings. Government electronics experts, however, assured Hunt and Stowe that Gladstone's portrait concealed nothing more sinister than the fitting of an earlier wall light, and that the Grand Old Man was in no sense a cover for espionage. An electronic device installed years earlier was, however, removed. Robert Armstrong, after guidance from the Prime Minister, saw Mrs Thatcher at Scotney Castle and then in Chelsea on 9 and 11 August 1977. On these occasions, she expressed 'misgivings' about Harold Wilson's 'reliability' although her evidence was wholly anecdotal, based on such matters as Wilson's visits to Russia thirty years earlier, and his employment of figures such as Geoffrey Goodman (on whom MI5 had a file) whose political reliability she evidently questioned. However, she did not believe the bugging story and accepted Callaghan's suggestion that he issue a public statement rather than have a full inquiry. The Prime Minister reported publicly on 23 August that he was convinced that there had been no bugging of No. 10 during Harold Wilson's premiership in 1974–6, but that there were no grounds for doubting Wilson's loyalty either. He had conveyed the essence of his statement to the former Prime Minister in a private meeting but no suggestion for further leads emerged. Wilson acknowledged that he might well have misunderstood matters. On the face of it, the affair implied a rebuke of his predecessor by the Prime Minister. One of his main concerns, however, was to protect Wilson who was already showing signs of the illness that was to dog his latter years. There was some criticism that the inquiry, conducted from within Whitehall by the Secretary of the Cabinet assisted by the directors of MI5 and MI6 with the head of GCHQ and one or two others, must have been perfunctory in the extreme. Hunt himself commented long afterwards that his investigations did reveal some reactionary elements within MI5 who were hostile to the Labour government.[55] But there the matter rested for several years until the *Spycatcher* revelations. One of the odder features of the inquiry instituted by Callaghan is that Peter Wright had every opportunity to offer evidence to the 1977 inquiry but chose not to do so.

Many of the more colourful rumours were apparently rebutted at this time. A brief flurry surrounded Judith Hart, a blameless if left-wing minister. It ended when it emerged that she was being confused perhaps with Jenifer Hart, an Oxford history don who had been accused of links with Soviet agents many years earlier, or alternatively with Mrs Judith Tudor Hart, the wife of a well-known south Wales Communist. However, Callaghan did not regard MI5 and its associated appendages as a model of administrative effectiveness. Nor could Harold Wilson's claims that there had been attempts by the secret service to destabilize his regime be casually dismissed. One alarming feature of the previous two years had been a sequence of apparently co-ordinated burglaries directed against members of Wilson's advisory staff. Marcia Williams, Bernard Donoughue, and Geoffrey Goodman (three times) were some of a dozen or so who suffered mysterious break-ins, thefts, or searches through their private papers. So evidently did Harold Wilson himself. No evidence on those responsible ever emerged.

In executive terms, the secret service had been responsible for a sequence of blunders of which the failure to take action against Blunt was perhaps the most astonishing. Here truly was the establishment at work. In addition there were problems that arose from MI5's practice of direct recruitment of personnel. Callaghan had a low opinion of the current head of MI5, Sir Michael Hanley, whom he disliked and whom Wilson himself had sharply criticized, and indeed shouted at. 'I was quite unhappy with the way in which [he] was conducting its affairs and when he was due to retire I determined to bring someone into the office from a different culture', Callaghan recalled for the *Guardian* in 1996. He was also aware of private information about the loyalty of key personnel in MI5 and MI6;

one embarrassing figure was Maurice Oldfield, the head of MI6, who was said to be open to pressure because of undesirable associates resulting from his homosexuality. Later on, his positive vetting certificate was to be withdrawn. As it happened, Callaghan quite liked him and used him for obtaining information on Argentina and other potentially hostile countries. The Prime Minister also received other evidence from a covert intermediary he had used when providing secret assistance to Mario Soares in Portugal at the time of the revolution in that country in 1975. The upshot was that Callaghan saw Hanley and Oldfield, the heads of MI5 and MI6, together and that both were removed in the course of 1978. Callaghan felt there was 'laxity' under Hanley as head of MI5 and that institutional reform was needed, especially to purge any reactionary elements lurking within.

After some suggestions that the intelligence service be placed under the Cabinet Office, it was kept as a distinct department with Callaghan appointing Sir Howard Smith, the current ambassador to Moscow, to head it. Of course, he came from outside MI5 and would 'institute closer control, better management and more acceptable and accountable methods of recruitment'.[56] Callaghan had admired his realism about the Soviet Union during his time as ambassador, and had also seen him at work in Northern Ireland. In addition, Callaghan liked the fact that Smith came from a humbler background than men like Hanley and Hollis; he was the son of a hard-up schoolmaster who had worked his way up to Cambridge via Regent Street Polytechnic. MI5 was alarmed at his appointment but it had to swallow it. However, when Callaghan proposed, remarkably, that Smith, before his departure from Moscow, should tell Gromyko, the Soviet Foreign Minister with whom Callaghan had good relations, that he was going to head the British security services, this was done, despite bitter resistance by MI5 to the appointment being publicly gazetted. There the matter rested, and Smith remained head of MI5 until the time of Mrs Thatcher's premiership when he attempted to persuade her to open up the security services. He retired in 1981 having failed to move Mrs Thatcher, and not until 1992 when Stella Rimington was personally identified was even the name of the head of MI5 known to the public at large. Security was a dormant issue for the rest of Callaghan's premiership. He declined many opportunities to follow up journalists' leads on security issues, and his own reputation remained unaffected by the excitements about surveillance that accompanied the *Spycatcher* trial in Australia and the last stages of the cold war. The trial did, however, lead to a dispute with Mrs Thatcher who felt that Callaghan was trying to make some political capital whereas she felt she had been restrained during their earlier dealings on security in 1977. The truth, perhaps, was that, in this area as in others, Callaghan was a stronger champion of open government than she was.

Europe and its alliance systems had provided the central theme of Callaghan's time during his time as Foreign Secretary. While his premiership saw his attention range over a wide mass of global issues, European issues still loomed large even after the confirmation of British membership of the Common Market. Some of these European issues were bilateral matters of debate or dissent with individual states. The sale and purchase of aircraft, and measures to assist the dormant British aircraft industry, were the nub of some of them. There was some difficulty with the French over the involvement of British Aerospace with the European airbus project and further disputes over Nimrod reconnaissance aircraft. In the end, however, Callaghan, Giscard, and Schmidt together were able to reach agreement on a joint European airbus which symbolized a collective defence of the European aeroplane industry in the face of a severe challenge from the Americans in general and Boeing in particular. Years later, during the Westland debate in 1986, Callaghan was able to show how he had stood up to the Americans over aircraft manufacture in 1978 whereas the Thatcher government, he claimed, had surrendered to the American Sikorski option.[57] The needs of British aircraft manufacture also provided the context for one of the more embarrassing episodes of the Callaghan years, the official state visit of President Ceauşescu of Romania in June 1978. In the course of this the latter received an honour, and also a hunting rifle with a telescopic sight from the Queen. Subsequent events made this seem an unfortunate initiative. It originated from the need for an agreement for the Romanians to have a British BAC I–II airliner built, although whether Ceauşescu would have paid for it is a matter for debate.[58] Still, 1978 was not 1990 and the needs of British industry might have seemed a reasonable justification for the Romanian President's visit, quite apart from the belief that he was a useful dissenter against Soviet orthodoxy in east–west relations.

But the main area of European involvement was in working out the consequences of British membership of the Common Market. Here, for all the solid majority in favour of continuing in the Community in the referendum in 1975, progress was slow. The British people had embraced their Continental neighbours only with reluctance—what some of those neighbours called a 'pis-aller'—and by 1978 the opinion polls showed a significant majority hostile to Europe and the bureaucracy of Brussels. This was fully reflected in the viewpoint of the Labour government. It was forced to sanction direct European elections, to be held in June 1979,[59] but on all major aspects of European co-operation, economic or political, it was a drag on the wheel. Callaghan himself continued to be cool on British membership. In a talk to the Fabian Society at the 1975 Labour Party conference at Blackpool, subsequently published, while he waxed enthusiastic about British involvement at the United Nations or in east–west negotiations about détente, he added, 'I always feel uneasy about some of the rhetoric used about the future of Europe.'[60] Helmut Schmidt felt that the European vision never meant anything to him and that he remained mired in Britain's historic role. Giscard felt him to be 'too English' with an unequivocally 'non-continental attitude'.[61] Therefore, while he enormously welcomed association with Schmidt, Giscard, and other European heads of state, and used it to good effect on a range of world issues, his approach was the traditional British view from the time of Bevin onwards, pragmatic, functional, down to earth. The British people were going to be slow and steady in evolving a European viewpoint and their Prime Minister was not going to rush them along.

This emerged most clearly in the major attempt in this period to take European integration a stage further, by promoting a European monetary system. This idea emerged quite suddenly in the heads of government meeting at Copenhagen in April 1978 when Schmidt, who had been converted by Giscard, sprang it on his British colleague unexpectedly over breakfast at the French embassy.[62] In effect he was suggesting a European initiative to promote monetary stability which would lead to a European monetary system with perhaps in time a common currency. Callaghan reacted in unenthusiastic fashion. He feared it might add to Britain's monetary problems and merely enhance Germany's industrial strength. Copenhagen was a gloomy occasion and the (no doubt lavish) breakfast at the French embassy singularly lacking in *joie de vivre*. Roy Jenkins has memorably described the meeting of Schmidt and Callaghan as comparable to two friendly ships passing one another at night with neither showing recognition of the proximity of the other.[63] The British line was to express some support in general for the idea: after all, Callaghan had every interest in measures to promote stable exchange rates. At Copenhagen he mentioned the problem of 'monetary disorder'. At the same time, he questioned and criticized the notion of an EMS in detail.

At a further conference of European heads of government at Bremen in July 1978 he appeared to show somewhat greater sympathy for the idea of a European zone of stability. Beforehand, at a private meeting with Schmidt in the Chancellor's bungalow near Bonn, he heard the German

Chancellor describe the benefits he believed an EMS, with its fixed but adjustable exchange rates, would bring to Britain. This was sufficient to alarm Edmund Dell, an opponent of EMS and general Eurosceptic—'this was Callaghan the world statesman, a worrying phenomenon'.[64] The British Cabinet as a whole was generally opposed to British membership of an EMS, as was the Treasury. In the Cabinet committee, GEN 136, which considered the question, only Harold Lever was in favour of British membership. Healey, Owen, Varley, Silkin, and Dell were all hostile, though not for identical reasons.[65] The stern opposition of the Labour Party National Executive, assuming that it would have understood the question, was reflected in the description of it by one of Callaghan's aides, David Lipsey, as 'little Englander', while Tony Benn was furious with the Prime Minister for showing weakness on it.[66] Callaghan was to tell Schmidt at a private meeting in October of the opposition to the Common Market felt in the trade unions and the opposition of 'many of the pundits' to the EMS as a concept.[67]

What seems to emerge is that Callaghan himself became somewhat more enthusiastic about joining a European monetary system than were his Cabinet colleagues, although not by a great margin. At best, it could perhaps be a revised basis for currency stability, a new Bretton Woods. He variously confirmed to Anker Jorgensen, the Danish Prime Minister, Giulio Andreotti of Italy, and Helmut Schmidt in November–December that he favoured an EMS in principle.[68] It was one of his more personal involvements in foreign affairs, just as Mrs Thatcher's flat opposition to it was one of hers. However he had reservations about the exchange regulation aspect of the 'snake' and would also want preconditions about the convergence of inflation rates, the symmetry of stronger and weaker currencies, and the reform of the Common Agricultural Policy, all of them pretty fundamental changes. He told Jorgensen that his problems with an EMS were 'practical' not 'philosophical'.[69] Most of the Cabinet took a tougher line. After six meetings of the Cabinet between 2 November and 14 December to discuss the issue, the British government decided that it was premature to arrive at a view. There was some sympathy for Denis Healey's proposal to think of joining the EMS but without membership of an exchange regulatory mechanism.[70] There the matter rested.

The Conservative government of Mrs Thatcher showed less inclination still to push the matter forward. Britain's eventual membership of the ERM at an excessively high exchange rate for the pound begun in October 1990 ended ingloriously in September 1992 in a way that discredited the Chancellor of the day, Norman Lamont, who was eventually to resign seven months later. On balance, the handling of the issue by the Callaghan government shows the usual picture of a British government being suspicious and reactive. The discussion on joining a European monetary system took place almost as though Britain had never joined the Common Market at all. Callaghan had to reassure Helmut Schmidt at their meetings in Bonn on 18–19 October that he did not intend to lead the United Kingdom out of the Common Market despite pressure from within his party.[71] The British had been reluctant Europeans when James Callaghan became Prime Minister in April 1976. When he fell from power three years on, their—and his—reluctance was still all too apparent.

The climax of the variegated challenges of the foreign policy of the Callaghan administration came to a colourful finale with the four-power heads of government conference in Guadeloupe between 4 and 7 January 1979. The Prime Minister was accompanied only by a personal entourage of Audrey Callaghan, his doctor Montague Levine, Sir John Hunt, the faithful two Toms, McNally and McCaffrey, and Roger Stott, the last-named to keep him posted on the parliamentary situation at home and by implication the grave industrial scene as well. As will be seen, Guadeloupe had major effects on the British Prime Minister's domestic reputation. But in its own right it was an important international occasion. It was also a rather odd one with the confusion of issues that it discussed and its somewhat indeterminate status in relation to the other roster of international gatherings at the time. The atmosphere in a tropical setting of a beautiful French West Indian island was almost incongruous in its mood of relaxation and informality, with the wives of the heads of governments sunning themselves by the pool. Roger Stott was much struck by the spectacle of Callaghan sailing a dinghy on his own far out to sea, and with much expertise, one afternoon, while Carter, scuba-diving in a wetsuit, was surrounded by a posse of armed security men. There was much agreeable creole food and rum punch; Helmut Schmidt loosened up to the extent of opening a coconut with a machete, apparently without sustaining or inflicting serious injury. The first day began characteristically with Callaghan actually waking Giscard d'Estaing up with a telephone call prior to the opening meeting.[72] But it also raised crucially important issues and on a whole range of matters had an important impact, sometimes positive, sometimes the reverse, on the whole fabric of international affairs. For the United Kingdom, it was to shape aspects of its foreign and more particularly defence policies for the remainder of the century.

The first session on 5 January raised a wide variety of issues, including a stimulus to world exports and the problems presented by the Japanese.

There followed a brief discussion of arms sales to China, now on the point of being recognized by the United States.[73] The British government had been approached by the Chinese to provide Harrier jump jets. There was some resistance from the Americans, but Callaghan got support from Schmidt after he had explained that the Harrier was not an offensive weapon. Giscard did not seem to mind greatly either way. In the event, the Harrier deal with the Chinese was not to be completed under Mrs Thatcher, although it did give Callaghan a special place in the affections of the Chinese leaders which was to last for the rest of his life.[74] There was analysis of the crisis in Iran where the deposition of the Shah appeared imminent. There was also a brief discussion of African matters, with special reference to Rhodesia and southern Africa generally, on which Callaghan led off. Here he and Carter were in particular accord, defending a policy of international sanctions against South Africa against French objections. The choice of Ambassador Andrew Young, a flamboyant but committed figure, to be the US representative at the UN and hence involved in Rhodesia affairs was testimony to the President's genuine moral abhorrence, albeit as a southern Baptist, of racial discrimination and the evil of apartheid.[75]

But the nub of the Guadeloupe meeting was a series of intense discussions on disarmament and security. Here, the whole nexus of themes that had produced so much agitation amongst the allies since 1977 was considered—a SALT II and SALT III treaty, the problem of the 'Grey Areas' including the French and British nuclear deterrents, a nuclear test ban treaty, the future of central Europe, and the security of Germany. These matters dominated the sessions. Conversely, it was agreed to leave all economic issues to the next economic summit to be held in Tokyo.[76] It was eventually agreed by all four that progress should be rapid towards a SALT II treaty which they would all endorse, although it was admitted that many crucial details of the formula on intercontinental ballistic missiles and 'backfire' bombers needed to be worked out. On the broader strategic issues there was however the familiar pattern of argument between Carter and Schmidt over both SALT II and SALT III, with Callaghan playing a particularly important role. Callaghan's notes read, 'Schmidt illogical, Giscard detached. We agree Carter would probe Brezhnev. Germany's emergence as a world power—the economic giant becomes politically adult.' On his return to Britain, Callaghan spelt out his conclusions to his Cabinet colleagues on 11 January 1979. He repeated his view that Schmidt's arguments lacked consistency. 'He was particularly anxious to see something done about the threat posed by the SS20 but he was not prepared to see new theatre nuclear weapons deployed by the Alliance on German territory unless another member of NATO was also prepared to have them.'[77] Schmidt's view was that a SALT II treaty might have the effect, by producing a nuclear stalemate between the United States and the Soviet Union, of making central Europe more vulnerable, especially with the advent of the SS 20. With a Russian preponderance in intermediate-range missiles, the prospect of the classic NATO strategy being fulfilled and a war being fought solely on German soil was enhanced.

Callaghan, assisted by Giscard, had to try to pour oil on these troubled waters. Carter and Schmidt were sharply at odds over the entire American proposal for a policy of 'graduated response'. Schmidt felt it would leave Germany, the country at most risk, alone in the line of fire in central Europe. Carter felt the German attitude was negative and self-contradictory. Callaghan's interventions proved therefore to be of much importance. He endorsed Schmidt's view that NATO conventional forces be strengthened, while pointing out again the effect on Britain's finances of the support costs of the British army on the Rhine. But he also agreed that the Americans might be asked to station ground-launched Cruise missiles to protect Europe. Britain would be prepared to station them on its soil. With reluctance Schmidt agreed that Germany would consider doing the same. He then gave his endorsement of SALT II.

But then there was SALT III. This generated more argument, about the 'Grey Areas' above all. Here was a matter of direct concern to the British since it might include the British Polaris system. Giscard intervened by suggesting that it might make it easier to achieve if all the so-called 'Grey Area' weapons were excluded from it. But Carter was disturbed by this since he was anxious to include the Russian SS 20s at the earliest stage. Callaghan argued successfully, however, that the issue be left open to allow for flexibility in Brezhnev's diplomatic stance in his discussions with the American President. He would be prepared to recommend to the British Cabinet that the 'Grey Areas', Polaris and all, were included in SALT III talks, provided Britain was a direct participant in them. He pointed out to Schmidt that Britain as well as Germany must be regarded as a priority target for the Russian missiles because of both the British deterrent and the basing of American nuclear forces there.

This discussion ended somewhat unsatisfactorily. Carter was anxious about the lack of precision for the context of his talks with Brezhnev. Schmidt complained of the Americans' previous reluctance to include SS 20s in them and of the overall prospect of delay. A broad agreement was finally reached on a flexible proposal that Carter brought forward on the morning of 6 January. This was that he would tell Brezhnev of his wish to have discussions on the deployment of the SS 20s, perhaps throwing in US forward base systems for discussion as well, but leaving it open whether these matters would be raised in SALT III or in separate negotiations. In the event, the Russians were to defer talks until the end of 1979, and much of the momentum was lost. Schmidt was to complain that the slowness of the Americans in ratifying SALT II was a major contributory factor.[78] There was by now growing doubt as to the nature of Russian strategic intentions in any case and the broad relevance of the nuclear weaponry of the west. Carter's presidency petered out at the end of the year with renewed bad blood between him and Schmidt over SALT II, rival approaches to Brezhnev, whether intermediate missiles in Europe should be frozen or related to wider strategic weapons, and many other issues. Rapport between the Americans and the Europeans was no nearer than it had been when Carter became President. It was truly a 'Grey Area' of its own.

On the other hand, the Guadeloupe discussions were not wholly sterile. They did mark a breakthrough in leading to what came in the 1980s to be known as the 'twin track' approach, with the deployment of American Cruise missiles in Europe (notably in Britain at Greenham Common which generated much protest from women's groups), and also simultaneous negotiations with the Russians to eliminate all intermediate-range missiles including the SS 20s. President Reagan was to develop it in his 'zero-zero option' policy. A consensus of a kind did therefore emerge, and Callaghan's interventions were important in achieving it. There was also some progress in the nature of the arms control package to be offered, with the emergence of what came to be called the Theatre Nuclear Force (TNF) proposal. Callaghan himself was much engaged in the deliberations on this sombre issue. A brief note of his reads, 'Have we got overkill? Do we need to add to it?' Unfortunately, the leaders of the west were to conclude that we did.

The issue at Guadeloupe of most direct concern to Callaghan was whether the Americans would be prepared to renew the British independent deterrent. For Callaghan it was vital for military and diplomatic reasons that Britain should remain a nuclear power and that its arsenal be then added to international arms limitation negotiations. As he told the Cabinet Nuclear Policy Group, 'To give up our status as nuclear weapon state would be a momentous step in British history', one that would deprive Britain of influence on, and access to, American decision-making. Ministers had considered whether it would not be more appropriate for

Britain to focus on building up its conventional forces. Large sections of the Labour movement, especially among the unions, were hostile to Britain's having nuclear weapons at all. Callaghan himself spells out in his memoirs the European case for the British deterrent, and the support of Helmut Schmidt for the view that France should not be the only nuclear military power in Europe.[79] But his career suggests that national considerations weighed equally strongly with him. Callaghan went to Guadeloupe to 'probe rather than negotiate': the issue would be considered by the Cabinet on his return.The preponderance of British scientific opinion was that the Trident C4 missiles would provide the most effective affordable option in the future. David Owen, however, along with other ministers such as William Rodgers, favoured the cheaper Cruise missiles launched from the navy's existing submarines. The Nuclear Defence Group had remained uncommitted to either system.

At a purely private meeting in Carter's beach hut on the afternoon of 5 January, the first day of full talks, Callaghan had a lengthy discussion with the American President on Britain's military future.[80] The 'walk on the beach', of which no formal record seems to exist, subsequently became a theme of legend and rumour. Callaghan was at his most persuasive and effective. Carter seems to have agreed readily with him on the need for Britain to find a successor system to Polaris, both for military reasons and to reinforce the west's bargaining position in SALT III talks when a counter to the Russian SS 20s would come into the negotiations. The usefulness of the British deterrent, from this and other points of view, lay in the fact that it would never be used. The general verdict was that Trident C4 submarines might prove the most effective form of technology transfer and that talks might be begun on this issue. Subsequently, Sir Ronald Mason and Clive Rose, respectively chief scientist at the Ministry of Defence and the Cabinet deputy secretary who had been involved in force reduction talks in central Europe, went to Washington in February, and discussions also began between Fred Mulley and Harold Brown, the defence ministers in Britain and the United States.[81] By the time Callaghan fell from power the idea of a new British nuclear weapon capability was being actively pursued.

But it was at this stage only an idea. Callaghan put it to the Cabinet on his return on 11 January only in terms of possible options. There was no British commitment to finding a successor to Polaris at the time of the general election in May 1979, and the scientific and technical inquiries into both Trident and Cruise were still under way. Callaghan has robustly defended in his memoirs the view that he committed Britain no further than he was entitled to do in terms of the mandate from his Cabinet and (indirectly) his party. He is correct in doing so. It would have been feasible for the next Labour government, had it been returned, to eliminate entirely Britain's involvement as a nuclear military power. Many wished that Britain's defence policy had taken a quite different turn from the late 1940s. Like the legendary Irishman, they preferred not to start from here.

Even so, Callaghan's discussions with Carter took the next stage of Britain's nuclear commitment, with all its military, environmental, and moral imponderables, a significant stage further. The early 1980s were to see renewed passionate debate on the rationale for nuclear weapons as a component of Britain's national and international defence. Mrs Thatcher's Committee MISC 7 then decided in favour of Trident, upgraded from C4 to D5. Hugely expensive though it was, it would seem clear that Callaghan supported it, the 1979 Labour election manifesto notwithstanding. The Polaris submarine was finally retired in 1996, by which time the four Trident vessels under highly expensive construction already secured a national defence capability hugely in excess of any conceivable need. But by then, of course, the cold war which had dominated Guadeloupe was ended.

The conference at Guadeloupe marked the climax of Callaghan's involvement in foreign affairs as Prime Minister. Major discussions on détente and arms limitation, and on a European monetary system, continued right down to the resignation of his government in early May. After his defeat in the general election, he was the more caught up in worldwide debate on key international issues. It provided much of the intellectual thrust of his public life in his retirement in the 1980s and 1990s. Many of the key themes of the 1970s were replayed in the meetings in Vail, Colorado, in which Ford, Schmidt, Giscard, and Callaghan participated to mutual pleasure. The general course of western, more particularly American, diplomacy in the later 1970s was not subsequently thought to be distinguished or effective. Balanced against the considerable successes like the Camp David talks was the failure of the western leaders to provide a coherent strategy in the face of the Russian combination of détente and rearmament. It was foreign policy that in large measure led to Jimmy Carter's defeat by Ronald Reagan in the 1980 presidential election, amidst the stalling of SALT II, the Russian engagement in Afghanistan, and the humiliation of the Americans in the Iran hostage crisis. There were Russian troops in Afghanistan, Cuban troops in Angola, and plenty of Chinese in Vietnam. The Soviet Union under Brezhnev seemed to have recaptured the aggressive momentum it had last displayed in the last years of Stalin. Coexistence no longer seemed peaceful. In all these respects,

Carter was criticized in the United States as being indecisive. It is the more surprising that he was to re-emerge under President Clinton in the early 1990s as an international troubleshooter from Haiti to North Korea to Bosnia. Even here, Helmut Schmidt unforgivingly observed, he was showing the same traits as in the late 1970s and doing unauthorized things behind Clinton's back.[82]

For James Callaghan, however, it is reasonable to strike a more positive note. He played a major role as honest broker between the Americans and the continental Europeans on détente, defence, and economic collaboration. He did so more openly than Wilson, less dogmatically than Heath, less confrontationally than Thatcher, and with more confidence and plausibility than Major. From the Downing Street summit to Guadeloupe, he could be seen, to use one of his favourite phrases, as 'a stabilizing force', on whom both Carter and Schmidt placed some reliance. More than the other participants, perhaps, he could draw particular satisfaction from the Guadeloupe summit, since important progress had been made on his two main objectives—the 'twin track' approach on disarmament, and the future of the British independent deterrent. In a post-imperial age, he was one of Great Britain's last significant international statesmen, respected across the world. In the Middle East, he played a major role as a dispassionate adviser of the US President, uncommitted to either Jews or Arabs. Even in Rhodesia the impasse was distinctly less hopeless by May 1979.

More broadly, he had given Britain a more intelligible, if still somewhat negative, role in Europe but had also strongly reaffirmed its close relationship to the government of the United States. He had sensed, and seized, the possibilities of Britain's role as an experienced international honest broker. At the same time, perhaps more than most, he was well aware of the severe limitations imposed on British influence through its declining economic and strategic power. Alan Bullock quotes Callaghan speaking as Prime Minister at a dinner in Bonn in 1976, given by Helmut Schmidt and the German government. 'The mistake we made', observed Callaghan, 'was to think we won the war.' This was a judgement which both the British and Germans present endorsed.[83] In terms of British defence interests, he had sustained British needs in terms of the conventional wisdom on defence priorities current in the late 1970s. And he had done so with a relatively united Cabinet, and in the face of endless sniping from the National Executive and grass-roots activists on the left.

On a personal level, he had emerged with considerable stature, in western Europe and the Commonwealth, as an adroit, uniquely experienced, and rational practitioner of power. Among other things he had shown a remarkable, though not unusual, capacity for intellectual adaptation, for example to the changed strategic context of the late 1970s or the economic development of Europe following the turmoil of the great inflation earlier in the decade. Much of British foreign policy in these years was reactive and not particularly inspired. But the Prime Minister's defence of the national interest would be a major factor in reinforcing his authority as the old sailor returned home from the calmer waters of international peace-making to the maelstrom of social and economic problems at home.

1. Telephone conversation between Callaghan and Governor Carter, 13 Jan. 1977 (Callaghan Papers, box 33); 'Exchange of Remarks between the President and Prime Minister Callaghan', Office of the White House Press Secretary, 10 Mar. 1977, box 2 (Jimmy Carter Library, Atlanta).

2. Telephone conversation between Callaghan and Schmidt, 16 Mar. 1977 (Callaghan Papers, box 33).

3. Interview with Lord Callaghan. On the Callaghan–Carter relationship, see Zbigniew Brzezinski, *Power and Principle* (London, 1983) pp. 165, 291.

4. Henderson, *Mandarin*, 143 ff.

5. Ibid. 213 ff.

6. Prime Minister's diaries, 1976–9 (Callaghan Papers, box 35).

7. Interview with Helmut Schmidt, 30 Nov. 1994.

8. Callaghan to Schmidt, 14 Oct. (three calls) and 16 Oct. 1977 (Callaghan Papers, box 33).

9. Interviews with Lee Kuan Yew and Sir Thomas McCaffrey. The star of 'The Muppets', a puppet show, was Kermit the frog.

10. Interview with Sir Bryan Cartledge; record of visit to India (Callaghan Papers, box 21A). I have been told by Sir Montague Levine that one moment of alarm during this Indian visit came when the *Sunday Times* journalist Anthony Holden was diagnosed as having contracted mumps while on board the Prime Minister's VC 10. Although he had no recollection of ever having had this illness himself, Callaghan survived his visit mumps-free.

11. Interview with Lee Kuan Yew.

12. Information from Sir Reginald Hibbert.

13. Material in Callaghan Papers (uncatalogued); Callaghan's speech in Falklands debate, *Parl. Deb.* 6th ser., vol. 27, 479–82 (8 July 1982).

14. Record of Kissinger mediation (Callaghan Papers, box 21A).

15. Kissinger to Callaghan, 18 Mar. 1976 (ibid., uncatalogued).

16. Record of Kissinger mediation (ibid., box 21A).

17. Ibid.; also Callaghan to Julius Nyerere, 23 Oct. 1976 (ibid., box 20).

18. Callaghan to Kaunda, 10 Feb. 1977 (ibid.); Owen, *Time to Declare*, 284.

19. Callaghan to Nyerere, 14 Aug. 1977, Callaghan to Kaunda, 7 Sept. 1977, MISC 77 (Callaghan Papers, box 20).

20. McNally to Callaghan, 8 July 1977 (ibid., box 21A).

21. McNally memo, 8 July 1977 (ibid.). Also McNally to Callaghan, 27 Feb. 1978 (ibid.).

22. Kaunda to Callaghan, 4 Dec. 1978, T254/78; Callaghan to Jorgensen, 1 Dec. 1978, T250A/78 (ibid., box 34).

23. Callaghan to Hughes, 22 Nov., 22 Dec. 1978 (ibid., box 21A); information from Lord Cledwyn.

24. Callaghan to Nyerere, 8 Mar. 1978, T49/78 (ibid.).

25. Callaghan to Nyerere, 22 Mar. 1978, MISC 78; Callaghan to Kaunda, 12 Apr. 1978 (ibid., box 20).

26. Callaghan to Desai, 10 Apr. 1978 (ibid.).

27. Record of meeting of Callaghan with Bishop Abel Muzorewa, 13 July 1979, and meeting with Miss L. P. Chibesakunda, 17 July 1979 (ibid., box 21A).

28. McNally memo, 8 July 1977 (ibid.).

29. Owen, *Time to Declare*, 381.

30. Telephone conversation between Callaghan and Schmidt, 16 Mar. 1977 (Callaghan Papers, box 33).

31. Ibid.

32. Ibid.

33. Jenkins, *A Life at the Centre*, 458–9.

34. Record of Economic Summit Conference, London, 5–8 May 1977, White House Central Files, box FO–43 (Jimmy Carter Library, Atlanta); telephone conversation between Callaghan and Carter, 20 May 1977 (Callaghan Papers, box 33).

35. Helmut Schmidt, *Men and Power: A Political Retrospective* (London, 1990), 185.

36. Callaghan to Carter, 30 June 1977; Carter to Callaghan, 7 July 1977 (Callaghan Papers, uncatalogued).

37. Interview with Helmut Schmidt.

38. Callaghan to Carter, 23 Mar. 1978 (Callaghan Papers, uncatalogued).

39. Callaghan to Carter, 26 May 1978 (ibid., box 34).

40. Material in Callaghan Papers, box 26 and uncatalogued.

41. Ibid.

42. Callaghan to Sir Robert Armstrong, 20 Dec. 1982, paper by Armstrong, 23 Jan. 1983 (Callaghan Papers, box 26).

43. Material in Callaghan Papers, uncatalogued.

44. Callaghan statement and answers to questions in the Commons, *Parl. Deb.*, 5th ser., vol. 931, 901–21 (9 May 1977). The Downing Street Declaration is printed on 915–21.

45. Telephone conversation between Callaghan and Carter, 17 Apr. 1978, T88B/78 (Callaghan Papers, box 34).

46. Callaghan memo, ? Apr. 1978, T61 2A/78 (ibid.).

47. See Jocelyn Statler, 'British Foreign Policy to 1985: The European Monetary System from Conception to Birth', *International Affairs*, 55 (1979) and Stephen George, *An Awkward Partner* (Oxford, 1990), on this.

48. Telephone conversation between Callaghan and Carter, 15 Feb. 1978, T36A/78 (Callaghan Papers, box 34).

49. Record of meeting of Callaghan and Begin, 3–4 Dec. 1977 (ibid., box 21A).

50. Record of meeting, 20 Dec. 1977 (ibid.), and telephone conversation of Callaghan and Begin, 26 Dec. 1977, T271/78 (ibid., box 33).

51. Record of meeting of Callaghan and Sadat, 14 Jan. 1978 (ibid., box 21A), and telephone conversation between Callaghan and Sadat, 26 Dec. 1977, T272/77 (ibid., box 33); Callaghan to Owen, 1 Jan. 1978, MI/78 (ibid., box 34).

52. Telephone conversation between Callaghan and Carter, 14 Jan. 1978, T11/78 (ibid., box 34).

53. Record of meeting of Callaghan and Begin, 22 Sept. 1978 (ibid., box 21A).

54. This account of security matters is largely based on Dorrill and Ramsay, *Smear!*, uncatalogued personal material in the Callaghan Papers, and an interview with Lord Hunt.

55. Dorril and Ramsay, *Smear!*, pp. 319 ff.

56. Material in Callaghan Papers (uncatalogued); see also Sir Howard Smith's obituary in *Guardian*, 10 May 1996, including some comments from Callaghan.

57. Callaghan to Schmidt and Giscard d'Estaing, 18 May 1978 (ibid., box 21A); Callaghan's speech in Westland debate, *Parl. Deb.*, 6th ser., vol. 89, 1110–11 (15 Jan. 1986).

58. Callaghan to John Sweeney, ? Sept. 1990, printed in *The Observer*, 10 Mar. 1991.

59. NEC/Cabinet paper on European elections, Aug. 1978, RE1798 (Callaghan Papers, box 10).

60. James Callaghan, *Challenges and Opportunities for British Foreign Policy* (Fabian Tract, 439, 1975), 13.

61. Henderson, *Mandarin*, 213–15; interview with Helmut Schmidt.

62. Material in Callaghan Papers, uncatalogued.

63. Jenkins, *A Life at the Centre*, 477. For much fascinating detail, see his *European Diary, 1977–81* (London, 1989).

64. Edmund Dell, 'Britain and the Origins of the European Monetary System', *Contemporary European History*, 3/1 (1994), 37.

65. Ibid. 39.

66. David Lipsey to Callaghan, 26 July 1977 (Callaghan Papers, box 10); Benn, *Conflicts of Interest*, 396 (25 Nov. 1978).

67. Notes of a meeting of Callaghan and Schmidt, Oct. 1977 (Callaghan Papers, uncatalogued).

68. Notes of conversation of Callaghan and Jorgensen, 1 Dec. 1978, T250A/78; Callaghan to Andreotti, 21 Dec. 1978, T263/78; telephone conversations of Callaghan and Schmidt, 16 Oct. 1978, T225A/78, and 26 Nov. 1978, T248A/78 (ibid., box 34).

69. Callaghan conversation with Jorgensen, loc. cit.

70. Dell, 'Britain and the Origins of the EMS', 50–4.

71. Record of meetings of Callaghan and Schmidt, 18–19 Oct. 1978 (Callaghan Papers, box 34).

72. This account of the Guadeloupe meeting is based on uncatalogued material and on material in box 26 in the Callaghan Papers, and the record of the Guadeloupe conference in the Jimmy Carter Library, Atlanta (White House Central Files, box FO-45).

73. Ibid.

74. Callaghan, *Time and Chance*, 546.

75. Uncatalogued material in the Callaghan Papers.

76. Ibid.

77. Ibid.

78. Schmidt, *Men and Power*, 39.

79. *Time and Chance*, 554–5.

80. Uncatalogued material in the Callaghan Papers.

81. Ibid.; *Time and Chance*, 557.

82. Interview with Helmut Schmidt.

83. Alan Bullock, *Ernest Bevin: Foreign Secretary* (London, 1983), 51 n.

26

ELECTION DEFERRED

LIKE all prime ministers, James Callaghan devoted immense care and attention to the question of getting back next time. He thought constantly about the timing of the next general election and how best to present himself and his government to the judgement of the voters. As with most politicians he assumed that this decision was the personal prerogative of the prime minister alone. In fact, this view followed a particular reading of the specific case of Lloyd George's decision to call the 'coupon election' in December 1918, one that academic political scientists might dispute. For Callaghan, it was a more powerful priority than for most since he was well aware that, through the accident of circumstances, he was the first Labour prime minister not to hold his position through the direct choice of the electorate. The timing of the next election was recognized as the ultimate test of the political skills of any prime minister. Callaghan had grown up as a young MP with the view that Attlee's timing had been wrong in both February 1950 and October 1951 and that this had very possibly cost Labour a further term in power. Much more recently, it was generally believed that had Edward Heath, as many of his ministers urged, opted for 7 February rather than 28 February 1974 for holding an election, he might well have been returned to power; in which case, Mrs Thatcher might have remained a footnote to history. On the other hand, Harold Wilson was generally praised for his astuteness in getting his electoral timing right, the unexpected defeat of June 1970 notwithstanding. Callaghan, generally admired as an almost legendary reader of the political entrails, was thought by most Labour MPs and party voters to be likely to get it right.

In practice, while the government could have remained in office (its parliamentary majority permitting, of course) until October 1979, the realistic choice was seen as lying between the autumn of 1978 and the spring of 1979. Planning for the next election campaign in fact began as early as July 1977, when Callaghan had been Prime Minister for only just over a year.

Tom McNally began offering suggestions for the campaign team for the next election; he proposed either John Harris, the former special assistant of Roy Jenkins, or Geoffrey Goodman, a respected industrial correspondent successively on the *Daily Herald*, *Sun*, and *Daily Mirror*, as political adviser, and Joe Haines, McCaffrey's predecessor as press secretary, as political speech writer.[1] The Labour Party had already retained Robert Worcester, the American director of the MORI organization, for conducting private opinion polls. Others suggested using the academic psephologist Ivor Crewe of the University of Essex, a Labour supporter who later backed the SDP in the early 1980s, to address the Campaign Committee.[2] A letter from Reg Underhill, the former national agent, probably in late 1977, made a point regarded as very important by many, that a new register would tend to favour Labour and perhaps give them six extra seats, whereas postal votes would, as usual, favour the Tories: this, of course, was an argument for delay since a new register would come into effect only in early 1979.[3] Other memos from McNally in January and March 1978 suggested the formation of an advertising team run by Edward Booth-Clibborn (chairman of the Designers and Arts Directors' Association), and passed on the views of Roger Carroll, political editor of the *Sun*. This claimed that in the next election Mrs Thatcher would 'play more dirty than most'. Her speeches were full of references to 'scroungers' to attack social security, 'Marxism' in relation to defence policy, and 'extremism' as regards law and order.[4] At a meeting with the Prime Minister's special advisers, headed by David Lipsey, on 17 March, Bob Worcester of MORI reported that the Tory lead had fallen dramatically in recent months. In particular, Labour was doing much better in Scotland where the SNP challenge appeared to be fading.[5]

In the end an election team was assembled and held its first meeting on 19 May 1978. Its chairman was Derek Gladwin, southern regional secretary of the General and Municipal Workers' Union and a long-serving member of the Labour conference arrangements committee. He had much experience of electoral organization going back to the North Lewisham constituency in the 1950s which included the Callaghans' home in Blackheath. Callaghan had offered him a post as Overseas Labour Officer during his time at the Foreign Office. The GMWU was a union with which Callaghan had close personal connections. He was actually a member of it and used the GMWU offices in Cardiff for his political surgeries. Its general secretary David Basnett was close to Callaghan and, as chairman of Trade Unionists for a Labour Victory, felt to be a major influence at that period. Derek Gladwin had with him a team of nine—Michael Foot and Merlyn Rees from the Cabinet; Tom McNally from the Political Office; Ron Hayward, Reg Underhill, and Percy Clark to represent Transport House and the party organization; Norman Willis for the TUC; Mike Molloy of the *Daily Mirror* for the press side; and Edward Booth-Clibborn for marketing and advertising. Others brought in from August 1978 were Tim Delaney and Trevor Eke on the advertising side, Roger Carroll of the *Sun* for speechwriting, and the Prime Minister's son Michael.[6] It was a balanced, though perhaps not inspired, group of people, with no obvious master-mind for key strategy. Former Harold Wilson followers like Joe Haines were excluded. No one had any particular experience of businesslike systems of management and delegation of authority, although this was in part supplied when the election came by Callaghan's son Michael, an executive with Ford Motors.

But in June–July 1978, with the opinion polls moving in Labour's direction at last, and the economic tidings still broadly favourable with no great sign of crisis on the horizon, this campaign team moved into more purposive action. There was a PR meeting at Transport House on 23 August to discuss personnel for party political broadcasts. It was agreed that the Prime Minister would be Labour's chief asset and that challenging Mrs Thatcher to a presidential-style televised debate might well be considered. The Booth-Clibborn group argued against using Michael Foot, but Percy Clark of Transport House 'said that, for political reasons, No 10 had indicated that he would have to be used'. Roy Mason would be dropped 'since he would remind people of the Northern Ireland problem'. Gladwin chaired a *Mirror* lunch to discuss election plans on 30 August, attended by Lipsey, McCaffrey, McNally, Geoffrey Goodman, Joe Haines, and Terry Lancaster. It was agreed that Labour needed to look for 'heart' in the campaign (the Health Service, education, and the youth vote were mentioned). Overall, Labour would base its appeal on the theme of 'Fairness'.

Many people in the Labour Party, including ministers ranging in viewpoint from Roy Hattersley to Tony Benn, were known to be sympathetic to an early appeal to the voters, probably in October. There were, however, two great imponderables which made the Prime Minister pause. The first was the parliamentary and constitutional mess over Scottish and Welsh devolution The second, and fundamentally more serious for the government and the country, was the future course of pay policy, with the apparent ending of the trade union commitment to pay restraint and thus a return to massive inflation which would throw the government irrevocably off course.

Devolution had been a headache for the government ever since Labour came to office in March 1974.[7] The success of Scottish Nationalist and Plaid Cymru candidates in by-elections in the period 1966–8 (in fact, not reproduced in the 1970 general election) had led to Harold Wilson appointing the Crowther Commission to consider the British constitutional structure and the prospects for devolution; when Lord Crowther died, he was replaced as chairman by Lord Kilbrandon. The Kilbrandon Commission reported in the autumn of 1973. It produced a range of options in a variety of reports, but the majority declared clearly in favour of an elected Scottish assembly with tax-raising powers, and a more limited elected Welsh assembly with a block grant mainly for expenditure on social matters from the Westminster government.

Callaghan himself had never viewed devolution with enthusiasm. Although he had come to support the creation of the Welsh Office in 1964 and indeed extended its powers significantly between 1976 and 1979, he took the traditional Labour view of endorsing a nationwide approach to social and economic planning and regarding devolution as a dangerous concession to parochial Celtic nationalism. This was traditionally the view of the members for, and citizens of, the capital city of Cardiff. In 1969, Callaghan had seen himself as the voice of 'Anglicized' Welshmen over the powers of the Welsh Office. In Wales, he shared little common ground with Plaid Cymru and viewed with revulsion the direct action of the youthful adherents of Cymdeithas yr Iaith Cymraeg (the Welsh Language Society), involving the defacing of English-only roadsigns, and attacks on post and tax offices and television masts. He wrote to Dr Norman Hunt, an Oxford academic prominent on the Kilbrandon Commission, on 7 February 1973 about his proposals for Welsh devolution, 'I would prefer to see the line drawn in a way that stripped as few functions as possible from Westminster. You will gather from all this that I am not enthusiastic and you would be right.'[8] Like almost all other Labour members, Callaghan was opposed to weakening the powers of the Scottish and Welsh Offices in favour of elected assemblies, believing that this would materially weaken the influence of the Scottish and Welsh on central decision-making. He was even more opposed to reducing the number of Scottish and Welsh MPs at Westminster in view of their crucial part in any Labour majority. Donoughue of the Policy Unit urged him to be more positive about devolution, especially in Scotland where Labour appeared 'old, complacent and resistant to change', as well as in some cases actually corrupt. Bruce Millan should inject some energy into the Scottish Office which appeared an Anglicizing influence, more focused on 'Tory Edinburgh than Labour Glasgow'.[9]

However, from October 1974, with Labour having a tiny majority dependent on the goodwill of the 11 Scottish Nationalist and 3 Plaid Cymru MPs, the government had no option other than to respond. In any case, some ministers regarded Scottish and Welsh devolution as a valuable reform in local democracy and accountability which should be welcomed. Shirley Williams, who chaired the Cabinet committee on Scottish devolution as Paymaster-General, warmly endorsed the idea of a Scottish parliament having taxing powers. The key figure was the leader of the House, Michael Foot, who was given the task of guiding proposals for devolution through his Commons. He pursued this goal with much dedication. Cledwyn Hughes, often in disagreement with him, was forced to comment that 'he has made a greater effort to understand us [the Welsh] and to meet Welsh aspirations than any non-Welsh politician I have ever known. He has stood up to cruel attacks which would have daunted lesser men. Foot has won an honourable place in Welsh history whatever may come of his bill.'[10] Michael Foot's view was in part formed by his intense regard for the radical Welsh political tradition although his particular hero, and predecessor as member for Ebbw Vale, Aneurin Bevan, was strongly hostile to devolution. Foot's deputy was to be an up-and-coming Scots barrister, John Smith, a protégé of Callaghan's who first made his mark in these debates. Although critical of Kilbrandon, which he saw as marking the death of the Scottish Office, in the March 1974 election, he was now to show himself as a strong and articulate devolutionist.[11]

The progress of Scottish and Welsh devolution, however, was anything but straightforward. As foreshadowed in a government white paper in 1975, *Our Changing Democracy: Devolution for Scotland and Wales* (Cmnd. 6348), a combined bill for Scottish and Welsh devolution was introduced in the autumn of 1976. Callaghan himself moved the second reading on 13 December 1976 and the bill went through with a government majority of 45, relatively comfortable for that parliament. However, the cross-voting in the Commons and especially the divided counsels on the Labour benches meant that devolution would have a particularly difficult passage into law. The Scottish Labour MPs were largely in favour of devolution, more emphatically so perhaps than the Scottish Secretary of State, Bruce Millan, and certainly more than his predecessor William Ross, prior to 1974. There was, however, at least one notable and difficult dissenter, Tam Dalyell (West Lothian), a thorn in the government's flesh in debates. Another Scottish critic was Robin Cook, while expatriate Scots, George Cunningham (Islington South and Finsbury) being prominent among them, also tended to be critical. The Welsh Labour MPs were much more divided, with six of them, a so-called 'gang of six' including Neil Kinnock (Bedwellty) and Leo Abse (Pontypool), being strongly opposed to a Welsh assembly on either socialist/centralist grounds or (in Abse's case) emotional prejudice against a proposal he saw as being the product of cultural pressure from semi-nationalist Welsh-speaking rural Wales and its Labour representatives such as Cledwyn Hughes and Elystan Morgan.[12] Even though the Wales TUC led by George Wright and the party organizers in Cardiff favoured devolution, opinion in Wales showed at best only a very shaky majority in favour; that was soon to disappear. The English MPs were either detached and bored or openly resentful; members for the north-east or north-west (including ministers such as William Rodgers) felt that Scotland and Wales would acquire advantages over their own regions which were not justified, and would also have their MPs able to vote on the affairs of other parts of Britain, while their own areas had protected status. Tam Dalyell's 'Mid-Lothian question' posed that question as starkly as A. V. Dicey had done over Gladstone's first Irish Home Rule Bill in 1886.

The government found the going very difficult over devolution in 1977–8. On 10 February John Smith announced that, to placate critics, there would be referendums in Scotland and Wales before the bills became law. Much procedural confusion followed, with Michael Foot central to it, as to whether these referendums were mandatory or merely consultative and not binding on the government. Shortly afterwards, a guillotine motion was lost by the government by 312 to 283 and the Scotland and Wales measure was thus dead and buried. There followed much anxious discussion about future policy (devolution was a key issue in the Lib–Lab pact agreed between Callaghan and David Steel on 21 March), with clear signs that, in Scotland at least, the Nationalists were benefiting from the government's indecision. In November, therefore, separate Scottish and Welsh devolution bills were introduced. They lurched their way hazardously through the committee stage, supported both by Nationalists who saw devolution as a stepping stone to self-government for the Celtic nations and by left-wing socialists such as Eric Heffer who rejected the idea totally. Two critical amendments were forced upon the government. One, moved by George Cunningham, spelt out that if less than 40 per cent of the electors (not just of those voting) in the referendums voted 'yes', orders in parliament would be laid down for the bills to be repealed. This doomed Welsh devolution at birth: the Abacus polling organization, commissioned by BBC (Wales), showed support in Wales for devolution on 15 September 1978 standing at just 27 per cent, the same figure as in December 1976, with 'noes' standing at 41 per cent. It also made Scottish devolution far more difficult to achieve. The other amendment was that referendums would have to follow within three months of a general election assuming that devolution was to go ahead. With relief more than exaltation in either Scotland or Wales, the two bills passed and received the Royal Assent on 31 July 1978. Rather unusually, Callaghan's speech to the national eisteddfod at Cardiff on 6 August followed a political tack by spelling out the need for an elected Welsh assembly. Even so the fulfilment of devolution in either nation remained most uncertain and an enormous potential blow to the government's prestige and capacity for survival lay at hand.

The crisis over the trade unions and pay restraint was more serious still. In effect, it raised the entire relationship of the industrial muscle of organized labour to the governmental process—what Edward Heath in 1974 had called the issue of 'who governs Britain?' There had been growing difficulties on industrial pay since the refusal of the unions in 1977 to continue the two-year wage freeze. In 1977–8 there was the process of a 'planned and orderly return to collective bargaining' as the formula went, which meant that wages crept upwards. When Jack Jones asked his own Transport Workers at their biennial delegate conference in July 1977 to continue the policy of restrictions on pay increases for a further year, even his great prestige did not prevent his suffering a serious defeat.

Throughout the early months of 1978 there were growing pressures for significant increases in wage levels from a variety of workers. These ranged from skilled workers in the car industry, notably in Ford Motors, who saw improvements in the economy leading to their wage levels falling behind others, to manual workers in the public services such as members of NUPE, GMW, and COHSE who felt the impact on jobs and wages of two years of squeeze on public expenditure. The prospects were not improved by developments on pay elsewhere. A variety of professional and other groups were given significant increases in pay of up to 40 per cent, including the doctors and dentists, the police, and the armed services. Less defensibly, the so-called 'Top People's' pay review body chaired by Lord Boyle recommended increases in salary for already highly remunerated people like judges, top civil servants, and the heads of nationalized industries. The government accepted the Boyle proposals which meant rises of an average of 30 per cent.[13] This did nothing for the persuasive powers of the government over ordinary workers in the public sector who had suffered a severe cut in real wages since 1975. Huge claims were being put forward that summer—40 per cent from the National Union of Mineworkers in late July, 25 per cent from the unions representing Ford car workers (resentful of the fact that they were on time rates and therefore doing less well than workers in British Leyland) on 24 August.[14] The autumn pay round was evidently going to be a most difficult and delicate affair.

The government's response was a highly personal one by the Prime Minister. He had long rejected the union shibboleth of leaving wage settlements to the free market. On 1 December 1977 he was to tell parliament, 'I ceased to worship free collective bargaining more than ten years ago.' He was utterly convinced that, both for economic and electoral reasons, the inflation rate must be kept in single figures for the remaining period that his government held office. The eventual overall figure for inflation in 1978 was to be 8.2 per cent, almost half that for 1977 (15.9 per cent), but there were already signs of growing inflationary pressure that summer. Indeed, wages rose by 15 per cent in 1977–8. A severe cut in pay rises, much less than the 10 per cent that was resulting from the TUC's voluntary formula for the year from August 1977, was inevitable. It would be sweetened by price stability, tax cuts, and a continuing fall in unemployment as economic recovery was maintained. As early as 22 December 1977, Callaghan put this approach to his Cabinet, but there was murmuring about being unduly rigid or provocative, and nothing firm resulted.[15]

However, in a BBC radio interview with Gordon Clough on 1 January 1978, Callaghan did offer the view that the pay norm for the next pay round should mean average increases of no more than 5 per cent. In effect, with wage drift, this would mean 7.5 per cent and enable the government to go to the country with inflation still in single figures. In his memoirs, Callaghan comments that this figure just 'popped out'.[16] If so, it was an unusual indiscretion by an invariably shrewd and calculating politician of great experience. It was in fact a personal initiative by a prime minister who took the Treasury formulations on board, and who felt, with much reason, that he had a better intuitive understanding of the psychology of the unions and the public at large than any other British politician. He had become convinced that it was the one practicable alternative to the failed strategy of a statutory incomes policy. Others were more sceptical. Sympathetic union leaders like David Basnett and Len Murray told him that they would be quite unable to maintain the position during the winter. In particular, workers in the public sector felt that they were being victimized and pay relativities destroyed. It was a view reinforced by industrial correspondents and other journalists whom Callaghan frequently saw in 10 Downing Street to discuss the future of the social contract. To them, Callaghan somewhat startlingly responded that he would appeal directly as national leader over the heads of union leaders to their rank and file members, calling for renewed wage restraint. Denis Healey supported his Prime Minister but felt at the time that 5 per cent was too rigid and inflexible to be satisfactory.[17] The Policy Unit had tended to counsel in favour of some flexibility also, although it recognized that there had to be stringency in assessing pay claims, and that even 5 per cent was by technical financial criteria too high. Perhaps a norm of zero per cent was what the country really required, apart from being what the IMF may have expected. Gavyn Davies pointed out that, even though unemployment might well rise rapidly up to 1982, despite the coming of North Sea oil, there was no provision in government policy for expanding public service employment. Tom McNally was inclined to support a 5 per cent norm, however, believing that for members of NUPE it would mean as much as 9 per cent which could hardly be described as a savage squeeze on pay.[18]

At a meeting with TUC leaders on 30 June, Callaghan addressed them boldly. He stated that single-figure pay increases for 1978–9 were essential, and formally proposed 5 per cent with another 2 per cent for anomalies, somewhat generally defined. The Cabinet in the main went along with a line which it had not formally discussed at all; the Prime Minister emphasized that it would be a policy collectively enforced, with much responsibility falling on individual ministers. Shirley Williams would have to pressurize the teachers, David Ennals the health workers, Peter Shore the water workers, and, no doubt, Tony Benn the power workers, which was inherently improbable. The government, therefore, retired for the summer recess with the high risk of a 5 per cent norm as its centrepiece. The government white paper *Winning the Battle against Inflation* published on 23 July set down formally the 5 per cent norm with room for adjustment in individual cases and the possibility of self-funding productivity deals which could produce a higher figure.[19] It was a limit which scarcely any of the major unions seemed disposed to observe.

A further complicating factor in the union world was the impact of personalities. The main agents in inducing the unions to accept the pay restraint policy in 1975–7 were neither Len Murray nor Callaghan's ally David Basnett, a weathercock union leader who overestimated his own influence, but Jack Jones of the Transport Workers and Hugh Scanlon. They were two veteran giants of the left who had helped throw out Barbara Castle's proposals in 1969 but who had been pivotal supporters of the Labour government and its social contract since Harold Wilson had returned to office. Now they were both gone. Scanlon retired early in 1978; his successor Terry Duffy, a devout Roman Catholic and loyalist right-winger, lacked his predecessor's tactical flair and prestige. The departure of Jack Jones as TGWU general secretary was far more serious. Not only was his retirement from the TUC and the Labour Party National Executive a major blow in itself. His successor turned out not to be Harry Urwin, his deputy whom Jones apparently ruled out on the grounds that he was only two years younger than himself and therefore too old, but a Welshman brought up in the Midlands, the TGWU regional organizer Moss Evans.[20] He had campaigned for the general secretaryship on the basis of a rejection of any formal interference with wage bargaining and a decentralist message that the central union leadership should defer to local plant representatives. In effect, he was content to give way to militant shop stewards as far as pay norms were concerned. At a very early meeting with the Prime Minister in April 1978 there was a dispute over whether the government should interfere in wage bargaining. Evans urged the government to 'back off' and have faith in the unions and the powers of leadership of men like himself.

The transition from Jack Jones to Moss Evans was not the only reason for the winter of discontent and the resultant humiliation and collapse of the Callaghan government. Evans himself consistently took the line that the demands of his men were reasonable and that it was government interference in trying to impose artificial restrictions on pay increases that was the cause of discontent.[21] But the advent of one who took an industry-centred view and hardly seemed to admit the seriousness of inflation as a cause of unemployment and economic difficulty was scarcely a bonus to a Labour government at this time. Harry Urwin would have had to retire in two years' time, but they were to prove two years of portentous significance. The consequence was to be eleven years of Thatcherism.

Even so, Callaghan retired to his Sussex farm still in the same confident mood he had felt for well over a year. He was cheered by the amiable character of meetings he held with TUC leaders and with their representatives on the Liaison Committee. They appeared ready to sustain the social contract which implied a continuation of their corporatist relationship to the Labour government. Moss Evans sounded co-operative at first. The Prime Minister was advised to spend time 'massaging his ego'.[22] In any case, Callaghan was convinced that his persuasive skills would manage to impress upon the TUC and the member unions the necessity for continued restraint and an acceptance of a 5 per cent norm. He felt himself to be an effective head of a successful government. He was to tell Helmut Schmidt at the end of August, 'I'm going to our trade union movement next week, and I'm going to make a powerful speech for no more than 5 per cent next year. I shall get a battering, of course, but I think we can pull off something like that. And if we can, it'll be a great help on inflation next year.'[23] As far as devolution was concerned, at least the Scottish and Welsh bills were on the statute book. In view of the decision to have local referendums, it was that symbolic achievement rather than the actual giving effect to devolution measures after the next general election that counted. In any case, until the Scots and Welsh had their referendums on devolution put in train, the fourteen Nationalist MPs had no option but to keep Callaghan in office.

It was the rival arguments for soldiering on as against an early general election that seemed to provide the key to Callaghan and the government's strategy. As the economic news continued to be mainly good, with a significant balance of payments surplus of £224m. for June recorded in mid-July, the expectation grew that the Prime Minister must call an early general election, probably for October. This was, indeed, the view of Donoughue and the Policy Unit. At the end of the previous year, it had spelt out the favourable economic indicators for the latter half of 1978—growth of 2.5–3 per cent of GDP, static unemployment around 6 per cent, price inflation falling to 9 per cent, real personal disposable income increasing by 6–7 per cent, and a balance of payments surplus of about £1 bn. in 1978. It seemed almost axiomatic that a general election should be timed for the autumn. The only uncertain factors appeared to be whether October or November was the more suitable month, and the matter of timing the election in relation to the Scottish devolution referendum.[24] If this scenario were to result, and an election take place, then surely the unions would swallow 5 per cent, indeed almost any figure that Callaghan proposed, for the sake of the social contract and keeping the dreaded Mrs Thatcher at bay. This linkage between a tough pay policy and an immediate election was made by the vast majority of political commentators and, more significantly, trade union and business leaders.

Callaghan went back to his farm in Sussex on 3 August. His summer reading would consist not of the historical biographies or Trollope novels beloved of earlier prime ministers, but the *Parliamentary Companion*, *The Times House of Commons*, David Butler's Nuffield election surveys, and sheaves of materials from Robert Worcester of MORI analysing the state of opinion and the likely outcome of the next general election, with special reference to English marginal seats.

Before retiring to Upper Clayhill Farm, he had had a series of key strategic meetings.[25] In late July he had seen David Steel who asked for a meeting with the Prime Minister on 11 September prior to the annual

Liberal Party conference. Even though the Lib–Lab pact was officially ended, relations between the two party leaders were still close and cordial. Steel expected an autumn election and had been given no indication from the Prime Minister that there would not be one. On 25 July an inner group of ministers had an informal meeting to discuss possible political outcomes; on this occasion Michael Foot for the first time seems to have raised the possibility of carrying on beyond the autumn. This also appeared to be the view of Michael Cocks, the chief whip. But Callaghan gave them no obvious encouragement. There was a strategy meeting at 7.15 p.m. on 31 July, just before the House went into recess, at which Callaghan discussed possibilities over drinks with his trusted group of private allies, Merlyn Rees, Jack Cunningham, Gregor MacKenzie, and Roger Stott. Finally on 3 August, just before he was driven to the farm, he had a talk with Kenneth Stowe who reported on a meeting with Michael Foot with particular reference to the Ulster Unionists. Foot had declared that if the Queen's Speech included proposals to bring forward a Northern Ireland Representation of the People Bill, in effect to give Ulster more MPs, the Unionists would not assist in bringing down the government. Gwynfor Evans, the president of Plaid Cymru, had already told John Morris, the Welsh Secretary, that his group of three Welshmen would also back the government on the Queen's Speech; the Scottish Nationalists were divided in their views and clearly could not be relied upon.[26] These intelligences, of varying degrees of reputableness, were largely tending to sway the Prime Minister's mind in favour of staying on. But his own options at this stage were wide open.

Callaghan spent the period from 4 to 28 August almost continuously at the farm, meditating and contemplating the options. He was genuinely open-minded about the decision that he must take. He enjoyed being Prime Minister, he felt his government was going well, and he was reluctant to jeopardize its and his subsequent reputation by a premature appeal to the people. On the other hand, he greatly resented the constraints of minority government. There was a particular area of uncertainty in Rhodesia, with the likelihood of talks between Ian Smith and Joshua Nkomo of the Patriotic Front, which a sudden British general election might severely jeopardize. However, things seemed to be going as well economically as they had ever done, while there were the prospects of much industrial turmoil looming up in the winter. There was, in the much-used phrase, a 'window' when all the economic indices, for growth, employment, trade, and inflation, seemed to be favourable at one and the same time. Living standards showed a rate of annual advance of 6 per cent.

Thomas Balogh had quoted the views of Nicky Kaldor—'it may be a submerged peak but it is a peak nevertheless'.[27] Other than Rhodesia, there were no particular crises overseas to deflect him from running an effective election campaign. Tom McNally, perhaps his closest adviser, felt sure that Callaghan was moving towards an October election, and peppered him with advice—to have his hair cut before he made his broadcast announcing an election, to have a spare jacket with a smart electioneering suit. A variety of particular factors were brought into play for consideration in choosing the precise day in October for the election—the start of the university terms, the advent of the Jewish holidays (which Jack Diamond mentioned), the date of Mrs Thatcher's birthday (13 October) all suggested problems about Thursday, 12 October.[28] But the 5th or the 19th would be all right. At least there was no football World Cup, or indeed any particular sporting event, to worry about this time around. All in all, the 'Octobrists' seemed to be winning.

But the more Callaghan brooded in his little study overlooking the Dutch barn or strolled down to the water meadow at Upper Clayhill Farm, the more he detected problems. There were dangerous signs of regional variations, notably in the sensitive West Midlands seats where Labour was not doing well. To Callaghan these local variations were more significant than the national findings of opinion polls. He told Helmut Schmidt at the end of the month, when some polls gave Labour a lead of as much as 4 per cent, 'I don't trust them. I don't believe in them.'[29] He worked out his own conclusions, seat by seat, and concluded that a possible result would be Labour 303, Conservatives 304. He had already decided that a further period of minority government, a hung parliament governed by the whims of small groups of Liberals, Unionists, and Nationalists, would be impossible. The unpredictable nature of the handful of Liberals during the existence of the pact had not impressed him. His own reading of the evidence suggested that Labour might not even get a majority at all. Nor was this calculation at all irrational. The material he consulted does indeed lead one to the conclusion that a Labour victory was at best a matter of hazard. Robert Worcester of MORI suggested in a private poll of 4 September that his findings envisaged a Tory lead of 47 per cent to 45 per cent. 'The Trade Union vote is significantly less solid than it was in 1973.'[30]

The Prime Minister seems to have reached his conclusion entirely on his own. He became irritated in September when Robert Worcester appeared to suggest in the *Daily Express* that it was his own advice that led Callaghan to decide against holding an early election. Callaghan felt that Worcester 'made an ass of himself' over this issue.[31] In fact, Worcester had to write to *The Times* to say that he had not seen Callaghan since the Penistone and Moss Side by-elections in July and that the most he had done was to supply Callaghan's staff with a preview of the next MORI poll which in fact showed the Tories two points ahead of Labour.[32] Callaghan was a cautious man but even if he were not the evidence before him suggested that an autumn election was the highest of high-risk strategies.

Callaghan was to tell the *Daily Mirror* in September that he had decided as early as 17 August not to hold an autumn election.[33] On the 18th, he invited himself to tea with his Sussex neighbour, the Chancellor, Denis Healey, at Alfriston. Healey gave the opinion that the balance of economic argument was neutral as between having the election in the autumn and in the spring, perhaps a surprising judgement given the rising inflationary pressures in the economy. Callaghan in return told him he had decided to soldier on until the spring. This meeting was part of a process of consultation of Cabinet colleagues. But the ministers consulted, and the order in which Callaghan did so, suggests strongly that he was engaged in confirming a decision already taken. He consulted four ministers initially—the wrong four in the view of Roy Hattersley, an advocate of an early election.[34] They were Merlyn Rees, a naturally cautious politician like Callaghan himself, Denis Healey, who wanted to give the economy more time to improve, David Owen, who wanted a settlement in Rhodesia, and Michael Foot, who was in touch with nervous MPs in marginal constituencies. All four gave their views, it would appear, in favour of soldiering on. There is some uncertainty about this. Healey's view was not a particularly emphatic one, and he warned that the improvement in living standards might slow down during the winter. There is a note from 'David', perhaps the Foreign Secretary, on 1 September stating, 'Go now—we cannot possibly be sure of surviving the winter.' However in his memoirs Owen states that he believed that Labour could not win that autumn, and that his own Devonport constituency was precarious; this may perhaps be taken as his considered view.[35] When Callaghan returned to Downing Street on 30 August, looking well and relaxed, and waving cheerily to the assembled crowds, an episode taken by journalists as a sign of an imminent declaration by an electioneering premier, his mind was already moving the other way.

He also prudently decided to take soundings from all members of the Cabinet and on 31 August–1 September almost all of them replied. Most of the younger ministers were in favour. Of those whose written views are available in Callaghan's papers, ten favoured an October election—Benn, Hattersley, Varley, Rodgers, and Mulley (all suggesting 12 October), Dell (no later than 5 October), Ennals, Barnett, Orme, and Shirley Williams, a scattering of right and left. So did Lord Diamond whom Callaghan also consulted as an old colleague. Albert Booth, the Labour minister, felt that the prospects of reaching agreement with the TVC on a non-statutory policy durign the winter were uncertain and that this consideration 'did not justify delaying a general election'. Those against included Callaghan, Foot, Rees, Owen, Lever, Peart, Morris, and probably Healey, eight in all. Shore was content to leave it to the Prime Minister's judgement; on balance he would have preferred to carry on. The opinions of Lord Elwyn-Jones, Roy Mason, and Bruce Millan do not emerge. The numbers showed a majority for an early poll but, probably in Callaghan's judgement, a balance in terms of Cabinet weight for delay.[36]

However, so private was his method of reaching a decision that the general view (other than those of ministers in the know like Healey and Foot) continued to be confident that there would indeed be an early poll. Callaghan's closest advisers were quite ignorant of what he would conclude. Bernard Donoughue and the Policy Unit were kept in the dark.[37] So, too, were Tom McNally and Tom McCaffrey; they were told merely that an announcement would be made on 7 September. They assumed that it would give the date of the October election and both began briefing friendly journalists like Terence Lancaster of the *Daily Mirror* to this effect.[38] The press began building up an atmosphere of election fever. There was one shrewd cautionary note, by Louis Heren, the well-informed political correspondent of *The Times*. He suggested on 30 August that Callaghan, as a cautious man, might well yield to the temptation of staying on in office after all. He cited evidence from Bob Worcester about Labour's shaky electoral prospects, the hope that a new electoral register in February would be helpful to Labour, and a belief that the economy might not deteriorate by the spring. But Heren's view was felt to be a somewhat maverick one at this particular time of political excitement. His *Times* colleague Fred Emery wrote on 3 September that many ministers would 'be taken aback' if an election were not called and Callaghan decided to slog on through the winter. He noted that the Prime Minister and Mrs Callaghan were due to stay with the Queen at Balmoral on 7 September.[39]

The views of Cabinet colleagues and party workers were, obviously, of much importance. So, too, were the views of whips like Michael Cocks, Walter Harrison, and Ann Taylor, all fearful of an early election.[40] But perhaps of even greater importance was the viewpoint of the leading trade unionists, since clearly Labour would go to the country on the basis of a renewed social contract and its close relationship to organized labour. The image successfully spread abroad of the Heath years was of strikes, power cuts, states of emergency, and the three-day week. Mrs Thatcher, it was claimed, would be even worse. Labour, by contrast, strove to portray itself as the party of conciliation and partnership, of moderation rather than confrontation. It had ended the miners' strike and set up ACAS. Apart from the firemen, there had been no significant strike for three years. This image of co-operative partnership was the particular speciality of the Prime Minister. His style suggested ressurance, tranquillity, and a safe pair of hands.

Much importance therefore was attached to a key meeting, held unusually over dinner at Upper Clayhill Farm in Ringmer, on 1 September, four days before Callaghan was due to address the TUC at Brighton on a special invitation conveyed by David Basnett.[41] The guests were all members of the so-called 'Neddy Six', the TUC General Council, and Trade Unionists for a Labour Victory—Len Murray, David Basnett, Lord Allen, Moss Evans, Hugh Scanlon (in his swansong), and Geoffrey Drain of NALGO. It was a wholly amicable domestic occasion, on a lovely summer's evening, with a superb dinner provided by Audrey Callaghan and served by their young granddaughter Tamsin Jay, to a background of the beauty of the Sussex Downs.

But the outcome has been the subject of intense debate. Callaghan's own notes state that he spent the evening arguing the case against an October election. Certainly he voiced scepticism about the union leaders' approach since they appeared to be arguing for an immediate election to pre-empt a wages explosion over the next twelve months as union members tossed appeals for renewed wage restraint aside. But the TUC leaders appear to have understood matters differently. Moss Evans later stated emphatically that Callaghan had suggested that the Cabinet was divided about an early election but that he gave no indication of his own view one way or the other. Len Murray was to say later in a television interview that while Callaghan did indeed present electoral reasons against going to the country, five of the six trade unionists present argued strongly for an autumn poll. (It later emerged that Hugh Scanlon was the odd man out.) The evening ended, in Murray's view, with no clear conclusion emerging. Indeed he himself felt embarrassed as a trade unionist to have to give a view on a supremely political matter like the timing of an election.[42] David Basnett, a sensitive man, who led Trade Unionists for a Labour Victory and felt he had a special relationship with the Prime Minister, was still totally convinced that the announcement of an early election was a matter of days away. He felt that he and his colleagues had persuaded the Prime Minister of the necessity of an early appeal to the country.

He and his colleagues remained of that opinion after Callaghan's speech to the TUC on 5 September. This was a skilful but also distinctly baffling occasion. *The Times* praised both speech and speaker. Callaghan, it declared, 'the best professional Prime Minister since Mr. Macmillan', was 'a hard man to beat'. Its leading article adopted a highly technical cricketing analogy. Callagan's speech 'reminded one of [Geoffrey] Arnold's bowling in the Gillette Cup, not deadly but shrewd, consistent, experienced and extraordinarily difficult for the opposition to hit'.[43] The Prime Minister's political equivalent of 'length and line' was therefore thought impressive. He included a thoughtful overview of the economy, part of which was an argument of the case for a 5 per cent pay norm. After referring to the £3.5 bn. tax cuts, and increases in benefits and pensions, he noted that earnings had risen by over 10 per cent. 'I say to you that if you accept 5 per cent insofar as other factors remain constant, then inflation will probably be lower by the end of 1979 than it is today.' Otherwise it would rise again. Any negotiated reduction in working hours, he added, must be part of a settlement that was self-financing or else offset against the 5 per cent guidelines.[44]

These views were greeted without enthusiasm (and, indeed, with scattered heckling) but without any major indication of dissent. What did attract most attention was his reference to the possibility of a general election. He told the delegates that he would not be revealing his intention that day. Then, extraordinarily, he burst into an old music-hall song, much as he had done, to Ian Bancroft's astonishment, before a group of businessmen at a time of economic crisis back in 1965. He sang a verse of a song 'by Marie Lloyd', which went as follows:

There was I waiting at the Church, waiting at the Church, waiting at the Church,
When I found he'd left me in the lurch, Lor' how it did upset me
All at once he sent me round a note, Here's the very note, This is what he wrote,
'Can't get away to marry you today, My wife won't let me!'

This musical interlude was greeted with cheerful enthusiasm by the more elderly and distinctly chauvinist delegates, some of whom remembered the great days of George Robey and even Marie Lloyd with clarity. But the import of the song led to much confusion. It would appear that the point of the rendition was to imply that Mrs Thatcher was being kept waiting in vain while the Prime Minister declared his intentions in his own way and in his own time. But the song could also suggest that it was the TUC itself that was left in the lurch. Callaghan had intended to imply that an election was being delayed. The TUC drew the exact opposite conclusion. There was even a historical inaccuracy. The song was not sung by Marie Lloyd at all, as the television comedian Roy Hudd wrote to the Prime Minister, but by Vesta Victoria. Callaghan replied that he did indeed know that, but felt that Marie Lloyd would be better known to the audience.[45] This unscholarly explanation somehow reinforced the baffling nature of the occasion. If politicians decide to borrow from popular culture, ambiguity is a dangerous thing. There is no doubt that most of the delegates were left with the firm impression that an autumn election was still on course. Callaghan was always at his most assured in TUC conferences, amongst his own kind. One TUC leader later privately reflected of these occasions, 'He was always a cheeky bugger.' The next day, with qualified enthusiasm, the TUC voted to endorse a £1m. election fund. *The Times* reported that the Cabinet on 7 September would result in the election date being announced, almost certainly 5 October, and that the preparations for Labour's election manifesto were already well under way.[46]

In fact the Cabinet, held at 10.30 a.m. on Thursday 7 September, provided a sensation of a different kind. Whereas Tony Benn, in common with almost all ministers, expected the Prime Minister to announce an immediate general election, what they heard was Callaghan stating briskly that he had decided, after consulting with Foot, Healey, and a few others, not to call an election that autumn, adding that he had written to the Queen the previous evening to tell her so. (In fact, his letter was handwritten and, while his handwriting was usually extremely clear, the Queen found difficulty in making out the word 'hung' attached to the word 'parliament'.[47]) While it was a personal decision, he gave some general reasons—the timing of the devolution referendums, the fact that Labour voters did not want an election, and that Labour's prospects would be stronger after the economy had had some more months to show an improvement. He said that he did not propose to write to the Queen a second time and then moved briskly on to the Bingham report on sanctions breaking in Rhodesia in the late 1960s. Cabinet ministers were astounded by the news. Edmund Dell, sometimes twitted by the Prime Minister for political naivety, was appalled and resigned from the government not long afterwards. Tony Benn, who learnt shortly that Callaghan had decided as early as 17 August not to have an election (as is indeed confirmed in *Time and Chance*),[48] was justifiably angry that there had been a *fait accompli*, that the consultation of Cabinet ministers was a purely cosmetic exercise, and that he, and indeed the majority of his colleagues, had been taken for granted. William Rodgers told friends that they had now lost the next election.[49] It was an unexpected and unwelcome demonstration of prime ministerial power.

Later that day, Callaghan gave a broadcast to the nation on television and radio in which he confirmed that there would be no autumn election. He outlined the case for continued economic recovery, talked much of the national interest, and concluded, in tones reminiscent of the Ministry of Information during the Second World War, 'Let us pull through together.' The astonishment of Cabinet ministers was reflected in the country. David Steel was 'astounded' at the news. Labour colleagues and party workers were said to be 'baffled'. The *Financial Times* declared that the political world was 'astounded' and felt that Callaghan had 'seriously miscalculated'. A close associate like his PPS Roger Stott was 'dumbfounded' and believed that Callaghan had placed too much faith in the reliability of the MORI polling. Most serious of all, TUC leaders were said to be extremely angry at being kept in the dark and ultimately at being misled. David Basnett, a 'proud and ineffective man' according to Peter Shore, was believed to be apoplectic with rage.[50] Almost all Callaghan's likely allies reacted in a negative or hostile way. Conversely, the Conservatives were delighted at a possible reprieve. James Prior, who had convened a special gathering of Conservative trade unionists during the TUC conference, anticipating an immediate election, was flabbergasted, and felt that it made a Tory election victory the more probable. Norman Tebbitt felt that Callaghan's decision only showed up his indecisiveness. He was a timid politician at bottom and he would certainly lose whenever the election came.[51] The only people to react favourably, in fact, were the financiers on the stock market. There was a massive bullish reaction in share prices and sterling strengthened on the news that industrial production had been 5 per cent higher in July than it had been twelve months earlier.[52]

Callaghan's decision not to hold an election signified not a release from pressure but an intensification of it. He had much else to preoccupy him over the next few weeks, notably the flight to Kano to meet President Kaunda of Zambia over the Rhodesian situation, followed by a meeting with President Obasanjo of Nigeria, on 21–2 September. But the industrial problems created by the ending of pay restraint were always looming in the background. While he was in Nigeria, the Ford car workers, members of the Transport Workers, began an open-ended official strike when an offer from the company had to be withdrawn because it breached the government's 5 per cent pay guidelines. Moss Evans, the new general secretary, and Ron Todd, the newly appointed TGWU national organizer, affirmed their endorsement of the workers' claim for a 25 per cent improvement in wages, especially in the light of Ford's recently declared profits of close to £600m. Ron Todd declared his opposition to observing a national incomes policy or anything like it.[53] At the same time, however illogically, union leaders were pleading the case for flexibility in pay guidelines for the sake of the lower paid, a group which manifestly did not include the toolmakers and other skilled workers at Ford's.

The Labour Party conference at Blackpool on 2–6 October proved to be another disaster for the leadership. Under the tolerant chairmanship of Joan Lestor, the left-wing tide in the unions and the constituencies was in full flood. Pressure both for an end to any kind of wages policy, and for internal party democracy in the reselection of candidates, the election of the shadow Cabinet, and the drawing up of the party manifesto, was intense. The Campaign for Labour Party Democracy did much active lobbying. On the very first day of the conference, a motion to throw out the 5 per cent limit, and indeed to reject pay restraint in any form, was overwhelmingly carried by 4,017,000 to 1,924,000, despite a stirring plea from Michael Foot for a Labour government to be supported. Another motion, by Alan Fisher, the left-wing spokesman for NUPE, was passed which called for a £60 per week minimum wage for public sector workers such as his own. Callaghan's own speech the next day, 3 October, was a powerful one. He had discussed its main themes with McNally, McCaffrey, Lipsey, and other No. 10 staff on 19 September; its main purpose, it was agreed, would be 'getting the adrenalin flowing after the postponement of the election'.[54] Much of the speech was a broad statement of the government's achievements—keeping down prices; restoring fuller employment; employment subsidies and work training; the reduction of working hours; the need for greater participation in education; housing tenancies; and Scottish and Welsh government. There was reassertion of 'the traditional values of our movement', including the family and law and order, and frequent reference to democratic socialism which was said to be about quality as well as equality (the tenants' charter in housing was mentioned specifically here). The underlying message, so the meeting of 20 September had concluded, was managing the process of change and 'moving from a centralising vision to one that emphasised the role, rights and responsibilities of the individual citizen'.

But the most significant passage by far was one added late on which dealt with inflation. Callaghan noted that speeches in the debate on pay the previous day had said almost nothing about inflation. (Moss Evans and Alan Fisher, leading speakers then, had ignored the subject entirely.) He repeated that pay increases of more than 5 per cent would see inflation going up again, and the government might have to take offsetting measures through monetary and fiscal policies. He appealed to trade unions to help the government in keeping pay settlements down and to reflect on how most effectively and constructively to exercise their power.[55] But, other than exhortation and a broad view that unions, employers, and government should come together to create a framework for pay and prices on a corporate basis, he did not offer clear proposals on how this might be done. Penal sanctions, of course, were not mentioned; they had been on the back burner since the failure of *In Place of Strife* nine years earlier. Tony Benn was generous about Callaghan's speech—'the best speech I had ever heard from a party leader at Conference'—and wrote him a private note to say so.[56]

But the conference as a whole was a dismal preliminary to a difficult autumn on the wages front, and a clear defeat for the government. Callaghan spoke subsequently in sombre terms to Helmut Schmidt (in a conversation partly concerned with the proposed Henry Moore sculpture for the German Chancellery in Bonn). The Prime Minister declared, 'I'm in terrible trouble' with the party conference having rejected the 5 per cent pay policy. 'We've got a difficult winter but it may not turn out to be as bad as people say', he added hopefully. 'I want a strong sterling and I want a tight monetary policy . . . Whether I shall be allowed to do it or whether I shall get chucked out first I don't quite know.'[57] Already, it seemed, the Prime Minister, in the private words of one of his Cabinet colleagues, was 'playing for history'.[58]

Callaghan's decision not to call an election in the autumn of 1978 has widely been seen as a great blunder. Roy Hattersley and many others felt that a golden opportunity had been thrown away and that the initiative had been passed to others for good.[59] Even Bernard Donoughue, loyal to his master, has pointed out that in October the polls showed a Labour lead of 7 per cent,[60] although he does not add that in August and early September their findings generally favoured the Conservatives. More generally, the decision to defer an election is seen as a period of successive political errors by Callaghan, starting in July with the rigidity of the 5 per cent pay norm which the unions predictably rejected almost to a man and woman, and ending with the failure to persuade the party conference in October to endorse pay restraint. There followed a further catalogue of mistakes throughout the winter of discontent, culminating in the passivity in February–March which saw the government forced out of office. The great political master had quite suddenly, and unaccountably (since he was still in excellent physical and mental fettle), lost his touch. Over seventeen years of right-wing Conservative rule were the result. However, it was not a 'sea change' in favour of Mrs Thatcher, monetarism, and privatization that caused the transformation but avoidable tactical and strategic errors by Labour's previously dominant leader.

In fact, each and every one of Callaghan's decisions, taken individually, had sound justification if taken in its own terms and without reference to the wider context. The pay policy of 5 per cent was in strictly economic terms quite correct if the object was to keep inflation down, or at least within manageable limits of single-figure dimensions. Inflation was rising again and was to reach a level of nearly 12 per cent in 1979 after the final rejection of pay restraint guidelines. This meant higher costs, economic decline, a sharp rise in unemployment, and diminished living standards for working people and their families, especially the low paid of whom so much was heard at the time. Callaghan could not accept the cynical view of union officials like Clive Jenkins who called for an early election to pre-empt the deluge of a pay explosion after the polls. This would have been a purely short-term political stratagem which would undermine the long-term economic recovery he believed was under way. Had the views of union leaders such as Moss Evans, Clive Jenkins, and Alan Fisher prevailed unchallenged, the rise in inflation would have been even more severe. Britain would have fallen even further behind industrial competitors such as the Germans, French, Italians, Swedes, and Dutch who managed things far more coherently, quite apart from the intense challenge posed by the Japanese and the Pacific Rim. Old admirers of the British labour movement such as Lee Kuan Yew beheld Britain's plight with dismay and were not surprised that Mrs Thatcher was returned to power.[61] Compared with the scenarios on offer, Callaghan's view that there should be a rigid norm, under which wage drift would increase by a further 2–3 per cent balanced by mild policies on tax, prices, and employment, with some flexibility for special cases, seems much the most reasonable. After all, the cries from ministers such as Foot or even Healey for 'reasonable' and 'flexible' approaches to pay meant in effect a surrender to stark pressure from union power, and a sectional rather than a national approach to economic management. This would mean a further bout of the 'British disease' of which even Anglophile overseas commentators like J. K. Galbraith complained.

Equally Callaghan had justification in rejecting the call for an autumn general election. He variously cited the situation in Rhodesia with the coming talks between Ian Smith and Joshua Nkomo (which, as it happened, never took place), the need for a new electoral register, the possible dates for the devolution referendums, the prospects of further improvements in the economy to which the voters would respond, and the drain of advertising costs on Tory resources.[62] He urged his followers to take the long view.

But the real reason why he rejected an election is that he did not feel that Labour would win it. Even if the Prime Minister's amateur attempts at electoral psephology might not carry total conviction, the evidence as it presented itself to him during his weeks on the Sussex farm in August surely argued for caution. The one professional psephologist that Callaghan did consult, Bob Worcester—himself somewhat tarnished by the episode—also suggested that Labour might well lose. The message from Transport House was that Labour electoral campaigning machinery was rusty and in poor repair, while from the constituencies the word was that party workers were either disillusioned loyalists or doctrinaires with their own militant agenda that bore little relation to Callaghan's calculations. There is no firm evidence at all from the polls (mostly showing a small Tory lead in September) that Labour had firm expectations of an overall majority. At best, endless horse-trading with small splinter groups, which meant plunging back into the quagmire of Celtic devolution or the troubles of Northern Ireland, or fencing with the Liberals on the arcane details of PR, lay ahead. Since more time could always mean, in Micawberish terms, something hopeful turning up, in particular the growing benefits of North Sea oil which was already worth £2 bn. to the economy, the case for a prime minister to hold on was a powerful one. If he were 66 years of age, the case might seem stronger still.

Finally, Callaghan's decision to confront his critics, however emollient his tone, at the party conference in October was inevitable. There was a mass flight from economic reality in the tone of the debate, fuelled in part, to be fair, by much particularist grievance at the fall in real living standards amongst the working population, skilled and unskilled. The Callaghan government might be greeted with jubilation in the stock market, but on the shop floor, and even more amongst low-paid council or other public sector workers, it raised little enough enthusiasm. Even so, the case for fighting inflation head-on, indeed making it the main target through a combination of monetary, budgetary, and planning policies, was a powerful one and foreshadowed by Callaghan's pronouncements since his somewhat ambiguous anti-Keynesian speech to conference in October 1976. Of all the speeches made on economic themes at the party conference in Blackpool in 1978, Callaghan was much the most balanced and far-sighted.

But if Callaghan's case was a solid one in each case, the way he presented it was a different matter. There can be little doubt that he made his task almost impossible on each occasion. His government had succeeded because of the highly personal stamp imposed on it by the Prime Minister, a credible and authoritative figure who inspired respect overseas. By the same token, it ran into difficulties because of Callaghan's highly personal style. Denis Healey reflected, as befitted a Balliol classicist, on the hubris, the overweening pride that afflicted great men and great governments when they became overmighty or perhaps overconfident. Hubris led inevitably to nemesis as in a Greek tragedy.[63] Callaghan took the decision to enforce the 5 per cent norm very much on his own, even in some isolation from the Chancellor of the Exchequer, and imposed his view on a somewhat cowed Cabinet in the course of 1978. It did not add to his popularity amongst them. He certainly took the decision about not calling a general election in a highly personal, even secretive, fashion. He did so in a way that left even his closest advisers, such as Tom McNally and Tom McCaffrey, in the lurch and unawares. He made it all too evident to his Cabinet colleagues that his consultation with them about their views was a cosmetic exercise only and it left Tony Benn amongst others in understandable anger and frustration.

Above all, he fatally antagonized the unions, or at least his closest supporters like David Basnett, Alf Allen, and Len Murray. This showed itself in the hostile reception he met with at the party conference in October. Given the way he intended to run the next election, in tandem with the unions, financed by their funds, and with Derek Gladwin, a leading trade unionist, as his campaign manager, this was a disastrous turn of events. At several points, he had committed errors in tactics or presentation quite unexpected in such a political grand master. His statement (or rather non-statement) of his case in the TUC conference in early September was highly unfortunate in the impression that it left. The TUC leaders, several of whom were hardly free from the sin of pride, felt that they had been almost humiliated. The decision to transmit his message in an old music-hall song was a misconceived attempt to convey a political point with a populist cultural note. In its way it was as fatal as the 'showbiz' style of Neil Kinnock's Sheffield rally in the 1992 general election, and far more unexpected. He had taken his authority over the union leaders, demonstrated time and again in the golden period from early 1977, for granted, and assumed that respect could be equally assumed from the rank and file. It was a very serious miscalculation, from which the roots of his downfall could be eventually traced.

All was far from lost for Callaghan's Labour government in October 1978. The opinion polls were not unhopeful. Few believed that the trade unions would commit hara-kiri with a general election imminent which might see the return of the dreaded Mrs Thatcher. But it was worryingly apparent for Labour's strategists that things were starting to unravel. The Prime Minister, instead of being the solution for it, was himself part of the problem. The supreme apostle of the Labour alliance with the trade unions and a former union official himself, he had greatly antagonized them over both the 5 per cent pay norm and the handling of the general election issue. The great exponent of collective Cabinet government who had handled matters with such suave effectiveness during the IMF crisis, he had now annoyed his colleagues and perhaps made some of them less willing to be co-operative in any wages difficulties that lay ahead. The master puppeteer at party conference, whose performances there had reduced Richard Crossman to awe and admiration in the past, almost in spite of himself, had now met a succession of severe rebuffs. Instead of being a triumphalist forum, as David Basnett had vainly intended the TUC conference to be as well, it was now a lion's den. Young left-wing constituency activists in decayed inner-city branches, or public sector union delegates oblivious of political considerations and of the great bond of brotherhood between party and unions since the days of Keir Hardie, regarded him as a reactionary or proto-Tory, to be hounded at will. For over eighteen months, James Callaghan had straddled the public scene as a minor colossus, deemed to be amongst the most effective of British prime ministers since the era of Lloyd George. Now he seemed liable to be toppled from his pedestal, an architect and a victim of the politics of discontent.

1. McNally to Callaghan, 7 July 1977 (Callaghan Papers, box 19).
2. ? to McNally, 18 Nov. 1977 (ibid.).
3. Memo by Reg Underhill, 1977 (ibid.).
4. McNally to Callaghan, 9 Mar. 1978 (ibid.).
5. Record of meeting of special advisers, 17 Mar. 1978 (private papers).
6. Interview with Lord Gladwin of Clee; Callaghan's notes of 11 Sept. 1978 (uncatalogued). Much of the material here is drawn from the papers of the election Campaign Committee chaired by Lord Gladwin, to whom I am much indebted.
7. For devolution, see Vernon Bogdanor, *Devolution* (Oxford, 1979); Morgan, *Rebirth of a Nation: Wales 1880–1980*, ch. 14; Chris Harvie, *Scotland and Nationalism* (Edinburgh, new edn., 1994).
8. Callaghan to Hunt, 7 Feb. 1973 (Callaghan Papers, box 10).
9. Donoughue memo, 'Scotland and Mr. Millan' (PU 199), 9 July 1976 (private papers).

10. Information from Baroness Williams; Cledwyn Hughes diary, 22 Feb. 1978.

11. Andy McSmith, *John Smith: A Life, 1938–1994* (London, 1994 edn.), 76–7.

12. See David Foulkes, J. Barry Jones, and R A. Wilford, *The Welsh Veto* (Cardiff, 1982).

13. *The Times*, 24 June 1978.

14. Ibid. 5 July, 24 Aug. 1978; information from Jack Jones.

15. Benn, *Conflicts of Interest*, 266 (22 Dec. 1977).

16. Transcript of interview with Gordon Clough, *The World this Week-end*, 1 Jan. 1978 (Callaghan Papers, box 22); *Time and Chance*, 519.

17. Interviews with Jack Jones, Geoffrey Goodman, and Lord Healey.

18. Gavyn Davies memo, 'The Medium-Term Economic Outlook' (PU), 23 Mar. 1978 (private papers); interview with Tom McNally.

19. *The Times*, 24 July 1978.

20. See Urwin's obituary in the *Guardian* by Geoffrey Goodman, 22 Feb. 1996, and the note of dissent by Moss Evans, ibid. 26 Feb. 1996.

21. See his comments in 'The Winter of Discontent: A Symposium', *Contemporary Record*, 1/3 (autumn 1987), 34–41.

22. McNally memo, 13 Jan. 1978 (Callaghan Papers, box 22).

23. Telephone conversation between Callaghan and Helmut Schmidt, 30 Aug. 1978, T184/78 (ibid., box 34).

24. Memo by Donoughue, 'Pre-election Strategy—Prospects, Policies and Options for 1978/9' (PU 346), 22 Dec. 1977.

25. Callaghan notes, 11 Sept. 1978 (ibid., uncatalogued).

26. Ibid. Prime Minister's diary (ibid., box 35).

27. Kenneth O. Morgan, *The People's Peace* (Oxford, 1992 edn.), 416.

28. Material in Callaghan Papers, uncatalogued and box 19.

29. Telephone conversation of Callaghan and Schmidt, 30 Aug. 1978 (loc. cit.).

30. This view is based on my own reading of polling material in the Callaghan and Gladwin Papers; David Lipsey memo for the Prime Minister, 6 Sept. 1978 (Gladwin Papers).

31. Callaghan notes, 11 Sept. 1978.

32. *The Times*, 9 Sept. 1978.

33. Ibid.; *Daily Mirror*, 8 Sept. 1978.

34. Interview with Roy Hattersley.

35. 'David' to Callaghan, 1 Sept. 1978 (Callaghan Papers, uncatalogued); Owen, *Time to Declare*, 382; Healey, *The Time of my Life*, 462. 'David' could perhaps be Ennals.

36. Material in Callaghan Papers, uncatalogued; Albert Booth to the author, 27 Feb. 1997.

37. Donoughue, *Prime Minister*, 159–60. The author says that, in a strategic green paper written during the previous Christmas recess, he had argued for a general election in Nov. 1978 because child benefits and other welfare benefits would be payable then. Callaghan, in fact, thought that the advent of child benefit might be disadvantageous to Labour because it was paid to the mother and was thus transferred from the wallet to the purse. He had clashed with Barbara Castle over this issue. Later, however, he saw its political value in opening up the theme of the 'family'.

38. Interviews with Tom McNally and Tom McCaffrey.

39. *The Times*, 30 Aug., 3 Sept. 1978.

40. Material in Callaghan Papers, uncatalogued.

41. Ibid.

42. Ibid. Moss Evans in *Contemporary Record*, 1/3 (autumn 1987), 37. Lord Murray, who was present at this symposium but apparently did not comment on this point, gave his recollections in *The Twentieth Century Remembered*, a BBC interview with Geoffrey Goodman, on 10 Feb. 1987. The estimate of Hugh Scanlon's view was given by Goodman. (Transcript of interview in Callaghan Papers, BLPES, box 7.) He added in the course of this interview that he considered Callaghan to be the second best prime minister since the war, next to Macmillan. In an interview with the present writer in 1996, Lord Murray confirmed to me that all the union leaders except Hugh Scanlon (usually a 'chancer' but cautious on this occasion) wanted an immediate election, but that they left with no indication of Callaghan's personal view.

43. *The Times*, 6 Sept. 1978. Geoff Arnold was a fast-medium opening bowler for Surrey and England, thought to be steady rather than devastating.

44. Draft of speech, as amended, in Callaghan Papers, box 22.

45. Callaghan to Roy Hudd, 11 Sept. 1978 (ibid., box 21B). Geoffrey Goodman, who was consulted by Callaghan about his speech a few days before the Brighton TUC, tells me that it did not then contain the song. He warned him again then of the impracticability of insisting on a 5 per cent norm. Marie Lloyd died in 1922.

46. *The Times*, 7 Sept. 1978.

47. Callaghan notes, 11 Sept. 1978.

48. *Time and Chance*, 516.

49. Benn, *Conflict of Interest*, 334 (7 Sept. 1978); cf. Barnett, *Inside the Treasury*, 154.

50. *Financial Times* and *The Times*, 8 and 9 Sept. 1978; interview with Roger Stott MP; Shore, *Leading the Left*, 132.

51. Tebbitt, *Upwardly Mobile*, 198–200.

52. 'Winter of Discontent', 40.

53. *The Times*, 3 Oct. 1978.

54. David Lipsey, summary of meeting of Prime Minister and No. 10 staff, 19 Sept. 1978 (Gladwin Papers).

55. Draft of Callaghan's speech, as amended (Callaghan Papers, box 22).

56. Benn, *Conflicts of Interest*, 356 (3 Oct. 1978).

57. Telephone conversation between Callaghan and Schmidt, 16 Oct. 1978, T225A/78 (Callaghan Papers, box 34).

58. Interview with Roy Hattersley.

59. Hattersley, *Who Goes Home?*, 208 records that there was uneasy laughter after his statement which Callaghan promptly stifled by observing that if there was trouble with the unions that winter they would react differently.

60. Donoughue, *Prime Minister*, 164.

61. Interview with Lee Kuan Yew.

62. Callaghan note, of 11 Sept. 1978.

63. Healey, *The Time of my Life*, 462.

27

DISCONTENT AND DECLINE

AFTER the fall of the Callaghan government, commentators tended to assume that the autumn and winter of 1978–9 were overshadowed throughout by industrial conflict. That was not altogether how things presented themselves to the Cabinet for some time, perhaps until the end of November. Up to then, the industrial troubles, while undoubtedly serious, appeared likely to be confined to a few difficult cases, of which the Ford workers' strike, declared official by both TGWU and AEUW, was the most acute. In addition, the business of government went on. There were other priorities facing government ministers, not all of them by any means regarded as negative factors from the standpoint of an administration which had decided to soldier on for the time being. There was continuing involvement in Rhodesia with the prospect of all-party talks until Cledwyn Hughes reported on their impracticability in December. There were major international meetings over Europe, particularly over the creation of the EMS. There were crucial discussions over Britain's nuclear weaponry prior to the meeting at Guadeloupe.

Nearer home in Ireland, while Roy Mason's policy of Thorough, Strafford style, against the Provisional IRA went on with evidence of success, there was also great activity in attracting American investment into the province from firms such as General Motors and Goodyear. This included, though, the ill-starred decision to manufacture deLorean sports cars in Northern Ireland. On 26 July 1978 the Cabinet decided to go ahead and back the venture with public funds: Roy Mason told his colleagues that it 'would be a hammer blow to the IRA'. It appeared to be a major boost for the Ulster economy. In fact, the management consultants, McKinsey, had warned of the risks inherent in the venture and it led to much later trouble for the Thatcher administration in 1981–2. The company finally collapsed in 1982 with a loss of 2,000 jobs in Belfast after costing the taxpayer £77m. in subsidies.[1]

Northern Ireland was relatively quiescent at this time. Elsewhere in the United Kingdom, the government's prospects showed signs of advance. The devolution referendums for Scotland and Wales were fixed for 1 March, St David's Day, and campaigns to promote the 'yes' cause began to be organized by Labour officials in both nations. Callaghan's personal standing in opinion polls remained strong throughout the autumn. Most of them showed Labour ahead in October and early November. Its policy document *Into the Eighties* offered a realistic prospect of rising living standards, lubricated by North Sea oil.

But the troubles with the unions were never far away. That autumn, the leaders of organized labour, especially shop stewards and others at the local or plant level, were aware of two factors above all. First of all, their members' take-home pay had slumped over the last three years, notably amongst public sector workers whose wages were directly affected by central government. No more pay restraint was acceptable. Unrestricted collective bargaining, backed by the threat of strikes, official or unofficial, was the only possibility. Union leaders recognized that a rank and file revolt against pay curbs was inescapable; men like Alan Fisher and Moss Evans gave it positive encouragement. Len Murray offered wiser counsel, but as a realist he spelt out the detectable mood of industrial revolt. Lord McCarthy had spoken of a 'break-out year' for wages being inevitable, and 1978–9 was probably going to be that year.

Secondly, the unions had never been more powerful. Not only did they have unique access to the government and the Prime Minister, through NEDC and the various organs of the Labour Party itself. Their membership had risen to record levels in the 1970s, partly as a result of closed shop arrangements, partly from a desire from public sector workers to defend their living standards at a time of inflation. In 1970 union membership stood at 11,179,000, or 45.8 per cent of the labour force. It had risen steadily throughout the 1970s, adding a further 2 million to the total. In 1979, when the maximum figure was recorded, trade union members numbered 13,498,000, with their percentage of the labour force standing at 53.0.[2] In particular, service employees in the public sector, notably in local government and the health service, showed a spectacular rise. Alan Fisher's NUPE, David Basnett's GMWU, Clive Jenkins's ASTMS, and COHSE, the union of Health Service employees, all grew rapidly in line with public expenditure throughout the decades. In particular, NUPE, which included a growing number of women members, was the success story of the decade, growing to 600,000 members. It was committed to consistent left-wing positions on issues ranging from pay policy to unilateralism even though on the one occasion the rank and file was directly consulted, over the deputy leadership in 1981, the views of members were strongly in favour of the right-winger Denis Healey rather than the tribune of the left, Tony Benn. It was NUPE whose motion on behalf of a £60 a week minimum wage for local authority manual workers, crystallizing the pent-up resentment of public sector employees, had set the tone for the party conference in early October where the left was rampant.

The great focus of industrial conflict in October and November was the official TGWU strike at Ford Motors. This was a multinational conglomerate anxious not to be provocative to governments and willing to obey their edicts. Callaghan had good personal relations with Ford, especially in having helped persuade them in 1976–7 to create a major new £180m., 2,500-job car-making plant at Bridgend in south Wales, close to his Cardiff constituency.[3] On a personal level, of course, his son Michael was an executive with the company. Ford's had no record of prolonged industrial trouble over the years. However, its success had shown itself in huge profits, £246m. being announced in 1978. This led Moss Evans and his TGWU to claim that the company could easily afford a massive rise in weekly pay. The Ford men were resentful that their time-rate payment meant that they had lagged behind the car workers of British Leyland. The solution offered, barely credibly, by Moss Evans was for a 30 per cent increase for both groups of workers. Any call for pay restraint was either ignored or else condemned as 'outside interference' with the normal free-market practices of pay bargaining. Ford themselves were not anxious for a fight. Their chairman Terence Beckett, while sympathetic to government policies of pay restraint, was not in the strongest position to argue since he himself had recently had a salary rise of 80 per cent. At any rate, Ford did resist, offering the token 5 per cent only. On 25 September, just after the Prime Minister's return from seeing President Kaunda in Kano, 57,000 Ford workers were on strike, the dispute almost immediately being declared official by Moss Evans and the TGWU executive.

A direct challenge to the government's guidelines by so powerful a union in a key industry, inevitably, had very wide repercussions. It soon became clear that, with ample funds of its own and the capacity to borrow, the TGWU could readily stand a long strike. It was also clear that Ford themselves would sooner make a quick settlement rather than bear the loss of exports through a long strike. On 2 November, with the Ford strike now in its fifth week, the union rejected a 'final' offer of 17 per cent. By this time, Vauxhall Motors had become the fourth large firm to breach the pay guidelines by making an offer to its members of well over 5 per cent.[4]

Indeed, 15 per cent rather than 5 per cent seemed quite suddenly to have become the going rate. In the end, Ford decided to settle, come what may. On 22 November, after seven weeks, the Ford men returned to work, armed with a pay deal of around 17 per cent. Market forces had prevailed, as indeed the union leaders had insisted that they should. The government promptly announced its intention of imposing the relatively gentle sanctions attached to the 5 per cent pay guidelines. As Paul Roots, industrial director of Ford's, commented some years later, 'we were getting hammered from all directions . . . We were going downhill fast, losing sales to companies that were being subsidised by the Government up in Birmingham and we thought "enough is enough" and we decided to do a deal.'[5] The comparative weakness of the employers in relation to the unions was graphically shown thereby. So, too, was the weakness of the government. Callaghan later reflected that the Ford settlement of 17 per cent convinced him that the next general election was as good as lost. As a sign of failing confidence in some Cabinet circles, Edmund Dell, a consistently pessimistic right-wing minister, had earlier resigned as Trade and Industry Secretary to take up a post with the Guinness Peat merchant bank. He was succeeded by the more vigorous figure of Callaghan's protégé John Smith, but the spectacle of a Labour Cabinet minister exchanging office for the welcoming bosom of capitalists in the City was not a good omen.

On 30 November, a few days after the Ford strike was settled, another key sector of the workforce, the drivers of the oil tankers of four of the five main companies—Shell, BP, Esso, and Texaco (only Mobiloil had reached a settlement)—announced that they, too, might well begin a national strike from 2 January in support of a pay claim of 40 per cent. They were also members of the TGWU which was now, in the words of the Transport Minister William Rodgers, engaged in a 'frontal attack' on the government.[6] In addition, the workers from British Oxygen were also on the point of a national stoppage, while in a totally different sector of the labour market, the bakers were also poised for strike action. Many other groups of workers seemed close to joining in.

In these circumstances, Callaghan pinned some hope on the TUC itself monitoring the situation and providing its own voluntary mechanisms, as was laid down in the social contract and the understandings that flowed from it. The TUC did indeed try. There were regular meetings between the TUC Economic Committee and Denis Healey and Michael Foot throughout October. Moss Evans for one promised that they would endeavour to get pay increases below 10 per cent provided action could be taken by the Chancellor on controlling prices.[7] The 'Neddy Six' of six major union leaders, including Len Murray, then produced a document to be discussed at its general council on 14 November entitled 'Collective Bargaining, Costs and Prices'. Since the Neddy Six included such forceful critics as Moss Evans and Alan Fisher, it was unlikely to be a document which contained much rigour. Neither 5 per cent nor any other guideline was mentioned. There was talk of an analysis of pay comparability in the public sector which could be extremely inflationary if taken very far. However, it was a basis for future policy and perhaps an attempt to find a genuine compromise.

The TUC Economic Committee passed it almost perfunctorily on the morning of 14 November. But in the afternoon, at the full General Council of the TUC, things went disastrously wrong. There should have been a clear majority for the document, but a series of decisions by individual union leaders produced the opposite effect. Sid Weighell of the Railwaymen, a right-winger, was absent doing a broadcast. Bill Sirs of the Steelworkers, another right-winger, actually voted against the document because he did not wish to commit his union at this stage. Extraordinarily, Moss Evans, part author of the document, was another absentee, choosing this very moment to take a private holiday in Malta. It is hard to imagine Jack Jones, attached though he was to at least some aspects of Spanish life, deserting his post at this key moment. The outcome was a tied vote 14 : 14. The chairman Tom Jackson, another right-winger, refused to cast his chairman's vote, declaring that the rules forbade it. And so, through this melancholy series of mishaps, the TUC document failed to pass, and the unions had in effect no policy at all other than vague exhortation. The social contract had become almost devoid of meaning.

Len Murray, however, subsequently took a different view. Any decision would have been impossible to impose, especially one carried by a narrow margin, and he felt relieved at not having to take action.[8] Soon after, the Prime Minister held a secret meeting with seven key trade unionists at Downing Street on 20 November: they included Alan Fisher of NUPE, Ray Buckton of ASLEF, and Clive Jenkins of ASTMS. The title of this group, chaired by the unhappy David Basnett, was, with unintended irony, the Trade Union Committee for a Labour Victory.

By early December, the seriousness of the situation had become all the clearer. What Bernard Donoughue well describes as 'a curious feverish madness' had broken out,[9] with nationwide strikes at the turn of the year variously by oil tanker drivers, road haulage drivers, British Leyland production workers, water and sewage workers (whose industrial muscle was being appreciated for the first time), and a range of local authority manual workers. The claims ranged from 20 to 40 per cent or even higher. Callaghan, on the eve of a visit to Brussels, wrote to Healey on 4 December in alarm at the apparent weakening of the government's stance on public sector pay, and questioning whether any concessions need be made to the local authority manuals at all.[10]

The main onus of handling these manifold challenges fell at first on Michael Foot. But he found his appeals for unity falling on deaf ears and little interest being taken in the issue of inflation. He had more than one clash with Moss Evans as a result. But Callaghan himself inevitably was drawn in, too. He was the apostle of voluntarism and untrammelled collective bargaining. He had argued passionately and successfully for this in 1969 when Barbara Castle's bill fell through. This was the tradition in which he had grown up, the tradition of Bevin, and Lawther and Deakin; it was a creed lately given renewed force by the unlikely apostles of orthodoxy and disciplinary leadership, Jack Jones and Hugh Scanlon. But the union movement in 1978, decentralized, driven by the grass roots, oblivious to feelings of solidarity with a Labour government, almost apolitical, was different by far from the traditions of his younger days. In this, it should be said, the Prime Minister was no more at a loss than anyone else. The major unions seemed almost beyond constitutional control as the dam of pay restraint finally broke. In particular, the white-collar and service workers of NUPE had a totally different, more circumscribed outlook from the major manual unions of the past. Callaghan later felt that he had been 'too supine' in the emergency.

His instincts, as ever, were for moderation. There was no question of penal sanctions being introduced, even assuming there had been a parliamentary majority for them. The TUC's failure to endorse a policy meant that their ability to offer a lead in promoting a voluntarist approach had disappeared. There were only two other choices. One was to embark on a tough, counter-strike policy, involving troops with perhaps a state of emergency being declared. This was not the government even to consider such an option, at least initially, even if Attlee had done so in 1949. The other was to try to find less direct forms of pressure in an attempt to instil discipline into both sides of industry. That meant fining the employers for the excesses and indiscretions of the workers. Action was, therefore, taken against Ford through the withdrawal of government subsidies and other penalties, although this was clearly a policy that could only be taken so far in view of the crucial role of investment by the American multinational in Britain, including as has been seen in south Wales. This met with resistance by many Labour MPs, not all on the left. Michael Foot was told by several fellow members of the Tribune group that they could not support the government in the lobbies; they told him that Callaghan should recognize the massive conference vote against the 5 per cent pay limit and obey it. Thirty of them put down the so-called Tribune amendment rejecting the government's pay policy. There were hints that the various TGWU-sponsored Labour MPs might be instructed not to vote for the government.[11] The Emperor Evans seemed to have replaced the mythical Emperor Jones.

Parliamentary approval was in any case required for the financial sanctions on Ford Motors. Against the wishes of David Owen as recorded in his memoirs,[12] Callaghan and Foot decided not to make it an issue of confidence. On 13 December the motion in favour of the government's counter-inflationary policy was moved by Roy Hattersley, in what he has described as an incoherent speech since he had just been struck down by a painful illness. The Conservatives, whose own posture on pay restraint was highly erratic, naturally voted against, as did the Liberals now that the pact was well and truly over. So, too, did the Scottish Nationalists, who were antagonistic to the government in general, citing the failure to provide an early date for the Scottish and Welsh devolution referendums. The Ulster Unionists were also in the opposition lobby. The government, for whom Joel Barnett wound up, was supported only by the three-man group of Plaid Cymru, faithful to the Welsh radical heritage to the last. What was decisive was that a number of Tribune group members decided to abstain in protest at the pay policy. Callaghan had had a bad-tempered meeting with six of them (Ron Thomas, Eddie Loyden, Jo Richardson, Frank Allaun, Stan Thorne, and Martin Flannery) at 10 that morning. They had complained at the failure to call the Tribune amendment; Callaghan had sarcastically inquired 'which party they thought they belonged to'. In the end, they and others including Arthur Latham, Sid Bidwell, and John Prescott refused to vote, and the government was thus defeated by 285 votes to 279.[13] Callaghan announced that he would respect the views of the House and the financial penalties on Ford were promptly withdrawn. Even that policy option was now removed, and the government looked more naked than ever.

The following day Callaghan moved a vote of confidence which this time the government won, all the Tribunite defectors returning to the fold. The Liberals and (contrary to David Owen's memoirs) the Scottish Nationalists still voted against, but there was a majority of ten, 300 to 290, almost comfortable in that desperate, smoke-filled parliament. The government also had had the vote of Cledwyn Hughes, flown back from his talks with Ian Smith in Rhodesia, and one Liberal, Geraint Howells (Cardiganshire), who had co-operated closely with Michael Foot and John Smith over Welsh devolution to which he was passionately attached. Yet the government seemed to be in office but not in power since one policy option after the other had been removed from them. They were condemned to keep governing. David Owen says of the decision not to have the pay policy made an issue of confidence, 'I have no doubt that it was at this moment that the Labour Party lost the 1979 General Election.'[14] Before Christmas there was the spectacle of the oil tanker drivers of Shell and other companies being bought off by wage increases of 20 per cent on average, with the government almost helpless spectators. A threatened strike by electricians might actually deprive the nation of its Christmas television. Callaghan went off to Chequers for the festive season, in preparation for his visit to Guadeloupe, in depressed and angry mood. For their part, many trade union leaders professed to believe that a letter sent them by the Prime Minister prior to his departure implied an early resolution somewhat along on the lines of the later Clegg Commission on public sector pay, but these hopes were to be disappointed.

Callaghan flew to Guadeloupe on 4 January. Prior to his departure, he received the cheerful intelligence that an official strike of road haulage drivers had begun in Scotland. As he left the country he heard that it had spread all over England and Wales. In Northern Ireland, things were worse still and a state of emergency would shortly be declared there by Roy Mason, the Northern Ireland Secretary. Immediately there were stories of the food shelves of supermarkets and stores becoming emptied. There were rumblings of massive strike action too by public sector workers which would impinge on every family in the country. In a secret meeting with Denis Healey on the morning of 3 January, the Prime Minister had expressed acute concern at the tendency of employers to settle outside the pay guidelines, and for the prospects of massive strikes by local authority manual workers. 'It was essential that the Government should re-establish a firm grip on the pay situation to somehow ensure that the pay round did not "run away".'[15]

However, once in Guadeloupe, these grave domestic events could be set aside. The Prime Minister could throw himself into the stimulating discussions he enjoyed with President Carter, Chancellor Schmidt, and President Giscard d'Estaing and relax in the sunshine. He felt that the meeting had been successful from the British point of view. As noted above, he had gained the agreement of his fellow heads of state for the sale of Harrier jump jets to China. He had also won Jimmy Carter's crucial support for a renewal of the British independent nuclear deterrent in succession to Polaris, even if the choice between Trident and Cruise still needed to be made, and approved by the Cabinet. Guadeloupe in itself was a brief, successful, and colourful interlude. What appeared to be a mistake at such a time was to accept the invitation of Tom Adams, an old associate, to extend his visit to Barbados, where the Prime Minister was concerned over defence and security considerations. There was also some sightseeing across this particularly beautiful island. Callaghan was to write to the British High Commissioner in Bridgetown after he returned, 'Although the British press do not seem disposed to agree with me, I am entirely confident that the visit was a necessary and useful means of keeping our relations with Barbados in good repair.'[16]

Still, the press made what they could of Callaghan's visit to a beautiful Caribbean location at so critical a time (they did not include *The Times*, which was another victim of union strike action from the start of the year). There were tabloid attempts to depict Audrey Callaghan, in 'her wide-brimmed Margaret Rutherford-style hat',[17] sunning herself on the waterfront and to photograph the Prime Minister in the swimming pool in Sandy Lane (one newspaper introduced a bevy of nubile air hostesses into the water in order to make the pictures as compromising as possible). Even so, Callaghan got on to his British Airways VC 10 in good spirits, relaxed and convinced that it had all been thoroughly worth while.

What happened thereafter, however, only added to the Prime Minister's difficulties. He arose during the flight home, refreshed from one of his typical catnaps, and summoned McNally and McCaffrey to him.[18] He wanted their views on whether to hold a press conference at Heathrow on his return. McNally thought it would be a good idea; it would show the Prime Minister in authoritative posture, taking instant command on his return. Tom McCaffrey took the opposite view. He felt it would be better for Callaghan to return to No. 10, get thoroughly briefed there, and face the press when he was refreshed after the journey and able to respond to journalists in a considered manner. After some thought, Callaghan declared that he agreed with Tom McNally, and that he would hold a press conference after all. It was one of his most unfortunate decisions in that bleak era of discontent.

When he returned to Heathrow early on 10 January, he immediately held a press conference of about a quarter of an hour (not recorded for once in his Prime Minister's diary). In Tom McNally's view, he handled it badly in every way, breaking every rule of public relations and generally deserting his invariable considered style of dealing with journalists. His manner was alternately testy and light-hearted (for instance, in relation to questions about pictures of him swimming). He gave the impression of chatting informally to the newspapermen rather than addressing the nation via the television cameras. In one disastrous aside, when asked by a junior reporter about the sense of chaos over the wave of industrial strikes, he was dismissive. The journalist's view he described as 'parochial'. His response was famously described in the *Sun*'s headline the following day as 'Crisis? What Crisis?' Callaghan, in fact, said, much more guardedly, 'I don't think other people in the world will share the view that there is mounting chaos.'

Peter Shore, one Cabinet colleague, did not feel that this episode did any harm; it merely showed the Prime Minister being relaxed and reassuring as he invariably was.[19] But Callaghan later felt that his words were not well chosen and that the headlines the following day did broadly reflect the stance he seemed to take.[20] For a desperate people, facing food shortage and endless disruptions in public services during a particularly cold, snowy winter, the spectacle of a sun-tanned prime minister, back from the Caribbean, appearing to brush their problems aside or dismiss their concerns as parochial was hard to take. In fact, it was a temporary miscalculation and no more. Callaghan was always throughout his career particularly sensitive to the human needs of ordinary citizens and usually a master at conveying his concern. It would in normal circumstances have been the most temporary of *frissons* and immediately forgotten. But the scale of the industrial crisis, its length, and the menace and sometimes violence with which it was conducted, made Callaghan's words more than a miscalculation. It was a serious public relations error which gave easy ammunition to his critics. It suggested even to his friends that the master politician was showing again a lack of touch.

Immediately after his return, after discussing with the Cabinet the various options about the British nuclear deterrent, Callaghan was now deeply plunged into mounting industrial conflict. It was a particularly depressing time for him. All the disciplines and loyalties on which his union and social democratic background was based seemed to be dissolving. The lorry drivers of Moss Evans's TGWU were still on strike in pursuit of a 20 per cent pay claim. Indeed, on 11 January it was declared official by the union. Callaghan had an urgent telephone conversation with Moss Evans at 10.45 p.m. on the night of 10 January, just after his return. This followed a talk with Len Murray fifteen minutes earlier who reported that the TUC were quite unable to help. Callaghan told Moss Evans of the likely calamitous consequences of the road hauliers' strike being declared official and asked whether he might meet the TGWU Finance Committee. Even at this passage of time, the irresponsibility of Evans's response seems astonishing. 'The strike', he said, 'would not last that long. The employers would pay up. The union had withdrawn its demand for a shorter working week, so their demand was not as high as the 18–19 per cent it had been made out to be. Moreover, he had a problem of conscience—how could he allow his drivers not to get as little as £65 a week on their basic rate?' Callaghan replied that 'that was nonsense' and that the government might have to come into conflict with the union over such matters as secondary picketing. But Evans seemed immovable, and the prime minister of the day almost powerless to resist.[21]

But the road hauliers were only one problem. There were also stoppages by the railwaymen, seeking 20 per cent plus a bonus. The engine drivers, ASLEF, were soon to join in. The water workers were on strike and the sewage workers threatened to join them. There was a nationwide air of menace as industrial muscle was exercised in an apparently callous and brutal way. There was a serious shortage of food with ports and depots blocked by secondary picketing. Medical supplies were also curtailed. An aspect which particularly incensed William Rodgers, the Minister of Transport, was the failure to transport medical supplies of chemotherapy chemicals intended for cancer victims from Hull Docks.[21] His own mother was dying of cancer at the time. Callaghan himself had an angry exchange with Tony Benn about the impact on Great Ormond Street children's hospital, Audrey Callaghan's own cherished institution. On 17 January, Tom McCaffrey wrote, 'The industrial situation is deteriorating rapidly', and suggested a joint appeal by the premier and the TUC to the nation, but in vain.[23]

From 22 January there was even more comprehensive chaos. A million and half public sector service workers, many of them in NUPE, began haphazard stoppages on behalf of a £60 a week minimum wage. There followed selective stoppages by a variety of public sector workers in hospitals and local government. Sick patients went unattended; schools were closed because of strikes by school caretakers or cooks, or just because they were unheated in freezing weather; ambulance men were failing to answer 999 calls; frozen main roads were not being gritted; dustbins and refuse bags piled up in town centres in their tens of thousands, full of rotting and insanitary waste. There were secondary pickets all over the country preventing non-strikers getting through. An episode on 21 January which caused particular revulsion came with the strike of grave-diggers in

Liverpool, in fact by members of David Basnett's GMWU. Grieving relatives thus saw their loved ones unburied, although it should in justice be pointed out that grave-diggers were exceptionally badly paid.

Far from being a struggle by the poor and defenceless, it was the most vulnerable, the old, the sick, children, the disabled, the bereaved who were suffering most grievously. Newpapers carried pictures of defenceless, cancer-stricken children and elderly people suffering hypothermia. Jack Jones and other union leaders rightly claimed that the press exaggerated many of the stories, that the British people came nowhere near starvation in fact, and that essential supplies always got through. Jack Jones himself was reviled in the right-wing tabloids when a death occurred at a Midlands hospital he visited, at a time when there was industrial action by COHSE workers.[24] Nevertheless, the abiding impression for anyone who could see was trade unions on the rampage, out of control, their ideals and consciences set on one side. Mrs Thatcher was to be returned at the May general election on a wave of anti-union hatred. Her measures to curb the irresponsible power of the overmighty unions in the 1980s were perhaps her most popular ones. In the 1997 election, Tony Blair's Labour Party was as committed as were the Conservatives to their retention in full.

The response of the government was, of course, a collective one. Isolating and identifying the Prime Minister's particular role and viewpoint is not easy. His dismay, indeed anger, at the course of events was transparent. But he seemed becalmed in a kind of depression, almost *ennui*. The decisive, authoritative leader of 1976–8 seemed shrunken and inert. The Prime Minister had become the embodiment of Durkheim's *anomie*. He complained that colleagues and civil servants in department after department were giving way to union pressure in a spineless way (David Ennals at Health was a particular target) but he offered no alternative strategy and no lead. For a vital period of three weeks, 10 Downing Street was silent. The Prime Minister refused to respond to appeals that he address the nation on the economic realities. He appeared slumped in fatalism. After a Cabinet meeting in late January, he asked his press officer Tom McCaffrey almost pathetically, 'How do you announce that the Government's pay policy has completely collapsed?' He appeared in the unfamiliar guise of a prime minister asking others what he should now do. The Policy Unit ground to a standstill. Bernard Donoughue offered a suggestion on 25 January of a 'flexible/modified 5%'; the policy endorsed by Michael Foot and David Ennals for a new norm was described as 'at its worst an approach of pathetic self-delusion'. But the Prime Minister no longer seemed to be listening. Donoughue was later to describe the second half of January as the most depressing period he had ever known in government.[25] Callaghan later confirmed this himself in private conversation. He felt that he should have acted more resolutely in the face of union actions he knew to be morally wrong. He sadly confided to Kenneth Stowe, 'I let the country down.'

Political as well economic decision-making was equally on hold. Callaghan did not respond to suggestions by Derek Gladwin throughout January or February that they should meet to discuss future electoral arrangements. One aspect, no doubt, was that Gladwin was in a somewhat ambiguous position himself, both campaign organizer and chief negotiator with the local authorities on behalf of the striking public sector manual workers of the GMWU. David Lipsey, a key Downing Street aide, expressed concern about the haphazard nature of election planning. 'The picture is discouraging. We do not have any tight decision-taking centre. The White Drawing Room Group is a talking shop and Ron Hayward and the N.E.C. go their own sweet way.' Only the Prime Minister could change things, but until the concordat with the TUC was concluded nothing much could happen.[26]

The Prime Minister had no special relationship now with many union leaders, it seemed. Men like Alan Fisher of NUPE, bent on a national minimum wage, almost disregarded him. Even his remarkably generous entry in the *Dictionary of National Biography* concedes with reluctance of this period that Fisher 'could not quite escape some blame'. David Basnett of GMWU, a 'frustrated academic' in the view of one of his close aides, felt unable to check Fisher's extremism lest he appear to be too right-wing in the eyes of his angry rank and file members. Moss Evans, far from trying to curb the excesses of his TGWU members, was static and gave one dispute after another the seal of official union backing. Government seemed to be grinding to a halt, crushed by the momentum of union power. The flow of papers between departments dried up. Initiatives from the Political Office and the Policy Unit were not taken up. The Think Tank was marking time. There seemed nothing to do, perhaps even nothing to think about. Joel Barnett has commented on how the Prime Minister gave an impression of deep depression, almost helplessness, and the word spread like wildfire across Westminster and Whitehall.[27]

At least the beginning of a lead had come in a Prime Minister's statement on 16 January. The government in effect abandoned the 5 per cent pay limit by relaxing it for the low paid, those defined as earning less than £44.50 a week. The principle of 'comparability' of pay was adopted to enable some public employees to go above 5 per cent and a commission was to be set up to determine it.[28] The Price Commission's powers would be strengthened to abolish the safeguards by which some firms could claim immediate increases in prices. This was the start of a policy which eventually was to bring to an end what the press dubbed 'the winter of discontent'. Denis Healey was asked to begin a new round of talks with the TUC leaders to provide the framework for yet another version of the social contract, based on voluntarism with a tougher framework of enforcement. Kenneth Stowe was asked to produce a draft government statement, working in conjuction with David Lea of the TUC.

But the immediate need was somehow to stop the strikes which mounted relentlessly. They reached a massive climax on 22 January when the TGWU, GMWU, NUPE, and COHSE brought out a million and half workers in a simultaneous demonstration of industrial power, a 'day of action' or more precisely of inaction. The Cabinet spent much time in January discussing a variety of possible norms to replace the discredited 5 per cent, but whether any figure would be observed on the shop floor or by picketing workers was debatable. In addition, even in Callaghan's statement of 16 January there was no machinery or procedure suggested which would empower the government to compel trade unionists to accept some pay policy and, additionally, observe the law. From 15 January onwards, worried ministers considered the one general option not so far tried—a tough, militant policy of taking on the unions. This meant calling a state of emergency, with the use of troops. It was a course not followed by Labour since 1974, not even in the firemen's dispute, but adopted on several occasions by the Attlee government from 1948 onwards, with the staunch backing of the socialist hero Nye Bevan himself.[29] But, then, the relation of Bevan on the one hand, and the TUC on the other, to the Labour government of the day was clean different from that of Tony Benn and the General Council thirty years on. In a maelstrom of sectionalism, 'solidarity for ever' was a lost cause.

There was already an emergency system of administration in place to try to keep normal life going.[30] This was the body known as GEN 158, a secret committee of ministers and civil servants, chaired by the Home Secretary, Merlyn Rees, to co-ordinate the governmental response and to try to keep essential services in operation. It included front-line ministers like Peter Shore (Environment) and William Rodgers (Transport); a key figure turned out to be Gerald Kaufman, a junior minister under Eric Varley at the Department of Industry. The detailed administration and policy implementation were handled by the Civil Contingencies Unit, a body formed by the Heath government in 1972 to combat a possible dock strike and designed to cope with possible food shortages. It had the status of a standing Cabinet committee; its chairman in 1979 was Sir Clive Rose, the energetic and resourceful deputy Cabinet secretary. Eleven Regional Emergencies Committees were established, with civil servants and representatives of the local authorities, the police, and the military to cope with the effects of the industrial crisis. At a very local level, there were home defence emergency depots, intended to maintain food and other supplies in case of nuclear attack. These met daily to try to deal with aspects of picketing and consequent effects upon supplies and economic life in general. In practice, much of their activity lay in regular negotiations with TGWU representatives to try to ensure that the essential needs of schools, hospitals, and other agencies were met. Ironically in the circumstances, it was thought appropriate that the Regional Committees met with official TGWU figures like Alex Kitson rather than local shop stewards so as not to undermine the alleged authority of the central Transport Workers' leadership.

These, however, were essentially reactive policies of a civil service nature, designed to combat the effects of the strikes rather than to take any initiative. The Cabinet's discussions about a possible state of emergency from 15 January onwards offered the alternative prospect of a coherent attempt to break the strike, organized by central government. Callaghan was believed to have said at one point to the union leaders, much as Lloyd George did when talking to Bob Smillie and the Miners' Federation leaders at a time of a possible national coal strike in 1919, 'we are prostrate before you'. But a state of emergency would replace a posture of helplessness with a combative assertion of governmental power. In the initial discussions in Cabinet on 15 January, Callaghan asked what the objections were to a state of emergency being declared: in the view of Tony Benn, he was anxious to find reasons for not having one.[31] Ministers as various as Roy Mason, Albert Booth, Joel Barnett, Bruce Millan, and John Morris all gave such reasons, saying in effect that it was not necessary, as the oil tanker drivers' dispute showed. The use of troops would be provocative and inflame the passions of the strikers still further to the extent that major public disturbance might result. Booth felt that union co-operation on vital supplies made a state of emergency unnecessary. But the debate did not end there: some of the more hawkish ministers, who appear to have included Denis Healey, William Rodgers, Joel Barnett, and Peter Shore, wanted far more resolute action by the government. After all, such tasks as clearing refuse, driving long-distance lorries, or even digging graves could, however disagreeably, be undertaken by the armed forces, assuming that they could be spared from the Rhine and Northern Ireland.

Callaghan was, of course, by instinct totally opposed to a state of emergency as were almost all his ministers. It would not only be potentially inflammatory, but could be argued as being unnecessary since, as John Silkin, the Minister of Agriculture repeatedly pointed out, the actual food shortages were not serious. It would also probably be ineffective. He accepted the point made by Fred Mulley that, to counter the lorry drivers' strike for instance, the availability of 10,000 army drivers would make little impression on perhaps half a million stationary vehicles, and probably would merely add to the worries of the general public. However, by 23 January he does seem to have moved somewhat nearer a state of emergency in some form. It would at least strike an important psychological blow on behalf of the beleaguered general public.

William Rodgers, the Minister of Transport, he took to be a strong advocate of a state of emergency. But at a key series of committees there appears to have been a misunderstanding between Callaghan and Rodgers which saw them fatally at cross-purposes.[32] In their discussion, Rodgers stated that he might well have favoured a state of emergency in the earlier oil tankers' strike when vehicles would have had to be requisitioned. But in the case of the road haulage dispute there were already many suitable vehicles available for the armed services. A state of emergency was therefore unnecessary. However, Rodgers did favour the use of the services, including their vehicles, though without having to call a state of emergency. He urged a selective use of troops, and went so far as to calculate the numbers and location of army vehicles that could be used from Catterick to transport anti-cancer drugs from the docks at Hull. In due course, Merlyn Rees, Albert Booth (Employment), and Rodgers were instructed to see Moss Evans and tell him 'that if he did not ensure these goods moved, we would move them. I [Rodgers] have always assumed that Moss Evans understood this to be a threat of a state of emergency.'

Callaghan seems to have thought that Rodgers was arguing against the use of troops in any circumstances, but this was far from being the case. His view was that, while the troops much preferred the formalities of a state of emergency when they could present themselves as simply being under orders, they could have been legitimately used selectively, for instance to pick up the medical supplies at Hull or to move sand or grit for frozen roads. The real opponent of a state of emergency, he believed, was not Callaghan who was 'half hawkish' nor even Merlyn Rees, ever moderate, but Sir Clive Rose, the head of the CCU. He had made it known that the Cabinet Office was strongly against the use of troops. This would antagonize the far left and might cause complications with Mrs Thatcher when, as expected, the Conservatives came to office after the next general election. He infuriated Rodgers by observing, almost casually, 'It is not our job to keep the Government going, but to keep the country going.' Sir Clive Rose, in Rodgers's judgement, made little or no effort to transmit to the Prime Minister Rodgers's view that the machinery should be put in place for the use of troops without calling a state of emergency. He gave ministers the impression that he was already anticipating Labour's fall from power.

Rodgers had three meetings 'on or about 23 January 1979'. The Prime Minister's diary suggests that they were on 24 January. At the first he attended a meeting of ministers, probably chaired by Merlyn Rees. At the second, he attended a meeting with Callaghan and about half the Cabinet. At the third in the evening, Rees, Booth, and Rodgers met Moss Evans and Ron Todd of the TGWU and threatened them with the use of 'our own resources' to move certain items: this was a selective use of troops not a state of emergency although it is not clear that Evans and Todd would have known precisely which was intended at this stage. The hawkish Rodgers was the main ministerial spokesman; the pro-union Booth had little to say. In effect, the union seems to have responded sufficiently to avert the use of troops. In the end, the broad view of cautious civil servants and shattered Cabinet ministers prevailed, namely that a state of emergency would do more damage than good. A typical view was that of Sir Patrick Nairne, who had chaired the CCU in the past, to the effect that the government's concordat with the unions meant that it was far from paralysed. He and Sir Clive Rose insisted that their working agreements with groups as various as hospital staff, ambulance men, water workers, and electricity supply workers made a state of emergency quite unnecessary. Contingency plans would prevail to avoid disaster. The only case where no such plans existed was the limited one of the grave-diggers, according to Rose. Nowhere could the Prime Minister find any firm support to reinforce the view that a state of emergency, challenging the unions head-on, was essential.

The view of civil servants like Rose and Nairne was moderate and reasonable. It also meant the complete appeasement of the striking unions. It is a remarkable illustration of what can happen when a government in retreat is manipulated by an entrenched civil service machine at a time of crisis. This was how key officials like Edward Troup and John Anderson had governed the Home Office at times of industrial disorder between the troubles at Tonypandy and the General Strike in 1910–26. But they were pressing for firmness; their successors in 1979 were arguing for the opposite approach. In the last two days of January the lorry drivers went triumphantly back to work, having gained wage rises of up to 20 per cent. The water workers achieved their cherished 14 per cent. Callaghan told his Cabinet on 30 January that the surrender reminded him of Munich.[33] Meanwhile one group of public sector workers after another began strike action—the dustmen, NHS workers, nurses, and ambulance workers being followed on 1 February by school caretakers and maintenance men, along with canteen workers. These last strikes meant that schools were insufficiently heated and deprived of kitchen services, so that children could not attend them. Many lay-offs resulted from the lorry drivers' strike. The severe snowstorms in many parts of the country made matters worse. Municipal bus drivers now went on strike, as did dockers at Bristol, Grimsby, and Immingham. The strike contagion spread unabated. The total of unemployed rose sharply to 1.34m., the highest total for years. One grim episode came when the Lord Chancellor, Lord Elwyn-Jones, asked about the unburied bodies as a result of the strike action of grave-diggers and council crematorium workers who had been on strike in Liverpool for nearly a fortnight. Harold Lever's response spelt out the government's fatalism—'Let the dead bury their dead.'[34]

Somehow, since positive action had been largely ineffective, the government would have to proceed yet again, as Labour administrations had done since 1969, on the basis of a voluntary agreement with the union leaders, solemn and binding or no. They must hope that the unions could somehow find the authority with their members to make it stick. Discussions began with Len Murray from 16 January onwards, and on 29 January Callaghan had a meeting in Downing Street with all forty members of the TUC General Council.[35] He conceded that the 5 per cent guideline was 'over-ambitious', but took issue with Len Murray's view that no new pay norm of any kind was required. He put it to them that they should focus on two problems, namely a counter-inflation policy that would bring down inflation to 5 per cent and an agreed trade union code of conduct to control the methods by which strikes were conducted, especially in relation to picketing. The TUC were quiet and conciliatory. A moderate speech was made by Harry Urwin of the TGWU who many felt ought to have become general secretary in place of Moss Evans in the first place. Two working parties were set up by the TUC to consider broad economic policy and employment policy. The social contract, now to be rechristened a 'concordat', was back in business. Underlying the discussion was the imminence of a general election: on 5 February the Tory lead over Labour in Robert Worcester's MORI poll stretched to 19 per cent (55 per cent to 36 per cent).[36] The *Financial Times* noted that Callaghan was 'in buoyant form' in the Commons on 30 January after his previous 'defensive and tetchy performances', encouraged by the positive tone of his meeting with the TUC.[37] On 3 February, in a speech at Newcastle, Callaghan made a controversial speech in which he hinted at the setting up of a Comparability and Relativities Board to consider pay differentials and anomalies, although he later appeared to withdraw from it.[38] From this, however, the ill-starred Clegg awards for public sector workers were later to flow in profusion.

Eventually on 14 February the so-called St Valentine's Day concordat was unveiled by Callaghan and Len Murray, in a symbolic joint appearance in a press conference at Millbank at 4.30 p.m. following the Prime Minister's statement in the House. A government paper was produced, written under circumstances of much pressure, by Kenneth Stowe, in association with David Lea of the TUC and union representatives. When they began work the sheet was quite blank. It was laid down here that the government and the TUC had jointly agreed that the latter should give 'guidance' to unions on the conduct of strikes including strike ballots, the maintenance of essential services, the absence of intimidation by pickets, and other well-meaning objectives. Secondly, there would be an annual 'national assessment' by the government and both sides of industry. Thirdly, an annual rate of inflation of 5 per cent within three years was the declared objective. The document rejected the notion of 'a going rate' but it also came close to admitting that the 5 per cent pay limit had been misconceived.[39] It was this policy that the government would put before the electors in due time: it was now believed that Callaghan would actually try to soldier on throughout the spring and the summer, with the election to come in October, when the full five-year term of that parliament was completed. On 16 February, Callaghan wrote formally to Healey asking him to chair a group of ministers to flesh out the agreement with the TUC on pay comparability, a national assessment, pay relativities, the TUC procedures on the monitoring of strikes, and the devising of 'no strike agreements' in essential services.[40] Government was under way once again.

Gradually the public sector strikes petered out over the next few weeks, though not before a further wave of strikes took place by civil servants, chiefly from the CPSA, action which Callaghan publicly called 'unnecessary and unjustifiable'.[41] Not until the middle of March did NUPE local authority workers return to work, with an additional £1 a week on top of what was agreed, while the teachers bid for 36 per cent and the civil servants for up to 48 per cent. The Prime Minister and the Chancellor had a brief row in Cabinet when Callaghan appeared to call for increased pay for the nurses. He described them as 'the heroines of the hour'.[42] Still, by early March some of the worst was over. The Prime Minister, the press reported, was 'surfacing from a deep despair' as employment and the economy in general began to improve.[42]

If the terms of the Valentine's Day agreement were taken literally, they would appear reasonable enough. The unions would work constructively with government in assessing all the indices of economic policy and would discipline their members so that strikes were no longer irrational, unselective, or violent. It was this kind of permanent agreement which underlay the 'accord' between the Australian trade unions and the Labour governments of Hawke and Keating. This helped ensure well over a decade of Labour rule from 1983 to 1996, although admittedly it was bolstered by the much stronger tradition of arbitration in pay awards present in Australia. The 'concordat' was certainly preferable to the formal constraints of the law and a penal sanctions policy, whether of the modest type favoured by Barbara Castle in 1969 or the more rigorous cumulative curbs on the unions introduced by Mrs Thatcher's government from 1981 onwards.

But that was in a different, idealized world. In reality, the new social contract did not appear credible to the voters. They no longer believed that the unions could restrain their members. Moss Evans hardly symbolized the smack of firm leadership. Indeed, the very fact that the onus yet again was being placed on the overmighty unions seemed only to re-emphasize the paralysis of the elected constitutional government. Previous Labour governments had had their union difficulties. The Attlee government had to cope with a rash of unofficial strikes by dockers, railwaymen, electricians, and others in 1948–51, and did so forcefully. The Wilson government almost broke in the course of the disputes over *In Place of Strife*. But no government in British history, Labour or otherwise, had been so helpless in the face of the undisciplined brute force of union power. Lloyd George had responded to the Triple Alliance and the unprecedented labour troubles of 1918–21 (involving even the police) by using the armed forces and the Emergency Powers Act. Even Stanley Baldwin, one of Callaghan's youthful heroes, had confronted and faced down the challenge of the General Strike.

A variety of factors had contributed to the 'winter of discontent'—the growth of decentralized plant bargaining in place of national negotiations; the rise of new kinds of union, especially amongst the unskilled or semi-skilled in the public sector; the emergence of a different, politically less attuned union leadership on the model of Moss Evans and Alan Fisher.

Beneath all these lay the pent-up anger of millions of public sector service workers after three years of pay restraint. But the government had no answer to any of them. Further, there was a sense of impotence, of 'quiet despair' in Bernard Donoughue's words, at the heart of government.[44] All other policy came to a halt. Union power gripped the public mind. Britain, in the last phase of Labour corporatism, seemed close to being ungovernable.

For the next decade and a half the party and the unions were tarred with the consequences and the backlash of Conservative anti-union policies. Unemployment rose sharply after 1979. The unions' membership went down by almost half over subsequent years, from over 12 million in 1979 to less than 7 million in 1996. Research at the University of Warwick showed that whereas 71 per cent of employees were covered by collective bargaining as late as 1984, in 1996 only four in ten were so covered. The decline was most serious in newer companies and amongst younger employees. Only two in every ten employees in 1996 carried a union card. The authority of the unions had become steadily marginalized. Even apparently strong causes such as the denial of union membership to the staff of GCHQ in Cheltenham by the Thatcher government failed to arouse much public support beyond union ranks. Public opinion supported the violent defeat of the print unions by the Murdoch press at Wapping. Union leaders in the 'winter of discontent' moved on. Moss Evans left the Transport Workers in 1985; eleven years later, he resurfaced as mayor of King's Lynn. Clive Jenkins emigrated to Tasmania.

When Labour had come back to office in 1974, the public standing of the unions was still high in public esteem. Heath's three-day week had seen to that. The unions were central to Labour's election victories in the two general elections of that year. A popular song in early 1973 went 'They can't stop me, I'm part of the union'; the group who sang it, The Strawbs, took it to the top of the hit parade and were received in private audience, Vatican style, by Vic Feather. People like Jack Jones were widely popular, custodians of the cloth cap, their impersonation by Mike Yarwood on television a sign of a kind of affection. Five years later, even amongst working-class families, who were of course consumers, spouses, and parents as well as producers, they were targets of something close to hatred. When Tony Blair's 'New Labour' asserted itself in the mid-1990s, one of its fundamental premisses, as a sign of 'modernity', was that the Old Labour alliance which had survived from Keir Hardie to James Callaghan should, if not actually scrapped, be consigned to the dustbin of history—one as overflowing and putrid as those dumped in their tens of thousands in British cities during the winter of discontent.

The Prime Minister was the ultimate casualty. The belief that he enjoyed a unique relationship with the unions, and was a supremely effective agent of industrial partnership, collapsed. His reputation never began to recover during his remaining time in office. Other policy initiatives by him, on education after the Ruskin speech, on home ownership, on job training or law and order, also evaporated. The Policy Unit found it difficult to attract his interest on any subject unconnected with the unions and their pay claims. The election Campaign Committee seemed to languish, the closeness of the general election notwithstanding. Meetings of ministers and National Executive members dragged on inconsequentially. The Prime Minister's much-cherished initiatives in foreign policy had no opportunity to flourish. Judging from the records that survive, his telephone conversations with Presidents Carter and Giscard, and with Chancellor Schmidt, for instance, seem to have petered out.

He met Schmidt and Giscard d'Estaing for only two days in his final period, on 12–13 March 1979 at the Council of Europe in Paris. There was no particular movement on the EMS issue. This was one of the least stimulating of summits. Nico Henderson, with whom Callaghan had clashed at times in the past, found him in relaxed, almost elegiac mood, all passion spent.[44] Where Schmidt was grumpy, Callaghan expressed genuine enthusiasm for the architecture of the French embassy and appreciation of one of Lady Henderson's stylish dinners. 'I have never known him so benign', Henderson commented. The ambassador mentioned to the Prime Minister the art exhibitions displayed at the Grand and Petit Palais. 'How I look forward to being able to do that sort of thing,' the Prime Minister observed, 'to look at a few pictures for a change.' It was as though the senior statesman, with little-known but genuine cultural and aesthetic enthusiasms, and now within a few days of his 67th birthday, was renouncing the habits of a lifetime and calling it a day. Yet even now caution prevailed. He sensed in Henderson a possible political audience. So he added, 'But I must win the election first.'

1. *Independent*, *Guardian*, 17 Aug. 1996; *The Times*, 21–2 Oct. 1982. John de Lorean was arrested in Los Angeles and charged with financing a $24m. cocaine deal, but the case never came to court.
2. Robert Taylor, *The Trade Union Question in British Politics* (London, 1993), app. 5.
3. See *Western Mail*, 'Economic Review', 20 Jan. 1978.
4. *Financial Times*, 3–4 Nov. 1978.
5. Paul Roots's evidence in 'Winter of Discontent', 39.
6. Williams Rodgers, 'Government under Stress', *Political Quarterly*, 155/2 (1984), 173.
7. *Time and Chance*, 527.

8. Interview with Lord Murray of Epping Forest.

9. Donoughue, *Prime Minister*, 171.

10. Donoughue to Healey, 4 Dec. 1978 (private papers).

11. Material in Callaghan Papers, uncatalogued.

12. Owen, *Time to Declare*, 171.

13. Record (by Philip Wood) of meeting of Prime Minister and Tribune representatives, 13 Dec. 1978 (private papers); *Parl. Deb.*, 5th ser., vol. 690 (13 Dec. 1978); Hattersley, *Who Goes Home?*, 198. Hattersley was suffering from kidney failure.

14. Owen, *Time to Declare*, 382.

15. Callaghan to J. S. Arthur, 15 Jan. 1979 (Callaghan Papers, box 21B).

16. Prime Minister's private secretary to A. M. W. Battishill, Treasury, 4 Jan. 1979 (private papers).

17. *Financial Times*, 8 Jan. 1979.

18. Interviews with Tom McNally and Sir Tom McCaffrey.

19. Shore, *Leading the Left*, 118.

20. Interview with Lord Callaghan.

21. Callaghan conversations with Len Murray and Moss Evans, 10 Jan. 1979 (private papers).

22. Interview with Lord Rodgers.

23. Tom McCaffrey to Callaghan, 17 Jan. 1979 (Callaghan Papers, box 10).

24. Interview with Jack Jones.

25. Donoughue, *Prime Minister*, 176; interviews with Sir Kenneth Stowe and Lord Gladwin of Clee; memo by David Lipsey, 13 Feb. 1979 (Gladwin Papers).

26. MS note on Cabinet meeting, late Jan. 1979; Donoughue memo to Callaghan, 'The Next Ten Weeks', 25 Jan. 1979 (private papers).

27. Barnett, *Inside the Treasury*, 170 ff. Cf. entry on Alan Fisher by William McCarthy and C. S. Nicholls, in Nicholls (ed.), *Dictionary of National Biography*, supplement 1986–90 (Oxford, 1996), 136.

28. *Financial Times*, 17 Jan. 1979.

29. Morgan, *Labour in Power*, 374–7, 437–8.

30. Memo by Policy Unit for the Prime Minister, 7 Jan. 1979 (Callaghan Papers, box 10); Jeffery and Hennessy, *States of Emergency*, 243–4; information from Lord Rodgers.

31. Benn, *Conflicts of Interest*, 437 (15 Jan. 1979).

32. Rodgers to Callaghan, 26 July 1984; Callaghan to Rodgers, 1 Aug. 1984; Rodgers to Callaghan, 5 Sept. 1984 (private possession). I am very grateful to Lord Rodgers for copies of this correspondence. Also see Rodgers, 'Government under Stress', 173.

33. Benn, *Conflicts of Interest*, 446 (30 Jan. 1979).

34. Ibid. 448.

35. Record of meeting of the Prime Minister and TUC General Council, 29 Jan. 1979 (Callaghan Papers, box 10).

36. *Daily Telegraph*, 6 Feb. 1979.

37. *Financial Times*, 31 Jan. 1979.

38. Ibid. 5 Feb. 1979

39. Ibid. 15 Feb. 1979; 'The Economy, the Government and Trade Union Responsibilities: Joint Statement by the TUC and the Government' (HMSO, Feb. 1979).

40. Callaghan to Healey, 16 Feb. 1979 (Callaghan Papers, box 21B).

41. *Daily Telegraph*, 23 Feb. 1979.

42. Benn, *Conflicts of Interest*, 465 (1 Mar. 1979). Benn calls this 'a nasty exchange'. A small increase of £2 to £2.50 a week was announced by the Nurses and Midwives Whitley Council on 3 Apr.

43. *Financial Times*, 3 Mar. 1979.

44. Donoughue, *Prime Minister*, 176.

45. Henderson, *Mandarin*, 258–9.

28

DYING FALL

In late February 1979 there appeared to be ground for hope that the government was at last climbing out of its troubles. The more costly strikes were now over. The Valentine's Day concordat at least provided the government and the TUC with something tangible, a fairly credible scrap of paper to wave before the electorate, even if Len Murray himself privately felt it was meaningless. The Prime Minister's introspective gloom slowly evaporated. But on 1 March 1979 there was yet another massive blow. In the referendums in Scotland and Wales, the devolution measures for those two nations, which had occupied so much of parliamentary time since the end of 1976 and which were vital to the tactical manœuvres which ensured the government's survival, failed to pass. The news did not come to the Prime Minister and Cabinet as a huge surprise. They had ploughed the sands of Celtic nationalism with (in most cases) limited conviction or intellectual engagement. Scarcely any Cabinet minister who represented an English constituency was in the least sympathetic to devolution; William Rodgers, who came from Liverpool and sat for Stockton in Teesside, voiced the antipathy of the north-east towards a Scottish assembly, which he shared. Roger Stott annoyed Callaghan by pointing out that the response of the SNP members to John Smith's revised package on Scottish devolution was to fail to support the government in the vote on the Queen's Speech. The 'yes' campaigns on devolution organized in Scotland and Wales during that snowy winter had not gone well at any time. In January and February, inevitably, they turned into a plebiscite on the government's record as a whole during the 'winter of discontent'. Overflowing dustbins, closed schools, and undug graves did not assist the cause of devolution, or make the voters even of staunchly Labour Wales and Scotland love their government.

In Wales, as the Secretary for Wales John Morris had warned Callaghan in early February, morale was very low amongst party workers, with strong hostility towards devolution shown in much of Labour-held south Wales. An apparently successful rally in Swansea on 21 February, addressed by the Prime Minister and by Len Murray, did not change the overall pattern.[1] Opinion polls through the campaign showed a large and growing majority against devolution; this was not surprising since the Welsh had been consistently lukewarm or hostile towards home rule since the Cymru Fydd divisions involving Lloyd George in the mid-1890s. Things were no different now that Labour had supplanted the old Liberal ascendancy. Public declarations by the Welsh great and good, local meetings adorned by operatic tenors, television actresses, or star rugby players, were not going to sway the voters. The defeat of devolution in the principality was wholly predictable.

In Scotland, the strength of pro-devolution feeling was much greater: after all, there were eleven Nationalist MPs in Scotland, both in urban and rural areas, whereas there were a mere three in Wales. But Scottish Unionism was still a strong sentiment particularly in Edinburgh, despite the mildly devolutionist sentiments of Conservatives north of the border such as Alick Buchanan-Smith and Malcolm Rifkind. Labour had its dissentients, too. Tam Dalyell of West Lothian, fiercely anti-devolution with his jibes about 'Ally's Tartan Army' (the dejected football supporters who witnessed Scotland's humiliating defeats by various ill-regarded teams in the 1978 World Cup), was a host unto himself. The youthful Robin Cook feared that devolution would mean fewer Scottish MPs at Westminster. The most powerful exponent of Scottish devolution amongst the MPs, the academic professor John Mackintosh, had died unexpectedly of a heart attack in 1978. Helen Liddell of the Scottish Labour Party urged Callaghan to take some part in the campaign. The government's attitude, she felt, was seen as 'ambivalent'.[2] In fact, the Prime Minister himself paid only a fleeting one-day visit to Glasgow on 12 February. The polls in Scotland showed the majority in favour of devolution slowly shrinking and the entire campaign poisoned by the bitter antipathy of Labour and the SNP. The Nationalists were fiercely critical of a measure in which a Scottish assembly would have no control over Scotland's electricity, gas, coal, or oil. The Scottish Office did not appear unduly committed either way.

Nevertheless, the results of the referendums as they came through on 2 March were a considerable psychological blow to the Callaghan government. They seemed to herald its early end. In Wales, the outcome was a humiliation for Labour. Devolution was rejected by over four to one by the electors. The results showed that 243,048 Welsh voters (11.8 per cent of the total electorate) supported the devolution proposals, but that 956,330

(46.5 per cent) voted against. All parts of Wales were strongly opposed; even in Gwynedd in the mountainous north-west where the Welsh language and nationalist sentiment were strongest, there was a vote of almost two to one against devolution. The Welsh assembly, intended for a derelict coal exchange in Cardiff's dockland, was dead and buried. In Scotland, there was actually a majority in favour of devolution, although only a very narrow one on a fairly low poll of 63 per cent. Strathclyde, Central, and Fife (the Labour strongholds), together with Highlands and (narrowly) Lothian, voted 'yes'; Tayside, Borders, Grampian, and Orkney and Shetland voted 'no'. The result was that 32.85 per cent of the electorate voted for devolution and 30.78 per cent against.[3] The majority in favour of a Scottish assembly was far short of the 40 per cent required under George Cunningham's amendment. The government seemed unlikely to implement Scottish devolution, so the eleven Scottish Nationalist MPs no longer felt obliged to support the Callaghan administration as they had been doing since Christmas. In these circumstances, the minority government's early defeat in the Commons appeared preordained.

Bernard Donoughue has well described the eerie, unreal atmosphere in which politics were conducted for what remained of March. 'It was like being on the sinking *Titanic* without the music.' The business of government continued after a fashion. The remaining strikes in the public sector, now featuring massive pay claims from the civil servants and the schoolteachers as has been seen, slowly wound down. The members of Alan Fisher's NUPE were expensively bought off. Meanwhile the atmosphere in the House was increasingly frenetic. The skills of Walter Harrison, the deputy whip, were strained to the full, not least in paying heed to the variegated customers of Annie's Bar. This hospitable venue attained an almost legendary reputation in the final phase of the Callaghan government, especially for the social activities of the Scottish Nationalist members. The political columnist of the *Observer*, Alan Watkins, a convivial Welshman himself, coined the memorable phrase that, for them, every night was Burns night.[4]

The major new development, of ominous significance for the future, was the appointment of the standing commission on pay comparability in the public sector as foreshadowed in the Valentine's Day concordat. Its chairman, appointed after a meeting at 10 Downing Street on 26 March, would be Professor Hugh Clegg of the University of Warwick. He was a strong supporter of traditional patterns of industrial relations who had fought successfully to retain the voluntarist system of free collective bargaining on the Donovan Commission back in 1968. The Policy Unit had somewhat reluctantly accepted the idea of the standing committee as a way of providing some kind of scientific, objective yardstick for making sense of public sector pay rates. But it was anticipated that it would come into effect as part of a wider package as foreshadowed in the concordat, including a national assessment of the economy. What happened in reality was that, following the election of the Thatcher government in May, the Clegg Commission remained as a free-standing body virtually in charge of issuing undated cheques on behalf of public sector workers. The new Prime Minister had been equivocal about the Clegg Commission before taking office. In Mrs Thatcher's first year, the Prime Minister, the fierce advocate of monetary controls and cash limits, now found herself presiding over a series of staged Clegg awards which meant pay rises of between 16 per cent and 25 per cent. This imposed severe upwards pressure on price levels and meant that inflation was running at over 20 per cent at the end of 1979, over double that of a year earlier. It also meant that, with the Thatcher government's increases in VAT up to a uniform level of 15 per cent, the money supply actually went up instead of being severely cut back as Friedmanite monetarist economics dictated. Even beyond the grave, therefore, the legacy of the winter of discontent continued to haunt the nation.

Otherwise, Callaghan himself continued at work with an increasingly inert Whitehall machine gripped by an air of fatalism. As noted, he had two days in Paris on 12–13 March for what turned out to be a final session with Helmut Schmidt and Giscard d'Estaing. He was reported as having adopted a provocative tone in telling the EEC that the Agricultural Policy was a 'rake's progress' and that Britain might well be contributing £1,000m. net in the next year to the Community budget. This was taken as being for domestic consumption, playing to anti-European sentiment at home.[5] The Prime Minister also took time off on 17 March to see Wales play England in the rugby international at Cardiff Arms Park. The outcome was highly satisfactory, Wales winning over the old enemy by 27 points to 3, with a rash of tries in the final quarter. But the great rugby team of the 1970s was ageing, stars like Gareth Edwards and Barry John having retired. Both of them, along with other sporting and musical celebrities, had declared themselves in favour of devolution prior to its rejection. Welsh rugby, like Welsh politics, perhaps like the old corporatist Labour Party itself, was reaching the end of an era.

The main focus of attention in party politics now was on how the government would react to a vote of confidence following the failure of the devolution proposals. This meant resuming the thankless task of bartering among a variety of small groups, with the Scottish Nationalists the most unpredictable of all. This was the speciality of Michael Foot, always a far more enthusiastic devolutionist than his Prime Minister, and anxious to salvage something from the debris.

He rang Callaghan at the farm on the morning of Sunday, 4 March, suggesting an ingenious strategy for survival, through which the Commencement Order for the Scottish measure would not be implemented until the start of the next parliamentary session in October.[6] Callaghan was doubtful, but Foot brought this up formally at a meeting of ministers on the Monday morning, 5 March. He proposed the early rejection of the repeal of the Scottish Act, which followed from the failure of the Scottish measure to obtain a vote of 40 per cent of the electors but delaying the Commencement Order and having at the same time a vote of confidence. This would compel the SNP, he believed, to support the government in the interim. The proposal would mean, obviously, the election being deferred until the last possible moment, October–November 1979. Callaghan, however, rejected this as too convoluted. Battered and morally challenged by years of manœuvrings, he recalled the charges of gerrymandering the constituencies made against him when Home Secretary back in 1969 which had damaged his reputation for honesty. Instead, he proposed all-party talks to see if anything could be done to amend the Scotland Act. He was supported by Denis Healey, and also by the chief whip, Michael Cocks, who urged that they play for time and who added that the SNP were not anxious for an early election in which most of their eleven members would probably lose their seats.

It was agreed that Callaghan should see David Steel, the Liberal leader, at once, and in private. This meeting took place at 3.40 p.m. on Tuesday, 6 March. But it emerged that the Liberals would not support repeal nor would they back the government in the House. It was widely known that the Liberals now wanted an early election, partly because they feared they would be wiped out in the European elections in June but more urgently because the Jeremy Thorpe trial, involving not only homosexuality but charges of attempted murder, would begin in April and this would inevitably cast a somewhat lurid light on the Liberal Party of which he had so recently been the leader. At a Cabinet meeting on the 8th, Callaghan again urged the need for all-party talks to find a compromise on Scottish devolution. In the meantime, the government considered other ways of showing its continued sympathy for the national aspirations of Wales and Scotland. John Morris, the Welsh Secretary, won support for having more powers transferred to the Welsh Office, and administered in Cathays Park, Cardiff, not in Glyndwr House, Whitehall.[7] For Scotland, there was an interesting letter to Bernard Donoughue from the Oxford political scientist Vernon Bogdanor of Brasenose College. He suggested that the government buy time by either establishing a select committee on Scottish affairs meeting periodically in Scotland, or else creating an assembly of Scottish local authority representatives to debate Scottish matters.[8]

Between 14 and 18 March the position hardened. The Scottish Nationalists' leader Donald Stewart issued an ultimatum to Callaghan which demanded that Scottish devolution be again pursued and put before parliament.[9] This was something the Prime Minister was unable to deliver in party terms; nor did he have the emotional commitment to doing so. The Conservatives announced that they would be putting down a vote of confidence for 28 March, and now a government defeat did seem probable. On 21 March, Foot offered a further suggestion for manœuvre, putting forward a motion to propose all-party talks on Scotland with the Repeal Orders to be debated within the week beginning 7 May. Callaghan at first appeared to be sympathetic, but he rang Foot back at 11.30 p.m.—'a late hour for him', Foot later observed—saying that he did not feel it right to proceed in this way.[10] More and more the Prime Minister appeared almost above the mêlée, concentrating on the constitutional proprieties, and perhaps what history would conclude in future years about the way he and his colleagues had behaved.

Callaghan had a meeting with Foot again before the Cabinet on the morning of 22 March. 'His patience had suddenly smapped. He wanted to invite the election and the decision that would lead to it.' It was, Foot believed, 'a considerable error'. At the Cabinet later, Callaghan's statement to the House on devolution was discussed. It was agreed that talks would continue with the other parties for some time but that the government would lose on a vote to repeal the Scotland and Wales Act. An early election was regarded as almost a certainty now, with Callaghan—and 'all the pro-Europeans' as Benn put it[11]—wanting 7 May. Merlyn Rees was reported on 24 March as believing that the government were very likely to be defeated in the vote of confidence. After all, one Labour backbencher, Tom Swain, had recently been killed in a car crash, while another, Sir Alfred Broughton, member for Batley and Morley, was critically ill and most unlikely to make it to Westminster to cast his vote.

Private negotiations continued on various fronts, with Michael Foot and the government whip Michael Cocks in the thick of things. Callaghan himself seemed, in a tone of weariness, to be arguing for an end to all further talks in meeting with the Liaison Committee of the PLP and the TUC on the morning of 26 March, but Foot, Healey, Cocks, and Merlyn

Rees successfully urged that they should continue.[12] There seemed no point now in continuing talks with either the Liberals or the Scottish Nationalists, both of whom were committed to voting against the government. There were four other groups to be approached. There were two 'Scottish Labour' members, Jim Sillars and John Robertson, Labour MPs who had resigned the whip in July 1976 because of the government's perceived lukewarmness on Scottish devolution. Their socialism was still strong enough to lead them to support Labour, though with reluctance. There were the three Plaid Cymru members, more instinctively sympathetic to Labour than the Scottish Nationalists, who were sometimes contemptuously referred to as 'tartan Tories'. Apart from the fact that Welsh devolution would hardly find any sympathy in Tory ranks, there was a special local issue of much interest to Dafydd Wigley and Dafydd Elis Thomas, who represented Caernarfon and Merionydd with their old slate quarrying communities, namely a bill to compensate retired quarry workers (and also miners in south Wales) who were victims of silicosis or other lung disease. Here the government was sympathetic and a precious three votes might be gleaned.[13]

Then there was, as always, Ireland. The goverment, through Roy Mason, Foot, and also Roy Hattersley, approached once again the Ulster Unionists, represented by Enoch Powell and James Molyneaux. Here again there were grounds for hope. Powell himself was still sympathetic to Labour as the more critical party on Europe with its insistence on reform of the Common Agricultural Policy. There had already been agreement to increase the Ulster representation at Westminster from twelve to seventeen which was another positive sign for the Unionists. This followed the recommendations of the Speaker's Conference, even though Bernard Donoughue had warned of Irish voters in England being concerned with Roy Mason's apparent drift towards the Unionists.[14] Finally there was the quite different issue of a gas pipeline connecting Northern Ireland with the British mainland, a proposal for which there was a good deal to be said, quite apart from any party political considerations, and which indeed was implemented in the 1980s. It would be popular, for a different mix of reasons, with both Unionists and Nationalists in Northern Ireland. Callaghan, however, was reluctant to push forward with a decision to approve a pipeline without the normal consultation and investigation. Roy Hattersley told Austin Mitchell that 'Jim was going to go down like a noble Roman'. He was again perhaps 'playing for history'.[15]

There were, however, two Unionists, Harold McCusker and Johnny Carson, who were naturally sympathetic to Labour. They reached a rapid agreement with Roy Hattersley—formally signed on the evening of the decisive vote on 28 March, after the first draft had been inadvertently ripped up through injudicious use of a biro. The agreement committed the government to a special retail price index for Northern Ireland and an inquiry by the Price Commission into the higher cost of commodities in the province. While there were uncertainties right up to the time of voting, and much care taken of them in the tearoom and the lobbies to make sure that the aberrant Ulstermen did not abscond,[16] here again appeared to be two precious Irish votes to add in the government to Plaid Cymru's three and Scottish Labour's two.

The other two Northern Irish MPs, however, were an unexpected problem. Gerry Fitt, a brave and impulsive man, an old socialist who had broadly voted with the government through thick and thin in the past few years, had long been incensed by what he regarded as the Unionism of the Northern Irish Secretary Roy Mason. The last straw for him was the decision, to which he was not party, to increase Ulster's representation at Westminster, which he regarded as pandering to Unionism for party ends. Gerry Fitt's alienation was such that he might well abstain. A meeting with Callaghan on 19 March failed to sway him: he complained that the government were placating Unionists who had voted against them on issue after issue.[17] His Nationalist colleague Frank Maguire, 'Independent Republican', was almost inaccessible, seemingly immured in his pub in Fermanagh. He seldom turned up in Westminster at all. This time he might well do so, but, even more than in the case of Gerry Fitt, his presence was unlikely to be helpful to the government. Tension mounted rapidly as the days and hours ticked away prior to the vote of confidence. On 27 March, Callaghan was attacked by the press for horse-trading over an Ulster gas pipeline, compensation for Welsh quarrymen, and other issues. He seemed angry, almost rattled.[18] It was also his 67th birthday, and was not a happy anniversary.

On 28 March 1978, the debate took its course. Mrs Thatcher began in pedestrian style; Callaghan replied with dignity, pleading for fairness, but had little new to say. The three Plaid Cymru members announced that they would support the government. The SNP group of eleven announced that they would vote against them. So did the Liberals. Two crucial blows were confirmation that Sir Alfred Broughton was too ill even to be 'nodded through the lobbies' on his stretcher (in fact, he died shortly afterwards) and Gerry Fitt's declaration that he would abstain. Frank Maguire was said to be in the vicinity of Westminster, 'abstaining in person', having been insulted by Fitt when he intended to vote with Labour.

The main group of Ulster Unionists, eight in number headed by Enoch Powell, would vote against the government. The debate ended with a blazing, defiant debating performance by Michael Foot, pouring scorn and derision on all the other groups, and on 'the boy David', the Liberals' leader, in particular.

The division confirmed Merlyn Rees's gloomy predictions. The government was defeated by one vote, 310 to 311. The majority included 279 Conservatives, 13 Liberals, 11 SNP, and 8 Ulster Unionists. The minority included 303 Labour, 3 Plaid Cymru, 2 Scottish Labour, and Roy Hattersley's shepherded duo of Unionists, McCusker and Carson, who had been navigated safely home to port in the government lobby. Callaghan, dignified in defeat, announced an immediate meeting with the Queen to request a dissolution of parliament and a general election. It was later announced that it would take place on 3 May. There was an air of intense excitement now that a government had lost power through a vote in the House of Commons, the first time such a thing had happened since the first Labour government of Ramsay MacDonald was defeated over the Campbell case in October 1924. A group of left-wing MPs, led by Neil Kinnock, a keen member of male voice choirs, sang 'The Red Flag' in the division lobbies[19] just as far more Labour MPs, including the 33-year-old James Callaghan, had done back in August 1945. But this time it was very different. Labour's progress had come full circle. If 1945, in the eyes of enthusiasts, saw the advent of 'the new Jerusalem', 1979 was more like an action replay of the fate of the old Jericho.

After the government's defeat on 28 March, there were those such as Michael Foot and Roy Hattersley who argued that it could have manœuvred its way to victory on the critical vote, perhaps even to the extent that an autumn election might have been won.[20] The Scottish Nationalists might have been conciliated by the offer of an early date for the debate of the Repeal Order (Shirley Williams as well as Michael Foot took this line). The Ulster Unionists might have at least abstained had there been more movement on a gas pipeline. Gerry Fitt would not have been alienated had Roy Mason not appeared so hard-line. Even one or two Liberals could have been detached—perhaps Geraint Howells who had worked closely with the Welsh Office over an elected assembly for Wales and who was no Tory, perhaps Clement Freud whose private member's bill on the release of government official information had the sympathy of many members of the government including Tony Benn. (Callaghan is recorded by Benn as saying that he found the issue of open government 'unutterably boring'.[20]) Michael Foot's view was that the Tories' motion could have been challenged with a government variant of it on 26 March, after which the Tories would have been left isolated against all other parties. In the narrower tactical sense, these scenarios are plausible. There were complaints that the Prime Minister, in the words of one Cabinet colleague, had simply 'bottled out'.

But in the longer term, Callaghan's instinct that further manœuvres would be harmful and inflict further damage on a government sorely stricken after the winter of discontent was surely wise. The best hope for survival now was to take a longer, more statesmanlike perspective, make the best of the concordat with the unions, emphasize the recent improvements in the economy, and point to a further rise in living standards assisted by North Sea oil. That would not only be a dignified response. It might even be politically effective. In general the Cabinet agreed. Perhaps like Attlee's veteran team in September–October 1951 they were exhausted, as much emotionally as physically. It was British public opinion, not a range of small Celtic splinter groups, that had to be won over. The effort had to begin.

The effective election campaign was designedly a long one. Indeed it was to be five weeks in length, by far the longest since that of 1945 and matched by that of 1997. The idea was that a long campaign would help to remind the electors of the achievements of the government and the authority of the Prime Minister. It would put the winter of discontent into perspective as almost a local difficulty. At the same time, it would help to expose the raw, inexperienced nature of Mrs Thatcher's political background and probably force her into extremist indiscretions on the unions, Europe, law and order, or some other fortuitous issue. Her tendency to make policy on the hoof was known to be a source for concern for the largely Heathite Tory front-bench spokesmen such as Whitelaw, Prior, Walker, Pym, and Gilmour.

But first the Labour Party, as usual, had to fight not the Tories but itself. There was immense tension beneath the surface of the contents of the Labour Party election manifesto. A radical document had been drawn up by Geoff Bish of Transport House, after regular meetings of the NEC and the Cabinet. However, on 29 March, the day after the vote, a version of the manifesto emanated from No. 10, drafted by Tom McNally and David Lipsey. A very long meeting on the election manifesto began in the Cabinet room of No. 10 at 6.15 p.m. It went on until the small hours.[22] Those present were the drafting committee, Callaghan, Healey, Foot, Shore, and Benn for the Cabinet, Frank Allaun, Eric Heffer, Mrs Lena Jeger, and the railwaymen's leader Russell Tuck for the NEC. On the face of it, it was a body slanted to the left with no place for the Social Democrats of the future. Also present were Ron Hayward, the Labour Party general secretary, with Tom McNally and David Lipsey of the Prime Minister's personal staff, and Reg Underhill, Joyce Gould, Geoff Bish, and Jenny Little of Transport House. It was a spartan occasion. Drinks and sandwiches were brought in at 8 p.m. and further refreshments at midnight. There were no civil servants present because of the latest strike. The meeting broke up at 3.15 a.m.

The discussions focused on the two rival draft manifestos. After some argument, Callaghan's ('a meaningless document' in Benn's view[23]) was taken as the basic text for discussion. There followed a lengthy, and occasionally acrimonious, dialogue between Callaghan, supported by Healey and usually Foot, and Benn and Heffer, backed up by Allaun, over the more disputatious features of the draft. On issue after issue, Benn and Heffer insisted that radical, socialist commitments had either been watered down or thrown out altogether. On each occasion, Callaghan, playing the prime ministerial, elder statesman card with much effect, declared that he was a better judge of public opinion and that he would not allow radical proposals to be included. He was in particularly determined mood, more so in the end than Benn and Heffer. Indeed, Tony Benn, while dissenting frequently and at much length, seems to have been remarkably lacking in rancour, perhaps in part because his 54th birthday came halfway through the meeting and was duly celebrated in the usual way by a midnight rendition. His vigour may have been diminished also by a bout of poorish health including splitting headaches.

The outcome followed Callaghan's views in almost every instance. There would be no compulsory planning powers and no nationalization of the banks. The criticism of the European Common Market was greatly toned down. It was implied that Britain would retain nuclear weapons; certainly Allaun's insistence that nuclear weapons would be abandoned by Britain was brusquely rejected. The abolition of fox-hunting was removed (although that of deer-hunting did eventually find its way in). The most intense and angry debate of all came on something relatively marginal to most people's political priorities—the proposal to abolish the House of Lords. It had been an obstacle to many of the Labour left's objectives in 1974–9, including the nationalization of shipbuilding. Heffer angrily banged the table and accused Callaghan of being a dictator. In turn Callaghan, who had no personal affection for the Lords but was certain that the issue had no electoral appeal, flatly stated that as long as he was leader this item would not appear on a Labour manifesto.[24] In effect, he was challenging the left to remove him which, on the very eve of a general election, was impossible. In the end, Benn and Heffer caved in, and the abolition of the Lords, an objective discussed by many late-Victorian Liberals such as the young Lloyd George, was set aside. On every issue, Callaghan was victorious. As they left around 3.30 a.m., Geoff Bish told Tony Benn, 'We've given away a lot tonight.'[25]

Before the finalizing of the manifesto, Callaghan had a pre-election meeting with the TUC 'Neddy Six', headed by Len Murray, at 3 p.m. on 4 April. He urged them to make the campaign a 'crusade' on behalf of Labour's fundamental aspirations. This meant that the issue of trade union power had to be faced openly. Moss Evans made his distinctive contribution at this point by declaring that they should never apologize for the winter of discontent, but rather explain to the electors how good it was that a state of emergency had been averted. Not surprisingly, Callaghan rejected this out of hand. The public, he declared, would remember the closed hospital wards and the undug graves. On this occasion, Len Murray and Terry Duffy agreed with him. But it was not a reassuring insight into the political outlook of key members of the TUC.[26]

At the NEC/Cabinet meeting at No. 10 at 10 a.m. on 6 April, chaired by Allaun but dominated by the Prime Minister, Callaghan was in similarly determined mood.[27] He flatly rejected a proposal by Benn to include broad policies for statutory intervention in industry and planning agreements. After a fierce, almost violent argument, statements condemnatory of the Common Market were left out, leaving only a general reference to defending the Westminster parliament against the Common Market's institutions. The meeting was evidently fundamentally divided both on this and on nuclear weapons, where again Callaghan's views prevailed. As on 4 April, there was a fierce discussion on whether to include the ending of the House of Lords in the Labour manifesto. On a vote, there was a large majority of 11 to 4 in favour of abolition. The eleven included not only the left (including its most youthful member, Neil Kinnock) but also Michael Foot, Barbara Castle, and even John Smith. The minority of four were Callaghan, Shore, John Golding, and Michael Cocks, the chief whip. But again the noes had it. Callaghan issued a straight leader's veto on any mention of the abolition of the Lords and all that survived was a brief and semi-literate statement about the Lords being 'indefensible with [*sic*] its power and influence'.

Later that day the manifesto was formally unveiled. It bore the vaguely 1940s title *Labour's Way is the Better Way*, and was a distinctly moderate document. There were promises about 3 per cent annual growth and a cut in inflation to 5 per cent by 1982, together with various social benefits such as higher pensions and child benefit. The only vestige of radicalism was a proposal for a wealth tax to fall on those with wealth of more than £150,000, including private residential houses. In a memorandum a few days later, Gavyn Davies of the Policy Unit pointed out that twelve Continental countries already had a wealth tax, but added that a survey conducted by the University of Bath revealed that a wealth tax was an unpopular part of Labour's programme. At least, however, Tony Benn's phrase about a 'fundamental and irreversible shift of wealth and power in favour of working people and their families' was included. At the end of the meeting, Benn felt, 'I thought we had done rather well.'[28] More realistically, the press the next day represented the moderation of the document as a triumph for Callaghan over the left.

The preparation of the 1979 party manifesto later led to immense argument. There was fury on the left at what was called 'the leader's veto' and the consequently anodyne nature of the party's proposals was claimed to be a major cause in leading to the triumph of Mrs Thatcher. In particular, it was said to have depressed party activists. Callaghan, for his part, claimed flatly that he had not vetoed the manifesto proposals and, more cogently, that left-wing propositions of the kind favoured by Benn and his friends would have alienated the voters even more than the winter of discontent and the left-wing outlook of constituency activities had already done. There was no evidence at all that such extreme measures as massive further nationalization or planning agreements, the abolition of nuclear weapons, or leaving the Common Market four years after the referendum would have added to Labour's popularity.

The issue was one embedded in the historic structure of the Labour Party, like so much else in that difficult document the 1918 party constitution, over which commentators have so often pored with the academic concentration of medieval schoolmen. Under Clause 5 (originally Clause 4) of the constitution, the manifesto was traditionally produced in combination by the National Executive and the party leadership. This assumed, of course, that they were in broad harmony: the constitution offered no guidance on how to resolve a conflict. This had undoubtedly been so in the Attlee years between 1945 and 1951, and again in most of the Wilson period of 1964–70. Since the early 1970s, however, the essential conflict between grass-roots democracy and a leadership representative of the broad national view had surfaced time and again. It took the classic form of a left-wing, socialist constituency view opposed to a centre-right stance upheld by the leadership. In that case, the manifesto could emerge not through compromise, but with one side being forced to surrender to the other.

In this case, the original manifesto had been the work of the party's Home Policy Commitee, chaired by Tony Benn, with a strong left-wing representation. The revised version was the product of the prime minister's office and had never been revealed to the Cabinet, let alone the NEC or the Liaison Committee. The former was representative of the views of constituency activists. The latter reflected, or so it was claimed, the broad beliefs of Labour voters, and of the nation in general. Whether Callaghan had vetoed a properly drafted manifesto depended on what view one took of the legitimacy of either side. The Bennite version was endorsed by most activists in the constituencies; the Callaghan version was upheld in every opinion poll. Two versions of democracy, one internalized, the other parliamentary, were thus in conflict.[29] Years after their time, Kautsky and Bernstein were locked in conflict. The outcome was that the Prime Minister's view, in the particular circumstances prevailing in April 1979, inevitably triumphed, but at the cost of deepening the fissures already present over rival definitions of democratic socialism. The schisms that in two years' time were to see the party mechanisms dominated by Bennite versions of internal democracy and many in the centre-right hiving off to join the new SDP were already foreshadowed.

The campaign that followed lasted a full five weeks. It was intended as has been noticed to draw the sting of Mrs Thatcher. It began appallingly with the assassination of Airey Neave, Mrs Thatcher's campaign manager in 1975, by the INLA (an offshoot of the IRA) in a bombing incident. But it was thereafter a quiet affair. In the recent past, there had been much criticism that Labour's election campaigns had been unduly dominated by the personality of Harold Wilson as party leader. This had given the British elections almost the air of an American presidential election; indeed, some British academics were to argue that the centralization of party leadership together with the pressure of the media inevitably had turned British party politics into presidential politics. In Wilson's case, this emphasis had been very fruitful in 1966 and damaging in 1970. Callaghan had operated a far more collective style of leadership than Wilson. This had inspired trust and cohesion in his Cabinet, however wide the ideological gulf that separated, say, Tony Benn from Shirley Williams.

But the most striking feature of the 1979 election on the Labour side is how the personality and style of the Prime Minister dominated their campaign, too. He travelled around the country, engaging in friendly 'walkabouts' in shopping centres from Oxford to Glasgow and apparently enjoying relaxed banter with passers-by. His leisurely, purposeful progresses, as he ambled or prowled from housing estate to shopping mall to community centre in a variety of places, recalled his highly effective stalking of his Cardiff South-East constituency in election after election from proletarian Splott and Adamsdown to bourgeois Penarth. In public meetings, the preferred approach was for Callaghan and Audrey to walk slowly together through an election audience greeting individuals before he spoke, with aides like Derek Gladwin and David Lipsey walking a respectful distance behind. Not for Callaghan the theatrical spotlight entry on to the platform of later campaigns, if it could be avoided. His speeches were informal in style with few 'soundbites'. He tended to have 'an inside pocket speech' alongside his formal address given to the press, to make his interaction with his audience as direct and natural as possible. Derek Gladwin felt he conducted an outstanding, prime ministerial campaign. 'Jim was in top form throughout.'

His message, one of moderation and of reason, emphasizing Labour's commitment to partnership with the unions, the control of prices, and a judicious extension of welfare services, conformed with his avuncular style. Personal attacks on Mrs Thatcher and the Tories were studiously avoided. The Nuffield 1979 survey complained that his speeches 'did not strike an inspirational note' and were 'half-hearted' or perhaps 'elegiac'.[30] Perhaps it is fairer to say that there was a deliberate attempt to tone down Labour's message and to contrast it with the far more strident, dogmatic, and confrontational style that Mrs Thatcher could not help offering to the electors. Indeed, Tony Benn was to declare his enthusiasm for the Conservative leader's uninhibited note of commitment as opposed to what he saw as Callaghan's right-wing and reactionary appeal to moderation. Bernard Donoughue from the start wanted a more aggressive campaign—'Attack!' On 21 April he felt that, partly for this reason, the Labour campaign was not 'having a great impact so far' and he urged Callaghan not to be above 'Thatcher bashing' on occasion. Three key groups were identified where Labour had much ground to gain: women voters, the young, and electors in the Midlands. He also urged the use of pro-Labour celebrities—the *Mirror* 'agony aunt' Marjorie Proops, the Derby County football manager Brian Clough, and the pop singer Elton John to appeal to young voters (although it was noted that the last-named 'has a complicated image').[31]

Callaghan's was a 'one-nation' appeal. It was he, rather than Mrs Thatcher, who appeared as the heir to Disraeli (assuming, for the moment, that the latter had actually used the phrase in the first place). In speeches and election broadcasts, he used the rhetoric of Britain's becoming a co-operative, just, unified society. Social benefits such as nursery schools, improved pensions, the purchase of council housing, and job training programmes would integrate it all the more. Labour was projected as the defender of the weak in society, the promoter of industrial technology, the protector of jobs, and the champion of the national interest as opposed to the sectarian and partisan Tories. There was some talk of 'Tory extremism'. Not once did his speeches, as recorded in Transport House's press releases, mention the word 'socialist' or 'socialism'.[32] He was usually relaxed and genial in television interviews. ITN apologized to him on 3 May when an interview with David Rose on *News at Ten* led to a row because it concentrated on industrial relations alone.[33] Interrogated by Robin Day for the BBC, he cheerfully accepted the comparison with Stanley Baldwin calling for 'Peace in our time, O Lord'. He took fourteen of the eighteen Labour press conferences in London. Invariably he was flanked by representatives of moderate Labour, Denis Healey, Roy Hattersley, and increasingly Shirley Williams, whose pleasant, direct image was implicitly poised against the strident appeal of the female leader of the Conservative Party. An appearance at press conferences was also made by an attractive young woman MP, Helene Hayman, who sat for the highly marginal seat of Hemel Hempstead. As noted above, Labour feared they were doing badly amongst women voters once again. Michael Foot made few appearances, and Tony Benn fewer still. They were left to campaign in the constituencies where both were popular with party workers. Union leaders had an even lower profile, and Trade Unionists for a Labour Victory was relatively inactive. Labour's private findings showed that the activities of the unions during the winter of discontent were easily the heaviest cross that the government had to bear, and that the unions indeed were now unpopular with a majority of the electors.

In ethic and presentation, Callaghan largely was Labour's campaign. The fundamental reason was simply that he was far more popular than the party. Like John Major in 1997, the Prime Minister was seen as easily his party's strongest asset if, against all the odds, the government was to be returned. Throughout the campaign, the opinion surveys showed that, while Labour invariably lagged behind the Conservatives in Gallup, MORI, Marplan, and, to a lesser extent, NOP polls, Callaghan led Mrs Thatcher by around an average 20 points in polls on the party leaders and who would make the better prime minister. David Lipsey wrote to Callaghan on 28 April that on television 'the electric moments are when you personalize your faith, when you say "I", not just "we" or "Labour" '.[34] In polling taken on 28–30 April, near the end of the campaign, Callaghan's lead over Mrs Thatcher was as large as 24 points, 57 to 33, although it narrowed somewhat in the last few days. But his personal popularity was beyond doubt. When Mrs Thatcher declined his (carefully considered) challenge to her to take part in a televised public debate on the issues, it was felt that Callaghan had only emphasized further his personal ascendancy over her. For her part, the Conservative leader claimed in her memoirs to have been disappointed that her advisers persuaded her to decline: 'I believed that Jim C. was greatly overrated.'[35] But she was seen as anything but a superwoman at this stage in her career, while the violence of the vocabulary in her speeches was widely noted.

The election campaign was run by the Campaign Committee under the calm chairmanship of Derek Gladwin. There was a regular routine of business breakfasts at No. 10, followed by a meeting of the Campaign Committee at Transport House and a press conference at 9.30 a.m. Then Callaghan would return to Downing Street and take off for a variety of provincial centres. He visited Glasgow, Manchester, and Stockport, Ilford, Oxford, and Cinderford in the week starting 9 April; in the week 14–21 April, he was at Southampton and his native Portsmouth, Leicester, Birmingham, Hertfordshire, Cardiff, Manchester, Bolton, Liverpool, Leeds, Halifax, and Huddersfield; in the week starting 23 April he was in Uxbridge and parts of London, Milton Keynes, Coventry, Lichfield, Redditch, Manchester, and Cardiff (where he visited the science and language laboratories at Llanrumney High School in his constituency on 27 April); on 28 April he was at Edinburgh and Newcastle; in the final week from 30 April he was at Gravesend and Chatham, then Ealing, and finally (after some controversy within the campaign team) at Cardiff on 2 May for an eve of the poll rally. It was a strenuous but manageable campaign, even for a man of 67. It was designed to give the maximum personal exposure to the Prime Minister. Tom McNally and Roger Carroll had worked out a schedule well in advance to produce less travel, more use of local television and radio, and the use of modern communications methods. This was in contrast to the wishes of the national agent Reg Underhill, who preferred, it was said, 'the traditional "Midlothian" campaign' across the country.[36] There was careful attention to his regular haircut appointments at Simpson's and the choice of dark suits that would look well on television in the evening news transmissions. This visual aspect of image-making was one that the Prime Minister, an old television hand since the 1950s who had been actually offered a job with ITV news by Geoffrey Cox at that time, took seriously and with much expert insight.[37]

His Campaign Committee worked reasonably well and there were very few hitches. Derek Gladwin ensured that the Policy Unit would prepare material for his speeches after an 'early steer' by the Prime Minister. Roger Carroll from the *Sun* would add political spice, while David Lipsey would undertake a co-ordinating role to ensure that Callaghan got his speech on time each day.[38] Tom McNally, of course, was also an important figure, although he had his own objectives to pursue since he was now the Labour candidate for Stockport South. He had been nominated after a good deal of local acrimony in the constituency party following attempts by left-wingers on the party NEC such as Frank Allaun, Joan Lestor, Dennis Skinner, Joan Maynard, and Eric Heffer to frustrate his nomination which they saw as a piece of prime ministerial patronage.[39] There was always potential tension, as there is in most campaigns, between the campaigning/policy-making bodies and the organizations concerned with marketing and public relations. Back in early December, long before the election date was known, Tom McNally had told Callaghan that the party's media advisers were 'somewhat rudderless'. The Publicity Committee had asked a team of television advisers to produce the next party political broadcast because they felt the Booth-Clibborn group, including figures like Tim Delaney and Trevor Bell, had not produced a satisfactory party political on the previous occasion and had also overspent their budget by £3,000.[40] Some tension was recorded by the Nuffield election survey between Transport House's own publicity machine including media professional MPs such as Austin Mitchell and Phillip Whitehead, and the Booth-Clibborn wing of the Campaign Committee.[41] In the end, Callaghan took the advice of the latter on party political broadcasts, emphasizing broad national objectives under the general theme of 'Fairness to all'.

To the businessman's eye of Michael Callaghan, actively engaged in the campaign, it all looked somewhat disorganized and unbusinesslike. There seemed to be a lack of commitment, passion, and urgency, given the immensity of the issues at stake. However, his own skills were able to some degree to plug the gaps between the prime ministerial candidate, his father, and the Campaign Committee. Geoffrey Goodman, seconded from the *Mirror* to help with the campaign, urged Callaghan to adopt a more combative campaigning style, since he felt the election might be 'slipping away', but to no effect.[42] At any rate, very few mistakes were made, nothing comparable to Gaitskell's statement in 1959 that there would be no cuts in income tax, or Neil Kinnock's fatally triumphalist Sheffield rally in 1992, both much cited later on as serious miscalculations. There was some trouble with leftish pronouncements by Tony Benn, about Europe or in defence of the unions. David Lipsey warned Callaghan of the need to avoid 'possible contradictions' when talking on industrial policy.[43] A brief *frisson* arose when Harold Wilson made some rather unhelpful remarks, praising Mrs Thatcher, criticizing Callaghan for weakness towards the left, and including a suggestion that his wife, who was not a political person, might well vote Conservative. Rumours passed on by George Wigg, that Roy Jenkins and George Thomson, both former ministers, might not be voting Labour, were successfully defused. There was a brief spat with Paul Johnson, former editor of the *New Statesman* and now a far-right journalist, when he referred at a press conference on 26 April to the appointment as ambassador of Peter Jay. But otherwise nothing went wrong, and the Prime Minister's sang-froid seemed undisturbed.

One area which did not seem to offer difficulty was his Cardiff South-East constituency. Fighting for the eleventh time, he faced a new Conservative candidate, Alun Jones, a Welsh-speaking solicitor educated at the University College of Wales, Aberystwyth, and formerly candidate for Pontypridd. There were also a variety of lesser challengers, Eric Roberts (Plaid Cymru), a bus driver; Richard Spencer (Communist), a university lecturer at Cardiff and active nuclear disarmer; R. W. Aldridge, a distinctly obscure 'Severnside Libertarian', whatever that meant; and the colourful and highly committed figure of Pat Arrowsmith (Independent Socialist). Ms Arrowsmith had been a pivotal figure in the more militant wing of CND, the Direct Action Committee, and the Committee of 100. She had been jailed ten times as a political prisoner and had twice been adopted as a prisoner of conscience by Amnesty International. She made the Prime Minister her main target as himself the advocate of Britain's remaining a nuclear power and developing a successor to Polaris. There was no Liberal this time, Chris Bailey, the former candidate, having been expelled and now advising voters in Cardiff South-East to vote Tory. Even with Militant sniping in the wings, Callaghan faced little problem from these miscellaneous opponents. His constituency had lost Penarth and of its six wards, five—Grangetown, South, Adamsdown, Splott, and Rumney (including the large Llanrumney housing estate)—were habitually Labour, with only middle-class Roath tending to back the Conservatives. Even here there were many professionals, such as university lecturers or BBC and HTV employees, who were Labour voters.[44]

There was one only residual local problem facing Callaghan—the long-ailing East Moors steel works. Its coming closure had been announced by the chairman of British Steel as early as December 1972, with the loss of its 920,000 tonnes of annual production. It was too costly and technically obsolete. An ore furnace and continuous casting unit would be set up instead with the remainder of supplies coming from the BSC billet capacity at Scunthorpe.[45] Callaghan had a good deal of correspondence with Tony Benn on the East Moors works. The Secretary for Energy was anxious to speed up its closure. Callaghan urged that this be delayed until 1980 and that in the interim a joint venture of British Steel and GKN be pursued. Benn had set up a 'task force' on steel closures, which would involve job losses of 4,600 at Cardiff, another 4,600 at Ebbw Vale (Michael Foot's constituency), and a further 6,500 at Shotton in Deeside, together with lesser job losses at Workington and Hartlepool.[46] As recently as 7 July 1977 Callaghan had assured the Lord Mayor of Cardiff that BSC would not close East Moors before 1980 and he rebutted charges locally that he had not been consulting the workforce at East Moors; he urged his secretary Ruth Sharpe to be 'tactfully upset' on this issue.[47] In fact, the historic East Moors works closed its doors in the course of 1978, a decision made inevitable by the world recession which cut down the demand for steel and made even the future of the mighty works at Port Talbot unpredictable. However, East Moors was not an insuperable problem for Callaghan. It was but one industry among many; others were reasonably thriving, while the fact that Cardiff had development area status and the active role of the newly formed Welsh Development Agency in promoting the industrial infrastructure were positive omens for the future. Apart from East Moors in any case, all seemed well.

As the campaign went on, the parties' standing in the polls narrowed somewhat. Callaghan's references to Labour's ability to keep prices stable seemed to go down well with the voters, especially housewives. This was felt by Labour strategists to be of importance since women voters, along with under-25s and semi- and unskilled workers, were felt to be a major segment of the electorate where the party's standing had fallen since 1974. A Gallup poll published in the *Daily Telegraph* on 3 May showed the Conservative lead down to two points; two days earlier, an NOP poll in the *Daily Mail* actually showed Labour with a 1 per cent lead of 43.4 per cent to 42.5 per cent. Peter Jenkins in the *Guardian* wrote that 'it would no longer be amazing to see Mr. Callaghan win by a whisker'. Robert Worcester of MORI told Callaghan privately on 30 April that 'there is better news'. Labour had almost caught up with the Tories on having 'the best people' and 'best policies', and was far ahead in popular estimation of 'the best leaders'. Bernard Donoughue on 29 April urged, for all his private inner pessimism, that 'the genuineness of Labour's appeal was getting through' and that the campaign strategy was working. He added, 'But we must not let up. Harold made that mistake in 1970 and 1974. . . . We need one last big heave to get home.'[48]

But then from the final Sunday the polls moved away from Labour again. The final eve-of-poll findings by MORI were a Tory lead of 8 per cent; Gallup put it at 7.7 per cent, and ORC at 6 per cent. Callaghan was not surprised. He had never at any time expected to win. His views were reinforced by ten privately conducted 'quickie polls' by Robert Worcester of MORI, sent through early in the day to be considered at 7.30 a.m. breakfast meetings. Callaghan went through the entire campaign in relaxed and genial mood. His son Michael Callaghan hardly ever saw him giving any indication that he was reconciled to defeat. Only at the very end, after several polls had shown large Conservative leads, did he respond, when his son proposed some new initiative, 'What's the use?' He also confided to Derek Gladwin (who remained optimistic about a last-minute surge of support), at a private meeting the weekend before polling day, that he felt that defeat was inevitable.[49] He unburdened himself to Bernard Donoughue in a famous observation (later confirmed by Lord Donoughue to the present writer) near the end of the campaign when it looked as if Labour could still conceivably scrape home. 'There are times, perhaps once every thirty years, when there is a sea-change in politics. It then does not matter what you say or what you do. There is a shift in what the public wants and what it approves of. I suspect there is now such a sea-change—and it is for Mrs Thatcher.'[50]

The election results confirmed this fatalism. Callaghan held on to Cardiff South-East with much ease. There was a small swing to the Conservatives, well below the national average. He had a majority of 8,701 over the Conservative Alun Jones, while all the other four candidates had only a tiny poll, 1,200 between the four of them. Pat Arrowsmith gained 132 votes, 0.3 per cent of the poll. But in the country as a whole from the announcements of the first results it was clear that there was a substantial swing to the Conservatives as Callaghan had always anticipated. At 5.2 per cent, it was the highest swing to any party since the Second World War. The Conservatives gained 61 seats from Labour. The final result was that the Conservatives won 339, Labour 268, and the Liberals 11. The latter had clearly not benefited from the Lib–Lab pact; neither had the nationalist parties benefited from the devolution debate, since the SNP lost 9 of their 11 seats and Plaid Cymru 1 of their 3. The Conservatives' share of the poll was 43.9 per cent. Labour's was 36.9 per cent, the lowest the party had achieved since the débâcle of 1931. Callaghan conceded defeat early on, and left 10 Downing Street with all speed in the afternoon of 4 May. He made generous remarks to Mrs Thatcher, who arrived at 10 Downing Street somewhat incongruously quoting St Francis of Assisi's message of harmony and peace, doing so on the prompting of Sir Ronald Millar. The only emotion Callaghan showed publicly was on the defeat of Shirley Williams at Hertford and Stevenage, about which he said he was 'heart-broken'.[51] Tony Benn, also saddened by the loss of left-wing colleagues such as Audrey Wise and Doug Hoyle, condemned the leader for fighting a right-wing campaign. He decided to withdraw from Labour's shadow Cabinet and front bench in preparation for the ferocious internal battles that surely lay ahead.[52]

Meanwhile, to console him, Callaghan had a flood of warm personal letters from Helmut Schmidt, Henry Kissinger, Gerald Ford, Jimmy Carter, Pierre Trudeau, Richard Nixon, Morarji Desai, Lee Kuan Yew, Michael Manley, Garret FitzGerald, Yigal Allon, and, more remarkably, Colonel Gadaffi of Libya, amongst foreign dignitaries, and from domestic politicians who included Douglas Houghton, Roy Mason, William Rodgers, David Steel, and Enoch Powell. Two other letters are perhaps of interest. The philosopher A. J. Ayer sent warm commiserations and noted that Maud Reeves's classic *Round about a Pound a Week* had just been republished. 'I would send a copy to Mrs Thatcher if I thought she would read it.' And a distinguished Welsh academic congratulated Callaghan especially for his success over the economy and education. 'You will surely be as highly esteemed by tomorrow's historian as you are by the great majority of today's public' was the conclusion of Sir Goronwy Daniel, principal of the University College of Wales, Aberystwyth, married to the granddaughter of an earlier prime minister from Wales, David Lloyd George.[53]

Callaghan's dying fall was a dignified one. He himself emerged from the election campaign with his public reputation as a generally effective prime minister intact. The pundits concluded that his party had fallen from power not because of its leadership but because of the near industrial anarchy of the winter of discontent. Certainly, until the industrial troubles mounted up in mid-November 1978, Labour was still doing well enough in the polls, sufficiently so to give credibility to the Prime Minister's decision to soldier on through the winter. Then it all collapsed, and Mrs Thatcher became the people's agent of revenge against the trade unions. The next few years saw them meeting retribution in the fullest measure.

Whether the election represented something more than that is a theme much discussed. There was much debate in the press about the late 1970s marking a landmark in British social and economic decline. *Is Britain Dying?* was one characteristic volume produced at this period which focused heavily on the role of the trade unions, while 'decline' and 'eclipse' habitually featured in political and economic works of the period.[54] It was frequently Americans who engaged in this kind of political pathology. On the other hand, accounts that regarded the fall of the Callaghan government as marking the end of an era took a more positive line too. Callaghan's downfall was linked not just with the winding up of old-style corporatism between government and unions but with the end of the post-war consensus featuring full employment, a mixed economy, a welfare state, and a broad social balance. It was a consensus to which Conservatives like Churchill, Eden, Macmillan, Butler, and Heath had been as committed as had the Labour administration after 1945. This kind of analysis really reflected the advent of Mrs Thatcher who manifestly came to power determined to 'change everything' and wind up a system which involved (as she and Sir Keith Joseph saw it) an all-encroaching domination by the state, a welfare dependency culture, and a 'debilitating consensus' which damaged enterprise and weakened the moral fibre of the nation. Whether the election of 1979 would have seemed so traumatic a change had it seen the return of the Conservatives under the leadership of a more emollient leader such as Willie Whitelaw or James Prior is highly debatable. Even under Mrs Thatcher, the breaking of the post-war consensus with the new gospel of privatization and monetarism was a gradual, cautious affair down to the election of 1983. There was scant sign of 'taking on the unions' at this stage. Victory in the Falklands War in 1982 gave Mrs Thatcher's government a momentum and force it had previously seemed to lack, and an electoral landslide followed.

What is clear is that the defeated leader, James Callaghan, represented more clearly than perhaps any other living politician the full force of the post-1945 creed of moderation. He was the classic consensus man, the champion of partnership and the evangelist of fairness. The creed he spelt out before the electors in 1979 did not differ in fundamentals from what he had been preaching and practising ever since he first entered parliament in 1945. For the moment, perhaps for ever, he had lost the national battle in defending this legacy amongst the electors. But there remained, dear to the emotions of so committed and professional a party politician and social democrat (if not perhaps any longer a democratic socialist), the internal battle—to fight for the heart and soul of a riven party, in fundamental conflict within itself about both the direction of future policy and its own structure and constitution. Even in the later stages of an eventful career, therefore, James Callaghan's odyssey was not over. He was not about to withdraw from the struggle as Harold Wilson had done, perhaps forced to do so by ill-health. The priority remained to make the old unreformed Labour Party fit for opposition and perhaps later for government again. In the immediate wake of electoral disappointment, Callaghan now turned to new conflicts as passionate and as all-absorbing as any in the past.

1. J.M. [John Morris] to Callaghan, ? Feb. 1979 (Callaghan Papers, box 10).

2. Donoughue to Callaghan, 27 Nov. 1978, reporting the views of Ms Liddell (private papers).

3. Christopher Harvie, *No Gods and Precious Few Heroes* (London, 1981), 164.

4. Donoughue, *Prime Minister*, 183; interview with Alan Watkins.

5. *Daily Telegraph*, 13 Mar. 1979.

6. 'How the Government Fell: A Few Brief Notes' by Michael Foot, given to James Callaghan, Apr. 1986; record of meeting of ministers, 5 Mar. 1979 (Callaghan Papers, box 26).

7. Benn, *Conflicts of Interest*, 469 (8 Mar. 1979).

8. Bernard Donoughue to Callaghan, 13 Mar. 1979 (Callaghan Papers, box 26).

9. *Daily Telegraph*, 14 Mar. 1979.

10. 'How the Government Fell'.

11. Benn, *Conflicts of Interest*, 476 (22 Mar. 1979).

12. 'How the Government Fell'.

13. Personal knowledge.

14. Donoughue memo, 'Northern Ireland' (PU 366), 7 Mar. 1978 (private papers).

15. Kenneth Stowe to Sir John Hunt, 23 Mar. 1979 (Callaghan Papers, box 26); interview with Roy Hattersley. A very lively account is Austin Mitchell, 'More like a Night to Forget', *House Magazine* (15 Nov. 1993), 26–7.

16. Hattersley, *Who Goes Home?*, 209–10.

17. Material in Callaghan Papers (uncatalogued).

18. *Daily Telegraph*, 28 Mar. 1979.

19. Ibid., 29 Mar. 1979.

20. Interview with Roy Hattersley; 'How the Government Fell'.

21. Benn, *Conflicts of Interest*, 472 (15 Mar. 1979).

22. Ibid. 481–3 (2 Apr. 1979); materials in Callaghan Papers (uncatalogued).

23. Benn, *Conflicts of Interest*, 482.

24. Meeting of the Prime Minister and the drafting committee 10 Downing Street (private papers).

25. Benn, *Conflicts of Interest*, 482.

26. Meeting of Prime Minister and 'Neddy Six', 4 Apr. 1979 (private papers).

27. Benn, *Conflicts of Interest*, 485–8 (6 Apr. 1979).

28. Ibid. 488; memo by Gavyn Davies, 12 Apr. 1979 (Callaghan Papers, box 23).

29. For an interesting discussion of this point, see David Kogan and Maurice Kogan, *The Battle for the Labour Party* (London, 1982), 137–42.

30. David Butler and Denis Kavanagh, *The British General Election of 1979* (London, 1980), 184.

31. Donoughue memo, 'The Election Campaign—Some Thoughts', 6 Apr. 1979, and memo for the Prime Minister, 21 Apr. 1979 (private papers).

32. Appendix by Shelley Pinto-Duschinsky, in Howard R. Penman (ed.), *Britain at the Polls, 1979: A Study of the General Election* (American Enterprise Institute for Public Policy Research, Washington, 1981), 315 ff.

33. *Daily Telegraph*, 4 May 1979.

34. David Lipsey memo to Callaghan, 28 Apr. 1979 (Gladwin Papers).
35. Margaret Thatcher, *Downing Street Years* (London, 1993), 444.
36. Prime Minister's diary (Callaghan Papers, box 35); McNally memo (ibid., box 23).
37. Interview with Lord Callaghan.
38. Notes on meeting held by Derek Gladwin, 18 Apr. 1979 (Callaghan Papers, box 23). Here and elsewhere, I am much indebted to Lord Gladwin of Clee for use of his file of material on the 1979 election campaign, as well as for his own recollections.
39. 'Stockport South': memo by Tom McNally, 26 Feb. 1979 (Callaghan Papers, box 23).
40. Memo by Tom McNally for the Prime Minister, 7 Dec. 1978 (ibid.).
41. Butler and Kavanagh, *The British General Election of 1979*, 136.
42. Interviews with Michael Callaghan and Geoffrey Goodman.
43. Memo by David Lipsey, ? Apr. 1979 (Callaghan Papers, box 23).
44. Material gathered by the author as election commentator for BBC Wales, 1979.
45. Material in Callaghan Papers, box 5.
46. Callaghan to Benn, 27 Mar. 1974; Benn to Callaghan, 21 Jan. 1975 (ibid.).
47. Callaghan to Lord Mayor of Cardiff, 7 July 1977, Callaghan to Bill Tobbutt, ? May 1975, and note to Ruth Sharpe (ibid.).
48. *Guardian*, 2 May 1979; Lipsey memo for Prime Minister, 28 Apr. 1979, Worcester polling presentation to Labour Party, 1 May 1979, Donoughue memo to Prime Minister, 'Strategy: Last Three Days', 29 Apr. 1979 (Gladwin Papers). Donoughue added that the unions were still a great problem. 'We are still losing badly on the doorstep because of them and last winter.'
49. Interviews with Michael Callaghan, Lord Donoughue, and Lord Gladwin.
50. Donoughue, *Prime Minister*, 191. He also made a somewhat similar remark to Geoffrey Goodman of the *Daily Mirror* after the results were declared—'I suppose the country needs someone like Mrs Thatcher' (interview with Geoffrey Goodman).
51. *Daily Telegraph*, 5 May 1979.
52. Benn, *Conflicts of Interest*, 494 (4 May 1979) and 501–2 (10 May 1979).
53. Letters in Callaghan Papers (uncatalogued).
54. See R. Emmett Tyrell, *The Future that Doesn't Work: Social Democracy's Failures in Britain* (New York, 1977); James E. Alt, *The Politics of Economic Decline* (Cambridge, 1979); William B. Gwyn and Richard Rose, *Britain: Progress and Decline* (London, 1980); Isaac Kramnick, *Is Britain Dying? Perspectives on the Current Crisis* (London, 1979).

29

LAST PHASE OF LEADERSHIP

WHEN parliament reassembled after the election on 9 May, Callaghan was unanimously re-elected leader of the Labour Party. 'There is no vacancy for my job', he told the Labour MPs. Some people were surprised that he did not follow the example of other senior party leaders and resign after an electoral defeat. He spoke frequently to family and colleagues of his longing to go back to the farm. His son Michael wanted him to retire after the intense physical and psychological strain of the past few years. But there were other, public imperatives. A shoal of letters came in from Labour MPs of the centre-right urging him to stay on as leader. This was the view of one of his most devoted supporters, Dr Jack Cunningham. W. A. Wilkins, a colleague of Tony Benn as a Bristol MP, told Callaghan that 'the party needs you even more than before'.[1]

Left to his own inclinations, Callaghan would have resigned immediately. But his own instincts were not to jump ship at this critical moment. Labour was in danger of being torn apart by ideological rifts after a heavy election defeat, and he himself would be made the scapegoat. He feared the leftwards tide amongst constituency activists and the indiscipline of union leaders that had led to the calamitous winter of discontent. He was anxious to prevent Labour, perhaps under the charismatic influence of Tony Benn, being swept into radical and, he felt, deeply unpopular policies such as mass nationalization and a siege economy, withdrawal from Europe, and unilateral nuclear disarmament. Other left-wing postures that Callaghan felt would be disastrous included the 'Troops out' movement in Northern Ireland, irresponsible gesture politics from some Labour councils christened by the Tory press 'the loony left', and responding to the problem of mounting crime by attacking the police. These were the themes flowing from motions to conference from the constituency parties. Underlying them was a range of what he believed were anti-constitutional and sinister groups of which the most alarming was Militant

Tendency, a Trotskyist organization which as has been seen had since 1974 struck some roots in his own constituency in Cardiff. Even at the risk of renewed internal conflicts and fierce personal attacks on himself, Callaghan felt that the call of duty to lead his party on to more tranquil times was overwhelming.

There was also a crucial aspect of internal strategy, namely doing what he could to fix the succession to the leadership in favour of a credible, authoritative figure. In Callaghan's view, there was only one possible candidate, the former Chancellor, Denis Healey. While the relations between the two had always been respectful rather than intimate, he had immense regard for Healey's intellectual qualities and formidable energy. Further, with the death of Crosland, there was no other figure of comparable stature in the centre-right of the party, one who would appeal to the nation as a whole rather than to the doctrinaire core of grass-roots activists. Peter Shore did not carry the same authority and in any case was fanatically hostile to Europe. Of the younger figures, Shirley Williams had lost her seat at the election, while the time of others of that generation, Roy Hattersley and more particularly John Smith, a Callaghan supporter whose talents the Prime Minister had sought to nurture, might come on in the future. Over David Owen, with his authoritarian temper, Callaghan had more than a few doubts. So Denis it would have to be. In a somewhat obscure cricket metaphor, Callaghan let it be known that he would stay on for some time, 'taking the shine off the ball' for Denis. This presumably meant trying to neutralize left-wing critics until such time as they ran out of steam. Callaghan well recalled the precedent of Attlee who, at an age very similar to his own (68 to 67), had lingered on for four unsuccessful years from 1951 to 1955, largely in order to prevent Herbert Morrison succeeding him as leader. That period, which Callaghan felt had been lacking in direction, had seen the civil war between Bevanites and Gaitskellites reach boiling point and a Labour Party perceived to be hopelessly divided in the end remaining in Opposition for thirteen years. The timing would have to be right. Perhaps eighteen months would do it. But someone authoritative would have to stand up to the fanaticism and extremism, as he saw it, of the hard left and Militant Tendency and he alone had the prestige to do so.

There was one remaining legacy of his premiership which caused comment. This was his farewell honours list, published on 11 June.[2] Callaghan well recalled the sleazy impact made by Harold Wilson's 'lavender paper' honours list in 1976 which showered peerages and knighthoods, Lloyd George style, on a variety of rich businessmen, many of dubious reputation. Some of them, notably Joe Kagan and Eric Miller, had turned out to be criminals. Even allowing for the tinge of anti-Semitism which coloured some of the criticism of the Wilson list, it undoubtedly did much damage to the Labour Party and even more to the reputation of the shop-soiled former Prime Minister himself. Callaghan was anxious to avoid anything of the kind. Julian Hodge, for instance, whom Callaghan felt deserved a peerage for his charitable activities, did not appear in his list. His honorands were overwhelmingly political associates, Labour Party colleagues at the Commons, in Transport House, and in Wales. There were peerages for Michael Stewart, Harold Lever, Cledwyn Hughes, William Ross, and Lena Jeger, all old friends; Reg Underhill, Labour's national agent, also became a peer, while Jack Brooks who had carefully managed the Cardiff constituency for so long became Lord Brooks of Tremorfa. The knights included Tom McCaffrey, his press secretary (who had hoped for a peerage), Frank Barlow, the long-serving secretary of the parliamentary Labour Party, and two former leftish Labour MPs, J. W. Mallalieu and Raphael Tuck. Judith Hart (whom Tony Benn felt to be 'a violent anti-colonialist'[3]) became a Dame and Denis Healey a Companion of Honour. The only personal gift appeared to be a CBE for Gordon Denniss, his long-standing partner in the farm at Sussex, but his work as planner and architect was a decent enough qualification. The difference in tone between Wilson's patronage of businessmen and Callaghan's recognition of his lifelong ties with the party was striking and to the advantage of the latter. There was scant likelihood of any of his list ending up in jail. Tony Benn attacked the honours list, more or less on principle, but in general it helped restore morale in areas of the political world where the ex-Prime Minister felt it mattered most.

After resigning as Prime Minister, Callaghan retained his previous close ties with international affairs. His links with men like Schmidt, Carter, Ford, and Kissinger became, if anything, even closer as they all moved into the ranks of elder statesmen. Rhodesia was one area where he kept up his ties with Commonwealth leaders, trying to bring the position there to a peaceful resolution now that Ian Smith was no longer Prime Minister and the country since April had been under a coalition administration, of a flimsy kind, under Bishop Abel Muzorewa. The forthcoming meeting of Commonwealth prime ministers at Lusaka would clearly be crucial for the future of Rhodesia. Callaghan used his links with Julius Nyerere of Tanzania in particular to urge him to give moral support to the new Conservative prime minister, Mrs Thatcher. He and Nyerere were in close touch soon after the election when the Tanzanian president expressed his worries to Callaghan that the Thatcher government might be leaning to recognition of the Muzorewa government. Callaghan responded that he had urged Muzorewa to find a way of involving the Patriotic Front leaders, Nkomo and Mugabe, in his administration. He added, 'Finally, Julius, please remember that our prime minister, though inexperienced in African matters, is a quick learner, and I hope that you will be able to explain to her some of the intricacies of the continent of Africa that she has not yet mastered.' He spent some time in talks with Mugabe and other ZANU leaders during the course of the constitutional talks held in London that September and October. He was, indeed, remarkably generous in his private help for his successor. He wrote to Lee Kuan Yew, 'I think you will be very interested to meet Mrs Thatcher in Lusaka. She is undoubtedly the best man in the Conservative team.'[4]

On wider issues, Callaghan was ever the Atlanticist. He wrote anxiously to Henry Kissinger in September 1979 when the former Secretary of State appeared to suggest that western Europe could not necessarily rely on US strategic nuclear protection, and received some reassurance.[5] He continued to prime President Carter with his knowledge of the Middle East, after a visit to the region in October. In giving his views on the various roles of Begin, Sadat, and King Hussein, he suggested that Carter might try another Camp David-type summit. In a note he produced afterwards, he reflected on the danger for the developing world resulting from monetarist governments in the west.[6] In Europe, he continued to maintain his close links with the German SDP government. On 14–15 November 1979 he went to Bonn for a ceremony at which he would receive the German Order of Merit from Helmut Schmidt. With the Foreign Minister, Hans-Dietrich Genscher, another old friend, he variously discussed the position of Israel, energy problems, and German worries over the installation of nuclear weapons on German soil. In a talk with Schmidt on 14 November he urged him to do what he could to try to ensure the re-election of Jimmy Carter, his old adversary who was facing a difficult presidential contest against Ronald Reagan in the United States. Callaghan's main concern in these talks, however, was Britain's relationship with Europe. He urged Schmidt to try in Dublin to be helpful to Mrs Thatcher (in the event the German Chancellor was to find her adversarial and generally tiresome). 'It is not inconceivable', said Callaghan, 'that she would do something dramatic if she did not get satisfaction'—referring to the ongoing argument about British contributions to the Community budget.[7] One solace was that the SDP-led administration had a guaranteed existence at least until the end of 1982.

Here and later, Callaghan continued to be closely involved in discussions about détente, arms limitation, and international security issues in general. The world scene generally had darkened through 1979 with the tension generated by the Russian invasion of Afghanistan which led the Americans to pull out of the Moscow Olympics to the intense disapproval of the Europeans, the crisis in Iran with the holding of American hostages after the deposing of the Shah, and the slow progress made in the ratification of SALT II by the American Congress. One of Callaghan's concerns was that Britain should continue to use its influence in a constructive direction and not in the cold-war terms initially spelt out by Mrs Thatcher. The defeat of Jimmy Carter was an ominous sign for him in this area. In addition, Callaghan also was creating new personal ties with the Chinese, stemming from the negotiations for China to purchase British-made Harrier jump-jet aircraft. He shortly visited China for the first time; his companions included Ron Hayward and his doctor, Montague Levine.[8] The latter briefly startled his hosts by pointing out that some of the skeletons in some ancient prehistoric village were unusual since some males had female pelvises and vice versa, but the prospect of a Chinese version of Piltdown Man was averted. The party enjoyed such wonders as the Great Wall and sailing down the Yangtze as well as discussing more contemporary matters such as nuclear disarmament and the future of Hong Kong with Deng Xiao Ping. There was a temporary health scare, involving none of Callaghan's party but the *Times* journalist accompanying them, David Bonavia, who contracted severe pneumonia during their trip down the Yangtze. Callaghan took charge of matters personally and ensured that Bonavia was promptly transferred to a nearby hospital at Wuhan. Otherwise the tour was an enjoyable one. Callaghan was to keep in contact with the Chinese thereafter, and to go there again in 1980 and 1983. He kept a watchful eye in 1997 on the handover of Hong Kong.

Another notable international event was his major speech at the Universal Speakers' lunch in Toronto, Canada, on 2 April 1980, when he spoke on the international economy and its problems. There was an elegiac air to his reference to the effective work of the Group of Seven economic summits, especially that of 1978 which followed months of patient and private negotiation by the heads of government concerned.[9] Already, well before his actual retirement had taken place, James Callaghan was underlining his justified role as an international senior statesman, a role fortified by decades of experience of colonial, financial, defence, and diplomatic issues.

But Callaghan's scope for attending to international issues and foreign travel was always restricted by the continuing pressures of argument and conflict within the Labour Party. After the election, these reached a new fever pitch. It was not new for the Labour Party to react to election defeat with a swing to the left. This had happened after the landslide of 1931, which saw left-wing policies being adopted, and the rise of bodies like the Socialist League and the dominance of Sir Stafford Cripps as the voice of the far left. After 1951, the Bevanite movement had reached its maximum point of influence, with the domination of the constituency section of NEC by the supporters of the great Welsh socialist, and a virtual decade of civil war leading to the massive argument over CND in 1960. After the 1979 defeat, however, the problems were of a quite different order. The move to the left had been powerful ever since the defeat in 1970. Tony Benn was quite as charismatic a voice of protest as Mosley, Cripps, or Bevan had been in the past, and had the added authority of almost a decade as a Cabinet minister. Far more important and potentially serious, though, many left-wing activists now worked in conjunction with extra-parliamentary groups which had nothing in common with traditional mainstream Labour. Since 1973, the proscribed list which had historically debarred Trotskyists and fellow-travellers from party membership had been done away with. There was much complaint of inner-city constituency parties being invaded and taken over by 'bed-sit Trots'. As a result the party 'left' in 1980 was of a radically different nature from the essentially parliamentary Bevanites or Tribunites of the past. For the first time since the First World War, the anti-democratic left was to be found inside rather than outside the Labour Party.

Further, there were grounds for believing that the Labour Party now showed elements of structural decline not present in either the 1930s or the 1950s. The Labour vote had declined steadily since 1964. The old working class of the industrial heartlands and back-to-back terrace housing had declined in number with a consequent impact on party strength. Mrs Thatcher's election victory in 1979 was known to have shown a particular swing to the Conservatives amongst the so-called C2s, the skilled workers and technicians, previously solid for Labour but now anxious to own their homes and enjoy a more affluent lifestyle.[10] Relations with the unions, too, were difficult for Labour after the troubles of *In Place of Strife* and the winter of discontent. Nor was the ideological thrust of the party so clear any more. The only post-war successor to the intellectual giants of the past, the Webbs, Tawney, Laski, and Cole, was Tony Crosland, now dead. His *Future of Socialism* had, after all, been published almost a quarter of a century earlier. Neither Healey on the right, nor Benn on the left offered a doctrine of much ideological coherence or electoral appeal. The leadership of

Callaghan, many felt, represented Old Labour, a dying generation of old-style social democrats, or perhaps simply 'Labourism', an economist creed of support for the working class rather than a doctrine for the conquest and mobilization of power.

What contemporaries saw after the election was a series of increasingly fierce disputes between a socialist left and a centrist leadership, with little common ground. Even in the summer of 1979, there was speculation that a split was possible and that the gulf between the rival wings of the Labour Party seemed far wider than that between any of them and the Conservatives. Indeed, Tony Benn spoke warmly of Mrs Thatcher as a conviction politician but showed ill-disguised contempt for Callaghan, Healey, and what he saw as a reactionary leadership. The old battles resurfaced in an episode most embarrassing for Labour—the European elections which followed the general election in June 1979. Labour had not been looking forward to these at all. The party had long resisted having them, and had delayed them for as long as possible. While Callaghan himself became more committed to the European cause as his premiership went on, the Labour Party rapidly retreated to a hostile view. Many, not only left-wingers like Eric Heffer but more right-wing figures like Peter Shore or Douglas Jay, hoped that in 1979 the Labour manifesto would commit the party to withdrawal from the EEC altogether. Transport House poured out a sequence of documents criticizing not only agreed targets like the community budget, the Agricultural Plan, and the powers (and cost) of the Brussels bureaucracy, but also the very structure and purpose of the Community. Callaghan had himself published a letter to Ron Hayward, the party general secretary, during the party conference on 1 October 1977, making highly critical comments on the Common Market in general and calling for a curb to the expansion of its powers.[11]

Labour was bound to do very badly in the Euro elections. Indeed, one factor in holding the British general election in May rather than October 1979 was to diminish the damage, since heavy defeats in June would surely have compromised Labour's performance at the polls in an autumn contest. The party faced the June elections with its morale at a low ebb. The main point of contention between Callaghan and the NEC, which was broadly very anti-European, was the framing of the manifesto.[12] Callaghan and the Cabinet had played no part in it and left it to Transport House. In the event, the inevitable result was that the manifesto was strongly anti-Europe and came close to calling for Britain's withdrawal. It called for the British parliament to have the right to reject, repeal, or amend EEC legislation and to make British ministers directly accountable to the Commons on European issues. It pressed the case for 'democratic control of the economy'. Its demands included the right of British governments to nationalize key firms; conclude planning agreements; control prices, investment, and the location of jobs; and impose 'penetration ceilings' on imports.[13] By implication it appeared to criticize Wilson and Callaghan for advocating continued membership of the EEC in the 1975 referendum. When the manifesto was produced on 23 May, Callaghan had a fierce clash with Benn and Heffer at the NEC. In a widely publicized phrase, the leader protested that he was not 'a wheelhorse to be wheeled on to a platform when my support is needed'.[14] The public launch of the manifesto on 24 May by Callaghan, Benn, and Ron Hayward was a tense affair. Benn was remorselessly critical of the Community in all its aspects. Callaghan seemed almost to dissociate himself from proceedings altogether: he was heard to say *sotto voce*, 'It is not my manifesto.' Labour's divisions, as profound as those over Europe in the Conservative Party in the 1990s, were all too visible.

Thereafter, Callaghan took little part in the European campaign and distanced himself from a Labour stance which he regarded with distaste. He did take part in a Labour rally in Leeds in which he was accompanied on the platform by the French Socialist leader François Mitterrand, whose remarks had to be translated for the benefit of his Yorkshire audience. Callaghan also attended briefly a rally of European socialist leaders in Paris on 27 May. He made one party political broadcast, almost out of duty, and sent a message to Labour's Euro candidates which focused on the economic and social inadequacies of the Thatcher government. Conspicuously, he did not endorse the manifesto threat that Britain might withdraw from the EEC if sweeping and fundamental reforms were not made.[15] It was an election for which Labour had no heart and little hope. There was a mood of almost total apathy, with a poll of 31 per cent, below the level even of local government elections. The Conservatives ended up with 60 of the 81 seats and Labour only 17. Only in Wales, where three seats out of the four were captured, was Labour dominant. It was another humiliation and a demonstration of the immense ideological rifts and personal hatred within the people's party. Meanwhile Labour's opposition to Europe continued to build up, while the choice of Barbara Castle, obsessively anti-European by this time, as the head of the Labour representatives at Strasbourg, to the annoyance of other Labour MEPs, did not bode well.

Throughout the summer tension continued to grow. The main focus now was not so much left-wing demands for more socialism but the related pressure for more direct democracy. The Campaign for Labour

Party Democracy, under a young émigré Czech, Vladimir Dederer, was engaged in an effective grass-roots campaign for reinforcing the accountability of MPs and Cabinet ministers to the party. The main demands, all of which were taken up vigorously by Tony Benn and the left, were threefold. First, they wanted the mandatory reselection of Labour MPs instead of their being in effect representatives for life, unless electoral defeat intervened. Secondly, the party manifesto should be the work of the NEC alone, instead of being drawn up jointly by the NEC and Cabinet ministers, with the leader exercising an effective veto. Thirdly, the party leader and deputy leader ought to be elected not simply by fellow MPs but by an 'electoral college', comprising the trade unions and affiliated socialist organizations, the constituency parties, and Labour MPs in suitable proportions. The CLPD felt that this would prevent the frustration of the wishes of the party in the country by unaccountable leaders and MPs; they cited the way Labour had jettisoned socialism at the last election. It was also, they felt, a basic reason why Labour had lost it. They had made much progress in these directions in the past. Indeed, the mandatory reselection process for MPs, the most immediately popular of these proposals, would actually have been adopted at the 1978 party conference had not Hugh Scanlon of the AUEW, in his final appearance there, conveniently 'forgotten' to cast his vote as requested by his executive. When chided, Scanlon replied, 'You mind your business and I'll mind mine',[16] and left it at that. But it was clear that the 1979 party conference would be dominated by the subject, and that all three CLPD proposals would command widespread support.

This conflict over the nature of Labour Party democracy tore the movement apart, and left permanent scars. Callaghan felt that it was basically undemocratic, an attempt to make the party's MPs and leaders the creatures of left-wing constituency activists rather than answerable to the voters in the country as a whole. Direct democracy of this kind, he and most MPs felt, was really a way of riveting the hold of small, left-wing, or extremist management committees in the constituencies upon the independent minds and consciences of parliamentary representatives. It was a direct threat to parliamentary democracy. A traditional Bevanite left-winger like Michael Foot, dedicated for historical and cultural reasons to a free and independent parliament as the essential instrument for achieving democratic socialism, was almost as hostile as Callaghan to the new left's demands offered by 'brother Tony'. Like a latter-day Edmund Burke, he offered the riposte of the old left to the new. In theoretical and abstract terms, there was, he and others felt, every justification for Callaghan's views.

On the other hand, a situation in which MPs, or perhaps the leader alone in isolation, devised programmes, tactics, and policies was hardly satisfactory for democrats, left or right. Many felt the Callaghan–Foot view to be élitist and non-accountable. Younger activists, not necessarily at all on the left, felt that many of Callaghan's personal decisions were simply not acceptable. They instanced the announcement of a 5 per cent pay norm, the purely private decision on not holding an election in 1978, and the vetoing, as many saw it, of the terms of the manifesto in 1979 on his own fiat. The real answer, perhaps—one advanced somewhat cautiously by Callaghan himself in 1980, though rejected out of hand by the NEC—was to have party leaders voted for not by MPs alone, nor by small management caucuses, but by the party membership as a whole. This was the solution finally arrived at by John Smith and Tony Blair in 1993–4 when 'one member, one vote', applied also to trade union affiliates of the party, was adopted. This, it was felt, would, among other things, see the Labour Party conforming to the general practice of other left parties across the world, and ensure that the broadest possible range of approval was enlisted.[17] But in the context of 1979–80 it was the traditional version of parliamentary decision and the CLPD version of constituency control which were in conflict.

This conflict emerged with full passion in the party conference at Brighton in the first week of October 1979. It was an angry affair. The unforgiving chairman was the near-Stalinist Frank Allaun, whose opening address Peter Shore and Callaghan separately described as 'poisonous'.[18] No pity or mercy were spared for the fallen leader. In the debate on the very first day, Tom Litterick, a left-wing MP defeated at Selly Oak in the general election, turned on Callaghan with fury in what Benn termed 'a courageous speech'. He waved a clutch of policy papers, all of which he claimed Callaghan had vetoed. Quoting a popular television series featuring Jimmy Saville, he went on, ' "Jim will fix it", they said. Ay, he fixed it. He fixed all of us. He fixed me in particular.'[19] The delegates roared approval, and turned on their old idol Michael Foot when he tried to defend the leadership. Callaghan's speech on the next day, 2 October, went perhaps better than might have been expected. He took a moderate, almost quiet tone, but defended the government's policies with firmness and warned against constitutional changes. Tony Benn thought he did quite well—'but no socialist content whatever, of course'.[20]

Callaghan had anticipated defeat on the reselection of MPs and this duly occurred. There was a strong victory for the left, 4 million to 3 million. Henceforth in every parliament sitting MPs would be up for reselection by their constituency bodies. There was a similar margin of victory over a proposal for the 1980 conference for the manifesto to be the work of the National Executive alone. Only on the issue of the electoral college could the leadership take any comfort; the Engineers, led by their new secretary Terry Duffy, frustrated the proposal, but it also had gained massive support. A commission of inquiry would now look into the question with the object of providing new proposals for the next party conference. That an electoral college would come about seemed guaranteed. The left-wing steamroller seemed almost irresistible. Tony Benn was the dominant figure in the party. Jim Callaghan seemed old, lonely, the target of an embittered and determined left on every issue.

For the next few months, these disturbances in the Labour Party continued to erupt. Militant continued to grow. Indeed, it had been an active force in the Cardiff South-East constituency for several years. Andrew Price, a college lecturer, and Terry Burns, another avowed Trotskyist, had been waging a relentless war against Callaghan through the self-styled 'Socialist Education Association' and a broadsheet, the *Cardiff People's Paper*, since 1975. It required all the ingenuity and determination of stalwarts like Jack Brooks, Gordon Houlstead, and Alun Michael to keep it in control. However, a man like Brooks was not to be outmanœuvred, let alone overrun. He had told Callaghan in 1977 that 60 out of 75 members of the General Management Constituency were 'dependable'. Callaghan congratulated him on his 'splendid counter-activity'. After the 1979 election, Callaghan openly took on his Trotskyist critics. He was rewarded in 1980 when he was reselected from a short list of one. By 1983 his opponents in the constituency were in full and disorderly retreat.[21] As in many cases, often the spokesmen for Militant were not at all horny-handed sons and daughters of toil or spokesmen for an impoverished proletariat but what Alan Watkins in the *Observer* memorably called 'the polyocracy'—articulate professional people like university and polytechnic teachers, students, and public-sector white-collar employees. In Cardiff it was two lecturers in the arts faculty of the local university, married to each other as it happened, who were particularly troublesome as left-wing gadflies. No doubt this would have confirmed some of Callaghan's long-held instincts about parts of the middle-class intelligentsia.

But all over Britain, especially small, decayed inner-city areas where the party had collapsed along with the infrastructure of local government and community resources, left-wing groups were taking control. The rise of Ken Livingstone in London via the boroughs of Lambeth and Camden was a symptom of what was taking place. Another was the growing control of Militant in Liverpool, under the leadership of Tony Mulhearn and the youthful Derek Hatton. The moderates of Campaign for Labour Victory, the Manifesto group of Labour MPs, and union leaders like David Basnett and Terry Duffy were losing the initiative, and fast. New bodies emerged, such as the Rank and File Mobilizing Committee which recruited amongst the unions with success. This included Militant Tendency, the Revolutionary Socialist League, the Young Socialists, the National Organization of Labour Students, and the Labour Co-ordinating Committee along with other, mainly Trotskyist, splinter groups. A miscellany of far-left, mainly youthful protesters seemed at variance not only with the traditions of the Labour Party but with the very concept of representative parliamentary democracy. At this time the Soviet Union in the dying hands of Brezhnev was sunk in structural decay and economic collapse. Yet class-based socialism, almost Lenin's version of 'democratic centralism' operated by a revolutionary vanguard embodying socialist consciousness rather than spontaneity, seemed to be striking roots in Britain in a way unknown since the 1920s. Figures on the right began to talk of breaking away, Owen, Rodgers, and Shirley Williams prominent among them. Roy Jenkins, returning briefly from Brussels, in his Dimbleby lecture at the end of 1979 called openly for a new moderate party to be formed out of the ashes of Old Labour, and spoke of a great aeroplane taking off from the runway. He quoted Yeats to the effect that 'the best lacked all conviction and the worst were full of passionate intensity'. It was obviously the Labour Party, of which he was still notionally a member, that he had chiefly in mind.

For Callaghan it was deeply saddening and there seemed little he could do to strike back. He continued to lead the Labour Party in the House with experience and dignity. Threats of a breakaway were dismissed as 'mere fluff'. The Labour front bench were still an impressive team in debate, with new blood in the form of Neil Kinnock, appointed education spokesman by Callaghan and now showing signs of detaching himself from the Bennite left.[22] Callaghan had pursued the same tactic back in 1976 when he replaced Joan Lestor, who had resigned over education cuts, with the then far-left Margaret Jackson (Beckett) as junior Education Minister. Indeed, almost as an irrelevance, Labour's standing in the polls improved steadily and in the early months of 1980 it had built up a solid lead over the Conservatives. This was not because of its own performance, but rather the mass unemployment, surging inflation (standing at 21.8 per cent in May), and the decline of manufacturing industry which the first year of Mrs Thatcher witnessed. Britain was deindustrializing more rapidly than at any stage since the dawn of the industrial revolution. Indeed, had it not been for the Falklands War in 1982 it is possible that Thatcher might have been a one-term prime minister, defeated even by a riven and doctrinally divided Labour Party. But the party took little confidence from these developments. The electors noted rather the wounding attacks on the leader at constituency functions, the growth of the movement for immediate unilateral nuclear disarmament fostered by a revived CND, and a ferocious attack by Tony Benn at the NEC on 30 January 1980 on any commitment to a successor to Polaris or the stationing of Cruise missiles in Greenham Common.[23] This went down much better in the grassroots than it did in the parliamentary party. Labour appeared to be driven in a socialist, unilateralist, anti-European, almost anti-parliamentary direction, with no one able to stop it.

The party leaders were careful to keep their distance when the Iron and Steel Confederation, the steel union under Bill Sirs, a notoriously moderate body which had not been on strike since 1926, embarked on a national stoppage at the start of 1980 in protest against a poor pay offer and plant closures. With the international recession, they could not win, and after several months it emerged that the government had been able to take on a powerful union and come out victorious. The contrast with the recent helplessness of government in the face of union industrial muscle was all too apparent. Another bad episode for Labour came with a special policy conference at Wembley, held with almost perversely bad timing on 31 May. Callaghan made a low-key speech in which he dealt in gingerly fashion with Europe and unilateralism.[24] On the latter, he observed only that 'I cannot agree that we should take an insular view of our responsibilities.' David Owen was almost shouted down when he defended the British nuclear deterrent; Denis Healey was met with cries of 'Out, out!', while a remark about 'Toytown Trots' (a curious derivation from the *Children's Hour* of the 1940s) did not help his cause, even among his supporters. Buoyed up by massive feeling for socialism, unilateralism, and neutralism, the left was overjoyed. In a leading article entitled 'The World beyond Wembley' the *Guardian* reflected on how Mrs Thatcher's right-wing postures were providing a kind of reverse role model for the massed ranks of the Labour left.[25]

Callaghan seemed increasingly, many felt, out of date, a fixer from the past unable to point any new directions for the future. He faced many wounding personal attacks. At the party conference, on one occasion, he met with shouts and catcalls, with Neil and Glenys Kinnock prominent in the crowd. On another, he was met in his Cardiff constituency by cries for Kinnock to speak rather than himself.[26] A new London MP, Alf Dubs, member for Battersea and not particularly on the left, claimed that 'Mr. Callaghan was broadly quite unpopular, he was seen as sell-out merchant etcetera by the grassroots of the party.' When Dubs saw him as a new MP and told him he was interested in immigration and inner-city issues, Callaghan was reported by him as saying, 'Oh, God, another immigration and inner-city man—what we want is people interested in agricultural issues.' It is equally likely that Callaghan was trying to direct Dubs's energies to a more original area of concern. The story comes from uncorroborated testimony from a friend of Tony Blair, and may be regarded with some doubt. One consequence, though, was that the member for urban Battersea applied to join the parliamentary Labour Party's agricultural committee.[27] The comrades were not impressed. The strategy of lingering on to ensure the succession of Denis Healey, whose response to crisis appeared to be being rude to everybody, including his own putative allies, was not proving to be a success.

To resolve the issues of inner-party democracy, the NEC had set up a commission of inquiry after the Brighton conference, to look into new methods of appointing the party leader and the other constitutional issues raised. It was biased heavily towards the left, a majority of 10 : 4 in Tony Benn's gleeful judgement.[28] By no stretch of the imagination could it be called representative of Labour opinion across the spectrum. The seven NEC members (Benn, Heffer, Allaun, Jo Richardson, Joan Lestor, Norman Atkinson, and Alex Kitson of the TGWU) were all firmly on the left. Of the five trade unionists, Terry Duffy of the Engineers and Bill Keys of the print union SOGAT were in Callaghan's camp, but were more than balanced by Moss Evans of the Transport Workers and Clive Jenkins of ASTMS, with David Basnett a notional but basically weak Callaghan supporter. The other two were Callaghan and Foot, and it seemed unlikely that they could call on more than three reliable supporters at best, Duffy, Keys, and Basnett. To Callaghan, just back from his visit to China, it was a dismal homecoming.

After a number of sessions, the Commission determined on its conclusions in a meeting on 13–15 June in the agreeable ambience of Clive Jenkins's ASTMS Whitehall College, a country house located in Bishop's Stortford in Hertfordshire, and originally built for the Gilbey gin firm.[29] Tony Benn enjoyed himself in rural Hertfordshire where he could reflect on the physical evidence of the cultural degradation of capitalism, photograph Callaghan trying to relax in the swimming pool, and take part in a champagne party with Clive Jenkins and others. The formal business was much less agreeable. There was a great row over mandatory reselection of

MPs. David Basnett, in the chair, appeared to support Callaghan in wanting to defer the issue. In the end, the decision of conference was reaffirmed by 7 votes to 6. Callaghan then said that the question remained as to whether the reselection should be done by all members of a local party or by a General Management Committee on its own; he added that the Labour MPs would never accept it and then walked out. Benn believed that Callaghan and the union leaders had tried to defer the issue but Moss Evans of the TGWU, in another of his personal contributions to the Labour Party, let them down.

The main debate, however, came over the issue of an electoral college. David Basnett had tried to take the initiative here, by making his own proposal for the composition of a college to outflank the left, but his strategy came disastrously unstuck. Callaghan argued strongly against it. It would weaken the authority of MPs, elected by the whole electorate, it might lead to Labour having two rival leaders, and it would give the impression that the trade unions were running the country. Later he felt that he had been too tolerant and should have walked out of the conference altogether.[30] Michael Foot spoke strongly against from a traditional parliamentary standpoint. But Foot's proposal for retaining the status quo was heavily defeated, nine against and only himself, Callaghan, and Terry Duffy in favour. David Basnett and Bill Keys deserted the cause. After fierce argument, a proposal that a split membership for the college should be composed of 50 per cent for the parliamentary party, 25 per cent for the unions, 20 per cent for the constituency parties, and 5 per cent for the affiliated socialist societies—moved by Clive Jenkins and Moss Evans—was carried 7 : 6 as against a more radical version proposed by Heffer and supported by Benn.

For the left, it was perhaps a short-term tactical setback. The CLPD had wanted 50 per cent for the unions, 25 per cent each for the MPs and the constituency parties, and this is what Benn was to favour. But against this was the fact that the party leadership had had to accept the principle of the leader being elected by some outside body in which the MPs would have only a minor role. Activists might well impose a more radical figure on the party than members, ordinary unionists, and certainly the electors as a whole might want. Callaghan was in a hopeless position within the party. The left's dislike of him as a traitor to socialism was close to hatred. Now he was furiously assaulted by David Owen and, to a lesser extent, William Rodgers of the right, for committing the parliamentary party to an electoral college without any consultation of Labour MPs. Callaghan and Rodgers had their only major row in thirty years when the latter was accused of leaking the Bishop's Stortford decisions to the press. He felt that Callaghan should have attempted to rally the parliamentary party against the rampant leftists on the NEC. In the *Guardian*, Peter Jenkins, another future defector to the SDP, compared Bishop's Stortford to Munich and Callaghan to Neville Chamberlain, echoing Crossman's more improbable comparison at the time of devaluation in 1967.[31] The Labour right turned furiously on the leader for, in effect, selling out the rights of the parliamentary party. In riposte, Callaghan turned on Owen and Rodgers, for allegedly being in league with Roy Jenkins in producing schemes for a new party. Indeed, Owen, Rodgers, and Shirley Williams had on their own initiative produced a document earlier in June denouncing Labour's proposal to leave the European Community.

Callaghan seemed almost isolated. Michael Foot was never the man to pursue a nationwide campaign against the left. Denis Healey felt unable to oppose the Bishop's Stortford proposals publicly, however much he hated them, because he felt that to do so would repel fatally trade union leaders who supported them but who would also endorse him in a future leadership contest. He assured William Rodgers that he had 'told Jim to toughen up'. But there was no evidence of this. Healey himself was tough in style rather than in substance. Rodgers and other future members of the SDP were quite as disappointed by Healey as by Callaghan in this crisis. The former Chancellor was 'a limp rag'.[32] As for Callaghan, there was no doubt that, in the end, the old leader had given way at Bishop's Stortford, wearied beyond measure at the endless tide of party conflict. In the party conference on 30 September he was to plead with the delegates, quite in vain, 'For pity's sake, stop arguing.'[33]

He had made some effort to revive the forces of the right during the summer. In a speech to the Welsh Labour Party at Brecon on 5 July he spoke more aggressively than before on the constitutional changes proposed. He attacked the compulsory reselection of MPs, denounced leaving the NEC alone to decide the party's manifesto, and urged that the present method of electing the party leader be continued.[34] He also tried to mobilize his union supporters on Trade Unions for a Labour Victory to try to frustrate the dominant left at the last. But it was to little avail.

At the party conference there was an awareness that it was to be Callaghan's last appearance as party leader. That did not, however, lead to an outburst of sentiment or sympathy from the assembled militants. No 'Auld Lang Syne' here. His conference speech was a relatively low-key affair. Peter Shore noticed that he ignored the issues of mandatory reselection of MPs and of an electoral college for the leadership, as recommended by the Commission of Inquiry (which he did not mention).[35] Both he regarded as lost causes. The one area that was left was defence of the manifesto being drafted jointly by the shadow Cabinet and the NEC, and not the executive alone. He was successful in this narrow area, the conference voting by a small majority to continue the present system; a significant defection by Neil Kinnock helped the cause.

Benn wrote, almost patronizingly, of this farewell occasion, 'I felt almost affectionately disposed towards the old man.'[36] But mandatory selection of MPs was confirmed, and the electoral college was also passed by a narrow majority of 98,000. It was to be first adopted in the deputy leadership contest of 1981 in which Denis Healey narrowly defeated Tony Benn. It was last used in 1992 when John Smith easily won the leadership contest after Labour's fourth successive defeat. Tony Blair's reforms of 1994–5 killed it off. As a way of prolonging the agony of internal party division, apart from its extremely cumbersome and expensive procedures, it was almost a perpetual gift to the Conservatives. Callaghan had always argued against anything of the kind. But by confining his defence strictly to the present system of MPs alone making a choice in private conclave, rather than boldly advocating an election on a one-man, one-vote basis by all party members, he gave Labour supporters too limited a choice.

The entire conference was exceptionally unpleasant. On 1 October, a long speech by Tony Benn drove Callaghan to fury. He declared that the leader had personally struck out radical proposals such as a wealth tax from the election manifesto. Callaghan's lips visibly formed the world 'liar'. Indeed Benn was factually wrong on this particular issue, unlike, say, his reference to the House of Lords.[37] On 2 October there was what the press called 'a breakfast brawl' when, at a meeting at 8 a.m., the NEC voted by 13 to 7 to accept the CLPD proposal for a 40 : 30 : 30 split in the electoral college for the unions, the MPs, and the constituencies respectively.[38] Callaghan said that if this were implemented, he would withdraw and recommend to the parliamentary party that they elect their own leader. The MPs 'would never have Tony Benn foisted upon them'. The meeting ended inconclusively in a very sour atmosphere.[39] Callaghan wrote to Harold Lever just after it was all over, 'The conference was pretty beastly as you can imagine but I do not let it disturb me any more.'[40]

His resignation as leader now appeared imminent. The conference was under the control of the left. A breakaway to form a new party by right-wingers such as Owen and Rodgers, and perhaps many others (even, some vainly speculated, Callaghan himself), seemed imminent. There seemed little to be won by hanging on. A personal problem was that Audrey

Callaghan, on whom he so greatly depended, now went into hospital for a hip replacement operation and would be out of action for at least six weeks while her treatment took effect. Ironically, at this very late stage, left-wingers such as Eric Heffer and Alex Kitson who had spent the last two years denouncing Callaghan as a reactionary and class traitor now urged him to stay on as leader and declared what a fine prime minister he had been. This was because it was thought he would resign shortly, under the old electoral system and before a college had been put in place, to ensure the succession of Denis Healey, another right-winger and perhaps a more confrontational one.[41]

Michael Foot spent some time urging Callaghan to stay, too, and made a public appeal on 14 October. However, on the next day it was announced that Callaghan would not put himself forward as a candidate for the leadership election at the start of the next parliamentary session. He had had enough, and would retire to the backbenches. (Audrey's hip operation, which some journalists mentioned, was not a factor.) The following month the election to appoint his successor resulted, to much surprise, in the election of Michael Foot as leader, and the defeat of Denis Healey. Many on the left regarded the ageing Foot (only one year younger than Callaghan himself, after all) as a stalking-horse for the future succession of Tony Benn. It was believed that some putative defectors to the Social Democrats, such as Tom Ellis (Wrexham), had actually voted for Foot in order to magnify Labour's problems and perhaps make the desertions to a new centre-left party all the more numerous.[42] So even the succession had gone wrong, too. Instead of 'taking the shine off the ball' to ensure Denis Healey's election, the veteran opening batsman had left the Opposition fast bowlers in total command. The past fifteen months had resulted in the power of the left being all the more emphatic.

The last phase of Callaghan's party leadership was totally unsuccessful. It is, however, debatable whether anyone could have staved off disaster in Labour's ranks at this time, given the almost suicidal tendencies of both left-wing constituency parties and most of the major unions. The party seemed to have lost the urge for power in the quest for doctrinal purity. It was becoming more of a revivalist sect than a party with Tony Benn as its Savonarola. Many critics, from Bill Rodgers to Neil Kinnock, later argued that Callaghan could have 'taken on' the left and triumphed.[43] But this view, based on hindsight, perhaps demanded more than any leader, especially one aged 68, could have offered at the time. It took a far more calamitous electoral defeat in 1983 (when Labour's poll fell to 26 per cent, the lowest ever, and its tally of seats from 269 to 209) for Neil Kinnock to mobilize the mass support to challenge and expel Militant, and begin the process of modernization and revisionism. It was not until a fourth defeat in 1992, when Labour's percentage of the poll still stood at a mere 35 per cent, that first John Smith and more emphatically Tony Blair was able to make real progress. The base of the membership was now widened, and the historic wording of Clause 4, first invented by Sidney Webb in 1918, removed. This was strongly endorsed in a vote by party members. The party's outlook could be adapted to the economic realities of the contemporary world. Callaghan did not have these advantages. In hopeless circumstances, he did his best to fight, more consistently so than Denis Healey or others on the centre-right, while Owen and others were to jump ship altogether in disillusion or bitterness.

The press at the time in October 1980 took a wider perspective. In *The Times*, the historian Ian Bradley wrote a perceptive analysis which noted the traditional features in Callaghan's make-up, his views on the family and traditional values, and also his abiding commitment to partnership and to co-operation. He was described, not unfairly, as 'a conservative mediator who tried to run Labour by consent'. The paper's leading article, while noting the slump from October 1978, praised him for his achievements and his dignity in the face of adversity. For two and a half years he had been 'a successful prime minister'.[44] For middle of the road people, he conveyed a consoling image captured by 'Jen' in a novel by A. N. Wilson, set at the time of Callaghan's last phase. 'There *were* all kinds of hardship and injustices still and she felt Labour was the party to deal with them. All the same, it was reassuring that the Prime Minister, with his round chops and bluff manner and nice grey suits, seemed so reassuringly like a Conservative.'[45]

Callaghan himself felt his record, in a premiership which had been thrust upon him so unexpectedly, had been more than respectable nationally and internationally. As a party leader, structural and sociological changes had been against him, but he had kept the flag of Old Labour flying. The broad church had been sustained, while the traditional achievements of post-war Labour, social justice, welfare, industrial harmony, colonial freedom, had become part of the national fabric over thirty years. But, even for many whose sympathies were far from being with the left, the leadership appeared rooted in the past. In Ralf Dahrendorf's striking phrase, they symbolized the creed of 'a better yesterday'. There was still much to do, and much to fight for, however, especially as Thatcherism took hold. Callaghan remained intellectually in good fettle and prepared to bounce back from the desperate squabbles within his riven party. There were, to quote Jimmy Porter, 'good brave causes left' internationally, in economic collaboration and security issues in particular. There was also much unfinished business at home, particularly perhaps in education where the implications of his Ruskin speech had not begun to be followed up. Attlee after his retirement as leader in 1955 had played only a very marginal role in public life. Wilson was already showing signs of the debilitating illness that was to make his final years so painful. Callaghan, by contrast, still forceful and ambitious, and in good physical and mental health, was as ever in pursuit of great objectives. He would be an elder statesman, but an active one, loyal to his successors, but a constructive participant in public debate. The main part of the drama ended in October 1980, in acrimony and pain. But there was another act to come before the curtain fell.

1. Wilkins to Callaghan, 14 May 1979 (Callaghan Papers, box 2).

2. *Daily Telegraph*, 1 June 1979.

3. Benn, *Conflicts of Interest*, 152 (12 June 1979).

4. Nyerere to Callaghan, 10 July and 11 Aug. 1979; Callaghan to Nyerere, 19 July 1979 (Callaghan Papers, box 21A); Callaghan to Lee Kuan Yew, 21 May 1979 (ibid., box 2).

5. Kissinger to Callaghan, 20 Sept. 1979 (Callaghan Papers (BLPES), box 5).

6. Callaghan to Carter, 23 Oct. 1979 (ibid.). Cf. Callaghan's record of visit to Egypt, 10–13 Oct. 1979, and to Israel, 13–16 Oct. 1979 (ibid., box 21A).

7. Record of Callaghan's visit to Germany, and conversations with Schmidt and Genscher, 14–15 Nov. 1979 (ibid., box 21A).

8. Interview with Lord Callaghan; information from Sir Montague Levine.

9. Draft of speech at Toronto (Callaghan Papers, box 21A).

10. The MORI poll showed an 11% swing from Labour to Conservative amongst C2s between 1974 and 1979 (Butler and Donoughue, *The British General Election of 1979*, 346).

11. David Butler and David Marquand, *European Elections and British Politics* (London, 1981), 49 n.

12. Ibid., 59.

13. *Daily Telegraph*, 25 May 1979.

14. Ibid. 24 May 1979.

15. Ibid. 7 June 1979.

16. Phillip Whitehead, *The Writing on the Wall* (London, 1986), 348. This book contains many valuable interviews.

17. John Rentoul, *Tony Blair* (London, 1995), 302 ff.

18. Shore, *Leading the Left*, 128; interview with Lord Callaghan.

19. *The Times*, 2 Oct. 1979.

20. Ibid. 3 Oct. 1979; Benn, *Conflicts of Interest*, 543 (2 Oct. 1979).

21. Interviews with Lord Brooks of Tremorfa and Alun Michael MP; material in Callaghan Papers (BSPES), box 7.

22. Robert Harris, *The Making of Neil Kinnock* (London, 1984), 133–5.

23. *The Times*, 31 Jan. 1980; Benn, *Conflicts of Interest*, 574–6 (30 Jan. 1980).

24. *The Times*, 1 June 1980.

25. Owen, *Time to Declare*, 436–7.
26. Interview with Lord Callaghan.
27. Rentoul, *Tony Blair*, 67, citing Charles Falconer, a friend of Blair's.
28. Benn, *Conflicts of Interest*, 551 (24 Oct. 1979).
29. Tony Benn, *The End of an Era* (London, 1992), 5–10 (13–15 June 1980).
30. Interview with Lord Callaghan.
31. Owen, *Time to Declare*, 440–2; *The Guardian*, 18 June 1980.
32. Healey, *The Time of my Life*, 475–6; interview with Lord Rodgers.
33. *The Times*, 1 Oct. 1980.
34. Draft of speech in Callaghan Papers, box 17.
35. Shore, *Leading the Left*, 134.
36. Benn, *The End of an Era*, 31 (30 Sept. 1980).
37. *The Times*, 2 Oct. 1980.
38. Ibid. 3 Oct. 1980.
39. Benn, *The End of an Era*, 33–4.
40. Callaghan to Lever, 8 Oct. 1980 (Callaghan Papers, box 9).
41. *The Times*, 6 Oct. 1980.
42. Healey, *The Time of my Life*, 278–9.
43. Interviews with Lord Rodgers and Neil Kinnock.
44. *The Times*, 16 Oct. 1980.
45. A. N. Wilson, *Who was Oswald Fish?* (Harmondsworth, 1983), 157.

30

ELDER STATESMAN

In partial retirement, James Callaghan entered upon a phase of greater tranquillity, if still one of much activity. For the Labour Party, however, the period after his resignation as leader was anything but peaceful. It lurched into a phase of quite unprecedented turmoil. By 1983–4 it was widely predicted that the party, born in the backstreets of late Victorian Britain, was about to undergo the same kind of 'strange death' that the Liberal Party had suffered sixty years earlier. In Arthur Schlesinger Jr.'s terminology, British Labour had abandoned the politics of hope for the politics of memory. As noted above, Michael Foot defeated Denis Healey (for whom Callaghan, unlike Harold Wilson, voted in all ballots) in the leadership contest in November 1980. But the frail and gentle Foot, at the age of 67, was hardly one to impose the smack of firm government on his warring followers. On the contrary, the left-wing tide under Tony Benn reached full flood. The party was plunged into turmoil and confusion never previously experienced, even in the traumas after the crisis of 1931. A special party conference at Wembley on 31 January 1981 endorsed with acclamation the left-wing proposal for an electoral college to elect the leader and deputy leader. What made matters worse for most Labour MPs was that the trade unions would be given the largest share, 50 per cent of the voting proportions, with the MPs and the constituency parties sharing the rest.

The first test of the new electoral college, and the clearest indication of its destructive implications, was the contest for the deputy leadership between Denis Healey and Tony Benn. This went on for more or less the rest of the year. It resulted in Healey's extremely narrow victory, with 50.1 per cent of the vote after a divisive and bitter campaign. Labour now appeared more paralysed than ever. Its record in by-elections was appalling. The nadir was reached in the Bermondsey by-election in February 1982. In this old working-class stronghold on London's riverside, previously represented by Bob Mellish of the dockers with a huge majority, the Labour candidate, Peter Tatchell, an Australian far-left supporter of Militant Tendency and a crusader for homosexual rights, was crushed by the Liberal, Simon Hughes. A Labour majority of 11,000 became a Liberal majority of 9,000, a swing of nearly 48 per cent. By 1983, Michael Foot's Labour seemed a dispirited and ageing party, losing its old working-class mass support and dependent on a few client groups like public sector trade unions and the residents of council housing estates. It was as much a case of interest politics as were the operations of the franchise before the Reform Act of 1832.

The worst feature of this period for Labour was the serious split that ensued as right-wing MPs and supporters broke away from their cantankerous and divided comrades to form a new party. In March 1981 David Owen, Shirley Williams, and William Rodgers—the so-called 'Gang of Three'—joined forces with Roy Jenkins, now back from Brussels, to issue the so-called Limehouse Declaration on behalf of moderate Gaitskell-type social democracy. Shirley Williams repeatedly observed of her former comrades, 'This is not the Labour Party I joined.' The broad church had become an embittered, doctrinally narrow sect. Soon afterwards emerged the Social Democratic Party, a clear challenger for the traditional Labour role as main opponent of the Tories. Eventually twenty-eight Labour MPs and one Conservative defected, along with many influential figures in the country and the media.[1] There were spectacular by-election successes, notably Shirley Williams's triumph at Crosby, a hugely safe Conservative seat in Merseyside, in December 1981, and, less massive, Roy Jenkins's victory at Glasgow, Hillhead, in April 1982. Opinion polls seemed to show that the SDP attracted more support than the Labour Party. Its Alliance with the Liberals negotiated in the course of 1981 created a powerful third force. Until it lost momentum after the Falklands War it seemed that the landscape of British politics had been transformed, at the expense of the old Labour Party. To use the jargon of the day, the mould had perhaps been broken for good.

Callaghan witnessed the renewed conflicts within Labour ranks and the rise of the SDP with extreme dismay. The 28 Labour MPs who defected included some who had been amongst his campaign supporters in 1976 such as Dickson Mabon and James Wellbeloved. Owen, Shirley Williams, and Rodgers had, of course, been three of his Cabinet ministers, and with all of them he had close and friendly relations. Owen he had marked down as a possible future Labour leader. Most cruelly of all, after the October 1981 party conference, another dreadful occasion, Tom McNally, now

Labour MP for Stockport South, also joined the defectors, to the fury of former colleagues like Jack Cunningham and Roger Stott. Callaghan himself was never remotely likely to leave the Labour Party after fifty years' membership. But in terms of policies, the SDP, with its commitment to modified Keynesianism, social welfare, the mixed economy, NATO, membership of the EEC, and support for the British nuclear deterrent, was much closer to his own outlook and moderate instincts than was the rampaging, far-left Labour Party that Tony Benn and his supporters were trying to create.

He continued to play a significant part in politics even as a retired leader. He attracted some criticism, including from an old Treasury aide, Sir Bryan Hopkin, in September 1982 when he took the line in a BBC *Panorama* interview that trade unions had 'a contingent right' to flout 'bad laws'. Mrs Thatcher made valuable political capital out of this when she told the Tory Party conference on 8 October that you could not choose just to observe the laws that suited you. Callaghan, with some justice, was projected as a prisoner of his past.[2] Previously, he had some private communication with Mrs Thatcher over Irish terrorists whom President Mitterrand had told him were operating in France.[3] He made a strong impact in his intervention in a Falklands debate in July 1982, after the war had ended. He supported the Thatcher government's policy of recapturing the Falklands after the Argentine invasion. But he also contrasted his own watchful policy (negotiations backed up by a hunter-killer submarine, plus MI5), which had avoided a war, with the negligence of the Conservatives in allowing the islands to appear undefended. He, after all, had refused to withdraw the *Endurance* from Falklands waters and had sharply criticized Mrs Thatcher for doing so in early 1982. She had sneered, in the course of the Falklands debate, that Labour would have never fired a shot. 'I tell the right hon. Lady, if we had been in power, we would not have needed to.'[4] He took the same line, with much effect, in giving evidence to the Franks Commission later appointed to inquire into the circumstances that led to the war, but which merely covered up Mrs Thatcher's own errors of judgement.

He largely kept his own counsel on the passionate debates over policy between Bennites and their opponents that continued to beset the Labour Party under the gentle leadership of Michael Foot. However, he had ample evidence of it at first hand. Militant Tendency continued to be aggressive and vocal in his Cardiff South-East constituency, and he and supporters like Jack Brooks and Alan Michael were constantly at war with them. Callaghan's monthly reports to the General Management

Committee were contributions to an ongoing ideological war, fought as much with professional people from the middle-class Roath ward as with working-class spokesmen from Splott or Adamsdown. The atmosphere in General Management Committee meetings in Cardiff was poisonous, even violent. Trotskyite agitators would line the steps of the Transport Workers' headquarters in Charles Street, Cardiff, shouting aggressively as supporters of Callaghan turned up, with a crescendo reached when the member himself appeared. One person present recalled 'a bilious atmosphere of distrust and intimidation'. However, Callaghan himself had never in fifty years been one to buckle under in the face of threats from left-wing extremists, while supporters like Jack Brooks were equally strong-minded. Even so, it was only after the 1983 general election that the war of attrition against Militant began to be won after almost a decade of infighting. Its leader retired from the scene after suffering a nervous breakdown.

On one issue, however, Callaghan, even though broadly supportive of Michael Foot and even more of Denis Healey, his deputy, was outspoken and confrontational. This was on the issue of nuclear disarmament to which Labour had been committed since 1981: indeed, Foot himself was a famous member of CND, as was his successor Neil Kinnock. Callaghan regarded the unilateral renunciation of nuclear weapons by Britain as irresponsible and almost suicidal. In a speech to the Cardiff Fabians on 18 November 1982, he strongly upheld collective security and multilateral disarmament. He decried Labour's avowed programme of scrapping Polaris, refusing to store Cruise missiles, and closing down the Polaris base at Holy Loch.[5] During the 1983 general election, he spoke in Cardiff on 25 May strongly against unilateralism, which he regarded as a policy of dismantling Britain's nuclear shield 'for nothing in return'. Polaris should not be given up unilaterally. 'The principal significance of nuclear weapons is political.' It was a speech which, somewhat unusually, he wrote out entirely on his own, and it caused his party much political embarrassment shortly before polling day.[6] On the other hand, he threw his support in favour of Cruise as its replacement; he forecast (wrongly) that Trident would be cancelled on grounds of cost. Later that year, in a fringe meeting at the 1983 party conference at Brighton, he condemned a reckless decision to abandon the commitment to multilateral disarmament to which Labour had adhered for the past eleven elections since 1945. Unilateralism, he declared, was deeply unpopular with the voters and made Labour appear irresponsible and doctrinaire; the opinion polls all confirmed this view. Callaghan's views met with furious assault from the left. Benn, Heffer, Alex Kitson, and others denounced him as a traitor.

It did not help his cause at the general election of May 1983, held when the Thatcherite tide was in full flood. Even loyalists like Alun Michael and Jack Brooks felt it was unnecessary to be so directly provocative when the manifesto had been carefully revised to exclude some of the more extreme possible statements on defence.[7] But Callaghan was unapologetic. He felt that the manifesto was an absurd and extremist document ranging over everything from the abolition of the Lords to the ending of fox-hunting. Gerald Kaufman was said to be the author of a phrase that it was 'the longest suicide note in history'. Callaghan had a much tougher fight on his hands this time anyhow, his constituency now being renamed Cardiff South and Penarth since it again reclaimed the latter town, a middle-class seaside resort with many elderly voters. His majority reflected the massive swing to Conservatism in this election. Mrs Thatcher ended up with 397 seats, a larger total even than Attlee in 1945, although this represented only 42.9 per cent of the poll. The Liberals and Social Democrats' Alliance won 26 per cent of the poll, which netted them only 23 seats (17 Liberal and 6 SDP) under the prevailing voting system. Labour put up by far its worst performance since it had become a nationwide party in 1918. Its tally of seats fell to 209 and its share of the poll to 27.6 per cent, just ahead of the Alliance, a slump of about 7.5 points since Callaghan's election in 1979. Michael Foot resigned immediately after the poll. In Cardiff, Callaghan's majority fell to 2,276 (5.4 per cent) over David Tredinnick, the Conservative, an Old Etonian property developer, with Winston Roddick, chairman of the Welsh Liberals, claiming 20.9 per cent and Sian Edwards (Plaid Cymru) losing her deposit. The four seats in Cardiff (following redistribution) taken together showed a swing to the Conservatives of 4 per cent compared with 1979. It was Callaghan's last electoral stand and almost his least successful. In every respect, the post-1945 world in which he had made his career had turned full circle.

He continued to intervene frequently in Commons debates after 1983. He was now the father of the House. On 1 January 1987 he became Sir James Callaghan as a Knight of the Garter, an honour which he greatly treasured. The advent of Neil Kinnock as party leader in October 1983 did not fill him with enthusiasm, since Kinnock had been one of the left-wing critics on the NEC in the late 1970s who had made his life almost impossible. Kinnock, a member of CND and a socialist of the left, appeared to be a rerun of Michael Foot. Callaghan voted for his opponent Roy Hattersley, who eventually became deputy leader. However, his attitude towards Kinnock became much more positive as the new leader engaged on a sweeping programme of revisionism after the national miners' strike of 1984–5. Kinnock's powerful demolition of Militant in the 1985 party conference, much assisted by the mood of hopelessness in the party after the polls, achieved what Callaghan and Healey had never found the resources to do in earlier years. He became a strong supporter of Kinnock henceforth, went out of his way to be friendly, and gave him practical assistance, for instance in enabling him to talk privately to the heads of the security services. He noted that Mrs Thatcher was far less forthcoming to Kinnock than he himself had been to Mrs Thatcher when she had been Opposition leader.[8]

He took part in major setpiece debates as a highly respected and experienced senior figure treated with much deference. He spoke powerfully in the debates on the US attack on Libya in April 1986 and somewhat startled the house by observing that, were he prime minister, he would not have given the Americans permission to launch their bombing raids against Colonel Gadaffi. He also endorsed the views of Edward Heath who recorded how he had refused the Americans the use of British bases in Cyprus during the 1973 Yom Kippur War.[9] Callaghan again spoke with authority during the debates on Westland helicopters earlier that same year, far more effectively than Kinnock as it happened. This was a crisis which saw Michael Heseltine leave the government and Mrs Thatcher herself come remarkably near to having to resign. With the stature of a former premier, Callaghan compared his own defence of British aerospace interests in developing the joint European airbus in 1978 in the face of the challenge from Boeing, with the appeasement of the US Sikorski option and the neglect of Europe by the Thatcher government. It was a highly effective performance which added to the Prime Minister's discomfiture.[10]

There was also a flash of Callaghan's old animosity towards the Labour left in a speech to the House on 9 March 1987. Labour still had a stance of unilateral nuclear disarmament, although highly modified to the point of almost total confusion. Callaghan then spoke out against it in a defence debate in the Commons and vehemently declared his support now for Trident submarines as the British nuclear deterrent, although he added that they should be thrown into any future negotiations as a bargaining counter. Only thus, he believed, could Britain be a realistic participant in any future disarmament talks. This led to a famous 'tearoom row' in the Commons with the left-wing MP for Hull, John Prescott. He accused Callaghan, whom he said had lost Labour two elections in a row, of 'leading us like lambs to the bloody slaughter'.[11] There was a brief outcry from the left, and a huge correspondence for Callaghan, both for and against his views, usually passionately so. Opinion polls demonstrated that he reflected the views of the majority of Labour voters, but it did not help the party's cause in the May 1987 general election. In the event, Neil Kinnock was able to improve Labour's results by winning 229 seats with 30.8 per cent of the vote, significantly ahead of the Alliance (with the SDP now close to extinction after its brief blaze of glory) but far behind the Conservatives' 376. This, of course, fell far below what Labour had managed in 1979.

On balance, despite his continuing capacity to enrage the far left, Callaghan was widely regarded as a comparatively reassuring figure by now, seen with much affection. The harsh reality of Thatcherism, with its privatization, monetarism, and glorification of private wealth-creation at the expense (many felt) of public service and social justice, was a shock to middle Britain. It was a reversion to what R. H. Tawney had called 'the acquisitive society'. Callaghan by contrast seemed a relaxed symbol of a kinder, gentler world when no prime minister could be represented (or perhaps misrepresented) as claiming that 'there was no such place as society'. Even Tony Benn, his most savage critic, was moved by Callaghan's appearance on a television interview with Brian Walden. The former premier was 'progressive, liberal, straight and reassuring. It . . . was comforting to feel that this old man was on our side. It . . . was friendly and comfortable, and I think that's what people want.'[12] It was perhaps unfortunate that this insight had not struck the diarist much earlier.

Callaghan still embodied values that the community revered and trusted. He had retired from the House after 1987, and Alun Michael succeeded him as member for Cardiff South as he had hoped. But he would remain a parliamentarian, since he now received his due as a baron. He had long held the Lords in some contempt as an old man's club and a political irrelevance. But it would enable him to remain in political life, and offered a platform for him to air his views, especially on international matters. Over the next ten years, he was to be amongst the most respected and influential of the peers, whose views, delivered to a generally ill-attended upper house, frequently commanded national attention. It was a transition that, combined with the move from party leader to senior backbencher, appeared subtly to modify not only his political outlook but even his personality, making him less abrasive and partisan, more self-assured and reflective.

He was now settled into the comparatively relaxed life of an elder statesman. He was not in the least put out by police security measures forced upon him after his name had appeared on an IRA 'hit list' found in the bombed house of a murdered Conservative MP, Ian Gow. He spent much more of his time at the Sussex farm. Well into his eighties, he took the closest interest in the practical and financial details of its management. His progress around the farm was sometimes assisted by a four-wheel Honda motor bicycle. A neighbour acted as contractor for doing the farm work, although the former Prime Minister was physically involved in some of the detailed operations, including in the lambing season. He took a keen interest in the gardens where Audrey helped him extend his knowledge of flowers. In 1986 the Callaghans bought a new London house off West Square, a Georgian development dating from 1791. The bicentenary of the Square in 1991 saw them involved in community celebrations. The house was conveniently located about ten minutes' drive from the Houses of Parliament (as a former prime minister, Callaghan had the permanent services of an official car and a new chauffeur, Alan Currie, to succeed his prime ministerial driver Joe Hazard in 1990). The house in Temple West Mews was a small modern one with a tiny study. It necessitated a good deal of climbing up and down stairs which was not altogether convenient as the Callaghans became older, but it had a pleasant view of the late-eighteenth-century enclosed square, its terraces and flower-beds. It was a political enclave with Merlyn Rees, Denis Healey, and their wives among close neighbours, along with the Conservative peer Lord Peyton. As his private secretary from 1981 to 1983 Callaghan took on Nigel Bowles, a young graduate student in politics from Nuffield College, Oxford, previously his researcher from January 1980. He helped look after the office, wrote speeches, and acted as all-purpose lightning-conductor at times of stress. Callaghan's main administrative support, as for nearly thirty years past, was his constituency secretary, the faithful Ruth Sharpe. She continued to look after political and constituency affairs with grace and efficiency, and without arousing any of the suspicion that other personal assistants to leading politicians could generate. Her sudden death from a heart attack at the end of 1981 was greatly lamented in the political world and was a severe personal loss to Callaghan himself. In the 1990s, the secretarial role was in the capable hands of Gina Page.

Family life became more and more pleasant as grandchildren multiplied. By 1994 the Callaghans had ten grandchildren and there were also two great-grandchildren. There was a consequent abundance of parties and anniversaries to celebrate, and Christmas became complicated. A less agreeable aspect of the family's life was the divorce of Peter and Margaret Jay after their time in the embassy in Washington. But both remarried and Peter Jay remained close and warm towards his former father-in-law. Margaret Jay bought a house in the west of Ireland and the Callaghans immensely enjoyed visits there each summer, revelling in the green Irish countryside and the company of congenial neighbours such as the eminent film producer (and Labour Party member) David Putnam and his wife.

Callaghan's health remained remarkably good. He had an operation to remove his gall bladder in January 1985, and there was the scare of a minor heart attack during a memorial service in October 1988. But he soon recovered, and well into the 1990s maintained a most active lifestyle including immense amounts of foreign travel. He took regular exercise on the farm and drank nettle tea to help his arthritis. It was a disappointment for him in 1996 when a temporary spasm of poorer health caused him to miss for the first time for years Gerald Ford's annual get-together in Vail, Colorado. However he went again in June 1997. Audrey Callaghan's health was also generally good; she recovered after a particularly unpleasant mugging in London which caused her husband immense anxiety, and was able to accompany him on worldwide trips to China, India, America, and elsewhere. His mental alertness until his mid-eighties was astonishing: his memory and capacity to absorb detail were razor-sharp.

All in all, the Callaghans greatly enjoyed life. Social activities in Wales were especially jolly: Callaghan always liked the Welsh with their capacity for spontaneous enjoyment. The resignation of his Cardiff seat was followed by the presidency of the University College of Swansea, in succession to Lord Harlech, which afforded further opportunities for involvement in Welsh life. A particularly pleasant event for Callaghan was the annual Royal Welsh Show at Builth Wells each July, at which he was the guest of Harlech Television, and when he could indulge to the full his passion for farming, including regular inspections of Welsh Blacks. The national eisteddfod, with its aura of nationalism and insistence on the all-Welsh rule, he found much less appealing. He was able to indulge his leisure interests more fully now. Although this was not immediately apparent to some personal advisers, some of these were cultural. He now had time to go to art galleries in Europe and America; visits to the special showings of the Royal Academy were a notable delight. The Academy's exhibition of the portraits of Franz Hals in 1992 gave him particular pleasure, and he also took a keen interest in sculpture. The opera and the theatre were also much more possible now. He was a frequent patron of the Welsh National Opera in Cardiff. His 80th birthday in March 1992 was celebrated with a mass family outing to Stratford to see *The Taming of the Shrew* and Shakespeare was always a favourite. It was all rather different from the highly charged way that Lady Thatcher chose to spend her retirement, focusing on highly paid ideological crusades, mostly in America and the Far East, and keeping relentlessly busy.

He continued to enjoy sport, including regular visits to Welsh rugby internationals, tempered by the fact that Wales was infinitely less successful than at the time of his premiership. Chess was also another passion, with visits to the Hastings and other tournaments, and occasional participation in matches, including a brisk demolition by the world champion, Gary Kasparov, in a simultaneous display at Simpson's in the Strand. He also found more time for reading, including the historical biographies which most retired politicians appear to find appealing. Anthony Howard's life of R. A. Butler (1987) was one he enjoyed, while Ben Pimlott's and Philip Ziegler's massive biographies of Harold Wilson in 1992 and 1993 (for each of which he had himself given an interview to the author) he found engrossing. He read again some of the works of his old television sparring partner Alan Taylor, to gain historical perspective on the problems of the Balkans. He also did some reading up on Lloyd George (for whose social reforms he had much admiration) prior to the opening of the Lloyd George museum at Llanystumdwy in December 1990. On a much wider range, indeed, he read vastly more than was commonly supposed. His bookshelves included many works of poetry, Russian authors from Tolstoy to Kuznetsov, political philosophy from Burke to Russell, and much on the history of art. All in all, for a man who often dismissed himself as someone without hobbies or interests, his range of cultural and intellectual interests in retirement was highly impressive.

These private indulgences were set against a background of wider involvement in international conferences and organizations as befitted a respected elder statesman. He visited thirty-seven countries in the period from 1979, including annual visits to the United States, sometimes simply for tourism but usually with some official or public business to fulfil. In many prestigious lectures, and in articles in journals and newspapers, Callaghan devoted much care and effort to communicating his analysis of world problems and possible solutions. In particular, he focused on international economic issues as they affected the developing world, a major concern of his since his time as Chancellor in the mid-1960s, and a fusion of his interest in the global economy and the problems of Africa. In a preview of the economic summit in Mexico in the autumn of 1981, he strongly endorsed the conclusion of the Brandt report in favour of the transfer of resources to developing countries, and called for much of third-world debt to be written off.[13] While he dealt with other themes such as energy and price stabilization, his main emphasis was on a global food programme, especially on the need to develop cereals, which required fewer energy inputs than did animal products.

He also delivered two prestigious lectures in New Delhi in late 1981 on 'Democracy and Leadership in our Interdependent World', with Mrs Gandhi in the chair.[14] He stressed the need for immediate action on fulfilling the aspirations of the Brandt report and again called for a world food programme. He pointed out that 40 per cent of the pre-school children in the developing world were showing signs of suffering from clinical malnutrition. In 1985 he again returned to these themes. Official development assistance had dropped by almost $4 bn. in 1981–3 and private capital investment had been vastly inadequate. The developing countries should free themselves from a miasma of debt; trade credits to them should be unfrozen, and capital and interest payments to the third world should be immensely speeded up.[15]

Africa was always a particular speciality of his. In January 1993 he chaired a major conference held in Cape Town of leading politicians, economists, and churchmen in that country, to consider the political, economic, and social difficulties in South Africa, and the way ahead.[16] The massive shortfall in development finance was again spelt out. But, as he had done as shadow Colonial Secretary, he also emphasized the need for Africans to help themselves and not be merely passive recipients. They should acquire technological skills and embark on policies of population control. Callaghan intervened frequently as chairman, usually in agreement with the speakers, though he had a sharp exchange with Barney Desai of the militant Pan African Congress. 'History shows that extremism breeds extremism', Callaghan observed. West Africa similarly engaged his attention. He commented in severe terms on the critical situation in Nigeria in 1995 with the coexistence of a corrupt and despotic government with a collapse of the economic infrastructure and worried about the fate of General Obasanjo.[17] Here he appeared as a figure of genuinely worldwide authority and stature. So did he in India, where he was made an honorary member of the Bhavan alongside men like Pandit Nehru and Dr Radakrishnan in the past. He received a degree from Sardar Patel University. A 'Callaghan colony' was named after him in the district of Medak.[18]

If world poverty and development were perhaps his dominant themes, others emerged with great force also. One was international leadership, political and otherwise, a theme he developed both in India and in delivering the Hubert Humphrey memorial lecture in Minneapolis in 1982. In New Delhi, he repeated his criticisms of the recent constitutional changes in the Labour Party. He added a quotation from Bagehot on the role of the leader—'he must make us hear what otherwise we would not.'[19] Elsewhere, he attended the Institute of Jewish Affairs in New York for a presentation to Dr Kissinger,[20] and in October 1993 spoke in New York to the Interaction Council on 'Where next for the United Nations?', to mark the 75th birthday of Helmut Schmidt.[21] Here he focused on the changing approach of the UN towards questions of national sovereignty, citing evidence from Yugoslavia and Iraq to illustrate his argument about the need for extending UN jurisdiction into new areas. In 1992 he spoke on international co-operation in the twenty-first century at Cardiff, on 'Prospects for the Political Integration with the European Community' before the economics faculty in Rome, and to the US navy in Annapolis, Maryland, on international security and the prospects for world disarmament.[22] He called here for a new attempt at a non-nuclear proliferation treaty. A particularly searching address was one to a conference at Bakersfield, California, in October 1994, discussing the impact on the Euro-American alliance of the internal changes in Russia, the unification of Germany, and the post-Maastricht European Community. He noted in manuscript, 'This raises more questions than it answers', but the confident synoptic sweep reads impressively.[23] Elsewhere, he appeared in conferences on international themes, from San Francisco to Tokyo. As vice-president of the Anglo-Chinese Society, he visited China twice more, in 1986 and in 1993, when his son Michael accompanied him. In May 1993 he had an extended talk with President Jiang on smoothing away the problems prior to the Chinese takeover of Hong Kong in 1997. He was himself invited by the British government to attend the handing over of the former British colony in that year, though he chose not to go. However he was active in the spring of 1997 in trying to arrange Chinese representation on the Interaction Council.

Many of the events specified above were individual occasions, when a lecture was delivered to a distinguished audience, or a conversation held with a particular leader, with no very obvious follow-up. Some lectures were highly paid—for example one half-hour performance in Los Angeles. But many were given gratis, often to low-profile local audiences. One regular feature of Callaghan's period in retirement, noted earlier, was his involvement in the Vail Interaction group, so called. In this, ex-President Ford invited ex-premier Callaghan, ex-Chancellor Schmidt, ex-President Giscard, and sometimes Malcolm Fraser of Australia, and others, a gathering of the great men of the 1970s reflecting on the problems of mankind and the handling or mishandling of them by their successors. They and their wives met every summer for some weeks in the mountain resort of Vail, Colorado. Their meetings were commemorated in 1995 in a group portrait by an Italian artist, later placed on display in the Congress building in Washington. There was always a more leisurely or convivial aspect, too, once a boat trip along the coast of Alaska, once a boat trip from Kiev to the Black Sea and Crimea (somewhat complicated by passport difficulties between the new Russia and the Ukraine). On occasion, the Vail group produced its own public declarations on world issues, and its own diagnoses of problems, especially world poverty and the need to revitalize the economies of the developing nations.

This background of international activity and evangelism did not, however, deflect Callaghan from close and consistent participation in affairs at home. Indeed, his new role in the House of Lords consorted well with his growing reputation as an elder stateman for whom the world was his parish. In the Lords Callaghan spoke with growing regularity and always with powerful effect. He was able to use his long-standing associations with Conservative peers such as Lords Whitelaw or Peyton, or with eminent former civil servants such as Lord Bancroft or Lord Allen of Abbeydale. He spoke on the Gulf War and on Europe. He defended the Maastricht treaty in June 1993 in a speech which *The Times* called 'magnificently Olympian',[24] and expressed constructive concern on Bosnia. With his extraordinary background of public service, there was hardly an issue on which he could not pronounce with authority, whether it be the EMS, defence, education, the criminal justice system, Northern Ireland, southern Africa, or China. His words were often conveyed far beyond the silent and somnolent benches of the House of Lords. He gave evidence before the Nolan Committee on standards in public life in 1994, with much impact on that austere gathering of judges, politicians, and academics. In the press he urged the need for a new public code of ethics, for civil servants as well as for politicians.[25] Civil liberties often exercised him to good effect. In condemning the Police Bill, with its widespread powers given to the chief constables to approve police bugging and surveillance, in January 1997, he was challenging the Labour shadow Home Secretary, Jack Straw, as well as the Tory government. His speech was a notable feature of the Lords' debate on the bill which saw the government's measure rejected by a majority of 64.

These pronouncements, delivered without notes to a small house of mainly very elderly peers, were not of merely academic significance. On several of them the government was forced to retreat. It was in some measure the informed contribution to public debate made by senior figures like Lord Callaghan that defused some of the Labour criticism of the Lords in the later 1980s and the early 1990s. Labour's proposals for reform in 1996 concentrated on abolishing the hereditary element in the Lords, rather than destroying the entire house altogether, an issue on which Callaghan and Tony Benn had famously clashed before the 1979 election. In the language of the pre-1914 Liberals, they would mend it, not end it.

Honours were showered on him. There were honorary degrees from Wales, Birmingham, and Sussex (along with Sardar Patel in India and Meisei in Japan), the freedoms of Portsmouth, Sheffield, and Swansea, to go with that of Cardiff. In July 1996 he gained two more honorary degrees, both links with his past, from Liverpool where David (now Lord) Owen was chancellor, and from the Open University for whose foundation he had guaranteed the funding when Chancellor of the Exchequer in 1965. He was being transmuted from man into institution. Of course, a respected senior figure like a former prime minister almost inevitably sees his reputation elevated to a more timeless, non-partisan plane as he grows old. By the mid-1990s Tony Benn himself had become a kind of affectionately regarded licensed rebel, regularly invited on to television chat shows. But the politician can also help create his own reception and shape his own historical reputation. Callaghan's contribution lay not only in prestigious lectures across the world, but in speeches to the Lords and incisive appearances on television and radio, ranging from *Panorama* to the Jimmy Young show.

There was also his lengthy autobiography, *Time and Chance*, published in 1987. His private papers for his career since the early 1930s had been meticulously preserved by his secretary Ruth Sharpe. Queries about their future location by the Cabinet Office were brushed aside, for which scholars would later be grateful. The Callaghan papers were sorted out for almost four years by his young secretary Nigel Bowles, who helped greatly with the research. From 1983 similar duties were carried out by Caroline Anstey. The Callaghan archive, which spanned his career in much detail since his first trade union activities in the early 1930s, was of much scholarly interest, indeed unusually so for a recent political leader. In addition to the usual reports and records of meetings, there were extensive papers from his personal office, diaries, accounts of foreign travels, contemporary *aide-mémoires* on key crises, and transcripts of conversations with foreign leaders. There were none of the problems here that surrounded the papers of other prime ministers, from Lloyd George to Harold Wilson. There was neither a Frances Stevenson nor a Marcia Falkender to be squared this time. Callaghan, with much reluctance for a relatively inexperienced author (his study on Northern Ireland in 1973 was his only previous book), took the advice of his friend, the former publisher William Collins, and embarked on his autobiography. It cost him immense intellectual and physical effort over some years. He worked hard on all aspects of it: his aged sister Dorothy sent in some reminiscences on their early life in Portsmouth and Brixham. It was finally published by Collins in 1987. Its reception was respectful rather than rapturous. It lacked the literary elegance of Jenkins or the intellectual panache of Healey. A former parliamentary colleague, Brian Walden, ex-Labour now Thatcherite, writing in the *Sunday Times*, was critical—'there was no resolution, no vision, no fitting sense of the gravity of the sickness afflicting the Labour Party and the nation'. Conversely, the *Times* journalist and later Professor Peter Hennessy wrote sympathetically that 'history would be kind to him'.[26] This autobiography had none of the overtones of alleged adultery, conspiracy, and espionage that, for instance, featured in biographies of Harold Wilson. Julian Hodge is not mentioned.

The tone is solemn and much of Callaghan's generally buoyant and outgoing personality is suppressed. He did not find writing the book a particularly satisfying activity and the style somewhat reflects the fact. At the same time, *Time and Chance* is certainly worth much more close attention than some have given it credit for. It is lucid, meticulously accurate, and covers wide swathes of British domestic and international history. Callaghan drew on his own government materials with care and precision. It is a sound, serious book, much cited in scholarly articles in learned journals. On the other hand, it focuses on Callaghan the statesman rather than Callaghan the man. Apart from a moving account of his childhood, it is somewhat bloodless in tone. There are set sections on his work as Chancellor, Home Secretary, Foreign Secretary, and Prime Minister. His activities as a party political figure, his personal contacts and friendships loom less prominently, and large numbers of them are left out. The fact that the book ends with the 1979 election also tends to give it an official prime ministerial air. It conveys, as intended, the marmoreal public image of the national and international statesman, on display if not exactly on a pedestal. It is Cardiff's version of the Lincoln Memorial. Lytton Strachey, let alone Freud, has not spoken yet. It provides a valuable but incomplete insight into his career.

Callaghan maintained many other public interests in these years of retirement. Indeed, as the 1980s merged into the 1990s, these seemed to increase and multiply. Instead of turning to lucrative directorships or business consultancies as so many former Conservatives ministers tended to do, he concentrated largely on charitable and educational good causes which brought him scant personal remuneration. Thus he was president of a Housing Association in Cardiff (which led to 'Callaghan Court' being built), he retained his links with the Wiener Library and Chatham House, he served on the Forte Trust over many years to distribute funds to good causes, and was heavily engaged in discussions in 1995–6 when the Forte Trust Houses were bought up by the Granada group. One bonus was that he could lunch in style at the Café Royal. One remarkable personal achievement in 1987 came when he persuaded Lord Young to include in companies' legislation a provision for the royalties from Barrie's *Peter Pan* to go to assist Audrey's beloved Great Ormond Street children's hospital. Callaghan's initiative added massively to its income, while disproving the pessimism of the lawyers about whether the idea was feasible.

Two particular interests predominated—the environment and education. In environmental and ecological matters, he had in many ways been a pioneer in his early concern. His interest in the protection of the sea from oil and other pollution, and the recycling of waste, became part of the common culture with the growing passion for 'green issues' in the 1980s and 1990s. So, too, did his love of wildlife and the countryside, where the threats from human depredation became all the more serious. Here he was, as a practising farmer, particularly interested in the issue of striking a balance between the productive needs of agriculture and the preservation of natural resources. ACOPS continued to thrive and in the 1990s an annual Callaghan lecture was launched.[27] Over education, he noted the way in which his 1976 Ruskin speech on educational standards became in the 1980s something close to the conventional wisdom. On 16 October 1996, twenty years on from his Ruskin address, when he was well into his eighty-fifth year, he delivered a bold speech to the London University Institute of Education calling for a massive, long-term, multi-billion programme of educational reform. He addressed his observations particularly to the members of the likely future Labour government. There was also an external aspect to this passion for education. He was very active, as a bencher of the Inner Temple, in organizing overseas scholarships for young would-be lawyers from Commonwealth countries. Another initiative, on which he was approached by Mrs Jean Floud, the principal of Newnham College, was the Cambridge-based Overseas Trust, for which a fund of over £12m. was eventually accumulated, affording opportunities for graduate work in Cambridge and elsewhere for hundreds of young overseas scholars, many of them from the smaller Commonwealth countries. Callaghan's immense range of personal contacts was helpful in mounting direct approaches to heads of state and others. In Zimbabwe, for instance, he paid a personal visit to ensure the signature to the agreement of President Robert Mugabe. Another interest was the Appeal Committee for the British Museum.

Probably none of these good causes, however, engaged him as intensely as did his appointment in 1986 as president of the University College of Swansea.[28] He was appointed somewhat unexpectedly after the president-designate, Lord Harlech, had been killed in a car crash, but he seized the opportunity with great enthusiasm. It combined two elements dear to his heart—higher education and continuing contact with old friends in south Wales. The presidency of one of the Welsh university colleges would commonly be thought of as largely ceremonial, especially since at Swansea the chairmanship of the college council was undertaken by Callaghan's good friend, the banker Emrys Evans. But he threw himself into his new role with immense enthusiasm and gusto. He attended councils and degree ceremonies faithfully and evidently enjoyed them, looking a commanding figure in his robe and braided academic hat.

During his eight years as president, Swansea developed considerably, almost doubling from 4,037 full-time students in 1985–6 to 7,412 in 1994–5, with 1,351 part-time students as well. Callaghan took care to keep in touch with staff and student activities during this expansion. Some, indeed, found it somewhat intimidating to have a former prime minister, with strong opinions of his own, imposing himself on the college and its administration. But there can be little doubt that it was much the stronger for it, especially in its public image. It was by no means a trouble-free assignment. Callaghan needed all his political skills to help settle a difficult dispute in 1991 when two philosophy lecturers launched serious criticisms, later largely vindicated, about the running of a graduate course in the philosophy department and alleged plagiarism by a student. They were suspended but later reinstated. In time, the president's influence managed to defuse matters. There were other activities of a far more positive kind. For instance, Callaghan took a close interest in the Swansea students' community work for local good causes, and there was the continuing education department, run by Dr Hywel Francis, the son of a famous Welsh miners' leader with whom Callaghan had stayed back in 1947. When a new initiative of a 'university for the valleys', granting part-time degrees, was launched, Callaghan went up to Onllwyn to participate in its activities by giving his reflections on the events of 1945. After he retired as president in late 1995, the new humanities building on the main Singleton Park campus was named the 'James Callaghan building' and opened formally by him in October 1996. There was also an annual Callaghan lecture inaugurated in January 1996 as part of Swansea's celebration of its seventy-fifth anniversary. The first such lecture was on the topic of the eponymous ex-Prime Minister.[29]

He also became much involved in the labyrinthine activities of the federal University of Wales. He supported moves to try to promote academic direction at the centre, and was brusque with some of the college principals who he felt were recalcitrant. But he came to realize that centralist measures could hardly succeed, since for decades the essential initiative had lain in the individual colleges who had their own direct access to the funding bodies, and to whom 98 per cent of public funding went. Callaghan's objective was one of balance, trying to preserve the university as a collaborative institution for research purposes, while protecting the autonomy of individual institutions such as Swansea. Federalism, the dualism between central control and local autonomy, was a thorny subject as he well knew from the Labour Party, not to mention his central African experience. But the University of Wales functioned better than many he had known and had strong public roots in the sentiments of the Welsh people. On public occasions, Callaghan was without doubt a superb ambassador both for Swansea and for the entire university. His speech of welcome at Swansea to the Commonwealth vice-chancellors in the summer of 1993 was a model of its kind, not least because he knew at first hand every country represented there so well. Delivered as usual without notes, it offered a wide-ranging analysis of the relationship between higher education and the needs of the developing world. His address in presenting the President of Ireland, Mrs Mary Robinson, for a doctorate during the university's centenary honorary degree ceremony in November 1993 was equally memorable, not least for the way he drew on his own experience of Irish affairs. Only he could have done it with such authority.

In many ways, therefore, his nine years as president in Swansea helped fulfil some of Callaghan's lifelong impulses for advanced education and training, providing opportunities which he had himself been denied by time and chance. Nor did the sedate academic ambiance of Swansea neuter Callaghan's abiding political subtlety. As with the Labour Party, he spent some time in trying to secure the succession for a chosen candidate. He wanted Swansea's president to remain a Labour man, to avoid the prospect of the position falling to the Tory Lord Howe, originally from Aberavon across Swansea Bay. Cardiff's president was a Tory peer, Lord Crickhowell, and Callaghan did not want another in Swansea. He attempted to promote Neil Kinnock as his successor, but in the end was well pleased with another Welshman, Lord Richard of Ammanford. He had been, as Ivor Richard, his minister at the UN and one-time messenger to Rhodesia, and was now leader of the Labour peers in succession to Lord Cledwyn. Unlike Dr Johnson, Callaghan ensured that, once again, the Whig dogs had the best of it.

If Swansea showed the possibilities for a benevolent senior politician, another of his activities, the Cambridge Overseas Trust, illustrated the possible pitfalls. For much of the funding for it, initially at least, came from a Middle Eastern financial operator, Agha Hassan Abedi, to whom he had been introduced by ex-President Jimmy Carter. Following a number of meetings and meals at the Athenaeum, Abedi gave Callaghan in all £3m. to fund the Overseas Trust. In return Callaghan signed his British naturalization papers after consulting with the Bank of England.[30] Later, however, it transpired that Abedi's millions had come from highly improper sources, including involvement in the international arms and drugs markets. The Bank of Credit and Commerce International was finally brought down in 1991 when it was successfully prosecuted in America for money-laundering, fraud, and racketeering charges. Abedi's Bank collapsed, and thousands of small savers in Middle East countries especially lost their savings. $13 bn. went missing and Abedi himself took refuge in Pakistan where he died in 1995 still immune from prosecution. His Bank was fundamentally corrupt and irregularly run. There were hints of Mafia associations. Unfortunately, somewhat as in the case of Julian Hodge, Callaghan's enthusiasm for a good cause—in this case, a perfectly proper scheme for bringing young Commonwealth scholars to study at Cambridge University—had led to problems. He had spoken with warmth on behalf of BCCI in the Lords in April 1990, commending its directors as 'people of the highest integrity and probity' whose purpose and philosophy were 'honourable'.[31] In view of the money-laundering and other activities of BCCI this enthusiasm was gravely misplaced. Callaghan (like Jimmy Carter for whose institute to aid the third world Abedi had also donated substantial sums) had been badly misled. Abedi, indeed, had focused on eminent politicians with an interest in the third world, such as Carter, Callaghan, David Owen, and Denis Healey, to try to promote his often dubious causes.

However, Callaghan, it emerged, had also been temporarily employed as an adviser by BCCI and it came out, too, that in his last few months as an MP in 1987 he had received £12,500 for travel and other expenses for secretarial work in connection with the Commonwealth Trust. In addition, he had not formally declared them in the register of members' interests in the Commons.[32] At a time when he was commending to the Nolan Committee openness and the maximum of integrity in public life, this technicality afforded some grist to the mill of Conservative newspapers who had suffered repeated Labour attacks on Tory MPs receiving private hospitality or cash for questions, or else acting on behalf of financial interests without declaring them. Certainly there was absolutely no hint of personal corruption in this. Callaghan's abiding priority, without doubt, was the cause of higher education in the Commonwealth. Abedi's plans to establish a bank to promote third-world development excited him. But carelessness of methods in finance had led him astray on matters of detail, no doubt an occupational hazard of the fund-raiser. In the case of BCCI, from whose activities so many innocent investors suffered, Callaghan's activities did not amount to anything resembling a crime, but they added up to at least a series of avoidable embarrassments.

As Callaghan reached the milestone of his 80th birthday on 27 March 1992, he seemed almost inseparable from the history of his times. No one living better embodied the course of later twentieth-century Britain. A television documentary by Michael Cockerell at the time depicted him in a benign, almost heroic light, man and monument combined. There was a party in the Cholmondely room in the Lords, attended by Lord Wilson of Rievaulx and Baroness Castle; Neil Kinnock, Lord Cledwyn, and Callaghan himself all made rousing speeches, at a time when a Labour election victory appeared a strong possibility. He was invariably brought into radio or television studios to comment on past events or personalities, especially at times of anniversaries. He offered his reminiscences of Bevin and Attlee, of Nixon and Mitterrand. He seemed to have met and known everybody. At the anniversary of VE Day in May 1995, he went to Berlin where he took a vigorous part in a multinational discussion chaired by Melvin Bragg.

His contemporaries offered their own kinds of reflection upon him. Tony Benn's successive volumes of diaries published throughout the 1980s combined scathing attacks on Callaghan as a non-socialist with genial remarks on his personality and his fairness as Prime Minister. Callaghan was invited to attend Benn's book launches but could not bring himself to associate with one he regarded as the main author of Labour's recent disasters. The memoirs of Denis Healey, David Owen, and, up to a point, Roy Jenkins depicted his premiership in very positive terms. Healey thought him the best premier since Attlee. Only Barbara Castle's were remorsely critical of an old enemy. A more unexpected source of criticism—the only one that Callaghan confessed brought him some pain—were the memoirs published in 1985 of George Thomas, recently the House Speaker and now Lord Tonypandy.[33] These revealed a remarkable degree of spite, amounting to envy, directed against an old colleague with whom he had worked so intimately for forty years. Michael Foot and Cledwyn Hughes were also amongst Thomas's targets. *The Times* felt moved to criticize the former Speaker in a leading article for behaviour unbecoming so major a public figure. More serious than the personal animosity was Thomas's use of his confidential knowledge of conversations behind the Speaker's chair to spice the book up, in a manner that was indiscreet and perhaps unconstitutional. Michael Foot declared that there was a better case against George Thomas for disclosing official secrets than there had been against Clive Ponting.[34] Callaghan replied with dignity and denied that there had been 'mutual antipathy' between the two Cardiff colleagues. He merely felt 'deeply sorry' that he had written in such a way to try to sell his book. Shortly afterwards, he visited Tonypandy in hospital where he had throat cancer, apparently dying. Thomas apologized, Callaghan forgave him, and they parted, Callaghan believing that they would presumably not meet again. Unexpectedly, Thomas recovered from his cancer and returned to the Lords, but no doubt charitable thoughts continued to prevail.

Contemporaries passed away one after the other, Douglas Jay being the latest in March 1996. His old union leader Douglas Houghton also died that spring at the great age of 98. The death that most affected Callaghan was undoubtedly that of Harold Wilson, always an enigma but in his fashion a comrade-in-arms over many decades and in four administrations. Callaghan went to the funeral service in the Scillies after Wilson's death in 1995, and delivered a warm memorial address at Westminster Abbey. He felt that some of the obituaries of the former Prime Minister were too severe. Lord Home, another former premier, died some time afterwards. There were still three prime ministers alert and highly active. Ted Heath was still in the Commons in 1997, himself the father of the House now, tough and opinionated especially on Europe. Lady Thatcher spent much time and energy on itinerant worldwide evangelism on behalf of her Foundation, but paid occasional visits to the Lords, notably to defend the government over the 'Arms to Iraq' affair. But only Callaghan appeared to have achieved the unique balance of Olympian detachment and party involvement to give his political interventions wider effect. He showed, many felt, how a former prime minister ought to behave.

The politics of the time now reflected a different mood. Old Labour fought on, but Neil Kinnock's final bid for power in the April 1992 general election failed again and he resigned. His successor as leader was none other than Callaghan's former protégé, John Smith, and he witnessed his modernizing activities and success in introducing 'one member, one vote' with much pleasure. However, Smith's cruelly unexpected death in May 1994 brought it all to an abrupt conclusion. Among other things, it meant that all three of the projected Labour leaders in the late 1970s, Smith, Owen, and Hattersley, had in some sense fallen by the wayside. The new leader was Tony Blair, elected to parliament only in 1983 and a young man of 41 whom Callaghan scarcely knew. There were speculations that he might have favoured his old sparring partner John Prescott, a former trade union official whom he felt had 'come on a lot' but in fact he voted for Blair, and for Prescott as his deputy. At the state funeral of President Mitterrand in Paris in January 1996, Callaghan was astonished to hear Tony Blair tell him he had never met Harold Wilson at all.[35] It was truly a generational divide.

The creed of 'New Labour' subsequently proclaimed, with the emphasis on markets, privatization, low taxation, tough social policies, and no commitments in raising public expenditure, seemed to draw a clear line, distancing Blair not only from the Callaghan government of the 1970s but even from the Attlee government of 1945. To adapt a famous speech of Manny Shinwell after 1945, the working class, redefined out of existence, did not seem to matter a tinker's cuss. Tony Blair's speech to the Fabians in July 1995 on the occasion of the fiftieth anniversary of the election of the 1945 Labour government, seemed to suggest that the Attlee administration and the present Labour front bench were ideologically far apart, with only perhaps the National Health Service as a mutual point of reference. Nationalization, universalized welfare benefits, full employment, active regional policies, redistributive taxation, the commitment to equality—all the priorities of the young Callaghan in 1945—belonged to that seemingly very distant era. In the cleansing atmosphere of the 'stakeholder society', it would be goodbye to all that. The emphasis now would be on generalized 'values' rather than on detailed policies. *The Blair Revolution*, written jointly by Blair's election organizer Peter Mandelson, and published in February 1996, was a straw in the wind. It dismissed, almost brusquely, any talk of a social contract or the kind of relationship between government and unions that the Callaghan administration had nurtured in the mid-1970s. Indeed the authors seemed to visualize no particular point of contact between the Labour Party and unions at all: this was the more startling since Mandelson was the grandson of one famous apostle of the old alliance, namely Herbert Morrison.

These revisionist views were apparently upheld during the 1996 TUC annual conference. Here one of Labour's more obscure front-bench spokesmen, Stephen Byers, appeared to suggest that the formal ties with the unions, already weakened by the removal of the block vote at party conference and the establishment of 'one member, one vote', should be scrapped altogether after almost a century of partnership. This caused Callaghan great alarm since he believed that the TUC under John Monks's secretaryship had returned to the traditional moderate, centrist role it had exercised in the pre-Frank Cousins days in the 1940s and early 1950s. He resisted pressures from some friends to speak out publicly against the party's apparent drift to the right. But he conveyed his concern privately to the leadership, and rejected their invitation to take up the cudgels against his old adversary Barbara Castle on the issue of pensions at party conference. The ideological roots of the new spokesmen and spin doctors, so feared many Labour activists, by no means all of them on the left, appeared to lie more with the SDP defectors of the early 1980s than with traditional Labour. For some Blair supporters, the Labour governments of 1964–79 were a chronicle of almost consistent failure.[36] Centrist figures like Wilson and Callaghan, along with evangelists like Keir Hardie and George Lansbury, no longer seemed to belong to Labour's usable past. Callaghan, however, for long refused to join in internal party wrangling over the unions or the meaning of socialism. When asked, he offered his advice to Blair on how an incoming Labour government should manage the levers of power. He felt that each generation of leaders had to lead in his (or, conceivably, her) own fashion, making a break with the past where necessary and stamping his own personality on the movement as he himself had done in his own time. That did not rule out 'a quiet word' with the new leader as circumstances allowed.

Somewhat unexpectedly, in December 1996, he intervened more directly. An interview in the *New Statesman*, while nowhere directly critical of the party leadership, warned of the dangers of 'New Labour' disavowing its past, and especially of breaking with the unions. He described himself as neither Old nor New, but as 'original' Labour. His guarded remarks struck a chord in many sections of the party, especially in its old heartlands in the north and the Celtic fringe.[37] For the moment, both for financial and administrative reasons, the unions retained a central role. Callaghan's sense of party had still something to offer as a source of organization and shared values and ideas.

Above all, its old leader was still not merely physically alive, but active, a symbol of forty years of conmmunal endeavour. As the main issues unfolded during the 1997 general election campaign—the economy; relations with Europe; peace in Northern Ireland; remodelling education and the welfare state; law and order; integrity in public life—one great survivor spanned them all. He actually knew what it was like to be in government, whereas New Labour was innocent of ministerial experience after eighteen years of Conservative rule. Callaghan was in one sense no more than

Labour's last prime minister. Prior to Tony Blair, many had long thought he might be perhaps the last ever as the 'long march' ended in its appointed *cul de sac*. But in another respect he was both a custodian of Labour's traditional values and a guide to its approach to the operations of power. He spanned the worlds of Attlee and Blair and had footholds in both.

On a brilliantly sunny morning on 2 May, Callaghan relaxed benignly in a BBC television studio, offering the viewers his thoughts on Labour's stupendous election victory. It followed a lengthy campaign, in which, for the first time since 1931, he had played no part. With 419 seats and an overall majority of 179, Tony Blair had achieved an astonishing transformation, one that promised to change the political landscape for years, perhaps decades. The Conservatives lost scores of suburban strongholds. They won nothing in Birmingham, Liverpool, Manchester, Sheffield, or Leeds. They ended up with no seats at all in either Scotland or Wales. The party of the Union was confined to England. Compared with the post-war landslide that had brought Callaghan to Westminster for the first time, Labour's share of the poll was 48% in 1945, 44.5% in 1997; there were 203 Labour gains in the former election, 146 in the latter. But in terms of the tally of seats, the size of the overall majority and of the national swing, Labour's colossal victory on May Day 1997 was unique in its history. The rout of the Tories was comparable with that of the Duke of Wellington in 1832. In Cardiff South and Penarth, Alun Michael's majority was almost 14,000, much more than his predecessor had ever achieved.

The day after the deluge, Callaghan was generous and serene, full of warm praise for the dynamic leadership of the 43-year-old Tony Blair, a man almost half his age. He spoke calmly of how Blair and his colleagues had 're-invented the Labour Party', making it credible and contemporary in a way that the divided party he himself had led in the later 1970s could never be. A swathe of Labour gains in southern England was testimony to a quality of electability in New Labour which the old corporatist, class-based movement in which he had spent his career had long ceased to possess. He praised Neil Kinnock for instigating the process of change and modernization in his battles with the left in the 1980s. Tony Blair he applauded for his realism in committing himself to a precise, limited programme which could be achieved in the lifetime of a parliament. No far-left 'suicide note' this time around.

Yet by his very presence, Callaghan reminded the party of its traditions and its roots. While it had transformed its structure and policies, Labour was still founded on a sense of community and solidarity as old as industrialization itself. To Callaghan, the trade unions were still essential vehicles of it. In its moment of triumph, New Labour should not proclaim 'an end to history' as Fukuyama had done of the cold war. No party could erase its memories or engage in instant amnesia. The past was an inspiration not an albatross. The values and objectives which underpinned the Blair government sprang from the demonstrable injustices of a living society, the hard unequal world in which Jim Callaghan grew up. They would never be forgotten. At the age of 85, therefore, he remained an active participant in a dialogue still unfinished.[38]

1. See Crewe and King, *SDP*, 104 ff.
2. Material in Callaghan Papers (BLPES), box 4.
3. Callaghan to Thatcher, 9 Dec. 1982; Thatcher to Callaghan, 13 Dec. 1982 (ibid.).
4. *Parl. Deb.*, 6th ser., vol. 27 (8 July 1982). Tony Benn in *The End of an Era*, 217–18, describes him as 'an old Tory warmonger'.
5. Callaghan, 'Defence and Disarmament: We Need to Think Again' (address to Cardiff Fabian Society, 18 Nov. 1982).
6. *The Times*, 26 May 1983; interview with Nigel Bowles.
7. Interviews with Lord Brooks and Alun Michael MP.
8. Interview with Lord Callaghan.
9. *Parl. Deb.*, 6th ser., vol. 95, 893–7 (16 Apr. 1986).
10. *Parl. Deb.*, 6th ser., vol. 89, 1107–14 (15 Jan. 1986).
11. *The Times*, 10 Mar. 1987; material in Callaghan Papers (BLPES), box 4; Frank Field to Callaghan, n.d. (ibid.).
12. Benn, *The End of an Era*, 500–1 (17 Apr. 1987).
13. L. J. Callaghan, 'The World Summit in Mexico', *Round Table* (Commonwealth Journal of International Affairs) (July 1981), 208–15.
14. Rajaji Centenary National Committee lectures, 24–5 July 1981 (published by Bharatiya Vidya Bhavan, Bombay, 1982).
15. 'Meeting the Challenge of the Third World' (Grindlays Bank lecture, 1985).
16. *Towards a New South Africa*, proceedings of meetings by high-level group chaired by Lord Callaghan of Cardiff with South African leaders, Cape Town, 21–3 January 1993 (Interaction Council, New York, 1993), 122–3. See also Callaghan's articles in *Guardian*, 16 Feb. 1993, and 'An Example for the Rest of Africa', *Financial Times*, 5 May 1994.
17. Article in *New York Times*, July 1995 (personal copy).
18. Paper by S. Ramakrishnan sent to Lord Callaghan, 10 Nov. 1994 (personal copy).
19. 'Democracy and Leadership: Our Interdependent World', 20.
20. Callaghan notes, 26 Oct. 1993 (personal copy).
21. This appeared, in a somewhat different form, as the Earl Mountbatten lecture to the Cambridge Union Society, 27 Oct. 1993.
22. Speech to Sealink 92 Symposium, Annapolis, Md., 18 June 1992 (personal copy).
23. Speech to the Tenth Annual Bakersfield Business Conference, 15 Oct. 1994.
24. House of Lords, *Official Report*, vol. 546, no. 149, 732–4 (7 June 1993); *The Times*, 8 June 1993.
25. *Observer*, 6 Nov. 1994.

26. Peter Hennessy, review in *Listener*, 16 Apr. 1987.

27. 'Maintaining Wildlife Balance' (Sussex FWAG conference, 14 Jan. 1995); Callaghan's Presidential message in *ACOPS Newsletter*, issue 1 (May 1997). He had been president of ACOPS since retiring as chairman in 1963.

28. Personal knowledge. I am grateful for information from Ms Margaret Park, University Registry, Swansea.

29. Kenneth O. Morgan, *'Steady as she Goes': Writing the Biography of Lord Callaghan* (Swansea, 1996). The second Callaghan lecture in Feb. 1997 was given by the Cambridge chemist Sir John Meurig Thomas FRS.

30. Interview with Lord Callaghan; Peter Truell and Larry Gurwin, *BCCI* (London, 1991), 87 ff.

31. House of Lords, *Official Report*, vol. 518 (23 Apr. 1990), 415–17.

32. *Mail on Sunday*, 6 Nov. 1994.

33. Thomas, *Mr Speaker*; see Callaghan's letter to *The Times*, 27 Feb. 1985, and leading article, 26 Feb. 1985.

34. *The Times*, 27 Feb. 1985. See also Foot, *Loyalists and Loners*, 65–77, 'Brother George', for some blistering comments

35. Information from Michael Callaghan.

36. Mandelson and Liddle, *The Blair Revolution*.

37. Interview with Steve Richards, *New Statesman*, 21 Dec. 1996.

38. After the election, Tony Blair did not consult Callaghan for advice about the forthcoming European summit at Noordwijk. In November 1990, just after becoming Premier, John Major had called in Callaghan to discuss a European heads of government meeting at Rome the following month. In May 1997 Blair ignored Callaghan but had a private discussion with Lady Thatcher instead (*Independent*), 26 May 1997).

31
CONCLUSION

RALPH WALDO EMERSON said of Abraham Lincoln, 'He is the true history of the American people in his time.' Much the same could be said of James Callaghan, as a representative figure in the history of the British people for most of the second half of the twentieth century. His career spanned the whole gamut of British historical experience from the Second World War onwards. Like many of his generation, he found wartime service a formative experience. It offered a new impetus for collective reconstruction after a 'people's war' and also gave his political and economic ideas a new international dimension. After the war, he regarded Attlee's consensus as his abiding point of reference and always took it as his ideological starting point thereafter. It was the political expression of the wartime mood of partnership and solidarity. At the same time, he was simultaneously both a frequent critic of post-war policies, especially in relation to the cold war, and a force for reconciliation in the party after the fierce conflicts between Gaitskellites and Bevanites. The epitome of 'Keep Calm', he stood somewhat detached from both. It made him the more credible as a coming leader.

In the 1960s, he shared both in the excitement of Harold Wilson's advent to power as a new-born modernizer and in the disillusion that accompanied Labour's failure to achieve its planning objectives. He was central to that experience, both through his having to devalue the pound and in his fateful opposition to change in industrial relations. More positively, he was a creative force in the peaceful winding up of empire, especially in Africa, and in promoting new forces for change in Northern Ireland. In the 1970s, he was central both to the national and party compromise which brought Britain into Europe, and to the decline of corporatism brought about by the changing outlook of the unions. He embodied national faith in the imperatives of planning, welfare, and state direction in the 1940s, and the public questioning of them in the 1970s. At the time of his fall from power, he was commonly linked—and indeed associated himself—with the culture of national decline. The 'winter of discontent' threatened to destroy his reputation as it had shattered his morale. But in his long and constructive retirement, he came in the 1980s to symbolize traditional communal objectives as the competitive ethic of Thatcherism began to lose its sheen.

All the great themes of post-war Britain—economic struggle and decline; the potentialities and limitations of the post-imperial state; the challenge of social and educational inequality; crises of law and order; relations between government and both sides of industry; the new tensions involving race and the upsurge of Celtic nationalism, on both sides of the Irish Sea; relations with the North Atlantic alliance, Europe, and a changing and newly liberated Commonwealth; the adaptation of an historic civic culture to new intellectual, moral, and sexual norms, and to generational change—all of them found their echo in James Callaghan's career. In each case, he played a major part in the political nation's response, positive or innovative, enthusiastic or resigned. It is scarcely possible to examine any major aspect of Britain's comparative adjustment to recent political, social, economic, and international change without reference to Callaghan's part in it.

His career went through many remarkable fluctuations. In 1945 he was but one of many ambitious unknown spear-carriers in Attlee's army. Thereafter, his career had five significant landmarks. He first made his mark as a significant politician of real stature in his important phase as shadow Colonial Secretary in 1956–61. Here he showed himself to be a genuinely authoritative voice of constructive anti-colonialism, and also built up partnerships with a whole generation of third-world leaders, notably in Africa, which helped to provide a platform for his future advance. As Chancellor in the mid-1960s, a time of much trauma, he was most prominently associated with the devaluation of the pound which led to his resignation and kindled a belief that his career as a mainline figure might be over. But his positive achievements as Chancellor, and his standing in the party, not least as its treasurer, meant that he remained a major figure, always available for the party leadership. His real recovery came not from the infighting over *In Place of Strife* (even though his cool judgement of what the party and the unions would take proved to be correct all along the line) but over Northern Ireland. Here he achieved some brilliant executive successes in that graveyard for British politicians and confirmed himself as Wilson's probable successor. Many felt at the time that, had he stayed on in the Home Office after 1970, a long-term settlement of the dilemmas of modern Ireland would have been achieved.

His stature was reinforced by a fourth phase, his role in promoting a national consensus over the terms of entry into the Common Market. His diplomacy effectively snuffed out Europe as a source of national contention for a decade and a half. It also made him Prime Minister, able to win support across broad sections of the party and the movement. Finally, there was his premiership which confirmed him as a dominant leader. He presided over a notable phase of economic recovery and established himself as a major force in international diplomacy at the time of détente. It also saw his precipitate decline in the face of uncontrolled union power, but still left his reputation as one of the more effective post-war prime ministers comparatively secure. His was a career of remarkable turbulence and undulations, but strength of will and a perceived strength of character saw him rebound from periods of disappointment and demonstrate his capacity in meeting the challenges of the highest post of all.

The office of prime minister is not achieved by being universally amiable. In politics as in sport, nice guys tend to come last. Callaghan had many critics, including within his own party and Cabinet, who viewed him as a bully or worse. Roy Jenkins saw him as an aggressive pike eating up the minnows, with a brooding air of menace. Harold Wilson and Barbara Castle saw him as devious and manœuvring, 'a snake in the grass' in the latter's words—although in that he was merely the recipient of standard criticisms in the supremely unfraternal party that was Labour in the 1960s and perhaps most other times. He was found by some journalists and aides to be unduly touchy and insecure, perhaps reflective of his tough childhood and limited formal education. His circle of friends was not large, with the amiable Merlyn Rees perhaps the closest; some said he attracted a coterie of lesser politicians rather than real intimates. He could be a terrifyingly hard man; he could threaten with a barely concealed hint of menace. Critics would be threatened with total oblivion, their careers reduced to tatters. One of the less appropriate sobriquets for this sometimes difficult and bad-tempered man was 'Sunny Jim'. In that, he resembled a predecessor, Arthur Henderson, 'Uncle Arthur', whose avuncular qualities were not too often on public display.

But he was always capable of relaxing in a remarkably unstuffy and even cheerful way, especially in a gathering when he felt himself among friends. Tony Benn was struck by his naturalness when Prime Minister at a dinner during a trade union gathering. The premier got up to entertain those present with a rollicking version of an old music-hall song:

> I'm the man, the very fat man, who waters the workers' beer.[1]

As MP and as party leader, he could show warmth and thoughtfulness He aroused feelings of genuine affection among colleagues from Hattersley to Tony Benn. He could be spontaneously kind to younger associates when they were plunged into private distress. Prime ministerial official visits to distant lands were notable for his concern for travelling companions, including journalists, when they fell ill or experienced other misfortune. He was quick to commune, slow to condemn. He showed humanity to younger figures like Owen and Hattersley when they were in personal difficulties, just as he did to his old patron Hugh Dalton when he was becoming a marginalized, neglected figure in the twilight of his career. He was often encouraging to the young, consoling and sympathetic to constituents however humble. In the later phase of his career from the election defeat of 1979, a defining moment in his view of the world and himself, he gave a genuine impression of pursuing wider national and international objectives, on grounds of principle, rather than party or personal advantage. He was a generous patron of younger men like John Smith and charitably forgave close friends like Tom McNally who deserted him for the abortive SDP. In his later period he spent much time in promoting good causes, especially educational. Long before the time of his retirement, he had won a general reputation for wise statesmanship, combined with much humanity and common sense.

He had not always been unduly fussy about his associates—the links with his constituent Julian Hodge and later with BCCI showed evidence of carelessness at least. But particularly by contrast with Harold Wilson, he conveyed an air of dignity and integrity which endured to the end. He was certainly anything but a timid man. There was a tough streak of independence of judgement from his time as young rebel in the Inland Revenue Staff Federation, through his clashes with giants like Morrison and Shinwell in the Attlee years, down to his throwing down the gauntlet to the Prime Minister and Chancellor over trade union reform in 1969. But he was never independent-minded for its own sake and always kept lines of recovery open. The roles of poacher and gamekeeper were never irreconcilably distant. The young leader of the New Entrants in the IRSF became a major official of the union three years later. The outspoken critic and temporary pariah who challenged *In Place of Strife* was to end up as Labour's unchallenged leader and prime minister. He was also a brave man, physically as in Northern Ireland in 1969, morally as in upholding the ideas of the Atlantic alliance and British nuclear capability in the face of the left-wing tide in the 1980s. He was nobody's punchball. He would stand up to the most aggressive of adversaries—Manny Shinwell, Roy Welensky,

George Brown, Robert MacNamara, John Prescott—and trade blow for blow.

At the same time, his fundamental talent was as a reconciler and a philosopher of partnership. That, he felt, was his predestined role in the movement. He played his major part in harmonizing the differing perspectives of Gaitskellites and Bevanites in the early 1960s, reconciling different views on Europe in the 1970s, and, less successfully, in keeping Labour's left and right within his administration, creating an effective troika of himself and those two past adversaries, Denis Healey and Michael Foot. He was also a powerful reconciler in the Commonwealth, a major educative force for a generation of African and Asian leaders, and in world affairs a respected honest broker between Kissinger and Carter on the one hand, and Schmidt, Giscard, and European leaders on the other. He helped give the west a credible perspective on international security in Europe and the Middle East, finding a creative response which would combine the needs of collective defence with strategic disarmament. He was a little-known background force behind the Camp David Agreement between Israel and Egypt. Throughout he was one of the major communicators of his time, a crisp and confident speaker, good in committee, at home with the new media, though at times defensive and unduly guarded in meeting bodies of professionals, including academics. He bridged the transition from the street corner meeting through the impact of television and Commons formal debates to the sedate gentility of the House of Lords. He was equally effective in all of them.

Callaghan was wont to write himself down intellectually. This probably reflected a feeling of defensiveness arising from the fact that he never went to university.[2] It was a fact that weighed on him, needlessly but repeatedly. It was the first thing he mentioned to Cledwyn Hughes in the emotional aftermath of being elected party leader in 1976. In some ways, he echoed the thoughts and self-assessment of Stanley Baldwin, someone he admired in his youth and who was inclined to observe, 'I am not a clever man.' Indeed, Baldwin cleverly constructed an image of himself as a simple-minded country philosopher, most at home looking at pigs and Herefordshire cattle and reading the homespun novels of Mary Webb (even though he was himself a Cambridge graduate from an industrial background as an ironmaster). It was a major component of his political appeal. Like Callaghan, he reinvented himself as a plain farmer. 'Honest Stan' was contrasted with the devious methods of Lloyd George to whom Tories were inclined to attach Lord Salisbury's remark about Iain Macleod, that he was 'too clever by half'. Callaghan's was in fact a powerful, if untrained, mind. He deeply impressed the civil servants in every department in which he worked by his analytical powers in getting to grips with a question, absorbing rapidly large quantities of detailed and technical information, pursuing officials and colleagues relentlessly. He had a Socratic method of posing seminal questions but would then reach a clear and decisive conclusion. Ian Bancroft over Treasury finance, Brian Cubbon over penal reform, Bryan Cartledge on east–west relations, Sir Ronald Mason over nuclear weaponry, Sir Kenneth Stowe over prime ministerial leadership—all university-trained mandarins of great intellectual power—testified to Callaghan's qualities in these respects. Bernard Donoughue considered him more formidable than Harold Wilson himself in the way he challenged and interrogated advisers and officials in determining policy.

He may have had an analytical rather than a creative or truly innovative mind. But the intellectual force he showed in such arcane and complex areas as international liquidity and special drawing rights, communal relations in Northern Ireland, or nuclear deterrence and international security in the late 1970s commanded respect. The accounts by Crossman and others sometimes contain contemptuous or patronizing remarks by Gaitskell, Crossman himself, Wilson, and Gordon Walker, all former Oxford dons, about the limitations of Callaghan's intelligence. These perhaps reflect on the social and cultural assumptions of those who made them. The Labour governments between 1964 and 1979 were full of immensely able people, however ineffective in office some of them may have been, but there is never any sign of Callaghan being left behind. On the contrary, he was perhaps those governments' most consistently effective force in relating policy objectives to political practicalities. It might be noted, too, that his close friends and admirers included variously Douglas Jay, Evan Durbin, John Strachey, and Tony Crosland, four of the intellectual giants of British socialism by any standards. Kissinger and Schmidt, two more admirers, were among the most cerebral of international statesmen, while other supporters of his were American savants such as Dick Neustadt and John Kenneth Galbraith. Oxford may have thrown up its critics and failed to offer Callaghan an honorary degree: perhaps he was a victim of Mrs Thatcher's rejection by the university in 1985. But even Oxford might have noted that he was a long-time Fellow of Nuffield. Intellectually, Jim Callaghan was nobody's poodle.

Trying to place Callaghan in the complex typology of British Labour leaders, as was attempted in the past by Continental political scientists such as Robert Michels, Egon Wertheimer, or Max Weber, is not a straightforward exercise. But his own definitions of political leadership provide useful evidence here, in setting him in the context of Labour leadership from Keir Hardie to Tony Blair. It is easiest to state what Callaghan was not. He was never Weber's 'charismatic leader', never a Keir Hardie or Nye Bevan or Michael Foot. He never reached out for the inspirational Celtic revivalism of MacDonald or even Kinnock; indeed it was alien to his more pragmatic temperament. The behaviour of Tony Benn in the 1970s aroused his impatience or even his contempt. Nor was he a socialist intellectual on the model of Gaitskell or Crosland, or for that matter Schmidt or Mitterrand. He was critical of the Continental style of abstract theorizing. There is no one text, either an article or a speech, in which he sets out an ideologically path-breaking credo. Perhaps his brief chapter on 'Equality' in *Socialism: The British Way* (1948) comes closest to it. Neither was he a technocrat on the model of Wilson or perhaps Jay. He was never especially involved with policy-making in the years of opposition. In government he was more interested in identifying problems or else placing them in a broad global setting than in finding the technical machinery to provide the linkage in between. This led Barbara Castle, somewhat extraordinarily, to allege that Callaghan felt in later life he was not really interested in politics at all (she seems to assume he meant political theory).[3] He was inclined to criticize himself as being a 'generalist', able to turn his hand to anything home or away, rather than someone with a specialist expertise in any one area.

Nor was he an organizer on the model of Herbert Morrison. Indeed, while able to keep the party machine in Cardiff in excellent repair, he remained detached from Transport House and he was far less exercised than Wilson over plots, leaks, or internal machinations. As a young MP he was not an apparatchik but a signed-up member of the awkward squad. He moved up the party hierarchy through his hold over parliament and his empathy for the unions, not through the centralizing imperatives of a mass political organization. Whatever Callaghan's career embodies, therefore, it does not illustrate Michels's theory of the 'iron law of oligarchy' (which was, after all, the theory of a distinctly disillusioned German Social Democrat). His origins did not lie in local government either, as Morrison's did. Although pre-eminently a union man, he was not exactly a trade union politician: the Inland Revenue Federation was a minor, white-collar union relatively unimportant in Labour circles. His background as a union official left a legacy of a distinctive negotiating style which his civil servants noticed when he was a Cabinet minister. But it was not until he became party treasurer in 1967 that he developed a close and permanent relationship with the major trade unions. A Welsh colleague like Jim Griffiths, a former miners' agent, represented a very different point of departure. A coalface worker from the Amman valley inherited a sociological frame of reference that contrasted sharply with that of the *déraciné* Inland Revenue tax clerk. Callaghan was always the voice of something much more than bread-and-butter 'economism' or, in its native version, 'Labourism'. He stood, therefore, on the margin of the classic Bevin-type view of the Labour Alliance. At the same time, his roots in the movement and its institutions were such that he did not easily identify either with Tony Blair's New Labour of the 1990s with its attempt to draw a line under the whole of Labour's history prior to the Sedgfield election of 1983. Jim Callaghan belongs neither to the 'long march' nor to the 'long goodbye' interpretation of British socialism.

What perhaps he best symbolizes is something more familiar to German and Scandinavian political tradition—the classic, professional social democratic politician, on the model of Germany's Herbert Wehner, France's Pierre Mauroy, or Sweden's Per Albin Hansson. Hugh Gaitskell's description of Herbert Morrison—'the nearest we have to a Scandinavian Socialist leader'[4]—applies perhaps even more directly to Jim Callaghan. This quality gave him a reassuring solidity that was a close personal bond between himself and Helmut Schmidt. Indeed, Callaghan's stature in Germany in the 1980s was perhaps higher than in his own country. Egon Wertheimer, writing on Snowden, Clynes, or Jimmy Thomas in 1929, would have recognized him immediately.[5] He was propelled immediately from a minor trade union into the House of Commons and it was there, in conjunction with his Cardiff base, where he used the skills of the American 'ward-heeler' without the corruption, that he built up his ascendancy. With a network of local allies, he ensured that Militant in Cardiff were confronted and outmanœuvred. Nationally, he had a instinctive rapport with the political movement at all levels, from the local management meeting to the parliamentary lobby. He was a great Commons tearoom operator, with a gift for appealing to the most humdrum, insignificant backbencher and making him a friend for life. He was almost always outstanding in his command of the party conference. The Labour Party was for him a complete universe, almost a church, from his entry into parliament until he became father of the House. It was his strong tower of refuge after he left the Baptist Church. In the party, he never neglected a detail, never miscalculated the votes, never forgot a face. He seemed to know in minute detail the background of every backbencher, every constituent, every grandchild. Journalists have said that he became party leader because of his total identification with the movement at its most humdrum—the drab committee rooms, the peeling wallpaper, the stale tea. 'Jim loves that kind of thing.'

But his ability to enter into that world, with genuine humanity and without the patronizing quality that some of his Oxbridge-trained colleagues conveyed when they met ordinary voters, was central to his progress. He was in that sense the most complete and representative Labour figure since Arthur Henderson, whom by temperament and outlook he part resembled. Henderson indeed was in some ways a role model for him when he encountered the serried ranks of the mandarins of the Foreign Office. Like Uncle Arthur, Big Jim insisted that they read the Labour Party manifesto on his arrival amongst them. He would show them who was in charge, where the buck really stopped. After all, as he told Roger Stott, the two of them had been elected by the people. He emerged (and felt himself to have done so) from an authentic, rooted working class. This was not the Oxford world of Wilson or the Hampstead clique of Gaitskell, not the journalistic *demi-monde* of Foot, not the university student politics of Kinnock, not the Scottish advocate's domain of John Smith, certainly not the fashionable chattering-class world of London chic, but the genuine human and financial deprivation of a broken family in the backstreets of Portsmouth. Callaghan himself felt, as perhaps John Major also did in the 1990s, that he had risen up through the ranks of the dispossessed, a world of hard knocks and hard lessons, shaped by childhood poverty and a wide experience of life in peace and in war. It was something of a bond between the two men. He knew his own people. As Prime Minister, he could tell middle-class colleagues, with an air of authority, 'That's not what they are saying in the working men's clubs',[6] and they took his word.

Like Eric Hoffer's *True Believer*, Callaghan could project himself, perfectly credibly, as Labour's unknown soldier, symbolic of the revolution of our time. He believed implicitly in Labour as a 'movement'. Like Arthur Henderson, inventor of the famous phrase 'This Great Movement of Ours', he had deep roots in the unions and regarded the unbreakable unity of the old Labour alliance of the socialist bodies and the trade unions as essential for social progress. Only with the near-anarchy of the public sector unions, and their new style of leadership, during the winter of discontent, did he see that the world had changed and that the party must adapt with it. He recognized the end of the block vote, and promoting 'one member, one vote', as pursued by Kinnock, Smith, and Blair as inevitable, although he viewed them without undue enthusiasm. The unions, he felt, had been a force for stability in an agitated and rootless world.

Finally, like Arthur Henderson again, he fits into the typology of Labour leaders by linking political professionalism and the union alliance with a wider international vision. This is a genuinely pioneering aspect of Callaghan's political outlook, which links him with a much earlier phase of Labour's history, the 'brave new world' ethos of MacDonald and the UDC after the First World War. It was stimulated by Spain and the challenge of fascism in the 1930s, then by wartime service in the Far East. It was reinforced by his understanding of African nationalism in the 1950s and his knowledge of the Middle East, crystallized further by his ties with American political and financial circles when in government, and demonstrated anew by his new European alliances in the 1970s and his contacts with the Chinese after his retirement. Each phase of his governmental experience drove home the essential connection between domestic change and a changing international scene in which the settlements of Potsdam and Bretton Woods were being left behind. At times, he could seem among the most insular of British politicians. Lee Kuan Yew, a stern critic, thought his lack of feel for Singapore, with its teeming crowds, was very noticeable,[7] while his 'language of Chaucer' rhetoric during the Common Market debates seemed just a crude pandering to insular prejudice. He did not give a lead to the British public on Europe, even though he handled the 'renegotiation' of membership terms in 1974–5 with immense skill. He had no great grasp of foreign languages or culture.

Yet a genuine and deeply informed concern with foreign and colonial issues was for him not just the classic elder statesman's form of self-indulgence, but a real key to understanding an interdependent world. It was above all the aspect of his career on which he liked to dwell when he met former civil service aides on social occasions during his retirement, and with reason. From his time as a courageous backbencher in the late 1940s, he was anything but an unthinking cold-warrior. As Prime Minister thirty years later, he was a natural participant in a world of détente and disengagement. In his retirement, his pronouncements on the global economy, on international indebtedness, and the roots of regional and continental instability showed this important dimension to his thinking. Like most British politicians, for Callaghan politics like charity began at home. But they did not stay there. In his later years, he was widely thought to compare favourably with his immediate predecessor and with his successor in playing the role of ex-prime minister. He neither milked the media through television series or well-paid works of reminiscence, nor did he travel the globe as an itinerant ideologue. He focused on practical themes in public debate, drew on his experience to show their historical roots and wider significance, and was always on hand to offer advice to his successors. As a senior figure, Callaghan, controversial and often condemned in his earlier political days, was a model of his kind.

The usual stereotype of his political outlook was that he was a conservative figure. Dick Leonard once described him as 'Labour's Conservative';[8] Tony Benn would often dismiss him as an old Tory reactionary although admittedly he extended this description to almost all the Labour leadership at the time. Without doubt Callaghan approached life from a traditional moral standpoint. The imperial background of the navy and of Portsmouth, the social quiescence preached by the Baptist chapel brethren in his childhood, public-spirited though they were, did not create an adventurous outlook. They lent his every instinct a deep, almost unquestioned patriotism. He seemed robustly British in office, a kind of pacific Palmerston, most at home in defending British interests and institutions from the criticisms of unthinking Europeans or complaining African nationalists, but free from the bellicosity of a Morrison or a Shinwell over Iran or Suez. He wanted to retain British influence in the world, mainly in diplomatic and economic terms; but he also stood for no surrender on Gibraltar, Belize, and most of all the Falklands. He often felt depressed in his old age that his career had coincided with a relentless history of national decline. In the exciting, headlong years of his early period as a backbencher after 1945, Britain was one of the Big Three, taking the lead in NATO and the European Western Union, granting independence to the Indian subcontinent, creating the National Health Service, nationalizing the coal mines and the railways, offering an example to the world of a middle way of social democratic change while playing Greece to America's Rome. Those days were a world we had lost.

He was conservative in his views on many public issues. He was slow to revise his diagnosis of the British economy, especially of the international role of the pound, although criticisms of the failure to devalue in 1964 have invariably been superficial and coloured by hindsight. On the trade unions, on devolution for Scotland and Wales, on entry into Europe, he was instinctively resistant to change. But he was also quick to adapt, as over the Common Market where he ended up almost an enthusiast. In industrial relations, he was cautious in trying to reform a traditional adversarial system in stark contrast to the co-determination of Germany or even the accord of Australia. His failing lay not in opposing the 1969 Industrial Relations Bill (which was unworkable in a way that Jack Jones and Len Murray understood and that *bienpensant* middle-class academics have usually failed to recognize) but in not presenting any alternative, and also perhaps in not throwing sufficient weight behind the Bullock report on industrial democracy. The traditional stereotype of British leaders of workers and bosses, Us and Them, with the twain never meeting, was unwittingly reinforced. Furthermore, the changed character of British unionism, part of what Vernon Bogdanor has identified as the destructive 'new individualism' of Britain in the 1970s, replacing the harmonies and disciplines of Callaghan's social democratic Britain with an almost anarchic self-centredness,[9] was beyond his experience or power to control. His message of partnership and co-operation, 'pulling through together' as in 1940, seemed a requiem to a lost world. It took the bludgeon of Mrs Thatcher's 1980s legislation to provide an undoubtedly effective alternative.

Again, Callaghan was not down to the 1970s an advocate of sweeping changes in the machinery of government, the Commons, local government, a new status for Scotland and Wales, the civil service, a bill of rights, freedom of information, least of all the monarchy. In the the 1980s and 1990s, he was deeply antipathetic to thoughts of republicanism and deplored the damaging effects on the common weal of the royal troubles in the 1990s. He felt thoroughly at home with the comfortable conventions of an unwritten constitution. Britain, he liked to say, was 'a back of the envelope country'. By the 1990s, though, his views had progressed through changing circumstances, notably on Scottish devolution. Perhaps the most fateful aspect of this institutional caution was the inability in his last phase to reform or update the Labour Party. He left it riddled by entryism, a prey to often anti-parliamentary inner caucuses, increasingly out of touch with the electors both in its inflated industrial and its diminishing political wings. Constituency Labour parties like Bermondsey had turned into client-run rotten boroughs. Critics argued that in sabotaging the attempt to reform the unions in 1969 and reinforcing the corporate mould he had made matters worse. Eighteen years of Thatcherite and post-Thatcherite hegemony were the indirect outcome. At least, though, Callaghan understood the dangers, and articulated them even in his advanced years. As Prime Minister he was a consistent, if often unsuccessful, educator. Labour's failure to react was a collective one, with responsibility shared by influential figures such as Healey and Crosland, not to mention Harold Wilson, along with others who fled the battlefield to find a temporary bolthole in the Social Democratic Party or else left politics altogether.

He found many of the wider cultural changes of the time hard to accept. An unlikely symbol of the 1960s, he became the unwitting celebrant of a more liberal culture to which in some ways he had led a principled resistance. For all his empathy for young people, the rebelliousness of the young, not just their methods of violent disruption, but their long hair, untidiness, and dabbling in drugs, were alien to him. Here was a Home Secretary particularly opposed to permissiveness, one indeed who became the champion of the silent majority rejecting experimental or anarchic lifestyles. The Baptists of Portsmouth were fighting back. Here, too, was a natural spokesman for the Police Federation. On race relations, he tilted the scales in the direction of the exclusion of black and brown Commonwealth immigrants, and the change stuck. He also did not adjust easily to the agenda of sexual and social change heralded by Roy Jenkins's time at the Home Office. Aspects of feminism he found hard to take, which may have spilled over indirectly into his relations with women politicians like Barbara Castle or Margaret Thatcher. On social policy, he was slow to respond to the woman's view on child benefit payments. Like most men of his generation he held a broadly traditional view of the role of women, and feared for the impact upon society of broken homes, single mothers, divorce, and unrestrained sexual emancipation. But in this he probably reflected the views of the majority of the party and the nation, not the man and woman on the legendary omnibus but the prime-time viewer in the living room. The partial reaction that set in against permissiveness from the 1970s, notably amongst the middle-class educated young who rejected protest for professional advancement, was a victory for Callaghan's vision of Britain, or more appropriately England.

But he had the flexibility, the basic humanity and decency, to move with the times. He had the supreme politician's virtue of being able to adapt. He did not like some of the cultural phenomena of the day especially among young people, but he accepted them with tolerance and good grace. He was invariably very effective with student audiences. In some areas he had strong reforming instincts, too. The Kenyan Asians episode notwithstanding, his personal instincts were also strongly opposed to racial prejudice, as his experience in Cardiff shows. As Home and Foreign Secretary, he made a positive contribution to good race relations, from the Race Relations Board to the ending of sporting and other contacts with South Africa. His premiership saw in 1976 Britain's most important measure to combat racial discrimination, with the setting up of the Commission on Racial Equality. Again, he was always a powerful opponent of capital punishment, prepared to stand up to the mighty Herbert Morrison on the issue when it might have cost him political advancement. As Home Secretary he ensured that the rope disappeared from British history for ever. The relationship with the Police Federation did not lead him in any way to soften his views on humanitarian issues. He was repelled by the political persecution of homosexuals. He hated violent activity like bull-fighting, professional boxing, and fox-hunting. He transcended the narrow religious constraints of his upbringing. Indeed he became a notable exponent of a more tolerant approach to communal confessionalism in Northern Ireland, while his breadth of vision made him an important bridge between Arabs and Jews in the 1970s. A very English figure, he became a warm supporter of the cultural values and national identity of his adopted Wales. He was much the most influential Englishman in Welsh politics since Gladstone was in residence at Hawarden Castle.

Just as his political and cultural instincts were in some ways deeply conservative and patriotic, he could also be dramatically innovative. He had a strong commitment to civil liberties, shown in Britain when he was Home Secretary handling student protest and as Foreign Secretary in relation to the revolution in Portugal. He kept the activities of the security services in check after the excitements of the Wilson period, and imposed his authority over MI5. At times, he could be the almost single-handed motor of policy change. Over African nationalism, over Northern Ireland especially, over the prophetic Ruskin speech on educational standards in 1976, in the handling of economic policy from 1976 including the invention of the Lever seminars, in the re-examination of Keynesianism, he could be an agent of quite startling originality. Indeed, by comparison with many of his political contemporaries, it is his reforming zeal rather than stand-pat complacency that stands out. It has abiding legacies in everyday life from 'Cats eyes' on roads to decimal coinage. In merging a rooted commitment to patriotic values with a willingness to experiment through the interventionist role of the state, he made an important contribution to British social democracy, and thereby to the stability of his country in the later twentieth century.

The ultimate justification for Callaghan's career lies in the view one takes of the much-maligned British democratic socialist tradition. Cautious and pragmatic though he was by temperament, Jim Callaghan's career shows that there was in his day a long-term British ideological impulse that felt itself to be not just progressive but genuinely socialist. Recent research has shown how the Attlee government, along with its supporters such as Callaghan after 1945, felt itself to be a socialist administration, partly generated by the wartime consensus in the undogmatic British fashion. This belief straddled leftists such as Bevan, centrists such as Dalton, and right-wingers such as Morrison.[10] Callaghan's abiding lifelong creed embodied this kind of socialism. For him, as for Jim Griffiths, 1945 was 'Year One'. It was his abiding historical marker and reference point as Ernest Bevin's was 1926, Attlee's was 1918, and the warm-hearted Citizen Foot's appeared at times to be 1789.

British Labour's dominant ethos, reinforced in the war, and increasingly popular in the New Labour rhetoric of the 1990s, was that of 'community'. It sprang from an amalgam of Fabian 'efficiency' and late Victorian social Christianity, an abiding touchstone from Keir Hardie to Tony Blair. Its rhetorical keywords in Callaghan's speeches were such words as 'partnership' and 'co-operation'. It embodied a kind of moral cohesion, a social contract writ large. In the 1970s, when its energy was in manifest decay, this creed contrasted with the kind of confrontation personified variously by Margaret Thatcher and Tony Benn and foreshadowed the imperatives of New Labour in the 1990s. It was founded on the premiss that there was indeed such a thing as society. It showed that, contrary to Roy Jenkins's Dimbleby lecture in 1979, the decent centre could indeed hold in the face of the passionate intensity of extremists on right and left. Its roots were ultimately ethical and egalitarian rather than economic. Its original inspiration lay in the late nineteenth-century nonconformist radicalism symbolized variously by Keir Hardie and Lloyd George, rather than in the Keynesian programme of the 1930s planners. It was this aspect that made Evan Durbin, himself a Keynesian-style economist of much distinction, but also the son of the Baptist manse who had been named after Evan Roberts, the Welsh revivalist of 1905, more congenial to Callaghan than other contemporaries such as Gaitskell, Meade, or perhaps Jay.

But it was a sense of community rooted not in abstract centrism such as that taken up briefly by the SDP or some versions of 1990s 'New Labour' but in real structures and living organisms—families, neighbourhoods, regions, communal loyalties, embodying those kinder, gentler values of which the celebrant was George Orwell during the war in *The Lion and the Unicorn*, or perhaps J. B. Priestley in his radio *Postscripts*. At the same time, Callaghan was tough-minded and tough-spirited enough to see that these old virtues needed the vigorous stimulus of positive government. Amongst his formative reading, none is more important than the writings of Harold Laski, a libertarian socialist committed to both pluralism and public leadership, erratic prophet and visionary of the 'revolution of our time'. As Prime Minister, Callaghan was the heir of the young idealist who had gone with Audrey to listen to Laski in the Kingsway Hall or Friends' House in the 1930s, or excitedly plunged into the bulky pages of *The Grammar of Politics* while munching his sandwiches on Tower Hill.

Jim Callaghan is a major agent of the continuities and achievements of the British socialist tradition. He is a key exhibit in the alternative version of our history that it provides, one that is seldom included in the historical core curriculum invented in the Thatcher era. This tradition, the social democratic 'middle way' absorbed by Liberals and One-Nation Tories too, is perhaps Britain's main ideological contribution to the world in the twentieth century. Perhaps it has been of more enduring significance in history than British resistance in two world wars, which after all reflected a very different system of values and international power systems. It has powerfully influenced world civilization in a way the fiercely self-critical British have often underestimated.

Callaghan's heritage of socialism took its often unacknowledged point of origin from the New Liberals at the turn of the century, associated with men like Hobson, Hobhouse, Masterman, and Chiozza Money. This sought to give Liberalism a collectivist rather than an individualist ethic, and to generate a more positive view of the state and a Darwinian, evolutionary view of society. It focused on the social injustice, the poverty, malnutrition, ignorance, and unemployment, that unregulated Victorian capitalism had left largely untouched. It directed the attention of concerned middle-class Christians to 'how the other half lived'. But British social democratic socialism, especially through the writings of the Fabians and later Tawney, pressed on where the New Liberals left off. The latter had very little to say about industrial relations, the role of the unions, or the redistribution of political and economic power. They had to yield to the fledgeling and disregarded Labour Party over the 1906 Trades Disputes Act. Their economics and their sociology were half-developed. The developmental potential of the state was largely ignored.

In consequence, it is striking that Callaghan and his major contemporaries were in a sense ideologically self-contained. Callaghan for one never referred to his Liberal or progressive inheritance. He did not express retrospective endorsement for the Lloyd George brand of radicalism, and never echoed Tony Blair's enthusiasm for a rainbow coalition of progressives going back to the New Liberalism of pre-1914. His creed was uniquely that of the British non-Marxist ethical socialist tradition, Morris and Blatchford, Laski and Tawney, embellished by Shaw and Wells, with a residual flavouring of Dickens and the New Testament. For men and women of Callaghan's generation, the themes that marked them off from Edwardian Liberalism were decisive. This meant moving on from the contributory insurance schemes and partial arbitration boards of Lloyd George-style reformism, and creating a truly comprehensive welfare state, new forms of industrial dialogue, a dynamic role for the state in the ownership and management of industry and public utilities, alongside a peaceful and civilized retreat from empire in a spirit of interracial partnership and development. It also implied, in changing attitudes to the rise of the trade unions, a different perception of the relationship of the political process to the phenomenon of class.[11] For well over a generation, from the late 1930s to the late 1970s, this reformist creed dominated British public rhetoric, on the right as well as the centre-left. Some called it a consensus.

More important still, through its massive impact on the new generation of third-world leaders with whom Callaghan's ties were particularly close, it made Labour Britain the international symbol of the democratic socialist 'middle way' between capitalism and communism. It thus provided an ideological vanguard for future generations across the world. Daniel Moynihan, the American sociologist and Democratic senator, noticed this in the early 1960s. He pointed to the combined roles of the Fabian Society, the *New Statesman*, and the London School of Economics (to which others would add Bush House). Laski, Tawney, and Rita Hinden, with men like Brailsford or Brockway in reserve, were agents of ideological change in Africa, Asia, and the Caribbean when old advocates of empire, from Churchill downwards, were regarded as anachronistic and irrelevant. The Churchillian ethos, removed from the drawer for public veneration at the time of the anniversaries of VE and VJ days, stirred nostalgic English nationalists and evoked past imperial glories, but it was never meant for export. Churchill, after all, had never actually visited most of his cherished empire since the death of Queen Victoria. For all his passion for India, he never set foot in the country after 1897; he never saw an African colony after 1908. By contrast, the more subdued message of the consensual democrats of British Labour, and their intellectual heirs, had contemporary relevance and meaning. It was potentially a dynamic creed, and the impact of even a naturally cautious man like Callaghan almost inspirational in the third world.

Conversely, politicians like Callaghan were after 1945 able to blend these values at home with highly traditional views on law and order, permissiveness, institutions of all kinds, and to give them an aura of patriotism. The symbols and myths of national identity were prised away from the grip of the racialist and imperialist right.[12] Unlike the bitter aftermath of 1914–18, which Attlee and his colleagues well recalled, this time a people's peace had followed a people's war. It was a somewhat circumscribed programme, and in the late 1970s appeared to be falling into total discredit amidst a mass of evidence of British ungovernability that some Americans even compared with that in Chile. If the British wished to celebrate a people's peace, they did not feel that Moss Evans or Arthur Scargill were particularly appropriate symbols of it. Yet the socialist tradition did play an important part in keeping Britain as a remarkably stable, internally peaceful society in a disintegrating world, when crises and violence racked almost every other nation from France to the United States. The unions, the co-ops, and Labour-run local authorities were vital agents of it. So in time were leftish pressure groups like Shelter. Great Britain, in its own fashion, managed to avoid both internal insurrection and Bonapartism. It threw up neither Malcolm X nor President de Gaulle. Confronted with Danny the Red and Colonel Stirling, the flesh of the average British citizen positively refused to creep. In the 1980s, when the passion of the extra-parliamentary left and the dogmatism of the free-market Thatcherites both began to recede, and the new panacea of the SDP dissolved almost overnight, it was from within the revisionist democratic socialist tradition, as variously redefined by Kinnock, Smith, and especially Tony Blair, that the counter-culture of the centre-left managed to rebuild and kindle a spark of hope.

Callaghan, like all contemporary politicians, made mistakes, sometimes from overconfidence. Many of them came in 1978–9, and they cost him his job. He suffered from holding the supreme office at a time of especial difficulty when he was perhaps too old to strike out against his adversaries. Of his performance during the 'winter of discontent' he was later fiercely critical. He would say sadly, 'I let the country down.' Despite successes in economic and foreign policy, his government heralded almost two decades of Labour in Opposition.

For all that, his career was one of achievement, not so much in dramatic legislative action but in helping to consolidate the public mood of a lifetime. Macaulay's *History of England* had seen the events of 1688 and 1832 as Britain's two preserving revolutions in political and constitutional terms. They generated strategic change in order to conserve. In his way, Jim Callaghan also embodied Macaulay's credo. He was a key figure in Britain's preserving social revolution of the later twentieth century. After the confrontational politics of the late 1970s and the 1980s, his legacy seemed more attractive, and it had been built up without his personal reputation being seriously tarnished as had happened with Harold Wilson. His life was in itself a marvellous story of how a poor boy from the working-class backstreets of a provincial town could emerge from relative poverty and a broken home to capture supreme political power. More even than Lloyd George, his life is a triumph for the 'cottage-bred man'. But it is also a parable of and commentary on his country's recent history. It tells us in human terms precisely how, why, and when England arose. It illustrates the schizoid quality of *fin de siècle* Britain, its commitment to the past and its capacity to renew. It shows how both have been reconciled in an ageless Burkean continuity. Through the career of one tough, humane individual, it offers an explanation for both the inertia and the stability of the British people in times like these.

1. Tony Benn broadcast, reading excerpts from his diary, BBC Radio Four, 6 June 1994.

2. Edmund Dell, my predecessor but one at Queen's, Oxford, emphasizes this point in *The Chancellors*, 305.

3. Castle, *Fighting All the Way*, 492–3.

4. *The Diary of Hugh Gaitskell*, 332 ('1952–4 continued').

5. Egon Wertheimer, *Portrait of the Labour Party* (London, 1929).

6. *Guardian*, 4 Mar. 1978, in which Callaghan is reported as rebuking Barbara Castle over her wish to raise government expenditure.

7. Interview with Lee Kuan Yew, Istana Negara, Singapore, 21 Sept. 1993.

8. Dick Leonard, 'Labour's Conservative', *The Economist*, 28 Apr. 1979.

9. See Vernon Bogdanor, 'The Fall of the Heath Government and the End of the Post-war Settlement', in Anthony Seldon and Stuart Ball, *The Heath Government* (London, 1996).

10. See Stephen Brooke, *Labour's War* (Oxford, 1992); id., 'Evan Durbin: Reassessing a Labour "Revisionist" ', *20th Century British History*, 7/1 (1996); Martin Francis, *Ideas and Policies under Labour, 1945–1951, Building A New Britain* (Manchester, 1997); Geoffrey Foote, *The Labour Party's Political Thought: A History* (Beckenham, 1986), 191 ff.; Nick Tiratsoo (ed.), *The Attlee Years* (London, 1991); idem, *From Blitz to Blair* (1997).

11. On the growing gulf between Progressive Liberals and socialists between the wars, see the excellent discussion in Michael Freeden, *Liberalism Divided* (Oxford, 1986), esp. 177–222.

12. For a superb (and successful) attempt to reclaim patriotism and national identity for the British left, see Raphael Samuel (ed.), *Patriotism*, 3 vols., History Workshop series (London, 1991) and idem, *Theatres of Memory* (London, 1994).

Select Bibliography

The Callaghan Papers originally consisted of two substantial collections. The main archive was the 38 boxes deposited in the House of Lords Record Office, which cover all aspects of Lord Callaghan's career from the 1930s to 1980. There was also a lesser collection of 17 boxes covering his activities from his retirement as party leader in November 1980 onwards, deposited in the British Library of Political and Economic Science. Both collections (together with a few smaller items) were in 1996 brought together, to be catalogued and put on permanent deposit in the Bodleian Library, Oxford. In my footnotes, I have cited references to the HLRO and the BLPES but these, of course, will in time be superseded.

A. MANUSCRIPT COLLECTIONS

I. PRIVATE PAPERS

Lord Attlee papers (Bodleian Library, Oxford, and Churchill College, Cambridge).
Lord Boyd of Merton papers (Bodleian Library, Oxford).
Sir Alec Cairncross diary (private possession, courtesy of Sir Alec Cairncross).
Lord Cledwyn papers (National Library of Wales, Aberystwyth).
Frank Cousins papers (Modern Records Centre, University of Warwick).
Arthur Creech Jones papers (Rhodes House Library, Oxford).
Anthony Crosland papers (British Library of Political and Economic Science).
Hugh Dalton papers (British Library of Political and Economic Science).
Desmond Donnelly papers (National Library of Wales, Aberystwyth).
Hugh Gaitskell papers (formerly at Nuffield College, Oxford).
Lord George-Brown papers (Bodleian Library, Oxford).
Lord Gladwin of Clee papers (private possession, courtesy of Lord Gladwin).
Anthony Greenwood papers (Bodleian Library, Oxford).
James Griffiths papers (National Library of Wales, Aberystwyth).
Professor Ian Little papers (private possession, courtesy of Professor Little).
Lord Tonypandy papers (National Library of Wales, Aberystwyth).
Sir Roy Welensky papers (Rhodes House Library, Oxford).

The Harold Wilson papers in the Bodleian Library, Oxford, were being catalogued and were not available to researchers.

2. PUBLIC RECORDS

Jimmy Carter Library, Atlanta, Georgia
White House Central Files: name files.

Gerald R. Ford Library, Ann Arbor, Michigan
Presidential papers: Kissinger-Scowcroft files, Savage files, Seidman files.

Lyndon Baines Johnson Library, Austin, Texas
Secretary Henry T. Fowler papers.
Presidential papers: President's personal papers, Cabinet papers, National Security files.
Oral History and Audio-Visual History collections.

Public Record Office, Kew
Admiralty: ADM 1; ADM 167 (Board of Admiralty).
Cabinet Office: CAB 128 (Cabinet Conclusions, 1945–51, 1964–6); CAB 129 (Cabinet papers, 1945–51, 1964–6); CAB 130 (Cabinet Economic Affairs Committee, 1964–6); CAB 134 (Cabinet Emergencies Committee, 1948–9).
Colonial Office: CO 926.
Dominions Office: DO 121.
Foreign Office: FO 800 (Bevin papers).
Ministry of Transport: MT 108 (Road Safety Committee).
Prime Minister's Office: PREM 8 (1945–51); PREM 11, 13 (1964–6).
Treasury: T 171 (Budget and Finance Bill papers); T 225 (Defence Policy and Materials Division).

3. OTHER PAPERS

Bank of Wales papers (courtesy of Mr Gerald Rees).
Confederation of British Industry papers (Modern Records Centre, University of Warwick).
Inland Revenue Staff Federation papers (Douglas Houghton House, London (courtesy of Mr Clive Brooke), and MRC, University of Warwick).
Labour Party: National Executive Committee minutes (Labour Party headquarters, now at Museum of Labour History, Manchester).

B. OFFICIAL PAPERS

Hansard, *Parliamentary Debates*, 5th and 6th series.
Hansard, *House of Lords, Official Report*.
Return of the Expenses of Each candidate at the General Election of July 1945 in Great Britain and Northern Ireland, H. of C. 1945–6 (128), xix. 539.
Parliamentary Constituencies (Electors), England, Wales and Northern Ireland, 26 February 1946, H. of C. 1945–6 (88), xx. 547.

Boundary Commission for Wales: Initial Report (Cmd. 7274), H. of C. 1947–8, xv. 895.

Federation of Rhodesia and Nyasaland, Constitution Amendment Bill, 1957 (Cmnd. 298), H. of C. 1957–8, xxiv. 145.

Royal Commission on the Police, 1960: Minutes of Evidence and Interim Report (Cmnd. 1222) and *Final Report* (Cmnd. 1728), H. of C. 1960–1, xx. 333, and 1961–2, xx. 515 (Willink report).

Financial Statement for 1964–5 (179), H. of C. 1963–64, xxi. 239.

Children in Trouble (Cmnd. 3601), H. of C. 1967–8, xxix. 149.

Advisory Council on the Penal System, 'The Regime for Long Term Prisoners in Conditions of Maximum Security' (HMSO, 1968) (Radzinowicz report).

Report of the Race Relations Board for 1969–70 (309), H. of C. 1969–70, xv. 145.

Advisory Committee on Drug Dependence, Sub-Committee Report, 1968 (non-parliamentary, Home Office, HMSO, 1969) (Wootton report on cannabis).

Renegotiation of the Terms of Entry into the EEC, 1974 (Cmnd. 5593) H. of C. 1974, iv. 829.

Democracy and Devolution (Cmnd. 5732), H. of C. 1974, v. 85.

Membership of the European Community, Statement by the Prime Minister, 18 Mar. 1975 (Cmnd. 5999), H. of C. 1974–5, ix. 549.

Our Changing Democracy: Devolution in Scotland and Wales (Cmnd. 6348), H. of C. 1975–6, xiv.

Second Amendment to the Articles of Agreement of the International Monetary Fund (Cmnd. 6705), H. of C. 1976–7, viii. 331.

Committee of Inquiry into Industrial Democracy (Cmnd. 6706), H. of C. 1976–7, xvi. 231 (Bullock report).

'The Economy, the Government and Trade Union Responsibilities: Joint Statement by the TUC and the Government', 14 Feb. 1979 (non-parliamentary, Department of Employment, HMSO, 1979).

Falkland Islands Review, Report of a Committee of Privy Counsellors (Cmnd. 8787), H. of C. 1982–3 (Franks report).

Standards in Public Life (Cm. 2850–II), H. of C. 1994–5 (Nolan report).

C. NEWSPAPERS, PERIODICALS, AND REPORTS

1. NEWSPAPERS

Aberdare Leader, *Belfast Telegraph*, *Birmingham Post*, *Cardiff District News*, *Daily Express*, *Daily Herald*, *Daily Guardian* (Freetown, Sierra Leone), *Daily Mirror*, *Daily Telegraph*, *Evening News*, *Evening Standard*, *Financial Times*, *Guardian (Manchester Guardian)*, *Independent*, *Mail on Sunday*, *Manchester Evening News*, *News Chronicle*, *New York Times*, *Northern Echo*, *Observer*, *Penarth News*, *People*, *Portsmouth Evening News*, *Reynolds News*, *South Wales Evening Post*, *Sunday Telegraph*, *Sunday Times*, *Sunderland Echo*, *The Times*, *Wall Street Journal*, *Western Mail*, *Women's Sunday Mirror*.

2. PERIODICALS

AUEW Journal, *African Affairs*, *Ashore and Afloat*, *Banker*, *Bank of England Quarterly Bulletin*, *Cardiff People's Paper*, *Central African Examiner*, *Clarion*, *The Economist*, *Foreign Affairs*, *Forward*, *Labour Bulletin*, *Lloyds Bank Review*, *New Statesman*, *Pergamon Chess Monthly*, *Private Eye*, *Rebecca*, *Socialist Commentary*, *South Wales Echo*, *Spectator*, *Taxes*, *Tribune*, *West African Review*, *Young Socialist*.

3. REPORTS

Annual or quarterly reports of the following organizations:

Bank of Wales (1971–4), British Medical Association (Portsmouth conference, 1923), Chatham House, Labour Party (1944–80), Trades Union Congress (1945–80), University of Wales, Swansea (1987–94), Wiener Library.

D. PUBLISHED BOOKS, PAMPHLETS, AND ARTICLES BY LORD CALLAGHAN

The Enemy Japan., twelve talks, edited with notes for discussion group leaders (Personal Services Department, Admiralty, 1944).

'Trade Unions in Czechoslovakia', in S. G. Duff *et al.*, *Czechoslovakia: Six Studies in Reconstruction* (Fabian Society, London, 1947), 46–54.

'The Approach to Social Equality', in Donald Munro (ed.), *Socialism: The British Way* (London, 1948), 127–52.

'Taxation and the National Debt', in Herbert Tracey (ed.), *The British Labour Party*, vol. ii (London, 1948), 223–38.

Whitleyism: A Study of Joint Consultation in the Civil Service (Fabian Society, London, 1953).

A House Divided: The Dilemma of Northern Ireland (London, 1973).

A Commemorative Symposium on Adam Smith (Kirkcaldy, 1973), 77–81.

Challenges and Opportunities for British Foreign Policy (Fabian Society, London, 1975).

'The Ruskin Speech', *Education*, 22 Oct. 1976.

Foreword to Granville Eastwood, *Harold Laski* (London, 1977), vii–ix.

'Der Demokratische Sozialismus und die Wiedergeburt Grossbritanniens' (Democratic Socialism and the Rebirth of Britain) in Richard Lowenthal (ed.), *Demokratischer Sozialismus in den achtziger Jahren* (Cologne, 1979), 79–102 (festschrift for Willy Brandt's 65th birthday, including chapters by Schmidt, Palme, Gonzales, den Uyl, Peres, Soares, Kreisky, Mitterrand, Craxi, etc.).

'The World Summit in Mexico', *Round Table* (July 1981), 208–15.

'Cumber and Variableness', in *The Home Office: Perspectives on Policy and Administration* (Royal Institute of Public Administration, London, 1982), 9–20.

The Political Leader, foreword by Walter Mondale (Minneapolis, 1982).

Democracy and Leadership: Our Interdependent World (Bharatiya Vidya Bhavan, Bombay, 1982).

Defence and Disarmament: We Need to Think Again (Cardiff Fabian Society, 1982).

The Individual and the Institution (St George's House, Windsor, lecture, 1983).
Trade Unions, Decision-Making and Democracy, Ernest Bevin Memorial Lecture, (Mirror Group Newspapers, London, 1985).
Meeting the Challenge of the Third World (Grindlay's bank address, St Helier, 1985).
Time and Chance (London, 1987) (autobiography).
'The Education Debate I', in Michael Williams, Richard Daugherty, and Frank Banks (eds.), *Continuing the Education Debate* (Cassell Educational, London, 1992), 9–16.
Making Education Britain's Top Priority, Ruskin speech twentieth anniversary lecture (University of London Institute of Education, 1996).
'Address given at the new Lloyd George Museum', in *David Lloyd George: The Llangstumdwy Lecture, 1990–1996* (Caernarfon, 1997), pp. 1–5.

In addition, Lord Callaghan wrote many hundreds of more ephemeral articles in newspapers, periodicals, etc.

E. BIOGRAPHIES, MEMOIRS, AND DIARIES

Place of publication London unless otherwise stated.

Abse, Leo, *Private Member* (1973).
Barnett, Joel, *Inside the Treasury* (1982).
Benn, Tony, *Years of Hope: Diaries, Papers and Letters, 1940–1962*, ed. Ruth Winstone (1994).
—— *Out of the Wilderness: Diaries, 1963–67*, ed. R. Winstone (1987).
—— *Office without Power: Diaries, 1968–72*, ed. R. Winstone (1988).
—— *Against the Tide: Diaries, 1973–76*, ed. R. Winstone (1989).
—— *Conflicts of Interest: Diaries, 1977–80*, ed. R. Winstone (1990).
—— *The End of an Era: Diaries, 1980–90*, ed. R. Winstone (1992).
Brivati, Brian, *Hugh Gaitskell* (1996).
Brown, Colin, *Fighting Talk: The Biography of John Prescott* (1997).
Brown, George, *In my Way* (1971).
Brzezinski, Zbigniew, *Power and Principle. Memoirs of the National Security Advisor, 1977–81* (1983).
Burns, Sir Alan, *Colonial Civil Servant* (1949).
Campbell, John, *Nye Bevan and the Mirage of British Socialism* (1987).
—— *Edward Heath* (1993).
Carter, Jimmy, *Keeping Faith: Memoirs of a President* (New York, 1982).
Castle, Barbara, *The Castle Diaries, 1964–70* (1984).
—— *The Castle Diaries, 1974–76* (1980).
—— *Fighting All the Way* (1994).
Cole, John, *As it Seemed to Me* (1995).
Crosland, Susan, *Tony Crosland* (1982).
Crossman, Richard, *The Backbench Diaries of Richard Crossman, 1951–64*, ed. Janet Morgan (1981).

—— *Diaries of a Cabinet Minister*, ed. Janet Morgan, 3 vols. (1979).

Dalton, Hugh, *Memoirs: High Tide and After* (1962).

—— *The Political Diary of Hugh Dalton, 1918–40; 1945–60*, ed. Ben Pimlott (1986).

Dalyell, Tam, *Dick Crossman: A Portrait* (1990).

Dell, Edmund, *A Hard Pounding* (1991).

—— *The Chancellors* (1996).

Dimbleby, Jonathan, *The Prince of Wales: A Biography* (1994).

Foot, Michael, *Aneurin Bevan*, vol. ii (1973).

—— *Loyalists and Loners* (1986).

Gaitskell, Hugh, *The Diary of Hugh Gaitskell 1945–1956*, ed. Philip Williams (1983).

Goodman, Geoffrey, *The Awkward Warrior* (1979).

Gordon Walker, Patrick, *Political Diaries, 1932–1971*, ed. Robert Pearce (1991).

Gormley, Joe, *Battered Cherub* (1982).

Hailsham, Lord, *A Sparrow's Flight: Memoirs* (1990).

Harris, Kenneth, *The Prime Minister Talks to the Observer* (1979).

—— *Attlee* (1982).

Harris, Robert, *The Making of Neil Kinnock* (1984).

—— *Good and Faithful Servant* (1990).

Hattersley, Roy, *Who Goes Home?* (1995).

Hayes, Maurice, *Minority Verdict* (Dublin, 1995).

Healey, Denis, *The Time of my Life* (1989).

Henderson, Sir Nicholas, *Mandarin: The Diaries of Nicholas Henderson* (1994).

Hennessy, Peter, *The Sea-Changer: James Callaghan, 1976–79* (1997).

Hills, Dennis, *Tyrants and Mountains* (1994).

Horne, Alastair, *Harold Macmillan*, vol. ii (1989).

Jones, Mervyn, *Michael Foot* (1994).

Jay, Douglas, *Change and Fortune: A Political Record* (1980).

Jay, Peggy, *Loves and Labours: An Autobiography* (1990).

Jenkins, Roy (ed.), *European Diary, 1977–81* (1989).

—— *A Life at the Centre* (1991).

Jones, Jack, *Union Man* (1986).

Kellner, Peter, and Hitchens, Christopher, *Callaghan: The Road to Number Ten* (1976).

King, Cecil, *The Cecil King Diary, 1965–70* (1972).

Kissinger, Henry, *Years of Upheaval* (Boston, 1982).

Lawson, Nigel, *The View from No. 11: Memoirs of a Tory Radical* (1992).

Longford, Lord, *Eleven at Number Ten* (1984).

MacDougall, Donald, *Don and Mandarin: Memoirs of an Economist* (1987).

McSmith, Andy, *John Smith: A Life 1938–1994* (1994).

Marsh, Richard, *Off the Rails* (1978).

Maudling, Reginald, *Memoirs* (1978).

Mikardo, Ian, *Backbencher* (1988).

Morgan, Austen, *Harold Wilson* (1992).

Morgan, Kenneth O., *'Steady as she Goes': Writing the Biography of Lord Callaghan* (Swansea, 1996).

MORRIS, ROGER, *Uncertain Greatness: Henry Kissinger and American Foreign Policy* (1977 edn.).
OWEN, DAVID, *Time to Declare* (1991).
PATERSON, PETER, *Tired and Emotional: The Life of Lord George-Brown* (1993).
PIMLOTT, BEN, *Hugh Dalton* (1985).
—— *Harold Wilson* (1992).
—— *The Queen* (1996).
REES, MERLYN, *Northern Ireland: A Personal View* (1985).
RENTOUL, JOHN, *Tony Blair* (1995).
ROLL, ERIC, *Crowded Hours* (1985).
ROUTLEDGE, PAUL, *Madam Speaker: A Biography* (1995).
SCHMIDT, HELMUT, *Men and Power: A Political Retrospective* (1990).
SHEPHERD, ROBERT, *Iain Macleod: A Biography* (1994).
SHINWELL, EMANUEL, *Conflict without Malice* (1955).
SILVER, ERIC, *Vic Feather TUC* (1973).
STEEL, DAVID, *Against Goliath* (1989).
SULLIVAN, TIMOTHY, *Julian Hodge: A Biography* (1981).
TEBBITT, NORMAN, *Upwardly Mobile* (1989).
THATCHER, MARGARET, *The Path to Power* (1995).
THOMAS, GEORGE (Lord Tonypandy), *Mr Speaker* (1985).
THOMAS, HUGH, *John Strachey* (1973).
THORPE, D. R., *Alec Douglas-Home* (1996).
WEBBER, ALAN M., interview, 'James Callaghan: The Statesman as CEO', *Harvard Business Review* (Nov.–Dec. 1986).
WELENSKY, ROY, *Welensky's 4000 Days* (1964).
—— *The Welensky Papers*, ed. J. R. T. Wood (Durban, 1983).
WHITELAW, WILLIAM, *The Whitelaw Memoirs* (1989).
WHITTAKER, DAVID J., *Fighter for Peace* (York, 1989).
WILLIAMS, MARCIA, *Inside Number Ten* (1972).
WILLIAMS, PHILIP, *Hugh Gaitskell* (1979).
WILSON, HAROLD, *The Labour Government, 1964–70: A Personal Memoir* (1971).
—— *Final Term: The Labour Government, 1974–1976* (1979).
YOUNG, HUGO, *One of Us* (1989).
ZIEGLER, PHILIP, *Wilson: The Authorized Life* (1993).
ZUCKERMAN, SOLLY, *Men, Monkeys and Missiles* (1988).

F. OTHER SECONDARY WORKS

Place of publication London unless otherwise stated.

ARTIS, MICHAEL, and COBHAM, DAVID, *Labour's Economic Policies, 1974–79* (Manchester, 1991).
ASCOLI, DAVID, *The Queen's Peace* (1971).

BAILEY, VICTOR (ed.), *Forged in Fire: The History of the Fire Brigades Union* (1992).

BAIN, GEORGE, *The Growth of White Collar Unionism* (Oxford, 1970).

BARNES, DENIS, and REID, EILEEN, *Government and Trade Unions: The British Experience, 1964–79* (1980).

BAYLIS, JOHN (ed.), *British Defence Policy in a Changing World* (1977).

BECKERMAN, WILFRED (ed.), *The Labour Government's Economic Record, 1964–1970* (1972).

BLACKABY, F. (ed.), *British Economic Policy, 1960–74* (Cambridge, 1978).

BLACKSTONE, TESSA, and PLOWDEN, WILLIAM, *Inside the Think Tank: Advising the Cabinet, 1971–1983* (1988).

BLAKE, ROBERT, *A History of Rhodesia* (1977).

BOGDANOR, VERNON, *Devolution* (Oxford, 1979).

BRITTAN, SAMUEL, *The Treasury under the Tories* (Harmondsworth, 1969).

BRIVATI, BRIAN, and JONES, HARRIET (eds.), *From Reconstruction to Integration: Britain and Europe since 1945* (Leicester, 1993).

BROWN, E. H. PHELPS, *The Origins of Trade Union Power* (Oxford, 1983).

BURK, KATHY, *The First Privatisation* (1988).

—— and CAIRNCROSS, ALEC, *'Goodbye Great Britain': The 1976 IMF Crisis* (Newhaven, 1992).

BUTLER, DAVID, *The British General Election of 1951* (1952).

—— *The British General Election of 1955* (1955).

—— and KAVANAGH, DENIS, *The British General Election of February 1974* (1974).

—— —— *The British General Election of October 1974* (1975).

—— —— *The British General Election of 1979* (1980).

—— —— *The British General Election of 1983* (1984).

—— and KING, ANTHONY, *The British General Election of 1964* (1965).

—— —— *The British General Election of 1966* (1967).

—— and KITZINGER, UWE, *The 1975 Referendum* (1976).

—— and MARQUAND, DAVID, *European Elections and British Politics* (1981).

—— and PINTO-DUSCHINSKY, MICHAEL, *The British General Election of 1970* (1971).

—— and ROSE, RICHARD, *The British General Election of 1959* (1960).

—— and SLOMAN, ANNE, *British Political Facts, 1900–1979* (1980).

CAIRNCROSS, ALEC, *Years of Recovery: British Economic Policy, 1945–52* (1985).

—— *Managing the British Economy in the 1960s: A Treasury View* (1996).

—— and EICHENGREEN, BARRY, *Sterling in Decline* (1983).

CAIRNCROSS, FRANCES, and CAIRNCROSS, ALEC (eds.), *Britain's Economic Prospects Reconsidered* (1983).

CARSWELL, JOHN P., *Government and the Universities in Britain: Programme and Performance, 1960–1980* (Cambridge, 1985).

COCKERELL, MICHAEL, *Live from Number Ten: Prime Ministers and Television* (1988).

CREWE, IVOR, and KING, ANTHONY, *SDP: The Birth, Life and Death of the Social Democratic Party* (Oxford, 1994).

DARWIN, JOHN, *Britain and Decolonisation: The Retreat from Empire in the Post-war World* (1988).

DAVIS, WILLIAM, *Three Years' Hard Labour: The Road to Devaluation* (1968).

DOCKRILL, MICHAEL, *British Defence since 1945* (Oxford, 1988).

DONOUGHUE, BERNARD, *Prime Minister: The Conduct of Policy under Harold Wilson and James Callaghan* (1988).

DORRILL, STEPHEN, and RAMSAY, ROBIN, *Smear!* (1992).

ELBAUM, BERNARD, and LAZOWICK, WILLIAM (eds.), *The Decline of the British Economy* (Oxford, 1986).

FARR, DIANA, *Five at Ten: Prime Minister's Consorts since 1957* (1985).

FREEDMAN, LAWRENCE, *Britain and the Falklands War* (Oxford, 1988).

Furzeham School, Brixham, 1889–1989: A Centenary Booklet (Brixham, 1989).

GEORGE, STEPHEN, *An Awkward Partner* (Oxford, 1990).

GUPTA, PARTHA S., *Imperialism and the British Labour Movement, 1914–1964* (1975).

HAINES, JOE, *The Politics of Power* (1972).

HARVIE, CHRISTOPHER, *No Gods and Precious Few Heroes* (1981).

—— *Scotland and Nationalism* (? 1994 edn.).

—— *Fools' Gold: The Story of North Sea Oil* (1994).

HASELER, STEPHEN, *The Gaitskellites* (1969).

HENNESSY, PETER, *Cabinet* (Oxford, 1986).

—— *Whitehall* (1989).

—— *Never Again: Britain 1945–1951* (1992).

—— *The Hidden Wiring* (1995).

—— and SELDON, ANTHONY (eds.), *Ruling Performance: British Governments from Attlee to Thatcher* (1987).

HOLLINGSWORTH, MARK, and NORTON-TAYLOR, RICHARD, *Blacklist: The Inside Story of Political Vetting* (1988).

HOLMES, MARTIN, *The Labour Government, 1974–1979: Political Aims and Economic Reality* (1985).

JAY, DOUGLAS, *Sterling: A Plea for Moderation* (1985).

JEFFERY, KEITH, and HENNESSY, PETER, *States of Emergency: British Governments and Strikebreaking since 1919* (1983).

JENKINS, PETER, *The Battle of Downing Street* (1970).

JONES, BETI, *Etholiadau Seneddol yng Nghymru* (Talybont, 1977).

JUDGE, ANTHONY, *The First Fifty Years: The Story of the Police Federation* (1968).

KAVANAGH, DENIS (ed.), *The Politics of the Labour Party* (1982).

KELLEY, KEVIN J., *The Longest War: Northern Ireland and the IRA* (Westport, Conn., 1988 edn.).

KOGAN, DAVID, and KOGAN, MAURICE, *The Battle for the Labour Party* (1982).

KRAMNICK, ISAAC (ed.), *Is Britain Dying? Perspectives on the Current Crisis* (1979).

LAMB, RICHARD, *The Macmillan Years, 1957–1963: The Emerging Truth* (1995).

LOUIS, WILLIAM ROGER, and BULL, HEDLEY (eds.), *The Special Relationship: The Anglo-American Relationship since 1945* (Oxford, 1986).

MCCALLUM, R. B., and READMAN, ALISON, *The British General Election of 1945* (Oxford, 1947).

MCKENZIE, R. T., *British Political Parties* (1963 edn.).

MARTIN, J. P., and WILSON, GAIL, *The Police: A Study in Manpower* (1969).

MIDDLEMAS, R. K., *Power, Competition and the State*, ii: *Threats to the Postwar Settlement, 1961–74* (1990).

MINKIN, LEWIS, *The Labour Party Conference* (Manchester, 1980).
MORGAN, KENNETH O., *Rebirth of a Nation: Wales 1880–1980* (Oxford, 1981).
—— *Labour in Power, 1945–1951* (Oxford, 1984).
—— *Labour People: Leaders and Lieutenants, Hardie to Kinnock* (Oxford, 1992 edn.).
—— *The People's Peace: British History, 1945–1990* (Oxford, 1992 edn.).
MORRIS, TERENCE, *Crime and Criminal Justice since 1945* (Oxford, 1989).
O'MALLEY, PADRAIG, *The Uncivil Wars: Ireland Today* (Belfast, 1983).
OVENDALE, RITCHIE, *British Defence Policy since 1945* (1994).
PEDEN, G. C., *British Economic Policy, Lloyd George to Margaret Thatcher* (Deddington, 1985).
PELLEW, JILL, *The Home Office, 1848–1914* (1982).
PENNIMAN, HOWARD (ed.), *Britain at the Polls: A Study of the General Election* (Washington, 1981).
PIMLOTT, BEN, and COOK, CHRIS (eds.), *Trade Unions in British Politics* (1991 edn.).
POLLARD, SIDNEY, *The Development of the British Economy, 1914–1980* (1983).
POLYVIOU, P. G., *Cyprus: Conflict and Negotiation, 1960–1980* (1980).
ROLL, ERIC, *Where did We Go Wrong?* (1995).
SADDEN, JOHN, *Keep the Home Fires Burning: The Story of Portsmouth and Gosport in World War I* (Portsmouth, 1990).
SASSOON, DONALD, *One Hundred Years of Socialism: The West European Left in the Twentieth Century* (1996).
SCHNEER, JONATHAN, *Labour's Conscience: The Labour Left, 1945–1951* (1988).
SCOTT, L. V., *Conscription and the Attlee Governments: Policy and Politics, 1945–1951* (Oxford, 1993).
SELDON, ANTHONY, *Churchill's Indian Summer: The Conservative Government, 1951–55* (1981).
SHORE, PETER, *Leading the Left* (1993).
STEWART, MICHAEL, *The Jekyll and Hyde Years: Politics and Economic Policy since 1964* (1977).
STRANGE, SUSAN, *Sterling and British Policy* (Oxford, 1971).
TAYLOR, ROBERT, *The Fifth Estate: Britain's Unions in the Seventies* (1978).
—— *The Trade Union Question in British Politics: Government and Unions since 1945* (Oxford, 1993).
TRUELL, PETER and GURWIN, LARRY, *BCCI* (London, 1992).
TYRELL, R. EMMETT, JR., *The Future that Doesn't Work: Social Democracy's Failures in Britain* (New York, 1977).
VERRIER, ANTHONY, *The Road to Zimbabwe* (1986).
WHITELEY, PAUL, *The Labour Party in Crisis* (1983).
WICKHAM-JONES, MARK, *Economic Strategy and the Labour Party: Politics and Policy-Making 1970–83* (1996).
WILLIAMS, MARCIA (Lady Falkender), *Inside Number Ten* (1972).
—— *Downing Street in Perspective* (1983).
WILLIAMS, SHIRLEY, *Politics is for People* (1981).
WINDRICH, ELAINE, *The Politics of Rhodesian Independence* (1978).

WORSWICK, G. N., and ADY, P. (eds.), *The British Economy in the Nineteen-Fifties* (Oxford, 1962).

G. ARTICLES

BALE, TIM, ' "A Deplorable Episode"? South African Arms and the Statecraft of British Social Democracy', *Labour History Review* (forthcoming).

BUCHANAN, TOM, 'Divided Loyalties: The Impact of the Spanish Civil War on Britain's Civil Service Trade Unions, 1936–9', *Historical Research*, 65/156 (Feb. 1992).

BURK, KATHY, 'The Americans, the Germans, and the British: The 1976 IMF Crisis', *20th Century British History*, 5/3 (1994).

DELL, EDMUND, 'Britain and the Origins of the European Monetary System', *Contemporary European History*, 3/1 (1994).

—— 'The Chrysler UK Rescue', *Contemporary Record*, 6/1 (summer 1992).

—— and HUNT, Lord, of Tanworth, 'The Failings of Cabinet Government in the Mid to Late 1970s', *Contemporary Record*, 8/3 (winter 1994).

DENHAM, ANDREW, and GARNETT, MARK, 'The Nature and Impact of Think Tanks in Contemporary Britain', *Contemporary British History*, 10/1 (spring 1996).

JUST, PETER D., 'Ex-Prime Ministers and Parliament: A Riposte to Mythology', Research Papers in Legislative Studies 4/96 (University of Hull) (courtesy of the author).

KANDIAH, MICHAEL DAVID (ed.), 'Witness Seminar: The Number 10 Policy Unit', Contemporary British History, 10/1 (spring 1996).

MCKIBBIN, ROSS, 'Homage to Wilson and Callaghan', *London Review of Books*, 24 Oct. 1991, 65/156 (Feb. 1992).

MARSH, IAN, 'Liberal Priorities, the Lib–Lab Pact and the Requirements for Policy Influence', *Parliamentary Affairs* (July 1990).

OVENDALE, RITCHIE, 'Macmillan and the Wind of Change in Africa, 1957–1960', *Historical Journal*, 38/2 (1995).

RODGERS, WILLIAM, 'Government under Stress: Britain's Winter of Discontent', *Political Quarterly*, 55/2 (1984).

ROSE, RICHARD, 'A Crisis of Confidence in British Party Leaders?', *Contemporary Record*, 9/2 (autumn 1995).

STATLER, JOCELYN, 'British Foreign Policy to 1985: The European Monetary System from Conception to Birth', *International Affairs*, 55 (1979).

'The British Referendum on Europe', Contemporary British History 10/3 (autumn 1996).

'The Winter of Discontent: A Symposium', *Contemporary Record*, 1/3 (autumn 1987).

H. AUDIO-VISUAL MATERIAL

British Broadcasting Corporation, London: transcripts of interviews (courtesy of Mr Peter Morgan and Professor Peter Hennessy).
Jimmy Carter Library, Atlanta, Georgia.
Gerald R. Ford Library, Ann Arbor, Michigan.
Inland Revenue Staff Federation, London.
Lyndon Baines Johnson Library, Austin, Texas.
Miners' Library, Swansea (courtesy of Professor Hywel Francis).
National Library of Wales, Aberystwyth.

Index